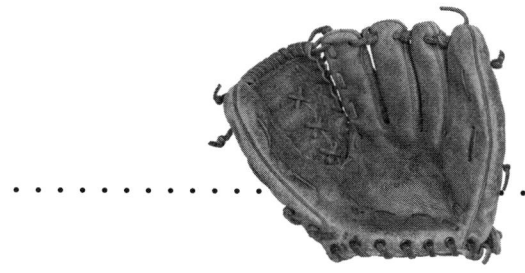

THE GIANTS ENCYCLOPEDIA

Tom Schott
and
Nick Peters

Sports Publishing L.L.C.
Champaign, Illinois

Director of Production: Susan Moyer
Interior Design and Layout: Michelle R. Dressen/
Greg Hickman (update)
Dustjacket Design: Julie L. Denzer/
Kenneth J. O'Brien (update)

ISBN:1-58261-693-0

Printed in Canada.

SPORTS PUBLISHING L.L.C.
www.SportsPublishingLLC.com

To my mother, Bobette; my sister, Debbie; my brother, Steve;
and my wife, Jane, who always cheer with me and for me.
— T.S.

To Lise, Lisa, Anamarie, Melanie, and Briana—
and to Sandy King, who was a giant of a fan.
— N.P.

TABLE OF CONTENTS

ACKNOWLEDGMENTS

The authors would like to thank Tom James for his assistance in compiling the career statistics of all the Giants' batters and pitchers. In addition, our appreciation goes out to Bob Rose and Missy Mikulecky of the San Francisco Giants' media relations/publications department; Bill Francis, Frank Vito and Tim Wiles of the National Baseball Library and Archive (Cooperstown, New York); Mary Brace of Brace Photo (Chicago, Illinois); and Mark Rucker of Transcendental Graphics (Boulder, Colorado). We also would like to acknowledge Mike Pearson, Susan Moyer, Julie Denzer, Michelle Dressen and Michelle Garrett of Sports Publishing L.L.C. for helping make this book a reality.

CHAPTER ONE

THROUGH
THE YEARS

		1883	
46-50	**.479**	**6th Place (-16)**	**—**
		John Clapp	

The National League expanded into New York, as well as Philadelphia, in 1883 after folding its franchises in Troy, New York, and Worchester, Massachusetts. New York's team, whose corporate name was the National Exhibition Company, was owned by John B. Day, a well-to-do tobacco merchant in New York City who also operated the New York Metropolitans of the American Association. The team was known as the Gothams from 1883-85. John Clapp, who previously managed the Indianapolis Browns (1878), Buffalo Bisons (1879), Cincinnati Red Stockings (1880) and Cleveland Blues (1881), was the Gothams' first manager and also a reserve catcher and outfielder.

On May 1 the Gothams played their inaugural game and defeated the Boston Red Stockings 7-5 at the first Polo Grounds, located at 110th Street and Sixth Avenue in New York. Former U.S. president Ulysses S. Grant was among the 15,000 spectators in the stands. Two days later John Montgomery Ward pitched for New York and belted two home runs in a 10-9 victory over the Red Stockings at the Polo Grounds.

John Clapp was the first manager of the New York Gothams in 1883 and also served as a backup catcher and outfielder. (Transcendental Graphics)

The Gothams finished their debut season with a respectable 46-50 record, for sixth place, 16 games behind the champion Red Stockings. Catcher Buck Ewing topped the N.L. with 10 home runs, while first baseman Roger Connor batted a team-high .357 and left fielder Pete Gillespie had 62 RBI. The squad's top pitcher was right-hander Mickey Welch, who came to New York from Troy and posted a 25-23 record with a 2.73 ERA. He completed 46 of the 52 games he started while allowing 431 hits in 426.0 innings.

1884			
62-50	.554	T4th Place (-22)	—
Jim Price/John Montgomery Ward			

Jim Price, a native of New York who had never played or managed in the major leagues, was appointed manager for the 1884 season. He piloted the Gothams to a 56-42 record before being replaced by pitcher-infielder-outfielder John Montgomery Ward.

The eventual champion Providence Grays handed New York a 19-5 loss at the Polo Grounds in New York on May 24 in a game that Gothams' right fielder Mike Dorgan committed five errors. Dorgan batted .276 for the season and also pitched in 14 games with an 8-6 record.

Once again, the ace of the pitching staff was right-hander Mickey Welch, who went 39-21 with a 2.50 ERA. He completed 62 of his 65 starts while throwing a whopping 557.1 innings with 345 strikeouts (all franchise records). On August 28 he struck out the first nine batters he faced against the Cleveland Blues at the Polo Grounds: first baseman Bill Phillips, right fielder Pete Hotaling and third baseman George Pinckney in the first inning; left fielder Ernie Burch, third baseman Mike Muldoon and right fielder Jake Evans in the second inning; and second baseman Germany Smith (who reached first base when catcher Loughran misplayed the ball), pitcher John Henry and catcher Jerrie Moore in the third.

Amazingly, Welch had been injured in his two previous starts, and ironically, the streak went unrecorded for more than 50 years because the official scorer did not credit Welch with striking out Smith because he reached base. Baseball historian Harry Simmons pointed out the error in 1941. The feat stood for nearly 86 years until Tom Seaver of the New York Mets fanned 10 in a row against the San Diego Padres on April 22, 1970.

When asked to explain his success as a pitcher, the carefree Welch, who was one of the great beer drinkers of the time, offered this cheery couplet:
"Pure elixir of malt and hops,
"Beats all the drugs and all the drops."
The Gothams posted the first winning season in franchise history (62-50) and finished tied for fourth place with the Chicago White Stockings, 22 games behind Providence. Roger Connor, who played second base, third base and outfield, was the team's leading batter with a .317 average, four home runs and 82 RBI. Catcher Buck Ewing led the National League with 20 triples, and first baseman Alex McKinnon drove in 73 runs.

1885			
85-27	.759	2nd Place (-2)	—
Jim Mutrie			

Recognizing that the National League had greater potential than the American Association, owner John B. Day moved star right-handed pitcher Tim Keefe, as well as third baseman Dude Esterbrook, from the New York Mets (A.A.) to the New York Gothams (N.L.). Manager Jim Mutrie also was switched. The moves paid huge dividends as New York posted a stunning 85-27 record (a franchise-best .759 winning percentage) but still finished two games behind the pennant-winning Chicago White Stockings.

Keefe won his first start 1-0 over the Providence Grays at the Polo Grounds on May 9. He allowed only one hit while outdueling

Charles "Old Hoss" Radbourn. On May 27 the Gothams banged out 29 hits en route to a 24-0 beating of the Buffalo Bison. On June 3 New York defeated the Philadelphia Phillies 8-7 in 11 innings at Recreation Park in Philadelphia to improve its record to 19-5. As legend has it, after the game an enthusiastic Mutrie proclaimed: "My big fellows! My Giants! We are the people." The nickname caught on immediately and has remained to this day.

New York still had a chance to catch Chicago late in the season but lost back-to-back games at West Side Park in Chicago, 7-4 on September 29 and 2-1 on September 30.

Right-handed pitcher Mickey Welch con-tinued his fine work, winning 17 straight games from July 18-September 4 and finishing with a 44-11 record and a 1.66 ERA. The 44 wins are a franchise record. Keefe had a 32-13 record with an N.L.-best 1.58 ERA.

First baseman Roger Connor led the league with a .371 batting average and had 65 RBI, while right fielder Mike Dorgan (.326), catcher Buck Ewing (.304) and center fielder Jim O'Rourke (.300) all batted at a .300 clip or better. O'Rourke topped the league with 16 triples.

The 1885 Giants featured six future Hall of Famers: Connor, Ewing, Keefe, O'Rourke, Welch and shortstop John Montgomery Ward.

The 1885 Giants featured six future Hall of Famers: first baseman Roger Connor, catcher Buck Ewing, pitcher Tim Keefe, center fielder Jim O'Rourke, shortstop John Montgomery Ward and pitcher Mickey Welch. (National Baseball Library and Archive)

1886
75-44 .630 3rd Place (-12½) — Jim Mutrie

The Giants put together their second straight banner season with a 75-44 record, but it only was good enough for third place behind the Chicago White Stockings (90-34) and Detroit Wolverines (87-36).

Right-handers Tim Keefe and Mickey Welch compiled more lofty numbers, Keefe finishing 42-20 with a 2.53 ERA and Welch going 33-22 with a 2.99 ERA. Keefe paced the National League in wins, games pitched (64), innings pitched (535.0) and complete games (62).

Offensively, first baseman Roger Connor (.355, league-leading 20 triples and 71 RBI); catcher Buck Ewing (.309); and shortstop John Montgomery Ward (81 RBI) were the stalwarts.

During this era, teams utilized 12-player rosters, so keeping healthy was paramount. On May 13 the Giants lost at Chicago by the score of 7-3 with just seven able-bodied players.

1887
68-55 .553 4th Place (-10½) — Jim Mutrie

Offense was the watchword as New York finished with a 68-55 record and in fourth place, 10½ games behind the Detroit Wolverines.

First baseman Roger Connor was the first player in franchise history to total 100 RBI (104) while batting .285 with 26 doubles, 22 triples and 17 home runs. Shortstop John Montgomery Ward batted at a team-leading .338 clip to go with a franchise-record and National League-leading 111 stolen bases (from 1886-97 a base runner was credited with a stolen base for advancing a base on a hit or an out made by a teammate).

The Giants had numerous big games. They scored 12 runs in the third inning against the Philadelphia Phillies at the Philadelphia Baseball Grounds on June 7 (but lost 15-14) and plated 11 runs in the first inning against the Phillies at the Polo Grounds en route to a 26-2 onslaught four days later. In the victory, second baseman Danny Richardson became the first player in franchise history to collect six hits in a game. On June 15 outfielder Mike Tiernan set a National League record by scoring six runs in a 29-1 bombing of the Phillies.

On the flip side, left-handed pitcher Bill George established a baseball record with 16 walks in the first game of a double-header against the Chicago White Stockings at the Polo Grounds on May 30. New York led 11-5 heading into the ninth inning, but four walks helped Chicago score seven runs and win 12-11.

Right-hander Tim Keefe posted a 35-19 record with a 3.10 ERA, while right-hander Mickey Welch went 22-15 with a 3.36 ERA.

On July 12 Ward was replaced as field captain by Ewing. Club management indicated that several players had been hostile to Ward,

Second baseman Danny Richardson became the first player in franchise history to collect six hits in a game against the Philadelphia Phillies on June 11, 1887. (Transcendental Graphics)

but four days later Ward released a letter he had written to N.L. president Nicholas Young detailing a series of abuses to which teams had been subjecting their players (including the reserve clause that bound a player to a particular team forever). Ward would go on to become one of the principal figures in the development of the Players League that operated during the 1890 season.

1888			
84-47	.641	1st Place (+9)	—
		Jim Mutrie	

The Giants won their first National League pennant with an 84-47 record, nine games ahead of the Chicago White Stockings, and then defeated the St. Louis Browns, champions of the American Association, in the World Series six games to four.

Along the way, first baseman Roger Connor belted three home runs against the Indianapolis Hoosiers at Seventh Street Park in Indianapolis on May 9, right-handed pitcher Tim Keefe set a franchise record with 19 consecutive wins from June 23-August 10 and right fielder Mike Tiernan became the first player in franchise history to hit for the cycle against the Philadelphia Phillies at the Polo Grounds in New York on August 25.

New York clinched the pennant with a 1-0 victory over Chicago at the Polo Grounds on October 4. Left-hander Ed Crane threw a one-hitter and struck out four batters in the fifth inning. The Giants scored their lone run in the fifth on a bases loaded wild pitch by Chicago pitcher John Tener, who would go on to serve as president of the N.L. from 1913-18.

Catcher Buck Ewing paced the Giants with a .306 batting average and 53 stolen bases, followed by Tiernan (.293 and 52 RBI) and Connor (.291, 14 home runs and 71 RBI). Keefe went 35-12 with a 1.74 ERA, topping the N.L. in wins, ERA, shutouts (8 — tied) and strikeouts (335). Right-hander Mickey Welch was 26-19 with a 1.93 ERA.

1889			
83-43	.659	1st Place (+1)	—
		Jim Mutrie	

On February 4 New York City announced it would be tearing down the Polo Grounds to build the area known as Douglass Circle. Giants' owner John B. Day offered to donate $10,000 to local charities if his team could use the grounds for one more season, but the city rejected the good-will gesture and sent Day searching for a new home for the Giants. They opened the season at Oakland Park in New Jersey (two games) and then moved to St. George Grounds in Staten Island (23 games) before taking up residency in the Second Polo Grounds at 155th Street and 8th Avenue on July 8, 1889.

Despite the constant change of address, the Giants repeated as National League champions with an 83-43 record, edging the Boston Beaneaters by one game. New York also defended its world championship by defeating the cross-town rival Brooklyn Bridegrooms of the American Association six games to three. It was the first meeting between the two franchises that have remained combatants to the present day.

Right-handed pitcher Ed Crane threw the first no-hitter in franchise history against the Washington Senators at the Polo Grounds on September 28. The 3-0 victory was cut to seven innings due to darkness.

After right-handers Tim Keefe (28-13, 3.31 ERA) and Mickey Welch (27-12, 3.02) were splendid during the regular season, the Giants got boosts from Crane and right-hander Hank O'Day in the World Series. Crane was 4-1, while O'Day went 2-0, including a 3-2 win in the decisive Game 9 at the Polo Grounds on October 29.

Five regulars batted .300 or better: right fielder Mike Tiernan (.335), catcher Buck Ewing (.327), left fielder Jim O'Rourke (.321), first baseman Roger Connor (.317) and center fielder George Gore (.305). Connor also contributed 32 doubles, 17 triples, 13 home runs

and a league-high 130 RBI, while second baseman Danny Richardson drove in 100 runs. Tiernan scored a franchise-record 147 runs to lead the N.L.

The Brotherhood of Professional Base Ball Players (a players' union), led by New York shortstop John Montgomery Ward, succeeded in organizing the Players League, which would make its debut in 1890.

1890			
63-68	.481	6th Place (-24)	60,667
		Jim Mutrie	

The Players League virtually wiped out the Giants. New York lost two crucial court rulings that allowed catcher Buck Ewing and shortstop John Montgomery Ward to join other teams. Both jumped to the P.L., Ewing as player-manager of the New York Giants and Ward as player-manager of the Brooklyn Wonders.

Only three players from the 1889 National League Giants remained in 1890: pitcher Mickey Welch, outfielder Mike Tiernan and reserve catcher Pat Murphy. The Giants filled their roster with rookies and castoffs, including six players from the now-defunct Indianapolis Hoosiers.

The biggest pickup from Indianapolis was hard-throwing right-handed pitcher Amos Rusie. He managed just a 29-34 record with a 2.56 ERA in 1890 but topped the N.L. with 341 strikeouts. He would become a big-time winner for the Giants down the road. Welch went 17-14 with a 2.99 ERA.

Shortstop Jack Glasscock, also from Indianapolis, led the league with a .336 batting average to go with 66 RBI and 54 stolen bases. Rookie outfielder and part-time pitcher Jesse Burkett batted .309 with 60 RBI, and Tiernan batted .304 with 25 doubles, 21 triples, 13 home runs (tied for the N.L. lead), 59 RBI and a team-leading 56 stolen bases.

Meanwhile, the P.L. Giants, who played their home games adjacent to the Polo Grounds, made the competition for fans fierce.

The N.L. team billed itself as "the real Giants," while the P.L. squad (made up of many transplanted N.L. Giants) called itself "the big Giants."

In one of the most exciting games of the season May 12, Tiernan blasted a home run with one out in the bottom of the 13th inning to give the Giants a 1-0 victory over the Boston Beaneaters at the Polo Grounds. Adding drama to the homer was the fact that after the ball cleared the center field fence it bounded up against the outside fence of adjoining Brotherhood Park, where the P.L. Giants were playing host to the Boston Red Stockings. Tiernan was applauded by fans in both ballparks as he trotted around the bases.

On September 27 Glasscock banged out six singles in six at-bats in a 15-3 victory over the Cincinnati Reds at the Polo Grounds.

The Giants finished with a 63-68 record, in sixth place, 24 games behind the pennant-winning Brooklyn Bridegrooms in their first year in the N.L.

1891			
71-61	.538	3rd Place (-13)	210,568
		Jim Mutrie	

With the Players League having folded after just one season, the Giants took over their home ball park at 157th Street and 8th Avenue and renamed it the New Polo Grounds. New York also got back some of its key players from the 1888 and 1889 championship teams, including first baseman Roger Connor, catcher Buck Ewing, pitcher Tim Keefe, left fielder Jim O'Rourke and second baseman Danny Richardson.

Outfielder Mike Tiernan batted at a .306 clip with 30 doubles, 12 triples, 16 home runs (tied for the National League lead), 73 RBI and 53 stolen bases, while O'Rourke batted .295 with 95 RBI and Connor batted .290 with 94 RBI.

Right-hander Amos Rusie pitched a no-hitter against the Brooklyn Bridegrooms on

July 31, winning 6-0 at the Polo Grounds. He went on to finish 33-20 with a 2.55 ERA and paced the N.L. with six shutouts and 337 strikeouts. Right-hander John Ewing went 21-8 with a league-best 2.27 ERA. Father Time began to catch up with right-handers Tim Keefe and Mickey Welch. The 34-year-old Keefe was 1-5 with a 5.24 ERA before moving on the Philadelphia Phillies, and the 31-year-old Welch was 7-10 with a 4.28 ERA.

The P.L. hurt Giants' owner John B. Day financially, and he had been forced to sell shares of stock in his team to survive. Over time from 1890-92 Day sold shares to Edward Talcott, a New York lawyer who had operated the P.L. Giants. As part of the transactions, Talcott insisted that Jim Mutrie be replaced as manager, and he was November 7 after the Giants finished in third place with a 71-61 record, 13 games behind the champion Boston Beaneaters.

1892		
31-43	.419	10th Place (-21)
40-37	.519	6th Place (-13½)
71-80	.470	8th Place (-31½) 130,566
	Pat Powers	

The American Association folded following the 1891 season, leaving the National League as the only professional baseball circuit. In order to still have a postseason championship, the N.L. divided its season into two halves, with the first-half champion to play the second-half champion in the World Series.

New York, under new manager Pat Powers, finished 10th in the 12-team league in the first half with a 31-43 record, 21 games behind the Boston Beaneaters. The Giants improved some in the second half, going 40-37 to place sixth, 13½ games behind the Cleveland Spiders.

The season actually started out in fine fashion as right-hander Amos Rusie defeated former New York pitcher Tim Keefe and the Philadelphia Phillies by the score of 5-4 on

April 12. Rusie won both games of a doubleheader (6-4 and 9-5) against the Washington Senators at the Polo Grounds in New York on October 4.

Catcher Buck Ewing paced the Giants with a .310 batting average and 76 RBI, while left fielder Jim O'Rourke batted .304 with 28 doubles and 56 RBI. Doyle, Ewing and second baseman Eddie Burke each stole 42 bases. Rusie had a 31-31 record with a 2.88 ERA, and right-hander Silver King was 23-24 with a 3.24 ERA.

1893			
68-64	.515	5th Place (-19½)	290,000
	John Montgomery Ward		

The Giants rung in 1893 with a new owner (C.C. Von Cott) and a new manager (John Montgomery Ward). They posted a winning record at 68-64 but still limped home in fifth place, 19½ games behind the Boston Beaneaters.

Five regulars batted .300 or better: third baseman George Davis (.355), second baseman Ward (.328), catcher-outfielder Jack Doyle (.321), right fielder Mike Tiernan (.309) and first baseman Roger Connor (.305). Three players drove in 100 or more runs: Davis (119), Connor (105) and Tiernan (102). Davis set a franchise record with 27 triples. Left fielder Eddie Burke topped the team with 54 stolen bases.

Davis, who had been acquired from the Cleveland Spiders during the offseason in exchange for catcher Buck Ewing, established a franchise record with a 33-game hitting streak from August 3-September 9. Ironically, the streak was snapped by Cleveland pitcher Cy Young at League Park in Cleveland on September 11.

Right-hander Amos Rusie was 33-21 with a 3.23 ERA while leading the National League with 56 appearances, 482.0 innings pitched, 50 complete games, four shutouts (tied) and

208 strikeouts. Right-hander Mark Baldwin finished 16-20 with a 4.10 ERA.

1894			
88-44	.667	2nd Place (-3)	387,000
John Montgomery Ward			

Behind the pitching of right-handers Amos Rusie and Jouett Meekin, the Giants finished in second place in 1894 with an 88-44 record, just three games behind the Baltimore Orioles. From 1894-97, the National League scheduled a postseason best-of-seven championship series between the regular season's first- and second-place teams. The winner was awarded the Temple Cup, a lavish silver cup presented by William Chase Temple, a major stockholder in the Pittsburgh Pirates. New York stunned Baltimore by sweeping the series.

Rusie was 36-13 with a 2.78 ERA, leading the N.L. in wins, ERA, shutouts (3 — tied) and strikeouts (195), while Meekin went 33-9 with a 3.70 ERA. Both pitchers won two games in the Temple Cup.

Offensively, first baseman Jack Doyle batted .367 with 30 doubles, 100 RBI and 42 stole bases. Center fielder George Van Haltren batted .331 with 104 RBI and 43 stolen bases. Third baseman George Davis batted at a .352 clip.

In what has to be considered one of the finest all-around performances in franchise history, Meekin pitched a six-hitter and collected three triples in a 4-3 win over the Cleveland Spiders in the morning game of a double-header at League Park in Cleveland on July 4. Meekin was aided by the ground rules that permitted three bases on fair balls hit into the overflow crowd.

1895			
66-65	.504	9th Place (-21½)	240,000
George Davis/Jack Doyle/Harvey Watkins			

The 1895 season marked the beginning of the controversial and tumultuous eight-year

reign of Andrew C. Freedman as owner of the Giants. Freedman was known for his revolving door of managers (12 in eight years, including two with two different stints) and run-ins with players, umpires and the media.

Freeman employed three managers during his first season: third baseman George Davis (16-17 record), first baseman Jack Doyle (32-31) and Harvey Watkins (18-17), an actor who was working for Barnum and Bailey's circus at the time of his appointment. Davis made his managerial debut April 18—a 7-4 loss to the Brooklyn Bridegrooms at the Polo Grounds in New York—at the age of 24, becoming the youngest manager in major league history.

Through the three skippers, New York managed a respectable 66-65 record but finished in ninth place, 21½ games behind the Baltimore Orioles.

Davis, who had six hits (three singles, two doubles and a triple) against the Philadelphia Phillies at the Baker Bowl in Philadelphia on August 15, batted .340 for the season with 36 doubles, 101 RBI and 48 stolen bases. The team's leading batter was right fielder Mike Tiernan at .347 with 23 doubles, 21 triples, seven home runs and 70 RBI, while center fielder George Van Haltren batted at a .340 clip with eight homers and 103 RBI.

Right-hander Amos Rusie was 23-23 with a 3.73 ERA and topped the National League with four shutouts (tied) and 201 strikeouts. Right-hander Dad Clarke went 18-15 with a 3.39 ERA.

On August 20 shortstop Shorty Fuller recorded 11 putouts in a 3-2 win over the St. Louis Browns at the Polo Grounds. That total remains tied for a baseball record to this day.

1896			
64-67	.489	7th Place (-27)	274,000
Arthur Irwin/Bill Joyce			

New York was dealt a blow in 1896 when star right-handed pitcher Amos Rusie refused to sign a contract over a dispute with owner

Andrew C. Freedman. Rusie sat out the entire season before returning in 1897.

In the meantime, the Giants used two managers, Arthur Irwin (36-53), a 13-year major league shortstop, and reserve third baseman Bill Joyce (28-14) en route to totaling a 64-67 record and placing seventh, 27 games behind the Baltimore Orioles.

Outfielder Mike Tiernan led New York with a .369 batting average to go with 24 doubles, 16 triples, seven home runs and 89 RBI. Outfielder George Van Haltren batted .351 and tied for the National League lead with 21 triples, while infielder George Davis contributed a .320 batting average, 99 RBI and 48 stolen bases. In Rusie's absence, right-hander Jouett Meekin was 26-14 with a 3.82 ERA.

1897			
83-48	.634	3rd Place (-9½)	390,340
		Bill Joyce	

Somehow player-manager Bill Joyce survived the offseason and returned as manager for the 1897 season. Even more remarkable is the fact that he lasted the entire campaign. The Giants were vastly improved—to the tune of an 83-48 record, good for third place, 9½ games behind the Boston Beaneaters.

Joyce also was New York's third baseman, and he tied a major league record with four triples in an 11-5 victory over the Pittsburgh Pirates at Exposition Park in Pittsburgh on May 18. George Strief of the Philadelphia Athletics (American Association) set the standard with four triples June 25, 1885.

On June 3 left-hander Cy Seymour pitched two complete-game victories in a double-header sweep of the Louisville Colonels at the Polo Grounds in New York. The Giants won 6-1 and 10-6 in seven innings due to darkness. Seymour allowed just three hits in the first game and four hits in the second game.

Shortstop George Davis paced New York with a .353 batting average, 31 doubles, 136 RBI (best in the National League) and 65 stolen

bases. Outfielders Mike Tiernan and George Van Haltren both batted .330, and second baseman Kid Gleason drove in 106 runs.

Right-hander Amos Rusie returned from his year-long holdout to post a 28-10 record with a league-leading 2.54 ERA. Right-hander Jouett Meekin went 20-11 with a 3.76 ERA, and Seymour finished 18-14 with a 3.37 ERA.

1898			
77-73	.513	7th Place (-25½)	206,700
	Bill Joyce/Cap Anson/Bill Joyce		

The 1898 season was typical for Giants' owner Andrew C. Freedman. After first baseman Bill Joyce piloted New York to a 22-21 record to start the year, he was replaced by future Hall of Famer Cap Anson, a standout with the Chicago White Stockings and Colts from 1876-97. The players were not happy with Joyce's dismissal and after Anson mustered just a 9-13 record, Joyce reclaimed his old job.

New York went 46-39 the rest of the way to finish 77-73, but that record meant only a seventh-place finish, 25½ games behind the Boston Beaneaters.

On July 25 Freedman became embroiled in one of his infamous controversies, the Ducky Holmes incident. Holmes, an outfielder who played for the Giants in 1897 before joining the Baltimore Orioles, struck out with the bases loaded in the fourth inning and returned to the bench to the heckling of a New York fan at the Polo Grounds. Holmes let loose with a racial slur in reference to Freedman ("But I'm glad I don't have to work for no Sheeny no more," it was reported in the New York Times). Although such comments were not so politically incorrect in those days as they are today, Freedman took exception and tried to attack Holmes on the field (with the support of his private group of policemen). When Freedman refused to clear the field, umpire Tom Lynch forfeited the game to the Orioles. Freedman issued refunds to the spectators in attendance, but he stopped payment on Baltimore's check for its share of

the gate receipts.

Outfielder George Van Haltren was the Giants' leading batter at .312 with 28 doubles, 16 triples and 36 stolen bases. Shortstop George Davis batted .307 with 86 RBI, while Joyce and third baseman Fred Hartman had 91 and 88 RBI, respectively.

Left-hander Cy Seymour replaced right-hander Amos Rusie as the team's top winner with a 25-19 record and a 3.18 ERA. He paced the National League with 239 strikeouts, as well. Rusie was 20-11 with a 3.03 ERA.

1899			
60-90	.400	10th Place (-42)	121,384
		John Day/Fred Hoey	

Without question, the 1899 season was one of the ugliest in the franchise's storied history. It began with the hiring of John Day as manager. Day was owner of the Giants from 1883-92 but at the age of 53 was in serious financial straits and searching for work. He led New York to a respectable 29-35 record before being dismissed.

Day, who had been popular with the players, was replaced by Fred Hoey, whose greatest athletic claim to fame was as a competing pigeon shooter. Then the wheels fell off as the Giants went 31-55 under Hoey to finish 60-90 and in 10th place, a whopping 42 games behind the Brooklyn Superbas.

On August 12 New York sold right-handed pitcher Jouett Meekin to the Boston Beaneaters in a surprise move.

Bright spots in an otherwise dismal season included the batting of center fielder George Van Haltren (.301 and 58 RBI), first baseman Jack Doyle (.299 and 76 RBI) and left fielder Tom O'Brien (.297 and 77 RBI). Right-hander Bill Carrick "led" the pitching staff with a 16-27 record and a 4.65 ERA while tying for the National League lead with 40 complete games. Left-hander Ed Doheny was 14-17 with a 4.51 ERA, and left-hander Cy Seymour went 14-18 with a 3.56 ERA.

Seymour had an unusual game against the Cincinnati Reds at League Park in Cincinnati on May 24. He had two singles and two doubles but issued 13 walks, including the game-winner with the bases loaded in the bottom of the ninth inning as the Giants dropped a 7-6 decision.

1900			
60-78	.435	8th Place (-23)	190,000
		Buck Ewing/ George Davis	

New York owner Andrew C. Freedman celebrated the turn of the century with two more managers, former catcher Buck Ewing (21-41) and shortstop George Davis (39-37), who returned for his second go-around. When the 1900 season came to an end, the Giants were in eighth place with a 60-78 record, 23 games behind the Brooklyn Superbas.

On June 7 the Giants sent wild left-hander Cy Seymour to Worcester after he surrendered 10 hits and 11 walks in a 10-3 win over the St. Louis Perfectos at the Polo Grounds in New York. He had led the National League in walks in 1897, 1898 and 1899.

Right-hander Christy Mathewson, who had a 20-2 record with Norfolk (Va.), made his New York debut July 17 against Brooklyn at Washington Park in Brooklyn. The 19-year-old replaced left-hander Ed Doheny in the fifth inning and hit three batters and walked two as the Superbas rallied for a 13-7 win. Mathewson pitched in six games with an 0-3 record and a 5.08 ERA before being sent back to Norfolk. He was drafted by the Cincinnati Reds after the season but returned to the Giants in a trade for pitcher Amos Rusie on December 15. The deal ranks as perhaps the most lopsided in baseball history as Mathewson would go on to win 373 games, while Rusie did not record another victory.

New York's top pitchers were right-handers Bill Carrick (19-22, 3.53 ERA and N.L.-leading 45 appearances) and Pink Hawley (18-18, 3.53 ERA and league-high 34 complete

games). The leading batters were left fielder Kip Selbach (.337, 29 doubles, 12 triples and 68 RBI); Davis (.319); center fielder George Van Haltren (.315, 30 doubles and 51 RBI); and third baseman Charlie Hickman (.313 and 91 RBI). Van Haltren tied for the top spot in the N.L. with 45 stolen bases.

1901			
52-85	.380	7th Place (-37)	297,650
		George Davis	

The 1901 Giants, under player-manager George Davis, foundered with a 52-85 record that left them in seventh place, 37 games behind the Pittsburgh Pirates.

Nevertheless, there were several highlights. On June 9 New York banged out 31 hits in a 25-13 football-like victory over the Cincinnati Reds at League Park in Cincinnati. Left fielder Kip Selbach led the way with six hits (four singles and two doubles), while right fielder Charlie Hickman and center fielder George Van Haltren both had five hits. On July 15 right-handed pitcher Christy Mathewson fired a no-hitter against the St. Louis Cardinals at Robison Field in St. Louis, winning by the score of 5-0.

Two Giants batted at least .300, Van Haltren (.334 with 65 RBI) and Davis (.301). First baseman John Ganzel drove in 66 runs, while third baseman Sammy Strang stole 40 bases. Mathewson led the way with a 20-17 record and a 2.41 ERA, and right-hander Dummy Taylor, a deaf mute, was 18-27 with a 3.18 ERA. The 27 losses are a franchise record. Taylor tied for the National League lead with 45 appearances.

1902			
48-88	.353	8th Place (-53½)	302,875
		Horace Fogel/Heinie Smith/John McGraw	

No year was more important to the long-term growth and success of the Giants than

1902. But it didn't start out that way. First, New York limped through two more managers, Horace Fogel (18-23), who previously managed the Indianapolis Hoosiers in 1887, and second baseman Heinie Smith (5-27). Fogel considered moving budding star right-handed pitcher Christy Mathewson to first base, and Smith thought of switching him to shortstop. Smith served merely as a figurehead as Fogel continued to direct the team from behind the scenes. From June 23-July 6, the Giants lost a franchise-record 13 consecutive games.

But then owner Andrew C. Freedman made his best decision by luring away John McGraw from the Baltimore Orioles of the two-year old American League to take over as player-manager of the Giants. On July 16—

John McGraw came to New York from the Baltimore Orioles on July 16, 1902, and piloted the Giants to 10 National League pennants and three World Series championships before retiring June 3, 1932. (National Baseball Library and Archive)

with New York owning a 23-50 record—McGraw signed a four-year contract that would pay him $6,500 annually.

Not only did McGraw bring an aggressive, winning attitude, he also brought several key players: pitchers Joe McGinnity and Jack Cronin, catcher Roger Bresnahan, first baseman Dan McGann and outfielder Steve Brodie. McGraw won his first game in New York over the Brooklyn Superbas 4-1 at the Washington Park in Brooklyn on July 23. Although the Giants improved to 25-38 under McGraw, they wound up 48-88 and in last place, 53½ games behind the Pittsburgh Pirates.

On September 9 the Giants got their second big lift when Freedman agreed to sell controlling interest in the franchise to John T. Brush, a wealthy clothing manufacturer in Indianapolis who had owned the Indianapolis Hoosiers from 1887-89 and the Cincinnati Reds from 1891-1902. Brush gave McGraw the complete authority to do whatever it took (and spend as much money as necessary) to build the Giants into a winning team.

Mathewson was New York's leading pitcher with a 14-17 record and a 2.11 ERA while tying for the National League lead with eight shutouts. McGann batted .300 after coming over from Baltimore, while third baseman Billy Lauder collected a team-best 44 RBI.

1903			
84-55	.604	2nd Place (-6½)	579,530
		John McGraw	

In John McGraw's first full season as manager, the Giants made tremendous strides and finished the 1903 season in second place with an 84-55 record, just 6½ games behind the Pittsburgh Pirates.

Right-hander Joe McGinnity was the big story in the month of August as he pitched complete games in both games of three double-headers: August 1 against the Boston Beaneaters, August 8 against the Brooklyn

Superbas and August 31 against the Philadelphia Phillies. The three "daily doubles" set baseball season and career records.

McGinnity and fellow right-hander Christy Mathewson gave New York a quality 1-2 punch. Mathewson was 30-13 with a 2.26 ERA and McGinnity went 31-20 with a 2.43 ERA. McGinnity led the National League in and set modern-day franchise records (since 1900) for games started (48), complete games (44) and innings pitched (434.0), while Mathewson had a modern-day high of 267 strikeouts (tops in the league). McGinnity also paced the N.L. in wins and appearances (55).

They were supported offensively by center fielder/first baseman/catcher Roger Bresnahan, who batted .350 with 30 doubles and 55 RBI; right fielder George Browne, who batted .313; and left fielder Sam Mertes, who drove in a league-leading 104 runs to go with a .280 batting average, 32 doubles (tied for the N.L. lead), 14 triples, seven home runs and 45 stolen bases.

On September 7 Brooklyn engaged in one of the episodes that would represent the tremendous rivalry with the Giants. In the fifth inning of the first game of a double-header at Washington Park in Brooklyn, left fielder Jimmy Sheckard of the Superbas stuck up his bat to interfere with a throw by Giants' catcher Frank Bowerman attempting to throw out third baseman Sammy Strang trying to steal second base. The Giants figured interference would be called and did not go after the ball that had ricocheted up the first base line. Meanwhile, Strang came all the way around to score the tying run. Umpire Tim Hurst did not call interference, leading to an argument from the Giants that resulted in Bowerman being ejected. Justice was belatedly served as New York scored two runs in the eighth inning to win the game 6-4.

Right-hander Red Ames made his major league debut September 14 and held the St. Louis Cardinals hitless for five innings before the game (the second of a double-header) was called because of darkness. New York swept

the twin-bill 8-2 and 5-0 at Robison Field in St. Louis.

McGraw made one of his key trades when he acquired shortstop Bill Dahlen from Brooklyn in exchange for shortstop Charlie Babb and pitcher Jack Cronin on December 12.

1904			
106-47 .693	1st Place (+13)		609,826
	John McGraw		

In dominating fashion, the 1904 Giants rolled to the National League pennant with a sizzling 106-47 record, a whopping 13 games better than the runner-up Chicago Cubs. The 106 victories established a franchise record. But because owner John T. Brush and manager John McGraw regarded the American League as an inferior league, New York refused to play the A.L. champion Boston Pilgrims in the modern World Series that had been instituted a year earlier. The following year the National Commission of baseball adopted Brush's rules for postseason play, which included a best-of-seven format, umpires from both leagues and a revenue-sharing formula for the two teams involved.

From June 17-July 4, the Giants reeled off an 18-game winning streak, capped by a 4-1 and 11-3 double-header sweep of the Philadelphia Phillies at the Polo Grounds

Christy Mathewson established himself as one of baseball's most prolific pitchers during his career with the Giants from 1900-16.

in New York. It tied the 1894 Baltimore Orioles for the longest streak in baseball history and stood until the Giants won 26 in a row during the 1916 season.

Looking for some added depth, the Giants acquired outfielder Mike Donlin from the Cincinnati Reds in exchange for outfielder Moose McCormick and cash on July 3.

Following a 6-1 and 4-3 double-header sweep of the Boston Beaneaters at the Polo Grounds on September 6, jubilant Giants' fans stormed the field and attempted to carry McGraw off the field. But they dropped him, walked over him and left him with a badly sprained ankle.

Right-handed pitchers Christy Mathewson and Joe McGinnity both posted banner seasons. Mathewson finished 33-12 with a 2.03 ERA and an N.L.-high 212 strikeouts. McGinnity went 35-8 with a 1.61 ERA, leading the league in wins, ERA, appearances (51), innings pitched (408.0) and shutouts (9). McGinnity opened the season by winning his first 14 decisions from April 15-June 8, and Mathewson set a franchise record with 16 strikeouts against the St. Louis Cardinals at Robison Field in St. Louis on October 3. Right-hander Dummy Taylor contributed a 21-15 record with a 2.34 ERA, and rookie left-hander Hooks Wiltse set a baseball record by winning his first 12 decisions from May 29-September 1

en route to going 13-3 with a 2.84 ERA.

New York clinched the pennant with a 7-5 victory over the Cincinnati Reds at the Polo Grounds in the first game of a double-header September 22. In the game, 54-year-old Jim O'Rourke, who last played in the majors in 1893, was the Giants' catcher. He went 1-for-4 with a single and a run scored while becoming the oldest individual to play a full game.

First baseman Dan McGann, who set a franchise record with five stolen bases against the Brooklyn Superbas at the Polo Grounds on May 27, was the Giants' leading batter at .286 with 71 RBI, while shortstop Bill Dahlen paced the N.L. with 80 RBI and left fielder Sam Mertes drove in 78 runs. Both players had 47 stolen bases. On October 4 Mertes hit for the cycle against St. Louis at the Polo Grounds. Right fielder George Browne led the league with 99 runs scored.

1905			
105-48	.686	1st Place (+9) John McGraw	552,700

Proving they were not a one-hit wonder, the Giants successfully defended their National League championship in 1905 with a 105-48 record, nine games better than the Pittsburgh Pirates. New York then won a pitching-dominated World Series over the Philadelphia Athletics four games to one.

On May 21 manager John McGraw was involved in the infamous "Hey, Barney" episode in which he accused Pittsburgh owner Barney Dreyfuss of having influence over the N.L. office and its umpires. Dreyfuss responded by issuing a formal complaint to the league office about McGraw, including his offering publicly to wager $10,000 that the Giants would win that day's game. After the N.L. fined McGraw $150 and suspended him for 15 games, some 12,000 Giants' fans signed a petition to have the punishment dropped. In the meantime, Dreyfuss went public with a description of arguments he had engaged in with

McGraw on their betting activities. The league responded by exonerating McGraw and reprimanding Dreyfuss. McGraw ignored the fine and suspension and got away with it.

On the field, right-hander Christy Mathewson authored the second no-hitter of his career against the Chicago Cubs at the West Side Grounds in Chicago on June 13. He out dueled Mordecai "Three Finger" Brown by the score of 1-0 as the Giants parlayed four consecutive singles into a run in the ninth inning.

Five pitchers won at least 15 games for New York: Mathewson (31-9, 1.28 ERA); right-hander Red Ames (22-8, 2.74 ERA); right-hander Joe McGinnity (21-15, 2.87 ERA); right-hander Dummy Taylor (16-9, 2.66 ERA); and left-hander Hooks Wiltse (15-6, 2.47 ERA). Mathewson led the N.L. in wins, ERA, shutouts (8) and strikeouts (206), while McGinnity tied for the top spot with 46 games pitched.

Outfielder Mike Donlin was the team's top batter with a .356 average, 31 doubles, 16 triples, seven home runs and 80 RBI. He topped the N.L. with 124 runs scored. Outfielder Sam Mertes had 108 RBI and 52 stolen bases, while third baseman Art Devlin stole 59 bases to tie for the league lead.

On November 10 McGraw signed a contract to manage the Giants through 1908.

1906			
96-56	.632	2nd Place (-20) John McGraw	402,850

Despite a snappy 96-56 record, the Giants finished as runners-up to the Chicago Cubs by 20 games in 1906. In a microcosm of the campaign, Chicago walloped New York by the score of 19-0 in a game at the West Side Grounds in Chicago on June 7.

On other days, the Giants' pitching fared better. Left-hander Hooks Wiltse struck out seven batters over two innings, including four in the fifth, en route to a 4-1 victory over the

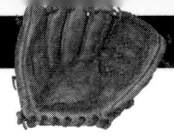

Cincinnati Reds at the Palace of the Fans in Cincinnati on May 15. Right-handers Red Ames and George Ferguson pitched 3-0 and 2-0 shutouts, respectively, in a double-header sweep of the St. Louis Cardinals at the Polo Grounds in New York on October 1.

Right-hander Joe McGinnity was involved in a mighty brawl with Pittsburgh catcher Heinie Peitz at Exposition Park in Pittsburgh on July 24. The two had been going at one another verbally when Peitz began cussing McGinnity in the fourth inning. McGinnity responded by chasing after Peitz, and the two rolled on the ground and exchanged punches. National League president Harry C. Pulliam fined McGinnity $100 and suspended him for 10 games for "attempting to make the ball park a slaughterhouse." Peitz was fined $50 and suspended for five games, and umpire Hank O'Day, formerly a Giants' pitcher in 1889, was fined $50 for not stopping the "disgraceful affair."

On October 5, right-handed Henry Mathewson, younger brother of Christy, made his major league debut against the Boston Beaneaters at the Polo Grounds and issued a franchise modern-day record (since 1900) of 14 walks in a 7-1 loss.

Outfielder Cy Seymour led the Giants with a .320 batting average and four home runs, while third baseman Art Devlin batted at a .299 clip with a team-high totals of 23 doubles, eight triples, 65 RBI and 54 stolen bases. McGinnity topped the pitching staff with a 27-12 record and a 2.25 ERA, pacing the National League in wins and innings pitched (339.2). Christy Mathewson went 22-12 with a 2.97 ERA.

		1907	
82-71	.536	4th Place (-25½)	538,350
		John McGraw	

Despite a quick start, the Giants wound up the 1907 season in fourth place with an 82-71 record, 25½ games behind the Chicago

Cubs. New York opened the year by winning 24 of its first 27 games, including a 17-game winning streak from April 25-May 18.

As usual, right-handed pitcher Christy Mathewson was the team's big winner, going 24-12 with a 2.00 ERA. He topped the National League in wins, shutouts (8—tied) and strikeouts (178). Right-hander Joe McGinnity went 18-18 with a 3.16 ERA. The Giants' leading batters were first baseman Dan McGann with a .298 average and center fielder Cy Seymour with a .294 mark, 25 doubles and 75 RBI. Third baseman Art Devlin had 38 stolen bases. Left fielder Spike Shannon scored a league-best 104 runs.

Catcher Roger Bresnahan made history for being the first player to wear shin guards while catching and a helmet while batting.

Twice, the fans made news. More than 10,000 fans raced onto the field at the Polo Grounds in New York following a 3-2 loss to Chicago on May 21 to protest several calls made against the Giants. Umpires Hank O'Day and Bob Emslie, aided by policemen with drawn revolvers, were able to leave the field unharmed. And on July 12 a fan insisted on keeping a foul ball (before the popular practice was allowed at the Polo Grounds), raising the ire of club secretary Fred Knowles, who announced after the game that in the future anyone who refused to return a foul ball would be arrested.

On August 29 the Giants purchased first baseman Fred Merkle from Tecumseh of the Southern Michigan League for $2,500.

		1908	
98-56	.636	T2nd Place (-1)	910,000
		John McGraw	

The 1908 season ranks as one of the most disappointing in New York history. On September 19 the Giants held a 3½ game lead over the Chicago Cubs with just over two weeks to play. But two surprising events down the stretch left the Giants and Cubs tied for first

place at the end of the regular season and forced a one-game playoff.

First was the historic "Merkle Incident." On September 23 at the Polo Grounds in New York, the Giants and Chicago were tied 1-apiece in the bottom of the ninth inning, and the Giants had left fielder Moose McCormick on third base and first baseman Fred Merkle on first. Shortstop Al Bridwell singled off Cubs' pitched Jack Pfiester that apparently scored McCormick with the winning run. Merkle, meanwhile, ran off the field without touching second base—a typical action of the day—but Chicago second baseman Johnny Evers supposedly retrieved the ball and declared that Merkle should be forced out and McCormick's run should not count. Base umpire Bob Emslie did not call Merkle out, but home plate umpire Hank O'Day did that evening in his hotel room. N.L. president Harry C. Pulliam concurred, and the game was ruled a 1-1 tie.

Then on September 29 after right-hander Christy Mathewson won the first game of a double-header against the Philadelphia Phillies at the Polo Grounds by the score of 6-2, the Giants lost the second game 7-0 to relative unknown Philadelphia rookie pitcher Harry Coveleski, who became known as the "Giant Killer" for his surprise victory.

Chicago went on to win the one-game playoff 4-2 at the Polo Grounds on October 8 to capture the pennant. Merkle was blamed for the Giants' misfortune and forever was unfairly saddled with the nickname "Bonehead." New York wound up with a 98-56 record and tied the Pittsburgh Pirates for second place.

Mathewson went 37-11 with a 1.43 ERA, setting modern-day franchise records (since 1900) for wins and shutouts (11) and leading the National League in both categories as well as ERA, appearances (56), innings pitched (390.2), complete games (34) and strikeouts (259). Left-hander Hooks Wiltse, who pitched a 10-inning no-hitter against Philadelphia at the Polo Grounds on July 4, wound up 23-14 with a 2.24 ERA.

New York's leading batter was right

fielder Mike Donlin, who returned to the team after sitting out the 1907 season to work in vaudeville and compiled a .334 average with 26 doubles, 13 triples, six home runs, 106 RBI and 30 stolen bases. Second baseman Larry Doyle batted .308, center fielder Cy Seymour drove in 92 runs and first baseman Fred Tenney topped the N.L. with 101 runs scored.

On September 18 the Giants swept the Pirates in a double-header 7-0 and 12-7 before some 35,000 fans at the Polo Grounds, the largest crowd in baseball history up to that point. New York drew a record 910,000 fans for the season.

Left-hander Rube Marquard, purchased from Indianapolis of the American Association for a record sum of $11,000, made his major league debut September 25 against the Cincinnati Reds at the Polo Grounds and lost 7-1 to earn the nickname the "$11,000 Lemon." He had sweeter days ahead.

The Giants traded catcher Roger Bresnahan to the St. Louis Cardinals on December 13 in exchange for outfielder Red Murray, pitcher Bugs Raymond and catcher Admiral Schlei.

1909			
92-61	.601	3rd Place (-18½)	783,700
	John McGraw		

During a season in which the Giants had an impressive 92-61 record but finished in third place, 18½ games behind the Pittsburgh Pirates, there were several notable individual performances.

On April 15 right-hander Red Ames pitched a perfect game against the Brooklyn Dodgers at the Polo Grounds in New York for 9.1 innings before losing the game 3-0 in 13 innings and settling for a four-hitter. Outfielder Bill O'Hara stole second, third and home in the eighth inning of a 3-0 victory over the St. Louis Cardinals at Robison Field in St. Louis on August 8. On August 18 player-coach Arlie Latham, 49 years old, stole second against the

On August 18, 1909, at the age of 49, player-coach Arlie Latham became the oldest major leaguer to steal a base against the Philadelphia Phillies at the Baker Bowl in Philadelphia.

Philadelphia Phillies at the Baker Bowl in Philadelphia, the oldest major leaguer ever to steal a base. Right-hander Christy Mathewson out dueled Mordecai "Three Finger" Brown 1-0 at the West Side Grounds in Chicago on September 16 with president William Howard Taft in attendance.

Mathewson went on to post a 25-6 record with a franchise-record and National League-low 1.14 ERA. Left-hander Hooks Wiltse was 20-11 with a 2.00 ERA, and right-hander Bugs Raymond went 18-12 with a 2.47 ERA. Raymond, however, was a heavy drinker whose favorite practice was trading baseballs for drinks at bars near the ballpark. He pitched for the Giants in 1910 and 1911 before succumbing to his alcohol problem September 7,

1912, at the age of 30. Offensively, second baseman Larry Doyle batted .302 with 27 doubles, while right fielder Red Murray had 12 triples, a league-high seven home runs, 91 RBI and 48 stolen bases.

1910			
91-63	.591	2nd Place (-13)	511,785
		John McGraw	

Another successful season was not good enough for the Giants in 1910. They went 91-63 but were runners-up to the Chicago Cubs by 13 games.

On May 7 New York signed Wee Willie Keeler of "Hit 'em where they ain't" fame after he was released by the New York Highlanders of the American League. Keeler and Giants' manager John McGraw had been teammates with the Baltimore Orioles from 1894-98. Keeler, who broke in with the Giants in 1892 and 1893, was 3-for-10 at the plate in his final go-around in the major leagues.

Outfielder Fred Snodgrass was the Giants' leading batter at .321, followed by left fielder Josh Devore at .304. Right fielder Red Murray totaled 87 RBI and 57 stolen bases, while first baseman Fred Merkle contributed a .292 batting average, 35 doubles, 14 triples and 70 RBI. No fewer than five pitchers won in double figures: right-hander Christy Mathewson (27-9, 1.89 ERA); right-hander Doc Crandall (17-4, 2.56 ERA); left-hander Hooks Wiltse (14-12, 2.72 ERA); right-hander Louis Drucke (12-10, 2.47 ERA); and right-hander Red Ames (12-11, 2.22 ERA). Mathewson was the National League's top winner and tied for the top spot with 27 complete games.

Following the season, the Giants and Highlanders, who finished second in the A.L. with an 88-63 record, took part in an exhibition World Series. The Giants won the series four games to two behind the pitching of Mathewson, who had three wins and a save. Each of the winning players received $1,100.

On December 13 Dan McGann, the Gi-

Bugs Raymond pitched for the Giants from 1909-11, going 18-12 with a 2.47 ERA during the 1909 season. A heavy drinker whose favorite practice was trading baseballs for drinks at bars near the ballpark, he succumbed to his alcohol problem September 7, 1912, at the age of 30.

ants' first baseman from 1902-07, shot himself in a Louisville hotel.

		1911	
99-54	.647	1st Place (+7½)	675,000
		John McGraw	

New York's National League championship season of 1911 did not start off particularly well. In the early morning hours of April 14, a fire destroyed the Polo Grounds. As a re-

sult, the Giants used the New York Highlanders' home grounds, Hilltop Park, at 168th Street and Broadway as their temporary residence until they could return to the partially rebuilt Polo Grounds on June 28. Right-hander Christy Mathewson downed the Boston Beaneaters 3-1 in the Giants' first game back home.

While the Polo Grounds was under construction, on May 3 Giants' owner John T. Brush obtained a long-term lease ("for the life of the National League") from Harriet G. Coogan, owner of the Polo Grounds site commonly referred to as Coogan's Bluff.

In one of the wildest games in franchise history, New York scored 13 runs in the bottom of the first inning—including a major league record of 10 before the first out was recorded—en route to a 19-5 blitzing of the St. Louis Cardinals at Hilltop Park on May 13. First baseman Fred Merkle drove in six runs in the inning with a home run and a triple. Mathewson started the game but in order to be saved for another day was replaced by left-hander Rube Marquard, who set a major league record with 14 strikeouts as a reliever over the final eight innings.

The Giants went on to capture the N.L. pennant with a 99-54 record, 7½ games ahead of the Chicago Cubs. They set a major league record with 347 stole bases, led by left fielder Josh Devore (61) and center fielder Fred Snodgrass (51). New York lost the World Series to the Philadelphia Athletics four games to two in a rematch of the 1905 championship.

Mathewson finished the year with a 26-13 record and a league-leading 1.99 ERA, while Marquard went 24-7 with a 2.50 ERA and an N.L.-high 237 strikeouts. Second baseman Larry Doyle batted .310 with 25 doubles, 25 triples (tops in the circuit), 13 home runs and 77 RBI. Catcher Chief Meyers had a .332 average and first baseman Fred Merkle drove in 84 runs.

The 1911 season marked the arrival of Charlie "Victory" Faust, who showed up when the Giants were in St. Louis to play the Cardi-

nals early in the season. He informed manager John McGraw that a fortune-teller had told him if he pitched for the Giants they would win the pennant. The right-handed Faust remained with the team for the balance of the season, was paid by McGraw and appeared in two meaningless games while the fortune-teller's prediction came true.

Following the campaign, the Giants participated in a Barnstorming trip to Cuba. On November 30 after the final game, manager John McGraw and umpire Cy Rigler became involved in an alcohol-induced fight with Cuban fans, and the two were arrested.

1912			
103-48	.682	1st Place (+10)	638,000
		John McGraw	

The Giants' dynasty was well in the making as they rolled to their second straight National League pennant with a 103-48 record, 10 games better than the Pittsburgh Pirates. But New York again lost in the World Series, this time to the Boston Red Sox four games to three.

On April 19 the Giants formally dedicated the enlarged and redesigned Polo Grounds (a double-decked, concrete and steel-supported grandstand with a seating capacity of 34,000) and defeated the Brooklyn Dodgers by the score of 6-2.

Catcher Chief Meyers, outfielder Josh Devore and pitcher Jeff Tesreau provided three individual highlights. Meyers hit for the cycle against the Chicago Cubs at the Polo Grounds on June 10, Devore equalled the franchise record with five stole bases (including second and third twice in the ninth inning) against the Boston Beaneaters at the South End Grounds in Boston on June 20 and Tesreau fired a 3-0 no-hitter against the Philadelphia Phillies in the first game of a double-header at the Baker Bowl in Philadelphia on September 6.

In between, the Giants assembled a 16-game winning streak from June 19-July 3, and left-hander Rube Marquard tied the franchise record (set by Tim Keefe in 1888) with 19 straight victories at the start of the season from April 11-July 3. Under present-day scoring rules, Marquard would have had 20 consecutive wins because Tesreau was credited with a victory April 20 when the Giants rallied after Marquard came into the game as a reliever.

On June 20 right-hander Ernie Shore made his major league debut in the bottom of the ninth inning at Boston. He came into the game with New York leading 21-2 and proceeded to give up eight hits and 10 runs (though just three earned). Shore did not pitch again for New York and achieved his greatest acclaim with the Boston Red Sox on June 23, 1917, when he relieved left-hander Babe Ruth (ejected for arguing after walking the first batter), saw the runner thrown out attempting to steal and proceeded to retire the next 26 batters.

Second baseman Larry Doyle received the Chalmers Award as the N.L. Most Valuable Player after batting .330 with 33 doubles, eight triples, 10 home runs, 90 RBI and 36 stolen bases. Meyers batted at a .358 clip, while right fielder Red Murray had 92 RBI and left fielder Fred Snodgrass came up with 43 stolen bases. Marquard wound up with a 26-11 record (tying for the N.L. lead in wins) and a 2.57 ERA, right-hander Christy Mathewson went 23-12 with a 2.12 ERA and topped the league in innings pitched (310.0). Tesreau had an impressive rookie season at 17-7 with a league-best 1.96 ERA.

Following the 1912 World Series, Brush headed by train to Southern California and its warm weather. On November 26, he passed away in his private car, the Oceanic, in Louisiana, Missouri, at the age of 67. The Giants became the property of Brush's wife, Elsie, and their daughters, Eleanor Brush Hempstead and Natalie Brush. Harry N. Hempstead, husband of Eleanor and a longtime director of the Giants, took over day-to-day operations of the team.

Prominent Giants from the early 20th century included (left to right): first baseman Fred Merkle, second baseman Larry Doyle, pitcher Christy Mathewson, manager John McGraw and outfielder Fred Snodgrass.

1913			
101-51 .664	1st Place (+12½)	630,000	
	John McGraw		

New York made it 3-for-3 in National League pennants but the same in lost World Series. The Giants captured the league flag with a 101-51 record, 12½ games ahead of the Philadelphia Phillies, then were beaten in postseason play by the Philadelphia Athletics four games to one.

On May 22 New York acquired right-handed pitcher Art Fromme from the Cincinnati Reds in exchange for pitcher Red Ames, outfielder Josh Devore and infielder Heinie Groh.

The Giants featured three 20-game winners on the mound: right-hander Christy Mathewson (25-11, N.L.-best 2.06 ERA); left-hander Rube Marquard (23-10, 2.50 ERA) and right-hander Jeff Tesreau (22-13, 2.17 ERA). Along the way, Mathewson pitched a remarkable 68 innings without issuing a walk. The streak ended July 18 when Mathewson walked St. Louis Cardinals' first baseman Ed Konetchy in the eighth inning of a game at the Polo Grounds in New York.

Only one player batted better than .300 (catcher Chief Meyers at .312). Second baseman Larry Doyle topped the team with 75 RBI, while first baseman Fred Merkle totaled 30 doubles and 13 triples, and left fielder George Burns stole 40 bases.

Following the season, the Giants and Chicago White Sox embarked on a 44-game world tour to Japan, China, the Philippines, Australia, Ceylon, Egypt, Italy, France and England. The trip started in October 18 and ran into February.

A key element to the on-going rivalry with the Brooklyn Dodgers transpired October 30 when Giants' manager John McGraw let go pitching coach and longtime friend Wilbert Robinson after the pair's relationship soured, and Robinson was hired as Brooklyn's manager.

1914			
84-70	.545	2nd Place (-10½)	364,313
		John McGraw	

On July 4, 1914, the Giants were in first place and seeking to win their fourth straight National League pennant. The Boston Braves were nestled in last place, 15 games off the pace. But Boston went 50-14 in August, September and October to win the league title and become known as the "Miracle Braves." New York finished as runners-up, 10½ games out, with an 84-70 record.

Right-hander Jeff Tesreau just missed pitching the second no-hitter of his career when he yielded a two-out, ninth-inning single to Pittsburgh Pirates' center fielder Joe Kelly at Forbes Field in Pittsburgh on May 16. Tesreau was forced to settle for a one-hitter and a 2-0 victory. The Giants and Pirates later hooked up in a 21-inning game won by New York 3-1 in Pittsburgh on July 17. New York left-hander Rube Marquard and Pittsburgh right-hander Babe Adams both worked all 21 innings.

Left fielder George Burns topped the Giants with a .303 batting average, 35 doubles, 10 triples and a modern-day franchise record (since 1900) of 62 stolen bases. He paced the N.L. in stolen bases and runs scored (100). First baseman Fred Merkle hit seven home runs, and shortstop Art Fletcher had 79 RBI.

Tesreau led the pitching staff with a 26-10 record, 2.37 ERA and eight shutouts (tops in the league), while right-hander Christy Mathewson went 24-13 with a 3.00 ERA.

1915			
69-83	.454	8th Place (-21)	391,850
		John McGraw	

The 1915 season was marked by transition for the Giants, who finished in last place for the only time in John McGraw's 31-year tenure as manager with a 69-83 record, 21 games behind the champion Philadelphia Phillies but only 3½ games behind the fourth-place Chicago Cubs.

New York bid farewell to two stalwarts of their pennant-winning clubs, outfielder Fred Snodgrass was released August 19 and left-handed pitcher Rube Marquard was released August 26. In between, on August 20, the Giants purchased first baseman George Kelly from the Victoria (British Columbia) team. Kelly, though, would not begin to make major contributions to the Giants for several years.

Before Marquard was let go he authored a 2-0 no-hitter against the Brooklyn Dodgers at the Polo Grounds in New York on April 15. Ironically, Marquard had signed the Brooklyn Tip-Tops of the second-year Federal League during the offseason but returned to the Giants. Following his release, he signed with the Dodgers and helped them win the National League pennant in 1916.

Right-hander Christy Mathewson, at age 36, slipped to an 8-14 record with a 3.58 ERA. New York's top pitchers were right-handers Jeff Tesreau (19-16, 2.29 ERA) and Sailor Stroud (11-9, 2.79 ERA).

Second baseman Larry Doyle enjoyed another solid offensive season by batting an N.L.-leading .320 with 40 doubles (also tops in the league), 10 triples, four home runs and 70 RBI. Shortstop Art Fletcher drove in 74 runs, while left fielder George Burns had 27 stolen bases.

On September 1 outfielder Jim Thorpe, just recalled from Harrisburg (Pennsylvania) for his third go-around with the Giants, went 3-for-3 in a 6-5 win over Philadelphia at the Polo Grounds. The outstanding Indian athlete and 1912 Olympic Games star could not learn

to hit the curve ball and did not make it as a regular.

	1916		
86-66	.566	4th Place (-7)	552,056
	John McGraw		

On December 22, 1915, Organized Baseball and the Federal League signed a peace treaty that ended their two-year war and disposed of the fledgling circuit. The Giants took advantage of the open market of players, signing pitcher Fred Anderson from the Buffalo Buffeds; outfielder Benny Kauff from the Brooklyn Tip-Tops; and third baseman Bill McKechnie, catcher Bill Rariden and outfielder Edd Roush from the Newark Peppers.

Early on it looked as though New York would be in for a repeat of its cellar-dwelling 1915 season. The Giants were 2-13 and once again saddled in last place May 9 before going on a nifty 17-game winning streak (all on the road) that left them 19-13 and just 1½ games behind the Pittsburgh Pirates on May 29. The 17-game road winning streak is tied for the longest in baseball history with the 1984 Detroit Tigers.

With his team in the thick of a pennant race, manager John McGraw made several trades as the season progressed. First, he dealt 37-year-old right-hander Christy Mathewson, McKechnie and Roush

Pol Perritt pitched two complete-game victories over the Philadelphia Phillies on September 9, 1916, at the Polo Grounds, winning by the scores of 3-1 and 3-0.

to the Cincinnati Reds in exchange for third baseman Buck Herzog and outfielder Red Killefer on July 20. This deal was made largely so Mathewson, McGraw's good friend, could take over as player-manager of the Reds, but McGraw also wanted Herzog, traded from the Giants twice before, to steady his erratic club. Next, McGraw traded first baseman Fred Merkle to the Brooklyn Dodgers for catcher Lew McCarty on August 20. Finally, McGraw sent second baseman Larry Doyle, infielder Herb Hunter and outfielder Merwin Jacobson to the Chicago Cubs for infielder Mickey Doolan and third baseman Heinie Zimmerman on August 28. The Giants also acquired left-handed pitcher Slim Sallee from the St. Louis Cardinals for $10,000 on July 23.

Coincidence or not, New York caught fire and set a major league record with a 26-game winning streak (all at home) from September 7-30. But the Giants could not catch Brooklyn for the National League championship. The Giants finished 86-66 for fourth place, seven games behind the Dodgers.

Twice during the year New York orchestrated double-header shutout victories, July 31 against Pittsburgh (Sallee 7-0 and right-hander Jeff Tesreau 7-0) at the Polo Grounds in New York and September 28 against the Boston Braves (Tesreau 2-0 and left-hander Ferdie Schupp 6-0) at the Polo Grounds. In addition, right-hander Pol Perritt pitched two complete-game victories over the Philadelphia Phillies on

September 9 at the Polo Grounds, winning by the scores of 3-1 and 3-0.

Perritt went on to post an 18-11 record with a 2.62 ERA, while left-hander Rube Benton was 16-8 with a 2.87 ERA. Right fielder Dave Robertson was the Giants' leading batter at .307 with 12 home runs (tied for the National League top spot) and 69 RBI, and Kauff, who was regarded as the "Ty Cobb of the Federal League," topped the team with 15 triples, 74 RBI and 40 stolen bases from center field. Left fielder George Burns led the league with 105 runs scored.

1917			
98-56	.636	1st Place (+10)	500,264
		John McGraw	

Manager John McGraw signed a five-year contract with the Giants for $40,000 per year plus bonuses March 25, making him the highest paid individual in the game. Then the Giants went out and won their fourth National League pennant in seven years and their sixth in McGraw's 16 years at the helm with a 98-56 record, 10 games better than the Philadelphia Phillies. But New York could not overcome its World Series jinx, dropping its fourth straight postseason series to the Chicago White Sox four games to two.

Five pitchers won at least 13 games for the Giants: left-hander Ferdie Schupp (21-7, 1.95 ERA); left-hander Slim Sallee (18-7, 2.17 ERA); right-hander Pol Perritt (17-7, 1.88 ERA); left-hander Rube Benton (15-9, 2.72 ERA); and right-hander Jeff Tesreau (13-8, 3.09 ERA). Sallee won 10 straight games from June 30-August 16. Right-hander Fred Anderson led the league with a 1.44 ERA despite having just an 8-8 record.

Third baseman Heinie Zimmerman collected an N.L.-best 102 RBI and batted at a .297 clip, while center fielder Benny Kauff and left fielder George Burns batted .308 and .302, respectively. Kauff added 68 RBI, and Burns led the league with 103 runs scored to go with 40

Outfielder Dave Robertson tied for the National League home run lead in both 1916 and 1917.

stolen bases. Right fielder Dave Robertson clubbed 12 home runs to tie for the league lead for the second straight season.

On September 25 New York wrapped up the pennant with a 2-1 win over the St. Louis Cardinals in the first game of a double-header at Robison Field in St. Louis, and outfielder Ross Youngs made his major league debut in the second game by going 0-for-4.

Of course, the season would not be complete without controversy and confrontation. McGraw was fined $150 and suspended for two weeks after punching umpire Bill Byron in the face following a 2-1 loss to the Cincinnati Reds at Crosley Field in Cincinnati on June 8. Giants' shortstop Art Fletcher and Brooklyn Dodgers' right fielder Casey Stengel brawled in the second game of a double-header at the Polo Grounds in New York on August 14. And

Ferdie Schupp posted a 21-7 record with a 1.95 ERA to lead the 1917 pennant-winning Giants.

Art Fletcher, a shortstop for the Giants from 1909-20, played in four World Series (1911, 1912, 1913 and 1917).

New York suspended second baseman and team captain Buck Herzog on September 18 for refusing to accompany the squad on a road trip. Herzog returned a few days later without explanation but was traded by the Giants for the third time to the Boston Braves in exchange for right-hander Jesse Barnes and second baseman Larry Doyle on January 8, 1918.

1918			
71-53	.573	2nd Place (-10½)	256,618
	John McGraw		

The 1918 Giants could not defend their National League championship, finishing in second place with a 71-53 record, 10½ games behind the Chicago Cubs.

Center fielder Benny Kauff topped New York with a .315 batting average, while right fielder Ross Youngs batted .302. Third baseman Heinie Zimmerman totaled 56 RBI, and left fielder George Burns had 22 doubles, 51 RBI and 40 stolen bases. Anchoring the pitching staff were right-handers Pol Perritt (18-13, 2.74 ERA) and Red Causey (11-6, 2.79 ERA).

On July 25 New York purchased right-handed pitcher Fred Toney from the Cincinnati Reds, and after posting a 6-2 record with a 1.69 ERA in 11 games he was sentenced to four months in jail December 31 after pleading guilty to violating the Mann Act which prohibited the interstate transportation of women for immoral purposes.

Tragedy struck the Giants on October 5 when infielder Eddie Grant was killed while leading his infantry unit in the Argonne Forest near Verdun, France. Grant was the first major leaguer killed in World War I, and a memorial was erected in center field of the Polo Grounds.

On October 5, 1918, infielder Eddie Grant was killed while leading his infantry unit in the Argonne Forest near Verdun, France. He was the first major leaguer killed in World War I, and a memorial was erected in center field of the Polo Grounds.

		1919	
87-53	.621	**2nd Place (-9)**	708,857
		John McGraw	

On the way to a second-place finish with an 87-53 record, nine games behind the Cincinnati Reds, the Giants made several headlines during the 1919 season.

First, the franchise was sold by Harry N. Hempstead on January 14 to a group headed by New York stockbroker Charles A. Stoneham, Giants' manager John McGraw and New York City magistrate Francis X. McQuade. Stoneham was named president, McGraw vice president (while remaining manager) and McQuade treasurer.

On March 7 former star right-hander Christy Mathewson, who had been traded in order to become manager of the Cincinnati Reds in 1916 and subsequently served in World War I, was brought back to the Giants as pitching coach and heir apparent to McGraw as manager. The latter never materialized.

Sunday baseball was legalized in New York, and the Giants played their game on the Sabbath on May 4, a 4-3 loss to the Philadelphia Phillies at the Polo Grounds.

Over the course of the season, the Giants acquired several players who would prove to be key contributors to their dynasty from 1921-24. Infielder Frankie Frisch was signed out of Fordham College and made his major league debut June 17; catcher Frank Snyder was acquired from St. Louis in exchange for left-hander Ferdie Schupp on July 16; right-hander Phil Douglas was acquired from the Chicago Cubs for outfielder Dave Robertson on July 25; and left-hander Art Nehf was acquired from the Boston Braves for right-handers Red Causey, Johnny Jones and Joe Oeschger, catcher Mickey O'Neil and $55,000 on August 15.

In September first baseman Hal Chase and third baseman Heinie Zimmerman failed to play in a number of games and were sent home by McGraw without public explanation. A year later, during the investigation of the Chicago Black Sox scandal from the 1919 World Series, McGraw testified that he had dismissed Chase and Zimmerman for throwing games and for attempting (unsuccessfully) to get pitcher Rube Benton, center fielder Benny Kauff and pitcher Fred Toney to do so, as well.

Several Giants enjoyed successful campaigns on the field. Right fielder Ross Youngs batted .311 with a National League-leading 31 doubles, left fielder George Burns batted at a .303 clip with 30 doubles and a league-best 40 stolen bases and Kauff hit 10 home runs with 67 RBI. Burns also scored an N.L.-high 86 runs. Right-hander Jesse Barnes finished 25-9 to top the N.L. in wins with a 2.40 ERA, including a 3-1 one-hitter against the Philadelphia Phillies in the first game of a double-header at the Baker Bowl in Philadel-

Third baseman Heinie Zimmerman, who led the National League with 102 RBI in 1917, was dismissed from the Giants (along with first baseman Hal Chase) by manager John McGraw in September of 1919 for throwing games.

phia on July 4. Benton went 17-11 with a 2.63 ERA, and Toney was 13-6 with a 1.84 ERA.

On September 28 the Giants downed Philadelphia 6-1 at the Polo Grounds in 51 minutes, the fastest nine-inning game in major league history.

1920			
86-68	.558	2nd Place (-7)	929,609
		John McGraw	

In 1920 New York was still a year away from its string of four straight National League pennants and finished in second place with an 86-68 record, seven games behind the crosstown rival Brooklyn Dodgers.

The season was highlighted by some lofty offense. On May 11 right fielder Ross Youngs legged out three triples (one shy of the major league record) against the Cincinnati Reds at Crosley Field in Cincinnati. The Giants had five triples as a team but lost the game 9-4. Shortstop Dave Bancroft, who was acquired from the Philadelphia Phillies in exchange for shortstop Art Fletcher, right-handed pitcher Bill Hubbell and a reported $100,000 on June 8, collected six singles in six at-bats against his former teammates at the Baker Bowl in Philadelphia on June 28. And left fielder George Burns hit for the cycle and added a double against the Pittsburgh Pirates at the Polo Grounds in New York on September 17.

Left-hander Rube Benton pitched a remarkable 17-inning shutout against the Pirates at Forbes Field on July 16. New York won the game 7-0 with an offensive explosion in the final frame that featured eight hits, including three consecutive triples by second baseman Frankie Frisch (with the bases loaded), first baseman George Kelly and center fielder Lee King.

Youngs topped the team with a .355 batting average and had 78 RBI. Kelly stroked 11 home runs and had 94 RBI to tie for the league lead, while Frisch totaled 34 stolen bases. Left fielder George Burns led the N.L. with 115 runs scored.

Three pitchers won 20 or more games: right-hander Fred Toney (21-11, 2.65 ERA); left-hander Art Nehf (21-12, 3.08 ERA); and right-hander Jesse Barnes (20-15, 2.64 ERA). Right-hander Phil Douglas contributed a 14-10 record with a 2.71 ERA.

Manager John McGraw received his fair share of headlines. He was suspended by N.L. president John Heydler for five games after engaging in a game-long argument with umpires Bill Klem and Charlie Moran against the Chicago Cubs at Cubs Park on May 19 (an 8-6, 12-inning New York win), and he reportedly injured two visitors to his New York City apartment in separate incidents on August 8 and September 18.

Rube Benton pitched a remarkable 17-inning shutout against the Pittsburgh Pirates at Forbes Field in Pittsburgh on July 16, 1920.

1921			
94-59	.614	1st Place (+4)	973,477
		John McGraw	

A late-season charge propelled the 1921 Giants to the first of four straight National League pennants with a 94-59 record, four games better than the Pittsburgh Pirates. New York went on to snap its World Series losing streak at four (1911, 1912, 1913 and 1917) by defeating the cross-town rival Yankees five games to three. It was the first of seven postseason series between the two foes. From 1919-21 the World Series was played under a best-of-eight format.

On August 24 the Giants trailed the front-running Pirates by 7½ games as the two clubs opened a five-game series at the Polo Grounds in New York. The Giants won all five games (10-2, 7-0, 5-2, 2-1 and 3-1) to cut the deficit to 2½ games and gain momentum. They took over first place September 11 with an 11-3 victory over the Brooklyn Dodgers at Ebbets Field in Brooklyn.

Two keys to the turnabout in New York's fortune were the acquisitions of second baseman Johnny Rawlings and outfielder Irish Meusel in separate trades with the Philadelphia Phillies. The Giants got Rawlings and outfielder Casey Stengel in exchange for outfielder Lee King, third baseman Goldie Rapp and infielder Lance Richbourg on June 30 and obtained Meusel for catcher Butch Henline, outfielder Curt Walker, pitcher Jesse Winters and $30,000 on July 25.

Third baseman Frankie Frisch paced the Giants with a .341 batting average and 49 stolen bases (tops in the N.L.), right fielder Ross Youngs batted at a .327 clip and first baseman George Kelly blasted 23 home runs to lead the league. Kelly, Youngs and Frisch became the second trio in franchise history to collect 100 or more RBI each with 122, 102 and 100, respectively. Shortstop Dave Bancroft hit for the cycle against Philadelphia in the first game of a double-header at the Polo Grounds on June 1 en route to a .318 batting average for season.

Meanwhile, the New York Yankees of the American League, who had shared the Polo Grounds with the Giants since 1913, were becoming the more popular tenants thanks in large part to the acquisition of the legendary Babe Ruth from the Boston Red Sox. On May 14 the Giants informed the Yankees that their lease would not be renewed after the 1920 season, then rescinded the eviction order a week later. But the Yankees began searching for a new home ballpark anyway and moved into Yankee Stadium across the Harlem River in the Bronx in 1923.

On October 29 the Giants signed Hughie Jennings as a coach. Jennings and manager John McGraw had been teammates with the Baltimore Orioles from 1893-98.

In 1921 first baseman George Kelly topped the National League with 23 home runs to go with a .308 batting average and 122 RBI.

Left-hander Art Nehf posted a 20-10 record with a 3.63 ERA and was one of four Giants' pitchers to win at least 15 games, along with right-hander Fred Toney (18-11, 3.61 ERA); right-hander Jesse Barnes (15-9, 3.10 ERA); and right-hander Phil Douglas (15-10, 4.22 ERA and a league-best three shutouts).

Not one to rest on his laurels, manager John McGraw acquired third baseman Heinie Groh from the Cincinnati Reds in exchange for outfielder George Burns, catcher Mike Gonzalez and $100,000 on December 7.

		1922	
93-61	.604	1st Place (+7)	945,809
		John McGraw	

Manager John McGraw signed a five-year contract to remain with the Giants on January 20 and then went out and piloted his team to its second straight National League pennant with a 93-61 record, seven games better than the Cincinnati Reds. The frosting on the cake was a second straight World Series championship over the American League champion New York Yankees by a count of four games to none with one tie.

Early in the season, the Giants pulled off three of baseball's greatest achievements nine days apart. On April 29 first baseman George Kelly hit two inside the park home runs and right fielder Ross Youngs hit for the cycle against the Boston Braves at Braves Field. Then on May 7 right-hander Jesse Barnes spun a 6-0 near-perfect no-hitter against the Philadelphia Phillies at the Polo Grounds in New York. He faced the minimum of 27 batters, allowing only a leadoff fifth-inning walk to Philadelphia center fielder Cy Williams and then seeing him get erased one out later on a double play.

New York bolstered its pitching staff with the acquisition of right-hander Hugh McQuillan from Boston in exchange for right-handers Larry Benton and Fred Toney and $100,000 on July 30. Toney refused to report and remained with the Giants.

Future standout shortstop Travis Jackson made his debut September 27 against Philadelphia at the Polo Grounds.

In one of the truly great misfortunes in franchise history, right-handed pitcher Phil Douglas was banned from baseball for life by commissioner Kenesaw Landis after receiving a tongue-lashing from manager John McGraw on August 17, drinking heavily and writing a letter to St. Louis Cardinals' catcher Les Mann suggesting he would "go fishing" for the balance of the season if the price was right and help St. Louis win the pennant. Mann turned the letter over to Cardinals' manager Branch Rickey, who informed McGraw and Landis. The misfortune of the story surrounds the fact that when Douglas sobered up he asked Mann to destroy the letter, but it was too late.

Left-hander Art Nehf went 19-13 with a 3.29 ERA, while right-hander Rosy Ryan finished 17-12 with a 3.01 ERA and Barnes went

Pitcher Phil Douglas was banned from baseball for life by commissioner Kenesaw Landis in 1922. Douglas was 11-4 with a National League-leading 2.63 ERA prior to his dismissal.

was completely enclosed by stands with the construction of covered, double-decked grandstands extending into the outfield. The seating capacity now reached its maximum of 55,987, with only a section of wooden bleachers for some 4,600 spectators being uncovered.

By this time, the Giants were well on their way to establishing their dynasty. They won their third National League pennant in as many years with a 95-58 record, $4\frac{1}{2}$ games better than the Cincinnati Reds. But in their third consecutive World Series against the New York Yankees, the Giants were beaten four games to two.

On June 1 New York became the first team in the 20th century to score in every inning en route to a 22-8 drubbing of the Philadelphia Phillies at the Baker Bowl in Philadelphia. Three Giants collected five hits apiece: third baseman Heinie Groh, center fielder Jimmy

13-8 with a 3.51 ERA. Douglas was 11-4 with a league-leading 2.63 ERA prior to his dismissal.

Seven of the Giants' eight regulars batted better than .300: center fielder Casey Stengel (.368), catcher Frank Snyder (.343), left fielder Irish Meusel (.331), Youngs (.331), Kelly (.328), second baseman Frankie Frisch (.327) and shortstop Dave Bancroft (.321). Kelly had 17 home runs and 107 RBI, and Meusel contributed 16 homers and 132 RBI. Frisch stole 31 bases.

1923			
95-58	.621	1st Place (+4½)	820,780
		John McGraw	

The Polo Grounds underwent its final major expansion in 1923 when the playing field

Casey Stengel was an outfielder for the Giants from 1921-23 before going on to a Hall of Fame managerial career with the New York Yankees.

O'Connell and right fielder Ross Youngs. O'Connell had a single, three doubles and a home run. New York totaled 23 hits as a team.

Shortstop Travis Jackson drove in eight runs with two singles, a double and a home run against the Cincinnati Reds at Crosley Field in Cincinnati on August 4, and first baseman George Kelly socked three consecutive home runs while going 5-for-5 against the Chicago Cubs at Cubs Park on September 17.

On September 30 future standout first baseman and manager Bill Terry played his first major league game and was 1-for-3 against the Boston Braves at the Polo Grounds.

For the second time in three years, three Giants had 100-plus RBI: left fielder Irish Meusel (N.L.-leading 125), second baseman Frankie Frisch (111) and Kelly (103). The trio belted 19, 12 and 16 home runs, respectively.

Rosy Ryan led the 1923 National League pennant-winning Giants with a 16-5 record and a 3.49 ERA and tied teammate Claude Jonnard for the league lead with 45 appearances.

Frisch posted team highs of a .348 batting average and 29 stolen bases, while outfielder Ross Youngs batted at a .336 clip and paced the league with 121 runs scored.

Right-hander Rosy Ryan compiled a 16-5 record with a 3.49 ERA, right-hander Jack Scott was 16-7 with a 3.89 ERA and right-hander Hugh McQuillan went 15-14 with a 3.40 ERA. Ryan and right-hander Claude Jonnard tied for the N.L. lead with 45 appearances.

Manager John McGraw helped out his friend, former pitcher Christy Mathewson who now was president of the Boston Braves, by trading shortstop Dave Bancroft and outfielders Bill Cunningham and Casey Stengel to Boston in exchange for pitcher Joe Oeschger and outfielder Billy Southworth on November 12.

1924		
93-60 .608 1st Place (+1½) 844,068		
John McGraw/Hughie Jennings		

Same song, different verse. The 1924 Giants won their fourth consecutive National League pennant, this time edging out the Brooklyn Dodgers by 1½ games. No N.L. team before or since has recorded a four-peat. New York finished with a 93-60 record, then lost a heart-breaking World Series to the Washington Senators four games to three.

For the first time since 1902, someone other than John McGraw managed the Giants, on a temporary basis. A knee injury kept McGraw from the bench for 44 games early in the season. Coach Hughie Jennings filled in and compiled a 32-12 record.

First baseman George Kelly enjoyed a monster offensive campaign, batting .324 with 27 home runs and a league-best 136 RBI. He hit three home runs in one game for the second time in his career against the Cincinnati Reds at the Polo Grounds in New York on June 14 and set an N.L. record (since tied by three other players) with seven homers over a six-game stretch from July 11-16.

On September 10 shortstop Frankie Frisch banged out six hits (five singles and a home run) in seven at-bats against the Boston Braves at the Polo Grounds. He went on to bat .328 with 22 stolen bases and tied for the league lead with 121 runs scored. Right fielder Ross Youngs batted at a .356 clip, while left fielder Irish Meusel contributed a .310 average with 102 RBI.

Third baseman Fred Lindstrom made his debut with the Giants against the Brooklyn Dodgers at the Polo Grounds on April 15.

Coach Hughie Jennings (1921-25) filled in for ailing manager John McGraw during both the 1924 and 1925 seasons.

O'Connell admitted his involvement to commissioner Kenesaw Landis and at the same time said teammates Frisch, Kelly and Youngs and coach Cozy Dolan put him up to the act. After questioning all five individuals, Landis banned O'Connell and Dolan from the game and cleared Frisch, Kelly and Youngs.

Following the season, the Giants and Chicago White Sox made a European tour that included a game played at Stamford Bridge in front of King George V.

Left-hander Jack Bentley topped New York pitchers with a 16-5 record and a 3.78 ERA. He clinched the pennant with a 5-1 victory over the Philadelphia Phillies at the Polo Grounds on September 27. Right-hander Virgil Barnes was 16-10 with a 3.06 ERA, left-hander Art Nehf went 14-4 with a 3.62 ERA and right-hander Hugh McQuillan finished 14-8 with a 2.69 ERA.

Five years after first baseman Hal Chase and third baseman Heinie Zimmerman were banned from baseball for throwing games, the Giants were hit with more scandal. On September 27 New York led Brooklyn by one game with three to play. The Giants' final series was against Philadelphia at the Polo Grounds, while the Dodgers finished up against the Boston Braves. Before the first game, Phillies' shortstop Heinie Sand told his manager, former New York shortstop Art Fletcher, that Giants' outfielder Jimmy O'Connell had offered him $500 "if he wouldn't bear down too hard" that day.

1925			
86-66	.566	2nd Place (-8½)	778,993
	John McGraw/Hughie Jennings		

The Pittsburgh Pirates made sure New York's string of dominance in the National League would come to an end by capturing the 1925 pennant by 8½ games over the Giants, who compiled an 86-66 record.

After getting off to a 10-4 start, the Giants played the next 32 games without manager John McGraw, who was sidelined for the second year in a row, this time with abdominal problems. Coach Hughie Jennings piloted the team to a 21-11 mark in McGraw's absence.

New York trailed Pittsburgh by three games heading into a double-header against the Pirates at the Polo Grounds in New York on August 22. Before a record crowd of 55,000—with some 30,000 more trying to gain admittance—the Pirates won both games, 8-1 and 2-1 to take a five-game lead. The following

day, the two teams split a double-header—New York winning the first game 7-4 and Pittsburgh taking the second 3-2—before another record gathering of 58,000. But the Giants still were five games out of first place and did not catch up.

In comings and goings, right-hander Freddie Fitzsimmons made his debut against the Pirates at Forbes Field in Pittsburgh on August 12. Earlier in the month, the Giants let go of outfielder Hack Wilson, who went to enjoy a Hall of Fame career with the Chicago Cubs.

Left fielder Irish Meusel led the Giants in batting average (.321), home runs (21) and RBI (111), while George Kelly batted .309 with 20 homers and 99 RBI in his first season at second base. Infielder Frankie Frisch, no longer a regular, had 21 stolen bases. Right-hander Virgil Barnes was the team's big winner with a 15-11 record and a 3.53 ERA. Right-hander Jack Scott was 14-15 with a 3.15 ERA, and right-hander Kent Greenfield went 12-8 with a 3.88 ERA.

On October 7 McGraw and the rest of the Giants' family was dealt a major blow as former standout pitcher Christy Mathewson passed away in Saranac Lake, New York, following a battle with tuberculosis.

1926			
74-77	.490	5th Place (-13½)	700,362
		John McGraw	

For the first time in a decade, the Giants stumbled home with a losing record in 1926. They were 74-77 for fifth place, 13½ games behind the St. Louis Cardinals.

It proved to be a definite year of transition. Right-handed pitcher Art Nehf, suffering from a sore arm, was sold to the Cincinnati Reds on May 11. Nehf was bothered by the fact that Giants' manager John McGraw did not inform the Reds of his ailment, and the two did not speak to one another for six years. On September 16 New York released third baseman Heinie Groh and allowed outfielder Irish Meusel to buy out his release in order to make a deal for himself. He wound up signing with the Brooklyn Dodgers. Then on December 20 the Giants traded infielder Frankie Frisch and right-handed pitcher Jimmy Ring to the St. Louis Cardinals in exchange for second baseman Rogers Hornsby. Frisch, the Giants' team captain, had left the club during an August road trip to St. Louis after receiving a tongue-lashing from McGraw.

Meanwhile, outfielder Mel Ott made his

Christy Mathewson passed away October 7, 1925, in Saranac Lake, New York, following a battle with tuberculosis. His good friend and former manager, John McGraw, was one of the pallbearers.

major league debut against the Philadelphia Phillies at the Baker Bowl in Philadelphia on April 27.

Right-hander Freddie Fitzsimmons paced New York with a 14-10 record and a 2.88 ERA. Right-handers Kent Greenfield and Jack Scott went 13-12, 3.96 and 13-15, 4.34, respectively. Scott topped the National League with 50 appearances. Shortstop Travis Jackson was the squad's leading batter with a .327 average, while Kelly, back at first base, had 13 home runs and 80 RBI. Frisch stole 23 bases.

1927			
92-62	.597	3rd Place (-2)	858,190
John McGraw/Rogers Hornsby			

The Giants nearly made it five National League pennants in six years in 1927—the year Charles Lindbergh made his historic flight across the Atlantic Ocean—before winding up in third place with a 92-62 record, two games behind the Pittsburgh Pirates. The St. Louis Cardinals finished second in a tight, three-team race.

There was plenty of news before the season began, beginning with off-season acquisition Rogers Hornsby, who had led the Cardinals to the 1926 World Series championship as player-manager, signing a two-year contact for $40,000 a year January 8 that made him the second-highest paid player in all of baseball behind the legendary Babe Ruth of the New York Yankees at $55,000. Hornsby also was named team captain. On February 1 N.L. president John Heydler ordered Hornsby to sell his stock in the Cardinals before playing for the Giants. After Hornsby and Cardinals' owner Samuel Breadon could not agree on a price per share and McGraw threatened to sue baseball, the six other N.L. owners got involved and helped complete the transaction.

New York acquired right-handed spitball pitcher Burleigh Grimes from the Brooklyn Dodgers in a three-way deal January 9 and re-acquired outfielder Edd Roush from the Cincinnati Reds in exchange for first baseman George Kelly on February 9.

On March 9 it was announced that outfielder Ross Youngs would miss the entire campaign with a serious kidney ailment. He ultimately lost his life to Bright's disease on October 22.

The Giants celebrated manager John McGraw's 25 years at the helm with John McGraw Day at the Polo Grounds in New York on July 19, but the Chicago Cubs ruined the party with an 8-5 victory. For the third time in four years, health issues kept McGraw from managing a full season, so Hornsby filled in and had a 22-10 record.

In a classic case of "everyone has 15 minutes of fame," left fielder Heinie Mueller enjoyed a banner double-header against the Cubs at the Polo Grounds on August 29. He stroked a pinch-hit home run in the third inning of the first game and came to bat again in the same frame and had a two-run single. In the second game he broke a 1-1 tie with a bases loaded single that scored two runs. The Giants swept the twin-bill 8-7 and 4-1. Mueller was the uncle of future Giants' outfielder Don Mueller.

Grimes, who won 13 straight decisions from July 15-September 19, went on to post a 19-8 record with a 3.54 ERA. Right-hander Freddie Fitzsimmons was 17-10 with a 3.72 ERA, right-hander Virgil Barnes went 14-11 with a 3.98 ERA and right-hander Larry Benton finished 13-5 with a 3.95 ERA.

Hornsby, the Giants' second baseman, paced the offense with a .361 batting average, 26 home runs, 125 RBI and 133 runs scored (tied for the league lead), while first baseman Bill Terry batted .326 with 20 homers and 121 RBI. Shortstop Travis Jackson contributed a .318 batting average, 13 homers and 98 RBI, and Roush stole 18 bases.

In 1927—his only season with the Giants—second baseman Rogers Hornsby batted .361 with 26 home runs, 125 RBI and 133 runs scored (tied for the National League lead).

1928				
93-61	.604	2nd Place (-2)		916,191
		John McGraw		

While Roger Hornsby assembled lofty numbers in 1927 (.361 batting average, 26 home runs and 125 RBI), he proved to be a "team owner" rather than a "team player," often threatening the Giants' status quo. So on January 10, 1928, while manager John McGraw was in Havana, Cuba, owner Charles A. Stoneham traded Hornsby to the Boston Braves in exchange for catcher Shanty Hogan and outfielder Jimmy Welsh.

Then, at Stoneham's urging, the Giants traded right-handed pitcher Burleigh Grimes to the Pittsburgh Pirates for right-hander Vic Aldridge on February 11.

The two deals meant the Giants opened the 1928 season minus their top batter and pitcher from the previous campaign. Amazingly, they remained in the National League race until late in the year before finishing in second place with a 93-61 record, just two games behind the St. Louis Cardinals. In the first game of a double-header against the Chicago Cubs at the Polo Grounds in New York on September 27, a controversial non-interference call kept a run from scoring in the bottom of the sixth inning and led to a 3-2 Giants' loss that effectively ruined New York's chance of capturing the flag.

Four highlights of the season included the opener being broadcast on radio for the first time ever on New York City stations WOR and WEAF with Graham McNamee calling the action April 11, first baseman Bill Terry hitting for the cycle and driving in six runs against the Brooklyn Dodgers at Ebbets Field in Brooklyn on May 27, third baseman Fred Lindstrom tying a major league record with nine hits in a double-header (shared with eight others) against the Philadelphia Phillies at the Baker Bowl in Philadelphia on June 25 and left-hander Carl Hubbell making his major league debut against the Pittsburgh Pirates at the Polo Grounds on July 26.

Six regulars batted .300 or better for the Giants: Lindstrom (.358), Hogan (.333), Terry (.326), right fielder Mel Ott (.322), left fielder Lefty O'Doul (.319) and Welsh (.307). Lindstrom added 14 home runs, 107 RBI and 15 stolen bases, while Terry had 36 doubles, 11 triples, 17 homers and 101 RBI. New York had two 20-game winners on the mound, right-handers Larry Benton (25-9, 2.73 ERA) and Freddie Fitzsimmons (20-9, 3.68 ERA). Benton tied for the N.L. top spot in wins and complete games (28).

Finishing the year the way they started—by trading a bona fide star—the Giants sent O'Doul and cash to Philadelphia for outfielder Fred Leach on October 29.

1929			
84-67	.556	3rd Place (-13½)	868,806
		John McGraw	

During a season in which New York finished in third place with an 84-67 record, 13½ games behind the Chicago Cubs, there were plenty of individual accomplishments.

The highlights started May 8 when left-hander Carl Hubbell, in his first full season in the big leagues, authored an 11-0 no-hitter against the Pittsburgh Pirates at the Polo Grounds in New York. The gem ended with a nifty double play started by Hubbell. Right fielder Mel Ott hit two home runs in the game, providing a glimpse of things to come.

On May 16 Ott hit for the cycle against the Boston Braves at Braves Field, on June 19 he had four doubles and two homers in a double-header against the Philadelphia Phillies at the Baker Bowl in Philadelphia and on June 20 he drove in a run for the 11th consecutive game. On October 5—the second-to-last day of the season—Ott and Philadelphia right fielder Chuck Klein were tied for the National League lead with a record of 42 home runs. The two players and their teams played a double-header in Philadelphia, and Klein homered in his first at-bat. After getting a single and a walk in the first game and a single in his first at-bat of the second game, Ott was intentionally walked his next five trips by Phillies' manager Burt Shotton and his club. The following day in Boston, Ott was held to two singles and lost the home run chase to Klein 43-32.

There was more offense from the Giants. First baseman Bill Terry tied the baseball record with nine hits in a double-header against the Brooklyn Dodgers at Ebbets Field on June 18. Terry went on to bat .372 with 39 doubles, 14 home runs and 117 RBI. Ott finished with a .328 batting average, 37 doubles and a franchise-record 151 RBI. Center fielder Edd Roush batted at a .324 clip.

Hubbell wound up with an 18-11 record and a 3.69 ERA, while right-hander Freddie Fitzsimmons was 15-11 with a 4.10 ERA and

left-hander Bill Walker went 14-7 with a National League-low 3.09 ERA.

The year and decade ended with the Giants bringing suit against Francis X. McQuade, dismissed as team treasurer over a year and a half earlier, for attempting to "wreck and destroy" the National Exhibition Company (the Giants' corporate name). McQuade responded by filing a suit of his own that cited his termination as a violation of the contract he, president Charles A. Stoneham and vice president John McGraw had signed when the trio purchased the franchise in 1919. The New York Supreme Court ruled that the Giants pay McQuade his back salary but did not order his reinstatement. The Giants protested the payment and ultimately were upheld by the Court of Appeals.

1930			
87-67	.565	3rd Place (-5)	868,714
		John McGraw	

In a word, the 1930 season was offensive. The Giants set a baseball record with a .319 team batting average, while the entire National League batted at a .303 clip.

Leading the onslaught was first baseman Bill Terry with a franchise-record and league-leading .401 average and a franchise-best and N.L. record-tying 254 hits (also left fielder Lefty O'Doul of the Philadelphia Phillies in 1929). Terry is the last player in the Senior Circuit to bat .400. He had 39 doubles, 15 triples, 23 home runs and 23 RBI. In addition, third baseman Fred Lindstrom batted .379 (the second-highest mark in Giants' history) with 39 doubles, 22 homers, 106 RBI and 15 stolen bases, and right fielder Mel Ott contributed a .349 average, 34 doubles, 25 homers and 119 RBI. Those three players are one of just six trios in Giants' history to collect 100 RBI.

The offensive explosion, however, was only good enough for a third-place finish with an 87-67 record, five games behind the St. Louis Cardinals. But that's not to suggest New

York had poor pitching. Right-hander Freddie Fitzsimmons posted a 19-7 record with a 4.25 ERA, left-hander Carl Hubbell was 17-12 with a 3.87 ERA (second in the N.L.) and left-hander Bill Walker was 17-15 with a 3.93 ERA (third in the N.L.). The league team ERA was 4.97.

It clearly was a batters' year. On May 8 Lindstrom hit for the cycle and added a single in a 13-10 win over the Pittsburgh Pirates at Forbes Field in Pittsburgh. From July 28-August 23, he hit in 23 consecutive games. Ott belted three home runs against the Boston Braves in the second game of a double-header at the Polo Grounds in New York on August 31.

Other notable occurrences included the Giants playing their first-ever night game April 6 against their Bridgeport (Connecticut) farm

First baseman Bill Terry posted a franchise-record and National League-leading .401 batting average in 1930 and was named the league Most Valuable Player. He is the last player in the Senior Circuit to bat at a .400 clip. Terry managed the Giants from 1932-41.

team in Bridgeport (10 years before the Polo Grounds was equipped with lights), the acquisition of second baseman Hughie Critz from the Cincinnati Reds in exchange for right-hander Larry Benton on May 21; the debut of Ladies' Day (free admission to women for Friday games) on July 21 and the signing of manager John McGraw to a five-year contract September 3 amid rumors he would leave the Giants at the conclusion of the campaign.

1931			
87-65	.572	2nd Place (-13)	812,163
		John McGraw	

New York first baseman Bill Terry nearly made it two straight National League batting titles in 1931 but lost out on the last day of the season to St. Louis Cardinals' outfielder Chick Hafey by an ever-so-slim .3489-.3486 margin. Terry finished with 43 doubles, 20 triples (tops in the league), nine home runs, 112 RBI and 121 runs scored (tied for the N.L. lead).

Those two players' teams finished the same way in the standings as the Giants were 87-65, 13 games behind the Cardinals. On September 5—with just over three weeks to play—New York had closed to within 5½ games after sweeping the Brooklyn Dodgers by the scores of 5-1 and 10-1 at the Polo Grounds in New York. In the seventh inning of the first game, right-hander Freddie Fitzsimmons was hit in the stomach on a ground ball by Brooklyn pitcher Fred Heimach and then hit in the head on a pitch by Cy Moore. Fitzsimmons subsequently collapsed in the clubhouse and was diagnosed with a ruptured blood vessel in his head. Amazingly, he missed only one start.

Center fielder Mel Ott supported Terry with a .292 batting average, 23 doubles, eight triples, 29 home runs and 115 RBI. Shortstop Travis Jackson batted .310 with 13 stolen bases. Fitzsimmons topped the pitching staff with an 18-11 record and a 3.05 ERA. He was one of four pitchers to win at least 13 games, joining left-handers Bill Walker (16-9, league-

best 2.26 ERA); Carl Hubbell (14-12, 2.65 ERA); and Clarence Mitchell (13-11, 4.07 ERA). Walker authored an N.L. high of six shutouts.

The Giants shut out the Boston Braves twice on Bill Terry Day at the Polo Grounds on May 26, 3-0 behind Hubbell in the first game and 6-0 behind Walker in the second game. Between games Terry was recognized for his outstanding 1930 season. On July 11 New York beat up on the Philadelphia Phillies 23-5 in the opener of a double-header at the Baker Bowl in Philadelphia. The Giants banged out 28 hits, including seven doubles and five home runs.

1932			
72-82	.468	6th Place (-18)	484,868
	John McGraw/Bill Terry		

It is true that all good things must come to an end. On June 3, 1932, the most successful era in Giants' history came to an end as an ailing and aging John McGraw stepped down as manager after a double-header against the Philadelphia Phillies at the Polo Grounds in New York was rained out. He named first baseman Bill Terry as his replacement.

The Giants were 17-23 when McGraw called it quits and improved to 55-59 under Terry, winding up 72-82 for sixth place, 18 games behind the Chicago Cubs.

Highlights were few and far between. In the first game of a double-header August 13 Terry, right fielder Mel Ott and center fielder Fred Lindstrom hit home runs on three consecutive pitches in the fourth inning off the Brooklyn Dodgers at the Polo Grounds but went on to lose 18-9. Brooklyn third baseman Joe Stripp, left fielder Lefty O'Doul and second baseman Tony Cuccinello returned the favor against Giants' right-hander Waite Hoyt in the second game and completed the sweep with a 5-4 win.

On September 12 Terry signed a two-year contract as player-manager, and he made his first trade October 10 by obtaining catcher Gus Mancuso and right-hander Ray Starr from the St. Louis Cardinals in exchange for outfielder Ethan Allen, left-hander Jim Mooney, catcher Bob O'Farrell and left-hander Bill Walker. Then on December 12 the Giants traded Lindstrom, who was perturbed at not being selected as McGraw's replacement, to the Pittsburgh Pirates in a complicated three-way transaction that sent outfielder Kiddo Davis (from the Philadelphia Phillies) and pitcher Glenn Spencer (from the Pirates) to the Giants and outfielders Gus Dugan (from the Pirates) and Chick Fullis (from the Giants) to the Phillies.

Terry led New York with a .350 batting average and 42 doubles to go with 28 home runs and 117 RBI. Right fielder Mel Ott batted .318 with 38 homers (tied for the National League lead) and 123 RBI. Left-hander Carl Hubbell was the team's only dependable pitcher with an 18-11 record and a 2.50 ERA.

The eight N.L. teams donned numbers on their uniforms for the first time during the 1932 season, with the Giants making their numerical debut June 23 against St. Louis at the Polo Grounds. The New York Yankees of the American League had been the first club to use numbers three years earlier.

1933			
91-61	.599	1st Place (+5)	604,471
	Bill Terry		

In its 1933 preseason poll, the Associated Press picked the Giants to finish in sixth place in the National League. But New York proved the prognosticators wrong, capturing the pennant with a 91-61 record, five games better than the Pittsburgh Pirates. Not satisfied, the Giants went on to win the World Series over the Washington Senators four games to one. Essentially, the N.L. race was over June 10 when New York took over first place for good.

A new-style dead ball was put into use in 1933, and the Giants took advantage of it behind a solid pitching staff. Left-hander Carl Hubbell was the ace, posting a 23-12 record with a snappy 1.66 ERA en route to being

named the N.L. Most Valuable Player. He paced the league in wins, ERA, innings pitched (308.2) and shutouts (10). Right-hander Hal Schumacher, just 22 years old, was 19-12 with a 2.16 ERA, while right-hander Freddie Fitzsimmons was 16-11 with a 2.90 ERA and right-hander Roy Parmelee went 13-8 with 3.17 ERA.

How dominating was New York's pitching? Twice the Giants authored double-header shutouts, May 7 against the Cincinnati Reds (Hubbell 1-0 and Schumacher 5-0) at the Polo Grounds in New York and July 2 against the St. Louis Cardinals (Hubbell 1-0 in 18 innings and Parmelee 1-0) at the Polo Grounds. Hubbell went on to pitch a franchise-record 46.1 consecutive scoreless innings from July 13 (seventh inning)-August 1 (fifth inning). In a 2-0, 10-inning victory over the Boston Braves in the first game of a double-header at Braves Field on September 1 he not only did not walk a batter but did not fall behind a single hitter. He also drove in the game-winning running with a

Pitcher Carl Hubbell was named the National League Most Valuable Player in both 1933 and 1936. (Brace Photo)

10th-inning single off Boston right-hander Fred Frankhouse.

On a day off June 12, the entire New York team accompanied Schumacher to St. Lawrence University where he received his diploma. The Giants acquired left-handed pitcher Watty Clark and outfielder Lefty O'Doul, who previously played for them in 1928, from the Brooklyn Dodgers in exchange for first baseman Sam Leslie on June 16. Catcher Harry Danning made his major league debut July 8.

First baseman-manager Bill Terry was the team's leading batter at .322, while outfielder Mel Ott batted .283 with 36 doubles, 23 home runs and 103 RBI. The only other player to reach double figures in homers was third baseman Johnny Vergez with 16 to go with 72 RBI. Center fielder Kiddo Davis stole 10 bases.

The first All-Star Game was played July 6 at Comiskey Park in Chicago, and four Giants were selected for historic event: Hubbell, O'Doul, Schumacher and Terry, plus former manager John McGraw (1902-32) to pilot the N.L. team. It was McGraw's last appearance in a major league dugout in an official capacity.

Terry, often a troublesome sort when it came to agreeing to contractual terms, was rewarded with a five-year, $40,000 a year pact to remain as the Giants' player-manager October 9.

		1934	
93-60	.608	2nd Place (-2)	730,851
		Bill Terry	

The Giants nearly made it back-to-back National League pennants in 1934 before losing out with a 93-60 record, two games behind the St. Louis Cardinals. But it was the Brooklyn Dodgers who got the last laugh. New York had led St. Louis and the Chicago Cubs by six games on Labor Day, but by mid-September the Giants were faltering and the "Gas House Gang" Cardinals were rolling. The two teams

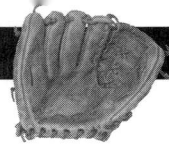

were tied with two games to play when Brooklyn got involved.

First, a flashback to the N.L. meetings in New York on February 6 when Roscoe McGowen, a writer for the *New York Times*, asked Giants' player-manager Bill Terry how he thought Brooklyn would do in 1934. Referring to the Dodgers' inability to make any offseason trades, Terry responded: "Is Brooklyn still in the league? I haven't heard from them." It was an unintentional slap in the face, but the Dodgers got revenge by beating the Giants the last two games of the season at the Polo Grounds in New York, 5-1 on September 29 and 8-5 on September 30. Many Brooklyn fans were in attendance hanging banners that read "Bill Who?" and "Yeah, We're Still in the League." Meanwhile, the Cardinals won their final two games over the Cincinnati Reds to capture the flag.

On February 23 former manager John McGraw (1902-32) passed away in New Rochelle, New York, following a bout with prostate cancer.

Third baseman Johnny Vergez hit a home run and a double in a six-run eighth inning as the Giants topped the Boston Braves 14-5 at the Polo Grounds on June 7. Right fielder Mel Ott tied the modern-day major league record (since 1900) with six runs scored in a 21-4 New York win over the Philadelphia Phillies at the Baker Bowl in Philadelphia in the second game of a double-header August 4.

Left-handed pitcher Carl Hubbell started for the N.L. in the All-Star Game at the Polo Grounds on July 10 and achieved his legendary status by striking out five consecutive future Hall of Famers: Babe Ruth, Lou Gehrig and Jimmie Foxx to end the first inning and Al Simmons and Joe Cronin to begin the second.

Ott led the Giants with 35 home runs (tied for the league lead) and 135 RBI (tops in the circuit) to go with a .326 batting average. Terry was the team's top batter with a .354 average, while shortstop Travis Jackson drove in 101 runs. Left fielder Joe Moore batted .331 and

Pitcher Carl Hubbell (left) and New York Yankees' legendary first baseman Lou Gehrig. Hubbell was the starting pitcher for the National League in the 1934 All-Star Game at the Polo Grounds and achieved his legendary status by striking out five consecutive future Hall of Famers: Babe Ruth, Gehrig and Jimmie Foxx to end the first inning and Al Simmons and Joe Cronin to begin the second.

paced the squad with five stolen bases. The Giants had just 19 steals as a team.

Right-hander Hal Schumacher had a 23-10 record with a 3.18 ERA, Hubbell was 21-12 while leading the N.L. with a 2.30 ERA and 25 complete games. Right-hander Freddie Fitzsimmons went 18-14 with a 3.04 ERA.

New York made a key trade with the acquisition of shortstop Dick Bartell from Philadelphia in exchange for left-handed pitcher Pretzels Pezzullo, infielder Blondy Ryan, third baseman Johnny Vergez, outfielder George Watkins and cash November 1.

1935			
91-62	.595	3rd Place (-8½)	748,748
		Bill Terry	

After a World Series championship in 1933 and a near-miss National League title in 1934, the Giants appeared primed for more success in 1935. And they were in first place in the N.L. from the start of the season until August 25 before winding up in third place with a 91-62 record, 8½ games behind the Chicago Cubs. Chicago reeled off a franchise-record 21-game winning streak from September 4-27.

The season began with the return of the legendary Babe Ruth to New York with the Boston Braves. On April 16 Ruth had a run-producing single and a three-run homer as Boston defeated the Giants 4-2 at the Polo Grounds.

New York provided its own highlights, including a 3-0 one-hitter by right-hander Hal Schumacher against the Philadelphia Phillies at the Polo Grounds on April 28 (the lone hit was of the scratch variety by pitcher Orville Jorgens in the third inning); a double-header shutout sweep of the Brooklyn Dodgers at Ebbets Field in Brooklyn on July 28 (6-0 by left-hander Carl Hubbell and 1-0 by right-hander Slick Castleman); and two doubles, a triple and a home run by center fielder Hank Leiber against the Cincinnati Reds at the Polo Grounds on August 18.

First baseman-manager Bill Terry batted .341, followed by Leiber (.331) and right fielder Mel Ott (.322). Leiber topped the team with 37 doubles to go with 22 home runs and 107 RBI, and Ott was the leader with 31 homers and 114 RBI. Left-hander Carl Hubbell posted a 23-12 record with a 3.27 ERA, while Schumacher went 19-9 with a 2.89 ERA. Right-hander Freddie Fitzsimmons tied for the N.L. lead with four shutouts.

On November 14 the Giants purchased right-handed pitcher Dick Coffman from the St. Louis Browns, and they obtained second baseman Burgess "Whitey" Whitehead from the Cardinals in exchange for right-hander Roy Parmelee and first baseman Phil Weintraub on December 9.

1936			
92-62	.597	1st Place (+5)	837,952
		Bill Terry	

New York returned to the National League penthouse in 1936, fashioning a 92-62 record to finish five games ahead of the Chicago Cubs. However, on July 15 the Giants were a season-high 11 games behind the Cubs before a nifty 39-8 surge propelled them to their second pennant in player-manager Bill Terry's fifth season at the helm. The Giants squared off against the cross-town rival Yankees in the World Series for the fourth time and were beaten for the second time four games to two.

Before the campaign began, owner Charles A. Stoneham passed away January 6 and was succeeded by his son, Horace C. Stoneham, at just 32 years of age. On February 15 Eddie Brannick, a team employee since the early days of former manager John McGraw (1902-32), replaced Jim Tierney as the Giants' secretary.

It didn't take long for the Giants and the Brooklyn Dodgers to resume their rivalry. On April 15 en route to a 5-3 New York victory, Giants' shortstop Dick Bartell and Dodgers' pitcher Van Lingle Mungo brawled after Mungo jolted Bartell on a play at first base. Then two combatants, finally pried apart by umpire John "Beans" Reardon, were immediately ejected and subsequently fined by N.L. president Ford Frick.

In perhaps the most wild game of the season, right fielder Mel Ott blasted a three-run homer with two outs in the ninth inning to give New York a 13-12 victory over the Philadelphia Phillies at the Baker Bowl in Philadelphia on May 11. Ott also collected a single and a double with eight RBI.

One of the key hits of the year came from Terry as a pinch-hitter with a bases-loaded single in the 14th inning to break a 1-1 tie

against the Pittsburgh Pirates at Forbes Field in Pittsburgh on August 28. The Giants won 7-2 for their 15th consecutive victory. Two days later Ott banged out seven hits in a double-header sweep of the Chicago Cubs at Wrigley Field in Chicago.

Left-hander Carl Hubbell won his last 16 decisions from July 17-September 23 and finished with a 26-6 record and a 2.31 ERA (leading the league in wins and ERA) to earn his second N.L. Most Valuable Player Award. Left-hander Al Smith was 14-13 with a 3.78 ERA and four shutouts (tied for the league lead), while right-hander Harry Gumbert went 11-3 with a 3.90 ERA.

Offensively, Ott batted .328 with a league-leading 33 home runs and 135 RBI, while left fielder Joe Moore and catcher Gus Mancuso batted at .316 and .301 clips, respectively, with 63 RBI apiece. First baseman Sam Leslie hit for the cycle against Philadelphia at the Polo Grounds in New York on May 24.

Outfielder Mel Ott spent his entire 22-year playing career with the Giants from 1926-47.

On December 18 the Giants purchased the Albany (New York) club from the International League for $60,000 and transferred it to Jersey City, New Jersey. Former New York star infielder Travis Jackson (1922-36) was named the team's manager.

1937			
95-57	.625	1st Place (+3)	926,887
		Bill Terry	

Trailing the first-place Chicago Cubs by seven games August 3, the 1937 Giants stormed back to take over the top spot by the end of the month and then held off the Cubs to capture their second straight National League pennant by three games with a 95-57 record. But also for the second straight year, the Giants lost the World Series to the cross-town rival Yankees four games to one.

Bill Terry ended his playing career following the 1936 season, and on January 8, 1937, he signed his first contract as a manager only for a reported $27,500 annually. He would be ejected from a game for the first time in his 15-year career with the Giants in a 6-3 loss to the Philadelphia Phillies at the Baker Bowl in Philadelphia on July 12 by veteran umpire Bill Klem.

Once again, the story of the season was the pitching of left-hander Carl Hubbell. He won his first eight decisions of the campaign from April 23-May 27 to run his two-year winning streak to 24, a major league record. The amazing run ended with a 10-3 loss to the Brooklyn Dodgers in the first game of a Memorial Day double-header May 31 before 61,756 fans at the Polo Grounds, the second-largest in the ballpark's history. Roger Clemens of the Toronto Blue Jays and New York Yankees threatened the streak with 20 consecutive wins in 1998 and 1999. Hubbell went up against fellow future Hall of Famer Dizzy Dean of the St. Louis Cardinals for the final time June 27 and won 8-1 at Sportsman's Park in St. Louis. The two stalwarts faced one another 11 times dur-

ing their careers with Hubbell winning eight of the meetings. Hubbell went on to post a 22-8 record (leading the N.L. in wins) with a 3.20 ERA and a league-best 159 strikeouts.

Terry made perhaps his worst trade when he dealt right-handed pitcher Freddie Fitzsimmons to Brooklyn in exchange for right-hander Tom Baker on June 11.

Rookie left-hander Cliff Melton gave New York a lift by going 20-9 with a team-leading 2.61 ERA. Right-hander Slick Castleman was 11-6 with a 3.31 ERA.

The Giants' top offense producers were right fielder Mel Ott (.294 batting average, 31 home runs—tied for the N.L. lead, 95 RBI); center fielder Jimmy Ripple (.317, 66 RBI); and left fielder Joe Moore (.310, 37 doubles, 10 triples, 57 RBI). Moore, Ott, and second baseman Burgess Whitehead each stole seven bases.

On September 7 Terry signed a five-year, $40,000 per year contract as general manager/manager amid speculation that the Cleveland Indians had offered him a lucrative deal.

		1938	
83-67	.553	3rd Place (-5) Bill Terry	799,633

At the 1938 All-Star break, the Giants were in first place and appeared headed to three consecutive National League pennants. But elbow injures to the anchors of the pitching staff—left-hander Carl Hubbell and right-hander Hal Schumacher—proved too much to overcome, and New York finished third with an 83-67 record, five games behind the Chicago Cubs.

Before the duo was sidelined, both authored masterful games. Schumacher pitched a 1-0, one-hitter against the Brooklyn Dodgers at Ebbets Field in Brooklyn on April 24, and Hubbell threw an 11-0, one-hitter against the Philadelphia Phillies at the Polo Grounds in New York on May 28. Schumacher finished with a 13-8 record and a 3.50 ERA,

while Hubbell went 13-10 with a 3.07 ERA.

The Giants' two big winners were right-hander Harry Gumbert (15-13, 4.01 ERA) and left-hander Cliff Melton (14-14, 3.89 ERA). Right-hander Dick Coffman tied for the N.L. top spot with 51 appearances while posting an 8-4 record and a 3.48 ERA.

Mel Ott played both right field and third base during the season. On August 18 a cereal company announced the results of a contest to determine the most popular player at each position. Ott received the most votes at both of his spots. He was awarded with two gorgeous blue sedans for the dual winnings but accepted only one as a right fielder and asked the company to present the other one to popular Cubs' third baseman Stan Hack. Ott led New York with a .311 batting average, 36 home runs (tops in the N.L.), 116 RBI and 116 runs scored (also the league best).

Catcher Harry Danning, who was suspended for a week in July for refusing to play after missing several games with a kidney ailment, batted .306 with 60 RBI. Not surprisingly, his relationship with manager Bill Terry was forever uneasy. Left fielder Joe Moore batted at a .302 clip, center fielder Hank Leiber had 12 homers and 65 RBI and utility infielder George Myatt stole 10 bases.

There were three major offseason announcements. First, the Giants traded Leiber, shortstop Dick Bartell and catcher Gus Mancuso to the Cubs in exchange for outfielder Frank Demaree, shortstop Billy Jurges and catcher Ken O'Dea on December 6. Then, on December 11 New York acquired first baseman Zeke Bonura from the Washington Senators for pitcher Tom Baker, minor league first baseman Jim Carlin and $20,000. Lastly, the Giants and New York Yankees announced December 16 that all of their 1939 home games except Sundays would be broadcast on radio station WABC in New York with Mel Allen and Arch McDonald. The Giants, Yankees and Brooklyn Dodgers had had a long-standing agreement that none of the teams would broadcast games—although many major league clubs

were—but the Dodgers earlier announced that all of their home and away games would be carried in 1939.

1939			
77-74	**.510**	**5th Place (-18½)**	**702,457**
		Bill Terry	

Not only did New York slip to fifth place in 1939 with a 77-74 record, 18½ games behind the Cincinnati Reds, but the Giants wound up below the hated Brooklyn Dodgers (third place) for the first time since 1932 and for only the second time since 1920.

New York got an early boost with the return of left-handed pitcher Carl Hubbell following elbow surgery in August of 1938. At the age of 36, the future Hall of Famer compiled an 11-9 record with a 2.75 ERA in 29 games.

The story of the season was the Giants' home run hitting prowess. Twice they belted seven round-trippers in one game, June 6 against the Cincinnati Reds at the Polo Grounds in New York (including a major league record of five in the fourth inning) and August 13 against the Philadelphia Phillies in the first game of a double-header at the Polo Grounds. New York won the two games 17-3 and 11-2, respectively.

Five players finished in double figures in homers: right fielder Mel Ott (27), catcher Harry Danning (16), first baseman Zeke Bonura (11), center fielder Frank Demaree (11) and left fielder Joe Moore (10). Bonura topped the team with a .321 batting average and 85 RBI but set a major league record by grounding into five double plays in two consecutive games against the Dodgers at Ebbets Field in Brooklyn on July 8-9. Danning batted .313 with 74 RBI, while Ott batted .308 with 80 RBI.

Leading the pitching staff was right-hander Harry Gumbert with an 18-11 record and a 4.32 ERA.

On July 15 the Giants lost to Cincinnati by the score of 8-4 at the Polo Grounds in a controversial game to began a nine-game losing

streak that effectively removed New York from the pennant race. New York led 4-3 in the top of the eighth inning when Reds' center fielder Harry Craft hit a low, curving line drive into the lower left field stands at the foul pole. Home plate umpire Lee Ballanfant ruled it a two-run homer, which drew a huge argument from the Giants. Danning, Moore and shortstop Bill Jurges all were ejected. Jurges and second base umpire George Magerkurth really came to blows, with spit and punches flying. Both were fined $150 and suspended for 10 days. National League president Ford Frick subsequently required that two-foot screens be installed inside all four poles to prevent future disputable calls.

In a bizarre story, second baseman Burgess Whitehead was suspended by the Giants on August 16 and the next day asked New York Yankees' manager Joe McCarthy for permission to work out with the team. McCarthy turned him down and Whitehead rejoined the Giants a few days later but subsequently left the team in mid-September and was suspended for the balance of the campaign. He returned in 1940.

On November 14 the Giants announced plans to install lights at the Polo Grounds at a projected cost of $150,000.

1940			
72-80	**.474**	**6th Place (-27½)**	**747,852**
		Bill Terry	

The new decade didn't bring any cause for celebration in New York as the Giants slipped to a 72-80 record for sixth place in the National League, a whopping 27½ games behind the pennant-winning Cincinnati Reds. It marked the Giants' first losing season since 1932 (72-82) and the farthest they finished out of first place since 1902 (53½ games).

Looking to bolster its pitching staff, New York signed right-hander Paul "Daffy" Dean (the younger brother of Hall of Famer Dizzy) on March 19 following his release by the St. Louis Cardinals. But Daffy mustered just a 3-3

record with a 5.17 ERA and was traded back to the Cardinals on May 14, 1941.

The Giants played the first-ever night game at the Polo Grounds in New York on May 24 and defeated the Boston Braves by the score of 8-1 behind the pitching of right-hander Harry Gumbert and home runs by left fielder Joe Moore, shortstop Billy Jurges and catcher Harry Danning.

Despite the sub-par team showing, there were some individual highlights. Left-hander Carl Hubbell, at age 37, fired a 7-0 one-hitter against the Brooklyn Dodgers in the first game of a double-header at Ebbets Field in Brooklyn on May 30, Danning hit for the cycle (including an inside-the-the-park home run that wound up 483 feet from home plate behind the Eddie Grant memorial in center field) against the Pittsburgh Pirates at the Polo Grounds on June 15 and center fielder Johnny Rucker collected seven of his season total of 23 RBI in two innings against Boston at the Polo Grounds on September 29 (he hit a grand slam in the second inning and a three-run homer in the third).

Right fielder Mel Ott began suffering from eyesight difficulties and wore glasses for a few weeks before forgoing the experiment. He was honored with Mel Ott Night at the Polo Grounds on August 7 en route to batting .289 with a team-high 19 home runs and 79 RBI.

Center fielder Frank Demaree led the Giants with a .302 batting average, while first baseman Babe Young had 101 RBI to go with a .286 average and 17 homers. Danning contributed a .300 average, 13 homers and 91 RBI.

No starting pitcher had a winning record with right-hander Hal Schumacher going 13-13 with a 3.25 ERA. Gumbert went 12-14 with a 3.76 ERA, and Hubbell finished 11-12 (his first and only losing mark in 16 major league seasons) with a 3.65 ERA.

The tide continued to turn between the area's two N.L. teams as Brooklyn had an 88-65 record and finished in second place.

The Giants signed former player-manager and future Hall of Famer Gabby Hartnett of the

Chicago Cubs to be a player-coach November 13.

1941			
74-79	.484	5th Place (-25½)	763,098
		Bill Terry	

Not only did the Giants post a 74-79 record during the 1941 season, and not only did they finish in fifth place, 25½ games out, but the Brooklyn Dodgers won the National League pennant. It marked Brooklyn's first title since 1920 and just their fourth in the 20th century.

New York tried its mightiest to keep the Dodgers from capturing the flag and temporarily knocked them out of first place with a 4-3 and 5-1 double-header sweep at the Polo Grounds in New York on August 30. But Brooklyn came back to edge out the St. Louis Cardinals by 2½ games.

Right-handed pitcher Bill Lohrman had a no-hitter for 8.1 innings against the Boston Braves in the first game of a double-header at the Polo Grounds on May 10 before center fielder Johnny Cooney singled to center field. Lohrman held on to win the game by the score of 4-2.

The Giants pulled off an unpopular trade May 14 by sending right-handers Daffy Dean and Harry Gumbert and cash to the Cardinals in exchange for right-hander Bill McGee. After reporting to New York overweight, McGee went just 2-9 with a 4.92 ERA, while Gumbert was 11-5 with a 2.74 ERA for St. Louis.

As the war in Europe continued to make headlines, the Giants' game against Boston at the Polo Grounds in New York on May 27 was delayed 45 minutes for the broadcasting of one of U.S. president Franklin D. Roosevelt's famous "fireside chats" over the loudspeakers atop the center field clubhouse. Ironically, New York's game against the Pittsburgh Pirates at Forbes Field in Pittsburgh on June 18 also was temporarily halted so fans could listen to the boxing title fight between Joe Louis and local

favorite Billy Conn. The game then had to be suspended in the 11th inning with the two teams tied because of local regulations that forbid starting an inning after 11:50 p.m. local time. Said an angry Giants' manager Bill Terry afterwards: "I can see holding up a game so we can hear a presidential speech, but, hell, not for a prize fight. They might as well hold up the game to listen to a Jack Benny or Bob Hope radio show."

The greatest individual milestone came from right fielder Mel Ott, who hit his 400th career home run and collected his 1,500 career RBI against the Cincinnati Reds at the Polo Grounds on June 1. Ott finished the season with a .286 batting average, 27 home runs and 90 RBI.

First baseman Babe Young had 25 homers and 104 RBI, while shortstop Dick Bartell, back with the Giants after helping the Detroit Tigers win the 1940 American League pennant, batted at a .303 clip. Outfielder Sid Gordon, a native of Brooklyn, made his major league debut September 20 against Boston at the Polo Grounds.

Right-hander Hal Schumacher led the pitching staff with a 12-10 record and a 3.36 ERA, right-hander Bob Carpenter was 11-6 with a 3.83 ERA and left-hander Carl Hubbell went 11-9 with a 3.57 ERA .

On December 2 Ott was named to replace Terry as manager. Ott received given a two-year, $25,000 per year contract as player-manager, while Terry was given a two-year, $30,000 per year deal as general manager in charge of the farm teams and scouting operations. Speculation had swirled that Terry desired to relinquish his onfield duties, but the selection of Ott was a complete surprise. Ott was a hugely popular with everyone but quiet and easy-going and without any managerial experience.

It didn't take long for Ott to make a move and increase his stock. The Giants acquired first baseman Johnny Mize from the Cardinals for Lohrman, first baseman Johnny McCarthy, catcher Ken O'Dea and $50,000.

1942			
85-67	.559	3rd Place (-20)	779,621
		Mel Ott	

Mel Ott's first season as player-manager clearly was a case of good news, bad news. The Giants, after two sub-.500 campaigns, went 85-67 to place third in the National League standings but were 20 games behind the pennant-winning St. Louis Cardinals, who set a franchise-record with a 106-48 mark. The Brooklyn Dodgers were second with a 104-50 record, marking the fourth straight season they finished ahead of the Giants.

New York's success was the result of monster offensive seasons by Ott, the right fielder, and newly-acquired first baseman Johnny Mize. Ott batted .295 with an N.L.-best 30 home runs, 93 RBI and 118 runs scored (tops in the league), while Mize had a .305 batting average, 26 homers and a league-high 110 RBI. The Giants' next-best batter for average was catcher Harry Danning at .279, and

Mel Ott served as manager of the Giants from 1942-48.

center fielder Willard Marshall was next with 11 homers and 59 RBI.

At the same time, the Giants' pitching was decent but not spectacular. Right-hander Bill Lohrman posted a 13-4 record with a 2.56 ERA, but New York's next biggest winner was right-hander Hal Schumacher at 12-13 with a 3.04 ERA. Three pitchers won 11 games: left-hander Cliff Melton (11-5, 2.63 ERA); left-hander Carl Hubbell (11-8, 3.95 ERA at 39 years of age); and right-hander Bill Carpenter (11-10, 3.15 ERA). Right-hander Ace Adams was 7-4 with a 1.84 ERA out of the bullpen while topping the league with 61 appearances.

Ott reached two milestones during the season, collecting his N.L.-record 1,583rd RBI against the Chicago Cubs at Wrigley Field in Chicago on June 4 and picking up his 2,500th hit in Chicago on August 30. Pinch hitter Babe Young had a double and a triple in a 10-run eighth inning of a 12-6 Giants' win over the Cincinnati Reds at the Polo Grounds in New York on May 14.

With the Giants having wrapped up third place and unable to move up September 25, outfielder Hank Leiber made his first and only major league appearance as a pitcher and threw a complete game but lost 9-1 to the Philadelphia Phillies at the Polo Grounds. Leiber surrendered nine hits and five walks with five strikeouts.

On November 30 Bill Terry resigned as farm system director to enter private business. The Giants had dropped off from nine farm clubs at the start to 1942 to just two, Jersey City (New Jersey) and Fort Smith (Arkansas).

1943			
55-98	.359	8th Place (-49½)	466,095
		Mel Ott	

When the Giants opened spring training in 1943, they were without catcher Harry Danning, outfielder Willard Marshall, first baseman Johnny Mize and outfielder Babe Young, who had been called into service for World War II. New York conducted spring training in Lakewood, New Jersey, as all major league clubs were required to stay close to their home cities because of the transportation and fuel shortages caused by the war.

It didn't take long for the undermanned Giants (they seemed to lose more regulars than any other team) to sink into the bottom half of the National League. They ended up in last place with a 55-98 record, an almost unbelievable 49½ games behind the St. Louis Cardinals.

On April 27 the Giants acquired catcher Frank Lombardi from the Boston Braves in exchange for catcher Hugh Poland and infielder Connie Ryan. Lombardi went on to bat .305 (second on the team) with 10 home runs (second) and 51 RBI (third). Second baseman Mickey Witek topped the team with a .314 batting average, while right fielder-manager Mel Ott socked 18 homers and infielder Sid Gordon drove in 63 runs.

Forty-year-old left-handed pitcher Carl Hubbell, in his final major league season, won his 250th career game by the score of 5-1 on a one-hitter against the Pittsburgh Pirates at Forbes Field in Pittsburgh on June 5. He finished 4-4 with a 4.91 ERA before retiring with 253 victories and taking over as the Giants' farm system director. New York's top pitcher was right-handed reliever Ace Adams with an 11-7 record and a 2.82 ERA in a league-high 70 appearances. Left-hander Cliff Melton was the most prolific starter at 9-13 with a 3.19 ERA.

On July 6 New York obtained outfielder Joe Medwick from the Brooklyn Dodgers for $50,000. Shortstop Buddy Kerr made his major league debut September 8 against the Philadelphia Phillies at the Polo Grounds in New York and became the first player in franchise history to hit a home run in his first at-bat.

Ott received a vote of confidence and a new three-year contract to continue as manager September 9.

1944			
67-87	.435	5th Place (-38)	674,483
		Mel Ott	

The 1944 Giants went 67-87 to finish in fifth place in the National League, 38 games behind the St. Louis Cardinals, who won the third of their three consecutive pennants. Combined with its 1943 record of 55-98, New York owned a two-year mark of 122-185, a lowly .397 winning percentage.

Before the season, former player, manager and farm system director Bill Terry (1923-42) announced he was quitting baseball for good to become a partner in a business firm.

The year got off to a record-breaking start as first baseman Phil Weintraub set the franchise standard with 11 RBI in a 26-8 win over the Brooklyn Dodgers at the Polo Grounds in New York on April 30. He had two doubles, a triple and a home run. Catcher Ernie Lombardi drove in seven runs, while right fielder-manager Mel Ott equalled his records of five walks and six runs scored. The Giants drew 17 walks from Brooklyn pitchers in the most lopsided victory in franchise history.

During World War II, night baseball had been disallowed, but with the situation improving in 1944 the Giants were allowed to play their first game under the lights since 1941 on May 23 against Brooklyn at Ebbets Field in Brooklyn. New York led the Dodgers 2-1 with two on and two outs in the bottom of the ninth when Brooklyn outfielder Lloyd Waner hit a routine fly ball to right center for what appeared to be the final out. But just as the ball landed in center fielder Johnny Rucker's glove, right fielder Charlie Mead, ironically inserted for defensive purposes, bumped into Rucker and knocked the ball loose. Both Brooklyn runners scored, and the Dodgers won the game by the score of 3-2.

On June 21 Ott passed Honus Wagner of the Louisville Colonels and the Pittsburgh Pirates (1897-1917) for career runs scored with his 1,741st against the Dodgers at Ebbets Field.

In an effort to raise money for war bonds, the Giants, Dodgers and New York Yankees played against each other in a six-inning contest at the Polo Grounds on June 26. Each team played successive innings against the other two teams, then sat out an inning. The final score was Dodgers 5, Yankees 1, Giants 0. More than 50,000 fans were on hand, and $6.5 million was raised.

New York tied the franchise record with 13 straight losses from August 9-20 (also from June 23-July 6, 1902). Right-hander Bill Voiselle snapped the skid with a 3-1 win over the St. Louis Cardinals in the second game of a double-header at Sportsman's Park in St. Louis on August 20. Voiselle went on to post a 21-16 record with a 3.02 ERA while topping the league with 312.2 innings pitched and 161

Catcher Ernie Lombardi collected seven RBI in a 26-8 victory over the Brooklyn Dodgers at the Polo Grounds in New York on April 30, 1944. First baseman Phil Weintraub set with the franchise record with 11 RBI in the same game. (Brace Photo)

strikeouts. He was the first Giants' pitcher to reach the 20-victory plateau since left-handers Carl Hubbell (22) and Cliff Melton (20) in 1937. Right-hander Ace Adams led the N.L. with 65 appearances.

Ott bounced back to bat .388 with 26 home runs and 82 RBI, while left fielder Joe Medwick batted .337 with 85 RBI, Weintraub batted .316 with 13 homers and 77 RBI and shortstop Buddy Kerr had 14 stolen bases.

For the first time since 1938, the Giants fared better in the standings than the Dodgers, who wound up in seventh place with a 63-91 record.

1945			
78-74	.513	5th Place (-19)	1,016,468
		Mel Ott	

Although the Giants finished the 1945 season in fifth place, 19 games behind the Chicago Cubs, they managed a winning record at 78-74 and reached a major milestone by drawing one million fans for the first time in franchise history (1,016,468). They passed the million mark September 26, but the Brooklyn Dodgers spoiled the party with an 8-1 victory.

New York made a strong start out of the gate and was in first place by 3½ games after splitting a double-header with the Pittsburgh Pirates at the Polo Grounds in New York on May 20. Four days later the Giants beat the Cincinnati Reds 7-6 on outfielder Danny Gardella's pinch hit home run at Crosley Field in Cincinnati. Before the game, the colorful Gardella shocked his road roommate, third baseman Nap Reyes, by writing a suicide note ("life is too much for me") and leaving the hotel room window opened. Reyes had been out and upon his return discovered the note and immediately rushed to the window, where Gardella was hanging onto the window and grinning from ear to ear. Reyes was still shaking when he arrived at the ball park.

Right fielder-manager Mel Ott continued to make headlines by breaking the National League record of 4,888 total bases (established by Honus Wagner of the Louisville Colonels and the Pittsburgh Pirates from 1897-1917) in the first game of a double-header against the Chicago Cubs at Wrigley Field in Chicago on May 30. Then on August 1 he belted his 500th career home run against right-hander Johnny Hutchings of the Boston Braves at the Polo Grounds. At the time, only Babe Ruth of the Boston Red Sox, New York Yankees and Boston Braves (1914-35) with 714 and Jimmie Foxx of the Philadelphia Athletics, Red Sox, Chicago Cubs and Philadelphia Phillies (1925-45) with 527 had more lifetime homers, and the second-highest total by an N.L. player was just 302 by Rogers Hornsby of the St. Louis Cardinals, Giants, Braves and Cubs (1915-33).

Ott also was in the news for fining right-hander Bill Voiselle $500 for not wasting an 0-2 pitch to St. Louis right fielder Johnny Hopp in the bottom of the ninth inning that helped rally the Cardinals from a 3-1 deficit to a 4-3 victory at Sportsman's Park in St. Louis on June 1. Ott subsequently recanted the fine, but Voiselle never seemed to get over the incident.

On June 16 New York traded outfielder Joe Medwick and left-hander Ewald Pyle to the Braves for catcher Clyde Kluttz.

Outfielder Whitey Lockman homered in his first major league at-bat against the Cardinals at the Polo Grounds on July 5.

The popular Ott, despite two fifth-place and two eight-place finishes the last four seasons, was given a five-year contract at a "substantial boost" to continue as manager September 27.

1946			
61-93	.396	8th Place (-36)	1,219,873
		Mel Ott	

Things were looking up in 1946, the first post-World War II season. On January 5 the Giants purchased catcher Walker Cooper from the St. Louis Cardinals for $175,000, by far the

largest sum of money they had paid for a player.

But New York's fortunes changed drastically as several players left the team to play in the Mexican League (organized by Jorge Pasquel), which was paying grande pesos. During a six-week period, the Giants lost pitchers Ace Adams, Harry Feldman, Sal Maglie and Adrian Zabala; first baseman Roy Zimmerman; second baseman George Hausmann; third baseman Nap Reyes; and outfielder Danny Gardella. None of the other seven National League teams suffered losses anywhere near so severe, and the Giants were doomed. Not surprisingly, they limped to a 61-93 record for eighth place, 36 games behind the St. Louis Cardinals, who won a best-of-three playoff series against the Brooklyn Dodgers to capture the National League pennant.

In the season opener April 16, 37-year-old player-manager Mel Ott hit his 511th and final home run against Philadelphia Phillies' left-hander Oscar Judd at the Polo Grounds in New York. But the following day Ott injured his knee diving after a fly ball and played sparingly and ineffectively the rest of the season.

Brooklyn manager Leo Durocher's infamous phrase, "Nice guys finish last" had its origin July 5 during an interview with Dodgers' broadcaster Red Barber. One day earlier the Dodgers and Giants split a double-header at the Polo Grounds with New York socking five home runs. Barber remarked to Durocher that with the Giants hitting so many home runs, Brooklyn was fortunate to gain a split in the two games. "Hell, they were nothing, just cheap Polo Grounds specials," Durocher responded. Said Barber, "Come on, Leo, be a nice guy and give credit where it's due." Snapped back Durocher: "Nice guys! Do you know a nicer guy than Mel Ott? Or any of the other Giants? And where are they? The nice guys over there are in last place!" Needless to say, the rest is history.

On September 9 future Giants' star and American icon Bobby Thomson made his major league debut against the Philadelphia Phillies at Shibe Park in Philadelphia.

Shortstop Buddy Kerr established two National League fielding records as the season mercifully came to an end. He broke the mark for consecutive chances handled by a shortstop without an error (252) against the Boston Braves at the Polo Grounds on September 26 and set the standard for consecutive errorless games (52) against Philadelphia at the Polo Grounds on September 29. Kerr still holds the record for consecutive chances without an error at 383 during a 68-game span from July 28 (1), 1946-May 25, 1947.

First baseman Johnny Mize led the Giants with a .337 batting average, 22 home runs and 70 RBI. Left fielder Sid Gordon batted .293, and second baseman Buddy Blattner had 12 stolen bases. Left-hander Dave Koslo was the only pitcher to reach double figures in wins, yet he was merely 14-19 with a 3.63 ERA. Right-hander Ken Trinkle paced the N.L. with 48 appearances.

On the positive side, the Giants surpassed the 1,000,000 mark in home attendance for the second straight season with a record draw of 1,219,873 spectators.

1947			
81-73	.526	4th Place (-13)	1,600,793
		Mel Ott	

The addition of three young players—right-handed pitcher Larry Jansen, second baseman Bill Rigney and center fielder Bobby Thomson—instilled some life into the Giants in 1947 and helped them rebound from their last-place showing the year before to go 81-73 and finish fourth, 13 games behind the Brooklyn Dodgers.

But the big story of the year was New York's home run hitting prowess that earned the team the nickname "Windowbreakers." The Giants blasted 221 homers, shattering the baseball record of 182 set by the New York

First baseman Johnny Mize led the National League with 51 home runs and 138 RBI during the 1947 season. (Brace Photo)

Yankees in 1936. New York's total remains a record for a 154-game season, tied by the Cincinnati Reds during the 1956 campaign.

First baseman Johnny Mize set the tone for the power spree by clouting three consecutive homers against the Boston Braves at Braves Field on April 24. Right fielder Willard Marshall duplicated the feat against the Cincinnati Reds at the Polo Grounds in New York on July 18. The Giants hit 55 homers in the month of July, a total that is still a National League record. The American League mark is 58 by the Baltimore Orioles in May of 1987. Mize added a homer in the All-Star Game against New York Yankees' right-hander Spec Shea in the fourth inning at Wrigley Field in Chicago.

At season's end, Mize had 51 homers (tied for the league lead), followed by Marshall (36), catcher Walker Cooper (35), Thomson (29) and Rigney (17). Mize batted .302 with N.L. highs of 138 RBI and 137 runs scored, Copper batted

.305 with 122 RBI and Marshall batted .291 with 107 RBI. Those three players are one of just six trios in Giants' history to collect 100 RBI. They were the last group until second baseman Jeff Kent (121), first baseman J.T. Snow (104) and left fielder Barry Bonds (101) in 1997.

The other news item of the year was the pitching of Jansen, who went 21-5 with a 3.16 ERA. Left-hander Dave Koslo had a 15-10 record with a 4.39 ERA, while right-hander Ken Trinkle was 8-4 with a 3.75 ERA and paced the league with 62 appearances.

Player-manager Mel Ott made his final appearance as a player—popping out to short-stop as a pinch hitter—against the Pittsburgh Pirates at Forbes Field in Pittsburgh on June 11. The Giants acquired right-handed pitcher Mort Cooper from the Boston Braves in exchange for right-hander Bill Voiselle and cash June 13. Mort reformed a battery with his younger brother, Walker, that previously existed with the St. Louis Cardinals from 1940-45.

For the third straight year, attendance reached an all-time high as the Giants attracted 1,600,793 fans to the Polo Grounds.

1948			
78-76	.506	5th Place (-13½)	1,459,269
	Mel Ott/Leo Durocher		

There are shockers, and then there are shockers. Giants' owner Horace C. Stoneham pulled a huge one July 16, 1948. With his team in a 37-38 funk, Stoneham chose to dismiss manager Mel Ott. Stoneham was interested in Brooklyn Dodgers' coach Burt Shotton, but when club president and general manager Brach Rickey mentioned that manager Leo Durocher was available, Stoneham chose him. That's right. Durocher went from manager of the cross-town rival Dodgers to manager of the Giants. The news stunned everyone in Flatbush and Gotham, not to mention the entire baseball world.

"The thought of Leo Durocher coming to manage the Giants was the furthest thing from anybody's mind," right fielder Willard Marshall recalled. "Nobody ever imagined it would happen. It definitely was a surprise and added to what already was quite a rivalry between the two ball clubs."

New York improved slightly to 41-38 under Durocher, a fiery competitor who was the complete opposite of the easy-going Ott, to wind up 78-76 overall for fifth place, 13½ games behind the Boston Braves.

"Leo was a great manager," right-handed pitcher Larry Jansen said. "He was always thinking ahead and that allowed him to make quick decisions, like when to bunt or hit and run or steal. When the game is going on, you don't have a lot of time to make decisions, but Leo was always a step ahead of the opposition. Mel Ott was a great guy, but because he had been an outfielder and not close to the action, I think he had a tough time making quick decisions."

Home runs again were the biggest on-the-field story for the Giants. On May 21 outfielder Les Layton socked a pinch hit homer in his first major league at-bat against the Chicago Cubs at the Polo Grounds in New York. New York paced the National League with 164 round-trippers. First baseman Johnny Mize led the way with 40 (tied for the league top spot) while batting .289 with 125 RBI, and third baseman Sid Gordon had 30 homers to go with a .299 batting average and 107 RBI. Seven of

In one of the most surprising moves in baseball history, the Giants hired Leo Durocher (left) from the cross-town rival Brooklyn Dodgers to replace Mel Ott (right) as manager on July 16, 1948.

New York's eight everyday position players hit at least 10 home runs with the lone exception being shortstop Buddy Kerr, who ironically had none.

Jansen enjoyed his second straight banner season, going 18-12 with a 3.61 ERA. Right-hander Sheldon Jones was 16-8 with a 3.35 ERA.

Stoneham had told Durocher to evaluate everyone, and at season's end Durocher offered his succinct recommendation, "Horace, back up the truck." In other words, wholesale changes were on the way.

1949			
73-81	.474	5th Place (-24)	1,218,446
		Leo Durocher	

The year 1949 began and ended with major news for the Giants. On January 28 New York signed its first black players, outfielder Monte Irvin and pitcher Ford Smith, and assigned them to their farm team in Jersey City, New Jersey.

Irvin and infielder Hank Thompson became the first blacks to join the Giants on July 5 and three days later became the first to play for them against the Brooklyn Dodgers at Ebbets Field in Brooklyn. Smith never made it to the major leagues.

Through it all, New York continued to hit home runs. Left fielder Whitey Lockman, third baseman Sid Gordon and right fielder Willard Marshall belted consecutive homers in the sixth inning against the Cincinnati Reds at the Polo Grounds in New York on June 13. Left-handed pitcher Monte Kennedy got in on the act with a grand slam en route to a 16-0 shutout of the Brooklyn Dodgers at the Polo Grounds on July 3. The Giants batted around in both the first and seventh innings. And Gordon became the third player in franchise history to sock two homers in one inning when he

Outfielder Monte Irvin (left) and infielder Hank Thompson (above) were the first blacks to join the Giants on July 5, 1949, and three days later became the first to play for them against the Brooklyn Dodgers at Ebbets Field in Brooklyn. (Brace Photo)

First baseman Sid Gordon hit two home runs in the second inning of the second game of a double-header against the Cincinnati Reds at Crosley Field in Cincinnati on July 31, 1949. (Brace Photo)

One of the keys to the Giants' improvement under manager Leo Durocher was the acquisition of second baseman Eddie Stanky from the Boston Braves on December 14, 1949. (Brace Photo)

accomplished the feat in the second inning of the second game of a double-header against Cincinnati at Crosley Field in Cincinnati on July 31. The other two were Hack Wilson at Philadelphia (July 1, 1925—2nd game) and Hank Leiber against Chicago (August 24, 1935). New York swept the double-header via the shutout, 10-0 behind right-hander Larry Jansen and 9-0 behind left-hander Adrian Zabala.

Center fielder Bobby Thomson was the Giants' most productive batter to the tune of a .309 average, 27 home runs and 109 RBI. Gordon batted at a .284 clip with 26 homers and 90 RBI, while Lockman had 12 stolen bases. Right-hander Sheldon Jones topped the pitching staff with a 15-12 record and a 3.34 ERA. Jansen was 15-16 with a 3.85 ERA. Left-hander Dave Koslo led the National League with a 2.50 ERA but managed just an 11-14 record.

Manager Leo Durocher, who signed a two-year contract extension May 13, didn't

like the makeup of his team. He preferred a team built on aggressiveness and speed, rather than power. So, as promised, he began to make changes as the Giants limped home with a 73-81 record and a second straight fifth-place finish, 24 games behind the, ugh, Brooklyn Dodgers.

First, New York sold first baseman Johnny Mize to the New York Yankees for $40,000 on August 22. Then in the deal that would drastically alter the landscape of the Giants' lineup, shortstop Alvin Dark and second baseman Eddie Stanky were obtained from the Boston Braves for Gordon, Marshall and shortstop Buddy Kerr on December 14. Kerr would return to the Giants as a scout and signed future Hall of Famer right-handed pitcher Juan Marichal on September 17, 1957.

"Leo wanted a ball club that could run, hit and run, hit to the opposite field," Jansen recalled. "The Giants were not a fast ball club, and Leo could not stand that. He just couldn't

put up with it, so he went out and traded for his type of players. We started playing a different kind of baseball for sure and became a pretty good team."

1950			
86-68	.558	3rd Place (-5)	1,008,878
		Leo Durocher	

Three off-season deals revitalized the club and placed it in position for its great pennant run of 1951. The Giants acquired the double-play combination of second baseman Eddie Stanky and shortstop Alvin Dark from the Boston Braves and acquired pitchers Sal Maglie and Jim Hearn.

Although Dark would go on to a better career and later would manage the Giants, Stanky batted .300 and scored 115 runs in his Giants' debut. The right-handed Maglie, who had jumped to the Mexican League, was 18-4 with a 2.21 ERA. Hearn, also a right-hander, went 11-3.

The newcomers changed the complexion of a sagging old team and took off in the second half, climbing from seventh place on Memorial Day to a solid third-place finish with an 86-68 record, five games behind the Philadelphia Phillies. Rookie outfielder Monte Irvin contributed a .299 average and 15 home runs in 105 games.

Center fielder Bobby Thomson, one year away from carving his niche in Giants' history, hit a team-leading 25 home runs. Catcher Wes Westrum added 23 homers, and third baseman Hank Thompson hit 20 homers. One year later, the club proved fast finishes were no fluke.

1951			
98-59	.624	1st Place (+1)	1,059,539
		Leo Durocher	

Outfielder-third baseman Bobby Thomson culminated his dream season with a historic playoff home run against the cross-town rival Brooklyn Dodgers. That was the dramatic punctuation of a great comeback which started after the Giants trailed Brooklyn by 13½ games on August 11. Shortstop Alvin Dark batted .303 with 41 doubles.

The Giants started their spree with a 16-game winning streak and finished the regular season winning 12 of their last 13 games. They wound up 98-59 after winning a best-of-three playoff series against the Dodgers two games to one.

Thomson was a standout prior to the playoffs, too, batting .293 with a team-leading 31 homers and 101 RBI. Left fielder Monte Irvin emerged as a star, contributing a team-high .312 average, 24 homers and 121 RBI. Center fielder Willie Mays, playing 68 games as a rookie, overcame a 1-for-25 start and finished with 20 home runs in a dazzling preview of what was to come.

The pitching was in the trusted hands of starters Sal Maglie, Larry Jansen and Jim Hearn, who combined for 63 victories and merely 26 defeats. The right-handed Maglie led the way with a 23-6 record and a 2.93 ERA, slightly better than fellow right-handers Jansen (23-11, 3.03) and Hearn (17-9).

1952			
92-62	.597	2nd Place (-4½)	984,940
		Leo Durocher	

Outfielder Willie Mays was in military service and outfielder Monte Irvin fractured an ankle in a spring training game, but the momentum of the 1951 miracle and manager Leo Durocher's deft guidance enabled the Giants to remain in the race and post a 92-62 record. New York finished in second place, 4½ games behind the Brooklyn Dodgers.

Third baseman Bobby Thomson continued where he left off the previous season, leading the way with 108 RBI. He also had a rare triple-double with 29 doubles, a league-leading 14 triples and 24 home runs. Shortstop Alvin Dark was the team batting leader at .301.

Pitcher Hoyt Wilhelm was perhaps the first great relief specialist in the National League. In 1952 he posted a 15-3 record with 11 saves while leading the league in appearances (71), winning percentage (.833) and ERA (2.43). (Brace Photo)

The pitching was solid, aided by the addition of right-handed knuckleballer Hoyt Wilhelm, perhaps the first great relief specialist in the National League. The future Hall of Famer appeared in a league-high 71 games, posting a 15-3 record with 11 saves and an N.L.-best 2.43 ERA.

Wilhelm also was tops in winning percentage (.833), supporting a solid rotation. Right-hander Sal Maglie was 18-8 with a 2.92 ERA as the ace. The "Barber" was complemented by right-hander Jim Hearn's 14-7 record. Spot starters Dave Koslo, Al Corwin and Bill Connelly were a combined 21-8.

1953			
70-84	.455	5th Place (-35)	811,518
		Leo Durocher	

The lull before the storm. Still minus outfielder Willie Mays, the Giants stayed around .500 much of the year, but faltered over the final two months and finished 14 games below

the break-even mark at 70-84 and in fifth place, 35 games behind the champion Brooklyn Dodgers.

Center fielder Bobby Thomson once again was solid with 26 home runs and 106 RBI, and the team boasted of four .300 hitters: right fielder Don Mueller (.333), left fielder Monte Irvin (.329), third baseman Hank Thompson (.302) and shortstop Alvin Dark (.300). Irwin rebounded from his ankle injury with 21 homers and 97 RBI.

Dark contributed 41 doubles and 23 home runs. Thompson hit 24 home runs, and utility man Daryl Spencer provided 20 homers off the bench. But the pitching was woeful, topped by right-hander Ruben Gomez's meager 13-11 record and right-hander Hoyt Wilhelm's 15 saves and a 3.04 ERA.

1954			
97-57	.630	1st Place (+5)	1,155,067
		Leo Durocher	

Center fielder Willie Mays' remarkable return and the acquisition of pitchers Johnny Antonelli and Marv Grissom placed the Giants back on track. San Francisco won the National League pennant with a 97-57 record, five games ahead of the Brooklyn Dodgers.

Outfielder Dusty Rhodes' power off the bench added a big boost, including two home runs in a World Series sweep of the mighty Cleveland Indians.

The incomparable Mays wasted no time finding his groove in his first full season following a two-year Army hitch. He batted a National League-leading .345 with 33 doubles, 13 triples, 41 home runs, 119 runs and 110 RBI as the envy of stickball players in New York.

Right fielder Don Mueller finished right behind the "Say Hey Kid" with a .342 average and a league-leading 212 hits. Third baseman Hank Thompson added 26 home runs and 86 RBI. Rhodes, in the equivalent of half a season, contributed a .341 average, 15 home runs and 50 RBI in 82 games and 164 at-bats.

The pitching staff had a league-best 3.09 ERA, and much of the credit went to Antonelli and Grissom. The left-handed Antonelli was 21-7 with an N.L.-leading 2.29 ERA. The right-handed Grissom had 19 saves and a 2.36 ERA. Right-handers Ruben Gomez (17-9), Sal Maglie (14-6) and Hoyt Wilhelm (12-4) also excelled.

1955			
80-74	.519	3rd Place (-18½)	824,112
		Leo Durocher	

Center fielder Willie Mays was at it again with another triple-double, but his supporting cast dropped off appreciably. Wondrous Willie batted .319 with 18 doubles, 13 triples and a National League-leading 51 home runs. He also scored 123 runs and knocked in 127.

Right fielder Don Mueller slipped to .306 and outfielder Dusty Rhodes batted .305 off the bench, but there wasn't much power to aug-ment what Mays provided. Third baseman Hank Thompson was second on the club with 17 homers, and left fielder Whitey Lockman added 15 for a lackluster offense.

The pitching didn't come close to approaching its 1954 totals. Left-hander John Antonelli and right-hander Jim Hearn both were a disappointing 14-16, and right-hander Sal Maglie's final fling before he was traded to the Brooklyn Dodgers was a 9-5 record. Right-hander Don Liddle was a solid 10-4.

New York wound up with an 80-74 record, good for a third-place finish, 18½ games behind Brooklyn.

1956			
67-87	.435	6th Place (-26)	629,179
		Bill Rigney	

Center fielder Willie Mays added a league-leading 40 stolen bases to his remarkable repertoire, but his other numbers weren't

In 1955 center fielder Willie Mays led the major leagues with 51 home runs. Here he displays the bat and ball used for hitting No. 51 against Robin Roberts of the Philadelphia Phillies at the Polo Grounds in New York on September 26. (AP/Wide World Photos)

First baseman Bill White played for New York in 1956. He served as president of the National League from 1989-94. (Brace Photo)

so imposing by his standards: .296 average, 36 home runs and 84 RBI. Newcomers Jackie Brandt (.299) and Red Schoendienst (.296) had solid seasons in left field and second base, respectively.

Rookie first baseman Bill White, who would become president of the National League, showed promise with 22 home runs and 59 RBI, but soon would be expendable because of Orlando Cepeda's presence. Outfielder Dusty Rhodes lost his magic, slipping to .217 as a reserve.

Left-handed pitcher Johnny Antonelli was the only Giants' pitcher to stand out in a miserable year. He was 20-13 with a 2.86 ERA on a club that had nobody else win so many as eight games. Right-hander Steve Ridzek was a decent 6-2, and right-hander Marv Grissom posted a 1.56 ERA in relief.

The end result was sixth place in the standings with a 67-87 record, 26 games behind the Brooklyn Dodgers.

1957			
69-85	.448	6th Place (-26)	653,923
		Bill Rigney	

If you thought 1956 was bad, 1957 was even worse (despite two more victories) because there was season-long grumbling about the club's move to Minneapolis or San Francisco. It all came down to a sad final day at the Polo Grounds on September 29, a 9-1 loss to the Pittsburgh Pirates before a mere 11,606 fans.

There wasn't much fun prior to the final curtain, either. Center fielder Willie Mays, as usual, led the way with a .333 average, 35

The Giants head to their clubhouse beyond center field after playing their final game at the Polo Grounds in New York on September 29, 1957—a 9-1 loss to the Pittsburgh Pirates before a mere 11,606 fans. (National Baseball Library and Archive)

home runs, 97 RBI and a National League-leading 38 stolen bases. Left fielder Hank Sauer, formerly a Most Valuable Player with the Chicago Cubs, added 26 homers.

A generous pitching staff featured right-hander Ruben Gomez (15-13) and left-hander Johnny Antonelli (12-18), who both posted a 3.78 ERA. Right-hander Curt Barclay was next at 9-9, and right-hander Marv Grissom was effective with 14 saves and a 2.60 ERA.

But there was little positive about 1957 at the Polo Grounds, as the Giants bid farewell with a 69-85 record, 26 games behind the Milwaukee Braves.

1958			
80-74	.519	3rd Place (-12)	1,272,625
		Bill Rigney	

The Giants' first season on the West Coast was a breath of fresh air for the franchise. Attendance nearly doubled from the final year at the Polo Grounds, despite bandbox Seals Stadium (capacity 22,900), and the club jumped from sixth to third with an 80-74 record, 12 games behind the Milwaukee Braves.

Center fielder Willie Mays was the main attraction with his career-best .347 batting average, but the fans were as enchanted by four newcomers who landed on the all-rookie team: first baseman Orlando Cepeda, right fielder Willie Kirkland, third baseman Jim Davenport and outfielder Leon Wagner.

Cepeda was unanimous Rookie of the Year after batting .312 with 25 home runs and 96 RBI. Mays had 29 homers and 96 RBI, barely losing the batting title to Richie Ashburn of the Philadelphia Phillies (.350-.347). Left-hander Johnny Antonelli was the pitching ace at 16-13 with a 3.28 ERA.

But the pitching favorite was right-hander Ruben Gomez, who shut out the transplanted Los Angeles Dodgers by the score of 8-0 in the historic West Coast opener

April 15. The Giants won 16 of 22 games with the dreaded Dodgers that year and were a surprising first-place team as late as July 29.

1959			
83-71	.539	3rd Place (-4)	1,442,130
		Bill Rigney	

One of the tightest races in National League history found the Giants, Los Angeles Dodgers and Milwaukee Braves in contention up to the final weekend. The Giants held a two-game lead with eight games remaining before winning merely one game the rest of the way.

Going into the final day, the Giants needed a double-header sweep of the St. Louis Cardinals and losses by the Dodgers and

The scene is Montgomery Street as the Giants are welcomed to San Francisco with a downtown parade April 14, 1958. (San Francisco Chronicle/SPI Archives)

Ruben Gomez delivers the first pitch in San Francisco Giants' history against the Los Angeles Dodgers at Seals Stadium on April 15, 1958. The batter is center fielder Gino Cimoli, the catcher is Valmy Thomas and the umpire is Jocko Conlin. (Dick Dobbins/SPI Archives)

Braves for a tie. The Dodgers won to clinch, and the Giants lost both games to finish third with an 83-71 record after being ahead much of the season.

A solid rotation was the key to success. Right-handed newcomer Sam Jones tied Warren Spahn of the Braves for the victory lead at 21-15 and was the league ERA champion at 2.83, edging right-handed teammate Stu Miller's 2.84. Left-hander Johnny Antonelli complemented Jones with a 19-10 record.

On June 12 left-hander Mike McCormick pitched a five-inning, rain-shortened no-hitter against the Philadelphia Phillies at Shibe Park in Philadelphia, and Jones held the St. Louis Cardinals hitless for seven innings before the rains came at Sportsman's Park in St. Louis on September 26.

The offensive highlight was first baseman Willie McCovey's smashing 4-for-4 debut against Robin Roberts of the Philadelphia Phillies. "Big Mac" was Rookie of the Year after batting at a .354 clip. Mays batted .313 with 34 home runs and 104 RBI. Cepeda matched him at .317 with 27 homers and 105 RBI.

1960			
79-75	.513	5th Place (-16)	1,795,356
Bill Rigney/Tom Sheehan			

The Giants shifted to brand-new Candlestick Park and immediately established a new franchise attendance record at 1,795,356. But it was a season of turmoil. Manager Bill Rigney was fired June 18 with the team in second place.

Successor Tom Sheehan, a longtime crony of owner Horace Stoneham, took over and the team dived to a fifth-place finish with a 79-75 record, 16 games behind the Pittsburgh Pirates. The famous winds of Candlestick Park sapped the team of its power, and there was frequent grumbling about the conditions at the new ball park.

All wasn't gloomy, however. Vice president Richard Nixon threw out the ceremonial first pitch and right-hander Sam Jones' three-hitter downed the St. Louis Cardinals 3-1 in the Candlestick opener April 12. Left fielder Orlando Cepeda had all three RBI and finished the season with 24 home runs and 96 RBI.

Center fielder Willie Mays was the offensive standout with a .319 batting average, 29 homers and 103 RBI despite winds that weren't to his advantage. Right-hander Juan Marichal made his debut July 19 at Candlestick, pitching a one-hit shutout over the Philadelphia Phillies en route to a 6-2 record in 11 starts.

1961			
85-69	.552	3rd Place (-8)	1,390,679
Alvin Dark			

It was a highly-offensive season, aided by the expansion Houston Colt .45s and New York

Stan Musial of the St. Louis Cardinals (left) and Willie Mays are two of the game's most-celebrated players.

Mets, but the Giants didn't get sufficient starting pitching to sustain their dangerous lineup. No starter won more than 13 games. Right-handed swing man Stu Miller was the big winner at 14-5. San Francisco finished a solid 85-69 for third place, eight games behind the Cincinnati Reds.

The best and worst of the season were compacted in an April weekend at Milwaukee's County Stadium. Two days after Warren Spahn pitched the first-ever no-hitter against San Francisco, center fielder Willie Mays became the ninth player in baseball history to hit four home runs in one game.

Mays finished with a .308 average, 40 homers and 123 RBI but was somewhat obscured by first baseman/outfielder Orlando Cepeda, who enjoyed his finest year with the Giants. The "Baby Bull" batted .311 with 46 home runs and a San Francisco-record that still stands: 142 RBI.

The Giants hosted the 30th All-Star Game, one of two played that season. Mays scored the winning run on a 10th-inning single by Roberto Clemente of the Pittsburgh Pirates, but much of the attention went to a wind gust that nudged Miller into a costly balk.

1962			
103-62	.624	1st Place (+1)	1,556,551
		Alvin Dark	

Arguably the finest team in San Francisco history won a dramatic three-game playoff with the Los Angeles Dodgers and took the vaunted New York Yankees down to a seventh game in the World Series before losing 1-0. The 103 victories (against 62 losses) were the Giants' most since 1905.

It was a mini version of the great 1951 race, what with the Giants trailing the Dodgers by four games on September 16. The Giants went 7-6 the rest of the way, earning a tie because Los Angeles slipped to 3-10 down the stretch.

Center fielder Willie Mays had a National League-leading 49 home runs and 141 RBI. First baseman Orlando Cepeda added 35 homers and 114 RBI. Right fielder Felipe Alou batted .316 with 25 homers and 98 RBI. Catchers Tom Haller and Ed Bailey combined for 35 homers and 100 RBI. Left fielder Harvey Kuenn batted at a .304 clip, and third baseman Jim Davenport contributed a .297 average.

The four-man pitching rotation combined for a dazzling 77-38 record, paced by right-hander Jack Sanford's 16 consecutive victories and a 24-7 mark. Left-handers Billy O'Dell (19-14) and Billy Pierce (16-6) and right-hander Juan Marichal (18-11) followed. Right-hander Stu Miller registered 19 saves.

1963			
88-74	.543	3rd Place (-11)	1,568,965
		Alvin Dark	

It was a breakthrough year for right-handed pitcher Juan Marichal and left fielder Willie McCovey and included two of the greatest games in the history of Candlestick Park. But it was more a season of personal success than team accomplishment for the underachieving defending National League champions. The Giants posted an 88-74 record, finishing in third place, 11 games behind the Los Angeles Dodgers.

Marichal clearly was the highlight. The high-kicking "Dominican Dandy" was 25-8 with a 2.41 ERA, pitched the Giants' first nine-inning no-hitter since Carl Hubbell in 1929 and went the distance in a dramatic, 1-0 victory over Warren Spahn of the Milwaukee Braves in 16 innings.

McCovey signaled the demise of Orlando Cepeda as a Giant by hitting 44 home runs with 102 RBI in his first season as a regular.

Juan Marichal was one of the premier pitchers in the National League during the 1960s but somehow never earned the Cy Young Award.

Cepeda batted .316 with 34 homers and 97 RBI. Center fielder Mays contributed a .314 average, 38 homers and 103 RBI.

The first San Francisco no-hitter was notched by Marichal against the Houston Colt .45s at Candlestick Park on June 15. Two weeks later Mays' 16th-inning homer won a Candlestick classic. On September 15 three brothers—Felipe, Matty and Jesus Alou—played in a major league outfield for the first time.

1964			
90-72	.556	4th Place (-3)	1,500,883
		Alvin Dark	

It was a deceptive fourth-place finish for a club that was embroiled in a four-team race up to the final weekend. San Francisco wound up 90-72 for fourth place, just three games behind the St. Louis Cardinals. Crucial injuries played a significant role for the first time since the Giants shifted westward from New York.

Right-hander Juan Marichal was a solid 21-8, but back spasms forced him to miss six starts, and the Giants dropped 8½ games behind before they regrouped down the stretch. Cracked ribs, muscle pulls and sore knees limited left fielder Willie McCovey to a .220 batting average, 18 home runs and 54 RBI.

On a positive note, center fielder Willie Mays was the National League home run champion with 47 to go with 111 RBI, and rookies Jim Ray Hart and Jesus Alou made favorable first impressions at third base and right field, respectively. Hart set a Giants' rookie record with 31 home runs, and Alou matched the club mark with six hits against the Chicago Cubs at Wrigley Field in Chicago on July 10.

There was a historic 32-inning doubleheader against the New York Mets at Shea Stadium in New York on May 31, the Giants winning the opener 5-3 in nine innings and the second game 8-6 in 23 innings. In all the two teams played for 9 hours and 52 minutes.

Left-hander Masonari Murakami became the first Japanese native to pitch in the majors when he made the jump from Class-A Fresno in September.

1965			
95-67	.586	2nd Place (-2)	1,542,588
Herman Franks			

The Giants were eliminated on the next to the last day of the season for the second year in a row, yet it stands as the third winningest season (95-67) in San Francisco history, largely because of a sensational season by incomparable center fielder Willie Mays.

Wondrous Willie was voted the National League Most Valuable Player after his .317 batting average, career-high 52 home runs and 112 RBI nearly pushed the Giants over the top. First baseman-outfielder Orlando Cepeda missed most of the season with injury. First baseman Willie McCovey broke out with 39 homers and 92 RBI.

Mays blasted 17 home runs in August to give pennant hopes impetus. The Giants took over first place on September 7 and remained there for three weeks with the help of a 14-game winning streak, a San Francisco record. The Dodgers won 13 in a row in September.

Los Angeles went 15-1 down the stretch to edge the Giants by two games. Right-handed pitcher Juan Marichal's nine-game suspension for attacking Dodgers' catcher John Roseboro with a bat at Candlestick Park in San Francisco on August 22 proved costly. Marichal was 22-13 with a 2.14 ERA, 240 strikeouts and 10 shutouts.

1966			
93-68	.578	2nd Place (-1½)	1,651,293
Herman Franks			

Falling barely short a third consecutive year, the Giants rode the sturdy right arms of Juan Marichal (25-6) and Gaylord Perry (21-8).

Marichal fashioned a 2.23 ERA and was the winning pitcher in the All-Star Game after entering it 12-1.

Marichal, who struck out 15 Philadelphia Phillies on July 22, and Perry combined for a 46-14 record, but other starters Bob Bolin, Ron Herbel and Ray Sadecki were a combined 18-22. The left-handed Sadecki, acquired in a controversial early-season trade for first baseman-outfielder Orlando Cepeda, was a 3-7 flop.

The good news was the offense. Center fielder Willie Mays (37), first baseman Willie McCovey (36), third baseman Jim Ray Hart (33) and catcher Tom Haller (27) combined for 133 home runs, powering a September surge that nearly captured a pennant. The club was five games behind on September 20 but went 8-1 thereafter.

A 7-4 victory over Pittsburgh on the final day kept the Giants in contention. If the Dodgers had lost that day, the Giants would have gone to Cincinnati for a makeup game. But the Dodgers defeated Philadelphia by the score of 6-3 for the pennant. San Francisco wound up with a 93-68 record.

On August 22, 1965, pitcher Juan Marichal attacked Los Angeles Dodgers' catcher John Roseboro with a bat. Marichal was suspended for nine games.

1967			
91-71	.562	2nd Place (-10½)	1,237,119
	Herman Franks		

It was an era of superior pitching, and the Giants came up with a bonus when they re-acquired left-hander Mike McCormick from the Washington Senators and he became the only Cy Young Award winner in San Francisco history.

Right-hander Juan Marichal, who never earned pitching's most coveted honor, pitched only once after August 4 because of a hamstring injury. McCormick picked up the slack with a 22-10 record and 2.85 ERA, becoming the first Giants' lefty to win 20 games since Johnny Antonelli in 1956.

The pitching staff topped the National League with a 2.92 ERA, and right-hander Frank Linzy was the league's finest reliever with seven wins, 17 saves and a 1.51 ERA.

Meanwhile, a power-packed lineup wasn't devoid of some offensive highlights. First baseman Willie McCovey had 31 home runs and 91 RBI, hitting three grand slams at Candlestick Park. Third baseman Jim Ray Hart contributed 29 homers and 99 RBI. Center fielder Willie Mays slipped to 22 homers and 70 RBI.

The club was 21-7 down the stretch to wind up 91-71, but the St. Louis Cardinals won the pennant by 10½ games.

Mike McCormick pitched for the Giants from 1956-62 and then for the Baltimore Orioles (1963-64) and Washington Senators (1965-66) before returning to San Francisco from 1967-70. He won the National League Cy Young Award in 1967, the only player in franchise history to earn pitching's most coveted honor.

1968			
88-74	.543	2nd Place (-9)	833,594
	Herman Franks		

Manager Herman Franks made it four consecutive second-place finishes, but a spirited September drive fell two games short of the St. Louis Cardinals, and he made good on his promise to retire if the Giants failed to win the pennant. San Francisco finished with an 88-74 record.

It was a season of great personal achievement. On the same September weekend at Candlestick Park, right-handed pitcher Gaylord Perry pitched a no-hitter over the Cardinals in a tidy 1 hour and 40 minutes. The next day, Ray Washburn of St. Louis improbably pitched a no-hitter against the Giants.

The pitching staff established a San Francisco record with a 2.71 ERA. Right-hander Juan Marichal led the way with a 26-9 record and a 2.43 ERA. Right-hander Bob Bolin, the fifth starter, was a solid 10-5 and posted a 1.99 ERA, best in San Francisco history. Right-hander Frank Linzy had a 2.08 ERA.

Offensively, first baseman Willie McCovey led the league with 36 home runs and 105 RBI. Right fielder Bobby Bonds was impressive as a rookie with power and speed. His debut against the Los Angeles Dodgers featured a grand slam homer for his first hit. That achievement had not been done since 1898.

1969
90-72   .556   2nd Place (-3)   870,341
Clyde King

The Giants increased their chances to advance when divisional play was introduced, but they finished second again, this time under manager Clyde King. But they made it interesting, reaching the final weekend before elimination. San Francisco wound up 90-72, three games behind the Atlanta Braves in the National League West Division.

First baseman Willie McCovey attained career highs with 45 home runs, 126 RBI and a .656 slugging percentage, leading the league in each category. He also batted .320, his highest full-season average, and was voted the N.L. Most Valuable Player. Right fielder Bobby Bonds came into his own during his first full season. He used his sprinter speed for 45 stolen bases, adding 32 home runs and 90 RBI.

The pitching was dominated by right-hander Juan Marichal, who registered a career-best 2.10 ERA, leading the league, and going 21-11. Right-hander Gaylord Perry was 19-14 with a 2.49 ERA.

1970
86-76   .531   3rd Place (-16)   728,498
Clyde King/Charlie Fox

The club featured a high-octane offense, but a lack of pitching depth caused early trouble. With a 19-23 record in late May, King was fired and replaced by Charlie Fox, who went 67-53 the rest of the way but couldn't climb higher than third place. San Francisco's overall record was 86-76, 16 games behind the Cincinnati Reds.

First baseman Willie McCovey enjoyed his third consecutive dominating season with 39 home runs and 126 RBI. Dick Dietz had the best season ever by a San Francisco catcher, batting .300 with 22 homers and 107 RBI. Cen-

ter fielder Willie Mays had 28 homers (including No. 600 of his career) and his 3,000th hit.

Right fielder Bobby Bonds set a San Francisco record with 134 runs scored, leading the league in the process, and became the second San Francisco batter with 200 hits while batting at a .302 clip. Utility man Jim Ray Hart hit for the cycle against the Atlanta Braves at Atlanta-Fulton County Stadium on July 8.

Right-handed workhorse Gaylord Perry pitched four consecutive shutouts in September and was 23-13 with a 3.20 ERA.

1971
90-72   .556   1st Place (+1)   1,088,083
Charlie Fox

The "Year of the Fox" produced the first division title in Giants' history, but it came at a costly price. The club took the division lead with an 18-5 April but faltered down the stretch (8-16) and required a final-day victory in San Diego to clinch with a 90-72 record, one game better than the Los Angeles Dodgers.

With the help of a home run from rookie first baseman-outfielder Dave Kingman, Marichal posted a 5-1 victory and finished 18-11. But the last-day assignment, though rewarding, kept him from facing the Pittsburgh Pirates twice in the National League Championship Series, and Pittsburgh won three out of four to advance to the World Series.

The Giants won a championship without a .300 batter or a 20-game winner, the first time any major league team did so since 1876. Right fielder Bobby Bonds made merely two errors afield and paced the offense with 33 home runs, 110 runs and 102 RBI.

Rookie shortstop Chris Speier provided leadership, and Fox was named Manager of the Year. Marichal and right-hander Gaylord Perry (16-12) were the staff aces, and right-hander Jerry Johnson provided solid relief with 12 wins, 18 saves and a 2.97 ERA.

Gaylord Perry pitched four consecutive shutouts in September of 1970. (S.F. Giants Archives)

Jerry Johnson provided solid relief pitching with 12 wins, 18 saves and a 2.97 ERA for the 1971 pennant-winning Giants. (S.F. Giants Archives)

		1972	
69-86	.445	5th Place (-26½)	637,327
		Charlie Fox	

High hopes were dashed early in the strike-shortened season when first baseman Willie McCovey broke his right arm in the fourth game of the year in San Diego. McCovey missed much of the season and contributed merely 14 home runs and 35 RBI to the first losing season in San Francisco. The Giants wound up 69-86 for fifth place, 26½ games behind the Cincinnati Reds.

It suddenly turned into a rebuilding year. Right-handed pitcher Jim Barr set a major league record by retiring 41 consecutive batters over two starts. Left-hander Ron Bryant showed promise with a 14-7 record and a 2.90 ERA, compensating for Gaylord Perry's loss and Juan Marichal's 6-16 record.

The offense was puny by Giants' standards. Shortstop Chris Speier was the leading batter at .269. Utility man Dave Kingman hit 29 home runs to go with 83 RBI, just ahead of right fielder Bobby Bonds' 26 homers and 80 RBI. Kingman hit for the cycle against the Houston Astros at the Astrodome on April 16. Catcher Dave Rader, center fielder Garry Maddox and Barr were outstanding as rookies.

		1973	
88-74	.543	3rd Place (-11)	834,193
		Charlie Fox	

A temporary rebirth preceded four straight down years for the franchise. The Giants went 88-74 to finish in third place, 11 games behind the Cincinnati Reds.

Right fielder Bobby Bonds and left-handed

Wondrous Willie Mays, who patrolled center field for the Giants from 1951-52 and from 1954-72, arguably is the greatest player in National League history. He was the Most Valuable Player in 1954 and 1965.

pitcher Ron Bryant led the way, being named Player of the Year and Pitcher of the Year, respectively, for the major leagues by *The Sporting News,* an unusual double for a non-contender.

Bonds, in his perhaps his finest all-around season, just missed becoming the major's first-ever 40-40 player with 39 home runs and 43 stolen bases. As an All-Star Game reserve, he entered the game in Kansas City and earned Most Valuable Player honors with a winning homer.

Bryant, nicknamed "Bear," became the winningest left-hander in San Francisco history with a 24-12 record. He was the leader of a staff that received outstanding relief from right-handers Elias Sosa (10-4, 18 saves), Randy Moffitt (14 saves) and Don McMahon (4-0, 1.50 ERA).

Left fielder Gary Matthews earned Rookie of the Year honors with a .300 batting average. Second-year star center fielder Garry Maddox

batted .319. First baseman Willie McCovey contributed 29 homers and 75 RBI in merely 383 at-bats. Third baseman Ed Goodson (.302) gave the club three .300 hitters for the first time since 1962.

1974			
72-90	.444	5th Place (-30)	519,991
	Charlie Fox/Wes Westrum		

First baseman Willie McCovey and right-handed pitcher Juan Marichal joined the exodus of Sixties superstars, and the franchise started falling on hard times with a 72-90 season for fifth place, 30 games behind the Los Angeles Dodgers.

The year started off poorly when left-hander Ron Bryant was injured in a spring training swimming pool accident that ruined his career.

Manager Charlie Fox was replaced by former Giants' catcher Wes Westrum at mid-season, but there was no improvement. Injuries contributed to an inept offense (catcher Dave Rader was the batting leader at .291), but left fielder Gary Matthews had a solid sophomore season with 16 home runs and 82 RBI.

The pitching, however, was respectable. Left-hander Mike Caldwell provided a bonus with a 14-5 record and a 2.95 ERA. Right-hander Jim Barr logged a 13-9 record with a 2.74 ERA. Right-hander John D'Acquisto was *The Sporting News* National League Rookie Pitcher of the Year at 12-14.

1975			
80-81	.497	3rd Place (-27½)	522,925
	Wes Westrum		

The 1975 season hit rock bottom for the Stoneham era, but the club barely missed a winning season (80-81) with the help of unexpected sources: right-handed pitcher John Montefusco, first baseman Willie Montanez and center fielder Von Joshua all made great first impressions.

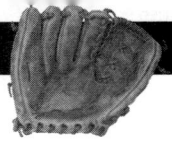

Ron "Bear" Bryant posted a 24-12 record in 1973 to become the winningest left-handed pitcher in San Francisco Giants' history.

Montefusco brashly gave the club a breath of fresh air, backing his boastfulness with a 15-9 record, a 2.88 ERA and 215 strikeouts, most by a National League rookie since 1911. Right-handed teammate Ed Halicki pitched a no-hitter against the New York Mets at Candlestick Park in San Francisco on August 24.

Montanez, acquired for outfielder Garry Maddox, batted .305. Joshua led the club with a .318 average. Right fielder Bobby Murcer, replacing Bobby Bonds in the first trade ever involving $100,000 players, batted .298 with a team-leading 91 RBI.

San Francisco finished in third place, 27½ games behind the Cincinnati Reds.

1976			
74-88	.457	4th Place (-28)	626,868
		Bill Rigney	

The Giants' rebirth under new owner Bob Lurie's regime was not an instant success. In fact, the club played better the previous year. San Francisco finished the 1976 season with a 74-88 record, 28 games behind the Cincinnati Reds.

But there was an emotional high when Lurie and co-owner Bud Herseth saved the team from the clutches of Toronto. Lurie, who eventually bought out Herseth, embraced a nostalgia theme in his efforts to stir attendance and interest, hiring Bill Rigney to manage.

The offensive talent was minimal with right fielder Bobby Murcer's 23 home runs and 90 RBI leading the way. Center fielder Larry Herndon batted .288 and earned some Rookie of the Year distinction. Right-handed pitcher John Montefusco was the ace at 16-14 with a 2.84 ERA, throwing a no-hitter against the Atlanta Braves at Atlanta-Fulton County Stadium on September 29. Right-hander Jim Barr was 15-12 with a 2.89 ERA. Right-hander Randy Moffitt and left-hander Gary Lavelle recorded 14 and 12 saves, respectively.

1977			
75-87	.463	4th Place (-23)	700,056
		Joe Altobelli	

The refurbished Giants had a new manager (Joe Altobelli), a former batting champion (third baseman Bill Madlock), a blossoming rookie (right fielder Jack Clark) and an old favorite (first baseman Willie McCovey) during a season of change that produced excitement but not results. San Francisco was 75-87 for fourth place, 23 games behind the Los Angeles Dodgers.

McCovey, ostensibly washed up, earned Comeback Player of the Year honors with a .280 batting average, a team-leading 28 home runs and 86 RBI at age 39. Madlock's San Francisco debut produced a .302 average. Clark contributed 13 homers and 51 RBI as a swaggering newcomer.

The pitching was dominated by Gary Lavelle's impeccable relief. The left-handed closer set a franchise record with 20 saves to go with a 7-7 record and a minuscule 2.06 ERA. Right-hander Ed Halicki enjoyed his best season, going 16-12 with a 3.31 ERA.

1978			
89-73	.549	3rd Place (-6)	1,740,480
		Joe Altobelli	

The 1978 season was a breakthrough year for the Giants, who remained in the thick of the race and surpassed one million in attendance for the first time since 1971. San Francisco was in first place at the All-Star break before winding up third with an 89-73 record, six games behind the Los Angeles Dodgers. Joe Altobelli was named National League Manager of the Year.

General manager Spec Richardson was Executive of the Year for assembling a club that was extremely competitive until it lost 10 of 11 in early September and dropped out of the race. Richardson's coup was adding left-handed pitcher Vida Blue and first baseman Mike Ivie in trades.

Blue crossed the bay in a blockbuster trade with the Oakland Athletics at the end of spring training and won 10 in a row from June 10-August 4 en route to an 18-10 season. He had a 2.79 ERA and became the first pitcher to start an All-Star Game for both leagues. Left-hander Bob Knepper was 17-11 with a 2.63 ERA.

Ivie, who joined the Giants from the San Diego Padres, batted .308 and provided four home runs as a pinch hitter, including two grand slams. Right fielder Jack Clark enjoyed his finest season with the Giants, batting .306 with 25 homers and 98 RBI while setting San Francisco franchise records with 46 doubles and a 26-game hitting streak from June 30-July 25.

1979			
71-91	.438	4th Place (-19½)	1,456,392
		Joe Altobelli/Dave Bristol	

A regression to the depths of the division cost manager Joe Altobelli his job in early September, but replacement Dave Bristol fared no better in a season of major disappointment. Few individuals played up to their 1978 form, and it showed as the Giants went 71-91 for fourth place, 19½ games behind the Cincinnati Reds.

San Francisco led the league in runs at the All-Star break, but an 8-19 August and a general pitching collapse sealed the club's doom. Left-hander Vida Blue, for instance, was the staff ace, yet merely had a 14-14 record and a 5.01 ERA to show for it.

First baseman-outfielder Willie McCovey, who had two stints with the Giants (1959-73 and 1977-80), ranks as one of the most popular players in franchise history. (S.F. Giants Archives)

Mike Ivie, playing more as Willie McCovey's replacement at first base, attained career highs with 27 home runs and 89 RBI. Right fielder Jack Clark added 26 homers and 86 RBI. McCovey passed Ott, Ernie Banks and Eddie Mathews on baseball's all-time home run list.

1980			
75-86	.466	5th Place (-17)	1,096,115
		Dave Bristol	

Hard hit by injuries, the Giants never recovered down the stretch. The club was 60-60 when right fielder Jack Clark was plunked on the wrist by a pitch, short-circuiting the batting order. The Giants went 15-26 thereafter to wind up with a 75-86 record and in fifth place, 17 games behind the Houston Astros. Nine different players went on the disabled list.

Clark missed one month, yet still finished with 22 home runs, 82 RBI and a National League-leading 18 game-winning RBI. First baseman Willie McCovey became a four-decade player and, at age 42, played his final game July 6. Third baseman Darrell Evans contributed 20 homers and 78 RBI.

Left-hander Vida Blue rebounded from his 1979 disappointment to go 14-10 with a 2.97 ERA, but there wasn't much help in the rotation. There was depth and quality in the bullpen with left-handers Al Holland and Gary Lavelle and right-hander Greg Minton combining for 35 saves.

1981			
27-32	.458	5th Place (-10)	
29-23	.558	3rd Place (- 3½)	
56-55	.505	4th Place (-11½)	632,276
		Frank Robinson	

Frank Robinson became the first African-American manager in the National League, and his leadership rallied a veteran club in the second half of a strike-shortened season.

The Giants were 27-32 and in fifth place, 10 games behind the Los Angeles Dodgers, when the strike occurred June 12 and knocked 51 games off their schedule. After play resumed August 10, the club went 29-23 in the second half and wasn't eliminated until October 1 before finishing third, 3½ games behind the Houston Astros.

Milt May batted .302, a San Francisco record for catchers, and backup first baseman Jeff Leonard batted at a .307 clip after being acquired from Houston.

But it was the pitching that carried the club, as evidenced by a 3.28 team ERA. Right-handed newcomer Doyle Alexander provided a big boost by posting an 11-7 record with a 2.90 ERA. Right-hander Greg Minton set the franchise record with 21 saves.

1982			
87-75	.537	3rd Place (-2)	1,200,948
		Frank Robinson	

A 20-7 September placed the Giants in the division race until the final weekend. The club was 32-42 on June 27, but its 55-33 mark over the last 88 games was the best in baseball. The Giants wound up 87-75, two games behind the Atlanta Braves.

Veterans Joe Morgan and Reggie Smith provided the spark. Second baseman Morgan, at age 39, batted .289 and joined Giants' lore by eliminating the Los Angeles Dodgers from the race with a home run on the final day of the season at Candlestick Park in San Francisco. First baseman Smith, 37, contributed 18 home runs and a .284 average.

Right fielder Jack Clark was the offensive leader with 27 homers, 103 RBI and a National League-leading 21 game-winning hits. He had help from rookie center fielder Chili Davis, who had 19 homers and 76 RBI. Tough in the clutch, the club won 27 games in its final at-bat.

A solid bullpen also made the late heroics possible. Right-hander Greg Minton went 10-4

with a 1.83 ERA and a then franchise-record 30 saves. He was complemented by left-handers Gary Lavelle (10-7, 2.67 ERA) and Al Holland (7-3). Right-handed San Francisco native Fred Breining (11-6, 3.08 ERA) was the best starter.

Manager Frank Robinson was inducted into the National Baseball Hall of Fame on August 1.

1983			
79-83	.488	5th Place (-12)	1,251,530
	Frank Robinson		

This team was a mystery, going 20-10 against division champions Los Angeles (West) and Philadelphia (East), yet a mere 59-73 against everyone else. It all added up to a 79-83 record for fifth place, 12 games behind the Dodgers. First baseman Reggie Smith didn't return and second baseman Joe Morgan was traded to the Phillies, so the club missed their leadership.

Left-handed pitcher Atlee Hammaker was the National League ERA leader at 2.25, but he was shaken by Fred Lynn's grand slam homer in the All-Star Game at Comiskey Park in Chicago and went 1-5 thereafter. Right fielder Jack Clark had 20 home runs and 66 RBI. Left fielder Jeff Leonard came through with 21 homers, 87 RBI and 21 stolen bases. Utility man Joel Youngblood batted a team-high .292 with 17 homers.

The Giants enjoyed a 19-7 May behind N.L. Player and Pitcher of the Month Darrell Evans and Bill Laskey, respectively. Evans, primarily a first baseman, batted .423 with nine homers and 23 RBI for the month, while Laskey was 6-0 with a 2.83 ERA.

San Francisco came from nowhere to nearly win the National League West Division title in 1982, thanks in large part to the play of veterans Joe Morgan (left) and Reggie Smith (right). (S.F. Giants Archives)

1984			
66-96	.407	6th Place (-26)	1,001,545
Frank Robinson/Danny Ozark			

The offense had the most hits in the National League (1,499), but it was betrayed by shaky pitching and porous defense. Things got so bad that manager Frank Robinson was fired August 4 with a 42-64 record and was replaced by coach Danny Ozark. The club went 24-32 the rest of the way to wind up 66-96 for sixth place, 26 games behind the San Diego Padres.

One of the few bright spots was center fielder Dan Gladden, who was tearing up the Pacific Coast League for Phoenix (.397 batting average) before finishing with the Giants and batting at a .351 clip.

Left fielder Jeff Leonard had a solid year with a .302 average, 21 home runs and 86 RBI, but right fielder Chili Davis and catcher Bob Brenly represented the club in the All-Star Game at Candlestick Park in San Francisco. Davis batted .315 with 21 homers and 81 RBI, while Brenly batted .291 with 20 homers and 80 RBI.

Joel Youngblood, playing out of position at third base, made 37 errors.

1985			
62-100	.383	6th Place (-33)	818,697
Jim Davenport/Roger Craig			

The Giants thought they hit rock bottom in 1984, but they plumbed new depths one year later by losing a franchise-record 100 games. The final mark was 62-100 for sixth place, 33 games behind the Los Angeles Dodgers. Rookie manager (and former infielder) Jim Davenport didn't last the season, replaced by Roger Craig with 18 games to go.

San Francisco's .233 batting average was the lowest in the major leagues, and other facets weren't so hot, either. Nobody batted above .271 or had more than 62 RBI, and nobody

won more than eight games in the Giants' most futile year since the 1943 club lost 98 games.

Highlights were rare. Catcher Bob Brenly led the club with 19 home runs, while rookie third baseman Chris Brown batted .271 with 16 homers and 61 RBI. Left fielder Jeff Leonard hit for the cycle against the Cincinnati Reds at Riverfront Stadium in Cincinnati on May 27. Right-handed pitcher Scott Garrelts won nine games and posted a 2.30 ERA.

But help was on its way, thanks to Craig and general manager Al Rosen.

1986			
83-79	.512	3rd Place (-13)	1,528,748
Roger Craig			

The Giants retooled following the 1985 debacle, and results were immediate. Remarkably, they were in first place at the All-Star break and became just the ninth team in history to post a winning record following a 100-loss season. Their final mark of 83-79 was good enough for third place, 13 games behind the Houston Astros.

A spring decision paid huge dividends. General manager Al Rosen and manager Roger Craig elected to go with first baseman Will Clark and second baseman Robby Thompson, neither of whom played Triple-A baseball. Clark's first major league swing produced a home run off future Hall of Fame fire-baller Nolan Ryan of the Astros.

The club slumped to 35-39 in the second half, but pride and confidence had been restored. The Giants won 26 games in their final at-bat, partly because of 10 homers and 59 RBI from pinch hitters. Clark batted .287 and Thompson .271.

Right-hander Mike Krukow had his finest season, going 20-9 with a 3.05 ERA, being named to the National League All-Star team and winning his 100th career game. Left-hander Vida Blue also reached a milestone,

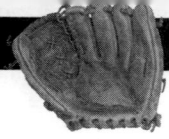

En route to losing a franchise-record 100 games during the 1985 season, Giants' owner Bob Lurie hired Al Rosen (left) as general manager and Roger Craig (right) as field manager September 18. Rosen and Craig restored pride and confidence and led San Francisco to the National League West Division championship in 1987 and to the World Series in 1989. (S.F. Giants Archives)

posting his 200th victory during a 10-10 season. Candy Maldonado had 18 home runs and 85 RBI in a reserve role.

		1987	
90-72	.556	1st Place (+6)	1,917,863
		Roger Craig	

A San Francisco-record 205 home runs powered the Giants to their first National League West Division title in 15 years. The Giants went 90-72 to beat out the Cincinnati Reds by six games.

First baseman Will Clark, shrugging off the sophomore jinx, led the way with a career-high 35 home runs and added 91 RBI and a .308 batting average.

Center fielder Chili Davis was second with 24 home runs, followed by right fielder Candy Maldonado (20) and left fielder Jeffrey Leonard

(19). Maldonado hit for the cycle against the St. Louis Cardinals at Busch Stadium in St. Louis on May 4. Reserve Mike Aldrete batted a career-high .325.

The club also had the pitching to match its hitting, thanks to general manager Al Rosen's wheeling and dealing during the summer. On July 4 he acquired left-handers Dave Dravecky and Craig Lefferts and third baseman Kevin Mitchell from the San Diego Padres, and it turned the season around. Right-hander Don Robinson was added in a July 31 trading deadline deal, and right-hander Rick Reuschel came on board August 21, both from the Pittsburgh Pirates. The new pitchers combined to post a 20-12 record.

They fueled a 37-7 stretch drive. Mitchell helped, too. He homered twice in his first game with the Giants against the Chicago Cubs at Wrigley Field in Chicago and batted .306 with his new club. Right-hander Mike LaCoss, a rec-

Pitcher Mike Krukow enjoyed his finest season in 1986 with a 20-9 record and a 3.05 ERA.

Pitcher Don Robinson was one of general manager Al Rosen's key acquisitions during the Giants' 1987 National League West Division championship run. (S.F. Giants Archives)

lamation project of pitching-guru manager Roger Craig, was the big winner at 13-10, followed by fellow right-handers Kelly Downs (12-9) and Scott Garrelts (11-7).

1988			
83-79	.512	4th Place (-11½)	1,786,482
		Roger Craig	

It was a season of tragedy for the Giants, not for a failure to repeat, but because of the death of shortstop Jose Uribe's wife, Sara, during childbirth in mid-season, and left-handed pitcher Dave Dravecky's surgery to remove a cancerous tumor from his left arm. Those two events overshadowed an 83-79 record and fourth-place finish, 11½ games behind the Los Angeles Dodgers.

First baseman Will Clark enjoyed another banner season with 29 home runs and a league-leading 109 RBI. "Thrill" was exceptional in June, earning National League Player of the Month honors with a .329 batting average, eight homers and 29 RBI.

Third baseman Kevin Mitchell, in his first full season with the club, had 19 homers and 80 RBI. Newcomer center fielder Brett Butler was solid at the leadoff spot, batting .287 with 109 runs, 97 walks and 43 steals. Chris Speier, filling in for injured second baseman Robby Thompson, hit for the cycle against the St. Louis Cardinals at Candlestick Park in San Francisco on July 8. Newcomer outfielder Donnell Nixon batted .346.

Pitching was quite respectable, topped by right-hander Rick Reuschel with a 19-12

Three different Giants led the National League in RBI from 1988-90: first baseman Will Clark (109) (left), left-fielder Kevin Mitchell (127) (not pictured) and third baseman Matt Williams (122). (S.F. Giants Archives)

record and a 3.12 ERA. Right-hander Don Robinson was 10-5 with a 2.45 ERA and pitched a one-hitter against the Houston Astros. Right-hander Kelly Downs was 13-9.

		1989	
92-70	.568	1st Place (+3)	2,059,829
		Roger Craig	

Left fielder Kevin Mitchell flourished during a Most Valuable Player season, and first baseman Will Clark wasn't far behind as the Giants' 1-2 punch knocked out the National League. The Giants won the West Division championship with a 92-70 record, three games ahead of the San Diego Padres, and defeated the Chicago Cubs in the National League Championship Series four games to one.

In its first World Series appearance since 1962, San Francisco fell to the Oakland A's four games to none in a series that was marred a 7.0 earthquake prior to Game 3 at Candlestick Park.

Mitchell had 31 home runs by the All-Star break and finished with a league-leading 47 homers and 125 RBI. Clark's .333 batting average was the highest for a player with Candlestick Park as a home field. He lost the batting title to San Diego's Tony Gwynn (.336) on the final weekend. Third baseman Matt Williams returned from the minors to hit 11 homers in August and 18 overall. Infielder Ken Oberkfell paced a strong bench and batted .318 with 18 pinch hits.

Right-hander Rick Reuschel was 17-8 with a 2.94 ERA. Right-hander Scott Garrelts was the league ERA champ at 2.28 and posted a 14-5 record. Right-hander Steve Bedrosian was acquired in mid-summer from the Philadelphia Phillies to shore up the bullpen, complementing left-hander Craig Lefferts' 20 saves. Right-handed reliever Jeff Brantley was 7-0.

It was an emotional season in many ways. Left-hander Dave Dravecky miraculously returned for two games but broke his arm pitching in Montreal and would never pitch again following an amputation.

		1990	
85-77	.525	**3rd Place (-6)**	1,975,571
		Roger Craig	

Injuries took their toll on a club that used 26 pitchers among 51 players in an attempt to repeat. The disabled list was used 15 times, so the club rarely had its starting lineup intact and played well on a consistent basis briefly.

The Giants raised expectations by winning 16 of their first 17 games in June, but they were a mediocre 69-76 the rest of the time and finished 85-77 for third place, six games behind the Cincinnati Reds, despite some potent offensive production from their 1989 standouts.

Third baseman Matt Williams joined first baseman Will Clark and left fielder Kevin Mitchell as a force with 33 home runs and 122 RBI. He became the third Giant in three years to lead the league in RBI, joining Clark (1988) and Mitchell (1989). Center fielder Brett Butler set the table with 192 hits.

Pitcher Dave Dravecky captured the hearts of everyone by coming back from cancer surgery in his throwing arm to defeat the Cincinnati Reds 4-3 at Candlestick Park in San Francisco on August 10, 1989. (S.F. Giants Archives)

Mitchell's encore included a .290 batting average, 35 homers and 93 RBI. Clark followed at .295 with 19 homers and 95 RBI. Right-hander John Burkett, previously a non-descript minor leaguer, led the staff with 14 wins. Right-hander Scott Garrelts and left-hander Trevor Wilson both pitched one-hitters.

		1991	
75-87	.463	**4th Place (-19)**	1,737,479
		Roger Craig	

The first taste of failure by the Rosen-Craig regime started with a poor decision. Center fielder Brett Butler, arguably the best leadoff hitter in the National League, was allowed to sign with the dreaded Los Angeles Dodgers and sorely was missed.

The Giants got off to a 12-28 start, their worst in San Francisco history, and never recovered en route to finishing 75-87 for fourth place, 19 games behind the Atlanta Braves.

Nevertheless, there were some respectable performances. Second baseman Robby Thompson's 19 home runs, for instance, were the most ever by a San Francisco second baseman. He hit for the cycle against the San Diego Padres at Candlestick Park in San Francisco on April 22. First baseman Will Clark had his last great season with the Giants, batting .301 with 29 homers and 116 RBI. Third baseman Matt Williams continued to improve with 34 home runs.

Left-handed pitcher Trevor Wilson blossomed into the staff ace with a 13-11 record and a 3.56 ERA.

		1992	
72-90	.444	**5th Place (-26)**	1,560,998
		Roger Craig	

The 1992 season essentially was a bummer because of the fear the club would be leaving Northern California for Tampa-St. Pe-

Trevor Wilson paced the 1991 Giants with a 13-11 record and a 3.56 ERA. (S.F. Giants Archives)

tersburg. Owner Bob Lurie sold the Giants, following the failure to erect a new stadium at any of numerous Bay Area locations.

Talk of the team's move served as a distraction down the stretch, affecting performance. First baseman Will Clark was the only successful batter with a .300 average, 16 home runs and 73 RBI. A nine-game losing streak at the end of August sealed the club's doom. The Giants mustered just a 72-90 record and finished in fifth place, 26 games behind the Atlanta Braves.

Bright spots included a new investors' group—led by Peter A. Magowan—saving the Giants from the clutches of Florida, right-handed pitcher Bill Swift going 10-4 with a National League-leading 2.08 ERA and right-hander Rod Beck emerging as the closer of the future with 17 saves and a 1.56 ERA.

1993				
103-59	.636	2nd Place (-1)		2,606,354
		Dusty Baker		

It was a storybook season except for a disappointing final chapter. There was a re-birth under new ownership, which made hiring Dusty Baker as manager and acquiring left fielder Barry Bonds top priorities, and they developed into the signings of the year.

With career years abounding, the Giants tied the franchise record with 103 victories (against 59 losses), falling merely one game short of the champion Atlanta Braves on the final day. Bonds won his third National League Most Valuable Player trophy and Baker, a rookie, was named Manager of the Year.

The Giants trailed by 3½ games on September 15 but went 14-3 down the stretch to make it interesting. Bonds was the catalyst in his San Francisco debut, coming home to attain career highs with a .336 batting average, 46 home runs and 123 RBI.

Others were at their best, too. Right-handed pitchers John Burkett (22-7, 3.65 ERA) and Bill Swift (21-8, 2.82 ERA) formed a mighty 1-2 punch; right-hander Rod Beck saved a franchise-record 48 games; center fielder Darren Lewis didn't make an error; second baseman Robby Thompson batted .312 with 19 homers; and shortstop Royce Clayton batted at a .282 clip.

1994				
55-60	.478	2nd Place (-3½)		1,704,608
		Dusty Baker		

A strike-shortened season abruptly halted the momentum of third baseman Matt Williams and the entire ball club following a spirited second-half showing with newly-acquired outfielder Darryl Strawberry.

When the season was called off in mid-August, the Giants didn't feel like losers. They had won nine in a row and 17 of their last 21 games in July and were playing well when the season came crashing down. San Francisco's final record of 55-60 was good for second place, 3½ games behind the Los Angeles Dodgers.

Perhaps nobody was affected greater than Williams, who was on pace for 61 home runs (then the major league record, set by the New York Yankees' Roger Maris in 1961) after 115 games. He also had 96 RBI in the 112 games he played and, along with left fielder Barry Bonds, clearly was heading for a prodigious season. Bonds batted .312 with 37 homers and 81 RBI. Right-hander Rod Beck easily was the most effective pitcher, setting a record with 28 saves in 28 opportunities.

1995			
67-77	.465	4th Place (-11)	1,241,500
		Dusty Baker	

A broken foot suffered on a foul tip was third baseman Matt Williams' menace this time, limiting him to 76 games. He still mustered 23 home runs and 65 RBI to accompany a .336 batting average while rapidly becoming one of the best hitters in the game.

Pitcher Rod Beck set a franchise record with 48 saves during the 1993 season. (S.F. Giants/Stanton)

Left fielder Barry Bonds complemented Williams with 33 homers and 104 RBI, while right fielder Glenallen Hill contributed 24 homers and 86 RBI. First baseman Mark Carreon batted .301, and Mike Benjamin tied the franchise record with six hits against the Chicago Cubs at Wrigley Field in Chicago on June 14.

Right-handed newcomer Mark Portugal, who dominated the Giants when he was with the Houston Astros, lost some of his magic once he joined them, posting an 11-10 record. Right-hander John Burkett was the best pitcher, going 10-4, and right-hander Rod Beck saved 33 games, nearly half of the team's 67 wins.

San Francisco wound up 67-77 for fourth place, 11 games behind the Los Angeles Dodgers.

1996			
68-94	.420	4th Place (-23)	1,413,687
		Dusty Baker	

Left fielder Barry Bonds became baseball's second 40-40 player with 42 home runs and 40 steals—following Jose Canseco of the Oakland Athletics in 1988—but it couldn't prevent the Giants from having their third consecutive losing season at 68-94 for fourth place, 23 games behind the San Diego Padres. Bonds also batted .308 with 129 RBI and 151 walks.

Long losing streaks proved costly for a team sorely deficient in pitching. There was an 0-10 plunge in June and 0-7 struggles in both July and August. The club also dropped 14 of 16 at one point in September, making it obvious that change was necessary.

One of the few offensive highlights was rookie third baseman Bill Mueller's .330 batting average after replacing Matt Williams, whose season ended with shoulder surgery. Right-handed newcomer Mark Gardner was the most effective starter, posting a 12-7 record.

1997			
90-72	.556	1st Place (+2)	1,690,831
		Dusty Baker	

The Giants staged a remarkable turn-around following a controversial winter trade that sent popular third baseman Matt Williams to the Cleveland Indians for second baseman Jeff Kent, shortstop Jose Vizcaino and right-handed pitcher Julian Tavarez.

Before long, nobody was complaining. That's because the Giants became merely the fourth team to win a division title following a last-place finish. They wound up 90-72, two games better than the Los Angeles Dodgers.

Kent came through with 29 home runs and 129 RBI. First baseman J.T. Snow, another new-comer, added 28 homers and 104 RBI. They gave the club a solid heart of the order because left fielder Barry Bonds had 40 homers and 101 RBI. Catcher Brian Johnson had the hit of the year, a 12th-inning homer to edge the Dodgers at 3Com Park at Candlestick Point in San Francisco on September 18, tying Los Angeles for the division lead.

Left-hander Shawn Estes, in his first full season, was 19-5 with a 3.18 ERA and a perfect 9-0 record following losses. Another left-hander, Kirk Rueter, went 13-6, and reinforcements came when general manager Brian Sabean traded prospects to the Chicago White Sox for left-hander Wilson Alvarez and right-handers Roberto Hernandez and Danny Darwin prior to the July 31 trading deadline.

1998			
89-74	.546	2nd Place (-9½)	1,925,634
		Dusty Baker	

A fantastic rally down the stretch produced a wild-card tie and a losing playoff game to the Chicago Cubs at Wrigley Field in Chicago, diminishing a solid season fueled by an 11-game winning streak in early June and second baseman Jeff Kent's incredible second half following a knee injury.

The Giants won nine out of 10 to move into a tie and were in a position to win the wild card with a victory over the Colorado Rockies at Coors Field in Denver on the final day of the regular season. Instead, they squandered a 7-0 lead and were defeated 9-8. San Francisco lost the playoff game 5-3 and wound up with an 89-74 record to finish second in the National League West Division, 9½ games behind the San Diego Padres.

Kent, who missed nearly a month, came back with 79 RBI in the second half. He finished with a .297 batting average, 31 home runs and 128 RBI. Left fielder Barry Bonds reached a milestone by becoming the only player ever with at least 400 home runs and 400 stolen bases. He batted .303 with 44 doubles, 37 homers and 122 RBI.

Outfielder Ellis Burks joined the Giants in a trade with the Colorado Rockies and batted at a .306 clip. Marvin Benard, the new center fielder, batted .371 in his last 65 games. Left-hander Kirk Rueter was 16-9, while right-hander Mark Gardner went 13-6, including 5-0 down the stretch.

1999			
86-76	.531	2nd Place (-14)	2,078,365
		Dusty Baker	

One of the greatest offensive outputs in San Francisco Giants' history ended in disappointment for a club which battled the division-champion Arizona Diamondbacks down to the final two weeks following a 22-6 run between August 18-September 17. But that impressive stretch, which included winning streaks of eight and seven games, gained merely 2½ games in the standings. The Giants were in first place for the last time July 23, going 34-31 the rest of the way as injuries mounted and the bullpen faltered. They wound up 86-76, 14 games behind the second-year Diamondbacks.

Left fielder Barry Bonds, despite in-season elbow surgery, had 34 home runs and 83 RBI

in 355 at-bats; Jeff Kent, with a bum toe, drove in 100-plus runs (101) for the third straight year and batted .290; Ellis Burks contributed 31 homers and 96 RBI on gimpy knees; and Rich Aurilia set San Francisco franchise records for a shortstop with 22 homers and 80 RBI.

The Giants scored 872 runs, their second-most since 1930, and set a franchise record with 307 doubles, including 40 by Kent. Center fielder Marvin Benard scored 100 runs, while first baseman J.T. Snow drove in 98. Catcher Brent Mayne batted at a .301 clip.

Aurilia, Bonds, Burks, Kent (23) and Snow (24) became only the third 20-home run quintet in the Giants' 117-year history, along with the 1953 and 1963 squads. They became the first fivesome to collect 80 RBI. But injuries

took their toll as Bonds, Burks, Kent and Snow were in the lineup at the same time in only 48 games. Kent hit for the cycle against the Pittsburgh Pirates on May 3 at Three Rivers Stadium in Pittsburgh.

Right-hander Russ Ortiz, in his first full major league season, went 18-9 with a 3.81 ERA. Left-hander Kirk Rueter was 15-10, and right-hander Robb Nen recorded 37 saves.

On September 30 the Giants played their final game at Candlestick/3Com Park and lost to the Los Angeles Dodgers 9-4 before a regular-season record crowd of 61,389. San Francisco went over 2,000,000 in home attendance for the third time in franchise history with 2,078,365.

2000			
97-65	.599	1st Place (+11)	3,315,330
		Dusty Baker	

The power-packed Giants moved into their new downtown digs and rewarded their tremendous fan support at glistening Pacific Bell Park with a runaway division title. A prodigious heart of the order helped the champions establish a franchise record with 226 home runs, and a 41-19 stretch run beginning July 31 left the rest of the N.L. West lagging far behind.

A nine-game winning streak, Aug. 30-Sept. 7, proved decisive, expanding the division lead from 21/2 to 81/2 games. Right-hander Russ Ortiz and left-hander Shawn Estes each won two games during that crucial stretch, and The Big Three of Barry Bonds, Jeff Kent and Ellis Burks terrorized pitchers throughout the season.

For the first time since 1962, the Giants produced the best record in the major leagues, and they did it after falling nine games behind the Arizona Diamondbacks on May 28. In fact, their final 111/2-game edge represented their biggest lead since the franchise moved to San Francisco in 1958.

With capacity crowds urging them on—the club set its all-time attendance record with

Left fielder Barry Bonds posted two of the greatest back-to-back seasons in history in 2001-02, winning two more MVP awards in the process. In 2001, he set major league records with 73 home runs, 177 walks and an .863 slugging percentage. In 2002, he won his first batting title (.370) and set ML marks with 198 walks and a .582 on-base percentage. (S.F. Giants Archives)

3,315,330 paying customers—the Giants overcame a 0-6 start at Pac Bell to finish 55-26 at home, where the pitching and fielding flourished. The pitchers posted a league-leading 3.45 home ERA and the team made merely 33 errors at home while setting franchise records with 93 total errors and a .985 fielding percentage.

That was complemented with an offensive attack that vaulted Jeff Kent to MVP distinction with a .334 average, 33 home runs and 125 RBI. Barry Bonds was the MVP runnerup with a solid season that included a .306 average, 49 home runs and 106 RBI. Ellis Burks, limited to 393 at-bats by injuries, still mustered 24 home runs and 96 RBI with a .344 average.

Among the pitchers, right-hander Livan Hernandez enjoyed his first full season with the club, going 17-11. Estes was a solid 15-6, and Ortiz turned a 6-0 August into a winning 14-12 season. Right-handers Robb Nen and Felix Rodriguez became a formidable one-two relief punch - Nen notching 41 saves and a 1.50 ERA while Rodriguez worked 76 games in a setup role.

		2001	
90-72	.556	2nd Place (-2)	3,307,686
		Dusty Baker	

Bolstered by newcomers Andres Galarraga and Jason Schmidt, the Giants made their move in late July and early August, winning nine in a row to pull within one-half game of the Diamondbacks' division lead. But Arizona never fell behind, prevailed by two games and went on to win the World Series. That and the Sept. 11 tragedy placed a damper on a remarkable season by Barry Bonds, one which ranks among the best ever.

Bonds, at the ripe age of 37, soared past several Hall of Famers and raised his home run total to 567 with a record-shattering 73 homers, erasing Mark McGwire's three-year-old standard of 70. He also toppled two of Babe Ruth's major league marks with an .863 slug-

ging percentage and 177 walks, and finished with a career-high 137 RBI and an unprecedented fourth MVP award.

His pursuit of the home run record accelerated with three homers at Coors Field, Sept. 9, lifting his season total to 63 with 18 games remaining. The terrorist attack placed his chase on hold, but when play resumed, so did Bonds' slugging spree. He added 10 homers in the final 16 games, including a pair against the Dodgers, Oct. 5, to break a tie with McGwire.

Bonds' phenomenal season guised a career year for Rich Aurilia, who joined an elite list of slugging shortstops with 37 home runs and 97 RBI. Batting second ahead of Bonds, he also scored 114 runs, led the league with 206 hits and posted a .324 average. Jeff Kent added a franchise-record 49 doubles, batted .298 and had 106 RBI. Galarraga, playing 49 games with his new club, batted .288 with 35 big RBI

But the right-handed Schmidt was the best of the in-season acquisitions, going 7-1 with a 3.39 ERA in 11 starts after coming from Pittsburgh in a trade for Armando Rios and Ryan Vogelsong. Right-hander Russ Ortiz earned ace status with a 17-9 record and a 3.29 ERA. Right-handers Robb Nen and Felix Rodriguez again were the bullpen stalwarts, Nen with a career-high 45 saves and Rodriguez with a 9-1 record and a 1.68 ERA in 80 games.

		2002	
95-66	.590	2nd Place (-2½)	3,253,203
		Dusty Baker	

Beginning the season 6-0 and ending it 8-0, the Giants registered what ultimately would be their most successful season in 40 years. They didn't win a division championship, but the point was moot when they entered the playoffs as the National League wild card, won their first pennant since 1989 and took at Anaheim Angels to a seventh game before losing the World Series.

In a stretch drive reminiscent of 1951, the Giants rallied from 111/2 games behind the division-champion Diamondbacks on Aug. 25 to make it a tight finish and wrest the wild card from the Dodgers, who held a 41/2-game lead that day. The Giants did it by going 25-8 the rest of the way behind new sparkplug Kenny Lofton, workhorse catcher Benito Santiago and the incomparable Bonds.

As an encore to his staggering 2001 season, Bonds went on yet another record romp. He shattered his year-old walks mark with 198, won his first batting title with a San Francisco-best .370, obliterated Ted Williams' 51-year-old on-base percentage standard with a .582 and was a unanimous winner of his fifth MVP award. Bonds also hit 46 home runs and joined Hank Aaron, Babe Ruth and Willie Mays in the 600-homer club.

A mid-season move by manager Dusty Baker conributed to the team success. He flopped Bonds and Jeff Kent in the batting order, and Kent batted .337 in the third spot. Kent had a league-leading 23 homers after the All-Star break and finished with a career-high 37 to accompany a .313 average, 42 doubles and 108 RBI. Santiago, at age 37, provided a bonus with solid catching, a .278 average and 74 RBI.

General manager Brian Sabean, as was his custom, provided a boost by acquiring Lofton by the July 31 trading deadline to solve the club's leadoff woes. Following a slow start, Lofton batted .322 the final month and was a key in the NLCS. David Bell (20 homers, 73 RBI) and Reggie Sanders (23-85) also made contributions in their only seasons with the club.

Pitching and fielding were also vital to success, especially at home. The Giants set a franchise record with merely 90 errors, and their pitchers ranked second in the league with a 3.54 ERA. There were no big winners, but a balanced rotation had five starters with at least one dozen victories, topped by left-hander Kirk Rueter's 14-8 record and 3.23 ERA. Right-handed closer Robb Nen saved 43 games and became the club's career leader with 206 saves. Right-hander Tim Worrell was 8-2 with a 2.25 ERA in 80 games.

CHAPTER TWO
OWNERS AND EXECUTIVES

OWNERS

John B. Day (1883-92)

The founding father of Giants baseball is John B. Day, who owned the franchise from its beginning in 1883 through 1892.

Originally from Colchester, Connecticut, and a well-to-do tobacco merchant in New York City, Day first dabbled in baseball by organizing a semi-pro team in Orange, New Jersey, in 1879. After a game against the Brooklyn Metropolitans in which Day pitched and was roughed up, the player-owner met Jim Mutrie, a smooth-talking baseball aficionado who had operated a ballclub of his own in his home state of Massachusetts. The brazen pair talked for a while and decided they could—and would—put baseball on the map in New York with the founding of the Metropolitan Exhibition Company. With Day providing the finances and Mutrie the baseball knowledge, the original "Dynamic Duo" of Gotham City was confident it had a sure thing.

Day and Mutrie debuted an independent club (which they named the Metropolitans or Mets for short) in 1880 and played games whenever they could be scheduled. The Mets' home games were played in Brooklyn, and fans not living in the borough had a nearly-impos-

John B. Day (Transcendental Graphics)

sible time getting there. Attendance was low, and Day (on the advice of a bootblack) moved his team to a large rectangular plot of land at 110th Street and Sixth Avenue in New York (where the wealthy partook in the sport of polo). City dwellers responded by showing up at the Polo Grounds in droves, and baseball became a bona fide hit.

In 1882 the American Association (the other organized professional circuit besides the National League) invited Day and Mutrie to join its league. The two declined because they felt the A.A. was inferior and represented a lower class with its beer-drinking fans. Then on December 7, 1882, at the baseball winter meetings in Providence, Rhode Island, the cities of New York and Philadelphia were awarded "honorary membership" into the N.L. Subsequently, Day and Alfred J. Reach, proprietor of a semi-pro team in Philadelphia, applied for full-fledged member. With the Troy Trojans and Worchester Brown Stockings having been expelled from the league (both teams struggled on the field and at the gate), the N.L. eagerly added New York and Philadelphia.

However, Day pulled a shocker when he announced that he also would take up the offer to join the A.A. He placed the Mets in the A.A. and developed an entirely new team for the N.L. Day bought out the Trojans, and divided the roster between his two teams, with most of the more talented players being assigned to the new squad (named the Gothams). Mutrie stayed with the Mets, and John Clapp was hired as manager of the N.L. entity.

Having adequately filled both rosters, the next step was to come up with an additional field of play. No problem as the Polo Grounds was big enough for two surfaces. Day gave the existing field to the N.L. team and built a new domain for the A.A. squad. The adjacent fields were separated by a large piece of canvas, although from certain vantage points it was possible to watch two games simultaneously.

By 1885 it was clear that the N.L. had greater potential than the A.A. As a result, Day transferred Mutrie and some of his marquee players from the Mets to the N.L. team. Towards the end of the calendar year Day sold the Mets to an amusement park operator by the name of Erasmus Wiman.

Day attempted to be a "19th-century Branch Rickey" in 1888 when he purchased George Stovey, a fire-balling left-handed pitcher from Newark of the International League who happened to be black. But word leaked out of the impending transaction, and after it was suggested that some opponents would not play a team that had a black player, the Giants (as Mutrie first named them in 1885) passed on signing Stovey.

Everything was going along tremendously for the Giants under Day (they won world championships in 1888 and 1889) when the Brotherhood of Professional Base Ball Players, organized by Giants' shortstop John Montgomery Ward, founded the Players League in 1890. The P.L. put a team in New York, called it the Giants and filled the roster with virtually all the key players from the N.L. squad. With two professional teams in New York (both Giants) and three more in Brooklyn (the Bridegrooms in the N.L., Gladiators in the A.A. and Wonders in the P.L.), the competition for fans was stiff, and every franchise struggled financially.

Day, who continually was pouring money from his tobacco business into the Giants (including building a new ball park in 1889), told the N.L. that he would have to file for bankruptcy and sell out to the Brotherhood if the N.L. didn't come to his rescue. League president Albert Spalding, club owners Arthur H. Soden of Boston and Reach of Philadelphia and Brooklyn principal stockholder Ferdinand A. Abell lent Day $62,500. In addition, John T. Brush, former owner of the Indianapolis Hoosiers who sold Day several players to fill his roster, canceled an outstanding $25,000 debt. Each contributor was given stock in the Giants.

Despite the collapse of the P.L. after just one season, Day still was looking for additional revenue and sold stock in his team to Edward Talcott, a New York lawyer who had operated the P.L. Giants. As part of the trans-

action, Talcott insisted that Mutrie be dismissed as manager. The arrangement was put off for a year but further bewildered a dispirited Day, and within another year he sold his remaining shares of stock to Talcott.

In 1899, at the age of 53 and never having recovered from his financial woes, Day was searching for work and returned to the Giants as manager. He was the seventh of 12 managers employed by owner Andrew C, Freedman during his eight years at the helm from 1895-1902 and lasted just 66 games (29-35 record) before being dismissed.

Little was heard from Day for nearly a quarter of a century when he was found gravely ill in 1923. Unable to care for himself or his wife, who was dying of cancer, the Giants organized a benefit game on Day's behalf. The game was played October 3, 1923, with the Giants defeating the minor league Baltimore Orioles 9-0 at the Polo Grounds. Babe Ruth of the cross-town rival Yankees played for the Giants and hit a home run over the right field roof.

Day passed away January 25, 1925, in Cliffside, New Jersey, at the age of 77.

Andrew C. Freedman (1895-1902)

After nearly destroying the New York Giants during his eight years as owner from 1895-1902, Andrew C. Freedman saved it in his final days.

Personally, Freedman was an arrogant and selfish individual. Professionally, he had the reputation of being a dishonest real estate lawyer who had close ties with the corrupt New York City Democratic Organization (more commonly referred to as Tammany Hall after the name of its headquarters) that controlled municipal business with institutionalized thievery.

Freedman officially completed the purchase of the Giants on January 24, 1895. But Freedman actually had been acquiring shares of the franchise for some time, acting as a business representative for James A. Bailey (who later made circus fame with P.T.

Barnum). Bailey had no knowledge of the transactions because Freedman was making the purchases strictly for himself. When the sale was finalized, it was estimated that Freedman paid just $48,000 for an operation worth a quarter of a million dollars.

Upon taking control of the Giants, Freedman started a revolving door of 12 different managers (including two with two different stints). George Steinbrenner would have been proud. The rundown follows:

- John Montgomery, who had managed the Giants in 1893 and 1894, was fired immediately and replaced by third baseman George Davis.
- Davis managed for 33 games (16-17 record) in 1895 before being fired and replaced by first baseman Jack Doyle.
- Doyle didn't like Freedman (few people did) and was fired after 64 games (32-31

Andrew C. Freedman (Transcendental Graphics)

record). Then Freedman hired Harvey Watkins, unquestionably the most unqualified manager in baseball history. Watkins was an actor who was at the least adjacently associated with Tammany Hall and was working for Bailey's circus at the time of his appointment. Watkins somehow managed an 18-17 record over the duration of the 1895 season, but the Giants wound up in ninth place in the National League.

- Arthur Irwin, who played shortstop in the major leagues for 13 seasons, was brought on board in 1896 and lasted 90 games (36-53 record) before being replaced by third baseman Bill Joyce. New York finished in seventh place.

- Joyce survived the offseason and the entire 1897 campaign as the Giants were 83-48, good for third place in the N.L. (9½ games behind the Boston Beaneaters). Joyce remained at the helm for 43 games (22-21 record) in 1898 before finally being dismissed.

- Next up was Cap Anson, the future Hall of Fame first baseman who had a 22-year playing career with the Chicago White Stockings and Colts from 1876-97. Anson lasted 22 games (9-13 record) before quitting when he no longer could tolerate Freedman. Then Joyce returned for the final 92 games (46-39 record) as the Giants ended up in seventh place.

- In 1890 Freedman hired former owner John B. Day (1883-92), who had yet to recover from the financial beating he took while running the franchise from its inception. Day lasted just 66 games (29-35 record) before being fired. He was replaced by Fred Hoey, an unqualified Freedman crony who had never managed before and never would again. Hoey lasted the remaining 87 games (31-55 record), and New York dropped to 10th place, a whopping 42 games behind the champion Brooklyn Superbas.

- Buck Ewing, who played for the Giants

from 1883-89 and again from 1891-92, was brought back as manager in 1900 for 63 games (21-41 record). He was replaced by George Davis. Not only had Ewing been traded for Davis in 1892, but (in case you have lost track) Davis was Freedman's first manager five years previously. The Giants wound up in eighth place (finishing last for the first time ever). Davis was retained in 1901 and had a 52-85 record for seventh place.

- The 1902 season began with Horace Fogel as manager. Fogel previously had managed the Indianapolis Hoosiers in 1897. He tinkered with the idea of moving budding star pitcher Christy Mathewson to first base. After 41 games (18-23 record), Freedman replaced Fogel on the surface with second baseman Heinie Smith, who envisioned moving Mathewson to shortstop. Fogel, in truth, remained in charge of the club's decisions from behind the scenes. Smith's tenure consisted of a mere 32 games (5-27 record) before Freedman made his best decision.

- Meet John McGraw. A hard-nosed shortstop with a brilliant baseball mind, McGraw was player-manager of the Baltimore Orioles in 1901 but constantly clashed with American League president Ban Johnson. He accepted Freedman's offer to join the Giants on July 16, 1902. As the saying goes, "The rest is history," as McGraw managed New York for 31 seasons.

There was more to Freedman than managerial comings and goings. He constantly was at odds with players (both his own and the opposition's) and the press. The New York fans certainly did not like what he was doing to the franchise either and attendance suffered.

Among the lowlights was the infamous Ducky Holmes incident of July 25, 1898. Holmes, an outfielder who played for the Giants in 1897 before joining the Baltimore Orioles, struck out with the bases loaded in the fourth inning and returned to the bench to the

heckling of a New York fan at the Polo Grounds. Holmes let loose with a racial slur in reference to Freedman ("But I'm glad I don't have to work for no Sheeny no more," it was reported in the *New York Times*). Although such comments were not so politically incorrect in those days as they are today, Freedman took exception and tried to attack Holmes on the field (with the support of his private group of policemen). When Freedman refused to clear the field, umpire Tom Lynch forfeited the game to the Orioles. Freedman issued refunds to the spectators in attendance, but he stopped payment on Baltimore's check for its share of the gate receipts.

Freedman's most significant conflict with one of his own players involved star pitcher Amos Rusie, who sat out the 1896 season over a contract dispute. Rusie filed a lawsuit demanding to become a free agent. In March of 1897 other N.L. team owners, concerned that Rusie's suit could drastically change the economics of the game, pooled together a reported $3,000 (to cover an earlier fine from Freedman, his salary for 1896 and the difference in his salary for 1897 between what he sought and what Freedman was willing to pay) for him to go back to the Giants.

Then there was the press. Freedman did not appreciate the press corps taking shots at him for essentially destroying the once-proud New York franchise. Specifically, Freedman revoked the press credentials of Sam Crane of the *New York Commercial Advertiser.* Crane, a former major league player (including the 1890 season with the Giants) and manager, responded by purchasing a ticket for each game in order to write a story. Freedman then instructed his ticket sellers to not make any sales to Crane. When other scribes came to Crane's defense, Freedman responded by prohibiting entire newspapers from covering his team. One particular target was the *New York Sun,* against whom Freedman filed some two dozen libel suits (none of which he won). Freedman once punched a reporter from the *New York Times.* One of Freedman's critics was Henry Chadwick

of the *Brooklyn Eagle,* who originated the box score, was a member of baseball's Rules Committee and is enshrined in the National Baseball Hall of Fame. When Freedman attempted to have Chadwick's $500 annual pension from the National League discontinued, Chadwick responded by boycotting the Polo Grounds and urging Giants fans to do the same.

Having wreaked havoc on the Giants, Freedman capped his baseball career by attempting to do the same on the game. In August of 1901 he conceived a plan to operate the National League as a gigantic trust. It was called "syndicate baseball" and was based on a plan in which the money made by the league be put into stock and paid out to the eight teams on the following basis: New York 30 percent; Boston, Cincinnati and St. Louis 12 percent each; Chicago and Philadelphia 10 percent apiece; Pittsburgh 8 percent; and Brooklyn 6 percent. In addition, the players would be owned by a central league office and assigned to teams on a year-by-year basis. Fortunately, Freedman's idea did not receive universal support (not surprisingly from the four owners who were at the bottom half of the scale) and failed.

On September 9, 1902, Freedman sold the Giants to John T. Brush. Freedman passed away December 4, 1915, in New York, at the age of 55. A lifelong bachelor who had accumulated an estimated $7 million fortune at his death, the bulk of his estate was used to build a home for the aged in the Bronx.

John T. Brush (1902-12)

Although John T. Brush did not take control of the New York Giants until September 9, 1902, he had been very much involved with the franchise for more than a decade.

A native of Clintonville, New York, who became a wealthy clothing manufacturer in Indianapolis, Brush was owner of the Indianapolis Hoosiers of the National League from 1887-89. Following the 1889 season, with the Hoosiers struggling and the Giants being depleted by the formation of the Players League,

the N.L. worked out an arrangement to have Brush sell six of his players to the Giants. When New York owner John B. Day was fighting off bankruptcy at the end of the 1890 campaign, N.L. president Albert Spalding mandated that in place of the remaining $25,000 Brush was owed by Day, he be given stock in the Giants.

Ironically, Brush played a role in the development of the P.L. In 1889 he attempted to implement the Classification Plan by which every player was rated on a scale of A to E—based on ability, morality and performance—and

John T. Brush (Transcendental Graphics)

Even before the transaction was completed, Brush was working to build the Giants. On December 15, 1900, he traded budding star pitcher Christy Mathewson from the Reds to the Giants in exchange for aging and disgruntled pitcher Amos Rusie. Later Brush became involved in getting McGraw to come to New York from the Baltimore Orioles, and at one point Brush held stock in the American League franchise.

Brush gave McGraw the complete authority to do whatever it took (and spend as much money as necessary)

paid a uniform salary. Not surprisingly, the players opposed the plan, as well as the reserve clause that bound a player to a particular team forever, and responded by forming their own league.

Brush was owner of the Cincinnati Reds from 1891-1902. In those days, it was not uncommon for an individual to have interests in more than one franchise, as Brush did. Meanwhile, after the Giants were nearly destroyed during the tumultuous rein of owner Andrew C. Freedman from 1895-1902, he pulled off an 11th-hour rescue with the hiring of John McGraw as manager on July 16, 1902. Then the Giants got an added lift when Freedman finalized the sale of the team to Brush, who was serving as chairman of the executive committee of the N.L. Brush purchased the franchise for $100,000.

to build the Giants into a winning team. In 1904 New York captured the N.L. pennant with a 106-47 record, 13 games better than the second-place Chicago Cubs. The 106 victories are the most in franchise history. However, Brush and McGraw refused to play in the World Series against the A.L. champion Boston Pilgrims because they considered the A.L. an inferior league. There was talk of New York playing a postseason series against the Cubs (reviving the Temple Cup championship) but nothing materialized.

Because he brought baseball back to life in New York, Brush was aptly referred to as "the savior of the National League." Although the oldest owner in the N.L. in terms of age, he was regarded as the youngest in ideas and methods. The Giants repeated as N.L. champions in 1905 and defeated the Philadelphia Ath-

letics in the World Series four games to one.

By 1911 Brush was in failing health—a victim of locomotor ataxia and rheumatism for many years—and confined to a wheelchair. After midnight April 14, 1911, the Giants' home ballpark, the Polo Grounds, caught fire and was destroyed. Brush was determined to build a new park, a concrete and steel structure with a seating capacity of 34,000, at the same location of 157th Street and Eighth Avenue. Original plans called for the rebuilt park to be named Brush Stadium, but by the time it opened June 28 against the Boston Braves (a 3-1 win) the common name of Polo Grounds was being used.

The Giants, who played at Hilltop Park (home of the cross-town rival Highlanders) while their home was under construction, won N.L. crowns in 1911 and 1912 but lost to Philadelphia (four games to two) and the Boston Red Sox (four games to three with one tie) in the respective World Series. In September of 1912 Brush suffered a hip injury when he was thrown from his automobile that skidded on a wet street.

Following the 1912 World Series, Brush headed by train to Southern California and its warm weather. On November 26, he passed away in his private car, the Oceanic, in Louisiana, Missouri, at the age of 67. The Giants became the property of Brush's wife, Elsie, and their daughters, Eleanor Brush Hempstead and Natalie Brush. Harry N. Hempstead, husband of Eleanor and a longtime director of the Giants, took over day-to-day operations of the team.

Harry N. Hempstead (1912-19)

Though his rein as owner of the New York Giants lasted just over six years from 1912-19, Harry N. Hempstead witnessed definite success by his ball club. The Giants captured National League pennants in 1913 and 1917 (but lost in the World Series to the Philadelphia Athletics and Chicago White Sox, respectively) and finished second in 1914 and 1918. They averaged nearly 85 wins per season.

Harry N. Hempstead (Transcendental Graphics)

Hempstead was married to Eleanor Brush Hempstead, daughter of former Giants' owner John T. Brush by his first wife, Agnes. Harry, who took over day-to-day operations of the Giants upon Brush's death November 26, 1912, previously served as a vice-president of the franchise and was being groomed to take over as president. Hempstead was actively involved in supervising the construction of the new grandstand being built at the Polo Grounds in 1911 to replace the one that had burned down earlier that year.

A native of Philadelphia and a collegiate baseball player at Lafayette College, Hempstead took over Brush's clothing store in Indianapolis in 1902 and served as president until retiring in 1922. Hempstead divided his time between Indianapolis and New York before moving to New York permanently in the summer of 1913. Upon Brush's death, rumors circulated that the heirs to the estate would sell the Giants, but Hempstead was quick to

dismiss those notions. Hempstead enjoyed the sports side of baseball but was less than enthralled with the business of it and in many ways treated the Giants as a hobby.

On January 14, 1919, Hempstead sold the majority of his interests in the Giants to a group headed by New York broker Charles A. Stoneham. Hempstead passed away March 26, 1938, in New York at the age of 69 following a stroke.

Charles A. Stoneham (1919-36)

The New York Giants reign of Harry N. Hempstead from 1912-19 was frustrating for manager John McGraw. Even though the Giants won National League pennants in 1913 and 1917 (but lost to the Philadelphia Athletics and Chicago White Sox in the World Series, respectively), McGraw generally was not consulted regarding player personnel decisions. Rather, Hempstead depended heavily on club secretary John B. Foster.

So when word got out that Hempstead was looking to sell the Giants after the 1918 season, McGraw most certainly was pleased. In fact, he yearned to get involved in the ownership of the franchise. A press conference as called for January 14, 1919, at which time it was expected that Hempstead would announce the sale of the Giants to George Loft, founder of a New York-based candy company.

But instead the Giants became the control of Charles A. Stoneham, who bought 1,300 shares of stock for $1.3 million. Francis X. McQuade, a city magistrate who in 1918 orchestrated the campaign that led to baseball being played on

Charles A. Stoneham (S.F. Giants Archives)

Sunday, and McGraw both acquired 70 shares for $50,000 apiece. McGraw was named vice-president and McQuade was named treasurer. McGraw was a double winner, having gained interest in the team and regaining control of baseball-related decisions. Hempstead and N. Ashley Lloyd of Cincinnati retained some stock.

Little was known about Stoneham when he was introduced as the Giants' new owner. He was head of the firm Charles A. Stoneham & Co., a bucket shop that took orders to buy and sell stocks, bonds and commodities but did not actually execute the orders. It was legal business prior to the stock market crash of 1929 but nevertheless considered a form of gambling in which the firm sought to profit by purchasing shares on margin and betting on the rise and fall of their prices. Stoneham also had Tammany Hall connections (the corrupt New York City Democratic Organization that controlled municipal business with institutionalized thievery), adding to the questions that surrounded him. He also was a close friend of McGraw's and a baseball fan.

McGraw, who was given the freedom to spend money lavishly for players, managed the Giants into the 1932 season and piloted the team to four consecutive National League championships from 1921-24 and back-to-back World Series titles in 1921 and 1922 over the cross-town rival Yankees.

Early in his ownership reign, Stoneham had limited activity in day-to-day baseball decisions, but as he became more familiar with the games affairs he took a more prominent role. The change resulted in friction among Stoneham, McGraw and McQuade

and ultimately led to McQuade being forced out in 1928. When McGraw resigned as manager in 1932, the reason given was failing health; however, some believe it was the result of conflict with Stoneham. Known for his old-fashioned views on baseball, Stoneham was vehemently opposed to night games.

Bill Terry succeeded McGraw as manager and led the Giants to the World Series championship in 1933 over the Washington Senators.

Stoneham was involved in more than just baseball while at the Giants' helm. He had interests in the New York Nationals soccer club and in a summer opera company, as well as Havana race track and a racing stable. Stoneham also was plagued by litigation throughout his professional life, from law suits over the practices of his bucket shop to mail fraud to a widow trying to collect salary and bonuses after the death of her husband who was a jockey that was killed at Jamaica race track while riding one of Stoneham's horses. Stoneham was acquitted in some cases and found guilty in others.

Stoneham eventually dropped everything but the Giants. Commissioner Kenesaw Landis was particularly opposed to the race track holding. On several occasions, Stoneham was rumored to be on the verge of selling his interest in the franchise. In 1925, it was reported that circus owner John Ringling would take over majority control, but the transaction never materialized.

Another rumor—which was denied by Stoneham—had Branch Rickey of the St. Louis Cardinals joining the Giants as executive advisor and chief scout in September of 1932. A reported trade of Terry, outfielder Fred Lindstrom and third baseman Johnny Vergez to the Cardinals in exchange for first baseman/outfielder Rip Collins, infielder Frankie Frisch and outfielder Pepper Martin also was denied by Stoneham.

In December of 1935, Stoneham became ill and contracted a severe kidney ailment called Bright's disease. He passed away January 6, 1936, in Hot Springs, Arkansas, at the age of 59. Stoneham's son, Horace, assumed the presidency of the Giants on January 15, 1936.

Horace C. Stoneham (1936-75)

The Giants' longtime owner was reared in a baseball family, so Horace Stoneham was a natural to succeed his father, Charles Stoneham, when he died in 1936, 17 years after purchasing the club in 1919. Horace was 32 at the time and held control of the Giants longer than anyone—until the National League intervened in 1975 when the parent National Exhibition Co. was in dire financial straits.

Stoneham, born of privilege, unquestionably was a spoiled brat as a youngster. He bounced in and out of boarding schools and colleges while immersed in his father's wealth. Charles decided to teach his son some humility and the lessons of life by sending him to work in a copper mine he owned in California's Mother Lode.

"I don't exactly know what Pop expected to happen, but when it came to handling liquor, those boys in that camp really completed my education—they were the greatest collection of two-fisted drinkers you could find anywhere," Horace recalled, perhaps why he earned a reputation as the perfect host and as a man who later outfoxed other owners with his staying power.

Fellow owner Bill Veeck once wrote: "Horace Stoneham has two occupations in life—he owns the Giants and he drinks. Horace's great attraction to us is that he looks so innocent and vulnerable, and that he is so well and favorably known for his drinking habits that he inspires baseball operators with an almost missionary zeal to get him drunk and steal him blind."

Veeck noted that the advantage more often than not was Stoneham's because he had the capacity to outdrink everyone. Still, young Horace emerged from his mining venture more mature and responsible. His partying was legendary, and his drinking buddies included

Horace C. Stoneham (S.F. Giants Archives)

Jackie Gleason, Toots Shor and numerous Giants.

He also was shy, disdaining personal publicity. He disliked public places and would usually watch games from his office above the clubhouse in center field at the Polo Grounds. But his proclivity for a good time with the boys never interfered with a sharp baseball mind. He okayed a myriad of deals that brought the Giants pennants in 1951, 1954 and 1962.

Horace is regarded as the franchise's finest owner, a man who enjoyed the high life and was eager to keep his players, especially the superstars, happy. Perhaps his motivation was different than that of Branch Rickey, but Stoneham quickly followed the Dodgers in integrating baseball with the likes of Monte Irvin, Hank Thompson and Willie Mays.

He also was a pioneer in mining the rich talent of the Dominican Republic, using scout Horacio Martinez to sign Juan Marichal, Manny Mota and the three Alous. But Horace created a stir by hiring Leo Durocher away

from the cross-town rival Brooklyn Dodgers to manage the Giants in 1948, a sacrilege to stout New York fans. The criticized move was justified when the "Lip" produced pennants in 1951 and 1954. It might have started a trend because former Dodgers Herman Franks, Roger Craig and Dusty Baker all became successful Giants' managers.

There is a popular misconception that Stoneham could have beaten Walter O'Malley to the riches of Los Angeles, but Horace was either going to move to Minneapolis or San Francisco. Prior to O'Malley announcing his shift from Brooklyn to Los Angeles, Stoneham told a Congressional committee investigating baseball and the anti-trust laws that the Giants were moving regardless of what the Dodgers did.

"The city of New York cannot support three clubs," Stoneham explained. It must have been a painful admission. As a New York schoolboy, he loved the Giants long before his father purchased the club. As a 12-year-old Loyola student, Horace asked to write an essay on what he would do with one million dollars. His composition began, "If I had a million dollars, I'd buy the Giants."

His father complied by purchasing the club a few years later, explaining that he did it to make certain his son someday could realize his dream. "My dad used to take me to the Polo Grounds when I was a kid," Horace recalled. "I went to my first game in 1908. I remember the old park and the old wooden stands, and us coming in through the speedway entrance. It was a July 4 double-header, and Matty (Christy Mathewson) pitched and Chief Meyers caught.

"Dad came home one night in the fall of 1918, and I remember him saying we might have a ballclub. Pop was always a fan and he was a close friend of John McGraw. After Dad bought the club, he and Mr. McGraw would come home after a game and they'd sit around for hours just gabbing. Mr. McGraw was the greatest individual figure this game has ever seen, the greatest offensive manager."

Charles was in the brokerage business and predicted the Great Depression, insulating the Giants against it. At age 59, Charles had Bright's disease and went to Hot Springs, Arkansas, for treatment, lapsed into a coma and died. Horace encountered success immediately with back-to-back pennants under manager Bill Terry in 1936 and 1937.

It was more of the same in 1951 and 1954, where his pride of Coogan's Bluff swept the mighty Cleveland Indians in the World Series. The Giants attracted 1.55 million fans that championship season, but dipped to 824,112 in 1955 and dwindled to 629,179 in 1956. It didn't take much convincing by Dodgers' owner O'Malley to have Horace move westward with him.

"We're going to San Francisco in 1958," Stoneham declared at a Polo Grounds press conference August 19, 1957. The New York Giants wuz dead. When Horace was told that kids in the Bronx loved the Giants and would miss them, the owner reportedly said, "Yes, but I haven't seen many of their fathers at the games lately."

Stoneham was anticipating a future in sophisticated San Francisco, and legend has it that he preferred the Bay Area to the abundant riches of Southern California because San Francisco was more like his beloved New York City. "I'm glad this thing is over," he said following the final game at the Polo Grounds. "It's tough leaving here, but there's more to this than my feelings. Why are we going? Lack of attendance."

Stoneham had announced the move first, but the Dodgers previously staked claim to Los Angeles. Until March of 1957, in fact, it was believed the Giants would shift to Minneapolis, home of their Triple-A team. San Francisco mayor George Christoper, who was reared a few blocks from the new Pacific Bell Ballpark, is credited with giving O'Malley the idea that the Giants and the Dodgers could extend their rivalry to California, where San Francisco and Los Angeles already were natural rivals.

The Giants then moved to Seals Stadium,

a beautiful minor league park, where they played for two years before $15-million Candlestick Park was built. Shortly after it opened in 1960, the park was the object of scorn because of playing conditions which rankled opponents and exposed fans to the frigid elements.

Stoneham knew he needed a winner to attract paying customers, so he rashly fired manager Bill Rigney, and close friend, scout Tom "Clancy" Sheehan, completed the season. It was all part of a master plan. Stoneham loved Alvin Dark as the fiery captain of the 1951 champions, and he envisioned "Blackie" as an ideal manager.

Dark, then 38, was ending his career with the Milwaukee Braves at the time, and was traded after the 1960 season to the Giants for young shortstop Andre Rodgers. Dark began his managerial career in 1961. Stoneham was wise during his early years in San Francisco to have his new fans develop a strong identity with young standouts who had no ties to the New York years. Mays was the exception, of course, but those early teams included future Hall of Famers Orlando Cepeda, Willie McCovey, Marichal and Gaylord Perry.

The owner had the pleasure of one more pennant in 1962 and a division title in 1971, but mostly there was disappointment as the franchise slowly fell into disarray. One of his final positive gestures was making sure his beloved Mays was well taken care of, so he sold the aging superstar to the New York Mets, allowing the "Say Hey Kid" to finish his Hall of Fame career where it started.

By then, Perry already was gone and Marichal and McCovey were heading out the door. After Bobby Bonds and Tito Fuentes completed the housecleaning by 1974, minority stockholders clamored for his resignation. A local columnist called Stoneham "hopelessly out of touch with the times." He soon settled into retirement in Scottsdale, Arizona, and had little to do with the Giants. Shy and reclusive, he died at age 86 in 1990.

Robert A. Lurie (1976-92)

Just like Peter Magowan and his ownership group did 16 years later, Bob Lurie saved the San Francisco Giants from the clutches of another city when they were sold to a Toronto brewery with the intent of bringing major league baseball to Ontario before the expansion Blue Jays in 1977. Lurie and Arizona meat packer Bud Herseth, with the help of San Francisco mayor George Moscone, made a last-ditch offer which was accepted.

"In 1975, I had my first feelings about buying the club," Lurie recalled. "But it was Horace Stoneham's life, and I would never ask him about it. When the club was for sale, I went after it." But the board voted to sell the club to Toronto. Labatt's Brewery made an offer which was accepted, but it was stopped by a court injunction. Then a deal with Bob Short fell through, so it didn't look good. But Herseth came through with $4 million, enabling Lurie to beat the deadline and keep the Giants in San Francisco. The club experienced a rebirth in

Robert A. Lurie (S.F. Giants Archives)

1976, was a contender by 1978 and flourished when Lurie had the wisdom to place general manager Al Rosen and manager Roger Craig in charge at the end of a 100-loss season in 1985.

The club's fortunes changed instantly, and National League West Division titles followed in 1987 and 1989. Lurie, son of wealthy San Francisco financier Louis Lurie, ran the team with style and made use of his connections to throw a great All-Star Game party in 1984, using various landmark buildings like City Hall to entertain guests.

Lurie was educated in Chicago but spent most of his life in the Bay Area. He was chairman of the Lurie Corp., a commercial real estate firm, and was active in civic affairs. When the Giants moved west in 1958, he was named to the club's board of directors, beginning an association with owner Stoneham and general manager Chub Feeney.

His two biggest disappointments as owner were the failure to win a World Series—the 1989 Giants were runners-up—and an inability to get voter approval *anywhere* in the Bay Area for a new stadium. With the club's lease at Candlestick Park expiring in 1994 and Lurie vowing not to renew, he sold the club to Tampa-St. Petersburg interests in 1992, and it seemed the Giants were destined to beat the Devil Rays to Florida's Gulf Coast.

Lurie didn't win any friends with his final act as owner, but nobody could really blame his frustration over not securing a new stadium. Finally, he contributed a $10-million loan toward selling the franchise to Magowan's group. An avid golfer, Lurie frequently participates in the prestigious AT&T Pro-Am on the Monterey Peninsula.

Peter A. Magowan (1993-present)

Like Sir Galahad, Peter A. Magowan came to the rescue of a foundering franchise in 1992 and came up with enough money to keep the Giants in San Francisco. His reward was instant success—103 victories in 1993 with Barry Bonds, his hand-picked choice for resident superstar, leading the way under rookie manager

Dusty Baker.

Magowan had a deep-rooted interest in the Giants long before they headed westward. He was reared in New York's fashionable East Side and attended games at the Polo Grounds, where he idolized Willie Mays, and he frequently listened to games on radio, including the famous 1951 playoff with the Dodgers. That partly explains why the Giants' new downtown stadium, Pacific Bell Park, is graced with a huge statue of Mays at the main entrance.

Magowan's family moved to the Bay Area at about the same time as did the Giants, and he received his degree in English from Stanford in 1964. Peter later attended Oxford and the Johns Hopkins School of Advanced International Studies, intending to join the Foreign Service.

Then he more or less was steered into the family "grocery" business. Charlie Merrill, of the prestigious Merrill Lynch brokerage firm, was his grandfather and the biggest shareholder in Safeway. Magowan became the CEO of Bay Area-based Safeway Inc. at age 37 in 1980, a job previously held for 15 years by his father.

"I was given the opportunities to go to the finest schools and receive the finest education," Magowan recalled. "I'm sure I was given what some people might consider unfair advantages because of my last name. But, if anything, I think I had to work twice as hard *because* of my background."

Magowan relinquished Safeway duties shortly after acquiring the Giants, and his lasting legacy will be his ability to build a long-awaited downtown stadium. While others failed in their efforts, Magowan viewed a new baseball-only ballpark as the Giants' salvation. In December of 1995, Magowan unveiled a popular plan to build a 42,000-seat stadium adjacent to the bay in China Basin.

The primary selling point was no public funding, so there was an overwhelming victory for Proposition B in a 1996 election.

Peter A. Magowan (S.F. Giants Archives)

Magowan's grand accomplishment was Pacific Bell Park, which opened its doors to rave reviews in 2000 and produced three consecutive years of more than three million in attendance, a division championship (2000) and a pennant (2002)—a "splash homer" in every sense of the word.

GENERAL MANAGERS

Charles (Chub) Feeney (1946-68)

Among the last of the National League diehards, Charles (Chub) Feeney served the Giants and the league for many years. His mother was owner Horace Stoneham's sister, and Chub selected a life in baseball after a three-year Navy hitch during World War II. "I started going to the Polo Grounds as an 11-year-old," Feeney recalled. "We lived in Jersey, but I had a pass from uncle Horace."

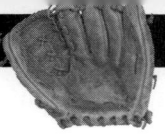

Charles (Chub) Feeney (S.F. Giants Archives)

Fenney attended Dartmouth and Fordham Law School before admission to the New York Bar Association. When he married wife, Margaret, in 1948, the newlyweds went from the church to celebrate at the Polo Grounds before taking a brief honeymoon while boyhood idol Mel Ott was fired as the manager. He worked his way through the Giants' front office in a 24-year career with the club that began in 1946.

By 1950 he was vice president and general manager, titles he held until he was asked to become president of the N.L. in 1969. His best trade was among his first. The boy wonder acquired Alvin Dark and Eddie Stanky from the Boston Braves, a move that produced the improbable pennant of 1951. In 1954, he again dealt with the Braves and acquired Johnny Antonelli, who won 21 games for the pennant winners that year.

Feeney's swaps for Billy Pierce, Billy O'Dell and Harvey Kuenn helped San Francisco win a pennant in 1962, but some failures followed. He allowed Felipe Alou (Braves), Matty Alou (Pirates) and Orlando Cepeda (Cardinals) to slip away, and all went on to productive careers after departing the Giants.

A humorous anecdote had Feeney visiting the Candlestick Park construction site shortly after the club moved west. He had heard so much about the furious winds in the area, and his interest peaked when paper and dust were swirling that day. Feeney asked a workman, "Is it this windy all the time?" The reply stunned him. "No," the worker said, "just from 1 till 5 p.m." Of course, that's exactly when the Giants played day games.

Feeney presided over the Giants and the N.L. when the league was in its glory, dominating the American League in All-Star games and in attendance with superstars like Mays, Hank Aaron, Roberto Clemente, Pete Rose, Bob Gibson, Sandy Koufax and Marichal. Strong league feelings made him a vocal opponent of interleague play 30 years before it transpired. "The World Series is baseball's strength," he said. "Why water it down?"

Feeney made an easy adjustment to San Francisco once the Giants moved west, and shifted N.L. offices from Cincinnati to downtown San Francisco when he succeeded Warren Giles as N.L. president. Feeney later served as president of the San Diego Padres, but he left his heart in San Francisco, where he retired. Daughter Katy, one of five offspring, presently is a N.L. vice president, carrying on the family tradition.

Spec Richardson (1976-81)

Spec Richardson assumed the responsibility of running the San Francisco Giants in an unconventional manner. When the Horace Stoneham regime hit the skids in 1975, and the Giants were on their way out of town, the National League appointed the former Houston Astros' general manager to run the Giants.

Spec Richardson (S.F. Giants Archives)

Al Rosen (S.F. Giants Archives)

He was capable enough at his job to earn Executive of the Year honors in 1978 for turning a rag-tag team into a contender, primarily because of a spring training swap with the crossbay Oakland A's for Vida Blue. Richardson was a throwback general manager, doing much of his work in hotel lobbies.

Richardson made perhaps his greatest trade with the Giants by acquiring Jeff Leonard from the Astros for troubled Mike Ivie. Leonard went on to have success for several years while Ivie faded from baseball. Curiously, that deal was made by then-Houston general manager Al Rosen, who regarded it as the worst trade of his career.

Richardson, an avid baseball fan, often made the drive from his Columbus. Georgia, home to watch games in Atlanta. A veteran of more than 30 years in baseball administration when he retired, Richardson returned to where

his career started as concessions manager of the Columbus minor league team in 1946. He became general manager of Houston's Triple-A team and was instrumental in the city acquiring an expansion franchise and in the construction of Colt Stadium and the Astrodome. He was vice president and general manager of the Astros and served the franchise for 14 years.

Al Rosen (1985-92)

Long before he became a great president and general manager for the Giants, Al Rosen was a slugging third baseman for the Cleveland Indians and a decent boxer. In 1950, his first full season as a major leaguer, "Flip" was the American League home run leader with 37. By 1953 he was the league Most Valuable Player for a season which included a .336 average and a league-leading 43 home runs, 115 runs and 145 RBI.

Rosen went into the brokerage business after his retirement, serving Bache and Co. as vice president of its Cleveland office. He was coaxed back into baseball by George Steinbrenner, who made him president of the New York Yankees. He moved to a similar post with the Houston Astros in 1980, but attained his greatest fame as a baseball executive when he was given control of reshaping a Giants' club which had lost 100 games in 1985.

The Giants showed a drastic improvement in 1986 and won the National League West Division title in 1987 following a bold July trade that brought Kevin Mitchell, Dave Dravecky and Craig Lefferts from San Diego. Later that season, Rosen acquired pitchers Rick Reuschel and Don Robinson and was named Executive of the Year by *The Sporting News*.

"Best trade I ever made, but I had no idea Mitchell would be so good for us," Rosen said of the 1989 MVP. Rosen did it again that year, trading for reliever Steve Bedrosian of the Philadelphia Phillies, the closer required to win the Giants' first pennant in 27 years.

Bob Quinn (S.F. Giants Archives)

Rosen also had the vision in 1986 of promoting minor leaguers Will Clark and Robby Thompson, a pair of future stars who never played Triple-A baseball. "We had nowhere to go but up after 100 losses, so there really was nothing to lose," he reasoned.

Rosen remained with the Giants through 1992 and currently makes his home in Rancho Mirage, California.

Bob Quinn (1993-96)

Bob Quinn continued a legacy of baseball leadership his grandfather, J.A. Quinn, started as a general manager of four major league teams early in the 20th century. Bob's father, John, carried the torch as the general manager of the Braves and Phillies for a combined 36 years.

"Dad encouraged me, but only if I wanted to go out and learn the business at the minor league level," Quinn said. "He didn't feel it was appropriate to summarily give his son a job in the Braves' front office. He wanted me to learn the business from the ground up."

Quinn worked his way up through player development and earned his first general manager's job with the Yankees in 1988, when he first worked with present Giants' general manager Brian Sabean, a protégé. He joined the Cincinnati Reds in 1990 and immediately produced a World Series champion to earn Executive of the Year honors from *The Sporting News*.

When Sabean was elevated to general manager late in the 1996 season, Quinn briefly served as an advisor and later was named the Giants' director of Arizona operations, overseeing the club's training facilities and Scottsdale Stadium. Born in Boston when his father was the general manager of the Braves, Quinn attended Marquette University, where he co-captained the track and field squad.

"I began thinking seriously about a baseball career when I got to high school," he recalled. "We moved to Milwaukee when I was 16 and the franchise shifted from Boston. I had

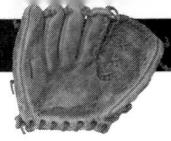

Brian Sabean (S.F. Giants Archives)

Sabean began shaping the Giants of the future early in the 1996 season and officially was named vice president and general manager September 30, 1996. His impact was immediate, beginning with a stunning November trade which sent popular slugger Matt Williams to Cleveland Indians for Jeff Kent, Jose Vizcaino, Joe Roa and Julian Tavarez.

That bold deal was criticized at the time, but Sabean enjoyed the last laugh when Kent alone had a better year than Williams and the Giants won the National League West before losing in the playoffs. "Sabes" also acquired J.T. Snow and Brian Johnson, whose dramatic September homer helped to overtake the Dodgers He also obtained pitchers Wilson Alvarez, Roberto Hernandez and Danny Darwin for the stretch run in 1997, and it paid off.

The 1998 Giants fell short in a one-game playoff - and it wasn't from lack of trying. Sabean replaced popular closer Rod Beck with powerful Robb Nen, and later added Ellis Burks, Joe Carter and Jose Mesa in a bid for the wild card. Nen and Burks were prominent in the 2000 success, and Sabean's magic produced Andres Galarraga and Jason Schmidt as a bid to win the division fell two games shy in 2001.

The active GM added David Bell and Reggie Sanders at the start of the 2002 season, dropped Kenny Lofton, Tom Goodwin and Scott Eyre into the mix and was rewarded with a pennant. Thanks to his moves within the constraints of a middle-level budget, the Giants have been competitive on an annual basis, and economics dictated more tweaking when Ray Durham, Edgardo Alfonzo, Damian Moss, Jose Cruz Jr. and Neifi Perez were added for 2003.

Sabean, known for possessing a keen eye for talent, was graduated from Eckerd College of St.Petersburg, Fla., in 1978. He began his career as a college coach, guiding the Univerity of Tampa to the NCAA tournament in 1984 before joining the Yankees, where he held various positions until he joined the Giants in 1993.

great foot speed as a semipro player, but I convinced myself I wasn't going anywhere as a player."

He eventually became Milwaukee's director of minor league operations in 1971, shortly after that franchise moved from Seattle. In 1973, he bean a 12-year association with the Cleveland Indians, rising to the position of vice president of player development and scouting.

Brian Sabean (1996-present)

Among the young lions running baseball operations, Brian Sabean served as an assistant to Bob Quinn when Peter Magowan's ownership group purchased club in 1993. His background was in the scouting department of the New York Yankees, where he first met Quinn. By mid-season in 1996, management realized it had better secure Sabean, or lose him to another organization seeking a bright and energetic general manager.

Edward Brannick (S.F. Giants Archives)

SIGNIFICANT OTHERS

Edward Brannick (1905-71)

Eddie Brannick was employed 65 years by the Giants when he retired before the 1971 season at age 77. He was reared in the tough Hell's Kitchen neighborhood of New York and was hired in 1905, at age 12, to help work the scoreboard in the original Madison Square Garden, re-creating games for the public.

Later that year, he witnessed Christy Mathewson's three shutouts in the 1905 World Series and became an errand boy for invalid owner John T. Brush, relaying messages between the boss and manager John McGraw. The club's all-purpose office boy began sitting on the bench next to McGraw in 1907 and became full-time road secretary in 1936 after Horace Stoneham succeeded his late father, Charles, as the club owner.

"Charles was a fan before he bought the club, and he always looked out for the fan,"

Brannick recalled. "Mr. Stoneham indoctrinated Horace at an early age to his way of thinking."

Brannick regarded the 1921 team as the best Giants' squad he watched, and there was a definite fondness for McGraw.

"Mr. McGraw loved life and he loved people," Brannick said. "He was rough in the clubhouse and rough on the bench, bursting with enthusiasm to get a job done. But he had a genuine, tender affection for many people when he was off the field."

Brannick's trademark was an old-fashioned straw hat with a bright band. The dapper gentleman refrained from alcoholic beverages but made sure newspapermen were well supplied. He resisted leaving his beloved New York when the franchise moved west, but he finally relented and resumed duties with San Francisco.

Brannick was in tears on the final day at the Polo Grounds, but he willingly moved west. "I love Horace, and I loved his father before him," Brannick said. "Anything anyone named Stoneham wants to do is all right with me."

Brannick unquestionably was one of the finest traveling secretaries in the history of the game, a pioneer who was perfect for the Giants. He was known to like *everything* but the rival Dodgers. "There's something about them that I can't stand," he summed up in typical Giant fashion.

Walter Mails (1958-72)

One of the more colorful characters in major league and San Francisco history bears mentioning because of his link with the club and the city. Born at San Quentin in 1895, Walter Mails was an eccentric left-hander who

turned a modest career into a lifetime occupation with his bravado and boastfulness.

He nicknamed himself "The Great" and was known by that moniker long after his playing days concluded. He attended St.Mary's College and enjoyed early success as a minor leaguer, winning 24 games for Seattle of the Northwest League in 1915. He then helped the 1920 Cleveland Indians win a pennant after posting 19 wins for Sacramento of the Pacific Coast League in 1919.

Mails won seven in a row for the Indians down the stretch and the club won the pennant by two games. He pitched 6⅔ innings of scoreless relief in the World Series before his 1-0 shutout in Game 7 of the eight-game series. He soon returned to the Pacific Coast League, finishing his pitching career with San Francisco in 1937.

From there, Mails launched his second career as the Seals' publicity and promotions director. His flamboyance and knowledge of the Bay Area served him well, and he was retained by the Giants as the head of their speakers' bureau when the club moved west in 1958. Mails had to be a great P.R. man because he gained fame in the game despite a mere 32-25 major league record.

Miguel (Mike) Murphy (1958-present)

The ubiquitous "Murph" was as much a fixture at Candlestick Park as the notorious wind and cold. When the stadium closed its baseball doors in September of 1999, Mike Murphy was the Giants' employee with the longest service with the club.

His loyalty dates to 1958, when the Giants moved from New York to the West Coast. Murphy, a native San Franciscan, served as a batboy for the club's first two years in San Francisco at Seals Stadium. Veteran equipment manager Eddie Logan took a liking to him. So, when Candlestick Park opened in 1960, Murphy was made a visitors' clubhouse attendant, serving in that capacity for 20 years and building friendships with players like Stan Musial, Pete Rose, Hank Aaron and Frank Robinson.

In 1980 he was promoted to equipment manager of the Giants and began 20 more years of serving his beloved team. Consequently, there was a degree of sadness when Candlestick hosted its final Giants' game on September 30, 1999. It had been his home away from home for 40 years.

"A lot of memories are going with me," Murphy said. "I've met a lot of great players and a lot of great people through this job. I've been very fortunate. Mr. Logan kind of taught me the ropes and looked after me.

"The 1962 World Series was a big thrill, getting to meet Mickey Mantle, Roger Maris and Yogi Berra. But Willie Mays is the greatest I ever saw. Besides being the best ballplayer, he would do anything for you. The day he was traded was my worst."

Murphy lists the 16-inning Juan Marichal-Warren Spahn game in 1963; the Gaylord Perry-Ray Washburn back-to-back no-hitters in 1968; and watching Giants Hall of Famers Orlando Cepeda, Willie McCovey, Marichal, Mays and Perry play among his top memories.

But "Murph," a former sandlot first baseman who was deficient defensively, looked forward to moving into Pacific Bell Park in 2000. It was his first exclusively baseball clubhouse since his days at Seals Stadium.

"It won't be as windy, and it will be more comfortable there," he said. "And there will be no more football. Sharing space with the 49ers made it tough at Candlestick, and it also tore up the field."

Murphy loved the Giants so much he spurned college to work with the team. Over the years, he has made a lot of friends whose autographed photos graced his cramped clubhouse office—Frank Sinatra, Joe DiMaggio and presidents Reagan and Bush among them.

Garry Schumacher (1946-71)

One of the last of the old breed of base-

ball publicists, Garry Schumacher became involved with the game he loved quite by accident. A Brooklyn native, born in 1900, young Schumacher attended night school at New York University and took a once-a-week course in journalism taught by the city editor of the *New York Globe*.

He was so fascinated with newspapers he would visit the city room after concluding his day job as a bank clerk. The newspaper was short-staffed one particular night in 1920, and Schumacher was dispatched to answer an alarm. Instead of a fire, however, it was a major disaster. The Sixth Avenue elevated train plunged 30 feet to the street. He arrived at the scene, called for reinforcements and was offered a job as a cub reporter.

"I was so excited, I never let the bank know I wasn't coming back," Schumacher said in his typically thick Brooklyn accent. By age 22, he was sports editor of the Brooklyn section of the *New York Journal*. In 1924 he began covering the Dodgers and the Yankees, a job that lasted until 1946, when "Guv" was hired as an assistant to Giants' owner Horace Stoneham, specializing in public relations.

Schumacher gained immediate respect from his peers for his integrity and assistance at a time when service was the emphasis for P.R. people. He was helpful to old and young reporters alike and was a master storyteller on a variety of subjects. The postgame press gatherings, a thing of the past, were graced by his presence.

A history buff, Schumacher especially was fond of the Civil War. Once, when asked why the Confederate Army was defeated, he promptly replied, "They were a lousy road team." Discussing Napoleon, Schumacher summed up, "He couldn't win on the road, either."

Schumacher once aptly described junk ball pitcher Stu Miller as, "He throws a Wells Fargo pitch—it comes up to the plate in stages." Everything seemed to revolve around baseball for "Guv," one of the game's first great publicity directors.

Eddie Logan (1931-79)

When Eddie Logan succeeded his father as the Giants' equipment manager in 1947, he began a 32-year career at that position until he retired in 1979 and protege Mike Murphy succeeded him. Murphy began working for his father as the assistant equipment manager at the Polo Grounds in 1931.

When his father died, he took over the reins and was the diminutive dynamo of the clubhouse through the turbulent 1950s, a decade which included the highs of the 1951 pennant race and the 1954 World Series sweep and the lows of the Giants leaving New York after the 1957 season.

Logan, along with traveling secretary Eddie Brannick and publicist Garry Schumacher, reluctantly left their beloved Manhattan and headed westward to begin a new chapter in the club's history. The move cost Logan his first marriage because his wife didn't want to leave New York.

"Those guys didn't want to move, but they came out and grew to love the Bay Area," Murphy said. "Everybody loved Logan. He was close to a lot of players, and we'd sit around and hear all the stories about the New York days. He taught me a lot about the business."

In Mike Mandel's fine oral history of the Giants, Logan recalled some of the highlights of his career shortly before his retirement. He fondly remembered the long barnstorming spring traning trainrides, adventures involving colorful pitcher Ruben Gomez and the famous Juan Marichal-John Roseboro altercation in 1965, perhaps the ugliest incident in Candlestick Park history.

Because the Dodgers were leaving town after the ballgame, a bloodied Roseboro was escorted to the airport early to avoid any postgame trouble. But the wounded catcher realized the patch covering his head - compliments of Marichal's bat - was unsightly and that his cap was still on the field.

"We couldn't find Roseboro's cap, so we gave him an S.F. cap," Logan told Mandel. "He

put it on and rode to the airport with the S.F. cap on. Can you imagine Johnny Roseboro walking around the airport with an S.F. cap on his head right after he gets banged up by Marichal?"

Larry Baer (1993-present)

The primary mover behind the Pacific Bell Park project, the ambitious Baer is a fourth-generation San Franciscan who has served as club president Peter Magowan's top lieutenant ever since the ownership group saved the Giants from a shift to Florida in 1993. Baer was the club's executive vice president until he was named chief operating officer of the franchise in 1996.

Whereas efforts to build the Giants a new ballpark failed under the previous regime, Baer was the driving force behind Pacific Bell Park when he was named president of the China Basin Ballpark Corporation in 1996. Previously, he was a key member in assembling the ownership group that kept the Giants in San Francisco and vowed to build a stadium far removed from the wind and cold of Candlestick Point.

His "baby" has been a rousing success, including more than 3 million in attendance in each of the first three years. Baer's love of the Giants was fostered as a schoolboy and continued at Cal-Berkeley, where he was Phi Beta Kappa and interested in broadcasting. In fact, he was hired by Charlie Finley to announce Oakland A's games.

After he was graduated from Cal, Baer joined the Giants as marketing director. He departed in 1983 to enter Harvard Business School, and was special assistant to CBS chairman Laurence Tisch before rejoining the Giants. In 1996, he received the San Francisco Distinguished Leadership Award for his community involvement.

Pat Gallagher (1976-present)

A fixture under two regimes of Giants' ownership, Gallagher was hired as the club's marketing director when Bob Lurie assumed control in 1976 and was among the few employees retained when the new ownership group took over in 1993. When the 2002 season concluded, Gallagher was president of Giants Enterprises, a business dedicated to developing non-baseball opportunities for Pacific Bell Park.

Under Gallagher's guidance, the new downtown ballpark now hosts the annual East-West Shrine Game for college football seniors, various concerts and various private, corporate and convention events. Previously, he served the club as senior vice president for business operations, which included marketing, promotion, advertising, sales and public relations.

Prior to joining the Giants, Gallagher was a marketing executive for Marine World/Africa USA and Sea World before leaving the popular theme parks to begin an award-winning business career in baseball. One of his most memorable promotions was the "Croix de Candlestick" pin for fans surviving extra-inning night games at Candlestick. He refuses to take credit for the short-lived "Crazy Crab" mascot.

Gallagher's expertise was used in several phases of Pacific Bell Park planning, especially the development of a successful marketing plan, corporate sponsorship, ballpark naming rights and means to defray the enormous debt of the privately-financed jewel-by-the-bay.

CHAPTER THREE
PROMINENT MANAGERS

Jim Mutrie (1885-91)

The nickname "Giants" for New York's National League baseball franchise is traced to Jim Mutrie.

In 1885 Mutrie was named the third full-time manager of the New York Gothams (as they were known from their origin two years earlier). A smooth-talking baseball aficionado, Mutrie had known New York owner John B. Day for several years. In 1883 and 1884 Mutrie was manager of the New York Metropolitans (or Mets for short), who also were owned by Day and played in the American Association. Day and Mutrie first got involved in baseball together in 1880 when they founded the Metropolitan Exhibition Company that fielded an independent team in New York.

On June 3, 1885, New York defeated the Philadelphia Phillies 8-7 in 11 innings at Recreation Park in Philadelphia to improve its record to 19-5. As legend has it, after the game an enthusiastic Mutrie proclaimed: "My big fellows! My Giants! We are the people." The nickname caught on immediately and has remained to this day. New York finished the season with an 85-27 record (a franchise-best .759 winning percentage) but was two games behind the pennant-winning Chicago White Stockings.

In Mutrie's day, a team's manager was more closely associated with today's general manager or business manager. Always formally dressed—complete with black top hat—"Truthful Jim" would divide his time between counting gate receipts and leading cheers from the grandstands. Meanwhile, today's field manager duties were handled by the team captain.

By 1888 Day and Mutrie put together a championship-caliber team that featured six future members of the National Baseball Hall of Fame (first baseman Roger Connor, catcher Buck Ewing, pitcher Tim Keefe, outfielder Jim O'Rourke, shortstop John Montgomery Ward and pitcher Mickey Welch). The Giants won their first N.L. pennant with an 84-47 record and faced the St. Louis Browns, winners of the A.A., for the world championship. New York captured the title six games to two (they played best-of-nine) before the Browns were victorious in two additional exhibition games.

The Giants repeated as N.L. champions in 1889 with an 83-43 record, one game better than the Boston Beaneaters. New York clinched the title on the final day of the season (October 5) with a 5-3 win over the Cleveland Spiders at the Polo Grounds in New York, while Boston

lost to the Pittsburgh Alleghenys 6-1 at Exposition Park in Pittsburgh. The Giants then beat the Brooklyn Bridegrooms of the A.A. six games to three for their second straight world championship.

When the Players League virtually depleted the Giants' roster in 1890, Day began absorbing financial losses. He sold shares of stock in his team to Edward Talcott, who wanted Mutrie to be relieved of his duties. The latter part of the deal was put off for a year, and Mutrie was dismissed November 7, 1891. Mutrie's seven-year record was 529-345. His snappy .605 winning percentage is the best among full-time Giants' managers, and he trails only John McGraw (2,583), Bill Terry (823), Leo Durocher (637) and Roger Craig (586) in victories.

Counting his 129-74 record with the Mets, Mutrie's lifetime mark was 658-419 for a .611 winning percentage that ranks second in baseball history to Joe McCarthy (.615 with the Chicago Cubs from 1926-30, New York Yankees from 1931-46 and Boston Red Sox from 1948-50). Mutrie is credited with being the founder of postseason play in 1884 when he arranged for the Mets to play the Providence Grays of the N.L. in a three-game series. Providence won all three games (6-0, 3-1 and 11-2) behind future Hall of Fame pitcher Charley "Old Hoss" Radbourn.

Mutrie passed away January 24, 1938, in New York at the age of 88.

John McGraw (1902-32)

With a nickname like "Little Napoleon," it's simple to figure out what type of man-

Jim Mutrie (Transcendental Graphics)

ager—and man—John McGraw was during his tenure with the New York Giants from 1902-32. Demonstrative. Fiery. Intense. And, oh yes, ultra successful.

McGraw earned his first win at the helm of the Giants on July 23, 1902, with a 4-1 victory over the cross-town rival Brooklyn Superbas at Washington Park in Brooklyn. During the next 31 seasons McGraw compiled a 2,583-1,790 record (.591 winning percentage). He piloted New York to a whopping 10 National League pennants and three World Series championships.

Immediately upon taking over the last-place Giants, McGraw made numerous personnel changes and began orchestrating what soon would become a dynasty. In 1904 New York captured the National League pennant with a franchise-best 106-47 record, 13 games ahead of the second-place Chicago Cubs. But McGraw and club owner John T. Brush refused to play the American League champion Boston Pilgrims in the World Series because they considered the A.L. to be an inferior league. The following year the Giants repeated as league champions, and defeated the Philadelphia Athletics in the World Series four games to one.

McGraw, widely regarded as a baseball genius and true teacher of the game, led New York to pennants in 1911, 1912, 1913 and 1917 but lost the World Series each year. In 1919 he became a minority stockholder in the ball club under new owner Charles A. Stoneham and began serving as a vice president, as well. McGraw became the first—and to this day only—manager to win four consecutive league

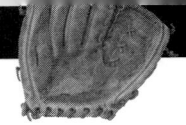

titles from 1921-24, and the Giants won back-to-back World Series crowns over the cross-town rival New York Yankees in 1921 and 1922. Throughout all his triumphs, McGraw was at odds with umpires, was levied his share of fines and suspensions and was embroiled in conflict and controversy.

McGraw's health began to decline in his latter years as the Giants' manager, and he re-signed June 3, 1932, after a double-header against the Philadelphia Phillies at the Polo Grounds in New York was rained out. He was replaced by first baseman Bill Terry.

From 1891-1906 McGraw enjoyed a pro-ductive 16-year playing career as an infielder and outfielder with the Baltimore Orioles (1891-99 and 1901-02), St. Louis Perfectos (1900) and Giants (1902-06). In 1,099 games he batted .334 with 462 RBI and 436 stolen bases. "Mugsy," with his 5-foot-7, 155-pound frame, was known for his scrappy play, ability to foul off pitches and willingness to get hit by pitches. His career on-base percentage of .466 ranks third on baseball's all-time list behind Hall of Famers Ted Williams (.483) and Babe Ruth (.474). McGraw had an on-base percentage of .547 in 1899, the second-best mark ever for a single season (behind Williams' .551 in 1941).

In 1899 McGraw became player-manager of the Orioles, and he returned to that po-sition in 1901 fol-lowing his one-year stint with the Per-

John McGraw (AP/Wide World Photos)

fectos. But McGraw and A.L. president Ban Johnson constantly clashed, and McGraw moved on to New York a year later. McGraw's overall managerial record was 2,763-1,948 (.586 winning percentage). Only Connie Mack (3,731 wins) has more victories as a big league skipper.

McGraw was stricken with prostate can-cer late in life and passed away February 25, 1934, in New Rochelle, New York, at the age of 60. He was inducted into the National Baseball Hall of Fame in 1937 and later had the letters "NY" retired in his honor by the Giants (since he did not wear a uniform number).

Leo Durocher (1948-55)

On July 16, 1948, the unbelievable, un-imaginable and unthinkable occurred. Leo Durocher, set to be replaced as manager of the cross-town rival Brooklyn Dodgers, was hired to manage the New York Giants.

The news stunned everyone in Flatbush and Gotham and sent shockwaves through-out baseball. How could Durocher manage a group of players he had tried so hard to beat for the previous nine years? How could Gi-ants' fans cheer for a "villain" they had been trained to hate?

After being sus-pended by baseball commissioner A.B. "Happy" Chandler for the entire 1947 season (reportedly for associating with gamblers and for marrying actress Laraine Day before she had divorced),

Leo Durocher (Brace Photo)

Durocher returned to the Dodgers in 1948 but was at constant odds with club president and general manager Branch Rickey. By mid-July, Rickey decided to oust Durocher and, at the same time, Giants' owner Horace C. Stoneham was looking to replace his manager, Mel Ott. Stoneham asked Rickey for permission to talk with coach Burt Shotton, but when Rickey mentioned that Durocher was available, Stoneham willingly opted for the proven manager.

Not only was Durocher making a bold decision in moving cross town, but he also was replacing a popular figure in Ott. Everyone liked Ott and his easy-going style; however, the Giants were foundering in fourth place in the National League with a lukewarm 37-38

record. Durocher was the direct opposite of Ott. Fiery. Intense. Rambunctious.

With his team in a funk, Stoneham told Durocher to evaluate everyone. The Giants went 41-38 with Durocher at the helm, and at the end of the season he made a succinct recommendation to Stoneham, "Horace, back up the truck." In other words, Durocher felt the Giants needed to make wholesale changes.

Over the next year, Durocher molded his type of squad. The Giants became quicker, scrappier and more aggressive (the way the "Lip" played as a shortstop with the New York Yankees, Cincinnati Reds, St. Louis Cardinals and Dodgers in 1925, 1928-41, 1943 and 1945) with the acquisition of players like shortstop Alvin Dark and second baseman Eddie Stanky from the Boston Braves on December 14, 1949.

In 1951 New York pulled off one of the greatest comebacks in baseball annuals. Trailing the Dodgers by 13½ games August 12, the Giants roared back to force a three-game playoff and ultimately captured the pennant on Bobby Thomson's dramatic three-run home run (the "Shot Heard 'Round The World") in the bottom of the ninth inning of the third and deciding game. The Giants lost to the Yankees in the World Series four games to two.

The Giants were N.L. champions again in 1954 with a 97-57 record, five games ahead of the Dodgers. In the World Series they upset the Cleveland Indians (with their splendid 111-43 regular-season record) four games to none.

Durocher managed the Giants through the 1955 season, compiling a 637-523 record (.549 winning percentage). He subsequently managed the Chicago Cubs (1966-72) and Houston Astros (1972-73) before retiring with a 24-year career record of 2,008-1,709 (.540). He ranks seventh on baseball's all-time games managed (3,739) and games won lists.

Known for his snazzy fashion sense, love for living life in the fast lane and enjoyment in mingling with the high-society crowd, Durocher passed away October 7, 1991, in Palm Springs, California, at the age of 86. He

was inducted into the National Baseball Hall of Fame in 1994 by the Veterans Committee.

Bill Rigney (1956-60, 1976)

"Rig" was a natural to become the first manager of the San Francisco Giants in 1958, and not merely because he was at the helm in 1957, their last year at the Polo Grounds. Born in crossbay Alameda, Rigney was a Bay Area native who loved the region and was steeped in its rich baseball tradition, but it wasn't an easy transition.

"I remember how difficult it was to move from New York, and I was a native," Rigney recalled. "I was the manager of the New York Giants, and there was a lot of tradition back there. It was traumatic for me, even though I was coming home."

Rigney learned the game from his father, George, a distinguished semi-pro player in the Bay Area. His son rose from the sandlots, the minors and World War II to join the Giants after serving as a physical training instructor at the Navy pre-flight school at nearby St. Mary's College.

He was a string bean shortstop in 1946 and managed 17 home runs among the club's record total of 221 in 1947. That success and a quick start the following year earned him All-Star Game selection in 1948, but he was primarily a reserve thereafter. "You know the phrase, 'good-field, no-hit'? Well, it might have been invented to describe me," said Rigney, who was part of the Giants' 1951 miracle.

"We were 13½ games behind the

Bill Rigney (S.F. Giants Archives)

Dodgers on August 12, but I thought we were still in the race," he said. "Why? Because we were in second place and didn't have to jump over anybody. As a player, Rigney was called "Cricket" by his Giants' teammates for his constant chatter in the infield. But his calling was more as a manager than as a player.

Curiously, he picked up a lot of pointers on managing when Alvin Dark and Eddie Stanky joined the Giants. Rigney was relegated to the bench, so he observed the two field leaders. The year after he was fired as manager of the Giants, Dark took over the reins.

Rigney started managing in the minors and was promoted to the Giants in 1956, succeeding Leo Durocher after winning a pennant with Triple-A Minnesota at 92-62 in 1955. "It was the fulfillment of a dream," said Rigney, who kept the Giants' job until June of the 1960 season, when he was replaced by longtime scout Tom Sheehan, a Horace Stoneham confidant.

"I'd kept telling them to bring Juan Marichal up at the *beginning* of the season, but they said he wasn't ready," Rigney said. "Then they bring him up right after I'm fired. My top thrills were that opening day at Seals Stadium in 1958 and Willie McCovey's (4-for-4) debut."

The latter occurred in 1959 and was followed by regret. The Giants held a two-game lead over the Dodgers but crumpled down the stretch, and Los Angeles won the pennant. "We just couldn't hold on," Rigney said. "I might have overworked Sam Jones a bit. If I had managed

109

as well for the Giants in '59 as I did with the Angels in '62, we'd have won it."

Pitcher Stu Miller didn't see it that way, explaining: "Rigney was the best manager I ever played for. He was great. He'd manage 25 players. He made them all feel part of the team. It was a travesty when he got fired. We were eight games over .500 and two games out of first, and he got fired."

Rigney's big regret was being given the boot shortly before Marichal made his debut with a one-hitter. He wasn't disappointed for long, however. Named the first manager of the expansion Los Angeles Angels in 1961, he guided the 1962 version to an 86-76 record—best ever for an expansion club in its second year.

He also won a division crown with the Minnesota Twins in 1970 after taking over for Billy Martin as manager. Rigney resurfaced as the Giants' manager in 1976 for sentimental reasons when Bob Lurie purchased the club but lasted only one year. "That wasn't much fun," he said. "I hadn't wanted to manage anymore. I'd had enough. But Bob asked me if I would because he didn't want to worry about finding a manager if he got the club."

Rigney worked with A's prior to that nostalgia trip, and resumed working with Oakland as

Alvin Dark (S.F. Giants Archives)

a broadcaster, administrative assistant and ambassador until the 1990s. A noted storyteller with a facile mind, Rigney is one of the Bay Area's most beloved baseball personalities. Bay Area baseball writers annually present the most accommodating players on the Giants and A's with the Bill Rigney Good Guy Award.

Alvin Dark (1961-64)

The most controversial manager in San Francisco history produced a dramatic pennant-winner in 1962 and took the mighty Yankees down to the last out of Game 7 in the World Series. Alvin Dark was credited with fusing the Giants' diverse racial mix into a 103-win champion in 1962.

Yet a controversial ratings system in 1963 and insensitive remarks in 1964 pushed him out of the job. Dark's strong religious beliefs were questioned by the arch-rival Dodgers in 1961, after he ordered the base paths at Candlestick Park soaked to shut down the fleet Maury Wills.

He also concocted a plus-minus points system to determine which of his players were best under pressure, and there was a flap because Jim Davenport rated way ahead of Orlando Cepeda. "The guy who really messed up the Giants was Alvin Dark, I don't now why they fired Bill Rigney," declared Cepeda, who had 46 home runs

and a club-record 142 RBI in 1961, yet was a minus in Dark's point system.

Felipe Alou wasn't as vehement, but he let his feelings be known after Dark forbade the club's many Latin ballplayers from speaking Spanish. Later, "Blackie" allegedly told a reporter that African-American and Hispanic players were slackers and were the reason the club fell short in 1963 and 1964. He supposedly told the reporter minority players weren't as mentally alert or as dedicated to winning as their white counterparts.

Dark insisted the quotes were distorted, and some minority players and prominent journalists vouched for him, but the damage had been done. Repercussions followed, and he was fired at end of 1964 season when his Baptist preachings had worn out their welcome. Dark went on to manage Kansas City, Cleveland and Oakland with no further racial controversy.

Actually, he made an effort to bridge the cultural gaps between whites, blacks and Hispanics when he became Giants' manager in 1961, attempting to break up cliques by having the lockers of different ethnic mixes next to each other in the clubhouse. He is the most successful manager in San Francisco history with a .569 winning percentage on 366 victories and 277 defeats.

Herman Franks (1965-68)

Herman Franks should have been nicknamed "Avis," because he was always second and trying harder. He managed the Giants merely four years (1965-68) and finished second each time. The Giants may have had the best National League team over those years, but the Los Angeles Dodgers (1965-66) and the St. Louis Cardinals (1967-68) were better in given years.

Franks' .567 winning percentage (367-280) is bettered only by Alvin Dark (.569) among San Francisco skippers. Franks bemoaned the lack of a great double-play combo dragging the club down in those days, failing to win once despite five Hall of Famers: Willie

Herman Franks (S.F. Giants Archives)

Mays, Willie McCovey, Juan Marichal, Gaylord Perry and, briefly, Orlando Cepeda.

"I have great memories of those teams, but it's still hard to take that we didn't win a pennant," he said. Franks was especially close with Mays, who enjoyed a Most Valuable Player season in 1965 with a franchise-record 52 home runs. That was Franks' rookie season and the Giants won 95 games.

"Herman was a good man," Cepeda said. "He understood the Latin players." The club's victory totals decreased to 93, 91 and 88 before Franks was fired for finishing second too many times. Herman's gruff exterior didn't win many friends among sportswriters, but he was well liked by intimates.

He didn't respond well to negative publicity, and a Philadelphia columnist wrote, "Franks carries around newspaper clippings the way some people carry bad checks—as souvenirs of misplaced trust."

A catcher, Franks had success in the minors, and then played briefly with the Cardinals, Dodgers, A's and Giants. He batted .199 in 188 major league games and appeared in the 1941 World Series with the Dodgers before beginning military duty. Franks began a coaching career with the Giants in 1949 and was on Bill Rigney's staff when the franchise moved west in 1958.

Franks, a native of Utah, also managed the Chicago Cubs briefly following his Giants' days. He was educated at the University of Utah and became a shrewd businessman, becoming highly successful with investments and real estate. He still resides in Salt Lake City.

Charlie Fox (1970-74)

As a youngster in the Bronx, Charlie Fox dreamt of playing with his beloved Giants. He was a New York American Legion star, attracting the attention of the Yankees, but spurned them because his family rooted for the Giants. He got his wish in 1942, reaching the majors and batting .429 with three hits in seven at-bats for New York before World War II interrupted his brief major league career.

After spending three years in the Navy, including dangerous missions in the North Atlantic, Fox returned in 1946 and was on a veteran-stocked Manchester (Massachusetts) team in the New England League. The manager couldn't handle the players, so Fox, then merely 24, got his first managerial job late that season.

He finished third that year, launching a career which led him to the majors as the Giants' manager 24 years later. Curiously, Walter Alston guided Nashua to second place for the Dodgers in 1946, and Fox returned the favor by beating Alston and Los Angeles for the National League Western Division title in 1971.

That was the "Year of the Fox," easily his finest as a major league manager. Fox earned Manager of the Year distinction. That rookie-laden team started strong but nearly squandered the lead down the stretch. Juan Marichal had to be used the final day to stave off the

Charlie Fox (S.F. Giants Archives)

Dodgers, and it proved costly in the playoffs because Marichal could pitch merely once. The Pirates won three out of four and reached the World Series.

A long minor league career prepared Fox for the Giants' job. He was with Triple-A Phoenix in Portland, Oregon, and heard the good news after Clyde King's Giants dropped a 17-16 decision on May 23, 1970. He also was a hit on the banquet circuit with his Irish tenor voice. Fox currently owns a restaurant, Bertolucci's, a few miles south of Candlestick Park.

Joe Altobelli (1977-79)

Joe Altobelli had a mediocre major league playing career (.210 batting average in 166 games) as a first baseman, but he found his niche managing and reaped the benefits of a 1978 San Francisco Giants' resurgence which landed him Manager of the Year honors. He re-

placed Bill Rigney in 1977 and went 75-87, a one-game improvement over the previous year.

But in 1978, the spring acquisition of pitcher Vida Blue led to a resurgence on the field and at the gate. The 1978 Giants were a division-leading 52-34 at the All-Star break and finished 89-73 for a 14-game gain over the previous year. Before the 1979 season concluded, however, the Giants had fallen on hard times again and Altobelli was replaced by coach Dave Bristol.

"Alto" had one more moment of glory, guiding the 1983 Baltimore Orioles to a World Series championship. He paid his dues, spending 11 years as a minor league manager with the Orioles. He produced four pennants and won three Manager of the Year Awards.

He was a solid minor league player following an outstanding prep career in Detroit. He was best known for his fancy glove work and continued to work with first basemen during his coaching and managing career. As a Florida State League rookie in 1951, Altobelli hit safely in 36 consecutive games.

Frank Robinson (1981-84)

The great Hall of Famer Frank Robinson was a much better player than he was a manager, but he had the great distinction of being the first man of African-American heritage to manage in both leagues—with the 1975 Cleveland Indians in the American League and with the Giants in 1981.

Displaying the same determination and toughness that made him a superstar, Robinson kept the Giants competitive during a strike-shortened 56-55 season in 1981. The addition of veteran first baseman Reggie Smith helped the club contend in 1982, finishing two games out of the lead with an 87-75 record.

When "Robby" guided back-to-back winners in 1981-82, it was a first for the Giants since 1970-71. He directed the club to a 10-game winning streak and 45 comeback victories in 1982, landing UPI Manager of the Year honors. But Robinson fell on hard times thereafter.

Partly because of a lack of administrative support, he was doomed by 1984, when owner Bob Lurie fired him during the Olympic Games in Los Angeles, keeping adverse publicity to a minimum. Robinson was vindicated when the 1985 Giants dropped a franchise-record 100 games without him.

Robinson ranks among the great superstars of the 1950s and 1960s, holding his own while competing with the likes of Willie Mays, Hank Aaron, Roberto Clemente and Ernie Banks. He attended Oakland's McClymonds High School, where he was a basketball teammate of the unheralded Bill Russell.

Robinson signed with the Cincinnati Reds, whom he joined in 1956, and tied the rookie record of 38 home runs while leading the league with 122 runs scored. By 1961 he was the N.L. Most Valuable Player for taking the Reds to the World Series. He led the N.L. in slugging percentage three straight years, 1960-

Joe Altobelli (S.F. Giants Archives)

Frank Robinson (S.F. Giants Archives)

62, and had a league-leading 51 doubles and 134 RBI, both career highs, in 1962.

Robinson joined the Baltimore Orioles in a controversial trade for pitcher Milt Pappas and promptly powered the O's to a World Series title by winning the Triple Crown with a .316 average, 49 homers and 122 RBI. He also became the first player to win MVP awards in both major leagues. He also played for the Dodgers and the Angels before joining the Indians in 1974.

One year later, he integrated the majors as a player-manager, winning that historic first game with a dramatic home run. Following his Giants' career, he served in various jobs with the Orioles, including manager from 1988-91, going 87-75 for second place in 1989. Robinson was the commissioner of the Arizona Fall League and a special consultant to commissioner Bud Selig in 1998.

Roger Craig (1985-92)

No one can accuse Roger Craig of being afraid to accept a good, old-fashioned chal-

lenge. Rather, the former San Francisco Giants' manager is one of those people who seems to thrive in a difficult situation, one who would likely jump at the opportunity to cut down a redwood tree with a pocket knife.

When Craig was hired late in the 1985 season, the Giants were on their way to becoming the first team in franchise history (including the New York years) to lose 100 games. One year earlier they had suffered 96 defeats. Craig was hand-picked by new general manager Al Rosen, and the duo was given a "mandate for change" by owner Bob Lurie.

A first-rate challenge, to say the least. But Rosen and Craig quickly went to work and by Opening Day of 1986 had assembled a new-look team that was eager to win. Craig sold the players—a well-meshed combination of veterans (like Bob Brenly and Mike Krukow) and rookies (like Will Clark and Robby Thompson)—on his positive attitude that included such catchy phrases as "Humm Baby" and "Don't get your dauber down."

The Giants were the talk of the baseball world and as late as July 18, 1986, were in first place in the National League West Division. San Francisco ended up in third place, 13 games behind the Houston Astros, with an 83-79 record. It marked a 21-game improvement from the previous year and provided a clear indication that a winning foundation had been laid. The Giants became just the ninth team in history to post a winning season following a 100-loss season.

In 1987 the Giants captured their first division championship since 1971 with a 90-72 record before suffering a heart-breaking seven-game loss to the St. Louis Cardinals in the National League Championship Series. Craig was named National League Manager of the Year by the Associated Press.

San Francisco won its second division crown in three years in 1989 with a 92-70 record and then defeated the Chicago Cubs four games to one for the N.L. pennant. The Giants were World Series bound for the first time since 1962. The powerful Oakland Athlet-

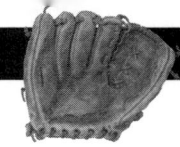

ics went on to sweep the Fall Classic that was marred by a 7.0 earthquake prior to the start of Game 3 (5:04 p.m. local time) at Candlestick Park in San Francisco.

The Giants appeared ready to repeat in 1990, but a serious rash of injuries proved too much to overcome down the stretch. They finished in third place at 85-77, six games behind the eventual world champion Cincinnati Reds.

Craig, a Lyndon B. Johnson lookalike with a grandfatherly presence, managed the club through a tumultuous 1992 season, after which he held San Francisco records for most games managed (1,252) and won (586). Those marks were then exceeded by his protege, Dusty Baker, who was Craig's batting coach in 1988-92. The Giants posted a .509 winning percentage under "The Humm Baby," including five winners in seven years.

A 12-year major league pitcher from 1955-66 (with the Brooklyn and Los Angeles

Roger Craig (S.F. Giants Archives)

Dodgers, New York Mets, St. Louis Cardinals, Cincinnati Reds and Philadelphia Phillies), Craig employed a hands-on approach with his San Francisco pitching staffs. He is widely-regarded as the guru of the split-fingered fastball and taught the pitch to a majority of his hurlers. The Giants compiled a nifty 3.63 ERA under Craig's tutelage.

Dusty Baker (1993-2002)

Dusty Baker convincingly disproved the theory that good ballplayers don't succeed as managers. He concluded a 10-year career at the 2002 World Series with the most wins (840) in San Francisco Giants' managerial history, trailing only the legendary John McGraw on the franchise list; joined Roger Craig as the only S.F. skippers with two division titles, and earned an unprecedented three Manager of the Year awards from the baseball writers.

And, after posting merely one postseason victory in his first nine years, he guided the 2002 club to a pennant and the seventh game of the World Series during a 10-7 run as the National League wild card. Baker, a Riverside, Cal., native, was a four-sport standout as a Sacramento prep who began his baseball career after attending American River Junior College.

Baker signed with Atlanta Braves and made a big splash by batting .321 in his first full season as a major leaguer in 1972. He learned from idols like Hank Aaron, Felipe Alou and Orlando Cepeda, and increased his power after joining the Dodgers. He homered on the last day of the 1977 season for a career-high 30, giving Los Angeles four players with at least 30 home runs, an unprecedented feat.

Baker finished his career with the Giants in 1984 and with the Oakland Athletics in 1985 and 1986. He posted a .278 lifetime average with 242 home runs in a 16-year career, and excelled in the National League playoffs, batting .371 with a .597 slugging percentage in 17 games with the Dodgers.

He was in private business in 1987, but was convinced by Bob Lurie and Al Rosen to

become a coach, serving the Giants in that capacity from 1988-92. Baker was credited with Kevin Mitchell's Most Valuable Player success of 1989 as the batting coach of a pennant-winner.

Despite concerns over a lack of managerial experience, Baker was signed to manage under the new ownership group in 1993 and posted a remarkable 103 victories, tying the franchise record. The team lost on the final day in Los Angeles, finishing one game behind the Atlanta Braves in the N.L. West Division before the wild card came into existence.

Dusty Baker (S.F. Giants Archives)

He had the Giants on the rise again in 1994 when the strike cut the season short. His ability to relate to players kept Baker popular despite losing seasons in 1995-96, and he bounced back to win a division title in 1997.

The Giants lost a one-game wild-card playoff to the Cubs, who Baker managed in 2003, in 1998, but he wasn't denied in 2000 or 2002. His 2000 club topped the majors with 97 victories and was division champion. After finishing two games behind champion Arizona in 2001, his 2002 Giants reached the World Series as the wild card by stunning Atlanta and St. Louis in the playoffs. He finished with a final 840-715 log (.540) as the Giants' manager, and added 11 postseason wins.

But Baker's value wasn't based on wins and losses as much as it was for his manner in handling diverse groups, utilizing his entire roster, having players realize their roles and keeping aging veterans fresh to maximize their potential down the stretch. That perhaps explains why only the Braves posted more victories while the Giants were under his watch, or why the club played merely 11 games that didn't have playoff implications since the 1997 season.

CHAPTER FOUR
PLAYERS ROLL CALL

Felipe Alou, Outfielder (1958-63)

It took 40 years, but Felipe Alou finally made it back to the Giants at age 68 when he signed on as the Giants' manager for 2003. Coming full circle after starring with the 1962 pennant-winning club, Felipe had some big shoes to fill as Dusty Baker's replacement on a reshuffled World Series club, but after establishing himself as an exemplary leader as a ballplayer and as manager of the Montreal Expos, he seemed equal to the task.

The eldest of the ballplaying Alous, Felipe was born in the Dominican Republic and was signed by the Giants as Felipe Alou Rojas, named after his father. But a minor league manager figured it was easier to pronounce Alou instead of Rojas, so his mother's surname stuck.

Felipe signed with the Giants for a $200 bonus and, playing for Cocoa in the Florida State League, won the batting title with a .380 average. After starting out 1958 with a .319 average for 55 games in Triple-A, he was called up to the infant San Francisco Giants.

"The day I joined the Giants was one of the most important days of my life," he recalled. "That was the day my new teammate, Al Worthington, introduced me to Jesus Christ. I don't believe in accidents. I believe that was a man who was waiting for me."

Alou soon impressed sufficiently to win the right field job from heralded Willie Kirkland, who eventually was traded. Felipe's best year in San Francisco was 1962, as the Giants won the pennant. He batted .316 with 25 home runs. At the time, manager Alvin Dark claimed he was the National League's second-best outfielder. "After you get past Willie Mays, he's as good as anyone," Dark said.

The eldest Alou had fond memories of 1962, his first real taste of success as a major leaguer. "That was the biggest year of my baseball life, winning the pennant and playing the Yankees in the World Series," he said. "It wasn't only that, but everything that happened that year. It was my first .300 year, my first big year, my first pennant and one of the richest spiritual experiences of my life. It was like a miracle."

Felipe was traded to the Milwaukee Braves in 1963 and it wasn't truly a surprise. "I knew I was going to go," he said. "I was one of the voices raising certain issues relating to Latin players and to my Christian stand. I was committed to what I believe."

He finished his career with more than 2,000 hits and 200 home runs, leading the league in hits for Atlanta in 1966 and 1968. "I've never seen any player hit so consistently

Felipe Alou (S.F. Giants Archives)

all season long," teammate Henry Aaron said of Felipe's 31 homers and .327 average in 1966. "We all thought Felipe should have been the MVP."

Braves catcher Joe Torre concurred, adding: "Everything he hit was hard, everything was a line drive. You can't imagine some of the shots that were caught." Felipe's lifetime average was .286 after he finished his career with the 1974 Milwaukee Brewers. When he retired, his 2,101 hits were the most by a native of the Dominican Republic, but he was surpassed by Julio Franco. Alou's 98 RBI with the 1962 Giants served as a record for Dominicans until his son, Moises, had 115 for the 1998 Astros, yet Moises was born in Atlanta.

"I was surprised I got traded by the Giants," he said. "I'm not afraid to say that they made a mistake. I became a better player after that. When I came up, the Giants were a very special team because of their understanding and acceptance of Latin ballplayers."

Felipe became the highly-successful manager of the Montreal Expos in recent years, known for his handling of young players and for getting the most out of a low-budget roster. Only Tom Kelly (Minnesota Twins) and Bobby Cox (Atlanta Braves) managed their teams longer through the 1999 season. With his 521st victory August 19, 1998, in Arizona, he broke a tie with Buck Rodgers as the winningest manager in Expos' history.

Loyal to a fault, Felipe spurned a lucrative offer to become the Los Angeles Dodgers' manager in 1999 and remained with the Expos. He managed 12 minor league teams for the Expos from 1977-91 and had three championships and nine second-place finishes, including split seasons. He began his Montreal managing career in 1992 and posted two runner-up finishes, going 94-68 in 1993. He had the Expos in first place in 1994 when the strike ended a 74-40 season and denied the club an opportunity to reach the playoffs.

Felipe was named Manager of the Year, however, and guided the N.L. to victory in the 1995 All-Star Game. Very athletic as a youth, he represented the Dominican Republic in the 1954 Pan American Games as a baseball player and in the javelin. He became the second Dominican to reach the majors, following Ozzie Virgil, also with the Giants.

Jesus Alou, Outfielder (1963-68)

Youngest of the Alou brothers (eight years younger than Felipe), Jesus reached the Giants in 1963 and played in the same outfield with his two brothers—an unprecedented feat—on September 10 at the Polo Grounds against the Mets. The three Alous first performed the feat in the 1961 Dominican Winer League.

Felipe and Matty were gone in 1964 and Jesus remained with the Giants. He was called Jay Alou by some reporters apparently uncomfortable with Jesus. "What is wrong with my real name—Jesus?" he asked. "It is a common name in Latin America. My parents named me Jesus, and I'm proud of my name. This Jay, I do not like. It is not my name."

Jesus Alou (S.F. Giants Archives)

The rookie set a San Francisco record with six hits in one game July 10, 1964, against the Chicago Cubs. He hit five singles and a home run against six different pitchers in the Giants' 10-3 romp. It was tied by Mike Benjamin on June 14, 1995, also against the Cubs.

Jesus encountered Don Drysdale during his rookie season, and it wasn't pleasant. The youngest Alou had a nervous tick that frequently had him twitching his neck and shoulders. Drysdale, unaware of the affliction, thought Jesus was doing it to distract him, and promptly knocked him down with a brushback pitch.

The youngest Alou also was known as a bad-ball hitter, once hitting a home run off Sandy Koufax on a fastball heading for his head. He enjoyed his best season with the Giants in 1965, batting .298. He batted .292 in 1967 with the Giants, and improved to .306 with the 1970 Houston Astros, concluding his career with a .280 lifetime average.

Jesus didn't have the same interest in baseball that his brothers shared in the Dominican Republic. He signed for a $1,500 bonus at age 16 and started as a pitcher, but switched to the outfield. "I grew up playing with my brothers in the Dominican," he said. "We pitched to each other until somebody struck out. That was about the only baseball I played. I never played on an organized team until the Giants signed me in 1958."

He was signed as a pitcher, but his career didn't take off until he concentrated on hitting. Jesus never batted below .323 in five minor league seasons. "We decided that all Alous belong in the outfield," Giants farm director Carl Hubbell said, explaining why Alou was permanently removed from the pitcher's mound.

Matty Alou, Outfielder (1960-65)

Mateo Alou enjoyed his best years after leaving Giants, for whom he couldn't attain regular status. As a Pittsburgh regular, he led the National League with a .342 average in 1966, proving to be a Giant mistake. He showed flashes of hitting ability with a .310 average in 81 games for the 1961 Giants, but couldn't crash their talent-laden outfield.

"I signed one year after Felipe, but he never told me about Willie Mays—and I was a center fielder," Matty remembered. His big break was a trade to the Pirates, where manager Harry Walker and future Hall of Famer Roberto Clemente were credited with changing his batting stance and making him use a heavier bat. He choked up on the bat for better control and was a great bunter, helping him to become the first native of the Dominican Republic to win a batting title.

"When I signed, I was 16 years old, 5-foot-7 and 135 pounds," Mateo recalled. "I wasn't a good size for a ballplayer, but it came natural. Nobody taught me how to play. Nobody told me how to hit. But I practiced, I had good reflexes and I had good eyes."

He batted at least .331 four consecutive years with Pirates from 1966-69. Felipe was second in the 1966 N.L. batting race (.327),

Matty Alou (S.F. Giants Archives)

marking the first time brothers finished 1-2. Mateo, easily the smallest of the Alous, had so much promise in his early days with the Giants, but his inability to find a spot in a crowded outfield was frustrating.

"Mousey" batted .333 for the Giants in six games of the 1962 World Series but still couldn't find regular work until 1965 and was traded one year later, his big break. In 1969 he led the league with 231 hits and 41 doubles, also setting a major league record with 698 at-bats. He joined the Waner brothers, Paul and Lloyd, as the only Bucs with at least 230 hits.

The diminutive Dominican batted above .300 in six full major league seasons and finished with a .307 lifetime mark after merely batting .260 with the Giants before he was traded for Joe Gibbon and Ozzie Virgil. Among his highlights in baseball was playing in the Giants' outfield along with his two brothers in 1963 at the Polo Grounds.

"I pinch hit and then went to center field," he said. "I didn't know that all three of us were playing until I checked to my left and to my right. That was the only time with the Giants that we all played together, but in winter ball we played together every game for about 10 years." Mateo, who also played in Japan, subsequently headed the Giants' scouting operations in his native Dominican Republic.

Red Ames, Pitcher (1903-13)

In his major league debut September 14, 1903, New York Giants' right-handed pitcher Leon "Red" Ames held the St. Louis Cardinals hitless for five innings before the game (the second of a double-header) was called because of darkness. Ames and the Giants won the game 5-0 at Robison Field in St. Louis.

From 1903-13, Ames was a consistent performer for the Giants, but he constantly lived in the shadows of more-celebrated pitchers like Christy Mathewson and Joe McGinnity. Ames enjoyed his best season in 1905 when he compiled a 22-8 record with a 2.74 ERA and 198 strikeouts in 262.2 innings pitched. Those numbers, while certainly impressive, paled in comparison to Mathewson's (31-9, 1.28 ERA and 206 strikeouts).

Ames struggled with control early in his career, and in 1905 he set a modern-day major league record (since 1900) with 30 wild pitches.

The Giants won the 1905 World Series over the Philadelphia Athletics four games to one. Ames was the only relief pitcher used by either team in the series when he hurled a scoreless ninth inning in Game 2 after McGinnity was pinch hit for by Sammy Strang. Mathewson pitched shutouts in Games 1, 3 and 5 and McGinnity did the same in Game 4. Meanwhile, the Athletics got two complete games apiece from Chief Bender (including a shutout in Game 2) and Eddie Plank and one from Andy Coakley.

Ames led the Giants with 156 strikeouts in 1906 and with three shutouts in 1910. He was 15-10 with a 2.69 ERA in 1909 and 11-5 with a 2.46 ERA in 1912.

On opening day of the 1909 season April 15, Ames pitched 9.1 hitless innings against the

Brooklyn Dodgers at the Polo Grounds in New York before giving up seven hits over the next 3.2 innings and suffering a 3-0 defeat. The Giants managed just three hits off the Dodgers' Kaiser Wilhelm. New York outfielders recorded no putouts. It was tough-luck performances such as that one which earned Ames the nickname "Kalamity" by sportswriter Charley Dryden.

In Game 5 of the 1911 World Series against Philadelphia, Ames pitched four scoreless innings in relief of Rube Marquard as the Giants rallied from a 3-0 deficit for a 4-3 victory. Ames then started Game 6 the following day and surrendered five runs (two earned) in four innings as the Athletics won 13-2 to win the championship four games to two.

Ames was traded to the Cincinnati Reds along with outfielder Josh Devore, infielder Heinie Groh and $20,000 in exchange for pitcher Art Fromme and infielder Eddie Grant on May 22, 1913. In his 11 seasons in New York, Ames compiled a 108-77 record with a 2.45 ERA in 282 games. On the Giants' franchise lists, he ranks fourth in ERA, eighth in

Leon "Red" Ames

strikeouts (1,169) and 10th in walks (620). Ames averaged 5.84 strikeouts per nine innings, the best ratio among New York Giants pitchers and the seventh-best ratio in franchise history. Opponents batted just .234 against Ames, the fifth-lowest average in franchise history.

After pitching for the Reds from 1913-15, Ames went to the Cardinals from 1915-19 and concluded his playing days with the Philadelphia Phillies in 1919. His 17-year career statistics included a 183-167 record, 2.63 ERA and 1,702 strikeouts in 533 games. He was known as a cold-weather pitcher who did his best work when the temperature was low. Ames spent time in the minor leagues in 1921 and 1922 and subsequently became a minor league manager.

Ames passed away October 8, 1936, in Warren, Ohio, at the age of 54 following a long illness. His son, Leon Jr., was a minor league pitcher.

Johnny Antonelli, Pitcher (1954-60)

When the New York Giants acquired left-handed pitcher Johnny Antonelli from the Milwaukee Braves on February 1, 1954, the trade was not exactly welcomed with open arms in Gotham. After all, Antonelli had won just 17 games during his first three-plus seasons, and the principal player going to Milwaukee was popular third baseman/outfielder Bobby Thomson. (The Giants also sent catcher Sam Calderone to the Braves and received infielder Billy Klaus, pitcher Don Liddle, catcher Ebba St. Claire and $50,000.)

But during his seven seasons with the Giants from 1954-60, Antonelli was one of baseball's most consistent performers. He averaged 15 wins and just under 230 innings pitched per year. Only once did he allow more hits than innings pitched.

Antonelli, who originally made headlines by receiving the biggest signing bonus ($65,000) in baseball history from the Boston Braves as an 18-year-old in 1948, wasted no time making a name for himself in New York.

Johnny Antonelli (S.F. Giants Archives)

He fashioned a 21-7 record with a National League-leading 2.30 ERA in 1954. In 258.2 innings pitched he surrendered just 209 hits while limiting the opposition to a league-low .219 batting average. He also topped the Senior Circuit with six shutouts to go with 18 complete games.

After winning the N.L. pennant by five games over the cross-town rival Brooklyn Dodgers with a 97-57 record, the Giants squared off against the American League champion Cleveland Indians and their gaudy 111-43 record in the World Series. Antonelli started Game 2 at the Polo Grounds in New York and went the distance, allowing a mere one run on eight hits with six walks and nine strikeouts en route to a 3-1 victory. Then just two days later in Game 4 at Municipal Stadium in Cleveland, Antonelli was brought in out of the bullpen with one out, two runners on base and the tying run at the plate. He worked out of the jam and went on to retire the Indians in

the ninth inning to earn the save. The Giants won the game 7-4 and the World Series four games to none.

In 1956 Antonelli finished 20-13 with a 2.86 ERA and a league-leading six shutouts. He was 16-13, 3.28 ERA in 1958 and 19-10, 3.10 ERA and a league-best four shutouts in 1959.

Antonelli was a five-time N.L. All-Star with the Giants (1954, 1956, 1957, 1958 and 1959). He tossed four scoreless innings to earn the save in the 1956 game at District of Columbia Stadium in Washington and was the winning pitcher in the first of two games played in 1959 at Forbes Field in Pittsburgh, picking up the victory in relief after retiring future Hall of Famer Al Kaline of the Detroit Tigers on the only pitch he threw.

On December 3, 1960, the Giants traded Antonelli and outfielder Willie Kirkland to Cleveland in exchange for outfielder Harvey Kuenn. The Indians subsequently sent Antonelli back to the Braves for cash July 4, 1961. The Braves then dealt Antonelli and pitcher Ken MacKenzie to the expansion New York Mets for cash October 11, 1961, but Antonelli opted to retire.

In 280 games with the Giants (219 starts), Antonelli posted a 108-84 record and a 3.13 ERA with 86 complete games, 21 shutouts and 19 saves. He had 919 strikeouts in 1,600.2 innings pitched. Antonelli's 12-year career numbers included a 126-110 record and a 3.34 ERA in 377 games (268 starts).

Following his playing days, Antonelli managed in the Mets' minor league system for the Class AA Memphis Blues (1969-72) and the Class AAA Tidewater Tides (1973-74). He currently makes his home in Pittsford, New York.

Rich Aurilia, Shortstop (1995-present)

The Giants probably didn't realize what they were getting when they traded former ace John Burkett to the Texas Rangers on Dec. 24,

1994, for obscure minor league shortstop Rich Aurilia. What a Christmas present it turned out to be. Within five years, the Brooklyn native blossomed into an offensive force at his position.

It wasn't a sudden transformation. There were growing pains as the club brought in Shawon Dunston, Jose Vizcaino and Rey Sanchez to share the position while he patiently awaited his turn. The learning process paid off when Aurilia became the fulltime starter in 1999, beginning a four-year run that produced an average of 23.5 homers and 79.3 RBI.

And while establishing himself as the National League's sluggingest shortstop, Aurilia gradually improved his defense. His error totals were reduced each season - from a league-worse 28 in 1999 to a league-leading 11 in 2002, when he topped N.L. shorstops with a .980 fielding percentage.

Aurilia's defensive accomplishments, however, were obscured by his hitting. In 2001, for instance, he became the first N.L. shortstop since Dave Concepcion 20 years previously to lead his position in home runs and RBI three straight seasons. That year, he and Jeff Kent became the first double-play combo in history with three consecutive 20-homer seasons each.

Switched to the No. 2 spot in the batting order in 2001, Aurilia thrived while hitting in front of Barry Bonds. He was part of several homeplate home run celebrations because he constantly was on base during a career year that included a league-leading 206 hits, most by a Giant since Willie Mays set the S.F. standard with 208 in 1958.

Such staggering production from a shortstop produced a .324 batting average, 37 doubles, 37 home runs, 114 runs and 97 RBI. Only Hall of Famer Ernie Banks hit more homers in one season as a N.L. shortstop, and Aurilia joined Banks and Barry Larkin as the only N.L. shortstops to surpass 30 home runs.

Elbow surgery reduced his offednsive effectiveness in 2002, limiting him to 15 homers and 61 RBI, but Aurilia picked up the pace with a .293 average and 18 RBI the final month and continued to produce in October, including a .333 average and two homers in the NLCS and two homers and five RBI in the World Series.

Rich Aurilia (S.F. Giants)

Dave Bancroft, Shortstop (1920-23, 1930)

The New York Giants were coming off back-to-back second-place finishes (1918 and 1919) in the National League when they acquired shortstop Dave "Beauty" Bancroft from the Philadelphia Phillies in exchange for shortstop Art Fletcher, pitcher Bill Hubbell and a reported $100,000 on June 8, 1920.

Bancroft, who played for the Giants from 1920-23 and returned as a player-coach in 1930, paid immediate dividends when he tied the franchise record (shared with seven others) with six hits (all singles in six at-bats) against

Dave Bancroft (Brace Photo)

the Philadelphia Phillies at the Baker Bowl in Philadelphia on June 28, 1920. New York won 18-3 in a game that took just 1 hour and 58 minutes to complete.

Although the Giants finished second again in 1920, they put together a string of three consecutive N.L. pennants from 1921-23 thanks in large part to the competitive, energetic and inspirational Bancroft, who was appointed team captain by manager John McGraw.

In 1921 Bancroft batted .318 with 26 doubles and career highs of 15 triples, 67 RBI and 17 stolen bases. On June 1, in the second game of a double-header, he hit for the cycle against the Phillies in Philadelphia. New York went on to win the World Series over the cross-town rival Yankees five games to three.

The switch-hitting Bancroft continued to provide offensive fireworks in 1922 as he posted personal bests of a .321 batting average and 41 doubles to go with 60 RBI and 16 stolen

bases. Defensively, he established a major league record that still stands today with 984 total chances, while setting franchise records for putouts (405) and assists (579). The Giants repeated as World Series champions over the Yankees four games to none.

New York completed its N.L. pennant-winning three-peat in 1923 with Bancroft batting .304 with 33 doubles and 31 RBI. The Yankees, though, got revenge in the postseason by winning the World Series four games to two. Bancroft had been stricken with pneumonia in June, and his legs had troubled him several times during the season, so Travis Jackson had been groomed as a replacement. On November 12, 1923, the Giants traded Bancroft to the Boston Braves along with outfielders Bill Cunningham and Casey Stengel in exchange for pitcher Joe Oeschger and outfielder Billy Southworth.

Bancroft took over as player-manager of the Braves, whose president was former Giants' pitcher Christy Mathewson. He remained in Boston through the 1927 season before moving on to the Brooklyn Dodgers (as a player only) in 1928 and 1929 and then returning to New York in 1930. Bancroft retired as a player following the 1930 campaign and remained with the Giants as a coach in 1931 and 1932.

In five years with the Giants, Bancroft batted .310 with 130 doubles, 30 triples, 11 home runs, 189 RBI and 48 stolen bases in 534 games. His 16-year career statistics included a .279 batting average with 320 doubles, 77 triples, 32 home runs, 591 RBI and 145 stolen bases in 1,913 games. He topped N.L. shortstops in total chances and putouts four times (1918, 1920, 1921 and 1922), assists three times (1920, 1921 and 1922) and fielding percentage twice (1920 and 1925) and had a lifetime fielding percentage of .944. Bancroft compiled a 249-363 managerial record (.407 winning percentage).

Bancroft was inducted into the National Baseball Hall of Fame in 1971 by the Veterans Committee. He passed away October 7, 1972,

in Superior, Wisconsin, at the age of 81. Bancroft was given the nickname "Beauty" in the minor leagues because he had the habit of shouting "Beauty" every time the pitcher on his team threw a good-looking pitch.

Jesse Barnes, Pitcher (1918-23)

The New York Giants faced the cross-town rival Yankees in six World Series (1921, 1922, 1923, 1936, 1937 and 1951). No Giants' pitcher experienced more success against the Yankees than hard-throwing right-hander Jesse Barnes.

Barnes pitched in six games against the Yankees in the 1921, 1922 and 1923 World Series and posted a 2-0 record with a sparkling 1.45 ERA. He pitched 31 innings and surrendered just 22 hits with eight walks and 28 strikeouts.

In the 1921 Fall Classic, Barnes won two games with masterful relief pitching. He relieved Fred Toney in Game 3 at the Polo

Jesse Barnes

Grounds and allowed just one run over the final seven innings as the Giants rallied for a 13-5 victory. Barnes also took over for Toney in Game 6 at the Polo Grounds and gave up two runs in 8.1 innings as the Giants posted an 8-5 comeback win. The Giants captured the championship five games to three.

The following autumn, Barnes started Game 2 at the Polo Grounds and was hooked up with Bob Shawkey in a 3-3 deadlock in the 10th inning when home-plate umpire George Hildebrand opted to call the game on account of darkness even though the sun was still prominent in the sky. Barnes allowed eight hits and two earned runs with two walks and six strikeouts. The Giants went on to take the series four games to none.

Barnes hurled 4.2 innings of scoreless relief in the 1923 World Series, giving up four hits with no walks and four strikeouts. The Yankees took the title four games to two.

But there was more to Barnes than being the "Yankee killer." He was a solid contributor for the Giants from 1918-23 after being acquired from the Boston Braves along with second baseman Larry Doyle in exchange for infielder Buck Herzog on January 8, 1918. Barnes began his career with the Braves from 1915-17.

In 1918 Barnes led the National League in wins, going 25-9 with a 2.40 ERA. He finished 20-15 with a 2.64 ERA the following year. On May 7, 1922, Barnes authored a 6-0 no-hitter against the Philadelphia Phillies at the Polo Grounds. He faced the minimum of 27 batters —allowing only a fourth-inning walk to center fielder Cy Williams, who was erased in a double play. Philadelphia manager Art Fletcher, a former New York shortstop, challenged Barnes by sending up three consecutive pinch-hitters—Lee King, Cliff Lee and Russ Wrightstone—in the ninth inning. Each of them hit the ball solidly, but their drives were caught by Giants' outfielders.

New York traded Barnes back to Boston along with catcher Earl Smith in exchange for catcher Hank Gowdy and pitcher Mule Watson

on June 7, 1923. In six seasons with the Giants, Barnes compiled an 82-43 record with a 2.92 ERA in 181 games. His .656 winning percentage ranks fourth on the franchise all-time list. Barnes pitched for the Braves through the 1925 season before finishing his career with the Brooklyn Dodgers in 1926 and 1927. His 13-year totals included a 152-150 record with a 3.22 ERA in 422 games.

Barnes' younger brother, Virgil, pitched for the Giants from 1919-28 and for Boston the second half of the 1928 campaign. The two faced one another on 10 occasions. Jesse had a 5-3 record and Virgil a 3-4 mark in those games. A third brother, Clark, pitched in the minor leagues from 1925-29.

Jesse served as a captain in the El Dorado (Kansas) police department for 17 years following his playing days. He passed away September 9, 1961, in Santa Rosa, New Mexico, while on a family vacation at the age of 69.

Jim Barr, Pitcher (1971-78, 1982-83)

Jim Barr joined the Giants' organization as a second-round draft pick after helping a star-studded 1970 Southern California team to the NCAA championship. He was primarily a reliever (only 14 minor league starts) when he first came up with the Giants in 1971 and helped them to a division crown.

When he became a starter in 1972, Barr turned in a record-setting performance in his first full season by retiring 41 consecutive batters over a two-game span. He pitched a shutout against Pittsburgh on August 23, retiring the last 21 batters. Then he blanked the Cardinals on August 9, retiring the first 20 batters for a total of 41. That's the equivalent of 13-plus hitless innings. The previous major league high of 38 batters in a row was established by Harvey Haddix in 1959.

"That's what I cherished the most," Barr said of his streak. "It started against Pittsburgh at Candlestick Park, and the pitcher led off the third inning with a hit. Then I retired them the rest of the way, striking out Roberto Clemente for the last out. Then we went back to St.

Jim Barr (S.F. Giants Archives)

Louis, and I got everybody out until there were two outs in the seventh inning. Bernie Carbo came up and hit a double. I had no idea what I'd done. I just knew I put two pretty good games back to back."

Barr finished with a 2.87 ERA that season despite a so-so 8-10 record. He was regarded as a throwback pitcher in an era of growing specialization, posting complete games when it wasn't popular, including a high of 12 in 1975. His winningest season was 1976, when he went 15-12 with a 2.89 ERA for a losing team.

He finished as the winningest Giants' pitcher of the 1970s, going 81-90. Then he pitched two years for the Angels before returning to close out his career with San Francisco, going 9-6 as a spot starter and reliever in 1982-83. The comeback was impressive considering he'd spent the entire 1981 season in the minors.

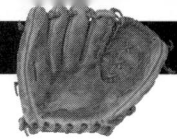

"Gentleman Jim" won 101 games with a respectable 3.56 career ERA. The durable right-hander taught in the off season and later settled down in Sacramento, California, where he ran fast-food franchises. He also served as the pitching coach at Sacramento State while continuing to pitch in senior hardball leagues into his 50s.

Dick Bartell, Shortstop (1935-38, 1941-43, 1946)

Dick Bartell was one of those players that teammates loved and opponents hated. He was aggressive, intense and raucous. His nickname "Rowdy Richard" fit perfectly.

Bartell had three separate stints with the New York Giants—1935-38, 1941-43 and 1946—primarily as a shortstop. He had a passion for baseball and viewed it not as a game or a job but as life. He ate, slept and breathed it. As a result, Bartell often came across as overzealous, but no one could argue with his success.

After spending the first eight years of his major league career with the Pittsburgh Pirates (1927-30) and the Philadelphia Phillies (1931-34), the Giants acquired Bartell in exchange for pitcher John Pezzulo, infielder Blondy Ryan, third baseman Johnny Vergez, outfielder George Watkins and cash November 1, 1934. The Giants were a foundering ball club in need of a jolt, and Bartell was the tonic.

Bartell was instrumental in the Giants capturing National League pennants in 1936 and 1937. New York's leadoff hitter, he batted .298 with 31 doubles, eight home runs and 42 RBI during the 1936 season and .306 with a career-high 38 doubles, a career-high tying 14 home runs and 62 RBI during the 1937 campaign. The Giants dropped both World Series to the cross-town rival Yankees, four games to two in 1936 and four games to one in 1937. Bartell slugged a home run in the fifth inning of the opening game in 1936 against the Yankees' Red Ruffing.

Bartell was selected to the 1937 All-Star Game and was 1-for-4 at Griffith Stadium in

Dick Bartell (Brace Photo)

Washington D.C. He previously played in the inaugural Midsummer Classic in 1933 at Comiskey Park in Chicago.

On December 6, 1938, the Giants traded Bartell along with outfielder Hank Leiber and catcher Gus Mancuso to the Chicago Cubs in exchange for outfielder Frank Demaree, shortstop Bill Jurges and catcher Ken O'Dea. Bartell played for the Cubs in 1939 and the Detroit Tigers in 1940 (they won the American League pennant) and 1941 before returning to New York on May 15, 1941. He was inserted at third base and batted at a .303 clip.

Bartell continued with the Giants in 1942 and 1943, then served in the U.S. Navy for two years and concluded his career with a five-game stint in New York in 1946. In eight seasons with the Giants, Bartell posted a .279 batting average with 167 doubles, 60 home runs and 293 RBI in 835 games. His 18-year career totals included a .284 batting average

with 2,165 hits and 442 doubles in 2,016 games. Bartell led N.L. shortstops in total chances six times, assists and double plays four times apiece and putouts three times. He had a lifetime .953 fielding percentage. Ironically, though, Bartell did not have a single fielding chance in a 10-inning game between the Giants and Phillies on July 3, 1935.

An aggressive base runner, Bartell often was (negatively) compared with legendary Hall of Famer Ty Cobb since both players made habits of sliding hard into bases with spikes flashing in the air. Opponents responded with similar hard-nosed tactics that led to Bartell battling a variety of leg ailments. Many times his head was the target of opposing pitchers. Bartell simply viewed the actions as part of the game.

Bartell was a minor league manager with Sacramento (Pacific Coast League) in 1947, Kansas City (American Association) in 1948 and Montgomery-Knoxville (South Atlantic League) in 1956. He coached for the Tigers from 1949-52 and with the Cincinnati Reds in 1954 and 1955. Bartell passed away August 4, 1995, in Almeda, California, at the age of 87.

Rod Beck, Pitcher (1991-97)

Among the most popular of the new-era Giants, Rod Beck became the Giants' closer during the 1992 season and shattered the franchise record with 48 saves in 1993. He used impeccable control for success, but created anguish for the Giants and their fans with a tendency to get into ninth-inning jams he usually escaped.

He was nicknamed "Shooter" for his ability to gun down batters, and his menacing glare and Fu Man Chu mustache gave him a nasty demeanor that belied his fun-loving and humorous personality. When management didn't think Beck would be a good long-term investment because of added pounds and dwindling velocity, they decided on Robb Nen for 1998.

Not to worry, Beck signed with the Chicago Cubs and posted a club-record 51 saves

Rod Beck (S.F. Giants Archives)

while registering the last out of a one-game playoff victory over San Francisco that enabled the Cubbies to advance. He was the A's 13th-round draft choice after a prep career in Southern California (Van Nuys), and primarily was a starter in his minor league days.

The Giants acquired him from Oakland for minor league pitcher Charlie Corbell in 1988, and it was a steal for San Francisco and a break for Beck, who no longer had Dennis Eckersley in his path. He showed the Giants potential as a starter by going a combined 18-5 at Clinton and Shreveport in 1989. He followed with a 14-10 record at Shreveport and Phoenix in 1990, including a four-hitter against Calgary in his Triple-A debut.

Beck started the 1991 season as a starter for Phoenix, but switched to the bullpen in an early stint with the Giants before returning to the minors and concentrating on relief. He relinquished one earned run in his first 17 appearances of 1992 and eased into the closer role by the end of the season, going 3-3 with a 1.76 ERA and 17 saves.

His breakthrough year of 1993 included 48 saves in 52 opportunities, a National

League record 24 consecutive saves, a 3-1 record and a 2.16 ERA. The 48 saves shattered the previous franchise record by 18—Greg Minton had 30 in 1982. Beck was the N.L. Rolaids Relief champion in strike-shortened 1994, finishing with 28 saves without a blown save, erasing his one-year-old record.

Beck extended his major league consecutive saves record to 41 early in the 1995 season, one in which his effectiveness soon faltered. He finished with a 4.45 ERA and 33 saves, and slumped further in 1996, going 0-9 with 35 saves. He improved to 37 saves for the 1997 division champions, but Roberto Hernandez was acquired to share closer duties, and Beck's days as the Giants' bullpen ace were numbered.

Vida Blue, Pitcher (1978-81, 1985-86)

Consider these nifty numbers regarding pitcher Vida Blue: One no-hitter, five one-hitters, four two-hitters, seven three-hitters and 27 four-hitters.

One of the most popular athletes in Bay Area sports history, Blue spent 15 of his 17 major league seasons with the Oakland Athletics (1969-77) and the San Francisco Giants (1978-81, 1985-86).

After throwing a 6-0 no-hitter against the Minnesota Twins at the Oakland Coliseum on September 21, 1970, Blue burst onto the scene in 1971, posting a 24-8 record, American League-leading 1.82 ERA, 24 complete games, eight shutouts and 301 strikeouts in 312 innings pitched. He earned both the American League Cy Young and Most Valuable Player awards. The fire-balling left-hander later went 20-9, 3.28 ERA in 1973 and 22-11, 3.01 ERA in 1975.

The Athletics traded Blue to the Giants in exchange for seven players (catcher Gary Alexander, infielder/designated hitter Mario Guerrero, pitcher Dave Heaverlo, outfielder/first baseman Gary Thomasson and three minor league pitchers) plus $390,000 on March 15, 1978. In January, Oakland owner Charles O. Finley had attempted to send Blue to the

Vida Blue (S.F. Giants Archives)

Cincinnati Reds for minor league first baseman Dave Revering and $1.75 million, but baseball commissioner Bowie Kuhn voided the deal after Finley had ignored Kuhn's directive that he be consulted on any transaction involving at least $400,000.

With the Giants, Blue went 18-10 with a 2.79 ERA during the 1978 season. Two years later he finished 14-10 with a 2.97 ERA.

Blue was selected to five All-Star Games (1971, 1975, 1977, 1978 and 1981). He started for the American League in 1971 at Tiger Stadium in Detroit and for the National League in 1978 at Jack Murphy Stadium in San Diego, becoming the first pitcher in baseball history to earn the starting assignment for both leagues.

On March 30, 1982, the Giants traded Blue and pitcher Bob Tufts to the Kansas City

Royals in exchange for pitchers Craig Chamberlain, Atlee Hammaker and Rene Martin and infielder Brad Wellman. Blue pitched in Kansas City for two seasons before returning to San Francisco as a free agent in 1985 and making the team as a non-roster invitee to spring training. In 1986, at the age of 36, he posted a 10-10 record with a 3.27 ERA while helping the "Humm Baby" Giants make a serious run at the National League West Division championship just one year after losing 100 games.

Blue's overall numbers with the Giants included a 72-58 record and a 3.52 ERA. He pitched in 179 games totaling 1,131.1 innings with 31 complete games, seven shutouts and 704 strikeouts. On San Francisco's career lists, Blue ranks eighth in wins and strikeouts, ninth in innings pitched and tied for ninth in complete games.

In 502 career outings, Blue was 209-161 with a 3.27 ERA, 143 complete games, 37 shutouts and 2,175 strikeouts. He allowed an average of just 7.90 hits per nine innings pitched.

Blue, who was inducted in the Bay Area Sports Hall of Fame in 1996, has worked in the Giants' front office as a community representative since 1991. He makes personal appearances on behalf of the club, acts as a liaison to the Giants Alumni Association and serves as commissioner of the "Junior Giants" youth baseball program. Blue lives in Sonora, California.

Bobby Bolin, Pitcher (1961-69)

Underrated and hard-throwing, Bobby Bolin was obscured by fellow right-handers Juan Marichal and Gaylord Perry during his heyday in the pitching-dominated 1960s. Remarkably, Bolin is the Giants' record-holder for ERA by a starter, posting a 1.99 along with a 10-5 record in 1968. That was same season Bob Gibson set the major league record with a minuscule 1.12 ERA.

"BB" joined the Giants in 1961 and was 7-3 for the 1962 pennant winners, starting and relieving. "I was never classified as a starter or

Bobby Bolin (S.F. Giants Archives)

as a reliever," he said, "so I mostly sat on a tarp between the bullpen and the dugout because I didn't know which one I'd be doing."

He pitched perhaps his finest game against the Cubs in 1963, tying the Giants' record with 14 strikeouts June 12. His winningest season was 1965, when he went 14-6 with a 2.76 ERA. He finished his Giants' career 73-56 with a 3.26 ERA, fifth on the San Francisco career charts. Later he played with the Brewers and the Red Sox and had an 88-75 record and a 3.40 ERA.

Bobby signed with the Giants out of Hickory Grove, South Carolina, and relied on a live fastball when he first played pro ball. But he was content to be a farmer after originally signing with the Pirates only to have it voided by Commissioner Ford Frick because he was under age.

"One day, not long after that, I was plowing with a mule back on the farm," he recalled.

"A Giants' scout drove up in a big Buick and damn near scared my mule to death. I figured anybody that come that far looking for somebody to play ball ought to go ahead and play with him. There was a $4,000 limit on what you can sign for, but I went ahead and did it."

Bolin was wildly effective as a minor leaguer, walking a ton of batters and striking out even more. He pitched seven-inning no-hitters in 1957 and 1959. As a rookie with Michigan City in 1957, he went 15-9 despite 172 walks in 199 innings. Two years later, with Eugene, he was a brilliant 20-8 with 271 strikeouts in 225 innings. They called him "BB," which also could have been a reference to all his bases on balls.

Bolin once gave this apt description of the difficulty of playing baseball: "You can take all the big football players, beef 'em up and get them to weigh 300 pounds. Let 'em grunt and groan and push guys around, and they're stars. But let 'em walk up to home plate trying to hit that little white rat going 95 miles an hour, not knowing whether it's going to go at you, or down, or out, or up—that takes a very special ability."

Barry Bonds, Outfielder (1993-present)

Barry Bonds ranks with Hall of Famer Willie Mays, his godfather, as the greatest player to wear a San Francisco Giants uniform. Nobody has done it better than this gifted athlete ever since he became a Giant in 1993 and sparked a turnaround that produced a franchise-tying 103 victories. Like a premium Napa Valley cabernet, Bonds has mellowed and improved with age.

In his first 10 years with the Giants, he finished a glorious 2002 season with a .311 batting average accompanied by 115.8 runs, 43.7 home runs, 109.6 RBI and 131.1 walks per season in San Francisco. In 1998, he became the first player in baseball history with at least 400 home runs and 400 stolen bases, beginning 2003 seven steals shy of 500-500 distinction.

After being named Player of the Decade for the 1990s, Bonds was even more productive as the Giants' centerpiece following the shift to Pacific Bell Park in 2000. His first three years in the new ballpark, ostensibly not conducive to prodigious hitting, produced an average of 56 home runs, 125 runs, 117.7 RBI and 164 bases on balls, along with a .333 batting average.

Bonds joined Jimmie Foxx, Joe DiMaggio, Stan Musial, Roy Campanella, Yogi Berra, Mickey Mantle and Mike Schmidt as the only three-time Most Valuable Players when he was rewarded following his maiden season with the Giants. Following remarkable back-to-back campaigns in 2001-02, he added two more MVP awards to his trophy case.

They weren't difficult choices for the voting baseball writers, who also rated him the runner-up in 1991 (Terry Pendleton) and 2000 (teammate Jeff Kent). In 2001, Bonds simply raised the bar for slugging excellence, setting major league records with 73 home runs, an .863 slugging percentage, 177 walks and one homer per 6.52 at-bats. One year later, he raised the walks record to 198 and had the

Barry Bonds (© S.F. Giants)

best on-base percentage (.582) ever.

As if that weren't enough, Bonds exorcized his postseason demons in 2002. Entering with one home run in 97 postseason at-bats, a source of stinging criticism, he erupted with eight homers in 45 at-bats, including four in a World Series in which he batted .471 with a record 13 walks. This was a stronger Bonds model than the fleet youngster who joined father Bobby as the only players with five 30-30 (homers-steals) seasons.

"I really can't explain what's happening," a humbled Bonds said during his 2001 pursuit of Mark McGwire's home run record. "There are some things I can't understand right now. The balls that used to go off the wall are just flying out. I've tried to figure it out, and I can't. If I knew what was happening, I'd have done it sooner. I just feel lucky to have played as long as I have played. I feel great to have accomplished the things I've accomplished."

Barry grew up playing in the Giants' clubhouse and watching his father perform for the club from 1968-74. He was a three-sport prep star at Serra High School, south of San Francisco, where he batted .404 over three seasons, including .467 as a senior All-American. He was drafted by the Giants in 1992, but they couldn't afford to pay him, so he enrolled at Arizona State and posted career numbers of a .347 average, 45 homers and 175 RBI in three years, earning All-America honors as a junior in 1985. He was named to the all-time College World Series team in 1996.

The first-round draft choice of the Pittsburgh Pirates, Bonds required merely 115 games of minor league seasoning before reaching the majors to stay in 1986. He wasn't an immediate success as a center fielder and leadoff batter, but found his groove by 1990 and drove the Pirates to the playoffs three consecutive years while winning two MVP Awards.

That year he joined Eric Davis as the only two players ever with at least 30 home runs and 50 steals in the same season, stealing a career-high 52 bases and hitting 33 home runs. He also won his first of eight Gold Gloves for fielding excellence. Barry made the first of eight N.L. All-Star teams in 1990 and entered 2000 with a .300 average in 20 All-Star at-bats.

The only downside in his Pittsburgh years was a failure to reach the World Series and a .191 average in 20 NLCS games. Bonds truly hit his stride after signing with the Giants' new ownership group in 1993. That was his first great season: .336, 129 runs, 38 doubles, 46 homers, 123 RBI and 126 walks.

The average, runs and homers all were career highs, and his .336 average was the highest ever recorded by a player whose home games were at Candlestick Park. His .677 slugging percentage set a Giants' franchise record. In addition to MVP honors, Bonds was winner of the S. Rae Hickok Award as the nation's top professional athlete and was named the Associated Press Major League Player of the Year.

He was on pace to match the 1993 power numbers when the 1994 season abruptly ended with a strike in mid-August. Barry bounced back with a career-high 129 RBI and 151 walks in 1996, joining Jose Canseco in the exclusive 40-40 club with 42 homers and 40 steals. Alex Rodriguez also did it in 1998, so Bonds remains the only N.L. player with such distinction. His 151 walks established the N.L. record.

The 1997 season was regarded as a down year because of a .291 average, but his 40 home runs powered the Giants to a division championship. He belted a career-high 44 doubles in 1998, helping the Giants reach a one-game wild card playoff. Bonds was off to a hot start with four home runs in the first two weeks of the 1999 season when surgery to remove bone spurs and repair a tendon in his left elbow made him miss most of the first half. Before being sidelined he passed Hank Aaron with his 294th career intentional walk, a major league record. Bonds returned in June and collected career hit No. 2,000 against Tom Glavine of the Atlanta Braves at 3Com Park in San Francisco on September 11.

Bonds amassed 361 home runs during the 1990s, bettered only by McGwire (405) and Ken Griffey Jr. (382). He collected 1,076 RBI, topped only by Albert Belle (1,099) and Griffey (1,091). The best was yet to come. By the end of the 2001 season, Bonds was rated as a prime contender to surpass Hank Aaron's record 755 home runs. During 2002, he joined Aaron, Babe Ruth and Mays as the only member of The 600 Home Run Club.

Bobby Bonds, Outfielder (1968-74)

Talk about making a grandiose entrance.

In his first game with the San Francisco Giants on June 25, 1968, Bobby Bonds socked a grand slam in the sixth inning off Jack Purdin of the rival Los Angeles Dodgers at Candlestick Park. A star was born.

Bonds spent the first seven seasons (1968-74) of his 14-year major league career with the Giants. A fixture in right field, he totaled 20 or more home runs and 70-plus RBI in each of his six full campaigns and recorded at least 40 stolen bases on five occasions.

In 1973 Bonds was named *The Sporting News'* National League Player of the Year after batting .283 with a career-high 39 home runs, 96 RBI and 43 stolen bases. In the All-Star Game on July 24, 1973, he hit a two-run homer off Bill Singer of the California Angels in the fifth inning and later turned a single into a crowd-pleasing double to earn Most Valuable Player honors in the N.L.'s 7-1 victory at Royals Stadium in Kansas City, Missouri.

Bonds set the major league record with 11 leadoff home runs during the 1973 season and finished with 35 for his career, second only to Rickey Henderson on baseball's all-time list.

Other personal bests for Bonds during his Bay Area days included a .302 batting average, a San Francisco season-record 134 runs and 48 stolen bases in 1970 and 102 RBI in 1971. He was selected to the 1971 All-Star Game and earned Gold Glove awards in 1971, 1973 and 1974.

Bonds is San Francisco's career leader with 263 stolen bases (ninth on the franchise list, including the New York years) and ranks in the top 10 in runs (third, 765); triples (third, 42); home runs (sixth, 186); hits (seventh, 1,106); at-bats (eighth, 4,047); doubles (eighth, 188); and RBI (eighth, 552). His home run total is eighth on the franchise list. He had a .273 batting average in 1,014 games.

San Francisco traded Bonds to the New York Yankees in exchange for Bobby Murcer on October 22, 1974. Bonds went on to play for the Angels (1976-77), Chicago White Sox (1978), Texas Rangers (1978), Cleveland Indians (1979), St. Louis Cardinals (1980) and Chicago Cubs (1981). He was an American League All-Star in 1975 and had 37 home runs, a career-high 115 RBI and 41 stolen bases in 1977.

For his career Bonds amassed 332 home runs, 1,024 RBI and 461 stolen bases while batting at a .268 clip. He is one of just four players in baseball history with 300 home runs and 300 stolen bases (also his son, Barry; Andre Dawson; and Willie Mays). Bobby and

Bobby Bonds

133

Barry share the Major League record with five seasons of 30 homers and 30 steals apiece.

In 1993 Bonds joined the Giants as a coach under manager Dusty Baker and was in that capacity through the 1996 season. Barry signed with San Francisco as a free agent December 8, 1992, after playing the first seven seasons of his big league career with the Pittsburgh Pirates. He is an eight-time All-Star. Bobby and Barry lead all Major League father-son tandems in home runs (777 through 1999), RBI (2,322) and stolen bases (921).

Bobby, who makes his home in San Carlos, California, served as a special assistant in player personnel for the Giants' minor league system from 1997-99.

Bob Brenly, Catcher (1981-88, 1989)

Presently a color commentator for Fox and the Arizona Diamondbacks, Bob Brenly was a colorful and glib catcher during the Giants' revival in the mid-1980s. He was a college All-American at Ohio University, where he tied Mike Schmidt's single-season home run record with 10. Signed by the Giants as a free agent, he first displayed pro power with a career-high 22 home runs for Cedar Rapids in 1977.

"BB" joined the Giants to stay after batting .292 for Triple-A Phoenix in 1981. He was selected to the 1984 All-Star squad off a .316 first half and was hitless in one at-bat in the game at Candlestick Park. That was his finest major league season: .291, 20 homers and 80 RBI. He averaged 18.3 homers from 1984-87.

Primarily a catcher, Brenly filled in at third base in 1986, and he will never forget it. He became merely the fourth player since 1900 to make four errors in one inning, but he redeemed himself nicely with three hits and four RBI. He beat the Braves with his second home run, a two-out shot in the bottom of the ninth off Paul Assenmacher.

When he hit 19 home runs in 1985, he became the first catcher to lead the club since Buck Ewing in 1885. Brenly showed off his broadcasting potential by hosting "The Bob

Bob Brenly (S.F. Giants Archives)

Brenly Show" on radio following Giants' games. His candor got him in trouble, and he was coaxed into temporarily giving up his radio career. Brenly coached for the Giants when he was hired to work Cubs' games on radio, and the rest is history.

Roger Bresnahan, Catcher/Infielder/Outfielder (1902-08)

Which of the following statements about the New York Giants' Roger Bresnahan is true?

A. He often was the Giants' leadoff hitter.
B. He was Christy Mathewson's favorite catcher.
C. He was the first catcher to wear shin guards.
D. All of the above.

The correct answer is D. Bresnahan spent seven seasons in New York from 1902-08. A versatile performer with good speed, he was a catcher, an infielder and an outfielder. When John McGraw left the Baltimore Orioles to become manager of the Giants in 1902, he brought several players with him, including Bresnahan. The two belligerent Irishmen be-

Roger Bresnahan

lieved in winning at all costs and developed into close friends.

During his first three years with the Giants, Bresnahan saw action at virtually every position (catcher, first base, second base, shortstop, third base and the outfield). In 1903 he was the team's leadoff hitter and compiled a career-high .350 batting average to finish fourth in the National League. Bresnahan also had personal bests of 30 doubles, 55 RBI and 34 stolen bases that season.

Bresnahan became the starting catcher (and Mathewson's preferred batterymate) in 1905 and batted .302 with 46 RBI. The Giants won the N.L. pennant with a 105-48 record and defeated the Philadelphia Athletics in the World Series four games to one. Bresnahan was behind the plate for four New York shutouts, three by Mathewson and one by Joe McGinnity. Bresnahan also batted .313 (5-for-16) with two doubles and an RBI.

In 1907 Bresnahan began donning a pair of "cricket leg guards" while he was catching. He was the subject of much harassing from opponents, but N.L. president Harry Pulliam approved the shin guards. Previously, Bresnahan had experimented with a batting helmet (though he found the football helmet-like head gear to be too bulky), and later he was the first player to add padding to his catcher's mask.

The "Duke of Tralee" (his family originally came from Ireland) led the N.L. with a career-high 83 walks in 1908 while batting at a .283 clip with 25 doubles and 54 RBI. He had a nifty .985 fielding percentage, as well. The Giants traded Bresnahan to the St. Louis Cardinals in exchange for outfielder Red Murray, pitcher Bugs Raymond and catcher Admiral Schlei on December 12, 1908. Bresnahan's statistics with New York included a .293 batting average with 135 doubles, 15 home runs, 291 RBI and 118 stolen bases in 751 games.

With the Cardinals, Bresnahan was a player-manager from 1909-12. He then concluded his career with the Chicago Cubs from 1913-15, serving as player-manager the final year. In 17 major league seasons (which began in 1897 with the Washington Senators, followed by a season with the Chicago Orphans in 1900 and a year-plus with the Orioles) Bresnahan batted .279 with 218 doubles, 26 home runs, 530 RBI and 212 stolen bases in 1,446 games. He appeared in 974 games at catcher, 281 in the outfield, 42 at third base, 33 at first base, 28 at second base and eight at shortstop. Bresnahan also pitched in nine games (none with the Giants) and posted a 4-1 record with a 3.95 ERA. His five-year managerial record was 328-432 (.432 winning percentage).

Bresnahan returned to the Giants as a coach under McGraw from 1925-28.

On December 4, 1944, Bresnahan passed away in his hometown of Toledo, Ohio, at the age of 65. He was inducted into the National Baseball Hall of Fame in 1945 by the Veterans Committee.

Ron Bryant, Pitcher (1967, 1969-74)

A very promising career was cut short by a freak spring training pool accident in 1974. Ron Bryant never regained the form which made him *The Sporting News'* Pitcher of the Year in 1973 with a 24-12 record, the most wins by a Giants' left-hander since Carl Hubbell posted 26 victories in 1936.

Nobody else came close in the National League, as Tom Seaver and Jack Billingham finished second with 19 wins. He was nicknamed "Bear" by longtime equipment manager Mike Murphy, and not because of the legendary Alabama football coach. "Ron looked like a bear with his chunky build, his way of walking and his curly hair," Murphy explained.

Bryant's career took off in 1972, when he brought a three-foot stuffed bear to the dugout. Murphy dressed it in a Giants' uniform with Bryant's No. 32 on the back. "We were going out to eat in Chicago, when we saw this young girl on the street with the stuffed bear," he recalled. "She said she was a Cubs' fan. I offered her $25 for the bear, but she wanted $30, so Dave Rader chipped in, and I had the thing."

Bryant showed promise that season with a 14-7 record and a 2.90 ERA before becoming the winningest lefty in San Francisco history for one season in 1973. His major league career took off just before the 1972 All-Star Game when he reeled off six complete-game victories—three of them shutouts—in a span of seven starts.

Success would have been even greater were it not for a bout with pneumonia which hospitalized him and knocked him out of action for the first three weeks of August. "I won't be satisfied with 14 wins next year." he prophetically declared after the season. "I'm going to spring training with the attitude that I've got to win a starting job all over again."

His stuffed bear ran into trouble in 1973 when it was run over by an airport baggage cart in Houston early in the season, but there was no stopping Bryant in his career year. After his first 10 starts, he was 6-3 with a 2.31 ERA, including a 1-0 loss to Don Sutton in which the run was unearned.

Bryant joined Mike McCormick as the only lefty 20-game winners in San Francisco history by downing the Mets in New York, and there was some disbelief over his accomplishment. "I just didn't believe I had the ability to do that when I turned pro," Bryant said. "I didn't think I had a good enough fastball, or anything else.

"It's hard for me to realize the significance of 20 wins. You can't call me a spectacular pitcher. I have a decent fastball now and can sometimes overpower hitters. I'd never had a curve to amount to anything until Larry Jansen got me started on one and Don McMahon helped me polish it. I also studied a lot of film of me pitching."

Ron Bryant (S.F. Giants Archives)

Disappointment followed shortly. His 24 victories didn't bring a Cy Young Award (Seaver got it), and his career essentially concluded in a Palm Springs swimming pool during spring training of 1974. It was March 15, and that night he tried a slide into the hotel pool, struck the edge and tore up his right side. An estimated 30 stitches were required to close the wound.

"Mentally, I had trouble after that," Bryant said after missing more than one month and struggling through a 3-15 season. "It kind of preyed on my mind that the club relied on me as a winner." By spring training of 1975, Bryant relinquished his $50,000-plus salary and retired. "I'm not really enjoying playing baseball the way I did in the past," he summed up.

Bryant was scouted by accident when Ed Montague, the man who signed Willie Mays, went to Davis, California, to evaluate Bob Heise. Ron pitched a no-hitter for Davis High School that day and was signed for a small bonus as part of the first-ever June amateur draft in 1965. His tough luck began as a prep when he didn't allow an earned run as a senior, yet lost five games, including that no-hitter. He attracted the Giants' attention with a 12-10 record and 2.97 ERA for Class-A Fresno in 1967.

He retired with the thought of running a golf pro shop because he was particularly fond of that sport. He learned the game from his father at age five. The elder Bryant was good friends with Gail Stockton, father of golfer Dave Stockton and also Ron's Little League coach in San Bernardino, California.

John Burkett, Pitcher (1987, 1990-94)

The Giants' biggest winner of the 1990s with a 67-42 record, John Burkett reached the majors by accident following an undistinguished Triple-A career. He was the last man in the Phoenix rotation in 1990 when a Giants' starter went down, so he was promoted as an emergency starter who soon would be back in the minors.

Instead, "Burkey" seized the opportunity by winning his April 30 debut and finishing with a 14-7 record in 204 innings. Only John Montefusco, with 15, ever posted more victories among San Francisco rookies. With less than one year of major league experience, he started the 1991 opener, and he was a solid 13-9 in 1992, but he didn't help himself with the bat. His 1-for-55 (.018) was the eighth-lowest average ever for a player with at least 50 at-bats.

It all came together for Burkett in 1993, when his 22 victories placed him fourth in the Cy Young Award voting and represented the most wins by a Giant since Ron Bryant's 24 in 1973. He was the All-Star Game loser after posting a 13-3 first-half record. His 7-0 start that season was the best since Juan Marichal went 10-0 in 1966. He pitched 231.2 innings, the most by a Giant in the 1990s.

John Burkett (S.F. Giants Archives)

Burkett slipped to 6-8 in 1994 after his career-best 22-7 season, and ultimately helped the Giants in a trade with the Texas Rangers that included prospect Rich Aurilia, the Giants' starting shortstop in 1999. Oft-injured, Burkett never regained his touch with the Rangers or the Florida Marlins, except for a 1996 playoff victory with Texas. He is an avid bowler with 300 games to his credit, and once contemplated a PBA career.

Ellis Burks, Outfielder (1998-2000)

Ellis Burks was with the Giants barely two seasons, yet he made a great impact with his play and his leadership, becoming an instant hit with his teammates and being sorely missed when the club parted company with the brittle outfielder over health concerns following the championship season of 2000.

The power-hitting right fielder provided the pop to complement Barry Bonds and Jeff Kent while helping the Giants to their most productive season in years. When he reluctantly departed for Cleveland in 2001, the offense was short-circuited and runs were reduced drastically.

Providing much-needed sock in the No. 5 slot, Burks played 284 games with the Giants, and in the equivalent of two seasons produced a .312 average with 60 home runs and 214 RBI. He was at his best in 2000, batting .344 with 24 homers and 96 RBI before continuing his success with the Indians, mostly as a DH.

It didn't take long for Ellis to become a solid member of the Giants after he joined the club in a trading-deadline deal with Colorado that sent Darryl Hamilton to the Rockies in 1998. The newcomer batted .306 over the final two months and added 31 homers and 96 RBI in 1999 after having both knees surgically repaired.

Burks, who hit his 10th career grand slam in 1999, acquired his power stroke as the star center fielder of the Colorado Rockies in 1994 until he was traded just prior to the July 31 trading deadline in 1998.

Ellis Burks (S.F. Giants Archives)

In 1996 he batted .344 for the Rockies and also attained career highs with 211 hits, 142 runs, 45 doubles, 40 homers, 128 RBI and 32 stolen bases as a solid Most Valuable Player candidate. He finished third in the voting after joining Hall of Famer Hank Aaron as the only players with at least 40 homers, 200 hits and 30 steals in one season. (Alex Rodriguez joined the elite list in 1998.)

Injuries limited him to 115 games, a .290 average and 32 home runs in 1997 before the Rockies regarded him and his hobbled knees expendable. He expressed a desire to save wear and tear on his knees by switching from center to right and definitely overachieved in 1999. His production was especially impressive considering the sore knees made it difficult for him to plant his feet.

Burks was a No. 1 Boston Red Sox draft pick when he reached the majors in 1987 and

promptly batted .272 with 30 doubles and 20 homers as a rookie. By 1990 he was an All-Star with the Red Sox and later with the Rockies in 1996. Following a season with the White Sox in 1993, he joined the Rockies and began a career of .300 batting in the National League.

His fielding prowess, especially on healthy legs, earned Burks a Gold Glove in 1990. He also has won Silver Slugger awards in both leagues as the best offensive center fielder in 1990 and 1996. Burks tied a major league record with two home runs in one inning for Boston against the White Sox at Comiskey Park in Chicago on August 27, 1990.

George Burns, Outfielder (1911-21)

During an 11-year career with the New York Giants from 1911-21, outfielder George Burns was one of baseball's most-complete performers. He was a quality hitter, fielder and runner, and Giants' manager John McGraw rated Burns the second-best player he ever managed (behind Hall of Fame pitcher Christy Mathewson).

During his first two seasons in New York, Burns saw limited action as McGraw wanted to carefully groom him. A converted catcher, Burns took over as the Giants' regular left fielder and leadoff hitter in 1913. He went on to establish a modern National League record (since 1900) for outfielders by playing in 459 consecutive games from April 14, 1915-September 24, 1917. The current standard is 897 by Chicago Cubs' Hall of Famer Billy Williams from 1963-69.

The speedy Burns set a modern-day Giants' franchise record with a league-leading 62 stolen bases during the 1915 season. He had 40 steals in three consecutive campaigns from 1918-20 and led the circuit in 1920. Burns stole home 27 times during his career, an N.L. record since broken by Max Carey (1910-29) of the Pittsburgh Pirates and Brooklyn Dodgers. Burns had five steals of home in 1918. The N.L.

record is seven by Pete Reiser of Brooklyn in 1946. Hall of Famer Ty Cobb holds both major league marks with eight thefts in 1912 and 50 for his career.

Burns led the N.L. in runs on five occasions, including a career-high 115 in 1920. He topped the league with a .396 on-base percentage in 1919 and paced all outfielders with a .990 fielding percentage. Burns batted a personal-best .303 in both 1915 and 1919.

On September 17, 1920, Burns hit for the cycle and added a double for good measure against Pittsburgh in a 10-inning game at the Polo Grounds in New York. Burns moved to center field in 1920 and with left fielder Irish Meusel and right fielder Ross Youngs gave the Giants the N.L.'s premium outfield.

The Giants captured three N.L. pennants during Burns' playing days (1913, 1917 and 1921). In the 1921 World Series against the cross-town rival Yankees, he batted .333 (11-for-33) with four doubles. He was 4-for-6 in

George Burns (Brace Photo)

Game 3 and drove in the go-ahead run in Game 4 with an eighth-inning double off the Yankees' Carl Mays. The Giants won the championship five games to three after losing the 1913 series to the Philadelphia Athletics four games to one and the 1917 series to the Chicago White Sox four games to two.

New York traded Burns and catcher Mike Gonzalez, along with $100,000, to the Cincinnati Reds in exchange for third baseman Heinie Groh on December 7, 1921. Burns' statistics with the Giants included a .290 batting average with 267 doubles, 82 triples, 458 RBI and 334 stolen bases in 1,362 games. On the franchise career lists, he ranks fourth in stolen bases, sixth in walks (631), seventh in doubles, ninth in runs (877) and 10th in games and at-bats (5,311). Burns is third in putouts (2,848) and sixth in assists (144) among all-time Giants' outfielders.

Burns played for the Reds from 1922-24 before concluding his career with the Philadelphia Phillies in 1925. Over 15 seasons, he batted at a .287 clip with 1,188 runs, 362 doubles, 872 walks and 383 stolen bases in 1,853 games. He led the N.L. in walks five times (four with the Giants and once with the Reds). His lifetime fielding percentage was .970.

From 1926-30, Burns served as a player-manager for numerous minor league teams. He returned to the Giants as a coach for the 1931 season under McGraw.

Burns passed away August 15, 1966, in Gloversville, New York, following a long illness at the age of 75.

Brett Butler, Outfielder (1988-90)

Al Rosen regards it as his biggest mistake as Giants' general manager when he allowed Brett Butler to slip away to the Los Angeles Dodgers as a free agent following the 1990 season. "Bugsy" played only three years with the Giants, but clearly was the best pure lead-off hitter to ever wear a San Francisco uniform from 1988-90.

He signed with the Giants as a free agent after the 1997 season and was an immediate

success with a league-leading 109 runs in 1988. That marked the first time a Giant had reached triple digits in runs since Bobby Bonds' 131 in 1973. He also led the club with a .287 average, 43 steals, 94 walks and a .393 on-base percentage.

Butler also had a league-leading 21 bunt singles and improved to 23 in 1989. He helped the club to the 1989 World Series with 100 runs and 31 steals, patrolling center field deftly. He made it three solid seasons in a row when he batted .308 with 108 runs, 90 walks and 51 stolen bases in 1990.

That final season with San Francisco included a .397 on-base percentage and 192 hits that tied Len Dykstra for the league lead. It was the first time a Giant led the league in that category since Willie Mays in 1960. He didn't hit into a double play all season, and his 51 steals were the second highest total in San Francisco history, exceeded only by Bill North's 58 in 1979.

"Bugsy" probably got his nickname because he was pesky like a gnat, constantly getting under the skin of opponents with his threat on the base paths and by doing the little

Brett Butler (S.F. Giants Archives)

things to win. Somehow, he was deemed expendable and signed with the Dodgers, for whom he was a spark plug until cancer cut short his career.

Orlando Cepeda, First Baseman/ Outfielder (1958-66)

Orlando Cepeda is synonymous with the early days of the San Francisco Giants. Cepeda made his major league debut in 1958, the same year the Giants first played in the Bay Area.

In fact, Cepeda started at first base in the Giants' inaugural game April 15, 1958, at Seals Stadium in San Francisco, and he homered in an 8-0 victory over the rival Los Angeles (formerly Brooklyn) Dodgers. Cepeda went on to earn National League Rookie of the Year honors after batting .312 with 25 home runs and a Giants' rookie-record 96 RBI.

For the next six seasons, Cepeda was a fixture in the Giants' lineup at first base or in the outfield. He topped the league with career highs of 46 home runs and 142 RBI (a San

Orlando Cepeda (S.F. Giants Archives)

Francisco record) to go with a .311 batting average in 1961. The following year he batted .306 with 35 homers and 114 RBI. Cepeda, nicknamed "Baby Bull" and "Cha Cha," played in six All-Star Games from 1959-64.

On July 4, 1961, Cepeda tied a San Francisco record (also held by Hall of Famer Willie Mays) by driving in eight runs against the Chicago Cubs at Wrigley Field in Chicago. He had two singles, two doubles and a homer in the Giants' 19-3 victory. Cepeda drove in the tying run in the ninth inning of the Giants' thrilling come-from-behind 6-4 win over the Dodgers in the deciding game of their three-game playoff October 3, 1962, at Dodger Stadium in Los Angeles that brought San Francisco its first National League pennant.

A knee injury limited Cepeda to just 33 games in 1965, and the Giants ultimately traded him to the St. Louis Cardinals in exchange for pitcher Ray Sadecki on May 8, 1966. Cepeda batted .303 with 17 home runs and 58 RBI for his new team and was named the National League Comeback Player-of-the-Year. He received the National League Most Valuable Player Award in 1967 after batting .325 with 25 homers and a league-leading 111 RBI.

Cepeda later played for the Atlanta Braves (1969-72), Oakland Athletics (1972), Boston Red Sox (1973) and Kansas City Royals (1974). He finished his 17-year career with a .297 batting average, 2,351 hits, 379 home runs and 1,365 RBI.

On San Francisco's career lists, Cepeda ranks third in hits (1,286) and RBI (767), fifth in doubles (226) and home runs (226), sixth in at-bats (4,178), seventh in runs (652) and tied for seventh in games (1,114). He is sixth in homers and ninth in RBI on the franchise's career lists, including the New York years. Cepeda batted at a .308 clip with the Giants.

In 1993, in his 15th and final year of eligibility for the National Baseball Hall of Fame (on the Baseball Writers' Association of America ballot), Cepeda missed being inducted by a mere seven votes. It stands as the fifth-

narrowest margin in history. Cepeda ultimately was inducted into the Hall of Fame in 1999 by the Veterans Committee. His uniform No. 30 has been retired by the Giants.

Cepeda has worked in the Giants' front office as a community representative since 1990. In that capacity he visits inner-city schools and speaks to "at-risk" students about the dangers of alcohol and drug abuse. Cepeda is recognized nationally for his humanitarian efforts as an ambassador for baseball. He makes his home in Suisun City, California.

Jack Clark, Outfielder (1975-84)

During his decade with the San Francisco Giants from 1975-84, Jack Clark was one of the most-feared right-handed batters in the game.

The 6-foot-2, 205-pound package of power averaged 21 home runs and 77 RBI over the course of his seven full seasons in the Bay Area (including the strike-shortened 1981 campaign). The "Ripper" led San Francisco in home runs and RBI on four occasions.

Regarded as a "can't-miss prospect," Clark came into his own during the 1978 season, batting .306 with a franchise-record 46 doubles, 25 home runs and 98 RBI. From June 30-July 25 he assembled a San Francisco-record 26-game hitting streak. The following year Clark batted at a team-leading .273 clip with 26 homers and 86 RBI. He was selected to both the 1978 and 1979 All-Star Games. Clark was the initial recipient of the Giants' Willie Mac Award in 1980 (presented annually to the player who best exemplifies the spirit and leadership displayed by Hall of Famer Willie McCovey throughout his career).

In 1982 Clark was instrumental in San Francisco remaining in the National League West Division race until the final weekend of the season. He batted .274 with 30 doubles, 27 home runs and 103 RBI (a San Francisco record for right fielders) in a career-high 157 games. He established a franchise standard and shared the N.L. lead with 21 game-winning RBI (tied

Jack Clark (S.F. Giants Archives)

with Keith Hernandez of the St. Louis Cardinals). Clark got off to a banner start in 1984 with a .320 batting average, 11 home runs and 44 RBI in 57 games before suffering torn cartilage in his right knee that required surgery and sidelined him for the remainder of the season.

The Giants traded Clark to the Cardinals in exchange for first baseman/outfielder David Green, pitcher Dave LaPoint, first baseman/outfielder Gary Rajsich and shortstop Jose Gonzalez (later Jose Uribe) on February 1, 1985. Clark played for the Cardinals from 1985-87—he had career highs of 35 home runs and 106 RBI in 1987—and later donned uniforms of the New York Yankees (1988), San Diego Padres (1989-90) and Boston Red Sox (1991-92). Clark was an N.L. All-Star in 1985 and 1987.

Clark developed the reputation for being a bit on the surly side in San Francisco, but much of that tagging can be attributed to the fact that he was an intense performer who demanded excellence from himself and everyone around him.

On San Francisco's career lists, Clark ranks seventh in doubles (197) and RBI (595), eighth in runs (597) and home runs (163), ninth in hits (1,034) and 10th in at-bats (3,731) and triples (30). His home run total ranks 10th on the franchise list (including the New York

Will Clark (S.F. Giants Archives)

years). He batted .277 in 1,044 games. Clark was selected the right fielder on the Giants' Silver Anniversary Dream Team, commemorating 25 years in San Francisco, in a vote by the fans at the conclusion of the 1981 season.

Clark's 18-year career totals included a .267 batting average, 340 home runs and 1,180 RBI in 1,994 games. He currently lives in Pleasanton, California.

Will Clark, First Baseman (1986-93)

It didn't take long for the San Francisco Giants' Will Clark to live up to his nickname, "Thrill." In his first major league game, on his first swing (a 1-1 pitch), Clark belted a home run against fire-balling future Hall of Famer Nolan Ryan of the Houston Astros at the Astrodome in Houston on April 8, 1986.

Previously, Clark had homered on his first professional swing with Class-A Fresno (California) in 1985, and he went on to hit a round-tripper in his inaugural game at Candlestick

Park in San Francisco against Houston's Bob Knepper on April 15, 1986.

Clark was the Giants' first baseman from 1986-93 after being the second overall selection (behind B.J. Surhoff, who was picked by the Milwaukee Brewers) in the June 1985 free-agent draft. Clark was a member of the 1984 U.S. Olympic team and received the 1985 Golden Spikes Award as the best collegiate player in the country as a junior at Mississippi State University.

His youthful enthusiasm was instrumental in San Francisco going from a franchise-worst 62-100 in 1985 to 83-79 just one year later. In 1987 Clark fully emerged and batted .308 with a career-high 35 home runs and 91 RBI as the Giants won the National League West Division championship. The left-handed batter with the oh, so sweet swing became the first San Francisco player to bat .300 with at least 30 homers since first baseman Willie McCovey in 1969, and Clark's 35 home runs were the most by a Giant since outfielder Bobby Bonds had 39 in 1973. Clark crowned his campaign by batting .360 (9-for-25) with a homer and three RBI in the NLCS against the St. Louis Cardinals.

Over the next five seasons, Clark was the league's premier first baseman and played in the All-Star Game each year. In 1988 he topped the N.L. with 109 RBI and 100 walks while batting .282 with 29 home runs. The following year he scored a league-high 104 runs to go with a career-high .333 batting average, 23 homers and 111 RBI en route to finishing as

runner-up for N.L. Most Valuable Player honors to teammate Kevin Mitchell.

San Francisco returned to postseason play in 1989, and Clark was named the NLCS MVP after batting a robust .650 (13-for-20) with two home runs and eight RBI as the Giants defeated the Chicago Cubs four games to one. His batting average and hit total are records for a five-game series. He socked a grand slam off Greg Maddux in the fourth inning of Game 1 at Wrigley Field in Chicago and came up with a game-winning two-run single in the fifth and deciding game off Mitch (Wild Thing) Williams at Candlestick Park.

In 1991 Clark led the N.L. with a .536 slugging percentage and paced league first basemen with a .997 fielding average. He batted .301 with 29 home runs and a career-high 116 RBI. Clark blasted a three-run homer in the 1992 All-Star Game in the eighth inning off Rick Aguilera of the Minnesota Twins at Jack Murphy Stadium in San Diego.

Following the 1993 season, Clark became a free agent and signed with the Texas Rangers on November 22. In eight seasons with the Giants, Clark batted .299 with 249 doubles, 176 home runs and 709 RBI in 1,160 games. On the franchise career lists, including the New York years, he ranked ninth in homers and 10th in doubles. Among San Francisco players only, he was third in doubles; fourth in batting average and hits (1,278); fifth in games, at-bats (4,269), runs (687), walks (506), RBI and on-base percentage (.373); sixth in slugging percentage (.499); and seventh in homers.

Clark played with Texas from 1994-98 before joining the Baltimore Orioles as a free agent December 7, 1998.

Roger Connor, First Baseman (1883-89, 1891, 1893-94)

By today's standards, Roger Connor's career total of 137 home runs certainly is modest. But in the 19th century, it was exorbitant. Fact is, Connor was baseball's all-time leader in homers until the legendary Babe Ruth passed him during the 1921 season.

Roger Connor (Transcendental Graphics)

Connor, primarily a first baseman, had three different stints with the Giants: 1883-89, 1891 and 1893-94. He began his career with the Troy (New York) Trojans from 1880-82 and belted the first-ever grand slam in major league history September 10, 1881, off Lee Richmond of the Worcester Ruby Legs in Albany, New York. When Troy was dispatched from the National League following the 1882 season, John B. Day purchased the rights to the players and divided them between his two franchises, the New York Gothams (who would be named the Giants in 1885) of the N.L. and the New York Metropolitans of the American Association. Connor was assigned to the Gothams.

Literally a "giant" for his time, the 6-foot-3, 230-pound Connor batted over .300 each of his first four seasons in New York, including a career-high and league-leading .371 average in 1885. He was the Giants' first-ever batting champion. That year New York finished with an 85-27 record (a franchise-best .759 winning percentage) but wound up two games behind

the pennant-winning Chicago White Stockings. The following year Connor topped the N.L. with 20 triples while batting at a .355 clip.

In 1887 Connor blossomed as a home run hitter with a career-high 17 round-trippers. He finished second in the league in both homers and RBI (104) behind Billy O'Brien of the Washington Statesmen (19) and Sam Thompson of the Detroit Wolverines (166), respectively. Connor also came up with 22 triples that season, the third-greatest total in franchise history.

New York captured N.L. pennants and world championships in both 1888 and 1889, and Connor was instrumental in the winning ways. He batted .291 with 14 home runs and 71 RBI in 1888 and .317 with 13 homers and a career-high and league-leading 130 RBI in 1889. He topped the circuit with a .528 slugging percentage in 1889, as well. On May 9, 1888, Connor slammed three home runs against the Indianapolis Hoosiers at Seventh Street Park in Indianapolis.

In 1890 Connor was one of 12 Giants who jumped to the newly-formed Players League, which was organized by New York's John Montgomery Ward. Connor, who ironically played for the New York Giants, led the league with 14 home runs and a .548 slugging percentage while batting .349 with 103 RBI. He hit for the cycle July 21 against the Buffalo Bisons in Buffalo, the only individual to accomplish the feat in the one-year existence of the Players League. Connor returned to the N.L. Giants in 1891, played for the Philadelphia Phillies in 1892, again returned to the Giants for all of 1893 and part of 1894 before concluding his 18-year career with the St. Louis Cardinals from 1894-97. On June 1, 1895, Connor collected six hits in six at-bats against the Giants at the Polo Grounds in New York. He managed the Cardinals for 46 games during the 1896 campaign.

On the Giants' franchise lists, Connor ranks third in triples (131—behind Mike Tiernan and Willie Mays), sixth in batting average (.319) and seventh in runs (946). Connor

had 76 home runs and 786 RBI in 1,120 games. In 1,998 career games over 18 seasons, he batted .317 with 233 triples (fifth on baseball's all-time list) and 1,125 RBI.

Connor passed away January 4, 1931, in Waterbury, Connecticut, at the age of 73. He was inducted into the National Baseball Hall of Fame in 1976 by the Veterans Committee. Connor's younger brother, Joe, played in the major leagues in 1895, 1900-01 and 1905.

Harry Danning, Catcher (1933-42)

Harry Danning was supposed to make his major league debut during the 1932 season. One of Bill Terry's first moves upon taking over as manager of the New York Giants on June 3, 1932, was to bring up Danning from the minor leagues.

Danning was about to take the field for a game with Bridgeport (Connecticut) of the Eastern League when word reached him of his recall. He played in the game and was stricken by a line drive as a base runner at third base. The result was a broken jaw and subsequent infection that hospitalized him and delayed his arrival in the big leagues until the following season.

The added time in the minor leagues proved to be a blessing. Playing for Buffalo (New York) of the International League in 1933, Danning learned a great deal about catching from Hall of Famer Ray Schalk, who was managing the Buffalo club. Danning went on to have a 10-year career as a catcher for the Giants from 1933-42.

Danning saw limited playing time his first five years while backing up Gus Mancuso. Nevertheless, Danning was a member of the Giants' National League pennant-winning teams in 1936 and 1937. Then Mancuso suffered a broken finger in 1938 that paved the way for Danning to take over as the starter. In an added bit of irony, Danning was selected to the N.L. All-Star team that year when Brooklyn Dodgers' catcher Babe Phelps suffered a broken thumb from a foul tip off Danning's bat just prior to the Mid-Summer Classic at

Crosley Field in Cincinnati. Danning finished the year batting .306 with nine home runs and 60 RBI.

In 1939 Danning posted career highs of a .313 batting average and 16 home runs to go with 74 RBI. He batted at a .300 clip with 13 homers and personal bests of 34 doubles and 91 RBI in 1940. On June 15, 1940, Danning hit for the cycle against the Pittsburgh Pirates at the Polo Grounds in New York. His home run was an inside-the-park blast that sailed 460 feet on the fly into center field. After not signing his

Harry Danning (Brace Photo)

1941 contract until March 5, Danning faced a move to left field by Terry, but the experiment proved to be a failure and Danning returned to catcher.

A right-handed batter, Danning used an exaggerated closed stance that he felt allowed him pull inside pitches and drive outside deliveries down the right field line.

Danning, who earned the reputation of being the third-best catcher of his day behind future Hall of Famers Gabby Harnett of the Chicago Cubs and Bill Dickey of the New York Yankees, was an N.L. All-Star in 1939, 1940 and 1941. In the 1940 All-Star Game, Danning contributed a run-scoring single to a 4-0 N.L. win at Sportsman's Park in St. Louis.

Prior to the start of the 1943 season, Danning went into the U.S. Army. He suffered from an arthritic knee condition that prevented him from returning to baseball following World War II. Danning's career statistics included a .285 batting average with 162 doubles, 57 home runs and 397 RBI in 890 games. His

fielding percentage of .985 is tied for third on the franchise all-time list among catchers (with Wes Westrum, 1947-57 and Dave Radar, 1971-76), behind Tom Haller (1961-67) at .992 and Kirt Manwaring (1987-96) at .991.

Broadcaster Ted Husing gave Danning the nickname "Harry the Horse" during the 1936 World Series against the cross-town rival Yankees because Danning appeared to work like a horse (and in those days with about as much grace). The moniker stuck in part because of its alliteration and also because there was a fictional Broadway character named Harry the Horse.

Danning was a minor league coach for Hollywood (California) of the Pacific Coast League following his playing days. He currently makes his home in Valparaiso, Indiana.

Alvin Dark, Shortstop (1950-56)

The son of an oil driller, Alvin Dark was born in Oklahoma and lived in Texas before settling down in Lake Charles, Louisiana. He was a three-sport star in high school and played baseball, football and basketball at Louisiana State, attaining some All-America halfback mention when he attended Southwestern Louisiana as a Marine Corps trainee.

"We didn't have a baseball team in high school, so I was more proficient in football," he recalled. "We had an undefeated football team at LSU in '42, beating Fordham at the Polo Grounds." He was a 19-year-old sophomore in the same backfield with future NFL great Steve

Van Buren, but his greatest gridiron fame came during his service time.

In the 1944 Oil Bowl, Dark scored a touchdown, passed for another and kicked three extra points and a field goal against Arkansas A&M. He led the school to an undefeated season and outplayed Bob Waterfield in a 20-7 victory over Fort Benning (Georgia) and matched Glenn Dobbs in a big upset over Randolph, including a booming punt to the loser's 1-yard line.

Dark eventually served at Pearl Harbor and in China before returning in 1946. Pro football scouts were eager to sign him, and Philadelphia Eagles' coach Greasy Neale compared Dark favorably with quarterback Norm Van Brocklin, but Alvin opted for a $40,000 bonus with the Boston Braves.

Playing for Milwaukee of the American Association, he batted .303 in 1947 with a league-leading 49 doubles and 121 runs scored. By 1948 he was the Braves' regular shortstop, batting .322 as a rookie and helping Boston to the National League pennant. After

Alvin Dark (Brace Photo)

the Braves fell below .500 in 1949, Dark and double-play partner Eddie Stanky were traded to the New York Giants for Sid Gordon and Buddy Kerr.

They were hand-picked by manager Leo Durocher as the gritty players who would transform the Giants from sluggers into contenders. That deal may have been consummated sooner, but the Giants weren't willing to part with Bobby Thomson, which was a good thing two years later. Dark also was a deft golfer at the time, winning the Baseball Players Golf Tournament in Miami in February of 1951.

It was a good omen, perhaps, because he also starred for the 1951 pennant winners, batting .303 with a league-leading 41 doubles. In an anticlimactic World Series loss to the Yankees, "Captain" Dark batted .417 with three doubles and a home run among 10 hits. He batted .293 in 1954 and a sizzling .412 in the World Series sweep against the great Cleveland pitching staff. He ended his playing career with a .323 average in 16 World Series games.

Jim Davenport, Infielder (1958-70)

There may be no individual more closely associated with the history of the San Francisco Giants than Jim Davenport. A bold statement, for sure, with names like Mays and McCovey, but Davenport has done it all with the organization: played, coached and managed.

Davenport spent his entire 13-year playing career with the Giants from 1958-70, has had three coaching stints (1970, 1976-82, 1996) and was the team's manager during the 1985 season. He also has served as a scout and as a minor league manager, coach and instructor.

Davenport debuted in San Francisco the same year the Giants first played in the Bay Area and batted .256 with 12 home runs and 41 RBI in 134 games. In 1961 he posted career highs of 25 doubles and 65 RBI while batting at a .278 clip with 12 homers. The following year he recorded personal bests of a .297 batting average and 14 home runs to go with 58 RBI.

Davenport was named a National League All-Star in 1962, and in the first of two All-Star Games played that summer he helped provide an insurance run with an eighth-inning single in the N.L.'s 3-1 victory at District of Columbia Stadium in Washington.

In the deciding game of their three-game playoff against the rival Los Angeles Dodgers at Dodger Stadium on October 3, 1962, Davenport drew a bases loaded walk off Stan Williams that forced home Felipe Alou with the go-ahead run in the top of the ninth inning as the Giants rallied from a 4-2 deficit to win 6-4 and bring San Francisco its first N.L. pennant.

Primarily a third baseman, Davenport also saw action at second base and shortstop, plus first base and the outfield. He is regarded as the finest defensive infielder in San Francisco history. Davenport topped N.L. third basemen in fielding percentage in 1959 (.978), 1960 (.961) and 1961 (.965) and won a Gold Glove at third base in 1962 (.952 fielding percentage and 28 double plays). During the 1964 season

Jim Davenport (S.F. Giants Archives)

he committed a mere 11 errors while playing 64 games at shortstop, 41 at third base and 30 at second base, and in 1967 he put together a string of 64 consecutive games without committing a miscue.

On San Francisco's career lists, Davenport ranks third in games (1,501), fourth in at-bats (4,427), sixth in hits (1,142), tied for sixth in triples (37) and 10th in runs (552) and doubles (177). He was a .258 lifetime batter with 77 home runs and 456 RBI. Davenport was selected the third baseman on the Giants' Silver Anniversary Dream Team, commemorating 25 years in San Francisco, in a vote by the fans at the conclusion of the 1981 season.

Davenport makes his home in San Carlos, California.

Chili Davis, Outfielder (1981-87)

A fan favorite when he started his career with the Giants, the switch-hitting Charles "Chili" Davis was allowed to slip away too early, as was the case with George Foster, Garry Maddox and Gary Matthews in the 1970s. After playing six seasons with the Giants, he was signed as a free agent by the California Angels following the 1987 season and enjoyed American League success as an outfielder and a designated hitter through the 1999 season.

Davis, a native of Jamaica, was reared in Los Angeles, where he was a prep catcher. Drafted in the 11th round by the Giants in 1978, he didn't take long to grab the club's attention. Playing for Triple-A Phoenix in 1981, he batted .350 with 40 stolen bases and soon was a major leaguer to stay.

An ankle surgery reduced his speed thereafter, but he was an All-Star by 1984, playing in the game at Candlestick Park. The switch-hitting Chili batted .315 that season and had a career-high 18-game hitting streak. He suffered a dislocated left shoulder in 1995, slipping down the dugout steps in Cincinnati. He never approached his 1994 form again with Giants, for whom he hit 24 home runs in their drive toward the 1987 division title.

Chili Davis (S.F. Giants Archives)

Serving exclusively as a designated hitter, he had a career-high 112 RBI for the 1993 Angels. He batted .311 for them in 1994 and .318 in 1995 before providing 30 homers and 90 RBI for the Kansas City Royals in 1997. Injuries cut short his 1998, but the professional was performing at a high level at age 39 for the New York Yankees in 1999.

George Davis, Shortstop (1893-1901, 1903)

In 1893 the New York Giants traded popular catcher Buck Ewing to the Cleveland Spiders in exchange for a young utility player by the name of George Davis. The deal was not popular among the fans in Gotham City.

But soon all was forgotten. Davis, a shortstop for the Giants from 1893-1901 and in 1903, became the first player in major league history to hit a home run and a triple in the same inning (fourth) against the Chicago Colts at the Polo Grounds in New York on June 14, 1893. From August 3-September 9, 1893, Doyle hit in a franchise-record 33 consecutive games. He finished the season with career

highs of a .355 batting average, 27 triples (also a franchise best) and 11 home runs with 119 RBI. The following year Davis batted .352 while leading the second-place Giants to a four-game sweep of the champion Baltimore Orioles in the Temple Cup series.

Davis took over as player-manager in 1895 after the controversial Andrew C. Freedman succeeded C.C. Van Cott as club president. At age 24, Davis was the youngest major league manager up to that time, and he posted just a 16-17 record before being replaced by first baseman Jack Doyle. Davis remained a player and batted .340 with a career-high 36 triples, 101 RBI and 48 stolen bases. On August 15 he tied the franchise record of six hits (shared by seven other players) against the Philadelphia Phillies at the Baker Bowl in Philadelphia.

The Giants floundered under the ownership of Freedman—finishing in seventh place or lower in the National League in seven of eight seasons from 1895-1902—but Davis provided his fair share of positives. He led the N.L. with a career-high 136 RBI (tied for fifth on the Giants' single-season list) while batting .353

George Davis (Transcendental Graphics)

with a personal-best 65 stolen bases (second on the season list) in 1897, and he was the league's top fielding shortstop in 1899 and 1900.

Davis got a second opportunity as player-manager in July of 1900 and piloted the Giants to a 39-37 record over the balance of the season. He continued at the helm for the entire 1901 campaign even though New York went 52-85 for seventh place. Davis batted .301 in 1901, the ninth time in nine seasons with the Giants he finished with a better-than-.300 batting average.

During the 1901-02 offseason, Davis moved to the Chicago White Stockings of the newly-formed American League. The N.L. and A.L. competed for players and attention in those days and ultimately signed a "peace treaty" in 1903. Part of the agreement prevented teams from taking players from teams in the other league, but Davis violated the policy when he returned to the Giants for the 1904 season. White Stockings' owner Charles Comiskey obtained a court injunction (defeating Davis' attorney and friend, John Montgomery Ward, a former teammate in New York) that resulted in Davis playing in just four games with the Giants in 1903 and going back to Chicago in 1904. Davis played for the White Stockings through 1909.

In his decade with the Giants, Davis batted .332 with 227 doubles, 98 triples, 53 home runs, 816 RBI and 354 stolen bases in 1,096 games. On the franchise all-time lists, the switch-hitter ranks second in batting average and stolen bases, seventh in triples and RBI and 10th in runs (838). His managerial record was 107-139 (.435 record). Davis' 20-year career statistics (he played in Cleveland from 1890-92) included a .295 batting average and 616 stolen bases (15th on baseball's all-time list) in 2,368 games. He pitched in three games (0-1 record) in 1891.

From 1913-18 Davis served as head coach at Amherst (Massachusetts) College. He also was a scout for the New York Yankees (1915) and St. Louis Browns (1917).

Davis passed away October 17, 1940, in Philadelphia at the age of 70. He was inducted into the National Baseball Hall of Fame in 1998 by the Veterans Committee.

Josh Devore, Outfielder (1908-13)

None of baseball's all-time stolen base leaders accomplished what Josh Devore did. Not Rickey Henderson. Not Lou Brock. Not Billy Hamilton.

On June 20, 1912, Devore, an outfielder for the New York Giants from 1908-13, stole a record four bases in the ninth inning against the Boston Beaneaters at the South End Grounds in Boston. Twice he singled and swiped both second and third base against the Beaneaters' battery of Brad Hogg and Gil Whitehouse. Devore finished with a franchise-record tying five steals while New York had a modern-day National League record (since 1900) of 11 thieves in a 21-12 win.

Devore's voyage into the record books was an interesting one. In 1906 he was turned down for a position with Meriden (Mississippi) of the Cotton States League because manager Sy Sample felt he was too small at 5-foot-6 and 160 pounds. But Devore's older brother, Bill, was so confident in Josh's ability that he gave Sample $100 to cover the costs for a tryout. Devore made the team, led the league in batting and was purchased by the Giants' organization.

In his major league debut September 25, 1908, against the Cincinnati Reds at the Polo Grounds in New York, Devore entered the game as a pinch-runner and was picked off first base.

Devore made a living out of reaching base via bunts and walks. He batted at a career-high .304 clip in 1910 with a personal best 10 triples and 43 stolen bases (fifth in the N.L.). The following year the leadoff-hitter extraordinaire batted .280 with career bests of 19 doubles, 10 triples, three home runs, 50 RBI, 61 stolen bases (second in the N.L. and fifth on the Giants' single-season list) and 81 walks.

After batting .275 with 27 stolen bases and 51 walks during the 1912 season, Devore saved Game 3 of the World Series against the Boston Red Sox. The Giants led 2-1 in the bottom of the ninth inning at Fenway Park in Boston, and the Red Sox had runners at second and third when catcher Hick Cady hit a line drive to right center that would have scored the tying and winning runs. Devore ran back for the ball, threw up his bare (left) hand, knocked the ball down and juggled it twice before holding onto it for the final out. Boston went on to win the championship four games to three with one tie.

Josh Devore

Over the first 16 games of 1913, Devore managed just a .190 batting average before bring traded to the Reds along with pitcher Red Ames, infielder Heinie Groh and $20,000 in exchange for pitcher Art Fromme and infielder Eddie Grant on May 22. In six seasons in New York, Devore batted .283 with 45 doubles, 27 triples, seven home runs, 118 RBI, 141 stolen bases and 184 walks in 431 games.

Devore played in 66 games with the Reds, then was dealt to the Philadelphia Phillies. He opened the 1914 season with the Phillies and was swapped to Boston in July. The Braves, who were 15 games behind the first-place Giants on July 4, won 34 of their final 44 games to capture the N.L. pennant and then took the World Series over the Philadelphia Athletics four games to none. Devore was released following the season. His seven-year career sta-

tistics included a .277 batting average with 160 stolen bases in 601 games.

Though his major league playing days were over (he attempted a comeback with the Phillies in 1916), Devore continued his career in the minor leagues for several years both before and after serving in World War I. He coached at Marietta (Ohio) College in 1918 and for a minor league team in Grand Rapids (Michigan) from 1920-24.

Devore passed away October 6, 1954, in Chillicothe, Ohio, at the age of 66.

Dick Dietz, Catcher (1966-71)

Dick Dietz had a brief career with the Giants, but he gained distinction by enjoying the greatest season ever by a San Francisco catcher. He played 149 games in 1970 and batted .300 with 36 doubles, 22 home runs and 107 RBI, forming a 1-2 punch with Willie McCovey.

By 1972 manager Charlie Fox elected to go with youngsters Dave Rader and Fran Healy, so Dietz was out of a job and moved on to the Dodgers. One reason for the demotion was his fielding, including a league-leading 25 passed balls in 1970. Still, it was one helluva 1970 before Fox succeeded Clyde King and made changes. The 1970 dream season included homering off Catfish Hunter after entering the All-Star Game.

"Mule" was batting in the May 31, 1968, game in which Don Drysdale of the Dodgers

established a record of 58 consecutive scoreless innings. Dietz was hit by a Drysdale pitch with the bases loaded, but home plate umpire Harry Wendelstedt ruled the batter made no effort to get out of the way, enabling the Dodgers' ace to remain scoreless.

"It was a 2-2 count on me, and Drysdale threw a spitball," Dietz recalled. "I was protecting the plate, and he hit me on the elbow. All I had time to do was flinch. I took two steps toward first base, and Wendelstedt said, `No!' I said, `No, what?' And he said, `You didn't try to get out of the way of it.' I was hot. He had to kick me out of the game for what I said to him. It was the worst call, without a doubt, that I have ever seen."

Following a great prep baseball and football career in Greensville, South Carolina, Dietz signed a six-figure bonus with the Giants and had outstanding power numbers throughout his minor league career. His best season was 1963 with El Paso, where he batted .354 with 35 home runs and 101 RBI in 134 games as the league batting champion and Most Valuable Player. At first, the Giants wanted to make an outfielder out of Dietz, but then he settled into catching and the club eventually traded Tom Haller to make room for him.

Dick Dietz (S.F. Giants Archives)

Mike Donlin, Outfielder
(1904-06, 1908, 1911, 1914)

Had Mike Donlin not forgone baseball for an acting career, he might very well have been one of the game's premier players.

Donlin was an outfielder for the Giants from 1904-06 and in 1908, 1911 and 1914. He was a flamboyant personality on and off the field who earned the nickname "Turkey Mike" because of a strutting walk. New York fans loved him.

So did Giants' manager John McGraw. In 1899 Donlin began his major league career with the St. Louis Perfectos, and the following year he and McGraw became teammates. When McGraw went to the Baltimore Orioles as player-manager in 1901, Donlin joined him. Donlin was the first-ever American League player to get six hits in a game when he accomplished the feat against the Detroit Tigers on June 24, 1901. Donlin played for the Cincinnati Reds from 1902-04 before being traded to the Giants on August 7, 1904, in exchange for outfielder Moose McCormick and cash. Donlin batted .280 in 42 games as the Giants won the National League pennant.

In 1905 the left-handed swinging Donlin posted career highs of a .356 batting average (10th on the Giants' season list) and 124 runs (tops in the N.L.) to go with 31 doubles, 16 triples, seven home runs, 80 RBI and 33 stolen (tied for his personal best). New York defended its N.L. championship and defeated the Philadelphia Athletics in the World Series four games to one.

Donlin was limited to 37 games in 1906 after suffering a broken leg, and he sat out the 1907 campaign over a contract dispute. He returned in 1908 to bat .334 with 26 doubles, 13 triples, seven home runs, a career-high 106 RBI and 30 stolen bases.

Then Donlin, who married actress and vaudeville star Mabel Hite on April 10, 1906, spent 1909 and 1910 performing on the vaudeville circuit. New Yorkers pleaded for his return:

Mike Donlin (Transcedental Graphics)

"If Donlin would only join the Giants
"The fans would drink his health in pints."
On June 28, 1911, Donlin came back to the Giants, but after appearing in just 12 games he was sold to the Boston Beaneaters on August 1. He finished the campaign with the Beaneaters and then was dealt to the Pittsburgh Pirates for the 1912 season. In December of 1912 the Philadelphia Phillies attempted to claim Donlin on waivers, but he refused and returned to vaudeville. He also played 36 games for Jersey City (New Jersey) of the International League. Donlin returned for his final stint in the majors as a pinch-hitter with the Giants in 1914.

Thereafter, Donlin concentrated on vaudeville and movies. Hite passed away in 1912, and Donlin married another vaudevillian, Rita Ross, on October 20, 1914. Donlin was manager of Memphis of the Southern Association in 1917 and the following year was a scout

for the Boston Braves. Donlin never became a bona fide star actor, but he did receive numerous small parts and earned decent reviews.

In six seasons with the Giants, Donlin batted .333 with 70 doubles, 34 triples, 18 home runs, 218 RBI and 75 stolen bases in 431 games. His 12-year career numbers included a .333 batting average in 1,049 games (an average of just 87 games per season). He pitched in four games (0-1 record) in 1899 and 1902. Aggression and alcohol often got Donlin in trouble. He was arrested on more than one occasion for everything from assault to refusing to pay a taxi cab bill.

Donlin passed away September 24, 1933, in Hollywood, California, at the age of 55 after suffering a heart attack.

Jack Doyle, First Baseman (1892-95, 1898-1900, 1902)

If you can't beat 'em, join 'em.

Such must have been the sentiment of Jack Doyle, a first baseman for the New York Giants from 1892-95, 1898-1900 and 1902. After a playing career that was notorious for his run-ins with umpires, Doyle became an arbiter himself.

But first things first. A native of Killorglin, Ireland, Doyle broke into the major leagues with the Columbus Colts of the American Association in 1889-90. He then played for the Cleveland Spiders in 1891-92 before joining the Giants.

In 1894 Doyle established career highs of a .367 batting average (the sixth-highest mark in franchise history), 30 doubles and eight triples to go with 100 RBI. The Giants finished in second place in the National League and upset the pennant-winning Baltimore Orioles in the Temple Cup series four games to none. Early the following year Doyle replaced shortstop George Davis as player-manager, but Doyle didn't like club president Andrew C. Freedman and was replaced as manager after posting a 32-31 record.

Doyle moved on to Baltimore in 1896 and 1897 and played on two Temple Cup-champi-

onship teams. He had personal bests of 101 RBI and 73 stolen bases (fifth in the N.L.) during the 1896 campaign while batting at a .339 clip. Doyle began the 1898 season as a player-manager with the Washington Senators (8-9 record) before returning to the Giants. Manager John Day selected Doyle team captain in 1899.

Stint No. 2 with the Giants lasted until February of 1901 when Doyle was traded to the Chicago Orphans in exchange for infielder Sammy Strang. Then in February of 1902 Doyle and infielder Jim Delahanty were sold to New York. But after 42 games Doyle was off again to Washington, and he subsequently donned uniforms for the Brooklyn Superbas (1903-04), Philadelphia Phillies (1904) and New York Highlanders (1905).

Throughout his career "Dirty Jack" had the reputation of being an aggressive and scrappy player with a fiery temper. The deadball era was characterized by close, low-scoring games, and Doyle knew every run was important, so he played with reckless abandon. Doyle also was known for his confrontations with umpires. One of his most famous run-ins came with Tom Lynch in 1897 when Doyle played for Baltimore. Doyle was arrested after assaulting Lynch, and the incident led to Orioles' manager Ned Hanlon getting rid of Doyle. Lynch went on to be president of the N.L. from 1910-13 and, ironically, hired Doyle as an umpire in 1911.

Doyle's eight-year statistics with the Giants included a .306 batting average, 157 doubles, 28 triples, 16 home runs, 476 RBI and 254 stolen bases (10th on the franchise all-time list) in 741 games. In 17 seasons as a big leaguer, the right-handed swinger batted .299 with 315 doubles, 968 RBI and 516 stolen bases (29th on baseball's all-time list) in 1,564 games. Doyle compiled a 40-40 managerial record.

Following his playing days, Doyle played and managed in the minor leagues from 1905-07 and then served as police commissioner of Holyoke, Massachusetts, in 1908 and 1909. He subsequently returned to baseball as an um-

Jack Doyle (Transcendental Graphics)

pire, primarily in the minors. His only year in the majors was 1911. From 1920-38 Doyle was a scout for the Chicago Cubs, and he is credited with discovering Hall of Fame catcher Gabby Hartnett. Doyle also is said to have recommended Hall of Famer Hack Wilson to the Cubs after the Giants failed to protect him against the draft.

Doyle passed away December 31, 1958, in Holyoke at the age of 89.

Larry Doyle, Second Baseman (1907-16, 1918-20)

As his nickname would suggest, "Laughing Larry" Doyle was a good-humored and good-natured guy with a captivating smile.

A second baseman for the New York Giants from 1907-16 and 1918-20, Doyle loved the game of baseball, and it showed with his play on the field. He was a key ingredient to the Giants' back-to-back-to-back National League pennants in 1911, 1912 and 1913.

Nevertheless, Doyle had an inauspicious debut with New York. Upon being purchased by the team from Springfield (Illinois) of the Three I League in July of 1907, Doyle arrived in Gotham City and hopped aboard the wrong El train which made him late for his first game. Manager John McGraw started Doyle at second base (he had primarily played third in the minors) in his debut July 22 against the Chicago Cubs, and he committed a mental error (allowing the winning run to score from third on a groundout instead of throwing the ball home) in a 2-0 New York loss. Doyle expected to be released, but McGraw gave him a vote of confidence.

The rest, as they say, is history. Doyle became a fixture at second base and served as team captain from 1908-16. In 1909 he led the N.L. with 172 hits while batting at a .302 clip. He topped the league with 25 triples (second on the franchise single-season list) in 1911. One day that year the 25-year-old Doyle made his famous comment, "It's great to be young and a Giant."

Doyle put together a banner 1912 season that culminated with him receiving the Chalmers Award as the N.L.'s Most Valuable Player. He posted career highs of a .330 batting average and 90 RBI to go with 33 doubles, eight triples, 10 home runs and 36 stolen bases.

On July 17, 1914, Doyle hit a game-winning, two-run inside-the-park homer in the 21st inning against Babe Adams of the Pittsburgh Pirates at Forbes Field in Pittsburgh. New York won 3-1 in what was the longest game in major league history up to that point.

The left-handed swinger topped the N.L. in batting average (.320), hits (career-high 189) and doubles (career-high 40) during the 1915 season. But the Giants traded Doyle along with infielder Herb Hunter and outfielder Merwin Jacobson to the Cubs in exchange for infielder Mickey Doolan and third baseman Heinie Zimmerman on August 28, 1916.

After playing for Chicago in 1917, Doyle returned to the Giants in a three-way deal that

Larry Doyle

sent pitcher Lefty Tyler from the Cubs to the Boston Braves for Doyle, catcher Art Wilson and $15,000 on January 4, 1918, and then sent Doyle and pitcher Jesse Barnes to the Giants for infielder Buck Herzog four days later. Doyle played three more seasons in New York before retiring.

During his 13 seasons with the Giants, Doyle batted .292 with 275 doubles, 117 triples, 67 home runs, 725 RBI and 291 stolen bases in 1,622 games. On the franchise all-time lists, he ranks fourth in triples; sixth in games, at-bats (5,995) and doubles; seventh in hits (1,751) and stolen bases; eighth in runs (906) and RBI; and ninth in walks (576). He leads all Giant second basemen in career putouts (3,316) and assists (4,272). Doyle's 14-year career statistics included a .290 batting average. He stole home 17 times (tied for 14th on baseball's all-time list), including twice in a game (tied for the major league record) against the Pirates at Forbes Field on September 18, 1911.

Upon his retirement, Doyle was a minor league manager and a scout for the Giants. In 1942 he was diagnosed with tuberculosis. Doctors determined he contracted the disease from former teammate Christy Mathewson, who was his roommate with the Giants. Doyle was given four of five months to live, but he beat the tuberculosis and lived until March 1, 1974, when he passed away in Saranac Lake, New York, at the age of 87.

Dave Dravecky, Pitcher (1987-89)

Dave Dravecky won only 11 games for the San Francisco Giants from 1987-89, but he always will occupy a special place in the hearts of Bay Area fans.

Dravecky's story is about more than wins. It's about courage, faith and inspiration. On October 7, 1988, Dravecky had a malignant tumor removed from his left (throwing) arm. Over the next two and a half years the cancer resurfaced on multiple occasions, and he ultimately had his left arm amputated June 18, 1991. In between, Dravecky provided the game of baseball with one of its most stirring stories ever.

Following the initial surgery that removed half of his deltoid muscle, Dravecky was told by doctors that, barring a miracle, he would never pitch again. That ray of hope was all Dravecky, a devout Christian, needed to hear. By June of 1989, Dravecky was throwing batting practice, and the following month he was working his way up through the Giants' minor league system on a rehabilitation assignment. Then August 10 he was back on the mound at Candlestick Park in San Francisco for a start against the Cincinnati Reds. Prior to throwing his first pitch, Dravecky paused to say, "Thank you, Lord, for this miracle."

Dravecky received numerous tear-jerking ovations from the crowd of 34,810, and he authored a one-hit shutout through seven innings. He surrendered a three-run homer to Luis Quinones in the eighth but still was the winning pitcher in a 4-3 San Francisco victory.

Five days later Dravecky started (and

won) against the Montreal Expos at Olympic Stadium in Montreal. But in the sixth inning, as he prepared to deliver a pitch, the humerus bone in his left arm broke and Dravecky fell to the ground in excruciating pain. On October 9, as the Giants celebrated their five-game victory over the Chicago Cubs in the National League Championship Series, Dravecky bumped into a teammate and broke his arm again. Dravecky announced his retirement November 13, 1989. He underwent two more operations before finally having his limb removed.

After starting out in the Pittsburgh Pirates organization, Dravecky spent the first six seasons of his major league career with the San Diego Padres. He was selected to the 1983 All-Star Game at Comiskey Park in Chicago. On July 4, 1987, Dravecky was traded to the Giants along with pitcher Craig Lefferts and infielder/outfielder Kevin Mitchell in exchange for third baseman Chris Brown and pitchers Keith Comstock, Mark Davis and Mark Grant.

Dave Dravecky (S.F. Giants Archives)

Dravecky went 6-2 with a 2.68 ERA (including three shutouts and 21.1 consecutive scoreless innings) in his first 13 starts with the Giants. He finished 7-5, 3.20 ERA as San Francisco captured its first division crown since 1971. In the NLCS against the St. Louis Cardinals, Dravecky fired a 5-0, two-hit gem in Game 2 at Busch Stadium in St. Louis on October 7 and was a tough-luck 1-0 loser in Game 6 on October 13. Counting his appearances with San Diego in the 1984 playoffs, Dravecky allowed just one run in 25.2 innings of postseason play.

In 27 games with the Giants, Dravecky posted an 11-5 record with a 3.22 ERA. His eight-year career totals included a 64-57 record with a 3.13 ERA in 226 games.

Since his retirement from baseball Dravecky has written several books, including *Comeback, When You Can't Come Back* and *The Worth of a Man*. He and his wife, Jan, founded the Outreach of Hope non-for profit ministry with a mission to "offer hope and encouragement through Jesus Christ to those suffering from cancer or amputation." Dave, Jan and their children, Tiffany and Jonathan, live in Monument, Colorado.

Shawn Estes, Pitcher (1996-2001)

"As Estes goes, so go the Giants" was a popular theme for the club during an erratic S.F. career that featured equal parts of brilliance and failure. It was no coincidence that his two finest seasons in a Giants' uniform produced division championships in 1997 and 2000, or that his lackluster performances contributed to team disappointment.

One thing was certain: When Estes' talent was properly channeled, he ranked with the best pitchers in the National League. When management tired of his inconsistency, he was traded to the New York Mets for Tsuyoshi Shinjo and Desi Relaford following the 2001 season. That move also paid dividends because Relaford was swapped for David Bell, who helped the Giants reach the 2002 World Series.

Shawn Estes (S.F. Giants Archives)

So, Estes had a hand in three playoff teams, not bad following a change-of-scenery trade with the Seattle Mariners for fellow bad boy Salomon Torres, May 20, 1995. Torres was soon out of baseball (he made a comeback in 2002), and Estes blossomed in his first full major league season with the Giants in 1997.

At age 24, he posted a 19-5 record and 3.18 ERA, and was named to the National League All-Star team. His 19 victories were the most by a Giants' lefty since Ron Bryant won 24 in 1973. Estes also had a career-high 181 strikeouts in 201 innings, and was a star on the rise until injuries and self-doubt prefaced a downfall.

Estes slumped to 7-12 with a 5.06 ERA in 1998 and wasn't much better in 1999. But the good Shawn resurfaced in 2000, and his 15-6 record helped the Giants to a division title. But his bad luck returned in Game 2 of the playoffs with the Mets, when he injured his ankle on clumsy base-running and was knocked out after three innings.

After one more year with the Giants, he was gone along with his solid 64-50 career record with the club he followed as a promising Nevada prep. After turning down a Stanford scholarship to sign with Seattle, the first-round draft choice got off to a bad start in the Mariners' farm system before turning into a steal for the Giants.

Darrell Evans, Infielder (1976-83)

Darrell Evans was nicknamed "Doody" because of his resemblance to the famous TV puppet. A journeyman slugger if there ever was one, Evans finished with 414 home runs and twice hit at least 40 in one season. But not with the Giants, where Candlestick Park's wind helped him lead the league in warning-track outs. "Just missed it," was a favorite saying.

Evans joined the Giants in 1976 and was dependable for 20-plus homers and 70-plus RBI per season, not star quality but solid numbers for a major leaguer. He increased his value with an excellent season with the 1983 Giants, batting .277 with 30 home runs, including three in one game against Houston at Candlestick. That led the Detroit Tigers to take a chance on him, and he responded with a league-leading 40 home runs in 1985.

He hit 41 homers with Atlanta in 1973, joining Hank Aaron and Davey Johnson as the only three teammates ever with the same 40-plus season. "I hit 19 homers the year before, and all of a sudden I'm hitting 40," Evans said. "Maybe I thought I was too good. After awhile, I started thinking I had the weight of the world on my shoulders."

Evans was a versatile player who performed adequately at third base, first base and the outfield, and even filled in at shortstop in an emergency when Johnnie LeMaster was injured in 1982. He enjoyed a memorable debut for the Giants after joining the club in a 1976 trade that sent malcontent Willie Montanez to Atlanta.

"I had been doing poorly in Atlanta," he recalled. "But on my first day at Candlestick, it was a double-header and I hit home runs in

Darrell Evans (S.F. Giants Archives)

both games to win both games. There was a pretty good-sized crowd and it was a great feeling to make a good first impression and to show the Giants they didn't make a mistake."

A native of Pasadena, California, Evans attended Pasadena City College and played on championship baseball and basketball junior college teams. He signed with the Braves after attending L.A. State and reached the big club after hitting 20 homers for Triple-A Richmond in 1970. Although his .248 lifetime average doesn't indicate it, Evans had a good eye at the plate, drawing 1,605 walks—eighth on baseball's all-time list—to balance 1,410 strikeouts.

Buck Ewing, Catcher (1883-89, 1891-92)

Most, if not all, baseball historians agree that William "Buck" Ewing was the greatest player of the 19th century. He was an all-

around talent—batting, fielding, running and thinking.

Ewing played for the New York Giants from their entry into the National League in 1883 (as the Gothams) through 1889 and from 1891-92. He began his career with the Troy (New York) Trojans in 1880. When John B. Day was granted New York franchises in both the N.L. (Gothams) and the American Association (Metropolitans) for the 1883 season, he bought out the Trojans, who were being dispatched from the N.L., and divided the roster between his two teams. Ewing, chiefly a catcher, was assigned to the Gothams (who became the Giants in 1885).

In his first season in New York, the right-handed batting Ewing topped the N.L. with a career-high 10 home runs, and the following year he led the league with 20 triples (also a personal best and tied for seventh on the franchise list).

Although not exceptionally fast, Ewing generally batted leadoff and was a smart base runner. One day in the 10th inning of a scoreless game at the Polo Grounds in New York he stole second base and third base, then announced, "I'm going to steal home" and proceeded to do so. The play became the subject of a popular lithograph entitled "Ewing's Famous Steal."

In 1888 the Giants captured their first World Series championship. Ewing, who succeeded John Montgomery Ward as team captain (a position similar to today's manager), led the squad with a .306 batting average and a career-high 53 stolen bases. New York repeated as champions in 1889 as Ewing batted at a .327 clip with 87 RBI and 34 stolen bases.

Ewing was one of the founders of the Brotherhood of Professional Base Ball Players, which served as a protection agency for the players against the owners, and he jumped to the Players League in 1890 as player-manager of the New York Giants. But the league folded after one season, and Ewing returned to the N.L. Giants at a team-high $5,500 salary. An

arm injury limited him to 14 games in 1891, and he primarily played first base in 1892 while pacing the team with a .310 batting average and 76 RBI and 42 stolen bases (tied with Eddie Burke and Jack Doyle).

Prior to the 1893 season Ewing was traded to the Cleveland Spiders in exchange for infielder/outfielder George Davis. His nine-year statistics with the Giants included a .306 batting average, 905 hits, 122 doubles, 109 triples (sixth on the franchise list), 47 home runs, 459 RBI and 178 stolen bases in 734 games.

Ewing played for Cleveland for two seasons, then joined the Cincinnati Reds as player-manager in 1895. He retired as a player in 1897 but remained as manager through 1889. In 1890 he was hired as manager of the Giants, who were in a state of disarray under owner Andrew C. Freedman. Ewing compiled a 21-41 record before being dismissed with the team in last place.

Buck Ewing

During his 18-year career, Ewing batted .303 with 1,625 hits, 250 doubles, 178 triples, 71 home runs, 883 RBI and 354 stolen bases in 1,315 games. He possessed a rifle arm and is credited with being the first catcher to throw from a crouched position. Ewing was a versatile performer who played all nine positions on the field, including nine games as a pitcher (2-3 record, 3.45 ERA). His seven-year managerial record was 489-395 (.553 winning percentage).

Following his baseball days Ewing enjoyed a fairly wealthy lifestyle as the result of some successful real estate investments. He developed diabetes, however, and passed away October 20, 1906, in Cincinnati at the age of 47. He was inducted into the National Baseball Hall of Fame in 1939 by the Veterans Committee.

Freddie Fitzsimmons, Pitcher (1925-37)

Freddie Fitzsimmons isn't in the National Baseball Hall of Fame, and he never was selected to the All-Star Game. But the right-handed pitcher who played for the New York Giants from 1925-27 was memorable, popular and successful.

After joining the Giants in August of 1925, "Fat Freddie" (5-foot-11, 200-215 pounds) won in double figures in each of the next eight seasons. He threw a hard knuckleball that resembled a spitball and spun around to turn his back on the batter before delivering his pitch. In 1928 Fitzsimmons went 20-9 (establishing a career

Freddie Fitzsimmons (Brace Photo)

high for victories) with a 3.68 ERA and 16 complete games. Two years later he topped the National League with a .731 winning percentage (19-7 record) with a 4.25 ERA and 17 complete games.

New York captured the 1933 N.L. pennant as Fitzsimmons posted a 16-11 record with a 2.90 ERA. He lost Game 3 of the World Series against the Washington Senators 4-0 as Earl Whitehill fired a five-hit shutout. It was the Giants' lone setback in the series as they won the championship four games to one.

Fitzsimmons tied for the league lead with four shutouts in 1935 and the following year helped the Giants capture another N.L. championship by going 10-7 with a 3.32 ERA. In Game 2 of the 1936 World Series against the cross-town rival Yankees, Fitzsimmons was a tough-luck 2-1 loser after allowing just four hits in eight innings. He was beaten in the decisive Game 6 by the score of 13-5 as the Yankees won the series four games to two.

With Fitzsimmons appearing to be on the decline, Giants' manager Bill Terry traded him to the Brooklyn Dodgers in exchange for pitcher Tom "Rattlesnake" Baker on June 11, 1937. Fitzsimmons' compiled a 170-114 record (.599 winning percentage) with a 3.54 ERA in 403 games during his 13 seasons in New York. On the franchise's all-time lists, he ranks sixth in innings pitched (2,514.1), tied for sixth in games started (329), seventh in wins and 10th in games. An economical worker, he averaged just 2.4 walks and 2.5

strikeouts per nine innings. Fitzsimmons is fourth all-time among Giants' pitchers with a .974 career fielding percentage.

The deal turned out to be one of the worst in Giants' history. Baker won his only decision for New York in 1937 but was let go after appearing in two games in 1938. Fitzsimmons, who initially wasn't too keen about the trade, led the N.L. with an .899 winning percentage (16-2 record) in 1940 and returned to the World Series in 1941. But in Game 3 against the Yankees he was knocked out of a scoreless duel in the seventh inning when Yankees' pitcher Marius Russo scorched a line drive off his left knee. Fitzsimmons suffered a bad bruise and a ruptured blood vessel and never recovered. He pitched in 10 games in 1942 and 1943 before retiring.

During his 19-year career, Fitzsimmons had a 217-146 record (.598 winning percentage) with a 3.51 ERA in 513 games. He was a lifetime .200 batter with 14 home runs.

From 1943-45 Fitzsimmons served as manager of the Philadelphia Phillies but had just a 105-181 record (.367 winning percentage). He subsequently was a coach for the Boston Braves (1948), Giants (1949-55), Chicago Cubs (1957-59, 1966) and Kansas City Athletics (1960). He and Giants' manager Leo Durocher were fined $500 apiece and Fitzsimmons was suspended for a month of spring training in 1949 by baseball commissioner A.B. "Happy" Chandler, who ruled that Fitzsimmons was still under contract with the Braves when he contacted Durocher about a position with the Giants. Fitzsimmons later was general manager of the Brooklyn Dodgers of the All-America Football Conference.

Fitzsimmons passed away November 18, 1979, in Yucca Valley, California, at the age of 78.

Frankie Frisch, Infielder (1919-26)

Plain as day, Frankie Frisch was a winner.

During his eight seasons with the New York Giants from 1919-26, Frisch played on two World Series championship teams (1921

Frankie Frisch

and 1922), two other National League championship teams (1923 and 1924) and three N.L. runner-up squads (1919, 1920 and 1925).

A native of New York, Frisch joined the Giants immediately out of Fordham University in June of 1919. His college coach, Art Devlin, was a former New York third baseman (1904-11) and recommended Frisch to manager John McGraw. The "Fordham Flash" played shortstop in college but generally was used at second base and third base with the Giants.

Frisch became a regular in 1920 and the following year began a string of 11 consecutive seasons in which he batted at better than a .300 clip. The switch-hitter topped the Giants in batting four times (.341 in 1921, career-high .348 in 1923, .331 in 1925 and .314 in 1926) and led the way in stolen bases every year from 1920-26, including an N.L. high and career best of 49 thefts in 1921. Frisch topped the league with career highs of 223 hits in 1923 and 121 runs in 1924.

Six times in franchise history the Giants have had three players record at least 100 RBI in the same season, and Frisch is apart of two of the trios—1921 (George Kelly 122, Ross Youngs 102 and Frisch 100) and 1923 (Irish Meusel 125, Frisch 111 and Kelly 103).

On September 10, 1924, Frisch went 6-for-7 (reaching safely in his first six at-bats before being retired attempting to bunt for his seventh hit) with a home run in the first game of a double-header against the Boston Braves at the Polo Grounds in New York. He is one of only eight players in franchise history to collect six hits in a game, along with Danny Richardson (1887), Jack Glasscock (1890), George Davis (1895), Kip Selbach (1901), Dave Bancroft (1920), Jesus Alou (1964) and Mike Benjamin (1995).

In four World Series with the Giants, Frisch compiled a robust .363 batting average (37-for-102) in 26 games. New York defeated the cross-town rival Yankees in both 1921 and 1922, then lost to the Yankees in 1923 and the Washington Senators in 1924.

For awhile it appeared as though Frisch was being groomed to replace McGraw as the Giants' manager. But the two hard-nosed and outspoken individuals had a falling out, and New York traded its team captain to the St. Louis Cardinals along with pitcher Jimmy Ring in exchange for second baseman Rogers Hornsby on December 20, 1926. Frisch's statistics with New York included a .321 batting average (fourth on the franchise list), 180 doubles, 77 triples, 54 home runs, 524 RBI and 224 stolen bases in 1,000 games.

Frisch played for the Cardinals from 1927-37, served as player-manager from 1933-37 and was full-time manager in 1938. He was the N.L. Most Valuable Player in 1931 and was a member of two World Series championship teams (1931 and 1934) and two other N.L. championship squads (1928 and 1930). His career statistics included a .316 batting average, 2,880 hits, 466 doubles, 138 triples, 105 home runs, 1,244 RBI and 419 stolen bases in 2,311 games. Frisch was a broadcaster for the

Braves in 1939, then went back to the dugout as manager of the Pittsburgh Pirates (1940-46) and Chicago Cubs (1949-51). His 16-year managerial record was 1,138-1,078, a .514 winning percentage.

From 1947-49, Frisch returned to New York as a broadcaster for the Giants. He was elected to the National Baseball Hall of Fame in 1947. Frisch passed away March 12, 1973, in Wilmington, Delaware, at the age of 74 following an automobile accident.

Tito Fuentes, Second Baseman (1965-67, 1969-74)

Rigoberto (Tito) Fuentes, a native of Havana, ranks among the most colorful players in San Francisco history. He played the game with flair and zest while continuing the Giants' tradition of developing outstanding Latin talent. Tito was known for his flamboyance afield and a fistful of flashy rings, being called "Hot Dog" by opponents while hearing chants of "Tito! Tito! Tito!" from adoring fans.

"Outside of Bill Mazeroski, I think Tito has the quickest hands in the National League," manager Herman Franks said after Fuentes joined the Giants in 1966. He didn't hit his stride until he teamed with rookie Chris Speier as a double-play combination in 1971. He was adept at knocking down balls going up the middle and flipping to the shortstop, who would throw to first for the out.

"I'd been in the game a long time, and I'd never seen anybody do that," manager Charlie Fox recalled. "Tito had a lot of talent—he could really play. We always had trouble turning the double play until Tito and Speier got together and hit it off right away."

Fuentes suffered a setback while with Triple-A Phoenix in 1968 by breaking a leg and tearing ligaments on a slide at second base May 9, and he was out the remainder of the season. He was named second baseman on the Giants' 25th Anniversary dream team in 1982, and was the lone member of the club's all-decade team of the 1960s who wasn't on the 1962 pennant winner.

Little Tito, then 15, spurned a 1959 Giants' offer to sign him during the pre-Castro days. He instead played on a telephone company team that won the Cuban championship. He signed with the Kansas City A's, but his father had the contract voided because Tito was under age. The Giants called again, and he was signed out of Cuba as an 18-year-old in 1962.

"It was difficult because I didn't know the language and I had no money in a new country—I was living on corn flakes and Kool-Aid," recalled Fuentes, who batted .320 for Decatur in 1963. Making it into professional baseball wasn't easy for a youngster in the poverty of Havana.

Tito Fuentes

"We had to use rocks, rags—anything—for bases," he said. "We didn't see too many real baseballs. We bought tape, 25 cents a roll, and kept wrapping it into a ball. Maybe it would last four or five games. We were pretty poor, but somehow we managed to play, sometimes all day, everyday. And we had fun."

He improved to .347 at Double-A El Paso in 1964 and reached the majors with a .302 average and 20 home runs for Phoenix in 1965. Tito didn't hit well early in his San Francisco career, so he was sent back to Phoenix, where he thrived in 1968-69, batting .329 and .340, respectively.

Fuentes especially enjoyed 1971 because the Giants were division champions. He contributed to the lone playoff victory over the Pirates with a two-run homer off Steve Blass that gave the club a lead in a 5-4 victory at Candlestick Park. "That was the greatest year," Tito said. "We didn't have a super team, but we had great, great fun. There was tremendous teamwork, and we had so much confidence because we never lost first place."

The 1973 season was his finest with the Giants, including a .277 average, a 16-game hitting streak and a National League record with only six errors and a .993 fielding percentage by a second baseman. A back injury reduced is effectiveness in 1974, and a spat with owner Horace Stoneham prefaced a trade to the San Diego Padres with pitcher Butch Metzger for fellow infielder Derrel Thomas prior to the 1975 season.

Tito played two years with San Diego, batting .280 in 1975, and he spent his final two years in American League, where he enjoyed success with 1977 Detroit Tigers, batting .309 with 10 triples. The Tigers didn't invite him back, and Fuentes soon drifted out of baseball and became a Bay Area baseball broadcaster for an Hispanic radio station.

"My problem was that I was outspoken, and in my later years I complained when things weren't right," said Fuentes, who finally settled down in Reno, Nevada. "I guess they resented me, but I wasn't going to change just

to please somebody. I played with four organizations, and not one compared to the Giants."

Scott Garrelts, Pitcher (1982-91)

Right-handed pitcher Scott Garrelts essentially enjoyed two distinct careers with the San Francisco Giants from 1982-91. At different times he filled the roles of both stopper out of the bullpen and ace of the starting rotation.

Primarily a starter plagued by control problems early on (6.8 walks per nine innings pitched), Garrelts took over as the Giants' short reliever in 1985 when Greg Minton was sidelined with a variety of injuries and illnesses. Garrelts began pitching exclusively out of the stretch and responded by posting a 9-6 record with a team-leading 13 saves and a 2.30 ERA in a career-high 74 games (third in the National League). Most impressive was the fact that he issued just 58 walks in 105.2 innings pitched (4.9 per nine innings) to go with 106 strikeouts. Garrelts was selected to the 1985 All-Star Game at the Metrodome in Minneapolis, though he did not pitch.

Garrelts continued his quality relief work over the next three seasons, topping the team with 10 saves in 1986, 12 saves in 1987 and 13 saves in 1988. He also started 18 games during the 1986 season and had a 13-9 overall record with a 3.11 ERA. Garrelts, whose arsenal featured a fastball, slider and nasty split-fingered fastball, finished 11-7 with a 3.22 ERA and a career-high 127 strikeouts in 106.1 innings pitched during the 1987 campaign. He limited opponents to a league-low .192 batting average.

In 1989, with the Giants in need of a starter and with Craig Lefferts established as the closer, Garrelts took over a spot in the rotation. He emerged as the staff ace with a 14-5 record and a league-leading 2.28 ERA. Garrelts also topped N.L. pitchers with a .260 opponent's on-base percentage and an average of just 9.1 hits and walks allowed per nine innings. He was tied for third with a .212 opponent's batting average.

Scott Garrelts (S.F. Giants Archives)

Garrelts was the winning pitcher in the opening game of the 1989 National League Championship Series against the Chicago Cubs, going seven innings and allowing eight hits and three runs with one walk with six strikeouts as the Giants rolled to an 11-3 victory at Wrigley Field in Chicago. San Francisco went on to win the series four games to one. Garrelts started (and lost) two games in the earthquake-marred World Series against the Oakland Athletics, who swept the Giants four games to none.

On July 29, 1990, Garrelts fired a one-hitter against the Cincinnati Reds, winning 4-0, at Candlestick Park in San Francisco. The only hit he allowed was Paul O'Neill's two-out single in the ninth inning. Garrelts is the last San Francisco pitcher to throw a one-hitter. He finished 12-11 that season but then fell victim to arm

woes that limited him to eight appearances in 1991 and ultimately forced him to retire.

His 10-year numbers with the Giants included a 69-53 record (.566 winning percentage) with 48 saves (ninth on the franchise list, including the New York years) and a 3.29 ERA. In 352 games (89 starts), Garrelts pitched 959.1 innings and amassed 703 strikeouts. He ranks seventh on San Francisco's career list in saves, eighth in games and ninth in wins and strikeouts.

San Francisco's first-round pick in the June 1979 free-agent draft, Garrelts once struck out 22 batters in a seven-inning game as a junior at Buckley-Loda High School in Buckley, Illinois. He currently makes his home in Louisiana.

Ruben Gomez, Pitcher (1953-58)

Ruben Gomez's name will forever be etched in San Francisco Giants' history because he was the pitcher in the first major league game ever played on the West Coast. It was April 15, 1958, at Seals Stadium, and Gomez hooked up with the dreaded Dodgers, posting an 8-0 shutout en route to a mediocre 10-12 season, his last with the Giants.

"I'm glad I was the first pitcher on the West Coast," Gomez recalled in a 1998 reunion. "I also was the first Latin to win a World Series game (1954), and I pitched for 31 years. I finished my major league career in 1967, but I pitched in Puerto Rico until 1979."

In that historic San Francisco opener, Gomez constantly worked out of trouble while yielding six singles and six walks. Pee Wee Reese, Duke Snider and Gil Hodges, the 2-3-4 batters, were a combined zero for nine.

"I liked Ruben and I liked his ability," manager Bill Rigney recalled. "Ruben was not just a marvelous pitcher, but a marvelous athlete. He could have played left or center. He could have played anywhere. He had quality ability, and he never had a sore arm in his life. I think he could have been a great reliever, but he didn't like relieving."

A well-educated native of Puerto Rico, Gomez was in the minors (1949-52) before becoming a member of the New York Giants' rotation. He was 13-11 as a rookie in 1953 and enjoyed his finest season with the 1954 World Series champions, going 17-9 with a 2.88 ERA despite extraordinary wildness. That year, he walked a league-leading 109 batters while striking out 106.

All was forgiven in the World Series. Gomez started Game 3 in Cleveland and yielded two runs in 7.1 innings of a 6-2 victory that helped the Giants sweep the series over the record-setting Indians. He also helped the Giants give the Polo Grounds some final highlights in 1957, posting a 15-13 record in the Giants' last season in New York.

"I was sad and I didn't feel it was a good move," Ruben recalled. "But the welcome we got in San Francisco was really beautiful, like a dream. We had a helluva ball club that first year, too. We were very close."

The dashing Ruben also helped the Giants when he was traded to the Philadelphia Phillies

Ruben Gomez (S.F. Giants Archives)

for Jack Sanford in 1959. Long after Gomez was an effective pitcher, Sanford won 24 games to help San Francisco reach the 1962 World Series.

Gomez later served as player-manager of the Santurce Crabbers in the Puerto Rican Winter League, once fining Dusty Baker $1,000 for missing a sign. Gomez was a serious zero-handicap golfer who lived in Puerto Rico during the winter and served as a golf pro in Quebec during the summer months.

Heinie Groh, Third Baseman (1912-13, 1922-26)

When Heinie Groh joined the New York Giants as a 22-year old rookie in 1912, many fans believed the 5-foot-8, 158-pounder was the team's batboy. Ironically, it was Groh's unique bottle-shaped bat that distinguished his career.

Groh had two stints with the Giants—1912-13 and 1922-26—primarily as a third baseman. New York manager John McGraw told Groh he needed to use a heavier bat in order to overcome his slightly-built frame, so Groh proceeded to get a weightier piece of lumber and whittle down the handle to resemble the neck of a bottle. Groh also utilized a unique batting stance in which he essentially faced the pitcher, held his hands apart and up on the handle and then slid his hands down as the delivery was being made. He looked as though he was preparing to bunt on every pitch (a skill he mastered), and he was an expert at hitting the ball to all fields.

Heinie Groh

After appearing in just 31 games for the Giants in 1912 and 1913, Groh was traded to the Cincinnati Reds along with pitcher Red Ames, outfielder Josh Devore and $20,000 in exchange for pitcher Art Fromme and infielder Eddie Grant on May 22, 1913.

Groh blossomed into a star, initially at second base and later at third. The quintessential right-handed leadoff batter led the National League in on-base percentage in 1917 (.385) and 1918 (.395). He managed the Reds for the final 10 games of the 1918 campaign (7-3 record) after Christy Mathewson resigned to serve in the army. Groh then helped Cincinnati win the scandal-ridden 1919 World Series over the Chicago (Black) White Sox five games to three.

In 1921 Groh held out all of spring training and early in the season over a salary dispute with Reds' president August Hermann. Groh declared he would sign only when Cincinnati would agree to trade him. A deal was worked out with the Giants, but commissioner Kenesaw M. Landis nixed it under the circumstances. Groh reported to the Reds and batted a career-high .331.

McGraw still wanted Groh and ultimately acquired him in exchange for outfielder George Burns, catcher Mike Gonzalez and $100,000 on December 7, 1921. Giants' fans didn't like seeing the popular Burns depart in favor of the expensive and temperamental Groh.

But Groh responded to his critics by helping the Giants, who won the 1921 World Series, capture N.L. pennants in 1922, 1923 and 1924. He led the league's third basemen in fielding percentage each year, including an N.L.-record .983 mark during the 1924 season. In the 1922 World Series, Groh batted a robust .474 as the Giants defeated the cross-town rival Yankees four games to none with one tie. Groh later put the impressive batting average on his license plate.

Groh batted .290 and .281 in 1923 and 1924, respectively, but he suffered a knee injury late in the 1924 season and never was the same. He was released by the Giants on September 16, 1926, and concluded his career with the N.L.-champion Pittsburgh Pirates in 1927.

In seven seasons with New York, Groh batted .276 with 155 RBI in 451 games. His 16-year career batting average was .292 with 566 RBI in 1,676 games, and he had a lifetime .967 fielding percentage. Groh led N.L. third basemen in fielding percentage and double plays six times (both tied for league records).

Following his big league days, Groh played and managed in the minor leagues and was a scout for the Giants (1934-40) and Brooklyn Dodgers.

Groh passed away August 22, 1968, in Cincinnati at the age of 78. His older brother, Lew, played in two games for the Philadelphia Athletics in 1919.

Tom Haller, Catcher (1961-67)

Tom Haller was a much better player than he was a general manager during a stormy five-year career in the Giants' front office from 1981-85. The former University of Illinois quarterback signed with the Giants for a $50,000 bonus in 1958 and developed into the best catcher in San Francisco history.

He was in the majors by 1961, but not before returning $2,500 of his bonus to the Illini because he skipped his senior year to turn pro. As early as 1961, Haller was being favorably compared with former Yankees' catcher Bill Dickey because of his 6-foot-4 frame and grace.

"Haller was by far the best catcher I ever threw to," Stu Miller once said. "He was smart, very good defensively and had a good arm." Giants farm director Carl Hubbell called him "an intellectual behind the plate."

On the pennant-winning 1962 team, Haller platooned with Ed Bailey, and the pair combined for 35 home runs and 100 RBI. He enjoyed his best success in 1966 with 27 homers and 67 RBI but was traded to the arch-rival Dodgers in 1968, a year in which he set a National League record for a catcher with 23 double plays.

"Hatch" homered off Whitey Ford in the 1962 World Series, batting .286. He was a member of three All-Star teams (1966-68) and the younger brother of Bill Haller, a long-time American League umpire.

Haller served as San Francisco's general manager during the frugal years of Bob Lurie's ownership. The Giants of the early 1980s couldn't afford draft picks, the farm system was in disarray and Haller's relationship with manager Frank Robinson was on the cool side.

Tom Haller

When the club set a dubious franchise record of 100 defeats in 1985, Haller was whisked out in a major housecleaning. He later served in the Chicago White Sox front office and then left the game to run a business in Southern California. He listed his top thrill as catching for Detroit with brother Bill the plate umpire in the 1972 American League Championship Series against the A's.

Jim Ray Hart, Third Baseman (1963-73)

A slugging third baseman who was denied greatness by injuries, Jim Ray Hart came up through the Giants' fruitful farm system and received a rude awakening to major league baseball in 1963. In his second major league game July 7, he was struck on the left shoulder blade by a Bob Gibson fastball after he had helped the Giants post a 15-inning victory in the first game of a double-header.

The Gibson blazer broke the shoulder blade, prompting trainer Frankie Bowman to declare, "That ball must have been traveling 150 miles an hour." Hart returned to action in

Jim Ray Hart (S.F. Giants Archives)

August and faced St. Louis again. This time, Curt Simmons beaned him in the ninth inning with St. Louis ahead 13-0. Jim Ray was taken to the hospital for observation merely four days after he came off the disabled list.

But resilience was a strength for Hart, who batted .286 with 31 home runs and 81 RBI as a rookie in 1964. "Hart is a natural .300 hitter if I ever saw one," batting coach Hank Sauer said. "His power is beyond our fondest expectations." In a five-year period from 1964-68, Hart averaged 27.8 homers and 89.4 RBI as a vital cog behind Willie Mays and Willie McCovey.

Then injuries started taking their toll and Hart finished a relatively brief career as the Yankees' designated hitter in 1973. Hart signed with the Giants out of Lenoir, North Carolina, in 1960 and embarked on a solid minor league career: .355 with 24 homers and 14 triples at Class-A Fresno in 1961, .337 at Springfield in 1962 and .312 for Triple-A Tacoma in 1963. He retired in the Sacramento, California, area.

Buck Herzog, Infielder (1908-09, 1911-13, 1916-17)

On one hand, Buck Herzog's cantankerous attitude was the reason the New York Giants traded him three times. On the other hand, it was the reason they acquired him twice.

An infielder—primarily at second and third base—for the Giants from 1908-09, 1911-13 and 1916-17, Herzog was not the most talented player. However, he made up for his shortcomings with aggressiveness and intelligence.

Herzog burst onto the scene in 1908 by batting a career-high .300 in 64 games. But after appearing in just 42 games the following year, the Giants traded him to the Boston Beaneaters in exchange for outfielder Beals Becker in December. Herzog had gotten in the disfavor of Giants' manager John McGraw when he refused to play in an exhibition game while recovering from an injury. He was fined and suspended.

Buck Herzog

In Boston, Herzog became a regular and was named team captain. Then on July 22, 1911, with the Giants in the National League pennant race, they brought Herzog back in a deal that sent shortstop Al Bridwell and first baseman Hank Gowdy to the Beaneaters. New York set an N.L. record with 347 stolen bases (Herzog had 22 in 69 games) and captured the league crown.

For the 1912 season, Herzog moved to third base and batted .263 for another pennant winner. He batted .400 (12-for-30) in the World Series against the Washington Senators. His 12 hits are a Giants' World Series record and tied for the most in an eight-game series in baseball history with Joe Jackson of the Chicago (Black) White Sox in 1919. Three players have had 13 hits in a seven-game series. The Giants lost the series four games to three with one tie.

Herzog batted at a .286 clip in 1913, but the right-handed swinger generally only played against left-handed pitchers while platooning at third base with Tillie Shafer. Following the season the Giants and White Sox went on a four-month world tour. Herzog did not make the trip, and Giants' owner Harry N. Hempstead traded him to the Cincinnati Reds along with catcher Grover Hartley for outfielder Bob Bescher on December 12, 1913. Although McGraw had not been consulted on the deal, he wasn't particularly upset because of his dislike for Herzog's temperament.

Not only did Herzog take over as the Reds' shortstop, but he also was named manager. He held the dual roles for three seasons before being sent back to New York along with outfielder Red Killefer in exchange for pitcher Christy Mathewson (who took over as manager), infielder Bill McKechnie and outfielder Edd Roush on July 20, 1916. Herzog was named team captain, and from September 7-30, 1916, the Giants won a franchise-record 26 consecutive games.

On March 30, 1917, Herzog and future Hall of Famer Ty Cobb of the Detroit Tigers became embroiled in a famous fight during an exhibition game in Dallas which culminated in Cobb's hotel room that evening. New York won another N.L. flag in 1917, but in the fifth game of the World Series against the White Sox (Chicago won the Fall Classic four games to two), McGraw and Herzog got into an argument. So the Giants traded Herzog for the third time—back to Boston—for pitcher Jesse Barnes and second baseman Larry Doyle on January 8, 1918. Herzog concluded his big league career with the Braves (1918-19) and Cubs (1919-20).

In his three stints with the Giants over seven seasons, Herzog batted .259 with 131 stolen bases in 602 games. His 13-year career batting average also was .259 in 1,493 games. He compiled a 165-226 record (.422 winning percentage) in three seasons as manager.

Herzog passed away September 4, 1953, in Baltimore at the age of 68. He had been hospitalized with tuberculosis in January of 1953 after being found penniless.

Chuck Hiller (S.F. Giants Archives)

Chuck Hiller, Second Baseman (1961-65)

Chuck Hiller had an undistinguished major league career—.243 in 704 games—but he enjoyed an Andy Warhol moment of glory that most players dream about. It was Game 4 of the 1962 World Series at Yankee Stadium, the bases were loaded in the seventh inning and Hiller was facing Yankees' reliever Marshall Bridges, a left-hander.

A left-handed hitter, Hiller lined a drive into the right field stands for the first grand-slam homer by a National Leaguer in World Series history. It provided to be the winning runs in a 7-3 Giants' victory. He finished with a .269 average and a .500 slugging percentage in that World Series, clearly his major league highlight.

"Bridges kept throwing me fastballs," Hiller recalled. "I hit that ball and ran like hell. I was sure it was a home run, but it was the excitement of it. I didn't know it was the first one by a National Leaguer. I didn't care about that. It was just a thrill because it put us in the lead. I hit three home runs in six hundred and

some times up that year, and to be able to do that when all those super hitters were playing. A Punch and Judy like me, and to do that? Hell, it made me feel good."

During the heated Giants-Dodgers rivalry that year, entertainer Danny Kaye sang a cornball song entitled, "A Miller-Hiller-Haller Holler-lujah Twist." It referred to Hiller and teammates Tom Haller and Stu Miller, and it ends with those Giants fielding a bunt, to wit:

"Cepeda runs to field the ball.

"So does Hiller—so does Miller.

"Miller hollers, 'Hiller!' Hiller hollers, 'Miller!'

"Haller hollers, 'Hiller!'—points to Miller with his fist.

"And that's the Miller-Hiller-Haller Holler-lujah twist."

Chuck was sold to the Mets in 1965 and batted a career-high .280 for them in 1966. The native of McHenry, Illinois, got his chance with the Giants after a trade for Don Blasingame proved to be a bust. The second base job was regarded as crucial to the club's success and Hiller worked hard to become a regular. He credited coach Whitey Lockman for improving his fielding and teammate Harvey Kuenn for helping him to hit line drives to all fields.

Carl Hubbell, Pitcher (1928-43)

Long before Shawn Estes, Steve Carlton or Warren Spahn, Carl Hubbell held the distinction of being baseball's premier left-handed pitcher.

During a 16-year career with the New York Giants from 1928-43, Hubbell posted a 253-154 record (.622 winning percentage) with a 2.98 ERA. From 1933-37, he averaged 23 wins (and just under 300 innings pitched) per season to more than live up to his nicknames of "King Karl" and the "Meal Ticket."

Hubbell was a two-time winner of the National League Most Valuable Player Award—in 1933 (23-12, 1.66 ERA) and 1936 (26-6, 2.31 ERA). From July 17, 1936-May 27, 1937, he won 24 consecutive games to set a baseball

Carl Hubbell (Brace Photo)

record that still stands today. The first 16 of those wins came during the second half of the 1936 campaign and helped the Giants come from behind to capture the National League pennant.

Two of Hubbell's greatest single-game performances included a no-hitter against the Pittsburgh Pirates at the Polo Grounds in New York on May 8, 1929, and a nowadays unheard of 1-0, 18-inning six-hitter (with 12 strikeouts and no walks) over the St. Louis Cardinals at the Polo Grounds on July 2, 1933. Hubbell, in fact, hurled a Giants' franchise-record 46.1 consecutive scoreless innings during the 1993 season.

The author of a nasty screwball that he was encouraged to throw by manager John McGraw, Hubbell was equally brilliant pitching in the limelight. In the 1934 All-Star Game at the Polo Grounds, which he started for the N.L., Hubbell made headlines by striking out five consecutive future Hall of Famers: Babe Ruth, Lou Gehrig and Jimmie Foxx to end the

first inning and Al Simmons and Joe Cronin to begin the second. Hubbell was selected to five straight All-Star Games between 1933-37.

Hubbell pitched in three World Series (1933, 1936 and 1937) with a 4-2 record and a snappy 1.79 ERA. In the 1933 Fall Classic against the Washington Senators (won by the Giants four games to one), he earned a pair of complete-game victories (4-2 and 2-1) while not allowing an earned run in 20 innings pitched.

On the Giants' franchise lists, Hubbell ranks second in wins and innings pitched (3,590.1); third in games started (431) and shutouts (36); and fourth in games (535) and complete games (260) and strikeouts (1,677).

Following his retirement in 1943, Hubbell went to work in the Giants' front office, first in player development (1943-77) and subsequently in scouting (1978-85). He was inducted into the National Baseball Hall of Fame in 1947. Hubbell's No. 11 is one of just nine uniform numbers to be retired by the Giants' franchise.

Hubbell passed away November 21, 1988, in Scottsdale, Arizona, at the age of 85.

Monte Irvin, Outfielder (1949-55)

Like so many other African-American baseball players, Monte Irvin was a victim of the times. He did not reach the Major Leagues until the age of 30, with the New York Giants in 1949 (two years after Jackie Robinson became the first player to break the color barrier).

Irvin, an all-star with the Newark Eagles of the Negro Leagues, signed with the Giants on the recommendation of club vice president Chub Feeney. Both had attended Orange High School in New Jersey, where Irvin earned all-state honors in baseball, basketball and football. Irvin, primarily an outfielder for New York, was a superb, all-around player. He could hit for average and power, was a skilled fielder and possessed an outstanding arm.

On July 5, 1949, Irvin and infielder Hank Thompson were called up from the minor

Monte Irvin (S.F. Giants Archives)

World Series champion Giants, who swept the Cleveland Indians four games to none to capture the crown.

During his career with the Giants from 1949-55, Irvin batted .296 with 84 home runs and 393 RBI in 653 games. He played for the Chicago Cubs in 1956 and then retired.

Irvin, who attended Lincoln University in Oxford, Pennsylvania, for two years, had two stints in the Negro Leagues (1939-42 and 1946-48) and compiled a lifetime .345 batting average. He played in the Mexican League in 1943 and served in the U.S. Army from 1943-45.

Following his playing days, the popular Irvin worked as a public relations representative in the baseball commissioner's office. Irvin was inducted into the National Baseball Hall of Fame in 1973. He became the fourth player to be selected by a special committee on the Negro Leagues (following Satchel Paige, Josh Gibson and Buck Leonard). Irvin currently makes his home in Homosassa, Florida.

Travis Jackson, Infielder (1922-36)

Travis Jackson was a classic example of one person's misfortune being another's opportunity.

In June of 1923, New York Giants' shortstop Dave Bancroft was stricken with pneumonia. Jackson, who played for the Giants from 1922-36, was inserted into the starting lineup and became a fixture. On August 8, 1923, he drove in eight runs with two singles, a double and a home run against the Cincinnati Reds at Crosley Field in Cincinnati. Manager John McGraw was so impressed with Jackson that he traded Bancroft to the Boston Braves (along with outfielders Bill Cunningham and Casey Stengel in exchange for pitcher Joe Oeschger and outfielder Billy Southworth) on November 12, 1923.

Jackson had been recommended to McGraw by Kid Elberfeld, who was his minor league manager at Little Rock (Arkansas) in the Southern Association during the 1922 season. McGraw sent his personal confidant (and one-

leagues, and three days later they became the first African-Americans to play for the Giants in a game against the Brooklyn Dodgers at Ebbets Field in Brooklyn.

In 1951 Irvin was instrumental in New York winning the National League pennant. He topped the team with career highs in triples (11), home runs (24) and RBI (league-leading 121) to go with a .312 batting average. In Game 1 of the World Series against the cross-town rival Yankees, Irvin went 4-for-5 and stole home in the first inning. He went on to bat a series-best .458 (11-for-24), but it was not enough as the Giants lost the Subway Series four games to two.

A fractured right ankle suffered in a pre-season exhibition game in Denver limited Irvin to just 46 games during the 1952 campaign. He was selected to the All-Star Game at Shibe Park in Philadelphia but could not play because of the injury. The following year Irvin batted a career-high .329 with 21 home runs and 97 RBI. He hit 19 homers for the 1954

Travis Jackson

sively, "Stonewall" possessed great range with a strong arm and a quick release.

From 1925-27 Jackson was part of an infield that featured six future Hall of Famers: George Kelly and Bill Terry at first base; Kelly, Frankie Frisch and Rogers Hornsby at second; and Fred Lindstrom at third.

Jackson put together many productive seasons. He batted .327 in 1926 and .318 with 14 home runs and 98 RBI in 1927. The next two years he established career highs with 35 doubles and 21 home runs, respectively. He was named to *The Sporting News'* Major League All-Star team in 1927, 1928 and 1929. In 1930 Jackson batted at a career-best .339 clip and, along with Terry (.401), second baseman Hughie Critz (.265) and Lindstrom (.379), he was a member of the best-hitting infield in baseball history (a composite .349 average). Jackson paced National League shortstops in fielding percentage in 1929 (.969) and 1931 (.970). He led the way in assists four times, in total chances three times and in double plays twice.

Injuries to both knees limited Jackson to just 52 games in 1932 and 53 in 1933, but he came back strong the following year and was selected to the All-Star Game at the Polo Grounds in New York. He finished the season with 16 home runs and a career-high 101 RBI.

During his 15-year career in New York, Jackson batted .291 with 291 doubles, 86 triples, 135 home runs and 929 RBI in 1,656 games. He played 1,326 games at shortstop and 307 at third base, plus one at both second base and in the outfield. Jackson ranks among the franchise leaders in games (5th); at-bats (5th, 6,086); doubles (5th); RBI (5th); hits (6th, 1,768); and triples (10th). He is tops among shortstops with 2,877 putouts and 4,635 assists. Jackson was the Giants' team captain for several years.

Following his playing days Jackson served as a minor league manager as a coach for the Giants in 1939 and 1940 and again in 1947 and 1948. He battled tuberculosis for several years. Jackson was inducted into the National

man scouting department) Dick Kinsella to watch Jackson and by the end of the campaign the 18-year-old Jackson was in New York.

Jackson quickly fit into the Giants' winning formula (they won four consecutive National League pennants from 1921-24 and were world champions in 1921 and 1922) and developed into a quality, all-around performer. An accomplished bunter who also could hit for power, he batted over .300 on six occasions and had more than 70 RBI eight times. Defen-

Baseball Hall of Fame in 1982 by the Veterans Committee. He passed away July 27, 1987, in his hometown of Waldo, Arkansas, at the age of 83.

Larry Jansen, Pitcher (1947-54)

This underrated right-handed pitcher had a long and distinguished association with San Francisco and the Giants from 1941 through the 1971 season. Larry Jansen was a minor league pitching sensation with the defunct San Francisco Seals of the Pacific Coast League from 1941-46, pitched for the New York Giants in 1947-54 and served as a minor league coach until he became the Giants' pitching coach from 1961-71.

An Oregon native, Jansen became a pro at age 19 and promptly went 20-7 with a tidy 2.19 ERA for Salt Lake City of the Pioneer League in 1940. One year later, he was a precocious 16-10 for the Seals in a league regarded just a notch below major league quality.

"I kept pretty busy around the family farm and really didn't think that much about baseball," Jansen said. "I always was a good hitter, but pitching appealed to me more. I was born with control. When I was with the Seals, (manager) Lefty O'Doul developed my confidence and (catcher/coach) Larry Woodall helped me in the technique of pitching."

When post-war baseball boomed in 1946, Jansen posted one of the greatest seasons in modern minor league history. He was a remarkable 30-6 with a 1.57 ERA while working 321 innings for the champion Seals. "The Giants had an agreement with the Seals and had first call on my services," Jansen recalled. "They paid something like $75,000 and four players for me."

Major league success was instant, too. As a rookie in 1947, he led the National League with an .808 winning percentage, going 21-5 with a Giants' powerhouse in New York. "Jansen's control is so smooth that in achieving his reputation for an ability to place the ball where he aims, his other talents were glossed over," manager Mel Ott once said. "By the time he reached the Polo Grounds, people had him marked as a control pitcher only. But, as a matter of fact, he has a great deal of speed."

Jansen originally was a semi-pro shortstop, which partly explains why he was regarded as such a good hitter for a pitcher. All of Larry's talents were on display in the 1950 All-Star Game at Pittsburgh. He singled and worked five shutout innings, yielding one hit and no walks. His six strikeouts included Ted Williams, Larry Doby, George Kell and Jerry Coleman.

He averaged 19.2 victories in his first five seasons, peaking in 1951 with a 23-11 record and a 3.04 ERA for the pennant-winning Giants. But he was 0-2 as the Yankees won the World Series four games to two and gradually lost his effectiveness, finishing his Giants' career a solid 120-86.

As the San Francisco pitching coach, he was blessed with youngsters like Hall of Famers Juan Marichal, Gaylord Perry and Cy

Larry Jansen (S.F. Giants Archives)

Young Award winner Mike McCormick. He also guided crafty veterans Jack Sanford, Billy O'Dell and Billy Pierce to 59 victories as the Giants won their first San Francisco pennant in 1962.

Sam Jones, Pitcher (1959-61)

Called "Sad Sam" for his mournful appearance and "Toothpick" because he liked to pitch with one dangling from his mouth, Sam Jones became San Francisco's first 20-game winner by going 21-15 with a league-leading 2.83 ERA in 1959, the club's second year on the West Coast. He was the highest rated of the Giants in the Most Valuable Player voting.

Despite some success, he was known as a tough-luck pitcher. With the Giants in 1959, he would have had a no-hitter at the Los Angeles Coliseum on June 30, but official scorer Charlie Park stubbornly refused to change a questionable call. Jones carried a no-hitter into the eighth inning and had two outs when Jim Gilliam bounced a ball over the pitcher's head and charging shortstop Andre Rodgers misplayed the pickup. It was ruled a hit, creating a one-hitter in a 2-0 Giants' victory.

"If I fielded the ball cleanly, I would have thrown him out," Rodgers said. Park attempted to console the teary-eyed Jones, telling him: "I'm sorry, Sam, but if I had to call it again, I'd still call it a hit. Gilliam would have beaten the throw." Jones wasn't convinced, adding: "Man, I guess they just don't want no-hitters thrown here. Imagine anyone calling that one a hit."

In his final start of the season, Jones had one more chance. He held the St. Louis Cardinals hitless, at Busch Stadium on September 26, but it was an abbreviated no-hitter because a storm washed the game out with two outs in the eighth inning. In April of 1960, the trend continued. Jones pitched 7.2 hitless innings against the Chicago Cubs and had a string of 17 straight outs before pinch-hitter Walt Moryn connected for a home run.

Jones did pitch a nine-inning no-hitter, however, for the Chicago Cubs against the Pittsburgh Pirates on May 12, 1955. After joining the Giants in a trade for future National League president Bill White, Sam had the distinction of starting the first game at Candlestick Park, posting a 3-1 victory over the Cardinals, yielding a home run to Leon Wagner.

"Sad Sam" started his career in the Negro Leagues and reportedly learned to throw a wicked curve from Satchel Paige. His career was marked by wildness. In 1955, his first full N.L. season, he lost 20 games and led the league with 198 strikeouts and 185 walks, repeating in 1956 with 176 strikeouts and 115 walks. Jones' legendary wildness produced 822 walks in 1,643.1 innings, but he also had 1,376 strikeouts in a 102-101 career.

During his 1955 no-hitter against the Pirates, he walked the bases loaded with nobody out in the ninth inning and was almost re-

Sam Jones (S.F. Giants Archives)

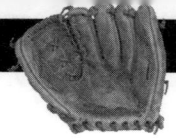
moved by manager Stan Hack. Then he struck out Dick Groat, Roberto Clemente and Frank Thomas. Jones' tough luck continued after his retirement. He died of cancer at age 45 in his native West Virginia.

Tim Keefe, Pitcher (1885-89, 1891)

Credit Tim Keefe for leading the New York Giants to their first world championship.

Keefe, a right-handed pitcher, was instrumental in the Giants winning the National League pennant in 1888 by going 35-12 with a 1.74 ERA. He paced the league in wins, ERA, winning percentage (.745), shutouts (8) and strikeouts (333) while pitching 434.1 innings. From June 23-August 10, Keefe won 19 consecutive games, a major league record since tied by Rube Marquard of the Giants during the 1912 season.

Then in the World Series against the St. Louis Browns, Keefe recorded four complete-game victories as the Giants captured the crown six games to four (they actually won six games to two, but the teams agreed to play two additional players' benefit contests). In 35 innings pitched, Keefe surrendered a mere 18 hits, two earned runs (for a minuscule 0.51 ERA) and nine walks with 30 strikeouts.

Keefe, nicknamed "Sir Timothy" for his royal-like pitching and mannerisms, played for the Giants from 1885-89 and in 1891. He began his career with the Troy (New York) Trojans from 1880-82, then joined the New York Metro-

politans in 1883 and 1884. He had a record-low 0.86 ERA in 1880 and won 41 games in 1883.

In 1885 Keefe was transferred from the Metropolitans of the American Association to the Giants (both teams were owned by John B. Day) and posted a 32-13 record (.711 winning percentage) with a league-leading 1.58 ERA. In 398 innings pitched, he allowed just 297 hits and 103 walks with 230 strikeouts. He completed 45 of the 46 games he started. New York finished with an 85-27 record (a franchise-best .759 winning percentage) but wound up two games behind the pennant-winning Chicago White Stockings.

The following year Keefe overtook Mickey Welch as the ace of the pitching staff and won a career-high 42 games (against 20 losses) to tie for the N.L. lead with Charles "Lady" Baldwin of the Detroit Wolverines. He topped the league with 62 complete games (in 64 starts) and 540 innings pitched while compiling a 2.53 ERA. Keefe went 28-13, 3.31 ERA in 1889 as the Giants repeated as world champions over the cross-town rival Brooklyn Bridegrooms.

In 1890 Keefe was one of 12 Giants who jumped to the newly-formed Players League, which was organized by New York's John Montgomery Ward. Keefe, who ironically played for the New York Giants, was named league secretary because he could take shorthand. That year he became the second pitcher to win 300 career games (joining Pud Galvin).

Tim Keefe (National Baseball Library and Archive)

But the Players League survived for only one season, and Keefe returned to the N.L. Giants the following year. He concluded his 14-year career with the Philadelphia Phillies from 1891-93.

Keefe's six-year statistics with the Giants included a 173-82 record (.678 winning percentage) with a 2.53 ERA in 272 games. He ranks among the franchise leaders in complete games (5th, 251); wins (6th); strikeouts (7th, 1,278); games started (9th, 269); innings pitched (9th, 2,270); and shutouts (10th, 22). On baseball's all-time lists, he is third in complete games (553), eighth in wins (341), 12th in innings pitched (5,052.1), 19th in games started (593) and 20th in strikeouts (2,521). Keefe is regarded as the originator of the change of pace delivery (changeup) and kept detailed records of opposing batters.

Following his playing days, Keefe worked as an N.L. umpire. He passed away April 23, 1933, in his hometown of Cambridge, Massachusetts, at the age of 76. Keefe was inducted into the National Baseball Hall of Fame in 1964 by the Veterans Committee.

George Kelly, First Baseman (1915-17, 1919-26)

George Kelly was the first modern-day power hitter for the New York Giants.

Primarily a first baseman for the Giants from 1915-17 and from 1919-26, Kelly appeared in just 109 games during his first four seasons in New York (he also played in eight games with the Pittsburgh Pirates in 1917). He initially got a chance to play on a regular basis late during the 1919 season when Giants' manager John McGraw became convinced that first baseman Hal Chase was throwing games.

Nicknamed "Highpockets" for his 6-foot-4, 190-pound frame, Kelly became a fixture and tied for the National League lead with 94 RBI in 1920 (with Rogers Hornsby of the St. Louis Cardinals). The following year he became the first player in franchise history to hit 20 home runs. He topped the N.L. with a career-high 23 and also had a personal best of 42 doubles to go with a .308 batting average and 122 RBI. Prior to 1921 the most homers hit by a New York player was 17 by Roger Connor during the 1887 campaign.

Over the next three seasons, Kelly batted a career-high .328 with 17 home runs and 107 RBI in 1922; .307 with 16 homers and 107 RBI in 1923; and .324 with 21 homers and a career-high and league-leading 136 RBI in 1924.

When Kelly first came to the Giants, McGraw considered making him a pitcher. Kelly, who pitched in one game in 1917 and won, had a decent fastball—but had difficulty throwing a curve—so McGraw had him take all the cutoff throws from the outfield. He struggled defensively early in his career but went on to develop into a solid performer. Kelly

George Kelly

led the N.L. in putouts and assists on three occasions, double plays twice and fielding percentage in 1926 (.993). He holds the N.L. record for putouts in a season with 1,759 in 1920.

Kelly sealed the Giants' 1921 world championship over the cross-town rival Yankees in the eighth game (they played best-of-nine) at the Polo Grounds in New York when he threw out Yankees' second baseman Aaron Ward attempting to go from first to third on a ground out with the tying run with two outs in the bottom of the ninth inning. The Giants won the game 1-0 and the World Series five games to three.

Among Kelly's top single-game performances were two inside-the-park home runs against the Boston Braves at Braves Field on April 29, 1922; three consecutive homers (in the third, fourth and fifth innings) as part of a 5-for-5 performance against the Chicago Cubs at Wrigley Field in Chicago on September 17, 1923; and three home runs with eight RBI against the Cincinnati Reds at the Polo Grounds on June 14, 1924. From July 11-16, 1924, Kelly set an N.L. record (since tied by three other players) with seven home runs over a six-game stretch.

With the emergence of first baseman Billy Terry, Kelly moved to second base in 1925. He returned to first in 1926 before being traded to the Reds along with $100,000 in exchange for outfielder Edd Roush on February 9, 1927. Kelly's statistics with the Giants included a .301 batting average, 1,270 hits, 218 doubles, 52 triples, 123 home runs and 762 RBI in 1,136 games. He ranks 10th on the Giants' career RBI list.

Kelly played for the Reds from 1927-30 and then for the Cubs (1930) and Brooklyn Dodgers (1932). In 16 seasons overall, he batted .297 with 148 home runs and 1,020 RBI in 1,622 games. Kelly served as a coach for the Reds (1935-37 and 1947-48) and Braves (1938-43). He was inducted into the National

Baseball Hall of Fame in 1973 by the Veterans Committee.

Kelly passed away October 13, 1984, in Burlingame, California, at the age of 89.

Jeff Kent, Second Baseman (1997-2002)

It's not often a "steal" when you trade away a superstar, but that's exactly what happened when the Giants swapped popular slugger Matt Williams to the Cleveland Indians following the 1996 season for pitcher Julian Tavarez, shortstop Jose Vizcaino and second baseman Jeff Kent—possibly in order of importance at the time.

Kent, who played college ball at the University of California, immediately felt right at home and instantly showed his appreciation. Proving to be a capable cleanup hitter behind Barry Bonds, he belted a career-high 38 doubles and had 29 homers and 121 RBI in 1997 as the replacement for Robby Thompson, who had started at second base since 1986.

For an encore, Kent improved in 1998 and attained career highs with a .297 average, 31 home runs and 128 RBI—despite missing nearly one month with a knee sprain. Only Hall of Famer Rogers Hornsby had more offensive success by a second baseman in back-to-back seasons than Kent, who accumulated 75 doubles, 60 home runs and 249 RBI in 1997-98.

He became the first second baseman since Jackie Robinson in 1949 to notch at least 120 RBI, and he did it three times with the Giants. Kent had 79 RBI in the second half of the 1998 season, more than Mark McGwire or Sammy Sosa during their record chase. He finished with a career-high 128 RBI in 137 games and continued to form one of the game's best one-two punches with Barry Bonds.

They were the Giants' most feared tandem over a longer period than the days of Willie Mays, Orlando Cepeda and Willie McCovey. In their six seasons as teammates, Kent and

Bonds averaged 225 RBI and 75.7 home runs. Kent, like Bonds, thrived when the club moved into Pacific Bell Park in 2000, excelling in a ballpark designed for pitching more than hitting.

Kent batted a career-high .334 in 2000 and added 33 home runs and 125 RBI while edging Bonds for MVP honors. Solid numbers followed in 2001, including a franchise-record 49 doubles, but Kent's 2002 was in doubt when a wrist injury suffered in a spring training motorcycle mishap knocked him out of the opener. With something to prove, he responded with a career-best 37 homers and a .313 average.

Differences with management contributed to his departure as a free agent following the World Series, but not before he set standards as a slugging second baseman. He had at least

Jeff Kent (S.F. Giants Archives)

100 RBI in each of his six seasons with the club, a streak exceeded only by Mays' eight straight in S.F. Giants' history. Only Tony Lazzeri and Charlie Gehringer, with seven, had more 100-RBI seasons as second basemen.

Kent's 689 RBI since 1997 were surpassed only by more heralded sluggers like Sosa (824), Manny Ramirez (752), Jeff Bagwell (732, Alex Rodriguez (728), Rafael Palmeiro (727) and Jason Giambi (693) over that span. Kent, who left to join Bagwell in the Houston Astros' lineup, has been an offensive force ever since he batted a school-record .500 as a prep senior at Huntington Beach, Cal.

But nobody could have imagined the extent of his prowess. Along with Hall of Famer Rogers Hornsby, Kent is the only second baseman with three 30-plus homer seasons. If he remains at the position, he would seriously threaten Ryne Sandberg's career home run record (277) for a second baseman and Gehringer's mark of 1,427 RBI. Kent, who owns a ranch near his new ballclub, left S.F. with 253 homers and 1,007 RBI.

He played shortstop on Cal team which reached the 1988 College World Series. He remembered his alma mater by donating $500 for each RBI to Cal's women's athletic department in 1998, also raising $64,000 for scholarships, not including matching contributions from others. He was selected in 20th round by the Toronto Blue Jays in 1989 and reached the majors with them in 1992 prior to a trade to the New York Mets for David Cone.

Jeff had a reputation as a hard-nosed player who wasn't especially popular in New York despite flashes off power. He had 21 homers and 80 RBI in 1993, batted .292 in 1994 and added 20 homers in 1995. He was batting .290 when the Mets traded him and Vizcaino to Cleveland for Carlos Baerga and Alvaro Espinoza in July of 1996. What were they thinking?

Dave Kingman, Infielder/Outfielder (1971-74)

"Kong" went on to a productive 442-homer major league career after hitting his first 77 with the Giants. The Illinois native was drafted by the club off an NCAA national championship Southern California team along with pitcher Jim Barr. Dave Kingman was an intimidating, 6-foot-6 college pitcher when he wasn't belting home runs. At the time, the legendary Rod Dedeaux labeled Kingman the finest player he had ever coached at USC.

Kingman reached the majors with the Giants late in the 1971 season after totaling 41 homers and 140 RBI over 165 minor league games with Amarillo and Phoenix over two seasons. He had 32 hits and 64 total bases in 115 at-bats for the Giants in 1971, helping them hold off the Dodgers for the division title.

Dave Kingman (S.F. Giants Archives)

His home run on the final day enabled Juan Marichal to defeat the host Padres, giving the Giants a one-game victory. The first of his six homers that season was a grand-slam off Dave Giusti of the Pirates. The next day, he hit two homers off Dock Ellis. Kingman's first full major league season produced a team-leading 29 homers and 83 RBI in 1972.

But his high strikeout totals and a lowly .225 average set the tone for a career that featured a lot more power than consistency. He concluded his career with the 1986 A's, appropriately hitting 35 home runs with a .210 average in an all-or-nothing finale.

At his best, Kingman delivered a league-leading 48 home runs and 115 RBI with a .288 average for the 1979 Chicago Cubs. He also led the N.L. with 37 homers for the 1982 Mets. An avid outdoorsman, Kingman retired to Lake Tahoe following a playing career that was full of pop and promise.

Mike Krukow, Pitcher (1983-89)

When the Philadelphia Phillies acquired Joe Morgan and Al Holland for Mark Davis and Krukow after the 1982 season, the Phillies reaped immediate benefits—a championship in 1983. But Krukow played a prominent role as the Giants' big winner (66-56) of the 1980s, including a career-topping 20-9 season with a 3.05 ERA in 1986.

He posted his 20th win against the Dodgers on the final day of the season, thanks partly to Candy Maldonado's grand slam homer. An ecstatic Krukow became the Giants' first 20-game winner since Ron Bryant in 1993 and the first San Francisco right-hander to do it since Gaylord Perry in 1970.

"That was a remarkable season because we turned it around and became a winner after losing 100 games in 1985," Krukow recalled. "Winning 20 has become more important to me through the years. I'm introduced as `20-game winner Mike Krukow.' They don't do that when you win 19."

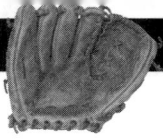

Mike Krukow (S.F. Giants Archives)

Harvey Kuenn, Outfielder (1961-65)

Harvey Kuenn started his career as a hot-hitting shortstop with the Detroit Tigers and finished it as manager of the 1982 pennant-winning Milwaukee Brewers, also known as "Harvey's Wallbangers." In between, he enjoyed five seasons with the Giants as an outfielder, helping them to a pennant in 1962.

Kuenn attended the University of Wisconsin and didn't require much minor league seasoning before hitting his stride with the Tigers. He batted .308 with a league-leading 209 hits in a Rookie of the Year campaign of 1953. He shifted to the outfield in 1958 and won a batting championship with a .353 average in 1959. Still, he was traded to Cleveland for Rocky Colavito prior to the 1960 season and was with the Giants one year later following a trade that sent Johnny Antonelli and Willie Kirkland to the Indians.

Injuries contributed to his decline thereafter, and "Kruke" was a mere 16-13 over the next three seasons despite being on division champions in 1987 and 1989. He then repaired to the broadcast booth, where he concluded his ninth season as an analyst for Giants' games in 1999. Krukow uses the same enthusiasm as a broadcaster that marked his playing career, which began when he was drafted in the eighth round by the Chicago Cubs in 1973.

The Long Beach, California, native spurned the California Angels, who made him a 32nd-round pick in 1970 and instead attended Cal Poly San Luis Obispo, where he was 25-7 with a 1.93 ERA during his college career. He pitched for the Cubs in parts of six seasons before having success with a 13-11 record and a 3.12 ERA for the 1992 Phillies.

Harvey Kuenn (S.F. Giants Archives)

181

Harvey, usually with a wad of tobacco in a bulging cheek, became a popular Giant and was a favorite of sportswriters because he had a ready quip. "He thinks and talks baseball all the time," owner Horace Stoneham observed. "He's aggressive and a team man. He has to be a great acquisition for us."

Kuenn recaptured some magic with a .304 average for the 1962 champions, but was a poor 1 for 12 in the World Series. A member of eight consecutive American League All-Star squads, Kuenn finished with a .303 lifetime average and 2,092 hits. Poor health in retirement cost him a leg amputation. He managed Milwaukee with a wooden leg and succumbed to cancer in 1988.

Hal Lanier, Infielder (1964-71)

Long before Barry Bonds played in the clubhouse while father Bobby starred afield, Hal Lanier was doing the same thing. His father, Max, was a pitcher for the New York Giants, and young Hal would dress in a uniform at the Polo Grounds and work out with the club. By 1961 Hal was a highly-touted prep athlete and received numerous scholarship offers.

In a package deal, however, the Laniers received a $50,000 bonus and Max secured a three-year scouting contract for Hal's services. He joined the Giants as a second baseman in 1964 and caught broadcaster Russ Hodge's eye. "The kid has more range at second base than any Giant

I've seen since Burgess Whitehead—more than Eddie Stanky, more than Davey Williams," Hodges said.

One year later, Lanier was switched to shortstop and was a regular there for five seasons until Chris Speier came along in 1971. He batted .274 in 1964, but that was his high point in a spotty career which resulted in a .228 lifetime average. He became a switch-hitter in 1968, but it didn't help.

Lanier made huge strides for epilepsy awareness. Hal had the disease, occasionally suffering seizures while switching from hot to cold water in showers. He wore a medal marked "epilepsy" and displayed it on a necklace, proving the disease wasn't a detriment to a professional athletic career. He later enjoyed a second career as a manager, mostly with the Houston Astros.

Gary Lavelle, Pitcher (1974-84)

Gary Lavelle was an unspectacular starter in the Giants' farm system but blossomed as a major league reliever one he reached the Giants in 1974. He holds the San Francisco record with 647 career appearances—110 more than Greg Minton's 537. He also had the Giants' career saves record with 127 until Rod

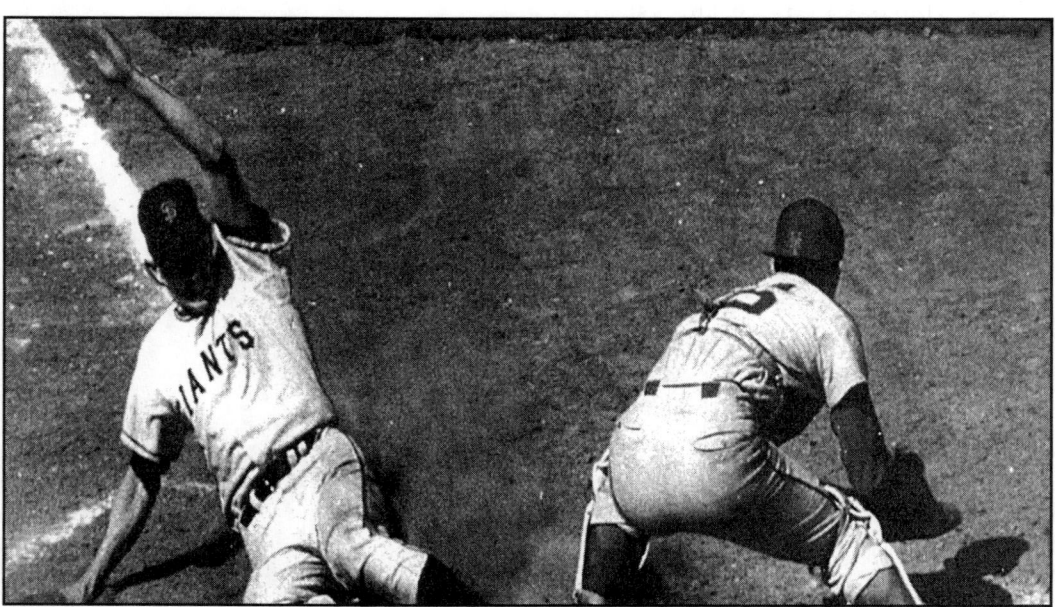

Hal Lanier

Gary Lavelle (S.F. Giants Archives)

Beck passed him and finished with 199. He started merely three major league games in a 14-year career that ended with the Blue Jays and the A's.

Lavelle played an integral role in the Giants' controversial Christian movement of the late 1970s, heading a group that included Jack Clark, Bob Knepper and Rob Andrews. "I found a great void in my life," he explained. "Something was really missing. I was playing winter ball in Venezuela in 1995, and I was born again. Back with the Giants, the guys noticed how I had changed, and guys began asking about the changes in my life. I got to share things with a few guys in our chapel program."

"Pudge" was drafted in 34th round by the Giants following a successful prep career in Bethlehem, Pennsylvania. In his third pro season, he pitched a no-hitter for Decatur against Clinton in the Midwest League and spent eight years in the minors before an 8-16 record and 5.24 ERA for Triple-A Phoenix convinced the Giants the left-hander was better suited to relief.

His bullpen success was immediate. He won at least 10 games out of the bullpen in three seasons with the Giants and posted ERA's under 3.00 on eight different occasions. Lavelle's 2.06 ERA in 73 games in 1977 was his stingiest, and he won a career-high 13 games over 67 appearances in 1978. Three times he collected 20 saves (1977, 1979 and 1983).

Hank Leiber, Outfielder (1933-38, 1942)

On June 6, 1941, the New York Giants donned protective batting helmets for the first time. It was four years too late for Hank Leiber.

An outfielder for the Giants from 1933-38 and in 1942, Leiber's career was curtailed by a severe beanball from hard-throwing rookie Bob Feller of the Cleveland Indians in an exhibition game in New Orleans on April 4, 1937. Leiber also was hit in the head with a pitch in 1941 as a member of the Chicago Cubs while facing former Giants' teammate Cliff Melton.

Leiber, an aggressive right-handed batter known for his plate-crowding stance, was discovered by former Giants' pitcher Art Nehf (1919-26) in Arizona. After seeing limited playing time his first two seasons in New York, Leiber became the Giants' regular center fielder in 1935. He responded by posting career highs of a .331 batting average, 37 doubles and 107 RBI (fifth in the National League) to go with 22 home runs. On August 24, 1935, Leiber belted two homers in the second inning of a game against the Chicago Cubs at the Polo Grounds in New York.

The following year Leiber dropped off to .279 with nine homers and 67 RBI as New York won the N.L. pennant. He rebounded with a solid spring training in 1937 before the initial beaning that left him plagued with severe headaches. Leiber appeared in just 51 games during the regular season but came on strong in the World Series against the cross-town rival Yankees by batting .364 with two RBI in three games. The Giants lost the series four games to one.

Leiber continued to be saddled in 1938 (.269 batting average in 98 games), but he still

was selected to the All-Star Game at Crosley Field in Cincinnati. He was retired as a pinch-hitter for N.L. starting pitcher Johnny Vander Meer in the bottom of the third inning.

On December 6, 1938, the Giants traded Leiber to the Chicago Cubs along with shortstop Dick Bartell and catcher Gus Mancuso in exchange for outfielder Frank Demaree, shortstop Bill Jurges and catcher Ken O'Dea. Leiber found new life with the Cubs and batted .310 with a career-high 24 home runs and 88 RBI in 1939 and .302 with 17 round-trippers and 86 RBI in 1940. He was selected to the All-Star Game in 1940 and 1941 but did not play in either Mid-Summer Classic. Then lightning struck for the second time when Melton's pitch resulted in Leiber sustaining a severe concussion and being hospitalized. Melton was so concerned for Leiber that he spent the entire night at the hospital waiting for his former teammate to regain consciousness. Leiber opened his eyes the following morning.

After an ineffective 1941 season, Leiber was traded back to the Giants for pitcher Bob Bowman on December 4, 1941. Former New York manager Bill Terry had fallen in disfavor with Leiber, but Terry was replaced by Mel Ott two days prior to the deal. Ott and Leiber had gotten along well as teammates during Leiber's first stint with the Giants.

But Leiber managed just a .218 batting average in 58 games in 1942 and retired at the conclusion of the campaign at just 31 years of age. Before hanging it up, though, he made the

Hank Leiber (Brace Photo)

only pitching appearance of his career September 25, 1912, against the Philadelphia Phillies at the Polo Grounds. The Giants had clinched third place and couldn't climb any higher, so Leiber went to the mound and threw a complete game in a 9-1 loss.

In seven seasons with the Giants, Leiber batted .287 with 53 home runs and 319 RBI in 531 games. His 10-year career statistics included a .288 batting average with 101 homers and 518 RBI in 813 games.

Leiber passed away November 8, 1993, in Tucson, Arizona, at the age of 82.

Johnnie LeMaster, Shortstop (1975-85)

A good-field, no-hit shortstop, Johnnie LeMaster might have been the best fielder at the position in San Francisco history. The rangy 6-foot-2 Ohio native was so highly-touted out of high school in Kentucky, he was the sixth player selected in the 1973 draft. His fielding prowess made him a minor league standout, and he was a Pacific Coast League (AAA) All-Star after batting a career-high .292 for Phoenix in 1975.

But he never came close to that average in the majors, attaining a high of .253 in 1981. His deft glove work kept him a regular from 1977-84 as a prototypical light-hitting defensive whiz. His skinny frame earned him the "Bones" nickname, and he definitely had a sense of humor.

Shortly after fans were riding him for lackluster play, he showed up at Candlestick Park with a uniform jersey that had "BOO" em-

Johnnie LeMaster (S.F. Giants Archives)

blazoned on the back. The fans got a kick out of the self-deprecating humor, but general manager Spec Richardson wasn't amused, banning that uniform.

One of LeMaster's few offensive highlights occurred in his first major league at-bat in 1975. "Bones" hit a home run, but what really made it unusual was that it was of the inside-the-park variety. It was his first of 22 lifetime homers. He was named the shortstop on the Giants' 25th Anniversary Dream Team in 1982.

Jeffrey Leonard, Outfielder (1981-88)

Perhaps the most important ingredient to the San Francisco Giants winning the 1987 National League West Division championship (just two years after losing a franchise-record 100 games) was left fielder Jeffrey Leonard.

Certainly the maturity of budding all-stars like first baseman Will Clark and second

baseman Robby Thompson was crucial, and the mid-season acquisitions of veteran pitchers like Dave Dravecky, Rich Reuschel and Don Robinson were vital, but Leonard's acceptance of manager Roger Craig's "Humm Baby" attitude was what landed the Giants in first place.

Leonard, who played for the Giants from 1981-88, essentially controlled the clubhouse and thrived on challenging the status quo. When Craig and general manager Al Rosen arrived in the Bay Area late in the 1985 season and were given a "mandate for change" by owner Bob Lurie, things most assuredly changed. Out was the country club atmosphere and losing mentality; in was a disciplined work ethic and positive frame of mind.

After buying into the changes and overcoming a right wrist injury in 1986, Leonard posted quality numbers in 1987: a .280 batting average with a career-high 29 doubles, 19 home runs and 63 RBI. He was a National League All-Star and was named the Most Valuable Player of the National League Championship Series against the St. Louis Cardinals (which the Giants lost four games to three) after batting .417 with four home runs and five RBI. Leonard, who made headlines with his methodical one-flap-down home run trot, became the first player in LCS history to homer in four consecutive games (the first four of the series); tied NLCS records with 10 hits, four homers and 22 total bases; and was the first NLCS MVP from a losing team.

A spray hitter early in his career, Leonard developed into a power threat under Giants' manager Frank Robinson. From 1977-81 with the Los Angeles Dodgers and Houston Astros, Leonard hit a grand total of three home runs in 248 games. San Francisco acquired Leonard from the Astros along with first baseman Dave Bergman in exchange for first baseman Mike Ivie on April 20, 1981, and Robinson convinced the 6-foot-4, 200-pounder that someone with his size and strength should be hitting the ball out of the park.

Leonard blasted 21 home runs and drove in 87 runs while batting at a .279 clip in 1983,

Jeffrey Leonard (S.F. Giants Archives)

From 1996-98 Leonard was a manager and coach in the Oakland Athletics' minor league system, and in 1999 he served as the Montreal Expos' roving hitting instructor. He makes his offseason home in Alpharetta, Georgia.

Sam Leslie, Pinch Hitter (1929-33, 1936-38)

Sam Leslie was a professional hitter.

In two stints with the New York Giants—1929-33 and 1936-38—Leslie was used primarily as a pinch hitter. Of the 438 games he played, "Sambo" appeared in the field just half of the time (219 games). When the left-handed swinging Leslie did take the field it was at first base, but he wasn't particularly adept at playing defense.

Between 1929-32 Leslie played in 133 games, all but nine as a pinch hitter. He established a Giants' franchise record that still stands with 22 pinch hits in 1932. It broke the major league record of 21 set by Doc Miller of the Philadelphia Phillies in 1913 and stood until Dave Philley of the Baltimore Orioles had 24 in 1961. The current mark is 28 pinch hits by the Colorado Rockies' John Vander Wal during the 1995 season.

Leslie batted .293 with 15 RBI in 1932. The following season his batting average stood at .321 with three home runs and 27 RBI through 40 games when the Giants traded him to the cross-town rival Brooklyn Dodgers in exchange for pitcher Watty Clark and outfielder Lefty O'Doul on June 16, 1933. It was the first deal between the two combatants in six and a half years when New York acquired pitcher Burleigh Grimes for catcher Butch Henline.

With the Dodgers, Leslie became the team's regular first baseman. He continued to excel at the plate to the tune of career highs of a .332 batting average, nine home runs and 102 RBI during the 1934 campaign. He batted .308 with 93 RBI in 1935.

On February 20, 1936, the Giants acquired Leslie from the Dodgers in exchange for

and the following year "Hac-Man" again socked 21 homers with 86 RBI and a career-high .302 batting average. Also in 1983 Leonard established a club record for left fielders with 17 assists. On June 27, 1985, Leonard hit for the cycle against the Cincinnati Reds at Riverfront Stadium in Cincinnati.

San Francisco traded Leonard to the Milwaukee Brewers in exchange for infielder Ernest Riles on June 8, 1988. In 789 games with the Giants, Leonard batted .275 with 99 home runs, 435 RBI and 115 stolen bases (seventh on San Francisco's career list). He originally went by the name "Jeff" before switching to "Jeffrey," and he donned three different uniform numbers (26, 20 and 00) during his Bay Area days. Leonard concluded his 14-year career with the Seattle Mariners in 1989 and 1990. His overall numbers included a .266 batting average with 144 homers, 723 RBI and 163 stolen bases in 1,415 games.

Sam Leslie (Brace Photo)

cash. He proceeded to split time at first base with player-manager Bill Terry. Leslie hit for the cycle against the Philadelphia Phillies at the Polo Grounds in New York on May 24, 1936. But the feat was overshadowed by New York Yankees' infielder Tony Lazzeri, who hit three home runs (including two grand slams) and collected an American League record 11 RBI. Leslie finished the campaign with a .295 batting average and 54 RBI as the Giants won the N.L. pennant. He was 2-for-3 as a pinch hitter in the World Series against the Yankees.

Leslie batted .309 in 1937 before retiring following the 1938 season. In eight seasons with the Giants, he compiled a .295 batting average with 53 doubles, 11 triples, 17 home runs and 148 RBI. He ranks second on the franchise all-time pinch hits list with 57, just one less than Joel Youngblood (1983-88). Leslie was a lifetime .304 batter with 389 RBI in 822 games over his 10 seasons in the big leagues.

Leslie passed away January 21, 1979, in Pascagoula, Mississippi, at the age of 73 following a lengthy illness.

Fred Lindstrom, Third Baseman/Outfielder (1924-32)

Here's a record that may never be broken. Fred Lindstrom of the New York Giants became the youngest player to appear in a World Series game when he started Game 1 of the 1924 Fall Classic at the tender age of 18 years, 10 months and 13 days.

Lindstrom spent the first nine seasons (1924-32) of his 13-year major league career with the Giants. He took over at third base late in his rookie season for the injured Heinie Groh and remained a regular for most of his time in New York.

In the 1924 World Series against the Washington Senators, Lindstrom gave a clear indication of things to come by batting .333 (10-for-30). The "Boy Wonder" was 4-for-5 with two RBI in Game 5 against future Hall of Fame pitcher Walter Johnson at the Polo Grounds in New York. Nevertheless, Lindstrom always will be remembered for two ground balls that he could not come up with after they took bad hops and were instrumental in Washington winning Game 7 and the championship.

Lindstrom batted over .300 for six straight seasons from 1926-31. He finished third in the National League with a .358 average in 1928 to go with a career highs of 39 doubles and 107 RBI and 14 home runs. Two years later he posted career bests of a .379 average (fifth in the N.L.) and 22 homers while equaling his personal best of 39 doubles and driving in 106 runs. Lindstrom moved to the outfield in 1931.

On June 25, 1928, Lindstrom tied a major league record (now shared with eight other players) by banging out nine hits in a doubleheader as New York swept the Philadelphia Phillies 12-4 and 8-2 at the Baker Bowl in Philadelphia. He hit for the cycle against the Pittsburgh Pirates on May 8, 1930, at Forbes Field in Pittsburgh.

For a while it appeared as though Lindstrom would replace John McGraw as the Giants' manager. But instead Bill Terry was

Fred Linstrom

given the reins midway through the 1932 season, and a perturbed Lindstrom demanded to be traded. New York dealt Lindstrom to the Pirates on December 12, 1932, in a complicated three-way transaction that sent outfielder Kiddo Davis (from the Phillies) and pitcher Glenn Spencer (from the Pirates) to the Giants and outfielders Gus Dugan (from the Pirates) and Chick Fullis (from the Giants) to the Phillies.

Lindstrom's .318 batting average ranks seventh on the Giants' franchise list. He collected 1,347 hits with 212 doubles, 63 triples, 91 home runs and 603 RBI in 1,087 games.

Lindstrom played for the Pirates in 1933 and 1934 before concluding his career with the Chicago Cubs (1935) and Brooklyn Dodgers (1936). The Cubs set a major league record by winning 21 consecutive games (without a tie) from September 4-27, 1935, and Lindstrom

drove in or scored the winning run seven times during the stretch.

In 1,438 career games, Lindstrom batted .311 with 301 doubles, 81 triples, 103 home runs and 779 RBI. He struck out only 276 times in 5,611 at-bats (once every 20.3 at-bats).

Lindstrom was inducted into the National Baseball Hall of Fame in 1976 by the Veterans Committee. He died October 4, 1981, in Chicago at the age of 75.

Frank Linzy, Pitcher (1963, 1965-70)

One of the first great relievers in San Francisco history, Frank Linzy posted a 2.71 ERA and 78 saves with the club before the latter were fashionable. He started his only game with the Giants in 1963 but was a reliever exclusively thereafter, using a nasty sinker as his out pitch.

"I just figured that if I wanted to stay in the big leagues, that was my job," he said of switching to the bullpen. Farm director Carl Hubbell endorsed the move because the Giants were coming off a season in which they had blown ninth-inning leads in 17 games.

"It might be asking a lot of him with his limited experience, but Frank has the temperament and the equipment for late-inning work," Hubbell said. "He's also one of the best fielding pitchers I've ever seen."

An avid bird hunter, Frank attended Oklahoma State and Northwestern State in his native Oklahoma when scout Billy McLean took a liking to him. His report: "I've just signed something, but I don't know what it is, outfielder or pitcher. The one thing I'm sure about is that it's a big league prospect at either position."

The scout, of course, was correct. In 1965, is first full year with Giants, Linzy registered 21 saves and a 1.43 ERA—lowest by a reliever in San Francisco history—and earned N.L. Rookie Pitcher of the Year distinction from *The Sporting News*. He followed with a 1.51 ERA in 1967 and a 2.08 ERA in 1968 en route to 308 games with the Giants. Linzy showed

Frank Linzy (S.F. Giants Archives)

promise early in the minors, going 41-24 in his first four years from 1960-63, mostly as a starter. He had 18 complete games with Springfield in 1963, posting a 16-6 record and a 1.55 ERA.

Whitey Lockman, Outfielder/First Baseman (1945, 1947-56, 1957-58)

Born Carroll Walter Lockman, he was nicknamed "Whitey" because of his blond hair. A precocious athlete, he played Triple-A baseball at age 16, and by 19 was with the Giants. Because of a player shortage during World War II, Lockman was accelerated to the majors and played in his first game with the New York Giants at age 18 in 1945—after serving on a transport ship in the Panama Canal and in the Pacific.

He homered in his first at-bat July 5 and batted .341 in 32 games. Then the veterans returned from military service and Lockman didn't become a regular again until 1948, one year after breaking his leg sliding in a 1947 exhibition game. He hit a career-high 18 home runs in 1948 and, despite owner Horace

Stoneham's reservations, was switched to first base in 1951.

That happened at manager Leo Durocher's urging in late May, and the Giants promptly staged a miracle comeback to catch the Dodgers and force a playoff. Whereas Bobby Thomson's title-clinching home run off Ralph Branca received all the attention, it was Lockman's ninth-inning double which knocked starter Don Newcombe out of the game and brought in Branca.

"The 1951 season was, without a doubt, the highlight of my career," he said. "I remember everything about that final playoff game. We trailed 4-1 in the bottom of the ninth, had runners on first and third with one out, and I was up as the tying run. I told myself I was going to try to jerk one out in right field. Newcombe was throwing smoke on the outside corner, so I went with the pitch, swung as hard as I could and doubled to left. Of course, you know what happened after that."

He also was involved in a World Series controversy as the third base coach of the 1962 Giants. It was Game 7 at Candlestick Park and the Giants were trailing the Yankees 1-0 in the ninth inning. Matty Alou led off with a drag bunt and Felipe Alou and Chuck Hiller struck out against Ralph Terry. Willie Mays lined an off-field double down the line in right.

Lockman was criticized for holding Alou at third base. It would have been a great risk, however, because Roger Maris made a great play in right to avoid further trouble. The Yankees emerged 1-0 winners and World Series champs, and Lockman took some of the heat.

"I was never questioned by any of the players or coaches about the call," he explained. "Maris made a good throw to the relay man (second baseman Bobby Richardson), and I immediately went into my hold-up sign. Richardson bounced the ball to (catcher) Elston Howard, but by then the play is over for us—I've already stopped Alou."

Whitey coached with the Giants until 1964 and then achieved success with the Chicago Cubs, being named a vice president in

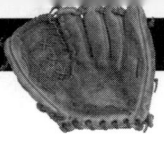

Whitey Lockman (S.F. Giants Archives)

1972 and replacing Durocher as manager at the All-Star break. He began a long and distinguished career as a semi-pro center fielder in Paw Creek, North Carolina, his hometown.

Garry Maddox, Outfielder (1972-75)

Garry Maddox received his first chance with the Giants in 1972, when Willie Mays was traded to the New York Mets. The club needed a center fielder, and the Mays deal was in the works, so the rangy youngster was promoted from Triple-A Phoenix and became a regular at age 22. Playing for Phoenix in 1971, he batted .299 with 30 homers and 106 RBI.

At the time of his promotion to the Giants one year later, he was terrorizing Pacific Coast League pitching for a .438 average, perhaps convincing owner Horace Stoneham that Mays was expendable. Maddox was called up the day after he hit a grand-slam homer for Phoenix in Salt Lake City.

He immediately noticed the difference, making his debut against Steve Carlton, who pitched a one-hitter with 14 strikeouts. "I was too anxious," he recalled. "It felt strange. I'm glad I didn't drop any fly balls."

Maddox's .319 average in his first full major league season, 1973, ranks among the highest for those who played home games at Candlestick Park. It has been exceeded three times—by Barry Bonds, Will Clark and Willie McCovey.

"The Giants had Bobby Bonds, so I had no idea I'd be the next center fielder after Mays," Maddox recalled. "I learned a lot over the years, but when I was younger, people would have a tendency to compare me with Mays. If a ball dropped in front of me, people would say that Willie would have caught it. I hit .319, and I would hear about Willie hitting .340 or something."

By 1975 Maddox was platooning with newcomer Von Joshua in center field. He soon was traded to Philadelphia in May of 1975 for Willie Montanez, who finished strong and then demanded a trade. Meanwhile, Maddox went on to enjoy a great Gold Glove career with the Phillies before going into broadcasting.

Garry Maddox (S.F. Giants Archives)

He was a great prep athlete in San Pedro, California, and attended Los Angeles Harbor Junior College. Garry signed with the Giants in 1968 and served a tour of duty in Vietnam before concentrating on baseball. He soured on the sport once he turned pro and was thinking about returning to school after his three-year hitch concluded.

But a family illness forced him to request an early discharge, and having a job was a prerequisite. Baseball was the option. It turned out to be a profitable and fulfilling one for the personable Maddox, who required merely one year of minor league seasoning before he reached the majors.

Sal Maglie, Pitcher (1945, 1950-54)

From 1950-52 Sal Maglie was as dominant as any pitcher in New York and San Francisco Giants history. Right up there with Mathewson, Hubbell and Marichal.

The right-handed Maglie initially joined the Giants in 1945, then after a four-year hiatus to the Mexican League returned to New York from 1950-54. He headed south of the border to get in on the grande pesos being handed out by Jorge Pasquel (organizer of the Mexican League) and after developing a wicked curve ball from former major league pitcher Dolph Luque came back to become a big-time winner in the United States.

Maglie actually was suspended from Major League Baseball by commissioner A.B. "Happy" Chandler when he signed with

Sal Maglie (Brace Photo)

the Mexican League but ultimately was reinstated. The Giants were thankful. From July of 1950 to May of 1952, Maglie won 45 games and lost merely seven. The impressive run included a franchise-record four straight shutouts (later equalled by Gaylord Perry in 1970) and 45 consecutive scoreless innings (1.1 shy of Carl Hubbell's club record) during the 1950 season.

The "Barber," nicknamed for his propensity to pitch batters so close they were given "a close shave," posted an 18-4 record with a 2.71 ERA in 1950. His .818 winning percentage led the Senior Circuit and ranks second on the Giants' single-season list behind Hoyt Wilhelm's .833 mark in 1952. Maglie started just 16 of the 47 games in which he appeared but had 12 complete games and five shutouts (tied for the league lead).

The following year Maglie was the winning pitcher for the N.L. in the All-Star Game at Briggs Stadium in Detroit (allowing two runs in three innings of relief) en route to going 23-6 (.793 winning percentage) with a 2.93 ERA. The 23 wins led the league and represented a personal best. After helping New York force a three-game playoff with the cross-town rival Brooklyn Dodgers for the 1951 N.L. pennant, Maglie stood to be the losing pitcher in the third and deciding game before Bobby Thomson hit the "Shot Heard 'Round The World."

Maglie was 18-8 (.692 inning percentage) with a 2.92 ERA in 1952. He was selected to the All-Star

191

Game but did not pitch in the rain-shortened contest. After battling back problems in 1953, Maglie bounced back to go 14-6 with a 3.26 ERA for the pennant-winning Giants in 1954. He had a no-decision in Game 1 of the World Series against the Cleveland Indians (and their 111-43 record). New York won the Fall Classic four games to none.

On July 31, 1955, the Giants sold Maglie to the Indians. In seven seasons in New York, he had a snappy 95-42 record with a 3.13 ERA. He is the franchise's all-time winning percentage leader at .693. Maglie pitched in 221 games totaling 1,297.2 innings with 654 strikeouts.

Maglie didn't win a game in 12 outings for Cleveland and was traded to the Dodgers early in the 1956 campaign. Believed to be washed up, Maglie rebounded with a 13-5 record and a 2.87 ERA as Brooklyn captured the N.L. flag. He no-hit the Philadelphia Phillies on September 25 and was the losing pitcher in Game 5 of the World Series against the New York Yankees as Don Larsen authored a perfect game. Maglie began the 1957 season with the Dodgers before going on to pitch for the Yankees (1957-58) and St. Louis Cardinals (1958). He was the last of a handful of players to don uniforms of the Giants, Dodgers and Yankees. Maglie's career statistics included a 119-62 record (.657 winning percentage) and a 3.15 ERA in 303 games.

Following his playing days, Maglie served as a pitching coach for the Boston Red Sox and Seattle Mariners. He underwent brain surgery July 24, 1982, and passed away December 28, 1982, in his hometown of Niagara Falls, New York, at the age of 75.

Gus Mancuso, Catcher
(1933-38, 1942-45)

The first trade Bill Terry orchestrated as manager of the New York Giants may well have been his best.

On October 10, 1932, the Giants acquired catcher Gus Mancuso and pitcher Ray Starr from the St. Louis Cardinals in exchange for

Gus Mancuso (Brace Photo)

outfielder Ethan Allen, pitcher Jim Mooney, catcher Bob O'Farrell and pitcher Bill Walker. Mancuso was the key to the deal as far as New York was concerned. Not only did he provide a solid bat, but he proved to be a quality handler of the pitching staff, which included Carl Hubbell, Hal Schumacher and Freddie Fitzsimmons.

Mancuso, who had been a backup in his first four seasons in the major leagues with the Cardinals (1928-32), played for the Giants from 1933-38 and 1942-45. He immediately took over as the everyday catcher and batted .264 with six home runs and 56 RBI during the 1933 season while helping New York win the World Series over the Washington Senators four games to one. "Blackie" earned a lion's share of the credit for the Giants' pitchers leading the National League with a snappy 2.71 ERA.

Along the way, Mancuso proved to be a durable performer. He was behind the plate for

all 27 innings of a double-header against the St. Louis Cardinals at the Polo Grounds in New York on July 2, 1933. New York won both games 1-0, the opener a remarkable 18-inning shutout by Hubbell and the second contest a nine-inning whitewash by Roy Parmelee.

In 1935 Mancuso was selected to the All-Star Game at Municipal Stadium in Cleveland en route to batting at a .298 clip with five home runs and 56 RBI. He posted career highs of a .301 batting average, nine homers and 63 RBI the following season as the Giants captured the N.L. pennant but lost the World Series to the cross-town Yankees four games to two.

Mancuso was named the Giants' team captain in 1937 and returned to the All-Star Game at Griffith Stadium in Washington D.C. New York repeated as N.L. champions before again falling to the Yankees in the World Series four games to one. Mancuso batted .279 for the season while splitting time with Harry Danning.

After batting .348 in just 52 games during the 1938 campaign, the Giants traded Mancuso to the Chicago Cubs along with shortstop Dick Bartell and outfielder Hank Leiber for outfielder Frank Demaree, shortstop Bill Jurges and catcher Ken O'Dea on December 6, 1938. Mancuso played for the Cubs in 1939, then moved on the Brooklyn Dodgers (1940) before returning to the Cardinals (1941-42).

The Giants re-acquired Mancuso from St. Louis for cash May 5, 1942. He platooned with Danning for the duration of the 1942 campaign and with Ernie Lombardi, who was obtained from the Boston Braves on April 27, 1943, in 1943 and 1944. Mancuso concluded his career with the Philadelphia Phillies in 1945.

In nine seasons with the Giants, Mancuso batted .270 with 105 doubles, 36 home runs and 328 RBI in 882 games. More impressive were his capacities to work well with pitchers, block pitches in the dirt and make snap throws from his crouched catching position. Mancuso's 17-year career batting average was .265

in 1,460 games. He had a lifetime .977 fielding percentage.

After leaving the big leagues, Mancuso was a minor league manager and subsequently a broadcaster in Texas.

Mancuso passed away December 26, 1984, in Houston, Texas, at the age of 78.

Juan Marichal, Pitcher (1960-73)

During the pitching-rich decade of the 1960s, Juan Marichal of the San Francisco Giants may very well have been at the head of the class.

Pretty heady talk, indeed, considering the Los Angeles Dodgers featured Sandy Koufax and the St. Louis Cardinals had Bob Gibson, but Marichal's numbers certainly stood out. He won 191 games during the 1960s, more than any other National League pitcher (Gibson was second with 164). Marichal posted 20 or more victories six times in seven seasons from 1963-69 and fashioned an ERA in the 2.00s every year.

Juan Marichal (S.F. Giants Archives)

Marichal's six 20-win campaigns came in 1963 (25-8, 2.41 ERA); 1964 (21-8, 2.48 ERA); 1965 (22-13, 2.13 ERA); 1966 (25-6, 2.23 ERA); 1968 (26-9, 2.43 ERA); and 1969 (21-11, 2.10 ERA). He led the National League in wins in 1963 (tied with Koufax) and 1968 and won the ERA title in 1969. In addition, he topped the Senior Circuit in complete games in 1964 (22) and 1968 (Giants-record 30) and in shutouts in 1965 (Giants-record 10) and 1969 (8). He also holds Giants season standards for wins (26) and strikeouts (248 in 1963). Despite his annual success, the Cy Young Award somehow eluded Marichal throughout his career.

On June 15, 1963, Marichal no-hit the Houston Colt .45s at Candlestick Park—throwing a mere 89 pitches—and later that season outdueled Warren Spahn of the Milwaukee Braves 1-0 in 16 innings at home July 2—allowing only eight hits.

Marichal was selected to nine All-Star Games and pitched in eight of them (tied for the most in baseball history with Jim Bunning, Don Drysdale and Tom Seaver) and was the winning pitcher in 1962 and 1965. He was named the Mid-Summer Classic's Most Valuable Player in 1965 after starting and pitching three scoreless innings, surrendering just one hit, at Metropolitan Stadium in Bloomington, Minnesota.

Chronic arthritis and severe back pain nearly ended his career in 1970, but Marichal bounced back to go 18-11 with a 2.94 ERA for the 1971 N.L. West Division champion Giants. The back problems continued in 1972, and he wound up finishing his career with the Boston Red Sox (1974) and Los Angeles Dodgers (1975). Marichal's 16-year numbers included a 243-142 record with a 2.89 ERA and 2,303 strikeouts.

A native of Laguna Verde, Dominican Republic, and aptly nicknamed the "Dominican Dandy," Marichal threw a fastball, slider and screwball but was most widely-known for his ability to deliver them overhand, sidearm and underhand (submarine-style). He fired a one-hit, 2-0 shutout in his major league debut against the Philadelphia Phillies on July 19, 1960, in San Francisco.

On the Giants' franchise career lists (including the New York years), Marichal ranks second in games started (446), shutouts (52) and strikeouts (2,281); fourth in wins (238); fifth in innings pitched (3,444); sixth in games (458) and complete games (244); and 10th in ERA (2.84). Among San Francisco pitchers only, he is first in each of those categories except ERA (tied for second) and games (fourth).

Marichal was inducted into the National Baseball Hall of Fame in 1983, and his uniform No. 27 has been retired by the Giants. In 1996 he was appointed sports minister in his native Dominican Republic.

Rube Marquard, Pitcher (1908-15)

In 1908 the New York Giants outbid a number of teams for the services of minor league left-handed pitcher Richard "Rube" Marquard. They paid the Indianapolis club of the American Association a record sum of $11,000 for the red-hot

Rube Marquard

prospect—who was labeled the "$11,000 Beauty"—in hopes of receiving an instant pay-back.

But Marquard was no bull market. From 1908-10 he managed just a 9-18 record with a 3.15 ERA in 43 games. The former Cleveland Indians' batboy was not living up to his advanced billing and became known as the "$11,000 Lemon."

Then things began to change drastically in 1911 as Marquard went 24-7 with a 2.50 ERA. He topped the National League in winning percentage (.774) and strikeouts (career-high 237) while helping New York capture the pennant.

The following year Marquard opened with 19 straight wins to tie the major league record set by the Giants' Tim Keefe in 1888. The streak ran from April 11-July 3 and included victories over all seven other N.L. teams. Under present-day scoring rules, Marquard would have had 20 consecutive wins because New York starting pitcher Jeff Tesreau was credited with a victory April 20 when the Giants rallied after Marquard came into the game as a reliever.

Marquard went on to finish the year 26-11 (establishing a career-high for victories and tying Larry Cheney of the Chicago Cubs for the N.L. top spot) with a 2.57 ERA and a team-leading 175 strikeouts. The Giants repeated as N.L. champions, and Marquard was brilliant in the World Series against the Boston Red Sox. He won Games 3 and 6, going the distance in both and surrendering just two earned runs for a minuscule 0.50 ERA. But Boston rallied in Game 8 (forever remembered for the misplayed fly ball by Giants' center fielder Fred Snodgrass) to win the series.

New York fashioned three 20-game winners en route to winning its third consecutive N.L. championship in 1913: Christy Mathewson (25), Marquard (23) and Tesreau (22). Marquard, also an amateur actor, compiled a 2.50 ERA with 151 strikeouts.

Marquard's record slipped to 12-22 in 1914 but with a respectable 3.06 ERA. On July 17, 1914, he pitched a 21-inning complete game to defeat the Pittsburgh Pirates 3-1 at Forbes Field in Pittsburgh. Then on April 15, 1915 (after a brief jump to the Federal League), he fired a no-hitter against the cross-town rival Brooklyn Dodgers, winning 2-0, at the Polo Grounds in New York. Ironically, Marquard was sold to the Dodgers on August 31 after he went unclaimed on waivers. His eight-year statistics with New York included a 103-76 record, 2.85 ERA and 897 strikeouts in 239 games. He had 99 complete games.

In 1916 Marquard went 13-6 with a career-low 1.58 ERA as Brooklyn won the N.L. pennant. Marquard pitched for the Dodgers through the 1920 season, then moved on to the Cincinnati Reds (1921) and Boston Braves (1922-25). In 18 years he compiled a 201-177 record, 3.08 ERA and 1,593 strikeouts in 536 games.

Marquard was given his nickname "Rube" in the minor leagues by a sportswriter who likened his resemblance to legendary left-handed pitcher George "Rube" Waddell.

Following his playing days, Marquard was a minor league coach and umpire. He was inducted into the National Baseball Hall of Fame in 1971 by the Veterans Committee. Marquard passed away June 1, 1980, in Baltimore at the age of 90 (although there are questions about his actual date of birth—October 9, 1886 or 1889—and he may have been 93 years old).

Willard Marshall, Outfielder (1942, 1946-49)

In 1947 the Marshall Plan was as big a hit in New York as it was in Europe.

Willard Marshall was an outfielder for the New York Giants in 1942 and from 1946-49. Although he enjoyed a solid career, it was the 1947 season that brought him his greatest fame. At the same time, the Marshall Plan was aiding the reconstruction of Europe following World War II. Marshall posted personal bests of 36 home runs and 107 RBI to go with a .291 batting average. That year the Giants set a major league record with 221 homers. The mark has since been broken by several clubs, and

the current standard is 264 by the Seattle Mariners in 1997. The National League record is 239 by the Colorado Rockies, also in 1997.

Not only did Marshall's home run and RBI totals not lead the N.L., they weren't even tops on his own team. Giants' first baseman Johnny Mize and Ralph Kiner of the Pittsburgh Pirates tied for home run supremacy (51), while Marshall ranked third. Marshall was fifth in the RBI chase behind Mize (138), Kiner (127), Giants' catcher Walker Cooper (122) and Bob Elliott of the Boston Braves (113).

Marshall wasted no time making a name for himself in the big leagues. He burst onto the scene in 1942, was selected to the All-Star Game at the Polo Grounds in New York and finished the season batting .257 with 11 home runs and 57 RBI. Following a three-year stint with the U.S. Marines, Marshall returned to the Giants in 1946, took over as the everyday right fielder for player-manager and future Hall of Famer Mel Ott and batted .282 with 13 homers and 48 RBI. Marshall was a solid defensive player, and the left-handed swinger frequently took advantage of the short 257-foot right field porch at the Polo Grounds.

Then came the breakthrough campaign. Along the way, Marshall was selected to his second All-Star Game at Wrigley Field in Chicago, and on July 18, 1947, he socked three consecutive home runs against the Cincinnati Reds at the Polo Grounds. That feat has been accomplished only 10 times in franchise history.

Willard Marshall (Brace Photo)

In 1948 Marshall's power numbers dropped to 14 home runs and 86 RBI, though he still batted at a decent .272 clip. On June 20 Mize, Marshall and Sid Gordon hit three consecutive round-trippers in the eighth inning against the St. Louis Cardinals at the Polo Grounds.

The biggest news of 1948, though, came on July 16 when Leo Durocher, set to be replaced as manager of the cross-town rival Brooklyn Dodgers, was hired to manage the Giants. Durocher proceeded to build a scrappier team that had speed and played solid defense.

Marshall didn't fit into Durocher's plans. He survived the 1949 season and was the starting right fielder for the N.L. All-Star team at Ebbets Field in Brooklyn. On June 4 he was part of another three-homer inning with Gordon and Whitey Lockman in the sixth against Cincinnati at the Polo Grounds. Marshall went on bat a career-high .307 with 12 home runs and 70 RBI.

New York traded Marshall along with Gordon and shortstop Buddy Kerr to Boston in exchange for shortstop Alvin Dark and second baseman Eddie Stanky on December 14, 1949. Marshall's five-year statistics with the Giants included a .283 batting average with 86 home runs and 370 RBI in 686 games. He played in Boston into the 1952 season, then donned uniforms for the Reds (1952-53) and Chicago White Sox (1954-55). In 11 big league seasons, Marshall batted .274 with 130 homers and 604 RBI in 1,246 games.

Following his playing days, Marshall entered the real estate and insurance business.

He currently makes his home in Rockleigh, New Jersey.

Christy Mathewson, Pitcher (1900-16)

Like apple pie and hot dogs, Christy Mathewson truly was an American icon.

Mathewson, who pitched for the New York Giants from 1900-16, was well-educated, well-groomed and well-mannered. He was a knight in shining armor and a bona fide super-star. Mathewson won 373 games during his 17-year career (an average of nearly 22 per year) to rank tied for third on baseball's all-time list (with Grover Cleveland Alexander). Only Cy Young (511) and Walter Johnson (417) have more victories. Mathewson lost just 188 games for a lofty .665 winning percentage (tied for sixth in baseball annals with Larry Corcoran) and compiled a snappy 2.13 ERA (fifth).

In 635 games, Mathewson hurled 4,780.2 innings (16th on baseball's all-time list) with 434 complete games (13th) and 79 shutouts (third). He amassed 2,502 strikeouts (21st) with only 844 bases on balls for a ratio of nearly 3:1. Mathewson is the Giants' franchise career leader in wins (372), ERA (2.12), games started (550), innings pitched (4,771.2), complete games (433), shutouts (79) and strikeouts (2,499) and ranks second in games (634, trailing only Gary Lavelle with 647).

Mathewson managed just a 34-37 record over his first three major league seasons before starting a stretch in which he won 20 or more games a National League-record 12 straight years (1903-14). He eclipsed the 30-victory plateau during four seasons: 1903 (30-13, 2.26 ERA); 1904 (33-12, 2.03); 1905 (31-9, 1.28); and 1908 (37-11, 1.43). Mathewson led the National League in wins four times and in ERA and strikeouts on five occasions. He posted career highs of 390.2 innings pitched and 259 strikeouts during the 1908 season. In 1913 he pitched 68 consecutive innings without walking a batter.

Mathewson fired two no-hitters during his career, 5-0 over the St. Louis Cardinals on July

Christy Mathewson

15, 1901, at Robison Field in St. Louis and 1-0 over the Chicago Cubs on June 13, 1905, at the West Side Grounds in Chicago.

Although he possessed a blazing fastball (which earned him the nickname "Big Six" because it reminded newspaper reporters of a famous New York fire engine by the same name), it was a nasty screwball, more aptly called a fadeaway, that was key to Mathewson's arsenal.

Mathewson's dominance and durability were showcased during the 1905 World Series against the Philadelphia Athletics. He authored three shutouts in a span of six days (a 3-0 four-hitter in Game 1, a 9-0 four-hitter in Game 3 and a 2-0 six-hitter in the championship-clinching Game 5). In 27 innings he surrendered a mere 14 hits and one walk with 18 strikeouts. "Matty" pitched in 11 Fall Classic games overall and went the distance in 10 of them while posting a 5-5 record with a minuscule 1.15 ERA.

On July 20, 1916, the Giants, who were

managed by Mathewson's best friend, John McGraw, traded the right-hander to the Cincinnati Reds along with infielder Bill McKechnie and outfielder Edd Roush in exchange for infielder Buck Herzog and outfielder Red Killefer, so Mathewson could take over as the Reds' player/manager. He concluded his playing career at the end of the 1916 season (he defeated Hall of Famer Mordecai "Three-Finger" Brown of the Cubs 10-8 in the final game for both pitchers in the second game of a doubleheader September 4, 1916, at Weeghman Park in Chicago) and was manager until late in the 1918 campaign. Mathewson later was general manager and part owner of the Boston Braves.

Mathewson was an All-America kicker for the football team at Bucknell University in 1900 and also was elected class president. He served as a U.S. Army captain during World War I and was involved in a gas chamber accident in France in December of 1918 that damaged his lungs. Mathewson later contracted tuberculosis, which in the end resulted in his death October 7, 1925, in Saranac Lake, New York, at the age of 45.

On February 2, 1936, Mathewson was one of the five original inductees into the National Baseball Hall of Fame by the Baseball Writers' Association of America (along with Johnson, Ty Cobb, Babe Ruth and Honus Wagner). Since numbers were not part of uniforms during his playing days, Mathewson has had the letters "NY" retired in his honor by the Giants.

Mathewson's younger brother, Henry, pitched briefly for the Giants in 1906 and 1907.

Gary Matthews, Outfielder (1972-76)

Gary Matthews was among the Giants' rising stars when he was allowed to slip away to the Atlanta Braves as a free agent following the 1976 season, one in which he had 20 homers and 84 RBI. Those were difficult financial times for the club, so he simply didn't fit in the budget.

Matthews was a first-round pick of the Giants in 1968 following a standout prep career in San Fernando, California. He batted

Gary Matthews (S.F. Giants Archives)

.322 for Decatur in his maiden pro season of 1969, and that was a career high. He sparkled in 1972, attaining all-star honors in the Pacific Coast League with a .313 average, 21 homers and a Phoenix-record 108 RBI.

Promoted to the Giants in September, he opened eyes with a .290 average and 14 RBI in 20 games. Rookie of the Year honors followed in 1973 when he batted .300 with 10 triples, forming a gifted young outfield with Bobby Bonds and Garry Maddox. "Gary accomplished things you really couldn't have expected from a first-year player," Bonds said. "He was very deserving of the rookie award."

By 1974 he demonstrated the power to go with the speed, batting .287 with 16 homers and 82 RBI, prompting manager Charlie Fox to say: "The big thing about Matthews is that he's aggressive. He's a free-swinger who makes contact and makes use of his great speed. He has developed self-assurance at bat and in the field."

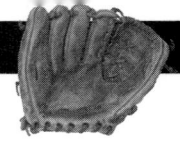

"Sarge" never batted below .279 in five seasons with the Giants, and continued to have success with Atlanta and Philadelphia. He batted .304 with 27 homers and 90 RBI, all career bests, with the 1979 Braves. He rejoined Maddox with the Phillies in 1981 and batted .301. Gary participated in 14 playoff games and batted .347 with six home runs in 49 at-bats, adding a home run in the 1983 World Series.

Willie Mays, Outfielder
(1951-52, 1954-72)

How good was Willie Mays?

In one of his first moves as president and managing general partner of the San Francisco Giants in 1993, Peter A. Magowan signed Mays to a lifetime contract ... at the age of 61.

Generally regarded as the best all-around player in baseball history, Mays wore a New York and San Francisco Giants uniform for 21 seasons (1951-52, 1954-72). He is the franchise's career leader in virtually every category, including games (2,857), at-bats (10,477), runs (2,011), hits (3,187), doubles (504) and home runs (646). He ranks second in triples (139—23 behind Mike Tiernan) and RBI (1,859—one behind Mel Ott) and third in stolen bases (336—behind Mike Tiernan and George Davis). Mays' batting average with the Giants was .304.

After going hitless in his first 12 major league at-

Willie Mays (S.F. Giants Archives)

bats, Mays hit a mammoth home run off Hall of Famer Warren Spahn of the Boston Braves at the Polo Grounds in New York on May 28, 1951. Mays went on to bat .274 with 20 home runs and 68 RBI in 121 games and was named the National League Rookie of the Year.

In 1952 Mays played in only 34 games before joining the service. He returned in 1954 and was the N.L. Most Valuable Player after leading the league with a .345 batting average to go with 41 home runs and 110 RBI. Mays earned his second Most Valuable Player Award in 1965 on the strength of a franchise-record and league-leading 52 homers, .317 batting average and 112 RBI. Mays also topped the N.L. in home runs in 1962 (49) and 1964 (47). He batted .300 or better on 10 occasions, including a personal best of .347 in 1958, and surpassed the 100 RBI plateau 10 times with a career-high 141 during the 1962 campaign.

On April 30, 1960, at Milwaukee's County Stadium, Mays clouted a franchise-record four home runs (the ninth player ever to do so) and had a San Francisco-record eight RBI. He collected the 3,000th hit of his career July 18, 1970, with a second-inning single off Mike Wegener of the Montreal Expos at Candlestick Park in San Francisco.

But Mays was more than a hitter. Much more. The "Say Hey Kid" paced the N.L. in stolen bases during four seasons, including a career-high 40 in 1956, and won 12 Gold Gloves (every

year from 1957-68). Mays has been idolized for his over-the-shoulder basket catch of Vic Wertz's drive to deep center field at the Polo Grounds (440 feet) in Game 1 of the 1954 World Series against the Cleveland Indians.

Mays appeared in 24 All-Star Games (tied for the most by any player with Hank Aaron and Stan Musial) and was named the Most Valuable Player in 1963 and 1968. He holds All-Star Game career records for hits (23) and stolen bases (6). At the 1965 game in Milwaukee, Mays robbed Boston Red Sox Hall of Famer Ted Williams of a home run.

San Francisco traded Mays, just past his 42nd birthday, to the New York Mets in exchange for pitcher Charlie Williams and reportedly $50,000 in cash May 11, 1972. Mays retired at the conclusion of the 1973 season.

On baseball's all-time lists, Mays ranks third in home runs (660), eighth in RBI (1,903) and 10th in hits (3,283). He was a lifetime .302 batter. Mays was the first player to record 300 homers and 300 stolen bases (338) and is one of just four individuals to accomplish the feat (also Barry Bonds, Bobby Bonds and Andre Dawson). Mays is baseball's all-time leader in outfield putouts (7,095).

Mays was inducted to the National Baseball Hall of Fame in 1979, becoming the ninth individual to make it in his first year of eligibility. His uniform No. 24 has been retired by the Giants.

Serving as a special assistant to the president with the Giants since 1986, Mays makes appearances on behalf of the club at a variety of charitable and civic events throughout the Bay Area. He resides in Atherton, California.

Mike McCormick, Pitcher
(1956-62, 1967-70)

Only one pitcher in San Francisco won the Cy Young Award, and you will never guess who. It was Mike McCormick, a left-hander whose Giants' career began as a $50,000 New York bonus baby, included the club's first five years on the West Coast and featured a fantastic comeback at Candlestick Park in 1967.

McCormick pitched in 16 different major league seasons from 1956-71, but he never came close to matching what he did in 1967 in an era of great pitching. One year before Bob Gibson's set the all-time ERA record of 1.12 and one year after Sandy Koufax retired, McCormick was the National League's best pitcher.

He rejoined the Giants in a trade that sent pitcher Bob Priddy and outfielder Cap Peterson to the Washington Senators and performed beyond expectations. That 1967 season included a league-leading 22-10 record and a 2.85 ERA in 262.1 innings. He completed 14 of 35 starts and pitched five shutouts in a dream season on a staff with future Hall of Famers Juan Marichal and Gaylord Perry.

Mike gained momentum with eight consecutive victories in June and July. Despite not winning his first game until May 4, McCormick was 11-3 at the All-Star break, yet wasn't selected for the N.L. squad. He was at his best

Mike McCormick

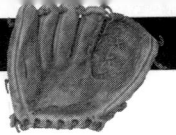

against the World Series champion St. Louis Cardinals that season, going 3-0 with a 0.86 ERA and two shutouts.

"There is no other answer but the screwball," farm director Carl Hubbell insisted. "When we traded him to Baltimore and he ended up with Rochester, you'd have thought Mike had had it. Now he's the Cy Young Award winner."

McCormick explained his 1967 success thusly: "I was on the team as a spot starter and long reliever, but somebody got hurt and I started a game in Houston. I went nine innings and won, so it warranted another start. Then I won eight in a row, and they couldn't get me out of the rotation. Really, there was a lot of luck involved."

Mike concluded his career with 134 major league victories, and is the San Francisco Giants' all-time lefty winner with 104, not including three victories when the club was in New York. His other big season with the Giants produced a 15-12 record and a league-leading 2.70 ERA as a 21-year-old phenom in 1960.

"I have never seen Mike flare up on the mound," catcher Hobie Landrith said at the time. "He never gets riled up. He's the most mature 21-year-old I ever saw, on and off the field."

A native of Pasadena, California, young Mike would pitch batting practice against Hollywood of the Pacific Coast League as a prep. Because the Stars were an affiliate of the Pittsburgh Pirates, he felt he might sign with the Bucs, but they already had bonus babies Paul Petit and the O'Brien twins, Johnny and Eddie. Mike also was a basketball star, receiving scholarship offers from USC and Stanford.

He enrolled at USC but took time to play for the U.S. in a pair of prep All-Star games in New York. Mike pitched six innings and struck out all 18 batters. The Giants' interest peaked, and he signed a bonus contract with the club at age 17 in 1956. "They were the first club to offer me a bonus, based on what Horace Stoneham saw in the All-Star game at the Polo Grounds," McCormick explained.

The phenom made it to the majors without any minor league experience because of a rule compelling teams to keep "bonus babies." He never played in the minors as a member of the Giants' organization but worked 29 games for Triple-A Rochester when he was with the Baltimore Orioles in 1964, receiving a shot of cortisone that revived his shoulder. McCormick was in the rotation of the original San Francisco Giants in 1958, going 11-8. One of his biggest disappointments was the sore arm which limited his participation during the 1962 pennant push and prefaced his first departure from the Giants.

"That was probably the most difficult season in my career," he said. "I had been among the leaders of the pitching staff for three or four years, and then came up with a sore arm. I was in some ways useless to the club. I won a couple of important games, but I never really felt like part of that team. When I left the Giants, I learned how to pitch, not just throw."

He was 59-59 with the Giants before going to the American League, where he posted a 25-32 record in four years. Upon his return to the Giants in 1967, he nearly approached his A.L. win total in one season. Mike suffered a back problem in 1970 and pitched briefly with the New York Yankees and the Orioles before retiring after the 1971 season. A Bay Area resident, McCormick is an annual visitor to spring training as a guest instructor with the club.

Willie McCovey, First Baseman/ Outfielder (1959-73, 1977-80)

It's easy to understand why Willie McCovey is one of the most popular players ever to wear a San Francisco Giants uniform. Not only did he perform, but he did so with class.

McCovey enjoyed two successful stints with the Giants (1959-73, 1977-80) as a first baseman and a left fielder. His 19 years with the organization are more than any other player in San Francisco history. Additionally, he is San Francisco's career leader in games (2,256), home runs (469) and RBI (1,388) and

ranks second behind Willie Mays in at-bats (7,214), runs (1,113), hits (1,974), doubles (308) and triples (45). On the franchise's all-time lists (including the New York years), McCovey is third in games, at-bats, home runs and RBI; fourth in hits and doubles; and fifth in runs. He was a .274 batter with the Giants.

On July 30, 1959, McCovey made a storybook debut at Seals Stadium in San Francisco, banging out four hits, including two triples, in four at-bats against Hall of Famer

Willie McCovey (S.F. Giants Archives)

Robin Roberts of the Philadelphia Phillies. McCovey went on to earn National League Rookie of the Year honors after batting .354 with 13 home runs and 38 RBI in 52 games.

Three times McCovey topped the National League in home runs (44 in 1963, 36 in 1968 and a career-high 45 in 1969). He also led the league in RBI in 1968 and 1969 (105 and a personal-best 126, respectively) to become just the fifth player in baseball history to capture back-to-back home run and RBI titles. McCovey batted .320 in 1969 and was named the National League Most Valuable Player. The following year McCovey drew a league-leading 137 walks, including a major league record of 45 intentional passes. He still batted at a .289 clip with 39 homers and a career-high tying 126 RBI.

Nicknamed "Stretch," for his ability to reach for errant throws from infielders while keeping one foot on first base, McCovey was a six-time All-Star (1963, 1966, 1968, 1969, 1970 and 1971) before injuries began to plague him. The Giants traded him to the San Diego

Padres along with outfielder Bernie Williams in exchange for pitcher Mike Caldwell on October 25, 1973. McCovey played for the Padres for two-plus seasons, then ended the 1976 campaign with the Oakland Athletics. He returned to the Giants as a free agent January 6, 1977, and on Opening Day received a standing ovation that brought him to tears. At age 39, McCovey batted .280 with 28 home runs and 86 RBI and was selected the N. L. Comeback Player of the Year.

McCovey retired in 1980 after a 22-year career. His 521 home runs are tied for 11th on baseball's career list with Ted Williams (ironically, his idol and minor league mentor). McCovey hit 439 round-trippers as a first baseman, more than any other player in N.L. annals. He holds the Senior Circuit record with 18 grand slams (only Lou Gehrig of the New York Yankees with 23 has hit more). His career batting average was .270 with 2,211 hits and 1,555 RBI.

One of only 22 major leaguers to play in four decades, McCovey became just the 16th individual to be inducted into the National Baseball Hall of Fame in his first year of eligibility (1986). His uniform No. 44 has been retired by the Giants.

In 1980 the Giants established the Willie Mac Award, presented annually to the player who best exemplifies the spirit and leadership displayed by McCovey throughout his career.

Following his retirement, McCovey worked for the Giants as a special assistant to the

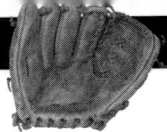

president and general manager, a member of the Giants Community Fund board of directors and an instructor in spring training. In September of 1999 he was appointed a Senior Advisor to the team, and the portion of San Francisco Bay behind right field at Pacific Bell Park was named McCovey Cove. McCovey currently resides in Woodside, California.

Joe McGinnity, Pitcher (1902-08)

Among the baseball records regarded as the least likely to be broken are Joe DiMaggio's 56-game hitting streak and Cal Ripken's 2,632 consecutive games played. Put this one at the top of the list: Joe McGinnity pitching complete games to win both games of a double-header on three occasions.

McGinnity, a right-handed pitcher for the New York Giants from 1902-08, was nicknamed "Iron Man" because he worked his father-in-law's iron mill. But the moniker was just as appropriate for his durability and stamina.

When John McGraw left the Baltimore Orioles to take over as player-manager of the Giants on July 16, 1902, he brought with him five players, including McGinnity. In fact, McGinnity was the starting pitcher for McGraw's first game in New York (a 4-3 loss to the Philadelphia Phillies at the Polo Grounds on July 19, 1902).

Amazingly, McGinnity pulled off his "triple-double" in one month during the 1903 season. He defeated the Boston Braves 4-1 and 5-2 at Braves Field on August 1; the Brooklyn Dodgers 6-1 and 4-3 at Washington Park in Brooklyn on August 8 (he stole home in the nightcap); and the Philadelphia Phillies 4-1 and 9-2 at the Polo Grounds on August 31. McGinnity also holds the record with five complete-game double-headers pitched (he split two with Baltimore in 1901).

McGinnity finished the 1903 campaign with 48 games started and 434 innings pitched, both National League records since 1900. He also topped the league with 55 games pitched, 44 complete games and 31

wins (against 20 losses) with a 2.43 ERA. It was more of the same the following year as he led the N.L. with 51 games pitched, 408 innings pitched, nine shutouts, 35 wins (against eight losses), a 1.61 ERA and five saves. McGinnity shared the lead with 46 games pitched in 1905 and was tops with 339.2 innings pitched and 27 wins (against 12 losses) in 1906 and with four saves in 1907. He and teammate Christy Mathewson tied for the N.L. lead with five saves in 1908.

From April 15-June 8, 1904, McGinnity won 14 consecutive games before losing 1-0 in 12 innings to the Chicago Cubs at the Polo Grounds on June 11. In the 1905 World Series against the Philadelphia Athletics, McGinnity

Joe McGinnity

lost the second game 3-0 (allowing three un-earned wins) to Chief Bender before winning the fourth game 1-0 over Eddie Plank. In his two outings, McGinnity surrendered just 10 hits and three walks with six strikeouts in 17 innings. The Giants won the championship four games to one.

In his seven seasons in New York, McGinnity compiled a 151-88 record with a 2.38 ERA in 300 games. On the Giants' fran-chise lists, he ranks second in ERA, seventh in complete games (186), ninth in shutouts (26) and wins and 10th in innings pitched (2,151.1). McGinnity's 10-year career statistics (he pitched for Baltimore in 1899, 1901 and 1902 and for the Brooklyn Superbas in 1900) in-cluded a 246-142 record and 2.66 ERA in 465 games.

Following his major league playing days, McGinnity continued to pitch, as well as man-age, in the minor leagues for more than 10 years before serving as a coach for the Brook-lyn Dodgers during the 1926 season. He later was an assistant baseball coach at Williams College in Williamstown, Massachusetts.

McGinnity, born McGinty, passed away November 14, 1929, in Brooklyn at the age of 58 following a battle against cancer. He was inducted into the National Baseball Hall of Fame in 1946 by the Veterans Committee.

Fred Merkle, First Baseman (1907-16)

One of the most famous moments in New York Giants' history is the "Merkle Incident."

The date was September 23, 1908, and the Giants were playing host to the Chicago Cubs at the Polo Grounds in New York. The National League pennant race was tight, with the Giants and Cubs virtually deadlocked for first place, a mere game and a half ahead of the Pittsburgh Pirates. New York and Chicago were tied 1-apiece in the bottom of the ninth inning, and the Giants had left fielder Moose McCormick on third base and first baseman Fred Merkle on first with two outs. Shortstop Al Bridwell singled off Cubs' pitched Jack Pfiester that apparently scored McCormick

with the winning run. Merkle, meanwhile, ran off the field without touching second base—a typical action of the day—but Chicago second baseman Johnny Evers supposedly retrieved the ball and declared that Merkle should be forced out and McCormick's run should not count. Base umpire Bob Emslie did not call Merkle out, but home plate umpire Hank O'Day did that evening in his hotel room. N.L. president Harry C. Pulliam concurred, and the game was ruled a 1-1 tie.

New York and Chicago wound up the regular season with identical 98-55 records, necessitating a one-game playoff at the Polo Grounds on October 8. The Cubs won 4-2 to win the pennant. Merkle was blamed for the Giants' misfortune and forever was unfairly saddled with the nickname "Bonehead."

Ironically, Merkle, who played for the Gi-ants from 1907-16, had been a substitute dur-ing his first two seasons but started on that fateful September day because regular first baseman Fred Tenney was sidelined with a sore back.

Fred Merkle

Just 19 years old at the time of the incident, Merkle was left void of his confidence and thought about quitting baseball. But manager John McGraw reassured him, and in 1910 Merkle became the Giants' regular first baseman. He batted .292 with 70 RBI and 23 stolen bases.

The following season Merkle batted at a .283 clip with career highs of 12 home runs, 84 RBI and 49 stolen bases as New York captured the N.L. flag. Along the way he drove in an N.L.-record six runs in the bottom of the first inning against the St. Louis Cardinals at the Polo Grounds on May 13. In 1912 Merkle posted a career-high .309 batting average while equaling his personal best of 84 RBI. The Giants repeated as N.L. champions and were on the verge of winning the World Series when center fielder Fred Snodgrass committed a two-base error in the bottom of the 10th inning that opened the door for Boston to score two runs and win the game 3-2 and the series four games to three with one tie. Merkle also had an error in the inning and was stricken again.

New York made it three consecutive pennants (but three consecutive World Series defeats, as well) in 1913, and Merkle continued to play everyday into the 1916 campaign. On August 20, 1916, the Giants traded Merkle to the cross-town rival Brooklyn Dodgers in exchange for catcher Lew McCarty. In his 10 seasons with the Giants, Merkle batted .272 with 192 doubles, 58 triples, 48 home runs, 508 RBI and 212 stolen bases in 1,105 games.

Merkle played for the Dodgers in 1916-17 before moving onto the Cubs from 1917-20. After five years in the minor leagues, Merkle joined the New York Yankees as a player-coach in 1925 and 1926. His 16-year career statistics included a .273 batting average, 60 home runs, 733 RBI and 272 stolen bases in 1,638 games. An intelligent individual, he enjoyed playing bridge and was one of the first baseball players to take up golf.

Following his playing days, Merkle essentially disappeared from the public eye. Finally in 1950 he returned to the Polo Grounds for an Old-Timers' Game but still heard shouts of "Bonehead." Merkle passed away March 2, 1956, in Daytona Beach, Florida, at the age of 67.

Sam Mertes, Outfielder (1903-06)

Despite playing for the New York Giants for just four seasons, outfielder Sam Mertes had some notable individual performances.

- On August 12, 1903, Mertes drew five walks against the St. Louis Cardinals at the Polo Grounds in New York. The total remains tied for a modern-day National League record (since 1900).

- Mertes became the first Giants' player to hit for the cycle in the 20th century (the second in franchise history after Mike

Sam Mertes (Transcendental Graphics)

Tiernan in 1888) when he accomplished the feat October 4, 1904, against the Cardinals at the Polo Grounds in New York.

- On July 24, 1905, Mertes turned an unassisted double play from left field against the Cincinnati Reds at the Polo Grounds. In the top of the second inning, with one out and Reds' center fielder Cy Seymour (a former and future Giants' player) on third base, catcher Admiral Schlei hit a short fly ball to left. Mertes raced in to make the catch and sprinted in to touch third before Seymour could return.

Mertes began his major league career with the Philadelphia Phillies in 1896 and subsequently played for the Chicago Orphans (1898-1900) and Chicago White Sox (1901-02) before joining the Giants.

In his first season in New York, Mertes topped the N.L. with 104 RBI and tied for the league lead with a career-high 32 doubles (with Fred Clarke of the Pittsburgh Pirates and Harry Steinfeldt of the Reds) to go with a .280 batting average. He also topped N.L. outfielders with a .973 fielding percentage. In 1904 the right-handed swinging Mertes batted at a .276 clip with 78 RBI, and the Giants won their first modern-day N.L. championship (but refused to play the Boston Pilgrims in the World Series).

The following year Mertes batted .279 with personal bests of 108 RBI and 52 stolen bases as New York repeated as league champions and defeated the Philadel-

phia Athletics in the World Series four games to one. Mertes doubled in the Giants' second run in the fifth inning of Game 1 (a 3-0 shutout by future Hall of Famer Christy Mathewson).

After playing in 71 games for the Giants during the 1906 campaign, Mertes was traded to the Cardinals along with catcher Doc Marshall in exchange for outfielder Spike Shannon on July 13, 1906. Mertes played the balance of the season in St. Louis before concluding his playing career in the minor leagues in 1907 and 1908. He returned to the game in 1912 as umpire in the Pacific Coast League.

Mertes' statistics with the Giants included a .273 batting average, 96 doubles, 48 triples, 17 home runs, 323 RBI and 165 stolen bases in 507 games. His 10-year lifetime batting average was .279 with 396 stolen bases in 1,190 games. He pitched in one game for the White Sox in 1902 and earned a victory with eight innings of relief work.

Nicknamed "Sandow," Mertes passed away March 11, 1945, in his hometown of San Francisco, California, at the age of 72 after suffering a heart attack.

Irish Meusel, Outfielder (1921-26)

When Bob Meusel helped put the New York Yankees on the baseball map in the early 1920s, New York Giants' manager John McGraw was not happy.

Never one to stand pat, McGraw fought fire with fire and acquired Meusel's younger brother, Emil, from the Philadelphia

Irish Meusel

Phillies in exchange for catcher Butch Henline, outfielder Curt Walker, pitcher Jesse Winters and $30,000 on July 25, 1921. Emil, who was better known as "Irish," starred for the Giants as an outfielder from 1921-26.

Upon arriving in New York, Irish took over in left field, the same position Bob played for the Yankees. Irish wasted little time impacting his new team. On August 24, 1921, the Giants were 7½ games out of first place at the start of a five-game series against the pace-setting Pittsburgh Pirates at the Polo Grounds in New York. Meusel proceeded to bang out seven hits in 16 at-bats (.438 average), including two doubles, a triple and a home run, and draw five walks as New York swept the series and went on to win the National League pennant. Meusel batted .329 with 36 RBI in 62 games for the Giants.

As fate would have it, the Giants' opponent in the World Series was the Yankees. Irish outhit Bob .345 (10-for-29) to .200 (6-for-20) and collected seven RBI (a Giants' record in World Series play) while leading his team to victory five games to three. Irish's 10 hits are tied for the fifth-most in franchise history.

In 1922 Meusel batted .331 with 17 triples, 16 home runs and a career-high 132 RBI (second in the N.L. to Rogers Hornsby of the St. Louis Cardinals with 152). The Giants repeated as league champions and squared off against the Yankees in the World Series. This time, Bob outhit Irish .300 (6-for-20) to .250 (5-for-20), but Irish equalled his franchise record of seven RBI as the Giants swept the series four games to none with one tie.

The right-handed swinging Meusel topped the N.L. with 125 RBI the following year while batting at a .297 clip with 14 triples and 19 home runs. He helped the Giants capture their third consecutive league flag and, once again, take on the Yankees in the World Series. Irish had a slight advantage in batting average at .280 (7-for-25) to .269 (7-for-26), but Bob drove in seven runs as the Yankees got revenge by winning the championship four games to two.

In the three World Series in which they faced one another, the demonstrative Irish batted .297 (22-for-74) with 16 RBI and the reserved Bob batted .288 (19-for-66) with 12 RBI.

The Giants made it four N.L. pennants in as many years in 1924. Meusel contributed to the cause with a .310 batting average and 102 RBI. In 1925 he reached the century mark in RBI for the fourth straight season (111) while establishing career highs in doubles (35) and home runs (21) and batting at a .328 clip. After batting .292 with 65 RBI the following year, Meusel was given his outright release September 16, 1926. In six seasons with the Giants, Meusel batted .314 (eighth on the franchise career list) with 148 doubles, 64 triples, 70 home runs and 571 RBI in 765 games.

In 1927 Meusel joined the cross-town rival Brooklyn Dodgers. He played in the minor leagues in 1928 and 1929, returned to the Giants as a coach under McGraw in 1930 and concluded his playing career in the minors in 1931. In 11 big league seasons (he appeared in one game for the Washington Senators in 1914 before playing for Philadelphia from 1918-21), Meusel batted .310 in 1,289 games. Bob played for Yankees from 1920-29 and for the Cincinnati Reds in 1930.

Meusel passed away March 1, 1963, in Long Beach, California, at the age of 69.

Chief Meyers, Catcher (1909-15)

When John "Chief" Meyers joined the New York Giants in 1909, he essentially was in a two-strike hole. First, as a full-blooded Indian, he was regarded as a second-class citizen at best, and second, he was being counted on to replace future Hall of Fame catcher Roger Bresnahan.

But Meyers, a Huyakawa Indian, didn't strike out. Rather, he enjoyed a distinguished career with the Giants through 1915. He came to New York as a 28-year-old rookie but lied about his age so it would not be held against him.

Chief Meyers

Meyers was not a power hitter, but he hit for a high average and drove in his fair share of runs. During the 1910 season, he had a career-high 62 RBI to go with a .285 batting average. The following year he batted .332 with nine triples and 61 RBI, and he batted at a career-high .358 clip with a personal-best six home runs and 54 RBI in 1912. On June 10, 1912, Meyers hit for the cycle against the Chicago Cubs at the Polo Grounds in New York.

Defensively, Meyers established a franchise record for catchers with 154 assists during the 1910 season. In 1912 he was behind the plate for all but one of pitcher Rube Marquard's major league record-tying 19 consecutive victories.

The right-handed swinging Meyers continued his efficient production in 1913 and 1914, batting .312 with 47 RBI and .286 with 55 RBI, respectively. He had 150 assists (the second-most in franchise history) in 1914 and 143 assists in 1913 (tied for fifth). Also during the 1913 season, outfielder Jim Thorpe, an Indian who arguably was the greatest all-around athlete of all time in the United States, joined

the Giants and was Meyers' roommate for three years.

Meanwhile, the Giants captured three consecutive National League pennants from 1911-13. Although they were beaten in each of the World Series (by the Philadelphia Athletics in both 1911 and 1913 and by the Boston Red in 1912), Meyers posted some impressive numbers. He batted .300 (6-for-20) in 1911 and .357 (10-for-28) in 1912 before appearing in just one game in 1913. His 10 hits during the 1912 series are tied for the fifth-most by a Giants' player in World Series play. Meyers totaled 12 assists in 1911, a major league record for a six-game series.

Meyers had the good fortune of handling some of the greatest pitchers in Giants' history, including future Hall of Famers Marquard, Christy Mathewson and Joe McGinnity. New York manager John McGraw thought so highly of Meyers that he refused to let him catch any pitcher who threw a spitball after Bugs Raymond, a notorious spitter, split one of Meyers' fingers on his ungloved hand with a delivery in 1910.

In 1915 Meyers slipped to a .232 batting average with 26 RBI, but he still led N.L. catchers with a .986 fielding percentage. He was sent to the cross-town rival Brooklyn Dodgers on waivers February 10, 1916, and played on another N.L. championship team. Meyers began the 1917 season in Brooklyn before finishing both the year and his career with the Boston Braves.

Meyers' seven-year statistics with the Giants included a .301 batting average, 103 doubles, 34 triples, 14 home runs and 335 RBI in 840 games. On the franchise career lists, he ranks first in assists by a catcher (827) and second in putouts (3,849). Meyers' nine-year career batting average was .291 with 393 RBI in 992 games. In the 1918 *Spalding Official Baseball Record*, a Grand National All-America Team for the period of 1871 (the beginning of professional baseball) to 1917 was named among players on championship teams, and Meyers was selected the catcher.

Meyers, who had attended Dartmouth College for a year before becoming a big leaguer, passed away July 25, 1971, in San Bernardino, California, four days shy of his 91st birthday.

Stu Miller, Pitcher (1957-62)

The well-traveled right-hander with the nasty change-up was San Francisco's first great reliever, but he also helped the club as a spot starter during their infancy on the West Coast. Unfortunately, Miller received the most attention because of the forces of nature. Pitching at Candlestick Park in one of the two 1961 All-Star games, the diminutive (5-foot-11, 172 pounds) pitcher was in his windup when a gust of wind nudged him off the mound and resulted in a balk that gave the American League the go-ahead run in the top of the ninth.

It was a true "blown" save, but the National League rallied in the 10th to win. Still, the big talk was of Candlestick's wind and Miller's dilemma, adding to the ballpark's growing reputation because it was viewed on national TV. "No, I *didn't* get blown off the mound," Miller recalled. "I went in and told the umpire (Stan Landes) that the wind just pushed me, that it *made* me balk. He said there was nothing he could do about it, rules are rules.

"The next day in the newspaper, it's (headline) not 'Miller Wins All-Star Game,' but, 'Miller Blown Off Mound.' I couldn't believe the wind that day." The sudden notoriety guised the fact Miller was an excellent pitcher with tantalizing off-speed stuff when he moved from New York with the club.

In that maiden San Francisco season, he led the N.L. with a 2.47 ERA, making 20 starts in 41 appearances and working 182 innings. Despite the windy All-Star Game incident, Miller fashioned an even better season in 1961. He topped all N.L. relievers with a 14-5 record and 17 saves in 63 games, posting a 2.66 ERA and being named Fireman of the Year by *The Sporting News*.

Stu Miller (S.F. Giants Archives)

"Stu is worth his weight in gold as a relief man," manager Alvin Dark said. "I've often thought about starting him, but if he went nine innings, I'd lose him for the bullpen for a couple of days. I can't afford that luxury." Ed Bailey, one of his catchers, used lines like, "Stu couldn't break an egg with his fastball," and "You could catch him with a pair of pliers."

Miller didn't mind his reputation as a crafty pitcher, noting: "I never had a good fastball, even in the minors. I relied mostly on deception and off-speed pitches." After notching a team-leading 19 saves for the 1962 N.L. champions, Miller was traded to Baltimore along with Mike McCormick in what was a big mistake for the Giants.

He had a league-leading 27 saves for the Orioles in 1963 and was 14-7 with a 1.89 ERA for them in 1965. Jack Fisher, Jim Coker and Billy Hoeft, the three players the Orioles shipped to San Francisco in the trade, did little for the Giants. More than 30 years later, he was named the reliever on the club's all-decade team of the 1960s.

Miller, a Massachusetts native, never played high school or college ball, but attended Davidson College and signed with the St. Louis Cardinals in 1949. He reached the majors in 1952 and posted a 105-103 record with a 3.24 ERA and 93 saves in 704 games. He retired in the Bay Area and owned a liquor store before moving to the Sierra foothills near Sacramento.

Greg Minton, Pitcher (1975-87)

No one knew it at the time, but a late spring training trade in 1973 brought the San Francisco Giants one of the greatest relief pitchers in the franchise's history.

On April 2, 1973, the Giants sent little-used catcher Fran Healy to the Kansas City Royals in exchange for minor leaguer Greg Minton. Six years later, Minton had mastered a

Greg Minton (S.F. Giants Archives)

wicked sinker pitch that made him one of baseball's premier closers of his day. He pitched in the Bay Area from 1975-87.

Minton's sinker propelled him to the majors, but he more or less fell into the Giants' right-handed stopper's role. When Randy Moffitt was diagnosed with a stomach disorder in 1979, manager Dave Bristol needed someone to fill the void and team with lefty reliever Gary Lavelle. Bristol found that someone in Minton, who already was making headlines with his "Moon Man" nickname and eccentric clubhouse antics.

After posting 19- and 21-save seasons in 1980 and 1981, respectively, Minton put it all together in 1982. He assembled a 10-4 record with a sparkling 1.83 ERA and a then club-record 30 saves. Minton was named to the National League All-Star team and pitched two-thirds of an inning at Olympic Stadium in Montreal. He went on to finish sixth in the balloting for the N.L. Cy Young Award.

Minton also pitched his way into the major league records book in 1982. From September 6, 1978-May 2, 1982, Minton pitched 269.1 innings and did not surrender a single home run. John Stearns of the New York Mets snapped the string with a round-tripper at Candlestick Park in San Francisco.

A home run of his own provided Minton with perhaps his least-known achievement. The switch-hitter, who had a total of 103 at-bats in 12-plus seasons with the Giants, connected off Atlanta side-armer Gene Garber, an accomplished reliever in his own right, while batting left-handed September 27, 1983, at Atlanta-Fulton County Stadium.

Minton was part of history again in 1983 when he and Lavelle gave San Francisco the first N.L. bullpen with two 20-save relief pitchers. Minton finished with 23, while Lavelle had 20. Minton had 19 saves during the 1984 campaign.

Minton's total of 125 saves with the Giants ranks third on the franchise's career list (including the New York years) behind Rod Beck (199) and Lavelle (127). He also is third

on the career games list with 552, trailing Lavelle (647) and Hall of Famer Christy Mathewson (634). Minton had a 45-52 record with a 3.23 ERA for San Francisco.

From 1987-90 Minton pitched for the California Angels. In 710 career games he compiled a 59-65 record with a 3.10 ERA and 150 saves.

In 1998 Minton was hired as pitching coach of the Class AAA Vancouver Canadians in the Angels' minor league system, and he spent the 1999 season with the Class A Cedar Rapids Kernels. He lives in Scottsdale, Arizona, during the offseason.

Kevin Mitchell, Outfielder (1987-91)

Kevin Mitchell had one great season in five years with the Giants, and it was one of the most outstanding in San Francisco history. That was 1989, and Mitchell was the National League Most Valuable Player while powering the Giants to the World Series with a league-leading 47 home runs, 125 RBI and a .635 slugging percentage.

He became the Giants' first MVP since Willie McCovey in 1969 and was named Major League Player of the Year by *The Sporting News*. Kevin thrived under batting coach Dusty Baker and kept on rolling after leading N.L. players with a .455 average and seven home runs in spring training. He batted .291 during the season and improved to .353 with two homers in the playoff series with the Chicago Cubs.

He also homered off Mike Moore of the Athletics in Game 4 of the World Series, where he batted .294. Injuries prevented Mitchell from regaining that form again, but he batted .341 for the Cincinnati Reds in 1993 and had 30 homers in 95 games for them in 1994 before moving on. He concluded a checkered career with Oakland in 1998.

A San Diego native, Mitchell signed with the New York Mets and began his pro career in 1981, batting .335 at Kingsport. By 1986 he was a key reserve on the World Series champions, playing six positions and batting .277. Partly because of some mild scrapes with the

Kevin Mitchell (S.F. Giants Archives)

law, the Mets gave up on "Mitch" that winter, shipping him (along with pitcher Kevin Brown) to San Diego in a deal that brought the Mets Kevin McReynolds.

Under the influence of his boyhood chums, an unsavory lot, "Mitch" didn't thrive in San Diego and was traded to the Giants in a July 4 blockbuster that included Dave Dravecky and Craig Lefferts for Chris Brown, Mark Davis, Mark Grant and Keith Comstock. Davis won Cy Young honors as a Padres' reliever, but the Giants got the far better of the megadeal, winning division titles in 1987 and 1989. Also nicknamed "Boogie Bear," he had an immediate impact on the Giants, hitting two home runs in his debut against the Cubs at Wrigley Field.

Playing mostly third base, he batted .306 with 15 homers and 44 RBI in 69 games with his new club. He switched to left field permanently in 1988 and had knee surgery following an unspectacular season. But he was good as new in 1989 and enjoyed a magnificent campaign. He also helped the Giants when he was traded to Seattle in 1991 for pitchers Bill Swift, Dave Burba and Mike Jackson, a swap which contributed to 103 wins in 1993.

Johnny Mize

Johnny Mize, First Baseman (1942, 1946-49)

The first man to hit 50 home runs in a Giants' uniform joined the New York Giants on December 11, 1941, in a trade with the St. Louis Cardinals. Johnny Mize was the National League batting champion with the Redbirds in 1939 with a .349 average, and he also led the league in home runs in 1939 and 1940. He batted .364 in 1938 and had 137 RBI in 1940, so his acquisition by the Giants was a major coup.

The Cardinals felt his arm was worthless, so it turned out to be a rare mistake by Branch Rickey, then the Cardinals' general manager, when the slugger was shipped to the Giants for $50,000 and two players. Mize returned from military service in 1946 and in 1947 set the franchise record of 51 home runs, since toppled by Willie Mays.

Mize's mark still stands as an N.L. record for a left-handed batter. He tied Ralph Kiner for Senior Circuit home run honors in 1947 and

1948 but was sold to Yankees for $40,000 in August 1949 because Leo Durocher wanted to build his team around speed and Mize was slowing down. But Mize still had some life left, proving to be a vital reserve on some great Yankees' teams.

In merely 90 games in 1950, for instance, Mize mustered 25 home runs and 72 RBI. He hit three home runs, one as a pinch hitter, in the 1952 World Series. The "Big Cat" was the Mark McGwire of his day, hitting three home runs in a game a record six times and registering 30 multiple-homer games. Mize finished with a .312 career average, 2,011 hits, 359 home runs and 1,337 RBI on way toward Hall of Fame induction.

He briefly served the Giants as a coach in New York before retiring from the game. Mize overcame odds to attain major league stardom. He was given a 50-50 chance of playing again when he had surgery to remove a bone spur high in his leg. The surgery, unusual at the time, was a success, and he soon launched a great career with the Cardinals.

John Montefusco, Pitcher (1974-80)

From 1974-76 the San Francisco Giants averaged a mere 6,871 spectators per game. Enter John Montefusco, whose flare for the dramatic provided a much-needed boost to sagging spirits.

A boastful and free-spirited right-handed pitcher for the Giants from 1974-80, Montefusco was drafted in June of 1973 and predicted he would be in the major leagues in two years. In truth, he arrived sooner, making his debut September 3, 1974, against the rival Los Angeles Dodgers at Dodger Stadium. The "Count" came in with the bases loaded and no outs in the first inning and the Giants trailing 3-2, worked out of the jam, belted a two-run homer in the third (his first at-bat of the season after playing in the Pacific Coast and Texas leagues which utilized the designated hitter) and finished the game to earn a 9-5 victory.

"I got drunk the night before when I learned I was going up, because they told me I

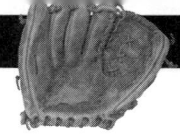

wouldn't pitch for at least a week," Montefusco recalled. "When they called my name with the bases loaded, I was ready to turn around and walk out of there. I was shaking, but I got a grounder and two strikeouts and got out of the inning. I hit a homer and I was the winner. I couldn't ask for anything better for breaking into the big leagues."

In 1975 Montefusco proved his coming-out party was not a fluke. He orchestrated a 1-0, 10-inning five-hitter against the Philadelphia Phillies at Veterans Stadium in Philadelphia on May 27; recorded a career-high 14 strikeouts in a 9-1 victory over the Montreal Expos at Candlestick Park in San Francisco on August 27; and had 13 strikeouts in a 5-4 win over the Phillies at Candlestick in his next start August 31. (The Giants' franchise record for strikeouts in a game is 16 by Christy Mathewson against the St. Louis Cardinals on October 3, 1904.)

Montefusco finished the campaign with a 15-9 record, 2.88 ERA, 215 strikeouts (second

John Montefusco (S.F. Giants Archives)

in the National League behind Tom Seaver of the New York Mets with 243), 10 complete games and four shutouts to earn N.L. Rookie of the Year honors by both the Baseball Writers Association of America and *The Sporting News*. His 15 victories were the most by a Giants' rookie since Larry Jansen won 21 games in 1947, while his strikeout total was the greatest by any newcomer in baseball since Herb Score of the Cleveland Indians fanned 245 batters in 1955. Both marks are San Francisco rookie records.

"I think I'm a pretty good pitcher," Montefusco boldly declared. "I could be rated with Tom Seaver or Don Sutton, I think. One of these days, I want to throw a no-hitter, too.

"Who am I hurting by popping off? I'm just having fun. What's the sense of keeping it in? I like to set goals and put pressure on myself. I like to go after the other team's big man. I figure it can help me because the hitters might try a little too hard against me."

The beat continued in 1976 as Montefusco was named to the N.L. All-Star team (pitching two scoreless innings with two strikeouts and two walks at Veterans Stadium) and fired a 9-0 no-hitter (remember the prediction) against the Atlanta Braves at Atlanta-Fulton County Stadium on September 29. The gem capped a season in which Montefusco went 16-14 with a 2.85 ERA, 172 strikeouts, 11 complete games and six shutouts (tied for the league lead with the Mets' Jon Matlack).

After a down 1977 season (7-12, 3.49 ERA), Montefusco returned to form by opening the following year with a 7-2 record through June 25. He wound up 11-9 with a 3.81 ERA but then mustered just three wins in 1979 and four in 1980. Upset about being removed from a game against the Mets at Candlestick on June 18, 1980, Montefusco got into a scuffle with manager Dave Bristol and wound up with a black eye. Montefusco, who also occasionally was at odds with teammates, was traded to the Braves along with minor league outfielder Craig Landis in exchange for pitcher Doyle Alexander on December 12, 1980.

On San Francisco's career lists, Montefusco ranks fifth in strikeouts (869), seventh in games started (175) and innings pitched (1,182.2) and eighth in shutouts (11). In 185 games he compiled a 59-62 record with 30 complete games.

After pitching for the Braves in 1981, Montefusco moved on the San Diego Padres (1982-83) and New York Yankees (1983-86). His 13-year career totals included a 90-83 record with a 3.54 ERA and 1,081 strikeouts in 298 games.

Montefusco subsequently worked in the Yankees' minor league system. He owned a thoroughbred as a player and went on to become a driver on the harness circuit. Trouble with the law landed him in jail in the 1990s. He currently makes his home in Colts Neck, New Jersey.

Joe Moore (Brace Photo)

Joe Moore, Outfielder (1930-41)

When left fielder Joe Moore hit a home run in the fourth inning against the Cincinnati Reds at the Polo Grounds in New York on June 6, 1939, he put himself and the New York Giants in the baseball record book.

Moore's blast was the Giants record-setting fifth homer of the inning, following catcher Harry Danning, center fielder Frank Demaree, second baseman Whitey Whitehead and pitcher Manuel Salvo. The mark has since been tied by the Philadelphia Phillies (1949), San Francisco Giants (1961) and Minnesota Twins (1966).

Later during the 1939 season, "Jo-Jo" was the final ingredient of a four-home run inning against Philadelphia at the Polo Grounds in the first game of a double-header August 13, along with first baseman Zeke Bonura, second baseman Alex Kampouris and pitcher Bill Lohrman. In both cases, Moore's homer was the third consecutive shot, and the Giants went on to finish with seven round-trippers.

Moore spent his entire 12-year career with the Giants from 1930-41. He played sparingly his first two seasons—while spending most of his time in the minor leagues—but one of manager Bill Terry's first acts upon replacing John McGraw as New York's manager on June 3, 1932, was to make Moore the everyday left fielder and leadoff batter.

In 1933 Moore batted .292 with 42 RBI as the Giants captured the National League pennant and defeated the Washington Senators in the World Series four games to one. The following year Moore posted career highs of a .331 batting average, 37 doubles and 15 home runs to go with 61 RBI. Along the way, he was selected to his first of six All-Star Games (1934, 1935, 1936, 1937, 1938 and 1940).

Nicknamed the "Thin Man" and the "Gause Ghost" (he was a starkly thin 5-foot-11 and 155 pounds and hailed from Gause, Texas), Moore was the epitome of consistency. He drove in a personal best of 71 runs to go with a .295 batting average and 15 home runs during the 1935 campaign, and batted at better

than .300 each of the next three campaigns. All the while, he was a deft fielder who played the caroms off the difficult left field wall at the Polo Grounds with definite aplomb.

The Giants won back-to-back N.L. flags in 1936 and 1937 but lost to the cross-town rival Yankees on both occasions. Moore contributed a .391 batting average (9-for-23) in the 1937 matchup while tying the record for hits in a five-game series.

Moore concluded his career with a .298 batting average, 258 doubles, 53 triples, 79 home runs and 513 RBI in 1,335 games. On the Giants' franchise lists, he ranks eighth in hits (1,615) and doubles and ninth in at-bats (5,427).

Moore currently resides in Bryan, Texas. He celebrated his 90th birthday on Christmas of 1998 and holds the distinction of being the oldest-living former Giants' player.

Joe Morgan, Second Baseman (1981-82)

Second baseman Joe Morgan only played for the San Francisco Giants in 1981 and 1982, but he provided one of the franchise's most memorable home runs.

On October 2, 1982—one day after the Giants were eliminated from the National League West Division race by the rival Los Angeles Dodgers—Morgan socked a game-winning, three-run homer in the bottom of the seventh inning off the Dodgers' Terry Forster at Candlestick Park in San Francisco. The Giants won the game 5-3 to knock out Los Angeles and give the division crown to the Atlanta Braves. (As an interesting aside, Forster went on to sign with Atlanta as a free agent during the offseason.)

Ironically, the game was Morgan's last in a Giants' uniform. He was traded to the Philadelphia Phillies along with pitcher Al Holland in exchange for pitchers Mark Davis and Mike Krukow and minor league outfielder Charles Penigar on December 14, 1982. Although Krukow would ultimately be a 20-game winner and Davis was a youngster with a promising future, the deal was regarded as the most con-

Joe Morgan

troversial in general manager Tom Haller's tenure.

Morgan had signed with San Francisco as a free agent February 9, 1981. Despite being 37 years old at the time, he was a proven winner who provided tremendous leadership while still being productive. Morgan batted only .240 during the 1981 season, but he was second in the N.L. with 66 walks, had a .374 on-base percentage and stole 14 bases.

In 1982 Morgan batted at a .289 clip with 14 home runs, 61 RBI and 24 stolen bases en route to being named the N.L. Comeback Player of the Year. He ranked third in the league with a snappy .402 on-base percentage (behind Mike Schmidt of the Philadelphia Phillies at .407 and Keith Hernandez of the St. Louis Cardinals at .404) and was sixth with 85 walks.

That year the Giants were foundering in fourth place, 13 games behind Atlanta on August 3 before making a huge surge that featured numerous late rallies. A 20-7 record in September left San Francisco just one game out with three games to play against Los Angeles, but the comeback came up just short.

Morgan, the 1965 N.L. Rookie of the Year, began his career with Houston from 1963-71 and achieved his greatest acclaim with the Cincinnati Reds from 1972-79. He earned back-to-back N.L. Most Valuable Player awards in 1975 and 1976 (one of only 10 players in baseball history to do so) as the Reds won the World Series both years. Morgan was a nine-time All-Star and won five consecutive Gold Glove awards from 1973-77. After playing for the N.L.-champion Phillies in 1983, Morgan concluded his career with the Oakland Athletics in 1984.

In his brief stint with the Giants, Morgan batted .270 with 22 home runs and 92 RBI in 314 games. His 22-year career statistics included a .271 batting average, 2,517 hits, 268 homers and 1,133 RBI in 2,649 games. Four times he paced the lead in on-base percentage. He ranks third in baseball history with 1,865 walks, trailing only Babe Ruth (2,056) and Ted Williams (2,019).

Morgan was inducted into the National Baseball Hall of Fame in 1990 (his first year of eligibility). He currently serves as color commentator on ESPN's Sunday Night Baseball telecasts and resides in Danville, California.

Don Mueller, Outfielder (1948-57)

Throughout his major league career, Don Mueller was known as a top-flight singles hitter. He earned the nickname "Mandrake The Magician" for his ability to seemingly guide base hits through holes on the infield.

But Mueller, an outfielder for the New York Giants from 1948-57, has his name in the baseball record book for clouting five home runs over a two-game span. He accomplished the feat against the cross-town rival Brooklyn Dodgers at the Polo Grounds in New York on

September 1-2, 1951, hitting three homers in the first game and two in the second contest. The fifth blast came moments after Mueller learned he had become a father. The achievement has been done 11 other times in the National League and on nine occasions in the American League.

The Giants won both of those games as part of their amazing comeback from 13 1/2 games behind Brooklyn on August 12 to force a three-game playoff. In the third and deciding game at the Polo Grounds on October 3, the Dodgers led 4-1 in the bottom of the ninth inning. Mueller contributed a key single to New York's rally but suffered a sprained left ankle sliding into third base on first baseman Whitey Lockman's double. Mueller had to be carried off the field on a stretcher and was in the clubhouse when third baseman Bobby Thomson won the game with his infamous "Shot Heard

Don Mueller (Brace Photo)

'Round The World." The injury sidelined Mueller for the World Series against the cross-town rival Yankees, who won the championship four games to two.

After playing sparingly for the Giants during his first two seasons, Mueller took over as the everyday right fielder in 1950 and batted .291 with a career-high 84 RBI. Of his 153 hits, 125 of them were singles. Mueller hit a personal best of 16 home runs during the pennant-winning 1951 campaign while batting at a .277 clip with 69 RBI.

In 1953 Mueller batted .333 with 60 RBI. He then compiled his best numbers a year later with career highs of a .342 batting average, 35 doubles and eight triples to go with 71 RBI. Entering the final day of the season, Mueller led the N.L. in batting but was overtaken by teammate Willie Mays (.345). Mueller did top the league with 212 hits (165 singles), the 10th-highest total in franchise history. Along the way, Mueller was selected to the All-Star Game at Municipal Stadium in Cleveland and came up with a pinch-hit RBI double. He hit for the cycle against the Pittsburgh Pirates at the Polo Grounds on July 11 and put together a 21-game hitting streak from August 22-September 11.

New York went on to capture the 1954 N.L. pennant and sweep the Cleveland Indians (with their eye-popping 111-43 record) in the World Series four games to none. The left-handed swinging Mueller batted at a .389 clip (7-for-19) and scored four runs in the series. His seven ties tied shortstop Alvin Dark for the most on the team.

Mueller returned to the All-Star Game in 1955 at County Stadium in Milwaukee as the N.L.'s starting right fielder and was 1-for-2. For the season, he batted .306 with 83 RBI. Mueller played two more seasons with the Giants before being sold to the Chicago White Sox for what was reported as slightly more than $20,000 on March 21, 1958.

In 10 seasons with the Giants, Mueller batted .298 with 134 doubles, 37 triples, 65 home runs and 504 RBI in 1,211 games. Some 81 percent of his hits were singles (1,012 of

1,248). Mueller saw limited playing time with the White Sox in 1958 and 1959 before retiring. His lifetime batting average was .296 with 520 RBI in 1,245 games.

Mueller currently resides in Maryland Heights, Missouri. His father, Walter, was an outfielder for the Pirates from 1922-24 and in 1926.

Masanori Murakami, Pitcher (1964-65)

Masanori Murakami didn't enjoy the success of many Giants omitted from these pages, but his two years with San Francisco in 1964 and 1965 were of historical significance. The 6-foot left-hander became the first Japanese native to pitch in the major leagues, although ties to his homeland limited him to those two years.

Coming to the United States as a 19-year-old, "Mashi" was an immediate success with Class-A Fresno in 1964. The baby Giants won the California League championship, and the impressive import was the main reason. Murakami posted a league-leading 1.78 ERA with an 11-7 record and 15 saves.

Masanori Murakami (S.F. Giants Archives)

He dazzled scouts with 159 strikeouts in merely 106 innings and earned a late-season promotion to the Giants. He pitched nine games and 15 innings for San Francisco, yielding a run in merely one of them to go 1-0 with a 1.80 ERA, striking out 15 and walking one. Murakami improved to 4-1 in 45 games in 1965, but the Giants lost a contract war with the Nankai Hawks, who owned his rights in Japan.

An agreement was reached so he could pitch for the Giants in 1965, but there were no guarantees for 1966 because the Hawks wanted him back. Commissioner Ford Frick entered the fracas and temporarily suspended relations between the United States and Japan until the Murakami matter could be decided. Family pressure made it easier for the pitcher to return to his homeland, and he never again pitched in the majors.

"Mashi's" father had a job with the Hawks, and it would have been in jeopardy had the pitcher ignored the team's wishes. The Giants missed him, not only because of his pitching ability but also because of his clubhouse presence. He often was the target of pranks by teammates, and he responded accordingly. In spring training, Murakami took an interest in the Western culture and wanted to buy some souvenirs to take back home, but he returned to the hotel empty-handed.

When asked why, he shook his hand and said: "No good. No good. Everything made in Japan." Later, during a game at Wrigley Field, manager Herman Franks was thrown out after a heated argument with umpire Mel Steiner, and Franks was stewing when he entered the dugout. A grinning Murakami innocently asked Franks why he was tossed. "I said nothing," Franks grumbled. Murakami's reply, "Maybe so, Mr. Herman, but I know what umpire say to you—take a hike!"

The dugout erupted in laughter and the phrase "Take a hike" was repeated many times thereafter. "Mashi" returned home, but he didn't stay away forever. As a Japanese journalist, he often visits the Giants and was honored by the club in 1994 on the 30th anniversary of his feat of breaking the barrier for Japan.

Art Nehf, Pitcher (1919-26)

Art Nehf, who pitched for the New York Giants from 1919-26, is the only pitcher in World Series history to win two games by the score of 1-0.

Interestingly, Nehf authored both of his masterpiece whitewashes against the crosstown rival Yankees. The left-hander blanked them in the eighth and deciding game of the 1921 series and in Game 3 of the 1923 series.

But those weren't the only postseason games Nehf won. He also defeated the Yankees in the fifth and deciding game of the 1922 World Series by the score of 5-3 and outlasted future Hall of Famer Walter Johnson and the Washington Senators in the opener of the 1924 series by the score of 4-3 in 12 innings. In the Giants' four World Series appearances from 1921-24, Nehf compiled

Art Nehf

only a 4-4 record but with a snappy 1.96 ERA. He pitched in 10 games totaling 78 innings and allowed merely 49 hits.

Nehf began his major league career with the Boston Braves from 1915-19 before being acquired by the Giants in exchange for pitchers Red Causey, Johnny Jones and Joe Oeschger; catcher Mickey O'Neil; and $55,000 cash of August 15, 1919. Nehf made an immediate impact, going 9-2 with a 1.50 ERA in 13 games.

The next two seasons were Nehf's best. He went 21-12, establishing a career high in wins, with a 3.08 ERA in 1920 and finished 20-10 with a 3.63 ERA in 1921. On August 24, 1921, the Giants trailed the first-place Pittsburgh Pirates by 7½ games. That day Nehf won the opener of a double-header and a five-game series against the Pirates 10-2 at the Polo Grounds in New York, and three days later helped the Giants complete the sweep with a 3-1 victory. New York went on to capture the National League pennant by four games over Pittsburgh.

From 1920-22 Nehf completely dominated the Pirates to the tune of a 15-3 record, including 12 consecutive wins (one in 1920, seven in 1921 and four in 1922). It was big-time revenge for a 2-0 loss Nehf suffered at the hands of Pittsburgh in 21 innings during his days with Boston during the 1918 campaign.

Nehf wound up 19-13 with a 3.29 ERA in 1922 and continued to win in double figures each of the next three years (13-10 in 1923, 14-4 in 1924 and 11-9 in 1925). He shutout the cross-town rival Brooklyn Dodgers 3-0 at the Polo Grounds on September 28, 1923, to clinch the Giants' third straight pennant.

After beginning the 1926 season in New York, Nehf was sold to the Cincinnati Reds on May 11. He was bothered by a sore arm, and when he found out Giants' manager John McGraw had not informed Cincinnati of his condition Nehf became furious and did not speak to McGraw for six years. In eight seasons in Gotham City, Nehf compiled a 107-60 record with a 3.45 ERA in 226 games. On the franchise career lists, he ranks sixth with a .641 winning percentage.

Nehf pitched for the Reds in 1926 and 1927 before concluding his career with the Chicago Cubs from 1927-29. His 15-year record was 184-120 with a 3.20 ERA in 451 games. "Artful Artie" issued only 640 walks in 2,707.2 innings (2.1 per nine innings).

A graduate of Rose Polytechnic Institute (Terre Haute, Indiana) with a B.S. in electrical engineering, the well-spoken Nehf worked in hotel management following his playing days and later got involved in the real estate business.

Nehf passed away December 18, 1960, in Phoenix, Arizona, at the age of 68.

Robb Nen, Pitcher (1998-present)

Rangy Robb Nen wasn't known for his ability to keep runners on base, so he found a solution during his first five seasons as the Giants' closer - keep them off base. Relying on a wicked slider that has baffled hitters for years, the 6-foot-5 Nen in 2002 fired past Rod Beck

Robb Nen (S.F. Giants Archives)

and became the franchise career saves leader with 206.

He did it with consistency, averaging 41.2 saves while never notching more than 45 nor fewer than 37. Nen has thrived at Pacific Bell Park, posting a career-best 1.50 ERA in 2000, a career-high 45 saves in 2001 and 43 saves with a 6-2 record and a 2.20 ERA in 2002, followed by seven postseason saves for the pennant-winners.

Nen made his debut with the Giants in 1998 and promptly posted 40 saves, the second-highest total in franchise history. Beck, who holds the single-season record with 48 in 1993, was not re-signed following the 1997 season to make room for the younger Nen, who threw harder and was more intimidating.

Rapid Robb raced to a sensational start with his new club, yielding one earned run the opening month, saving 10 games in May and entering his first All-Star Game with a 6-1 record, 25 saves and a 0.98 ERA. He became a fan favorite because of his success at home, going 4-2 with 23 saves and a 0.43 ERA at Candlestick/3Com Park. Victimized by a lack of opportunities in the second half, Nen finished 7-7 with a 1.52 ERA, limiting opponents to a .180 batting average and attaining career highs in games (78), innings (88.2) and strikeouts (110).

The son of former major leaguer Dick Nen, Robb was reared in Southern California and was a Los Alamitos High School teammate of Giants' first baseman J.T. Snow. Whereas Snow was a prep superstar, Nen mainly was a prospect. He was drafted in the 32nd round by the Texas Rangers in 1987 and was primarily a starter in six unspectacular minor league seasons (13-26) when he reached the Rangers in 1993.

When the Florida Marlins acquired him in July, he was switched to the bullpen and showed gradual improvement every year. Nen saved 15 games in 1994 after Marlins' closer Bryan Harvey was injured, saved 23 more in 1995 and had 35 saves in both 1996 and 1997.

He was 15-for-15 on saves opportunities to start his career. Nen went 5-1 with a 1.95 ERA in 1996 and helped the Marlins to a World Series championship in 1997.

He posted a 9-3 record with the Marlins and was flawless in the playoff series against the Giants and the Braves, going 1-0, saving two games and yielding only one hit and no runs in four innings. He added four saves in World Series against Cleveland despite being tagged for four runs in 4.2 innings. Then the Giants' derived the benefits of the Florida housecleaning.

Lefty O'Doul, Outfielder (1928, 1933-34)

Lefty O'Doul achieved as much off the field as on it as a long-time manager of the San Francisco Seals and as an ambassador who introduced baseball to Japan. He accompanied barnstorming American players, including Babe Ruth, to Japan in 1931 and 1934, establishing professional baseball there and returning with his 1949 Seals. O'Doul also escorted a 1951 All-Star team that included Joe DiMaggio to Japan and lined up the Giants' 1960 goodwill tour among his 30 trips to Japan.

"I'm not here to raid them (of players)," he said of his trips to the Orient. "I'm here to help them." O'Doul's major disappointment was not being elected to the Baseball Hall of Fame, to which he once said, "I would rather be elected to the Japanese Hall of Fame."

Lefty was a popular San Francisco restauranteur at, of course, "Lefty O'Doul's" near Union Square until his death at age 72 in 1969. To San Franciscans, he was a colorful character, born Francis Joseph O'Doul and nicknamed "Lefty." He also was known as "Marblehead" when he managed the hometown Seals, and as the "Man in the Green Suit" for his trademark green apparel and his snappy wardrobe.

Opponents viewed him differently during his playing days as one the greatest National League hitters despite a brief major league career. He began with the 1917 Seals after starring as a teen pitcher on a South San Francisco

semi-pro team. He was purchased by the Yankees as a pitcher in 1918, becoming one of only two players drafted out of the minors that year. He was seldom used in 1919-20, so he was optioned to Seals and went 25-9 with a 2.39 ERA in 1921.

Soon he joined Ruth in a successful conversion from the mound to the outfield. Lefty injured his arm while pitching for the Boston Red Sox in 1923 and was sold to Salt Lake City of the Pacific Coast League, where he blossomed as a hitter with a .394 average and a staggering 309 hits in 198 games in 1924. But he still couldn't land a major league job and was cut by the Chicago Cubs in 1926 despite 19 hits in 21 spring training at-bats.

Lefty O'Doul

So Lefty returned to his beloved P.C.L. and batted .338 with Hollywood in 1926, earning MVP honors, and batted .378 with the Seals in 1927. Drafted for $5,000, he reached the majors to stay with the 1928 Giants, batting .319, but he didn't stay long with one team. Lefty shifted to the Philadelphia Phillies in 1929 and was the N.L. batting champion at .398. Lefty also belted 254 hits, setting an N.L. record that was tied by Bill Terry the following year. It still stands.

"My greatest accomplishment and my greatest thrill," O'Doul said. "Rogers Hornsby held the old record, so I was very proud of what I did as a washed-up pitcher with a bad leg. What a season that was. The ball looked like a balloon." He followed with a .383 average for Philadelphia in 1930 before moving to Brooklyn in 1931 and winning his second batting title with the Dodgers at .368 in 1932. He batted .316 with the Giants in 1934, his final major league season. Lefty's lifetime average was .349, not far behind Ty Cobb (.367) and Hornsby (.358).

O'Doul had merely one World Series at-bat, and he made the most of it with the Giants against the Washington Senators in 1933. New York trailed 1-0 in the sixth inning of Game 2, and Lefty pinch hit with the bases loaded. His two-run single off Alvin Crowder placed the Giants ahead. After the game he was carried off the field by delirious fans. "I really was a hero that day," he said. "I'll never forget the feeling I had running down to first base. It was just like I was running on clouds."

He began his managerial career with pennant-winning Seals in 1935 and held the job through 1951 despite persistent rumors he would manage a major league team. "San Francisco is my home and the West Coast is my range," he explained. "Why move into a lot of trouble I don't have here?"

Lefty's 1946 club was among the P.C.L.'s greatest ever, going 115-68 and setting a minor league attendance record. Larry Jansen, who later gained pitching fame with the Giants, won 30 games for O'Doul in 1946. Lefty also was vice president of the Seals from 1948-51 and later managed San Diego, Oakland, Vancouver and Seattle in the P.C.L.

The biggest question remaining is why isn't he in the Hall of Fame, which has kept him out because he didn't have a long major league career. San Francisco will never forget him, however. A draw bridge in China Basin, adjacent to the new Pacific Bell Park, bears his name. Symbolically, it's located near the Butchertown neighborhood from where he crossed the bridge to stardom.

Jim O'Rourke, Outfielder (1885-89, 1891-92, 1904)

Jim O'Rourke spoke the English language eloquently and played the game of baseball splendidly.

Aptly nicknamed "Orator Jim" for his way with words, O'Rourke played for the New York Giants from 1885-89, 1891-92 and 1904. He primarily played in the outfield but also saw action at catcher, first base, second base and third base.

O'Rourke began his professional baseball career in the National Association with the Middletown (Connecticut) Mansfields in 1872 and the Boston Red Stockings from 1873-75. The present-day National League was formed in 1876, and the Red Stockings were a charter member. The N.L.'s inaugural game was played April 22, 1876, at 25th and Jefferson streets in Philadelphia, and with two outs in the first inning O'Rourke singled off the Athletics' Lon Knight for the first hit in N.L. history.

O'Rourke played for the Red Stockings through 1878, moved to the Providence Grays in 1879, returned to Boston in 1880 and moved to the Buffalo Bisons as player-manager from 1881-84. He finished second in the N.L. in batting in both 1879 (.348) and 1884 (.347) and was fourth in 1877 (career-high .362). O'Rourke was a member of three consecutive N.L. pennant-winning teams from 1877-79.

Prior to the 1885 season O'Rourke was traded to the Giants. He batted .300 with a league-leading 16 triples in 1885, .309 in 1886 and .321 (fourth in the N.L.) in 1889. The Giants won World Series championships in 1888

JAMES O'ROURKE, Right-fielder.

Jim O'Rourke (Transcendental Graphics)

and 1889. He jumped to the newly-formed Players League in 1890 and at the age of 39 posted career highs of nine home runs and 115 RBI with a .360 batting average for the New York Giants. The P.L. folded after one season, and O'Rourke returned to the N.L. Giants and topped the team with 95 RBI. In 1893 he moved to the Washington Senators as player-manager for one season before retiring.

Eleven years later, the 54-year-old O'Rourke asked Giants' manager John McGraw if he could play in one final game. McGraw agreed, and O'Rourke caught the first game of a double-header against the Cincinnati Reds at the Polo Grounds in New York on September 22, 1904. He went 1-for-4 with a single and a run scored while becoming the oldest individual to play a full game. Meanwhile, the Giants clinched the N.L. pennant with a 7-5 victory.

In 807 games with the Giants, O'Rourke batted .299 with 966 hits, 170 doubles, 60

triples, 21 home runs and 446 RBI. The right-handed batter's 19-year major league statistics included a .310 batting average with 2,304 hits, 414 doubles, 132 triples, 50 home runs and 1,010 RBI in 1,774 games. He played all nine positions on the field, including six games as a pitcher in 1883 and 1884. His five-year managerial record was 246-258 (.488 winning percentage).

In 1894 O'Rourke worked as an N.L. umpire, and he subsequently became player-manager of the Bridgeport team in the Connecticut League from 1897-1908. He served as league president from 1907-13. One day while catching O'Rourke got into an argument with an umpire and used some obscenities. He responded by announcing to the crowd that president O'Rourke was fining player-manager O'Rourke for his undiplomatic behavior.

On New Year's Day of 1919, O'Rourke, who had earned a law degree from Yale University, contracted pneumonia after walking to meet a client on a frigid day. He passed away January 8, 1919, in Bridgeport at the age of 68. O'Rourke was inducted into the National Baseball Hall of Fame in 1945 by the Veterans Committee. His older brother, John, and son, Queenie, both played in the major leagues.

Russ Ortiz, Pitcher (1998-2002)

The Giants probably wouldn't have reached the 2002 National League Championship Series, or even earned the wild card without Ortiz's clutch pitching down the stretch, so it came as a surprise when economics dictated his trade to the Atlanta Braves shortly after the World Series. It didn't seem possible to deal a young power pitcher who averaged 15.8 victories and 209 innings over four full major league seasons.

Ortiz's 63 victories over a four-year stretch were the most by a Giant since the days of Hall of Famers Juan Marichal and Gaylord Perry - and he did it in his first four full seasons, beginning with an eye-opening 18-9 record in 1999, his first year as a regular member of the rotation.

The former college (Oklahoma) and minor league closer was at his best down the stretch for the Giants, going 15-10 in August and 16-4 in September-October during his S.F. career. That included a 6-0 August in 2000 for N.L. Pitcher of the Month honors and a 5-0 final month in 2002. The club reached the playoffs both seasons.

One couldn't blame the Braves from pursuing Ortiz, perhaps their most significant acquisition since Greg Maddux in 1993. Russ was 3-0 against Atlanta in 2002, including two dazzling performances at Turner Field in the opening round. He yielded two runs in seven innings during an 8-5 victory in Game 1 and one run in the clinching 3-1 triumph in Game 5.

Ortiz also had the Giants on the verge of winning their first World Series in 48 years when he carried a two-hit shutout and a 5-0 lead into the bottom of the seventh inning at Anaheim in Game 6. The Giants were leading three games to two at the time, but the Game 6 lead was squandered after Ortiz was lifted and

Russ Ortiz (© S.F. Giants)

the Angels rallied to win the final two games in what was to be Ortiz's final game with the club.

A former fourth-round draft choice, Ortiz exceeded the Giants' expectations after beginning a promising career as a closer. In his first professional season, he yielded merely three earned runs in 401/3 innings for Bellingham (Wash.) and San Jose in 1995. One year later, he posted a combined 36 saves in 60 games with Class-A San Jose and Double-A Shreveport before being converted into a starter in 1997 and reaching the majors in 1998.

Mel Ott, Outfielder (1926-47)

San Francisco Giants left fielder Barry Bonds would know how Mel Ott felt. Like Bonds, Ott was routinely pitched around ... and with good reason.

Ott, who clubbed 511 home runs as a member of the New York Giants from 1926-47, drew 100 or more walks a National League-record 10 times during his 22-year career. When he retired he held the league record with 1,708 bases on balls (since broken by Joe Morgan). Ott led the N.L. in free passes during six seasons and was walked five times in a game on four occasions.

When he wasn't trotting to first base, Ott was moving runners around the bases. The first National Leaguer to hit 500 homers, he ranks 10th on baseball's all-time RBI (1,860) and runs scored (1,859) lists. He compiled a lifetime .304 batting average with 2,876 hits.

With a 5-foot-9, 170-pound frame, Ott clearly didn't have the stature of a prototype power hitter. But the left-handed swinger took advantage of the Polo Grounds' short 257-foot right field porch, belting 323 of his home runs there (63 percent), more than any other player has hit in a single park.

Ott utilized an unorthodox batting stance in which he raised his right foot at least six inches as the pitch was being delivered and then stepped toward the pitcher's mound, shifting his weight for maximum leverage. At the same time, he lowered his bat to an al-

Mel Ott (Brace Photo)

most-horizontal position that resulted in a beautiful fluid swing. New York manager John McGraw was worried that minor league skippers would try to alter Ott's stance, so Ott went straight to the majors after being signed as a 17-year-old out of high school.

In his fourth season (1929), at the ripe old age of 20, Ott became a full-time starter and responded with a .328 batting average and career highs of 42 home runs, 151 RBI (a franchise record) and 138 runs scored, along with 113 walks. Moreover, he struck out just 38 times and is one of only five players in baseball history to hit 40-plus homers without fanning on more than 40 occasions. Ott topped the Senior Circuit in home runs three times (1936, 1938, 1942) and shared the crown on three other occasions (1932, 1934, 1937). He hit a career-high .349 in 1930 and drove in 100 or more runs during nine seasons.

A deft outfielder, as well, Ott averaged 17 assists per season over the course of his career and was involved in a record 12 double plays during the 1929 campaign. He also played some third base.

Ott was instrumental in the Giants winning the 1933 World Series over the Washington Senators and, following pennant-winning seasons in 1936 and 1937, he took over as player-manager for Bill Terry in 1942. A pleasant and popular player, Ott attempted to emulate McGraw's fiery managerial style, but the "Little Napoleon" image did anything but suit him. Ultimately, Ott returned to his natural personality and managed into the 1948 season.

An 11-time N.L. All-Star, Ott is the Giants' career leader in RBI and walks and ranks second to Willie Mays in games (2,730), at-bats (9,456), runs, hits, doubles (488) and home runs. Following his playing and managing days, he worked in New York's front office. Ott was inducted into the National Baseball Hall of Fame in 1951 and later had his uniform No. 4 retired by the Giants. He passed away November 21, 1958, in New Orleans at the age of 49 following a serious automobile accident.

Jose Pagan, Shortstop (1959-65)

The unsung hero of the Giants' 1962 pennant race, Jose Pagan provided steady fielding and decent offense for the champions. He set a club record by playing in 164 games that season (team played 165 because of three-game playoff with Dodgers). Pagan led National League shortstops in fielding, batted .259 and excelled in the World Series.

Against the vaunted Yankees, he batted .368, including a homer off series Most Valuable Player Ralph Terry, despite going hitless the last two games with a sprained wrist. "He is the silent anchor of our infield," manager Alvin Dark said. Giants' publicist Garry Schumacher, a former sportswriter, said, "Pagan goes back into left field for pop flies and fouls better than any shortstop I've ever seen."

After injuries had taken their toll and Hal Lanier was becoming the regular, Pagan was traded to the Pittsburgh Pirates in 1965 and became a valuable utilityman. He reached the pinnacle with Pittsburgh in the 1971 World Series against the Baltimore Orioles. Game 7 was tied 1-1 in eighth inning with Willie Stargell on first base. Pagan's double scored him and the Pirates were world champions on the 2-1 victory.

Pagan's lifetime major league average was .251, but he improved to .324 in 11 World Series games. The son of a foreman in a sugarcane plantation, Pagan signed with the Giants along with fellow Puerto Rican Orlando Cepeda in 1955. Both were named to the Giants' all-decade team of the '60s in 1999.

Gaylord Perry, Pitcher (1962-71)

Gaylord Perry always will be memorialized for allegedly throwing the (illegal) spitball while pitching for eight major league teams. What also should be remembered is that his 22-

Jose Pagan forcing Pittsburgh's Roberto Clemente on a double play.

year career was born and began to flourish with the San Francisco Giants.

Perry pitched in the Bay Area from 1962-71, posting a 134-109 record with a 2.96 ERA. He ranks second on San Francisco's career lists for wins, games started (283), innings pitched (2,294.2), complete games (125), shutouts (21) and strikeouts (1,606); fourth in ERA; and seventh in games (367). On the franchise's career list (including the New York years), Perry ranks fifth in strikeouts and eighth in games started and innings pitched.

After learning to throw the spitball from veteran teammate Bob Shaw during the 1964 season, Perry developed into a big-time winner in 1966. He mastered the spitter to go with his own nifty slider and was 21-8 with a 2.99 ERA, 201 strikeouts and just 40 walks. On July 12, 1966, Perry was the winning pitcher in relief for the National League in the All-Star Game at Busch Stadium in St. Louis, and he recorded 15 strikeouts against the Philadelphia Phillies at Candlestick Park in San Francisco on July 22, 1966.

In 1967 Perry touted a 2.61 ERA and pitched a San Francisco-record 40 consecutive scoreless innings, but he suffered an amazing 10 one-run losses and finished with a 15-17 record. The following year the rule that allowed pitchers to put their fingers to their mouth on the mound (8.02 of the Official Baseball Rules) was amended, and Perry changed from using his own saliva to a lubricant that was placed someplace on his uniform and/or body. For the rest of his career, it appeared obvious that he was conducting an illegal activ-

Gaylord Perry

ity, but no one could catch Perry, and he thrived, if nothing else, at psyching out opposing batters.

On September 17, 1968, Perry fired a no-hitter against the St. Louis Cardinals at Candlestick Park, winning 1-0 on a Ron Hunt home run in the first inning, and the following day the Cardinals' Ray Washburn returned the favor against the Giants.

Perry topped the National League with 23 wins, 328.2 innings pitched, 23 complete games and five shutouts in 1970, was selected to his second All-Star Game and finished runner-up for the National League Cy Young Award to Bob Gibson of the Cardinals. Meanwhile, Perry's older brother, Jim, won 24 games for the Minnesota Twins and earned the American League Cy Young Award. Gaylord and Jim made baseball history by becoming the first brothers to both win 20 games in the same season.

San Francisco traded Perry and shortstop Frank Duffy to the Cleveland Indians in exchange for pitcher Sam McDowell on November 29, 1971. Perry later pitched for the Texas Rangers, San Diego Padres, New York Yankees, Atlanta Braves, Seattle Mariners and Kansas City Royals. He won the A.L. Cy Young Award with the Indians in 1972 and the N.L. Cy Young Award with the Padres in 1978 and is the only pitcher to receive the honor in both circuits.

Perry concluded his career in 1983 with a 314-265 record and a 3.11 ERA. He ranks 15th on baseball's all-time wins list and is sixth with 3,534 strikeouts. Gaylord and Jim's 529

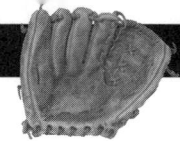

combined victories are second to Joe and Phil Niekro (539) among brother combinations.

In 1991 Perry was inducted into the National Baseball Hall of Fame. He currently lives on a farm in North Carolina.

Billy Pierce, Pitcher (1962-64)

The left-handed Billy Pierce was a well-established American League pitching ace with the Chicago White Sox when he caught a second wind and enjoyed a briefly successful career with the Giants. Although overshadowed by Jack Sanford's 24 wins, Pierce easily was the unsung hero of the Giants' pennant-winning season of 1962. Without him, there may not have been a playoff victory over the dreaded Dodgers. Without him, there wouldn't have been a Game 7 in the World Series.

The Giants acquired the veteran lefty and Don Larsen from the White Sox after the 1961 season for Ed Fisher, Dom Zanni, Vern Tiefenthaler and Bob Farley. Pierce performed beyond expectations for perhaps the greatest team in San Francisco history. He made a great first impression, winning his first eight decisions following a mediocre spring training.

He finished the regular season 15-6 and pitched his finest in Game 1 of the playoff series with the Dodgers. The Giants knocked Sandy Koufax out in the second inning and Pierce cruised 8-0 with a three-hitter. "It was a lovely ball game—everything went right," he said after remaining unbeaten at Candlestick Park.

When the best-of-three series shifted to Los Angeles, the Dodgers won Game 2, overcom-

Billy Pierce (S.F. Giants Archives)

ing a 5-0 deficit. In the deciding Game 3 at Dodger Stadium, the Giants rallied for four improbable runs in the top of the ninth, and a weary Pierce was summoned from the bullpen to nail down the win. He retired Maury Wills, Junior Gilliam and pinch hitter Lee Walls, giving the Giants the pennant.

"This was going to be the pennant, so you're ready," he said. "Your arm could be falling off, you're ready. You want to pitch. You don't want to sit there and do nothing. Those three hitters, that one inning, has got to be one of the prime moments in my baseball career."

Despite great success with the White Sox, including back-to-back 20-win seasons in 1956-57, his lone playoff appearance was with the Giants, and he made the most of it. Pierce finished the regular season 16-6 with a 3.49 ERA, but he wasn't done. After losing his first World Series start 3-2 in New York, Pierce was entrusted with keeping the Giants' hopes alive when play resumed in San Francisco for Game 6. Pierce was a 5-2 winner, squaring the series at 3-3.

"The sixth game was a game where you're on the spot a little bit," he said. "If you lose, the World Series is over. I was happy to pitch it and to do well. I had a no-hitter into the fifth. They got a run, and then Maris hit a home run." The victory at Candlestick wasn't surprising. During the regular season Pierce was 13-0 at home.

But his good fortune turned in 1963, when he went 3-11. He decided to retire after a 3-0 start in 1964, concluding a solid career with a 211-169 record and a 3.27 ERA. In those two World Series starts, he was 1-1 with a

1.89 ERA against the Yankees' powerhouse. The San Francisco Giants have had their share of one-year wonders, but none were as meaningful as what Pierce achieved in 1962.

Rick Reuschel, Pitcher (1987-91)

Not very exciting on or off the mound, Rick Reuschel was a workhorse who quietly helped the Giants to division titles in 1987 and 1989 as the ace of a nondescript pitching staff. His career took a positive turn in 1987 when he was traded to San Francisco for pitchers Jeff Robinson and Scott Medvin on August 12.

He was 5-3 in nine starts with his new club but was roughed up by the St. Louis Cardinals (0-1, 6.30 ERA) in two playoff starts. Reuschel's first full season with the Giants produced a 19-11 record, 3.12 ERA and 245 innings as the Giants' ace in 1988. He was 11-4 with a 2.90 ERA at the All-Star break but turned down an invitation so he could marry Barbara Thompson, sister of former teammate and agent Scot Thompson.

Rick started quickly in 1989, possibly his finest of 4½ seasons with the Giants. He posted 17-8 record and 2.94 ERA for a championship team, again getting off to a quick start with his assortment of off-speed pitches

Rick Reuschel (S.F. Giants Archives)

that kept baffled batters off balance. Named "Big Daddy" by Cubs' teammate Mike Krukow because of his 6-foot-3, 240-pound size, he was a 10-game winner by June 2—the quickest Giant to double-digit victories since Juan Marichal in 1966.

Reuschel was the National League Pitcher of the Month for May (6-0, 0.84 ERA) and became the first San Francisco pitcher since Vida Blue in 1978 to start an All-Star Game, taking a 12-3 record into the break. Bo Jackson greeted him with a monster homer, and he didn't fare well in post season play, either. He went 1-1 with a 5.19 ERA against the Cubs and 0-1 with an 11.20 ERA in his lone World Series start against the Athletics.

The veteran also notched his 200th career victory in 1989 and finished with a 214-191 record and a 3.37 ERA. An Illinois native, Reuschel attended Western Illinois University and reached the majors about the same time as his brother, Paul, also a pitcher. The right-handed Rick was a third-round draft choice of the Cubs in 1970 and was a mainstay two years later. Reuschel had several solid seasons with mediocre teams and reached his Chicago peak in 1977 with a 20-10 record and 2.79 ERA.

Reuschel's career was in jeopardy because of rotator cuff surgery that knocked him out of the entire 1982 season with the Yankees, but he gradually made it back with the Cubs and the Pirates before attaining success once again with the Giants. Despite a ponderous appearance, "Big Daddy" was a graceful athlete and a Gold Glove winner while also helping himself with the bat. He retired to his Illinois farm after the 1991 season.

Dusty Rhodes, Outfielder (1952-59)

Dusty Rhodes enjoyed a brief but glorious career with the Giants, emerging as the hero of the shocking 1954 World Series sweep of the Cleveland Indians with two home runs, one as a pinch hitter. He was born James Rhodes in Mathews, Alabama, and nicknamed "Dusty" as a youth. The left-handed hitter played for the

Dusty Rhodes (S.F. Giants Archives)

Giants from 1952-57 and again in 1959 after the club moved to San Francisco.

It was an otherwise nondescript career except for his moment of fame in the World Series. The Indians were heavy favorites because of their legendary pitching staff and a record 111 victories, but someone forgot to tell Dusty. It was hot and humid at the Polo Grounds, where 52,251 gathered to watch the two teams tied 2-2 after nine innings in Game 1.

Willie Mays walked in the bottom of the 10th and stole second. Hank Thompson was walked intentionally, bringing up Monte Irvin, who had yet to hit a ball out of the infield. Manager Leo Durocher pointed to Rhodes, who batted .341 during the season, mostly as a pinch hitter. Bob Lemon was the pitcher and his first fastball landed 260 feet and barely over the fence down the right field line for a 5-2 victory over the disbelieving Indians.

It was more of the same in Game 2. Early Wynn had a 1-0 lead when the Giants placed runners on first and second in the fifth inning.

Rhodes once again batted for Irvin and blooped a single to right for the tying run. Dusty stayed in the game and, with the Giants leading by one run, homered off Wynn deep into the right field seats to add to a New York victory.

When the action shifted to Cleveland for Game 3, the Giants were clinging to a 1-0 lead until Rhodes came off the bench to deliver a two-run single, and the Indians were doomed again by a man who couldn't crack the starting lineup. Dusty, who set a World Series record by going three for three as a pinch hitter, became a household name as the Giants produced an unthinkable 4-0 sweep.

Kirk Rueter, Pitcher (1996-present)

Unquestionably the most unheralded starter in San Francisco history, relative to his accomplishments and consistency over his first six full seasons with the club. Rueter, affectionately known as "Woody," in 2002 became the first Giants' left-hander since Johnny Antonelli (1954-59) to notch at least 10 victories six consecutive season.

He did it by quietly being the most effective starter (14-8, 3.23 ERA) on a pennant winner, and then thrusting the Giants into the World Series with six shutout innings in the clinching Game 5 victory over the St.Louis Cardinals at Pacific Bell Park. Rueter definitely has been taken for granted.

The Giants' version of Tom Glavine, through 2002, ranked among the active leaders with a .615 winning percentage (109-68). Among active lefties since 1980, only Randy Johnson, Andy Pettitte and Glavine had done better, and only Pedro Martinez (.727) had a better road record than Rueter's 60-29 (.674).

"Kirk is as good a competitor as I've been around - he keeps you in the game," manager Dusty Baker remarked during a 2002 season in which the Giants were a perfect 11-0 in his no-decisions and 25-8 overall in his 33 starts. The club had won 62.3 per cent of his starts (124 of 199) since he was acquired from Montreal in 1996.

Kirk Rueter (© S.F. Giants)

Rueter, who earned a degree in finance from Murray State (Ky.), was an 18th-round draft choice before making a rapid ascent through the Expos' farm system and making a big splash in his major league debut. He was 24-13 in three minor league seasons before his promotion, and was an immediate sensation.

He defeated the Giants in his first major league game, July 7, 1993, retiring 18 in a row at one juncture. He finished the season 8-0 for Rookie Pitcher of the Year honors, then won his first two decision in 1994 for a 10-0 start as a major leaguer. Only Hooks Wiltse of the 1904 Giants had done better as a starter, going 12-0.

Rueter, reunited with former Expos manager Felipe Alou in 2003, was traded for pitcher Mark Leiter on July 30, 1996, and went 13-6 for the division-champion Giants in 1997, his first full major league season. He worked seven innings, yielding one run, and wasn't involved in the decision against the Florida Marlins in the playoffs.

Amos Rusie, Pitcher (1890-95, 1897-98)

In 1893 the distance from the pitcher's mound to home plate was moved back from 50 feet to the current 60 feet, 6 inches. Some historians suggest that the reason for the switch was to nullify the blazing fastball of New York Giants' right-handed pitcher Amos Rusie.

A native of Mooresville, Indiana, the "Hoosier Thunderbolt" was one of the game's best during his eight-year career in New York from 1890-95 and 1897-98. Catcher Dick Buckley allegedly padded his glove with a thin sheet of lead to lessen the impact of Rusie's power.

Rusie began his career at the age of 17 with the Indianapolis Hoosiers in 1889. The franchise folded at the end of the season, and six players, including Rusie, were sold to the Giants. Rusie led the National League with a career-high 341 strikeouts in his first year in Gotham. Each of the next four seasons Rusie won 30-plus games. He topped the N.L. with 337 strikeouts in 1891; 50 complete games and 208 strikeouts in 1893; and a career-high 36 wins, 2.78 ERA and 195 strikeouts in 1894. Rusie authored two complete-game victories in the 1894 Temple Cup championship series as the Giants swept the Baltimore Orioles four games to none.

Control problems also characterized Rusie. He holds four of the top 10 season walks totals in baseball history: 289 (1st, 1890); 270 (3rd, 1892); 262 (4th, 1891); and 218 (10th, 1893).

On July 31, 1891, Rusie no-hit the Brooklyn Bridegrooms 6-0 at the Polo Grounds in New York. At 20 years and two months old, he is the youngest pitcher ever to throw a no-hitter. Twice in his career Rusie pitched two complete-game victories on the same

day—September 28, 1891, against Brooklyn at Eastern Park in Brooklyn (10-4 and 13-5 in six innings) and October 4, 1892, against the Washington Senators at the Polo Grounds (6-4 and 9-5).

Despite his success, Rusie often was at odds with club management. The difficulties began late in 1892 when the Giants released Rusie in order to save money but with the understanding that he would not join another team. Rusie, however, signed a contract with the Chicago White Stockings. New York ultimately bought out the contract and Rusie returned. In 1895 Rusie was fined for missing curfew and for making an obscene gesture at controversial owner Andrew C. Freedman in public. Rusie then refused to play in 1896 over a contract dispute and filed a lawsuit demanding to become a free agent. In March of 1897 other N.L. team owners, concerned that Rusie's suit could drastically change the economics of the game, pooled together a reported $3,000 (to cover his fine, his salary for 1896 and the

Amos Rusie (Transcendental Graphics)

difference in his salary for 1897 between what he sought and what Freedman was willing to pay) for him to go back to the Giants.

Rusie posted a league-leading 2.54 ERA in 1897, but he injured his arm making a pickoff throw in 1898 and subsequently left the Giants to be with his ailing wife in Washington. The Giants disciplined Rusie again, and he sat out the 1899 and 1900 campaigns.

New York traded Rusie to the Cincinnati Reds in exchange for pitcher Christy Mathewson (who had yet to pitch in the major leagues) on December 15, 1900. Rusie's eight-year statistics with the Giants included a 233-164 record with a 2.89 ERA. He ranks among the franchise's career leaders in complete games (3rd, 371); strikeouts (3rd, 1,819); innings pitched (4th, 3,522.2); shutouts (tied for 4th, 29); games started (5th, 403); wins (5th); and games (7th, 427). Rusie made just three appearances with the Reds before retiring. In 463 career games, Rusie was 246-174 with a 3.07 ERA and 1,950 strikeouts. He ranks seventh on baseball's all-time walks list with 1,707 and is 17th in complete games with 393 (among 427 starts).

On December 6, 1942, Rusie was killed in an automobile accident in Seattle at the age of 71. He was inducted into the National Baseball Hall of Fame in 1977 by the Veterans Committee.

Jack Sanford, Pitcher (1959-65)

The right-handed Jack Sanford enjoyed one great year for the Giants, and it was one of the most memorable in San Francisco history. Nobody did it better than Sanford in 1962, when his 24-7 record over 39 games and 265 innings helped to produce a pennant winner, the first for San Francisco in a span of 27 years. What made his year more remarkable is that he struggled with control and was 6-6 before he got rolling.

Sanford thereby went 18-1 the rest of the way, including a club-record 16 consecutive victories. "I guess I got mad after that," he said

of the sluggish start before losing only once after June 13. "I don't just throw my fastball anymore. I have an idea what I want to do with it, and I'm getting so I can do it. I could always throw hard, but I threw high."

No. 16 came in early September, a 2-0 blanking of the Pittsburgh Pirates in which he scattered eight hits. "A good bullpen and the breaks," he said modestly. "Sixteen in a row? This is ridiculous. Nobody wins 16 in a row." Success continued when Sanford gave San Francisco its first World Series victory, a three-hitter for a 2-0 triumph in Game 2 at Candlestick Park.

He was a 5-3 loser in Game 5 at Yankee Stadium, but five days of rain delays had him primed for Game 7 in San Francisco, where he was a 1-0 loser to series Most Valuable Player Ralph Terry when the Yankees scored on a double-play grounder in the fifth inning. "I never pitched better in my life," said Sanford, who was 1-2 in the World Series despite a 1.93

Jack Sanford (S.F. Giants Archives)

ERA. That loss really hurt, but maybe I proved something against the Yankees. Except for the very few (pitchers), nobody is going to overpower them, so I didn't try to. I was as surprised as anybody else at the year I had. Boy, what a year!"

He was nicknamed "Smiling Jack" because he was usually scowling, and he was also nervous and irritable. As a youngster in Wellesley, Massachusetts, Jack worked as a chauffeur for Lou Perini, owner of the Boston Braves, but he couldn't get a job with the Boston teams and signed with the Philadelphia Phillies for $125 a month in 1948 and began his slow climb to the majors. He was hit hard early on but made himself useful driving the team bus.

Sanford won at least 14 games in four different minor league seasons, yet still couldn't land with the Phillies. "I had to creep up the hard way," he recalled. "I spent seven years in the minors. They say if you can't make the majors in five years, you'd better quit. I almost did."

By 1956, at age 27, he was brought up to the big club with a reputation for wildness, a quick temper and a live fastball. In 1957 he was named Rookie of the Year with the Phillies after notching a league-leading 188 strikeouts to accompany a 19-8 record and 3.08 ERA.

Then he was traded to the Giants for catcher Valmy Thomas and pitcher Ruben Gomez but wasn't an overnight sensation. In fact, the club considered leaving him unprotected for the 1961 expansion draft, but manager Alvin Dark talked the brass out of it. Good thing. Sanford was an avid golfer, later becoming an instructor at Presidents Inn Country Club in West Palm Beach, Florida.

Benito Santiago, Catcher (2001-present)

Santiago joined players like Will Clark and Ellis Burks for making a significant impact on the Giants in a brief period of time. Like them, Santiago helped the club to the playoffs in his second season with the club, capping a dazzling comeback from a career-threatening auto

Benito Santiago *(© S.F. Giants)*

accident to become an All-Star and MVP of the National League Championship Series in 2002.

Such success at age 37 didn't seem possible for Santiago on Jan. 4, 1998, when he lay broken and battered in his crumpled Ferrari after crashing into a tree trunk near his Florida home. The collision left him unconscious with a broken pelvis, a damaged knee and stitches in his head. Some doctors told him he would never play again.

"It changed my life," Santiago said of his life-altering experience. "I've changed my attitude about a lot of things. I am more friendly with teammates, joking around and trying to be helpful. I'm also a lot closer to my (four) kids, making sure I stay in contact."

Santiago played later that year with Toronto, was a part-time catcher with the Cubs in 1999 and the Reds in 2000 and was out of

work in 2001 when the Giants called late in spring training. Dissatisfied with their young catchers, they whipped Benito into shape, and he became the starter by May, finishing with a .262 average in 133 games.

The comeback from obscurity to stardom was completed in 2002, when the durable Santiago reverted to the form that made him the National League's best catcher at the start of his career with the San Diego Padres in 1987-91. He batted .278 with 16 homers and 74 RBI in 126 games, and was at his best when it counted most.

Santiago batted .297 with 32 RBI in his last 52 games, knocked in several key runs as the No. 5 hitter in September and added 16 RBI in 17 postseason games. He was tough in the clutch in the NLCS, driving in four runs with a pair of singles and a homer in a 9-6 victory in Game 1, and giving the Giants a 4-3 decision with a two-out, two-run homer in the eighth inning of Game 4.

Then again, the Puerto Rico native was accustomed to success. Benito was a unanimous Rookie of the Year choice with the 1987 Padres, batting a career-best .300 with 18 home runs, 79 RBI and a rookie-record 34-game hitting streak. The five-time All-Star also was known for his rifle arm, often throwing out runners from his knees.

Hal Schumacher, Pitcher (1931-42, 1946)

How would you like to be a rookie pitcher and be called "another Christy Mathewson"? Hal Schumacher was by New York Giants' legendary Hall of Fame manager John McGraw, who saw Mathewson throughout his prime.

There were similarities. Both right-handers had dashing good looks, were college educated and featured a dominant pitch (Mathewson the fadeaway and Schumacher a sinker). Although Schumacher didn't match Mathewson's supremacy (nobody has), he was a winner throughout his major league career, which was spent entirely with the Giants from 1931-42 and 1946.

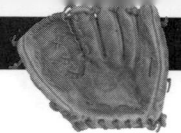

In the spring of 1931, Schumacher joined the Giants right off the campus of St. Lawrence University. He primarily was used out of the bullpen during his first two seasons before becoming a starter in 1933 and teaming with future Hall of Fame left-hander Carl Hubbell and right-handers Freddie Fitzsimmons and Roy Parmelee to give New York a quality four-man rotation. Hubbell and Schumacher were dubbed "King Karl" and "Prince Hal" in reference to their royal-like pitching.

Schumacher finished the season with a 19-12 record with a snappy and career-best 2.16 ERA. He was selected to the first-ever All-Star Game at Comiskey Park in Chicago but did not pitch. The Giants went on to win the National League pennant and defeat the Washington Senators in the World Series four games to one. Schumacher won Game 2 by the score of 6-1 on a complete-game five-hitter at the Polo Grounds in New York.

When Schumacher signed with New York he still had two semesters to go to receive his diploma from St. Lawrence. He made them up during the offseason and completed his degree in psychology. On June 12, 1993, Schumacher went through commencement exercises with the entire Giants' team in attendance on a day off for the club.

Schumacher went 23-10 with a 3.18 ERA in 1934 and 19-9 with a 2.89 ERA the following season. On April 28, 1935, he authored a one-hit, 3-0 shutout over the Philadelphia Phillies at the Polo Grounds. The lone safety was of the infield variety by Philadelphia pitcher Orville Jorgens with two outs in the third inning. New York shortstop Dick Bartell just missed throwing out Jorgens at first base on a bang-bang play. Schumacher subsequently was selected to his second All-Star Game and pitched four innings in relief (allowing one run with five strikeouts) at Municipal Stadium in Cleveland.

Although Schumacher slipped to an 11-13 record but with a respectable 3.47 ERA in 1936, the Giants won the N.L. pennant, and he pitched one of his most memorable games in

Hal Schumacher (Brace Photo)

the World Series against the cross-town rival Yankees. The Giants trailed the series three games to one, and Schumacher scattered 10 hits and six walks in 10 innings to earn a hard-fought 5-4 victory at Yankee Stadium. In the third inning, with the Giants leading 3-2 and the bases loaded with no outs, Schumacher struck out center fielder Joe DiMaggio and first baseman Lou Gehrig and retired catcher Bill Dickey on a fly ball.

Schumacher won 13 games each of the next four seasons, followed by a pair of 12-win campaigns. He then served in the U.S. Navy for three years before returning to the Giants in 1946. In 13 seasons in New York, Schumacher posted a 158-121 record with a 3.36 ERA in 391 games. On the franchise career lists, he ranks tied for fourth in shutouts (29), tied for sixth in games started (329), seventh in innings pitched (2,482.1) and eighth in wins.

Following his playing days, Schumacher helped found the Adirondack Bat Co. He passed away April 21, 1993, in Cooperstown, New York (where Mathewson is enshrined), at the age of 82.

Cy Seymour, Pitcher/Outfielder
(1896-1900, 1906-10)

Certainly the most famous pitcher-turned-position player in baseball history is immortal Hall of Famer Babe Ruth of the Boston Red Sox and New York Yankees. But years before Ruth made the switch, Cy Seymour of the New York Giants did. Seymour primarily was a pitcher for the Giants from 1896-1900 and later was a full-time outfielder from 1906-10.

A left-handed thrower and batter from Albany, New York, Seymour became a key member of the Giants' pitching staff during the 1897 season. He posted a 18-14 record with a 3.37 ERA and completed 28 of the 38 games he started. Opponents batted .242 against him, the best mark in the National League, and he ranked second with 149 strikeouts. But he also led the league with 164 walks, and lack of control became an on-going problem.

On June 3, 1897, Seymour authored two complete-game victories over the Louisville Colonels at the Polo Grounds in New York, winning by the scores of 6-1 and 10-6. He limited Louisville to three hits in the first game and four hits in the second game, which was called after seven innings due to darkness.

The following year, Seymour posted his best pitching numbers. He finished 25-19 (topping New York in wins) with a 3.18 ERA and 39 complete games among 45 starts. He paced the N.L. with 239 strikeouts but also with 213 walks (the fifth-most in franchise history) and 32 hit batters. He played 35 games in the outfield and had an overall .276 batting average.

In 1899 Seymour had a 14-18 record with a 3.56 ERA but for the third consecutive season led the N.L. in walks (170) while ranking second in strikeouts (142). Offensively, he batted at a .327 clip with 52 hits in 159 at-bats. On May 24 against the Cincinnati Reds at League Park in Cincinnati, Seymour collected two singles and two doubles but issued 13 walks, including one that forced in the winning run in a 7-6 loss.

Despite defeating the St. Louis Perfectos 10-3 at the Polo Grounds on June 7, 1900,

Seymour was sent to the minor leagues in Worcester, Massachusetts, after surrendering 10 hits and issuing 11 walks in the game. He subsequently joined the Baltimore Orioles in 1901 and later moved on to the Reds midway through the 1902 campaign.

By 1903 Seymour was solely an outfielder. In 1905 he led the N.L. with career highs in batting average (.377), hits (219), doubles (40), triples (21) and RBI (121). He was the only player besides future Hall of Fame shortstop Honus Wagner of the Pittsburgh Pirates to pace the league in batting from 1903-09. New York re-acquired Seymour for $12,000 on June 14, 1906. The price was costly, but the big-spending Giants were proud of the purchase and hung the framed canceled check in their offices.

Although he didn't match his 1905 output, Seymour was successful during his second stint with the Giants. He batted .294 with 25 doubles and 75 RBI in 1908 and .267 with 23

Cy Seymour

235

doubles and 92 RBI in 1909. Seymour played for the Giants through the 1910 season, then returned to the minor leagues before concluding his major league career with the Boston Braves in 1913.

As a pitcher for five years with New York, Seymour posted a 61-56 record with a 3.75 ERA in 139 games. He totaled 582 strikeouts in 1,026 innings pitched and ranks eighth on the franchise career list with 652 walks. His offensive numbers for 10 seasons with the Giants included a .285 batting average with 345 RBI in 727 games. Seymour's lifetime batting average was .303 with 799 RBI and 222 stolen bases in 1,528 games over 16 campaigns.

Seymour passed away penniless September 20, 1919, in New York at the age of 46.

Fred Snodgrass, Outfielder (1908-15)

Fred Snodgrass is universally blamed for the New York Giants losing the 1912 World Series to the Boston Red Sox but perhaps unfairly so.

The Giants led the eighth and deciding game 2-1 going into the bottom of the 10th inning at Fenway Park in Boston on October 16. Pinch hitter Clyde Engle led off for the Red Sox and hit a fly ball to left-center field that Snodgrass, who was playing center, dropped for a two-base error. The next batter, right fielder Harry Hooper, drove a fly ball to center that Snodgrass caught with a fantastic play. After second baseman Steve Yerkes walked, center fielder Tris Speaker hit a foul pop off first base that Giants' pitcher Christy Mathewson called for catcher Chief Meyers to catch even though it might have been an easier play for first baseman Fred Merkle. The ball landed uncaught. Given a second opportunity, Speaker proceeded to single in Engle with the tying run and send Yerkes to third. Two batters later, third baseman Larry Gardner plated the winning run with a sacrifice fly to right field. Boston won the series four games to three with one tie.

So Snodgrass, who played for the Giants from 1908-15, was left branded with having made the "$30,000 Muff," referring to the difference between the winners' and losers' total share of the World Series payoff. New York manager John McGraw, though, refused to put all the condemnation on Snodgrass and gave him a $1,000 raise the next season.

Snodgrass, nicknamed "Snow," enjoyed a respectable career in New York. He saw limited playing time his first two years before becoming the everyday center fielder. In 1910 he batted a career-high .321 with 22 doubles, eight triples, 44 RBI and 33 stolen bases. The following year he batted .294 with personal bests of 27 doubles, 10 triples, 77 RBI and 51 stolen bases as the Giants won the National League pennant (but lost to the Philadelphia Athletics in the World Series four games to two). In the series, the aggressive Snodgrass twice spiked Philadelphia third baseman Frank "Home Run" Baker, which raised the ire of the Athletics' fans.

Fred Snodgrass

Before the storied 1912 World Series, Snodgrass contributed 70 RBI and 43 stolen bases to the Giants' cause while batting at a .269 clip. He bounced back from an offseason full of criticism to compile a .291 batting average with 44 RBI and 27 stolen bases in 1913. New York captured its third consecutive N.L. flag but couldn't shake its World Series jinx, again falling to Philadelphia four games to one.

Two years had passed since Snodgrass was mde a scapegoat, but the play hardly had been forgotten. On September 7, 1914 (Labor Day), the Giants split a double-header with the Boston Braves at the South End Grounds in Boston. In the second game, Snodgrass drew a walk from Boston pitcher Lefty Tyler on four pitches all in the vicinity of Snodgrass' head. On his way to first base, Snodgrass went after Tyler, who ultimately retaliated by imitating Snodgrass' dropped fly ball. Then the crowd, a Boston record of some 34,000, got involved and threw bottles at Snodgrass. Finally, Boston mayor James Michael Curley went onto the field and got the rowdy spectators to calm down. The Braves went on to win the league title by 10½ games over the Giants, who had their three-year championship reign halted.

In 1915 Snodgrass slipped to a .194 batting average with 20 RBI and 11 stolen bases in 80 games before the Giants sold him, ironically, to the Braves on August 19. In eight seasons in New York, Snodgrass batted .278 with 128 doubles, 37 triples, 10 home runs, 345 RBI and 201 stolen bases in 788 games. He finished his major league career with the Braves a year later. Snodgrass' nine-year lifetime batting average was .275 with 351 RBI and 215 stolen bases in 923 games.

Snodgrass played in the minor leagues in 1917 and later became mayor of Oxnard, California. He passed away April 5, 1974, in his hometown of Ventura, California, at the age of 86.

J.T. Snow, First Baseman (1997-present)

A slick-fielding first baseman, J.T. Snow abandoned switch-hitting in 1999 and continued to be a productive hitter in his third year with the Giants. Despite some concern over his decision to bat strictly left-handed, Snow responded with success against lefties following a slow start and finished with 24 home runs and 98 RBI.

But Snow's batting is somewhat of a bonus. He's known primarily for his fielding and easily is the best defensive first baseman in San Francisco history. After winning Gold Gloves with the Anaheim Angels in 1995 and 1996, he duplicated the feat with the Giants in 1997-2002, making it six in a row

Snow, son of former NFL wide receiver Jack Snow, was a three-sport star at Los Alamitos High School in Southern California, where he was a schoolmate of present teammate Robb Nen. He attended the University of Arizona, where he teamed with Scott Erickson and Trevor Hoffman on a Pac-10 championship club.

A fifth-round draft choice of the New York Yankees in 1989, Snow played merely seven games for them in 1992 before he was traded

J.T. Snow (S.F. Giants Archives)

to Anaheim for pitcher Jim Abbott. By 1995 he began to suggest the Yankees might have made a mistake, batting .289 with 24 home runs and 102 RBI with the Angels.

He slumped in 1996 and was traded to the Giants for pitcher Allen Watson prior to the 1997 season. It was another big mistake. His maiden National League season produced a .281 average and career highs in doubles (36), home runs (28) and RBI (104). An off season in 1998 prompted giving up on switch-hitting.

Snow enjoyed a solid minor league season in his first taste of Triple-A with the Yankees' affiliate at Columbus in 1992. He won the International League batting title at .313 and was named the league Most Valuable Player, but it was his instinctive and sure-handed fielding at first base that made him a complete ballplayer.

Frank Snyder, Catcher (1919-26)

When the New York Giants captured four consecutive National League pennants from 1921-24, their roster was laden with future Hall of Famers like Dave Bancroft, Frankie Frisch, George Kelly and Ross Youngs.

But it took more than that talented bunch to pull off the four-peat, and one of the unsung heroes was catcher Frank "Pancho" Snyder. Not only did Snyder provide a decent bat, but he was a very good defensive player and a quality handler of the pitching staffs that did not feature anyone destined for Cooperstown.

After beginning his major league with the St. Louis Cardinals from 1912-19, Snyder was acquired by New York in exchange for pitcher Ferdie Schupp on July 16, 1919. Snyder went on to wear a Giants' uniform through the 1926 season.

Snyder split time behind the plate with Earl Smith in 1920 before essentially became the regular catcher the following season (although Smith still received his fair share of action). Snyder batted .320 with eight home runs and 45 RBI during the 1921 regular season and went on to post a team-leading .364 batting average (8-for-22) with one homer and three

Frank Snyder (Brace Photo)

RBI in the World Series as the Giants defeated the cross-town rival Yankees five games to three in the first-ever championship clash between the two Gotham City clubs. He collected four hits in Game 3 at the Polo Grounds, a record that stood until Paul Molitor of the Milwaukee Brewers had five safeties against the Cardinals in Game 1 of the 1982 World Series.

In 1922 the right-handed swinging Snyder batted at a career-high .343 clip with 21 doubles, five home runs and 51 RBI. Once again, he put together a stellar World Series by batting .333 (5-for-15) in the Giants' four game sweep of the Yankees.

Although his batting average slipped to .256 during the 1923 campaign, Snyder established a career high with 63 RBI and led N.L. catchers with a .990 fielding percentage. A year later he batted .302 with 53 RBI. The Giants lost the World Series both years, to the Yankees (four games to two) and to the Washington Senators (four games to three), respectively.

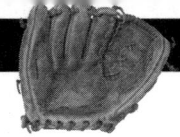

Snyder topped league receivers with a .985 fielding percentage in 1925 while hitting a career-high 11 home runs to go with 51 RBI. Following the 1926 season, he was released by the Giants and returned to the Cardinals for one year. In eight seasons in New York, Snyder batted .278 with 42 home runs and 317 RBI in 731 games. His total of 575 assists ranks fifth on the franchise all-time list for catchers. Snyder's 16-year career statistics included a .265 batting average in 1,392 games.

Following his big league days, Snyder was a successful player-manager in the minor leagues. He came back to the Giants as a coach under Bill Terry from 1933-41. Snyder is credited with helping in the development of pitchers Freddie Fitzsimmons, Carl Hubbell, Roy Parmelee and Hal Schumacher. Snyder subsequently returned to the minors as a manager until 1947.

Snyder passed away January 5, 1962, in his hometown of San Antonio, Texas, at the age of 68.

Chris Speier, Shortstop
(1971-77, 1987-89)

Chris Speier took over as Giants' shortstop in 1971 and immediately provided stability at the vital position with a solid glove, a strong arm and some pop in his bat. The Alameda, California, native was surrounded by veteran stars, yet his early leadership qualities and consistent play were regarded as crucial to a division championship, a contribution belying his .235 average.

The rookie batted .357 against Pittsburgh in the playoffs, and boosted his offense in 1972 (.269, 15 homers and 71 RBI) along with leading National League shortstops in assists. He played with the club until 1977 and was traded to Montreal for shortstop Tim Foli, who wasn't as good. Chris returned to the Giants in a utility role in 1987-88.

When Robby Thompson was injured after being named to the 1988 All-Star team, Speier stepped in at second base and hit for the cycle in a rout of the Cardinals. That prompted St. Louis and N.L. All-Star manager Whitey Herzog to say, "Maybe we took the wrong Giants' second baseman."

Speier went into coaching and managing after his retirement as a player and in 1999 piloted Triple-A Tucson in the Arizona Diamondbacks' farm system. He is the father of Justin Speier, who first pitched in the major leagues with the Cubs in 1998.

Chris was reared in the shadow of the Oakland Coliseum, so he mostly attended A's games as a youth and actually was a Dodgers' fan. After signing with the Giants out of UC-Santa Barbara, Chris' rise was swift, skipping Triple-A while wresting the job from Hal Lanier in 1971 spring training.

"I had been playing ball all winter to be really ready for spring training, and (manager) Charlie Fox took a liking to me," Speier recalled. "He told me to take charge of the infield because he said Willie McCovey didn't say too much and Tito Fuentes talked too much and you couldn't understand him. But it was some-

Chris Speier (S.F. Giants Archives)

thing to work with Tito. He was quick and flashy, and we really jelled together."

Partly to control his temper and to curb his aggressiveness, Chris converted to Catholicism in 1972, and later received communion from Pope John Paul II during a Papal Mass at Candlestick Park. Early in the 1977 season, Chris was a contract holdout and asked to be traded. General manager Spec Richardson dealt his stubborn shortstop to Montreal.

"I felt very hurt about leaving the Giants," he said. "I didn't want to leave—I wanted to play. But 1973 to 1976 in San Francisco was bad news. There were no people in the ballpark and the team was doing terribly. They were pinching pennies in the front office. It looked like Toronto was the answer."

If there were any ill feelings over his departure, they vanished when he came back 10 years later and was tough off the bench for manager Roger Craig.

Bill Swift, Pitcher (1992-94)

Another Giants' short-timer who made the most of his brief opportunity with the club, the right-handed Bill Swift went 39-19 in his three years with San Francisco from 1992-94. He joined the Giants in a trade involving Kevin Mitchell and immediately made his presence felt with a 10-4 record and a league-leading 2.08 ERA, the second-lowest ever by an San Francisco starter.

The Giants went 17-5 in his 22 starts, in which he yielded three runs or fewer in 19 of them. He won on opening day and bolted to a 6-0 start, making Mitchell's departure palatable. "Swifty" was even better in 1993, making 34 starts and going 21-8 with a 2.82 ERA in easily his finest season.

He went to spring training as a question mark that year because of injuries but teamed with John Burkett for the most victories (43) by two teammates. It also was the first time the Giants had two 20-game winners since Juan Marichal and Gaylord Perry in 1966.

"Swifty" enjoyed winning streaks of seven and six games, and yielded two runs or fewer in 20 starts while finishing second behind Greg Maddux in the Cy Young Award balloting. He was 17-5 in early August before hitting a wall and going winless for one month, but he rallied to go 4-0 down the stretch as the club finished with 103 victories.

He matched his win total with 21 hits, a San Francisco record for a pitcher. It surpassed Marichal, who had 20 in 1966. Injuries limited Swift to 17 games and an 8-7 record in 1994, and he signed with the Colorado Rockies as a free agent in 1995, never recapturing the magic which made him a successful Giant.

A native of Maine, Swift went 26-7 in four years at the University of Maine and pitched on the 1984 U.S. Olympic team that included Mark McGwire and Will Clark. He made it to the majors with Seattle in his first pro season in 1985 and won his debut at Cleveland with five shutout innings of relief. He was known for two things—an ability to induce ground balls and an assortment of injuries which curtailed a potentially great career.

Bill Swift (S.F. Giants Archives)

Luther "Dummy" Taylor, Pitcher (1900-01, 1902-08)

Mention the name Luther "Dummy" Taylor and what generally is remembered first is the fact that he was a deaf mute. Too bad because he also was one of the game's outstanding pitchers of the early 1900s.

Born deaf and dumb, Taylor played for the New York Giants in 1900-01 and 1902-08. The right-hander who mastered the drop ball was a key member of the pitching staffs that helped the Giants win their first two 20th century National League championships in 1904 and 1905.

Taylor burst into the limelight in 1901. He managed just an 18-27 record but was responsible for more than one-third of New York's 52 victories. In addition, he topped the N.L. with 43 games started and ranked second with 37 complete games.

Taylor jumped to the Cleveland Bronchos of the American League in 1902 because they were willing to pay him more money than New York. When the Giants realized they had lost an up-and-coming star, they sent catcher Frank Bowerman to Cleveland with explicit instructions not to return until Taylor came with him. Taylor settled on a deal and was back after pitching in just four games for the Bronchos. On May 16, the first and only time two deaf professional athletes competed against one another occurred when Taylor faced Cincinnati Reds' outfielder William "Dummy" Hoy at the Palace of the Fans in Cincinnati. Hoy collected two hits, but Taylor allowed no earned runs over eight innings in a 5-3 Giants' victory.

Later in 1902, John McGraw joined the Giants as player-manager, and with future Hall of Famers Christy Mathewson and Joe McGinnity as well as Taylor, New York had the makings of a seemingly unbeatable pitching trio. In 1904 all three hurlers won 20 games, one of only seven times an N.L. team has accomplished that feat since 1900 (also Pittsburgh in 1902, Chicago in 1903, New York in 1905, New York in 1913, New York in 1920 and Cincinnati in 1923). McGinnity and Mathewson won 35 and

Dummy Taylor

33 games, respectively, while Taylor finished 21-15 with a 2.34 ERA. The 21 wins were a career high, as were his 29 complete games (out of 36 starts), five shutouts and 138 strikeouts.

The following season Taylor was 16-9 with a 2.66 ERA. He didn't pitch in the World Series against the Philadelphia Athletics as Mathewson authored three shutouts and McGinnity added another. The Giants won the series four games to one.

Taylor posted a career-best 2.20 ERA during the 1906 season to go with a 17-9 record. He concluded his major league career following the 1908 campaign. In nine years with the Giants, Taylor compiled a 115-103 record with a 2.76 ERA in 270 games. He had 156 complete

games, 20 shutouts and 759 strikeouts while pitching 1,882.1 innings. On the franchise all-time lists, he ranks eighth in ERA and ninth in complete games.

Throughout his career Taylor proved to be somewhat of a court jester as he used sign language to berate umpires because he knew they couldn't understand him. But one day the last laugh was on Taylor when he used his antics on Hank O'Day, who had a deaf relative and knew sign language. O'Day threw Taylor out of the game and fined him $25. On road trips, Taylor kept his hotel room door open since he couldn't hear if somebody knocked. Taylor often visited with deaf people in other cities, and if these visits occurred at night one of his teammates' favorite pranks was to turn off the lights in his room.

Following his days with the Giants, Taylor pitched in the minor leagues and then became an umpire. He subsequently became a teacher, coach and administrator at various deaf schools in the midwest. Taylor passed away August 22, 1958, in Jacksonville, Illinois, at the age of 83.

Bill Terry, First Baseman (1923-36)

Few individuals in baseball history have experienced the success Bill Terry did as both a player and a manager.

As a first baseman for the New York Giants from 1923-36, Terry was a career .341 hitter with 154 home runs and 1,078 RBI. As the team's manager from 1932-41, he compiled a lofty .555 winning percentage and piloted the Giants to three National League pennants and the 1933 World Championship.

Following a two-year apprenticeship with the Giants in 1923 and 1924 (he platooned with future Hall of Famer George Kelly the latter season), Terry arrived on the scene as a regular in 1925. He was a fixture for the next decade and topped the team in batting for seven straight seasons from 1929-35.

Terry enjoyed his most successful campaign in 1930, when he paced the National League with a .401 batting average and 254

base hits (both Giants' records) to go with 129 RBI. He is the last Senior Circuit player to reach the .400 clip. Amazingly, on August 1, 1930, Terry's average stood at .396 and ranked fifth in the league.

The next two years Terry batted .349 (with 20 triples) and .350 (with 28 home runs), respectively. He was barely beaten out for a repeat of the batting title in 1931 by Chick Hafey of the St. Louis Cardinals (.3489 to .3486). Defensively, Terry led the National League in assists and putouts on five occasions.

Midway through the 1932 season, with his ballclub in a funk, Giants manager John McGraw approached Terry about taking over as skipper. New York breathed new life under Terry and in 1933 won the World Series in five games over the Washington Senators. Terry contributed a .322 batting average to the cause. The Giants were N.L. champions in both 1936 and 1937 but lost to the cross-town rival Yankees in the World Series both years.

Bill Terry (S.F. Giants Archives)

Terry, who was a starter in each of the first three All-Star Games from 1933-35, ranks high on many of the Giants' franchise lists: batting average (1st); hits (3rd, 2,193); doubles (3rd, 373); games (4th, 1,721); at-bats (4th, 6,428); runs (4th, 1,120); RBI (4th); and triples (5th, 112).

Times were not always so pleasant for Terry, whose professional career began as a minor league pitcher and included a no-hitter with Newnan (Georgia) of the Class D Georgia-Alabama League in June of 1915. After the 1917 season, Terry, battling financial strains, went to work for Standard Oil Company. He also played first base and served as manager of the company's baseball team and was spotted by McGraw, who signed Terry to a contract after three weeks of negotiations. Terry was sent to the Giants' farm team in Toledo, Ohio, where he played the 1992 and 1923 seasons and managed for part of the 1923 campaign, as well, before being called up to New York.

Following his playing and managing career, Terry spent one year (1942) as the Giants' farm director. He was inducted into the National Baseball Hall of Fame in 1954 and subsequently had his uniform No. 3 retired by the Giants.

Terry passed away January 9, 1989, in Jacksonville, Florida, at the age of 90.

Robby Thompson, Second Baseman (1986-96)

Second baseman Robby Thompson spent his entire 11-year major league career with the San Francisco Giants from 1986-96. He was the type of player everyone appreciates—selfless and steady. He could move runners along the bases or drive them home. He made all the plays in the field.

In 1986 Thompson earned a spot on San Francisco's roster coming out of spring training, despite not having played a single game of Triple-A ball. He was part of manager Roger Craig's enthusiastic "You Gotta Like These Kids" collection that included first baseman Will Clark, shortstop Jose Uribe and third

Robby Thompson (S.F. Giants Archives)

baseman Chris Brown, as well. Thompson batted .271 with seven home runs and 47 RBI and topped the team with 149 hits, 73 runs scored and 18 sacrifices en route to being named *The Sporting News'* National League Rookie of the Year.

The following year Thompson batted .262 with 10 home runs, 44 RBI and a career-high 16 stolen bases while helping San Francisco capture its first N.L. West Division crown since 1971. He batted at a .241 clip with a career-high and league-leading 11 triples, 13 home runs and 50 RBI for the 1989 N.L. champion Giants, who defeated the Chicago Cubs four games to one to capture the pennant. In Game 3 Thompson socked a game-winning, two-run homer over the left field fence in the seventh inning off Les Lancaster as the Giants came from behind for a 5-4 victory at Candlestick Park in San Francisco.

On April 22, 1991, Thompson hit for the cycle against the San Diego Padres at Candlestick Park. He tripled in the first inning,

homered in the third, singled in the sixth and doubled in the ninth. Thompson was the last Giants' player to accomplish the rare feat until Jeff Kent, also a second baseman, did so against the Pittsburgh Pirates at Three Rivers Stadium in Pittsburgh on May 3, 1999.

Thompson belted a career-high 19 home runs in 1991 and equalled that total in 1993, when he also posted personal bests of a .312 batting average, 30 doubles and 65 RBI. Defensively, he committed a mere eight errors and earned a Gold Glove Award. The Giants battled the Atlanta Braves for the West Division championship until the final day of the season before the Braves won the crown by one game.

A variety of injuries and ailments limited Thompson to an average of just 64 games played per year from 1994-96. Nevertheless, he tied the franchise record with three doubles against the Braves at Atlanta-Fulton County Stadium on June 21, 1996.

On San Francisco's career lists, Thompson ranks third in at-bats (4,612), fourth in games (1,304) and doubles (238), tied for fourth in triples (39), fifth in hits (1,187), sixth in runs (671) and eighth in stolen bases (103). He batted .257 with 119 home runs and 458 RBI.

Thompson, who was selected to the All-Star Game in 1988 and 1993, currently lives in his hometown of West Palm Beach, Florida. He became a roving instructor for the Giants' minor league system in 1999.

Bobby Thomson, Third Baseman/ Outfielder (1946-53, 1957)

Decades have passed since Bobby Thomson hit the "Shot Heard 'Round The World," but the home run remains baseball's most dramatic moment.

On October 3, 1951, in the bottom of the ninth inning of their third and deciding playoff game for the National League pennant, the New York Giants trailed the cross-town rival Brooklyn Dodgers by the score of 4-1. Then, with one run in and Clint Hartung on third base and Whitey Lockman on second with one out, Thomson launched Ralph Branca's no-

ball, one-strike pitch over the left field wall of the Polo Grounds for a miraculous 5-4 victory.

"The Giants win the pennant! The Giants win the pennant! The Giants win the pennant!"

Though remembered primarily for the home run, Thomson enjoyed a solid career with the Giants from 1946-53 and in 1957. After receiving a cup of coffee in September of 1946, Thomson burst onto the scene the following season. He batted .283 with 29 home runs and 85 RBI. That year New York clouted a franchise-record 221 homers (tied for the most in major league history for a 154-game schedule).

In 1949 Thomson was part of a New York outfield in which all three regulars batted at better than a .300 clip. He finished with a career-high and team-leading .309 average, plus 27 home runs and a personal best of 109 RBI as the center fielder, while Willard Marshall batted .307 in right and Lockman batted .301 in left.

Thomson slugged a career-high 32 homers in 1951 to go with a .293 batting average

Bobby Thomson (Brace Photo)

and 108 RBI. In May he was moved from center to third base by manager Leo Durocher to make room for a rookie by the name of Willie Mays. Ironically, Thomson belted a two-run homer off Branca in Game 1 of the playoff series in New York's 3-1 victory. The Giants, who stormed back from a 13½ -game deficit in mid-August to tie the Dodgers for first place and force the playoff, lost to the New York Yankees in the World Series four games to two.

The next two seasons Thomson again surpassed the century mark in RBI with 108 in 1952 and 106 in 1953. He led the N.L. with a career-high 14 triples in 1952. On February 1, 1954, New York traded Thomson and catcher Sam Calderone to the Milwaukee Braves in exchange for pitcher Johnny Antonelli, infielder Billy Klaus, pitcher Don Liddle, catcher Ebba St. Claire and $50,000.

Thomson played for the Braves from 1954-57 before being traded back to the Giants along with pitcher Ray Crone and infielder Danny O'Connell in exchange for future Hall of Fame second baseman Red Schoendienst on June 15, 1957.

But the "Staten Island Scot," as the native of Glasgow, Scotland, was nicknamed, had a short second stint in New York. The Giants dealt him to the Chicago Cubs in exchange for first baseman/outfielder Bob Speake and cash April 3, 1958. Thomson played for the Cubs in 1958 and 1959 before concluding his career with the Boston Red Sox and Baltimore Orioles in 1960.

On the Giants' franchise lists Thomson ranks seventh with 189 home runs. The three-time N.L. All-Star (1948, 1949 and 1952) batted .277 with 704 RBI in 1,135 games. He led New York in homers for five consecutive seasons from 1949-53 and in RBI in 1949, 1952 and 1953. Thomson's 15-year career numbers included a .270 batting average with 264 homers and 1,026 RBI in 1,779 games.

Thomson currently makes his home in Watchung, New Jersey. He and Branca are good friends and often appear together at baseball memorabilia shows and other events.

The home run is commemorated on a United States postage stamp that was issued in April of 1999.

Jim Thorpe, Outfielder (1913-19)

Regarded as the finest American athlete of the 20th century long after his death in 1953, Jim Thorpe was best known for his track and field achievements and his prowess as a football All-American at Carlisle College in 1911-12, placing the Pennsylvania Indian school on the map with victories over national powers under coach Pop Warner. He first enrolled there at age 19 in 1907, intending to become an electrician.

Thorpe had a brief and unsuccessful major league career, mostly with the New York Giants, with whom he spent parts of six seasons. A switch hitter, Thorpe batted merely .252 in 289 major league games with 10 home runs. A career total of 18 triples in limited playing time attested to his speed on the base paths.

When his Carlisle career concluded, Thorpe played *and* coached football with the Canton Bulldogs and spent his summers playing baseball. But he didn't get along with manager John McGraw of the Giants because of work habits the Giants' boss didn't appreciate once the star reported to spring training in Texas in 1913.

Thorpe reportedly arrived five minutes prior to an exhibition and was reprimanded by the tough-minded McGraw. To which the athlete responded: "I can hit, can't I? I can throw, can't I? I can run, can't I? What do you want to do—see me sweat?"

The rift widened during the season when Thorpe primarily was a pinch hitter. The two frequently argued, and Thorpe called his manager "a little wind trying to blow hard." He was demoted to the minors, returned to the majors and still was playing minor league baseball at age 40 in 1928.

His hitting problems enabled Thorpe to concentrate on his first love, football. He played professionally from 1915-26 and was

Jim Thorpe (S.F. Giants Archives)

the first president of the league that would become the NFL. At $500 per game, he was pro football's best-paid player.

The Oklahoma native, born in 1888 as a grandson of heroic Chief Black Hawk, became an athletic god by winning the grueling decathlon *and* the pentathlon at the 1912 Olympics in Stockholm, Sweden. When King Gustav V of Sweden told him, "You, sir, are the greatest athlete in the world," Thorpe was said to reply, "Thanks, King."

The Olympic medals were confiscated because of his professional standing in other sports—he made $15 per week playing semi-pro baseball in 1910—but eventually were returned to his family. "How was I to know playing baseball for money made me a professional in track?" he said. "I was just a dumb Indian kid."

At the least, he was extremely naive and honest. His early semi-pro baseball days where at Rocky Mount, North Carolina, and it was common practice in those days for collegians to hide their identity to retain their amateur standing. Thorpe, unaware of the potential repercussions, used his own name.

An early superstar of legendary proportions, Thorpe was named the greatest athlete of the half-century in an Associated Press poll, easily outdistancing Babe Ruth and Jack Dempsey while earning more first-place votes than all the others combined. He was accomplished in 11 sports—baseball, basketball, bowling, boxing, football, golf, lacrosse, shooting, swimming, track and field and wrestling.

Mike Tiernan, Outfielder (1887-99)

Like Theodore Roosevelt, the 26th president of the United States, Mike Tiernan spoke softly and carried a big stick.

An outfielder for the New York Giants from 1887-99, "Silent Mike" accounted for some of the greatest moments in the early days of the franchise and still holds several records.

- On June 15, 1887, Tiernan set a franchise record by scoring six runs in a 29-1 victory over the Philadelphia Phillies at the Polo Grounds in New York. More than 100 years later the run total still is tied for the National League record with nine other players, including Mel Ott of the Giants (the only player to do so twice). The major league record is seven by Guy Hecker of the Louisville Colonels (American Association) on August 15, 1886. Interestingly, Tiernan also pitched the final five innings of the game, allowing no hits.

- Tiernan was the first player in Giants' history to hit for the cycle when he accomplished the feat against the Phillies at the Huntington Street Grounds in Philadelphia on August 25, 1888. He drove in four runs in a 7-0 win.

- In the first world championship game the Giants ever played against the St. Louis Browns at the Polo Grounds on October 16, 1888, Tiernan drew a leadoff walk from pitcher Silver King in the bottom of the third inning with the score tied 1-apiece. Tiernan took off to steal second base and came all the way around to score what proved to be the winning run

when the throw from catcher Jack Boyle sailed past center fielder Harry Lyons.

- On May 12, 1890, Tiernan blasted a home run with one out in the bottom of the 13th inning to give the Giants a 1-0 victory over the Boston Beaneaters at the Polo Grounds. Adding drama to the homer was the fact that after the ball cleared the center field fence it bounded up against the outside fence of adjoining Brotherhood Park, where the New York Giants of the Players League were playing host to the Boston Red Stockings. Tiernan was applauded by fans in both ballparks as he trotted around the bases.

During his 13 seasons in New York, Tiernan batted over .300 on seven occasions. He led the N.L. with a franchise-record 147 runs in 1889 and twice shared the league lead

in home runs (13 in 1890 and a career-high 16 in 1891). Tiernan had two seasons in which he legged out a career-high 21 triples (1890 and 1895), five shy of the franchise record set by George Davis during the 1893 campaign. Other personal bests included 30 doubles in 1891, 102 RBI in 1893 and a .369 batting average in 1896. He batted .335 in 1889 to rank third in the league.

When the Players League was formed for the 1890 season, the teams raided N.L. and A.A. rosters for players. Only three members of the 1889 Giants returned in 1890: Tiernan, pitcher Mickey Welch and catcher Pat Murphy.

Tiernan's career totals included a .311 batting average, 1,834 hits, 256 doubles, 162 triples, 851 RBI and 428 stolen bases in 1,476 games. He is the Giants' all-time leader in triples and stolen bases (although when he played a stolen base was awarded if a player advanced an extra base on a hit or an out by a teammate). He ranks third in runs (behind Willie Mays with 2,011 and Ott with 1,859), fifth in hits, sixth in RBI, seventh in at-bats (5,906), ninth in games and doubles and 10th in batting average. Tiernan also pitched in five games during the 1887 season (1-2 record with one save and a 8.69 ERA).

Tiernan passed away November 7, 1918, in New York at the age of 51, following a lengthy bout with tuberculosis.

Jose Uribe, Shortstop (1985-92)

The popular Jose Uribe was the key player the Giants acquired from the St. Louis Cardinals in the Jack Clark trade February 1, 1985, that helped both clubs. Uribe, with Ozzie Smith no longer in his path, became the unsung hero of the 1987 and 1989 champions with his stellar play at shortstop that tightened a leaky defense.

Named the Giants' All-Decade shortstop of the 1980s, Uribe came up through the New York Yankees' and Cardinals' systems and was known as Jose Gonzalez before taking his mother's last name, Uribe, because "there are too many guys named Jose Gonzalez."

Mike Tiernan (Transcendental Graphics)

247

There also were too many shortstops from the Dominican Republic, and Uribe belonged among the elite while serving as the glue of a solid Giants' infield from the day he became a regular in 1985.

A lifetime .241 batter, Uribe enjoyed a career year in 1987, batting .291 and making merely 13 errors. It's no coincidence the Giants won their first division title in 16 years, and his two-run single in Game 5 of the playoffs produced a 3-2 victory over the Cardinals at Candlestick Park.

"Every time I look up to check my infield, Jose is exactly where he's supposed to be," former infield coach Bob Lillis said. "He is one of those players who instinctively does the right thing. You don't know whether somebody taught him, or he just came that way."

Joe Uribe (AP/Wide World Photos)

Uribe, a switch-hitter at the time, teamed with second baseman Robby Thompson to form one of the two great double-play combinations in San Francisco history along with Chris Speier and Tito Fuentes. They led the league in double plays in 1987, spearheading a defense that made the club a big winner.

But Uribe didn't have much time to celebrate his accomplishments. On June 1, 1988, his world was turned around. Wife, Sara, died of primary pulmonary hypertension which resulted in a heart attack shortly after giving birth to their first son, Rique, three weeks premature. They also had two daughters, Luzadriana and Jacqueline.

Manager Roger Craig gave his shortstop as much time off as he needed. The funeral was in their native Dominican Republic, and Uribe was anxious to return to work, taking his mind off the tragedy. He took a short break and was back doing the job he loved, finishing with a career-high seven triples in 1988.

"I try to keep going, working hard," Uribe explained. "I got three kids to take care of. I got to be father. I got to be mother. I got to be everything to them. You have to make your life keep going. You have to play baseball. I know the only way to take care of my children is to play baseball.

"This season has been like 20 years for me. It sometimes seems like it will never end. My body is sore and my mind is so tired. There are times when I feel I don't want to play. I have to keep my mind on baseball. It helps me."

Uribe, however, never regained his career-best form of 1987. He batted .221 for the pennant-winning Giants of 1989 and gradually had his playing time reduced as the club groomed former No. 1 draft choice Royce Clayton for the job. Uribe was traded to the Houston Astros in 1993, batting .245 in his final season.

George Van Haltren, Outfielder (1894-1903)

George Van Haltren was one of the New York Giants' finest players of the late 19th and early 20th centuries.

Primarily an outfielder, the hard-hitting Van Haltren donned a Giants' uniform from 1894-1903. Before settling in New York, he played for the Chicago White Stockings (1887-90), Brooklyn Wonders of the Players' League (1890), Baltimore Orioles (1891-92) and Pittsburgh Pirates (1892-93).

Upon signing with the Giants in 1894, Van Haltren took over as the regular center fielder and batted .331 with seven home runs, a career-high 104 RBI and 43 stolen bases. New York finished in second place in the National League and played the champion Orioles in the Temple Cup series. Van Haltren banged out seven hits in 14 at-bats as the Giants upset Baltimore four games to none. The following year Van Haltren batted at a .340 clip with eight homers, 103 RBI and 32 stolen bases.

In 1896 "Rip" continued to do just that to the baseball to the tune of a career-high .351 batting average. He topped the N.L. with 21 triples (also a personal best and tied for third on the Giants' single-season list) and drove in 74 runs. Van Haltren batted at better than a .300 clip each of the next five seasons, capped by a .335 mark during the 1901 campaign. He tied for the league lead with 45 stolen bases in 1900 (with outfielder Patsy Donovan of the St. Louis Perfectos).

Early in his career, Van Haltren was a pitcher as well as an outfielder. On June 21, 1888, he authored a six-inning no-hitter for Chicago against Pittsburgh at West Side Park in Chicago, winning by the score of 1-0. He posted a 15-10 record for Brooklyn in 1890. But Van Haltren's potent bat led to him essentially forgo pitching a year later. Nevertheless, he is credited with helping develop Giants' future Hall of Famer Christy Mathewson when the two were roommates in 1901. Van Haltren pitched in five games during his New York days

George Van Haltren (Transcendental Graphics)

and won his only decision during the 1896 season.

In 10 seasons with the Giants, Van Haltren batted .321 with 194 doubles, 88 triples, 29 home runs, 604 RBI and 320 stolen bases in 1,221 games. On the franchise all-time lists, he ranks fifth in batting average, sixth in runs (973) and stolen bases and ninth in hits (1,575) and triples. Defensively, he is second among outfielders with 224 assists and fifth with 2,440 putouts. He had a whopping total of 37 assists in 1896.

His 17-year career statistics included a .316 batting average, 2,532 hits, 1,014 RBI and 583 stolen bases (19th on baseball's all-time list) in 1,984 games. As a pitcher he had a 40-31 record with a 4.05 ERA. Van Haltren served as player-manager for Baltimore briefly in 1892 and had a 1-10 record.

Following his major league days, Van Haltren played and managed in the minors for several years. He subsequently was a scout for

Pittsburgh and a minor league umpire. Van Haltren passed away September 29, 1945, in Oakland, California, at the age of 79.

Bill Voiselle, Pitcher (1942-47)

In 1944 Bill Voiselle of the New York Giants became the only rookie in baseball history to win 20 games, pitch 300 innings and lead the league in strikeouts. He finished 21-16 with a 3.02 ERA while striking out 161 batters in 312.2 innings and was named *The Sporting News'* National League Pitcher of the Year.

Voiselle toiled for the Giants from 1942-47, but he appeared in only six games his first two seasons after coming up from New York's minor league teams in Oklahoma City and Jersey City, respectively. Therefore, the 1944 season was his official rookie year.

Expanding on Voiselle's achievement, only 11 rookies have led their respective league in strikeouts (since 1900), only 13 have won 20 games (since 1920) and only 23 have pitched 300 innings (since 1900).

On his way into the record book, Voiselle was selected to the National League All-Star team as a replacement for injured St. Louis Cardinals' pitcher Red Munger, but he did not appear in the game at Forbes Field in Pittsburgh. From August 9-20, the Giants lost 13 consecutive games, and Voiselle snapped the skid with a 3-1 victory in the second game of a double-header against the Cardinals at Sportsman's Park in St. Louis. Voiselle was the only Giants' starting pitcher with a winning record in 1944 as the team finished 67-87, for fifth place in the N.L., 38 games behind the pennant-winning Cardinals.

The right-handed Voiselle continued his fine work the following year with an 8-2 record heading into a game against St. Louis at Sportsman's Park on June 1, 1945. He was leading the Cardinals 3-1 in the bottom of the ninth inning with pinch-runner Dave Bartosch on first base and one out and right fielder Johnny Hopp at the plate. On an 0-2 pitch, Voiselle tried to waste a pitch that got away from him, and Hopp tripled to make the score 3-2. After center fielder Buster Adams grounded out (with Hopp holding at third), a terrific windstorm followed by a drizzling rain delayed the game for about an hour. When play resumed, Voiselle was sent back to the mound and gave up a single to first baseman Ray Sanders to tie the game and a triple to third baseman Whitey Kurowski to lose it. Afterwards, Giants' manager Mel Ott announced that he was fining Voiselle $500 for "disobeying pitching orders" by not wasting the 0-2 pitch. Usually, the fine for failing to waste a pitch was $100, but Ott was particularly upset about losing this game. Ott subsequently recanted the fine, but Voiselle never seemed to get over the incident. Voiselle went on the finish the season 14-14 with a 4.49 ERA.

Coincidence or not, Voiselle was not a consistent winner after being fined. On June 13, 1948, New York traded him to the Boston Braves in exchange for pitcher Mort Cooper and cash. Cooper joined his younger brother,

Bill Voiselle (Brace Photo)

Walker, a catcher for the Giants. In six seasons in New York, Voiselle compiled a 46-52 record with a 3.64 ERA in 137 games.

With Boston, Voiselle donned uniform No. 96 in honor of his hometown of Ninety-Six, South Carolina. In 1948 the Braves' slogan was "Spahn and Sain and pray for rain," in reference to pitchers Warren Spahn (a future Hall of Famer) and Johnny Sain. But Voiselle contributed a 13-13 record with a 3.63 ERA as Boston won the N.L. pennant. He was the losing pitcher in the sixth and deciding game of the World Series against the Cleveland Indians.

Nicknamed "Big Bill," the 6-foot-4 Voiselle concluded his major league career with the Chicago Cubs in 1950. His nine-year career totals included a 74-84 record with a 3.83 ERA in 245 games. He subsequently pitched in the minor leagues for several years.

Voiselle currently makes his home in Ninety Six, South Carolina.

John Montgomery Ward, Pitcher/Infielder (1883-89, 1893-94)

John Montgomery Ward was involved in virtually every aspect of the game of baseball: pitcher, position player, manager, executive, owner, union organizer and lawyer.

When the New York Gothams acquired Ward from the Providence Grays for their inaugural season in 1883, they figured to be getting one of the game's elite pitchers. After all, he led the National League with 47 wins in 1879 and pitched a perfect game against the Buffalo Bisons on June 17, 1880. However, a tired arm led to Ward being moved to the infield, and he became a premier second baseman and shortstop with the reputation of being a daring and dashing performer. "Monte" wore a New York uniform from 1883-89 and 1893-94.

In his first season with the Gothams, Ward had a 16-13 record with a 2.70 ERA. He pitched in nine games the following year (and served as manager for the final 16 contests) before taking over as New York's everyday shortstop in 1885. Ward put together his finest season in 1887 when he batted a career-high

John Montgomery Ward (National Baseball Library and Archive)

.338 (fourth in the N.L.) with a league-leading and franchise-record 111 stolen bases (although in those days a stolen base was awarded if a player advanced an extra base on a hit or an out by a teammate). He paced N.L. shortstops with a .919 fielding percentage, as well.

However, Ward also made headlines in 1887 for sending a letter to league president Nicholas Young on July 16 detailing a series of abuses to which teams had been subjecting their players (including the reserve clause that bound a player to a particular team forever). Interestingly, four days earlier Ward had been replaced as team captain in favor of Buck Ewing. Ward, who was elected president of the

Brotherhood of Professional Base Ball Players (a players' union) in 1885, went on to be the principle figure in the formation of the Players League in 1890.

On January 28, 1890, the U.S. Supreme Court ruled against an injunction that would have prevented Ward from playing for any other team except the Giants in 1890. As a result, Ward became player-manager of the Brooklyn Wonders of the P.L. When the league folded after one season he joined the Brooklyn Bridegrooms of the N.L. for the 1891 and 1892 campaigns. During this period, when betting was an accepted part of the game, Ward won 20 shares of stock in the Giants in a wager.

Ward desired to return to the Giants, and he did so as player-manager in 1893. The following year he piloted New York to second place with an 88-44 record, three games behind the pennant-winning Baltimore Orioles. The two teams then squared off in the Temple Cup championship, and the underdog Giants swept the Orioles four games to none.

In 1895 Andrew C. Freedman took over as the Giants' president and immediately fired Ward as manager. Ward, who had taken night classes at Columbia University to earn his law degree in 1885, retired from baseball at the age of 35 to pursue his second career. Much of his law practice involved ballplayers. In 1909 Ward made an unsuccessful run at becoming president of the N.L., and in 1911 he was part of a triumvirate that purchased the Boston Braves. His partners bought him out a year later. Ward subsequently served as business manager of the Brooklyn Tip-Tops of the Federal League and as a member of the Major League Baseball rules committee.

During his nine years with the Giants, Ward batted .279 with 546 RBI and 332 stolen bases (fifth on the franchise list) in 1,070 games. He pitched in 43 games in 1883 and 1884 with a 19-16 record and a 2.83 ERA. His managerial record was 162-116 (.583 winning percentage). Ward's 17-year career offensive totals included a .275 batting average, 867 RBI and 540 stolen bases in 1,825 games. On the mound he was 164-102 with a 2.10 ERA in 292 games over seven seasons. He compiled a 412-320 record as manager (.563 winning percentage).

Ward passed away March 4, 1925, in Augusta, Georgia, one day after his 65th birthday after contracting pneumonia. He was inducted into the National Baseball Hall of Fame in 1964 by the Veterans Committee.

Phil Weintraub, First Baseman/ Outfielder (1933-35, 1937, 1944-45)

They say everyone has 15 minutes of fame. Phil Weintraub, a first baseman and outfielder for the New York Giants, had a few hours.

On April 30, 1944, Weintraub had a franchise-record 11 RBI as the Giants crushed the cross-town rival Brooklyn Dodgers by the score of 26-8 in the first game of a double-header at the Polo Grounds in New York. He

Phil Weintraub (Brace Photo)

had two doubles, a triple, a home run and a bases-loaded walk. Afterwards, he was greeted in the clubhouse by legendary Hall of Famer Babe Ruth, who had witnessed the eye-popping performance from a front-row box alongside the Giants' dugout. The major league standard is 12 RBI by Jim Bottomley of the St. Louis Cardinals in 1924 and by Mark Whiten of the Cardinals in 1993.

A minor league pitcher until hurting his arm in 1930, Weintraub had three stints with the Giants: 1933-35, 1937 and 1944-45. He played sparingly his first three seasons for manager Bill Terry and was traded to St. Louis along with pitcher Roy Parmelee and cash in exchange for second baseman Burgess "Whitey" Whitehead on December 9, 1935.

It was the first of several moves for Weintraub, who resembled boxing heavyweight champion Max Baer, over the next seven years. He did not play for the Cardinals and joined the Cincinnati Reds in 1937 before returning to New York. Then he was sold to the Philadelphia Phillies and batted .311 with a career-high 23 doubles, four home runs and 45 RBI in 100 games during the 1938 campaign. After bouncing all around the minor leagues—from Minneapolis to Los Angeles to Rochester (New York) to Toledo (Ohio)—from 1939-43, Weintraub ultimately wound up back in New York, which was now being managed by Mel Ott, in 1944.

His record day at the plate set the tone for his best season as Weintraub went on to post personal bests of a .316 batting average, nine triples, 13 home runs and 77 RBI. The following year "Mickey" batted .272 with 10 homers and 42 RBI before retiring.

In six seasons with the Giants, the left-handed swinging Weintraub batted .293 with 34 doubles, 13 triples, 25 home runs and 142 RBI in 295 games. His seven-year lifetime batting average was .295 in 444 games. In 1982 Weintraub was inducted into the Chicago (his hometown) Jewish Athletes Hall of Fame.

Weintraub passed away June 21, 1987, in Palm Springs, California, at the age of 79 following a lengthy battle against cancer.

Mickey Welch, Pitcher (1883-92)

Mickey Welch was the first premier pitcher in the history of the Giants' franchise. He toiled for New York from its entry into the National League in 1883 through 1892 (the team was known as the Gothams before first being called the Giants my manager Jim Mutrie in 1885).

Welch, a right-hander known for his screwball, began his career with the Troy (New York) Trojans of the National League from 1880-82. In the era of "finishing what you start," he completed his first 105 starts over two-plus seasons. On July 4, 1881 (his 22nd birthday), Welch picked up two complete-game victories in a double-header against the Buffalo Bisons.

When John B. Day was granted New York franchises in both the National League (Gothams) and the American Association (Metropolitans) for the 1883 season, he bought out the Trojans, who were being dispatched from the N.L., and divided the roster between his two teams. Welch was assigned to the Gothams.

In his first season with the Gothams, Welch went 25-23 with a 2.73 ERA. He pitched 426 innings and walked a mere 66 batters (1.4 per nine innings). Welch was 39-21, 2.50 ERA with a career-high 345 strikeouts in 557.1 innings pitched in 1884. He completed 62 of the 63 games he started. On August 28, 1884, Welch began a game against the Cleveland Blues at the Polo Grounds in New York by striking out nine consecutive batters, a major league record that stood for nearly 86 years until Tom Seaver of the New York Mets fanned 10 in a row against the San Diego Padres on April 22, 1970.

Welch put together his finest season in 1885, finishing 44-11 for a league-leading .800 winning percentage with a 1.66 ERA. He surrendered just 372 hits in 492 innings pitched with 131 walks and 258 strikeouts. From July 18-September 4 he won 17 consecutive games, two shy of the major league standard. That

Mickey Welch (Transcendental Graphics)

year right-handed pitcher Tim Keefe was transferred from the Metropolitans to the Giants and won 32 games. Keefe and Welch, who previously were teammates with Troy from 1880-82, combined for 76 of New York's 85 victories. The Giants finished with an 85-27 record (a franchise-best .759 winning percentage) but wound up two games behind the pennant-winning Chicago White Stockings.

Keefe ultimately replaced Welch as the ace of the pitching staff. Still, Welch was 33-22 with a 2.99 ERA in 1886, and he finished 26-19 with a 1.93 ERA in 1888 as the Giants won their first World Series championship over the St. Louis Browns. In the World Series he was 1-1 with a 2.65 ERA. The following year Welch was 27-12, 3.02 ERA, and New York repeated as world champions over the cross-town rival Brooklyn Bridegrooms. On September 10, 1889, Welch served as the first-ever pinch hitter in the N.L. against the Indianapolis Hoo-

siers (the career .224 batter struck out).

"Smiling Mickey," as he was nicknamed because of the seemingly constant smile on his face, passed up the opportunity to join the newfound Players League in 1890, and that year he became the third pitcher in baseball history to win 300 career games (joining Pud Galvin and Keefe).

Welch's 10-year statistics with the Giants included a 240-145 record with a 2.69 ERA. He ranks among the franchise's career leaders in complete games (2nd, 391); wins (3rd); innings pitched (3rd, 3,579.0); games started (4th, 412); shutouts (6th, 28); strikeouts (6th, 1,570); ERA (7th); and games (8th, 426). On baseball's all-time lists, he ranks sixth in complete games (525), 14th in innings pitched (4,802), 18th in wins (307) and 24th in games started (549).

Following his playing career, Welch worked as a custodian at the Polo Grounds in New York. He passed away July 30, 1941, in Concord, New Hampshire, at the age of 82. Welch was inducted into the National Baseball Hall of Fame in 1973 by the Veterans Committee.

Hoyt Wilhelm, Pitcher (1952-56)

If Noah Webster were scribing the meaning of the word "durability" today, he undoubtedly would include a sketch of Hoyt Wilhelm with the definition. The right-handed pitcher, who began his career with the New York Giants from 1952-56, without question, fits the description of a durable performer. The knuckleballer appeared in 1,070 games over 21 seasons, more than any other pitcher in baseball history until Dennis Eckersley passed him in 1998. (Jesse Orosco passed both Wilhelm and Eckersley in 1999.)

Wilhelm burst onto the scene in 1952, going 15-3 with a National League-best 2.43 ERA and a team-leading 11 saves. He was the first rookie ever to lead the league in both winning percentage (.833) and ERA. In his major league debut April 23, 1952, Wilhelm hit a home run in his first at-bat in the fourth inning off Dick

Hoover of the Boston Braves at the Polo Grounds in New York. Wilhelm went on to pick up the win in relief.

The following year Wilhelm was selected to the All-Star Game at Crosley Field in Cincinnati (though he did not pitch) en route to recording a then Giants' record-tying 15 saves. Wilhelm was 12-4 with a 2.10 ERA and seven saves for the 1954 World Series champion Giants, who swept the Cleveland Indians four games to none to capture the crown. He paced New York with eight saves during the 1956 campaign.

The Giants traded Wilhelm to the St. Louis Cardinals in exchange for first baseman/ outfielder Whitey Lockman on February 26, 1957. Wilhelm's overall numbers with New York included a 42-25 record with a 2.98 ERA and 41 saves in 319 games (all in relief).

Wilhelm later pitched for the Indians (1957-58), Baltimore Orioles (1958-62), Chicago White Sox (1963-68), California Angels (1969), Atlanta Braves (1969-70 and 1971), Chicago Cubs (1970) and Los Angeles Dodgers (1971-72). He equalled his career high of 15

Hoyt Wilhelm (S.F. Giants Archives)

wins in 1959, recorded a career-high 27 saves in 1964 and posted a career-low 1.31 ERA in 1967. He was an American League All-Star in 1959, 1961 and 1962 and a National League All-Star in 1970.

Wilhelm started only 52 games over the course of his career (completing 20 of them). He made 27 starts in 1959, when he topped the American League with a 2.19 ERA. Wilhelm is the only pitcher to lead both leagues in ERA.

On September 20, 1958, Wilhelm authored a 1-0 no-hitter for the Orioles against the New York Yankees at Memorial Stadium in Baltimore. He broke Cy Young's record of 906 games pitched July 24, 1968, became the first pitcher in baseball history to earn 200 career saves May 3, 1969, and made his 1,000th career appearance May 10, 1970.

Wilhelm, who pitched until he was nearly 49 years old, posted a 143-122 career record with a 2.52 ERA and 227 saves. He holds all-time records for games won in relief (124) and games finished (651) and ranks seventh in hits allowed per nine innings (7.01). Wilhelm was inducted into the National Baseball Hall of Fame in 1985, becoming the first relief pitcher to receive the game's ultimate distinction. The recipient of a Purple Heart after being wounded while serving in the Army in World War II, Wilhelm currently resides in Sarasota, Florida.

Matt Williams, Third Baseman (1987-96)

The Giants have had their share of solid third baseman during the San Francisco years—Jim Davenport and Jim Ray Hart to name two—but none played the position as well as Matt Williams, a converted shortstop. "Matty" turned down the New York Mets following a solid prep career in Carson City, Nevada, and it was a wise choice.

As a junior at the University of Nevada-Las Vegas, Williams dazzled the scouts with a .351 average, 25 homers and 89 RBI as an All-America shortstop. That greatly increased his value, and he became the third overall pick in the draft, joining the Giants. Rushed to the ma-

jors because of injuries, he struggled at the start of his career, batting .188, .205 and .202 in parts of his first three years with the club from 1987-89.

Williams' power gained more attention in 1988, when he tied the Pacific Coast League record with four home runs for Phoenix against Albuquerque. That same year he reached the majors and hit a grand-slam homer off Nolan Ryan. By the end of 1989, "Matty" was in the majors to stay despite a failed first stint as the Giants' opening day third baseman.

Matt Williams (S.F. Giants Archives)

Optioned to Phoenix with a .130 average on May 1, he batted .320 with 26 home runs in 76 games, prompting a promotion July 23. Williams hit 11 home runs in August and finished with 18. Combining his Triple-A and Giants' totals, he had 44 homers and 111 RBI in 160 games. The home run total was surpassed only by teammate Kevin Mitchell's 47 in professional baseball.

Williams was a postseason standout, too, batting .300 with two home runs and setting a five-game N.L. Championship Series record with nine RBI against the Chicago Cubs before adding a World Series homer off Dave Stewart. In 1990, his first full season as a major leaguer, Williams led the N.L. with 122 RBI to accompany a .277 average and 33 home runs.

The RBI total set a record for San Francisco third basemen, shattering Hart's 99 and surpassing Mel Ott's franchise mark of 117 in 1938. "Matty" hit 34 home runs with 98 RBI in

1991, slipped to a .227 average and 20 homers in 1992 but bounced back with a solid 1993 while forming a 1-2 power punch with newcomer Barry Bonds. He ranked right behind Bonds in many offensive categories and won his second Gold Glove to nail Comeback Player of the Year honors from United Press International.

His numbers that year included a .294 average, 33 doubles, 38 home runs and 110 RBI. But the 1994 season unquestionably was his finest as Williams was in serious pursuit of Roger Maris' home run record (61) when play was halted because of the strike. "I don't know what I would have done, I don't know what I was capable of," Williams said after finishing with 43 home runs, tops in the majors, in merely 112 games.

Williams was runner-up to Jeff Bagwell in the Most Valuable Player voting after setting a pace that could have eclipsed the Giants' (Willie Mays, 52) and the N.L. (Hack Wilson, 56) home run records at the time. He started in the All-Star Game and went on a tear thereafter, heading into the strike with nine home runs and 21 RBI in 20 games.

His 33 homers at the All-Star break were the most ever by a National Leaguer. His 40 home runs through July 31 also set a new N.L. record previously held by Willie Stargell, Johnny Bench, Mike Schmidt and Mays at 36. He also set an N.L. record with the most home runs before July with 29. Williams also had a

career-high 16-game hitting streak and was a Gold Glove winner again.

There were strong indications that 1995 would become Williams' best year because he turned into more of a hitter than a player strictly with power. He batted a career-best .336 but was limited to 23 homers and 65 RBI in merely 76 games—roughly one-half season—because of a freak foot fracture suffered on a foul tip June 3, shortly after he was N.L. Player of the Month in May with a .405 average, 12 homers and 31 RBI.

Injury again struck him down in 1996, when shoulder surgery restricted him to a .302 average, 22 homers and 85 RBI in 105 games. The Giants were concerned about his physical condition and sent him to Cleveland in an unpopular trade that eventually brought them a division title in 1997. Williams had 32 homers and 105 RBI for the Indians in 1997, batting .385 in the World Series, but a divorce left him longing for his children in Arizona. He requested a trade to the Diamondbacks and was accommodated in a deal for fellow third baseman Travis Fryman.

"Matty" played 135 games for the expansion club in 1998, producing 20 homers and 71 RBI. He entered the 1999 season with a new wife, marrying actress Michelle "Blame It On Rio" Johnson. Blessed with a great sense of humor, Williams also is known for comical routines in which he impersonates the home run swings and trots of notable sluggers like Babe Ruth and Reggie Jackson.

Hooks Wiltse, Pitcher (1904-14)

Only four pitchers in major league baseball history have thrown 10-inning no-hitters, and George "Hooks" Wiltse of the New York Giants is one of them.

Wiltse, a left-hander for the Giants from 1904-14, spun his gem in the first game of a double-header against the Philadelphia Phillies at the Polo Grounds in New York on July 4, 1908. It would have been a perfect game had Wiltse not grazed Phillies' pitcher George

McQuillan on the arm with a pitch with two outs in the ninth inning. New York won the game by the score of 1-0.

The others who have authored extra-inning no-hitters are Sam Kimber of the Brooklyn Bridegrooms (American Association) against the Toledo Blue Stockings on October 4, 1884; Fred Toney of the Cincinnati Reds against the Chicago Cubs on May 2, 1917; and Jim Maloney of the Reds against the Cubs on August 19, 1965. Three additional times pitchers have thrown 10 or more hitless innings before having their "no-no" broken up.

Wiltse had the look of a winner from the beginning of his career. He won the first 12 games he started for the Giants from May 29-September 5, 1904, a streak that remains a major league record to this day. Wiltse went on to finish his rookie season with a 13-3 record and a 2.84 ERA as New York won its first modern-day N.L. pennant (since 1900). His .813 winning percentage ranked second in the league to teammate Joe McGinnity (.814) and is tied for fourth on the Giants' season list.

Hooks Wiltse

In 1905 Wiltse finished 15-6 with a 2.47 ERA while helping the Giants repeat as league championships. The following year he was 16-11 with a 2.27 ERA and a career-high 125 strikeouts. On May 15, 1906, Wiltse stuck out seven consecutive batters in the fourth and fifth innings against Cincinnati at the Palace of the Fans in Cincinnati. Third baseman Jim Delahanty of the Reds fanned to start the fifth but reached first base when Giants' catcher Roger Bresnahan mishandled the third strike. Wiltse wound up with 12 strikeouts in a 4-1 victory.

Wiltse's no-hitter in 1908 came en route to his best overall season. He posted a 23-14 record with a 2.24 ERA while establishing personal bests for wins, complete games (30) and shutouts (7) and surrendering a mere 266 hits in 330 innings pitched (7.3 per nine innings). In 1909 Wiltse went 20-11 with a career-best 2.00 ERA.

From 1911-13 Wiltse was a member of three consecutive pennant-winning New York teams. He pitched sparingly in the 1911 World Series and not at all in 1912 and 1913. Nevertheless, Wiltse was instrumental in New York winning Game 2 of the 1913 series against the Philadelphia Athletics at Shibe Park in Philadelphia when he took over for the injured Fred Snodgrass at first base (who was filling in for the injured Fred Merkle) and cut down two runners (center fielder Amos Strunk and shortstop Jack Barry) trying to score on groundouts in the ninth inning. The Giants went on to win 3-0 in 10 innings but lost the series four games to one. Wiltse merited the nickname "Hooks" for his fielding ability.

In 1915 Wiltse jumped to the Federal League and concluded his big league career with the Brooklyn Tip-Tops. In 11 seasons with the Giants, Wiltse had a 136-85 record with a 2.48 ERA in 339 games. On the franchise career lists, he ranks fifth in ERA, tied for seventh in shutouts (27) and 10th in wins and complete games (153). His 12-year career numbers included a 139-90 record with a 2.47 ERA (tied for 24th on baseball's all-time list) in 357 games.

Wiltse subsequently served as a player-manager in the minor leagues and then as a coach for the New York Yankees in 1925. He passed away January 29, 1959, in Long Beach, New York, at the age of 78. His older brother, Snake, pitched in the major leagues from 1901-03.

Ross Youngs, Outfielder (1917-26)

Ross Youngs was one of baseball's original superstars and also one of its early tragedies.

During a 10-year career with the New York Giants from 1917-26, Youngs compiled a lifetime .322 batting average (third on the franchise's career list behind Bill Terry at .341 and George Davis at .332) with 93 triples (eighth). He possessed great speed (he stole home 10 times), a strong throwing arm and was the consummate team player.

But Youngs suffered a severe kidney ailment called Bright's disease that ultimately took his life October 22, 1927, at just 30 years of age.

Youngs, nicknamed "Pep," was discovered by Dick Kinsella, a scout for the Giants and personal confidant of manager John McGraw. He became New York's everyday right fielder in 1918 and helped the Giants win four consecutive National League pennants from 1921-24. In 1921 the 5-foot-8, 162-pound left-handed swinger drove in a career-high 102 runs, and in 1924 he posted personal bests of a .356 batting average and 10 home runs.

A native of Texas and a one-time star halfback at West Texas Military Academy, Youngs hit for the cycle April 29, 1922, against the Boston Braves at Braves Field.

Youngs earned the reputation of being a "gamer," and it was clearly evident in his World Series play. In the seventh inning of Game 3 of the 1921 Fall Classic against the cross-town rival Yankees, Youngs became the first player in Series history to collect two hits

Ross Youngs (Transcendental Graphics)

in one inning. He banged out a double and a triple as part of a seven-run uprising that propelled the Giants to a 13-5 victory. The Giants went on to win the first-ever Subway Series (played under a best-of-nine format) five games to three. Youngs batted .375 and .348 in the 1922 and 1923 Series, respectively.

Youngs was hospitalized midway through the 1926 campaign with what was publicly called intestinal trouble. The illness was the result of an earlier throat malady that moved into his kidneys. He returned to the Giants (accompanied by a specialist) in mid-August and, despite being far from at full strength, managed to end the season with a .306 batting average in 95 games. But Youngs never played again.

In 1972, some 45 years after his death, Youngs was inducted into the National Baseball Hall of Fame by the Veterans Committee.

CHAPTER FIVE

FAMOUS BROADCASTERS

Russ Hodges (1949-70)

The last voice of the New York Giants and the first announcer for the San Francisco Giants was born June 18, 1910, in Dayton, Tennessee, a relatively obscure Dixie town until the famous "Scopes Trial" was held there in 1925. By then, the Hodges clan had moved to Kentucky, and Russ became a great sports fan because his father, a railroad telegrapher, took him to sporting events.

Hodges remembered attending the famous 1919 Dempsey-Willard heavyweight fight in Toledo, Ohio. The next year, the Hodges family moved to Covington, across the Ohio River from Cincinnati, so sporting events were abundant. But Russ' mother fan-

Russ Hodges (S.F. Giants Archives)

cied a singing career and had him take voice lessons, which he was to appreciate later.

His baseball hero was Edd Roush of the neighboring Reds, and he became a Giants' fan only after Roush was traded to them in 1927. Hodges was good enough as an athlete to earn a football scholarship to Kentucky, but a broken ankle suffered in the first game of his sophomore season soon placed his melodic baritone voice to use announcing the Kentucky-Tennessee game.

That eventually led to radio work as a hillbilly disc jockey, but his station began broadcasting Reds' games in 1932, and in the process Hodges was graduated from law school at the University of Cincinnati

and passed the bar examination. "But in those days," he pointed out, "lawyers were jumping out of windows."

Instead, he went to cover baseball in Chicago, but the station (WIND) soon turned to soap operas. Then there was a stint in Charlotte, North Carolina, recreating Washington Senators' games before the Yankees beckoned and partnered him with the great Mel Allen in 1946. Whereas he was an employee of the Yankees, Hodges was a diehard fan of the Giants and was hired by Horace Stoneham to do their games in 1949, an association that lasted 21 years.

Hodges also was broadcasting Columbia football games, those of New York in the defunct All-American Football Conference (AAFC) and top boxing matches. Hodges contacted Bell's palsy, which is the result of the pinching of a facial nerve but was cured in time to work the 1950 season.

One year later, he was to make a call that immortalized him, announcing the fabled "Shot Heard 'Round the World," Bobby Thomson's playoff-clinching home run against the Brooklyn Dodgers on October 3, 1951. Hodges didn't remember what he said during the greatest moment in Giants' history, but someone preserved it on tape and presented it to him. The famous call:

"Branca pitches, and Bobby Thomson takes a strike called, on the inside corner ... Branca throws again ... there's a long fly ... it's gonna be ... I believe ... the Giants win the pennant! ... the Giants win the pennant! ... the Giants win the pennant! ... the Giants win the pennant! ... Bobby hit it into the lower deck of the left field seats ... the Giants win the pennant and they're going crazy ... I don't believe it! ... I don't believe it! ... I will not believe it! ..."

Hodges worked the fateful ninth by luck of the draw. It was partner Ernie Harwell's turn to do TV, so Hodges was left with radio chores and called the historic homer. Harwell: "What did radio bring Russ? Immortality. What did coast-to-coast TV bring me? Nothing. It's fair

to say that TV was still not a household fact."

Hodges moved west with his beloved Giants in 1958 and, like Stoneham, embraced San Francisco. But it was an adjustment because he had a habit of referring to them as the "New York Giants" and making fans angry during the exhibitions. He was intent on kicking the habit and, in his memoirs, recalled taking the microphone for the historic West Coast opener April 15, 1958.

"Good afternoon, everyone," he said, "this is Russ Hodges with Lon Simmons about to bring you the first major league game ever played on the Pacific Coast—the opening game of the season between the San Francisco Giants and the Los Angeles Dodgers at the Polo Grounds ... I mean, Seals Stadium."

It was one of the few mistakes he ever made in a distinguished career that spanned six decades. Hodges also was known for his home run call: "It's bye-bye baby." Summing up his career, Hudges once said: "Rather dull, not imaginative. I don't believe in keeping the listeners on the edge of their seats."

Lon Simmons
(1958-73, 1976-78, 1996-present)

The popular and witty Lon Simmons and his rich baritone voice turned to broadcasting when his attempts to reach the majors as a pitcher in the Philadelphia Phillies' and Boston Braves' organizations failed. A back problem ended that career, and he briefly worked as a carpenter until he began broadcasting in Elko, Neveda. Simmons, half Cherokee, was born in Vancouver, Washington, and attended high school in Southern California before enrolling at Compton Junior College.

He was a miler and a pitcher good enough to fire a no-hitter for a Los Angeles semi-pro team against USC. "I signed a bonus contract," he recalled, "and I made my first pro start in Terre Haute (Indiana). I struck out the side in the first inning, but I threw out my back pitching to the first guy in the second inning and later hurt my shoulder as a result of that."

Simmons began his radio career in Elko,

in 1952 and worked in Yuba City/Marysville and Fresno in the great California valley before becoming sports director of KSFO radio in San Francisco. That was a big break because it became the Giants' flagship station one year later. He teamed with Russ Hodges from 1958 until Hodges' death in 1971, continued with the Giants through 1973 and returned from 1976-78.

Simmons began doing Oakland Athletics' broadcasts with Bill King in 1981 and rejoined the Giants on a limited basis in 1996. Simmons, also the San Francisco 49ers' radio voice for 24 consecutive years (1957-80), says "You can tell it goodbye" as his home run trademark, and that slogan was used as the theme for the Giants' final season at Candlestick Park in 1999.

"I had to come up with something." Simmons explained, "because Russ had his 'Bye-Bye Baby.' I wanted something low-key, too, so that's how that slogan developed." Simmons is indebted to Hodges for making it easy for him to break into big-league broadcasting. The pair became fast friends, and Simmons was defending Hodges long after his death to critics of Hodges' legendary call of Bobby Thomson's epic 1951 playoff home run.

Hodges briefly lost control while in a euphoric state, and Dodgers' announcer Red Barber accused him of not being professional. "It was baseball's greatest-ever call, part of Americana, a chapter in history," said Simmons, who fondly called Hodges, "The Fabulous Fatman." Simmons emphasizes that his most pleasant memories as a broadcaster

Lon Simmons (S.F. Giants Archives)

were spent working with Hodges.

"Russ had a fabulous sense of humor—we got along so great—and I never enjoyed working with anyone more," Simmons said. The relationship extended to the NFL, where Simmons did 49ers' games occasionally with Hodges as a partner. Bill Thompson, also a member of the Giants' broadcast team in the 1960s, was a teammate of Simmons' at Burbank High School, and they have remained friends for 60 years.

Another Simmons thrill came at Squaw Valley, California, in the 1960 Winter Olympics, when he broadcast the U.S. gold-medal hockey upset of the Soviet Union. "The success that I always felt I had with the Giants or the 49ers is that I sort of announce as though I'm sitting in the stands with the people," he summed up. "I sort of echo their feelings. I'm an interested fan."

That certainly was evident on the final day of the 1962 season. Simmons was working the 49ers' game against the Vikings at Kezar Stadium, while Hodges was a few miles away at Candlestick. The Giants needed a win to catch the Dodgers, and Simmons was listening to his transistor radio when Willie Mays hit a game-winning homer.

"There was a roar in the crowd because they had transistors, too," Simmons recalled. "The Vikings were just breaking out of their huddle when they heard this tremendous cheer. They just stopped and looked around. They were thinking what great fans, cheering a huddle. They couldn't understand it."

Hank Greenwald (1979-86, 1989-96)

Hank Greenwald was the Giants' version of Cal Ripken. When he retired after the 1996 season, he had worked 2,798 consecutive major league games, including a two-year stint with the New York Yankees (1987-88). A native of Detroit, he was born Howard Greenwald, but he went to his first Tigers' game with his parents in 1945 and was infatuated with Hank Greenberg, the great Jewish slugger.

Before long, he became Hank Greenwald, and the hero-worship continued when he named his son, Douglas, after Gen. Douglas MacArthur, his favorite military leader. Greenwald's family moved to Rochester, New York, and that's when his love of baseball truly blossomed. He would listen to radio broadcasts of the three New York teams, and any other broadcast he could pick up late at night.

"Russ Hodges did the Giants, Red Barber did the Dodgers and Mel Allen did the Yankees," he said admiringly. "I also could pick up the Cardinals, the White Sox and the Pirates. That began my fascination with the voices of baseball. It was magic. I knew pretty early that I'd never make it as a player, so I thought maybe there was another way."

Broadcasting immediately came to mind, so Greenwald attended Syracuse University, a breeding ground for several prominent announcers. He spent a few years doing minor league baseball before shifting to the Bay

Hank Greenwald (S.F. Giants Archives)

Area to work with Bill King on the San Francisco Warriors' games. An avid traveller, he had a yearning to go to the South Pacific, so he resettled briefly in Australia.

Before long, Hank was in Honolulu, broadcasting the Hawaii Islanders of the Pacific Coast League. Then the Giants hired him in 1979 to team with Lindsey Nelson, one of his boyhood heroes. That began a Giants' career highlighted by his pleasant anecdotal manner which kept fans entertained and informed even during the dullest ballgames.

"You're not there to create a sight, you're there to capture it," Greenwald said. "I try to make the dead spots of a game interesting. We can't make a (bad) game interesting, but we can make a broadcast interesting. A bad game doesn't have to be a bad broadcast."

Following a disagreement with his station management, Greenwald decided to return to New York and work the Yankees' broadcasts. The move saddened his Giants' fans, and it soon made Greenwald realize that he preferred the Bay Area, where George Steinbrenner *didn't* live.

"Steinbrenner is everything you've heard, maybe worse," Greenwald recalled. "The man yells at the little people. I'd walk through the Yankees' offices, and I could tell if he was in town or not from the fear level of the office workers."

Greenwald kept his home in San Francisco, so returning to the Giants in 1989 was convenient. But when the new Giants' ownership group didn't in-

vite partner Ron Fairly back in 1993, Greenwald became more and more disenchanted with the rigors of constant travel and the changing face of baseball. "Every person coming into this business should feel like it's a great life because it is," he said shortly before his retirement in 1996. "Players today are far and away better athletes, but the system now prevents them from being better players. They're rushed through a diminished system of farm clubs."

Although there was some bitterness at the end of a marvelous career, Greenwald will best be remembered for his sense of humor. Once, while broadcasting a game against Montreal, he broke out with a touch of Cole Porter. "It's a beautiful day for baseball here at Candlestick Park," he began. "It's delightful, it's delectable ... it's Delino DeShields leading it off for the Expos."

Jon Miller (1997-present)

Jon Miller was a natural to succeed Hank Greenwald as the Giants' lead announcer, even though he built a national reputation as the voice of the Baltimore Orioles. Miller was born in the Bay Area, in the Eastbay community of Hayward, and was an avid Giants' fan as a youngster. Unlike most youthful followers, Miller carried it to an extreme, honing his broadcasting skills at an early age.

In his memoirs, Miller recalled going to his first baseball game with his father. It was at Candlestick Park and the Giants clobbered the Dodgers 19-8 in 1962, the year of the first pennant for San Francisco. Shortly thereafter, he was so hooked on baseball that he played it in imaginary games.

Little Jon purchased his first Strat-O-Matic set, a game which used dice and cards to recreate an actual game. Soon, the fanatic Miller was playing entire major league schedules, using his vivid imagination to announce them as he was playing. He added his own twist by being an advocate of international baseball way ahead of his time, placing franchises in places

Jon Miller (S.F. Giants Archives)

like Rome, London and in the Peruvian Andes.

In fact, he's been known to still play the game in the sanctity of his hotel room during baseball trips but probably without the broadcasting. At age 14, Miller knew he wanted to become a broadcaster. With the help of a reel-to-reel recorder, he would tape his simulations as well as televised Warriors' and Giants' games with the sound down.

Soon, the Athletics moved from Kansas City to Oakland, not far from his home. The eager teenager would go to the Coliseum with his recorder, sit in the right field bleachers and do his broadcast. Miller grew up idolizing Giants' announcers Russ Hodges and Lon Simmons, so it was a thrill for him to visit the Giants' booth as a College of San Mateo project.

Simmons listened to the tape, offered encouragement and nearly 30 years later works with his protege on Giants' games. Miller considers him fortunate to learn his trade in the

Bay Area of the 1960s, where top-flight announcers like Bill King, Hodges, Simmons and Greenwald flourished. He drew from all of them, admiring the rapport of the Hodges-Simmons tandem, the game descriptions of the versatile King and the wit and humor of Greenwald.

Soon, the aspiring announcer went to work with Monte Moore on Athletics' games and learned the nuances of the game from manager Alvin Dark. Miller eventually teamed with Ken Coleman in 1979 to do Boston Red Sox games. Coleman exposed another side to Miller, and it made the young broadcaster instantly popular. During a rain delay, Coleman asked his partner to do impersonations, and Miller regaled the radio audience with bits on Vin Scully, Chuck Thompson and Bob Sheppard, the public address announcer at Yankee Stadium.

The response was so positive it made Miller popular on the banquet circuit, and he still brings down the house while mimicking various personalities. Miller began getting national exposure in 1986, working as a backup on the famous NBC Game of the Week and teaming with Tony Kubek.

Miller's longest stint was with the Baltimore Orioles (1983-96), and he had the privilege of broadcasting Cal Ripken's record consecutive games streak of 2,131. It was a strange call, devoid of drama, because it was set when Ripken merely walked out to his shortstop position September 6, 1995. "Ripken heads out to play shortstop to start the game ... He's there now ... and, that's the record," he said.

While with the O's, Miller also became the lead announcer for ESPN, primarily doing the Sunday night games with Joe Morgan. Miller, a Maryland resident, never wanted to leave the Orioles, but owner Peter Angelos made no attempt to retain him while the Giants were eager for a big-name broadcast personality once Greenwald announced his retirement following the 1996 season.

CHAPTER SIX
WORLD SERIES STORIES

1888 — GIANTS DEFEATED ST. LOUIS BROWNS 6 GAMES TO 4

The New York Giants captured their first National League pennant and world championship in 1888, just their sixth year of existence. They captured the league flag by nine games over the Chicago White Stockings and defeated the mighty St. Louis Browns, champions of the American Association, in the World Series six games to four. St. Louis, owned by Chris Von der Ahe and managed by first baseman Charlie Comiskey, won its fourth consecutive A.A. championship, a major league record that stood until the Giants won four straight N.L. titles from 1921-24. The New York Yankees of the American League ultimately bettered the mark with five crowns in a row from 1949-53 and again from 1960-64.

St. Louis, which won just one of its three previous world championship series, was dealt a blow prior to the start of the 1888 championship when Nat Hudson, the Browns' second-best pitcher with a 25-10 record and 2.54 ERA during the regular season, chose to skip the series and head to Hot Springs, Arkansas, to enjoy its fresh water baths. Hudson regularly came and went as he pleased without any control from management.

The series was set up for the first team to win six games being declared champions, but when the Giants did so in eight games, two additional exhibition contests were played. Right-handed pitcher Tim Keefe compiled a 4-0 record for New York with a minuscule 0.51 ERA (two earned runs in 35.0 innings pitched) and 30 strikeouts. Shortstop John Montgomery Ward batted .379 with six RBI and six stolen bases. The Giants stole 38 bases as a team.

Game 1: October 16 at New York (Polo Grounds)
New York 2, St. Louis 1

New York right-hander Tim Keefe won a classic pitching duel with Silver King of the Browns in Game 1 by the score of 2-1. Keefe allowed just three hits and one walk while striking out nine batters.

In the bottom of the second inning, first baseman Roger Connor and shortstop John Montgomery Ward singled, and Connor ultimately came around to score the first run of the game on a sacrifice fly by center fielder Mike Slattery.

The lead was short-lived as St. Louis scored its lone run in the top of the third on an RBI single by left fielder Tip O'Neill (who played for New York in 1883) that scored third

The 1888 New York Giants. (National Baseball Library and Archive)

baseman Arlie Latham. But the Browns could muster nothing more against Keefe.

New York tallied what proved to be the winning run in the bottom of the third. Right fielder Mike Tiernan drew a two-out walk, stole second and came around to score when catcher Jack Boyle's throw got past center fielder Harry Lyons and right fielder Tommy McCarthy's backup throw was wild at home.

King limited the Giants to two hits and one walk with three strikeouts.

Oct. 1											R	H	E
St. Louis	0	0	1	0	0	0	0	0	0	—	1	3	5
New York	0	1	1	0	0	0	0	0	x	—	2	2	4

W — Keefe (1-0). L — King (0-1). Attendance — 4,876.

Game 2: Oct. 17 at New York (Polo Grounds)
St. Louis 3, New York 0

The Browns evened the series one game apiece with a 3-0 blanking in Game 2. Twenty-year-old right-hander Elton Chamberlin shut out New York on six hits with three walks and two strikeouts. The Giants advanced a runner to third base on four occasions but couldn't come up with a timely hit. In the first and sixth innings, they had runners at second and third with two outs, but shortstop John Montgomery Ward was retired.

Meanwhile, New York pitcher Mickey Welch was nearly as stingy. The Browns scored one run in the second inning and then were held scoreless until pushing across two insurance runs in the ninth. First baseman Charlie Comiskey, catcher Jocko Milligan and right fielder Tommy McCarthy each had two hits. Welch surrendered seven hits and three walks while striking out two.

The Giants stole four bases, giving them eight in two games.

Oct. 17											R	H	E
St. Louis	0	1	0	0	0	0	0	0	2	—	3	7	4
New York	0	0	0	0	0	0	0	0	0	—	0	6	1

W — Chamberlin (1-0). L — Welch (0-1). Attendance — 5,575.

Game 3: Oct. 18 at New York (Polo Grounds)
New York 4, St. Louis 2

The Giants' Tim Keefe earned his second complete-game victory over Silver King 4-2 in Game 3 to give the Giants a two games to one lead in the series. Keefe allowed five hits while walking four and striking out eight.

New York scored twice in the bottom of the first inning on RBI singles by first baseman Roger Connor and shortstop John Montgomery Ward and added solo tallies in the fourth and seventh before St. Louis got on the scoreboard with runs in the eighth and ninth. Both of the Browns' runs were unearned.

St. Louis had a chance in the fifth as it loaded the bases with one out, but Keefe wiggled out of the jam by getting King to pop out to Connor and striking out third baseman Arlie Latham. In the seventh, the Browns loaded the bases with two outs, but Latham hit a ground ball to Ward that forced King at second.

Ward collected two of the Giants' five hits off King, who walked two and struck out two over eight innings. New York had six stolen bases, including two by Ward, running its three-game total to 14 (compared with two for the Browns).

Oct. 18												R	H	E
St. Louis	0	0	0	0	0	0	0	1	1	—		2	5	5
New York	2	0	0	1	0	0	1	0	x	—		4	5	2

W — Keefe (2-0). L — King (0-2). Attendance — 5,780.

Game 4: at Brooklyn (Washington Park)
New York 6, St. Louis 3

The Giants went up three games to one with a 6-3 victory in Game 4. Ed Crane, who compiled just a 5-6 record in 12 games during the season (but fired the first no-hitter in franchise history against the Washington Senators on September 27), pitched a complete game, allowing seven hits and two walks and striking out seven.

First baseman Roger Connor led New York's offensive attack with a double and a triple, the Giants' first extra base hits of the series, and two runs scored. Shortstop John Montgomery Ward also had two hits. The Giants stole five more bases.

New York scored in the first on a sacrifice fly by second baseman Danny Richardson, then added four runs in the third and one more in the fifth. The Browns tallied a single run in the third and two in the eighth. St. Louis catcher Jocko Milligan collected two hits.

Elton Chamberlin suffered the loss for the Browns.

Oct. 19												R	H	E
New York	1	0	4	0	1	0	0	0	0	—		6	8	2
St. Louis	0	0	1	0	0	0	0	2	0	—		3	7	4

W — Crane (1-0). L — Chamberlin (1-1). Attendance — 3,062.

Game 5: at New York (Polo Grounds)
New York 6, St. Louis 4 (8 innings)

The Giants erupted for five runs in the bottom of the eighth to win Game 5 by the score of 6-4 and go up four games to one in the series. The game was called after eight innings because of darkness. The crowd of 9,124 was the largest of the series.

St. Louis led 4-1 heading into the decisive eighth inning behind pitcher Silver King. The Giants' bats then came to life while the Browns' gloves went into hibernation. It was 4-2 when catcher Buck Ewing tripled in pitcher Tim Keefe, who reached on an error. Then Ewing scored the tying run on a comebacker by second baseman Danny Richardson that was mishandled by King. First baseman Roger Connor followed with a triple and came in to score the winning run when shortstop John Montgomery Ward's fly ball to short center that should have been caught fell between second baseman Yank Robinson and center fielder Harry Lyons.

With Robinson leading off the ninth inning, umpires John Gaffney and John Kelly declared it too dark to continue playing.

Keefe was the benefactor of the Giants' late heroics as he improved to 3-0 in the series

269

after giving up just five hits and two walks with two strikeouts. King fell to 0-3 despite allowing just one earned run. Connor and right fielder Mike Tiernan both had two hits for New York.

Oct. 20											R	H	E
St. Louis	0	0	3	0	0	1	0	0	-	—	4	5	5
New York	1	0	0	0	0	0	0	5	-	—	6	9	2

W — Keefe (3-0). L — King (0-3). Attendance — 9,124.

Game 6: at Philadelphia (League Park) New York 12, St. Louis 5 (8 innings)

En route to St. Louis, the Giants and Browns squared off in Philadelphia for Game 6. New York won 12-5 to take a commanding five games to one lead in the series. The game was called after eight innings on account of darkness.

St. Louis jumped out to a 4-0 lead through three innings against Mickey Welch before the New York bats came to life. The Giants scored one run in the fourth, three in the sixth, three in the seventh and five in the eighth.

Catcher Buck Ewing had three hits and scored two runs, while left fielder Jim O'Rourke and right fielder Mike Tiernan both collected two hits. Once again, the Giants took advantage of some shoddy St. Louis defense that committed seven errors.

Welch also was the victim of poor support behind him as all five runs scored by the Browns were unearned. He gave up just three hits and six walks with no strikeouts. Elton Chamberlin suffered his second straight loss for St. Louis.

Oct. 22											R	H	E
New York	0	0	0	1	0	3	3	5	-	—	12	13	5
St. Louis	3	0	1	0	0	0	0	1	-	—	5	3	7

W — Welch (1-1). L — Chamberlin (1-2). Attendance — 3,281.

Game 7: at St. Louis (Sportsman's Park) St. Louis 7, New York 5 (8 innings)

The Browns stayed alive in the series with an exciting, come-from-behind 7-5 victory in Game 7. For the third straight game, play was called after eight innings because of darkness.

The score was tied at 3-apiece after five innings when the Giants scored twice to take a 5-3 advantage. Third baseman Art Whitney plated first baseman Roger Connor with a triple and then scored himself on an out by pitcher Ed Crane. It was the third RBI and second run scored of the game for Whitney, who singled home left fielder Jim O'Rourke and center fielder Mike Slattery and subsequently scored in the second.

St. Louis erupted for four runs in the eighth off Crane, who suffered the loss, with the decisive blow being a two-run double by shortstop Bill White that scored right fielder Tommy McCarthy and center fielder Ed Herr.

In its half of the eighth (New York batted second), the Giants threatened as the skies darkened. They had runners at second and third with one out before St. Louis winning pitcher Silver King got Whitney and catcher Pat Murphy to pop out to catcher Jocko Milligan.

Oct. 24											R	H	E
New York	0	3	0	0	0	2	0	0	-	—	5	11	3
St. Louis	0	0	3	0	0	0	4	-	—	7	8	3

W — King (1-3). L — Crane (1-1). Attendance — 4,624.

Game 8: at St. Louis (Sportsman's Park) New York 11, St. Louis 3

Behind home runs from catcher Buck Ewing and right fielder Mike Tiernan and superb pitching by Tim Keefe, the Giants wrapped up their first world championship with an 11-3 victory in Game 8.

New York scored one run in the first inning, three in the third, one in the fourth and six in the ninth on the strength of 12 hits, all against Elton Chamberlin. Four players had two hits apiece: Ewing, center fielder Mike Slattery, shortstop John Montgomery Ward and third baseman Art Whitney. Ewing homered in the first and added a three-run triple in the third. Tiernan blasted a three-run homer in the ninth.

It was more than enough for Keefe, who won his fourth game of the series in 10 days.

He limited the Browns to five hits and two walks with 10 strikeouts. St. Louis center fielder Ed Herr fanned four times.

Oct. 25												R	H	E
New York	1	0	3	1	0	0	0	0	6	—	11	12	2
St. Louis	0	0	0	1	0	0	1	1	0	—	3	5	6

W — Keefe (4-0). L — Chamberlin (1-3). HR — Ewing (1), Tiernan (1). Attendance — 4,865.

Game 9: at St. Louis (Sportsman's Park) St. Louis 14, New York 11 (10 innings)

In the first of two exhibition games, the Browns won a slugfest 14-11 in 10 innings behind a 15-hit offensive attack against New York pitcher Bill George.

St. Louis left fielder Tip O'Neill provided the decisive blow with a three-run home run in the 10th inning.

The Giants, who led 8-5 after three innings, contributed to the St. Louis cause with five errors that led to six unearned runs. New York totaled 14 hits, including three by second baseman Danny Richardson, who also scored three runs. Four other players had two hits apiece. Jim Devlin earned the win with seven innings of effective relief work after starter Silver King went the first three innings.

Before the game, each member of the Giants was presented with a handsome scarf pin.

Oct. 26										R	H	E
St. Louis	1	4	0	0	2	0	2	0	2	3 —	14	15	4
New York	0	3	5	0	0	0	1	2	0	0 —	11	14	5

W — Devlin (1-0). L — George (0-1). HR — O'Neill (1). Attendance — 711.

Game 10: at St. Louis (Sportsman's Park) St. Louis 18, New York 7

The Browns hit two home runs to win another exhibition game 18-7 in the final game of the World Series. Left fielder Tip O'Neill blasted his second homer in as many days, while right fielder Tommy McCarthy connected on his first of the series.

Cannonball Titcomb pitched the first four innings, allowing six runs (three earned), before second baseman Gil Hatfield, who had not pitched in the major leagues up to this point, worked the final five innings and gave up 12 runs (seven earned). Hatfield went on to pitch in 13 games during his eight-year career. St. Louis banged out 17 hits, including four by third baseman Arlie Latham.

New York, playing without several of its regulars, still managed to collect 13 hits, including a home run by first baseman Bill George. The Giants committed eight errors that led to eight unearned runs.

Following the game, St. Louis owner Chris Von der Ahe turned over the Browns' championship flag to Giants' owner John B. Day.

Oct. 27										R	H	E
St. Louis	0	1	0	5	0	5	4	2	1	—	18	17	3
New York	3	1	0	0	0	0	0	2	1	—	7	13	8

W — Chamberlin (2-3). L — Titcomb (0-1). HR — George (1), McCarthy (1), O'Neill (2). Attendance — 412.

1889 — GIANTS DEFEATED BROOKLYN BRIDEGROOMS 6 GAMES TO 3

Despite having virtually the same team that won the world championship a year earlier, the New York Giants just edged out the Boston Beaneaters to win the National League pennant. The Giants finished 83-43, while Boston was 83-45. The race was not decided until the final day of the season. In the World Series, New York faced the Brooklyn Bridegrooms in the first meeting of what would become a heated rivalry between the two teams separated by the East River that has carried over to San Francisco and Los Angeles. The Bridegrooms (nicknamed such because several of their players had gotten married during the season) won the American Association championship by two games over the defending champion St. Louis Browns.

The series was the first featuring two teams from the east and was a best-of-11 format (in other words, the first team to win six games). Brooklyn, which was managed by Bill McGunnigle, won three of the four games be-

fore New York stormed back to win five straight games and capture the championship. With stalwart pitchers Tim Keefe and Mickey Welch having logged 364.0 and 375.0 innings during the season, respectively, and consequently being fatigued during the series, the Giants were given a huge boost by Ed Crane and Hank O'Day. Crane was 4-1, while O'Day, who later became a well-respected umpire, was 2-0 with a 1.17 ERA. Shortstop John Montgomery Ward batted .417 with seven RBI and first baseman Roger Connor batted at a .343 clip and drove in 12 runs. Second baseman Danny Richardson socked three home runs.

Game 1: at New York (Polo Grounds)
Brooklyn 12, New York 10 (8 innings)

The Bridegrooms rallied with four runs in the eighth inning before the game was called on account of darkness and won the opening game of the series 12-10. Through seven innings, the Giants led 10-8 as nightfall set in, but umpires Bob Ferguson and John Gaffney, both from the American Association, insisted that play continue. National League umpire Tom Lynch had refused to work the game over a financial squabble, and Ferguson took his place.

Brooklyn right fielder Oyster Burns hit a double over the head of Giants' center fielder George Gore to score second baseman Hub Collins with the winning run in the eighth, and Burns then scored himself on a double by first baseman Dave Foutz. Then play was called.

Neither team's pitcher was particularly effective, Tim Keefe of the Giants and Adonis Terry of the Bridegrooms. Keefe allowed 16 hits and Terry surrendered 12. Second baseman Danny Richardson led New York's offensive attack with three hits, including a triple and a two-run inside-the-park homer in the fourth inning.

The Bridegrooms led 6-2 after two innings and 6-5 through six before New York plated five runs in the seventh. Shortstop John Montgomery Ward had a two-run single in the up-

rising, and left fielder Jim O'Rourke capped the comeback with a run-producing triple.

Oct. 18										R	H	E
New York	0	2	0	2	1	0	5	0	-	—	10	12	2
Brooklyn	5	1	0	0	0	0	2	4	-	—	12	16	3

W — Terry (1-0). L — Keefe (0-1). HR — Collins (1), Richardson (1). Attendance — 8,848.

Game 2: at Brooklyn (Washington Park)
New York 6, Brooklyn 2

Thanks to some aggressive base running, the Giants evened the series at one game piece with a 6-2 win over Brooklyn. New York was credited with seven stolen bases, including three by left fielder Jim O'Rourke and two by center fielder George Gore. The Bridegrooms aided the cause by committing eight errors.

The teams traded runs in the first two innings before the Giants pulled away with single scores in the third and fourth and two tallies in the fifth. Gore, who finished with three of New York's 10 hits, scored what proved to be the winning run when Brooklyn shortstop Germany Smith failed to cleanly field a ball hit by catcher Buck Ewing.

It was more than enough for pitcher Ed Crane, who was 14-10 during the season and a year earlier spun the first no-hitter in franchise history against the Washington Senators. Crane limited Brooklyn to four hits (all singles) while issuing seven walks and striking out three. Both runs were unearned.

A crowd of 16,172 was on hand, the largest of the series.

Oct. 19										R	H	E
New York	1	1	1	1	2	0	0	0	0	—	6	10	4
Brooklyn	1	1	0	0	0	0	0	0	0	—	2	4	8

W — Crane (1-0). L — Caruthers (0-1). Attendance — 16,172.

Game 3: at New York (Polo Grounds)
Brooklyn 8, New York 7 (8 innings)

For the second time in three games, the Giants were affected by a controversial decision by the umpires and dropped an 8-7 eight-inning decision in Game 3 that enabled Brooklyn

to take a two games to one lead in the series.

In the ninth inning, New York had the bases loaded with one out when American Association umpire John Gaffney called the game because of darkness.

The Bridegrooms built a 6-2 lead after four innings before the Giants got a three-run homer from left fielder Jim O'Rourke in the fifth to cut the deficit to one run. Brooklyn came back with two runs in its half of the fifth, and New York scored twice in the sixth to remain close.

Mickey Welch suffered the loss after allowing 12 hits but just three earned runs over the first five innings. Center fielder Pop Corkhill homered in the fifth. Brooklyn's Mickey Hughes gave up 14 hits and six earned runs in seven innings and picked up the victory. Five Giants had multiple-hit games, led by shortstop John Montgomery Ward with three.

Oct. 20											R	H	E
New York	2	0	0	0	3	2	0	0	-	—	7	15	2
Brooklyn	0	2	3	1	2	0	0	0	-	—	8	12	3

W — Hughes (1-0). L — Welch (0-1). HR — Corkhill (1), O'Rourke (1). Attendance — 5,181.

Game 4: at Brooklyn (Washington Park) Brooklyn 10, New York 7 (6 innings)

A 10-7 victory in six innings gave the Bridegrooms a decisive three games to one lead in the series. Brooklyn led 7-2 after five when New York scored five runs to even the score. Winning pitcher Ed Crane tripled in a pair of runs, and a throwing error by Brooklyn catcher Bob Clark allowed two more runs to score.

New York catcher Buck Ewing had been on third base with shortstop John Montgomery Ward on first, and when Ward attempted to steal second, Clark tried to pick off Ewing at third. The throw was wild, and both runners came home as the throw in hit Jim O'Rourke while he was coaching third. A 20-minute argument over whether Ward should be sent back to third ensued and cut into the remaining daylight. The Giants won the argument but

lost the game in the bottom of the inning as Brooklyn right field Oyster Burns stroked a two-run double that turned into a three-run inside the park homer when O'Rourke failed to play the ball in left field. After that the game was called.

Adonis Terry picked up his second win of the series, while Crane fell to 1-1 after his teammates committed eight errors behind him.

Oct. 23											R	H	E
New York	0	0	1	1	0	5	-	-	-	—	7	9	8
Brooklyn	2	0	2	0	3	3	-	-	-	—	10	7	1

W — Terry (2-0). L — Crane (1-1). HR — Burns (1). Attendance — 3,045.

Game 5: at Brooklyn (Washington Park) New York 11, Brooklyn 3

The Giants more closely resembled the defending world champions they were with a lopsided 11-3 victory in Game 5, trimming the series deficit to three games to two.

Pitcher Ed Crane was the story. Not only did he pitch a complete game one day after working six innings, but he hit a double and a two-run homer, as well. Crane scattered eight hits and six walks while striking out eight.

New York collected 12 hits, including three apiece by catcher Willard Brown and third baseman Art Whitney. Brown blasted a home run in the ninth, while second baseman Danny Richardson hit a two-run round-tripper in the fifth.

Bob Caruthers was the losing pitcher for Brooklyn.

Oct. 24											R	H	E
New York	0	0	4	0	4	0	0	2	1	—	11	12	2
Brooklyn	0	0	0	1	1	1	0	0	0	—	3	8	2

W — Crane (2-1). L — Caruthers (0-2). HR — Brown (1), Crane (1), Richardson (2). Attendance — 2,901.

Game 6: at New York (Polo Grounds) New York 2, Brooklyn 1 (11 innings)

Pitcher Hank O'Day and shortstop John Montgomery Ward were the heroes as the Gi-

HENRY O'DAY.

Hank O'Day, who later became a well-respected umpire, was 2-0 with a 1.17 ERA during the 1889 World Series against the Brooklyn Bridegrooms. (Transcendental Graphics)

ants downed Brooklyn 2-1 in 11 innings to win Game 6 and even the series at three games apiece.

Day, who was 9-1 with a 4.27 ERA during the season for the Giants after going 2-10 with a 4.32 ERA for the Washington Senators, went the distance, scattering six hits (five of them singles) and four walks while striking out four. Brooklyn scored its only run in the second inning on an RBI single by losing pitcher Adonis Terry that plated catcher Joe Visner.

The Giants trailed 1-0 with two outs in the ninth when Ward singled to right field. He proceeded to steal both second and third base and came into score on a single by first baseman Roger Connor. In the 11th inning, center fielder Mike Slattery singled and advanced to second on an out by catcher Buck Ewing. Then Ward chopped a ball to shortstop Jumbo Davis and beat the throw to first while Slattery kept on running and scored the winning run.

Oct. 25												R	H	E
Brooklyn	0	1	0	0	0	0	0	0	0	0	0	— 1	6	4
New York	0	0	0	0	0	0	0	0	1	0	1	— 2	7	1

W — O'Day (1-0). L — Terry (2-1). Attendance — 2,556.

Game 7: at New York (Polo Grounds) New York 11, Brooklyn 7

An eight-run second inning propelled the Giants to an 11-7 victory in Game 7 and a four games to three lead in the series.

New York led 1-0 heading into the second inning before unleashing an offensive barrage against Brooklyn pitcher Tom Lovett. The Giants sent 12 batters to the plate and collected seven hits, including back-to-back home runs by second baseman Danny Richardson and left fielder Jim O'Rourke. Other big hits were delivered by right fielder Mike Tiernan (two-run single) and first baseman Roger Connor (RBI double).

The Bridegrooms rallied and closed the gap to 9-7 by scoring four runs in the third and three in the fifth. Giants' pitcher Ed Crane, starting his third game in four days, surrendered just five hits in seven innings but walked nine batters while striking out one. He earned the win to improve to 3-1 in the series before being relieved by Tim Keefe, who held Brooklyn hitless over the final three innings.

Catcher Buck Ewing paced New York's 14-hit attack with three singles.

Oct. 26										R	H	E
Brooklyn	0	0	4	0	3	0	0	0	0	— 7	5	3
New York	1	8	0	0	0	1	1	0	x	— 11	14	4

W — Crane (3-1). L — Lovett (0-1). HR — O'Rourke (2), Richardson (3). Attendance — 3,312.

Game 8: at Brooklyn (Washington Park) New York 16, Brooklyn 7

The Giants continued to pound the baseball, and the result was a 16-7 victory in Game 8, a five games to three lead in the series and one win away from repeating as world champions.

They started quickly with five runs in the first inning, highlighted by back-to-back, two-

run singles by first baseman Roger Connor and second baseman Danny Richardson. After Brooklyn scored twice in its half of the first, New York picked right back up with four more tallies in the top of the second. Connor collected two more RBI with a single.

The Giants continued to add to their run total with one in the third, two in the fourth and three in the sixth to make it 15-2. Brooklyn starting pitcher Adonis Terry lasted just four innings before being replaced by Dave Foutz, the Bridegrooms' first baseman.

Right fielder Mike Tiernan homered in the sixth for New York, which banged out 15 hits. Tiernan, Connor and shortstop John Montgomery Ward had three hits each. Ward also had a whopping five stolen bases.

It wasn't until the eighth inning that Brooklyn pushed across another run against New York pitcher Ed Crane, who won his fourth game in five decisions in the series. The Bridegrooms scored twice in the eighth (a two-run homer by right fielder Oyster Burns), but it was too little too late. Crane allowed a mere five hits to go with five walks and four strikeouts.

Oct. 28										R	H	E
New York	5	4	1	2	0	3	0	0	1	— 16	15	4
Brooklyn	2	0	0	0	0	0	2	3		— 7	5	4

W — Crane (4-1). L — Terry (2-2). HR — Burns (2), Foutz (1), Tiernan (1). Attendance — 2,584.

Game 9: at New York (Polo Grounds) New York 3, Brooklyn 2

The Giants put the finishing touches on their amazing comeback by winning Game 9 by the score of 3-2 for their fifth consecutive victory and a second straight world championship.

After Brooklyn scored its two runs in the top of the first inning, New York came back with a single tally in the bottom of the frame on a triple by shortstop John Montgomery Ward that plated right fielder Mike Tiernan.

New York continued to trail 2-1 heading the sixth when second baseman Danny

Richardson's sacrifice fly to center field scored Ward. The following inning center fielder Mike Slattery reached on a fielder's choice, stole second base and came around with what proved to be the winning run when catcher Buck Ewing struck out, but the third strike got away from Brooklyn catcher Doc Bushong.

Meanwhile, Hank O'Day held the Bridegrooms to four hits and five walks with five strikeouts to earn the win. Adonis Terry scattered eight hits with four walks and one strikeout but was the tough-luck loser.

Oct. 29										R	H	E
Brooklyn	2	0	0	0	0	0	0	0	0	— 2	4	2
New York	1	0	0	0	0	1	1	0	x	— 3	8	5

W — O'Day (2-0). L — Terry (2-3). Attendance — 3,067.

1894 — GIANTS DEFEATED BALTIMORE ORIOLES 4 GAMES TO 0

From 1894-97 the National League scheduled a postseason best-of-seven championship series between the regular season's first- and second-place teams. The winner was awarded the Temple Cup, a lavish silver cup presented by William Chase Temple, a major stockholder in the Pittsburgh Pirates.

The Baltimore Orioles, with future Giants' manager John McGraw and coaches Hughie Jennings and Wilbert Robinson on the roster, finished first in the N.L. with an 89-39 record, three games ahead of the New York Giants at 88-44. But the feisty Orioles needed victories in 24 of their final 25 games to surge past the defending champion Boston Beaneaters.

Original plans for the Temple Cup called for the winning team to receive two-thirds of the gate receipts and the losing team the remaining one-third. But the Orioles argued that as the championship team they should be guaranteed a better payoff. Giants' manager John Montgomery Ward—knowing his team was a substantial underdog in the series—agreed to a 50-50 split, but Temple objected to the revised plan on the premise that neither team would be motivated to win if both were earning the same payoff. So publicly the play-

ers agreed to compete under the original breakdown; however, many Baltimore players privately worked out 50-50 deals with members of the Giants.

After the wild regular-season finish, the Orioles, under manager Ned Hanlon, appeared to have little energy or interest left for the postseason. The Giants took advantage and swept the series four games to none. Right-handers Jouett Meekin and Amos Rusie, who had replaced Tim Keefe and Mickey Welch as the aces of New York's pitching staff, overmatched Baltimore. The two Indiana natives (Meekin from New Albany and Rusie from Terre Haute) both won two games, with Rusie posting a minuscule 0.50 ERA (one earned run in 18 innings) and Meekin right behind with a 1.59 ERA (three earned runs in 17 innings). Amazingly, Meekin also batted .556 (5-for-9) with three RBI, while Rusie batted .429 (3-for-7) and drove in one run.

Among the regulars, first baseman Jack Doyle paced the Giants with a .588 batting average (10-for-17), six RBI and six stolen bases. Center fielder George Van Haltren batted .500 (7-for-14) and Ward, the second baseman, drove in six runs.

Baltimore was without the services of its ace right-handed pitcher Sadie McMahon, who went 25-8 with a 4.21 ERA during the season but was shelved with a sore arm.

Game 1: at Baltimore (Oriole Park)
New York 4, Baltimore 1

Right-hander Amos Rusie shut down the high-flying Orioles on seven hits, and the Giants scored single runs in the fifth, sixth, seventh and eighth innings en route to a 4-1 victory in the opening game at Oriole Park in Baltimore. The Orioles' lone run came in the ninth.

Three of New York's runs came following hits that went past the ropes in the outfield which held back the fans. The ground rules designated such hits as triples. Center fielder George Van Haltren tripled to right field in the fifth and scored on a sacrifice fly by shortstop

Shorty Fuller, third baseman George Davis tripled down the left field line in the sixth and score on a single by first baseman Jack Doyle and Doyle tripled to right in the eighth and scored on a sacrifice hit by second baseman John Montgomery Ward.

Left fielder Eddie Burke had four of the Giants' 13 hits, while Doyle, Rusie and catcher Duke Farrell each had two hits. Rusie, who walked one and struck out three, helped his own cause by doubling in the seventh and scoring on a single by Burke.

Duke Esper suffered the loss for the Orioles.

The game was marked by a few run-ins between the players, and umpire Bob Emslie had be escorted off the field by police to avoid the wrath of Baltimore fans.

Oct. 4											R	H	E
New York	0	0	0	0	1	1	1	1	0	—	4	13	2
Baltimore	0	0	0	0	0	0	0	1	—		1	7	1

W — Rusie (1-0). L — Esper (0-1). Attendance — 9,000.

Game 2: at Baltimore (Oriole Park)
New York 9, Baltimore 6

The Giants and Baltimore were tied 5-apiece after eight innings in Game 2 at Oriole Park before New York tallied four runs in the top of the ninth inning and held on for a 9-6 victory and a two games to none advantage in the series.

Shortstop Shorty Fuller and catcher Duke Farrell led off the ninth with singles off starting and losing pitcher Kid Gleason before pitcher Jouett Meekin struck out. Then left fielder Eddie Burke hit a double play grounder to Baltimore shortstop Hughie Jennings, who bobbled the ball and got nobody out. Right fielder Mike Tiernan followed with a three-run triple and subsequently scored on a single by third baseman George Davis.

The Orioles loaded the bases on walks in the bottom of the ninth and scored a run on an error by first baseman Jack Doyle, but Meekin got center fielder Steve Brodie to ground out to first to end the game.

Tiernan banged out four hits, while Doyle, Meekin and second baseman John Montgomery Ward had two apiece. Meekin scattered seven hits and five walks with two strikeouts.

Oct. 5											R	H	E
New York	0	0	4	0	0	0	0	1	4	—	9	14	3
Baltimore	0	2	2	0	0	0	1	0	1	—	6	7	2

W — Meekin (1-0). L — Gleason (0-1). Attendance — 11,000.

Game 3: at New York (Polo Grounds) New York 4, Baltimore 1

Game 3 was a virtual repeat of Game 1 as right-hander Amos Rusie limited the Orioles to seven hits, and the Giants won 4-1 at the Polo Grounds in New York to take a commanding three games to none series lead.

Baltimore actually had runners on base in every inning except the first, but when Rusie got in a jam he "sent the ball over the plate with the speed of a rifle shot." He walked two batters and struck out six.

Rusie also broke a 1-apiece tie in the bottom of the fifth inning against Baltimore starting and losing pitcher George Hemming with a sacrifice that scored catcher Duke Farrell. The Giants added two runs in the sixth, highlighted by an RBI double by first baseman Jack Doyle that plated third baseman George Davis.

Left fielder Eddie Burke banged out two doubles, while Doyle and center fielder George Van Haltren both had two singles.

Oct. 6											R	H	E
Baltimore	0	0	0	1	0	0	0	0	0	—	1	7	4
New York	1	0	0	0	1	2	0	0	x	—	4	10	4

W — Rusie (2-0). L — Hemming (0-1). Attendance — 20,000.

Game 4: at New York (Polo Grounds) New York 16, Baltimore 3

Baltimore clearly had thrown in the towel as the Giants blitzed the Orioles 16-3 in Game 4 at the Polo Grounds to wrap up the inaugural Temple Cup series via the sweep. The game was played with threatening weather overhead and was called after eight innings because of darkness. The Giants became the talk—and toast—of the sporting world.

Baltimore scored two runs in the top of the first to take the early lead and was up 3-2 after three innings before New York exploded off Orioles' starting and losing pitcher Bill Hawke and reliever Kid Gleason. The Giants plated three runs in the fourth, five in the fifth, one in the sixth and five in the seventh.

Giants' right-hander Jouett Meekin not only held the Orioles to six hits with three walks and four strikeouts, but he had three hits of his own as part of New York's 20-hit barrage. First baseman Jack Doyle rapped out four hits, while catcher Duke Farrell, shortstop Shorty Fuller and center fielder George Van Haltren joined Meekin in the three-hit club. Farrell scored three runs. All nine New York starters had at least one hit and one run scored.

Oct. 8										R	H	E
Baltimore	2	0	1	0	0	0	0	-	—	3	6	3
New York	1	0	1	3	5	1	5	0	-	—	16	20	4

W — Meekin (2-0). L — Hawke (0-1). Attendance — 12,000.

1905 — GIANTS DEFEATED PHILADELPHIA ATHLETICS 4 GAMES TO 1

The New York Giants won their first National League championship of the 20th century in 1904, but owner John T. Brush and manager John McGraw refused to play the American League champion Boston Pilgrims in the modern World Series that had been instituted a year earlier because they regarded the A.L. as an inferior league. In 1905 the National Commission of baseball adopted Brush's rules for postseason play, which included a best-of-seven format, umpires from both leagues and a revenue-sharing formula for the two teams involved, and the Giants defended their N.L. crown with a 105-48 record, nine games better than the Pittsburgh Pirates. New York, donning brand-new black uniforms with white trim, de-

feated the Philadelphia Athletics in the World Series four games to one.

No series has been more dominated by pitching than the one in 1905. All five games were decided via a shutout, with Giants' right-hander Christy Mathewson authoring three of them. In 27 innings he allowed merely 14 hits and one walk with 18 strikeouts. Philadelphia, managed by the legendary Connie Mack, scored just three runs and had a meager .161 batting average (25-for-155) against New York pitchers.

Meanwhile, New York's leading batters were catcher Roger Bresnahan (.313 average) and first baseman Dan McGann (four RBI).

Philadelphia was without the services of ace left-handed pitcher Rube Waddell, who had led the A.L. with 27 wins and a 1.48 ERA during the season before suffering an injury to his left shoulder in a friendly scuffle with fellow pitcher Andy Cohen on September 1. Unsubstantiated reports during the World Series had the New York betting crowd paying for Waddell to spend time in a lush Manhattan apartment with a group of Broadway showgirls.

Winning Player's Share: $1,142
Losing Player's Share: $832

Game 1: at Philadelphia (Columbia Park)
New York 3, Philadelphia 0

Right-hander Christy Mathewson shutout the Athletics on four hits, and the Giants captured the opener 3-0 at Columbia Park in Philadelphia. Mathewson did not walk anyone and had six strikeouts.

Mathewson, who led the National League with 31 wins and a 1.28 ERA during the season, helped himself offensively by singling in the top of the fifth inning. Catcher Roger Bresnahan forced Mathewson at second base but then stole the base and scored the game's first run on a single by center fielder Mike Donlin. On the throw home, Donlin took second and came home on a double by left fielder Sam Mertes. The Giants added a tally in the

ninth as Bresnahan drove in second baseman Billy Gilbert, who had three of New York's 10 hits off Philadelphia starting and losing pitcher Eddie Plank.

Game 2: at New York (Polo Grounds)
Philadelphia 3, New York 0

The Athletics evened the series at one game apiece with a 3-0 victory over the Giants at the Polo Grounds in New York. Philadelphia's Chief Bender, a full-blooded Chippewa Indian, blanked New York on four hits with three walks and nine strikeouts.

In truth, New York right-hander Joe McGinnity was every bit as effective, allowing five hits and no walks with two strikeouts, but two Giants' errors led to three unearned runs. Philadelphia scored once in the third inning and twice in the eighth.

Center fielder Mike Donlin collected two hits, including a double, for New York, while Philadelphia center fielder Bris Lord had two hits and two RBI.

Game 3: at Philadelphia (Columbia Park)
New York 9, Philadelphia 0

Right-hander Christy Mathewson orchestrated his second shutout in four days, and the Giants rolled to a 9-0 victory in Game 3 at the Polo Grounds in New York to take a two games to one lead in the World Series. Mathewson's masterpiece resulted in four hits—all singles—with one walk and eight strikeouts.

Although New York roughed up Philadelphia starter and loser Andy Cohen for eight hits and drew five walks, only two of the Giants' runs were earned because of four Athletics' errors. New York first baseman Dan McGann was 3-for-5 with a double and four RBI.

The Giants scored two runs in the first inning, five in the fifth and two in the ninth.

Game 4: at New York (Polo Grounds)
New York 1, Philadelphia 0

Another day, another shutout. This time New York right-hander Joe McGinnity got in on the act and blanked the Athletics on five

singles with three walks and four hits. The Giants won the game 1-0 at the Polo Grounds in New York and took a commanding three games to one lead in the series.

In the bottom of the fourth inning, the Giants took advantage of some shoddy Philadelphia defense to score the game's lone run. Left fielder Sam Mertes reached on an error by shortstop Monte Cross, advanced to second one out later on a ground out by third baseman Art Devlin and scored when second baseman Billy Gilbert's grounder bounded away from third baseman Lave Cross for another error. Athletics' starting and losing pitcher Eddie Plank was every bit as effective as McGinnity, surrendering four hits and two walks with six strikeouts.

New York right fielder George Browne went 2-for-4 and was the only player on either team with more than one hit.

Game 5: at New York (Polo Grounds) New York 2, Philadelphia 0

Despite having just one day's rest, New York right-hander Christy Mathewson came back with his third shutout in six days as the Giants captured the World Series with a 2-0 win in Game 5 at the Polo Grounds in New York. Mathewson's third whitewash consisted of six hits and no walks with four strikeouts. He was strong even at game's end, retiring Philadelphia center fielder Bris Lord and first baseman Harry Davis on ground balls back to the pitcher's mound and third baseman Lave Cross on a grounder to shortstop Bill Dahlen.

Once again, the opposing starting pitcher was a tough-luck loser. Chief Bender allowed two runs on five hits with three walks and four strikeouts. The walks, though, proved costly. Giants' left fielder Sam Mertes and shortstop Bill Dahlen drew free passes to open the bottom of the fifth inning and moved up on a sacrifice by third baseman Art Devlin. Then a sacrifice fly by second baseman Billy Gilbert to left field scored Mertes. In the eighth Mathewson walked, advanced to third on a double by catcher Roger Bresnahan and came home on a ground out by right fielder George Browne.

Bresnahan had two hits for the Giants.

1905
Game 1 (Oct. 9)

New York	AB	R	H	RBI	Philadelphia	AB	R	H	RBI
Bresnahan, c	3	1	1	1	Hartsel, lf	4	0	1	0
Browne, rf	5	0	0	0	Lord, cf	4	0	0	0
Donlin, cf	5	1	2	1	Davis, 1b	4	0	1	0
McGann, 1b	3	0	1	0	L. Cross, 3b	4	0	0	0
Mertes, lf	4	0	1	1	Seybold, rf	3	0	0	0
Dahlen, ss	4	0	0	0	Murphy, 2b	3	0	1	0
Devlin, 3b	4	0	1	0	M. Cross, ss	3	0	0	0
Gilbert, 2b	4	1	3	0	Schreckengost, c	3	0	1	0
Mathewson, p	3	0	1	0	Plank, p	3	0	0	0
Totals	35	3	10	3	Totals	31	0	4	0

										R	H	E
New York	0	0	0	0	2	0	0	0	1	—	3	10	1
Philadelphia	0	0	0	0	0	0	0	0	0	—	0	4	0

E—Donlin. DP—New York 1. LOB—New York 9, Philadelphia 4. 2B—McGann, Mertes, Davis, Murphy, Schreckengost, Murphy, Davis. SB—Bresnahan, Donlin, Devlin, Gilbert. S—Mathewson.

New York	IP	H	R	ER	BB	SO
Mathewson (W, 1-0)	9	4	0	0	0	6

Philadelphia	IP	H	R	ER	BB	SO
Plank (L, 0-1)	9	10	3	3	2	5

WP—Mathewson. HBP—By Plank (Bresnahan). Umpires—Sheridan (A.L.), O'Day (N.L.). Time—1:46. Attendance—17,995.

Game 2 (Oct. 10)

Philadelphia	AB	R	H	RBI	New York	AB	R	H	RBI
Hartsel, lf	4	1	2	0	Bresnahan, c	4	0	1	0
Lord, cf	4	0	2	2	Browne, rf	4	0	0	0
Davis, 1b	4	0	0	0	Donlin, cf	4	0	2	0
L. Cross, 3b	3	0	0	0	McGann, 1b	3	0	0	0
Seybold, rf	4	0	0	0	Mertes, lf	4	0	0	0
Murphy, 2b	4	0	1	0	Dahlen, ss	3	0	0	0
M. Cross, ss	4	0	0	0	Devlin, 3b	3	0	1	0
Schreckengost, c	4	2	1	0	Gilbert, 2b	3	0	0	0
Bender, p	2	0	0	0	McGinnity, p	2	0	0	0
					Strang, ph	1	0	0	0
					Ames, p	0	0	0	0
Totals	33	3	6	2	Totals	31	0	4	0

										R	H	E
Philadelphia	0	0	1	0	0	0	0	2	0	—	3	6	2
New York	0	0	0	0	0	0	0	0	0	—	0	4	2

E—Murphy, Bresnahan, McGann, M. Cross. LOB—Philadelphia 5, New York 7. 2B—Hartsel, Bresnahan, Donlin. SB—Dahlen, Devlin. S—Bender.

Philadelphia	IP	H	R	ER	BB	SO
Bender (W, 1-0)	9	4	0	0	3	9

New York	IP	H	R	ER	BB	SO
McGinnity (L, 0-1)	8	5	3	0	0	2
Ames	1	1	0	0	0	1

Umpires—O'Day (N.L.), Sheridan (A.L.). Time—1:55. Attendance—24,992.

Game 3 (Oct. 12)

New York	AB	R	H	RBI	Philadelphia	AB	R	H	RBI
Bresnahan, c	3	2	0	0	Hartsel, lf	4	0	0	0
Browne, rf	5	2	1	0	Lord, cf	4	0	0	0
Donlin, cf	3	3	1	0	Davis, 1b	4	0	1	0
McGann, 1b	5	1	3	4	L. Cross, 3b	4	0	1	0
Mertes, lf	3	0	1	1	Seybold, rf	3	0	1	0
Dahlen, ss	3	1	0	1	Murphy, 2b	3	0	0	0
Devlin, 3b	4	0	1	1	M. Cross, ss	3	0	1	0
Gilbert, 2b	4	0	0	0	Schreckengost, c	2	0	0	0
Mathewson, p	4	0	1	0	Powers, c	1	0	0	0
					Coakley, p	2	0	0	0
Totals	35	9	8	7	Totals	30	0	4	0

											R	H	E
New York	2	0	0	0	5	0	0	0	2	—	9	8	1
Philadelphia	0	0	0	0	0	0	0	0	0	—	0	4	4

E—Devlin, Murphy 3, Hartsel. DP—New York 1, Philadelphia 2. LOB—New York 4, Philadelphia 5. 2B—McGann. SB—Browne 2, Donlin, Dahlen, Devlin, Hartsel.

New York	IP	H	R	ER	BB	SO
Mathewson (W, 2-0)	9	4	0	0	1	8

Philadelphia	IP	H	R	ER	BB	SO
Coakley (L, 0-1)	9	8	9	2	5	2

HBP—By Coakley (Bresnahan), By Mathewson (Coakley). Umpires—Sheridan (A.L.), O'Day (N.L.). Time—1:55. Attendance—10,991.

Game 4 (Oct. 13)

Philadelphia	AB	R	H	RBI	New York	AB	R	H	RBI
Hartsel, lf	1	0	0	0	Bresnahan, c	2	0	1	0
Lord, cf	4	0	0	0	Browne, rf	4	0	2	0
Davis, 1b	4	0	1	0	Donlin, cf	3	0	0	0
L. Cross, 3b	4	0	1	0	McGann, 1b	3	0	0	0
Seybold, rf	3	0	0	0	Mertes, lf	4	1	0	0
Murphy, 2b	3	0	1	0	Dahlen, ss	3	0	0	0
M. Cross, ss	4	0	1	0	Devlin, 3b	3	0	1	0
Powers, c	3	0	0	0	Gilbert, 2b	3	0	0	0
Hoffman, ph	1	0	0	0	McGinnity, p	3	0	0	0
Plank, p	3	0	1	0					
Totals	30	0	5	0	Totals	28	1	4	0

											R	H	E
Philadelphia	0	0	0	0	0	0	0	0	0	—	0	5	2
New York	0	0	0	1	0	0	0	0	x	—	1	4	0

E—M. Cross, L. Cross. LOB—Philadelphia 8, New York 7. 2B—Devlin. SB—Hartsel. S—Hartsel, Murphy, Donlin, McGann.

Philadelphia	IP	H	R	ER	BB	SO
Plank (L, 0-2)	8	4	1	0	2	6

New York	IP	H	R	ER	BB	SO
McGinnity (W, 1-1)	9	5	0	0	3	4

WP—Plank. Umpires—O'Day (N.L.), Sheridan (A.L.). Time—1:55. Attendance—13,598.

Game 5 (Oct. 14)

Philadelphia	AB	R	H	RBI	New York	AB	R	H	RBI
Hartsel, lf	4	0	2	0	Bresnahan, c	4	0	2	0
Lord, cf	4	0	0	0	Browne, rf	4	0	1	1
Davis, 1b	4	0	1	0	Donlin, cf	4	0	0	0
L. Cross, 3b	4	0	0	0	McGann, 1b	3	0	0	0
Seybold, rf	3	0	1	0	Mertes, lf	2	1	1	0
Murphy, 2b	3	0	0	0	Dahlen, ss	2	0	0	0
M. Cross, ss	3	0	1	0	Devlin, 3b	2	0	0	0
Powers, c	3	0	1	0	Gilbert, 2b	3	0	1	1
Bender, p	3	0	0	0	Mathewson, p	1	1	0	0
Totals	31	0	6	0	Totals	25	2	5	2

											R	H	E
Philadelphia	0	0	0	0	0	0	0	0	0	—	0	6	0
New York	0	0	0	0	1	0	0	1	x	—	2	5	1

E—Mathewson. DP—New York 1. LOB—Philadelphia 4, New York 4. 2B—Powers, Bresnahan. S—Devlin, Mathewson

Philadelphia	IP	H	R	ER	BB	SO
Bender (L, 1-1)	8	5	2	2	3	4

New York	IP	H	R	ER	BB	SO
Mathewson (W, 3-0)	9	6	0	0	0	4

Umpires—Sheridan (A.L.), O'Day (N.L.). Time—1:35. Attendance—24,187.

1911 — PHILADELPHIA ATHLETICS DEFEATED GIANTS 4 GAMES TO 2

In a rematch of the 1905 World Series, New York squared off against the Philadelphia Athletics in the 1911 series. Both clubs were under their same managerial leadership, John McGraw of the Giants and Connie Mack of the Athletics. This time, however, the Giants' pitching was not quite so dominant, and Philadelphia took the title four games to two. New York reached the series after capturing the National League pennant with a 99-54 record, 7½ games ahead of the Chicago Cubs.

After pitching three shutouts during the 1905 series, Giants' right-hander Christy Mathewson was merely mortal this time around. He was 1-2 with a 2.00 ERA and allowed 25 hits with two walks and 13 strikeouts in 27 innings. New York's leading batters were second baseman Larry Doyle (.304 average) and catcher Chief Meyers (.300 with two RBI).

Philadelphia third baseman Frank Baker, who had led the American League with 11 home runs during the regular season, earned his nickname "Home Run" in the series after stroking two decisive round-trippers in Games 2 and 3.

Winning Player's Share: $3,655
Losing Player's Share: $2,436

Game 1: at New York (Polo Grounds) New York 2, Philadelphia 1

The 1911 World Series opened the same way the 1905 one did with Giants' right-hander Christy Mathewson pitching a masterful 2-1 decision at the Polo Grounds in New York. Mathewson, who topped the National League with a 1.99 ERA during the season, limited the Athletics to six hits with one walk and five strikeouts.

Philadelphia starter Chief Bender essentially matched Mathewson, scattering five hits with four walks and 11 strikeouts.

The Athletics led 1-0 heading into the bottom of the fourth inning when Giants' center fielder Fred Snodgrass walked and streaked all the way around to score when Philadelphia second baseman Eddie Collins misplayed a hit and run grounder by New York right fielder

Red Murray. Snodgrass was hustling all the way while Collins hesitated to throw the ball. The Giants scored the winning run in the seventh on doubles by catcher Chief Meyers and left fielder Josh Devore.

Game 2: at Philadelphia (Shibe Park)
Philadelphia 3, New York 1

Philadelphia third baseman Frank Baker began his transformation into Home Run Baker as the Athletics evened the series one game apiece with a 3-1 victory at Shibe Park in Philadelphia. With the score tied at 1 and two outs in the bottom of the sixth inning, Philadelphia second baseman Eddie Collins doubled and Baker followed with a two-run homer off New York starting and losing pitcher Rube Marquard over the right field wall.

Then it was up to the Athletics' Eddie Plank to keep the Giants at bay, and he did just that. Plank scattered five hits—four of them singles—and walked no one to go with eight strikeouts while pitching a complete game. Marquard worked eight innings and allowed just four hits with no walks and four strikeouts.

Catcher Chief Meyers drove in New York's lone run in the second with a single that plated third baseman Buck Herzog, who had doubled. Center fielder Fred Snodgrass had two hits and also reached base after being hit by a Plank pitch.

Game 3: at New York (Polo Grounds)
Philadelphia 3, New York 2 (11 innings)

Frank Baker became Home Run Baker. The Philadelphia third baseman powered the Athletics to a 3-2 win in 11 innings in Game 3 at the Polo Grounds in New York and a two games to one lead in the series.

New York right-hander Christy Mathewson appeared headed for a 1-0 shutout victory with one out in the ninth inning when Baker hit a 2-1 pitch over the right field fence to tie the score. The Athletics later scored twice in the 11th inning and held off the Giants. In the bottom of the 11th, New York catcher Chief Meyers nearly tied the game with a two-run

homer that landed foul by a few feet. After an error by Philadelphia second baseman Eddie Collins allowed Giants' third baseman Buck Herzog to score and cut the deficit to one run, pinch hitter Beals Becker was thrown out attempting to steal second to end the game.

Both Mathewson and his Philadelphia counterpart, Jack Combs, pitched complete games. Mathewson scattered nine hits with no walks and three strikeouts, while Combs limited the Giants to three hits with four walks and seven strikeouts.

Game 4: at Philadelphia (Shibe Park)
Philadelphia 4, New York 2

Following six days of continuous rain, the World Series resumed at Shibe Park in Philadelphia with the Athletics winning Game 4 by the score of 4-2 to take a commanding three games to one lead.

The Giants jumped in front with two runs in the top of the first inning on an RBI triple by second baseman Larry Doyle that scored left fielder Josh Devore and subsequent sacrifice fly to left field by center fielder Fred Snodgrass. Then Philadelphia pitcher Chief Bender settled down. He pitched a complete game, allowing seven hits with two walks and four strikeouts.

Philadelphia broke through against New York starter and loser Christy Mathewson with three runs in the fourth and one more in the fifth. Mathewson surrendered 10 hits, including six doubles, with one walk and five strikeouts in eight innings.

Devore and shortstop Art Fletcher both had two hits for the Giants, while shortstop Jack Barry led the Athletics' offensive attack with three hits, including two doubles. Philadelphia third baseman Frank "Home Run" Baker also collected two doubles.

Game 5: at New York (Polo Grounds)
New York 4, Philadelphia 3 (10 innings)

With their backs against the wall, the Giants came from behind to win Game 5 by the score of 4-3 in 10 innings and cut Philadelphia's series lead to three games to two.

The Athletics appeared headed for victory with a 3-0 lead through six innings. Center fielder Rube Oldring accounted for all the scoring with a three-run homer in the top of the third off New York left-handed starter Rube Marquard. The Giants scored one run in the seventh and two in the ninth before pulling out the victory with a run in the 10th.

With Philadelphia ahead 3-1 and one out in the ninth, Giants' shortstop Art Fletcher doubled but remained their as catcher Chief Meyers lined out to shortstop. Then relief pitcher Doc Crandall doubled to score Fletcher and left fielder Josh Devore singled to score Crandall and tie the game. Interestingly, the general consensus was that Philadelphia would bring in Ed Plank to face Devore because Plank had struck out Devore four times in Game 2.

Plank ultimately got into the game in the 10th in what would have been the final inning regardless with darkness approaching. Second baseman Larry Doyle led off with a double and advanced to third when Plank unsuccessfully tried to retire him at third base on a sacrifice by center fielder Fred Snodgrass. After left fielder Red Murray flied out to short right field—with both runners holding—first baseman Fred Merkle hit a sacrifice fly to right. Doyle beat the throw home but didn't touch the plate. Philadelphia failed to appeal, and home plate umpire Bill Klem said afterwards he would have called Doyle out.

The right-handed Crandall earned the win after allowing just two hits over three scoreless innings. Marquard worked the first three frames (the three runs he allowed were unearned), followed by four scoreless innings by right-hander Red Ames.

Doyle banged out four of the Giants' nine hits.

Game 6: at Philadelphia (Shibe Park) Philadelphia 13, New York 2

After winning Game 5 in dramatic fashion and scoring in the top of the first inning of Game 6, the Giants figured ready for a major comeback in the series. But Philadelphia had other ideas and rolled to a 13-2 victory to take the series four games to two.

The game was tied 1-apiece after three innings before the Athletics scored four runs in fourth, one in the sixth and seven in the seventh. New York right-handed starting and losing pitcher Red Ames was touched for five runs (two earned) in four innings, and left-hander Hooks Wiltse was roughed up for eight runs (seven earned) in 2.1 innings. Philadelphia totaled 13 hits, including four by right fielder Danny Murphy and three by left fielder Bris Lord.

Meanwhile, Chief Bender pitched a complete game for the Athletics, scattering four hits with two walks and five strikeouts. New York's runs were scored by second baseman Larry Doyle and third baseman Buck Herzog.

1911

Game 1 (Oct. 14)

Philadelphia	AB	R	H	RBI	New York	AB	R	H	RBI
Lord, lf	4	0	0	0	Devore, lf	3	0	1	1
Oldring, cf	4	0	2	0	Doyle, 2b	3	0	1	0
Collins, 2b	3	0	0	0	Snodgrass, cf	2	1	0	0
Baker, 3b	4	1	2	0	Murray, rf	3	0	0	0
Murphy, rf	3	0	0	0	Merkle, 1b	4	0	1	0
Davis, 1b	4	0	1	1	Herzog, 3b	3	0	0	0
Barry, ss	3	0	0	0	Fletcher, ss	4	0	0	0
Thomas, c	3	0	0	0	Meyers, c	3	1	1	0
Bender, p	3	0	1	0	Mathewson, p	3	0	1	0
Totals	31	1	6	1	Totals	28	2	5	1

										R	H	E
Philadelphia	0	1	0	0	0	0	0	0	0	—	1	6	2
New York	0	0	0	1	0	0	1	0	x	—	2	5	0

E—Baker, Collins. LOB—Philadelphia 5, New York 8. 2B—Oldring 2, Devore, Meyers. SB—Doyle. S—Murphy, Murray.

Philadelphia	IP	H	R	ER	BB	SO
Bender (L, 0-1)	8	5	2	1	4	11

New York	IP	H	R	ER	BB	SO
Mathewson (W, 1-0)	9	6	1	1	1	5

HBP—By Bender (Snodgrass). PB—Meyers. Umpires—Klem (N.L.), Dinneen (A.L.), Brennan (N.L.), Connolly (A.L.). Time—2:12. Attendance—38,281.

Game 2 (Oct. 16)

New York	AB	R	H	RBI	Philadelphia	AB	R	H	RBI
Devore, lf	4	0	0	0	Lord, lf	4	1	1	0
Doyle, 2b	4	0	0	0	Oldring, cf	3	0	0	0
Snodgrass, cf	3	0	2	0	Collins, 2b	3	1	2	0
Murray, rf	4	0	0	0	Baker, 3b	3	1	1	2
Merkle, 1b	3	0	1	0	Murphy, rf	3	0	0	0
Herzog, 3b	3	1	1	0	Davis, 1b	3	0	0	0
Fletcher, ss	3	0	0	0	Barry, ss	3	0	0	0
Meyers, c	3	0	1	1	Thomas, c	3	0	0	0
Marquard, p	2	0	0	0	Plank, p	3	0	0	0
Crandall, ph-p	1	0	0	0					
Totals	30	1	5	1	Totals	28	3	4	2

										R	H	E
New York	0	1	0	0	0	0	0	0	0	—	1	5	3
Philadelphia	1	0	0	0	0	2	0	0	x	—	3	4	0

E—Devore, Merkle, Murray. LOB—New York 3, Philadelphia 2. 2B—Herzog, Collins. HR—Baker. S—Oldring.

New York	IP	H	R	ER	BB	SO
Marquard (L, 0-1)	7	4	3	2	0	4
Crandall	1	0	0	0	0	2

Philadelphia	IP	H	R	ER	BB	SO
Plank (W, 1-0)	9	5	1	1	0	8

HBP—By Plank (Snodgrass). WP—Marquard. Umpires—Connolly (A.L.), Brennan (N.L.), Klem (N.L.), Dinneen (A.L.). Time—1:52. Attendance—26,286.

Game 3 (Oct. 17)

Philadelphia	AB	R	H	RBI	New York	AB	R	H	RBI
Lord, lf	5	0	0	0	Devore, lf	4	0	0	1
Oldring, cf	5	0	0	0	Doyle, 2b	4	0	0	0
Collins, 2b	5	1	2	0	Snodgrass, cf	3	0	0	0
Baker, 3b	5	2	2	1	Murray, rf	2	0	0	0
Murphy, rf	5	0	0	1	Merkle, 1b	3	0	0	0
Davis, 1b	5	0	2	1	Herzog, 3b	3	1	1	0
Barry, ss	3	0	2	0	Fletcher, ss	4	0	0	0
Lapp, c	4	0	1	0	Meyers, c	4	1	1	0
Coombs, p	4	0	0	0	Mathewson, p	3	0	1	0
					Becker, ph	1	0	0	0
Totals	41	3	9	3	Totals	31	2	3	1

												R	H	E
Philadelphia	0	0	0	0	0	0	0	0	1	0	2	—	3	9	2
New York	0	0	1	0	0	0	0	0	0	0	1	—	2	3	5

E—Fletcher 2, Herzog 3, Collins 2. DP—New York 1. LOB—Philadelphia 6, New York 1. 2B—Barry, Herzog. HR—Baker. SB—Collins, Barry. S—Barry, Murray.

Philadelphia	IP	H	R	ER	BB	SO
Coombs (W, 1-0)	11	3	2	1	4	7

New York	IP	H	R	ER	BB	SO
Mathewson (L, 1-1)	11	9	3	1	0	3

Umpires—Brennan (N.L.), Connolly (A.L.), Klem (N.L.), Dinneen (A.L.). Time—2:25. Attendance—37,216.

Game 4 (Oct. 24)

New York	AB	R	H	RBI	Philadelphia	AB	R	H	RBI
Devore, lf	4	1	2	0	Lord, lf	4	0	1	0
Doyle, 2b	3	1	1	1	Oldring, cf	3	0	0	0
Snodgrass, cf	3	0	0	1	Collins, 2b	3	1	2	0
Murray, rf	4	0	0	0	Baker, 3b	3	1	2	1
Merkle, 1b	4	0	1	0	Murphy, rf	4	1	2	1
Herzog, 3b	4	0	0	0	Davis, 1b	4	1	1	1
Fletcher, ss	4	0	2	0	Barry, ss	4	0	3	0
Meyers, c	4	0	1	0	Thomas, c	3	0	0	1
Mathewson, p	1	0	0	0	Bender, p	4	0	0	0
Becker, ph	1	0	0	0					
Wiltse, p	0	0	0	0					
Totals	32	2	7	2	Totals	32	4	11	4

											R	H	E
New York	2	0	0	0	0	0	0	0	0	—	2	7	3
Philadelphia	0	0	0	3	1	0	0	0	x	—	4	11	1

E—Fletcher, Baker, Murray, Mathewson. DP—Philadelphia 1. LOB—New York 6, Philadelphia 8. 2B—Merkle, Meyers, Baker 2, Murphy 2, Davis, Barry 2. 3B—Doyle. S—Oldring, Collins. SF— Snodgrass, Thomas.

New York	IP	H	R	ER	BB	SO
Mathewson (L, 1-2)	7	10	4	4	1	5
Wiltse	1	1	0	0	0	1

Philadelphia	IP	H	R	ER	BB	SO
Bender (W, 1-1)	9	7	2	2	2	4

Umpires—Dinneen (A.L.), Klem (N.L.), Connolly (A.L.), Brennan (N.L.). Time—1:49. Attendance—24,355.

Game 5 (Oct. 25)

Philadelphia	AB	R	H	RBI	New York	AB	R	H	RBI
Lord, lf	5	0	0	0	Devore, lf	5	0	1	1
Oldring, cf	5	1	2	3	Doyle, 2b	5	1	4	0
Collins, 2b	3	0	0	0	Snodgrass, cf	4	0	0	0
Baker, 3b	4	0	0	0	Murray, rf	5	0	0	0
Murphy, rf	4	0	1	0	Merkle, 1b	2	1	0	1
Davis, 1b	4	0	0	0	Herzog, 3b	4	0	1	0
Barry, ss	4	0	1	0	Fletcher, ss	4	1	1	0
Lapp, c	4	1	1	0	Meyers, c	3	0	1	1
Coombs, p	4	1	2	0	Marquard, p	0	0	0	0
Strunk, pr	0	0	0	0	Becker, ph	1	0	0	0
Plank, p	0	0	0	0	Ames, p	1	0	0	0
					Crandall, ph-p	1	1	1	1
Totals	37	3	7	3	Totals	35	4	9	4

												R	H	E
Philadelphia	0	0	3	0	0	0	0	0	0	0	—	3	7	1
New York	0	0	0	0	0	0	1	0	2	1	—	4	9	2

Two outs when winning run scored.

E—Fletcher, Doyle, Collins. DP—Philadelphia 1, New York 1. LOB—Philadelphia 5, New York 8. 2B—Doyle 2, Fletcher, Crandall. HR—Oldring. SB—Collins, Barry, Doyle, Herzog. S—Snodgrass. SF—Merkle, Meyers.

Philadelphia	IP	H	R	ER	BB	SO
Coombs	9	8	3	2	2	9
Plank (L, 1-1)	0.2	1	1	1	0	0
New York	**IP**	**H**	**R**	**ER**	**BB**	**SO**
Marquard	3	3	3	0	1	2
Ames	4	2	0	0	0	2
Crandall (W, 1-0)	3	2	0	0	0	0

HBP—By Coombs (Merkle). WP—Crandall. Umpires—Klem (N.L.), Dinneen (A.L.), Connolly (A.L.), Brennan (N.L.). Time—2:33. Attendance—33,228.

Game 6 (Oct. 26)

New York	AB	R	H	RBI	Philadelphia	AB	R	H	RBI
Devore, lf	4	0	0	0	Lord, lf	5	1	3	1
Doyle, 2b	4	1	1	0	Oldring, cf	5	1	1	0
Snodgrass, cf	4	0	0	0	Collins, 2b	4	1	0	1
Murray, rf	3	0	0	0	Baker, 3b	5	2	2	1
Merkle, 1b	4	0	0	0	Murphy, rf	4	3	4	1
Herzog, 3b	4	1	1	0	Davis, 1b	4	2	1	2
Fletcher, ss	4	0	0	1	McInnis, 1b	0	0	0	0
Meyers, c	3	0	1	0	Barry, ss	2	2	1	2
Wilson, c	1	0	0	0	Thomas, c	3	1	1	0
Ames, p	1	0	1	0	Bender, p	4	0	0	0
Crandall, ph	0	0	0	0					
Wiltse, p	1	0	0	0					
Marquard, p	0	0	0	0					
Totals	33	2	4	1	Totals	36	13	13	8

										R	H	E
New York	1	0	0	0	0	0	0	0	1	—	2	4	3
Philadelphia	0	0	1	4	0	1	7	0	x	—	13	13	5

E—Barry 3, Merkle, Murray, Oldring, Ames, Murphy. LOB—New York 6, Philadelphia 3. 2B—Doyle, Lord 2, Murphy, Barry. SB—Herzog. S—Collins, Barry. SF—Barry.

New York	IP	H	R	ER	BB	SO
Ames (L, 0-1)	4	4	5	2	1	4
Wiltse	2.1	7	8	7	0	1
Marquard	1.2	2	0	0	0	2
Philadelphia	**IP**	**H**	**R**	**ER**	**BB**	**SO**
Bender (W, 2-1)	9	4	2	0	2	5

WP—Bender, Marquard. Umpires—Connolly (A.L.), Brennan (N.L.), Klem (N.L.), Dinneen (A.L.). Time—2:12. Attendance—20,485.

1912: BOSTON RED SOX DEFEATED GIANTS 4 GAMES TO 3 (1 TIE)

In one of the most dramatic World Series ever played, the Boston Red Sox defeated the Giants four games to three with one tie in the autumn of 1912. Certainly the series is best re-membered for New York center field Fred Snodgrass' dropped fly ball in the bottom of the 10th inning of Game 8 that helped Boston rally and win the championship.

The Giants won their second straight National League pennant with a 103-48 record, 10 games ahead of the Pittsburgh Pirates. The Red Sox of manager Jake Stahl were equally as dominant, capturing the American League flag with a 105-47 record, 14 games better than the Washington Senators.

In the series, New York batted .270 as a team, compared with a .220 average for Boston. Third baseman Buck Herzog led the Giants with a .400 mark (12-for-30) and five RBI, while catcher Chief Meyers batted .357 (10-for-28) and right fielder Red Murray batted .323 (10-for-31) with four RBI.

Left-hander Rube Marquard, who won 19 consecutive games during the season, won both of his series decisions with a minuscule 0.50 ERA. He pitched 18 innings, allowing 14 hits and one earned run with two walks and nine strikeouts. Right-hander Christy Mathewson was 0-2 despite a 1.26 ERA, and right-hander Jeff Tesreau was 1-2 with a 3.13 ERA. Tesreau and Mathewson ranked 1-2 in ERA during the season at 1.96 and 2.12, re-spectively.

Winning Player's Share: $4,025
Losing Player's Share: $2,566

Game 1: at New York (Polo Grounds) Boston 4, New York 3

A three-run rally in the seventh inning propelled Boston to a 4-3 victory in Game 1 at the Polo Grounds in New York.

The Giants took a 2-0 lead into the sixth after scoring twice in the third on a two-run single by right fielder Red Murray that plated left fielder Josh Devore and second baseman Larry Doyle, who earned the 1912 Chalmers Award as the National League Most Valuable Player. Boston cut the deficit in half in the sixth before erupting one inning later. Right fielder Harry Hooper provided the big blow with a two-run single and then scored on a hit by second baseman Steve Yerkes to put the Red Sox ahead 4-2. New York rallied in the bottom of the ninth, scoring once and having runners at second and third with one out, but shortstop Art Fletcher and pitcher Doc Crandall both struck out.

Boston right-hander Joe Wood, who went 34-5 with a 1.91 ERA during the season, pitched a complete game, scattering eight hits and two walks with 11 strikeouts. New York right-hander Jeff Tesreau suffered the loss.

Doyle and third baseman Buck Herzog both had two hits for the Giants.

Game 2: at Boston (Fenway Park) New York 6, Boston 6 (11 innings)

Game 2 of the series was called on ac-count of darkness by home plate umpire Silk O'Loughlin after 11 innings at Fenway Park in Boston. The Giants easily could have won the game but committed five errors that led to five unearned runs.

New York right-hander Christy Mathewson allowed 10 hits in 11 innings but walked nobody and struck out four. Third baseman Buck Herzog and right fielder-left fielder Red Murray both collected three of the Giants' 11 hits. Herzog had a double and a triple with three RBI.

It was 4-2 Boston after seven innings before the Giants scored three times in the top of the eighth—two runs coming home on a double by Murray—to take a 5-4 lead. But the Red Sox tied the score in their half of the inning. Both teams tallied a single run in the 10th.

Game 3: at Boston (Fenway Park)
New York 2, Boston 1

The Giants evened the series with a 2-1 victory in Game 3 at Fenway Park in Boston. Left-hander Rube Marquard limited the Red Sox to seven hits with one walk and six strikeouts while pitching a complete game.

Marquard, though, needed a spectacular catch by right fielder Josh Devore in the bottom of the ninth to preserve the victory. After the Red Sox scored their only run and had the tying run at second base, catcher Hick Cady hit a fly ball that Devore traveled some 30 feet to track down and end the game.

Boston right-hander Buck O'Brien was nearly as tough as Marquard, allowing six hits with three walks and three strikeouts over eight innings. New York scored runs in the second and fifth on a sacrifice fly by third baseman Buck Herzog and an RBI single by shortstop Art Fletcher, respectively.

Devore had two of the Giants' seven hits.

Game 4: at New York (Polo Grounds)
Boston 3, New York 1

Red Sox right-hander Joe Wood won his second game of the World Series with a 3-1 victory in Game 4 at the Polo Grounds in New York. As a result, Boston took a two games to one lead in the series.

Wood allowed nine hits in nine innings, but only one was for extra bases (a double by

shortstop Art Fletcher), and he did not walk anybody while recording eight strikeouts.

Meanwhile, the Red Sox scored single runs in the second, fourth and ninth innings. New York right-hander Jeff Tesreau pitched well, going eight innings and allowing just five hits and two runs with two walks and five strikeouts.

The Giants scored their lone run in the bottom of the seventh. With one out, third baseman Buck Herzog singled and, after catcher Chief Meyers lined out to center field, scored on Fletcher's double. Herzog had two hits in the game.

Game 5: at Boston (Fenway Park)
Boston 2, New York 1

The Red Sox took a convincing three games to one lead in the series with a 2-1 victory in Game 5 at Fenway Park in Boston.

For the second time in four days, New York right-hander Christy Mathewson deserved a better fate. He suffered the loss despite allowing just two runs on five hits with no walks and two strikeouts in eight innings. But Boston right-hander Hugh Bedient was a bit better, limiting the Giants to one run on three hits with three walks and four strikeouts in nine innings.

Boston scored both of its runs in the third inning. Right fielder Harry Hooper and second baseman Steve Yerkes legged out back-to-back triples, and Yerkes scored when Giants' second baseman fumbled a grounder by center fielder Tris Speaker.

In the seventh, New York parlayed two of its three hits into its lone run. First baseman Fred Merkle had a leadoff double and scored two outs later on a single by pinch-hitter Moose McCormick.

Game 6: at New York (Polo Grounds)
New York 5, Boston 2

With their backs against the wall, the Giants looked to left-hander Rube Marquard, and he did not disappoint. Marquard pitched his second complete game of the series as New

York posted a 5-2 win to cut the series deficit to three games to two.

Meanwhile, the Giants exploded for all five of their runs with two outs in the bottom of the first inning against Boston right-hander Buck O'Brien. The big hits were back-to-back doubles by first baseman Fred Merkle and third baseman Buck Herzog, and O'Brien committed a balk that plated a run.

Boston came back and tallied its two unearned runs in the top of the second, but Marquard shut down the Red Sox after that. He scattered seven hits with one walk and three strikeouts. Left-hander Ray Collins blanked the Giants over the final seven innings.

Merkle, catcher Chief Meyers and right fielder Red Murray each collected two of New York's 11 hits.

Game 7: at Boston (Fenway Park)
New York 11, Boston 4

After facing elimination and a three games to one deficit one day earlier, the Giants regained the momentum with an 11-4 pasting of the Red Sox in Game 7 at Fenway Park in Boston that evened the series at three games apiece.

New York wasted no time getting started, scoring six runs on seven hits in the top of the first inning off Red Sox right-hander Joe Wood. Center fielder Fred Snodgrass doubled home the first two runs, and pitcher Jeff Tesreau helped his own cause with a two-run single. The Giants, who banged out 16 hits, added one run in the second, two in the sixth (a two-run home run by second baseman Larry Doyle), one in the seventh and one in the ninth, all off right-handed reliever Sea Lion Hall.

Doyle and catcher Chief Meyers both had three hits for New York.

All the while, Tesreau was holding the Red Sox in check. He was not dominating but effective, allowing four runs (two earned) on nine hits with five walks and six strikeouts. Boston third baseman Larry Gardner reached him for a solo homer in the second inning.

Game 8: at Boston (Fenway Park)
Boston 3, New York 2 (10 innings)

The eighth and deciding game of the 1912 World Series came down to extra innings before the Red Sox won the championship with a 3-2 win in 10 innings at Fenway Park in Boston.

New York took a 2-1 lead in the top of the 10th when left fielder Red Murray doubled and scored on a single by first baseman Fred Merkle.

Then baseball lore was made. Pinch hitter Clyde Engle led off for the Red Sox and hit a fly ball to left-center field that center fielder Fred Snodgrass dropped for a two-base error. The next batter, right fielder Harry Hooper, drove a fly ball to center that Snodgrass caught with a fantastic play. After second baseman Steve Yerkes walked, center fielder Tris Speaker hit a foul pop off first base that Giants' right-handed pitcher Christy Mathewson called for catcher Chief Meyers to catch even though it might have been an easier play for first baseman Fred Merkle. The ball landed uncaught. Given a second opportunity, Speaker proceeded to single in Engle with the tying run and send Yerkes to third. Two batters later, third baseman Larry Gardner plated the winning run with a sacrifice fly to right field. So Snodgrass was left branded with having made the "$30,000 Muff," referring to the difference between the winners' and losers' share of the World Series payoff.

Mathewson's tough luck continued as he suffered the loss despite allowing just one earned run (three total) on eight hits with five walks and four strikeouts in 9.2 innings. Boston right-hander Joe Wood pitched the final three innings in relief of right-hander Hugh Bedient and gave up one run on three hits with one walk and two strikeouts to earn his third win of the series.

Murray had two doubles and third baseman Buck Herzog had a single and a double to pace New York's nine-hit attack.

1912

Game 1 (Oct. 8)

Boston	AB	R	H	RBI	New York	AB	R	H	RBI
Hooper, rf	3	1	1	1	Devore, lf	3	1	0	0
Yerkes, 2b	4	0	1	2	Doyle, 2b	4	1	2	0
Speaker, cf	3	1	1	0	Snodgrass, cf	4	0	1	0
Lewis, lf	4	0	0	1	Murray, rf	3	0	1	2
Gardner, 3b	4	0	0	0	Merkle, 1b	4	1	1	0
Stahl, 1b	4	0	0	0	Herzog, 3b	4	0	2	0
Wagner, ss	3	1	2	0	Meyers, c	3	0	1	1
Cady, c	3	0	1	0	Becker, pr	0	0	0	0
Wood, p	3	1	0	0	Fletcher, ss	4	0	0	0
					Tesreau, p	2	0	0	0
					McCormick, ph	1	0	0	0
					Crandall, p	1	0	0	0
Totals	31	4	6	4	Totals	33	3	8	3

											R	H	E
Boston	0	0	0	0	0	1	3	0	0	—	4	6	1
New York	0	0	2	0	0	0	0	0	1	—	3	8	1

E—Fletcher, Wagner. DP—Boston 1. LOB—Boston 6, New York 6. 2B—Hooper, Wagner, Doyle. 3B—Speaker. S—Hooper, Cady.

Boston	IP	H	R	ER	BB	SO
Wood (W, 1-0)	9	8	3	3	2	11

New York	IP	H	R	ER	BB	SO
Tesreau (L, 0-1)	7	5	4	4	4	4
Crandall	2	1	0	0	0	2

HBP—By Wood (Meyers). Umpires—Klem (N.L.), Evans (A.L.), Rigler (N.L.), O'Loughlin (A.L.). Time—2:10. Attendance—35,730.

Game 2 (Oct. 9)

New York	AB	R	H	RBI	Boston	AB	R	H	RBI
Snodgrass, lf-cf	4	1	1	0	Hooper, rf	5	1	3	0
Doyle, 2b	5	0	1	0	Yerkes, 2b	5	1	1	1
Becker, cf	4	1	0	0	Speaker, cf	5	2	2	0
Murray, rf-lf	5	2	3	1	Lewis, lf	5	2	3	0
Merkle, 1b	5	1	1	0	Gardner, 3b	4	0	0	1
Herzog, 3b	4	1	3	3	Stahl, 1b	5	0	1	2
Meyers, c	4	0	2	1	Wagner, ss	5	0	0	0
Shafer, pr-ss	0	0	0	0	Carrigan, c	5	0	0	0
Fletcher, ss	4	0	0	0	Collins, p	3	0	0	0
McCormick, ph	0	0	0	1	Hall, p	1	0	0	0
Wilson, c	0	0	0	0	Bedient, p	1	0	0	0
Mathewson, p	5	0	0	0					
Totals	40	6	11	6	Totals	44	6	10	4

											R	H	E
New York	0	1	0	1	0	0	0	3	0	1	0	—	6	11	5
Boston	3	0	0	0	1	0	0	1	0	1	0	—	6	10	1

E—Lewis, Fletcher 3, Wilson, Doyle. DP—New York 1. LOB—New York 9, Boston 6. 2B—Snodgrass, Murray, Herzog, Hooper, Lewis 2. 3B—Murray, Merkle, Herzog, Yerkes, Speaker. SB—Snodgrass, Herzog, Hooper 2, Stahl. S—Gardner. SF—Herzog, McCormick.

New York	IP	H	R	ER	BB	SO
Mathewson	11	10	6	1	0	4

Boston	IP	H	R	ER	BB	SO
Collins	7.1	9	5	3	0	5
Hall	2.2	2	1	1	4	0
Bedient	1	0	0	0	1	1

HBP—By Bedient (Snodgrass). Umpires—O'Loughlin (A.L.), Rigler (N.L.), Klem (N.L.), Evans (A.L.). Time—2:38. Attendance—30,148.

Game 3 (Oct. 10)

New York	AB	R	H	RBI		Boston	AB	R	H	RBI
Devore, rf	4	0	2	0		Hooper, rf	3	0	0	0
Doyle, 2b	3	0	0	0		Yerkes, 2b	4	0	1	0
Snodgrass, cf	4	0	1	0		Speaker, cf	4	0	1	0
Murray, lf	4	1	1	0		Lewis, lf	4	1	2	0
Merkle, 1b	3	0	0	0		Gardner, 3b	3	0	1	1
Herzog, 3b	2	1	1	1		Stahl, 1b	4	0	2	0
Meyers, c	4	0	1	0		Henriksen, pr	0	0	0	0
Fletcher, ss	3	0	1	1		Wagner, ss	4	0	0	0
Marquard, p	1	0	0	0		Carrigan, c	2	0	0	0
						Engle, ph	1	0	0	0
						Cady, c	1	0	0	0
						O'Brien, p	2	0	0	0
						Ball, ph	1	0	0	0
						Bedient, p	0	0	0	0
Totals	28	2	7	2		**Totals**	33	1	7	1

										R	H	E
New York	0	1	0	0	1	0	0	0	0	—	2	7	1
Boston	0	0	0	0	0	0	0	0	1	—	1	7	0

E—Merkle. DP—Boston 1. LOB—New York 6, Boston 7. 2B—Murray, Herzog, Gardner, Stahl. SB—Devore, Fletcher, Wagner. S—Merkle, Marquard, Gardner. SF—Herzog.

New York	IP	H	R	ER	BB	SO
Marquard (W, 1-0)	9	7	1	1	1	6

Boston	IP	H	R	ER	BB	SO
O'Brien (L, 0-1)	8	6	2	2	3	3
Bedient	1	1	0	0	0	0

HBP—By Bedient (Herzog). Umpires—Evans (A.L.), Klem (N.L.), O'Loughlin (A.L.), Rigler (N.L.). Time—2:15. Attendance—34,624.

Game 4 (Oct. 11)

Boston	AB	R	H	RBI	New York	AB	R	H	RBI
Hooper, rf	4	0	1	0	Devore, lf	4	0	1	0
Yerkes, 2b	3	0	1	0	Doyle, 2b	4	0	1	0
Speaker, cf	4	0	1	0	Snodgrass, cf	4	0	0	0
Lewis, lf	4	0	0	0	Murray, rf	4	0	1	0
Gardner, 3b	3	2	2	0	Merkle, 1b	4	0	1	0
Stahl, 1b	3	1	0	0	Herzog, 3b	4	1	2	0
Wagner, ss	3	0	0	0	Meyers, c	4	0	0	0
Cady, c	4	0	1	1	Fletcher, ss	4	0	1	1
Wood, p	4	0	2	1	Tesreau, p	2	0	1	0
					McCormick, ph	1	0	1	0
					Ames, p	0	0	0	0
Totals	32	3	8	2	Totals	35	1	9	1

											R	H	E
Boston	0	1	0	1	0	0	0	0	1	—	3	8	1
New York	0	0	0	0	0	0	1	0	0	—	1	9	1

E—Meyers, Wagner. DP—New York 1. LOB—Boston 7, New York 7. 2B—Speaker, Fletcher. 3B—Gardner. SB—Stahl, Merkle. S—Yerkes, Stahl.

Boston	IP	H	R	ER	BB	SO
Wood (W, 2-0)	9	9	1	1	0	8
New York	IP	H	R	ER	BB	SO
Tesreau (L, 0-2)	7	5	2	2	2	5
Ames	2	3	1	1	1	0

WP—Tesreau. Umpires—Rigler (N.L.), O'Loughlin (A.L.), Evans (A.L.), Klem (N.L.). Time—2:06. Attendance—36,502.

Game 5 (Oct. 12)

New York	AB	R	H	RBI	Boston	AB	R	H	RBI
Devore, lf	2	0	0	0	Hooper, rf	4	1	2	0
Doyle, 2b	4	0	0	0	Yerkes, 2b	4	1	1	1
Snodgrass, cf	4	0	0	0	Speaker, cf	3	0	1	1
Murray, rf	3	0	0	0	Lewis, lf	3	0	0	0
Merkle, 1b	4	1	1	0	Gardner, 3b	3	0	0	0
Herzog, 3b	4	0	0	0	Stahl, 1b	3	0	0	0
Meyers, c	3	0	1	0	Wagner, ss	3	0	1	0
Fletcher, ss	2	0	0	0	Cady, c	3	0	0	0
McCormick, ph	1	0	0	0	Bedient, p	2	0	0	0
Shafer, pr-ss	0	0	0	0					
Mathewson, p	3	0	1	0					
Totals	30	1	3	0	Totals	29	2	5	2

											R	H	E
New York	0	0	0	0	0	0	1	0	0	—	1	3	1
Boston	0	0	2	0	0	0	0	0	x	—	2	5	1

E—Gardner, Doyle. DP—Boston 1. LOB—New York 5, Boston 3. 2B—Merkle. 3B—Hooper, Yerkes.

New York	IP	H	R	ER	BB	SO
Mathewson (L, 0-1)	8	5	2	2	0	2
Boston	IP	H	R	ER	BB	SO
Bedient (W, 1-0)	9	3	1	0	3	4

Umpires—O'Loughlin (A.L.), Rigler (N.L.), Klem (N.L.), Evans (A.L.). Time—1:43. Attendance—34,683.

Game 6 (Oct. 14)

Boston	AB	R	H	RBI	New York	AB	R	H	RBI
Hooper, rf	4	0	1	0	Devore, lf	4	0	1	0
Yerkes, 2b	4	0	2	0	Doyle, 2b	4	1	1	0
Speaker, cf	3	0	0	0	Snodgrass, cf	4	0	1	0
Lewis, lf	4	0	0	0	Murray, rf	3	1	2	0
Gardner, 3b	4	1	0	0	Merkle, 1b	3	1	2	1
Stahl, 1b	4	1	2	0	Herzog, 3b	3	1	1	1
Wagner, ss	4	0	0	0	Meyers, c	3	1	2	0
Cady, c	3	0	1	0	Fletcher, ss	3	0	1	1
O'Brien, p	0	0	0	0	Marquard, p	3	0	0	0
Engle, ph	1	0	1	2					
Collins, p	2	0	0	0					
Totals	33	2	7	2	Totals	30	5	11	3

										R	H	E
Boston	0	2	0	0	0	0	0	0	0	—	2	7	2
New York	5	0	0	0	0	0	0	0	x	—	5	11	1

E—Cady, Yerkes, Marquard. DP—Boston 1, New York 1. LOB—Boston 5, New York 1. 2B—Merkle, Herzog, Engle. 3B—Meyers. SB—Speaker, Doyle, Herzog, Meyers.

Boston	IP	H	R	ER	BB	SO
O'Brien (L, 0-2)	1	6	5	3	0	1
Collins	7	5	0	0	0	1

New York	IP	H	R	ER	BB	SO
Marquard (W, 2-0)	9	7	2	0	1	3

BK—O'Brien. Umpires—Klem (N.L.), Evans (A.L.), O'Loughlin (A.L.), Rigler (N.L.). Time—1:58. Attendance—30,622.

Game 7 (Oct. 15)

New York	AB	R	H	RBI	Boston	AB	R	H	RBI
Devore, rf	4	2	1	0	Hooper, rf	3	0	1	1
Doyle, 2b	4	3	3	2	Yerkes, 2b	4	0	0	0
Snodgrass, cf	5	1	2	2	Speaker, cf	4	1	1	0
Murray, lf	4	0	0	0	Lewis, lf	4	1	1	0
Merkle, 1b	5	1	2	1	Gardner, 3b	4	1	1	2
Herzog, 3b	4	2	1	0	Stahl, 1b	5	0	1	0
Meyers, c	4	1	3	1	Wagner, ss	5	0	1	0
Wilson, c	1	0	1	0	Cady, c	4	1	0	0
Fletcher, ss	5	1	1	0	Wood, p	0	0	0	0
Tesreau, p	4	0	2	2	Hall, p	3	0	3	0
Totals	40	11	16	8	Totals	36	4	9	3

										R	H	E
New York	6	1	0	0	0	2	1	0	1	—	11	16	4
Boston	0	1	0	0	0	0	2	1	0	—	4	9	3

E—Devore, Gardner, Merkle, Speaker, Doyle 2, Hall. DP—New York 1, Boston 1. LOB—New York 8, Boston 12. 2B—Snodgrass, Lewis, Hall. HR—Doyle, Gardner. SB—Devore 2, Doyle. S—Murray. SF—Hooper.

New York	IP	H	R	ER	BB	SO
Tesreau (W, 1-2)	9	9	4	2	5	6

Boston	IP	H	R	ER	BB	SO
Wood (L, 2-1)	1	7	6	4	0	0
Hall	8	9	5	3	5	1

HBP—by Tesreau (Gardner). WP—Tesreau 2. Umpires—Evans (A.L.), Klem (N.L.), O'Loughlin (A.L.), Rigler (N.L.). Time—2:21. Attendance—32,694.

Game 8 (Oct. 16)

New York	AB	R	H	RBI	Boston	AB	R	H	RBI
Devore, rf	3	1	1	0	Hooper, rf	5	0	0	0
Doyle, 2b	5	0	0	0	Yerkes, 2b	4	1	1	0
Sndograss, cf	4	0	1	0	Speaker, cf	4	0	2	1
Murray, lf	5	1	2	1	Lewis, lf	4	0	0	0
Merkle, 1b	5	0	1	1	Gardner, 3b	3	0	1	1
Herzog, 3b	5	0	2	0	Stahl, 1b	4	1	2	0
Meyers, c	3	0	0	0	Wagner, ss	3	0	1	0
Fletcher, ss	3	0	1	0	Cady, c	4	0	0	0
McCormick, ph	1	0	0	0	Bedient, p	2	0	0	0
Shafer, ss	0	0	0	0	Henriksen, ph	1	0	1	1
Mathewson, p	4	0	1	0	Wood, p	0	0	0	0
					Engle, ph	1	1	0	0
Totals	38	2	9	2	Totals	35	3	8	3

												R	H	E
New York	0	0	1	0	0	0	0	0	0	1	—	2	9	2
Boston	0	0	0	0	0	0	1	0	0	2	—	3	8	5

Two outs when winning run scored.

E—Gardner 2, Snodgrass, Speaker, Doyle, Stahl, Wagner. LOB—New York 11, Boston 9. 2B—Murray 2, Herzog, Gardner, Stahl, Henriksen. SB—Devore. S—Meyers. SF—Gardner.

New York	IP	H	R	ER	BB	SO
Mathewson (L, 0-2)	9.2	8	3	1	5	4
Boston	IP	H	R	ER	BB	SO
Bedient	7	6	1	1	3	2
Wood (W, 3-1)	3	3	1	1	1	2

Umpires—O'Loughlin (A.L.), Rigler (N.L.), Klem (N.L.), Evans (A.L.). Time—2:37. Attendance—17,034.

1913: PHILADELPHIA ATHLETICS DEFEATED GIANTS 4 TO 1

New York and Philadelphia met in the World Series for the third time in nine years—the Giants winning in 1905 and the Athletics winning in 1911—and manager Connie Mack's Athletics captured the rubber series four games to one.

The Giants were making their third straight postseason appearance after winning the National League pennant with a 101-51 record, a whopping 12½ games ahead of the Philadelphia Phillies. But New York was short-handed in the series as injuries shelved catcher Chief Meyers (cut hand) and hampered second baseman Larry Doyle (automobile accident) first baseman Fred Merkle (sprained ankle) and center fielder Fred Snodgrass (leg cramp).

Right-handed pitcher Christy Mathewson, who led the N.L. with a 2.06 ERA during the season, had another solid series showing with a 0.95 ERA (two earned runs in 19 innings) but managed just a 1-1 record. He also was 3-for-5 at the plate. Among the regulars, replacement catcher Larry McLean batted .500 (6-for-12).

Winning Player's Share: $3,246
Losing Player's Share: $2,164

Game 1: at New York (Polo Grounds) Philadelphia 6, New York 4

Philadelphia third baseman Frank "Home Run" Baker, who earned his nickname in the 1911 World Series against New York, haunted the Giants in Game 1 of the 1913 series with a homer, two singles and three RBI as the Athletics took Game 1 by the score of 6-4 at the Polo

Grounds in New York.

Second baseman Eddie Collins also collected three hits and catcher Wally Schang drove in two runs for Philadelphia, which roughed up New York left-hander Rube Marquard to the tune of five runs and eight hits in five innings.

The Athletics led 5-1 heading into the bottom of the fifth when the Giants scored three runs to trim the deficit. After that, Philadelphia right-hander Chief Bender settled down and went on pitch a complete game, allowing four runs (three earned) on 11 hits with no walks and four strikeouts.

Four Giants rapped two hits each: second baseman Larry Doyle, shortstop Art Fletcher, first baseman Fred Merkle and right fielder Red Murray. Doyle had two RBI.

Game 2: at Philadelphia (Shibe Park)
New York 3, Philadelphia 0 (10 innings)

Flashback: 1905 World Series. New York right-hander Christy Mathewson authors three shutouts against Philadelphia. He did it again in Game 2 of the 1913 series, blanking the Athletics for 10 innings as the Giants evened the series with a 3-0 victory at Shibe Park in Philadelphia.

Mathewson, who scattered eight hits (all singles) with one walk and five walks, also was key offensively. In the top of the 10th, catcher Larry McLean led off with a single and pinch-runner Eddie Grant was sacrificed to second by Hooks Wiltse, a left-handed pitcher who was put in to play first base for the injured Fred Snodgrass. Then Mathewson singled to left-center field to score Grant. Mathewson and third baseman Buck Herzog later came home on a single by shortstop Art Fletcher.

Wiltse, meanwhile, saved the game in the bottom of the ninth by throwing out center fielder Amos Strunk and shortstop Jack Barry on back-to-back throws to the plate after fielding ground balls.

Fletcher, Mathewson and McLean each had two of the Giants' seven hits off Philadelphia left-hander Eddie Plank, who pitched all

10 innings.

Game 3: at New York (Polo Grounds)
Philadelphia 8, New York 2

The Athletics scored three runs in the first inning and two more in the second and coasted to an 8-2 win in Game 3 and a two games to one lead in the series.

Second baseman Eddie Collins was 3-for-5 with three RBI, while third baseman Home Run Baker drove in two runs and catcher Wally Schang hit a home run. Most of Philadelphia's damage came against New York right-hander Jeff Tesreau, who surrendered seven runs (six earned) on 11 hits with three strikeouts.

Philadelphia right-hander Joe Bush fashioned a complete game, scattering five hits with four walks and three strikeouts. The Giants scored single runs in the fifth (an RBI single by catcher Larry McLean) and seventh (an RBI single by right fielder Red Murray). No New York player had more than one hit.

Game 4: at Philadelphia (Shibe Park)
Philadelphia 6, New York 5

A late-game rally came up short, and the Giants lost Game 4 by the score of 6-5 at Shibe Park in Philadelphia and fell behind three games to one in the series.

The Athletics built a 6-0 lead with a run in the second, three in the fourth and two in the fifth. Catcher Wally Schang had a pair of two-run singles in the second and fifth. In the bottom of the fifth, Philadelphia left fielder Rube Oldring made a marvelous catch on a ball hit by New York pinch-hitter Moose McCormick that kept the Giants off the scoreboard.

But the Giants finally cashed in against Athletics' right-hander Chief Bender with three runs in the seventh and two in the eighth. First baseman Fred Merkle stroked a three-run homer in the seventh, while left fielder George Burns and center fielder Tillie Shafer recorded RBI with a double and a triple, respectively, in the eighth. Then with Shafer representing the tying run at third base, right fielder Red Murray lined out hard to second base.

Right-hander Al Demaree was saddled with the loss after giving up four runs (two earned) on seven hits with one walk and no strikeouts over the first four innings. Bender held on to pitch a complete game, allowing eight hits with one walk and five strikeouts.

Game 5: at New York (Polo Grounds) Philadelphia 3, New York 1

Philadelphia left-hander Eddie Plank outdueled New York right-hander Christy Mathewson as the Athletics won Game 5 by the score of 3-1 and captured the World Series championship four games to one.

Plank held the Giants to one unearned run on two hits (both singles) with one walk and one strikeout while pitching a complete game and facing merely 29 batters (two over the minimum). Mathewson also went the distance, allowing three runs (two earned) on six hits (all singles) with one walk and two strikeouts.

The Athletics scored once in the top of the first inning and twice in the third. Third baseman Home Run Baker accounted for two RBI with a sacrifice fly and a single. New York's lone tally came in the fifth when catcher Larry McLean singled home center fielder Tillie Shafer. Mathewson had the Giants' only other hit.

The Giants played in nine World Series under Hall of Fame manager John McGraw. (National Baseball Library and Archive)

1913

Game 1 (Oct. 7)

Philadelphia	AB	R	H	RBI	New York	AB	R	H	RBI
E. Murphy, rf	4	0	1	0	Shafer, cf	5	0	1	0
Oldring, lf	4	0	1	0	Doyle, 2b	4	1	2	2
Collins, 2b	3	3	3	0	Fletcher, ss	4	0	2	1
Baker, 3b	4	1	3	3	Burns, lf	4	0	1	1
McInnis, 1b	3	0	1	1	Herzog, 3b	4	0	0	0
Strunk, cf	4	1	0	0	Murray, rf	4	0	2	0
Barry, ss	4	1	1	0	Meyers, c	4	0	0	0
Schang, c	4	0	1	2	Merkle, 1b	4	2	2	0
Bender, p	4	0	0	0	Marquard, p	0	0	0	0
					McCormick, ph	1	1	1	0
					Crandall, p	1	0	0	0
					Tesreau, p	0	0	0	0
					McLean, ph	1	0	0	0
Totals	34	6	11	6	Totals	36	4	11	4

								R	H	E
Philadelphia	0	0	0	3	2	0	0	1	0	—	6	11	1
New York	0	0	1	0	3	0	0	0	0	—	4	11	0

E—Barry. DP—Philadelphia 1. LOB—Philadelphia 4, New York 6. 2B—McInnis, Barry, Burns. 3B—Collins, Schang. HR—Baker. SB—Collins. S—McInnis, Marquard.

Philadelphia	IP	H	R	ER	BB	SO
Bender (W, 1-0)	9	11	4	3	0	4

New York	IP	H	R	ER	BB	SO
Marquard (L, 0-1)	5	8	5	5	1	1
Crandall	2	3	1	1	0	1
Tesreau	2	0	0	0	1	1

Crandall pitched to three batters in the 8th.

Umpires—Klem (N.L.), Egan (A.L.), Rigler (N.L.), Connolly (A.L.), Time—2:06. Attendance—36,291.

Game 2 (Oct. 8)

New York	AB	R	H	RBI	Philadelphia	AB	R	H	RBI
Herzog, 3b	5	1	0	0	E. Murphy, rf	5	0	0	0
Doyle, 2b	4	0	0	0	Oldring, lf	5	0	1	0
Fletcher, ss	5	0	2	2	Collins, 2b	4	0	1	0
Burns, lf	4	0	0	0	Baker, 3b	5	0	2	0
Shafer, cf	5	0	0	0	McInnis, 1b	4	0	0	0
Murray, rf	4	0	0	0	Strunk, cf	3	0	1	0
McLean, c	4	0	2	0	Barry, ss	4	0	1	0
Grant, pr	0	1	0	0	Lapp, c	4	0	1	0
Wilson, c	0	0	0	0	Plank, p	4	0	1	0
Snodgrass, 1b	1	0	1	0					
Wiltse, pr-1b	2	0	0	0					
Mathewson, p	3	1	2	1					
Totals	37	3	7	3	Totals	38	0	8	0

										R	H	E
New York	0	0	0	0	0	0	0	0	0	3	—	3	7	2
Philadelphia	0	0	0	0	0	0	0	0	0	0	—	0	8	2

E—Baker, Doyle 2, Collins. LOB—New York 8, Philadelphia 10. S—Collins, Wiltse.

New York	IP	H	R	ER	BB	SO
Mathewson (W, 1-0)	10	8	0	0	1	5

Philadelphia	IP	H	R	ER	BB	SO
Plank (L, 0-1)	10	7	3	2	2	6

HBP—By Plank (Doyle). Umpires—Connolly (A.L.), Rigler (N.L.), Klem (N.L.), Egan (A.L.). Time—2:22. Attendance—20,563.

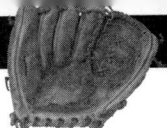

Game 3 (Oct. 9)

Philadelphia	AB	R	H	RBI	New York	AB	R	H	RBI
E. Murphy, rf	5	1	2	0	Herzog, 3b	4	0	0	0
Oldring, lf	5	3	2	0	Doyle, 2b	4	0	1	0
Collins, 2b	5	2	3	3	Fletcher, ss	2	0	1	0
Baker, 3b	4	1	2	2	Burns, lf	4	0	0	0
McInnis, 1b	4	0	0	0	Shafer, cf	3	1	1	0
Strunk, cf	4	0	0	0	Murray, rf	3	1	1	1
Barry, ss	4	0	1	0	McLean, c	2	0	1	1
Schang, c	4	1	1	1	Cooper, pr	0	0	0	0
Bush, p	4	0	1	0	Wilson, c	2	0	0	0
					Merkle, 1b	2	0	0	0
					Wiltse, pr-1b	0	0	0	0
					Tesreau, p	2	0	0	0
					Crandall, p	1	0	0	0
Totals	39	8	12	6	Totals	29	2	5	2

											R	H	E
Philadelphia	3	2	0	0	0	0	2	1	0	—	8	12	1
New York	0	0	0	0	1	0	1	0	0	—	2	5	1

E—Schang, Fletcher. DP—Philadelphia 3, New York 1. LOB—Philadelphia 4, New York 5. 2B—Shafer. 3B—Collins. HR—Schang. SB—Oldring, Collins, Baker, Fletcher, Murray, Cooper.

Philadelphia	IP	H	R	ER	BB	SO
Bush (W, 1-0)	9	5	2	1	4	3

New York	IP	H	R	ER	BB	SO
Tesreau (L, 0-1)	6.1	11	7	6	0	3
Crandall	2.2	1	1	1	0	1

HBP—By Bush (Fletcher). Umpires—Rigler (N.L.), Connolly (A.L.), Klem (N.L.), Egan (A.L.), Time—2:11. Attendance—36,896.

Game 4 (Oct. 10)

New York	AB	R	H	RBI	Philadelphia	AB	R	H	RBI
Snodgrass, cf	2	0	0	0	E. Murphy, rf	5	0	0	0
Herzog, 3b	2	0	1	0	Oldring, lf	4	0	2	0
Doyle, 2b	4	0	0	0	Collins, 2b	4	0	0	0
Fletcher, ss	4	1	0	0	Baker, 3b	4	0	0	0
Burns, lf	4	2	2	1	McInnis, 1b	4	1	1	0
Shafer, 3b-cf	4	0	1	1	Strunk, cf	2	2	1	0
Murray, rf	2	1	1	0	Barry, ss	4	2	3	1
McLean, c	2	0	2	0	Schang, c	2	1	2	4
Cooper, pr	0	0	0	0	Bender, p	4	0	0	1
Wilson, c	1	0	0	0					
Crandall, ph	1	0	0	0					
Merkle, 1b	4	1	1	3					
Demaree, p	1	0	0	0					
McCormick, ph	1	0	0	0					
Marquard, p	1	0	0	0					
Grant, ph	1	0	0	0					
Totals	34	5	8	5	Totals	33	6	9	6

											R	H	E
New York	0	0	0	0	0	0	3	2	0	—	5	8	2
Philadelphia	0	1	0	3	2	0	0	0	x	—	6	9	0

E—Merkle 2. LOB—New York 4, Philadelphia 7. 2B—Burns, Barry 2. 3B—Shafer, Oldring. HR—Merkle. SB—Burns, Murray, Collins. S—Strunk.

New York	IP	H	R	ER	BB	SO
Demaree (L, 0-1)	4	7	4	2	1	0
Marquard	4	2	2	2	2	2

Philadelphia	IP	H	R	ER	BB	SO
Bender (W, 2-0)	9	8	5	5	1	5

HBP—By Bender (Murray). PB—McLean. Umpires—Egan (A.L.), Klem (N.L.), Connolly (A.L.), Rigler (N.L.). Time—2:09. Attendance—20,568.

Game 5 (Oct. 11)

Philadelphia	AB	R	H	RBI	New York	AB	R	H	RBI
E. Murphy, rf	3	1	2	0	Herzog, 3b	4	0	0	0
Oldring, lf	4	2	0	0	Doyle, 2b	4	0	0	0
Collins, 2b	3	0	1	0	Fletcher, ss	3	0	0	0
Baker, 3b	3	0	2	2	Burns, lf	3	0	0	0
McInnis, 1b	2	0	0	1	Shafer, cf	2	1	0	0
Strunk, cf	4	0	0	0	Murray, rf	3	0	0	0
Barry, ss	4	0	0	0	McLean, c	3	0	1	1
Schang, c	4	0	1	0	Merkle, 1b	3	0	0	0
Plank, p	3	0	0	0	Mathewson, p	2	0	1	0
					Crandall, ph	1	0	0	0
Totals	30	3	6	3	Totals	28	1	2	1

											R	H	E
Philadelphia	1	0	2	0	0	0	0	0	0	—	3	6	1
New York	0	0	0	0	1	0	0	0	0	—	1	2	2

E—Burns, Doyle, Plank. DP—Philadelphia 2. LOB—Philadelphia 5, New York 1. S—Collins, McInnis. SF—Baker, McInnis.

Philadelphia	IP	H	R	ER	BB	SO
Plank (W, 1-1)	9	2	1	0	1	1

New York	IP	H	R	ER	BB	SO
Mathewson (L, 1-1)	9	6	3	2	1	2

Umpires—Klem (N.L.), Egan (A.L.), Rigler (N.L.), Connolly (A.L.). Time—1:39. Attendance—36,632.

1917: CHICAGO WHITE SOX DEFEATED GIANTS 4 GAMES TO 2

The 1917 Giants won their fourth National League pennant of the decade (also 1911, 1912 and 1913) but lost their fourth World Series, this time to the Chicago White Sox four games to two. New York captured the N.L. flag with a 98-56 record, 10 games ahead of the Philadelphia Phillies. The White Sox, managed by Pants Rowland, took the American League title in similar fashion, going 100-54 to better the Boston Red Sox by nine games.

Chicago's pitching staff, anchored by right-hander Red Faber, held the Giants to 17 runs in the six games (2.8 per game). Right fielder Dave Robertson, who tied for the N.L. lead with 12 home runs during the season, topped New York batters with a .500 average (11-for-22), while center fielder Benny Kauff had five RBI.

Winning Player's Share: $3,669
Losing Player's Share: $2,442

Game 1: at Chicago (Comiskey Park) Chicago 2, New York 1

In a classic pitchers' dual, Chicago right-hander Eddie Cicotte outdueled New York left-hander Slim Sallee by the score of 2-1 in Game 1 at Comiskey Park in Chicago. Cicotte, who featured a "shine ball" that was something between a slider and a spitter, scattered seven hits (six singles) with one walk and two strikeouts in nine innings, while Sallee allowed seven hits with no walks and two strikeouts.

The White Sox led 1-0 through three innings before center fielder Happy Felsch homered in the fourth for what proved to be the decisive run. New York scored its lone run in the fifth on an RBI single by Sallee that plated catcher Lew McCarty, who had tripled.

New York first baseman Walter Holke collected two hits.

Game 2: at Chicago (Comiskey Park) Chicago 7, New York 2

The White Sox won Game 2 by the score of 7-2 at Comiskey Park in Chicago to take a two games to none lead in the series. It was the

first World Series contest ever played on a Sunday.

It was 2-apiece heading into the fourth inning when Chicago parlayed six singles into five runs off Giants' right-handed relievers Fred Anderson and Pol Perritt. Left-handed starter Ferdie Schupp was knocked out after allowing two runs on four hits in 1.1 innings.

That support was more than enough for White Sox right-hander Red Faber, who pitched a complete game and allowed two runs on eight hits with one walk and one strikeout. Right fielder Dave Robertson was 2-for-3 for the Giants.

Chicago left fielder "Shoeless" Joe Jackson, two years away from becoming part of baseball lore for his association with the 1919 Black Sox scandal, was 3-for-3 with two RBI.

Game 3: at New York (Polo Grounds) New York 2, Chicago 1

In an 0-2 hole, the Giants got a huge lift from left-handed pitcher Rube Benton in Game 3 and won 2-0 at the Polo Grounds in New York to cut the deficit to two games to one. Benton, who was 15-9 with a 2.72 ERA and three shutouts during the season, blanked the White Sox on five hits (four singles and a double) with no walks and five strikeouts.

Chicago right-hander Eddie Cicotte nearly matched Benton, allowing eight hits with no walks and eight strikeouts over eight innings. The Giants scored both of their runs in the fourth inning. Right fielder Dave Robertson tripled and scored on a double by first baseman Walter Holke, who crossed the plate two outs later on a single by left fielder George Burns.

Robertson finished the game with three hits and a stolen base.

Game 4: at New York (Polo Grounds) New York 5, Chicago 0

Giants' left-hander Ferdie Schupp authored a seven-hit shutout, and the Giants captured Game 4 by the score of 5-0 at the Polo Grounds in New York to even the World

Series at two games apiece. Schupp, who topped New York with a 21-7 record and a 1.95 ERA during the season, walked one and struck out seven.

Sharing the headlines was center fielder Benny Kauff, who hit an inside-the-park home run to give the Giants a 1-0 lead in the fourth inning off Chicago right-handed starter and loser Red Faber and capped the scoring with a two-run outside-the-park homer in the eighth off left-handed reliever Dave Danforth. New York also plated single runs in the fifth and seventh.

Game 5: at Chicago (Comiskey Park) Chicago 8, New York 5

Leading 5-2 through six and a half innings, the Giants appeared headed to their third consecutive win. But Chicago bounced back with three runs in the seventh and three more in the eighth to take an 8-5 victory in Game 5 and a three games to two lead in the series.

In the seventh the White Sox loaded the bases with two outs. Then first baseman Chick Gandil hit a wind blown pop fly that landed among three Giants for a two-run double. Second baseman Buck Herzog subsequently fumbled right fielder Dave Robertson's relay throw, enabling Gandil to score with the tying run.

Chicago right fielder Shano Collins singled to lead off the eighth inning, was sacrificed to second by third baseman Fred McMullin and scored the go-ahead run on a single by second baseman Eddie Collins. A throwing error by New York third baseman Heinie Zimmerman allowed another White Sox run to cross the plate, as did an RBI single by center fielder Happy Felsch off right-handed reliever Pol Perritt.

Right-hander Red Faber, the White Sox fourth pitcher, worked the final two innings to pick up the win. New York left-handed starter Slim Sallee suffered the loss after allowing eight runs (seven earned) on 13 hits with four walks and two strikeouts in 7.1 innings.

One interesting side note is that famed Olympian Jim Thorpe was in the Giants' starting lineup as the right fielder, but when Chicago replaced left-handed starting pitcher Red Russell with right-handed reliever Eddie Cicotte in the first inning, New York pinch hit for the right-handed batting Thorpe with the left-handed swinging Robertson. As a result, Thorpe never officially appeared in a World Series game. Robertson and catcher Bill Rariden both had three of New York's 14 hits.

Game 6: at New York (Polo Grounds) Chicago 4, New York 2

The White Sox posted a 4-2 victory in Game 6 at the Polo Grounds to win the World Series four games to two.

New York aided the White Sox cause with some defensive lapses in the fourth inning. Errors by third baseman Heinie Zimmerman and right fielder Dave Robertson put Chicago runners at first and third with no outs. Then White Sox center fielder Happy Felsch hit a grounder to pitcher Rube Benton, who chased the runner at third (second baseman Eddie Collins) back to the base. When New York catcher Bill Rariden ran up the line for an anticipated rundown he left home plate unguarded, and Collins outran Zimmerman to score the game's first run. First baseman Chick Gandil followed with a two-run single, and the White Sox led 3-0.

In the fifth the Giants scored their two runs on a triple by second baseman Buck Herzog that plated Rariden and left fielder George Burns. But Chicago right-hander Red Faber blanked them the rest of the way. He surrendered just six hits with two walks and four strikeouts.

The left-handed Benton was a tough-luck loser, giving up three unearned runs on four hits with one walk and three strikeouts over the first five innings.

Zimmerman undeservedly was roasted afterwards, but he answered his critics with a bona fide question, "Who should I have thrown to? (Home plate umpire Bill) Klem?"

1917

Game 1 (Oct. 6)

New York	AB	R	H	RBI	Chicago	AB	R	H	RBI
Burns, lf	3	0	1	0	S. Collins, rf	4	1	3	0
Herzog, 2b	4	0	1	0	McMullin, 3b	3	0	1	1
Kauff, cf	4	0	0	0	E. Collins, 2b	3	0	0	0
Zimmerman, 3b	4	0	0	0	Jackson, lf	3	0	0	0
Fletcher, ss	4	0	0	0	Felsch, cf	3	1	1	1
Robertson, rf	4	0	1	0	Gandil, 1b	3	0	1	0
Holke, 1b	3	0	2	0	Weaver, ss	3	0	0	0
McCarty, c	3	1	1	0	Schalk, c	3	0	0	0
Sallee, p	3	0	1	1	Cicotte, p	3	0	1	0
Totals	32	1	7	1	Totals	28	2	7	2

											R	H	E
New York	0	0	0	0	1	0	0	0	0	—	1	7	1
Chicago	0	0	1	1	0	0	0	0	x	—	2	7	1

E—McCarty, Weaver. DP—Chicago 1. LOB—New York 5, Chicago 3. 2B—Robertson, S. Collins, McMullin. 3B—McCarty. HR—Felsch. SB—Burns, Gandil. S—McMullin.

New York	IP	H	R	ER	BB	SO
Sallee (L, 0-1)	8	7	2	2	0	2

Chicago	IP	H	R	ER	BB	SO
Cicotte (W, 1-0)	9	7	1	1	1	2

Umpires—O'Loughlin (A.L.), Klem (N.L.), Rigler (N.L.), Evans (A.L.),. Time—1:48. Attendance—32,000.

Game 2 (Oct. 7)

New York	AB	R	H	RBI		Chicago	AB	R	H	RBI
Burns, lf	3	0	1	0		S. Collins, rf	1	0	0	0
Herzog, 2b	4	0	0	0		Leibold, ph-rf	3	1	1	1
Kauff, cf	4	0	0	0		McMullin, 3b	5	1	1	1
Zimmerman, 3b	4	0	0	0		E. Collins, 2b	4	1	2	1
Fletcher, ss	4	0	1	0		Jackson, lf	3	1	3	2
Robertson, rf	3	1	2	0		Felsch, cf	4	1	1	0
Holke, 1b	3	1	1	0		Gandil, 1b	4	0	1	1
McCarty, c	1	0	1	1		Weaver, ss	4	1	3	1
Rariden, c	2	0	1	0		Schalk, c	4	1	1	0
Schupp, p	1	0	0	0		Faber, p	3	0	1	0
Anderson, p	0	0	0	0						
Perritt, p	1	0	1	0						
Wilhoit, ph	1	0	0	0						
Tesreau, p	0	0	0	0						
Totals	31	2	8	1		**Totals**	35	7	14	7

										R	H	E
New York	0	2	0	0	0	0	0	0	0	—	2	8	1
Chicago	0	2	0	5	0	0	0	0	x	—	7	14	1

E—Schalk, Fletcher. DP—New York 1, Chicago 3. LOB—New York 3, Chicago 7. SB—E. Collins 2, Jackson.

New York	IP	H	R	ER	BB	SO
Schupp	1.1	4	2	2	1	2
Anderson (L, 0-1)	2	5	4	4	0	3
Perritt	3.2	5	1	1	1	0
Tesreau	1	0	0	0	1	1
Chicago	IP	H	R	ER	BB	SO
Faber (W, 1-0)	9	8	2	2	1	1

PB—McCarty. Umpires—Evans (A.L.), Rigler (N.L.), Klem (N.L.), O'Loughlin (A.L.). Time—2:13. Attendance—32,000.

Game 3 (Oct. 10)

Chicago	AB	R	H	RBI		New York	AB	R	H	RBI
S. Collins, rf	4	0	0	0		Burns, lf	4	0	1	1
McMullin, 3b	4	0	0	0		Herzog, 2b	4	0	1	0
E. Collins, 2b	4	0	2	0		Kauff, cf	4	0	0	0
Jackson, lf	4	0	0	0		Zimmerman, 3b	4	0	1	0
Felsch, cf	3	0	1	0		Fletcher, ss	4	0	0	0
Gandil, 1b	3	0	0	0		Robertson, rf	4	1	3	0
Weaver, ss	3	0	2	0		Holke, 1b	4	1	1	1
Schalk, c	3	0	0	0		Rariden, c	2	0	1	0
Cicotte, p	3	0	0	0		Benton, p	3	0	0	0
Totals	30	0	5	0		**Totals**	33	2	8	2

										R	H	E
Chicago	0	0	0	0	0	0	0	0	0	—	0	5	3
New York	0	0	0	2	0	0	0	0	x	—	2	8	2

E—Holke, S. Collins 2, Fletcher, Cicotte. DP—New York 1. LOB—Chicago 4, New York 8. 2B—Weaver, Holke. 3B—Robertson. SB—Robertson. S—Rariden.

Chicago	IP	H	R	ER	BB	SO
Cicotte (L, 1-1)	8	8	2	2	0	8
New York	IP	H	R	ER	BB	SO
Benton (W, 1-0)	9	5	0	0	0	5

Umpires—Klem (N.L.), O'Loughlin (A.L.), Evans (A.L.), Rigler (N.L.). Time—1:55. Attendance—33,616.

Game 4 (Oct. 11)

Chicago	AB	R	H	RBI	New York	AB	R	H	RBI
S. Collins, rf	4	0	2	0	Burns, lf	4	0	1	0
McMullin, 3b	4	0	1	0	Herzog, 2b	3	1	1	0
E. Collins, 2b	3	0	1	0	Kauff, cf	4	2	2	3
Jackson, lf	4	0	0	0	Zimmerman, 3b	4	0	1	0
Felsch, cf	4	0	0	0	Fletcher, ss	4	1	2	0
Gandil, 1b	4	0	1	0	Robertson, rf	3	1	1	0
Weaver, ss	3	0	0	0	Holke, 1b	2	0	1	0
Schalk, c	3	0	2	0	Rariden, c	3	0	0	1
Faber, p	2	0	0	0	Schupp, p	3	0	1	1
Risberg, ph	1	0	0	0					
Danforth, p	0	0	0	0					
Totals	**32**	**0**	**7**	**0**	**Totals**	**30**	**5**	**10**	**5**

										R	H	E
Chicago	0	0	0	0	0	0	0	0	0	—	0	7	0
New York	0	0	0	1	1	0	1	2	x	—	5	10	1

E—Herzog. DP—New York 1, Chicago 1. LOB—Chicago 6, New York 3. 2B—E. Collins. 3B—Zimmerman. HR—Kauff 2. SB—E. Collins. S—Herzog.

Chicago	IP	H	R	ER	BB	SO
Faber (L, 1-1)	7	7	3	3	0	3
Danforth	1	3	2	2	0	2

New York	IP	H	R	ER	BB	SO
Schupp (W, 1-0)	9	7	0	0	1	7

HBP—By Faber (Holke). WP—Faber. Umpires—Rigler (N.L.), Evans (A.L.), O'Loughlin (A.L.), Klem (N.L.). Time—2:09. Attendance—27,746.

Game 5 (Oct. 13)

New York	AB	R	H	RBI	Chicago	AB	R	H	RBI
Burns, lf	4	2	1	1	S. Collins, rf	5	1	1	0
Herzog, 2b	5	0	1	0	McMullin, 3b	3	0	0	0
Kauff, cf	5	0	2	2	E. Collins, 2b	4	2	3	1
Zimmerman, 3b	5	1	1	0	Jackson, lf	5	2	3	0
Fletcher, ss	5	1	1	0	Felsch, cf	5	1	3	2
Thorpe, rf	0	0	0	0	Gandil, 1b	5	1	1	2
Robertson, ph-rf	5	0	3	1	Weaver, ss	4	1	1	0
Holke, 1b	5	0	0	0	Schalk, c	3	0	1	0
Rariden, c	3	1	3	1	Russell, p	0	0	0	0
Sallee, p	3	0	0	0	Cicotte, p	1	0	0	0
Perritt, p	0	0	0	0	Risberg, ph	1	0	1	1
					Williams, p	0	0	0	0
					Lynn, ph	1	0	0	0
					Faber, p	0	0	0	0
Totals	**40**	**5**	**12**	**5**	**Totals**	**37**	**8**	**14**	**6**

										R	H	E
New York	2	0	0	2	0	0	1	0	0	—	5	12	3
Chicago	0	0	1	0	0	1	3	3	0	—	8	14	6

E—Williams, Weaver 3, S. Collins, Gandil, Fletcher, Herzog, Zimmerman. DP—Chicago 2. LOB—New York 11, Chicago 10. 2B—Kauff, Fletcher, Felsch, Gandil. SB—Kauff, Schalk. S—Sallee, McMullin.

New York	IP	H	R	ER	BB	SO
Sallee (L, 0-2)	7.1	13	8	7	4	2
Perritt	0.2	1	0	0	0	0

Chicago	IP	H	R	ER	BB	SO
Russell	0	2	2	2	1	0
Cicotte	6	8	2	1	1	3
Williams	1	2	1	1	0	3
Faber (W, 2-1)	2	0	0	0	0	1

Russell pitched to three batters in the 1st.

Umpires—O'Loughlin (A.L.), Klem (N.L.), Rigler (N.L.), Evans (A.L.). Time—2:37. Attendance—27,323.

Game 6 (Oct. 15)

Chicago	AB	R	H	RBI	New York	AB	R	H	RBI
S. Collins, rf	3	0	0	0	Burns, lf	4	1	0	0
Leibold, ph-rf	2	0	1	1	Herzog, 2b	4	0	2	2
McMullin, 3b	5	0	0	0	Kauff, cf	4	0	0	0
E. Collins, 2b	4	1	1	0	Zimmerman, 3b	4	0	0	0
Jackson, lf	4	1	1	0	Fletcher, ss	4	0	1	0
Felsch, cf	3	1	0	0	Robertson, rf	3	0	1	0
Gandil, 1b	4	0	2	2	Holke, 1b	4	0	1	0
Weaver, ss	4	1	1	0	Rariden, c	3	1	0	0
Schalk, c	3	0	1	0	Benton, p	1	0	0	0
Faber, p	2	0	0	0	Wilhoit, ph	0	0	0	0
					Perritt, p	1	0	1	0
					McCarty, ph	1	0	0	0
Totals	34	4	7	3	Totals	33	2	6	2

											R	H	E
Chicago	0	0	0	3	0	0	0	0	1	—	4	7	1
New York	0	0	0	0	2	0	0	0	0	—	2	6	3

E—Schalk, Robertson, Zimmerman 2. LOB—Chicago 7, New York 7. 2B—Holke. 3B—Herzog. S—Faber.

Chicago	IP	H	R	ER	BB	SO
Faber (W, 3-1)	9	6	2	2	2	4

New York	IP	H	R	ER	BB	SO
Benton (L, 1-1)	5	4	3	0	1	3
Perritt	4	3	1	1	2	3

HBP—By Faber (Robertson). PB—Schalk. Umpires—Klem (N.L.), O'Loughlin (A.L.), Evans (A.L.), Rigler (N.L.). Time—2:18. Attendance—33,969.

1921: GIANTS DEFEATED NEW YORK YANKEES 5 GAMES TO 3

The New York Giants squared off against the cross-town rival Yankees in the 1921 World Series and snapped their four-series losing streak by winning the championship five games to three. From 1919-21 the World Series changed from a best-of-seven format to best-of-nine.

While the Giants captured their sixth National League pennant under manager John McGraw (also 1904, 1905, 1911, 1912, 1913 and 1917) with a 93-61 record, seven games ahead of the Cincinnati Reds, the Yankees of manager Miller Huggins won their first American League pennant in the franchise's 21-year history with a 98-55 record, 4 1/2 games better than the Cleveland Indians.

The Yankees were led by legend-in-the-making outfielder Babe Ruth, who had been acquired from the Boston Red Sox two years earlier. In 1921 Ruth led the major leagues with 59 home runs and 171 RBI to go with a .378 batting average (third in the A.L.). In the series Ruth batted .313 (5-for-16) with one homer and five RBI, but he was limited to a single pinch-hitting appearance over the last three games because of an arm injury.

Right-handers Jesse Barnes (2-0, 1.65 ERA) and Phil Douglas (2-1, 2.08 ERA) provided solid pitching for the Giants. Catcher Frank Snyder and left fielder Irish Meusel batted .364 (8-for-22) and .345 (10-for-29), respectively, with one homer apiece.

Since both teams played their home games at the Polo Grounds, the field was used for all eight contests with the squads alternating as home and visitor.

Winning Player's Share: $5,265
Losing Player's Share: $3,510

Game 1: at New York (Polo Grounds) Yankees 3, Giants 0

Right-hander Carl Mays pitched a five-hit shutout as the Yankees blanked the Giants 3-0 in Game 1. The submariner Mays, who was

27-9 with a 3.05 ERA during the season, walked none and struck out one. The only Giants' player to solve Mays was third baseman Frankie Frisch, who was 4-for-4 with a triple. Second baseman Johnny Rawlings collected the other hit.

Meanwhile, the Yankees scored one run in each of the first, fifth and sixth innings. Left fielder Babe Ruth singled in center fielder Elmer Miller in the first, third baseman Mike McNally stole home in the fifth and right fielder Bob Meusel drove in shortstop Roger Peckinpaugh in the sixth with an apparent triple, but Meusel missed first base and was called out when the Giants appealed.

Giants' right-hander Phil Douglas allowed all three tallies on five hits with four walks and six strikeouts in eight innings to absorb the loss.

Game 2: at New York (Polo Grounds) Yankees 3, Giants 0

The Giants were whitewashed for the second straight day, this time 3-0 by Yankees' right-hander Waite Hoyt. The win gave the Yankees a two games to none lead in the series.

Hoyt allowed merely two singles—by second baseman Johnny Rawlings in the third inning and third baseman Frankie Frisch in the ninth—with five walks and five strikeouts. Hoyt also drove in what proved to be the winning with an RBI groundout in the fourth inning. The Yankees added two insurance runs in the eighth.

Giants' left-hander Art Nehf gave up all three runs but only one was earned. He limited the Yankees to three hits (all singles) but issued seven walks, including three to left fielder Babe Ruth, to go with no strikeouts.

Game 3: at New York (Polo Grounds) Giants 13, Yankees 5

Things didn't look so good for the Giants after two and a half innings in Game 3. They trailed two games to none in the series and 4-0 the game. But then they came to life, scoring

four runs in the bottom of the third and erupting for eight more in the seventh en route to a 13-5 victory that cut the deficit to two games to one.

The Giants banged out 20 hits off four Yankees' pitchers to set a World Series record (tied by the St. Louis Cardinals against the Boston Red Sox in Game 4 of the 1946 series). Center fielder George Burns and catcher Frank Snyder led the assault with four hits apiece, while left fielder Irish Meusel had three. Right fielder Ross Youngs collected a double and a triple in the seventh-inning uprising and drove in a total of four runs. He was the first player in World Series history to have two hits in one inning.

Right-handed reliever Jesse Barnes was the benefactor of all the offense. He worked the final seven innings—after right-hander Fred Toney allowed four runs in two innings—and surrendered just one run on four hits with two walks and seven strikeouts.

Yankees' right-hander Jack Quinn suffered the loss in relief.

Game 4: at New York (Polo Grounds)
Giants 4, Yankees 2

The Giants evened up the World Series at two games apiece with a 4-2 win in Game 4.

Trailing 1-0 after seven innings, the Giants scored three runs in the top of the eighth. Second baseman Johnny Rawlings drove in the tying run with a single to score left fielder Irish Meusel, who had tripled, and center fielder George Burns later stroked a two-run double to drive in Rawlings and catcher Frank Snyder.

Right-hander Phil Douglas kept the Yankees at bay until the Giants' bats came alive. He authored a complete game, allowing seven hits with no walks and eight strikeouts and throwing 103 pitches. In the ninth inning, Yankees' left fielder Babe Ruth touched Douglas for a home run, the first of his 15 lifetime World Series round-trippers. That total ranks second in baseball history to Mickey Mantle of the Yankees with 18.

Yankees' right-hander Carl Mays went the distance, surrendering four runs on nine hits with no walks and one strikeout.

Game 5: at New York (Polo Grounds)
Yankees 3, Giants 1

After allowing an unearned run in the bottom of the first inning, Yankees' right-hander Waite Hoyt blanked the Giants the rest of the way as the Yankees won Game 5 by the score of 3-1 to take a three games to two lead in the World Series. Hoyt scattered 10 hits (eight of them singles) while walking two and striking out six.

Hoyt's teammates tied the game in the third and scored twice in the fourth. Left fielder Babe Ruth tallied what proved to be the winning run after reaching base on a bunt single and being driven home on a double by right fielder Bob Meusel. Giants' left-hander Art Nehf gave up merely six hits with one walk and five strikeouts in going the distance.

First baseman George Kelly, who led the National League with 23 home runs during the season, had three hits and an RBI for the Giants.

Game 6: at New York (Polo Grounds)
Giants 8, Yankees 5

First baseman George Kelly was 3-for-4 with three RBI to propel the Giants to an 8-5 win in Game 6 that evened the series at three games apiece.

The Yankees scored three runs in the bottom of the first inning to knock out Giants' right-handed starter Fred Toney. Right-hander Jesse Barnes relieved Toney and worked the final 8.1 innings, allowing two runs on four hits with four walks and 10 strikeouts.

Trailing 5-3 after three innings, the Giants scored four runs in the top of the fourth to take the lead for good at 7-5. Shortstop Dave Bancroft drove in two runs with a bases-loaded single, and Kelly also had a two-run single. Right-hander Bob Shawkey was the losing pitcher for the Yankees in relief of left-handed starter Harry Harper.

The Giants scored three runs in the second on a two-run homer by left fielder Irish Meusel and a solo shot by catcher Frank Snyder.

Yankees' left fielder Chick Fewster hit a two-run homer in the second. Fewster was playing for Babe Ruth, who was sidelined with an arm injury.

Game 7: at New York (Polo Grounds)
Giants 2, Yankees 1

The Giants took a four games to three lead in the 1921 World Series with a 2-1 victory in Game 7.

With the game deadlocked at 1-apiece in the bottom of the seventh inning, Giants' catcher Frank Snyder doubled home second baseman Johnny Rawlings with the winning run. Rawlings had reached on a error by Yankees' second baseman Aaron Ward.

Meanwhile, Giants' right-hander Phil Douglas outdueled Yankees' right-hander Carl Mays. Douglas scattered eight hits with one walk and three strikeouts, while Mays allowed six hits with no walks and seven strikeouts. Both pitchers went the distance.

Center fielder George Burns collected two doubles for the Giants.

Game 8: at New York (Polo Grounds)
Giants 1, Yankees 0

An unearned run in the first inning was all Giants' left-hander Art Nehf needed, as the Giants beat the Yankees 1-0 in Game 8 to capture the series five games to three. With one out, shortstop Dave Bancroft walked and one out later, right fielder Ross Youngs walked. Then first baseman George Kelly hit a grounder to Yankees' shortstop Roger Peckinpaugh, who let the ball roll through his legs and enabled Bancroft to score.

Then it was up to Nehf, who surrendered merely four hits (all singles) with five walks and three strikeouts. In the bottom of the ninth, Yankees' second baseman Aaron Ward drew a one-out walk. The next batter, third baseman Home Run Baker, hit a hard grounder between first and second base that Giants' second baseman Johnny Rawlings dove for and retired Baker. Inexplicably, Ward rounded second and was thrown out at third on a bullet throw from Kelly to third baseman Frankie Frisch to end the game and the series.

Yankees' right-hander Waite Hoyt deserved a better fate. He allowed six hits with four walks and seven strikeouts but absorbed the loss. In 27 World Series innings, Hoyt did not give up a single earned run.

Rawlings had a pair of doubles for the Giants.

1921

Game 1 (Oct. 5)

Yankees	AB	R	H	RBI	Giants	AB	R	H	RBI
Miller, cf	4	1	1	0	Burns, cf	4	0	0	0
Peckinpaugh, ss	3	1	1	0	Bancroft, ss	4	0	0	0
Ruth, lf	3	0	1	1	Frisch, 3b	4	0	4	0
B. Meusel, rf	4	0	0	1	Youngs, rf	3	0	0	0
Pipp, 1b	2	0	0	0	Kelly, 1b	4	0	0	0
Ward, 2b	3	0	1	0	I. Meusel, lf	3	0	0	0
McNally, 3b	4	1	2	0	Rawlings, 2b	2	0	1	0
Schang, c	2	0	0	0	Snyder, c	3	0	0	0
Mays, p	3	0	1	0	Douglas, p	2	0	0	0
					Smith, ph	1	0	0	0
					Barnes, p	0	0	0	0
Totals	28	3	7	2	Totals	30	0	5	0

											R	H	E
Yankees	1	0	0	0	1	1	0	0	0	—	3	7	0
Giants	0	0	0	0	0	0	0	0	0	—	0	5	0

DP—Giants 1. LOB—Yankees 5, Giants 5. 2B—McNally. 3B—Frisch. SB—McNally 2, Frisch. S—Peckinpaugh, Pipp, Schang, Youngs.

Yankees	IP	H	R	ER	BB	SO
Mays (W, 1-0)	9	5	0	0	0	1

Giants	IP	H	R	ER	BB	SO
Douglas (L, 0-1)	8	5	3	3	4	6
Barnes	1	2	0	0	0	1

HBP—By Mays (Rawlings). PB—Snyder. Umpires—Rigler (N.L.), Moriarty (A.L.), Quigley (N.L.), Chill (A.L.). Time—1:38. Attendance—30,203.

Game 2 (Oct. 6)

Giants	AB	R	H	RBI	Yankees	AB	R	H	RBI
Burns, cf	3	0	0	0	Miller, cf	3	0	0	0
Bancroft, ss	4	0	0	0	Peckinpaugh, ss	3	0	0	0
Frisch, 3b	4	0	1	0	Ruth, lf	1	1	0	0
Youngs, rf	2	0	0	0	B. Meusel, rf	4	1	1	0
Kelly, 1b	4	0	0	0	Pipp, 1b	3	0	0	1
I. Meusel, lf	2	0	0	0	Ward, 2b	4	1	1	0
Rawlings, 2b	3	0	1	0	McNally, 3b	3	0	0	0
Smith, c	3	0	0	0	Schang, c	2	0	0	0
Nehf, p	2	0	0	0	Hoyt, p	3	0	1	1
Totals	27	0	2	0	Totals	26	3	3	2

											R	H	E
Giants	0	0	0	0	0	0	0	0	0	—	0	2	3
Yankees	0	0	0	1	0	0	0	2	x	—	3	3	0

E—Frisch, Smith, Nehf. DP—Giants 2, Yankees 1. LOB—Giants 5, Yankees 6. 2B—Ruth 2, B. Meusel.

Giants	IP	H	R	ER	BB	SO
Nehf (L, 0-1)	8	3	3	1	7	0

Yankees	IP	H	R	ER	BB	SO
Hoyt (W, 1-0)	9	2	0	0	5	5

Umpires—Moriarty (A.L.), Quigley (N.L.), Chill (A.L.), Rigler (N.L.). Time—1:55. Attendance—34,939.

Game 3 (Oct. 7)

Yankees	AB	R	H	RBI	Giants	AB	R	H	RBI
Miller, cf	5	1	1	1	Burns, cf	6	1	4	0
Peckinpaugh, ss	3	1	0	0	Bancroft, ss	5	1	1	1
Ruth, lf	3	0	1	2	Frisch, 3b	2	3	2	0
Fewster, pr-lf	0	1	0	0	Youngs, rf	3	2	2	4
B. Meusel, rf	3	0	2	0	Kelly, 1b	3	1	0	1
Pipp, 1b	3	0	0	1	I. Meusel, lf	5	2	3	3
Ward, 2b	4	0	2	1	Rawlings, 2b	5	0	2	3
McNally, 3b	3	0	0	0	Snyder, c	5	1	4	1
Schang, c	2	1	1	0	Toney, p	0	0	0	0
DeVormer, c	1	0	0	0	Barnes, p	5	2	2	0
Shawkey, p	1	1	1	0					
Quinn, p	2	0	0	0					
Collins, p	0	0	0	0					
Rogers, p	0	0	0	0					
Baker, ph	1	0	0	0					
Totals	**31**	**5**	**8**	**5**	**Totals**	**39**	**13**	**20**	**13**

											R	H	E
Yankees	0	0	4	0	0	0	0	1	0	—	5	8	0
Giants	0	0	4	0	0	0	8	1	x	—	13	20	0

DP—Yankees 2. LOB—Yankees 5, Giants 10. 2B—B. Meusel, Burns, Youngs, I. Meusel. 3B—Burns, Youngs. SB—Burns, Frisch, I. Meusel. S—Pipp. SF—Bancroft.

Yankees	IP	H	R	ER	BB	SO
Shawkey	2.1	5	4	4	4	0
Quinn (L, 0-1)	3.2	7	4	4	2	2
Collins	0.2	5	4	4	1	0
Rogers	1.1	3	1	1	0	1

Giants	IP	H	R	ER	BB	SO
Toney	2	4	4	4	2	1
Barnes (W, 1-0)	7	4	1	1	2	7

Toney pitched to five batters in the 3rd.
Quinn pitched to four batters in the 7th.

HBP—By Barnes (McNally). WP—Barnes. Umpires—Quigley (N.L.), Chill (A.L.), Rigler (N.L.), Moriarty (A.L.). Time—2:40. Attendance—36,509.

Game 4 (Oct. 9)

Giants	AB	R	H	RBI	Yankees	AB	R	H	RBI
Burns, cf	4	0	2	2	Miller, cf	4	0	0	0
Bancroft, ss	4	0	0	0	Peckinpaugh, ss	4	0	1	0
Frisch, 3b	4	0	0	0	Ruth, lf	4	1	2	1
Youngs, rf	4	0	1	0	B. Meusel, rf	4	0	0	0
Kelly, 1b	4	1	1	0	Pipp, 1b	4	0	1	0
I. Meusel, lf	4	1	2	1	Ward, 2b	2	0	0	0
Rawlings, 2b	4	1	2	1	McNally, 3b	3	1	1	0
Snyder, c	4	1	1	0	Schang, c	3	0	2	1
Douglas, p	2	0	0	0	Mays, p	3	0	0	0
Totals	34	4	9	4	Totals	31	2	7	2

											R	H	E
Giants	0	0	0	0	0	0	0	3	1	—	4	9	1
Yankees	0	0	0	0	1	0	0	0	1	—	2	7	1

E—McNally, Bancroft. DP—Yankees 1. LOB—Giants 4, Yankees 3. 2B—Burns, Kelly. 3B—I. Meusel, Schang. HR—Ruth. S—Douglas, Ward.

Giants	IP	H	R	ER	BB	SO
Douglas (W, 1-1)	9	7	2	2	0	8

Yankees	IP	H	R	ER	BB	SO
Mays (L, 1-1)	9	9	4	4	0	1

Umpires—Chill (A.L.), Rigler (N.L.), Moriarty (A.L.), Quigley (N.L.). Time—1:38. Attendance—36,372.

Game 5 (Oct. 10)

Yankees	AB	R	H	RBI	Giants	AB	R	H	RBI
Miller, cf	3	0	1	1	Burns, cf	5	0	1	0
Peckinpaugh, ss	4	0	1	0	Bancroft, ss	4	1	1	0
Ruth, lf	4	1	1	0	Frisch, 3b	4	0	2	0
B. Meusel, rf	4	1	2	1	Youngs, rf	3	0	1	0
Pipp, 1b	3	0	0	0	Kelly, 1b	4	0	3	1
Ward, 2b	3	0	0	1	I. Meusel, lf	4	0	1	0
McNally, 3b	2	1	0	0	Rawlings, 2b	4	0	1	0
Schang, c	3	0	1	0	Smith, c	3	0	0	0
Hoyt, p	3	0	0	0	Nehf, p	3	0	0	0
					Snyder, ph	1	0	0	0
Totals	29	3	6	3	Totals	35	1	10	1

											R	H	E
Yankees	0	0	1	2	0	0	0	0	0	—	3	6	1
Giants	1	0	0	0	0	0	0	0	0	—	1	10	1

E—Frisch, McNally. LOB—Yankees 3, Giants 9. 2B—Miller, B. Meusel, Schang, I. Meusel, Rawlings. S—Pipp. SF—Miller, Ward.

Yankees	IP	H	R	ER	BB	SO
Hoyt (W, 2-0)	9	10	1	0	2	6

Giants	IP	H	R	ER	BB	SO
Nehf (L, 0-2)	9	6	3	3	1	5

Umpires—Rigler (N.L.), Moriarty (A.L.), Quigley (N.L.), Chill (A.L.). Time—1:52. Attendance—35,758.

Game 6 (Oct. 11)

Giants	AB	R	H	RBI	Yankees	AB	R	H	RBI
Burns, cf	3	1	1	0	Fewster, lf	3	2	1	2
Bancroft, ss	5	0	2	2	Peckinpaugh, ss	5	0	0	0
Frisch, 3b	4	2	0	0	Miller, cf	5	1	1	0
Youngs, rf	5	0	1	0	B. Meusel, rf	3	1	1	1
Kelly, 1b	4	1	3	3	Pipp, 1b	4	0	1	0
I. Meusel, lf	4	1	2	2	Ward, 2b	4	0	1	2
Rawlings, 2b	5	0	0	0	McNally, 3b	4	0	0	0
Snyder, c	4	2	2	1	Schang, c	2	0	1	0
Toney, p	0	0	0	0	Harper, p	0	0	0	0
Barnes, p	4	1	2	0	Shawkey, p	3	1	1	0
					Baker, ph	1	0	0	0
					Piercy, p	0	0	0	0
Totals	38	8	13	8	Totals	34	5	7	5

											R	H	E
Giants	0	3	0	4	0	1	0	0	0	—	8	13	0
Yankees	3	2	0	0	0	0	0	0	0	—	5	7	2

E—Ward, McNally. DP—Yankees 2. LOB—Giants 8, Yankees 7. HR—I. Meusel, Snyder, Fewster. SB—Frisch, Pipp. S—Burns.

Giants	IP	H	R	ER	BB	SO
Toney	0.2	3	3	3	1	0
Barnes (W, 2-0)	8.1	4	2	2	4	10

Yankees	IP	H	R	ER	BB	SO
Harper	1.1	3	3	3	2	1
Shawkey (L, 0-1)	6.2	8	5	3	2	5
Piercy	1	2	0	0	0	2

Umpires—Moriarty (A.L.), Quigley (N.L.), Chill (A.L.), Rigler (N.L.). Time—2:31. Attendance—34,283.

Game 7 (Oct. 12)

Yankees	AB	R	H	RBI
Fewster, lf	4	0	1	0
Peckinpaugh, ss	4	0	2	0
Miller, cf	3	0	0	0
B. Meusel, rf	4	0	0	0
Pipp, 1b	4	1	1	0
Ward, 2b	3	0	0	0
McNally, 3b	1	0	1	1
Baker, 3b	3	0	2	0
DeVormer, pr	0	0	0	0
Schang, c	4	0	1	0
Mays, p	3	0	0	0
Totals	33	1	8	1

Giants	AB	R	H	RBI
Burns, cf	4	0	2	0
Bancroft, ss	4	0	1	0
Frisch, 3b	4	0	0	0
Youngs, rf	3	1	1	0
Kelly, 1b	3	0	0	0
I. Meusel, lf	3	0	1	1
Rawlings, 2b	3	1	0	0
Snyder, c	3	0	1	1
Douglas, p	3	0	0	0
Totals	30	2	6	2

											R	H	E
Yankees	0	1	0	0	0	0	0	0	0	—	1	8	1
Giants	0	0	0	1	0	0	1	0	x	—	2	6	0

E—Ward. LOB—Yankees 7, Giants 4. 2B—Peckinpaugh, Pipp, Burns 2, Bancroft, Snyder. SB—Youngs. S—Ward.

Yankees	IP	H	R	ER	BB	SO
Mays (L, 1-2)	8	6	2	1	0	7

Giants	IP	H	R	ER	BB	SO
Douglas (W, 2-1)	9	8	1	1	1	3

WP—Douglas. Umpires—Quigley (N.L.), Chill (A.L.), Rigler (N.L.), Moriarty (A.L.). Time—1:40. Attendance—36,503.

Game 8 (Oct. 13)

Giants	AB	R	H	RBI
Burns, cf	4	0	1	0
Bancroft, ss	3	1	0	0
Frisch, 3b	4	0	0	0
Youngs, rf	2	0	1	0
Kelly, 1b	4	0	0	0
I. Meusel, lf	4	0	1	0
Rawlings, 2b	4	0	3	0
Snyder, c	2	0	0	0
Nehf, p	4	0	0	0
Totals	31	1	6	0

Yankees	AB	R	H	RBI
Fewster, lf	3	0	0	0
Peckinpaugh, ss	2	0	0	0
Miller, cf	4	0	1	0
B. Meusel, rf	4	0	0	0
Pipp, 1b	3	0	1	0
Ruth, ph	1	0	0	0
Ward, 2b	3	0	1	0
Baker, 3b	3	0	0	0
Schang, c	3	0	0	0
Hoyt, p	3	0	1	0
Totals	29	0	4	0

											R	H	E
Giants	1	0	0	0	0	0	0	0	0	—	1	6	0
Yankees	0	0	0	0	0	0	0	0	0	—	0	4	1

E—Peckinpaugh. DP—Giants 1. LOB—Giants 9, Yankees 7. 2B—Rawlings 2. SB—Youngs. S—Snyder 2.

Giants	IP	H	R	ER	BB	SO
Nehf (W, 1-2)	9	4	0	0	5	3

Yankees	IP	H	R	ER	BB	SO
Hoyt (L, 2-1)	9	6	1	0	4	7

WP—Nehf. Umpires—Chill (A.L.), Rigler (N.L.), Moriarty (A.L.), Quigley (N.L.). Time—1:57. Attendance—25,410.

1922: GIANTS DEFEATED NEW YORK YANKEES 4 GAMES TO 0 (1 TIE)

For the second straight year, the New York Giants and New York Yankees met in the World Series, with all games being played at the Polo Grounds. The Giants made it two straight series triumphs over their cross-town rivals managed by Miller Huggins, four games to none with a controversial 3-3, 10-inning tie in Game 2. After being played under a best-of-nine format from 1919-21, the series returned to the traditional best-of-seven in 1922.

The Giants won the National League pennant with a 93-61 record, seven games ahead of the Cincinnati Reds, while the Yankees captured the American League flag with a 94-60 record, one game better than the St. Louis Browns.

Giants' pitchers virtually shutdown the Yankees' batters, allowing just eight earned runs in 46 innings (1.57 ERA) to go with a .203 batting average (32-for-158). Left fielder Babe Ruth, after batting .315 with 35 home runs and 96 RBI, was limited to a .118 average (2-for-17) with one RBI.

Third baseman Heinie Groh paced the Giants' offense by batting at a .474 clip (9-for-19), while second baseman Frankie Frisch batted .471 (8-for-17) and left fielder Irish Meusel drove in seven of the team's 18 runs.

The 1922 World Series championship would prove to be the Giants' third and final one under legendary manager John McGraw.

Winning Player's Share: $4,470
Losing Player's Share: $3,225

Game 1: at New York (Polo Grounds) Giants 3, Yankees 2

The Giants erupted for three runs in the bottom of the eighth inning to edge the Yankees by the score of 3-2 in Game 1 of the series.

Trailing 2-0, shortstop Dave Bancroft, third baseman Heinie Groh and second baseman Frankie Frisch all singled to load the bases with no outs. Then left fielder Irish Meusel drove in Bancroft and Groh with a single that knocked out Yankees' right-hander starter and loser Joe Bush. Giants' right fielder Ross Youngs greeted right-handed reliever Waite Hoyt with a sacrifice fly that plated Frisch with the winning run.

Giants' right-handed reliever Rosy Ryan pitched two innings of one-hit relief with two strikeouts to earn the win. Left-hander Art Nehf worked the first seven innings, allowing two runs (one earned) on six hits with one walk and three strikeouts.

Groh had three of the Giants' 11 hits, including a triple.

Game 2: at New York (Polo Grounds) Giants 3, Yankees 3 (10 innings)

In one of the most bizarre games in World Series history, Game 2 was postponed on account of darkness after 10 innings with the Giants and Yankees tied 3-3. Home plate umpire George Hildebrand called the contest at 4:45 p.m. despite there being ample sunlight still available.

Not surprisingly, the participants were "thunderstruck" and the spectators angry that they did not see a complete game. Some 5,000 fans surrounded the field box where baseball commissioner Kenesaw Landis was seated, and Landis and his wife had to receive a police escort to leave the Polo Grounds. That evening, Landis announced that the $120,534 profit from the game would be given to a fund for disabled soldiers and to other New York charities.

The Giants scored their three runs in the top of the first inning on singles by third baseman Heinie Groh and second baseman Frankie Frisch and a home run by left fielder Irish Meusel. The Yankees scored single runs in the first, fourth and eighth innings.

Both starting pitchers—right-handers Jesse Barnes of the Giants and Bob Shawkey of the Yankees—worked all 10 innings.

Game 3: at New York (Polo Grounds)
Giants 3, Yankees 0

After being told during the offseason he would never pitch again because of a lame arm, right-hander Jack Scott authored a four-hit shutout en route to a 3-0 Giants' victory in Game 3 that gave them a two games to none lead in the series.

Scott, who joined the Giants after being released by the Cincinnati Reds over the winter and appeared in just 17 games (8-2 record, 4.41 ERA), walked one and struck out two while allowing just 10 balls to be hit out of the infield. The Yankees advanced runners to second and third with one out in the top of the eighth inning, but Scott struck out pinch-hitter Elmer Smith and retired shortstop Everett Scott to preserve the whitewash.

The Giants, meanwhile, scored two runs in the third on a sacrifice fly by second baseman Frankie Frisch and an RBI single by left fielder Irish Meusel. Frisch singled home the Giants' third run in the seventh. Right fielder Ross Youngs was 3-for-4.

Right-hander Waite Hoyt suffered the loss for the Yankees after allowing all three runs (one earned) on 11 hits with two walks and two strikeouts in seven innings.

Game 4: at New York (Polo Grounds)
Giants 4, Yankees 3

A four-run fifth inning propelled the Giants to a 4-3 win in Game 4 and a commanding three games to none lead in the series.

The Yankees took a 2-0 lead into the fifth before shortstop Dave Bancroft tied the game with a two-run singles. Shortstop Frankie Frisch drove in the go-ahead run with a sacrifice fly, and right fielder Ross Youngs singled to

plate Frisch with the decisive run.

After Giants' right-hander Hugh McQuillan gave up two runs in the bottom of the first, he settled down and allowed just a seventh-inning homer to Yankees' second baseman Aaron Ward the rest of the way. He finished with an eight-hitter while walking two and striking out four. McQuillan helped himself with a double in the Giants' fifth-inning uprising.

Bancroft, Youngs and catcher Frank Snyder each had two of the Giants' nine hits off Yankees' starter and loser Carl Mays, who worked the first eight innings.

Game 5: at New York (Polo Grounds)
Giants 5, Yankees 3

The Giants completed their 1922 World Series sweep of the Yankees with a come-from-behind 5-3 victory in Game 5.

Trailing 3-2 after seven and a half innings, the Giants put together a three-run rally in the bottom of the eighth. They loaded the bases with two outs following an intentional walk to right fielder Ross Youngs that Yankees' right-hander Joe Bush disputed. Then first baseman George Kelly singled in second baseman Frankie Frisch and left fielder Irish Meusel, and backup center fielder Lee King singled in Youngs.

Left-hander Art Nehf pitched a complete game for the Giants, allowing merely five hits (all singles) with two walks and three strikeouts. Bush absorbed the loss after giving up 10 hits with four walks and three strikeouts in eight innings.

The Yankees scored single runs in the first, fifth and seventh innings, while the Giants tallied two runs in the second.

Frisch, Kelly and third baseman Heinie Groh each had two hits for the Giants.

Juan
MARICHAL

Willie
McCOVEY

Orlando
CEPEDA

Barry
BONDS

©S.F. Giants

Barry Bonds rounds the bases after crushing his record-making 73rd home run.
Eric Risberg, AP/Wide World Photos

Barry Bonds watches as his 600th home run sails over the center field wall at Pacific Bell Park.
© S.F. Giants

Soon after joining the 500 career home run club, Barry Bonds would join the ranks of those who smashed 600 home runs in a career.
© S.F. Giants

Hank Aaron and Willie Mays were on hand to help the San Francisco Giants honor Barry Bonds after he became the fourth player

Willie Mays

PACIFIC BELL PARK

Opening Day April 2000

GIANTS

Pacific Bell Park

Pacific Bell

1922

Game 1 (Oct. 4)

Yankees	AB	R	H	RBI	Giants	AB	R	H	RBI
Witt, cf	4	0	1	0	Bancroft, ss	4	1	1	0
Dugan, 3b	4	1	1	0	Groh, 3b	3	1	3	0
Ruth, rf	4	0	1	1	Frisch, 2b	4	1	2	0
Pipp, 1b	4	0	1	0	I. Meusel, lf	4	0	1	2
B. Meusel, lf	4	1	2	0	Youngs, rf	3	0	0	1
Schang, c	2	0	1	0	Kelly, 1b	4	0	2	0
Ward, 2b	1	0	0	1	Stengel, cf	4	0	1	0
E. Scott, ss	3	0	0	0	Snyder, c	3	0	1	0
Bush, p	3	0	0	0	Nehf, p	2	0	0	0
Hoyt, p	0	0	0	0	Earl Smith, ph	1	0	0	0
					Ryan, p	0	0	0	0
Totals	29	2	7	2	Totals	32	3	11	3

											R	H	E
Yankees	0	0	0	0	0	1	1	0	0	—	2	7	0
Giants	0	0	0	0	0	0	0	3	x	—	3	11	2

E—Youngs, Nehf. DP—Yankees 1, Giants 3. LOB—Yankees 4, Giants 7. 3B—Witt, Groh. S—Schang 2. SF—Ward, Youngs.

Yankees	IP	H	R	ER	BB	SO
Bush (L, 0-1)	7	11	3	3	1	3
Hoyt	1	0	0	0	0	2

Giants	IP	H	R	ER	BB	SO
Nehf	7	6	2	1	1	3
Ryan (W, 1-0)	2	1	0	0	0	2

Bush pitched to four batters in the 8th.

PB—Schang. Umpires—Klem (N.L.), Hildebrand (A.L.), McCormick (N.L.), Owens (A.L.). Time—2:08. Attendance—36,514.

Game 2 (Oct. 5)

Giants	AB	R	H	RBI	Yankees	AB	R	H	RBI
Bancroft, ss	5	0	1	0	Witt, cf	5	0	1	0
Groh, 3b	4	1	1	0	Dugan, 3b	5	1	2	0
Frisch, 2b	4	1	2	0	Ruth, rf	4	1	1	0
I. Meusel, lf	4	1	1	3	Pipp, 1b	5	0	1	1
Youngs, rf	3	0	1	0	B. Meusel, lf	4	0	1	1
Kelly, 1b	4	0	0	0	Schang, c	4	0	0	0
Stengel, cf	1	0	1	0	Ward, 2b	4	1	1	1
Cunningham, pr-cf	2	0	0	0	E. Scott, ss	4	0	1	0
Earl Smith, ph	1	0	0	0	Shawkey, p	4	0	0	0
King, cf	0	0	0	0					
Snyder, c	4	0	1	0					
J. Barnes, p	4	0	0	0					
Totals	36	3	8	3	Totals	39	3	8	3

											R	H	E
Giants	3	0	0	0	0	0	0	0	0	—	3	8	1
Yankees	1	0	0	1	0	0	0	1	0	—	3	8	0

E—Bancroft. DP—Yankees 1. LOB—Giants 5, Yankees 8. 2B—Dugan, Ruth, B. Meusel. HR—I. Meusel, Ward. SB—Frisch.

Giants	IP	H	R	ER	BB	SO
J. Barnes	10	8	3	2	2	6

Yankees	IP	H	R	ER	BB	SO
Shawkey	10	8	3	3	2	4

WP—Shawkey. Umpires—Hildebrand (A.L.), McCormick (N.L.), Owens (A.L.), Klem (N.L.). Time—2:40. Attendance—37,020.

Game 3 (Oct. 6)

Yankees	AB	R	H	RBI		Giants	AB	R	H	RBI
Witt, cf	3	0	0	0		Bancroft, ss	3	2	0	0
Dugan, 3b	4	0	0	0		Groh, 3b	4	1	2	0
Ruth, rf	3	0	0	0		Frisch, 2b	2	0	2	2
Pipp, 1b	4	0	1	0		I. Meusel, lf	4	0	1	1
B. Meusel, lf	4	0	1	0		Youngs, rf	4	0	3	0
Schang, c	3	0	1	0		Kelly, 1b	3	0	1	0
Ward, 2b	2	0	0	0		Cunningham, cf	3	0	1	0
Elmer Smith, ph	1	0	0	0		Earl Smith, ph	4	0	1	0
McNally, 2b	0	0	0	0		J. Scott, p	4	0	1	0
E. Scott, ss	3	0	0	0						
Hoyt, p	2	0	1	0						
Baker, ph	1	0	0	0						
Jones, p	0	0	0	0						
Totals	**30**	**0**	**4**	**0**		**Totals**	**31**	**3**	**12**	**3**

										R	H	E
Yankees	0	0	0	0	0	0	0	0	0	—	0	4	1
Giants	0	0	2	0	0	0	1	0	x	—	3	12	1

E—Frisch, Ward. DP—Yankees 1. LOB—Yankees 5, Giants 9. 2B—Schang. SB—Pipp. S—Kelly. SF—Frisch.

Yankees	IP	H	R	ER	BB	SO
Hoyt (L, 0-1)	7	11	3	1	2	2
Jones	1	1	0	0	1	0

Giants	IP	H	R	ER	BB	SO
J. Scott (W, 1-0)	9	4	0	0	1	2

HBP—By J. Scott (Ruth). Umpires—McCormick (N.L.), Owens (A.L.), Klem (N.L.), Hildebrand (A.L.). Time—1:48. Attendance—37,630.

Game 4 (Oct. 7)

Giants	AB	R	H	RBI		Yankees	AB	R	H	RBI
Bancroft, ss	3	1	2	2		Witt, cf	4	1	2	0
Groh, 3b	4	1	1	0		Dugan, 3b	4	1	1	0
Frisch, 2b	3	0	0	0		Ruth, rf	3	0	0	0
I. Meusel, lf	4	0	1	1		Pipp, 1b	4	0	2	1
Youngs, rf	4	0	2	1		B. Meusel, lf	4	0	1	1
Kelly, 1b	4	0	0	0		Schang, c	4	0	1	0
Cunningham, cf	3	0	0	0		Ward, 2b	4	1	1	1
Snyder, c	4	1	2	0		E. Scott, ss	2	0	0	0
McQuillan, p	4	1	1	0		Mays, p	2	0	0	0
						Elmer Smith, ph	1	0	0	0
						Jones, p	0	0	0	0
Totals	**33**	**4**	**9**	**4**		**Totals**	**32**	**3**	**8**	**3**

										R	H	E
Giants	0	0	0	0	4	0	0	0	0	—	4	9	1
Yankees	2	0	0	0	0	0	1	0	0	—	3	8	0

E—Snyder. DP—Giants 1, Yankees 1. LOB—Giants 5, Yankees 4. 2B óMcQuillan, Witt, Pipp. HR—Ward. SB—B. Meusel. S—Frisch.

Giants	IP	H	R	ER	BB	SO
McQuillan (W, 1-0)	9	8	3	3	2	4

Yankees	IP	H	R	ER	BB	SO
Mays (L, 0-1)	8	9	4	4	2	1
Jones	1	0	0	0	0	0

Umpires—Owens (A.L.), Klem (N.L.), Hildebrand (A.L.), McCormick (N.L.),. Time—1:41. Attendance—36,242.

Game 5 (Oct. 8)

Yankees	AB	R	H	RBI	Giants	AB	R	H	RBI
Witt, cf	2	0	0	0	Bancroft, ss	4	0	0	0
McMillan, ph-cf	2	0	0	0	Groh, 3b	4	0	2	0
Dugan, 3b	3	1	1	0	Frisch, 2b	4	1	2	0
Ruth, rf	3	0	0	0	I. Meusel, lf	4	2	1	0
Pipp, 1b	4	0	1	1	Youngs, rf	2	2	0	0
B. Meusel, lf	4	1	1	0	Kelly, 1b	3	0	2	2
Schang, c	3	0	0	0	Cunningham, cf	2	0	1	2
Ward, 2b	2	1	0	0	Earl Smith, ph	1	0	0	0
E. Scott, ss	2	0	1	1	King, cf	1	0	1	1
Bush, p	3	0	1	1	Snyder, c	4	0	1	0
					Nehf, p	1	0	0	0
Totals	28	3	5	3	Totals	30	5	10	5

											R	H	E
Yankees	1	0	0	0	1	0	1	0	0	—	3	5	0
Giants	0	2	0	0	0	0	0	3	x	—	5	10	0

DP —Yankees 3. LOB—Yankees 4, Giants 6. 2B—Frisch. S—Ruth, Schang, Kelly. SF—E. Scott.

Yankees	IP	H	R	ER	BB	SO
Bush (L, 0-2)	8	10	5	5	4	3

Giants	IP	H	R	ER	BB	SO
Nehf (W, 1-0)	9	5	3	3	2	3

HBP—By Nehf (Dugan). WP—Nehf. Umpires—Klem (N.L.), Hildebrand (A.L.), McCormick (N.L.), Owens (A.L.). Time—2:00. Attendance—38,551.

1923: NEW YORK YANKEES DEFEATED GIANTS 4 GAMES TO 2

Amazingly, the New York Giants and New York Yankees faced one another in postseason play for the third consecutive time in the 1923 World Series. Two things were different this time around, though. First, the Yankees had moved out of the Polo Grounds and across the Harlem River to the Bronx and brand-new Yankee Stadium (making this series the first Subway Series). Second, the Yankees, after losing to the Giants in both the 1921 (five games to three) and 1922 (four games to none with one tie) series, were victorious in 1923 by a count of four games to two. It marked the first world championship for the Yankees.

The Giants won their third straight National League title with a 95-58 record, 4½ games ahead of the Cincinnati Reds, while the Yankees did the same in the American League with a 98-54 record, a whopping 16 games better than the Detroit Tigers. Right fielder Babe Ruth again was baseball's biggest story as he led the A.L. with 41 homers (tying Cy Williams of the Philadelphia Phillies for top honors in the major leagues) and 131 RBI and ranked second with a .393 batting average. Ruth's "counterpart" from the Giants, left fielder Irish Meusel, paced the N.L. with 125 RBI and was fourth with 19 homers.

The Giants were led in the series by center fielder Casey Stengel, who batted at a .417 clip (5-for-12) with two home runs and four RBI. Right-hander Rosy Ryan was the team's most effective pitcher, appearing in three games in relief with a 1-0 record and 0.96 ERA (one earned run in 11.1 innings).

Interestingly, prior to the start of the series, the Giants played an exhibition game against the Baltimore Orioles of the International League on October 3 to raise money for former club owner John B. Day. Ruth agreed to play for the Giants—although his uniform did not fit—and hit a mammoth home run over the right field roof of the Polo Grounds. It proved to be an indication of things to come.

Winning Player's Share: $6,143
Losing Player's Share: $4,113

Game 1: at New York (Yankee Stadium)
Giants 5, Yankees 4

The Giants took the 1923 World Series opener by the score of 5-4 at Yankee Stadium with a run in the ninth inning. With two outs and a three-ball, two-strike count, center fielder Casey Stengel, playing with an injured leg, hit a ball between left fielder Bob Meusel and center fielder Whitey Witt. Running like a man possessed and losing one of his shoes en route, Stengel came all the way around to score on an inside the park homer.

It capped a nice comeback for the Giants, who trailed 3-0 after two innings as the Yankees knocked out right-hander Mule Watson. The Giants put together a four-run third inning to go ahead 4-3. Third baseman Heinie Groh provided the big blow with a triple that right fielder Babe Ruth let get past him and scored two runs.

The Yankees tied the game in the seventh with their only run against right-hander reliever Rosy Ryan, who worked the final seven innings and scattered eight hits with one walk and two strikeouts to pick up the win. That set up Stencil's heroic blast of Yankees' right-handed reliever Joe Bush.

Groh and Stengel both had two of the Giants' eight hits.

Game 2: at New York (Polo Grounds)
Yankees 4, Giants 2

After being injured for the final three games of the 1921 World Series and batting just .118 with one RBI in the 1922 World Series, Yankees' right fielder Babe Ruth was determined to have a better showing in the 1923 series.

He did in Game 2, clouting two home runs to lead the Yankees to a 4-2 victory at the Polo Grounds. Not only did the Yankees even the series at one game apiece, they snapped an eight-game losing streak to the Giants, dating to Game 6 of the 1921 series.

Ruth's first homer came in the top of the fourth inning off Giants' right-handed starter and loser Hugh McQuillan, went over the right field roof (like his blast in the exhibition game October 3) and broke a 1-apiece deadlock. His second shot came an inning later off right-hander reliever Jack Bentley. Ruth, who also hit a hard drive in the ninth that was tracked down in deep center field by Casey Stengel, became the fourth player in World Series history to blast two home runs in a game and the first to do so in successive at-bats.

Yankees' second baseman Aaron Ward and Giants' left fielder Irish Meusel traded second-inning solo home runs prior to Ruth's power surge. That Giants scored their other run in the sixth on an RBI single by right fielder Ross Youngs.

Left-hander Herb Pennock pitched a complete game for the Yankees, allowing nine hits with one walk and one strikeout.

Game 3: at New York (Yankee Stadium)
Giants 1, Yankees 0

During the 1923 regular season, Giants' reserve outfielder Casey Stengel hit a total of five home runs, which was slightly above his 14-year major league average. In Game 3 of the World Series, the future Hall of Fame manager socked his second round-tripper of the postseason for the only run in a 1-0 Giants' victory at Yankee Stadium. Thus, the Giants grabbed a two games to one lead in the series.

Stengel, who had won Game 1 with an inside-the-park homer in the ninth inning, hit this one outside the park with one out in the seventh inning.

It was all Giants' left-hander Art Nehf needed. He authored a masterful complete game, scattering six hits (five of them singles) with three walks and four strikeouts. Nehf, who threw 123 pitches, previously blanked the Yankees 1-0 in Game 8 of the 1921 World Series at the Polo Grounds.

The Yankees had a rally going in the fourth with runners on first and second. Left fielder Bob Meusel was told to bunt, but he ignored the instruction and hit into a double play on the first pitch from Nehf.

Yankees' right-hander Sad Sam Jones made only the one mistake to Stengel. He worked the first eight innings and gave up four hits with two walks and three strikeouts. Second baseman Frankie Frisch had two (or half) of the Giants' hits.

Third baseman Heinie Groh made several key defensive plays in back of Nehf.

Game 4: at New York (Polo Grounds) Yankees 8, Giants 4

The Yankees evened the series at two games apiece with an 8-4 victory in Game 4 at the Polo Grounds.

A six-run second inning did in Giants' right-hander Jack Scott and his teammates. Shortstop Everett Scott (two-run single) and left fielder Bob Meusel (two-run triple) provided the major blows. The Yankees went on to lead 8-0 after three and a half innings before the Giants scored three runs in the eighth and one in the ninth. But it was too little too late.

Both teams totaled 13 hits. Right fielder Ross Youngs carried the Giants' biggest bat, going 4-for-5 with an inside-the-park home run in the ninth inning.

Scott was torched for four runs (three earned) on four hits with one strikeout in one-plus inning. He was followed by five other pitchers. Yankees' right-hander Bob Shawkey earned the win, despite giving up three runs on 12 hits with four walks and two strikeouts in 7.2 innings.

Game 5: at New York (Yankee Stadium) Yankees 8, Giants 1

The Yankees continued their torrid hitting with 14 hits in an 8-1 win in Game 5 at the Polo Grounds that put them ahead three games to two in the series. They wasted no time getting started, scoring three runs in the first inning and four more in the second to send Giants' left-hander Jack Bentley to an early shower.

Third baseman Joe Dugan led the onslaught with a 4-for-5 performance and three RBI. He hit a three-run inside-the-park homer in the second inning that got past center fielder Casey Stengel. Left fielder Bob Meusel also drove in three runs.

Yankees' right-hander Joe Bush hardly needed such support. He pitched a nifty three-hitter with two walks and three strikeouts. Left fielder Irish Meusel was the only Giants' player to solve him with a triple in the second inning, a double in the fourth and a single in the seventh. He grounded out to second base in the ninth.

Game 6: at New York (Polo Grounds) Yankees 6, Giants 4

For seven innings of Game 6 of the 1923 World Series at the Polo Grounds, the homestanding Giants appeared headed to a victory that would force Game 7. They held a 4-1 lead, and left-hander Art Nehf was cruising along with a one-hitter (right fielder Babe Ruth's first-inning home run).

Then Nehf tired, and the Yankees awoke. With one out, two singles and a walk loaded the bases. Another walk forced in a run and knocked out Nehf. Right-hander reliever Rosy Ryan issued yet another walk to make it 4-3 before striking out Ruth. But left fielder Bob Meusel followed with a two-run single that gave the Yankees the lead, and they added an insurance run on a throwing error by center fielder Bill Cunningham.

With the lead and the momentum, Yankees' right-hander reliever Sad Sam Jones blanked the Giants on one hit over the final two innings to preserve the victory. Left-hander Herb Pennock was credited with the win after giving up four runs on nine hits with no walks and six strikeouts over seven innings.

Second baseman Frankie Frisch was 3-for-4 in a losing cause, and catcher Frank Snyder hit a home run in the fifth inning.

Afterwards, Giants' manager John McGraw said: "I'm going to shake hands with everybody connected with the Yankees from (owner) Colonel Ruppert down to the bat boy. My hat's off to them."

1923

Game 1 (Oct. 10)

Giants	AB	R	H	RBI	Yankees	AB	R	H	RBI
Bancroft, ss	4	1	1	1	Witt, cf	5	0	1	2
Groh, 3b	4	1	2	2	Dugan, 3b	4	0	1	1
Frisch, 2b	4	0	1	1	Ruth, rf	4	1	1	0
Youngs, rf	3	0	0	0	B. Meusel, lf	4	0	1	1
I. Meusel, lf	4	0	0	0	Pipp, 1b	4	0	2	0
Stengel, cf	3	1	2	1	Ward, 2b	4	1	2	0
Cunningham, cf	0	0	0	0	Schang, c	3	1	2	0
Kelly, 1b	4	1	1	0	E. Scott, ss	2	0	0	0
Gowdy, c	0	0	0	0	Hendrick, ph	1	0	0	0
Maguire, pr	0	1	0	0	Johnson, ss	0	0	0	0
Snyder, c	2	0	0	0	Hoyt, p	1	0	0	0
Watson, p	0	0	0	0	Bush, p	3	1	2	0
Bentley, ph	1	0	1	0					
Gearin, pr	0	0	0	0					
Ryan, p	2	0	0	0					
Totals	**31**	**5**	**8**	**5**	**Totals**	**35**	**4**	**12**	**4**

											R	H	E
Giants	0	0	4	0	0	0	0	0	1	—	5	8	0
Yankees	1	2	0	0	0	0	1	0	0	—	4	12	1

E—Schang. DP—Giants 2, Yankees 2. LOB—Giants 2, Yankees 7. 2B—B. Meusel, Schang, Bush. 3B—Groh, Dugan, Ruth. HR—Stengel. SB—Bancroft. S—E. Scott.

Giants	IP	H	R	ER	BB	SO
Watson	2	4	3	3	1	1
Ryan (W, 1-0)	7	8	1	1	1	2

Yankees	IP	H	R	ER	BB	SO
Hoyt	2.1	4	4	4	1	0
Bush (L, 0-1)	6.2	4	1	1	2	2

WP—Ryan. Umpires—Evans (A.L.), O'Day (N.L.), Nallin (A.L.), Hart (N.L.). Time—2:05. Attendance—55,307.

Game 2 (Oct. 11)

Yankees	AB	R	H	RBI	Giants	AB	R	H	RBI
Witt, cf	5	0	0	0	Bancroft, ss	4	0	0	0
Dugan, 3b	4	0	1	0	Groh, 3b	3	1	1	0
Ruth, rf	3	2	2	2	Frisch, 2b	4	0	2	0
B. Meusel, lf	4	0	1	0	Youngs, rf	4	0	2	1
Pipp, 1b	3	1	1	0	I. Meusel, lf	4	1	2	1
Ward, 2b	4	1	2	1	Cunningham, cf	3	0	0	0
Schang, c	4	0	1	0	Gowdy, ph	1	0	0	0
E. Scott, ss	4	0	2	1	Stengel, cf	0	0	0	0
Pennock, p	3	0	0	0	Kelly, 1b	4	0	1	0
					Snyder, c	4	0	0	0
					McQuillan, p	1	0	0	0
					Bentley, p	2	0	1	0
					Jackson, ph	1	0	0	0
Totals	**31**	**4**	**10**	**4**	**Totals**	**35**	**2**	**9**	**2**

											R	H	E
Yankees	0	1	0	2	1	0	0	0	0	—	4	10	0
Giants	0	1	0	0	0	1	0	0	0	—	2	9	2

E—Youngs 2. DP—Yankees 1, Giants 2. LOB—Yankees 8, Giants 7. 2B—Dugan, Bentley. HR—Ruth 2, Ward, I. Meusel.

Yankees	IP	H	R	ER	BB	SO
Pennock (W, 1-0)	9	9	2	2	1	1

Giants	IP	H	R	ER	BB	SO
McQuillan (L, 0-1)	3.2	5	3	3	2	1
Bentley	5.1	5	1	1	2	0

HBP—By Bentley (Pennock). Umpires—O'Day (N.L.), Nallin (A.L.), Hart (N.L.), Evans (A.L.). Time—2:08. Attendance—40,402.

Game 3 (Oct. 12)

Giants	AB	R	H	RBI		Yankees	AB	R	H	RBI
Bancroft, ss	3	0	0	0		Witt, cf	4	0	1	0
Groh, 3b	4	0	0	0		Dugan, 3b	4	0	1	0
Frisch, 2b	4	0	2	0		Ruth, rf-1b	2	0	1	0
Youngs, rf	4	0	0	0		B. Meusel, lf	4	0	0	0
I. Meusel, lf	4	0	0	0		Pipp, 1b	2	0	0	0
Stengel, cf	3	1	1	1		Haines, rf	1	0	0	0
Kelly, 1b	3	0	0	0		Ward, 2b	4	0	1	0
Snyder, c	3	0	0	0		Schang, c	4	0	1	0
Nehf, p	3	0	1	0		E. Scott, ss	3	0	1	0
						Jones, p	2	0	0	0
						Hofmann, ph	1	0	0	0
						Bush, p	0	0	0	0
Totals	31	1	4	1		Totals	31	0	6	0

										R	H	E
Giants	0	0	0	0	0	0	1	0	0	—	1	4	0
Yankees	0	0	0	0	0	0	0	0	0	—	0	6	1

E—E. Scott. DP—Giants 2, Yankees 1. LOB—Giants 5, Yankees 7. 2B—Dugan. HR—Stengel.

Giants	IP	H	R	ER	BB	SO
Nehf (W, 1-0)	9	6	0	0	3	4

Yankees	IP	H	R	ER	BB	SO
Jones (L, 0-1)	8	4	1	1	2	3
Bush	1	0	0	0	0	0

Umpires—Nallin (A.L.), Hart (N.L.), Evans (A.L.), O'Day (N.L.),. Time—2:05. Attendance—62,430.

Game 4 (Oct. 13)

Yankees	AB	R	H	RBI		Giants	AB	R	H	RBI
Witt, cf	4	0	3	2		Bancroft, ss	5	0	1	0
Dugan, 3b	5	1	0	0		Groh, 3b	3	0	0	0
Ruth, rf	3	2	1	0		Frisch, 2b	5	0	2	0
B. Meusel, lf	5	0	1	2		Youngs, rf	5	2	4	1
Pipp, 1b	4	1	2	0		I. Meusel, lf	5	1	1	0
Ward, 2b	4	2	2	1		Stengel, cf	2	1	2	1
Schang, c	3	1	1	0		Cunningham, cf	1	0	0	0
E. Scott, ss	5	1	2	2		Kelly, 1b	5	0	2	1
Shawkey, p	3	0	1	1		Snyder, c	4	0	0	1
Pennock, p	1	0	0	0		J. Scott, p	0	0	0	0
						Ryan, p	0	0	0	0
						McQuillan, p	2	0	0	0
						Bentley, ph	1	0	1	0
						Maguire, pr	0	0	0	0
						Jonnard, p	0	0	0	0
						O'Connell, ph	0	0	0	0
						J. Barnes, p	0	0	0	0
Totals	37	8	13	8		Totals	38	4	13	4

											R	H	E
Yankees	0	6	1	1	0	0	0	0	0	—	8	13	1
Giants	0	0	0	0	0	0	0	3	1	—	4	13	1

E—J. Scott, Ruth. DP—Yankees 2. LOB—Yankees 10, Giants 12. 2B—Witt 2, Ruth. 3B—B. Meusel. HR—Youngs. S—Witt, Schange 2. SF—Shawkey.

Yankees	IP	H	R	ER	BB	SO
Shawkey (W, 1-0)	7.2	12	3	3	4	2
Pennock (S, 1)	1.1	1	1	1	0	1

Giants	IP	H	R	ER	BB	SO
J. Scott (L, 0-1)	1	4	4	3	0	1
Ryan	0.2	2	2	0	1	0
McQuillan	5.1	6	2	2	2	2
Jonnard	1	1	0	0	1	0
J. Barnes	1	0	0	0	0	2

J. Scott pitched to four batters in the 2nd.

HBP—By Shawkey (O'Connell). Umpires—Hart (N.L.), Evans (A.L.), O'Day (N.L.), Nallin (A.L.). Time—2:32. Attendance— 46,302.

Game 5 (Oct. 14)

Giants	AB	R	H	RBI	Yankees	AB	R	H	RBI
Bancroft, ss	4	0	0	0	Witt, cf	4	1	1	0
Groh, 3b	4	0	0	0	Dugan, 3b	5	3	4	3
Frisch, 2b	4	0	0	0	Ruth, rf	4	2	1	0
Youngs, rf	3	0	0	0	B. Meusel, lf	5	1	3	3
I. Meusel, lf	4	1	3	0	Pipp, 1b	3	0	0	2
Stengel, cf	3	0	0	1	Ward, 2b	4	0	2	0
Kelly, 1b	2	0	0	0	Schang, c	4	0	1	0
Gowdy, c	3	0	0	0	E. Scott, ss	4	0	1	0
Bentley, p	0	0	0	0	Bush, p	4	1	1	0
J. Scott, p	1	0	0	0					
J. Barnes, p	1	0	0	0					
O'Connell, ph	1	0	0	0					
Jonnard, ph	0	0	0	0					
Totals	30	1	3	1	Totals	37	8	14	8

											R	H	E
Giants	0	1	0	0	0	0	0	0	0	—	1	3	2
Yankees	3	4	0	1	0	0	0	x	—			8	14	0

E—Frisch, Kelly. DP—Giants 1. LOB—Giants 4, Yankees 9. 2B—I. Meusel. 3B—I. Meusel, B. Meusel. HR—Dugan. SB—Ward. S—Pipp.

Giants	IP	H	R	ER	BB	SO
Bentley (L, 0-1)	1.1	5	7	6	2	1
J. Scott	2	5	1	1	1	1
J. Barnes	3.2	4	0	0	0	2
Jonnard	1	0	0	0	0	1

Yankees	IP	H	R	ER	BB	SO
Bush (W, 1-0)	9	3	1	1	2	3

Umpires—Evans (A.L.), O'Day (N.L.), Nallin (A.L.), Hart (N.L.). Time—1:55. Attendance—62,817.

Game 6 (Oct. 15)

Yankees	AB	R	H	RBI	Giants	AB	R	H	RBI
Witt, cf	3	0	0	0	Bancroft, ss	4	0	0	0
Bush, ph	0	0	0	1	Groh, 3b	4	1	1	0
Johnson, pr	0	1	0	0	Frisch, 2b	4	2	3	0
Jones, p	0	0	0	0	Youngs, rf	4	0	2	1
Dugan, 3b	3	1	0	1	I. Meusel, lf	4	0	1	1
Ruth, rf	3	1	1	1	Cunningham, cf	3	0	1	1
B. Meusel, lf	4	0	1	2	Stengel, ph-cf	1	0	0	0
Pipp, 1b	4	0	0	0	Kelly, 1b	4	0	0	0
Ward, 2b	4	0	1	0	Snyder, c	4	1	2	1
Schang, c	4	1	1	0	Nehf, p	3	0	0	0
E. Scott, ss	4	1	1	0	Ryan, p	0	0	0	0
Pennock, p	2	0	0	0	Bentley, ph	1	0	0	0
Hofmann, ph	0	0	0	0					
Haines, pr-cf	0	1	0	0					
Totals	31	6	5	5	Totals	36	4	10	4

										R	H	E
Yankees	1	0	0	0	0	0	0	5	0	—	6	5	0
Giants	1	0	0	1	1	1	0	0	0	—	4	10	1

E—Cunningham. DP—Giants 1. LOB—Yankees 2, Giants 5. 3B—Frisch. HR—Ruth, Snyder.

Yankees	IP	H	R	ER	BB	SO
Pennock (W, 2-0)	7	9	4	4	0	6
Jones (S, 1)	2	1	0	0	0	0

Giants	IP	H	R	ER	BB	SO
Nehf (L, 1-1)	7.1	4	5	5	3	3
Ryan	1.2	1	1	0	1	1

Umpires—O'Day (N.L.), Nallin (A.L.), Hart (N.L.), Evans (A.L.). Time—2:05. Attendance—34,172.

1924: WASHINGTON SENATORS DEFEATED GIANTS 4 GAMES TO 3

The 1924 New York Giants tied a major league record by winning their fourth consecutive National League pennant. Previously, the St. Louis Browns captured four straight American Association flags from 1885-88. The standard stood until the New York Yankees won five American League titles in a row from 1949-53 and again from 1960-64.

The Giants' 10th and final league championship under manager John McGraw came with a 93-60 record, 1½ games ahead of the Brooklyn Dodgers. It marked the slimmest margin of any crown in the McGraw era. Meanwhile, the Washington Senators, a charter member of the A.L. in 1901, won its first-ever title with a 92-62 record, two games better than the New York Yankees, who had won three pennants in a row from 1921-23.

Washington, under player-manager Bucky Harris, won the World Series four games to three with the help of Mother Earth in the seventh and deciding game. Two bad-hop grounders over Giants' rookie third baseman Fred Lindstrom helped the Senators tie the game in the eighth inning and win it in extra innings. At the age of 18, the "Boy Wonder" became the youngest player ever to appear in a World Series. Lindstrom and second baseman Frankie Frisch both batted .333 (10-for-30) to lead the Giants' offensive attack.

It was a tightly-played series, to say the least. Only one game was decided by more than three runs, and both the opening and final contests took 12 innings to decide.

Winning Player's Share: $5,970
Losing Player's Share: $3,820

Game 1: at Washington
(Griffith Stadium)
New York 4, Washington 3 (12 innings)

The Giants grabbed the early upper hand by claiming a 4-3, 12-inning victory in Game 1 of the 1924 World Series at Griffith Stadium in Washington.

Both starting pitchers went the distance, left-hander Art Nehf of New York and right-hander Walter Johnson of Washington. Nehf allowed three runs (two earned) on 10 hits with five walks and three strikeouts, while Johnson gave up four runs (three earned) on 14 hits with six walks and 12 strikeouts. Johnson, the "Big Train," was making his first postseason appearance in his 18th major league season.

With the score tied 2-apiece after 11 innings, the Giants scored twice in the top of the 12th. They loaded the bases with no outs and, after second baseman Frankie Frisch forced out catcher Hank Gowdy at the plate, right fielder Ross Youngs delivered a single that scored Nehf, who earlier had singled. Then center fielder George Kelly hit a sacrifice fly to left field to plate pinch-runner Billy Southworth. New York needed the insurance tally as Washington scored once in its half of the inning. Left fielder Goose Goslin, who led the American League with 129 RBI during the season, grounded out to third base to end the game with the tying run on third.

Kelly hit a home run into the left field bleachers in the second inning to put the Giants ahead 1-0, and first baseman Bill Terry made it 2-0 in the fourth with a round-tripper of his own to left. Terry finished with three hits, as did Nehf. The Senators scored single runs in the sixth and ninth to force extra innings.

President Calvin Coolidge and his wife were among the 35,760 spectators in attendance.

Game 2: at Washington
(Griffith Stadium)
Washington 4, New York 3

A ninth-inning rally wasn't enough for the Giants, as Washington pulled out a 4-3 victory in Game 2 at Griffith Stadium in Washington to even the series at one game apiece. New York trailed 3-1 heading into the final frame before scoring two runs. Center fielder Hack Wilson tied the game with a single to right field that plated first baseman George Kelly.

But Washington answered the uprising by tallying the winning run in the bottom of the ninth. First baseman Joe Judge walked, moved to second on a sacrifice by third baseman Ossie Bluege and scored on a double by shortstop Roger Peckinpaugh.

Senators' right-handed reliever Firpo Marberry, who came into the game in the ninth inning and struck out the only batter he faced (shortstop Travis Jackson), picked up the victory. Left-hander Tom Zachary worked the first 8.2 innings and surrendered three runs on six hits with three walks and no strikeouts.

Left-hander Jack Bentley of the Giants took the loss, allowing four runs on six hits with four walks and six strikeouts in 8.1 innings. He served up a two-run home run to second baseman-manager Bucky Harris in the first inning and a solo shot to left fielder Goose Goslin in the fifth.

Game 3: at New York (Polo Grounds)
New York 6, Washington 4

The Giants withstood a late charge by Washington to win Game 3 by the score of 6-4 at the Polo Grounds in New York and take a two games to one lead in the series.

Trailing 6-3 in the top of the ninth inning, the Senators loaded the bases with no outs and knocked out New York right-handed reliever Rosy Ryan. Right-hander Claude Jonnard came in, proceeded to walk shortstop Ossie Bluege to force in a run and was removed in favor of right-hander Mule Watson. The seemingly nervous Watson must have had ice water in his veins as he retired third baseman Ralph Miller and catcher Muddy Ruel on grounders to save the day.

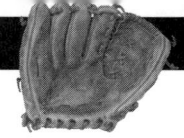

New York built a 2-0 lead in the second with the help of a botched double play and a wild pitch. It was 3-2 in favor of the Giants after three and a half innings when Ryan shocked everyone with a home run into the upper right field stands off right-handed reliever Allan Russell. The Giants tallied again in the sixth, and both teams scored in the eighth.

Despite working just 3.2 innings, New York right-handed starter Hugh McQuillan earned the victory. He gave up two runs on two hits with five walks and no strikeouts. Right-hander Firpo Marberry was the starter and loser for Washington.

Giants' catcher Hank Gowdy was 2-for-4 with two RBI.

Game 4: at New York (Polo Grounds)
Washington 7, New York 4

In Game 4 of the 1924 World Series, the Giants couldn't stop Washington left fielder Goose Goslin. They couldn't even contain him. Goslin went 4-for-4 with a home run and four RBI to lead the Senators to a 7-4 victory at the Polo Grounds in New York and even the series at two games apiece.

Goslin's biggest blow was a three-run homer in the top of the third inning that turned a 1-0 Washington deficit into a 3-1 lead. The Senators did not trail again, adding two runs in the fifth—one on an RBI single by Goslin—and two more in the eighth.

Meanwhile, New York couldn't break through Washington left-hander George Mogridge, who gave up three runs (two earned) on just three hits with five walks and two strikeouts in 7.1 innings. Right-hander Firpo Marberry finished up. The Giants scored single runs in the first, sixth, eighth and ninth. Third baseman Fred Lindstrom was 3-for-4.

Right-hander Virgil Barnes, the first of three Giants' pitchers, was saddled with the loss after giving up five runs on nine hits with three strikeouts in five innings.

Game 5: at New York (Polo Grounds)
New York 6, Washington 4

During the 1924 season, Washington right-hander Walter Johnson posted a 23-7 record with a 2.72 ERA. But the 36-year-old future Hall of Famer dropped to 0-2 in the World Series with a 6-4 setback to the Giants in Game 5 at the Polo Grounds in New York. With the victory, New York took a three games to two lead in the series.

Of the six runs Johnson allowed, only three were earned, but the Giants roughed him up for 13 hits to go with two walks and three strikeouts. Third baseman Fred Lindstrom led the onslaught with a 4-for-5 performance and two RBI.

New York broke a 1-apiece tie in the fifth inning when right-handed pitcher Jack Bentley socked a two-run homer into the right field stands. The Senators trimmed the deficit to 3-2 on left fielder Goose Goslin's home run in the eighth, but the Giants struck back with three runs in their half of the inning.

Bentley worked the first 7.1 innings, surrendering two runs on nine hits with three walks and four strikeouts, to earn the win. Right-hander Hugh McQuillan blanked the Senators the rest of the way.

Game 6: at Washington
(Griffith Stadium)
Washington 2, New York 1

Right-hander Tom Zachary pitched a nifty seven-hitter to lead the Senators to a 2-1 win in Game 6 at Griffith Stadium in Washington and even the series at three games apiece. Zachary walked none and struck out three.

Second baseman-manager Bucky Harris provided all the offense Zachary and the Senators needed with a fifth-inning two-run double that scored shortstop Roger Peckinpaugh and center fielder Earl McNeely.

New York left-hander Art Nehf was solid in defeat, giving up two runs on merely four hits (all singles) with four walks and four strikeouts.

First baseman George Kelly had an RBI single in the first inning to plate right fielder Ross Youngs with the Giants' lone run.

Game 7: at Washington
(Griffith Stadium)
Washington 4, New York 3 (12 innings)

The seventh and deciding game of the 1924 World Series was played at Griffith Stadium in Washington, and the Senators clearly took advantage of the home-field advantage. Washington won 4-3 in 12 innings to claim its first world championship.

A bad hop on a routine ground ball to Giants' third baseman Fred Lindstrom enabled the Senators to tie the game at 3-apiece in the bottom of the eighth inning, and another tough hop got past Lindstrom and allowed the winning run to cross the plate in the 12th.

New York scored three runs in the top of the sixth inning to take a 3-1 advantage. In the eighth, with the bases loaded and two outs, Washington manager-second baseman Bucky Harris hit a grounder that hopped over Lindstrom's head to score pinch-hitter Nemo Leibold and catcher Muddy Ruel and tie the game.

Then with one out in the 12th, Ruel doubled with one out after New York catcher Hank Gowdy tripped over his own mask attempting to catch a foul pop. An ensuing error by shortstop Travis Jackson on a grounder by right-handed reliever Walter Johnson put runners on first and second. The two miscues set the stage for center fielder Earl McNeely's hard grounder that skipped over Lindstrom's head and scored Ruel with the game- and series-winning run.

Johnson, 0-2 as a starter in the series, picked up the win after pitching four shutout innings of relief. The fourth Washington pitcher of the day allowed three hits with three walks and five strikeouts. Left-hander Jack Bentley, the Giants' fourth pitcher, was the tough-luck loser, giving up one run on three hits with one walk in 1.1 innings.

Washington started right-hander Curly Ogden to face right-handed batters Lindstrom and second baseman Frankie Frisch. After striking our Lindstrom and walking Frisch, Ogden was replaced by the intended starter, left-hander George Mogridge.

1924

Game 1 (Oct. 4)

New York	AB	R	H	RBI	Washington	AB	R	H	RBI
Lindstrom, 3b	5	0	0	0	McNeely, cf	5	1	1	0
Bentley, ph	0	0	0	0	Harris, 2b	6	0	2	1
Southworth, pr-cf	0	1	0	0	Rice, rf	5	0	2	1
Frisch, 2b-3b	5	0	2	0	Goslin, lf	6	0	1	0
Youngs, rf	6	0	2	1	Judge, 1b	4	0	1	0
Kelly, cf-2b	5	1	1	2	Bluege, 3b	5	1	1	0
Terry, 1b	5	1	3	1	Peckinpaugh, ss	5	0	2	1
Wilson, lf	6	0	2	0	Ruel, c	3	0	0	0
Jackson, ss	3	0	0	0	Johnson, p	4	0	0	0
Gowdy, c	3	0	1	0	Shirley, ph	1	1	0	0
Nehf, p	5	1	3	0					
Totals	43	4	14	4	Totals	44	3	10	3

														R	H	E
New York	0	1	0	1	0	0	0	0	0	0	0	2	—	4	14	1
Washington	0	0	0	0	0	1	0	0	1	0	0	1	—	3	10	1

E—McNeely, Jackson. DP—New York 1, Washington 2. LOB—New York 11, Washington 10. 2B—Frisch, Youngs, McNeely, Peckinpaugh. HR—Kelly, Terry. SB—Frisch, Rice, Peckinpaugh. S—Jackson. SF—Kelly.

New York	IP	H	R	ER	BB	SO
Nehf (W, 1-0)	12	10	3	2	5	3

Washington	IP	H	R	ER	BB	SO
Johnson (L, 0-1)	12	14	4	3	6	12

WP—Johnson. Umpires—Connolly (A.L.), Klem (N.L.), Dinneen (A.L.), Quigley (N.L.). Time—3:07. Attendance—35,760.

Game 2 (Oct. 5)

New York	AB	R	H	RBI	Washington	AB	R	H	RBI
Lindstrom, 3b	3	0	1	0	McNeely, cf	4	0	0	0
Frisch, 2b	3	1	1	0	Harris, 2b	3	1	1	1
Youngs, rf	4	0	1	0	Rice, rf	3	1	2	0
Kelly, 1b	3	2	1	1	Goslin, lf	4	1	1	2
Meusel, lf	4	0	1	0	Judge, 1b	2	1	1	0
Wilson, cf	4	0	1	1	Bluege, 3b	3	0	0	0
Jackson, ss	4	0	0	0	Peckinpaugh, ss	4	0	1	1
Gowdy, c	3	0	0	0	Ruel, c	3	0	0	0
Bentley, p	3	0	0	0	Zachary, p	2	0	0	0
					Marberry, p	0	0	0	0
Totals	31	3	6	2	Totals	28	4	6	4

										R	H	E
New York	0	0	0	0	0	0	1	0	2	—	3	6	0
Washington	2	0	0	0	1	0	0	0	1	—	4	6	1

One out when winning run scored.

E—Harris. DP—Washington 3. LOB—New York 4, Washington 5. 2B—Peckinpaugh. HR—Harris, Goslin. SB—Rice. S—Rice, Bluege.

New York	IP	H	R	ER	BB	SO
Bentley (L, 0-1)	8.1	6	4	4	4	6

Washington	IP	H	R	ER	BB	SO
Zachary	8.2	6	3	3	3	0
Marberry (W, 1-0)	0.1	0	0	0	0	1

Umpires—Klem (N.L.), Dinneen (A.L.), Quigley (N.L.), Connolly (A.L.). Time—1:58. Attendance—35,922.

Game 3 (Oct. 6)

Washington	AB	R	H	RBI
Leibold, cf	4	0	0	0
Harris, 2b	5	1	1	0
Rice, rf	3	1	1	0
Goslin, lf	5	0	1	0
Judge, 1b	5	1	3	0
Bluege, 3b-ss	3	1	1	0
Peckinpaugh, ss	1	0	0	0
Miller, 3b	2	0	1	1
Ruel, c	3	0	0	0
Marberry, p	1	0	0	0
Tate, ph	0	0	0	1
Russell, p	0	0	0	0
McNeely, ph	1	0	0	0
Martina, p	0	0	0	0
Shirley, ph	1	0	1	1
Speece, p	0	0	0	0
Totals	**34**	**4**	**9**	**3**

New York	AB	R	H	RBI
Lindstrom, 3b	4	0	1	1
Frisch, 2b	4	0	2	0
Youngs, rf	4	0	1	0
Kelly, cf	4	1	2	0
Southworth, cf	0	0	0	0
Terry, 1b	4	1	2	0
Wilson, lf	4	0	0	0
Jackson, ss	4	2	1	0
Gowdy, c	4	1	2	2
McQuillan, p	0	0	0	0
Ryan, p	2	1	1	1
Jonnard, p	0	0	0	0
Watson, p	0	0	0	0
Totals	**34**	**6**	**12**	**4**

											R	H	E
Washington	0	0	0	2	0	0	0	1	1	—	4	9	2
New York	0	2	1	1	0	1	0	1	x	—	6	12	0

E—Miller, Harris. DP—Washington 1, New York 1. LOB—Washington 13, New York 8. 2B—Judge, Linstrom. HR—Ryan. SB—Jackson. S—Ryan. SF—Miller.

Washington	IP	H	R	ER	BB	SO
Marberry (L, 1-1)	3	5	3	1	2	4
Russell	3	4	2	1	0	0
Martina	1	0	0	0	0	1
Speece	1	3	1	1	0	0

New York	IP	H	R	ER	BB	SO
McQuillan (W, 1-0)	3.2	2	2	2	5	0
Ryan	4.2	7	2	2	3	2
Jonnard	0	0	0	0	1	0
Watson (S, 1)	0.2	0	0	0	0	0

Jonnard pitched to one batter in the 9th.

HBP—By Marberry (Frisch). WP—Marberry. Umpires—Dinneen (A.L.), Quigley (N.L.), Connolly (A.L.), Klem (N.L.). Time—2:25. Attendance—47,608.

Game 4 (Oct. 7)

Washington	AB	R	H	RBI
McNeely, cf	5	2	3	0
Harris, 2b	5	2	2	0
Rice, rf	5	0	0	0
Goslin, lf	4	2	4	4
Judge, 1b	4	1	1	0
Bluege, ss	4	0	3	2
Ruel, c	3	0	0	0
Miller, 3b	4	0	0	0
Mogridge, p	4	0	0	0
Marberry, p	0	0	0	0
Totals	**38**	**7**	**13**	**6**

New York	AB	R	H	RBI
Lindstrom, 3b	4	1	3	1
Frisch, 2b	4	0	0	0
Youngs, rf	4	1	0	0
Kelly, 1b	5	1	1	0
Meusel, lf	2	0	0	0
Wilson, cf	4	0	1	2
Jackson, ss	4	0	0	0
Gowdy, c	4	1	1	0
Barnes, p	0	0	0	0
Terry, ph	1	0	0	0
Baldwin, p	0	0	0	0
Southworth, ph	1	0	0	0
Dean, p	0	0	0	0
Dean, p	0	0	0	0
Bentley, ph	1	0	0	0
Totals	**34**	**4**	**6**	**3**

											R	H	E
Washington	0	0	3	0	2	0	0	2	0	—	7	13	3
New York	1	0	0	0	0	1	0	1	1	—	4	6	1

E—Bluege, Miller, Rice, Meusel. LOB—Washington 5, New York 9. 2B—McNeely, Kelly, Wilson. HR—Goslin. S—Ruel.

Washington	IP	H	R	ER	BB	SO
Mogridge (W, 1-0)	7.1	3	3	2	5	2
Marberry (S, 1)	1.2	3	1	0	1	2

New York	IP	H	R	ER	BB	SO
Barnes (L, 0-1)	5	9	5	5	0	3
Baldwin	2	1	0	0	0	1
Dean	2	3	2	1	0	2

WP—Barnes. Umpires—Quigley (N.L.), Connolly (A.L.), Klem (N.L.), Dinneen (A.L.). Time—2:10. Attendance—49,243.

Game 5 (Oct. 8)

Washington	AB	R	H	RBI	New York	AB	R	H	RBI
McNeely, cf	4	0	1	0	Lindstrom, 3b	5	0	4	2
Harris, 2b	5	0	1	0	Frisch, 2b	5	0	1	0
Rice, rf	4	0	0	0	Youngs, rf	3	0	1	0
Goslin, lf	4	1	2	1	Kelly, cf	4	1	1	0
Judge, 1b	4	1	3	0	Terry, 1b	2	1	1	0
Bluege, ss	3	0	0	0	Wilson, lf	3	0	0	0
Ruel, c	2	0	0	0	Jackson, ss	3	1	1	1
Miller, 3b	3	0	1	1	Gowdy, c	4	2	1	0
Liebold, ph	1	0	0	0	Bentley, p	3	1	2	2
Johnson, p	3	0	1	0	McQuillan, p	1	0	1	1
Tate, ph	0	0	0	0					
Taylor, pr	0	0	0	0					
Totals	33	2	9	2	Totals	33	6	13	6

										R	H	E
Washington	0	0	0	1	0	0	0	1	0	—	2	9	1
New York	0	0	1	0	2	0	0	3	x	—	6	13	0

E—Johnson. DP—Washington 2. LOB—Washington 9, New York 8. 2B—Frisch. 3B—Terry. HR—Goslin, Bentley. S—Bluege, Wilson. SF—Jackson.

Washington	IP	H	R	ER	BB	SO
Johnson (L, 0-2)	8	13	6	3	2	3

New York	IP	H	R	ER	BB	SO
Bentley (W, 1-1)	7.1	9	2	2	3	4
McQuillan (S, 1)	1.2	0	0	0	1	1

HBP—By Johnson (Youngs). Umpires—Connolly (A.L.), Klem (N.L.), Dinneen (A.L.), Quigley (N.L.). Time—2:30. Attendance—49,271.

Game 6 (Oct. 9)

New York	AB	R	H	RBI	Washington	AB	R	H	RBI
Lindstrom, 3b	4	0	0	0	McNeely, cf	2	1	0	0
Frisch, 2b	4	0	2	0	Harris, 2b	4	0	1	2
Youngs, rf	4	1	0	0	Rice, rf	4	0	1	0
Kelly, 1b	4	0	2	1	Goslin, lf	4	0	0	0
Southworth, pr	0	0	0	0	Judge, 1b	3	0	0	0
Meusel, lf	4	0	0	0	Bluege, 3b-ss	3	0	0	0
Wilson, cf	4	0	2	0	Peckinpaugh, ss	2	1	2	0
Jackson, ss	3	0	0	0	Taylor, 3b	0	0	0	0
Gowdy, c	3	0	1	0	Ruel, c	2	0	0	0
Nehf, p	2	0	0	0	Zachary, p	3	0	0	0
Snyder, ph	1	0	0	0					
Ryan, p	0	0	0	0					
Totals	33	1	7	1	Totals	27	2	4	2

											R	H	E
New York	1	0	0	0	0	0	0	0	0	—	1	7	1
Washington	0	0	0	0	2	0	0	0	x	—	2	4	0

E—Kelly. DP—Washington 1. LOB—New York 5, Washington 7. 2B—Frisch. SB—McNeely, Bluege. S—Ruel.

New York	IP	H	R	ER	BB	SO
Nehf (L, 1-1)	7	4	2	2	4	4
Ryan	1	0	0	0	1	1

Washington	IP	H	R	ER	BB	SO
Zachary (W, 1-0)	9	7	1	1	0	3

Umpires—Klem (N.L.), Dinneen (A.L.), Quigley (N.L.), Connolly (A.L.). Time—1:57. Attendance—34,254.

Game 7 (Oct. 10)

New York	AB	R	H	RBI	Washington	AB	R	H	RBI
Lindstrom, 3b	5	0	1	0	McNeely, cf	6	0	1	1
Frisch, 2b	5	0	2	0	Harris, 2b	5	1	3	3
Youngs, rf-lf-rf	2	1	0	0	Rice, rf	5	0	0	0
Kelly, cf-1b	6	1	1	0	Goslin, lf	5	0	2	0
Terry, 1b	2	0	0	0	Judge, 1b	4	0	1	0
Meusel, ph-lf-rf-lf	3	0	1	1	Bluege, ss	5	0	0	0
Wilson, lf-cf	5	1	1	0	Taylor, 3b	2	0	0	0
Jackson, ss	6	0	0	0	Leibold, ph	1	1	1	0
Gowdy, c	6	0	1	0	Miller, 3b	2	0	0	0
Barnes, p	4	0	0	0	Ruel, c	5	2	2	0
Nehf, p	0	0	0	0	Ogden, p	0	0	0	0
McQuillan, p	0	0	0	0	Mogridge, p	1	0	0	0
Groh, ph	1	0	1	0	Marberry, p	1	0	0	0
Southworth, pr	0	0	0	0	Tate, ph	0	0	0	0
Bentley, p	0	0	0	0	Shirley, pr	0	0	0	0
					Johnson, p	2	0	0	0
Totals	45	3	8	1	Totals	44	4	10	4

												R	H	E
New York	0	0	0	0	3	0	0	0	0	0	0	—	3	8	3
Washington	0	0	0	1	0	0	0	2	0	0	1	—	4	10	4

E—Taylor, Jackson 2, Bluege 2. Judge, Gowdy. DP—New York 2, Washington 1. LOB—New York 14, Washington 8. 2B—Lindstrom, McNeely, Harris 2, Goslin, Judge, Ruel, Leibold. 3B—Frisch. HR—Harris. SB—Youngs. S—Lindstrom. SF—Meusel.

New York	IP	H	R	ER	BB	SO
Barnes	7.2	6	3	3	1	6
Nehf	0.2	1	0	0	0	0
McQuillan	1.2	0	0	0	0	1
Bentley (L, 1-2)	1.1	3	1	1	1	0
Washington	IP	H	R	ER	BB	SO
Ogden	0.1	0	0	0	1	1
Mogridge	4.2	4	2	1	1	3
Marberry	3	1	1	0	1	3
Johnson (W, 1-2)	4	3	0	0	3	5

Mogridge pitched to two batters in the 6th.

Umpires—Dinneen (A.L.), Quigley (N.L.), Connolly (A.L.), Klem (N.L.). Time—3:00. Attendance—31,667.

1933: GIANTS DEFEATED WASHINGTON SENATORS 4 GAMES TO 1

New York was picked to finish sixth in the National League by the Associated Press in 1933. But on June 10 the Giants took over first place for good, winning the pennant with a 91-61 record, five games ahead of the Pittsburgh Pirates. The Washington Senators, under the direction of player-manager Joe Cronin, took the American League flag with a 99-53 record, seven games better than the New York Yankees.

The Giants, in their first full season under player-manager Bill Terry, got revenge for their 1924 World Series loss to Washington by winning this one four games to one. Left-handed pitcher Carl Hubbell, who won the 1933 N.L. Most Valuable Player, continued his quality work in postseason play, going 2-0 and not allowing an earned run in 20 innings. He gave up 13 hits with six walks and 15 strikeouts. Right fielder Mel Ott anchored the offense with a .389 batting average (7-for-18), two home runs and four RBI.

Winning Player's Share: $4,257
Losing Player's Share: $3,010

Game 1: at New York (Polo Grounds) New York 4, Washington 2

Left-hander Carl Hubbell pitched a snappy five-hitter and right fielder Mel Ott went 4-for-4 with three RBI to lead the Giants to a series-opening 4-2 win over Washington at the Polo Grounds in New York.

The Senators managed merely five singles and two unearned runs against Hubbell, who walked two and struck out 10. Meanwhile, Ott got New York going with a two-run homer into the right field stands in the bottom of the first inning off Washington left-handed starter and loser Lefty Stewart. Ott made it 3-0 in favor of the Giants with an RBI single in the third that sent Stewart to an early shower.

New York banged out 10 hits (nine singles) against three Washington pitchers. The Senators scored single unearned runs in the four and ninth innings.

Game 2: at New York (Polo Grounds) New York 6, Washington 1

During the 1933 season, left-hander Carl Hubbell clearly was the Giants' ace with a 23-12 record and a 1.66 ERA en route to winning the National League Most Valuable Player Award. But right-hander Hal Schumacher was nearly as effective and provided New York with a stellar 1-2 punch, going 19-12 with a 2.16 ERA. The duo ranked first and third in ERA and first and fifth in wins in the league, respectively.

It was more of the same in the World Series. After Hubbell overwhelmed the Senators 4-2 in Game 1, Schumacher stopped them 6-1 in Game 2 at the Polo Grounds in New York. Schumacher limited Washington to five hits (four singles and right fielder Goose Goslin's third-inning home run) with four walks and two strikeouts.

Washington right-hander General Crowder kept the Giants off the scoreboard for five innings before they used a six-run uprising in the sixth to determine the game's outcome. With the bases loaded and one out, pinch-hitter Lefty O'Doul, who led the N.L. with a .368 batting average one year previously as a member of the Brooklyn Dodgers, lined a 1-2 pitch into center field to score second baseman Hughie Critz and first baseman-manager Bill Terry. It was O'Doul's only appearance in the series, and years later he admitted he stepped across the plate while swinging at the pitch and should have been called out.

The Giants tacked on four additional runs on RBI singles by third baseman Travis Jackson, catcher Gus Mancuso (a bunt), Schumacher and left fielder Joe Moore.

Game 3: at Washington
(Griffith Stadium)
Washington 4, New York 0

Perhaps inspired by president Franklin D. Roosevelt throwing out the first pitch, Washington left-hander Earl Whitehill authored a six-hit shutout as the Senators defeated the Giants by the score of 4-0 in Game 3 at Griffith Stadium in Washington and cut their series deficit to two games to one. Whitehill, who had gone 22-8 with a 3.33 ERA during the season, surrendered five singles and a double to go with two walks and two strikeouts.

The Senators scored two runs in the first inning, one in the second and one in the seventh to make a loser out of New York right-hander Freddie Fitzsimmons, who gave up nine hits and no walks with two strikeouts in seven innings. Washington second baseman Buddy Myer was 3-for-4 with a double and two RBI.

No New York batter managed more than one hit.

Game 4: at Washington
(Griffith Stadium)
New York 2, Washington 1 (11 innings)

Shortstop Blondy Ryan was the hero, driving in the winning run in the top of the 11th in-

ning for a 2-1 New York victory in Game 4 at Griffith Stadium in Washington. The victory gave the Giants a commanding three games to one lead in the series.

Third baseman Travis Jackson opened the decisive inning with a nifty bunt single along the third base line and moved to second on a sacrifice by catcher Gus Mancuso. Then Ryan, a .238 batter during the season, singled off Washington right-handed starter and loser Montie Weaver to plate Jackson.

Meanwhile, New York left-hander Carl Hubbell worked all 11 innings, allowing eight hits (all singles) with four walks and five strikeouts. The Senators loaded the bases with one out in their half of the 11th, but pinch-hitter Cliff Bolton grounded into a game-ending double play from Ryan to second baseman Hughie Critz to first baseman Bill Terry.

Terry gave the Giants a 1-0 lead in the fourth with a home run into the center field bleachers, and the Senators tied it with an unearned run in the seventh.

Game 5: at Washington
(Griffith Stadium)
New York 4, Washington 3 (10 innings)

Giants' right fielder Mel Ott socked a two-out home run in the 10th inning for a 4-3 win in Game 5 and a four games to one World Series championship.

New York held a 3-0 advantage through five and a half innings, highlighted by right-handed starting pitcher Hal Schumacher's two-run single in the second that scored third baseman Travis Jackson and catcher Gus Mancuso. In the sixth, Mancuso doubled home center fielder Kiddo Davis.

Appearing down and out, Washington was given a breath of life on center fielder Fred Schulte's three-run homer in the sixth. Later in the inning, Schumacher was replaced by 42-year-old right-hander Dolf Luque, who held the Senators to two hits and two walks with five strikeouts over the final 4.1 inning to earn the victory.

Ott's homer off Washington right-handed

reliever Jack Russell deflected off the glove of Schulte before landing in the temporary center field bleachers. The Senators put two runners on base in the bottom of the 10th, but Luque struck out first baseman Joe Kuhel on three pitches to end the game and the series.

1933

Game 1 (Oct. 3)

Washington	AB	R	H	RBI	New York	AB	R	H	RBI
Myer, 2b	4	1	1	0	Moore, lf	4	1	0	0
Goslin, rf	4	0	0	0	Critz, 2b	4	1	1	0
Manush, lf	4	1	0	0	Terry, 1b	4	1	1	0
Cronin, ss	4	0	2	1	Ott, rf	4	1	4	3
Schulte, cf	4	0	2	0	Davis, cf	4	0	2	0
Kuhel, 1b	4	0	0	1	Jackson, 3b	4	0	0	1
Bluege, 3b	4	0	0	0	Mancuso, c	4	0	0	0
Sewell, c	3	0	0	0	Ryan, ss	4	0	1	0
Stewart, p	1	0	0	0	Hubbell, p	3	0	1	0
Russell, p	1	0	0	0					
Harris, ph	0	0	0	0					
Thomas, p	0	0	0	0					
Totals	33	2	5	2	**Totals**	35	4	10	4

												R	H	E
Washington	0	0	0	1	0	0	0	0	1	—		2	5	3
New York	2	0	2	0	0	0	0	0	x	—		4	10	2

E—Ryan, Myer 3, Critz. DP—New York 1. LOB—Washington 6, New York 7. HR—Ott.

Washington	IP	H	R	ER	BB	SO
Stewart (L, 0-1)	2	6	4	2	0	0
Russell	5	4	0	0	0	3
Thomas	1	0	0	0	0	2
New York	**IP**	**H**	**R**	**ER**	**BB**	**SO**
Hubbell (W, 1-0)	9	5	2	0	2	10

Stewart pitched to three batters in the 3rd.

Umpires—Moran (N.L.), Moriarty (A.L.), Pfirman (N.L.), Ormsby (A.L.). Time—2:07. Attendance—46,672.

Game 2 (Oct. 4)

Washington	AB	R	H	RBI	New York	AB	R	H	RBI
Myer, 2b	3	0	0	0	Moore, lf	4	0	2	1
Goslin, rf	4	1	2	1	Critz, 2b	3	1	1	0
Manush, lf	3	0	1	0	Terry, 1b	4	1	1	0
Cronin, ss	4	0	0	0	Ott, rf	2	1	0	0
Schulte, cf	4	0	0	0	Davis, cf	2	0	1	0
Kuhel, 1b	3	0	0	0	O'Doul, ph	1	1	1	2
Bluege, 3b	2	0	0	0	Peel, cf	1	0	0	0
Harris, ph	1	0	0	0	Jackson, 3b	3	1	1	1
Sewell, c	3	0	0	0	Mancuso, c	4	1	1	1
Bolton, ph	1	0	0	0	Ryan, ss	4	0	1	0
Crowder, p	2	0	1	0	Schumacher, p	4	0	1	1
Thomas, p	0	0	0	0					
Rice, ph	1	0	1	0					
McColl, p	0	0	0	0					
Totals	31	1	5	1	**Totals**	32	6	10	6

										R	H	E
Washington	0	0	1	0	0	0	0	0	0	—	1	5	0
New York	0	0	0	0	0	6	0	0	x	—	6	10	0

DP—Washington 1, New York 1. LOB—Washington 7, New York 6. 2B—Terry. HR—Goslin. S—Jackson.

Washington	IP	H	R	ER	BB	SO
Crowder (L, 0-1)	5.2	9	6	6	3	3
Thomas	0.1	1	0	0	0	0
McColl	2	0	0	0	0	0

New York	IP	H	R	ER	BB	SO
Schumacher (W, 1-0)	9	5	1	1	4	2

WP—Schumacher. Umpires—Moriarty (A.L.), Pfirman (N.L.), Ormsby (A.L.), Moran (N.L.). Time—2:09. Attendance—35,461.

Game 3 (Oct. 5)

New York	AB	R	H	RBI	Washington	AB	R	H	RBI
Moore, lf	4	0	0	0	Myer, 2b	4	1	3	2
Critz, 2b	4	0	1	0	Goslin, rf	4	1	1	0
Terry, 1b	4	0	0	0	Manush, lf	4	0	0	0
Ott, rf	3	0	0	0	Cronin, ss	4	0	1	1
Davis, cf	4	0	1	0	Schulte, cf	4	0	2	1
Jackson, 3b	3	0	1	0	Kuhel, 1b	3	0	0	0
Mancuso, c	4	0	0	0	Bluege, 3b	3	1	1	0
Ryan, ss	3	0	0	0	Sewell, c	3	1	1	0
Fitzsimmons, p	2	0	1	0	Whitehill, p	3	0	0	0
Peel, ph	1	0	1	0					
Bell, p	0	0	0	0					
Totals	32	0	5	0	Totals	32	4	9	4

										R	H	E
New York	0	0	0	0	0	0	0	0	0	—	0	5	0
Washington	2	1	0	0	0	0	1	0	x	—	4	9	1

E—Cronin. DP—New York 1, Washington 1. LOB—New York 7, Washington 4. 2B—Jackson, Myer, Goslin, Schulte, Bluege. SB—Sewell.

New York	IP	H	R	ER	BB	SO
Fitzsimmons (L, 0-1)	7	9	4	4	0	2
Bell	1	0	0	0	0	0

Washington	IP	H	R	ER	BB	SO
Whitehill (W, 1-0)	9	5	0	0	2	2

WP—Whitehill. Umpires—Pfirman (N.L.), Ormsby (A.L.), Moran (N.L.), Moriarty (A.L.). Time—1:55. Attendance—25,727.

Game 4 (Oct. 6)

New York	AB	R	H	RBI	Washington	AB	R	H	RBI
Moore, lf	5	0	2	0	Myer, 2b	4	0	2	0
Critz, 2b	6	0	0	0	Goslin, rf-lf	4	0	1	0
Terry, 1b	5	1	2	0	Manush, lf	2	0	0	0
Ott, rf	4	0	2	0	Harris, rf	1	0	0	0
Davis, cf	4	0	1	0	Cronin, ss	5	0	1	0
Jackson, 3b	5	1	1	0	Schulte, cf	5	0	1	0
Mancuso, c	2	0	0	0	Kuhel, 1b	5	1	1	0
Ryan, ss	5	0	2	0	Bluege, 3b	3	0	0	2
Hubbell, p	4	0	1	0	Sewell, c	4	0	2	1
					Weaver, p	4	0	0	0
					Russell, p	0	0	0	0
					Bolton, ph	1	0	0	0
Totals	40	2	11	2	Totals	38	1	8	1

														R	H	E
New York	0	0	0	1	0	0	0	0	0	0	0	1	—	2	11	1
Washington	0	0	0	0	0	0	1	0	0	0	0	0	—	1	8	0

E—Hubbell. DP—Washington 1. LOB—New York 12, Washington 11. 2B—Moore. HR—Terry. S—Davis, Mancuso, Hubbell, Goslin, Bluege 2.

New York	IP	H	R	ER	BB	SO
Hubbell (W, 2-0)	11	8	1	0	4	5

Washington	IP	H	R	ER	BB	SO
Weaver (L, 0-1)	10	11	2	2	4	3
Russell	0.2	0	0	0	0	1

Umpires—Ormsby (A.L.), Moran (N.L.), Moriarty (A.L.), Pfirman (N.L.). Time—2:59. Attendance—26,762.

Game 5 (Oct. 7)

New York	AB	R	H	RBI	Washington	AB	R	H	RBI
Moore, lf	5	0	1	0	Myer, 2b	5	0	0	0
Critz, 2b	5	0	0	0	Goslin, rf	4	0	1	0
Terry, 1b	5	0	2	0	Manush, lf	5	1	1	0
Ott, rf	5	1	1	1	Cronin, ss	5	1	3	0
Davis, cf	5	1	2	0	Schulte, cf	4	1	2	3
Jackson, 3b	3	1	1	0	Kerr, pr	0	0	0	0
Mancuso, c	3	1	1	1	Kuhel, 1b	5	0	2	0
Ryan, ss	2	0	1	0	Bluege, 3b	4	0	1	0
Schumacher, p	3	0	1	2	Sewell, c	4	0	0	0
Luque, p	1	0	1	0	Crowder, p	2	0	0	0
					Russell, p	1	0	0	0
Totals	37	4	11	4	Totals	39	3	10	3

										R	H	E
New York	0	2	0	0	0	1	0	0	0	1	—	4	11	1
Washington	0	0	0	0	0	3	0	0	0	0	—	3	10	0

E—Jackson. DP—New York 1, Washington 1. LOB—New York 7, Washington 9. 2B—Davis, Mancuso. HR—Ott, Schulte. S—Jackson, Ryan.

New York	IP	H	R	ER	BB	SO
Schumacher	5.2	8	3	3	1	1
Luque (W, 1-0)	4.1	2	0	0	2	5

Washington	IP	H	R	ER	BB	SO
Crowder	5.1	7	3	3	2	4
Russell (L, 0-1)	4.2	4	1	1	0	3

WP—Crowder, Schumacher. Umpires—Moran (N.L.), Moriarty (A.L.), Pfirman (N.L.), Ormsby (A.L.). Time—2:38. Attendance—28,454.

1936: NEW YORK YANKEES DEFEATED GIANTS 4 GAMES TO 2

The New York Giants and the cross-town rival Yankees renewed old acquaintances in the 1936 World Series, and the Yankees captured the Battle of Broadway four games to two. Clearly, manager Joe McCarty's Yankees were the class of baseball after winning the American League pennant with a 102-51 record, a whopping 19½ games better than the Detroit Tigers. No fewer than five players collected at least 100 RBI: first baseman Lou Gehrig (152), center fielder Joe DiMaggio (125), second baseman Tony Lazzeri (109), catcher Bill Dickey (107) and right fielder George Selkirk (107). Gehrig also batted .354 with a league-leading 49 home runs to earn the A.L. Most Valuable Player Award. The Yankees topped the Junior Circuit with 1,065 runs scored.

Meanwhile, the Giants took the National League crown with a 92-62 record, five games ahead of the Chicago Cubs. Giants' left-handed pitcher Carl Hubbell earned his second N.L. Most Valuable Player Award in four years in 1936 after posting a 26-6 record with a 2.31 ERA. He paced the league in wins and ERA and won his last 16 decisions en route to setting the major league record of 24 consecutive victories in 1936-37. In the series, Hubbell went 1-1 with a 2.25 ERA. Shortstop Dick Bartell was the offensive catalyst with a .381 batting average (8-for-21) and three RBI. Player-manager Bill Terry drove in four runs, while right fielder Mel Ott batted at a .304 clip (7-for-23).

Winning Player's Share: $6,431
Losing Player's Share: $4,656

Game 1: at New York (Polo Grounds)
Giants 6, Yankees 1

Giants' left-hander Carl Hubbell continued his postseason dominance with a 6-1 victory in Game 1 at the Polo Grounds. He pitched a seven-hitter with one walk and eight strikeouts while not allowing a ball hit the outfield. In his previous World Series experience in 1924, Hubbell did not allow an earned run in 20 innings.

The only run Hubbell gave up in this game was a third-inning homer to Yankees' right fielder George Selkirk, and the blast gave the Yankees a 1-0 lead. After the Giants tied the game on a home run by shortstop Dick Bartell in the fifth, they took the lead for good with a run in the sixth and added four insurance tallies in the eighth. Second baseman Burgess Whitehead speared a hard line drive by center fielder Joe DiMaggio in the top of the eighth to start a double play and snuff out a Yankees' rally.

Yankees' right-hander Red Ruffing, who was 20-12 with a 3.85 ERA during the season, gave up all six runs (four earned) on nine hits with four walks and five strikeouts in eight innings. Four Giants picked up two hits each.

The loss ended a 12-game postseason winning streak for the Yankees (series sweeps in 1927, 1928 and 1932).

Game 2: at New York (Polo Grounds)
Yankees 18, Giants 4

The Yankees pounded five Giants' pitchers for 17 hits and coasted to an 18-4 victory in Game 2 at the Polo Grounds to even the series at one game apiece. The 18 runs set a World Series record. All nine starters had at least one hit and one run scored.

Catcher Bill Dickey and second baseman Tony Lazzeri both drove in five runs, while shortstop Frankie Crosetti scored a series record-tying four runs. Lazzeri blasted a grand slam (the second in World Series history) in the third inning and Dickey hit a three-run shot in the ninth. The Yankees scored two runs in the first, seven in the third, one in the sixth, two in the seventh and six in the ninth. They knocked out Giants' right-handed starter Hal Schumacher after two-plus innings and went to score against all four relievers.

Yankees' left-hander Lefty Gomez held the Giants to four runs on six hits with seven walks and eight strikeouts. First baseman-manager Bill Terry was 2-for-5 with two RBI.

Game 3: at New York (Yankee Stadium)
Yankees 2, Giants 1

Giants' right-hander Freddie Fitzsimmons was a tough-luck loser as the Yankees edged out a 2-1 victory in Game 3 at Yankee Stadium and took a two games to one lead in the series.

With the score tied 1-apiece in the bottom of the eighth inning, Yankees' shortstop Frankie Crosetti lined a two-out single on an 0-2 count off Fitzsimmons' glove to score left fielder Jake Powell with the winning run. The two teams traded solo home runs to account for the game's first two runs — first baseman Lou Gehrig for the Yankees in the second and center fielder Jimmy Ripple for the Giants in the fifth.

Fitzsimmons held the mighty Yankees to four hits with two walks and five strikeouts in eight innings. He also was 2-for-3 at the plate.

Yankees' right-hander Bump Hadley gave up 10 hits with one walk and two strikeouts over eight innings to earn the win before right-hander Pat Malone finished up.

Game 4: at New York (Yankee Stadium)
Yankees 5, Giants 2

The Yankees took a commanding three games to one lead in the series with a 5-2 win in Game 4 at Yankee Stadium. Giants' left-hander Carl Hubbell saw his 17-game winning streak snapped—he won his last 16 decisions of the season plus Game 1 of the World Series—while suffering his first-ever postseason defeat after three wins.

After taking a 1-0 lead in the bottom of the second inning, the Yankees took control with three runs in the third. Third baseman Red Rolfe had an RBI single and first baseman Lou Gehrig followed with a two-run homer. The Giants tallied single runs in the fourth and eighth, while the Yankees plated their final run in their half of the eighth.

Yankees' right-hander Monte Pearson authored a complete-game, allowing seven hits and two walks while striking out seven. Center fielder Jimmy Ripple of the Giants was 2-for-4 with an RBI. Hubbell gave up four runs (three earned) on eight hits with one walk and two strikeouts over seven innings.

Game 5: at New York (Yankee Stadium)
Giants 5, Yankees 4 (10 innings)

Facing elimination, the Giants lived to see another day with a 5-4, 10-inning victory in Game 5 at Yankee Stadium. In the 10th, left fielder Joe Moore hit a leadoff double against Yankees' right-handed reliever Pat Malone, was sacrificed to third by shortstop Dick Bartell and scored the winning run on a sacrifice fly to center field by first baseman-manager Bill Terry. It proved to be the second-to-last game of Terry's 14-year playing career.

Giants' right-hander Hal Schumacher battled all game long, pitching a complete game and giving up four runs (three earned) on 10 hits with six walks and 10 strikeouts. With the

Giants clinging to a 3-2 lead in the bottom of the third and the bases loaded with no outs, Schumacher struck out center fielder Joe DiMaggio and first baseman Lou Gehrig and retired catcher Bill Dickey on a fly ball to right.

The Giants opened a 3-0 lead in the first on RBI by Bartell, center fielder Jimmy Ripple and second baseman Burgess Whitehead before the Yankees ultimately tied the game at 4-apiece with a two-run fifth.

Yankees' right-hander Red Ruffing gave up four runs (three earned) on seven hits with one walk and seven strikeouts in six innings before giving way to Malone. Left fielder Joe Moore had two doubles and scored twice for the Giants.

Game 6: at Polo Grounds (New York)
Yankees 13, Giants 5

Too much Yankees' batting, not enough Giants' pitching. Such sums up the 1936 World Series, which the Yankees won four games to two with a 13-5 victory in Game 6 at the Polo Grounds. For the second time in the series, the Yankees totaled 17 hits.

The Giants led 2-0 after one inning on a two-run double by right fielder Mel Ott that scored left fielder Mel Ott and shortstop Dick Bartell, but the Yankees came back to take a 6-5 lead into the ninth and blew the game open with a seven-run uprising.

After pitching a four-hitter in Game 3, Giants' right-hander Freddie Fitzsimmons was roughed up for five runs on nine hits with one strikeout in 3.2 innings. The Yankees went on to score against all three Giants' relievers, including five runs off right-hander Dick Coffman, who didn't retire any of the six batters he faced in the ninth.

Center fielder Joe DiMaggio, second baseman Tony Lazzeri, left fielder Jake Powell and third baseman Red Rolfe each had three hits for the Yankees. Powell, who topped the team with a .455 batting average during the series (10-for-22), tied the game with a two-run homer in the second and finished with four RBI.

All the while, Yankees' left-hander Lefty

Gomez kept the Giants at bay. He worked the first 6.1 innings, giving up four runs (three earned) on eight hits with four walks and one strikeout. Right-hander Johnny Murphy pitched the final 2.2 innings.

Ott and Moore homered in the fifth and eighth innings, respectively.

1936

Game 1 (Sept. 30)

Yankees	AB	R	H	RBI	Giants	AB	R	H	RBI
Crosetti, ss	4	0	1	0	Moore, lf	5	0	0	0
Rolfe, 3b	3	0	1	0	Bartell, ss	4	1	2	1
DiMaggio, cf	4	0	1	0	Terry, 1b	4	1	2	0
Gehrig, 1b	3	0	0	0	Ott, rf	2	2	2	0
Dickey, c	4	0	0	0	Ripple, cf	2	0	0	0
Powell, lf	4	0	3	0	Mancuso, c	3	1	1	1
Lazzeri, 2b	3	0	0	0	Whitehead, 2b	3	1	0	1
Selkirk, rf	4	1	1	1	Jackson, 3b	4	0	0	1
Ruffing, p	3	0	0	0	Hubbell, p	4	0	2	1
Totals	32	1	7	1	Totals	31	6	9	5

										R	H	E
Yankees	0	0	1	0	0	0	0	0	0	—	1	7	2
Giants	0	0	0	0	1	1	0	4	x	—	6	9	1

E—Crosetti, Dickey, Hubbell. DP—Giants 1. LOB—Yankees 7, Giants 7. 2B—Crosetti, Powell, Ott. HR—Selkirk, Bartell. S—Rolfe, Ripple 2.

Yankees	IP	H	R	ER	BB	SO
Ruffing (L, 0-1)	8	9	6	4	4	5

Giants	IP	H	R	ER	BB	SO
Hubbell (W, 1-0)	9	7	1	1	1	8

HBP—By Hubbell (Gehrig). Umpires—Pfirman (N.L.), Geisel (A.L.), Magerkurth (N.L.), Summers (A.L.). Time—2:40. Attendance—39,415.

Game 2 (Oct. 2)

Yankees	AB	R	H	RBI	Giants	AB	R	H	RBI
Crosetti, ss	5	4	3	0	Moore, lf	5	0	0	0
Rolfe, 3b	4	3	2	1	Bartell, ss	3	0	1	1
DiMaggio, cf	5	2	3	2	Terry, 1b	5	0	2	2
Gehrig, 1b	5	1	2	3	Leiber, cf	4	0	0	0
Dickey, c	5	3	2	5	Ott, rf	4	0	0	0
Selkirk, rf	5	1	1	0	Mancuso, c	2	2	1	0
Powell, lf	3	2	2	0	Whitehead, 2b	4	0	0	0
Lazzeri, 2b	4	1	1	5	Jackson, 3b	4	1	1	0
Gomez, p	5	1	1	2	Schumacher, p	0	0	0	0
					Smith, p	0	0	0	0
					Coffman, p	0	0	0	0
					Davis, ph	1	1	1	0
					Gabler, p	0	0	0	0
					Danning, ph	1	0	0	0
					Gumbert, p	0	0	0	0
Totals	41	18	17	18	Totals	33	4	6	3

										R	H	E
Yankees	2	0	7	0	0	1	2	0	6	—	18	17	0
Giants	0	1	0	3	0	0	0	0	0	—	4	6	1

E—Jackson. DP—Giants 1. LOB—Yankees 6, Giants 9. 2B—DiMaggio, Bartell, Mancuso. HR—Dickey, Lazzeri. SB—Powell. SF—DiMaggio.

Yankees	IP	H	R	ER	BB	SO
Gomez (W, 1-0)	9	6	4	4	7	8

Giants	IP	H	R	ER	BB	SO
Schumacher (L, 0-1)	2	3	5	4	4	1
Smith	0.1	2	3	3	1	0
Coffman	1.2	2	1	1	0	1
Gabler	4	5	3	3	3	0
Gumbert	1	5	6	6	1	1

Schumacher pitched to three batters in the 3rd.

WP—Schumacher, Gomez. Umpires—Geisel (A.L.), Magerkurth (N.L.), Summers (A.L.), Pfirman (N.L.). Time—2:40. Attendance—43,543.

Game 3 (Oct. 3)

Giants	AB	R	H	RBI	Yankees	AB	R	H	RBI
Moore, lf	5	0	1	0	Crosetti, ss	4	0	1	1
Bartell, ss	3	0	1	0	Rolfe, 3b	4	0	0	0
Terry, 1b	4	0	1	0	DiMaggio, cf	3	0	1	0
Ott, rf	4	0	2	0	Gehrig, 1b	3	1	1	1
Ripple, cf	4	1	1	1	Dickey, c	2	0	0	0
Mancuso, c	4	0	1	0	Selkirk, rf	3	0	1	0
Whitehead, 2b	4	0	0	0	Powell, lf	2	1	0	0
Jackson, 3b	2	0	1	0	Lazzeri, 2b	2	0	0	0
Koenig, ph	1	0	0	0	Hadley, p	2	0	0	0
Fitzsimmons, p	3	0	2	0	Ruffing, ph	1	0	0	0
Leslie, ph	1	0	1	0	Johnson, pr	0	0	0	0
Davis, pr	0	0	0	0	Malone, p	0	0	0	0
Totals	35	1	11	1	Totals	26	2	4	2

											R	H	E
Giants	0	0	0	0	1	0	0	0	0	—	1	11	0
Yankees	0	1	0	0	0	0	0	1	x	—	2	4	0

DP—Giants 1, Yankees 1. LOB—Giants 9, Yankees 3. 2B—DiMaggio. HR—Ripple, Gehrig. S—Bartell, Lazzeri.

Giants	IP	H	R	ER	BB	SO
Fitzsimmons (L, 0-1)	8	4	2	2	2	5

Yankees	IP	H	R	ER	BB	SO
Hadley (W, 1-0)	8	10	1	1	1	2
Malone (S, 1)	1	1	0	0	0	1

Umpires—Magerkurth (N.L.), Summers (A.L.), Pfirman (N.L.), Geisel (A.L.). Time—2:01. Attendance—64,842.

Game 4 (Oct. 4)

Giants	AB	R	H	RBI	Yankees	AB	R	H	RBI
Moore, lf	3	0	1	0	Crosetti, ss	4	1	2	0
Bartell, ss	4	1	1	0	Rolfe, 3b	3	1	2	1
Terry, 1b	3	0	0	1	DiMaggio, cf	4	0	0	0
Ott, rf	4	0	0	0	Gehrig, 1b	4	2	2	2
Ripple, cf	4	0	2	1	Dickey, c	4	0	0	0
Mancuso, c	4	0	0	0	Powell, lf	4	1	1	1
Whitehead, 2b	3	0	0	0	Lazzeri, 2b	4	0	0	0
Koenig, ph	1	0	1	0	Selkirk, rf	3	0	1	1
Jackson, 3b	4	0	1	0	Pearson, p	4	0	2	0
Hubbell, p	2	0	0	0					
Leslie, ph	1	0	1	0					
Davis, pr	0	1	0	0					
Gabler, p	0	0	0	0					
Totals	33	2	7	2	Totals	34	5	10	5

										R	H	E
Giants	0	0	0	1	0	0	0	1	0	—	2	7	1
Yankees	0	1	3	0	0	0	0	1	x	—	5	10	1

E—Selkirk, Jackson. DP—Giants 1. LOB—Giants 6, Yankees 7. 2B—Crosetti, Gehrig, Pearson. HR—Gehrig.

Giants	IP	H	R	ER	BB	SO
Hubbell (L, 1-1)	7	8	4	3	1	2
Gabler	1	2	1	1	1	0

Yankees	IP	H	R	ER	BB	SO
Pearson (W, 1-0)	9	7	2	2	2	7

WP—Hubbell. Umpires—Summers (A.L.), Pfirman (N.L.), Geisel (A.L), Magerkurth (N.L.). Time—2:12. Attendance—66,569.

Game 5 (Oct. 5)

Giants	AB	R	H	RBI		Yankees	AB	R	H	RBI
Moore, lf	5	2	2	0		Crosetti, ss	5	0	0	1
Bartell, ss	4	1	1	1		Rolfe, 3b	5	0	2	0
Terry, 1b	5	0	0	1		DiMaggio, cf	4	0	1	0
Ott, rf	5	1	1	0		Gehrig, 1b	4	0	1	0
Ripple, cf	2	1	1	1		Dickey, c	5	0	1	0
Mancuso, c	3	0	2	0		Seeds, pr	0	0	0	0
Whitehead, 2b	4	0	1	2		Selkirk, rf	4	2	2	1
Jackson, 3b	4	0	0	0		Powell, lf	4	1	1	0
Schumacher, p	4	0	0	0		Lazzeri, 2b	3	1	1	1
						Ruffing, p	1	0	0	0
						Johnson, ph	1	0	0	0
						Malone, p	1	0	1	0
Totals	36	5	8	5		Totals	37	4	10	3

										R	H	E
Giants	3	0	0	0	0	1	0	0	0	1	—	5	8	3
Yankees	0	1	1	0	0	2	0	0	0	0	—	4	10	1

E—Crosetti, Bartell, Ott, Jackson. DP—Giants 3, Yankees 1. LOB—Giants 5, Yankees 9. 2B—Moore 2, Bartell, Mancuso, DiMaggio. HR—Selkirk. S—Bartell, Mancuso.

Giants	IP	H	R	ER	BB	SO
Schumacher (W, 1-1)	10	10	4	3	6	10

Yankees	IP	H	R	ER	BB	SO
Ruffing	6	7	4	3	1	7
Malone (L, 0-1)	4	1	1	1	1	1

WP—Schumacher. Umpires—Pfirman (N.L.), Geisel (A.L), Magerkurth (N.L.), Summers (A.L.). Time—2:45. Attendance—50,024.

Game 6 (Oct. 6)

Yankees	AB	R	H	RBI	Giants	AB	R	H	RBI
Crosetti, ss	4	0	0	1	Moore, lf	5	2	2	1
Rolfe, 3b	6	1	3	2	Bartell, ss	3	2	2	0
DiMaggio, cf	6	1	3	1	Terry, 1b	4	0	1	0
Gehrig, 1b	5	1	1	1	Leiber, cf	2	0	0	0
Dickey, c	5	2	0	0	Mayo, 3b	1	0	0	0
Selkirk, rf	5	2	2	0	Ott, rf	4	1	2	3
Powell, lf	5	3	3	4	Mancuso, c	3	0	0	0
Lazzeri, 2b	4	2	3	1	Leslie, ph	1	0	0	0
Gomez, p	3	0	1	1	Danning, c	1	0	0	0
Murphy, p	2	1	1	1	Whitehead, 2b	3	0	0	0
					Ripple, ph-cf	0	0	0	0
					Jackson, 3b	3	0	1	0
					Koenig, ph-2b	1	0	0	0
					Fitzsimmons, p	1	0	0	0
					Castleman, p	2	0	1	0
					Davis, ph	1	0	0	0
					Coffman, p	0	0	0	0
					Gumbert, p	0	0	0	0
Totals	45	13	17	12	Totals	35	5	9	4

											R	H	E
Yankees	0	2	1	2	0	0	0	1	7	—	13	17	2
Giants	2	0	0	0	1	0	1	1	0	—	5	9	1

E—DiMaggio, Danning, Rolfe. LOB—Yankees 11, Giants 10. 2B—Bartell, Ott. 3B—Selkirk. HR —Powell, Moore, Ott. S—Terry, Leiber.

Yankees	IP	H	R	ER	BB	SO
Gomez (W, 2-0)	6.1	8	4	3	4	1
Murphy (S, 1)	2.2	1	1	1	1	1
Giants	IP	H	R	ER	BB	SO
Fitzsimmons (L, 0-2)	3.2	9	5	5	0	1
Castleman	4.1	3	1	1	2	5
Coffman	0	3	5	5	1	0
Gumbert	1	2	2	2	3	1

Coffman pitched to six batters in the 9th.

Umpires—Geisel (A.L.), Magerkurth (N.L.), Summers (A.L.), Pfirman (N.L.). Time—2:50. Attendance—38,427.

1937: NEW YORK YANKEES DEFEATED GIANTS 4 GAMES TO 1

Only three different teams won National League pennants from 1928-38 (the St. Louis Cardinals in 1928, 1930, 1931 and 1934; the Chicago Cubs in 1929, 1932, 1935 and 1938; and the New York Giants in 1933, 1936 and 1937. A mere three of those squads went on to win the World Series: the 1931 Cardinals, 1933 Giants and 1934 Cardinals.

In other words, the decade was dominated by the American League. More specifically, by the New York Yankees, who won five pennants and five World Series. Twice they defeated the Giants in Subway Series, in six games in 1936 and in five games in 1937.

The Yankees of Joe McCarthy captured the 1937 A.L. flag with a 102-52 record, 13 games ahead of the Detroit Tigers. Their offensive juggernaut was led by three future Hall of Famers: center fielder Joe DiMaggio (.346 batting average, 46 home runs and 167 RBI); first baseman Lou Gehrig (.351, 37 homers and 159 RBI); and catcher Bill Dickey (.332, 29 homers and 133 RBI). They also had two 20-game winners in left-hander Lefty Gomez (21-11,

2.33 ERA) and right-hander Red Ruffing (20-7, 2.98 ERA). Gomez was 2-0 in the series, allowing only three runs while pitching two complete games for a 1.50 ERA.

Just south of the Harlem River, Bill Terry's Giants won the N.L. pennant with a 95-57 record, three games better than the Cubs. But the Yankees dominated postseason play, outscoring the Giants 28-12 in the five games. Left fielder Joe Moore paced the Giants' attack with a .391 batting average (9-for-23), while third baseman Mel Ott had three RBI.

Winning Player's Share: $6,471
Losing Player's Share: $4,490

Game 1: at New York (Yankee Stadium) Yankees 8, Giants 1

Giants' left-hander Carl Hubbell was coasting along with a one-hitter and a 1-0 lead into the bottom of the sixth inning before the Yankees erupted with a seven-run outburst and went on to win the series opener 8-1 at Yankee Stadium.

The decisive inning featured bases-loaded singles by center fielder Joe DiMaggio and right fielder George Selkirk. Second baseman Tony Lazzeri homered in the eighth inning for the Yankees' final run.

Hubbell, who was 22-8 with a 3.20 ERA during the season, was knocked out after allowing seven runs (four earned) on six hits with three walks and three strikeouts in 5.1 innings. At the same time, Yankees' left-hander Lefty Gomez pitched a six-hitter (five singles) with one walk and two strikeouts. The Giants scored their only run in the fifth inning when catcher Gus Mancuso hit into a double play that scored right fielder Jimmy Ripple.

Some miscommunication led to a bizarre sixth inning. Manager Bill Terry intended to replace Hubbell with right-hander Dick Coffman. But Mancuso, the team captain, informed home plate umpire Red Ormsby that right-hander Harry Gumbert was coming in, even though Gumbert had not been warming up. Once Gumbert was announced, he had to pitch

to at least one batter, and Lazzeri reached on an error by second baseman Burgess Whitehead. Gumbert then was removed in favor of Coffman.

Game 2: at New York (Yankee Stadium) Yankees 8, Giants 1

The proceedings of Game 2 were quite similar to Game 1, and the end result was exactly the same—an 8-1 win for the Yankees and a two games to none lead in the series.

This time, Giants' rookie left-hander Cliff Melton, who was 20-9 with a 2.61 ERA during the season, held the mighty Yankees scoreless on two hits for four innings before four straight hits in the bottom of the fifth led to two runs. Right-handed reliever Harry Gumbert stopped the bleeding but then gave up four runs on four hits in the sixth. Right fielder George Selkirk contributed a two-run double.

After surrendering a run in the top of the first inning—on a double by shortstop Dick Bartell and an RBI single by third baseman Mel Ott—Yankees' right-hander Red Ruffing kept the Giants off the scoreboard the rest of the game. He scattered seven hits with three walks and eight strikeouts in the route-going performance.

Melton gave up two runs on six hits with one walk and two strikeouts in four-plus innings to absorb the loss.

Game 3: at New York (Polo Grounds) Yankees 5, Giants 1

A change in venue didn't do anything to wake up the Giants' slumbering bats, as the Yankees rolled to a 5-1 victory in Game 3 and a commanding three games to none lead in the series. The Giants scored their lone run in the bottom of the seventh on a one-out single by right fielder Jimmy Ripple and an RBI double by first baseman Johnny McCarthy.

By then, the Yankees had a 5-0 lead with one run in the second, two in the third, one in the fourth and one in the fifth. All the damage was done against Giants' right-hander Hal Schumacher, who gave up nine hits and four

walks while striking out three in six innings.

Right-hander Monte Pearson was on the way to pitching the Yankees' third consecutive complete game, but he loaded the bases with two outs in the ninth and gave way to right-hander Johnny Murphy, who retired catcher Harry Danning to save the day.

Game 4: at New York (Polo Grounds)
Giants 7, Yankees 3

The Giants were kings for a day with a 7-3 win in Game 4 at the Polo Grounds that cut the Yankees' series lead to three games to one.

Trailing 1-0 heading into the bottom of the second inning, the Giants scored six runs (three more than their total output over the first three games). They strung together seven singles and a walk. Center fielder Hank Leiber opened the frame with a single and capped the scoring with a two-out, two-run single as the Giants batted around against Yankees' right-handed starter and loser Bump Hadley and right-handed reliever Ivy Andrews.

Catcher Harry Danning was 3-for-4 with a double and two RBI to pace the Giants' 12-hit attack.

Overshadowed by the offensive heroics was left-hander Carl Hubbell, who came back on two day's rest to author a complete game. He gave up three runs (two earned), including a ninth-inning homer to first baseman Lou Gehrig, on six hits with one walk and four strikeouts.

Game 5: at New York (Polo Grounds)
Yankees 4, Giants 2

The Yankees wrapped up their fifth World Series championship in 11 years with a 4-2 win over the Giants in Game 5 at the Polo Grounds, which had served as their home ballpark from 1913-22.

Home runs by left fielder Myril Hoag and center fielder Joe DiMaggio in the second and third innings, respectively, gave the Yankees a 2-0 lead. The Giants drew even on a two-run blast by third baseman Mel Ott in their half of the third.

Then it became the Lefty Gomez show. While the left-hander was blanking the Giants the rest of the way, he also drove in what proved to the series-deciding run in the fifth inning with a single to plate second baseman Tony Lazzeri, who had tripled. Gomez then scored on a double by first baseman Lou Gehrig. Gomez went the distance on the mound, scattering 10 hits and one walk while striking out six.

Giants' left-hander Cliff Melton was tagged with his second series setback after giving up four runs on six hits with three walks and five strikeouts in five innings.

Left fielder Joe Moore was 3-for-5 for the Giants.

Bill Terry piloted New York to three National League pennants (1933, 1936 and 1937) and the 1933 World Series championship. (Brace Photo)

1937

Game 1 (Oct. 6)

Giants	AB	R	H	RBI	Yankees	AB	R	H	RBI
Moore, lf	4	0	2	0	Crosetti, ss	4	1	1	0
Bartell, ss	4	0	1	0	Rolfe, 3b	4	1	1	1
Ott, 3b	4	0	0	0	DiMaggio, cf	4	0	2	2
Leiber, cf	4	0	0	0	Gehrig, 1b	2	1	0	0
Ripple, rf	3	1	1	0	Dickey, c	3	1	1	1
McCarthy, 1b	4	0	1	0	Hoag, lf	4	1	0	0
Mancuso, c	3	0	0	0	Selkirk, rf	4	1	1	2
Whitehead, 2b	3	0	1	0	Lazzeri, 2b	4	1	1	1
Hubbell, p	2	0	0	0	Gomez, p	2	1	0	0
Gumbert, p	0	0	0	0					
Coffman, p	0	0	0	0					
Berger, ph	1	0	0	0					
Smith, p	0	0	0	0					
Totals	**32**	**1**	**6**	**0**	**Totals**	**31**	**8**	**7**	**7**

										R	H	E
Giants	0	0	0	0	1	0	0	0	0	— 1	6	2
Yankees	0	0	0	0	0	7	0	1	x	— 8	7	0

E—Whitehead, Bartell. DP—Giants 1, Yankees 1. LOB—Giants 5, Yankees 6. 2B—Whitehead. HR—Lazzeri.

Giants	IP	H	R	ER	BB	SO
Hubbell (L, 0-1)	5.1	6	7	4	3	3
Gumbert	0	0	0	0	0	0
Coffman	1.2	0	0	0	4	0
Smith	1	1	1	1	0	0
Yankees	**IP**	**H**	**R**	**ER**	**BB**	**SO**
Gomez (W, 1-0)	9	6	1	1	1	2

Gumbert pitched to one batter in the 6th.

Umpires—Ormsby (A.L.), Barr (N.L.), Basil (A.L.), Stewart (N.L.). Time—2:20. Attendance—60,573.

Game 2 (Oct. 7)

Giants	AB	R	H	RBI	Yankees	AB	R	H	RBI
Moore, lf	5	0	2	0	Crosetti, ss	5	0	0	0
Bartell, ss	4	1	2	0	Rolfe, 3b	5	0	0	0
Ott, 3b	4	0	1	1	DiMaggio, cf	4	1	2	0
Ripple, rf	4	0	0	0	Gehrig, 1b	2	1	1	0
McCarthy, 1b	4	0	0	0	Dickey, c	4	1	2	1
Chiozza, cf	4	0	1	0	Hoag, lf	4	2	1	1
Mancuso, c	4	0	0	0	Selkirk, rf	4	2	2	3
Whitehead, 2b	3	0	1	0	Lazzeri, 2b	3	1	2	0
Melton, p	1	0	0	0	Ruffing, p	4	0	2	3
Gumbert, p	0	0	0	0					
Coffman, p	1	0	0	0					
Leslie, ph	0	0	0	0					
Totals	**34**	**1**	**7**	**1**	**Totals**	**35**	**8**	**12**	**8**

											R	H	E
Giants	1	0	0	0	0	0	0	0	0	—	1	7	0
Yankees	0	0	0	0	2	4	2	0	x	—	8	12	0

DP—Giants 1. LOB—Giants 9, Yankees 6. 2B—Moore, Bartell, Hoag, Selkirk, Ruffing.

Giants	IP	H	R	ER	BB	SO
Melton (L, 0-1)	4	6	2	2	1	2
Gumbert	1.1	4	4	4	1	1
Coffman	2.2	2	2	2	1	1

Yankees	IP	H	R	ER	BB	SO
Ruffing (W, 1-0)	9	7	1	1	3	8

Melton pitched to four batters in the 5th.

Umpires—Barr (N.L.), Basil (A.L.), Stewart (N.L.), Ormsby (A.L.). Time—2:11. Attendance—57,675.

Game 3 (Oct. 8)

Yankees	AB	R	H	RBI	Giants	AB	R	H	RBI
Crosetti, ss	4	0	0	0	Moore, lf	4	0	1	0
Rolfe, 3b	4	1	2	0	Bartell, ss	4	0	0	0
DiMaggio, cf	5	0	1	0	Ott, 3b	4	0	1	0
Gehrig, 1b	5	1	1	1	Ripple, rf	4	1	1	0
Dickey, c	5	1	1	1	McCarthy, 1b	3	0	1	1
Selkirk, rf	4	2	1	1	Chiozza, cf	3	0	1	0
Hoag, lf	4	0	2	0	Danning, c	4	0	0	0
Lazzeri, 2b	2	0	1	1	Whitehead, 2b	3	0	0	0
Pearson, p	3	0	0	0	Schumacher, p	1	0	0	0
Murphy, p	0	0	0	0	Berger, ph	1	0	0	0
					Melton, p	0	0	0	0
					Leslie, ph	1	0	0	0
					Brennan, p	0	0	0	0
Totals	36	5	9	4	Totals	32	1	5	1

											R	H	E
Yankees	0	1	2	1	1	0	0	0	0	—	5	9	0
Giants	0	0	0	0	0	0	1	0	0	—	1	5	4

E—Melton, McCarthy 2, Chiozza. DP—Giants 1. LOB—Yankees 11, Giants 6. 2B—Rolfe 2, McCarthy. 3B—Dickey. S—Hoag.

Yankees	IP	H	R	ER	BB	SO
Pearson (W, 1-0)	8.2	5	1	1	2	4
Murphy (S, 1)	0.1	0	0	0	0	0

Giants	IP	H	R	ER	BB	SO
Schumacher (L, 0-1)	6	9	5	4	4	3
Melton	2	0	0	0	2	0
Brennan	1	0	0	0	0	0

WP—Schumacher. Umpires—Basil (A.L.), Stewart (N.L.), Ormsby (A.L.), Barr (N.L.). Time—2:07. Attendance—37,385.

Game 4 (Oct. 9)

Yankees	AB	R	H	RBI	Giants	AB	R	H	RBI
Crosetti, ss	4	1	0	0	Moore, lf	5	1	1	1
Rolfe, 3b	4	1	2	0	Bartell, ss	5	1	1	1
DiMaggio, cf	4	0	0	1	Ott, 3b	5	0	1	0
Gehrig, 1b	4	1	1	1	Ripple, rf	2	0	1	0
Dickey, c	4	0	0	0	Leiber, cf	3	2	2	2
Hoag, lf	4	0	2	0	McCarthy, 1b	4	1	2	0
Selkirk, rf	3	0	0	0	Danning, c	4	0	3	2
Lazzeri, 2b	3	0	1	0	Whitehead, 2b	3	1	1	0
Hadley, p	0	0	0	0	Hubbell, p	4	1	0	1
Andrews, p	2	0	0	0					
Powell, ph	1	0	0	0					
Wicker, p	0	0	0	0					
Totals	33	3	6	2	Totals	35	7	12	7

									R	H	E
Yankees	1	0	1	0	0	0	0	0	1	—	3	6	0
Giants	0	6	0	0	0	0	1	0	x	—	7	12	3

E—Bartell 2, Ott. DP—Giants 2. LOB—Yankees 4, Giants 8. 2B—Danning. 3B—Rolfe. HR—Gehrig. SB—Whitehead.

Yankees	IP	H	R	ER	BB	SO
Hadley (L, 0-1)	1.1	6	5	5	0	0
Andrews	5.2	6	2	2	4	1
Wicker	1	0	0	0	0	0

Giants	IP	H	R	ER	BB	SO
Hubbell (W, 1-1)	9	6	3	2	1	4

Umpires—Stewart (N.L.), Ormsby (A.L.), Barr (N.L.), Basil (A.L.). Time—1:57. Attendance—44,293.

Game 5 (Oct. 10)

Yankees	AB	R	H	RBI	Giants	AB	R	H	RBI
Crosetti, ss	4	0	0	0	Moore, lf	5	0	3	0
Rolfe, 3b	3	0	1	0	Bartell, ss	4	1	1	0
DiMaggio, cf	5	1	1	1	Ott, 3b	3	1	1	2
Gehrig, 1b	4	0	2	1	Ripple, rf	4	0	2	0
Dickey, c	3	0	0	0	Leiber, cf	4	0	2	0
Hoag, lf	4	1	1	1	McCarthy, 1b	4	0	0	0
Selkirk, rf	4	0	1	0	Danning, c	4	0	0	0
Lazzeri, 2b	3	1	1	0	Whitehead, 2b	4	0	1	0
Gomez, p	4	1	1	1	Melton, p	1	0	0	0
					Ryan, ph	1	0	0	0
					Smith, p	0	0	0	0
					Mancuso, ph	1	0	0	0
					Brennan, p	0	0	0	0
					Berger, ph	1	0	0	0
Totals	34	4	8	4	Totals	36	2	10	2

									R	H	E
Yankees	0	1	1	0	2	0	0	0	0	—	4	8	0
Giants	0	0	2	0	0	0	0	0	0	—	2	10	0

DP—Yankees 1. LOB—Yankees 9, Giants 8. 2B—Gehrig, Whitehead. 3B—Gehrig, Lazzeri. HR—DiMaggio, Hoag, Ott. S—Rolfe.

Yankees	IP	H	R	ER	BB	SO
Gomez (W, 2-0)	9	10	2	2	1	6

Giants	IP	H	R	ER	BB	SO
Melton (L, 0-2)	5	6	4	4	3	5
Smith	2	1	0	0	0	1
Brennan	2	1	0	0	1	1

HBP—By Smith (Lazzeri). WP—Melton. Umpires—Ormsby (A.L.), Barr (N.L.), Basil (A.L.), Stewart (N.L.). Time—2:06. Attendance—38,216.

1951 — NEW YORK YANKEES DEFEATED GIANTS 4 GAMES TO 2

The cross-town rival Giants and New York Yankees squared off in the World Series for the sixth time in 1951, and the Yankees were victorious four games to two. It was the Yankees' fourth series win over the Giants.

While the Giants needed a three-game playoff victory over the Brooklyn Dodgers to win the National League pennant with a 98-59 record—after being 13½ games out on August 12—the Yankees captured the American League flag with a 98-56 record, five games ahead of the Cleveland Indians. The Yankees featured both the A.L. Most Valuable Player (catcher Yogi Berra) and Rookie of the Year (third baseman Gil McDougald).

After winning two of the first three games of the series, the Giants were beaten three straight. Left fielder Monte Irvin (.458 batting average) and shortstop Alvin Dark (.417) accounted for 21 of the Giants' 46 hits. The team batted just .237 overall, while Yankees' pitchers registered a 1.87 ERA (11 earned runs in 53 innings). Right-hander Jim Hearn was the Giants' most effective pitcher, winning Game 3 and posting a 1.04 ERA over two appearances (one earned run in 8.2 innings).

The series marked the final playing appearance for legendary Yankees' outfielder Joe DiMaggio, who retired during the offseason. He clearly went out with a bang, collecting six hits in his final 12 at-bats over the last three games.

Winning Player's Share: $6,446
Losing Player's Share: $4,951

Game 1: October 4 at New York (Yankee Stadium) Giants 5, Yankees 1

The day after third baseman Bobby Thomson's historic homer against the Brooklyn Dodgers, the Giants' momentum carried into the World Series opener at Yankee Stadium, where left fielder Monte Irvin's batting and running gave ample support to right-hander

Dave Koslo's complete-game 5-1 victory over right-hander Allie Reynolds.

Irvin's steal of home in the Giants' two-run first inning was the first such theft in a World Series game since Bob Meusel of the Yankees did it in 1928. Irvin finished with four hits in five at-bats, including a triple, to pace a 10-hit attack.

It was 2-1 entering the top of the sixth when shortstop Alvin Dark's three-run homer gave Koslo a four-run cushion. Yankees' shortstop Phil Rizzuto had two of the seven hits off Koslo, who also aided his cause with a pair of sacrifice bunts.

Game 2: October 5 at New York (Yankee Stadium) Yankees 3, Giants 1

Left fielder Monte Irvin erupted for three more hits, but the Giants were limited to five singles by left-hander Ed Lopat as the Yankees won Game 2 by the score of 3-1 at Yankee Stadium to square the series at one game apiece. First baseman Joe Collins of the Yankees had the only extra-base hit, a solo homer, in a game played before 66,018 spectators in a crisp 2 hours and 5 minutes.

Two bunt singles and a bloop single gave the Yankees a first-inning run off Giants' right-handed starter and loser Larry Jansen. The Yankees mustered merely six hits, one of them a run-scoring single by Lopat off right-handed reliever George Spencer in the eighth.

The Giants scored their lone run in the seventh on an RBI by pinch-hitter Bill Rigney that plated Irvin.

Despite the win, the Yankees' lost rookie right fielder Mickey Mantle for the balance of the series when he tore ligaments in his right knee while chasing a fly ball.

Game 3: October 6 at New York (Polo Grounds) Giants 6, Yankees 2

The Giants returned to the Polo Grounds for Game 3 and treated their fans among the 52,035 with a five-run fifth inning that featured

the hustle of second baseman Eddie Stanky. Right-hander Jim Hearn outdueled right-hander Vic Raschi by the score of 6-2, yielding one run on four hits in 7.2 innings and giving his team a two games to one lead in the series.

During the pivotal fifth, Stanky was an apparent out on a steal attempt of second base, but he kicked the ball out of shortstop Phil Rizzuto's glove with a hard slide, giving the rally impetus. Center fielder Willie Mays had his first two World Series hits and knocked in a run.

Fellow future Hall of Fame center fielder Joe DiMaggio of the Yankees helped the Giants take two of the first three games by going hit-less in 11 at-bats. The Yankees stranded 10 runners, aided by Hearn's eight walks.

Game 4: October 8 at New York (Polo Grounds) Yankees 6, Giants 2

Right-hander Allie Reynolds bounced back from his opening loss to go the distance, and center fielder Joe DiMaggio snapped his slump with a home run as the host Giants let the Yankees off the hook with a 6-2 victory in Game 4 at the Polo Grounds. The outcome evened the series at two games apiece.

Shortstop Alvin Dark doubled and left fielder Monte Irvin singled for a 1-0 Giants' lead in the first inning. The Yankees tied it in the second on left fielder Gene Woodling's double and a single by first baseman Joe Collins, and they went ahead in the fourth on Reynolds' RBI single.

Catcher Yogi Berra's single and DiMaggio's two-run homer off Giants' right-handed starter and loser Sal Maglie made it 4-1 in the fifth. The Giants scored their final run in the bottom of the ninth on right fielder Hank Thompson's walk, Irvin's single and a run-scoring single by third baseman Bobby Thomson.

Dark had three of the Giants' eight hits.

Game 5: October 9 at New York (Polo Grounds) Yankees 13, Giants 1

If there was a demoralizing game in the Subway Series, this one was it, and Yankees' center fielder Joe DiMaggio once again played a key role with three hits and three RBI. The Giants' only run off left-hander Eddie Lopat was unearned following a first-inning error by left fielder Gene Woodling. After that, the Yankees' bats erupted as they coasted to a 13-1 victory at the Polo Grounds for a three games to two series advantage.

The Yankees took the lead with a five-run third off right-hander Larry Jansen and kept piling it on. Second baseman Gil McDougald hit a grand slam in the third inning, and short-stop Phil Rizzuto homered and had three RBI. McDougald's slam was the third in World Series history, following Elmer Smith of the Cleveland Indians in 1920 and Tony Lazzeri of the Yankees in 1936. The Yankees' four-run seventh was punctuated by DiMaggio's two-run double.

Left fielder Monte Irvin had two of the Giants' five hits.

Game 6: October 10 at New York (Yankee Stadium) Yankees 4, Giants 3

The Giants were up to their old tricks, falling behind by two runs before rallying for two runs in the top of the ninth but falling short in Game 6 by the score of 4-3 at Yankee Stadium. Thus, the Yankees took the series four games to two.

The Yankees opened the scoring in the first on second baseman Jerry Coleman's single, catcher Yogi Berra's double and third baseman Gil McDougald's fly. The Giants tied it in the fifth on center fielder Willie Mays' single, a passed ball and fly balls by pitcher Dave Koslo and second baseman Eddie Stanky.

The decisive Yankees' sixth was triggered by Berra's one-out single and an error by Giants' right fielder Hank Thompson. Center fielder Joe DiMaggio was walked intentionally

and a wild pitch advanced the runners. First baseman Johnny Mize walked with two outs to load the bases, and they were cleared on a triple by right fielder Hank Bauer.

Of course, the Giants couldn't go quietly. Stanky opened the ninth with a single, shortstop Alvin Dark beat out a bunt and first baseman Whitey Lockman singled to center,

loading the bases. Left-hander Bob Kuzava replaced right-hander Johnny Sain, and left fielder Monte Irvin and third baseman Bobby Thomson hit run-scoring singles before Bauer made a great catch in right to deprive pinch-hitter Sal Yvars of extra bases.

Right-handed starter Vic Raschi earned the win, while Koslo took the loss.

1951

Game 1 (Oct. 4)

Giants	AB	R	H	RBI	Yankees	AB	R	H	RBI
Stanky, 2b	4	1	0	0	Mantle, rf	3	0	0	0
Dark, ss	5	1	2	3	Rizzuto, ss	4	0	2	0
Thompson, rf	3	1	0	0	Bauer, lf	4	0	0	0
Irvin, lf	5	1	4	0	DiMaggio, cf	4	0	0	0
Lockman, 1b	4	0	1	1	Berra, c	4	0	1	0
Thomson, 3b	3	0	1	0	McDougald, 3b	4	1	1	0
Mays, cf	5	0	0	0	Coleman, 2b	3	0	1	0
Westrum, c	3	1	2	0	Collins, 1b	3	0	1	0
Koslo, p	3	0	0	0	Mize, ph	1	0	0	0
					Reynolds, p	2	0	1	0
					Hogue, p	0	0	0	0
					Brown, ph	1	0	0	0
					Morgan, p	0	0	0	0
					Woodling, ph	1	0	0	0
Totals	35	5	10	4	Totals	34	1	7	0

									R	H	E
Giants	2	0	0	0	0	3	0	0	0	—	5	10	1
Yankees	0	1	0	0	0	0	0	0	0	—	1	7	1

E—McDougald, Thompson. DP—Yankees 1. LOB—Giants 13, Yankees 9. 2B—Lockman, McDougald. 3B—Irvin. HR—Dark. SB—Irvin. S—Koslo 2.

Giants	IP	H	R	ER	BB	SO
Koslo (W, 1-0)	9	7	1	1	3	3

Yankees	IP	H	R	ER	BB	SO
Reynolds (L, 0-1)	6	8	5	5	7	1
Hogue	1	0	0	0	0	0
Morgan	2	2	0	0	1	3

Umpires—Summers (A.L.), Ballanfant (N.L.), Paparella (A.L.), Barlick (N.L.), Stevens (A.L.), Gore (N.L.). Time—2:58. Attendance—65,673.

Game 2 (Oct. 5)

Giants	AB	R	H	RBI	Yankees	AB	R	H	RBI
Stanky, 2b	3	0	0	0	Mantle, rf	2	1	1	0
Dark, ss	4	0	1	0	Bauer, rf	2	0	0	0
Thomson, 3b	4	0	0	0	Rizzuto, ss	4	0	1	0
Irvin, lf	4	1	3	0	McDougald, 2b-3b	3	0	1	1
Lockman, 1b	4	0	1	0	DiMaggio, cf	3	0	0	0
Mays, cf	4	0	0	0	Berra, c	3	0	0	0
Westrum, c	2	0	0	0	Woodling, lf	3	0	0	0
Schenz, pr	0	0	0	0	Brown, 3b	3	0	1	0
Hartung, rf	1	0	0	0	Martin, pr	0	1	0	0
Thompson, rf	2	0	0	0	Coleman, 2b	0	0	0	0
Rigney, ph	1	0	0	1	Collins, 1b	3	1	1	1
Spencer, p	0	0	0	0	Lopat, p	3	0	1	1
Jansen, p	2	0	0	0					
Noble, ph-c	1	0	0	0					
Totals	32	1	5	1	**Totals**	29	3	6	3

										R	H	E
Giants	0	0	0	0	0	0	1	0	0	—	1	5	1
Yankees	1	1	0	0	0	0	0	1	x	—	3	6	0

E—Lockman. DP—Giants 1. LOB—Giants 6, Yankees 2. HR—Collins. SB—Irvin.

Giants	IP	H	R	ER	BB	SO
Jansen (L, 0-1)	6	4	2	2	0	5
Spencer	2	2	1	1	0	0

Yankees	IP	H	R	ER	BB	SO
Lopat (W, 1-0)	9	5	1	1	2	1

Umpires—Ballanfant (N.L.), Paparella (A.L.), Barlick (N.L.), Summers (A.L.), Gore (N.L.), Stevens (A.L.). Time—2:05. Attendance—66,018.

Game 3 (Oct. 6)

Yankees	AB	R	H	RBI	Giants	AB	R	H	RBI
Woodling, lf	4	1	1	1	Stanky, 2b	2	1	1	0
Rizzuto, ss	4	1	1	0	Dark, ss	4	1	1	1
McDougald, 2b	3	0	2	0	Thompson, rf	3	1	1	0
DiMaggio, cf	4	0	0	0	Irvin, lf	3	1	0	0
Berra, c	3	0	1	0	Lockman, 1b	4	1	1	3
Brown, 3b	3	0	0	0	Thomson, 3b	4	1	1	0
Collins, 1b	3	0	0	1	Mays, cf	4	0	2	1
Bauer, rf	4	0	0	0	Westrum, c	4	0	0	0
Raschi, p	1	0	0	0	Hearn, p	3	0	0	0
Hogue, p	0	0	0	0	Jones, p	0	0	0	0
Hopp, ph	0	0	0	0					
Ostrowski, p	0	0	0	0					
Mize, ph	1	0	0	0					
Totals	30	2	5	2	**Totals**	31	6	7	5

										R	H	E
Yankees	0	0	0	0	0	0	0	1	1	—	2	5	2
Giants	0	1	0	0	5	0	0	0	x	—	6	7	2

E—Westrum, Berra, Lockman, Rizzuto. DP—Yankees 1, Giants 2. LOB—Yankees 10, Giants 5. 2B—Thomson. HR—Woodling, Lockman.

Yankees	IP	H	R	ER	BB	SO
Raschi (L, 0-1)	4.1	5	6	1	3	3
Hogue	1.2	1	0	0	0	0
Ostrowski	2	1	0	0	0	1
Giants	IP	H	R	ER	BB	SO
Hearn (W, 1-0)	7.2	4	1	1	8	1
Jones (S, 1)	1.1	1	1	1	0	0

HBP—By Hearn (Rizzuto), By Raschi (Stanky). Umpires—Paparella (A.L.), Barlick (N.L.), Summers (A.L.), Ballanfant (N.L.), Stevens (A.L.), Gore (N.L.). Time—2:42. Attendance—52,035.

Game 4 (Oct. 8)

Yankees	AB	R	H	RBI		Giants	AB	R	H	RBI
Bauer, rf	4	0	2	0		Stanky, 2b	4	0	1	0
Rizzuto, ss	5	1	1	0		Dark, ss	4	1	3	0
Berra, c	5	1	1	0		Thompson, rf	3	1	0	0
DiMaggio, cf	5	1	2	2		Irvin, lf	4	0	2	1
Woodling, lf	4	2	1	0		Lockman, 1b	4	0	0	0
McDougald, 2b-3b	4	0	1	1		Thomson, 3b	2	0	2	1
Brown, 3b	4	1	2	0		Mays, cf	4	0	0	0
Coleman, 2b	0	0	0	0		Westrum, c	2	0	0	0
Collins, 1b	3	0	1	1		Maglie, p	1	0	0	0
Reynolds, p	4	0	1	1		Lohrke, ph	1	0	0	0
						Jones, p	0	0	0	0
						Rigney, ph	1	0	0	0
						Kennedy, p	0	0	0	0
Totals	38	6	12	5		Totals	30	2	8	2

										R	H	E
Yankees	0	1	0	1	2	0	2	0	0	—	6	12	0
Giants	1	0	0	0	0	0	0	0	1	—	2	8	2

E—Thomson, Stanky. DP—Yankees 3. LOB—Yankees 8, Giants 5. 2B—Woodling, Brown, Dark 3. HR—DiMaggio.

Yankees	IP	H	R	ER	BB	SO
Reynolds (W, 1-1)	9	8	2	2	4	7
Giants	IP	H	R	ER	BB	SO
Maglie (L, 0-1)	5	8	4	4	2	3
Jones	3	4	2	0	1	2
Kennedy	1	0	0	0	0	2

Umpires—Barlick (N.L.), Summers (A.L.), Ballanfant (N.L.), Paparella (A.L.), Gore (N.L.), Stevens (A.L.). Time—2:57. Attendance—49,010.

Game 5 (Oct. 9)

Yankees	AB	R	H	RBI		Giants	AB	R	H	RBI
Woodling, lf	3	3	1	0		Stanky, 2b	4	0	0	0
Rizzuto, ss	4	3	2	3		Dark, ss	4	1	2	0
Berra, c	4	2	1	0		Thomson, 3b	4	0	0	0
DiMaggio, cf	5	1	3	3		Irvin, lf	4	0	2	0
Mize, 1b	3	1	1	1		Lockman, 1b	4	0	0	0
Bauer, rf	1	0	0	0		Mays, cf	2	0	0	0
McDougald, 2b-3b	5	1	1	4		Hartung, rf	3	0	0	0
Brown, 3b	3	0	2	0		Westrum, c	3	0	1	0
Coleman, pr-2b	1	1	0	0		Jansen, p	0	0	0	0
Collins, rf-1b	5	1	1	0		Lohrke, ph	1	0	0	0
Lopat, p	5	0	0	0		Kennedy, p	0	0	0	0
						Rigney, ph	1	0	0	0
						Spencer, p	0	0	0	0
						Corwin, p	0	0	0	0
						Williams, ph	1	0	0	0
						Konikowski, p	0	0	0	0
Totals	39	13	12	11		Totals	31	1	5	0

										R	H	E
Yankees	0	0	5	2	0	2	4	0	0	—	13	12	1
Giants	1	0	0	0	0	0	0	0	0	—	1	5	3

E—Irvin, Hartung, Thomson, Woodling. DP—Yankees 1. LOB—Yankees 7, Giants 4. 2B—DiMaggio, Mize, Westrum. 3B—Woodling. HR—Rizzuto, McDougald.

Yankees	IP	H	R	ER	BB	SO
Lopat (W, 2-0)	9	5	1	0	1	3

Giants	IP	H	R	ER	BB	SO
Jansen (L, 0-2)	3	3	5	5	4	1
Kennedy	2	3	2	2	1	2
Spencer	1.1	4	6	6	3	0
Corwin	1.2	1	0	0	0	0
Konikowski	1	1	0	0	0	0

WP—Corwin. Umpires—Summers (A.L.), Ballanfant (N.L.), Paparella (A.L.), Barlick (N.L.), Stevens (A.L.), Gore (N.L.). Time—2:31. Attendance—47,530.

Game 6 (Oct. 10)

Giants	AB	R	H	RBI	Yankees	AB	R	H	RBI
Stanky, 2b	5	1	1	1	Rizzuto, ss	4	0	1	0
Dark, ss	3	1	1	0	Coleman, 2b	4	1	1	0
Lockman, 1b	5	0	3	0	Berra, c	4	1	2	0
Irvin, lf	4	0	0	1	DiMaggio, cf	2	1	1	0
Thomson, 3b	4	0	1	1	McDougald, 3b	4	0	0	1
Thompson, rf	3	0	1	0	Mize, 1b	2	1	1	0
Yvars, ph	1	0	0	0	Collins, 1b	1	0	0	0
Westrum, c	3	0	1	0	Bauer, rf	3	0	1	3
Williams, pr	0	0	0	0	Woodling, lf	3	0	0	0
Jansen, p	0	0	0	0	Raschi, p	1	0	0	0
Mays, cf	3	1	2	0	Sain, p	1	0	0	0
Koslo, p	2	0	0	0	Kuzava, p	0	0	0	0
Rigney, ph	1	0	1	0					
Hearn, p	0	0	0	0					
Noble, ph-c	1	0	0	0					
Totals	35	3	11	3	Totals	29	4	7	4

									R	H	E
Giants	0	0	0	0	1	0	0	0	2	—	3	11	1
Yankees	1	0	0	0	0	3	0	0	x	—	4	7	0

E—Thompson. DP—Giants 1, Yankees 3. LOB—Giants 12, Yankees 5. 2B—Lockman, Berra, DiMaggio. 3B—Bauer.

Giants	IP	H	R	ER	BB	SO
Koslo (L, 1-1)	6	5	4	4	4	3
Hearn	1	1	0	0	0	0
Jansen	1	1	0	0	0	0

Yankees	IP	H	R	ER	BB	SO
Raschi (W, 1-1)	6	7	1	0	5	1
Sain	2	4	2	2	2	2
Kuzava (S, 1)	1	0	0	0	0	0

Raschi pitched to two batters in the 7th.
Sain pitched to three batters in the 9th.

WP—Koslo. PB—Berra. Umpires—Ballanfant (N.L.), Paparella (A.L.), Barlick (N.L.), Summers (A.L.), Gore (N.L.), Stevens (A.L.). Time—2:59. Attendance—61,711.

1954: GIANTS DEFEATED CLEVELAND INDIANS 4 GAMES TO 0

Despite coming in as huge underdogs, the Giants swept the Cleveland Indians in the 1954 World Series four games to none. The Indians won the American League pennant with a then major league record of 11 wins (against 43 losses for a sizzling .721 winning percentage). It marked the end of a five-year reign for the New York Yankees, who finished as runners-up by eight games. Meanwhile, the Giants returned to postseason play after finishing fifth the previous year by winning the National League championship with a 97-57 record, five games better than the Brooklyn Dodgers.

The Giants won the series with batting heroics from an unlikely source (utility man Dusty Rhodes), solid pitching (a 1.46 team ERA) and highlight film-making defense (from center fielder Willie Mays). Rhodes had just six at-bats but produced a .667 batting average with two home runs and seven RBI. He was supported by shortstop Alvin Dark (.412), right fielder Don Mueller (.389) and third baseman Hank Thompson (.364). Left-hander Johnny Antonelli anchored the pitching staff with a 0.84 ERA in 10.2 innings.

Cleveland had one of the best teams ever assembled during the regular season with the likes of second baseman Bobby Avila (.341 batting average, 15 home runs and 67 RBI); third baseman Al Rosen (.300 average, 24 homers and 102 RBI); and right-handed pitchers Bob Lemon (23-7, 2.72 ERA) and Early Wynn (23-11, 2.73 ERA).

Winning Player's Share: $11,118
Losing Player's Share: $6,713

Game 1: September 29 at New York (Polo Grounds)
New York 5, Cleveland 2 (10 innings)

Just as Bobby Thomson's playoff homer in 1951 became one of baseball's most dramatic hits, the Giants won Game 1 by the score of 5-2 in 10 innings at the Polo Grounds in New York on one of the greatest catches in World Series history. It came in the eighth inning of a 2-2 tie.

The Indians had runners on first and second with no outs, and left-hander Don Liddle replaced right-handed starter Sal Maglie to face first baseman Vic Wertz, who sent a 440-foot drive toward the fence in center field. The incomparable Willie Mays sprinted and caught the ball over his left shoulder near the wall.

Mays stopped virtually on a dime and instantly made a great throw back to the infield. The stunned base runners couldn't advance, and right-hander Marv Grissom came in to preserve the tie until the Giants stirred in the bottom of the 10th off Indians' right-handed starter and loser Bob Lemon.

Mays walked with one out and promptly stole second. Third baseman Hank Thompson was walked intentionally and manager Leo Durocher sent Dusty Rhodes to bat for left fielder Monte Irvin. Rhodes hit Lemon's first pitch over the right field fence down the line, a 260-foot home run that gave the Giants a shocking opening victory. "Maybe it wasn't much of a hit, but you had to have a ticket to catch it," Durocher wisecracked.

Game 2: September 30 at New York (Polo Grounds)
New York 3, Cleveland 1

The emotion-filled opener set the tone for the upstart Giants, who took a two games to none lead in the series with a 3-1 win in Game 2 at the Polo Grounds in New York.

But Cleveland left fielder Al Smith's leadoff home run in the first inning put the Indians ahead of Giants' left-hander Johnny Antonelli. A great fielding play by third baseman Hank Thompson helped Antonelli, who scattered eight hits and six walks with nine strikeouts in a route-going performance.

Right-hander Early Wynn carried the 1-0 lead into the fifth, when New York center fielder Willie Mays led off with a walk and raced to third on Thompson's single to right. Dusty Rhodes was called upon as a pinch hitter and once again came through, this time

with a blooper to center for a 1-apiece tie.

Catcher Wes Westrum walked with one out, loading the bases. Antonelli hit a force grounder, but hustled to avoid the double play and the go-ahead run scored. Rhodes, who remained in the game, hit a towering homer to right in the seventh for the final scoring.

Game 3: October 1 at Cleveland (Municipal Stadium)
New York 6, Cleveland 2

The Indians returned home somewhat demoralized. Their American League powerhouse was short-circuited by the Giants' timely hitting, deft defense and solid pitching. Nothing changed when the scene shifted to Municipal Stadium before a crowd of 71,535 as New York took a commanding three games to none lead with a 6-2 victory.

After scoring a run in the first inning, the Giants pulled away with a three-run third off right-handed starter and loser Mike Garcia. Once again, Dusty Rhodes was prominent off the bench. With the bases loaded and one out, he again went to bat for left fielder Monte Irvin. Rhodes delivered a two-run single, and second baseman Davey Williams capped New York's scoring with a squeeze bunt for a 4-0 lead.

Cleveland first baseman Vic Wertz homered off a tiring right-hander Ruben

Gomez in the seventh, but right-hander Hoyt Wilhelm's 1.2 innings of shutout relief completed a four-hit collaboration.

Game 4: October 2 at Cleveland (Municipal Stadium)
New York 7, Cleveland 4

Cleveland right-hander Bob Lemon, who pitched so well in the Game 1 defeat, was clobbered in the deciding fourth game to the tune of a 7-4 New York win before 78,102 fans who attended the Indians' going-away party.

The Giants jumped to a 7-0 lead, more than enough for left-hander Don Liddle's exemplary start. Left fielder Monte Irvin's double and errors by first baseman Vic Wertz and right fielder Wally Westlake helped the Giants take a 2-0 lead in the second inning. Singles by shortstop Alvin Dark, right fielder Don Mueller and center fielder Willie Mays created a 3-0 lead in the third, and a four-run fifth landed the telling blow.

Irvin's two-run single was the key hit in the fifth off right-handed reliever Hal Newhouser. The Indians scored one earned run off Liddle in 6.2 innings (he gave up five hits with one walk and two strikeouts), and right-hander Hoyt Wilhelm and left-hander Johnny Antonelli pitched scoreless relief as the Giants completed a highly unexpected sweep.

This defensive play by center fielder Willie Mays—off the bat of Cleveland Indians' first baseman Vic Wertz in Game 1 of the 1954 World Series—is widely regarded as the best in baseball history. (National Baseball Library and Archive)

1954

Game 1 (Sept. 29)

Cleveland	AB	R	H	RBI	New York	AB	R	H	RBI
Smith, lf	4	1	1	0	Lockman, 1b	5	1	1	0
Avila, 2b	5	1	1	0	Dark, ss	4	0	2	0
Doby, cf	3	0	1	0	Mueller, rf	5	1	2	1
Rosen, 3b	5	0	1	0	Mays, cf	3	1	0	0
Wertz, 1b	5	0	4	2	Thompson, 3b	3	1	1	1
Regalado, pr	0	0	0	0	Irvin, lf	3	0	0	0
Grasso, c	0	0	0	0	Rhodes, ph	1	1	1	3
Philley, rf	3	0	0	0	Williams, 2b	4	0	0	0
Majeski, ph	0	0	0	0	Westrum, c	4	0	2	0
Mitchell, ph	0	0	0	0	Maglie, p	3	0	0	0
Dente, ss	0	0	0	0	Liddle, p	0	0	0	0
Strickland, ss	3	0	0	0	Grissom, p	1	0	0	0
Pope, ph-rf	1	0	0	0					
Hegan, c	4	0	0	0					
Glynn, ph-1b	1	0	0	0					
Lemon, p	4	0	0	0					
Totals	38	2	8	2	Totals	36	5	9	5

												R	H	E
Cleveland	2	0	0	0	0	0	0	0	0	0	—	2	8	0
New York	0	0	2	0	0	0	0	0	0	3	—	5	9	3

One out when winning run scored.

E—Irvin, Mueller 2. LOB—Cleveland 13, New York 9. 2B—Wertz. 3B—Wertz. HR—Rhodes. SB—Mays. S—Irvin, Dente.

Cleveland	IP	H	R	ER	BB	SO
Lemon (L, 0-1)	9.1	9	5	5	5	6

New York	IP	H	R	ER	BB	SO
Maglie	7	7	2	2	2	2
Liddle	0.1	0	0	0	0	0
Grissom (W, 1-0)	2.2	1	0	0	3	2

Maglie pitched to two batters in the 8th.

HBP—By Maglie (Smith). WP—Lemon. Umpires—Barlick (N.L.), Berry (A.L.), Conlan (N.L.), Stevens (A.L.), Wareneke (N.L.), Napp (A.L.). Time—3:11. Attendance—52,751.

Game 2 (Sept. 30)

Cleveland	AB	R	H	RBI	New York	AB	R	H	RBI
Smith, lf	4	1	2	1	Lockman, 1b	4	0	0	0
Avila, 2b	4	0	1	0	Dark, ss	4	0	1	0
Doby, cf	5	0	0	0	Mueller, rf	4	0	0	0
Rosen, 3b	3	0	1	0	Mays, cf	2	1	0	0
Regalado, pr-3b	1	0	0	0	Thompson, 3b	3	1	1	0
Wertz, 1b	3	0	1	0	Irvin, lf	1	0	0	0
Westlake, rf	3	0	1	0	Rhodes, ph-lf	2	1	2	2
Strickland, ss	3	0	0	0	Williams, 2b	3	0	0	0
Philley, ph	1	0	0	0	Westrum, c	2	0	0	0
Dente, ss	0	0	0	0	Antonelli, p	3	0	0	1
Hegan, c	4	0	1	0					
Wynn, p	2	0	1	0					
Majeski, ph	1	0	0	0					
Mossi, p	0	0	0	0					
Totals	34	1	8	1	Totals	28	3	4	3

											R	H	E
Cleveland	1	0	0	0	0	0	0	0	0	—	1	8	0
New York	0	0	0	0	2	0	1	0	x	—	3	4	0

LOB—Cleveland 13, New York 3. 2B—Hegan, Wynn. HR—Smith, Rhodes. S—Wynn.

Cleveland	IP	H	R	ER	BB	SO
Wynn (L, 0-1)	7	4	3	3	2	5
Mossi	1	0	0	0	0	0

New York	IP	H	R	ER	BB	SO
Antonelli (W, 1-0)	9	8	1	1	6	9

WP—Wynn. Umpires—Berry (A.L.), Conlan (N.L.), Stevens (A.L.), Barlick (N.L.), Wareneke (N.L.), Napp (A.L.). Time—2:50. Attendance—49,099.

Game 3 (Oct. 1)

New York	AB	R	H	RBI	Cleveland	AB	R	H	RBI
Lockman, 1b	4	1	1	0	Smith, lf	3	0	0	1
Dark, ss	4	0	1	0	Avila, 2b	2	0	0	0
Mueller, rf	5	2	2	0	Doby, cf	4	0	1	0
Mays, cf	5	1	3	2	Wertz, 1b	4	1	1	1
Thompson, 3b	3	2	1	0	Majeski, 3b	4	0	0	0
Irvin, lf	1	0	0	0	Philley, rf	3	0	1	0
Rhodes, ph-lf	3	0	1	2	Strickland, ss	3	0	0	0
Williams, 2b	2	0	0	1	Pope, ph	1	0	0	0
Westrum, c	4	0	1	1	Hegan, c	2	0	0	0
Gomez, p	4	0	0	0	Glynn, ph	1	1	1	0
Wilhelm, p	0	0	0	0	Naragon, c	0	0	0	0
					Garcia, p	0	0	0	0
					Lemon, ph	1	0	0	0
					Houtteman, p	0	0	0	0
					Regalado, ph	1	0	0	0
					Narleski, p	0	0	0	0
					Mitchell, ph	1	0	0	0
					Mossi, p	0	0	0	0
Totals	35	6	10	6	Totals	30	2	4	2

										R	H	E
New York	1	0	3	0	1	1	0	0	0	—	6	10	1
Cleveland	0	0	0	0	0	0	1	1	0	—	2	4	2

E—Strickland, Garcia, Dark. DP—New York 1, Cleveland 1. LOB—New York 9, Cleveland 5. 2B—Thompson, Glynn. HR—Wertz. S—Dark, Williams, Avilia.

New York	IP	H	R	ER	BB	SO
Gomez (W, 1-0)	7.1	4	2	2	3	2
Wilhelm (S, 1)	1.2	0	0	0	0	2

Cleveland	IP	H	R	ER	BB	SO
Garcia (L, 0-1)	3	5	4	3	3	3
Houtteman	2	2	1	1	1	1
Narleski	3	1	1	1	1	2
Mossi	1	2	0	0	0	1

WP—Garcia. Umpires—Conlan (N.L.), Stevens (A.L.), Barlick (N.L.), Berry (A.L.), Napp (A.L.), Wareneke (N.L.). Time—2:28. Attendance—71,555.

Game 4 (Oct. 2)

New York	AB	R	H	RBI	Cleveland	AB	R	H	RBI
Lockman, 1b	5	0	0	0	Smith, lf	3	0	0	0
Dark, ss	5	2	3	0	Pope, ph-lf	1	0	0	0
Mueller, rf	4	1	3	0	Mitchell, ph	1	0	0	0
Mays, cf	4	1	1	1	Avilia, 2b	4	0	0	0
Thompson, 3b	2	2	1	1	Doby, cf	4	0	0	0
Irvin, lf	4	1	2	2	Rosen, 3b	4	0	1	0
Williams, 2b	2	0	0	0	Wertz, 1b	4	1	2	0
Westrum, c	1	0	0	2	Westlake, rf	4	0	0	0
Liddle, p	3	0	0	0	Dente, ss	3	1	0	0
Wilhelm, p	1	0	0	0	Hegan, c	3	1	1	0
Antonelli, p	0	0	0	0	Lemon, p	1	0	0	0
					Newhouser, p	0	0	0	0
					Narleski, p	0	0	0	0
					Majeski, ph	1	1	1	3
					Mossi, p	0	0	0	0
					Regalado, ph	1	0	1	1
					Garcia, p	0	0	0	0
					Philley, ph	1	0	0	0
Totals	31	7	10	6	Totals	35	4	6	4

											R	H	E
New York	0	2	1	0	4	0	0	0	0	—	7	10	3
Cleveland	0	0	0	0	3	0	1	0	0	—	4	6	2

E—Liddle, Wilhelm, Williams, Westlake, Wertz. DP—New York 1, Cleveland 1. LOB—New York 7, Cleveland 6. 2B—Mays, Irvin, Wertz. HR—Majeski. S—Mueller, Williams, Westrum. SF—Westrum 2.

New York	IP	H	R	ER	BB	SO
Liddle (W, 1-0)	6.2	5	4	1	1	2
Wilhelm	0.2	1	0	0	0	1
Antonelli (S, 1)	1.2	0	0	0	1	3
Cleveland	IP	H	R	ER	BB	SO
Lemon (L, 0-2)	4	7	6	5	3	5
Newhouser	0	1	1	1	1	0
Narleski	1	0	0	0	0	0
Mossi	2	1	0	0	0	0
Garcia	2	1	0	0	1	1

Lemon pitched to three batters in the 5th.
Newhouser pitched to two batters in the 5th.

WP—Liddle. Umpires—Stevens (A.L.), Barlick (N.L.), Berry (A.L.), Conlan (N.L.), Wareneke (N.L.), Napp (A.L.). Time—2:52. Attendance—78,102.

1962: NEW YORK YANKEES DEFEATED GIANTS 4 GAMES TO 3

When the Giants and New York Yankees met in the 1962 World Series, it was not a matchup of cross-town rivals. No Battle of Broadway or Subway Series this time. The Giants had moved across the country from New York to San Francisco four years earlier and were appearing in postseason play for the first time in their new home.

It truly was a classic series, won by the Yankees four games to three, that was not decided until the final out. Just as they had prior to the 1951 World Series against the Yankees, the Giants posted a late-season rally and won a three-game playoff with the Los Angeles Dodgers to take the National League pennant with a 103-62 record. The Yankees won the American League pennant with a 96-66 record, five games ahead of the Minnesota Twins.

Neither team hit well in the series—the Giants .226 and the Yankees .199. San Fran-

cisco outscored New York by a 21-20 margin. Giants' shortstop Jose Pagan led all batters with a .368 average. In a pitching dominated series, San Francisco right-hander Jack Sanford had a 1.93 ERA (five earned runs in 23.1 innings) but managed just a 1-2 record. Yankees' big boppers Mickey Mantle (.120) and Roger Maris (.174) batted a combined .146, but it was small consolation.

Winning Player's Share: $9,883
Losing Player's Share: $7,291

Game 1: October 4 at San Francisco (Candlestick Park)
New York 6, San Francisco 2

The Giants snapped left-hander Whitey Ford's streak of 33.2 scoreless World Series innings, but he posted his record 10th victory in the Fall Classic with a 6-2 win in Game 1 at Candlestick Park in San Francisco.

A crowd of 43,852, delirious over the playoff triumph, barely settled in its seats before the Yankees struck. Second baseman Bobby Richardson and left fielder Tom Tresh singled with one out. After center fielder Mickey Mantle struck out, right fielder Roger Maris lined a two-run double to right that Felipe Alou nearly caught while keeping it from becoming a three-run homer.

Singles by Giants' center fielder Willie Mays and third baseman Jim Davenport were followed by shortstop Jose Pagan's bunt single that eluded

Pitcher Jack Sanford (center) is congratulated after pitching a masterful three-hitter in Game 2 of the 1962 World Series against the New York Yankees. The Giants won the game 2-0 to even the series at one game apiece. (AP/Wide World Photos)

Ford, breaking his scoreless streak in the second inning. Second baseman Chuck Hiller's single and right fielder Felipe Alou's double created a 2-2 tie in the third.

The deadlock persisted until third baseman Clete Boyer homered off Giants' left-handed starter and loser Billy O'Dell in the seventh. First baseman Dale Long's run-scoring single and Boyer's sacrifice pop added two runs in the eighth.

Ford survived constant trouble for the complete-game 10-hitter. Mays and Pagan had three hits apiece for the Giants.

Game 2: October 5 at San Francisco (Candlestick Park)
San Francisco 2, New York 0

Giants' right-hander Jack Sanford, pitching perhaps the most important game of his career (until the Series finale), responded with a dazzling three-hitter to edge right-hander Ralph Terry by the score of 2-0 in Game 2 and even the series at one game apiece.

A crucial first-inning play gave the Giants impetus. Second baseman Chuck Hiller, the leadoff batter, drilled a liner near the line in right. Roger Maris appeared to make a great shoetop catch, but the ball slipped out of his glove for a double. Right fielder Felipe Alou sacrificed Hiller to third, from where he scored on brother and left fielder Matty's grounder to second.

The 1-0 lead lasted until first baseman Willie McCovey hit a tape-

measure home run in the seventh. It was the longest of six San Francisco hits.

Sanford, pitching on two day's rest, was never better. He yielded a pop bunt by left fielder Tom Tresh in the first, a single by third baseman Clete Boyer in the fifth and a double by center fielder Mickey Mantle in the ninth. Sanford, who walked three and struck out six, regarded it the finest game he ever pitched.

Game 3: October 7 at New York (Yankee Stadium)
New York 3, San Francisco 2

The Giants returned to the Bronx and were greeted by 71,434 fans at Yankee Stadium, but right-hander Bill Stafford blanked them for the first eight innings and the Yankees won yet another well-pitched game, this one 3-2 to take a two games to one series lead. The Yankees mustered merely five hits, one more than the Giants.

San Francisco left-hander Billy Pierce, a longtime Yankees' nemesis from his days with the Detroit Tigers and Chicago White Sox, blanked the Bombers over the first six innings with the help of Felipe Alou's glove work in right field. New York had not scored for 15 innings when it erupted for all its scoring in the seventh.

Left fielder Tom Tresh led off with a single and went to third on center fielder Mickey Mantle's single. Mantle advanced on Alou's error, and right fielder Roger Maris followed with a two-run single that chased Pierce. Willie McCovey, playing right field, bobbled the ball for an error and Maris reached second.

Right-hander Don Larsen took over, and the Yankees scratched for what proved to be the winning run. Maris tagged and advanced on catcher Elston Howard's fly, first baseman Bill Skowron was struck by a pitch and Maris scored on a botched double-play grounder hit by third baseman Clete Boyer.

The Giants finally rallied in the ninth off Stafford, who had a one-hitter for seven innings. Stafford was struck on the shin by a

liner off the bat of Alou in the eighth, and he gave up two runs in the ninth on center fielder Willie Mays' single and a two-out homer by catcher Ed Bailey.

Game 4: October 8 at New York (Yankee Stadium)
San Francisco 7, New York 3

The most decisive victory of the series belonged to the Giants, a 7-3 decision in Game 4 at Yankee Stadium that evened the series at two games apiece.

A grand slam by second baseman Chuck Hiller—the first blast by a National Leaguer in World Series history—was the big blow. Hiller and catcher Tom Haller both had two of the Giants' nine hits before 66,607 spectators.

Curiously, it was October 8—the sixth anniversary of Don Larsen's perfect game for the Yankees against the Brooklyn Dodgers—and the right-hander was the winner in what started as a pitchers' duel between Giants' right-hander Juan Marichal and Yankees' left-hander Whitey Ford. Then an injury knocked Marichal from the game in the fifth. Attempting to bunt, he fouled a pitch off his right index finger.

The Yankees rallied for a 2-apiece tie in the sixth off right-handed reliever Bobby Bolin, whose first 20 pitches in relief of Marichal were strikes. Haller's two-run homer opened the scoring in the second.

In the sixth, center fielder Mickey Mantle and right fielder Roger Maris walked and first baseman Bill Skowron and third baseman Clete Boyer followed with run-scoring hits.

Right-hander Jim Coates replaced Ford and walked Davenport opening the seventh. Giants' manager Alvin Dark boldly had Matty Alou bat for shortstop Jose Pagan, his hottest hitter. Alou responded with a double to left. Left-hander Marshall Bridges took over and intentionally walked pinch hitter Bob Nieman. Then with two outs, Hiller drilled his historic homer to right for a 6-2 lead.

Larsen earned the win despite pitching just one-third of an inning, and left-hander Billy O'Dell allowed only one run over the final three innings to preserve the victory.

Game 5: October 10 at New York (Yankee Stadium)
New York 5, San Francisco 3

Right-handers Jack Sanford of the Giants and Ralph Terry of the Yankees were up to their old tricks as a crowd of 63,145 at Yankee Stadium roared its approval of a 5-3 win by the home team and a three games to two series lead.

The two starting pitchers were embroiled in a 2-apiece tie after seven innings when New York erupted for the winning rally in the eighth inning on left fielder Tom Tresh's three-run homer.

Before that, the Yankees had difficulty solving Sanford early, scoring their first two runs on a wild pitch and a passed ball. But shortstop Tony Kubek singled with one out in the eighth and second baseman Bobby Richardson followed with a single to left. Tresh followed with a homer to left for a 5-2 advantage.

Curiously, the Yankees had merely six hits—two apiece by Kubek, Richardson and Tresh at the top of the order. The rest of the team was hitless in 19 at-bats. That enabled Sanford to keep it close until Tresh's homer. Sanford worked the first 7.1 innings, allowing five runs (four earned) on six hits with one walk and 10 strikeouts.

Shortstop Jose Pagan's single and second baseman Chuck Hiller's double opened the Giants' scoring in the third and Pagan homered in the fifth. First baseman Willie McCovey's single and catcher Tom Haller's double scored the final run in the ninth.

Pagan and left fielder Felipe Alou both had two of the Giants' eight hits off Terry, who walked one and struck out seven while pitching a complete game.

Game 6: October 15 at San Francisco (Candlestick Park)
San Francisco 5, New York 2

Rain delayed the start of Game 6 for three days, but the wait was worth it for 43,948 partisans at Candlestick Park in San Francisco. Crafty left-hander Billy Pierce continued his mastery at home, and the Yankees were no exception while succumbing on three hits by the score of 5-2. Thus, the series again was tied, this time at three games apiece.

It was scoreless until the Giants tagged Yankees' left-hander Whitey Ford with three runs in the fourth inning. Right fielder Felipe Alou singled with one out and center fielder Mays walked. On an attempted pickoff at second, Alou scored and Mays reached third on Ford's throwing error. First baseman Orlando Cepeda's double and third baseman Jim Davenport's single made it 3-0. Cepeda's bad-hop single in the second had snapped an 0-for-29 slump by the "Baby Bull" in World Series and All-Star games.

Meanwhile, Pierce retired the first 12 batters. Then right fielder Roger Maris homered in the fifth to trim the deficit to 5-1 before the Giants quickly responded with two runs in the bottom half. Singles by left fielder Harvey Kuenn and second baseman Chuck Hiller placed the wheels in motion. Run-scoring singles by Alou and Cepeda made it 5-1. It was Cepeda's third hit.

Pierce had two walks and two strikeouts in his route-going performance.

Game 7: October 16 at San Francisco (Candlestick Park)
New York 1, San Francisco 0

Joe DiMaggio called it the best series game he ever saw as he assembled among a crowd of 43,948 at Candlestick Park in San Francisco for the deciding game of a World Series that featured alternating wins by each club. This time, it was the Yankees' turn 1-0 as right-hander Ralph Terry barely edged right-hander Jack Sanford.

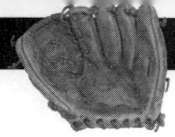

Terry went the distance on a four-hitter, surviving a tension-filled bottom of the ninth inning to earn series Most Valuable Player honors. The Yankees had seven hits in seven innings off Sanford, yet their only run came on a double-play grounder in the fifth inning.

First baseman Bill Skowron and third baseman Clete Boyer opened the fifth with singles and Terry walked on four pitches, loading the bases with no outs. Shortstop Tony Kubek then bounced into a double play and Skowron scored the game's lone run.

The Yankees loaded the bases again with one out in the eighth. Second baseman Bobby Richardson was safe on an error, left fielder Tom Tresh had an infield single and center fielder Mickey Mantle singled to right. Left-hander Billy O'Dell replaced Sanford and got right fielder Roger Maris to ground into a double play, setting the stage for a dramatic ninth inning.

Terry had a perfect game until Sanford singled with two away in the sixth. Left fielder Willie McCovey tripled in the seventh, and those were the only two runners off Terry until the Giants stirred in the controversial bottom of the ninth.

Pinch hitter Matty Alou beat out a bunt leading off. Terry promptly struck out right fielder Felipe Alou and second baseman Chuck Hiller. Center fielder Willie Mays followed with a double to right, but Maris recovered the ball quickly and fired it to Richardson who relayed it to catcher Elston Howard. Matty Alou properly was held at third by coach Whitey Lockman.

With first base open and the left-handed McCovey due to bat, manager Ralph Houk of the Yankees had the option of walking the original "Big Mac" and pitching to first baseman Orlando Cepeda. Terry preferred McCovey, whose sizzling liner to Richardson at second base ended a great series.

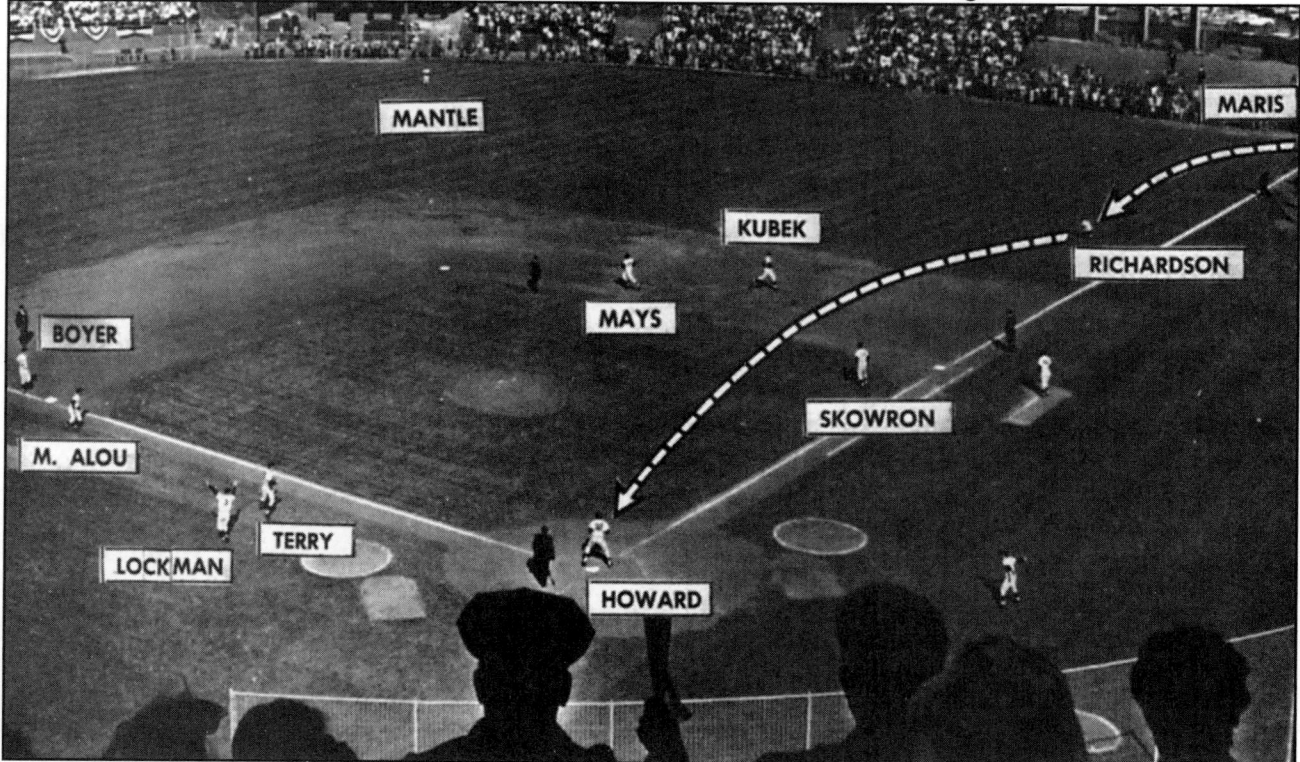

With two outs in the bottom of the ninth inning of Game 7 of the 1962 World Series—with the Yankees leading 1-0—the Giants' Willie Mays doubled to right field. New York's Roger Maris fielded the ball and made a perfect throw to second baseman Bobby Richardson, who relayed it to catcher Elston Howard. San Francisco third base coach Whitey Lockman held base runner Matty Alou at third. The next batter, Willie McCovey, lined out to Richardson to end the game and the series. (AP/Wide World Photos)

1962
Game 1 (Oct. 4)

New York	AB	R	H	RBI	San Francisco	AB	R	H	RBI
Kubek, ss	5	0	2	0	Kuenn, lf	5	0	0	0
Richardson, 2b	5	1	1	0	Hiller, 2b	4	1	1	0
Tresh, lf	5	2	2	0	F. Alou, rf	4	0	1	0
Mantle, cf	4	0	0	0	Mays, cf	4	1	3	1
Maris, rf	4	1	2	2	Cepeda, 1b	4	0	0	0
Howard, c	3	1	2	1	Davenport, 3b	2	0	1	0
Skowron, 1b	2	0	0	0	Bailey, c	4	0	0	0
Long, 1b	2	0	1	1	Miller, p	0	0	0	0
Boyer, 3b	3	1	1	2	Pagan, ss	4	0	3	1
Ford, p	3	0	0	0	O'Dell, p	3	0	1	0
					Larsen, p	0	0	0	0
					Orsino, c	1	0	0	0
Totals	36	6	11	6	Totals	35	2	10	2

											R	H	E
New York	2	0	0	0	0	0	1	2	1	—	6	11	0
San Francisco	0	1	1	0	0	0	0	0	0	—	2	10	0

DP—New York 2, San Francisco 1. LOB—New York 10, San Francisco 8. 2B—Maris, Hiller. HR—Boyer. SB—Tresh, Mantle. SF—Boyer.

New York	IP	H	R	ER	BB	SO
Ford (W, 1-0)	9	10	2	2	2	6

San Francisco	IP	H	R	ER	BB	SO
O'Dell (L, 0-1)	7.1	9	5	5	3	8
Larsen	1.0	1	1	1	1	0
Miller	0.2	1	0	0	1	0

HBP—By O'Dell (Howard). Umpires—Barlick (N.L.), Berry (A.L.), Landes (N.L.), Honochick (A.L.), Burkhart (N.L.), Soar (A.L.). Time—2:43. Attendance—43,852.

Game 2 (Oct. 5)

New York	AB	R	H	RBI	San Francisco	AB	R	H	RBI
Kubek, ss	4	0	0	0	Hiller, 2b	3	1	1	0
Richardson, 2b	4	0	0	0	F. Alou, rf	2	0	1	0
Tresh, lf	3	0	1	0	M. Alou, lf	4	0	1	1
Mantle, cf	4	0	1	0	Mays, cf	4	0	0	0
Maris, rf	3	0	0	0	McCovey, 1b	4	1	1	1
Berra, c	2	0	0	0	Haller, c	3	0	1	0
Long, 1b	3	0	0	0	Davenport, 3b	3	0	0	0
Boyer, 3b	3	0	1	0	Pagan, ss	1	0	0	0
Terry, p	2	0	0	0	Sanford, p	3	0	1	0
Blanchard, ph	1	0	0	0					
Daley, p	0	0	0	0					
Totals	29	0	3	0	Totals	27	2	6	2

											R	H	E
New York	0	0	0	0	0	0	0	0	—		0	3	1
San Francisco	1	0	0	0	0	0	1	0	x	—	2	6	0

E—Kubek. DP—San Francisco 1. LOB—New York 5, San Francisco 6. 2B—Mantle, Hiller. HR—McCovey. SB—Tresh. S—F. Alou, Pagan.

New York	IP	H	R	ER	BB	SO
Terry (L, 0-1)	7	5	2	2	1	5
Daley	1	1	0	0	1	0

San Francisco	IP	H	R	ER	BB	SO
Sanford (W, 1-0)	9	3	0	0	3	6

HBP—By Terry (Pagan). Umpires—Berry (A.L.), Landes (N.L.), Honochick (A.L.), Barlick (N.L.), Burkhart (N.L.), Soar (A.L.). Time—2:11. Attendance—43,910.

Game 3 (Oct. 7)

San Francisco	AB	R	H	RBI	New York	AB	R	H	RBI
F. Alou, rf	4	0	0	0	Kubek, ss	4	0	1	0
Hiller, 2b	3	0	0	0	Richardson, 2b	4	0	0	0
Mays, cf	4	1	1	0	Tresh, lf	4	1	1	0
McCovey, rf	3	0	0	0	Mantle, cf	3	1	1	0
Cepeda, 1b	4	0	0	0	Maris, rf	3	1	1	2
Bailey, c	4	1	1	2	Howard, c	3	0	1	0
Davenport, 3b	4	0	1	0	Skowron, 1b	2	0	0	0
Pagan, ss	3	0	1	0	Boyer, 3b	3	0	0	1
Pierce, p	2	0	0	0	Stafford, p	3	0	0	0
Larsen, p	0	0	0	0					
M. Alou, ph	1	0	0	0					
Bolin, p	0	0	0	0					
Totals	32	2	4	2	Totals	29	3	5	3

										R	H	E
San Francisco	0	0	0	0	0	0	0	0	2	—	2	4	3
New York	0	0	0	0	0	0	3	0	x	—	3	5	1

E—McCovey, F. Alou, Davenport, Boyer. DP—San Francisco 1. LOB—San Francisco 5, New York 3. 2B—Mays, Davenport, Kubek, Howard. HR—Bailey.

San Francisco	IP	H	R	ER	BB	SO
Pierce (L, 0-1)	6	5	3	2	0	3
Larsen	1	0	0	0	0	0
Bolin	1	0	0	0	0	1
New York	IP	H	R	ER	BB	SO
Stafford (W, 1-0)	9	4	2	2	2	5

Pierce pitched to five batters in the 7th.

HBP—By Larsen (Skowron). Umpires—Landes (N.L.), Honochick (A.L.), Barlick (N.L.), Berry (A.L.), Soar (A.L.), Burkhart (N.L.). Time—2:06. Attendance—71,434.

Game 4 (Oct. 8)

San Francisco	AB	R	H	RBI	New York	AB	R	H	RBI
Kuenn, rf	3	0	0	0	Kubek, ss	4	1	1	0
O'Dell, p	0	0	0	0	Richardson, 2b	4	0	1	0
Hiller, 2b	5	1	2	4	Tresh, lf	5	0	2	1
Mays, cf	5	0	1	0	Mantle, cf	4	1	0	0
F. Alou, lf	4	1	1	0	Maris, rf	3	1	0	0
Cepeda, 1b	4	0	0	0	Howard, c	4	0	0	0
Davenport, 3b	2	1	0	0	Skowron, 1b	4	0	3	1
Haller, c	4	1	2	2	Boyer, 3b	4	0	2	1
Pagan, ss	2	0	1	0	Ford, p	2	0	0	0
M. Alou, pr-rf	2	2	2	0	Berra, ph	0	0	0	0
Marichal, p	2	0	0	0	Coates, p	0	0	0	0
Bolin, p	0	0	0	0	Bridges, p	0	0	0	0
Larsen, p	0	0	0	0	Lopez, ph	1	0	0	0
Bailey, ph	0	0	0	0					
Nieman, ph	0	0	0	0					
Bowman, pr-ss	1	1	0	0					
Totals	34	7	9	6	Totals	35	3	9	3

										R	H	E
San Francisco	0	2	0	0	0	0	4	0	1	—	7	9	1
New York	0	0	0	0	0	2	0	0	1	—	3	9	1

E—Davenport, Richardson. DP—San Francisco 2, New York 1. LOB—San Francisco 5, New York 10. 2B—F. Alou, M. Alou. 3B—Skowron. HR—Hiller, Haller. S—O'Dell.

San Francisco	IP	H	R	ER	BB	SO
Marichal	4	2	0	0	2	4
Bolin	1.2	4	2	2	2	1
Larsen (W, 1-0)	0.1	0	0	0	1	0
O'Dell (S, 1)	3	3	1	1	0	0

New York	IP	H	R	ER	BB	SO
Ford	6	5	2	2	1	3
Coates (L, 0-1)	0.1	1	2	2	1	1
Bridges	2.2	3	3	2	2	3

Umpires—Honochick (A.L.), Barlick (N.L.), Berry (A.L.), Landes (N.L.), Soar (A.L.), Burkhart (N.L.). Time—2:55. Attendance—66,607.

Game 5 (Oct. 10)

San Francisco	AB	R	H	RBI		New York	AB	R	H	RBI
Hiller, 2b	3	0	1	1		Kubek, ss	4	1	2	0
Davenport, 3b	4	0	0	0		Richardson, 2b	4	2	2	0
M. Alou, rf	4	0	0	0		Tresh, lf	3	2	2	3
Mays, cf	4	0	0	0		Mantle, cf	3	0	0	0
McCovey, 1b	4	1	1	0		Maris, rf	3	0	0	0
F. Alou, lf	4	0	2	0		Howard, c	4	0	0	0
Haller, c	4	0	1	1		Skowron, 1b	3	0	0	0
Pagan, ss	4	2	2	1		Boyer, 3b	3	0	0	0
Sanford, p	2	0	1	0		Terry, p	3	0	0	0
Miller, p	0	0	0	0						
Bailey, ph	1	0	0	0						
Totals	34	3	8	3		Totals	30	5	6	3

											R	H	E
San Francisco	0	0	1	0	1	0	0	0	1	—	3	8	2
New York	0	0	0	1	0	1	0	3	x	—	5	6	0

E—McCovey, Hiller. DP—San Francisco 1. LOB—San Francisco 6, New York 4. 2B—Hiller, Haller, Tresh. 3B—F. Alou. HR—Pagan, Tresh. SB—Mantle. S—Sanford, Tresh.

San Francisco	IP	H	R	ER	BB	SO
Sanford (L, 1-1)	7.1	6	5	4	1	10
Miller	0.2	0	0	0	1	0

New York	IP	H	R	ER	BB	SO
Terry (W, 1-1)	9	8	3	3	1	7

WP—Sanford. PB—Haller. Umpires—Barlick (N.L.), Berry (A.L.), Landes (N.L.), Honochick (A.L.), Soar (A.L.), Burkhart (N.L.). Time—2:42. Attendance—63,165.

Game 6 (Oct. 15)

New York	AB	R	H	RBI		San Francisco	AB	R	H	RBI
Kubek, ss	4	0	1	1		Kuenn, lf	4	1	1	0
Richardson, 2b	4	0	0	0		M. Alou, lf	0	0	0	0
Tresh, lf	4	0	0	0		Hiller, 2b	4	1	2	0
Mantle, cf	4	0	0	0		F. Alou, rf	4	1	2	1
Maris, rf	3	1	1	1		Mays, cf	3	1	1	0
Howard, c	3	0	0	0		Cepeda, 1b	4	1	3	2
Skowron, 1b	3	0	0	0		Davenport, 3b	4	0	1	1
Boyer, 3b	2	1	1	0		Bailey, c	4	0	0	0
Ford, p	2	0	0	0		Pagan, ss	3	0	0	0
Coates, p	0	0	0	0		Pierce, p	3	0	0	0
Lopez, ph	1	0	0	0						
Bridges, p	0	0	0	0						
Totals	30	2	3	2		Totals	33	5	10	4

										R	H	E
New York	0	0	0	0	1	0	0	1	0	—	2	3	2
San Francisco	0	0	0	3	2	0	0	0	x	—	5	10	1

E—Davenport, Boyer, Ford. DP—New York 2, San Francisco 1. LOB—New York 3, San Francisco 5. 2B—Boyer, Cepeda. HR—Maris. SB—Mays.

New York	IP	H	R	ER	BB	SO
Ford (L, 1-1)	4.2	9	5	5	1	3
Coates	2.1	0	0	0	0	2
Bridges	1.0	1	0	0	0	0

San Francisco	IP	H	R	ER	BB	SO
Pierce (W, 1-1)	9	3	2	2	2	2

Umpires—Berry (A.L.), Landes (N.L.), Honochick (A.L.), Barlick (N.L.), Burkhart (N.L.), Soar (A.L.). Time—2:00. Attendance—43,948.

Game 7 (Oct. 16)

New York	AB	R	H	RBI	San Francisco	AB	R	H	RBI
Kubek, ss	4	0	1	0	F. Alou, rf	4	0	0	0
Richardson, 2b	2	0	0	0	Hiller, 2b	4	0	0	0
Tresh, lf	4	0	1	0	Mays, cf	4	0	1	0
Mantle, cf	3	0	1	0	McCovey, lf	4	0	1	0
Maris, rf	4	0	0	0	Cepeda, 1b	3	0	0	0
Howard, c	4	0	0	0	Haller, c	3	0	0	0
Skowron, 1b	4	1	1	0	Davenport, 3b	3	0	0	0
Boyer, 3b	4	0	2	0	Pagan, ss	2	0	0	0
Terry, p	3	0	1	0	Bailey, ph	1	0	0	0
					Bowman, ss	0	0	0	0
					Sanford, p	2	0	1	0
					O'Dell, p	0	0	0	0
					M. Alou, ph	1	0	1	0
Totals	32	1	7	0	Totals	31	0	4	0

										R	H	E
New York	0	0	0	1	0	0	0	0	0	—	1	7	0
San Francisco	0	0	0	0	0	0	0	0	0	—	0	4	1

E—Pagan. DP—San Francisco 2. LOB—New York 8, San Francisco 4. 2B—Mays. 3B—McCovey.

New York	IP	H	R	ER	BB	SO
Terry (W, 2-1)	9	4	0	0	0	4

San Francisco	IP	H	R	ER	BB	SO
Sanford (L, 1-2)	7	7	1	1	4	3
O'Dell	2	0	0	0	0	1

Sanford pitched to three batters in the 8th.

Umpires—Landes (N.L.), Honochick (A.L.), Barlick (N.L.), Berry (A.L.), Burkhart (N.L.), Soar (A.L.). Time—2:29. Attendance—43,948.

1989: OAKLAND ATHLETICS DEFEATED GIANTS 4 GAMES TO 0

The 1989 Bay Bridge Series, won by the Oakland Athletics over the Giants four games to one, always will be remembered for the 7.1 earthquake that rattled Candlestick Park in San Francisco prior to the start of Game 3.

When Mother Nature wasn't shaking up things, the Oakland batters were, to the tune of a .301 team batting average, nine home runs and an average of eight runs scored per game. Giants' pitchers had a combined 8.21 ERA (31 earned runs in 34 innings). The Athletics never trailed in the series.

Two years after losing the National League Championship Series to the St. Louis Cardinals and four years after losing 100 games, the Giants advanced to their first World Series since 1962. They won the N.L. West Division with a 92-70 record, three games ahead of the San Diego Padres, and defeated the Chicago Cubs in the NLCS four games to one. They were led during the regular season by N.L. Most Valuable Player Kevin Mitchell, who batted .291 with 47 home runs and 125 RBI. He was San Francisco's only consistent offensive threat against the Athletics with a .294 batting average (5-for-17), one homer and two RBI.

Across the bay, Oakland was winning the American League West Division with a 99-63 record, seven games in front of the Kansas City Royals. The Athletics downed the Toronto Blue Jays in the ALCS four games to one. Left fielder Rickey Henderson batted .474 during the World Series (9-for-19), while center fielder Dave Henderson belted two homers and catcher Terry Steinbach collected seven RBI.

Winning Player's Share: $114,252
Losing Player's Share: $83,529

Game 1: October 14 at Oakland (Oakland-Alameda Coliseum) Oakland 5, San Francisco 0

After smoking the Chicago Cubs for eight home runs in five National League Championship Series games, the Giants' offense was dormant against the Athletics in Game 1 of the World Series. Right-hander Dave Stewart pitched a five-hit shutout, winning 5-0, before 49,385 fans at Oakland-Alameda Coliseum.

The Athletics scored early and often off San Francisco right-handed starting and losing pitcher Scott Garrelts, erupting for three runs in the second inning. Center fielder Dave Henderson led off with a walk, catcher Terry Steinbach singled with one out and second baseman Tony Phillips lined a run-scoring single to right for a 1-0 advantage.

Steinbach was thrown out at the plate on shortstop Walt Weiss' grounder to first, but catcher Terry Kennedy dropped the ball for an error. Left fielder Rickey Henderson's single concluded the scoring. Designated hitter Dave Parker hit a solo homer in the third and shortstop Walt Weiss did likewise in the fourth.

There were no serious threats off Stewart until the ninth inning, when first baseman Will Clark and left fielder Kevin Mitchell opened with singles. Shortstop Matt Williams struck out and the runners advanced on a passed ball. Designated hitter Ernie Riles' strikeout and right fielder Candy Maldonado's grounder ended the game.

Stewart had one walk and six strikeouts. Clark and Mitchell both had two of the Giants' five hits.

Game 2: October 15 at Oakland (Oakland-Alameda Coliseum) Oakland 5, San Francisco 1

Right-hander Mike Moore nearly duplicated Dave Stewart's feat, yielding one run on four hits over seven-plus innings en route to a 5-1 Oakland win in Game 2 at Oakland-Alameda Coliseum and a two games to none lead in the series.

A crowd of 49,388 watched the Athletics take a 1-0 lead in the first off right-handed starter and loser Rick Reuschel on left fielder Rickey Henderson's leadoff walk, a steal and third baseman Carney Lansford's double.

Singles by catcher Terry Kennedy and center fielder Brett Butler followed by second baseman Robby Thompson's sacrifice fly tied the game in the third, but Oakland crushed Reuschel with a four-run fourth featuring designated hitter Dave Parker's run-scoring double and catcher Terry Steinbach's three-run homer to left.

The Giants were limited to one hit over the last five innings by Moore, left-hander Rick Honeycutt and right-hander Dennis Eckersley, Moore retiring 12 out of 13 batters at one point. Then the series shifted to San Francisco,

A 7.1 earthquake rocked Candlestick Park prior to the start of Game 3 of the 1989 World Series. (S.F. Giants Archives)

where a giant surprise was in store for everyone.

Game 3: October 17 at San Francisco (Candlestick Park)
Canceled

It was October 17, and a huge crowd was on hand for the Giants' first home World Series game since McCovey lined to Richardson in 1962. It was 5:04 p.m., about 30 minutes before the game was to start, and there was a rumble going through the stands.

Even when it was determined the shaking was caused by an earthquake, most fans shrugged it off and were eager to see a baseball game. When there were reports of extensive damage from a 7.1-magnitude earthquake, the attitude quickly changed.

Players poured out of the dugouts and sought out family members in the stands, many of the Giants and Athletics expressing fear. There was structural damage to Candlestick Park, so it was evacuated. Game 3 would not be played for another 10 days.

Game 3: October 27 at San Francisco (Candlestick Park)
Oakland 13, San Francisco 7

When play resumed, the Giants finally rediscovered their offense, but their pitching was no match for an Oakland club which erupted for 14 hits and 13 runs to disappoint 62,083 partisans at the newly-fortified Candlestick Park in San Francisco. The Athletics won 13-7 to take a commanding three games to none lead in the series.

Singles by third baseman Carney Lansford and right fielder Jose Canseco followed by center fielder Dave Henderson's double gave the Athletics a 2-0 first-inning lead off right-handed starter and loser Scott Garrelts.

Giants' shortstop Matt Williams homered off right-hander Dave Stewart in the second, and both teams scored twice in the fourth to make it 4-3 in favor of the Athletics. Oakland knocked out Garrelts with solo homers by Dave Henderson and second baseman Tony Phillips, and the Giants countered on catcher Terry Kennedy's two-run single with two outs.

Then the Athletics scored the next nine runs for a blowout. Canseco's three-run homer and a solo shot by Dave Henderson created a four-run fifth. Lansford homered in the sixth, and the four-run eighth featured run-scoring singles by Lansford and catcher Terry Steinbach off left-handed reliever Atlee Hammaker.

The Giants scored four runs in the ninth. Third baseman Ken Oberkfell led off with a walk, catcher Kirt Manwaring doubled with one out and pinch hitter Bill Bathe, formerly with the Athletics, hit a three-run homer. Center fielder Donnell Nixon's single and second baseman Greg Litton's double finished it.

Though not so sharp as in Game 1, Stewart earned the win after surrendering three runs on five hits with one walk and eight strikeouts in seven innings. Litton collected two of the Giants' 10 hits after entering the game as a pinch hitter.

Game 4: October 28 at San Francisco (Candlestick Park)
Oakland 9, San Francisco 6

The Athletics completed the series sweep with a 9-6 verdict in Game 4 at Candlestick Park in San Francisco.

They wasted no time moving in for the kill, jumping on San Francisco right-hander Don Robinson for a 4-0 lead after two innings. Left fielder Rickey Henderson homered on the third pitch of the game, and the rout was on. Oakland pitcher Mike Moore aided his cause with a two-run double and scored on Henderson's single in the second.

Oakland continued its onslaught against right-handed reliever Mike LaCoss with a three-run fifth that included a two-run, two-out triple by catcher Terry Steinbach and second baseman Tony Phillips' run-scoring double. Third baseman Carney Lansford's single built an 8-0 lead in the top of the sixth.

The 62,032 fans did not have much to cheer for until the home club scored twice in the sixth on first baseman Will Clark's two-out single and left fielder Kevin Mitchell's home run. The Giants added four runs in the seventh with second baseman Greg Litton contributing a two-run homer.

Moore was the winning pitcher after working the first six innings and allowing two runs on five hits with one walk and three strikeouts. Right-hander Dennis Eckersley pitched the ninth to earn the save. Robinson absorbed the loss.

1989

Game 1 (Oct. 14)

San Francisco	AB	R	H	RBI		Oakland	AB	R	H	RBI
Butler, cf	4	0	0	0		R. Henderson, lf	5	0	2	1
Thompson, 2b	4	0	0	0		Lansford, 3b	5	0	1	0
Clark, 1b	4	0	2	0		Gallego, 2b	0	0	0	0
Mitchell, lf	4	0	2	0		Canseco, rf	3	0	0	0
Williams, 3b-ss	4	0	0	0		Parker, dh	4	1	1	1
Riles, dh	4	0	0	0		Henderson, cf	3	1	0	0
Maldonado, rf	4	0	0	0		McGwire, 1b	4	0	3	0
Kennedy, c	3	0	0	0		Steinbach, c	4	1	1	0
Uribe, ss	2	0	1	0		Phillips, 2b-3b	4	1	2	1
Oberkfell, ph-3b	0	0	0	0		Weiss, ss	4	1	1	1
Totals	33	0	5	0		Totals	36	5	11	4

									R	H	E
San Francisco	0	0	0	0	0	0	0	0	0	—	0	5	1
Oakland	0	3	1	1	0	0	0	0	x	—	5	11	1

E—Kennedy, Stewart. LOB—San Francisco 7, Oakland 9. 2B—Clark. HR—Parker, Weiss.

San Francisco	IP	H	R	ER	BB	SO
Garrelts (L, 0-1)	4	7	5	4	1	5
Hammaker	1.2	3	0	0	0	2
Brantley	1.1	1	0	0	1	0
LaCoss	1	0	0	0	0	1

Oakland	IP	H	R	ER	BB	SO
Stewart (W, 1-0)	9	5	0	0	1	6

PB—Steinbach. Umpires—Garcia (A.L.), Runge (N.L.), Voltaggio (A.L.), Rennert (N.L.), Clark (A.L.), Gregg (N.L.). Time—2:45. Attendance—49,385.

Game 2 (Oct. 15)

San Francisco	AB	R	H	RBI	Oakland	AB	R	H	RBI
Butler, cf	2	0	1	0	R. Henderson, lf	3	1	3	0
Thompson, 2b	3	0	0	1	Lansford, 3b	3	0	1	1
Clark, 1b	4	0	0	0	Canseco, rf	2	1	0	0
Mitchell, lf	4	0	1	0	Parker, dh	4	1	1	1
Williams, 3b-ss	4	0	0	0	D. Henderson, cf	3	1	0	0
Riles, dh	3	0	0	0	McGwire, 1b	4	0	1	0
Maldonado, rf	3	0	0	0	Steinbach, c	4	1	1	3
Kennedy, c	3	0	1	0	Phillips, 2b	3	0	0	0
Uribe, ss	2	1	0	0	Weiss, ss	3	0	0	0
Oberkfell, ph-3b	1	0	1	0					
Totals	29	1	4	1	Totals	29	5	7	5

											R	H	E
San Francisco	0	0	1	0	0	0	0	0	0	—	1	4	0
Oakland	1	0	0	4	0	0	0	0	x	—	5	7	0

DP—San Francisco 2, Oakland 1. LOB—San Francisco 4, Oakland 5. 2B—Lansford, Parker, McGwire. 3B—R. Henderson. HR—Steinbach. SB—Butler 2, R. Henderson. SF—Thompson.

San Francisco	IP	H	R	ER	BB	SO
Reuschel (L, 0-1)	4	5	5	5	4	2
Downs	2	1	0	0	0	2
Lefferts	1	1	0	0	1	1
Bedrosian	1	0	0	0	0	2

Oakland	IP	H	R	ER	BB	SO
Moore (W, 1-0)	7	4	1	1	2	7
Honeycutt	1.1	0	0	0	0	1
Eckersley	0.2	0	0	0	0	0

Reuschel pitched to two batters in the 5th.
Moore pitched to one batter in the 8th.

WP—Moore 2. Umpires—Runge (N.L.), Voltaggio (A.L.), Rennert (N.L.), Clark (A.L.), Gregg (N.L.), Garcia (A.L.). Time—2:47. Attendance—49,388.

Game 3 (Oct. 27)

Oakland	AB	R	H	RBI
R. Henderson, lf	5	1	1	0
Nelson, p	0	0	0	0
Burns, p	0	0	0	0
Lansford, 3b	4	4	3	2
Honeycutt, p	0	0	0	0
Gallego, ph-3b	1	0	0	0
Canseco, rf	5	3	3	3
Javier, rf	0	0	0	0
McGwire, 1b	4	0	0	1
D. Henderson, cf	4	2	3	4
Steinbach, c	4	0	1	1
Phillips, 2b-3b-lf	5	1	1	1
Weiss, ss	5	1	1	0
Stewart, p	3	0	0	0
Blankenship, ph-2b	2	1	1	0
Totals	**42**	**13**	**14**	**12**

San Francisco	AB	R	H	RBI
Butler, cf	3	0	0	0
Nixon, ph-cf	2	1	1	0
Thompson, 2b	3	0	0	0
Litton, ph-2b	2	0	2	1
Clark, 1b	4	1	1	0
Mitchell, lf	5	1	1	0
Oberkfell, 3b	2	1	1	0
Williams, ss	4	1	1	1
Kennedy, c	3	0	1	2
Manwaring, c	1	1	1	0
Sheridan, rf	2	0	0	0
Brantley, p	0	0	0	0
Riles, ph	1	0	0	0
Hammaker, p	0	0	0	0
Lefferts, p	0	0	0	0
Bathe, ph	1	1	1	3
Garrelts, p	1	0	0	0
Downs, p	0	0	0	0
Maldonado, rf	3	0	0	0
Totals	**37**	**7**	**10**	**7**

										R	H	E
Oakland	2	0	0	2	4	1	0	4	0	—	13	14	0
San Francisco	0	1	0	2	0	0	0	0	4	—	7	10	3

E—Oberkfell, Lefferts, Mitchell. DP—San Francisco 1. LOB—Oakland 7, San Francisco 6. 2B—R. Henderson, D. Henderson, Litton, Manwaring. HR—Lansford, Canseco, D. Henderson 2, Phillips, Williams, Bathe. SB—R. Henderson 2.

Oakland	IP	H	R	ER	BB	SO
Stewart (W, 2-0)	7	5	3	3	1	8
Honeycutt	1	1	0	0	0	1
Nelson	0.2	3	4	4	1	1
Burns	0.1	1	0	0	1	0

San Francisco	IP	H	R	ER	BB	SO
Garrelts (L, 0-2)	3.1	6	4	4	0	3
Downs	1	2	4	4	2	1
Brantley	2.2	1	1	1	2	1
Hammaker	0.2	5	4	4	0	0
Lefferts	1.1	0	0	0	0	0

HBP—By Hammaker (D. Henderson). BK—Brantley. Umpires—Voltaggio (A.L.), Rennert (N.L.), Clark (A.L.), Gregg (N.L.), Garcia (A.L.), Runge (N.L.). Time—3:30. Attendance—62,038.

Game 4 (Oct. 28)

Oakland	AB	R	H	RBI	San Francisco	AB	R	H	RBI
R. Henderson, lf	6	2	3	2	Butler, cf	5	1	3	1
Lansford, 3b	4	1	2	1	Oberkfell, 3b	3	0	0	0
Canseco, rf	4	1	2	0	Thompson, ph-2b	1	0	1	1
McGwire, 1b	5	0	1	0	Bedrosian, p	0	0	0	0
D. Henderson, cf	3	2	1	0	Clark, 1b	4	1	1	0
Steinbach, c	4	1	1	3	Mitchell, lf	4	1	1	2
Phillips, 2b	5	0	1	1	Williams, ss-3b	4	0	1	0
Weiss, ss	3	1	0	0	Kennedy, c	3	1	0	0
Moore, p	3	1	1	2	Litton, 2b-3b-2b	4	1	1	2
Phelps, ph	1	0	0	0	Nixon, rf	3	0	0	0
Nelson, p	0	0	0	0	Robinson, p	0	0	0	0
Honeycutt, p	0	0	0	0	LaCoss, p	1	0	0	0
Burns, p	0	0	0	0	Bathe, ph	1	0	0	0
Parker, ph	1	0	0	0	Brantley, p	0	0	0	0
Eckersley, p	0	0	0	0	Downs, p	0	0	0	0
					Riles, ph	0	0	0	0
					Maldonado, ph	1	1	1	0
					Lefferts, p	0	0	0	0
					Uribe, ss	1	0	0	0
Totals	39	9	12	9	Totals	35	6	9	6

											R	H	E
Oakland	1	3	0	0	3	1	0	1	0	—	9	12	0
San Francisco	0	0	0	0	0	2	4	0	0	—	6	9	0

LOB—Oakland 10, San Francisco 4. 2B—D. Henderson, Phillips, Moore, Butler. 3B—R. Henderson, Steinbach, Maldonado. HR—R. Henderson, Mitchell, Litton. SB—Canseco.

Oakland	IP	H	R	ER	BB	SO
Moore (W, 2-0)	6	5	2	2	1	3
Nelson	0.1	1	2	2	1	0
Honeycutt	0.1	3	2	2	0	0
Burns	1.1	0	0	0	0	0
Eckersley (S, 1)	1	0	0	0	0	0

San Francisco	IP	H	R	ER	BB	SO
Robinson (L, 0-1)	1.2	4	4	4	1	0
LaCoss	3.1	4	3	3	3	1
Brantley	0.1	3	1	1	0	0
Downs	1.2	0	0	0	0	1
Lefferts	0.1	1	1	1	1	0
Bedrosian	1.2	0	0	0	2	0

Umpires—Rennert (N.L.), Clark (A.L.), Gregg (N.L.), Garcia (A.L.), Runge (N.L.), Voltaggio (A.L.). Time—3:07. Attendance—62,032.

2002: ANAHEIM ANGELS DEFEATED GIANTS 4 GAMES TO 3

The 2002 World Series was a bittersweet experience for the Giants, who were on the verge of their first championship since 1954 when they faltered at the finish after taking a 3-2 games lead when play returned to Anaheim following a record-shattering 16-4 romp at Pacific Bell Park in Game 5.

It seemed like a done deal when the Giants took a 5-0 lead in the top of the seventh inning of Game 6. The champagne was waiting in the clubhouse when the complexion of the game suddenly changed on a three-run homer by Scott Spiezio in the bottom of the seventh. Darin Erstad's solo homer and Series MVP Troy Glaus' two-run double produced a deflating 6-5 victory in the bottom of the ninth.

The Giants never recovered. They came out flat in Game 7, and were overwhelmed 4-1 on Garret Anderson's tie-breaking three-run double in the fourth inning. The dejection temporarily overshadowed the Giants' brilliant 25-8 stretch run for the National League wild card and stunning upsets of the Braves and Cardinals in the playoffs.

In retrospect, baseball's first Wild Card World Series spotlighted two hungry teams who entered the playoffs through the back door and emerged playing the most offense-minded Fall Classic in history, one which produced a record 21 home runs and 85 runs scored. The winning Angels were outhomered 14-7 and outscored 44-41.

The Giants' loss also dimmed the luster of Barry Bonds' postseason redemption. He smacked a record eight home runs, including four in the World Series despite being walked 13 times. And, after leading the National League with a .370 average, he batted .471 in the World Series. Jeff Kent had a team-high seven RBI for the Giants. Glaus and Spiezio each had eight for the champs.

Game 1: October 19 at Anaheim (Edison International Field) San Francisco 4, Anaheim 3

Relievers Felix Rodriguez, Tim Worrell and Rob Nen held the Angels hitless over the final 3 1/3 innings to nail down a 4-3 victory before 44,603 in Anaheim's first World Series appearance since the birth of the expansion franchise in 1961. The three relievers collectively retired 10 of the 11 batters they faced.

First baseman J.T. Snow, like Nen a former Orange County prep, provided the winning runs with a two-out, two-run homer off Angels' ace Jarrod Washburn in the top of the sixth inning. Barry Bonds, on his first World

Barry Bonds redeemed his postseason image in smashing style in 2002, sending eight balls into orbit—four in the World Series alone. (© S.F. Giants)

373

Series at-bat, gave the Giants a 1-0 lead with a leadoff homer off Washburn in the second.

Reggie Sanders also connected in the second for a 2-0 lead, and Troy Glaus got the Angels going with a solo homer off Jason Schmidt in the second. It remained 2-1 until Sanders singled with two outs in the sixth and Snow, a former Angel, expanded the lead to 4-1 with his homer.

Glaus opened the bottom of the sixth with his second home run, and Schmidt was lifted after a walk and Adam Kennedy's two-out single made it 4-3. Then the bullpen took over, fired zeroes and sealed the Giants' first World Series victory since Billy Pierce downed the Yankees 5-2 in Game 6 of 1962.

Game 2: October 20 at Anaheim (Edison International Field) Anaheim 11, San Francisco 10

The two clubs gave every indication that offense would prevail in a wild World Series when the Angels squeezed out an 11-10 triumph before 44,584 on Tim Salmon's second two-run homer of a three-hour, 57-minute donnybrook. It came off Felix Rodriguez with two outs in the bottom of the eighth and gave Anaheim an 11-9 lead.

Barry Bonds then sent a Troy Percival fastball into orbit in the top of the ninth for his second homer of the World Series and a final one-run deficit. The two teams combined for 28 hits and each batted around once in a game that featured the big inning, including a five-run first that didn't hold up for Anaheim.

Six of the first seven batters hit safely off Russ Ortiz as the Angels built a 5-0 lead. But Reggie Sanders' three-run homer followed by David Bell's solo quickly gave the Giants four runs off Kevin Appier in the second. Salmon's first homer made it 7-4, and Jeff Kent hit a leadoff homer off Appier in the third.

J.T. Snow's two-run single was the key blow in the Giants' four-run fifth for a 9-7 lead, but the Angels scored single runs in the fifth and sixth for a tie before David Eckstein's single and Salmon's second homer produced a

victory for rookie sensation Francisco Rodriguez, who retired all nine batters he faced, four on strikeouts.

Game 3: October 22 at San Francisco (Pacific Bell Park) Anaheim 10, San Francisco 4

The Angels threatened to obliterate World Series records when their second straight 16-hit outburst produced a 10-4 rout before 42,707 disappointed partisans. Darin Erstad paced the Anaheim attack with a double and two singles, but Scott Spiezio landed the big blows with a two-run triple and a run-scoring single for three RBI.

Kenny Lofton's leadoff walk, his steal of second and Benito Santiago's bases-loaded grounder enabled the Giants to scratch for a run in the first inning, but Livan Hernandez ran into big trouble in the third after escaping a bases-loaded jam in the second to protect the short-lived lead.

Spiezio's triple was the key blast in a four-run third, and Hernandez was chased as the Angels scored four more runs in the fourth for an 8-1 lead. Successive run-scoring singles by Spiezio, Adam Kennedy and Bengie Molina did the big damage off reliever Jay Witasick before the Giants stirred again.

They scored three runs in the bottom of the fifth off starter Ramon Ortiz. Rich Aurilia homered with one out, Jeff Kent lined a single to left and Barry Bonds homered for a third straight game, this one a 437-foot bolt to right-center. It was too little, too late. The Angels' bullpen fired one-hit relief over four innings to seal the deal.

Game 4: October 23 at San Francisco (Pacific Bell Park) San Francisco 4, Anaheim 3

David Bell's run-scoring single with one out in the bottom of the eighth inning cracked a tie as the Giants overcame a 3-0 deficit, dented rookie Francisco Rodriguez's armor and produced a series-squaring 4-3 victory before

Fans hoping to catch a Barry Bonds' homer gather in McCovey Cove during Game 3 of the 2002 World Series. (© S.F. Giants)

42,703. Rodriguez had retired 12 straight batters over two appearances before the decisive eighth.

After Rodriguez retired the Giants in order in the seventh, J.T. Snow opened the eighth with a sharp single to right. Reggie Sanders, attempting to sacrifice, fouled out before Snow advanced on catcher Bengie Molina's passed ball. Bell then lined a 1-0 pitch to center for the go-ahead run.

The Angels opened the scoring in the second on successive one-out singles by Benji Gil, Molina and pitcher John Lackey followed by David Eckstein's sacrifice fly. They made it 3-0 in the third on Glaus' two-run homer before Kirk Rueter settled down and pitched three shutout innings.

Rueter also ignited the Giants' comeback with a leadoff single in the fifth. Kenny Lofton then dropped a bunt single that hugged the

third base line and Rich Aurilia singled for 3-1. Jeff Kent's sacrifice fly cut the lead to one run and, after Barry Bonds was walked intentionally, Benito Santiago's single created a tie.

Game 5: October 24 at San Francisco (Pacific Bell Park)
San Francisco 16, Anaheim 4

Jeff Kent hit a pair of two-run homers and a double, scoring four runs and driving in four to power the Giants to a 16-4 romp before 42,713 satiated spectators. The home team closed out its Pac Bell season by bolting to a 6-0 lead after two innings and turning a 16-hit attack into a 3-2 World Series lead.

Angels ace Jarrod Washburn was roughed up for the second time, with four walks in the first inning contributing to his demise. Barry Bonds' double opened the scoring, and Benito

Santiago's sacrifice fly and David Bell's bases-loaded walk made it 3-0. Santiago added a two-run single in the three-run second.

Starter Jason Schmidt dominated the Angels with seven strikeouts through four innings, but Troy Glaus' run-scoring double crowned a three-run fifth. Anaheim added a run in the sixth, cutting the lead to 6-4, but the Giants' bullpen stopped the scoring and the hitters continued their rampage against the Angels' relievers.

Kent's first two-run homer created breathing room in the sixth. He connected again in a four-run seventh that also included a two-run triple by Kenny Lofton, who scored three runs. The Giants concluded their run-away with four unearned runs in the eighth, Rich Aurilia belting a three-run homer with two outs.

Game 6: October 26 at Anaheim (Edison International Field) Anaheim 6, San Francisco 5

In what turned out to be the pivotal game of the World Series, the Angels delighted 44,506 fans by rallying from a 5-0 deficit on their final two at-bats for a dramatic 6-5 victory that could have been scripted in nearby Hollywood. With Russ Ortiz in complete control, the Giants seemed destined to end their 48-year championship drought.

Ortiz, in what would be his final game as a Giant, was magnificent, shackling the Angels on two singles through six innings. Anaheim starter Kevin Appier kept pace until San Francisco cracked a scoreless tie in the sixth. David Bell singled to short with one out for the Giants' second hit of the game.

Veteran Shawon Dunston, used as the DH in the ninth spot, homered down the line in left for a 2-0 lead. Kenny Lofton's double, his steal, a grounder and Francisco Rodriguez's wild pitch made it 3-0. Barry Bonds' homer off Rodriguez added a run in the sixth for 4-0 entering the fateful seventh.

Jeff Kent flashed some rare emotion when his single made it 5-0 in the seventh, but the celebration was premature. Ortiz was lifted after Troy Glaus and Brad Fullmer hit one-out singles. Then the Giants' bullpen inexplicably collapsed. Felix Rodriguez gave up Scott Spiezio's three-run homer in the seventh and Tim Worrell and Robb Nen yielded big hits in the eighth, giving the Angels a stirring victory.

Game 7: October 27 at Anaheim (Edison International Field) Anaheim 4, San Francisco 1

The Giants' worst fears were realized on a lost weekend near Disneyland, where the Angels' magic carpet ride concluded with a 4-1 victory that touched off a wild celebration before 44,598 jubilant fans. There was little drama in the clincher because Livan Hernandez's horrid start gave the champions the early momentum.

While Anaheim completed its scoring on Garret Anderson's three-run double in the third inning, Angels starter John Lackey and relievers Brendan Donnelly and Francisco Rodriguez continually thwarted Giants' threats. San Francisco placed nine runners on base, yet only one scored.

That was in the second inning, when Reggie Sanders followed one-out singles by Benito Santiago and J.T. Snow with a sacrifice fly. Scott Spiezio's two-out walk and Bengie Molina's double quickly made it 1-1 in the bottom half. David Eckstein and Darin Erstad opened the third with singles.

Then Hernandez struck Tim Salmon with a pitch, loading the bases with no outs. Anderson, silent most of the series, unloaded them by lining a 1-1 pitch to right for a sudden 4-1. It was all the offense the Angels would require as they joined the 1997 Florida Marlins as the only wild cards to win baseball's biggest poker hand.

2002

Game 1 (Oct. 19 at Anaheim)

San Francisco	AB	R	H	RBI	BB	SO
K. Lofton, cf	3	0	0	0	0	1
R. Aurilia, ss	4	0	0	0	0	0
J. Kent, 2b	4	0	0	0	0	1
B. Bonds, lf	3	1	1	1	1	1
B. Santiago,c	4	0	1	0	0	1
R. Sanders, rf	3	2	2	1	1	1
J. Snow, 1b	3	1	1	2	1	0
D. Bell, 3b	4	0	0	0	0	1
T. Shinjo, dh	3	0	1	0	0	1
a-T. Goodwin, ph-dh	1	0	0	0	0	0
Totals	32	4	6	4	3	7

Anaheim	AB	R	H	RBI	BB	SO
D. Eckstein, ss	5	0	1	0	0	1
D. Erstad, cf	5	0	1	0	0	2
T. Salmon, rf	4	0	0	0	0	1
G. Anderson, lf	4	0	1	0	0	2
T. Glaus, 3b	4	2	2	2	0	1
B. Fullmer, dh	3	1	1	0	1	1
S. Spiezio, 1b	3	0	1	0	1	0
C. Figgins, pr	0	0	0	0	0	0
S. Wooten, 1b	0	0	0	0	0	0
B. Molina, c	3	0	0	0	0	0
b-O. Palmeiro, ph	1	0	0	0	0	0
J. Molina, c	0	0	0	0	0	0
A. Kennedy, 2b	4	0	2	1	0	1
Totals	36	3	9	3	2	9

											R	H	E
San Francisco	0	2	0	0	0	2	0	0	0	—	4	6	0
Anaheim	0	1	0	0	0	2	0	0	0	—	3	9	0

a-grounded to shortstop for T Shinjo in the 9th

b-fouled out to third for B Molina in the 8th

LOB—San Francisco 5, Anaheim 8. 2B—A Kennedy (1, J Schmidt); S Spiezio (1, J Schmidt). HR—B Bonds (1, 2nd inning off J Washburn 0 on, 0 out), T Glaus 2 (2, 2nd inning off J Schmidt 0 on, 1 Out, 6th inning off J Schmidt, 0 on, 0 out), R Sanders (1, 2nd inning off J Washburn 0 on, 1 out), J Snow (1, 6th inning off J Washburn 1 on, 2 out). SB—B Fullmer, K Lofton.

San Francisco	IP	H	R	ER	BB	SO
J. Schmidt (W, 1-0)	5.6	9	3	3	1	6
F. Rodriguez	1.3	0	0	0	0	1
T. Worrell	1	0	0	0	1	1
R. Nen (S, 1)	1	0	0	0	0	1

Anaheim	IP	H	R	ER	BB	SO
J. Washburn(L, 0-1)	5.6	6	4	4	2	5
B. Donnelly	1.6	0	0	0	0	0
S. Schoeneweis	0	0	0	0	1	0
B. Weber	1.6	0	0	0	0	2

S. Schoeneweis pitched to 1 batter in the 8th

Umpires: HP—Jerry Crawford, 1b—Angel Hernandez, 2b—Tim Tschida, 3b—Mike Winters, lf—Mike Reilly, rf—Tim McClelland.

Time—3:44.

Attendance—44,603.

Game 2 (Oct. 20 at Anaheim)

San Francisco	AB	R	H	RBI	BB	SO
K. Lofton, cf	5	0	1	0	0	1
R. Aurilia, ss	5	1	1	0	0	2
J. Kent, 2b	5	1	1	1	0	2
B. Bonds, lf	2	3	1	1	3	0
B. Santiago,c	5	1	1	0	0	1
J. Snow, 1b	4	2	2	2	0	0
R. Sanders, rf	4	1	2	3	0	2
D. Bell, 3b	4	1	2	2	0	0
S. Dunston	4	0	1	1	0	0
Totals	**38**	**10**	**12**	**10**	**3**	**8**

Anaheim	AB	R	H	RBI	BB	SO
D. Eckstein, ss	5	3	3	0	0	0
D. Erstad, cf	5	3	3	1	0	0
T. Salmon, rf	4	3	4	4	1	0
A. Ochoa, rf	0	0	0	0	0	0
G. Anderson, lf	5	1	2	2	0	0
T. Glaus, 3b	4	1	2	0	0	0
B. Fullmer, dh	3	1	2	1	1	0
S. Spiezio, 1b	3	0	1	2	0	0
B. Molina, c	4	0	0	0	0	0
A. Kennedy, 2b	4	0	0	0	0	0
Totals	**37**	**11**	**16**	**10**	**2**	**0**

										R	H	E
San Francisco	0	4	1	0	4	0	0	0	1	—	10	12	1
Anaheim	5	2	0	0	1	1	0	2	x	—	11	16	1

E— G Anderson, K Lofton LOB—San Francisco 4, Anaheim 5. 2B—R Aurilia (1, J Lackey); D Erstad (2, R Ortiz, C Zerbe); T Glaus (1, R Ortiz). HR—T Salmon 2 (2, 2nd inning off R Ortiz 1 on, 1 out, 8th inning off Fe Rodriguez 1 on, 2 out); R Sanders (2, 2nd inning off K Appier 2 on, 1 out); D Bell (1, 2nd inning off K Appier 0 on, 1 out), J Kent (1, 3rd inning off K Appier 0 on, 0 out), B Bonds (2, 9th inning off T Percival 0 on, 2 out). SB—S Spiezio, R Sanders. DP—2, (Ecktein-Spiezio), (Bell-Kent-Snow). SF—S Spiezio. PB—B Santiago.

San Francisco	IP	H	R	ER	BB	SO
R. Ortiz	1.6	9	7	7	0	0
C. Zerbe	4	4	2	1	0	0
J. Witasick	0	0	0	1	0	0
A. Fultz	.3	1	0	0	0	0
F. Rodriguez (L, 0-1)	1.6	2	2	2	1	0
T. Worrell	.3	0	0	0	0	0

Anaheim	IP	H	R	ER	BB	SO
K. Appier	2	5	5	5	2	2
J. Lackey	2.3	2	2	2	1	1
B. Weber	.6	4	2	2	0	1
F. Rodriguez (W, 1-0)	3	0	0	0	0	4
T. Percival (S, 1)	1	1	1	1	0	0

K Appier pitched to 2 batters in the 3rd
J Witasick pitched to 1 batter in the 6th

IBB— B Bonds (by J Lackey).

Umpires: HP—Angel Hernandez, 1b—Tim Tschida, 2b—Mike Winters, 3b—Mike Reilly, lf—Tim McClelland, rf—Jerry Crawford.

Time—3:57.
Attendance—44,584.

Game 3 (Oct. 22 at San Francisco)

Anaheim	AB	R	H	RBI	BB	SO	San Francisco	AB	R	H	RBI	BB	SO
D. Eckstein, ss	5	1	2	1	1	0	K. Lofton, cf	4	1	0	0	1	0
D. Erstad, cf	6	2	3	0	0	0	R. Aurilia, ss	5	1	2	1	0	2
T. Salmon, rf	4	2	1	1	2	1	J. Kent, 2b	4	1	2	0	0	0
S. Schoeneweis, p	0	0	0	0	0	0	B. Bonds, lf	2	1	1	2	2	1
G. Anderson, lf	6	0	1	1	0	0	B. Santiago, c	4	0	0	1	0	0
T. Glaus, 3b	5	2	2	1	1	0	J. Snow, 1b	4	0	1	0	0	0
S. Spiezio, 1b	5	2	2	1	1	0	R. Sanders, rf	4	0	0	0	0	1
A. Kennedy, 2b	5	1	2	1	0	2	D. Bell, 3b	1	0	0	0	3	0
B. Molina, c	2	1	2	1	3	0	L. Hernandez, p	0	0	0	0	0	0
R. Ortiz, p	3	0	0	0	0	2	J. Witasick, p	0	0	0	0	0	0
a-S. Wooten, ph	1	0	0	0	0	0	b-P. Feliz, ph	1	0	0	0	0	0
B. Donnelly, p	0	0	0	0	0	0	A. Fultz, p	0	0	0	0	0	0
c-B. Gil, ph	1	0	1	0	0	0	d-S. Dunston, ph	1	0	0	0	0	0
A. Ochoa, rf	0	0	0	0	0	0	F. Rodriguez, p	0	0	0	0	0	0
							S. Eyre, p	0	0	0	0	0	0
							e-R. Martinez, ph	1	0	0	0	0	1
Totals	43	10	16	9	8	5	**Totals**	31	4	6	4	6	5

										R	H	E
Anaheim	0	0	4	4	0	1	0	1	0	—	10	16	0
San Francisco	1	0	0	0	3	0	0	0	0	—	4	6	2

a—fouled out to first for R Ortiz in the 6th.
b—flied out to left for J Witasick in the 4th.
c—singled to left for B. Donnelly in the 8th.
d—flied out to left for A Fultz in the 6th.
e—struck out swinging for S Eyre in the 9th

E— D. Bell, B. Santiago. LOB—San Francisco 7, Anaheim 15. 2B—A Kennedy (2, L Hernandez), D Erstad (3, L Hernandez), T Salmon (1, Fe Rodriguez). 3B—S Spiezio (1, L Hernandez). HR—R Aurilia (1, 5th inning off R Ortiz 0 on, 1 out), B Bonds (3, 5th inning off R Ortiz 1 on, 1 out). SB—T Salmon, K Lofton. DP—2, (Eckstein-Kennedy-Spiezio), (Aurilia-Kent-Snow).

Anaheim	IP	H	R	ER	BB	SO
R. Ortiz (W, 1-0)	5	5	4	4	4	3
B. Donnelly	2	0	0	0	2	0
S. Schoeneweis	2	1	0	0	0	2

San Francisco	IP	H	R	ER	BB	SO
L. Hernandez (L, 0-1)	3.6	5	6	5	5	3
J. Witasick	.3	3	2	2	1	1
A Fultz	2	3	1	1	1	0
F. Rodriguez	1	1	0	0	0	0
S. Eyre	2	4	1	0	1	1

IBB— B Bonds (by R ORtiz), B Molina 2 (by L Hernandez), T Salmon (by S Eyre).
HBP— A Kennedy (by A Fultz).

Umpires: HP—Tim Tschida, 1b—Mike Winters, 2b—Mike Reilly, 3b—Tim McClelland, lf—Jerry Crawford, rf—Angel Hernandez.

Time—3:37.
Attendance—42,707.

Game 4 (Oct. 23 at San Francisco)

Anaheim	AB	R	H	RBI	BB	SO	San Francisco	AB	R	H	RBI	BB	SO
D. Eckstein, ss	3	0	0	1	0	0	K. Lofton, cf	4	1	3	0	0	0
D. Erstad, cf	4	0	0	0	0	0	R. Aurilia, ss	4	1	3	1	0	0
T. Salmon, rf	4	0	1	0	0	1	J. Kent, 2b	3	0	0	1	0	2
G. Anderson, lf	4	1	2	0	0	0	B. Bonds, lf	1	0	0	0	3	0
T. Glaus, 3b	4	1	1	2	0	0	B. Santiago, c	4	0	1	1	0	0
S. Spiezio, 1b	4	0	1	0	0	0	J. Snow, 1b	4	1	1	0	0	0
B. Gil, 2b	3	1	2	0	0	1	R. Sanders, rf	4	0	1	0	0	1
a—A. Kennedy, 2b	5	1	2	1	0	2	D. Bell, 3b	4	0	2	1	0	0
B. Molina, c	3	0	1	0	0	0	K. Reuter, p	2	1	1	0	0	0
b—B. Fullmer, ph	1	0	0	0	0	0	c—T. Goodwin, ph	0	0	0	0	1	0
J. Lackey, p	2	0	1	0	0	0	F. Rodriguez, p	0	0	0	0	0	0
B. Weber, p	0	0	0	0	0	0	T. Worrell, p	0	0	0	0	0	0
d—O. Palmeiro, ph	1	0	0	0	0	1	e—R. Martinez, ph	1	0	0	0	0	1
F. Rodriguez, p	0	0	0	0	0	0	R. Nen, p	0	0	0	0	0	0
Totals	34	3	10	3	0	3	Totals	31	4	12	4	4	4

										R	H	E
Anaheim	0	1	2	0	0	0	0	0	0	—	3	10	1
San Francisco	0	0	0	0	3	0	0	1	x	—	4	12	1

a—singled to right for B Gil in the 9th.
b—grounded to shortstop for B Molina in the 9th
c—walked for K Rueter in the 6th.
d—struck out swinging for B Weber in the 7th.
e—struck out swinging for T Worrell in the 8th.
E— T. Salmon, D Bell. LOB—San Francisco 8, Anaheim 5. 2B—R Aurilia (2, J Lackey). HR—T Glaus (3, 3rd inning off K Reuter 1 on, 1 out). SB—T Goodwin. DP—6, (Eckstein-Spiezio, Eckstein-Gil-Spiezio, B Molina-Gil), (Aurilia-Kent-Snow, Snow-Aurilia-Rueter, Aurilia-Snow). PB—B Molina. CS—D Bell.

Anaheim	IP	H	R	ER	BB	SO
J. Lackey	5	9	3	3	3	2
B. Weber	1	1	0	0	1	0
F. Rodriguez (L, 1-1)	2	2	1	0	0	2
San Francisco	**IP**	**H**	**R**	**ER**	**BB**	**SO**
K. Rueter	6	9	3	3	0	2
F. Rodriguez	1	0	0	0	0	1
T. Worrell (W, 1-0)	1	0	0	0	0	0
R. Nen (S, 2)	1	1	0	0	0	0

IBB— B Bonds 3 (by J Lackey).

Umpires: HP—Mike Winters, 1b—Mike Reilly, 2b—Tim McClelland, 3b—Jerry Crawford, lf—Angel Hernandez, rf—Tim Tschida.

Time—3:02.
Attendance—42,703.

Game 5 (Oct. 24 at San Francisco)

Anaheim	AB	R	H	RBI	BB	SO	San Francisco	AB	R	H	RBI	BB	SO
D. Eckstein, ss	4	1	2	1	1	1	K. Lofton, cf	6	3	3	2	0	0
D. Erstad, cf	4	0	1	1	0	1	S. Eyre, p	0	0	0	0	0	0
T. Salmon, rf	4	1	1	0	0	2	R. Aurilia, ss	6	2	2	3	0	1
A. Ochoa, rf	1	0	0	0	0	0	J. Kent, 2b	5	4	3	4	1	0
G. Anderson, lf	5	0	1	0	0	1	B. Bonds, lf	4	2	3	1	1	0
T. Glaus, 3b	4	0	1	1	0	3	B. Santiago, c	3	0	1	3	1	0
S. Spiezio, 1b	2	0	0	0	2	1	R. Sanders, rf	1	0	0	1	1	1
S. Shields, p	0	0	0	0	0	0	F. Rodriguez, p	0	0	0	0	0	0
A. Kennedy, 2b	4	0	0	0	0	1	a—S. Dunston, ph	1	0	0	0	0	1
B. Monlina, c	4	1	1	0	0	1	T. Worrell, p	0	0	0	0	0	0
J. Molina, c	0	0	0	0	0	0	b—P. Feliz, ph	1	0	0	0	0	0
J. Washburn, p	1	0	0	0	0	0	T. Goodwin, rf	0	0	0	0	0	0
c— O. Palmeiro, ph	1	1	1	0	0	0	J. Snow, 1b	4	2	2	0	1	1
B. Donnelly, p	0	0	0	0	0	0	D. Bell, 3b	3	2	2	1	1	0
d—B. Gil, ph	1	0	1	0	0	0	J. Schmidt, p	1	0	0	0	0	1
B. Weber, p	0	0	0	0	0	0	C. Zerbe, p	0	0	0	0	0	0
S. Wooten, 1b	1	0	1	0	0	0	T. Shinjo, rf-cf	2	1	0	0	0	1
Totals	36	4	10	3	3	11	Totals	37	16	16	15	6	6

											R	H	E
Anaheim	0	0	0	0	3	1	0	0	0	—	4	10	2
San Francisco	3	3	0	0	0	2	4	4	x	—	16	16	0

a—struck out swinging for F Rodriguez in the 6th.
b—flied out to right for T Worrell in the 8th.
c—doubled to right for J Washburn in the 5th.
d—doubled to center for B Donnelly in the 6th.
E— D Erstad, T Glaus. LOB—San Francisco 8, Anaheim 9. 2B—O Palmeiro (1, J Schmidt), T Glaus (2, J Schmidt), B Gil (1, C Zerbe), B Bonds 2 (2, J Washburn, B Weber), J Kent (1, J Washburn). 3b— K Lofton (1, B Weber). HR—J Kent 2 (3, 6th inning off B Weber 1 on, 2 out, 7th inning off S Shields 1 on, 2 out), R Aurilia (2, 8th inning off S Shields 2 on, 2 out). SB—D Eckstein.

Anaheim	IP	H	R	ER	BB	SO
J. Washburn (L, 0-2)	4	6	6	6	5	1
B. Donnelly	1	0	0	0	0	2
B. Weber	1.3	5	5	5	1	2
S. Shields	1.6	5	5	1	0	1
San Francisco	IP	H	R	ER	BB	SO
J Schmidt	4.6	7	3	3	3	8
C. Zerbe (W, 1-0)	1	2	1	1	0	0
F. Rodriguez	.3	0	0	0	0	0
T. Worrell	2	1	0	0	0	2
S. Eyre	1	0	0	0	0	1

WP—J Schmidt
IBB— R Sanders (by J Washburn), B Bonds (by J Washburn), B Santiago (by B Weber).
HBP—D Bell (by B Weber)

Umpires: HP—Mike Reilly, 1b—Tim McClelland, 2b—Jerry Crawford, 3b—Angel Hernandez, lf—Tim Tschida rf—Mike Winters.

Time—3:53.
Attendance—42,713.

Game 6 (Oct. 26 at Anaheim)

San Francisco	AB	R	H	RBI	BB	SO		Anaheim	AB	R	H	RBI	BB	SO
K. Lofton, cf	5	2	2	0	0	0		D. Eckstein, ss	4	0	0	0	0	0
R. Aurilia, ss	4	0	0	0	1	2		D. Erstad, cf	3	1	1	1	1	0
J. Kent, 2b	4	0	2	1	0	0		T. Salmon, rf	4	0	2	0	0	1
B. Bonds, lf	2	1	1	1	2	1		C. Figgins, pr	0	1	0	0	0	0
B. Santiago, c	3	0	0	0	1	1		A. Ochoa, rf	0	0	0	0	0	0
J. Snow, 1b	4	0	1	0	0	0		G. Anderson, lf	4	1	1	0	0	0
R. Sanders, rf	4	0	0	0	0	3		T. Glaus, 3b	3	1	2	2	1	0
D. Bell, 3b	4	1	1	0	0	2		B. Fullmer, dh	4	1	1	0	0	1
S. Dunston, dh	3	1	1	2	0	0		S. Spiezio, 1b	3	1	1	3	1	0
a—T. Goodwin, ph	1	0	0	0	0	1		B. Molina, c	2	0	0	0	0	0
								b—O. Palmeiro, ph	1	0	0	0	0	1
								J. Molina, c	0	0	0	0	0	0
								A. Kennedy, 2b	4	0	2	0	0	2
Totals	34	5	8	4	4	10		Totals	32	6	10	6	3	5

											R	H	E
San Francisco	0	0	0	0	3	1	1	0	0	—	5	8	1
Anaheim	0	0	0	0	0	0	1	3	x	—	6	10	1

a-struck out swinging for S Dunston in the 9th.
b-struck out swinging for B Molina in the 7th
E—B Bonds, B Molina. LOB—San Francisco 6, Anaheim 6. 2B—K Lofton (1, K Appier), T Glaus (3, R Nen). HR—S Dunston (1, 5th inning off K Appier 1 on, 1 out), B Bonds (4, 6th inning off F Rodriguez 0 on, 0 out), S Spiezio (1, 7th inning off F Rodriguez 2 on 1 out), D Erstad (1, 8th inning off T Worrell 0 on, 0 out) DP—2; (Kent-Aurilia-Snow), (Glaus-Kennedy-Spiezio).SB— K Lofton 2.

San Francisco	IP	H	R	ER	BB	SO
R. ORtiz	6.3	4	2	2	2	2
F. Rodriguez	.3	1	1	1	0	1
S. Eyre	0	1	0	0	0	0
T. Worrell (L, 1-1)	.3	3	3	2	0	0
R. Nen	1	1	0	0	1	2

Anaheim	IP	H	R	ER	BB	SO
K. Appier	4.3	4	3	3	3	2
F. Rodriguez	2.6	4	2	2	0	4
B. Donnelly (W, 1-0)	1	0	0	0	1	2
T. Percival (S, 2)	1	0	0	0	0	2

S Eyre pitched to 1 batter in the 7th
T Worrell pitched to 3 batters in the 8th

WP—Fr Rodriguez.
IBB—B Bonds (by K Appier), S Spiezio (by R Nen).

Umpires: HP—Tim McClelland, 1b—Jerry Crawford, 2b—Angel Hernandez, 3b—Tim Tschida, lf— MIke Winters, rf—Mike Reilly

Time—3:48.
Attendance—44,506.

Game 7 (Oct. 27 at Anaheim)

San Francisco	AB	R	H	RBI	BB	SO
K. Lofton, cf	4	0	0	0	1	0
R. Aurilia, ss	4	0	0	0	0	2
J. Kent, 2b	4	0	0	0	0	2
B. Bonds, lf	3	0	1	0	1	0
B. Santiago, c	3	1	2	0	1	1
J. Snow, 1b	4	0	3	0	0	0
R. Sanders, rf	1	0	0	1	0	0
a—T. Goodwin, ph-rf	2	0	0	0	0	1
D. Bell, 3b	3	0	0	0	1	1
P. Feliz, dh	3	0	0	0	0	2
b—T. Shinjo, ph-dh	1	0	0	0	0	1
Totals	32	1	6	1	4	10

Anaheim	AB	R	H	RBI	BB	SO
D. Eckstein, ss	3	1	1	0	1	0
D. Erstad, cf	3	1	1	0	0	1
T. Salmon, rf	2	1	0	0	1	1
A. Ochoa, rf	0	0	0	0	0	0
G. Anderson, lf	4	0	1	2	0	0
T. Glaus, 3b	2	0	0	0	2	2
B. Fullmer, dh	4	0	0	0	0	0
S. Spiezio, 1b	3	1	0	0	1	0
B. Molina, B, c	3	0	2	1	0	0
A. Kennedy, 2b	3	0	0	0	0	1
Totals	27	4	5	4	5	5

											R	H	E
San Francisco	0	1	0	0	0	0	0	0	0	—	1	6	0
Anaheim	0	1	3	0	0	0	0	0	x	—	4	5	0

a—struck out for R Sanders in the 6th.
b—struck out for P Feliz in the 9th.
LOB—San Francisco 9, Anaheim 6. 2B—J Snow (1, B Donnelly), B Molina, B 2 (2, L Hernandez, K Rueter), G Anderson (1, L Hernandez). DP—1 (Lofton-Kent)

San Francisco	IP	H	R	ER	BB	SO
L. Hernandez (L, 0-2)	2	4	4	4	4	1
C. Zerbe	1	0	0	0	0	0
K. Rueter	4	1	0	0	1	3
Worrell	1	0	0	0	0	1

Anaheim	IP	H	R	ER	BB	SO
J. Lackey (W, 1-0)	5	4	1	1	1	4
Donnelly	2	1	0	0	1	2
F. Rodriguez	1	0	0	0	1	3
T. Percival (S, 3)	1	1	0	0	1	1

L. Hernandez pitched to 5 batters in the 3rd.

IBB—T Glaus (by L Hernandez).
HBP—T Salmon (by L HErnandez).

Umpires: HP—Jerry Crawford, 1b—Angel Hernandez, 2b—Tim Tschida, 3b—Mike Winters, lf—Mike Reilly, rf—Tim McClelland.

Time—3:16
Attendance—44,598.

PLAYOFF PICTURES

1951 NATIONAL LEAGUE PLAYOFF — GIANTS DEFEATED BROOKLYN DODGERS 2 GAMES TO 1

Game 1: October 1 at Brooklyn (Ebbets Field)
New York 3, Brooklyn 1

Overlooked in the hysteria surrounding third baseman Bobby Thomson's "Shot Heard 'Round The World" in the dramatic and decisive Game 3, Thomson also hit a game-winning home run off ill-fated right-hander Ralph Branca in Game 1 before 30,707 at Ebbets Field. The Giants grabbed the opener by the score of 3-1.

The Dodgers bolted to a 1-0 lead in the bottom of the second when left fielder Andy Pafko connected for a solo homer. Thomson placed the Giants ahead to stay with a two-run homer in the fourth. New York left fielder Monte Irvin concluded the scoring with a solo homer in the eighth.

Right-hander Jim Hearn went the distance on a five-hitter, and the Giants' defense was superb, registering four double plays. The winners mustered merely six hits, two of them by second baseman Eddie Stanky in the first game since New York overcame a 13½-game deficit to tie Brooklyn.

Game 2: October 2 at New York (Polo Grounds)
Brooklyn 10, New York 0

The Dodgers had better luck when they switched to the Polo Grounds, where 38,609 paid to watch Brooklyn obliterate the Giants 10-0 behind a 13-hit attack. Second baseman Jackie Robinson and catcher Rube Walker were the batting heroes with three hits apiece, including home runs.

Robinson's two-run shot off right-hander Sheldon Jones in the first inning gave right-handed starter and winner Clem Labine a lead he never relinquished. Robinson's run-scoring single off right-hander George Spencer made it 3-0 in the fourth before the Dodgers' power turned it into a rout.

First baseman Gil Hodges, left fielder Andy Pafko and Walker hammered homers in the late innings, and the Giants' poor play included five errors. Labine pitched a complete-game six-hitter, setting the stage for a pivotal Game 3 on the same field.

Game 3: October 3 at New York (Polo Grounds)
New York 5, Brooklyn 4

The Dodgers seemed to gain momentum with their Game 2 blowout, scoring in the top

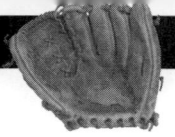

Third baseman Bobby Thomson hit the "Shot Heard 'Round The World" to win the decisive Game 3 of the 1951 National League playoff against the Brooklyn Dodgers. (National Baseball Library and Archive)

With Brooklyn ahead 4-1, 34,320 spectators braced for the seemingly inevitable. Instead, they witnessed arguably the most dramatic moment in baseball history. Shortstop Alvin Dark and right fielder Don Mueller opened the bottom of the ninth with singles off Newcombe.

Left fielder Monte Irvin popped out, but first baseman Whitey Lockman's double slashed the Dodgers' lead to 4-2. Then Brooklyn manager Chuck Dressen made a move that would be second-guessed for years, summoning right-hander Ralph Branca to replace Newcombe with third baseman Bobby Thomson coming to bat.

Branca fired a called strike, but his second pitch landed in the left field seats at 3:58 p.m. for a three-run homer, the most famous in postseason history. "The Giants win the pennant! The Giants win the pennant! The Giants win the pennant!" a delirious radio announcer Russ Hodges exclaimed. They certainly did, by the score of 5-4.

New York right-hander Larry Jansen was the winning pitcher after throwing a scoreless ninth inning.

of the first inning on second baseman Jackie Robinson's run-scoring single off right-hander Sal Maglie. Brooklyn right-hander Don Newcombe protected the 1-0 lead through six innings before the Giants tied it in the seventh.

Then the Dodgers erupted for three runs off Maglie in the eighth—one on a wild pitch and the others on run-scoring singles by left fielder Andy Pafko and third baseman Billy Cox. Shortstop Pee Wee Reese and center fielder Duke Snider triggered the rally with singles.

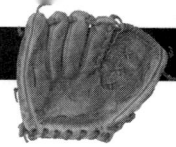

1962 NATIONAL LEAGUE PLAYOFF — GIANTS DEFEATED LOS ANGELES DODGERS 2 GAMES TO 1

Game 1: October 1 at San Francisco (Candlestick Park)
San Francisco 8, Los Angeles 0

The Giants were in the clubhouse when they gained a first-place tie on the Los Angeles Dodgers' final-day loss to the St. Louis Cardinals. When the best-of-three playoff opened before 32,660 fans at Candlestick Park in San Francisco the very next day, the Giants took care of business afield.

Left-hander Billy Pierce, unbeaten at home all season, performed his sorcery again, shackling the Dodgers on three hits for a brilliant shutout. Conversely, Los Angeles left-handed starter Sandy Koufax lasted one-plus innings, yielding four hits and three runs.

Right fielder Felipe Alou's two-out double and center fielder Willie Mays' homer gave the Giants a quick 2-0 lead in the first. Third baseman Jim Davenport homered off Koufax in the second, and Mays and first baseman Orlando Cepeda hit back-to-back homers off right-handed reliever Larry Sherry for a 5-0 lead after six.

"This game gave me the greatest satisfaction of my life," Pierce said following a convincing win. Koufax, meanwhile, remained winless since July 12 after injuring the index finger of his pitching hand. Mays' homers were his 48th and 49th of the season.

Game 2: October 2 at Los Angeles (Dodger Stadium)
Los Angeles 8, San Francisco 7

Only 25,321 showed up at Dodger Stadium, and they had little to cheer as the Giants bolted to a 5-0 lead off right-hander Don Drysdale. But a chain of events made it a tension-filled struggle that required 42 players and lasted a record four hours and 18 minutes.

First baseman Orlando Cepeda's single and right fielder Felipe Alou's double made it 1-0 in the second, and the Giants pounded

Drysdale with four runs in the sixth. Catcher Tom Haller walked and shortstop Jose Pagan doubled him to third. Pitcher Jack Sanford's squeeze bunt was fumbled by Drysdale, and Haller scored.

Run-scoring singles by second baseman Chuck Hiller and Davenport chased Drysdale, and left fielder Willie McCovey's single off right-handed reliever Ed Roebuck made it 5-0 while Sanford was extending the Dodgers' scoreless streak to 35 innings. It all ended so decisively.

The Dodgers erupted for seven runs in the bottom of the sixth, with pinch hitter Lee Walls' three-run double doing the biggest damage. San Francisco Pinch hitter Ed Bailey's run-scoring single and catcher John Orsino's sacrifice fly created a 7-7 tie in the eighth.

Then the Dodgers finally emerged victorious with last-ditch heroics. Manager Alvin Dark used four of his record eight pitchers in the bottom of the ninth, and the Dodgers finally ended their misery when first baseman Ron Fairly's sacrifice fly off left-hander Mike McCormick scored shortstop Maury Wills for the win.

Right-hander Stan Williams, the Dodgers' fifth pitcher, earned the win, while right-hander Bobby Bolin suffered the loss.

Game 3: October 3 at Los Angeles (Dodger Stadium)
San Francisco 6, Los Angeles 4

The Dodgers should have known better than to play the Giants on October 3, the date Bobby Thomson delivered his clinching 1951 homer. But here it was, the third day of October, and 45,692 fans jammed Dodger Stadium with the pennant—and the New York Yankees in the World Series—on the line.

It was a sloppy game at the outset, but it was saved by yet another dramatic Giants-Dodgers finish. Los Angeles went ahead 3-2 in the sixth on left fielder Duke Snider's single and third baseman Tommy Davis' homer off right-hander Juan Marichal. The Dodgers added a run in the seventh for a 4-2 advan-

The Giants celebrate after coming from behind to defeat the Los Angeles Dodgers by the score of 6-4 to win the third and deciding game of the 1962 National League playoff. (AP/Wide World Photos)

tage. Pesky Los Angeles shortstop Maury Wills singled and stole second and third before scoring on catcher Ed Bailey's throwing error.

The Giants spoiled the celebration with four runs in the ninth, a rally attributed to manager Walter Alston's refusal to use right-hander Don Drysdale.

Pinch hitter Matty Alou led off with a single and was forced at second by left fielder Harvey Kuenn. Right-handed reliever Ed Roebuck then walked pinch-hitter Willie McCovey and right fielder Felipe Alou to load the bases. Center fielder Willie Mays' liner was knocked down by Roebuck, but a run scored on the infield single to trim the deficit to 4-3.

Right-hander Stan Williams replaced Roe-

buck and first baseman Orlando Cepeda's sacrifice fly created a tie. Mays advanced on a wild pitch, and Bailey's intentional walk loaded the bases. Williams then walked third baseman Jim Davenport to give the Giants the lead.

The Giants added a final run off right-hander Ron Perranoski when second baseman Larry Burright fumbled shortstop Jose Pagan's grounder for an error. Right-hander Don Larsen pitched a scoreless eighth inning for the win, while left-hander Billy Pierce worked a scoreless ninth, triggering a wild celebration and a huge crowd awaiting the champs at the San Francisco Airport.

1971 NATIONAL LEAGUE CHAMPIONSHIP SERIES — PITTSBURGH PIRATES DEFEATED GIANTS 3 GAMES TO 1

Game 1: October 2 at San Francisco (Candlestick Park)
San Francisco 5, Pittsburgh 4

The Giants were riding high following their first division championship, and they were confident after winning nine of 12 games against the Pittsburgh Pirates during the regular season. That optimism continued when right-hander Gaylord Perry went the distance to win the opener by the score of 5-4 at Candlestick Park in San Francisco.

But it was false hope. Right-hander Juan Marichal had to be used in the final-day clincher—so could only make one start—and right fielder Bobby Bonds had a bruised rib cage. Dave Kingman, his replacement, misjudged a fly in right and the Pirates took a 2-0 lead in the second.

Shortstop Chris Speier's single, Perry's sacrifice and left fielder Ken Henderson's double made it 2-1 in the bottom half, and the Giants erupted with four runs off Pittsburgh right-handed starter and loser Steve Blass in the fifth. Second baseman Tito Fuentes, who merely homered four times during the season, provided the unexpected.

Speier singled and Fuentes followed with a homer to right for the go-ahead run. Then center fielder Willie Mays walked on four pitches and first baseman Willie McCovey homered to deep right for a 5-2 lead. The Pirates scored twice in the seventh, but Perry settled down and 40,977 fans went home happy.

Game 2: October 3 at San Francisco (Candlestick Park)
Pittsburgh 9, San Francisco 4

There was yet another surprise as the Pirates gained a split with a 9-4 victory. On October 3—the Giants' lucky day—first baseman Bob Robertson, homerless since August 25,

stunned San Francisco with three home runs and five RBI.

He homered to right in the fourth inning off left-handed starter and loser John Cumberland, hit a three-run shot to left off left-hander Ron Bryant in the seventh and crowned his career day with a blast to left-center off left-hander Steve Hamilton in the ninth.

Robertson went to work after the Giants scored singles runs in the first two innings off right-hander Dock Ellis, who escaped a bases-loaded, one-out jam in the first and went on to post the victory. Shortstop Chris Speier's double, Cumberland's sacrifice and left fielder Ken Henderson's single gave the Giants a 2-1 lead in the second.

Gaylord Perry won Game 1 of the 1971 National League Championship Series against the Pittsburgh Pirates by the score of 5-4, but the Pirates took the next three to capture the series and advance to the World Series.

Center fielder Gene Clines, the Giants' batting coach from 1997-99, homered for the Pirates in the fifth. His counterpart, center fielder Willie Mays, added a two-run homer and finished with three RBI to pace the Giants, who lost the home-field advantage in the best-of-five series by splitting at Candlestick Park.

Game 3: October 5 at Pittsburgh
(Three Rivers Stadium)
Pittsburgh 2, San Francisco 1

Giants' right-hander Juan Marichal finally got to start when the series moved to Pittsburgh, and he didn't disappoint. Hooked up with emergency Pirates' right-handed starter Bob Johnson, Marichal pitched a four-hitter but lost 2-1 on a pair of solo homers.

Pesky first baseman Bob Robertson connected in the second inning for a 1-0 lead, but the Giants tied it in the sixth with an unearned run on third baseman Richie Hebner's error. Hebner got even, homering to right off a Marichal screwball in the eighth inning.

Johnson limited the Giants to five singles over eight innings, striking out seven. Marichal, who struck out six and walked none, made two mistakes and they cost him. Hebner had half of the Pirates' hits. Right-hander Dave Giusti worked a scoreless ninth.

Game 4: October 5 at Pittsburgh
(Three Rivers Stadium)
Pittsburgh 9, San Francisco 5

The Giants felt good about squaring the series with right-hander Gaylord Perry on the mound and a four-run top of the second for a 5-2 lead. The visitors would not score again off Pittsburgh right-handed relievers Bruce Kison and Dave Giusti, and the Pirates celebrated a pennant-clincher at home with a 9-5 victory.

First baseman Willie McCovey's run-scoring single gave the Giants a 1-0 advantage in the first, but the Pirates snapped back with two in the bottom half on second baseman Dave Cash's single, third baseman Richie Hebner's double and right fielder Roberto Clemente's two-run single for a 2-1 lead.

Giants' shortstop Chris Speier promptly tied it with a leadoff homer off right-handed starter Steve Blass in the second. Left fielder Ken Henderson and second baseman Tito Fuentes then singled and McCovey hit a three-run homer for a four-RBI day. It wasn't enough. The Pirates scored three in the third to make it 5-5 and four more in the sixth.

Hebner's three-run homer stole the Giants' momentum, and the four-run sixth off Perry and right-hander Jerry Johnson finished them off. Clemente's run-scoring single and center fielder Al Oliver's three-run homer did the big damage.

Kison picked up the win with 4.2 scoreless innings, and Giusti worked the final 2.1 for his third save of the series. McCovey and Cash both had three hits.

1987 NATIONAL LEAGUE CHAMPIONSHIP SERIES — ST. LOUIS CARDINALS DEFEATED GIANTS 4 GAMES TO 3

Game 1: October 6 at St. Louis
(Busch Stadium)
St. Louis 5, San Francisco 3

Two years after a last-place finish, the jubilant Giants reached the playoffs for the first time in 16 years. A crowd of 55,331, the largest to ever watch a baseball game at Busch Stadium in St. Louis, saw left-handed pitcher Greg Mathews win 5-3 with his arm and his bat.

An error and a run-scoring grounder by right fielder Candy Maldonado staked right-hander Rick Reuschel to a 1-0 lead in the first, but the Cardinals tied it on left fielder Vince Coleman's single in the third. Left fielder Jeffrey Leonard's solo homer regained the lead for the Giants in the top of the fourth.

Shortstop Ozzie Smith's leadoff triple and center fielder Willie McGee's two-out single made it 2-2 in the bottom half before the Cardinals erupted for the decisive four runs in the sixth. Mathews' two-out single off Reuschel on a 1-2 pitch was the crushing blow.

Mathews was the winner, Reuschel took the loss and left-hander Ken Dayley retired the final four batters for the save.

Game 2: October 7 at St. Louis (Busch Stadium)
San Francisco 5, St. Louis 0

Left-hander Dave Dravecky, acquired during the season, never pitched better for the Giants. His brilliant 5-0 two-hitter smothered the St. Louis offense and tied the series behind a 10-hit attack that featured homers by first baseman Will Clark and left fielder Jeffrey Leonard.

St. Louis left-handed starter and loser John Tudor fell behind in the second on right fielder Candy Maldonado's leadoff single and Clark's one-out homer to right. Leonard led off the fourth with a homer, and the Giants added two unearned runs in the eighth on singles by Leonard and Maldonado and a rare Ozzie Smith error at shortstop.

Both hits off Dravecky were liners to center—by first baseman Jim Lindeman with two outs in the second and by second baseman Tom Herr following a leadoff walk in the fourth. Dravecky faced the minimum 18 batters thereafter.

Leonard had three hits for the Giants.

Game 3: October 9 at San Francisco (Candlestick Park)
St. Louis 6, San Francisco 5

When the Giants returned home, they were greeted by the largest crowd in San Francisco baseball history: 57,913. Candlestick Park was rocking with enthusiasm after the home club jumped on Cardinals' left-hander Joe Magrane for a 4-0 lead after three innings.

Center fielder Chili Davis' double, first baseman Will Clark's single, catcher Bob Brenly's double and a wild pitch made it 3-0 in the second. Then left fielder Jeffrey Leonard, who aggravated St. Louis fans with his "one flap down" home run trot, connected again in the third for a 4-0 advantage.

Then it turned sour for the Giants. Left-handed starter Atlee Hammaker entered the sixth with a three-hit shutout, but the Cardinals suddenly came to life. Shortstop Ozzie Smith's one-out single and first baseman Jim Lindeman's two-out homer ruined the shutout, and St. Louis added four runs in the seventh to steal a 6-5 victory.

Right fielder Jose Oquendo and pinch hitter Curt Ford opened with singles. Dan Driessen, pinch hitting, hit a run-scoring single off right-handed reliever Don Robinson, and left fielder Vince Coleman followed with a two-run single for the lead. Harry Spilman hit a pinch homer in the ninth for the final Giants' run.

Right-hander Bob Forsch, for many years the stalwart of the Cardinals' starting rotation, pitched two scoreless innings in relief to earn the win. Right-hander Todd Worrell allowed only Spilman's homer over the final three innings for the save. Robinson absorbed the loss.

Game 4: October 10 at San Francisco (Candlestick Park)
San Francisco 4, St. Louis 2

Down two games to one in the best-of-seven series, the Giants were in need of a victory. This time they fell behind 2-0 before rallying for a 4-2 win behind veteran right-hander Mike Krukow's pitching and left fielder Jeffrey Leonard's record fourth home run in four games to tie the Cardinals.

Krukow, in his finest playoff performance, went the distance on a nine-hitter. Four of them came in succession with one out in the second inning for a 2-0 St. Louis lead. Pitcher Danny Cox and left fielder Vince Coleman delivered run-scoring singles.

While three double plays pulled Krukow out of trouble, the Giants began chipping away before 57,997 spectators, the new San Francisco attendance record. Second baseman Robby Thompson hit a homer in the fourth, Leonard added a two-run blast in the fifth and catcher Bob Brenly connected in the eighth.

The right-handed Cox also authored a complete game but was the losing pitcher.

Winning pitcher Mike Krukow (center) whoops it up with catcher Bob Brenly (left) and first baseman Will Clark after beating the St. Louis Cardinals by the score of 4-2 in Game 4 of the 1987 National League Championship Series. The win evened the series at two games apiece. (AP/Wide World Photos)

Game 5: October 11 at San Francisco (Candlestick Park)
San Francisco 6, St. Louis 3

For the third game in a row, the Giants' home attendance record was shattered when 59,363 fans showed up and delighted in a dramatic victory that was spurred by left-handed reliever Joe Price's five innings of one-hit relief.

Left fielder Vince Coleman's double, shortstop Ozzie Smith's sacrifice and second baseman Tom Herr's sacrifice fly pushed the Cardinals ahead in the top of the first inning off right-handed starter Reuschel, but the Giants countered in the bottom half on second baseman Robby Thompson's walk and steal of second base and third baseman Kevin Mitchell's run-scoring single for a 1-apiece tie.

Three singles and Smith's sacrifice fly gave St. Louis the lead in the third, but the Giants again tied it in the bottom half on Mitchell's homer. Third baseman Terry Pendleton's triple and first baseman Will Clark's error gave the Cardinals an unearned run in the fourth and a 3-2 lead.

The Giants concluded the scoring with a four-run fourth that featured shortstop Jose

Uribe's two-run single, pinch hitter Mike Aldrete's sacrifice fly and Thompson's run-scoring triple. Cardinals' right-handed reliever Bob Forsch did not retire any of the four batters he faced in the fourth and was saddled with the loss.

Then Price took over—striking out six along the way—and the Giants headed to St. Louis with a series lead.

Game 6: October 13 at St. Louis (Busch Stadium)
St. Louis 1, San Francisco 0

Who was to know the Giants would not score again? While the Giants were hitless in seven at-bats with runners in scoring position, the Cardinals squeezed a run out of left-hander Dave Dravecky in the second inning, and it was enough for a 1-0 series-squaring victory.

Dravecky, who struck out eight and walked none, deserved better. The Cardinals scored following a leadoff triple by catcher

Tony Pena that right fielder Candy Maldonado lost in the lights. Maldonado's mishap proved costly when right fielder Jose Oquendo hit a sacrifice fly.

The Giants threatened frequently, but left-handed starter and winner Tudor pitched 7.1 scoreless innings. In his closest call, catcher Bob Melvin and shortstop Jose Uribe opened the fifth with singles, but Dravecky's bunt turned into a force at third, and they came up empty.

Game 7: October 14 at St. Louis (Busch Stadium)
St. Louis 6, San Francisco 0

This time it was St. Louis right-hander Danny Cox who extended the Giants' scoreless streak to the final 22 innings of a series that slipped away. The Giants had leadoff batters on base in four different innings but to no avail as the Cardinals celebrated before 55,331 fans.

Cox received all the support he required when the Cardinals bunched four consecutive

Left fielder Jeffrey Leonard became the first player from a losing team to earn National League Championship Series Most Valuable Player honors in 1987 after batting .417 with four home runs and five RBI. (AP/Wide World Photos)

one-out hits off left-hander Atlee Hammaker in the second inning for a 4-0 lead. Third baseman Terry Pendleton and catcher Tony Pena singled, center fielder Willie McGee's single made it 1-0 and right fielder Jose Oquendo homered on a 3-2 pitch.

The Giants' biggest threat came when shortstop Jose Uribe and pinch hitter Eddie Milner opened the third with singles. Right fielder Mike Aldrete grounded into a double play and third baseman Kevin Mitchell took a called third strike.

The losers' consolation was series Most Valuable Player honors for San Francisco left fielder Jeffrey Leonard, who batted .417 (10-for-24) with four home runs and five RBI.

1989 NATIONAL LEAGUE CHAMPIONSHIP SERIES — GIANTS DEFEATED CHICAGO CUBS 4 GAMES TO 1

Game 1: October 4 at Chicago (Wrigley Field)
San Francisco 11, Chicago 3

Chicago right-hander Greg Maddux was just another struggling young pitcher when he ran into a buzzsaw in the jam-packed (39,195) opener at Wrigley Field in Chicago. Giants' first baseman Will Clark had a double and two home runs for six RBI off the future Cy Young Award winner, and the Giants were ahead 8-3 after four innings en route to an 11-3 win.

The Giants wasted no time teeing off. Center fielder Brett Butler opened the game with a single, advanced on a sacrifice and a passed ball and scored on Clark's double. Left fielder Kevin Mitchell singled, and third baseman Matt Williams' two-run double concluded the three-run rally.

Second baseman Ryne Sandberg's double and first baseman Mark Grace's homer got two runs back off right-hander Scott Garrelts in the bottom of the first. Both teams scored in the third on solo homers by Clark and Sandberg, so it was 4-3 in favor of San Francisco entering

the fourth inning.

That's when Clark landed the telling blow. Right fielder Pat Sheridan and shortstop Jose Uribe opened with singles and Uribe stole second. Butler was walked intentionally with one out, loading the bases. After second baseman Robby Thompson popped out, Clark hit a grand slam homer to right. It was a monstrous blast, landing beyond the back wall.

For good measure, an error, Clark's walk and Mitchell's three-run homer placed the game out of reach in the eighth. Clark had four hits and a walk in his finest postseason performance.

Garrelts, who led the National League with a .737 winning percentage (14-5) and 2.28 ERA during the season, allowed three runs on eight hits with one walk and six strikeouts in seven innings to earn the victory.

Game 2: October 5 at Chicago (Wrigley Field)
Chicago 9, San Francisco 5

This one was over early. The Cubs pounced on right-handed starter and loser Rick Reuschel for six runs in the bottom of the first to gain a 9-5 win and a series split. Chicago sent 12 batters to the plate as Reuschel lasted two-thirds of an inning in a woeful performance against his former team.

Center fielder Jerome Walton led off the first with a single and second baseman Ryne Sandberg tripled. First baseman Mark Grace hit a run-scoring double with one out and scored on third baseman Luis Salazar's two-out single. Shortstop Shawon Dunston's single chased Reuschel, and right-handed reliever Kelly Downs walked catcher Joe Girardi to load the bases.

Pitcher Mike Bielecki's two-run single and Walton's run-scoring single concluded the scoring. Grace's three-run double off Downs in the sixth padded a 6-2 lead.

San Francisco left fielder Kevin Mitchell and third baseman Matt Williams both hit two-run homers, while second baseman Robby Thompson added a solo shot. Right-handed

First baseman Will Clark was named Most Valuable Player of the 1989 National League Championship Serier after batting a robust .650 against the Chicago Cubs. (S.F. Giants Archives)

Sutcliffe in the bottom half, despite not hitting the ball very hard.

Center fielder Brett Butler led off with a single, Thompson beat out a single to short and left fielder Kevin Mitchell was walked intentionally with one out, loading the bases. Third baseman Matt Williams' grounder to the mound started the scoring, right fielder Candy Maldonado walked with the bases loaded and shortstop Jose Uribe singled for a 3-2 advantage.

A botched bunt and a wild pitch enabled the Cubs to tie the game in the fourth. Sutcliffe's double, Uribe's error and Sandberg's sacrifice fly pushed the Cubs ahead in the seventh before Thompson came through in the bottom half.

Butler's one-out single off left-hander Paul Assenmacher set the scene for Thompson's game-winning blow to left. The Giants' bullpen of right-handers Jeff Brantley and Don Robinson, left-hander Craig Lefferts and right-hander Steve Bedrosian worked the final six innings without yielding an earned run. Robinson got the win, with Bedrosian recording the save.

reliever Les Lancaster allowed three runs over the final four innings but was credited with the win.

Game 3: October 7 at San Francisco (Candlestick Park)
San Francisco 5, Chicago 4

Giants' second baseman Robby Thompson stole the thunder from the big boys in this one, hitting a two-run homer off right-hander Les Lancaster in the seventh inning to overcome a 4-3 Cubs' lead. The dramatics and a 5-4 victory were witnessed by 62,065 fans, a record crowd for baseball in San Francisco.

Giants' right-handed starter Mike LaCoss fell behind 2-0 in the first on singles by second baseman Ryne Sandberg and left fielder Dwight Smith, followed by right fielder Andre Dawson's two-run single. The Giants rallied for three runs off right-handed starter Rick

Game 4: October 8 at San Francisco (Candlestick Park)
San Francisco 6, Chicago 4

First baseman Will Clark continued his pounding of Chicago right-hander Greg Maddux with two doubles and a single in the first five innings, but third baseman Matt Williams powered a 6-4 victory and a 3-1 series edge with a two-run homer and a two-run double for four RBI before a crowd of 62,048 at Candlestick Park.

Second baseman Ryne Sandberg's double, left fielder Dwight Smith's single and first baseman Mark Grace's sacrifice fly gave the Cubs a 1-0 lead off San Francisco right-handed starter Scott Garrelts in the first. Second baseman Robby Thompson's walk, Clark's single and left fielder Kevin Mitchell's force grounder created a tie in the bottom half off Maddux.

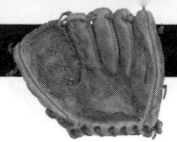

Chicago third baseman Luis Salazar led off the second with a home run, but the Giants answered with Williams' two-out, two-run bases loaded single in the third. Center fielder Jerome Walton's single, Grace's two-out triple and right fielder Andre Dawson's double made it 4-apiece in the fifth.

The Giants concluded the scoring on Clark's double and Williams' tie-breaking homer in the bottom of the fifth. Right-handed relievers Kelly Downs and Steve Bedrosian made it hold up with 4.1 combined innings of scoreless relief. Downs earned the win and Bedrosian the save.

Clark had three of the nine hits, going 6-for-6 against Maddux in two games.

Shortstop Jose Uribe was a member of the Giants' 1987 National League West Division championship team and the 1989 pennant-winning club. (S.F. Giants Archives)

Game 5: October 9 at San Francisco (Candlestick Park)
San Francisco 3, Chicago 2

The Giants hadn't clinched anything at home in their 32 years of existence in San Francisco, so this game truly was something special. A crowd of 62,084 assembled to watch the Giants win their first pennant since 1962. It was worth the wait.

The game was the best-pitched of an offense-minded series, with San Francisco right-hander Rick Reuschel being matched against Chicago right-hander Mike Bielecki. While Bielecki blanked the Giants on two hits over the first six innings, the Cubs scraped for an unearned run off Reuschel in the third.

With one out, left fielder Kevin Mitchell lost a ball in the sun and center fielder Jerome Walton reached second on the error. Second baseman Ryne Sandberg followed with a double for a 1-0 lead. Bielecki retired the first 11 batters and seemed in complete control entering the seventh.

That's when raging first baseman Will Clark led off with a triple off Andre Dawson's glove in right and left fielder Kevin Mitchell followed with a game-tying sacrifice fly. The Giants then took the lead with a rally that started with two outs and none on in the eighth.

Pinch hitter Candy Maldonado, center fielder Brett Butler and second baseman Robby Thompson walked in succession, loading the bases. Left-hander Mitch "Wild Thing" Williams replaced Bielecki to face the torrid Clark, who fell behind 0-2, took a ball and fouled off two pitches with the game on the line.

Williams' next pitch was lined to center for a two-run single that ultimately landed the Giants in a Bay Area World Series. Clark set a NLCS record with 13 hits in 20 at-bats, a .650 average. Williams set an NLCS record with nine RBI.

1997 NATIONAL LEAGUE DIVISION SERIES — FLORIDA MARLINS DEFEATED GIANTS 3 GAMES TO 0

Game 1: September 30 at Miami (Pro Player Stadium)
Florida 2, San Francisco 1

Giants' left-hander Kirk Rueter and Florida Marlins' right-hander Kevin Brown were locked in a scoreless pitching duel for the first six innings as the Marlins, an expansion team in their fifth season, entered the playoffs as the National League wild card. Florida won its first-ever postseason contest by the score of 2-1.

Third baseman Bill Mueller led off the seventh with a homer to right-center, giving the Giants a 1-0 lead over Brown, who had a no-hitter against them during the season. Florida catcher Charles Johnson returned the favor with a leadoff homer in the bottom half to tie the score.

After left-hander Dennis Cook held the Giants hitless for two innings in relief of Brown, the Marlins rallied off right-handers Julian Tavarez and Roberto Hernandez in the bottom of the ninth. Shortstop Edgar Renteria's two-out single through the right side with the bases loaded ended the game.

Cook earned the win, while Tavarez absorbed the loss.

Game 2: October 1 at Miami (Pro Player Stadium)
Florida 7, San Francisco 6

It was another walkoff victory for the Marlins, who overcame single runs by the Giants in each of the first four innings to take a 2-0 lead in the playoff with a 7-6 victory. The early scoring didn't help Giants' left-handed starter Shawn Estes, who yielded five runs in three innings.

The Giants moved into a 6-apiece tie in the top of the ninth off right-handed reliever Robb Nen, scoring an unearned run when center fielder Darryl Hamilton scored on a throw-ing error by second baseman Craig Counsell, trying for a double play on a force grounder by left fielder Barry Bonds.

Then the Marlins went to work against right-hander Roberto Hernandez. Right fielder Gary Sheffield singled and scored following left fielder Moises Alou's single to center when center fielder Dante Powell's throw hit the mound and bounced high.

Catcher Brian Johnson homered for the Giants.

Game 3: October 3 at San Francisco (3Com Park At Candlestick Point)
Florida 6, San Francisco 2

The Giants returned home, but no longer with an advantage. Still, 57,188 fans showed up to greet the National League West Division champions, who took a 1-0 lead after five innings thanks to a home run by second baseman Jeff Kent off right-hander Alex

Second baseman Jeff Kent batted at a .300 clip with two home runs in the Giants' three-game loss to the eventual world champion Florida Marlins in the 1997 National League Division Series. (S.F. Giants/Stanton)

397

Fernandez in the fourth. But the destined Marlins went on to sweep the series with a 6-2 victory en route to winning the N.L. pennant over the Atlanta Braves and the World Series over the Cleveland Indians.

Florida took a 4-1 advantage on center fielder Devon White's grand slam homer off left-handed starter and loser Wilson Alvarez in the sixth. Kent homered again in the bottom of the sixth for the Giants' final run. Then left-hander Dennis Cook and right-hander Robb Nen both pitched one inning of hitless relief to preserve the win for Fernandez.

Kent had three of the Giants' seven hits.

1998 NATIONAL LEAGUE WILD CARD ONE-GAME PLAYOFF — CHICAGO CUBS DEFEATED GIANTS 5-3

After squandering an opportunity to win the wild card outright on the final day of the season, blowing a 7-0 lead against the Colorado Rockies at Coors Field in Denver, the Giants entered a one-game playoff 24 hours later against the Chicago Cubs before 39,556 partisans at Wrigley Field. Chicago won the all-or-nothing game by the score of 5-3 to earn the right to face the Atlanta Braves in the National League Division Series.

Right-handed starters Mark Gardner of the Giants and Steve Trachsel of the Cubs fired zeroes until the bottom of the fifth, when left fielder Henry Rodriguez's leadoff single and third baseman Gary Gaetti's two-run homer on an 0-2 pitch placed the Cubs ahead to stay. Pinch hitter Matt Mieske added a two-run single in the sixth.

San Francisco right-handed reliever Jose Mesa's wild pitch gave the Cubs a 5-0 lead after eight innings, and ex-Giant Rod Beck earned the save and a wild card playoff berth by aborting a Giants' rally in the ninth.

Catcher Brent Mayne and third baseman Bill Mueller opened the ninth with singles, center fielder Stan Javier's RBI single averted a

shutout and left fielder Bonds' sacrifice fly scored the second run before Beck took over. Second baseman Jeff Kent hit a run-scoring force grounder before right fielder Joe Carter popped to first for the final out, ending the Giants' frantic dash down the stretch.

Trachsel and Gardner were the pitchers of record.

2000 NATIONAL LEAGUE DIVISION SERIES— NEW YORK METS DEFEATED GIANTS 3 GAMES TO 1

Game 1: October 4 at San Francisco (Pacific Bell Park) San Francisco 5, New York 1

The Giants finished the regular season with the major leagues' best record (97-65), so they were heavily favored to dispatch the wild card Mets in the opening playoff round. Game 1 before 40,930 partisans at Pacific Bell Park did nothing to dispell that notion, a 4-1 victory behind Livan Hernandez and Ellis Burks.

Bill Mueller's one-out double, Barry Bonds' single and Jeff Kent's grounder to short gave the Giants a 1-0 first-inning lead off Mike Hampton, a longtime regular-season nemesis. Mueller's two-out single, Bonds' triple, Kent's walk and Burks' homer to left added the club's final four runs in the third inning.

Hernandez, MVP of the 1997 NLCS and World Series for the Florida Marlins, continued his postseason success, improving to 5-0 with 72/3 strong innings. The Mets' lone run scored in the third on two-out singles by Mike Bordick and Hampton, Benny Agbayani's walk and Jay Payton's sacrifice fly. Robb Nen pulled Hernandez out of a bases-loaded jam in the eighth by striking out ex-Giant Darryl Hamilton.

Game 2: October 5 at San Francisco
(Pacific Bell Park)
New York 5, San Francisco 4 (10 innings)

There was high drama by the bay when pinch-hitter J.T. Snow's three-run homer off Mets closer Armando Benitez created a 4-4 tie and seemingly gave the Giants momentum for a two-game lead in the best-of-five series. But pinch-hitter Darryl Hamilton's two-out double and Jay Payton's single produced a 5-4 victory over Felix Rodriguez in the 10th.

Timo Perez's two-out, two-run single off Shawn Estes gave the Mets a 2-0 lead in the second, but the Giants got one back on Jeff Kent's single and Barry Bonds' double in the bottom half. New York staged a two-out rally off Rodriguez in the top of the ninth on Perez's single and Edgardo Alfonzo's homer off a 98-mph fastball for a 4-1 lead.

Then it got interesting. Bonds' leadoff double chased Mets starter Al Leiter in the bottom of the ninth. Kent, on a 1-2 pitch, greeted Benitez with a single to short. After Ellis Burks flied to short right, Snow came off the bench to provide one of the most memorable homers in S.F. history, albeit in a losing cause.

Game 3: October 7 at New York
(Shea Stadium)
New York 3, San Francisco 2 (13 innings)

Benny Agbayani's one-out home run off reliever Aaron Fultz in the bottom of the 13th inning provided the dramatics for the Mets, whose second consecutive exta-inning victory placed the Giants in a playoff hole. Each team had numerous chances in the late innings before Agbayani sent 56,270 fans home happy with one swing of the bat.

The Giants jumped on Rick Reed for two runs in the fourth inning after Ellis Burks and J.T. Snow opened with singles. Bobby Estalella singled with one out for 1-0 and Marvin Benard's two-out single made it 2-0. Russ Ortiz carried a no-hitter into the sixth before the Mets mounted their comeback.

A walk, pinch-hitter Darryl Hamilton's single and Timo Perez's run-scoring single cut the lead to 2-1. The Mets tied it in the bottom of the eighth when Mike Bordick was struck by an 0-2 Doug Henry pitch leading off. He was forced by pinch-hitter Lenny Harris, who scored on Edgardo Alfonzo's two-out double off Robb Nen for 2-2.

Game 4: October 8 at New York
(Shea Stadium)
New York 4, San Francisco 0

So far as the Giants were concerned, Bobby Jones couldn't have picked a worse time to pitch his greatest game. The Mets' right-hander, matched against Fresno buddy Mark Gardner, worked eight one-two-three innings and yielded merely a fifth-inning double to Jeff Kent in a 4-0 victory that knocked San Francisco out of the playoffs.

A crowd of 56,245 watched Jones flirt with perfection after the Mets gave him all the runs he required on Mike Piazza's two-out walk and Robin Ventura's 405-foot homer to right-center in the first inning. Jones struck out and reached first base on Gardner's wild pitch in the fifth before doubles by Timo Perez and Edgardo Alfonzo made it 4-0.

The Giants' lone threat came in the fifth. Kent doubled to left on a 1-2 pitch and went to third on Ellis Burks' fly to right. J.T. Snow and Doug Mirabelli walked around an out, but Gardner batted with the bases loaded and popped to second. As in the 1987 NLCS, when they failed to score in the final 18 innings at St. Louis, the Giants were scoreless the last 18 innings at Shea as the Mets took their first step toward a Subway Series.

2002 NATIONAL LEAGUE DIVISION SERIES — GIANTS DEFEATED ATLANTA BRAVES 3 GAMES TO 2

Game 1: October 2 at Atlanta (Turner Field)
San Francisco 8, Atlanta 5

J.T. Snow, Rich Aurilia and Benito Santiago each hit two-run doubles to support Russ Ortiz's sturdy pitching and the underdog Giants stunned the Braves 8-5 before 41,903 and a lot of empty seats at Turner Field. The visitors roughed up 18-game winner Tom Glavine for 10 hits and six runs in five innings.

One-out singles by Santiago and Reggie Sanders got the Giants going in the second inning. Snow's double down the line in right and David Bell's run-scoring single made it 3-0. Glavine's two-run single rallied the Braves in the bottom half, but the Giants scored three more in the fourth on two-out singles by Bell, Ortiz and Kenny Lofton, and Aurilia's double.

Santiago's double hiked the lead to 8-2 in the sixth, and Ortiz departed after holding the Braves to five hits and two runs in seven innings. Home runs by Gary Sheffield and Javy Lopez off reliever Tim Worrell made the score respectable in the eighth. Santiago powered a 12-hit attack - all in the first six innings - with three hits.

Game 2: October 3 at Atlanta (Turner Field)
Atlanta 7, San Francisco 3

Kirk Rueter, a crafty left-hander in the Tom Glavine mold, had a similar fate when the Braves battered him for seven runs in three-plus innings while rolling to a 7-3 victory before 47,167. Kevin Millwood worked six strong innings, yielding two runs while striking out seven and walking none.

Chipper Jones' single gave the Braves a 1-0 first-inning lead, but J.T. Snow's two-out homer created a tie in the second. Atlanta then scored three times in the bottom half on back-

J.T. Snow blasted a 2-out home run in the second inning of Game 2, but the Giants couldn't hold off the Braves' offense. (© S.F. Giants)

to-back homers by Javy Lopez and Vinny Castilla, Mark DeRosa's double and Rafael Furcal's single for a 4-1 lead.

They added three more in the fourth on Lopez' single, Castilla's walk and DeRosa's two-run triple. After Rueter departed, DeRosa scored on Benito Santiago's passed ball for a 7-1 lead. The Giants' final runs came on solo homers by Rich Aurilia in the sixth and Barry Bonds in the seventh.

Game 3: October 5 at San Francisco (Pacific Bell Park)
Atlanta 10, San Francisco 2

The Giants disappointed a record crowd of 43,643 with a lackluster performance in their home playoff opener. Greg Maddux prevailed over former Braves pitcher Jason

Schmidt with a 10-2 rout that gave Atlanta the series edge. It was a 1-1 game until Schmidt's wildness and a bullpen collapse doomed the home club.

With one out in the sixth, Gary Sheffield, Chipper Jones and Andruw Jones walked, loading the bases. Manny Aybar replaced Schmidt and the game became a debacle on his first two pitches. Vinny Castilla lined a two-run single on the first one, and Keith Lockhart followed with a three-run homer for a sudden 6-1 lead.

Barry Bonds homered in the bottom of the sixth, but the Braves' bullpen held the Giants hitless over the final three innings and Atlanta jumped on Tim Worrell, Aaron Fultz and Robb Nen with four more runs in the ninth. Andruw Jones' two-run single off Nen was the big blow.

Game 4: October 6 at San Francisco (Pacific Bell Park)
San Francisco 8, Atlanta 3

It was a game the Giants had to win to stay alive, and they had to do it with a weary bullpen. That's when Livan Hernandez reverted to his previous postseason mastery, working into the ninth inning for a series-squaring 8-3 victory. It came at the expense of Tom Glavine, who would be pitching his final game in a Braves' uniform.

Glavine was blasted for seven hits and seven runs in 2 2/3 innings. The Giants sent 22 batters to the plate in the first three innings, taking a 7-0 lead before 43,070, the largest baseball crowd in Pacific Bell Park history. By the end of three innings, Rich Aurilia had two singles, a homer, three runs and four RBI.

Hernandez blanked the Braves until the fifth, when a pair of singles and Rafael Furcal's double scored a run. They added two more in the sixth on Chipper Jones' single, Javy Lopez' double and Vinny Castilla's single. The two teams then took cross-country charter flights to Atlanta for the decisive fifth game without benefit of an offday.

Game 5: October 7 at Atlanta (Turner Field)
San Francisco 3, Atlanta 1

Who was to know that the two starters in this pivotal game, Russ Ortiz and Kevin Millwood, would be involved in an incredible twist of fate? Millwood would be pitching his final game with the Braves - being replaced by Ortiz in the 2003 Atlanta rotation. On this night, they battled to stave off elimination before 45,203 tomahawk-choppers.

The Giants jumped to a 2-0 lead behind Barry Bonds and held on for a 3-2 victory and their first playoff series triumph since the 1989 NLCS. Ortiz did his part by yielding merely one run in 5 1/3 innings and posting his second playoff victory over the Braves, who soon traded left-hander Damian Moss for him.

Bonds' leadoff single, Benito Santiago's groundout and Reggie Sanders' two-out single to center opened the scoring in the second inning. Bonds followed with a leadoff homer on a 3-2 Millwood pitch for a 2-0 lead in the fourth, and Ortiz carried a two-hit shutout into the sixth.

He was removed after Andruw Jones and Vinny Castilla singled, and Mark DeRosa greeted Aaron Fultz with a run-scoring single for 2-1. J.T. Snow's double, a pair of walks and Kenny Lofton's sacrifice fly in the seventh scored the Giants' third run. An error by Jeff Kent gave the Braves one last hope in the ninth before Robb Nen struck out Gary Sheffield and nailed Chipper Jones on a double play for his finest save.

The Giants celebrate after defeating the Braves in the 2002 National League Division Series. (© *S.F. Giants*)

2002 NATIONAL LEAGUE CHAMPIONSHIP SERIES — GIANTS DEFEATED ST. LOUIS CARDINALS 4 GAMES TO 1

Game 1: October 9 at St. Louis (Busch Stadium)
San Francisco 9, St. Louis 6

Pesky Kenny Lofton scored three runs in the first three innings and was center stage during a benches-clearing altercation as the Giants posted their first NLCS victory in 13 years with a 9-6 conquest of the Cardinals before 52,175. Benito Santiago chipped in with four RBI on a pair of run-scoring singles and a two-run homer.

Kirk Rueter, pitching the playoff opener against his favorite team as a youngster in Southern Illinois, staggered through the first five innings for the victory in a game dominated by offense. The two teams each had 11 hits, yet the outcome seldom was in doubt after the Giants jumped Cardinals ace Matt Mor-

ris for a 7-1 lead.

A pair of walks and Santiago's single placed the Giants ahead in the first inning, and they batted around while scoring four times in the second. Six consecutive two-out hits did the damage: Singles by Lofton, Rich Aurilia and Jeff Kent; Barry Bonds' two-run triple and singles by Santiago and J.T. Snow.

Solo homers by Lofton and David Bell preceded the flare-up when reliever Mike Crudale buzzed Lofton in the fifth inning. When order was restored, four more homers concluded the scoring. Santiago hit a two-run shot, as did the Cardinals' Albert Pujols and Miguel Cairo. Pinch-hitter J.D. Drew added a solo homer for St. Louis.

Game 2: October 10 at St. Louis (Busch Stadium)
San Francisco 4, St. Louis 1

Jason Schmidt shut out the Cardinals on three hits until the eighth inning and Rich Aurilia knocked in three runs on two homers

off Woody Williams as the Giants rolled to a 4-1 victory and a two-game edge in the series. A crowd of 52,195 didn't have much to cheer because of Schmidt's dominance and Aurilia's slugging.

Aurilia's first homer came with one out in the first inning for a 1-0 lead. Williams settled down until the fifth, when David Bell's leadoff single and Aurilia's two-out homer made it 3-0 for the hero-a-day Giants. They added their final run off Jason Isringhausen in the ninth on J.T. Snow's leadoff triple and Ramon Martinez's squeeze bunt.

Schmidt, shaking off the wildness which cost him in his previous playoff start, had five one-two-three innings among his first six, finishing with eight strikeouts and one walk. A double play started by center fielder Kenny Lofton preserved the shutout in the third, and Schmidt was chased after pinch-hitter Eduardo Perez homered with two down in the eighth.

Game 3: October 12 at San Francisco (Pacific Bell Park)
St. Louis 5, San Francisco 4

Eli Marrero's leadoff homer off reliever Jay Witasick in the sixth inning cracked a tie and the Cardinals' bullpen escaped late-inning trouble in a 5-4 victory before 42,177. The Giants loaded the bases in three different innings, scoring merely once and stranding a total of 11 runners.

The Giants scored first on successive no-out singles by J.T. Snow, David Bell and Russ Ortiz, followed by Rich Aurilia's sacrifice fly with one out. A double by Fernando Viña and solo homers by Mike Matheny and Jim Edmonds helped the Cardinals take a 4-1 lead off Ortiz, who was lifted in the fifth.

Aurilia's walk, Jeff Kent's single and Barry Bonds' three-run homer off Chuck Finley produced a 4-4 tie in the fifth before Marrero came through. After that homer, the Giants' bullpen retired the final 12 St. Louis batters, but the home club couldn't capitalize on a bases-loaded, one-out situation in the seventh.

Game 4: October 13 at San Francisco (Pacific Bell Park)
San Francisco 4, St. Louis 3

Benito Santiago's two-out, two-run homer off reliever Rick White in the bottom of the eighth snapped a tie and boosted the Giants to a dramatic 4-3 victory, preventing the Cardinals from moving into a series tie. Santiago's towering homer to left came on a 3-2 pitch after Barry Bonds was walked intentionally with nobody on base.

"Along with Brian Johnson's homer against the Dodgers (1997) and J.T. Snow's playoff homer against the Mets (2000), I can't think of any bigger homers since I've been managing," Dusty Baker said, echoing the sentiments of those who contend it might have been the Giants' most significant homer since Bobby Thomson's "Shot Heard 'Round the World" in the 1951 playoffs.

2002 National League Championship Series MVP Benito Santiago's homer sealed the Giants' victory in Game 4. (© S.F. Giants)

Santiago, who frequently made pitchers pay after walking Bonds down the stretch, embraced the glorious moment and summed up: "It was unbelievable, a dream come true. When I hit the ball, I knew I hit it hard. The time before that he (White) struck me out on the same pitch (an inside fastball). I tried to put the good side of the bat on the ball, and it happened."

A capacity crowd of 42,676 watched the Cardinals take a 2-0 first-inning lead off Livan Hernandez, who kept his unbeaten postseason streak intact. Fernado Viña's leadoff double and singles by J.D. Drew and Tino Martinez did the big damage, but St. Louis didn't score again until the ninth.

Andy Benes, in his final game before retiring, blanked the Giants until the sixth. He was lifted after Jeff Kent and Bonds walked with one out. White struck out Santiago, but J.T. Snow's double off the top of the fence in left-center made it 2-2 and set the stage for Santiago's heroics.

Then it was up to Nen to make it stand, and it nearly didn't happen. Leadoff batter Kerry Robinson struck out, but was safe on a wild pitch. Viña singled and Edgar Renteria's grounder placed both runners in scoring position. Jim Edmonds' single made it 4-3 before Nen struck out Albert Pujols and Drew for a hard-earned save.

Game 5: October 14 at San Francisco (Pacific Bell Park)
San Francisco 2, St. Louis 1

The Giants desperately didn't want to return to St. Louis, site of their 1987 nightmare, and Lofton again was the biggest culprit in a 2-1 walkoff victory that produced the third pennant in San Francisco history and a World Series date with the Anaheim Angels. The big night was witnessed by 42,673 partisans who partied deep into the night.

Held scoreless by Matt Morris for seven innings, the Giants rallied behind Lofton, who reached base on his final four NLCS at-bats. He singled with one out in the eighth, advanced when Rich Aurilia singled and Jeff Kent was struck by a Morris pitch, and scored the tying run on Barry Bonds' sacrifice fly to left.

After Tim Worrell worked a scoreless top of the ninth, the Giants staged a two-out rally to crown their season. Two-out singles by David Bell and Shawon Dunston chased Morris, and Steve Kline entered to face Lofton. He lined a first-pitch single to center, scoring Bell, ending a memorable game and sending fireworks skyward.

"I just happened to be there—it all comes down to opportunity," a giddy Lofton said after convincingly snapping a zero-for-16 series slump. "I was looking slider, and I got one. It's the biggest hit of my career, and I was happy because I knew we were going to the World Series. I just kept my focus."

Giants starter Kirk Rueter, as usual, was the unsung hero. He held the Cardinals scoreless for six hits before they opened the scoring off Felix Rodriguez in the seventh on Mike Matheny's leadoff double, a sacrifice and Fernando Viña's sacrifice fly. Catcher Benito Santiago, who along with Bonds had a series-high six RBI, was named MVP.

CHAPTER EIGHT
NO-HITTERS

Ed Crane vs. Washington Senators—September 27, 1888

Right-hander Ed Crane holds the distinction of throwing the first no-hitter in New York Giants' history. Under threatening skies that ultimately resulted in the game being called after seven innings due to darkness, "Cannonball" held the Washington Senators hitless in a 3-0 victory at the Polo Grounds in New York on September 27, 1888.

The Giants already had clinched their first National League championship, and the gathering of 2,000 fans was in a festive mood. Crane kept up their enthusiasm throughout the game. He retired six batters on ground balls to himself while striking out five and walking six.

Meanwhile, New York scored single runs in the third, fourth and sixth innings off Washington pitcher George Haddock. In the sixth, left fielder Elmer Foster was hit by a pitch, stole second base and came all the way around to score on a groundout by shortstop John Montgomery Ward. Center fielder Mike Slattery and right fielder Mike Tiernan had two hits apiece, while third baseman Art Whitney recorded the other hit. Slattery and Tiernan scored the other two runs. New York stole four bases, including one by Crane.

Ed Crane pitched the first no-hitter in Giants' history against the Washington Senators at the Polo Grounds in New York on September 27, 1888. (National Baseball Library and Archive)

Ed Crane vs. Washington Senators — September 27, 1888

Washington	AB	R	H	RBI	New York	AB	R	H	RBI
Hoy, cf	1	0	0	0	Tiernan, rf	4	1	2	0
Myers, 2b	3	0	0	0	Richardson, 2b	2	0	0	0
Dailey, rf	3	0	0	0	Connor, 1b	3	0	0	1
O'Brien, 1b	3	0	0	0	Foster, lf	2	1	0	0
Werden, lf	3	0	0	0	Ward, ss	3	0	0	1
Donnelly, 3b	2	0	0	0	Slattery, cf	3	1	2	0
Fuller, ss	1	0	0	0	Whitney, 3b	3	0	1	1
Arundel, c	3	0	0	0	Crane, p	3	0	0	0
Haddock, p	2	0	0	0	Brown, c	3	0	0	0
Banning, c	0	0	0	0					
Totals	21	0	0	0	Totals	26	3	5	3

										R	H	E
Washington	0	0	0	0	0	0	0	-	-	—	0	0	1
New York	0	0	1	1	0	1	0	-	-	—	3	5	0

E — Fuller. LOB — Washington 5, New York 4. 2B — Slattery. SB — Hoy, Fuller, Tiernan, Richardson, Whitney, Crane.
S — Whitney.

Washington	IP	H	R	BB	SO
Haddock (L)	7	5	3	1	3

New York	IP	H	R	BB	SO
Crane (W)	7	0	0	6	5

HP — Foster by Haddock. WP — Haddock 3. PB — Arundel, Brown 3. Umpire — Valentine. Time — 1:40.
Attendance — 2,000.

After beginning his career as an outfielder, Crane pitched for the Giants in 1888 and 1889 and in 1892 and 1893, compiling just a 37-44 record with a 3.79 ERA in 98 games. On October 4, 1888, he became the first pitcher in N.L. history to strikeout four batters in one inning against the Chicago White Stockings at the Polo Grounds. Crane's best season was 1889, when he finished 14-10 with a 3.68 ERA. He also pitched for the Boston Unions of the Union Association (1884), Senators (1886 and 1893), New York Giants of the Players League (1890), Cincinnati Kellys of the American Association (1891) and Cincinnati Reds (1891).

In the 1889 World Series, Crane posted a 4-1 record with a 3.72 ERA as the Giants defeated the cross-town rival Brooklyn Bridegrooms six games to three.

Unlike New York left-handed pitcher Ledell "Cannonball" Titcomb (1887-89), whose nickname stemmed from the velocity with which he could throw the ball, Crane's moniker was the result of his love to eat that resulted in a 5-foot-10, 204-pound frame.

Amos Rusie vs. Brooklyn Bridegrooms— July 31, 1891

On July 31, 1891, New York Giants' right-hander Amos Rusie no-hit the Brooklyn Bridegrooms 6-0 at the Polo Grounds in New York. At 20 years and two months old, he is the youngest pitcher ever to throw a no-hitter. Rusie was a bona fide fire-baller, and some historians suggest he was the reason the distance from the pitcher's mound to home plate was moved back from 50 feet to the current 60 feet, 6 inches in 1893.

Only one Brooklyn batter managed to hit the ball to the outfield (caught by center fielder George Gore) during Rusie's gem. There were eight groundouts to second baseman Danny Richardson, six to shortstop Jack Glasscock

and five to third baseman Charley Bassett. Rusie struck out four. Not surprisingly, he issued seven walks. Rusie was plagued by control problems throughout his career and holds four of the top 10 season walks totals in baseball history.

New York scored the only run Rusie would need in the first inning off Brooklyn pitcher Adonis Terry, then added two more in the sixth and three in the seventh. Left fielder Jim O'Rourke collected three hits and scored two runs, while catcher Dick Buckley had two hits and first baseman Roger Connor scored twice.

The crowd of 2,586 also was treated to a triple play turned by the Bridegrooms in the first inning from second baseman John O'Brien to shortstop John Montgomery Ward to first baseman Dave Foutz to catcher Con Daily to third baseman George Pinkney.

Nicknamed the "Hoosier Thunderbolt," Rusie finished the 1891 season with a 33-20 record and 2.55 ERA. He led the National

League with six shutouts and 337 strikeouts. Rusie pitched for the Giants from 1890-95 and from 1897-98 before being traded to the Cincinnati Reds in exchange for Christy Mathewson (who had yet to pitch in the major leagues) in 1900.

Rusie was inducted into the National Baseball Hall of Fame in 1977 by the Veterans Committee.

Christy Mathewson at St. Louis Cardinals—July 15, 1901

Without question, Christy Mathewson is the greatest pitcher ever to wear a New York or San Francisco Giants' uniform. So it is only fitting that he was the first hurler to orchestrate a no-hitter from the present-day distance of 60 feet, 6 inches from the pitcher's mound to home plate.

Mathewson no-hit the St. Louis Cardinals during a 5-0 victory July 15, 1901, at Robison Field in St. Louis. Only four balls were hit to

Amos Rusie vs. Brooklyn Bridegrooms — July 31, 1891

Brooklyn	AB	R	H	RBI	New York	AB	R	H	RBI
Ward, ss	3	0	0	0	Gore, cf	3	1	0	0
Foutz, 1b	4	0	0	0	Tiernan, rf	3	1	1	0
Pinkney, 3b	2	0	0	0	Bassett, 3b	3	0	0	0
Burns, rf	1	0	0	0	O'Rourke, lf	4	2	3	1
W. O'Brien, lf	4	0	0	0	Connor, 1b	3	2	1	2
Griffin, cf	3	0	0	0	Richardson, 2b	3	0	1	0
J. O'Brien, 2b	3	0	0	0	Glasscock, ss	4	0	0	0
Daily, c	2	0	0	0	Buckley, c	4	0	2	1
Terry, p	3	0	0	0	Rusie, p	4	0	0	0
Totals	25	0	0	0	Totals	31	6	8	4

								R	H	E
Brooklyn	0	0	0	0	0	0	0	0	0	—	0	0	1
New York	1	0	0	0	0	2	3	0	x	—	6	8	1

E — Daily, Richardson. DP — New York 2. TP — Brooklyn. LOB — Brooklyn 6, New York 7. 2B — Richardson, Buckley. 3B — Connor. SB — Ward (2), Griffin, Tiernan, O'Rourke. S — Connor.

Brooklyn	IP	H	R	ER	BB	SO
Terry (L)	8	8	6	2	6	5

New York	IP	H	R	ER	BB	SO
Rusie (W)	9	0	0	0	7	4

HP — Daily by Rusie. WP — Terry. PB — Buckley 2. Umpires — Powers, Beattin. Time — 1:47. Attendance — 2,586.

the outfield (two to center fielder George Van Haltren and one apiece to right fielder Algie McBride left fielder Kip Selbach). Van Haltren made a running attempt at catcher Jack Ryan's ball hit in the eighth inning but dropped the ball for a two-base error. Selbach preserved the no-hitter with a running catch of left fielder Jesse Burkett's fly ball in the ninth.

Mathewson, who walked four batters and also struck out four, helped himself defensively by catching two line drives and a pop up and fielding three ground balls.

The Giants scored twice in the first two innings

off St. Louis starting pitcher Willie Sudhoff and added their final run in the eighth. Four players had two hits apiece: shortstop Charlie Hickman, Selbach, second baseman Sammy Strang and Van Haltren.

The 22-year-old Mathewson, in his second major league season, went on to post a 20-17 record with a 2.41 ERA in 1901 en route to winding up in the National Baseball Hall of Fame.

Hall of Famer Christy Mathewson is the only Giants' pitcher to author two nine-inning no hitters, over the St. Louis Cardinals in 1901 and the Chicago Cubs in 1905.

Christy Mathewson at St. Louis Cardinals — July 15, 1901

New York	AB	R	H	St. Louis	AB	R	H
Van Haltren, cf	5	1	2	Burkett, lf	3	0	0
Selbach, lf	4	1	2	Donovan, rf	4	0	0
McBride, rf	3	1	1	Schriver, 1b	3	0	0
Davis, 3b	3	0	1	Padden, 2b	2	0	0
Ganzel, 1b	4	0	0	Wallace, ss	3	0	0
Hickman, ss	4	1	2	Kruger, 3b	3	0	0
Strang, 2b	4	1	2	Ryan, c	3	0	0
Warner, c	3	0	0	Nichols, cf	3	0	0
Mathewson, p	4	0	0	Sudhoff, p	3	0	0
Totals	34	5	10	Totals	27	0	0

											R	H	E
New York	2	2	0	0	0	0	0	1	0	—	5	10	1
St. Louis	0	0	0	0	0	0	0	0	0	—	0	0	1

E — Van Haltren, Wallace. LOB — New York 4, St. Louis 3. SB — Van Haltren. S — Davis, Warner.

New York	IP	H	R	ER	BB	SO
Mathewson (W)	9	0	0	0	4	4

St. Louis	IP	H	R	ER	BB	SO
Sudhoff (L)	9	10	5	4	2	3

Umpire — Dwyer. Time — 1:35. Attendance — n/a.

Red Ames at St. Louis Cardinals— September 14, 1903

The New York Giants' Leon "Red" Ames made his major league debut September 14, 1903, and held the St. Louis Cardinals hitless for five innings before the game (the second of a double-header) was called because of darkness. New York swept the twin-bill 8-2 and 5-0 at Robison Field in St. Louis.

Ames walked two batters—center fielder Homer Smoot and first baseman Ed Murphy—but faced only one over the minimum of 15 batters when second baseman Billy Gilbert and first baseman Dan McGann turned a double play. There were no balls hit to the outfield, and Ames recorded seven strikeouts. Gilbert and shortstop Charlie Babb took care of two ground balls apiece.

The Giants scored three runs in the first inning off St. Louis starting pitcher Mike O'Neill and added solo tallies in the second and fifth. New York collected only four hits

Leon "Red" Ames held the St. Louis Cardinals hitless for five innings (before the game was called on account of darkness) in his major league debut September 14, 1903, and he had a perfect game for 9.1 innings against the Brooklyn Dodgers on April 15, 1909, before giving up a hit and ultimately losing the game in 13 innings.

Red Ames at St. Louis Cardinals—September 14, 1903

New York	AB	R	H		St. Louis	AB	R	H
Browne, rf	3	1	1		Dunleavy, rf	2	0	0
Bresnahan, cf	3	1	1		Smoot, cf	1	0	0
McGann, 1b	3	0	0		Brain, ss	2	0	0
Mertes, lf	2	1	0		Burke, 3b	2	0	0
Babb, ss	1	1	0		Barclay, lf	2	0	0
Lauder, 3b	2	0	1		Ryan, c	2	0	0
Gilbert, 2b	3	0	0		Demont, 2b	1	0	0
Warner, c	3	1	1		Murphy, 1b	0	0	0
Ames, p	2	0	0		Hackett, 1b	1	0	0
					O'Neill, p	1	0	0
Totals	22	5	4		Totals	14	0	0

									R	H	E
New York	3	1	0	0	1	-	-	-	-	—	5	4	0
St. Louis	0	0	0	0	0	-	-	-	-	—	0	0	5

E—Demont 3, Murphy, Hackett. DP—New York 1. LOB—New York 6, St. Louis 1. 2B—Bresnahan. S—Babb, Lauder.

New York	IP	H	R	BB	SO
Ames (W)	5	0	0	2	7

St. Louis	IP	H	R	BB	SO
O'Neill (L)	5	4	5	2	2

Umpires—Moran, Johnstone. Time—1:04. Attendance—n/a.

(catcher Roger Bresnahan had a double) but took advantage of five Cardinals' errors.

Ames won his only other start of 1903 and went on to enjoy a distinguished 11-year career with the Giants before subsequently toiling for the Cincinnati Reds (1913-15), St. Louis (1915-19) and Philadelphia Phillies (1919).

Christy Mathewson at Chicago Cubs— June 13, 1905

In one of the truly historic pitching matchups the game of baseball has ever seen, the New York Giants' Christy Mathewson no-hit the Chicago Cubs and defeated Mordecai "Three-Finger" Brown 1-0 on June 13, 1905, under threatening skies at Wrigley Field in Chicago. It was Mathewson's second career no-hitter.

Mathewson did not issue a walk—while striking out two—and only a pair of New York errors (by shortstop Bill Dahlen and second baseman Billy Gilbert) prevented him from

pitching a perfect game. The Cubs grounded out five times to Gilbert, four times to Mathewson and three times to Dahlen. The hardest hit ball against Mathewson was by Chicago second baseman Johnny Evers in the fifth inning, a line drive caught by Giants' center fielder Mike Donlin.

Meanwhile, Brown was nearly as splendid. He surrendered just two hits through the first 8.1 innings before four consecutive singles by right fielder George Browne, first baseman Dan McGann, left fielder Sam Mertes and Dahlen pushed across McGann with the only run. Brown walked two and struck out three.

Mathewson was splendid throughout the 1905 season, to the tune of a 31-9 record with a 1.28 ERA. He led the National League in wins, ERA, shutouts (8) and strikeouts (206). Mathewson was simply dominating in the World Series that year, pitching three shutouts and allowing merely 14 hits and one walk with 18 strikeouts in 27 innings as the Giants defeated the Philadelphia Athletics four games to one.

Christy Mathewson at Chicago Cubs—June 13, 1905

New York	AB	R	H	RBI	Chicago	AB	R	H	RBI
Donlin, cf	4	0	1	0	Slagle, cf	4	0	0	0
Browne, rf	4	0	1	0	Schulte, lf	3	0	0	0
McGann, 1b	4	1	1	0	Maloney, rf	3	0	0	0
Mertes, lf	4	0	1	0	Chance, 1b	3	0	0	0
Dahlen, ss	4	0	2	1	Tinker, ss	3	0	0	0
Devlin, 3b	1	0	0	0	Evers, 2b	3	0	0	0
Gilbert, 2b	3	0	0	0	Casey, 3b	3	0	0	0
Bowerman, c	3	0	0	0	Kling, c	3	0	0	0
Mathewson, p	3	0	0	0	Brown, p	3	0	0	0
Totals	30	1	6	1	Totals	28	0	0	0

									R	H	E
New York	0	0	0	0	0	0	0	0	1	—	1	4	2
Chicago	0	0	0	0	0	0	0	0	0	—	0	0	2

E—Tinker, Kling, Dahlen, Gilbert. DP—New York 1. LOB—Chicago 1, New York 4. SB—Schulte, Dahlen.

New York	IP	H	R	ER	BB	SO
Mathewson (W)	9	0	0	0	0	2

Chicago	IP	H	R	ER	BB	SO
Brown (L)	9	6	1	1	2	3

BK—Brown. Umpires—Bauswine, Emslie. Time—1:25. Attendance—8,000.

Throughout their respective Hall of Fame careers, Mathewson and Brown squared off against one another 22 times, with Brown holding the upper hand by a 13-9 margin.

Hooks Wiltse vs. Philadelphia Phillies— July 4, 1908

The first New York Giants' left-handed pitcher to throw a no-hitter was George "Hooks" Wiltse, who celebrated Independence Day 1908 with a 1-0, 10-inning masterpiece against the Philadelphia Phillies in the first game of a double-header at the Polo Grounds in New York. He is one of only four pitchers in baseball history to author 10-inning no-hitters.

It would have been a perfect game had Wiltse not grazed opposing pitcher George McQuillan with a pitch with two outs in the ninth inning. On the previous delivery, McQuillan appeared to strike out, but umpire Cy Rigler said the pitch was a ball. Between games of the double-header, even McQuillan said the pitch should have been called a strike. Wiltse finished the game, which took a mere 1 hour and 45 minutes to complete, with five strikeouts.

New York managed eight hits off McQuillan, including two apiece by shortstop Al Bridwell, third baseman Art Devlin and first baseman Fred Tenney. Devlin scored the game's only run with no outs in the 10th inning. The Giants completed the double-header sweep with a 9-3 victory in Game 2.

Wiltse, who set a major league record that still stands by winning the first 12 games he started in his career during the 1904 season, had his best overall year in 1908. He posted a 23-14 record with a 2.24 ERA while establishing personal bests for wins, complete games (30) and shutouts (7).

Hooks Wiltse vs. Philadelphia Phillies—July 4, 1908

Philadelphia	AB	R	H		New York	AB	R	H
Grant, 3b	4	0	0		Tonney, 1b	4	0	2
Knabe, 2b	4	0	0		Doyle, 2b	3	0	0
Titus, rf	4	0	0		Bresnahan, c	4	0	0
Magee, lf	4	0	0		Donlin, rf	3	0	1
Bransfield, 1b	3	0	0		Seymour, cf	4	0	1
Osborne, cf	3	0	0		Devlin, 3b	4	1	2
Doolin, ss	1	0	0		Shannon, lf	2	0	0
Dooin, c	3	0	0		Bridwell, ss	4	0	2
McQuillan, p	2	0	0		Wiltse, p	1	0	0
Courtney, ss	2	0	0					
Totals	30	0	0		Totals	29	1	8

None out when winning run scored.

												R	H	E
Philadelphia	0	0	0	0	0	0	0	0	0	0	—	0	0	3
New York	0	0	0	0	0	0	0	0	0	1	—	1	8	0

E—Grant, Dooin, Courtney. DP—Philadelphia 2. LOB—Philadelphia 1, New York 7. SB—Donlin. S—Doyle, Wiltse (2), Shannon (2).

Philadelphia	IP	H	R	BB	SO
McQuillan (L)	9	8	1	0	1

New York	IP	H	R	BB	SO
Wiltse (W)	10	0	0	0	5

HP—McQuillen by Wiltse. Umpire—Rigler. Time: 1:45. Attendance—n/a.

McQuillan also enjoyed the best year of his decade-long career, going 23-17 with a 1.53 ERA, 32 complete games and seven shutouts.

Red Ames vs. Brooklyn Dodgers— April 15, 1909

On opening day of the 1909 season, the New York Giants' Leon "Red" Ames pitched a perfect game against the Brooklyn Dodgers at the Polo Grounds in New York for 9.1 innings before losing the game 3-0 in 13 innings.

Ames, a right-hander who authored a five-inning no-hitter in his major league debut against the St. Louis Cardinals in 1903, retired the first 28 batters he faced before second baseman Whitey Alperman doubled with one out in the 10th. Ames also gave up doubles in the 11th and 12th but kept the Dodgers off the scoreboard. Then in the 13th, player-manager Harry Lumley led off with a triple over the head of Giants' center fielder Bill O'Hara. After Ames

intentionally walked first baseman Tim Jordan, Brooklyn got consecutive run-producing singles from third baseman Ed Lennox, catcher Bill Bergen and left fielder Al Burch (a bunt base hit) to score three runs. Ames wound up allowing four hits and two walks with 10 strikeouts. New York outfielders recorded no putouts in the game.

Overshadowed by Ames' performance was Brooklyn pitcher Kaiser Wilhelm, who held the Giants without a hit until the eighth inning and finished with a three-hitter (singles by left fielder Buck Herzog, pinch hitter Chief Meyers and catcher Admiral Schlei). In the eighth, center fielder Jimmy Sebring threw out a runner at the plate, and in the 10th, New York advanced runners to second and third with two outs but couldn't come up with the big hit. Wilhelm did walk seven batters while striking out four.

It was tough-luck performances such as this one which earned Ames the nickname "Kalamity" by sportswriter Charley Dryden.

Red Ames vs. Brooklyn Dodgers—April 15, 1909

Brooklyn	AB	R	H	RBI	New York	AB	R	H	RBI
Burch, lf	6	0	1	1	Herzog, lf	6	0	1	0
Alperman, 2b	6	0	2	0	Fletcher, 2b	5	0	0	0
Hummel, ss	5	0	0	0	McCormick, ph	1	0	0	0
Sebring, cf	5	0	0	0	Murray, rf	5	0	0	0
Lumley, rf	5	1	1	0	Tenney, 1b	5	0	0	0
Jordan, 1b	4	1	1	0	O'Hara, cf	3	0	0	0
Lennox, 3b	4	1	1	1	Devlin, 3b	2	0	0	0
Bergen, c	5	0	1	1	Bridwell, ss	4	0	0	0
Wilhelm, p	5	0	0	0	Schlei, c	4	0	1	0
					Ames, p	4	0	0	0
					J. Meyers, ph	1	0	1	0
Totals	45	3	7	3	Totals	40	0	3	0

															R	H	E
Brooklyn	0	0	0	0	0	0	0	0	0	0	0	0	3	—	3	7	1
New York	0	0	0	0	0	0	0	0	0	0	0	0	0	—	0	3	2

E—Lennox, Fletcher, Schlei. DP — New York 1. LOB—Brooklyn 5. New York 8. 2B—Alperman 2, Jordan. 3B—Lumley.

Brooklyn	IP	H	R	ER	BB	SO
Wilhelm (W)	13	3	0	0	7	4

New York	IP	H	R	ER	BB	SO
Ames (L)	13	4	3	3	2	10

Umpires—Johnstone, Cuesack. Time—2:20. Attendance—30,000.

Ames went on to finish the 1909 season with a 15-10 record and a 2.69 ERA.

Jeff Tesreau at Philadelphia Phillies— September 6, 1912

New York Giants' rookie right-hander Jeff Tesreau was not given credit for his no-hitter against the Philadelphia Phillies in the first game of a double-header at the Baker Bowl in Philadelphia on September 6, 1912, until after the game.

Philadelphia center fielder Dode Paskert led off the bottom of the first inning by hitting a pop up along the first base line that either catcher Art Wilson or first baseman Fred Merkle easily could have caught. Both players got under the ball but then backed off for fear of a collision, and at the last instant Merkle stuck out his glove but had the ball hit off the tip and fall into fair territory. It originally was ruled a hit, but after the game Merkle admitted he touched the ball, and the official scorer changed the play to an error. Paskert advanced to second base and then tried to score on a wild pitch by Tesreau but was thrown out at the plate.

Only three other Phillies reached base against Tesreau—catcher Bill Killefer on an error by New York shortstop Art Fletcher in the third, Paskert on a walk in the third and third baseman John Dodge on a walk in the eighth.

The Giants banged out 10 hits against three Philadelphia pitchers but scored only three runs, two in the third and one in the fourth. Pinch hitter Doc Crandell provided the big blow with a two-run single in the third that scored Wilson and Fletcher. Three players had two hits apiece: second baseman Larry Doyle, Fletcher and Merkle.

New York won the second game of the double-header by the score of 9-8.

Tesreau went on to post a 17-7 record with a National League-leading 1.96 ERA for the Giants, who won the second of three straight N.L. pennants in 1912. Nicknamed

Jeff Tesreau no-hit the Philadelphia Phillies by the score of 3-0 at the Baker Bowl in Philadelphia on September 6, 1912. He nearly duplicated the feat against the Pittsburgh Pirates on May 16, 1914, before surrendering a hit with two outs in the ninth inning.

"Big Jeff" for his 6-foot-2, 218-pound frame and resemblance to fighter Jim Jeffries, Tesreau spent his entire seven-year major league career in New York and posted a 115-72 record with a 2.43 ERA in 247 games. On the franchise career lists, he ranks third in ERA and tied for seventh in shutouts (27).

Tesreau nearly threw another no-hitter against the Pittsburgh Pirates at Forbes Field in Pittsburgh on May 16, 1914, but center fielder Joe Kelly singled to center with two outs in the ninth inning. Tesreau was forced to settle for a one-hitter and a 2-0 victory.

Jeff Tesreau at Philadelphia Phillies—September 6, 1912

New York	AB	R	H	RBI	Philadelphia	AB	R	H	RBI
Devore, lf	1	0	0	0	Paskert, cf	3	0	0	0
Crandell, ph	1	0	1	2	Maugus, lf	4	0	0	0
Becker, lf-rf	2	0	0	0	Miller, rf	4	0	0	0
Doyle, 2b	5	0	2	0	Luderus, 1b	3	0	0	0
Snodgrass, cf	3	0	0	0	Walsh, 2b	3	0	0	0
Murray, rf-lf	4	0	1	0	Dooan, ss	3	0	0	0
Merkle, 1b	4	0	2	0	Dodge, 3b	2	0	0	0
Herzog, 3b	3	1	0	0	Killefer, c	3	0	0	0
Wilson, c	1	1	1	0	Rixey, p	1	0	0	0
Fletcher, ss	4	1	2	1	Magee, ph	1	0	0	0
Tesreau, p	3	0	1	0	Nicholson, p	0	0	0	0
					Cravath, ph	1	0	0	0
					Nelson, p	0	0	0	0
Totals	31	3	10	3	Totals	28	0	0	0

										R	H	E
New York	0	0	2	1	0	0	0	0	0	—	3	10	2
Philadelphia	0	0	0	0	0	0	0	0	0	—	0	0	4

E—Merkle, Fletcher, Killefer 2, Walsh 2. DP—Philadelphia 1. LOB—New York 11, Philadelphia 3. SB—Merkle (2), Becker, Herzog. S—Wilson, Tesreau.

New York	IP	H	R	ER	BB	SO
Tesreau (W)	9	0	0	0	2	2

Philadelphia	IP	H	R	ER	BB	SO
Rixey (L)	6	7	3	3	4	4
Nicholson	2	2	0	0	2	0
Nelson	1	1	0	0	1	1

WP—Tesreau, Rixey. PB—Killefer 2. Umpires—Klem, Orth. Time—1:55. Attendance—n/a.

Rube Marquard vs. Brooklyn Dodgers— April 15, 1915

After posting a 12-22 record for the New York Giants in 1914 (including a 12-game losing streak), Rube Marquard temporarily jumped to the Federal League with the Brooklyn Tip-Tops but then returned to the Giants. He celebrated by opening the 1915 season with a no-hitter against the Brooklyn Dodgers at the Polo Grounds in New York on April 15.

In the 2-0 victory, the right-handed Marquard faced 30 batters, three over the minimum. He walked two batters and a third reached on an error by Giants' shortstop Art Fletcher. Marquard had two strikeouts. Fletcher retired five Dodgers on groundouts, and third baseman Hans Lobert made several good defensive plays. Only three balls were hit to the outfield. It was reported that Marquard had such good control he could have "spun the ball over if the home plate was as small as a postage stamp."

With one out in the ninth inning, Brooklyn center fielder Hi Myers hit a fast roller over first base that Giants' first baseman Fred Merkle snared, fell down and crawled on his hands and knees to just beat Myers to the bag.

Marquard's opposing pitcher was Nap Rucker, who allowed eight hits in seven innings. New York scored one run in the fourth on a one-out single by Lobert and a two-out double by left fielder George Burns. In the seventh, Merkle reached on an infield single and went to second on a throwing error by short-

stop Gus Getz and wound up at third as the next two batters were retired. Then Marquard helped himself with a broken bat single to right field that plated Merkle with an insurance run.

Marquard went 9-8 with a 3.73 ERA in 27 games for the Giants before being released. Ironically, he signed with the Dodgers and helped them win the National League pennant in 1916 by going 13-6 with a 1.58 ERA (second in the N.L. to Grover Cleveland Alexander of the Philadelphia Phillies at 1.55).

Jesse Barnes vs. Philadelphia Phillies— May 7, 1922

En route to throwing a 6-0 no-hitter against the Philadelphia Phillies at the Polo Grounds in New York on May 7, 1922, New York Giants' right-hander Jesse Barnes faced the minimum of 27 batters. The only batter to

reach against him was center fielder Cy Williams, who drew a five-pitch walk leading off the top of the fifth inning but was erased one out later when shortstop Art Fletcher grounded into a double play from second baseman Johnny Rawlings to shortstop Dave Bancroft to first baseman George Kelly.

The middle of the infield was busy all afternoon. Rawlings fielded seven grounders, while Bancroft handled six chances. Only four balls were hit to the outfield, three to center fielder Ralph Shinners and one to left fielder Irish Meusel. Barnes finished with five strikeouts.

New York wasted no time jumping on Phillies' starting pitcher Lee Meadows, scoring two runs in the first inning. The first run came on an RBI single by Meusel that plated third baseman Heinie Groh. Then with right fielder

---

Rube Marquard vs. Brooklyn Dodgers—April 15, 1915

Brooklyn	AB	R	H	RBI	New York	AB	R	H	RBI
Schultz, 3b	4	0	0	0	Snodgrass, cf	2	0	1	0
Myers, cf	4	0	0	0	Doyle, 2b	4	0	1	0
Wheat, 1b	3	0	0	0	Lobert, 3b	4	1	2	0
Cutshaw, 2b	3	0	0	0	Fletcher, ss	4	0	0	0
Hummel, 1b	3	0	0	0	Burns, lf	4	0	1	1
Stengel, rf	1	0	0	0	Merkle, 1b	4	1	1	0
McCarty, ph	1	0	0	0	Thorpe, rf	2	0	0	0
Zimmerman, rf	0	0	0	0	Myers, c	3	0	1	0
Getz, ss	3	0	0	0	Marquard, p	3	0	1	1
Miller, c	3	0	0	0					
Rucker, p	2	0	0	0					
Egan, ph	1	0	0	0					
Ragan, p	0	0	0	0					
Totals	28	0	0	0	Totals	29	2	8	2

										R	H	E
Brooklyn	0	0	0	0	0	0	0	0	0	—	0	0	2
New York	0	0	0	1	0	0	1	0	x	—	2	8	1

E—Getz 2, Fletcher. LOB—Brooklyn 1, New York 7. 2B—Burns. SB—Snodgrass.

Brooklyn	IP	H	R	ER	BB	SO
Rucker (L)	7	8	2	1	3	1
Ragan	1	0	0	0	0	1

New York	IP	H	R	ER	BB	SO
Marquard (W)	9	0	0	0	2	2

WP—Rucker. Umpires—Rigler, Hart. Time—1:21. Attendance—n/a.

Ross Youngs at third and Meusel at first, the two attempted a double steal on which Meusel was thrown out at second as Youngs scored. The Giants knocked out Meadows in the second and capped a three-run inning with a Texas League single to left field by Groh off reliever George Smith that scored Barnes and Bancroft. Kelly finished the scoring in the fifth with a run-producing double that sent Youngs home.

In the ninth, Philadelphia pinch-hitter Lee King sent a 2-1 pitch to deep center that was chased down by Shinners for the first out. Next, pinch-hitter Cliff Lee grounded out to Rawlings, and finally, a third pinch-hitter, Russ Wrightstone, grounded out sharply to Bancroft.

Barnes' no-hitter and near perfect game came exactly one week after the Chicago White Sox' Charlie Robertson authored a perfect game against the Detroit Tigers at Tiger Stadium. It was the first no-hitter at the Polo Grounds since Ray Caldwell of the Cleveland Indians accomplished the feat against the New York Yankees on September 10, 1919.

Barnes posted a 13-8 record with a 3.51 ERA during the 1922 season.

Carl Hubbell vs. Pittsburgh Pirates— May 8, 1929

Carl Hubbell of the New York Giants was in complete control and received plenty of offensive support in an 11-0 no-hitter against the Pittsburgh Pirates at the Polo Grounds in New York on May 8, 1929.

The second-year left-hander walked one and struck out four. In the ninth inning, Pittsburgh pinch-hitter Harry Riconda led off and reached on an error by left fielder Chick Fullis.

Jesse Barnes vs. Philadelphia Phillies—May 7, 1922

Philadelphia	AB	R	H	RBI	New York	AB	R	H	RBI
LeBourveau, lf	3	0	0	0	Bancroft, ss	2	1	1	1
Rapp, 3b	3	0	0	0	Rawlings, 2b	4	0	0	0
Walker, rf	3	0	0	0	Groh, 3b	4	1	2	2
Williams, cf	2	0	0	0	Youngs, rf	4	2	2	0
Parkinson, 2b	3	0	0	0	Meusel, lf	4	0	1	1
Fletcher, ss	3	0	0	0	Kelly, 1b	4	1	3	1
Leslie, 1b	2	0	0	0	Shinners, cf	3	0	0	0
King, ph	1	0	0	0	E. Smith, c	3	0	0	0
Henline, c	2	0	0	0	J. Barnes, p	2	1	0	0
Lee, ph	1	0	0	0					
Meadows, p	0	0	0	0					
G. Smith, p	2	0	0	0					
Wrightstone, ph	1	0	0	0					
Totals	26	0	0	0	Totals	30	6	9	5

											R	H	E
Philadelphia	0	0	0	0	0	0	0	0	0	—	0	0	0
New York	2	3	0	0	1	0	0	0	x	—	6	9	0

DP—Philadelphia 1, New York 1. LOB—New York 4. 2B—Kelly 2. SB—Young 2.

Philadelphia	IP	H	R	ER	BB	SO
Meadows (L)	1.1	4	5	5	2	0
G. Smith	6.2	5	1	1	0	0

New York	IP	H	R	ER	BB	SO
J. Barnes (W)	9	0	0	0	1	5

HP—Shinners by Meadows, Bancroft by G. Smith. Umpires—Hart, O'Day, Emslie. Time—1:37. Attendance—30,000.

The next batter, second baseman Sparky Adams, hit a double play grounder to shortstop Travis Jackson, who booted the ball and got nobody out. After center fielder Lloyd Waner struck out, right fielder Paul Waner hit a ball between the mound and first base that Hubbell scooped up and whirled off balance to second base to start a fancy game-ending double play.

Only six balls were hit out of the infield against Hubbell (three to left field, two to right and one to center). Jackson threw out five batters from shortstop.

New York wasted no time scoring runs for Hubbell with two in each of the first three innings to chase Pittsburgh starting and losing

pitcher Jesse Perry (1.1 innings) and reliever Fred Fussell (1.1 innings). Ray Kremer allowed five runs over the final 5.1 innings. The Giants got two home runs from right fielder Mel Ott and one apiece from second baseman Andy Cohen and Fullis. Cohen collected three of the Giants' 12 hits.

Hubbell's no-hitter was the first in the major leagues since Ted Lyons of the Chicago White Sox against the Boston Red Sox on August 21, 1926; the first by a Giants' pitcher since Jesse Barnes against the Philadelphia Phillies on May 7, 1922; and the first by a left-hander since Hub Leonard of Boston against the Detroit Tigers on June 3, 1918.

Carl Hubbell vs. Pittsburgh Pirates—May 8, 1929

Pittsburgh	AB	R	H	RBI	New York	AB	R	H	RBI
Adams, 2b	3	0	0	0	Roush, cf	5	1	1	2
L. Waner, cf	3	0	0	0	Cohen, 2b	5	2	3	2
P. Waner, rf	4	0	0	0	Lindstrom, 3b	4	1	0	0
Traynor, 3b	3	0	0	0	Ott, rf	3	3	2	4
Stroner, 3b	0	0	0	0	Terry, 1b	4	0	1	0
Grantham, lf	1	0	0	0	Jackson, ss	4	0	1	0
Comorosky, lf	2	0	0	0	Fullis, lf	4	1	2	2
Sheely, 1b	3	0	0	0	O'Farrell, c	4	2	2	0
Bartell, ss	3	0	0	0	Hubbell, p	3	1	0	1
Hargreaves, c	3	0	0	0					
Petty, p	0	0	0	0					
Fussell, p	1	0	0	0					
Kremer, p	1	0	0	0					
Riconda, ph	1	0	0	0					
Totals	28	0	0	0	Totals	36	11	12	11

											R	H	E
Pittsburgh	0	0	0	0	0	0	0	0	0	—	0	0	2
New York	2	2	2	0	0	5	0	0	x	—	11	12	3

E—Traynor, Sheely, Jackson 2, Fullis. DP—New York 1. LOB—Pittsburgh 3, New York 3. 2B—O'Farrell. 3B—O'Farrell, Roush. HR—Ott 2, Fullis, Cohen. S—L. Waner, Hubbell.

Pittsburgh	IP	H	R	ER	BB	SO
Petty (L)	1.1	3	4	4	0	0
Fussell	1.1	3	2	2	1	0
Kremer	5.1	6	5	5	0	6

New York	IP	H	R	ER	BB	SO
Hubbell (W)	9	0	0	0	1	4

Umpires—Moran, McLaughlin, Quigley. Time—1:35. Attendance—8,000.

The Pittsburgh Pirates couldn't muster a hit against Carl Hubbell at the Polo Grounds in New York on May 8, 1929.

Mike McCormick at Philadelphia Phillies—June 12, 1959

An eye-popping defensive play didn't preserve 20-year-old left-hander Mike McCormick's no-hitter for the San Francisco Giants against the Philadelphia Phillies at Shibe Park in Philadelphia on June 12, 1959. Rather it was Mother Nature.

After holding the Phillies hitless through five innings, McCormick issued two walks and a single to center fielder Richie Ashburn in the bottom of the sixth. But before the inning was completed the heavens opened, and the game was rained out. Rules dictated that the game totals revert back to the last completed inning. At the time, National League president Warren C. Giles ruled that it was not a no-hitter, but now McCormick officially is recognized on the list of no-hitters of less than nine innings. It was the first no-hitter in San Francisco Giants' history.

The only runner to "officially" reach against McCormick was third baseman Gene Freese on a fourth-inning walk.

The Giants won the game 3-0. They scored a run in the first on a triple by third baseman Jim Davenport and an error by Phillies' first baseman Ed Bouchee on a grounder by right fielder Willie Kirkland. Shortstop Ed Bressoud doubled and catcher Hobie Landrith homered in the fifth for San Francisco's other two runs.

Philadelphia right-hander Jack Meyer, who allowed five hits in five innings, was the victim of McCormick's pitching and the weather.

McCormick finished the 1959 season with just a 12-16 record and a 3.99 ERA. But the following year he led the N.L. with a 2.70 ERA to go with a 15-12 mark.

Sam Jones at St. Louis Cardinals— September 26, 1959

When right-hander Sam Jones took the mound for the San Francisco Giants against the St. Louis Cardinals at old Busch Stadium (formerly Sportsman's Park) in St. Louis on September 26, 1959, he already was the author of one no-hitter (for the Chicago Cubs against the Pittsburgh Pirates on May 12, 1955) and another near-miss (a controversial one-hitter for the Giants against the Los Angeles Dodgers on June 30, 1959).

Jones held the Cardinals hitless for seven innings in the first game of what was to be a twi-night double-header. With two outs in the top of the eighth, umpire Frank Dascolli called time as heavy rains poured over the upper deck and high winds shredded the American flag flying in center field. After a 1 hour and 37 minute delay, the game was called. The second game was postponed and rescheduled as part of a double-header the next day.

The only two St. Louis batters to get on base against Jones were right fielder Joe

Mike McCormick at Philadelphia Phillies—June 12, 1959

San Francisco	AB	R	H	RBI	Philadelphia	AB	R	H	RBI
Davenport, 3b	3	1	2	0	Ashburn, cf	2	0	0	0
Alou, cf	3	0	0	0	Freese, 3b	1	0	0	0
Kirkland, rf	3	0	0	1	Bouchee, 1b	2	0	0	0
Cepeda, 1b	2	0	1	0	Post, rf	2	0	0	0
Spencer, 2b	2	0	0	0	H. Anderson, lf	2	0	0	0
Brandt, lf	2	0	0	0	Koppe, ss	2	0	0	0
Bressoud, ss	1	1	1	0	G. Anderson, 2b	2	0	0	0
Landrith, c	2	1	1	2	Thomas, c	1	0	0	0
McCormick, p	2	0	0	0	Meyer, p	1	0	0	0
Totals	20	3	5	3	Totals	15	0	0	0

								R	H	E
San Francisco	1	0	0	0	2	-	-	3	5	0
Philadelphia	0	0	0	0	0	-	-	0	0	1

E—Bouchee. LOB—San Francisco 3, Philadelphia 1. 2B—Bressoud. 3B—Davenport. HR—Landrith.

San Francisco	IP	H	R	ER	BB	SO
McCormick (W, 4-5)	5	0	0	0	1	2

Philadelphia	IP	H	R	ER	BB	SO
Meyer (L, 4-3)	5	5	3	3	1	3

Umpires—Burkhart, Donatelli, Venzon, Conlan. Time—1:35. Attendance—20,595.

Cunningham on a first-inning walk and shortstop Alex Grammas on a sixth-inning walk. Grammas the lone runner to reach second base. Jones struck out two to record his first win since September 12. It was a bit of sweet revenge for "Sad Sam," who was traded by the Cardinals to the Giants on March 25, 1959, in exchange for first baseman Bill White and third baseman Ray Jablonski.

San Francisco scored one run in the first on center fielder Willie Mays' 34th home run of the season off losing pitcher Vinegar Bend Mizell. The Giants added another tally in the third on an RBI double by left fielder Orlando Cepeda and two more in the seventh on a two-run homer by first baseman Willie McCovey.

National League president Warren C. Giles ruled the no-hitter was unofficial, but now Jones is on the list of no-hitters of less than nine innings. In any event, the no-hitter was the first one against the Cardinals since Hod Eller of the Cincinnati Reds on May 11, 1919.

Jones finished the season with a 21-15

record (he was the Giants' first 20-game winner in San Francisco) and an N.L.-leading 2.83 ERA. He tied for the league lead in wins (with Lew Burdette and Warren Spahn of the Milwaukee Braves) and ranked second with 209 strikeouts (behind Don Drysdale of the Los Angeles Dodgers with 242).

Juan Marichal vs. Houston Colt .45s—June 15, 1963

The San Francisco Giants' Juan Marichal simply overmatched the Houston Colt .45s en route to a 1-0 no-hitter at Candlestick Park in San Francisco on June 15, 1963. It was the Giants' first nine-inning no-hitter in 34 years, since Carl Hubbell against the Pittsburgh Pirates on May 8, 1929.

The "Dominican Dandy" allowed only six balls to be hit out of the infield. He retired the first 14 batters he faced before walking Houston left fielder Al Spangler with two outs in the fifth inning. The only other batter to reach against Marichal was third baseman Bob

419

Sam Jones at St. Louis Cardinals—September 26, 1959

San Francisco	AB	R	H	RBI	St. Louis	AB	R	H	RBI
Pagan, 3b	4	0	1	0	Blasingame, 2b	2	0	0	0
Alou, rf	4	0	0	0	Cunningham, rf	2	0	0	0
Mays, cf	3	2	2	1	Musial, 1b	3	0	0	0
McCovey, 1b	4	2	2	2	Boyer, 3b	3	0	0	0
Cepeda, lf	2	0	1	1	Cimoli, lf	3	0	0	0
Spencer, 2b	3	0	0	0	H. Smith, c	2	0	0	0
Bressoud, ss	4	0	0	0	Flood, cf	2	0	0	0
Schmidt, c	3	0	3	0	Grammas, ss	1	0	0	0
S. Jones, p	2	0	0	0	Mizell, p	1	0	0	0
					Shannon, ph	1	0	0	0
					Broglio, p	0	0	0	0
Totals	29	4	9	4	Totals	20	0	0	0

											R	H	E
San Francisco	1	0	1	0	0	0	2	-	-	—	4	9	0
St. Louis	0	0	0	0	0	0	0	-	-	—	0	0	3

E—Smith, Musial, Boyer. DP—St. Louis 2. LOB—San Francisco 7, St. Louis 2. 2B—Cepeda, Mays. HR—Mays, McCovey. S—S. Jones, Blasingame.

San Francisco	IP	H	R	ER	BB	SO
S. Jones (W, 21-15)	7	0	0	0	2	5

St. Louis	IP	H	R	ER	BB	SO
Mizell (L, 13-10)	6	8	2	2	2	0
Broglio	1.2	1	2	0	0	3

Umpires—Gorman, Secory, Landes, Dascoli. Time—1:15. Attendance—8,000.

Aspromonte on a one-out walk in the seventh. In the ninth, Marichal got pinch hitter Johnny Temple to foul out to first baseman Orlando Cepeda and then struck out pinch hitter Pete Runnells and center fielder Brock Davis. The right-hander finished with five strikeouts while throwing a mere 89 pitches in a game that took 1 hour and 41 minutes to play.

Only an infield single by San Francisco center fielder Willie Mays in the first inning stood between Houston right hander Dick Drott and a no-hitter of his own until the eighth. Then the Giants got a pair of doubles from third baseman Jim Davenport and second baseman Chuck Hiller to score the only run of the game. Drott finished with a three-hitter over eight innings.

Earlier in his career, Marichal threw two one-hitters —against the Philadlephia Phillies in his major league debut July 19, 1960, and against the Los Angeles Dodgers on August 2, 1961—and his no-hitter was the third of the 1963 season (following Sandy Koufax of Los Angeles against Marichal and the Giants on May 11 and Don Nottebart of Houston against Philadelphia on May 17). Marichal finished the year with a 25-8 record and a 2.41 ERA and probably would have won the Cy Young Award had it not been for Koufax (25-5 record, 1.88 ERA).

Gaylord Perry vs. St. Louis Cardinals—September 17, 1968

Hits were scare at Candlestick Park in San Francisco on the evening of September 17 and the afternoon of September 18, 1968. First, the

On June 15, 1963, Juan Marichal (center) fired a 1-0 no-hitter against the Houston Colt .45s at Candlestick Park in San Francisco. Second baseman Chuck Hiller (left) and third baseman Jim Davenport (right) hit doubles in the eighth inning to account for the game's only run.

Juan Marichal vs. Houston Colt .45s—June 15, 1963

Houston	AB	R	H	RBI	San Francisco	AB	R	H	RBI
Fazio, 2b	3	0	0	0	Hiller, 2b	3	0	1	1
Runnels, ph	1	0	0	0	F. Alou, rf	4	0	0	0
Davis, cf	4	0	0	0	Mays, cf	3	0	1	0
Aspromonte, 3b	2	0	0	0	McCovey, lf	2	0	0	0
Warwick, rf	3	0	0	0	Cepeda, 1b	3	0	0	0
Staub, 1b	3	0	0	0	Bailey, c	3	0	0	0
Spangler, lf	2	0	0	0	Davenport, 3b	3	1	1	0
Lillis, ss	3	0	0	0	Pagan, ss	1	0	0	0
Bateman, c	3	0	0	0	M. Alou, ph	1	0	0	0
Drott, p	2	0	0	0	Bowman, ss	0	0	0	0
Temple, ph	1	0	0	0	Marichal, p	3	0	0	0
Totals	27	0	0	0	Totals	26	1	3	1

											R	H	E
Houston	0	0	0	0	0	0	0	0	0	—	0	0	0
San Francisco	0	0	0	0	0	0	0	1	x	—	1	3	0

DP—Houston 1. LOB—Houston 2, San Francisco 4. 2B—Davenport, Hiller.

Houston	IP	H	R	ER	BB	SO
Drott (L, 2-4)	8	3	1	1	3	6

San Francisco	IP	H	R	ER	BB	SO
Marichal (W, 10-3)	9	0	0	0	2	5

Umpires—Sudol, Forman, Gorman, Landes. Time—1:41. Attendance—18,869.

Giants' Gaylord Perry threw a no-hitter against the St. Louis Cardinals, and the very next day the Cardinals' Ray Washburn returned the favor against San Francisco. It marks the only back-to-back no-hitters in major league history.

The right-handed Perry spun a 1-0 masterpiece. More surprising than the no-hitter was the fact that he won the game. Perry finished the 1968 season with a 16-15 record and a nifty 2.44 ERA, but of his 15 losses, three were by the score of 2-1 and three others were 2-0 setbacks. Light-hitting second baseman Ron Hunt made sure Perry had at least one run to work with when he homered off fire-balling future Hall of Famer Bob Gibson with one out in the bottom of the first inning.

Then it was up to Perry, who allowed only two Cardinals to reach base—third baseman Mike Shannon a two-out walk in the second and second baseman Phil Gagliano a two-out walk in the eighth. The only two difficult defensive chances came in the sixth when St. Louis shortstop Dal Maxvill hit a short bouncer leading off the inning that Perry pounced on, and two outs later when left fielder Bobby Tolan hit a shot to first baseman Willie McCovey, who made the stop and flipped the ball to Perry for the putout. Perry struck out nine batters while throwing 101 pitches. San Francisco catcher Dick Dietz said afterwards that Perry made only three bad pitches the entire game. Club owner Horace C. Stoneham rewarded Perry with a $1,000 bonus. Gibson, a 20-game winner, was nearly as tough, giving up just four hits and two walks with 10 strikeouts over eight innings. St. Louis, which won the 1967 World Series and the 1968 National League pennant, won Washburn's no-hitter 2-0 over the Giants' Bobby Bolin, who

Gaylord Perry vs. St. Louis Cardinals—September 17, 1968

St. Louis	AB	R	H	RBI	San Francisco	AB	R	H	RBI
Tolan, lf	4	0	0	0	Bonds, cf-rf	3	0	1	0
Flood, cf	4	0	0	0	Hunt, 2b	3	1	1	1
Maris, rf	3	0	0	0	Cline, rf	3	0	1	0
Cepeda, 1b	3	0	0	0	McCovey, 1b	3	0	0	0
McCarver, c	3	0	0	0	Hart, 3b	3	0	0	0
Shannon, 3b	2	0	0	0	Davenport, 3b	0	0	0	0
Gagliano, 2b	2	0	0	0	Marshall, rf	2	0	0	0
Maxvill, ss	2	0	0	0	Mays, cf	1	0	0	0
Edwards, ph	1	0	0	0	Dietz, c	2	0	0	0
Schofield, ss	0	0	0	0	Lanier, ss	3	0	1	0
Gibson, p	2	0	0	0	Perry, p	3	0	0	0
Brock, ph	1	0	0	0					
Totals	27	0	0	0	Totals	26	1	4	1

										R	H	E
St. Louis	0	0	0	0	0	0	0	0	0	—	0	0	0
San Francisco	1	0	0	0	0	0	0	0	x	—	1	4	0

DP—St. Louis 1. LOB—St. Louis 2, San Francisco 4. 2B—Lanier, Bonds. HR—Hunt. SB—Bonds. S—Hunt.

St. Louis	IP	H	R	ER	BB	SO
Gibson (L, 21-8)	8	4	1	1	2	10

San Francisco	IP	H	R	ER	BB	SO
Perry (W, 15-14)	9	0	0	0	2	9

Umpires—Wendlestedt, Jackowski, Secory, Burkhart. Time—1:40. Attendance—9,546.

gave up seven hits in eight innings. Legend has it that St. Louis trainer Bob Bauman predicted Washburn's masterpiece while working on him prior to the game.

Perry's no-hitter took 1 hour and 40 minutes to complete, while Washburn's lasted 2 hours and 19 minutes.

Less than a month earlier, on August 26, Perry took a no-hitter into the seventh inning against the Chicago Cubs at Candlestick Park before Glenn Beckert singled. Perry settled for a one-hitter and a 3-0 victory.

Ed Halicki vs. New York Mets— August 24, 1975

Not only did the 24,132 fans get their money's worth with a double-header between the San Francisco Giants and the New York Mets at Candlestick Park in San Francisco on August 24, 1975, they also were treated to a no-hitter by Ed Halicki in the second game. The Giants won the nightcap 6-0 after New York took the opener 9-5.

Halicki, a 6-foot-7 right-hander who debuted with the Giants in 1974, struck out 10 batters. Only three Mets reached base: right fielder Rusty Staub on an error by San Francisco second baseman Derrel Thomas leading off the fifth inning, pinch-hitter Mike Vail on a walk with one out in the sixth and center fielder Del Unser on a walk with one out in the ninth.

The Giants scored all the runs Halicki would need in their half of the first on a two-run single by first baseman Willie Montanez off New York starting pitcher Craig Swan. Center fielder Gary Thomasson collected three hits, including a triple, and had two RBI. Thomas, Thomasson and catcher Doug Rader each scored two runs. Thomas also stole three bases.

With the victory, Halicki improved his record to 8-10 en route to finishing the season 9-13 with a 3.49 ERA. In 1977 he topped the Giants with 16 wins (against 12 losses), a 3.32 ERA and 168 strikeouts. Halicki fired a one-hit-

Ed Halicki no-hit the New York Mets at Candlestick Park in San Francisco on August 24, 1975. (S.F. Giants Archives)

Ed Halicki vs. New York Mets—August 24, 1975

New York	AB	R	H	RBI	San Francisco	AB	R	H	RBI
Unser, cf	3	0	0	0	Thomas, 2b	2	2	0	0
Millan, 2b	4	0	0	0	Rader, c	3	2	1	0
Garrett, 3b	4	0	0	0	Thomasson, cf	4	2	3	2
Staub, rf	3	0	0	0	Matthews, lf	3	0	0	0
Kingman, 1b	3	0	0	0	Montanez, 1b	4	0	2	2
Milner, lf	3	0	0	0	Speier, ss	4	0	1	0
Phillips, ss	3	0	0	0	Ontiveros, rf	4	0	1	0
Stearns, c	3	0	0	0	Miller, 3b	3	0	0	0
Swan, p	1	0	0	0	Halicki, p	4	0	0	0
Vail, ph	0	0	0	0					
Baldwin, p	0	0	0	0					
Alou, ph	1	0	0	0					
Totals	28	0	0	0	Totals	31	6	8	4

										R	H	E
New York	0	0	0	0	0	0	0	0	0	—	0	0	0
San Francisco	2	0	0	0	2	0	2	0	x	—	6	8	1

E—Thomas. DP—New York 1. LOB—New York 3. San Francisco 6. 2B—Speier. 3B—Thomasson. SB—Thomas 3, Rader, Thomasson.

New York	IP	H	R	ER	BB	SO
Swan (L, 1-1)	5	4	4	4	3	5
Baldwin	3	4	2	2	2	1

San Francisco	IP	H	R	ER	BB	SO
Halicki (W, 8-10)	9	0	0	0	2	10

WP—Baldwin. Umpires—Froemming, A. Williams, Runge, Vargo. Time—2:15. Attendance—24,132.

ter against the Montreal Expos on June 12, 1978; a three-hitter against the Cincinnati Reds on June 21, 1978; and consecutive two-hitters against the Philadelphia Phillies and Houston Astros on May 12 and 17, 1979.

But just as he was reaching his peak, Halicki was struck with a bacterial infection that essentially ended his career. He pitched for the Giants until June of 1980, then concluded the year and his playing days with the California Angels.

John Montefusco at Atlanta Braves— September 29, 1976

On September 29, 1976, right-handed pitcher John Montefusco threw the first San Francisco Giants' no-hitter on the road in a 9-0 victory over the Atlanta Braves before a mere 1,369 spectators at Atlanta-County Stadium.

Only a leadoff walk to Atlanta third baseman Jerry Royster kept Montefusco from orchestrating a perfect game. The "Count" struck out four batters. He needed just 97 pitches (92 of which were fastballs) to dispose of the Braves, who were on their way to a 70-92 record and last-place finish in the National League West Division.

Meanwhile, the Giants erupted for four runs in the second inning off Atlanta starting pitcher Jamie Easterly. They added one run in the fourth, three in the fifth and one in the ninth while collecting 12 hits. Rookie shortstop Johnnie LeMaster provided the offensive fireworks with a double, triple and three RBI. First baseman Gary Thomasson drove in two runs.

It was the final start of the season for the brash and boastful Montefusco, who finished with a 16-14 record, 2.85 ERA, 11 complete

games and six shutouts (tied for the league lead with Jon Matlack of the New York Mets). Montefusco earlier had been named to the N.L. All-Star team and pitched two scoreless innings at Veterans Stadium in Philadelphia. He clearly avoided the "sophomore jinx" after being named N.L. Rookie of the Year in 1975.

After being named to the 1976 National League All-Star team—and meeting president Gerald R. Ford—John Montefusco authored a 9-0 no-hitter against the Atlanta Braves at Atlanta-Fulton County Stadium on September 29.

John Montefusco at Atlanta Braves—September 29, 1976

San Francisco	AB	R	H	RBI	Atlanta	AB	R	H	RBI
Herndon, cf	5	0	2	1	Royster, 3b	3	0	0	0
Perez, 2b	5	0	0	0	Gilbreath, 2b	3	0	0	0
Matthews, lf	5	2	2	0	Montanez, 1b	3	0	0	0
Muncer, rf	4	2	2	1	May, lf	3	0	0	0
Alexander, c	4	2	1	0	Asselstine, cf	3	0	0	0
Thomasson, 1b	4	0	2	2	Paciorek, rf	3	0	0	0
Thomas, 3b	4	1	1	1	Murphy, c	3	0	0	0
LeMaster, ss	3	2	2	3	Chaney, ss	2	0	0	0
Montefusco, p	4	0	0	1	Capra, p	0	0	0	0
					Wynn, ph	1	0	0	0
					Easterly, p	0	0	0	0
					Hanna, p	1	0	0	0
					Camp, p	0	0	0	0
					Rockett, ph-ss	1	0	0	0
					Gaston, ph	1	0	0	0
Totals	38	9	12	9	Totals	27	0	0	0

										R	H	E
San Francisco	0	4	0	1	3	0	0	0	1	—	9	12	0
Atlanta	0	0	0	0	0	0	0	0	0	—	0	0	2

E — Royster, Murphy. DP — Atlanta 1. LOB — San Francisco 5, Atlanta 1. 2B — LeMaster, Matthews, Murcer. 3B — LeMaster. SF — LeMaster.

San Francisco	IP	H	R	ER	BB	SO
Montefusco (W, 16-14)	9	0	0	0	1	4

Atlanta	IP	H	R	ER	BB	SO
Easterly (L, 1-1)	1.2	6	4	4	0	1
Hanna	2.1	4	4	3	2	0
Camp	2	0	0	0	0	1
Capra	3	2	1	1	0	2

Umpires — Davidson, Colosi, Olsen, Weyer. Time — 1:59. Attendance — 1,369.

C H A P T E R N I N E
BALLPARKS AND STADIUMS

First Polo Grounds (1883-88)

The first home park for New York's National League entity was located at 110th Street and Sixth Avenue in Manhattan. The grounds had been used by James Gordon Bennett Jr.—son of the founder and publisher of the *New York Herald*—and his society pals to play polo, and that is the genesis of the name Polo Grounds.

John B. Day, owner of the N.L. ball club, also owned an independent team, the New York Metropolitans (or Mets for short) from 1880-82, who played their games in Brooklyn but whose attendance struggled because the location of the parks (Union Grounds and Capitoline Grounds) only was convenient for Brooklyn residents and not for Manhattan dwellers. Day was tipped off to the polo grounds at 110th and Sixth (now along the northern edge of Central Park) by a bootblack and leased it from Bennett.

In December of 1882, Day accepted invitations to join both the N.L. and the other major league of the day, the American Association. He put the Mets in the A.A. and assembled a new team, which would be named the Gothams until first being called the Giants in 1885, for the N.L. Both squads played on adjoining fields at the Polo Grounds with a piece of canvas separating the two. The N.L.

team took up residence on the better field with a fine grandstand for the middle-class citizens who paid half a dollar to gain admittance. Meanwhile, the A.A. team attracted working-class fans for a quarter who enjoyed drinking beer as much as watching baseball, maybe more. The two fields were compared as the penthouse and the outhouse.

Nevertheless, the Mets fared better on the field and won the A.A. championship in 1884. But Day knew the long-term success of professional baseball would be in the N.L., so the following year he moved manager Jim Mutrie, future Hall of Fame pitcher Tim Keefe and third baseman Dude Esterbrook from the Mets to the Giants. Later in 1885 Day sold the Mets.

The Giants, who went on to win their first world championship in 1888, remained at the Polo Grounds until February of 1889 when New York City took over the site to build the area known as Douglass Circle at 110th Street and 5th Avenue. Day offered to donate $10,000 to local charities if the Giants could use the grounds for one more season, but the city rejected the good-will gesture and sent Day searching for a new home for the Giants.

Second Polo Grounds (1889-90)

The Giants' second home was located at 155th Street and Eighth Avenue, in the Harlem

flats uptown from the First Polo Grounds. The plot of land—New York City Plot 2006, Lot 100—previously had been a section of farmland that was granted by King George I to an Englishman by the name of John Lion Gardiner in the early 1700s. One of Gardiner's descendants, Harriet, married James J. Coogan, who became Manhattan's first borough president after the consolidation of the five boroughs into the City of New York in 1898. His remaining area of farmland was called Coogan's Hollow, and the overlooking rocky cliffs became known as Coogan's Bluff.

Giants' owner John B. Day contracted for the construction of a horseshoe-shaped wooden grandstand to be completed by the start of the 1889 season. But the work was not completed on time, and the Giants began the year at Oakland Park in New Jersey. After two games there, they moved to St. George Grounds in Staten Island for their next 23 games before finally moving into the Second Polo Grounds on July 8, 1889. The vagabond Giants went on to repeat as world champions.

In 1890 the Players League was formed by the Brotherhood of Professional Base Ball Players (a players' union), and New York fielded a team that played across the street from the Second Polo Grounds at Brotherhood Park, situated at 157th Street and Eighth Avenue. It goes without saying that the competition for fans was fierce. The National League team billed itself as "the real Giants," while the P.L. squad (made up of many transplanted N.L. Giants) called itself "the big Giants." The P.L., though, folded after one season, and the N.L. Giants took over Brotherhood Park—leasing it from the Coogan family—and renamed it the New Polo Grounds. The Second Polo Grounds was renamed Manhattan Field.

Third (New) Polo Grounds (1891-1957)

When the Players League closed its doors after the 1890 season, the owner of the National League's New York Giants, John B. Day, purchased Brotherhood Park (where the New York Giants of the P.L. played), which was located at 157th Street and Eighth Avenue, across the street from the Second Polo Grounds. Brotherhood Park became the Third (New) Polo Grounds and served as the Giants' home for their remaining 67 years in New York (1891-1957).

For opening day of 1891, the shallow, two-decked wooden grandstand shaped like a horseshoe from first around to third base was given a fresh coat of paint. The grandstand rose halfway up overlooking Coogan's Bluff, leaving plenty of free-standing room. Bleachers adorned both foul lines. The total seating capacity was 17,300. Prior to the first game played at the Third Polo Grounds against the Boston Braves on April 22, a ceremony took place where the Giants of the N.L. and the former Giants of the P.L. gathered and fraternized at second base in a show of unity. A banner hanging from the clubhouse balcony in the right field corner summed up the emotions of the day, "United, Greater and Stronger Than Ever." On July 31 pitcher Amos Rusie provided the first historic performance of the new park with a 6-0 no-hitter of the cross-town rival Brooklyn Bridegrooms.

Baseball legend has it that the term "hot dog" was first used at the Polo Grounds early in the 20th century. During a cold April game, concessionaire Harry M. Stevens was disappointed with ice cream sales and sent out for sausages and rolls that he promoted as "red shot dachshund sausages." The new treat was an instant hit, and when a sports cartoonist drew a sausage barking inside a bun but couldn't spell the word "dachshund" he captioned his work of art, "Hot Dog!" People have been eating hot dogs at games ever since.

The Polo Grounds virtually remained unchanged until the early morning hours of April 14, 1911, when a fire destroyed the ballpark. As a result, the Giants used the cross-town rival New York Highlanders' home grounds, Hilltop Park at 168th Street and Broadway, as their temporary residence until they could return to the partially rebuilt Polo Grounds on June 28,

1911. Christy Mathewson downed the Boston Beaneaters 3-1 in the Giants' first game back home. The park's reconstruction was fully completed by the start of the following season and dedicated April 19, 1912, with a seating capacity of 34,000. It had been the dream of aging Giants' owner John T. Brush to have his team play in a facility with a double-decked, concrete and steel-supported grandstand, and the dream came true. For awhile there was talk of renaming the park Brush Stadium but Polo Grounds stuck. The additional seating all but eliminated viewing the field from Coogan's Bluff, although from one isolated location it was possible to see second base and part of the outfield.

From 1913-22 the Giants shared the Polo Grounds with the New York Yankees (formerly Highlanders) of the American League. The two teams from opposing leagues managed to co-exist without incident until, quite frankly, the Yankees developed into a quality team thanks largely to the purchase of Babe Ruth from the Boston Red Sox in 1920. The Yankees got better on the field and more popular at the gate, which led to friction with the Giants and ultimately an eviction notice being issued to the Yankees by the Giants on May 14, 1920. The N.L. team softened its stance shortly thereafter, but Yankees' owner Jacob Ruppert still went searching for a location for his own park. He selected a plot of land at 161st Street and River Avenue in the Bronx, across the Harlem River from the Polo Grounds, and Yankee Stadium opened in 1923.

The Polo Grounds underwent its next—and final—major expansion in 1923 when the playing field was completely enclosed by stands with the construction of covered, double-decked grandstands extending into the outfield. The seating capacity now reached its maximum of 55,987, with only a section of wooden bleachers for some 4,600 spectators being uncovered.

In 1940 the Polo Grounds was equipped for night baseball, and the Giants defeated

Boston 8-1 in their first game under the lights on a chilly, foggy May 24. Harry Gumbert authored a five-hitter, while Joe Moore, Bill Jurges and Al Glossop hit home runs. The lighting system was set in eight towers above the grandstand roof and consisted of 836 bulbs of 1,500 watts each for a total of 200,000,000 candle-power brilliance. It was said to be the best lighting possible next to daylight.

The Giants remained at the Polo Grounds through the 1957 season. On July 17 owner Horace C. Stoneham announced that he would move his club out of the aging ballpark with limited (at best) parking availability unless either a new city-owned stadium was built or the Giants could share Yankee Stadium with the Yankees. Neither possibility came to fruition, attendance continued to drop and the Giants headed to San Francisco. They played their final game September 29, 1957, and lost to the Pittsburgh Pirates 9-1 before a sparse gathering of 11,606 spectators. Before the game, many former Giants' greats were introduced and Blanche S. McGraw, wife of the late Hall of Fame manager John, was presented with a bouquet of roses. Immediately following the final out, the crowd went on a souvenir-hunting rampage that sent the Giants' players sprinting for their center field clubhouse. A two-foot square piece of sod was shipped to San Francisco and planted in Candlestick Park.

Certainly the Polo Grounds played most to many memorable moments, but the park itself was special with its horseshoe shape and unique dimensions. The highly-unusual layout consisted of 257 feet down the right field line, 279 feet down the left field line and 483 feet to straight-away center field. Bona fide pull hitters thrived because of the short distances down the lines, but the distances increased quickly heading to center field. Both the home and visiting clubhouses were behind the outfield walls, while the bullpens were in the outfield corners. The outfield walls were among the most difficult to play in the major leagues because they had a variety of angles that made

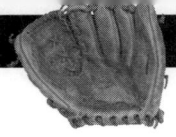

The Polo Grounds during the 1923 World Series against the New York Yankees. (Transcendental Graphics)

Fans go souvenir hunting following the Giants' final game at the Polo Grounds on September 29, 1957, a 9-1 loss to the Pittsburgh Pirates. (National Baseball Library and Archive)

Polo Grounds postcard. (Transcendental Graphics)

caroms tough to judge. Outfielders relied on the lettering on advertisements (GEM razor blades, Stahl-Meyer frankfurters, Botany clothes, etc.) to figure out rebounds, but the ads were replaced by solid green paint (to match the overall color scheme of the park) in 1948. In addition, in left field the upper deck facade extended well beyond the lower deck, meaning balls hit that just missed the upper deck were temporarily out of sight for outfielders. Left field also was the sun field.

One tragic piece of history was a granite marker erected in 1921 in memory of former Giants' infielder Eddie Grant, who was the first major leaguer to be killed in World War I.

The Polo Grounds was more than the home of the Giants. It also was the site of professional and college football games (the Four Horsemen of Notre Dame were christened by sportswriter Grantland Rice there in 1924) and

boxing matches (Jack Dempsey successfully defended his heavyweight title against Luis Firpo in one of the most savage and controversial fights of all-time there in 1923).

When the New York Mets joined the N.L. as an expansion team in 1962, they played in the Polo Grounds before moving to Shea Stadium in Flushing, New York, two years later. On April 10, 1964, demolition of the Polo Grounds began, and a $30 million, low-rent housing project subsequently was built on the site. Appropriately, the 11 men of the Wrecking Corporation of American hired to demolish the Polo Grounds showed up for their first day on the job wearing Giants' uniforms.

Seals Stadium (1958-59)

When the San Francisco Seals of the Pacific Coast League set a minor league attendance record in 1946, their ballpark was

Seals Stadium

regarded among the most beautiful in the land. The San Francisco Giants were a distant dream.

When the first major league game was played on the West Coast in 1958, Seals Stadium still was a precious jewel of a ballpark, up to big-league standards in every category except seating capacity. There were merely some 23,500 seats, but sight lines were great, there were no obstructed views and the downtown location was ideal—minus ample parking.

The field dimensions also were favorable to those at the Polo Grounds, where it was 257 feet to the right field foul pole and a gaudy 449 feet to the alley in right. Seals Stadium was beautifully proportioned: 355 (right) and 365 feet down the lines, 375 feet in the alleys and 412 feet in right-center.

It was a fair ballpark with somewhat milder climate than that of Candlestick Point. The original San Francisco Giants averaged just under 17,000 customers that first year, so the ballpark actually was big enough to sustain major league baseball, but a new ballpark already was in the works.

Those who loved Seals Stadium and its central location proposed a second deck to bring the ballpark up to major league standards, but the plan gained little momentum. (Curiously, the Giants didn't average more than 23,741 at Candlestick Park until 1987, their 28th year there.)

Seals Stadium was built at a cost of $600,000 by Charles Graham, George Putnam and Charles (Doc) Strub, owners of the hometown Seals. Interestingly, the 15th and Bryant site was a mine, and the original deed had it named Home Plate Mine.

The ballpark was opened in April of 1931, with the Seals defeating the Detroit Tigers 5-2 in an exhibition featuring three hits by San Francisco native Frankie Crosetti, a future standout for the New York Yankees. The first home run to sail out of Seals Stadium was hit by Gabby Hartnett of the Chicago Cubs in an exhibition against the Pittsburgh Pirates.

Jerry Donovan, who would become president of the Seals and later a Giants' executive, hit the first home run that counted at the ballpark, connecting in the 1931 PCL opener against the Portland Beavers. The Seals and the San Francisco Missions shared Seals Stadium until the Missions became the Hollywood Stars in 1938.

At the time of their demise in 1957, the Seals played in the largest uncovered ballpark in the United States. Nostalgic fans hated to see the team go, and the fact they were PCL champions that year as a Boston Red Sox farm club made it even tougher. Most of the tears dried, however, with the prospect of major league baseball.

There was great enthusiasm for the Giants when they took the field for the historic April 15 opener against the Los Angeles Dodgers in 1958. Pitcher Ruben Gomez made it a joyous occasion with an 8-0 victory in which Giants' shortstop Darryl Spencer blasted the first home run and future Hall of Famer Orlando Cepeda hit his first of his career.

The final game at Seals Stadium was played September 29, 1959, a 6-2 Dodgers' victory over the Giants. A wrecking ball soon demolished the cozy ballpark, and thoughts turned to the "major league" stadium a few miles away, one which was much larger and far less intimate—or comfortable.

Candlestick Park (1960-99)

Thanks to the efforts of San Francisco mayor George Christopher, who lured the Giants west with a promise of a new 40,000-plus capacity ballpark, Candlestick Park became a glistening reality. It all started with voters ap-

proving a $5 million bond issue in 1954 to finance a new stadium—providing a major league team would be acquired within five years.

There was speculation the St. Louis Browns or the Washington Senators would shift westward, but Christopher became mayor in 1956 and set his sights on the Giants, who were considering a move to Minneapolis. The fact that the Brooklyn Dodgers also were about to abandon the New York area made it an easier chore.

After the Giants moved to Seals Stadium, the next decision would be where to build a new ballpark. With a 40,000-plus capacity a necessity, considerable land would be needed, and there was merchant opposition to a downtown stadium. Moreover, it would have required $33 million to purchase property downtown, compared with the $2.7 million paid to contractor Charles Harney for his Candlestick site.

The final cost was $14,855,990, of which merely $6 million went into the stadium. There were flaws from the start, but it was the first stadium built since The Depression, and there were no standards by which to compare. (The Dodgers, by comparison, had Candlestick Park as a model when they opened shortly thereafter.)

Candlestick Park became reality when 42,269—the largest crowd ever to watch a baseball game in the Bay Area—enthusiastically showed up for Opening Day 1960. It was April 12, and the new state-of-the-art stadium was the toast of the town. Minor flaws were guised by the excitement over the major's first all-concrete stadium.

"San Francisco can say this is the finest ballpark in America," vice president Richard Nixon declared after throwing the ceremonial first pitch. "A Dazzling Diamond Palace," was among the gushing headlines. A *San Francisco Examiner* reporter called Candlestick "a symphony of gray concrete and steel."

Left fielder Orlando Cepeda's two-run triple in the bottom of the first inning was the

Candlestick Park on July 11, 1961, when it played host to the All-Star Game. (AP/Wide World Photos)

Giants' first hit, giving pitcher Sam Jones all the support he required in a 3-1 victory over the St. Louis Cardinals. Ex-Giant Leon Wagner had the distinction of hitting the first home run at Candlestick and earned a $100 prize.

It didn't take long for some sour notes to create The Stick's mystique. On July 15, 1958, for instance, a thick fog interrupted a 5-3 Dodgers' victory for 24 minutes. "It was an exciting time," Hall of Famer Willie Mays recalled. "We didn't complain about the weather. It affected the other teams more. We were just happy to be playing baseball."

But the notorious wind continued to command national attention. Stu Miller of the Giants, pitching in the 1961 All-Star Game at Candlestick, was nudged off the mound by a powerful gust while winding up in the ninth inning and was charged with a balk. Miller's misfortune remained a hot topic of conversation long after Mays' run-scoring double and Roberto Clemente's game-winning single produced a 5-4 National League victory in 11 innings.

One year later, the Giants won their first pennant in San Francisco, doing so in dramatic fashion. It was the California version of the famed 1951 Giants-Dodgers playoff, and with the same result. The Giants won the third game of the best-of-three series in dramatic fashion in Los Angeles and returned home to face the mighty New York Yankees the next day.

The World Series came down to Game 7, and a record 49,948 fans showed up for a duel between San Francisco's Jack Sanford and the Yankees' Ralph Terry. Tony Kubek's double-play grounder gave the Yankees a 1-0 lead in the fifth. That would be the game's only run, but there was tension and drama in the Giants' bottom of the ninth.

With runners on second and third and two outs, left fielder Willie McCovey strode to the plate. The original "Big Mac" worked the

count to 1-1 before hitting a viscous drive. Second baseman Bobby Richardson made the catch of the sinking liner for a stunning 1-0 victory as the crowd gasped. The Giants wouldn't reach the Fall Classic again until 1989.

But there were plenty of thrills in between. The 1963 season, for example, produced arguably the two finest pitching performances in the rich history of Candlestick Park. Juan Marichal was at the forefront during a 25-8 season. On June 15 he pitched a 1-0 no-hitter against Houston, the Giants' first nine-inning gem since Carl Hubbell did it in 1929.

What Marichal would do for an encore was answered 2½ weeks later. On the night of July 2 Marichal and Warren Spahn of the Milwaukee Braves combined for undeniably the last great pitchers' duel in the history of modern baseball. The future Hall of Famers battled for more than four hours until Mays' homer in the bottom of the 16th inning produced a magnificent 1-0 victory at 12:31 a.m.

Mays, on the final day of the season in 1965, hit his 52nd home run, a franchise record. He was the National League Most Valuable Player, and in 1966 he broke the N.L. record with his 512th homer off the Dodgers' Claude Osteen.

The Beatles created the greatest buzz at The Stick in 1966, playing what would be their final concert ever on August 29. The teeny-boppers paid up to $6.50 for tickets and interrupted their shrieking to listen to 40 minutes of hits from "Rock and Roll Music" to "Long Tall Sally."

John Lennon, who earlier created controversy by boldly suggesting The Beatles were more popular than Jesus, was proven wrong—at Candlestick, at least—on September 18, 1987. That's when Pope John Paul II commanded more than 70,000 worshipers for a 90-minute Pontifical Mass. It was a prodigious undertaking because the Giants played the day before and the day after. A baseball field was

transformed into a cathedral in less than 24 hours.

In between the rock and the religion, Karl "The Great" Wallenda walked on a tightrope high above the playing field May 8, 1977, long before bizarre promotions became commonplace. But it was the grand old game that kept bringing fans back to The Stick. The Giants posted five consecutive second-place finishes from 1965-69 under manager Herman Franks.

On September 17, 1968, Gaylord Perry required merely one hour and 40 minutes for a 1-0 no-hitter against the Cardinals. Light-hitting second baseman Ron Hunt belted a first-inning homer off Bob Gibson. But the laughter turned to sorrow less than 24 hours later. In a day game following Perry's nocturnal gem, Ray Washburn of the Cardinals turned the tables with a 2-0 no-hitter.

Division play was introduced in 1969, and the Giants won their first N.L. West title in 1971. The Pirates rallied from a 1-0 deficit to win the series with three consecutive victories, and it would be 16 years before the Giants reached the playoffs again. The biggest accomplishment in between was owner Bob Lurie saving the Giants from a Toronto future in 1976.

Recognizing the determination and loyalty that fans displayed by venturing to frigid Candlestick, the Giants in 1983 began issuing Croix de Candlestick badges to those individuals who styed until the end of an extra-inning night games. The orange pins said, "Vini•Vidi•Vixi"—"I came, I saw, I survived" and featured a snow-capped S.F. logo.

Some hard times followed. One year after hosting the 1984 All-Star Game, the Giants set a dubious franchise record of 100 defeats, a finish that cried for change. It occurred in the form of general manager Al Rosen, manager Roger Craig, first baseman Will Clark and second baseman Robby Thompson. The Giants became instant contenders.

In 1986 they improved by 21 games and went 83-69, finishing third. One year later they were back in the playoffs behind Clark's hitting

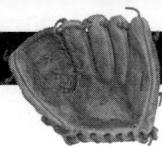

Candlestick Park (S.F. Giants Archives)

and newcomers Kevin Mitchell and Dave Dravecky. The St. Louis Cardinals fired shut-outs in the last two games to win the pennant, but the Giants wouldn't be denied in 1989.

In perhaps the most dramatic at-bat in Candlestick history, Clark fouled off a pair of 0-2 fastballs before lining a tie-breaking single off Mitch Williams of the Cubs for a clinching 2-1 NLCS victory. The Giants finally had returned to the World Series following a 27-year absence. There was little joy thereafter because of a four-game sweep by the Oakland Athletics and "The Earthquake."

At 5:04 p.m. on October 17, as fans settled in their seats for Game 3, a 7.0 earthquake struck, shaking the stadium, causing devastation and delaying the World Series for more than one week.

There was another scare three years later. Failed in his efforts to build a new stadium, Lurie agreed to sell the Giants to a Tampa-St. Petersburg group during the 1992 season. With Peter Magowan and other investors throwing a lifesaver, however, the Giants remained in San Francisco and began a new era with rookie manager Dusty Baker and newcomer Barry Bonds in 1993.

Candlestick succumbed to corporate naming rights in 1996, becoming known as 3Com Park at Candlestick Point. A few months later, inspired by a bold trade by general manager Brian Sabean, the Giants were division champions for the first time in eight years.

One of the most memorable moments in Candlestick history occurred on September 18, 1997. Bonds' homer helped pitcher Kirk Rueter defeat the Dodgers the previous day, pulling the Giants to within one game of Los Angeles. The series finale went into the 12th inning tied 1-1. Then catcher Brian Johnson, in his moment of fame, homered off Bill Guthrie leading off the 12th for a poignant 2-1 victory to tie the rival Dodgers.

Football, of course, also has been an integral part of Candlestick history—and will continue to do so as the exclusive home of the San

Francisco 49ers once the Giants move in 2000. Candlestick also has hosted the East-West Shrine Game and Oakland Raiders. It was the first major league stadium for the infant AFL team in 1960 before Al Davis took over.

The fledgling Raiders made their Candlestick debut December 20, 1960, and were crushed 41-17 by the Los Angeles Chargers before 12,061. They played six home games there in 1961 and then shifted to Oakland. Excepting the 1967 East-West Game, there was no football at Candlestick for nine years. The promise of a facelift, which enclosed the stadium and increased football seating to 62,000, lured the 49ers in 1971.

One of their defining moments occurred in 1982. The Dallas Cowboys held a 27-21 lead with less than five minutes left. The 49ers were backed up to their 11-yard-line. It looked hopeless. But quarterback Joe Montana drove to the Dallas 6 and fired high to the end zone. Dwight Clark soared for "The Catch" with 51 seconds to go. Ray Wersching kicked the 49ers into their first Super Bowl.

Three more NFC championship victories were produced at Candlestick: 23-0 over the Chicago Bears in 1985, 30-3 over the Los Angeles Rams in 1990 and 38-28 over Dallas in 1995. The final home game of the 1998 season, on January 3, 1999, continued the tradition. The Green Bay Packers were ahead 27-23 with less than two minutes remaining and the 49ers on their own 24-yard-line. Presto, Steve Young connected on six of eight passes, but the 49ers were in trouble, facing third-and-three at the Packers' 25. A crowd of 66,506 could hardly stand the tension. Young calmly dropped back, stumbled and recovered to throw a tight spiral. It evaded several Green Bay defenders and landed in Terrell Owens' hands for "The Catch II" and a 30-27 victory with three ticks left.

It might be a lot more comfortable for the fans and better for the ballplayers come April of 2000 at Pacific Bell Park, but it definitely won't be the same without Candlestick to kick around. Candlestick Park will live forever in the minds of those who braved the elements to enjoy the major league's version of the Arctic Circle. The Stick will never be forgotten.

Pacific Bell Park (2000-present)

Former owner Bob Lurie became exasperated when voters defeated four referendums that would have kept the Giants in the immediate Bay Area. His frustration led to the sale of his beloved ballclub to an ownership group which learned from the mistakes of the well-meaning Lurie regime.

Three seasons after acquiring the Giants in 1993, club president Peter Magowan announced plans for the first privately financed stadium in the United States since Dodger Stadium was erected in 1962. A campaign was launched to gain voter approval, and it passed with 67 percent of the vote in March of 1996.

A China Basin site—about one mile from Seals Stadium, as the seagull flies—was decided upon, and the wheels were set in motion to raise money for the $357 million stadium without use of public funds. Nearly half of that amount was raised by selling naming rights to Pacific Bell for $50 million, charter seat rights for $55 million and corporate sponsorship.

HOK Sports, the architectural firm which created Camden Yards in Baltimore, Coors Field in Denver and Jacobs Field in Cleveland, went to work designing an old-feel ballpark on a relatively small 13-acre bayfront site at Third and King streets, seven blocks south of the city's main artery, Market Street.

The glistening new ballpark, which began taking shape in 1998, features panoramic views of downtown San Francisco and the Bay Bridge from many seats, and a promise of less wind and cold, according to weather studies. The capacity is approximately 41,500, with virtually all 28,000 season tickets being sold for the first three years.

"We have a good start for the future," Magowan said. "There's a long-term lease at Pac Bell Park. The Giants are here to stay. Success isn't automatic just because you're in a new stadium, but I think we've proven our

commitment to win. And if we can do it at Candlestick, why not in the new park?

"We have people committed for the long haul, selling luxury boxes and suite seats for up to nine years. We think Pac Bell Park will be a lot more than a curiosity."

"I look at it like getting a new car," second baseman Jeff Kent said. "You just get excited going for the ride. There are no guarantees, but a downtown stadium will create excitement. Look at places like Cleveland and Baltimore. It also might enable the Giants to acquire some good players who might have been discouraged by The Stick. It's an extra perk for players."

The great anticipation for the beautiful new ballpark-by-the-bay was rewarded with unbridled success by the Giants in their new home, with rave reviews from the media and with enthusiasm for fans who were able to watch games in comfort. They showed their appreciation by filling Pac Bell to capacity most of the time, averaging 40,643 in per-game attendance over the first three years.

Players, happy to be away from the capricious climate of Candlestick Point, responded with a division championship (2000) and a pennant (2003) in their new digs. Barry Bonds captivated the fans by turning a tough hitters' park into his personal playground, splashing home runs into McCovey Cove.

And whereas Pac Bell is regarded as more conducive to pitching than hitting, Bonds, Jeff Kent and Rich Aurilia all enjoyed career years while taking their cuts in the new stadium. Combining that hitting prowess with solid pitching and defense, the Giants posted a glistening 154-89 home record in their first three years there.

![Pacific Bell Park aerial photograph](aerial view of Pacific Bell Park with San Francisco skyline)

Pacific Bell Park (© S.F. Giants)

BIBLIOGRAPHY

Alexander, Charles C. *John McGraw*. Lincoln, NE, and London: University of Nebraska Press, 1988.

Antonucci, Thomas J., and Eric Caren (Ed.). *Newspaper Reports on Big League Baseball in the Big Apple: The New York Giants*. Verplanck, NY: Historical Briefs, Inc., 1995.

Bitker, Steve. *The Original San Francisco Giants: The Giants of '58*. Champaign, IL: Sports Publishing Inc., 1998.

Bucek, Jeanine, et al (Ed.). *The Baseball Encyclopedia*. New York: Macmillan, 1996.

Carter, Craig (Ed.). *Complete Baseball Record Book*. St. Louis: The Sporting News, 1999.

Carter, Craig, and Dave Sloan (Ed.). *Baseball Guide*. St. Louis: The Sporting News, 1999.

Chadwick, Bruce, and David M. Spindel. *The Giants: Memories and Memorabilia from a Century of Baseball*. New York: Abbeville Press, Inc., 1993.

Dickey, Glenn. *San Francisco Giants: 40 Years*. San Francisco: Woodford Press, 1997.

Graham, Frank. *The New York Giants*. New York: G. P. Putnam's Sons, 1952.

Hodges, Russ, and Al Hirshberg. *My Giants*. Garden City, NY: Doubleday & Company, Inc., 1963.

Hynd, Noel. *The Giants of the Polo Grounds: The Glorious Times of Baseball's New York Giants*. New York: Doubleday, 1988.

James, Bill, et al (Ed.). *All-Time Baseball Sourcebook*. Skokie, IL: STATS Publishing, 1998.

New York Times, Oakland Tribune, San Francisco Chronicle, San Francisco Examiner and *The Sporting News*. Various Articles.

Peters, Nick. *San Francisco Giants Almanac*. Berkeley, CA: North Atlantic Books, 1988.

San Francisco Giants. Various Media Guides and Yearbooks.

Solomon, Burt. *The Baseball Timeline*. New York: The Stonesong Press, Inc., 1997.

Stang, Mark, and Linda Harkness. *Baseball by the Numbers: A Guide to the Uniform Numbers of Major League Teams*. Lanham, MD, and London: The Scarecrow Press, Inc., 1997.

Stein, Fred, and Nick Peters. *Giants Diary*. Berkeley, CA: North Atlantic Books, 1987.

Thomson, Bobby, Lee Heiman, and Bill Gutman. *"The Giants Win the Pennant! The Giants Win the Pennant!"* New York: Kensington Publishing Corp., 1991.

Thorn, John, et al (Ed.). *Total Baseball: The Official Encyclopedia of Major League Baseball*. New York: Penguin Books USA Inc., 1997.

Williams, Peter. *When the Giants were Giants: Bill Terry and the Golden Age of New York Baseball*. Chapel Hill, NC: Algonquin Books, 1994.

APPENDIX A
YEAR-BY-YEAR
DATA

NEW YORK/SAN FRANCISCO GIANTS YEAR-BY-YEAR RECORD

Season	Manager	Record	Pct.	Finish	Games Ahead/ Behind
1883	John Clapp	46-50	.479	6th	-16
1884	Jim Price	56-42	.571	—	—
	John Montgomery Ward	6-8	.429	—	—
	Totals	*62-50*	*.554*	*T4th*	*-22*
1885	Jim Mutrie	85-27	.759	2nd	-2
1886	Jim Mutrie	75-44	.630	3rd	-12$^1/_2$
1887	Jim Mutrie	68-55	.553	4th	-10$^1/_2$
1888	Jim Mutrie	84-47	.641	1st	+9
1889	Jim Mutrie	83-43	.659	1st	+1
1890	Jim Mutrie	63-68	.481	6th	-24
1891	Jim Mutrie	71-61	.538	3rd	-13
1892 (First Half)	Pat Powers	31-43	.419	10th	-21
1892 (Second Half)	Pat Powers	40-37	.519	6th	-13$^1/_2$
	Totals	*71-80*	*.470*	*8th*	*-31$^1/_2$*
1893	John Montgomery Ward	68-64	.515	5th	-19$^1/_2$
1894	John Montgomery Ward	88-44	.667	2nd	-3
1895	George Davis	16-17	.485	—	—
	Jack Doyle	32-31	.508	—	—
	Harvey Watkins	18-17	.514	—	—
	Totals	*66-65*	*.504*	*9th*	*-21$^1/_2$*
1896	Arthur Irwin	36-53	.404	—	—
	Bill Joyce	28-14	.667	—	—
	Totals	*64-67*	*.489*	*7th*	*-27*
1897	Bill Joyce	83-48	.634	3rd	-9$^1/_2$
1898	Bill Joyce	22-21	.512	—	—
	Cap Anson	9-13	.409	—	—
	Bill Joyce	46-39	.541	—	—
	Totals	*77-73*	*.513*	*7th*	*-25$^1/_2$*

Season	Manager	Record	Pct.	Finish	Games Ahead/Behind
1899	John Day	29-35	.453	—	—
	Fred Hoey	31-55	.360	—	—
	Totals	*60-90*	*.400*	*10th*	*-42*
1900	Buck Ewing	21-41	.339	—	—
	George Davis	39-37	.513	—	—
	Totals	*60-78*	*.435*	*8th*	*-23*
1901	George Davis	52-85	.380	7th	-37
1902	Horace Fogel	18-23	.439	—	—
	Heinie Smith	5-27	.156	—	—
	John McGraw	25-38	.397	—	—
	Totals	*48-88*	*.353*	*8th*	*-53$\frac{1}{2}$*
1903	John McGraw	84-55	.604	2nd	-6$\frac{1}{2}$
1904	John McGraw	106-47	.693	1st	+ 13
1905	John McGraw	105-48	.686	1st	+ 9
1906	John McGraw	96-56	.632	2nd	-20
1907	John McGraw	82-71	.536	4th	-25$\frac{1}{2}$
1908	John McGraw	98-56	.636	T2nd	-1
1909	John McGraw	92-61	.601	3rd	-18$\frac{1}{2}$
1910	John McGraw	91-63	.591	2nd	-13
1911	John McGraw	99-54	.647	1st	+ 7$\frac{1}{2}$
1912	John McGraw	103-48	.682	1st	+ 10
1913	John McGraw	101-51	.664	1st	+ 12$\frac{1}{2}$
1914	John McGraw	84-70	.545	2nd	-10$\frac{1}{2}$
1915	John McGraw	69-83	.454	8th	-21
1916	John McGraw	86-66	.566	4th	-7
1917	John McGraw	98-56	.636	1st	+ 10
1918	John McGraw	71-53	.573	2nd	-10$\frac{1}{2}$
1919	John McGraw	87-53	.621	2nd	-9
1920	John McGraw	86-68	.558	2nd	-7
1921	John McGraw	94-59	.614	1st	+ 4
1922	John McGraw	93-61	.604	1st	+ 7
1923	John McGraw	95-58	.621	1st	+ 4$\frac{1}{2}$
1924	John McGraw	16-13	.552	—	—
	Hughie Jennings	32-12	.727	—	—
	John McGraw	45-35	.563	—	—
	Totals	*93-60*	*.608*	*1st*	*+ 1$\frac{1}{2}$*
1925	John McGraw	10-4	.714	—	—
	Hughie Jennings	21-11	.656	—	—
	John McGraw	55-51	.519	—	—
	Totals	*86-66*	*.566*	*2nd*	*-8$\frac{1}{2}$*
1926	John McGraw	74-77	.490	5th	-13$\frac{1}{2}$
1927	John McGraw	70-52	.574	—	—
	Rogers Hornsby	22-10	.688	—	—
	Totals	*92-62*	*.597*	*3rd*	*-2*
1928	John McGraw	93-61	.604	2nd	-2
1929	John McGraw	84-67	.556	3rd	-13$\frac{1}{2}$
1930	John McGraw	87-67	.565	3rd	-5

Season	Manager	Record	Pct.	Finish	Games Ahead/ Behind
1931	John McGraw	87-65	.572	2nd	-13
1932	John McGraw	17-23	.425	—	—
	Bill Terry	55-59	.482	—	—
	Totals	*72-82*	*.468*	*T6th*	*-18*
1933	Bill Terry	91-61	.599	1st	+5
1934	Bill Terry	93-60	.608	2nd	-2
1935	Bill Terry	91-62	.595	3rd	-8$^1/_2$
1936	Bill Terry	92-62	.597	1st	+5
1937	Bill Terry	95-57	.625	1st	+3
1938	Bill Terry	83-67	.553	3rd	-5
1939	Bill Terry	77-74	.510	5th	-18$^1/_2$
1940	Bill Terry	72-80	.474	6th	-27$^1/_2$
1941	Bill Terry	74-79	.484	5th	-25$^1/_2$
1942	Mel Ott	85-67	.559	3rd	-20
1943	Mel Ott	55-98	.359	8th	-49$^1/_2$
1944	Mel Ott	67-87	.435	5th	-38
1945	Mel Ott	78-74	.513	5th	-19
1946	Mel Ott	61-93	.396	8th	-36
1947	Mel Ott	81-73	.526	4th	-13
1948	Mel Ott	37-38	.493	—	—
	Leo Durocher	41-38	.519	—	—
	Totals	*78-76*	*.506*	*5th*	*-13$^1/_2$*
1949	Leo Durocher	73-81	.474	5th	-24
1950	Leo Durocher	86-68	.558	3rd	-5
1951	Leo Durocher	98-59	.624	1st	+1
1952	Leo Durocher	92-62	.597	2nd	-4$^1/_2$
1953	Leo Durocher	70-84	.455	5th	-35
1954	Leo Durocher	97-57	.630	1st	+5
1955	Leo Durocher	80-74	.519	3rd	-18$^1/_2$
1956	Bill Rigney	67-87	.435	6th	-26
1957	Bill Rigney	69-85	.448	6th	-26
1958	Bill Rigney	80-74	.519	3rd	-12
1959	Bill Rigney	83-71	.539	3rd	-4
1960	Bill Rigney	33-25	.569	—	—
	Tom Sheehan	46-50	.479	—	—
	Totals	*79-75*	*.513*	*5th*	*-16*
1961	Alvin Dark	85-69	.552	3rd	-8
1962	Alvin Dark	103-62	.624	1st	+1
1963	Alvin Dark	88-74	.543	3rd	-11
1964	Alvin Dark	90-72	.556	4th	-3
1965	Herman Franks	95-67	.586	2nd	-2
1966	Herman Franks	93-68	.578	2nd	-1$^1/_2$
1967	Herman Franks	91-71	.562	2nd	-10$^1/_2$
1968	Herman Franks	88-74	.543	2nd	-9
1969	Clyde King	90-72	.556	2nd West	-3
1970	Clyde King	19-23	.452	—	—
	Charlie Fox	67-53	.558	—	—
	Totals	*86-76*	*.531*	*3rd West*	*-16*

Season	Manager	Record	Pct.	Finish	Games Ahead/ Behind
1971	Charlie Fox	90-72	.556	1st West	+ 1
1972	Charlie Fox	69-86	.445	5th West	-26$\frac{1}{2}$
1973	Charlie Fox	88-74	.543	3rd West	-11
1974	Charlie Fox	34-42	.447	—	—
	Wes Westrum	38-48	.442	—	—
	Totals	*72-90*	*.444*	*5th West*	*-30*
1975	Wes Westrum	80-81	.497	3rd West	-27$\frac{1}{2}$
1976	Bill Rigney	74-88	.457	4th West	-28
1977	Joe Altobelli	75-87	.463	4th West	-23
1978	Joe Altobelli	89-73	.549	3rd West	-6
1979	Joe Altobelli	61-79	.436	—	—
	Dave Bristol	10-12	.455	—	—
	Totals	*71-91*	*.438*	*4th West*	*-19$\frac{1}{2}$*
1980	Dave Bristol	75-86	.466	5th West	-17
1981 (First Half)	Frank Robinson	27-32	.458	5th West	-10
1981 (Second Half)	Frank Robinson	29-23	.558	3rd West	-3$\frac{1}{2}$
	Totals	*56-55*	*.505*	*4th West*	*-11$\frac{1}{2}$*
1982	Frank Robinson	87-75	.537	3rd West	-2
1983	Frank Robinson	79-83	.488	5th West	-12
1984	Frank Robinson	42-64	.396	—	—
	Danny Ozark	24-32	.429	—	—
	Totals	*66-96*	*.407*	*6th West*	*-26*
1985	Jim Davenport	56-88	.389	—	—
	Roger Craig	6-12	.333	—	—
	Totals	*62-100*	*.383*	*6th West*	*-33*
1986	Roger Craig	83-79	.512	3rd West	-13
1987	Roger Craig	90-72	.556	1st West	+ 6
1988	Roger Craig	83-79	.512	4th West	-11$\frac{1}{2}$
1989	Roger Craig	92-70	.568	1st West	+ 3
1990	Roger Craig	85-77	.525	3rd West	-6
1991	Roger Craig	75-87	.463	4th West	-19
1992	Roger Craig	72-90	.444	5th West	-26
1993	Dusty Baker	103-59	.636	2nd West	-1
1994	Dusty Baker	55-60	.478	2nd West	-3$\frac{1}{2}$
1995	Dusty Baker	67-77	.465	4th West	-11
1996	Dusty Baker	68-94	.420	4th West	-23
1997	Dusty Baker	90-72	.556	1st West	+ 2
1998	Dusty Baker	89-74	.546	2nd West	-9$\frac{1}{2}$
1999	Dusty Baker	86-76	.531	2nd West	-14
2000	Dusty Baker	97-65	.599	1st West	+ 11
2001	Dusty Baker	90-72	.556	2nd West	-2
2002	Dusty Baker	95-66	.590	2nd West*	-2$\frac{1}{2}$

*National League Wild Card

New York Totals (75 seasons)		6,067-4,898	.553
San Francisco Totals (45 seasons)		3,704-3,431	.519
Totals (120 seasons)		9,771-8,329	.540

NEW YORK/SAN FRANCISCO GIANTS ALL-TIME MANAGERS RECORDS

Manager	Seasons	Years	Games	Record	Pct.
Joe Altobelli	1977-79	3	464	225-239	.485
Cap Anson	1898	1	22	9-13	.409
Dusty Baker	1993-99	10	1,555	840-715	.540
Dave Bristol	1979-80	2	183	85-98	.464
John Clapp	1883	1	98	46-50	.479
Roger Craig	1985-92	8	1,152	586-566	.509
Alvin Dark	1961-64	4	644	366-277	.569
Jim Davenport	1985	1	144	56-88	.389
George Davis	1895, 1900-01	3	252	107-139	.435
John Day	1899	1	66	29-35	.453
Jack Doyle	1895	1	64	32-31	.508
Leo Durocher	1948-55	8	1,163	637-523	.549
Buck Ewing	1900	1	63	21-41	.339
Horace Fogel	1902	1	41	18-23	.439
Charlie Fox	1970-74	5	675	348-327	.516
Herman Franks	1965-68	4	649	367-280	.567
Fred Hoey	1899	1	87	31-55	.360
Rogers Hornsby	1927	1	33	22-10	.688
Arthur Irwin	1896	1	90	36-53	.404
Hughie Jennings	1924-25	2	76	53-23	.697
Bill Joyce	1896-98	3	316	179-122	.595
Clyde King	1969-70	2	204	109-95	.534
John McGraw	1902-32	31	4,373	2,583-1,790	.591
Jim Mutrie	1885-91	7	905	529-345	.605
Mel Ott	1942-48	7	1,004	464-530	.467
Danny Ozark	1984	1	56	24-32	.429
Pat Powers	1892	1	153	71-80	.470
Jim Price	1884	1	100	56-42	.571
Bill Rigney	1956-60, 1976	6	836	406-430	.486
Frank Robinson	1981-84	4	541	264-277	.488
Tom Sheehan	1960	1	98	46-50	.479
Heinie Smith	1902	1	32	5-27	.156
Bill Terry	1932-41	10	1,496	823-661	.555
John Montgomery Ward	1884, 1893-94	3	291	162-116	.583
Harvey Watkins	1895	1	35	18-17	.514
Wes Westrum	1974-75	2	247	118-129	.478
Totals		*120*		*9,771-8,329*	*.540*

NEW YORK/SAN FRANCISCO GIANTS ALL-TIME SERIES RECORDS

Opponent	New York	San Francisco	Overall
Anaheim	—	11-5	11-5
Arizona	—	37-38	37-38
Baltimore	43-58	1-2	44-60
Boston / Milwaukee / Atlanta	832-668	357-370	1,189-1,038
Brooklyn / Los Angeles	722-671	377-402	1,099-1,073
Buffalo	31-14	—	31-14
Chicago (Cubs)	777-740	320-292	1,097-1,032
Cincinnati	798-600	369-360	1,167-960
Cleveland	116-69	—	116-69
Colorado	—	80-57	80-57
Detroit	58-42	—	58-42
Florida	—	55-34	55-34
Houston	—	331-317	331-317
Indianapolis	42-15	—	42-15
Kansas City	15-3	—	15-3
Louisville	67-35	—	67-35
Milwaukee	—	24-18	24-18
Montreal	—	200-184	200-184
New York (Mets)	—	281-226	281-226
New York (Yankees)	—	1-2	1-2
Oakland	—	16-16	16-16
Philadelphia	892-604	319-274	1,211-878
Pittsburgh	786-666	311-281	1,097-947
Providence	20-26	—	20-26
San Diego	—	279-250	279-250
Seattle	—	9-7	9-7
St. Louis	754-632	297-295	1,051-927
Tampa Bay	—	2-1	2-1
Texas	—	9-7	9-7
Toronto	—	2-1	2-1
Washington	114-55	—	114-55
Totals	*8,067-4,898* (.553)	*3,704-3,431* (.519)	*9,771-8,329* (.540)

NEW YORK/SAN FRANCISCO GIANTS OPPONENT NICKNAMES

Anaheim
Angels (1997-present)

Arizona
Diamondbacks (1998-present)

Atlanta
Braves (1966-present)

Baltimore
Orioles (1892-present)

Boston
Red Stockings (1883-88)
Beaneaters (1889-1912)
Braves (1913-52)

Brooklyn
Bridegrooms (1890-98)
Superbas (1899-1904)
Dodgers (1905-57)

Buffalo
Bisons (1883-85)

Chicago
White Stockings (1883-90)
Colts (1891-97)
Orphans (1898-1901)
Cubs (1902-present)
White Sox (2003-present)

Cincinnati
Reds (1890-present)

Cleveland
Blues (1883-84)
Spiders (1889-99)

Colorado
Rockies (1993-present)

Detroit
Wolverines (1883-88)
Tigers (2003-present)

Florida
Marlins (1993-present)

Houston
Colt .45s (1962-65)
Astros (1966-present)

Indianapolis
Hoosiers (1887-89)

Kansas City
Cowboys (1886)
Royals (2003-present)

Los Angeles
Dodgers (1958-present)

Louisville
Colonels (1892-99)

Milwaukee
Braves (1953-65)
Brewers (1998-present)

Minnesota
Twins (2003-present)

Montreal
Expos (1969-present)

New York
Mets (1962-present)
Yankees (2002-present)

Oakland
Athletics (1997-present)

Philadelphia
Phillies (1883-present)

Pittsburgh
Alleghenys (1887-89)
Innocents (1890)
Pirates (1891-present)

Providence
Grays (1883-85)

San Diego
Padres (1969-present)

Seattle
Mariners (1997-present)

St. Louis
Maroons (1885-86)
Browns (1892-98)
Perfectos (1899-1900)
Cardinals (1901-present)

Tampa Bay
Devil Rays (2002-present)

Texas
Rangers (1997-present)

Toronto
Blue Jays (2002-present)

Washington
Senators (1886-89, 1892-99)

NEW YORK/SAN FRANCISCO GIANTS
YEAR-BY-YEAR RECORD AGAINST ALL OPPONENTS

Season	Boston	Brooklyn	Chicago	Cincinnati	Colorado	Florida	Houston	Montreal	New York	Philadelphia	Pittsburgh	San Diego	St. Louis	Totals
1883	7-7	—	5-9	—	—	—	—	—	—	12-2	—	—	—	46-50
	Buffalo (5-8) / Cleveland (6-7) / Detroit (6-8) / Providence (5-9)													
1884	8-8	—	4-12	—	—	—	—	—	—	11-5	—	—	—	62-50
	Buffalo (11-5) / Cleveland (11-5) / Detroit (14-2) / Providence (3-13)													
1885	13-3	—	10-6	—	—	—	—	—	—	11-5	—	—	12-4	85-27
	Buffalo (15-1) / Detroit (12-4) / Providence (12-4)													
1886	11-6	—	8-10	—	—	—	—	—	—	8-8	—	—	15-3	75-44
	Detroit (7-11) / Kansas City (15-3) / Washington (11-3)													
1887	10-7	—	6-11	—	—	—	—	—	—	7-10	12-6	—	—	68-55
	Detroit (8-10) / Indianapolis (15-3) / Washington (10-8)													
1888	12-8	—	8-11	—	—	—	—	—	—	14-5	10-7	—	—	84-47
	Detroit (11-7) / Indianapolis (14-5) / Washington (15-4)													
1889	6-8	—	13-5	—	—	—	—	—	—	12-7	12-7	—	—	83-43
	Cleveland (14-4) / Indianapolis (13-7) / Washington (13-5)													
1890	8-11	8-10	6-13	6-14	—	—	—	—	—	6-11	17-3	—	—	63-68
	Cleveland (12-6)													
1891	5-15	11-8	13-5	13-5	—	—	—	—	—	9-10	7-12	—	—	71-61
	Cleveland (13-6)													
1892	3-11	7-7	4-10	6-8	—	—	—	—	—	5-9	4-10	—	9-4	71-80
	Baltimore (9-5) / Cleveland (5-8) / Louisville (10-4) / Washington (9-4)													
1893	4-8	6-6	5-7	6-6	—	—	—	—	—	7-5	4-8	—	8-4	68-64
	Baltimore (8-4) / Cleveland (6-6) / Louisville (7-5) / Washington (7-5)													
1894	6-6	7-5	11-1	7-5	—	—	—	—	—	5-7	8-4	—	7-5	88-44
	Baltimore (6-6) / Cleveland (9-3) / Louisville (12-0) / Washington (10-2)													
1895	4-8	3-9	8-4	8-4	—	—	—	—	—	3-8	4-8	—	11-1	66-65
	Baltimore (3-9) / Cleveland (5-7) / Louisville (9-3) / Washington (8-4)													
1896	5-7	8-4	7-5	6-6	—	—	—	—	—	3-8	4-8	—	9-3	64-67
	Baltimore (3-9) / Cleveland (5-7) / Louisville (8-4) / Washington (6-6)													
1897	4-8	9-3	7-5	5-7	—	—	—	—	—	7-5	8-3	—	12-0	83-48
	Baltimore (7-5) / Cleveland (9-3) / Louisville (6-6) / Washington (9-3)													
1898	4-10	11-3	5-9	8-6	—	—	—	—	—	6-7	5-9	—	10-3	77-73
	Baltimore (3-10) / Cleveland (8-6) / Louisville (8-6) / Washington (9-4)													
1899	2-12	2-10	6-7	5-9	—	—	—	—	—	4-10	6-7	—	4-10	60-90
	Baltimore (4-10) / Cleveland (13-1) / Louisville (7-7) / Washington (7-7)													
1900	7-11	10-10	8-12	13-7	—	—	—	—	—	7-13	9-11	—	6-14	60-78
1901	6-14	6-11	9-11	12-8	—	—	—	—	—	8-12	4-16	—	7-13	52-85
1902	3-16	10-10	10-10	6-14	—	—	—	—	—	6-12	6-13	—	7-13	48-88
1903	12-8	12-7	12-8	8-12	—	—	—	—	—	15-5	10-10	—	15-5	84-55
1904	20-2	19-3	11-11	12-10	—	—	—	—	—	17-4	12-10	—	15-7	106-47
1905	19-3	15-7	12-10	16-5	—	—	—	—	—	14-8	12-10	—	17-5	105-48
1906	15-6	13-9	7-15	16-5	—	—	—	—	—	15-7	11-11	—	19-3	96-56
1907	13-9	12-10	6-16	13-9	—	—	—	—	—	11-10	10-12	—	17-5	82-71
1908	16-6	16-6	11-11	14-8	—	—	—	—	—	16-6	11-11	—	14-8	98-56
1909	14-8	15-7	11-11	13-9	—	—	—	—	—	12-10	11-11	—	16-5	92-61

Season	Boston	Brooklyn	Chicago	Cincin-nati	Colorado	Florida	Houston	Montreal	New York	Phila-delphia	Pitts-burgh	San Diego	St. Louis	Totals
1910	16-6	14-8	8-14	14-8	—	—	—	—	—	15-7	12-10	—	12-10	91-63
1911	15-7	16-5	11-11	14-8	—	—	—	—	—	12-10	16-6	—	15-7	99-54
1912	18-3	16-6	9-13	16-6	—	—	—	—	—	17-5	12-8	—	15-7	103-48
1913	14-8	14-8	14-7	17-5	—	—	—	—	—	14-8	14-8	—	14-7	101-51
1914	11-11	13-9	13-9	13-9	—	—	—	—	—	12-10	13-9	—	9-13	84-70
1915	9-13	8-12	14-8	13-9	—	—	—	—	—	7-15	8-14	—	10-12	69-83
1916	10-11	7-15	12-10	16-5	—	—	—	—	—	9-13	17-5	—	15-7	86-66
1917	15-7	13-9	15-7	11-11	—	—	—	—	—	14-8	16-6	—	14-8	98-56
1918	15-1	12-8	6-14	7-12	—	—	—	—	—	10-3	8-11	—	13-4	71-53
1919	14-6	12-8	14-6	8-12	—	—	—	—	—	14-6	11-9	—	14-6	87-53
1920	12-10	7-15	15-7	16-6	—	—	—	—	—	12-10	13-9	—	11-11	86-68
1921	13-8	10-12	14-8	14-8	—	—	—	—	—	16-6	16-6	—	11-11	94-59
1922	14-8	14-8	14-8	12-10	—	—	—	—	—	15-7	11-11	—	13-9	93-61
1923	16-6	11-11	12-10	10-12	—	—	—	—	—	19-3	13-9	—	14-7	95-58
1924	17-5	14-8	13-9	13-9	—	—	—	—	—	14-7	9-13	—	13-9	93-60
1925	11-11	12-10	15-7	13-9	—	—	—	—	—	13-8	10-12	—	12-9	86-66
1926	10-12	13-9	8-14	15-7	—	—	—	—	—	12-7	6-16	—	10-12	74-77
1927	15-7	12-10	12-10	15-7	—	—	—	—	—	15-7	11-11	—	12-10	92-62
1928	16-6	13-9	8-14	14-8	—	—	—	—	—	17-5	11-11	—	14-8	93-61
1929	13-9	7-14	10-12	12-10	—	—	—	—	—	16-5	13-8	—	13-9	84-67
1930	11-11	9-13	12-10	15-7	—	—	—	—	—	16-6	14-8	—	10-12	87-67
1931	16-6	10-10	10-12	15-7	—	—	—	—	—	14-8	12-10	—	10-12	87-65
1932	11-11	7-15	7-15	15-7	—	—	—	—	—	11-11	7-15	—	14-8	72-82
1933	10-12	14-8	13-9	17-4	—	—	—	—	—	15-6	13-9	—	9-13	91-61
1934	15-7	14-8	10-11	16-6	—	—	—	—	—	15-7	14-8	—	9-13	93-60
1935	16-5	13-9	8-14	14-8	—	—	—	—	—	12-10	14-8	—	14-8	91-62
1936	13-9	13-9	11-11	13-9	—	—	—	—	—	17-5	15-7	—	10-12	92-62
1937	10-10	16-6	10-12	14-8	—	—	—	—	—	15-7	16-6	—	14-8	95-57
1938	14-8	14-8	10-12	9-12	—	—	—	—	—	16-5	9-13	—	11-9	83-67
1939	11-10	10-12	11-11	11-11	—	—	—	—	—	14-7	11-11	—	9-12	77-74
1940	15-7	5-16	10-12	7-15	—	—	—	—	—	12-10	12-10	—	11-10	72-80
1941	16-6	8-14	13-9	7-15	—	—	—	—	—	16-6	8-14	—	6-15	74-79
1942	12-8	8-14	13-9	13-9	—	—	—	—	—	17-5	15-7	—	7-15	85-67
1943	11-11	8-14	9-12	6-16	—	—	—	—	—	8-14	9-13	—	4-18	55-98
1944	13-9	12-10	12-10	7-15	—	—	—	—	—	10-12	7-15	—	6-16	67-87
1945	10-10	7-15	11-11	16-6	—	—	—	—	—	17-5	11-11	—	6-16	78-74
1946	9-13	7-15	5-17	8-14	—	—	—	—	—	12-10	10-12	—	10-12	61-93
1947	9-13	8-14	15-7	9-13	—	—	—	—	—	12-10	15-7	—	13-9	81-73
1948	11-11	11-11	11-11	12-10	—	—	—	—	—	14-8	12-10	—	7-15	78-76
1949	10-12	8-14	12-10	15-7	—	—	—	—	—	11-11	12-10	—	7-15	73-81
1950	9-13	10-12	17-5	11-11	—	—	—	—	—	12-10	16-6	—	11-11	86-68
1951	14-8	11-14	15-7	17-5	—	—	—	—	—	16-6	14-8	—	11-11	98-59
1952	13-9	14-8	12-10	16-6	—	—	—	—	—	10-12	15-7	—	12-10	92-62
Milwaukee														
1953	8-14	7-15	13-9	13-9	—	—	—	—	—	9-13	11-11	—	9-13	70-84
1954	12-10	13-9	15-7	15-7	—	—	—	—	—	16-6	14-8	—	12-10	97-57
1955	8-14	9-13	10-12	13-9	—	—	—	—	—	10-12	17-5	—	13-9	80-74
1956	5-17	8-14	15-7	8-14	—	—	—	—	—	11-11	13-9	—	7-15	67-87
1957	9-13	10-12	9-13	10-12	—	—	—	—	—	10-12	13-9	—	8-14	69-85
Los Angeles														
1958	6-16	16-6	10-12	11-11	—	—	—	—	—	14-8	10-12	—	13-9	80-74
1959	10-12	8-14	10-12	14-8	—	—	—	—	—	13-9	12-10	—	16-6	83-71
1960	8-14	12-10	13-9	11-11	—	—	—	—	—	14-8	8-14	—	13-9	79-75
1961	11-11	12-10	17-5	10-12	—	—	—	—	—	14-8	12-10	—	9-13	85-69
1962	11-7	11-10	12-6	11-7	—	—	11-7	—	14-4	13-5	11-7	—	9-9	103-62
1963	8-10	9-9	8-10	10-8	—	—	10-8	—	12-6	10-8	13-5	—	8-10	88-74
1964	8-9	12-6	9-9	11-7	—	—	11-7	—	11-7	8-10	10-8	—	9-9	90-72
1965	8-10	8-10	12-6	12-6	—	—	15-3	—	13-5	10-8	7-11	—	10-8	95-67
Atlanta														
1966	10-8	9-9	12-6	10-7	—	—	12-6	—	9-9	8-10	11-7	—	12-6	93-68
1967	8-10	13-5	8-10	10-8	—	—	12-6	—	13-5	10-8	10-8	—	7-11	91-71
1968	9-9	9-9	9-9	10-8	—	—	10-8	—	11-7	9-9	11-7	—	10-8	88-74
1969	9-9	13-5	6-6	8-10	—	—	8-10	11-1	4-8	9-3	7-5	12-6	3-9	90-72

Season	Atlanta	Los Angeles	Chicago	Cincin-nati	Colorado	Florida	Houston	Montreal	New York	Phila-delphia	Pitts-burgh	San Diego	St. Louis	Totals
1970	11-7	9-9	5-7	9-9	—	—	8-10	6-6	6-6	4-8	8-4	13-5	7-5	86-76
1971	11-7	6-12	9-3	9-9	—	—	9-9	5-7	8-4	6-6	9-3	13-5	5-7	90-72
1972	11-7	9-9	5-7	5-10	—	—	5-13	6-6	4-8	6-6	3-9	10-4	5-7	69-86
1973	10-8	9-9	10-2	8-10	—	—	7-11	6-6	7-5	7-5	7-5	11-7	6-6	88-74
1974	10-8	6-12	6-6	7-11	—	—	8-10	8-4	6-6	4-8	4-8	7-11	6-6	72-90
1975	9-8	8-10	7-5	5-13	—	—	15-5	7-5	4-8	5-7	7-5	10-8	5-7	80-81
1976	9-9	10-8	4-8	9-9	—	—	8-10	5-7	5-7	6-6	3-9	10-8	5-7	74-88
1977	10-8	4-14	3-9	8-10	—	—	9-9	6-6	5-7	3-9	10-2	10-8	7-5	75-87
1978	7-11	7-11	8-4	6-12	—	—	12-6	7-5	9-3	6-6	8-4	10-8	9-3	89-73
1979	7-11	4-14	4-8	12-6	—	—	11-7	5-7	4-8	6-6	3-9	10-8	5-7	71-91
1980	6-11	5-13	7-5	11-7	—	—	7-11	5-7	9-3	6-6	4-8	8-10	7-5	75-86
1981	7-5	5-7	5-5	5-9	—	—	6-9	5-2	4-2	3-4	7-3	7-6	2-3	56-55
1982	10-8	9-9	6-6	12-6	—	—	13-5	8-4	8-4	2-10	6-6	8-10	5-7	87-75
1983	9-9	13-5	8-4	8-10	—	—	6-12	4-8	7-5	7-5	6-6	7-11	4-8	79-83
1984	8-10	8-10	3-9	6-12	—	—	6-12	5-7	8-4	4-8	6-6	5-13	7-5	66-96
1985	8-10	7-11	6-6	6-12	—	—	3-15	5-7	4-8	6-6	9-3	6-12	2-10	62-100
1986	11-7	10-8	6-6	9-9	—	—	9-9	7-5	5-7	3-9	8-4	10-8	5-7	83-79
1987	10-8	8-10	7-5	11-7	—	—	8-10	7-5	3-9	10-2	6-6	13-5	7-5	90-72
1988	13-5	6-12	7-5	7-11	—	—	11-7	5-7	8-4	5-7	4-8	10-8	7-5	83-79
1989	12-6	8-10	6-6	10-8	—	—	10-8	5-7	9-3	8-4	7-5	10-8	7-5	92-70
1990	13-5	10-8	5-7	11-7	—	—	8-10	5-7	5-7	4-8	4-8	11-7	9-3	85-77
1991	9-9	10-8	6-6	8-10	—	—	9-9	5-7	6-6	6-6	5-7	7-11	4-8	75-87
1992	7-11	11-7	4-8	8-10	—	—	6-12	7-5	2-10	9-3	6-6	7-11	5-7	72-90
1993	6-7	6-7	6-6	11-2	10-3	8-4	10-3	9-3	8-4	8-4	7-5	10-3	4-8	103-59
1994	1-5	5-5	4-5	2-7	7-3	4-2	2-8	7-5	6-6	8-4	5-1	2-5	2-4	55-60
1995	1-7	5-8	7-5	3-3	5-8	3-5	3-5	6-7	8-5	6-6	6-6	7-6	7-6	67-77
1996	5-7	6-7	5-7	4-9	8-5	7-5	4-8	4-9	6-6	6-6	4-8	2-11	7-6	68-94
1997	4-7	6-6	6-5	7-4	8-4	6-5	8-3	5-6	8-3	8-3	3-8	8-4	3-8	90-72

Anaheim (3-1) / Oakland (2-2) / Seattle (3-1) / Texas (2-2)

Season	Atlanta	Los Angeles	Chicago	Cincin-nati	Colorado	Florida	Houston	Montreal	New York	Phila-delphia	Pitts-burgh	San Diego	St. Louis	Totals
1998	2-7	6-6	3-7	7-2	5-7	9-0	3-6	6-3	5-4	6-2	7-2	4-8	7-5	89-74

Arizona (7-5) / Milwaukee (4-5) / Anaheim (2-1) / Oakland (2-2) / Seattle (2-1) / Texas (2-1)

Season	Atlanta	Los Angeles	Chicago	Cincin-nati	Colorado	Florida	Houston	Montreal	New York	Phila-delphia	Pitts-burgh	San Diego	St. Louis	Totals
1999	5-4	5-8	7-1	5-4	9-4	5-4	4-5	5-4	2-7	6-2	5-4	7-5	6-3	86-76

Arizona (3-9) / Milwaukee (5-4) / Anaheim (2-1) / Oakland (3-3) / Seattle (2-1) / Texas (0-3)

Season	Atlanta	Los Angeles	Chicago	Cincin-nati	Colorado	Florida	Houston	Montreal	New York	Phila-delphia	Pitts-burgh	San Diego	St. Louis	Totals
2000	3-6	5-7	5-4	6-3	7-6	5-3	3-6	6-3	5-3	7-2	6-2	7-2	5-4	97-65

Arizona (7-6) / Milwaukee (6-3) / Anaheim (1-2) / Oakland (3-3) / Seattle (1-2) / Texas (3-0)

Season	Atlanta	Los Angeles	Chicago	Cincin-nati	Colorado	Florida	Houston	Montreal	New York	Phila-delphia	Pitts-burgh	San Diego	St. Louis	Totals
2001	2-4	8-11	3-3	2-4	10-9	4-3	2-4	5-2	4-3	3-3	5-1	3-3	3-3	90-72

Arizona (9-10) / Milwaukee (4-5) / Anaheim (3-0) / Oakland (4-2) / Seattle (1-2) / Texas (2-1)

Season	Atlanta	Los Angeles	Chicago	Cincin-nati	Colorado	Florida	Houston	Montreal	New York	Phila-delphia	Pitts-burgh	San Diego	St. Louis	Totals
2002	3-3	11-8	3-3	4-2	11-8	3-4	5-1	2-4	6-0	3-3	4-2	14-5	2-4	95-66

Arizona (11-8) / Milwaukee (5-1) / Oakland (2-4) / Baltimore (1-2) / New York Yankees (1-2) / Tampa Bay (2-1) / Toronto (2-1)

NEW YORK/SAN FRANCISCO GIANTS MONTH-BY-MONTH RECORD

Season	April	May	June	July	August	September	October
1883	—	6-12	12-10	9-13	12-7	7-8	—
1884	—	17-8	12-11	11-8	10-9	9-9	3-5
1885	—	17-4	15-5	18-7	18-3	13-6	4-2
1886	—	15-8	16-5	16-9	14-8	9-11	5-3
1887	2-1	14-11	14-9	11-11	13-9	12-11	2-3
1888	5-3	12-9	13-11	18-5	16-8	13-8	7-3
1889	3-1	14-11	12-7	15-10	18-9	17-4	4-1
1890	3-6	13-10	9-16	11-17	13-11	14-6	0-2
1891	3-5	13-10	17-6	10-11	12-11	15-16	1-2
1892	6-6	11-12	10-17	12-13	10-14	16-11	6-7
1893	1-1	12-15	12-12	12-14	19-7	12-15	—
1894	3-5	13-11	15-8	18-7	20-8	19-5	—
1895	3-3	12-12	11-12	15-9	14-14	11-15	—
1896	1-10	13-11	10-12	10-16	18-10	12-8	—
1897	2-5	13-8	18-8	14-10	20-7	16-9	0-1
1898	3-6	16-9	10-16	18-9	16-9	9-17	5-7
1899	4-8	11-14	15-10	5-18	14-13	8-18	3-9
1900	3-5	8-15	8-13	11-12	11-15	14-14	5-4
1901	2-3	13-6	12-12	7-20	8-20	10-22	0-2
1902	7-5	8-16	5-15	7-19	12-14	8-15	1-4
1903	8-3	17-8	12-10	11-15	21-10	15-9	—
1904	9-2	16-9	19-5	18-8	22-8	20-11	2-4
1905	8-3	22-6	17-10	20-6	16-9	19-9	3-5
1906	12-3	14-12	16-8	16-9	16-11	19-11	3-2
1907	11-3	17-7	8-11	18-13	15-14	13-18	0-5
1908	8-6	10-9	19-12	16-10	16-8	24-8	5-3
1909	4-6	13-11	16-6	18-12	18-11	19-11	4-4
1910	9-3	14-11	13-8	15-14	16-12	19-11	5-4
1911	8-5	17-9	16-10	15-12	16-8	19-6	8-4
1912	8-3	20-4	22-4	17-13	15-12	19-9	2-3
1913	8-4	12-12	20-7	25-6	18-9	14-11	4-2
1914	4-4	17-7	16-12	15-12	11-15	17-18	4-2
1915	3-9	11-10	12-11	17-15	12-16	13-18	1-4
1916	1-8	20-6	9-15	15-14	11-15	29-5	1-3
1917	8-4	12-7	18-11	19-8	19-12	19-13	3-1
1918	11-1	14-10	16-9	16-16	13-16	1-1	—
1919	3-2	18-6	15-11	20-7	16-16	15-11	—
1920	3-7	12-14	15-14	17-10	20-11	18-11	1-1
1921	7-6	20-8	13-12	20-11	18-13	15-9	1-0
1922	12-3	14-12	17-9	15-14	16-10	18-12	1-1
1923	10-4	20-7	15-10	18-13	17-13	15-9	0-2
1924	9-2	16-12	19-8	17-12	14-15	18-11	—
1925	9-4	18-8	13-14	17-13	16-18	13-7	0-2

Season	April	May	June	July	August	September	October
1926	9-6	11-16	14-13	14-14	12-15	14-13	—
1927	11-4	11-13	11-16	21-14	16-5	20-10	2-0
1928	7-4	16-11	16-11	15-14	14-13	25-8	—
1929	4-4	13-13	21-12	17-16	12-12	15-9	2-1
1930	7-3	10-19	17-10	21-12	16-11	16-12	—
1931	9-4	14-9	15-14	13-16	22-11	14-11	—
1932	5-8	12-14	13-11	15-20	14-17	13-12	—
1933	8-4	13-12	19-9	17-12	16-11	18-13	—
1934	8-3	17-13	17-9	19-11	19-10	13-14	—
1935	7-3	19-6	18-9	16-15	16-14	15-15	—
1936	8-5	17-12	12-14	16-14	24-3	15-14	—
1937	5-2	18-13	15-10	16-13	17-9	22-9	2-1
1938	10-1	15-10	15-13	14-15	13-16	14-12	2-0
1939	3-6	14-15	18-7	9-18	15-12	17-16	1-0
1940	4-4	15-8	18-10	12-17	13-19	10-22	—
1941	8-6	12-11	17-13	8-15	15-21	14-13	—
1942	8-8	15-15	14-12	15-12	19-11	14-9	—
1943	2-4	13-17	9-19	11-18	9-20	11-17	0-3
1944	7-3	11-17	15-11	13-19	11-17	9-19	1-1
1945	8-4	18-7	10-19	14-17	17-10	11-17	—
1946	5-7	12-14	11-18	15-15	10-18	8-21	—
1947	4-7	17-7	13-13	15-15	15-20	17-11	—
1948	7-4	13-10	12-16	18-13	10-17	17-14	1-2
1949	6-5	16-13	11-16	16-12	14-16	10-17	0-2
1950	1-6	11-14	19-11	14-16	20-10	20-11	1-0
1951	3-12	18-9	17-11	18-12	20-9	20-5	2-1
1952	7-4	20-6	17-12	14-13	16-16	18-11	—
1953	5-9	14-10	15-14	18-10	10-25	8-16	—
1954	8-6	15-13	24-4	18-14	17-10	15-10	—
1955	6-8	18-13	10-17	20-12	14-13	12-11	—
1956	5-6	10-15	11-17	8-20	16-16	17-13	—
1957	7-6	11-17	18-13	8-21	18-13	7-15	—
1958	9-5	18-12	10-17	17-11	14-17	12-12	—
1959	9-7	17-12	17-14	14-12	16-13	10-13	—
1960	10-5	16-11	11-16	13-11	12-19	15-13	2-0
1961	10-6	16-10	15-15	13-15	15-11	15-11	1-1
1962	15-5	20-10	16-13	16-11	18-10	16-12	2-1
1963	11-9	19-9	14-15	16-14	14-14	14-13	—
1964	8-3	18-14	19-11	14-16	14-15	15-11	2-2
1965	7-9	19-11	14-13	15-10	17-14	21-9	2-1
1966	11-7	19-9	18-12	13-16	17-11	12-13	3-0
1967	7-9	17-10	16-16	14-15	16-14	20-7	1-0
1968	10-7	16-14	14-16	12-15	21-10	15-12	—
1969	15-6	9-16	15-14	18-11	17-12	16-13	—

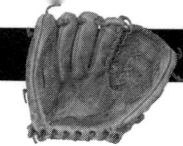

Season	April	May	June	July	August	September	October
1970	10-12	14-14	12-12	13-14	20-11	17-13	—
1971	18-5	19-9	13-15	15-14	14-13	11-16	—
1972	6-10	9-21	13-15	16-8	12-16	13-13	0-3
1973	18-6	14-14	13-14	15-12	13-13	15-15	—
1974	11-12	16-13	7-20	14-13	12-15	11-16	1-1
1975	10-11	13-11	14-17	15-14	15-15	13-13	—
1976	7-10	11-20	13-17	15-11	10-18	18-10	0-2
1977	8-11	13-16	14-16	12-15	15-14	12-14	1-1
1978	10-10	20-6	17-13	16-14	14-13	12-16	0-1
1979	9-14	16-12	13-13	14-16	8-19	11-17	—
1980	6-14	13-13	15-13	16-11	16-13	7-19	2-3
1981	9-12	16-13	2-7	—	12-8	16-13	1-2
1982	9-11	12-18	14-13	14-12	17-12	20-7	1-2
1983	7-14	19-7	12-16	13-16	12-17	14-13	2-0
1984	7-16	9-13	14-16	10-17	16-16	10-18	—
1985	7-12	10-16	10-20	13-14	11-14	9-20	2-4
1986	13-8	12-15	16-12	12-14	12-16	16-11	2-3
1987	16-7	11-15	11-16	14-13	18-11	18-8	2-2
1988	11-12	14-14	14-11	17-11	14-15	12-15	1-1
1989	12-12	17-10	18-10	14-12	14-14	17-11	0-1
1990	8-12	11-17	19-8	17-10	12-17	17-11	1-2
1991	8-12	8-20	17-10	15-9	14-16	10-18	3-2
1992	12-10	15-11	7-19	16-12	9-19	11-17	2-2
1993	15-9	18-9	19-9	18-8	15-11	16-12	2-1
1994	12-11	13-16	8-19	19-8	3-6	—	—
1995	2-3	16-13	12-14	9-18	15-14	13-14	0-1
1996	14-12	12-14	10-17	10-17	12-15	10-19	—
1997	17-7	14-14	16-13	12-15	16-13	15-10	—
1998	14-13	19-11*	15-12	10-15	16-13	15-10	—
1999	16-8	11-16	16-11	13-13	15-13	13-14	2-1
2000	10-13	15-12	13-13	19-8	19-10	20-9	1-0
2001	12-12	14-15	17-10	15-12	16-12	12-9	4-2
2002	15-11	15-12	15-12	14-13	18-10	18-8	—
N.Y. Totals	426-334 (.561)	1,074-809 (.570)	1,084-846 (.562)	1,121-976 (.525)	1,150-928 (.553)	1,104-887 (.554)	108-118 (.478)
S.F. Totals	481-430* (.528)	663-588 (.530)	618-625 (.497)	630-566 (.527)	646-612 (.514)	643-568 (.531)	43-42 (.506)
Overall Totals	907-764* (.543)	1,737-1,397 (.554)	1,702-1,471 (.536)	1,751-1,542 (.532)	1,796-1,542 (.538)	1,747-1,455 (.546)	151-160 (.486)

* includes 1-0 record in March.

NEW YORK/SAN FRANCISCO GIANTS WIN-LOSS BREAKDOWNS

Season	Home	Road	Day	Night	Pre-All-Star	Post-All-Star
1883	28-19	18-31	46-50	—	—	—
1884	34-22	28-28	62-50	—	—	—
1885	45-10	40-17	85-27	—	—	—
1886	47-12	28-32	75-44	—	—	—
1887	36-27	32-28	68-55	—	—	—
1888	44-23	40-24	84-47	—	—	—
1889	47-15	36-28	83-43	—	—	—
1890	37-27	26-41	63-68	—	—	—
1891	39-28	32-33	71-61	—	—	—
1892	42-36	29-44	71-80	—	—	—
1893	49-20	19-44	68-64	—	—	—
1894	49-17	39-27	88-44	—	—	—
1895	40-27	26-38	66-65	—	—	—
1896	39-26	25-41	64-67	—	—	—
1897	51-19	32-29	83-48	—	—	—
1898	45-28	32-45	77-73	—	—	—
1899	35-38	25-52	60-90	—	—	—
1900	38-31	22-47	60-78	—	—	—
1901	30-38	22-47	52-85	—	—	—
1902	24-44	24-44	48-88	—	—	—
1903	41-27	43-28	84-55	—	—	—
1904	56-26	50-21	106-47	—	—	—
1905	54-21	51-27	105-48	—	—	—
1906	51-24	45-32	96-56	—	—	—
1907	45-30	37-41	82-71	—	—	—
1908	52-25	46-31	98-56	—	—	—
1909	44-33	48-28	92-61	—	—	—
1910	52-26	39-37	91-63	—	—	—
1911	49-25	50-29	99-54	—	—	—
1912	49-25	54-23	103-48	—	—	—
1913	54-23	47-28	101-51	—	—	—
1914	43-36	41-34	84-70	—	—	—
1915	37-38	32-45	69-83	—	—	—
1916	47-30	39-36	86-66	—	—	—
1917	50-28	48-28	98-56	—	—	—
1918	35-21	36-32	71-53	—	—	—
1919	46-23	41-30	87-53	—	—	—
1920	45-35	41-33	86-68	—	—	—
1921	53-26	41-33	94-59	—	—	—
1922	51-27	42-34	93-61	—	—	—
1923	47-30	48-28	95-58	—	—	—
1924	51-26	42-34	93-60	—	—	—
1925	47-29	39-37	86-66	—	—	—

Season	Home	Road	Day	Night	Pre-All-Star	Post-All-Star
1926	43-33	31-44	74-77	—	—	—
1927	49-25	43-37	92-62	—	—	—
1928	51-26	42-35	93-61	—	—	—
1929	39-37	45-30	84-67	—	—	—
1930	47-31	40-36	87-67	—	—	—
1931	50-27	37-38	87-65	—	—	—
1932	37-40	35-42	72-82	—	—	—
1933	48-27	43-34	91-61	—	44-27	47-34
1934	49-26	44-34	93-60	—	48-28	45-32
1935	50-27	41-35	91-62	—	50-21	41-41
1936	52-26	40-36	92-62	—	40-32	52-30
1937	50-25	45-32	95-57	—	42-26	53-31
1938	43-30	40-37	83-67	—	46-26	37-41
1939	41-33	36-41	77-74	—	40-33	37-41
1940	33-43	39-37	64-76	8-4	40-26	32-54
1941	38-39	36-40	71-72	3-7	39-32	35-47
1942	47-31	38-36	80-62	5-5	40-37	45-30
1943	34-43	21-55	55-90	0-8	31-46	24-52
1944	39-36	28-51	53-70	14-17	37-39	30-48
1945	47-30	31-44	64-60	14-14	41-36	37-38
1946	38-39	23-54	53-74	8-19	33-41	28-52
1947	45-31	36-42	67-61	14-12	37-30	44-43
1948	37-40	41-36	65-60	13-16	36-37	42-39
1949	43-34	30-47	58-61	15-20	38-38	35-43
1950	44-32	42-36	61-53	25-15	34-39	52-29
1951	50-28	48-31	70-46	28-13	43-36	55-23
1952	50-27	42-35	61-44	31-18	47-26	45-36
1953	38-39	32-45	52-54	18-30	45-37	25-47
1954	53-23	44-34	64-39	33-18	57-27	40-30
1955	44-35	36-39	50-46	30-28	42-41	38-33
1956	37-40	30-47	44-53	23-34	31-44	36-43
1957	37-40	32-45	46-49	23-36	37-43	32-42
1958	44-33	36-41	55-40	25-34	41-38	39-36
1959	42-35	41-36	47-45	36-26	46-35	37-36
1960	45-32	34-43	47-36	32-39	40-38	39-37
1961	45-32	40-37	52-36	33-33	44-39	41-30
1962	61-21	42-41	67-31	36-31	57-31	46-31
1963	51-31	37-43	46-39	42-35	48-37	40-37
1964	44-37	46-35	54-33	36-39	47-31	43-41
1965	51-30	44-37	56-33	39-34	45-38	50-29
1966	47-34	46-34	52-40	41-28	54-33	39-35
1967	51-31	40-40	46-43	45-28	45-38	46-33
1968	42-39	46-35	48-43	40-31	42-42	46-32
1969	52-29	38-43	52-36	38-36	54-42	36-30

Season	Home	Road	Day	Night	Pre-All-Star	Post-All-Star
1970	48-33	38-43	43-30	43-46	41-44	45-32
1971	51-30	39-42	50-31	40-41	55-35	35-37
1972	34-43	35-43	32-46	37-40	41-52	28-34
1973	47-34	41-40	47-29	41-45	56-43	32-31
1974	37-44	35-46	39-42	33-48	45-53	27-37
1975	46-35	34-46	42-37	38-44	41-47	39-34
1976	40-41	34-47	39-39	35-49	35-52	39-36
1977	38-43	37-44	33-38	42-49	43-51	32-36
1978	50-31	39-42	46-31	43-42	52-34	37-39
1979	38-43	33-48	34-40	37-51	45-48	26-43
1980	44-37	31-49	35-30	40-56	37-43	38-43
1981	29-24	27-31	18-27	38-28	27-32	29-23
1982	45-36	42-39	35-26	52-49	42-46	45-29
1983	43-38	36-45	35-32	44-51	39-40	40-43
1984	35-46	31-50	30-39	36-57	33-50	33-46
1985	38-43	24-57	39-52	23-48	33-55	29-45
1986	46-35	37-44	40-37	43-42	48-40	35-39
1987	46-35	44-37	42-24	48-48	44-44	46-28
1988	45-36	38-43	39-28	44-51	46-39	37-40
1989	53-28	39-42	39-26	53-44	51-36	41-34
1990	49-32	36-45	33-30	52-47	44-39	41-38
1991	43-38	32-49	34-27	41-60	35-46	40-41
1992	42-39	30-51	36-32	36-58	43-44	29-46
1993	50-31	53-28	54-26	49-33	59-30	44-29
1994	29-31	26-29	30-31	25-29	39-50	16-10
1995	37-35	30-42	37-34	30-43	33-36	34-41
1996	38-44	30-50	35-43	33-51	38-48	30-46
1997	48-33	42-39	41-33	49-39	51-36	39-36
1998	49-32	40-42	41-28	48-46	52-37	37-37
1999	49-32	37-44	40-34	46-42	50-38	36-38
2000	55-26	42-39	37-29	60-36	46-39	51-25
2001	49-32	41-40	30-26	60-46	46-42	44-32
2002	50-31	45-35	35-30	60-36	49-38	46-28
N.Y.	3,301-2,184	2,766-2,714	5,762-4,584	305-314	1,018-848	987-979
Totals	(.602)	(.505)	(.557)	(.493)	(.546)	(.502)
S.F.	2,016-1,555	1,688-1,876	1,862-1,542	1,842-1,889	2,002-1,849	1,702-1,584
Totals	(.565)	(.474)	(.547)	(.494)	(.520)	(.518)
Overall	5,317-3,739	4,454-4,590	7,624-6,126	2,147-2,203	3,020-2,697	2,689-2,563
Totals	(.587)	(.492)	(.554)	(.494)	(.528)	(.512)

NEW YORK/SAN FRANCISCO GIANTS YEAR-BY-YEAR BATTING TOTALS

Season	G	AB	R	H	2B	3B	HR	RBI	BB	SO	SB	AVG	OBP	SLG
1883	98	3,524	530	900	139	69	24	371	127	297	—	.255	.281	.354
1884	116	4,124	693	1,053	149	67	23	497	249	492	—	.255	.298	.341
1885	112	4,029	691	1,085	150	82	16	464	221	312	—	.269	.307	.359
1886	124	4,298	692	1,156	175	68	21	527	237	410	155	.269	.307	.356
1887	129	4,516	816	1,259	167	93	48	651	361	326	415	.279	.339	.389
1888	138	4,747	659	1,149	130	76	55	487	270	456	314	.242	.287	.336
1889	131	4,671	935	1,319	208	77	52	742	538	386	292	.282	.360	.393
1890	135	4,832	713	1,250	208	89	25	563	350	479	289	.259	.315	.354
1891	136	4,833	754	1,271	189	72	46	630	438	394	224	.263	.329	.360
1892	153	5,291	811	1,326	173	85	39	645	510	474	301	.251	.320	.338
1893	136	4,858	941	1,424	182	101	61	768	504	281	299	.293	.366	.410
1894	137	4,806	940	1,446	197	96	43	789	476	217	319	.301	.368	.414
1895	132	4,605	852	1,324	191	90	32	699	454	292	292	.288	.355	.389
1896	133	4,661	829	1,383	159	87	40	720	439	271	274	.297	.364	.394
1897	137	4,844	895	1,449	188	84	31	759	404	327	328	.299	.361	.392
1898	157	5,349	837	1,422	190	86	34	712	428	372	214	.266	.328	.353
1899	152	5,092	734	1,431	161	65	23	607	387	360	234	.281	.337	.352
1900	141	4,724	713	1,317	177	61	23	564	369	343	236	.279	.335	.357
1901	141	4,839	544	1,225	167	46	19	458	303	575	133	.253	.303	.318
1902	139	4,571	401	1,088	147	34	6	337	252	530	187	.238	.283	.289
1903	142	4,741	729	1,290	181	49	20	569	379	—	264	.272	.338	.344
1904	158	5,150	744	1,347	202	65	31	564	434	—	283	.262	.328	.344
1905	155	5,094	780	1,392	191	88	39	642	517	—	291	.273	.351	.368
1906	153	4,768	625	1,217	162	53	15	513	463	—	288	.255	.343	.321
1907	155	4,874	574	1,222	160	48	23	475	516	—	205	.251	.331	.317
1908	157	5,006	652	1,339	182	43	20	562	494	—	181	.267	.342	.333
1909	158	5,218	623	1,327	173	68	26	510	530	—	234	.254	.329	.328
1910	155	5,061	715	1,391	204	83	31	623	562	489	282	.275	.354	.366
1911	154	5,006	756	1,399	225	103	41	651	530	506	347	.279	.358	.390
1912	154	5,067	823	1,451	231	89	47	702	514	497	319	.286	.360	.395
1913	156	5,218	684	1,427	226	71	30	580	444	501	296	.273	.338	.361
1914	156	5,146	672	1,363	222	59	30	566	447	479	239	.265	.330	.348
1915	154	4,982	584	1,162	167	50	31	459	570	669	198	.251	.317	.305
1916	155	5,152	597	1,305	188	74	42	500	356	558	206	.253	.307	.343
1917	158	5,211	635	1,360	170	71	39	544	373	533	162	.261	.317	.343
1918	124	4,164	480	1,081	150	53	13	400	271	365	130	.260	.310	.330
1919	140	4,664	605	1,254	204	64	40	505	328	407	157	.269	.322	.366
1920	155	5,309	682	1,427	210	76	46	590	432	545	131	.269	.327	.363
1921	153	5,278	840	1,575	237	93	75	748	469	390	137	.298	.359	.421
1922	156	5,454	852	1,661	253	90	80	756	448	421	116	.305	.363	.428
1923	153	5,452	854	1,610	248	76	85	790	487	406	106	.295	.356	.415
1924	154	5,445	857	1,634	269	81	95	781	467	479	82	.300	.358	.432
1925	152	5,327	736	1,507	239	61	114	682	411	494	79	.283	.337	.415

Season	G	AB	R	H	2B	3B	HR	RBI	BB	SO	SB	AVG	OBP	SLG
1926	151	5,167	663	1,435	214	58	73	617	339	420	94	.278	.325	.384
1927	155	5,372	*817*	1,594	251	62	109	765	461	462	73	.297	.356	.427
1928	155	5,459	807	1,600	276	59	118	758	444	376	62	.293	.349	.430
1929	152	5,388	897	1,594	251	47	136	829	482	405	85	.296	.358	.436
1930	154	5,553	959	1,769	264	83	143	880	422	382	59	.319	.369	.473
1931	153	5,372	768	1,554	251	64	101	727	383	395	83	*.289*	.340	.416
1932	154	5,530	755	1,527	263	54	116	718	348	391	31	.276	.322	.406
1933	156	5,461	636	1,437	204	41	82	598	377	477	31	.263	.312	.361
1934	153	5,396	760	1,485	240	41	126	716	406	526	19	.275	.329	.405
1935	156	5,623	770	1,608	248	56	123	703	392	479	32	.286	.336	.416
1936	154	5,449	742	1,529	237	48	97	687	431	452	31	.281	.337	.395
1937	152	5,329	732	1,484	251	41	111	677	412	492	45	.278	.334	.403
1938	152	5,255	705	1,424	210	36	125	672	465	528	31	.271	.334	.396
1939	151	5,129	703	1,395	211	38	116	651	498	499	26	.272	.340	.396
1940	152	5,324	663	1,423	201	46	91	614	453	478	45	.267	.329	.374
1941	156	5,395	667	1,401	248	35	95	625	504	518	36	.260	.326	.371
1942	154	5,210	675	1,323	162	35	109	632	558	511	39	.254	.330	.361
1943	156	5,290	558	1,309	153	33	81	518	480	470	35	.247	.313	.335
1944	155	5,306	682	1,398	191	47	93	644	512	480	39	.263	.331	.370
1945	154	5,250	668	1,439	175	35	114	626	501	457	38	.269	.336	.379
1946	154	5,191	612	1,326	176	37	121	576	532	546	46	.255	.328	.374
1947	155	5,343	830	1,446	220	48	221	790	494	568	29	.271	.335	.454
1948	155	5,277	780	1,352	210	49	164	733	599	648	51	.256	.334	.408
1949	156	5,308	736	1,383	203	52	147	690	613	523	43	.261	.340	.401
1950	154	5,238	735	1,352	204	50	133	684	627	629	42	.258	.342	.392
1951	157	5,360	781	1,396	201	53	179	734	671	624	55	.260	.347	.418
1952	154	5,229	722	1,337	186	56	151	663	536	672	30	.256	.329	.399
1953	155	5,362	768	1,452	195	45	176	739	499	608	31	.271	.336	.422
1954	154	5,245	732	1,386	194	42	*186*	701	522	561	30	.264	.341	.424
1955	154	5,288	702	1,377	173	34	169	643	497	581	38	.260	.334	.402
1956	154	5,190	540	1,268	192	45	145	497	402	659	67	.244	.306	.382
1957	154	5,346	643	1,349	171	54	157	612	447	669	64	.252	.318	.393
1958	154	5,318	727	1,399	250	42	170	682	531	817	64	.263	.339	.422
1959	154	5,281	705	1,377	239	35	167	660	473	875	81	.261	.329	.414
1960	156	5,324	671	1,357	220	62	130	622	467	846	86	.255	.323	.393
1961	155	5,233	773	1,379	219	32	183	709	506	764	79	.264	.337	.423
1962	165	5,588	878	1,552	235	32	204	807	523	822	73	.278	.349	.441
1963	162	5,579	725	1,442	206	35	197	680	441	889	55	.258	.322	.414
1964	162	5,535	656	1,360	185	38	165	608	505	900	64	.246	.317	.382
1965	163	5,495	682	1,384	169	43	159	623	476	844	47	.252	.319	.385
1966	161	5,539	675	1,373	195	31	181	627	414	860	29	.248	.307	.392
1967	162	5,524	652	1,354	201	39	140	604	520	978	22	.245	.318	.372
1968	163	5,441	599	1,301	162	33	108	566	508	904	50	.239	.315	.341
1969	162	5,474	713	1,325	187	28	136	657	711	1,054	71	.242	.341	.361

Season	G	AB	R	H	2B	3B	HR	RBI	BB	SO	SB	AVG	OBP	SLG
1970	162	5,578	**831**	1,460	**257**	35	165	**773**	**729**	1,005	83	.262	**.357**	.409
1971	162	5,461	706	1,348	224	36	140	653	**654**	1,042	101	.247	.335	.378
1972	155	5,245	662	1,281	211	36	**150**	600	480	964	123	.244	.316	.384
1973	162	5,537	739	1,452	212	**52**	161	684	590	913	112	.262	.341	.407
1974	162	5,482	634	1,380	228	38	93	568	548	869	107	.252	.326	.358
1975	161	5,447	659	1,412	235	45	84	606	604	775	99	.259	.341	.365
1976	162	5,442	595	1,340	211	37	85	552	518	778	88	.246	.320	.345
1977	162	5,497	673	1,392	227	41	134	624	568	842	90	.253	.331	.383
1978	162	5,364	613	1,331	240	41	117	576	554	814	87	.248	.325	.374
1979	162	5,395	672	1,328	192	36	125	616	580	925	140	.246	.327	.365
1980	161	5,368	573	1,310	199	44	80	539	509	840	100	.244	.317	.342
1981	111	3,766	427	941	161	26	63	399	**386**	543	89	.250	.326	.357
1982	162	5,499	673	1,393	213	30	133	631	**607**	915	130	.253	.334	.376
1983	162	5,369	687	1,324	206	30	142	638	619	990	140	.247	.333	.375
1984	162	**5,650**	682	**1,499**	229	26	112	646	528	980	126	.265	.335	.375
1985	162	5,420	556	1,263	217	31	115	517	488	962	99	.233	.304	.348
1986	162	5,501	698	1,394	269	29	114	637	536	1,087	148	.253	.328	.375
1987	162	**5,608**	783	1,458	274	32	205	731	511	1,084	126	.260	.330	.430
1988	162	5,450	670	1,353	227	44	113	629	550	1,023	121	.248	.327	.368
1989	162	5,469	699	1,365	241	52	141	647	508	1,071	87	.250	.322	**.390**
1990	162	5,573	719	1,459	221	35	152	681	488	973	109	.262	.330	.396
1991	162	5,463	649	1,345	215	48	141	605	471	973	95	.246	.314	.381
1992	162	5,456	574	1,330	220	36	105	532	435	1,067	112	.244	.309	.355
1993	162	5,557	808	1,534	269	33	168	759	516	930	120	**.276**	.348	**.427**
1994	115	3,869	504	963	159	32	123	472	364	719	114	.249	.324	.402
1995	144	4,971	652	1,256	229	33	152	610	472	1,060	138	.253	.327	.404
1996	162	5,533	752	1,400	245	21	153	707	**615**	1,189	113	.253	.338	.380
1997	162	5,485	784	1,415	266	37	172	746	642	1,120	121	.258	.347	.414
1998	163	5,628	845	1,540	292	26	161	800	**678**	1,040	102	.274	.353	.421
1999	162	5,563	872	1,507	307	18	188	828	696	1,028	109	.271	.356	.434
2000	162	5,519	925	1,535	304	44	336	889	**709**	1,032	79	.278	.362	**.472**
2001	162	5,612	799	1,493	304	40	**235**	775	**625**	1,090	57	.266	.342	.460
2002	162	5,497	783	1,465	300	35	198	751	616	961	74	.267	.344	**.442**

bold type denotes led National League (fewest for strikeouts).
bold italic type denotes tied for N.L. lead.

NEW YORK/SAN FRANCISCO GIANTS YEAR-BY-YEAR PITCHING TOTALS

Season	G	CG	ShO	IP	H	R	ER	HR	BB	SO	W-L	SV	ERA
1883	98	87	5	866.0	907	577	283	19	170	323	46-50	0	2.94
1884	116	111	4	1,014.0	1,011	623	351	28	326	567	62-50	0	3.12
1885	112	109	16	994.0	758	370	190	11	265	516	85-27	1	1.72
1886	124	119	3	1,062.0	1,029	558	338	23	280	588	75-44	1	2.86
1887	129	123	5	1,113.2	1,096	723	442	27	373	415	68-55	1	3.57
1888	138	133	20	1,208.0	907	479	263	27	307	726	84-47	1	1.96
1889	131	118	6	1,151.0	1,073	708	444	38	523	558	83-43	3	3.47
1890	135	115	6	1,177.0	1,029	698	400	14	607	612	63-68	1	3.06
1891	136	117	11	1,204.0	1,098	711	400	26	593	651	71-61	3	2.99
1892	153	139	5	1,322.2	1,165	826	484	32	635	650	71-80	1	3.29
1893	136	111	6	1,211.1	1,271	845	578	36	581	395	68-64	4	4.29
1894	137	111	5	1,212.0	1,292	789	516	37	539	395	88-44	5	3.83
1895	132	115	6	1,147.1	1,359	834	575	34	415	409	66-65	1	4.51
1896	133	104	30	1,136.2	1,303	821	574	33	403	312	64-67	2	4.54
1897	137	118	8	1,187.1	1,214	695	458	26	486	456	83-48	3	3.47
1898	157	141	9	1,353.2	1,359	800	517	21	587	558	77-73	1	3.44
1899	152	138	4	1,278.1	1,454	863	610	19	628	397	60-90	0	4.29
1900	141	113	4	1,207.1	1,423	823	531	26	442	277	60-78	0	3.96
1901	141	118	11	1,232.0	1,389	755	530	24	377	542	52-85	1	3.87
1902	139	118	11	1,226.1	1,193	590	384	16	332	501	48-88	1	2.82
1903	142	115	8	1,262.2	1,257	567	413	20	371	628	84-55	8	2.94
1904	158	127	21	1,396.2	1,151	476	337	36	349	707	106-47	15	2.17
1905	155	117	18	1,370.0	1,160	505	364	25	364	760	105-48	15	2.39
1906	153	105	19	1,334.1	1,207	510	369	13	394	639	96-56	18	2.49
1907	155	109	22	1,371.0	1,219	510	373	25	369	655	82-71	13	2.45
1908	157	95	25	1,411.0	1,214	456	336	26	288	656	98-56	18	2.14
1909	158	105	17	1,440.2	1,248	546	364	28	397	735	92-61	15	2.27
1910	155	96	9	1,391.2	1,290	567	414	30	397	717	91-63	10	2.68
1911	154	95	19	1,368.0	1,267	542	409	33	369	771	99-54	13	2.69
1912	154	93	8	1,369.2	1,352	571	393	36	338	652	103-48	15	2.58
1913	156	82	12	1,422.0	1,276	515	383	38	315	651	101-51	17	2.42
1914	156	88	20	1,390.2	1,298	576	455	47	367	563	84-70	9	2.94
1915	155	78	15	1,385.0	1,350	628	479	40	325	637	69-83	9	3.11
1916	155	88	22	1,397.1	1,267	504	404	41	310	638	86-66	12	2.60
1917	158	92	18	1,426.2	1,221	457	360	29	327	551	98-56	14	2.27
1918	124	74	18	1,111.2	1,002	415	326	20	228	330	71-53	11	2.64
1919	140	72	11	1,256.0	1,153	470	377	34	305	340	87-53	13	2.70
1920	155	86	18	1,408.2	1,379	543	439	44	297	380	86-68	9	2.80
1921	153	71	9	1,372.1	1,497	637	542	79	295	357	94-59	18	3.55
1922	156	76	7	1,396.1	1,454	658	536	71	393	388	93-61	15	3.45
1923	153	62	10	1,378.0	1,440	679	597	82	424	453	95-58	18	3.90
1924	154	71	4	1,378.2	1,464	641	554	77	392	406	93-60	21	3.62
1925	152	80	6	1,354.0	1,532	702	593	73	408	446	86-66	8	3.94

Season	G	CG	ShO	IP	H	R	ER	HR	BB	SO	W-L	SV	ERA
1926	151	61	4	1,341.2	1,370	668	562	70	427	419	74-77	15	3.77
1927	155	65	7	1,381.2	1,520	720	609	77	453	442	92-62	16	3.97
1928	155	79	7	1,394.0	1,454	653	568	77	405	399	93-61	16	3.67
1929	152	68	9	1,372.0	1,536	709	605	102	387	431	84-67	13	3.97
1930	154	64	6	1,363.1	1,546	814	699	117	439	522	87-67	19	4.61
1931	153	90	17	1,360.2	1,341	599	499	71	422	570	87-65	12	3.30
1932	154	57	3	1,375.1	1,533	706	585	112	387	506	72-82	16	3.83
1933	156	75	23	1,408.2	1,280	515	424	61	400	555	91-61	15	2.71
1934	153	68	13	1,370.0	1,384	583	486	75	351	499	93-60	30	3.19
1935	156	76	10	1,403.2	1,433	675	590	106	411	524	91-62	11	3.78
1936	154	60	12	1,385.2	1,458	621	532	75	401	500	92-62	22	3.46
1937	152	67	11	1,361.0	1,341	602	519	85	404	653	95-57	17	3.43
1938	152	59	8	1,349.0	1,370	637	543	87	389	497	83-67	18	3.62
1939	151	55	6	1,319.0	1,412	685	596	86	477	505	77-74	20	4.07
1940	152	57	11	1,360.1	1,383	659	573	110	473	606	72-80	18	3.79
1941	156	55	12	1,391.2	1,455	706	610	90	539	566	74-79	18	3.94
1942	154	70	12	1,370.2	1,299	600	504	94	493	497	85-67	13	3.31
1943	156	35	6	1,394.2	1,474	713	633	80	626	588	55-98	19	4.08
1944	155	47	4	1,363.2	1,413	773	650	116	587	499	67-87	21	4.29
1945	154	53	13	1,374.2	1,401	700	620	85	528	530	78-74	21	4.06
1946	154	47	8	1,353.1	1,313	685	589	114	660	581	61-93	13	3.92
1947	155	58	6	1,363.2	1,428	761	673	122	590	553	81-73	14	4.44
1948	155	54	15	1,373.0	1,425	704	599	122	556	527	78-76	21	3.93
1949	156	68	10	1,374.1	1,328	693	584	132	544	516	73-81	9	3.82
1950	154	70	19	1,375.0	1,268	643	567	140	536	596	86-68	15	3.71
1951	157	64	9	1,412.2	1,334	641	546	148	482	625	98-59	18	3.48
1952	154	49	12	1,371.0	1,282	639	547	121	538	655	92-62	31	3.59
1953	155	46	10	1,365.2	1,403	747	645	146	610	647	70-84	20	4.25
1954	154	45	19	1,390.0	1,258	550	478	113	613	692	97-57	33	3.09
1955	154	52	6	1,386.2	1,347	673	581	155	560	721	80-74	14	3.77
1956	154	31	9	1,378.0	1,287	650	578	144	551	765	67-87	28	3.78
1957	154	35	9	1,398.2	1,436	701	623	150	471	701	69-85	20	4.01
1958	154	38	7	1,389.1	1,400	698	614	166	512	775	80-74	25	3.98
1959	154	52	12	1,376.1	1,279	613	530	139	500	873	83-71	23	3.47
1960	156	55	16	1,396.0	1,288	631	534	107	512	897	79-75	26	3.44
1961	155	39	9	1,388.0	1,306	655	582	152	502	924	85-69	30	3.77
1962	165	62	10	1,461.2	1,399	690	616	148	503	886	103-62	39	3.79
1963	162	46	9	1,469.0	1,380	641	546	126	464	954	88-74	30	3.35
1964	162	48	17	1,476.1	1,348	587	523	118	480	1,023	90-72	30	3.19
1965	163	42	17	1,465.1	1,325	593	521	137	408	1,060	95-67	42	3.20
1966	161	52	14	1,476.2	1,370	626	531	140	359	973	93-68	27	3.24
1967	162	64	17	1,474.1	1,283	551	478	113	453	990	91-71	25	2.92
1968	163	77	20	1,469.0	1,302	529	442	86	344	942	88-74	16	2.71
1969	162	71	15	1,473.2	1,381	636	534	120	461	906	90-72	17	3.26

Season	G	CG	ShO	IP	H	R	ER	HR	BB	SO	W-L	SV	ERA
1970	162	50	7	1,457.2	1,514	826	729	156	604	931	86-76	30	4.50
1971	162	45	14	1,454.2	1,324	644	536	128	471	831	**90-72**	30	3.32
1972	155	44	8	1,386.1	1,309	649	569	130	507	771	69-86	23	3.69
1973	162	33	8	1,452.1	1,442	702	612	145	485	787	88-74	*44*	3.79
1974	162	27	11	1,439.0	1,409	723	604	116	559	756	72-90	25	3.78
1975	161	37	9	1,432.2	1,406	671	595	92	612	856	80-81	24	3.74
1976	162	27	*18*	1,461.2	1,464	686	573	**68**	518	746	74-88	31	3.53
1977	162	27	10	1,459.0	1,501	711	608	114	529	854	75-87	33	3.75
1978	162	42	*17*	1,455.0	1,377	594	534	84	553	840	89-73	29	3.30
1979	162	25	6	1,436.0	1,484	751	664	143	577	880	71-91	34	4.16
1980	161	27	10	1,448.1	1,446	634	556	92	492	811	75-86	35	3.46
1981	111	8	9	**1,009.1**	970	414	368	57	393	561	56-55	*33*	3.28
1982	162	18	4	1,465.1	1,507	687	592	109	466	810	87-75	45	3.64
1983	162	20	9	1,445.2	1,431	697	594	127	520	881	79-83	47	3.70
1984	162	9	7	1,461.0	1,589	807	713	125	549	854	66-96	38	4.39
1985	162	13	5	1,448.0	1,348	674	581	125	572	985	62-100	24	3.61
1986	162	18	10	1,460.1	1,264	618	541	121	591	992	83-79	35	3.33
1987	162	19	10	**1,471.0**	1,407	**669**	*601*	146	547	1,038	**90-72**	38	**3.68**
1988	162	25	13	1,462.1	1,323	626	550	99	422	875	83-79	42	3.39
1989	162	12	16	1,457.0	1,320	600	535	120	471	802	**92-70**	47	3.30
1990	162	14	6	1,446.1	1,477	710	655	131	553	788	85-77	45	4.08
1991	162	10	10	1,442.0	1,397	697	646	143	544	905	75-87	45	4.03
1992	162	9	12	1,461.0	1,385	647	586	128	502	927	72-90	30	3.61
1993	162	4	9	1,456.2	1,385	636	585	168	442	982	103-59	50	3.61
1994	115	2	4	1,025.1	1,014	500	455	122	372	655	55-60	33	3.99
1995	144	12	5	1,293.2	1,368	776	699	173	505	801	67-77	34	4.86
1996	162	9	8	1,442.1	1,520	862	755	194	570	997	68-94	35	4.71
1997	162	5	9	1,446.0	1,494	793	712	160	578	1,044	**90-72**	45	4.43
1998	163	6	6	1,477.0	1,457	739	686	171	562	1,089	89-74	44	4.18
1999	162	6	3	1,456.1	1,486	831	762	194	655	1,076	86-76	42	4.71
2000	162	9	*15*	1,444.1	1,452	747	675	151	623	1,076	**97-65**	47	4.21
2001	162	3	8	1,463.1	1,437	748	680	145	579	1,080	90-72	47	4.18
2002	162	10	13	1,437.1	1,349	616	566	116	523	992	95-66	43	3.54

bold type denotes led National League (fewest for hits, runs, earned runs, home runs and walks) or won N.L. pennant and/or West Division.
bold italic type denotes tied for N.L. lead.

NEW YORK/SAN FRANCISCO GIANTS YEAR-BY-YEAR FIELDING TOTALS

Season	G	PO	A	E	TC	DP	PCT
1883	98	2,564	1,181	468	4,213	52	.889
1884	116	3,014	1,379	514	4,907	69	.895
1885	112	3,001	1,359	331	4,691	85	.929
1886	124	3,183	1,496	359	5,038	70	.929
1887	129	3,317	1,650	431	5,398	82	.920
1888	138	3,632	1,609	432	5,673	76	.924
1889	131	3,418	1,574	437	5,429	90	.920
1890	135	3,507	1,709	449	5,665	104	.921
1891	136	3,611	1,731	384	5,726	104	.933
1892	153	3,965	1,911	565	6,441	97	.912
1893	136	3,632	1,834	432	5,898	95	.927
1894	137	3,627	1,721	443	5,791	101	.924
1895	132	3,438	1,728	438	5,604	106	.922
1896	133	3,404	1,647	365	5,416	90	.933
1897	137	3,556	1,733	397	5,686	109	.930
1898	157	4,053	2,099	447	6,599	113	.932
1899	152	3,830	2,107	433	6,370	140	.932
1900	141	3,617	2,029	439	6,085	124	.928
1901	141	3,691	1,884	348	5,923	81	.941
1902	139	3,675	1,814	330	5,819	104	.943
1903	142	3,802	1,743	287	5,832	87	.951
1904	158	4,176	2,147	294	6,617	93	.956
1905	155	4,108	2,057	258	6,423	93	.960
1906	153	3,984	2,120	233	6,337	84	.963
1907	155	4,089	1,893	232	6,214	75	.963
1908	157	4,218	2,088	250	6,556	79	.962
1909	158	4,306	2,066	307	6,679	99	.954
1910	155	4,183	1,958	291	6,432	117	.955
1911	154	4,090	1,925	256	6,271	86	.959
1912	154	4,098	1,934	280	6,312	123	.956
1913	156	4,252	1,936	254	6,442	107	.961
1914	156	4,165	2,032	254	6,451	119	.961
1915	155	4,151	1,969	256	6,376	119	.960
1916	155	4,184	2,031	217	6,432	108	.966
1917	158	4,274	2,085	208	6,567	122	.968
1918	124	3,328	1,664	152	5,144	78	.970
1919	140	3,755	1,997	216	5,968	96	.964
1920	155	4,232	2,240	210	6,682	137	.969
1921	153	4,111	2,128	187	6,426	155	.971
1922	156	4,181	2,083	194	6,458	145	.970
1923	153	4,131	1,988	176	6,295	141	.972
1924	154	4,130	2,031	186	6,347	160	.971
1925	152	4,078	1,999	199	6,276	129	.968

Season	G	PO	A	E	TC	DP	PCT
1926	151	4,029	1,941	186	6,156	150	.970
1927	155	4,138	2,041	195	6,374	160	.969
1928	155	4,180	2,028	178	6,386	175	.972
1929	152	4,117	2,008	158	6,283	163	.975
1930	154	4,079	1,976	164	6,219	144	.974
1931	153	4,076	1,772	159	6,007	126	.974
1932	154	4,126	1,898	191	6,215	143	.969
1933	156	4,224	2,087	178	6,489	156	.973
1934	153	4,107	2,031	179	6,317	141	.972
1935	156	4,211	1,874	174	6,259	129	.972
1936	154	4,154	2,068	168	6,390	164	.974
1937	152	4,083	1,984	159	6,226	143	.974
1938	152	4,043	1,920	168	6,131	147	.973
1939	151	3,964	1,893	153	6,010	151	.975
1940	152	4,081	1,896	139	6,116	132	.977
1941	156	4,177	1,800	160	6,137	144	.974
1942	154	4,108	1,816	138	6,062	128	.977
1943	156	4,189	1,892	166	6,247	140	.973
1944	155	4,095	1,797	179	6,071	128	.971
1945	154	4,124	1,844	166	6,134	112	.973
1946	154	4,056	1,742	159	5,957	121	.973
1947	155	4,095	1,775	155	6,025	136	.974
1948	155	4,106	1,711	156	5,973	134	.974
1949	156	4,121	1,675	161	5,957	134	.973
1950	154	4,124	1,779	137	6,040	181	.977
1951	157	4,238	1,785	171	6,194	175	.972
1952	154	4,113	1,750	158	6,021	175	.974
1953	155	4,097	1,721	151	5,969	151	.975
1954	154	4,170	1,734	154	6,058	172	.975
1955	154	4,160	1,732	142	6,034	165	.976
1956	154	4,134	1,660	144	5,938	143	.976
1957	154	4,196	1,811	161	6,168	180	.974
1958	154	4,168	1,707	152	6,027	156	.975
1959	154	4,129	1,645	152	5,926	118	.974
1960	156	4,188	1,614	166	5,968	117	.972
1961	155	4,164	1,513	133	5,810	126	.977
1962	165	4,385	1,649	142	6,176	153	.977
1963	162	4,407	1,613	156	6,176	113	.975
1964	162	4,428	1,718	159	6,305	136	.975
1965	163	4,396	1,706	148	6,250	124	.976
1966	161	4,429	1,816	168	6,413	131	.974
1967	162	4,425	1,902	134	6,460	149	.979
1968	163	4,406	1,834	162	6,402	125	.975
1969	162	4,421	1,928	169	6,518	155	.974

Season	G	PO	A	E	TC	DP	PCT
1970	162	4,373	1,774	170	6,317	153	.973
1971	162	4,364	1,750	179	6,293	153	.972
1972	155	4,159	1,659	156	5,974	121	.974
1973	162	4,357	1,753	163	6,273	138	.974
1974	162	4,317	1,826	175	6,318	153	.972
1975	161	4,298	1,768	146	6,212	164	.976
1976	162	4,385	1,940	186	**6,511**	153	.971
1977	162	4,377	1,749	179	6,305	136	.972
1978	162	4,365	1,705	146	6,216	118	.977
1979	162	4,308	1,806	163	6,277	138	.974
1980	161	4,345	1,825	159	6,329	124	.975
1981	111	**3,028**	1,313	102	4,443	102	.977
1982	162	4,396	1,909	173	6,478	125	.973
1983	162	4,337	1,775	171	6,283	109	.973
1984	162	4,383	1,843	173	6,399	134	.973
1985	162	4,344	1,773	148	6,265	134	.976
1986	162	4,381	1,794	143	6,318	149	.977
1987	162	**4,413**	1,861	129	**6,403**	183	.980
1988	162	4,387	1,796	129	6,312	145	.980
1989	162	4,371	1,725	114	6,210	135	*.982*
1990	162	4,339	**1,825**	107	**6,271**	148	*.983*
1991	162	4,326	1,753	109	6,188	**151**	*.982*
1992	162	4,383	1,782	113	6,278	**174**	.982
1993	162	4,370	1,733	**101**	6,204	**169**	.984
1994	115	3,076	1,275	**68**	4,419	113	.985
1995	144	3,881	1,548	108	5,537	142	.980
1996	162	4,327	1,637	136	6,100	165	.978
1997	162	4,338	1,799	125	6,262	157	.980
1998	163	4,431	**1,806**	101	**6,338**	157	.984
1999	162	4,369	1,629	105	6,103	155	.983
2000	162	4,333	1,644	**93**	6,070	173	.985
2001	162	**4,390**	1,650	118	6,158	170	.981
2002	162	4,312	1,630	90	6,032	166	.985

bold type denotes led National League (fewest for errors).
bold italic type denotes tied for N.L. lead.

NEW YORK/SAN FRANCISCO GIANTS YEAR-BY-YEAR BATTING LEADERS

1883
Batting Average — Roger Connor (.357)
Runs — Buck Ewing (90)
Hits — Roger Connor (146)
Doubles — Roger Connor (28)
Triples — Roger Connor (15)
Home Runs — **Buck Ewing (10)**
RBI — Pete Gillespie (62)
Stolen Bases — not recorded

1884
Batting Average — Roger Connor (.317)
Runs — Roger Connor, John Montgomery Ward (98)
Hits — Roger Connor (151)
Doubles — Roger Connor (28)
Triples — **Buck Ewing (20)**
Home Runs — Roger Connor, Alex McKinnon (4)
RBI — Roger Connor (82)
Stolen Bases — not recorded

1885
Batting Average — **Roger Connor (.371)**
Runs — Jim O'Rourke (119)
Hits — **Roger Connor (169)**
Doubles — Roger Connor (23)
Triples — **Jim O'Rourke (16)**
Home Runs — Buck Ewing (6)
RBI — Roger Connor (65)
Stolen Bases — not recorded

1886
Batting Average — Roger Connor (.355)
Runs — Jim O'Rourke (106)
Hits — Roger Connor (172)
Doubles — Roger Connor (29)
Triples — **Roger Connor (20)**
Home Runs — Roger Connor (7)
RBI — John Montgomery Ward (81)
Stolen Bases — John Montgomery Ward (36)

1887
Batting Average — John Montgomery Ward (.338)
Runs — John Montgomery Ward (114)
Hits — John Montgomery Ward (184)
Doubles — Roger Connor (26)
Triples — Roger Connor (22)
Home Runs — Roger Connor (17)
RBI — Roger Connor (104)
Stolen Bases — **John Montgomery Ward (111)**

1888
Batting Average — Buck Ewing (.306)
Runs — Roger Connor (98)
Hits — Roger Connor (140)
Doubles — Buck Ewing (18)
Triples — Roger Connor (17)
Home Runs — Roger Connor (14)
RBI — Roger Connor (71)
Stolen Bases — Buck Ewing (53)

1889
Batting Average — Mike Tiernan (.335)
Runs — **Mike Tiernan (147)**
Hits — Mike Tiernan (167)
Doubles — Jim O'Rourke (36)
Triples — Roger Connor (17)
Home Runs — Roger Connor (13)
RBI — **Roger Connor (130)**
Stolen Bases — John Montgomery Ward (62)

1890
Batting Average — **Jack Glasscock (.336)**
Runs — Mike Tiernan (132)
Hits — *Jack Glasscock (172)*
Doubles — Jack Glasscock (32)
Triples — Mike Tiernan (21)
Home Runs — *Mike Tiernan (13)*
RBI — Jack Glasscock (66)
Stolen Bases — Mike Tiernan (56)

1891
Batting Average — Mike Tiernan (.306)
Runs — Roger Connor (112)
Hits — Mike Tiernan (166)
Doubles — Mike Tiernan (30)
Triples — Roger Connor (13)
Home Runs — *Mike Tiernan (16)*
RBI — Jim O'Rourke (95)
Stolen Bases — Mike Tiernan (53)

1892
Batting Average — Buck Ewing (.310)
Runs — Eddie Burke (81)
Hits — Jim O'Rourke (136)
Doubles — Jim O'Rourke (28)
Triples — Buck Ewing (15)
Home Runs — Buck Ewing, Denny Lyons (8)
RBI — Buck Ewing (76)
Stolen Bases — Eddie Burke, Jack Doyle, Buck Ewing (42)

1893

Batting Average — George Davis (.355)
Runs — John Montgomery Ward (129)
Hits — George Davis (195)
Doubles — John Montgomery Ward (27)
Triples — George Davis (27)
Home Runs — Mike Tiernan (14)
RBI — George Davis (119)
Stolen Bases — Eddie Burke (54)

1894

Batting Average — Jack Doyle (.367)
Runs — Eddie Burke (121)
Hits — Eddie Burke, George Van Haltren (172)
Doubles — Jack Doyle (30)
Triples — George Davis (19)
Home Runs — George Davis (8)
RBI — George Van Haltren (104)
Stolen Bases — George Van Haltren (43)

1895

Batting Average — Mike Tiernan (.347)
Runs — Mike Tiernan (127)
Hits — George Van Haltren (177)
Doubles — George Davis (36)
Triples — Mike Tiernan (21)
Home Runs — George Van Haltren (8)
RBI — George Van Haltren (103)
Stolen Bases — George Davis (48)

1896

Batting Average — Mike Tiernan (.369)
Runs — George Van Haltren (136)
Hits — George Van Haltren (197)
Doubles — George Davis (25)
Triples — *George Van Haltren (21)*
Home Runs — Mike Tiernan (7)
RBI — George Davis (99)
Stolen Bases — George Davis (48)

1897

Batting Average — George Davis (.353)
Runs — Mike Tiernan (123)
Hits — George Van Haltren (186)
Doubles — George Davis (31)
Triples — Bill Joyce (13)
Home Runs — George Davis (10)
RBI — **George Davis (136)**
Stolen Bases — George Davis (65)

1898

Batting Average — George Van Haltren (.312)
Runs — George Van Haltren (129)
Hits — George Van Haltren (204)
Doubles — George Van Haltren (28)
Triples — George Van Haltren (16)
Home Runs — Bill Joyce (10)
RBI — Bill Joyce (91)
Stolen Bases — George Van Haltren (36)

1899

Batting Average — George Davis (.337)
Runs — George Van Haltren (117)
Hits — George Van Haltren (182)
Doubles — George Davis, Tom O'Brien,
            George Van Haltren (21)
Triples — Tom O'Brien (10)
Home Runs — Tom O'Brien (6)
RBI — Tom O'Brien (77)
Stolen Bases — Jack Doyle (35)

1900

Batting Average — Kip Selbach (.337)
Runs — George Van Haltren (114)
Hits — George Van Haltren (180)
Doubles — George Van Haltren (30)
Triples — Charlie Hickman (17)
Home Runs — Charlie Hickman (9)
RBI — Charlie Hickman (91)
Stolen Bases — *George Van Haltren (45)*

1901

Batting Average — George Van Haltren (.335)
Runs — Kip Selbach (89)
Hits — George Van Haltren (182)
Doubles — Kip Selbach (29)
Triples — George Davis (7)
Home Runs — George Davis (7)
RBI — John Ganzel (66)
Stolen Bases — Sammy Strang (40)

1902

Batting Average — Steve Brodie (.281)
Runs — Heinie Smith (46)
Hits — Heinie Smith (129)
Doubles — Billy Lauder (20)
Triples — Dan McGann (7)
Home Runs — Steve Brodie (3)
RBI — Billy Lauder (44)
Stolen Bases — Heinie Smith (32)

1903
Batting Average — Roger Bresnahan (.350)
Runs — George Browne (105)
Hits — George Browne (185)
Doubles — *Sam Mertes (32)*
Triples — Sam Mertes (14)
Home Runs — Sam Mertes (7)
RBI — **Sam Mertes (104)**
Stolen Bases — Sam Mertes (45)

1904
Batting Average — Dan McGann (.286)
Runs — **George Browne (99)**
Hits — George Browne (169)
Doubles — Sam Mertes (28)
Triples — Sam Mertes (11)
Home Runs — Dan McGann (6)
RBI — **Bill Dahlen (80)**
Stolen Bases — Bill Dahlen, Sam Mertes (47)

1905
Batting Average — Mike Donlin (.356)
Runs — **Mike Donlin (124)**
Hits — Mike Donlin (216)
Doubles — Mike Donlin (31)
Triples — Sam Mertes (17)
Home Runs — Bill Dahlen, Mike Donlin (7)
RBI — Sam Mertes (108)
Stolen Bases — *Art Devlin (59)*

1906
Batting Average — Sammy Strang (.319)
Runs — Art Devlin (76)
Hits — Art Devlin (149)
Doubles — Art Devlin (23)
Triples — Art Devlin, Dan McGann (8)
Home Runs — Cy Seymour, Sammy Strang (4)
RBI — Art Devlin (65)
Stolen Bases — Art Devlin (54)

1907
Batting Average — Cy Seymour (.294)
Runs — **Spike Shannon (104)**
Hits — Spike Shannon (155)
Doubles — Cy Seymour (25)
Triples — George Browne (10)
Home Runs — George Browne (5)
RBI — Cy Seymour (75)
Stolen Bases — Art Devlin (38)

1908
Batting Average — Mike Donlin (.334)
Runs — **Fred Tenney (101)**
Hits — Mike Donlin (198)
Doubles — Mike Donlin (26)
Triples — Mike Donlin (13)
Home Runs — Mike Donlin (6)
RBI — Mike Donlin (106)
Stolen Bases — Mike Donlin (30)

1909
Batting Average — Larry Doyle (.302)
Runs — Larry Doyle (86)
Hits — **Larry Doyle (172)**
Doubles — Larry Doyle (27)
Triples — Red Murray (12)
Home Runs — **Red Murray (7)**
RBI — Red Murray (91)
Stolen Bases — Red Murray (48)

1910
Batting Average — Fred Snodgrass (.321)
Runs — Larry Doyle (97)
Hits — Larry Doyle (164)
Doubles — Fred Merkle (35)
Triples — Larry Doyle, Fred Merkle (14)
Home Runs — Larry Doyle (8)
RBI — Red Murray (87)
Stolen Bases — Red Murray (57)

1911
Batting Average — Chief Meyers (.332)
Runs — Larry Doyle (102)
Hits — Larry Doyle (163)
Doubles — Red Murray, Fred Snodgrass (27)
Triples — **Larry Doyle (25)**
Home Runs — **Larry Doyle (13)**
RBI — Fred Merkle (84)
Stolen Bases — Josh Devore (61)

1912
Batting Average — Chief Meyers (.358)
Runs — Larry Doyle (98)
Hits — Larry Doyle (184)
Doubles — Larry Doyle (33)
Triples — Red Murray (20)
Home Runs — Fred Merkle (11)
RBI — Red Murray (92)
Stolen Bases — Fred Snodgrass (43)

1913

Batting Average — Chief Meyers (.312)
Runs — George Burns (81)
Hits — George Burns (173)
Doubles — George Burns (37)
Triples — Fred Merkle (13)
Home Runs — Larry Doyle, Tillie Shafer (5)
RBI — Larry Doyle (73)
Stolen Bases — George Burns (40)

1914

Batting Average — George Burns (.303)
Runs — **George Burns (100)**
Hits — George Burns (170)
Doubles — George Burns (35)
Triples — George Burns (10)
Home Runs — Fred Merkle (7)
RBI — Art Fletcher (79)
Stolen Bases — **George Burns (62)**

1915

Batting Average — **Larry Doyle (.320)**
Runs — Larry Doyle (86)
Hits — **Larry Doyle (189)**
Doubles — **Larry Doyle (40)**
Triples — George Burns (14)
Home Runs — Larry Doyle, Fred Merkle (4)
RBI — Art Fletcher (74)
Stolen Bases — George Burns (27)

1916

Batting Average — Dave Robertson (.307)
Runs — **George Burns (105)**
Hits — Dave Robertson (180)
Doubles — George Burns, Larry Doyle (24)
Triples — Benny Kauff (15)
Home Runs — *Dave Robertson (12)*
RBI — Benny Kauff (74)
Stolen Bases — Benny Kauff (40)

1917

Batting Average — Benny Kauff (.308)
Runs — **George Burns (103)**
Hits — George Burns (180)
Doubles — George Burns (25)
Triples — George Burns (13)
Home Runs — *Dave Robertson (12)*
RBI — *Heinie Zimmerman (102)*
Stolen Bases — George Burns (40)

1918

Batting Average — Ross Youngs (.302)
Runs — George Burns (80)
Hits — Ross Youngs (143)
Doubles — George Burns (22)
Triples — Heinie Zimmerman (10)
Home Runs — George Burns (4)
RBI — Heinie Zimmerman (56)
Stolen Bases — George Burns (40)

1919

Batting Average — Ross Youngs (.311)
Runs — **George Burns (86)**
Hits — George Burns (162)
Doubles — **Ross Youngs (31)**
Triples — Larry Doyle (10)
Home Runs — Benny Kauff (10)
RBI — Benny Kauff (67)
Stolen Bases — **George Burns (40)**

1920

Batting Average — Ross Youngs (.351)
Runs — **George Burns (115)**
Hits — Ross Youngs (204)
Doubles — George Burns (35)
Triples — Ross Youngs (14)
Home Runs — George Kelly (11)
RBI — *George Kelly (94)*
Stolen Bases — Frankie Frisch (34)

1921

Batting Average — Frankie Frisch (.341)
Runs — Dave Bancroft, Frankie Frisch (121)
Hits — Frankie Frisch (211)
Doubles — George Kelly (42)
Triples — Frankie Frisch (17)
Home Runs — **George Kelly (23)**
RBI — George Kelly (122)
Stolen Bases — **Frankie Frisch (49)**

1922

Batting Average — Irish Meusel,
               Ross Youngs (.331)
Runs — Dave Bancroft (117)
Hits — Dave Bancroft (209)
Doubles — Dave Bancroft (41)
Triples — Irish Meusel (17)
Home Runs — George Kelly (17)
RBI — Irish Meusel (132)
Stolen Bases — Frankie Frisch (31)

1923
Batting Average — Frankie Frisch (.348)
Runs — **Ross Youngs (121)**
Hits — **Frankie Frisch (223)**
Doubles — Dave Bancroft, Ross Youngs (33)
Triples — Irish Meusel (14)
Home Runs — Irish Meusel (19)
RBI — **Irish Meusel (125)**
Stolen Bases — Frankie Frisch (29)

1924
Batting Average — Ross Youngs (.356)
Runs — *Frankie Frisch (121)*
Hits — Frankie Frisch (198)
Doubles — George Kelly (37)
Triples — Frankie Frisch (15)
Home Runs — George Kelly (21)
RBI — **George Kelly (136)**
Stolen Bases — Frankie Frisch (22)

1925
Batting Average — Frankie Frisch (.331)
Runs — Frankie Frisch (89)
Hits — George Kelly (181)
Doubles — Irish Meusel (35)
Triples — Fred Lindstrom (12)
Home Runs — Irish Meusel (21)
RBI — Irish Meusel (111)
Stolen Bases — Frankie Frisch (21)

1926
Batting Average — Frankie Frisch (.314)
Runs — Fred Lindstrom (90)
Hits — Frankie Frisch (171)
Doubles — Frankie Frisch (29)
Triples — Irish Meusel (10)
Home Runs — George Kelly (13)
RBI — George Kelly (80)
Stolen Bases — Frankie Frish (23)

1927
Batting Average — Rogers Hornsby (.361)
Runs — *Rogers Hornsby (133)*
Hits — Rogers Hornsby (205)
Doubles — Fred Lindstrom (36)
Triples — Bill Terry (13)
Home Runs — Rogers Hornsby (26)
RBI — Rogers Hornsby (125)
Stolen Bases — Edd Roush (18)

1928
Batting Average — Fred Lindstrom (.358)
Runs — Bill Terry (100)
Hits — **Fred Lindstrom (231)**
Doubles — Fred Lindstrom (39)
Triples — Billy Terry (11)
Home Runs — Mel Ott (18)
RBI — Fred Lindstrom (107)
Stolen Bases — Fred Lindstrom (15)

1929
Batting Average — Bill Terry (.372)
Runs — Mel Ott (138)
Hits — Bill Terry (226)
Doubles — Bill Terry (39)
Triples — Travis Jackson (12)
Home Runs — Mel Ott (42)
RBI — Mel Ott (151)
Stolen Bases — Travis Jackon, Freddy Leach,
            Fred Lindstrom, Bill Terry (10)

1930
Batting Average — **Bill Terry (.401)**
Runs — Bill Terry (139)
Hits — **Bill Terry (254)**
Doubles — Fred Lindstrom, Bill Terry (39)
Triples — Bill Terry (15)
Home Runs — Mel Ott (25)
RBI — Bill Terry (129)
Stolen Bases — Fred Lindstrom (15)

1931
Batting Average — Bill Terry (.349)
Runs — *Bill Terry (121)*
Hits — Bill Terry (213)
Doubles — Bill Terry (43)
Triples — **Bill Terry (20)**
Home Runs — Mel Ott (29)
RBI — Mel Ott (115)
Stolen Bases — Chick Fullis, Travis Jackon (13)

1932
Batting Average — Bill Terry (.350)
Runs — Bill Terry (124)
Hits — Bill Terry (225)
Doubles — Bill Terry (42)
Triples — Bill Terry (11)
Home Runs — *Mel Ott (38)*
RBI — Mel Ott (123)
Stolen Bases — Fred Lindstrom, Mel Ott (6)

1933
Batting Average — Bill Terry (.322)
Runs — Mel Ott (98)
Hits — Mel Ott (164)
Doubles — Mel Ott (36)
Triples — Johnny Vergez (6)
Home Runs — Mel Ott (23)
RBI — Mel Ott (103)
Stolen Bases — Kiddo Davis (10)

1934
Batting Average — Bill Terry (.354)
Runs — Mel Ott (119)
Hits — Bill Terry (213)
Doubles — Joe Moore (37)
Triples — Mel Ott (10)
Home Runs — *Mel Ott (35)*
RBI — **Mel Ott (135)**
Stolen Bases — Joe Moore (5)

1935
Batting Average — Bill Terry (.341)
Runs — Mel Ott (113)
Hits — Hank Leiber, Bill Terry (203)
Doubles — Hank Leiber (37)
Triples — Travis Jackson (12)
Home Runs — Mel Ott (31)
RBI — Mel Ott (114)
Stolen Bases — Mel Ott, Bill Terry (7)

1936
Batting Average — Mel Ott (.328)
Runs — Mel Ott (120)
Hits — Joe Moore (205)
Doubles — Dick Bartell, Burgess Whitehead (31)
Triples — Joe Moore (9)
Home Runs — **Mel Ott (33)**
RBI — Mel Ott (135)
Stolen Bases — Burgess Whitehead (14)

1937
Batting Average — Jimmy Ripple (.317)
Runs — Mel Ott (99)
Hits — Joe Moore (180)
Doubles — Dick Bartell (38)
Triples — Joe Moore (10)
Home Runs — *Mel Ott (31)*
RBI — Mel Ott (95)
Stolen Bases — Joe Moore, Mel Ott,
          Burgess Whitehead (7)

1938
Batting Average — Mel Ott (.311)
Runs — **Mel Ott (116)**
Hits — Mel Ott (164)
Doubles — Dick Bartell, Harry Danning (26)
Triples — Joe Moore, Mel Ott (6)
Home Runs — **Mel Ott (36)**
RBI — Mel Ott (116)
Stolen Bases — George Myatt (10)

1939
Batting Average — Zeke Bonura (.321)
Runs — Mel Ott (85)
Hits — Frank Demaree (170)
Doubles — Harry Danning (28)
Triples — Billy Jurges (11)
Home Runs — Mel Ott (27)
RBI — Zeke Bonura (85)
Stolen Bases — Joe Moore (5)

1940
Batting Average — Frank Demaree (.302)
Runs — Mel Ott (89)
Hits — Burgess Whitehead (160)
Doubles — Harry Danning (34)
Triples — Frank Demaree, Burgess Whitehead (6)
Home Runs — Mel Ott (19)
RBI — Babe Young (101)
Stolen Bases — Burgess Whitehead (9)

1941
Batting Average — Billy Jurges (.293)
Runs — Johnny Rucker (95)
Hits — Johnny Rucker (179)
Doubles — Johnny Rucker (38)
Triples — Johnny Rucker (9)
Home Runs — Mel Ott (27)
RBI — Babe Young (104)
Stolen Bases — Johnny Rucker (8)

1942
Batting Average — Johnny Mize (.305)
Runs — **Mel Ott (118)**
Hits — Johnny Mize (165)
Doubles — Johnny Mize (25)
Triples — Babe Barna, Johnny Mize (7)
Home Runs — **Mel Ott (30)**
RBI — **Johnny Mize (110)**
Stolen Bases — Bill Werber (9)

1943
Batting Average — Mickey Witek (.314)
Runs — Mickey Witek (68)
Hits — Mickey Witek (195)
Doubles — Joe Medwick (20)
Triples — Sid Gordon (11)
Home Runs — Mel Ott (18)
RBI — Sid Gordon (63)
Stolen Bases — Mel Ott (7)

1944
Batting Average — Joe Medwick (.337)
Runs — Mel Ott (91)
Hits — Joe Medwick (165)
Doubles — Buddy Kerr (31)
Triples — Phil Weintraub (9)
Home Runs — Mel Ott (26)
RBI — Joe Medwick (85)
Stolen Bases — Buddy Kerr (14)

1945
Batting Average — Mel Ott (.308)
Runs — George Hausmann (98)
Hits — George Hausmann (174)
Doubles — Mel Ott (23)
Triples — Johnny Rucker (11)
Home Runs — Mel Ott (21)
RBI — Mel Ott (79)
Stolen Bases — George Hausmann,
        Johnny Rucker (7)

1946
Batting Average — Sid Gordon (.293)
Runs — Johnny Mize (70)
Hits — Willard Marshall (144)
Doubles — Buddy Kerr (20)
Triples — Buddy Blattner (6)
Home Runs — Johnny Mize (22)
RBI — Johnny Mize (70)
Stolen Bases — Buddy Blattner (12)

1947
Batting Average — Walker Cooper (.305)
Runs — **Johnny Mize (137)**
Hits — Johnny Mize (177)
Doubles — Johnny Mize, Bobby Thomson (26)
Triples — Walker Cooper, Sid Gordon (8)
Home Runs — *Johnny Mize (51)*
RBI — **Johnny Mize (138)**
Stolen Bases — Bill Rigney (7)

1948
Batting Average — Sid Gordon (.299)
Runs — Whitey Lockman (117)
Hits — Whitey Lockman (167)
Doubles — Sid Gordon, Johnny Mize (26)
Triples — Whitey Lockman (10)
Home Runs — *Johnny Mize (40)*
RBI — Johnny Mize (125)
Stolen Bases — Buddy Kerr (9)

1949
Batting Average — Bobby Thomson (.309)
Runs — Bobby Thomson (99)
Hits — Bobby Thomson (198)
Doubles — Bobby Thomson (35)
Triples — Bobby Thomson (9)
Home Runs — Bobby Thomson (27)
RBI — Bobby Thomson (109)
Stolen Bases — Whitey Lockman (12)

1950
Batting Average — Eddie Stanky (.300)
Runs — Eddie Stanky (115)
Hits — Alvin Dark (164)
Doubles — Alvin Dark (36)
Triples — Bobby Thomson (7)
Home Runs — Bobby Thomson (25)
RBI — Hank Thompson (91)
Stolen Bases — Alvin Dark, Eddie Stanky (9)

1951
Batting Average — Monte Irvin (.312)
Runs — Alvin Dark (114)
Hits — Alvin Dark (196)
Doubles — **Alvin Dark (41)**
Triples — Monte Irvin (11)
Home Runs — Bobby Thomson (32)
RBI — **Monte Irvin (121)**
Stolen Bases — Alvin Dark, Monte Irvin (12)

1952
Batting Average — Alvin Dark (.301)
Runs — Whitey Lockman (99)
Hits — Alvin Dark (177)
Doubles — Alvin Dark, Bobby Thomson (29)
Triples — **Bobby Thomson (14)**
Home Runs — Bobby Thomson (24)
RBI — Bobby Thomson (108)
Stolen Bases — Alvin Dark (6)

1953
Batting Average — Don Mueller (.333)
Runs — Alvin Dark (126)
Hits — Alvin Dark (194)
Doubles — Alvin Dark (41)
Triples — Hank Thompson (8)
Home Runs — Bobby Thomson (26)
RBI — Bobby Thomson (106)
Stolen Bases — Alvin Dark (7)

1954
Batting Average — **Willie Mays (.345)**
Runs — Willie Mays (119)
Hits — **Don Mueller (212)**
Doubles — Don Mueller (35)
Triples — **Willie Mays (13)**
Home Runs — Willie Mays (41)
RBI — Willie Mays (110)
Stolen Bases — Willie Mays (8)

1955
Batting Average — Willie Mays (.319)
Runs — Willie Mays (123)
Hits — Willie Mays, Don Mueller (185)
Doubles — Don Mueller (21)
Triples — *Willie Mays (13)*
Home Runs — **Willie Mays (51)**
RBI — Willie Mays (127)
Stolen Bases — Willie Mays (24)

1956
Batting Average — Willie Mays (.296)
Runs — Willie Mays (101)
Hits — Willie Mays (171)
Doubles — Willie Mays (27)
Triples — Jackie Brandt, Willie Mays (8)
Home Runs — Willie Mays (36)
RBI — Willie Mays (84)
Stolen Bases — **Willie Mays (40)**

1957
Batting Average — Willie Mays (.333)
Runs — Willie Mays (112)
Hits — Willie Mays (195)
Doubles — Daryl Spencer (31)
Triples — **Willie Mays (20)**
Home Runs — Willie Mays (35)
RBI — Willie Mays (97)
Stolen Bases — **Willie Mays (38)**

1958
Batting Average — Willie Mays (.347)
Runs — **Willie Mays (121)**
Hits — Willie Mays (208)
Doubles — Orlando Cepeda (38)
Triples — Willie Mays (11)
Home Runs — Willie Mays (29)
RBI — Orlando Cepeda, Willie Mays (96)
Stolen Bases — Willie Mays (31)

1959
Batting Average — Orlando Cepeda (.317)
Runs — Willie Mays (125)
Hits — Orlando Cepeda (192)
Doubles — Willie Mays (43)
Triples — Jackie Brandt, Willie Mays,
          Willie McCovey (5)
Home Runs — Willie Mays (34)
RBI — Orlando Cepeda (105)
Stolen Bases — **Willie Mays (27)**

1960
Batting Average — Willie Mays (.319)
Runs — Willie Mays (107)
Hits — **Willie Mays (190)**
Doubles — Willie Mays (36)
Triples — Willie Mays (12)
Home Runs — Willie Mays (29)
RBI — Willie Mays (103)
Stolen Bases — Willie Mays (25)

1961
Batting Average — Orlando Cepeda (.311)
Runs — **Willie Mays (129)**
Hits — Orlando Cepeda (182)
Doubles — Willie Mays (32)
Triples — Joey Amalfitano, Orlando Cepeda,
          Jim Davenport, Harvey Kuenn (4)
Home Runs — **Orlando Cepeda (46)**
RBI — **Orlando Cepeda (142)**
Stolen Bases — Willie Mays (18)

1962
Batting Average — Felipe Alou (.316)
Runs — Willie Mays (130)
Hits — Orlando Cepeda (191)
Doubles — Willie Mays (36)
Triples — Jose Pagan (6)
Home Runs — **Willie Mays (49)**
RBI — Willie Mays (141)
Stolen Bases — Willie Mays (18)

1963
Batting Average — Orlando Cepeda (.316)
Runs — Willie Mays (115)
Hits — Willie Mays (187)
Doubles — Orlando Cepeda (33)
Triples — Felipe Alou (9)
Home Runs — *Willie McCovey (44)*
RBI — Willie Mays (103)
Stolen Bases — Felipe Alou (11)

1964
Batting Average — Orlando Cepeda (.304)
Runs — Willie Mays (121)
Hits — Willie Mays (171)
Doubles — Orlando Cepeda (27)
Triples — Willie Mays (9)
Home Runs — **Willie Mays (47)**
RBI — Willie Mays (111)
Stolen Bases — Willie Mays (19)

1965
Batting Average — Willie Mays (.317)
Runs — Willie Mays (118)
Hits — Jim Ray Hart, Willie Mays (177)
Doubles — Jim Ray Hart (30)
Triples — Hal Lanier (9)
Home Runs — **Willie Mays (52)**
RBI — Willie Mays (112)
Stolen Bases — Matty Alou (10)

1966
Batting Average — Willie McCovey (.295)
Runs — Willie Mays (99)
Hits — Jim Ray Hart (165)
Doubles — Willie Mays (29)
Triples — Willie McCovey (6)
Home Runs — Willie Mays (37)
RBI — Willie Mays (103)
Stolen Bases — Tito Fuentes (6)

1967
Batting Average — Jesus Alou (.292)
Runs — Jim Ray Hart (98)
Hits — Jim Ray Hart (167)
Doubles — Jim Ray Hart (26)
Triples — Jim Ray Hart (7)
Home Runs — Willie McCovey (31)
RBI — Jim Ray Hart (99)
Stolen Bases — Willie Mays (6)

1968
Batting Average — Willie McCovey (.293)
Runs — Willie Mays (84)
Hits — Willie McCovey (153)
Doubles — Willie Mays (20)
Triples — Bobby Bonds, Willie Mays (5)
Home Runs — **Willie McCovey (36)**
RBI — **Willie McCovey (105)**
Stolen Bases — Bobby Bonds (16)

1969
Batting Average — Willie McCovey (.320)
Runs — *Bobby Bonds (120)*
Hits — Bobby Bonds (161)
Doubles — Willie McCovey (26)
Triples — Bobby Bonds (6)
Home Runs — **Willie McCovey (45)**
RBI — **Willie McCovey (126)**
Stolen Bases — Bobby Bonds (45)

1970
Batting Average — Bobby Bonds (.302)
Runs — Bobby Bonds (134)
Hits — Bobby Bonds (200)
Doubles — Willie McCovey (39)
Triples — Bobby Bonds (10)
Home Runs — Willie McCovey (39)
RBI — Willie McCovey (126)
Stolen Bases — Bobby Bonds (48)

1971
Batting Average — Bobby Bonds (.288)
Runs — Bobby Bonds (110)
Hits — Bobby Bonds (178)
Doubles — Bobby Bonds (32)
Triples — Tito Fuentes, Ken Henderson,
            Chris Speier (6)
Home Runs — Bobby Bonds (33)
RBI — Bobby Bonds (102)
Stolen Bases — Bobby Bonds (26)

1972
Batting Average — Chris Speier (.269)
Runs — Bobby Bonds (118)
Hits — Bobby Bonds (162)
Doubles — Tito Fuentes (33)
Triples — Garry Maddox (7)
Home Runs — Dave Kingman (29)
RBI — Dave Kingman (83)
Stolen Bases — Bobby Bonds (44)

1973
Batting Average — Garry Maddox (.319)
Runs — Bobby Bonds (131)
Hits — Garry Maddox (187)
Doubles — Bobby Bonds (34)
Triples — Garry Maddox, Gary Matthews (10)
Home Runs — Bobby Bonds (39)
RBI — Bobby Bonds (96)
Stolen Bases — Bobby Bonds (43)

1974
Batting Average — Gary Matthews (.287)
Runs — Bobby Bonds (97)
Hits — Gary Matthews (161)
Doubles — Garry Maddox (31)
Triples — Bobby Bonds (8)
Home Runs — Bobby Bonds (21)
RBI — Gary Matthews (82)
Stolen Bases — Bobby Bonds (41)

1975
Batting Average — Von Joshua (.318)
Runs — Derrel Thomas (99)
Hits — Von Joshua (161)
Doubles — Chris Speier (30)
Triples — Von Joshua (10)
Home Runs — Gary Matthews (12)
RBI — Bobby Murcer (91)
Stolen Bases — Derrel Thomas (28)

1976
Batting Average — Gary Matthews (.279)
Runs — Gary Matthews (79)
Hits — Gary Matthews (164)
Doubles — Gary Matthews (28)
Triples — Gary Thomasson (5)
Home Runs — Bobby Murcer (23)
RBI — Bobby Murcer (90)
Stolen Bases — Larry Herndon, Gary Matthews,
          Bobby Murcer (12)

1977
Batting Average — Bill Madlock (.302)
Runs — Derrel Thomas (75)
Hits — Bill Madlock (161)
Doubles — Bill Madlock (28)
Triples — Derrel Thomas (10)
Home Runs — Willie McCovey (28)
RBI — Willie McCovey (86)
Stolen Bases — Gary Thomasson (16)

1978
Batting Average — Bill Madlock (.309)
Runs — Jack Clark (90)
Hits — Jack Clark (181)
Doubles — Jack Clark (46)
Triples — Larry Herndon (9)
Home Runs — Jack Clark (25)
RBI — Jack Clark (98)
Stolen Bases — Bill Madlock (16)

1979
Batting Average — Jack Clark (.273)
Runs — Bill North (87)
Hits — Jack Clark (144)
Doubles — Jack Clark (25)
Triples — Roger Metzger (8)
Home Runs — Mike Ivie (27)
RBI — Mike Ivie (89)
Stolen Bases — Bill North (58)

1980
Batting Average — Jack Clark (.284)
Runs — Jack Clark (77)
Hits — Darrell Evans (147)
Doubles — Darrell Evans (23)
Triples — Larry Herndon (11)
Home Runs — Jack Clark (22)
RBI — Jack Clark (82)
Stolen Bases — Bill North (45)

1981
Batting Average — Milt May (.310)
Runs — Jack Clark (60)
Hits — Lary Herndon (105)
Doubles — Enos Cabell (20)
Triples — Larry Herndon (8)
Home Runs — Jack Clark (17)
RBI — Jack Clark (53)
Stolen Bases — Bill North (26)

1982
Batting Average — Joe Morgan (.289)
Runs — Jack Clark (90)
Hits — Chili Davis (167)
Doubles — Jack Clark (30)
Triples — Chili Davis (6)
Home Runs — Jack Clark (27)
RBI — Jack Clark (103)
Stolen Bases — Chili Davis, Joe Morgan (24)

1983
Batting Average — Jeff Leonard (.279)
Runs — Darrell Evans (94)
Hits — Darrell Evans (145)
Doubles — Darrell Evans (29)
Triples — Jeff Leonard (7)
Home Runs — Darrell Evans (30)
RBI — Jeff Leonard (87)
Stolen Bases — Johnnie LeMaster (39)

1984
Batting Average — Chili Davis (.315)
Runs — Chili Davis (87)
Hits — Chili Davis (157)
Doubles — Bob Brenly (28)
Triples — Chili Davis (6)
Home Runs — Chili Davis, Jeff Leonard (21)
RBI — Jeff Leonard (86)
Stolen Bases — Dan Gladden (31)

1985
Batting Average — Chris Brown (.271)
Runs — Dan Gladden (64)
Hits — Chili Davis (130)
Doubles — Chili Davis (25)
Triples — Dan Gladden (8)
Home Runs — Bob Brenly (19)
RBI — Jeff Leonard (62)
Stolen Bases — Dan Gladden (32)

1986
Batting Average — Chris Brown (.317)
Runs — Robby Thompson (73)
Hits — Robby Thompson (149)
Doubles — Candy Maldonado (31)
Triples — Mike Aldrete, Chris Brown, Chili Davis,
        Jeffrey Leonard, Candy Maldonado,
        Luis Quinones, Robby Thompson (3)
Home Runs — Candy Maldonado (18)
RBI — Candy Maldonado (85)
Stolen Bases — Dan Gladden (27)

1987
Batting Average — Will Clark (.308)
Runs — Will Clark (89)
Hits — Will Clark (163)
Doubles — Will Clark, Jeffrey Leonard (29)
Triples — Will Clark, Robby Thompson,
        Jose Uribe (5)
Home Runs — Will Clark (35)
RBI — Will Clark (91)
Stolen Bases — Chili Davis, Jeffrey Leonard,
        Robby Thompson (16)

1988
Batting Average — Brett Butler (.287)
Runs — **Brett Butler (109)**
Hits — Brett Butler (163)
Doubles — Will Clark (31)
Triples — Brett Butler (9)
Home Runs — Will Clark (29)
RBI — **Will Clark (109)**
Stolen Bases — Brett Butler (43)

1989
Batting Average — Will Clark (.333)
Runs — *Will Clark (104)*
Hits — Will Clark (196)
Doubles — Will Clark (38)
Triples — **Robby Thompson (11)**
Home Runs — **Kevin Mitchell (47)**
RBI — **Kevin Mitchell (125)**
Stolen Bases — Brett Butler (31)

1990
Batting Average — Brett Butler (.309)
Runs — Brett Butler (108)
Hits — *Brett Butler (192)*
Doubles — Matt Williams (27)
Triples — Brett Butler (9)
Home Runs — Kevin Mitchell (35)
RBI — **Matt Williams (122)**
Stolen Bases — Brett Butler (51)

1991
Batting Average — Willie McGee (.312)
Runs — Will Clark (84)
Hits — Will Clark (170)
Doubles — Will Clark (32)
Triples — Will Clark (7)
Home Runs — Matt Williams (34)
RBI — Will Clark (116)
Stolen Bases — Mike Felder (21)

1992
Batting Average — Will Clark (.300)
Runs — Will Clark (69)
Hits — Will Clark (154)
Doubles — Will Clark (40)
Triples — Kirt Manwaring, Matt Williams (5)
Home Runs — Matt Williams (20)
RBI — Will Clark (73)
Stolen Bases — Darren Lewis (28)

1993
Batting Average — Barry Bonds (.336)
Runs — Barry Bonds (129)
Hits — Barry Bonds (181)
Doubles — Barry Bonds (38)
Triples — Darren Lewis (7)
Home Runs — **Barry Bonds (46)**
RBI — **Barry Bonds (123)**
Stolen Bases — Darren Lewis (46)

1994
Batting Average — Barry Bonds (.312)
Runs — Barry Bonds (89)
Hits — Barry Bonds (122)
Doubles — Barry Bonds (18)
Triples — *Darren Lewis (9)*
Home Runs — **Matt Williams (43)**
RBI — Matt Williams (96)
Stolen Bases — Darren Lewis (30)

1995
Batting Average — Barry Bonds (.294)
Runs — Barry Bonds (109)
Hits — Barry Bonds (149)
Doubles — Barry Bonds (30)
Triples — Barry Bonds (7)
Home Runs — Barry Bonds (33)
RBI — Barry Bonds (104)
Stolen Bases — Barry Bonds (31)

1996
Batting Average — Barry Bonds (.308)
Runs — Barry Bonds (122)
Hits — Barry Bonds (159)
Doubles — Barry Bonds (27)
Triples — Marvin Benard (4)
Home Runs — Barry Bonds (42)
RBI — Barry Bonds (129)
Stolen Bases — Barry Bonds (40)

1997
Batting Average — Barry Bonds (.291)
Runs — Barry Bonds (123)
Hits — Barry Bonds (155)
Doubles — Jeff Kent (38)
Triples — Jose Vizcaino (7)
Home Runs — Barry Bonds (40)
RBI — Jeff Kent (121)
Stolen Bases — Barry Bonds (37)

1998
Batting Average — Barry Bonds (.303)
Runs — Barry Bonds (120)
Hits — Barry Bonds (167)
Doubles — Barry Bonds (44)
Triples — Barry Bonds (7)
Home Runs — Barry Bonds (37)
RBI — Jeff Kent (128)
Stolen Bases — Barry Bonds (28)

1999
Batting Average — Jeff Kent (.334)
Runs — Barry Bonds (129)
Hits — Jeff Kent (196)
Doubles—— Jeff Kent (41)
Triples — Marvin Benard (6)
Home Runs—— Barry Bonds (49)
RBI — Jeff Kent (125)
Stolen Bases — Marvin Benard (22)

2000
Batting Average — Jeff Kent (.334)
Runs — Barry Bonds (129)
Hits — Jeff Kent (196)
Doubles—— Jeff Kent (41)
Triples — Marvin Benard (6)
Home Runs—— Barry Bonds (49)
RBI — Jeff Kent (125)
Stolen Bases — Marvin Benard (22)

2001
Batting Average — Barry Bonds (.328)
Runs—— Barry Bonds (129)
Hits — **Rich Aurilia (206)**
Doubles — Jeff Kent (49)
Triples — Jeff Kent (6)
Home Runs — **Barry Bonds (73)**
RBI — Barry Bonds (137)
Stolen Base — Barry Bonds (13)

2002
Batting Average — **Barry Bonds (.370)**
Runs — Barry Bonds (117)
Hits — Jeff Kent (195)
Doubles—— Jeff Kent (42)
Triples — Reggie Sanders (6)
Home Runs — Barry Bonds (46)
RBI — Barry Bonds (110)
Stolen Bases — Reggie Sanders (18)

bold type denotes led National League.

bold italic type denotes tied for N.L. lead

NEW YORK/SAN FRANCISCO GIANTS YEAR-BY-YEAR PITCHING LEADERS

1883
Games — Mickey Welch (54)
Innings Pitched — Mickey Welch (426.0)
Complete Games — Mickey Welch (46)
Shutouts — Mickey Welch (4)
Strikeouts — Mickey Welch (144)
Wins — Mickey Welch (25)
ERA — John Montgomery Ward (2.70)
Saves — none

1884
Games — Mickey Welch (65)
Innings Pitched — Mickey Welch (557.1)
Complete Games — Mickey Welch (62)
Shutouts — Mickey Welch (4)
Strikeouts — Mickey Welch (345)
Wins — Mickey Welch (39)
ERA — Mickey Welch (2.50)
Saves — none

1885
Games — Mickey Welch (56)
Innings Pitched — Mickey Welch (492.0)
Complete Games — Mickey Welch (55)
Shutouts — Tim Keefe, Mickey Welch (7)
Strikeouts — Mickey Welch (258)
Wins — Mickey Welch (44)
ERA — **Tim Keefe (1.58)**
Saves — Mickey Welch (1)

1886
Games — **Tim Keefe (64)**
Innings Pitched — **Tim Keefe (535.0)**
Complete Games — **Tim Keefe (62)**
Shutouts — Tim Keefe (2)
Strikeouts — Tim Keefe (297)
Wins — *Tim Keefe (42)*
ERA — Tim Keefe (2.56)
Saves — Jim Devlin (1)

1887
Games — Tim Keefe (56)
Innings Pitched — Tim Keefe (476.2)
Complete Games — Tim Keefe (54)
Shutouts — Tim Keefe, Mickey Welch (2)
Strikeouts — Tim Keefe (189)
Wins — Tim Keefe (35)
ERA — Tim Keefe (3.12)
Saves — *Mike Tiernan (1)*

1888
Games — Tim Keefe (51)
Innings Pitched — Tim Keefe (434.1)
Complete Games — Tim Keefe (48)
Shutouts — Tim Keefe (8)
Strikeouts — Tim Keefe (335)
Wins — Tim Keefe (35)
ERA — Tim Keefe (1.74)
Saves — Ed Crane (1)

1889
Games — Tim Keefe (47)
Innings Pitched — Mickey Welch (375.0)
Complete Games — Tim Keefe, Mickey Welch (39)
Shutouts — Tim Keefe, Mickey Welch (3)
Strikeouts — Tim Keefe (225)
Wins — Tim Keefe (28)
ERA — Mickey Welch (3.02)
Saves — Mickey Welch (2)

1890
Games — Amos Rusie (67)
Innings Pitched — Amos Rusie (548.2)
Complete Games — Amos Rusie (56)
Shutouts — Amos Rusie (4)
Strikeouts — **Amos Rusie (341)**
Wins — Amos Rusie (29)
ERA — Amos Rusie (2.56)
Saves — Amos Rusie (1)

1891
Games — Amos Rusie (61)
Innings Pitched — Amos Rusie (500.1)
Complete Games — Amos Rusie (52)
Shutouts — **Amos Rusie (6)**
Strikeouts — **Amos Rusie (337)**
Wins — Amos Rusie (33)
ERA — **John Ewing (2.27)**
Saves — Amos Rusie, Jack Sharrott,
        Mickey Welch (1)

1892
Games — Amos Rusie (65)
Innings Pitched — Amos Rusie (541.0)
Complete Games — Amos Rusie (59)
Shutouts — Ed Crane, Amos Rusie (2)
Strikeouts — Amos Rusie (304)
Wins — Amos Rusie (32)
ERA — Amos Rusie (2.84)
Saves — Ed Crane (1)

1893
Games — **Amos Rusie (56)**
Innings Pitched — **Amos Rusie (482.0)**
Complete Games — **Amos Rusie (50)**
Shutouts — *Amos Rusie (4)*
Strikeouts — **Amos Rusie (208)**
Wins — Amos Rusie (33)
ERA — Amos Rusie (3.23)
Saves — *Mark Baldwin (2)*

1894
Games — Amos Rusie (54)
Innings Pitched — Amos Rusie (444.0)
Complete Games — Amos Rusie (45)
Shutouts — *Amos Rusie (3)*
Strikeouts — **Amos Rusie (195)**
Wins — **Amos Rusie (36)**
ERA — **Amos Rusie (2.78)**
Saves — Jouett Meekin (2)

1895
Games — Amos Rusie (49)
Innings Pitched — Amos Rusie (393.1)
Complete Games — Amos Rusie (42)
Shutouts — *Amos Rusie (4)*
Strikeouts — *Amos Rusie (201)*
Wins — Amos Rusie (23)
ERA — Dad Clarke (3.39)
Saves — Dad Clarke (1)

1896
Games — Dad Clarke (48)
Innings Pitched — Dad Clarke (351.0)
Complete Games — Jouett Meekin (34)
Shutouts — Dad Clarke (1)
Strikeouts — Jouett Meekin (110)
Wins — Jouett Meekin (26)
ERA — Jouett Meekin (3.82)
Saves — Dad Clarke, Charlie Gettig (1)

1897
Games — Amos Rusie, Cy Seymour (38)
Innings Pitched — Amos Rusie (322.1)
Complete Games — Amos Rusie (35)
Shutouts — Jouett Meekin, Amos Rusie,
          Cy Seymour (2)
Strikeouts — Cy Seymour (149)
Wins — Amos Rusie (28)
ERA — **Amos Rusie (2.54)**
Saves — Mike Sullivan (2)

1898
Games — Cy Seymour (45)
Innings Pitched — Cy Seymour (356.2)
Complete Games — Cy Seymour (39)
Shutouts — Amos Rusie, Cy Seymour (4)
Strikeouts — **Cy Seymour (239)**
Wins — Cy Seymour (25)
ERA — Amos Rusie (3.03)
Saves — Amos Rusie (1)

1899
Games — Bill Carrick (44)
Innings Pitched — Bill Carrick (361.2)
Complete Games — **Bill Carrick (40)**
Shutouts — Bill Carrick (3)
Strikeouts — Cy Seymour (142)
Wins — Bill Carrick (16)
ERA — Cy Seymour (3.56)
Saves — none

1900
Games — **Bill Carrick (45)**
Innings Pitched — Bill Carrick (341.2)
Complete Games — **Pink Hawley (34)**
Shutouts — Pink Hawley (2)
Strikeouts — Pink Hawley (80)
Wins — Bill Carrick (19)
ERA — Bill Carrick, Pink Hawley (3.53)
Saves — none

1901
Games — *Dummy Taylor (45)*
Innings Pitched — Dummy Taylor (353.1)
Complete Games — Dummy Taylor (37)
Shutouts — Christy Mathewson (5)
Strikeouts — Christy Mathewson (221)
Wins — Christy Mathewson (20)
ERA — Christy Mathewson (2.41)
Saves — Bill Phyle (1)

1902
Games — Christy Mathewson (34)
Innings Pitched — Christy Mathewson (276.2)
Complete Games — Christy Mathewson (29)
Shutouts — *Christy Mathewson (8)*
Strikeouts — Christy Mathewson (159)
Wins — Christy Mathewson (14)
ERA — Joe McGinnity (2.06)
Saves — Tully Sparks (1)

1903
Games — **Joe McGinnity** (55)
Innings Pitched — **Joe McGinnity** (434.0)
Complete Games — **Joe McGinnity** (44)
Shutouts — Christy Mathewson, Joe McGinnity (3)
Strikeouts — **Christy Mathewson** (267)
Wins — **Joe McGinnity** (31)
ERA — Christy Mathewson (2.26)
Saves — *Roscoe Miller (3)*

1904
Games — **Joe McGinnity** (51)
Innings Pitched — **Joe McGinnity** (408.0)
Complete Games — **Joe McGinnity** (38)
Shutouts — **Joe McGinnity** (9)
Strikeouts — **Christy Mathewson** (212)
Wins — **Joe McGinnity** (35)
ERA — **Joe McGinnity** (1.61)
Saves — **Joe McGinnity** (5)

1905
Games — *Joe McGinnity (46)*
Innings Pitched — Christy Mathewson (338.2)
Complete Games — Christy Mathewson (32)
Shutouts — **Christy Mathewson** (8)
Strikeouts — **Christy Mathewson** (206)
Wins — **Christy Mathewson** (31)
ERA — **Christy Mathewson** (1.28)
Saves — **Claude Elliot** (6)

1906
Games — Joe McGinnity (45)
Innings Pitched — **Joe McGinnity** (339.2)
Complete Games — Joe McGinnity (32)
Shutouts — Christy Mathewson (6)
Strikeouts — Red Ames (156)
Wins — **Joe McGinnity** (27)
ERA — Dummy Taylor (2.20)
Saves — **George Ferguson** (7)

1907
Games — Joe McGinnity (47)
Innings Pitched — Christy Mathewson (315.0)
Complete Games — Christy Mathewson (31)
Shutouts — *Christy Mathewson (8)*
Strikeouts — **Christy Mathewson** (178)
Wins — **Christy Mathewson** (24)
ERA — Christy Mathewson (2.00)
Saves — **Joe McGinnity** (4)

1908
Games — **Christy Mathewson** (56)
Innings Pitched — **Christy Mathewson** (390.2)
Complete Games — **Christy Mathewson** (34)
Shutouts — **Christy Mathewson** (11)
Strikeouts — **Christy Mathewson** (259)
Wins — **Christy Mathewson** (37)
ERA — **Christy Mathewson** (1.43)
Saves — *Christy Mathewson, Joe McGinnity (5)*

1909
Games — Bugs Raymond (39)
Innings Pitched — Christy Mathewson (275.1)
Complete Games — Christy Mathewson (26)
Shutouts — Christy Mathewson (8)
Strikeouts — Red Ames (156)
Wins — Christy Mathewson (25)
ERA — **Christy Mathewson** (1.14)
Saves — Doc Crandall (6)

1910
Games — Doc Crandall (42)
Innings Pitched — Christy Mathewson (318.1)
Complete Games — *Christy Mathewson (27)*
Shutouts — Red Ames (3)
Strikeouts — Christy Mathewson (184)
Wins — **Christy Mathewson** (27)
ERA — Christy Mathewson (1.89)
Saves — Doc Crandall (5)

1911
Games — Rube Marquard, Christy Mathewson (45)
Innings Pitched — Christy Mathewson (307.0)
Complete Games — Christy Mathewson (29)
Shutouts — Rube Marquard, Christy Mathewson (5)
Strikeouts — **Rube Marquard** (237)
Wins — Christy Mathewson (26)
ERA — **Christy Mathewson** (1.99)
Saves — Doc Crandall (5)

1912
Games — Rube Marquard, Christy Mathewson (43)
Innings Pitched — Christy Mathewson (310.0)
Complete Games — Christy Mathewson (27)
Shutouts — Jeff Tesreau (3)
Strikeouts — Rube Marquard (175)
Wins — *Rube Marquard (26)*
ERA — **Jeff Tesreau** (1.96)
Saves — Christy Mathewson (4)

1913
Games — Rube Marquard (42)
Innings Pitched — Christy Mathewson (306.0)
Complete Games — Christy Mathewson (25)
Shutouts — Rube Marquard, Christy Mathewson (4)
Strikeouts — Jeff Tesreau (167)
Wins — Christy Mathewson (25)
ERA — **Christy Mathewson (2.06)**
Saves — Doc Crandall (6)

1914
Games — Jeff Tesreau (42)
Innings Pitched — Jeff Tesreau (322.1)
Complete Games — Christy Mathewson (29)
Shutouts — **Jeff Tesreau (8)**
Strikeouts — Jeff Tesreau (189)
Wins — Jeff Tesreau (26)
ERA — Jeff Tesreau (2.37)
Saves — Art Fomme, Rube Marquard,
        Christy Mathewson (2)

1915
Games — Jeff Tesreau (43)
Innings Pitched — Jeff Tesreau (306.0)
Complete Games — Jeff Tesreau (24)
Shutouts — Jeff Tesreau (8)
Strikeouts — Jeff Tesreau (176)
Wins — Jeff Tesreau (19)
ERA — Jeff Tesreau (2.29)
Saves — Jeff Tesreau (3)

1916
Games — Pol Perritt, Jeff Tesreau (40)
Innings Pitched — Jeff Tesreau (268.1)
Complete Games — Jeff Tesreau (23)
Shutouts — Pol Perritt, Jeff Tesreau (5)
Strikeouts — Rube Benton, Pol Perritt (115)
Wins — Pol Perritt (18)
ERA — Pol Perritt (2.62)
Saves — Fred Anderson, Rube Benton,
        Christy Mathewson, Pol Perritt, Jeff Tesreau (2)

1917
Games — Fred Anderson (38)
Innings Pitched — Ferdie Schupp (272.0)
Complete Games — Ferdie Schupp (25)
Shutouts — Ferdie Schupp (6)
Strikeouts — Ferdie Schupp (147)
Wins — Ferdie Schupp (21)
ERA — **Fred Anderson (1.44)**
Saves — **Slim Sallee (4)**

1918
Games — Pol Perritt (35)
Innings Pitched — Pol Perritt (233.0)
Complete Games — Pol Perritt (19)
Shutouts — Pol Perritt (6)
Strikeouts — Pol Perritt (60)
Wins — Pol Perritt (18)
ERA — Slim Sallee (2.25)
Saves — *Fred Anderson (3)*

1919
Games — Jesse Barnes (38)
Innings Pitched — Jesse Barnes (295.2)
Complete Games — Jesse Barnes (23)
Shutouts — Jesse Barnes, Fred Toney (4)
Strikeouts — Jesse Barnes (92)
Wins — **Jesse Barnes (25)**
ERA — Fred Toney (1.84)
Saves — Jean Dubuc, Jesse Winters (3)

1920
Games — Phil Douglas (46)
Innings Pitched — Jesse Barnes (292.2)
Complete Games — Jesse Barnes (23)
Shutouts — Art Nehf (5)
Strikeouts — Fred Toney (81)
Wins — Art Nehf, Fred Toney (21)
ERA — Jesse Barnes (2.64)
Saves — Rube Benton, Phil Douglas,
        Pol Perritt (2)

1921
Games — Jesse Barnes, Fred Toney (42)
Innings Pitched — Art Nehf (260.2)
Complete Games — Art Nehf (18)
Shutouts — *Phil Douglas (3)*
Strikeouts — Art Nehf (67)
Wins — Art Nehf (20)
ERA — Jesse Barnes (3.10)
Saves — Jesse Barnes (6)

1922
Games — Rosy Ryan (46)
Innings Pitched — Art Nehf (268.1)
Complete Games — Art Nehf (20)
Shutouts — Art Nehf (3)
Strikeouts — Rosy Ryan (75)
Wins — Art Nehf (19)
ERA — **Phil Douglas (2.63)**
Saves — **Claude Jonnard (5)**

1923
Games — *Claude Jonnard, Rosy Ryan (45)*
Innings Pitched — Hugh McQuillan (229.2)
Complete Games — Hugh McQuillan (15)
Shutouts — Hugh McQuillan (5)
Strikeouts — Jack Bentley (80)
Wins — Rosy Ryan, Jack Scott (16)
ERA — Hugh McQuillan (3.40)
Saves — **Claude Jonnard (5)**

1924
Games — Rosy Ryan (37)
Innings Pitched — Virgil Barnes (229.1)
Complete Games — Virgil Barnes (15)
Shutouts — Virgil Barnes, Jack Bentley,
        Hugh McQuillan, Mule Watson (1)
Strikeouts — Art Nehf (72)
Wins — Virgil Barnes, Jack Bentley (16)
ERA — Hugh McQuillan (2.69)
Saves — Claude Jonnard, Rosy Ryan (5)

1925
Games — Jack Scott (36)
Innings Pitched — Jack Scott (239.2)
Complete Games — Jack Scott (18)
Shutouts — Jack Scott (2)
Strikeouts — Jack Scott (87)
Wins — Virgil Barnes (15)
ERA — Jack Scott (3.15)
Saves — Jack Scott (3)

1926
Games — **Jack Scott (50)**
Innings Pitched — Jack Scott (226.0)
Complete Games — Jack Scott (13)
Shutouts — Virgil Barnes (2)
Strikeouts — Jack Scott (82)
Wins — Freddie Fitzsimmons (14)
ERA — Freddie Fitzsimmons (2.88)
Saves — **Chick Davies (6)**

1927
Games — Dutch Henry (45)
Innings Pitched — Burleigh Grimes (259.2)
Complete Games — Burleigh Grimes (15)
Shutouts — Virgil Barnes, Burleigh Grimes (2)
Strikeouts — Burleigh Grimes (102)
Wins — Burleigh Grimes (19)
ERA — Burleigh Grimes (3.54)
Saves — Dutch Henry (4)

1928
Games — Larry Benton (42)
Innings Pitched — Larry Benton (310.1)
Complete Games — *Larry Benton (28)*
Shutouts — Larry Benton, Joe Genewich (2)
Strikeouts — Larry Benton (90)
Wins — *Larry Benton (25)*
ERA — Larry Benton (2.73)
Saves — Larry Benton (4)

1929
Games — Larry Benton, Carl Hubbell (39)
Innings Pitched — Carl Hubbell (268.0)
Complete Games — Carl Hubbell (19)
Shutouts — Freddie Fitzsimmons (4)
Strikeouts — Carl Hubbell (106)
Wins — Carl Hubbell (18)
ERA — **Bill Walker (3.09)**
Saves — Carl Mays (4)

1930
Games — Hub Pruett (45)
Innings Pitched — Bill Walker (245.1)
Complete Games — Freddie Fitzsimmons,
        Carl Hubbell (17)
Shutouts — Carl Hubbell (3)
Strikeouts — Carl Hubbell (117)
Wins — Freddie Fitzsimmons (19)
ERA — Carl Hubbell (3.87)
Saves — Joe Heving (6)

1931
Games — Bill Walker (37)
Innings Pitched — Freddie Fitzsimmons (253.2)
Complete Games — Carl Hubbell (21)
Shutouts — **Bill Walker (6)**
Strikeouts — Carl Hubbell (155)
Wins — Freddie Fitzsimmons (18)
ERA — *Bill Walker (2.26)*
Saves — Joe Heving, Carl Hubbell, Bill Walker (3)

1932
Games — Sam Gibson (41)
Innings Pitched — Carl Hubbell (284.0)
Complete Games — Carl Hubbell (22)
Shutouts — Sam Gibson, Jim Mooney,
        Hal Schumacher (1)
Strikeouts — Carl Hubbell (137)
Wins — Carl Hubbell (18)
ERA — Carl Hubbell (2.50)
Saves — Dolph Luque (5)

1933
Games — Carl Hubbell (45)
Innings Pitched — **Carl Hubbell (308.2)**
Complete Games — Carl Hubbell (22)
Shutouts — **Carl Hubbell (10)**
Strikeouts — Carl Hubbell (156)
Wins — **Carl Hubbell (23)**
ERA — **Carl Hubbell (1.66)**
Saves — Hi Bell, Carl Hubbell (5)

1934
Games — Carl Hubbell (49)
Innings Pitched — Carl Hubbell (313.0)
Complete Games — **Carl Hubbell (25)**
Shutouts — Carl Hubbell (5)
Strikeouts — Carl Hubbell (118)
Wins — Hal Schumacher (23)
ERA — **Carl Hubbell (2.30)**
Saves — **Carl Hubbell (8)**

1935
Games — Carl Hubbell (42)
Innings Pitched — Carl Hubbell (302.2)
Complete Games — Carl Hubbell (24)
Shutouts — *Freddie Fitzsimmons (4)*
Strikeouts — Carl Hubbell (150)
Wins — Carl Hubbell (23)
ERA — Hal Schumacher (2.89)
Saves — Al Smith, Allyn Stout (5)

1936
Games — Frank Gabler, Al Smith (43)
Innings Pitched — Carl Hubbell (304.0)
Complete Games — Carl Hubbell (25)
Shutouts — **Al Smith (4)**
Strikeouts — Carl Hubbell (123)
Wins — **Carl Hubbell (26)**
ERA — **Carl Hubbell (2.31)**
Saves — Dick Coffman (7)

1937
Games — Cliff Melton (46)
Innings Pitched — Carl Hubbell (261.2)
Complete Games — Carl Hubbell (18)
Shutouts — Carl Hubbell (4)
Strikeouts — **Carl Hubbell (159)**
Wins — Carl Hubbell (22)
ERA — Cliff Melton (2.61)
Saves — *Cliff Melton (7)*

1938
Games — *Dick Coffman (51)*
Innings Pitched — Cliff Melton (243.0)
Complete Games — Harry Gumbert (14)
Shutouts — Hal Schumacher (4)
Strikeouts — Carl Hubbell (104)
Wins — Harry Gumbert (15)
ERA — Carl Hubbell (3.07)
Saves — **Dick Coffman (12)**

1939
Games — Cliff Melton (41)
Innings Pitched — Harry Gumbert (243.2)
Complete Games — Harry Gumbert (14)
Shutouts — Harry Gumbert, Cliff Melton (2)
Strikeouts — Cliff Melton (95)
Wins — Harry Gumbert (18)
ERA — Carl Hubbell (2.75)
Saves — Jumbo Brown (7)

1940
Games — Jumbo Brown (41)
Innings Pitched — Harry Gumbert (237.0)
Complete Games — Harry Gumbert (14)
Shutouts — Bill Lohrman (4)
Strikeouts — Hal Schumacher (123)
Wins — Hal Schumacher (13)
ERA — Hal Schumacher (3.25)
Saves — *Jumbo Brown (7)*

1941
Games — Cliff Melton (42)
Innings Pitched — Hal Schumacher (206.0)
Complete Games — Hal Schumacher (12)
Shutouts — Cliff Melton, Hal Schumacher (3)
Strikeouts — Cliff Melton (100)
Wins — Hal Schumacher (12)
ERA — Cliff Melton (3.01)
Saves — **Jumbo Brown (8)**

1942
Games — **Ace Adams (61)**
Innings Pitched — Hal Schumacher (216.0)
Complete Games — Bob Carpenter, Bill Lohrman,
    Cliff Melton, Hal Schumahcer (12)
Shutouts — Hal Schumacher (3)
Strikeouts — Carl Hubbell, Cliff Melton (61)
Wins — Bill Lohrman (13)
ERA — Bill Lohrman (2.56)
Saves — Ace Adams (11)

1943
Games — **Ace Adams (70)**
Innings Pitched — Cliff Melton (186.1)
Complete Games — Cliff Melton (6)
Shutouts — Cliff Melton, Van Mungo (2)
Strikeouts — Ken Chase (86)
Wins — Ace Adams (11)
ERA — Cliff Melton (3.19)
Saves — Ace Adams (9)

1944
Games — **Ace Adams (65)**
Innings Pitched — **Bill Voiselle (312.2)**
Complete Games — Bill Voiselle (25)
Shutouts — Johnny Allen, Harry Feldman,
        Rube Fischer, Bill Voiselle (1)
Strikeouts — **Bill Voiselle (161)**
Wins — Bill Voiselle (21)
ERA — Bill Voiselle (3.02)
Saves — **Ace Adams (13)**

1945
Games — Ace Adams (65)
Innings Pitched — Bill Voiselle (232.1)
Complete Games — Bill Voiselle (14)
Shutouts — Bill Voiselle (4)
Strikeouts — Bill Voiselle (115)
Wins — Van Mungo, Bill Voiselle (14)
ERA — Van Mungo (3.20)
Saves — *Ace Adams (15)*

1946
Games — **Ken Trinkle (48)**
Innings Pitched — Dave Koslo (265.1)
Complete Games — Dave Koslo (17)
Shutouts — Dave Koslo (3)
Strikeouts — Dave Koslo (121)
Wins — Dave Koslo (14)
ERA — Monte Kenndey (3.42)
Saves — Junior Thompson (4)

1947
Games — Ken Trinkle (62)
Innings Pitched — Larry Jansen (248.0)
Complete Games — Larry Jansen (20)
Shutouts — Dave Koslo (3)
Strikeouts — Larry Jansen (104)
Wins — Larry Jansen (21)
ERA — Larry Jansen (3.16)
Saves — Ken Trinkle (10)

1948
Games — Sheldon Jones (55)
Innings Pitched — Larry Jansen (277.0)
Complete Games — Larry Jansen (15)
Shutouts — Larry Jansen (4)
Strikeouts — Larry Jansen (126)
Wins — Larry Jansen (18)
ERA — Sheldon Jones (3.35)
Saves — Ken Trinkle (7)

1949
Games — Hank Behrman (43)
Innings Pitched — Larry Jansen (259.2)
Complete Games — Larry Jansen (17)
Shutouts — Monte Kennedy (4)
Strikeouts — Larry Jansen (113)
Wins — Larry Jansen, Sheldon Jones (15)
ERA — **Dave Koslo (2.50)**
Saves — Dave Koslo (4)

1950
Games — Sal Maglie (47)
Innings Pitched — Larry Jansen (275.0)
Complete Games — Larry Jansen (21)
Shutouts — *Jim Hearn, Larry Jansen,*
        Sal Maglie (5)
Strikeouts — Larry Jansen (161)
Wins — Larry Jansen (19)
ERA — **Jim Hearn (2.49)**
Saves — Andy Hansen, Larry Jansen, Dave Koslo (3)

1951
Games — George Spencer (57)
Innings Pitched — Sal Maglie (298.0)
Complete Games — Sal Maglie (22)
Shutouts — Larry Jansen, Sal Maglie (3)
Strikeouts — Sal Maglie (146)
Wins — *Larry Jansen, Sal Maglie (23)*
ERA — Sal Maglie (2.93)
Saves — George Spencer (6)

1952
Games — **Hoyt Wilhelm (71)**
Innings Pitched — Jim Hearn (223.2)
Complete Games — Sal Maglie (12)
Shutouts — Sal Maglie (5)
Strikeouts — Sal Maglie (112)
Wins — Sal Maglie (18)
ERA — **Hoyt Wilhelm (2.43)**
Saves — Hoyt Wilhelm (11)

1953
Games — **Hoyt Wilhelm (68)**
Innings Pitched — Ruben Gomez (204.0)
Complete Games — Ruben Gomez (13)
Shutouts — Ruben Gomez, Sal Maglie (3)
Strikeouts — Ruben Gomez (113)
Wins — Ruben Gomez (13)
ERA — Ruben Gomez (3.40)
Saves — Hoyt Wilhelm (15)

1954
Games — Hoyt Wilhelm (57)
Innings Pitched — Johnny Antonelli (258.2)
Complete Games — Johnny Antonell (18)
Shutouts — **Johnny Antonelli (6)**
Strikeouts — Johnny Antonelli (152)
Wins — Johnny Antonelli (21)
ERA — **Johnny Antonelli (2.30)**
Saves — Marv Grissom (19)

1955
Games — Hoyt Wilhelm (59)
Innings Pitched — Johnny Antonelli (235.1)
Complete Games — Johnny Antonelli (14)
Shutouts — Ruben Gomez (3)
Strikeouts — Johnny Antonelli (143)
Wins — Johnny Antonelli, Jim Hearn (14)
ERA — Johnny Antonelli (3.33)
Saves — Marv Grissom (8)

1956
Games — Hoyt Wilhelm (64)
Innings Pitched — Johnny Antonelli (258.1)
Complete Games — Johnny Antonelli (15)
Shutouts — Johnny Antonelli (5)
Strikeouts — Johnny Antonelli (145)
Wins — Johnny Antonelli (20)
ERA — Johnny Antonelli (2.86)
Saves — Hoyt Wilhelm (8)

1957
Games — Marv Grissom, Al Worthington (55)
Innings Pitched — Ruebn Gomez (238.1)
Complete Games — Ruben Gomez (16)
Shutouts — Johnny Antonelli (3)
Strikeouts — Johnny Antonelli (114)
Wins — Ruben Gomez (15)
ERA — Curt Barclay (3.44)
Saves — Marv Grissom (14)

1958
Games — Al Worthington (54)
Innings Pitched — Johnny Antonelli (241.2)
Complete Games — Johnny Antonelli (13)
Shutouts — Mike McCormick (2)
Strikeouts — Johnny Antonelli (143)
Wins — Johnny Antonelli (16)
ERA — **Stu Miller (2.47)**
Saves — Marv Grissom (10)

1959
Games — Stu Miller (59)
Innings Pitched — Johnny Antonelli (282.0)
Complete Games — Johnny Antonelli (17)
Shutouts — *Johnny Antonelli, Sam Jones (4)*
Strikeouts — Sam Jones (209)
Wins — *Sam Jones (21)*
ERA — **Sam Jones (2.83)**
Saves — Stu Miller (8)

1960
Games — Stu Miller (47)
Innings Pitched — Mike McCormick (253.0)
Complete Games — Mike McCormick (15)
Shutouts — **Jack Sanford (6)**
Strikeouts — Sam Jones (190)
Wins — Sam Jones (18)
ERA — **Mike McCormick (2.70)**
Saves — Johnny Antonelli (11)

1961
Games — Stu Miller (63)
Innings Pitched — Mike McCormick (250.0)
Complete Games — Mike McCormick (13)
Shutouts — Juan Marichal, Mike McCormick (3)
Strikeouts — Mike McCormick (163)
Wins — Stu Miller (14)
ERA — Mike McCormick (3.20)
Saves — *Stu Miller (17)*

1962
Games — Stu Miller (59)
Innings Pitched — Billy O'Dell (280.2)
Complete Games — Billy O'Dell (20)
Shutouts — Juan Marichal (3)
Strikeouts — Billy O'Dell (195)
Wins — Jack Sanford (24)
ERA — Juan Marichal (3.36)
Saves — Stu Miller (19)

1963
Games — Bobby Bolin (47)
Innings Pitched — **Juan Marichal (321.1)**
Complete Games — Juan Marichal (18)
Shutouts — Juan Marichal (5)
Strikeouts — Juan Marichal (248)
Wins — *Juan Marichal (25)*
ERA — Juan Marichal (2.41)
Saves — Billy Pierce (8)

1964
Games — Bob Shaw (61)
Innings Pitched — Juan Marichal (269.0)
Complete Games — **Juan Marichal (22)**
Shutouts — Juan Marichal (4)
Strikeouts — Juan Marichal (206)
Wins — Juan Marichal (21)
ERA — Juan Marichal (2.48)
Saves — Bob Shaw (11)

1965
Games — Frank Linzy (57)
Innings Pitched — Juan Marichal (295.1)
Complete Games — Juan Marichal (24)
Shutouts — **Juan Marichal (10)**
Strikeouts — Juan Marichal (240)
Wins — Juan Marichal (22)
ERA — Juan Marichal (2.13)
Saves — Frank Linzy (21)

1966
Games — Lindy McDaniel (64)
Innings Pitched — Juan Marichal (307.1)
Complete Games — Juan Marichal (25)
Shutouts — Bobby Bolin, Juan Marichal (4)
Strikeouts — Juan Marichal (222)
Wins — Juan Marichal (25)
ERA — Juan Marichal (2.23)
Saves — Frank Linzy (16)

1967
Games — Frank Linzy (57)
Innings Pitched — Gaylord Perry (2.93)
Complete Games — Juan Marichal,
        Gaylord Perry (18)
Shutouts — Mike McCormick (5)
Strikeouts — Gaylord Perry (230)
Wins — **Mike McCormick (22)**
ERA — Gaylord Perry (2.61)
Saves — Frank Linzy (17)

1968
Games — Frank Linzy (57)
Innings Pitched — **Juan Marichal (326.0)**
Complete Games — **Juan Marichal (30)**
Shutouts — Ray Sadecki (6)
Strikeouts — Juan Marichal (218)
Wins — **Juan Marichal (26)**
ERA — Bobby Bolin (1.99)
Saves — Frank Linzy (12)

1969
Games — Frank Linzy (58)
Innings Pitched — **Gaylord Perry (325.1)**
Complete Games — Juan Marichal (27)
Shutouts — **Juan Marichal (8)**
Strikeouts — Gaylord Perry (233)
Wins — Juan Marichal (21)
ERA — **Juan Marichal (2.10)**
Saves — Frank Linzy (11)

1970
Games — Don McMahon (61)
Innings Pitched — **Gaylord Perry (328.2)**
Complete Games — Gaylord Perry (23)
Shutouts — **Gaylord Perry (5)**
Strikeouts — Gaylord Perry (214)
Wins — **Gaylord Perry (23)**
ERA — Gaylord Perry (3.20)
Saves — Don McMahon (19)

1971
Games — Jerry Johnson (67)
Innings Pitched — Gaylord Perry (280.0)
Complete Games — Juan Marichal (18)
Shutouts — Juan Marichal (4)
Strikeouts — Juan Marichal (159)
Wins — Juan Marichal (18)
ERA — Gaylord Perry (2.76)
Saves — Jerry Johnson (18)

1972
Games — Jerry Johnson (48)
Innings Pitched — Ron Bryant (214.0)
Complete Games — Ron Bryant (11)
Shutouts — Ron Bryant (4)
Strikeouts — Sam McDowell (122)
Wins — Ron Bryant (14)
ERA — Jim Barr (2.87)
Saves — Jerry Johnson (8)

1973
Games — Elias Sosa (71)
Innings Pitched — Ron Bryant (270.0)
Complete Games — Juan Marichal (9)
Shutouts — Jim Barr (3)
Strikeouts — Ron Bryant (143)
Wins — **Ron Bryant (24)**
ERA — Ron Bryant (3.53)
Saves — Elias Sosa (18)

1974
Games — Elias Sosa (68)
Innings Pitched — Jim Barr (239.2)
Complete Games — Jim Barr (11)
Shutouts — Jim Barr (5)
Strikeouts — John D'Acquisto (167)
Wins — Mike Caldwell (14)
ERA — Jim Barr (2.74)
Saves — Randy Moffitt (15)

1975
Games — Gary Lavelle (65)
Innings Pitched — Jim Barr (244.0)
Complete Games — Jim Barr (12)
Shutouts — John Montefusco (4)
Strikeouts — John Montefusco (215)
Wins — John Montefusco (15)
ERA — John Montefusco (2.88)
Saves — Randy Moffitt (11)

1976
Games — Gary Lavelle (65)
Innings Pitched — John Montefusco (253.1)
Complete Games — John Montefusco (11)
Shutouts — *John Montefusco (6)*
Strikeouts — John Montefusco (172)
Wins — John Montefusco (16)
ERA — John Montefusco (2.85)
Saves — Randy Moffitt (14)

1977
Games — Gary Lavelle (73)
Innings Pitched — Ed Halicki (257.2)
Complete Games — Ed Halicki (7)
Shutouts — Jim Barr, Ed Halicki, Bob Knepper (2)
Strikeouts — Ed Halicki (168)
Wins — Ed Halicki (16)
ERA — Ed Halicki (3.32)
Saves — Gary Lavelle (20)

1978
Games — Randy Moffitt (70)
Innings Pitched — Bob Knepper (260.0)
Complete Games — Bob Knepper (16)
Shutouts — **Bob Knepper (6)**
Strikeouts — John Montefusco (177)
Wins — Vida Blue (18)
ERA — Bob Knepper (2.83)
Saves — Gary Lavelle (14)

1979
Games — Gary Lavelle (70)
Innings Pitched — Vida Blue (237.0)
Complete Games — Vida Blue (10)
Shutouts — John Curtis, Bob Knepper (2)
Strikeouts — Vida Blue (138)
Wins — Vida Blue (14)
ERA — Bob Knepper (4.64)
Saves — Gary Lavelle (20)

1980
Games — Greg Minton (68)
Innings Pitched — Vida Blue (224.0)
Complete Games — Vida Blue (10)
Shutouts — Vida Blue (3)
Strikeouts — Vida Blue (129)
Wins — Vida Blue (14)
ERA — Vida Blue (2.97)
Saves — Greg Minton (19)

1981
Games — Greg Minton (55)
Innings Pitched — Doyle Alexander (152.1)
Complete Games — Tom Griffin (3)
Shutouts — Doyle Alexander, Tom Griffin,
    Ed Whitson (1)
Strikeouts — Tom Griffin (83)
Wins — Doyle Alexander (11)
ERA — Vida Blue (2.45)
Saves — Greg Minton (21)

1982
Games — Greg Minton (78)
Innings Pitched — Bill Laskey (189.1)
Complete Games — Bill Laskey (7)
Shutouts — Jim Barr, Atlee Hammaker,
    Bill Laskey (1)
Strikeouts — Rich Gale, Atlee Hammaker (102)
Wins — Bill Laskey (13)
ERA — Bill Laskey (3.14)
Saves — Greg Minton (30)

1983
Games — Greg Minton (73)
Innings Pitched — Fred Breining (202.2)
Complete Games — Atlee Hammaker (8)
Shutouts — Atlee Hammaker (3)
Strikeouts — Mike Krukow (136)
Wins — Bill Laskey (13)
ERA — **Atlee Hammaker (2.25)**
Saves — Greg Minton (22)

1984
Games — Gary Lavelle (77)
Innings Pitched — Bill Laskey (207.2)
Complete Games — Mike Krukow (3)
Shutouts — Mike Krukow, Jeff Robinson,
    Frank Williams (1)
Strikeouts — Mike Krukow (141)
Wins — Mike Krukow (11)
ERA — Bill Laskey (4.33)
Saves — Greg Minton (19)

1985
Games — Mark Davis (77)
Innings Pitched — Dave LaPoint (206.2)
Complete Games — Mike Krukow (6)
Shutouts — Atlee Hammaker, Mike Krukow,
    Dave LaPoint, Roger Mason (1)
Strikeouts — Mike Krukow (150)
Wins — Scott Garrelts (9)
ERA — Mike Krukow (3.38)
Saves — Scott Garrelts (13)

1986
Games — Mark Davis (67)
Innings Pitched — Mike Krukow (245.0)
Complete Games — Mike Kurkow (10)
Shutouts — Mike Krukow (2)
Strikeouts — Mike Krukow (178)
Wins — Mike Krukow (20)
ERA — Mike Krukow (3.05)
Saves — Scott Garrelts (10)

1987
Games — Scott Garrelts (64)
Innings Pitched — Kelly Downs (186.0)
Complete Games — Kelly Downs,
    Dave Dravecky (4)
Shutouts — Kelly Downs, Dave Dravecky (3)
Strikeouts — Kelly Downs (137)
Wins — Mike LaCoss (13)
ERA — Atlee Hammaker (3.58)
Saves — Scott Garrelts (12)

1988
Games — Scott Garrelts (65)
Innings Pitched — Rick Reuschel (245.0)
Complete Games — Rick Reuschel (7)
Shutouts — Kelly Downs (3)
Strikeouts — Don Robinson (122)
Wins — Rick Reuschel (19)
ERA — Don Robinson (2.45)
Saves — Scott Garrelts (13)

1989
Games — Craig Lefferts (70)
Innings Pitched — Rick Reuschel (208.1)
Complete Games — Don Robinson (5)
Shutouts — Scott Garrelts, Bob Knepper,
    Don Robinson (1)
Strikeouts — Scott Garrelts (119)
Wins — Rick Reuschel (17)
ERA — **Scott Garrelts (2.28)**
Saves — Craig Lefferts (20)

1990
Games — Steve Bedrosian (68)
Innings Pitched — John Burkett (204.0)
Complete Games — Scott Garrelts,
    Don Robinson (4)
Shutouts — Scott Garrelts, Trevor Wilson (2)
Strikeouts — John Burkett (118)
Wins — John Burkett (14)
ERA — John Burkett (3.79)
Saves — Jeff Brantley (19)

1991
Games — Jeff Brantley (67)
Innings Pitched — Bud Black (214.1)
Complete Games — Bud Black, John Burkett (3)
Shutouts — Bud Black (3)
Strikeouts — Trevor Wilson (139)
Wins — Trevor Wilson (13)
ERA — Trevor Wilson (3.56)
Saves — Dave Righetti (24)

1992
Games — Mike Jackson (67)
Innings Pitched — John Burkett (189.2)
Complete Games — John Burkett, Bill Swift (3)
Shutouts — Bill Swift (2)
Strikeouts — John Burkett (107)
Wins — John Burkett (13)
ERA — **Bill Swift (2.08)**
Saves — Rod Beck (17)

1993
Games — **Mike Jackson (81)**
Innings Pitched — Bill Swift (232.2)
Complete Games — John Burkett (2)
Shutouts — John Burkett, Bill Swift (1)
Strikeouts — Bill Swift (157)
Wins — *John Burkett (22)*
ERA — Bill Swift (2.82)
Saves — Rod Beck (48)

1994
Games — Dave Burba (57)
Innings Pitched — John Burkett (159.1)
Complete Games — Mark Portugal,
          Salomon Torres (1)
Shutouts — none
Strikeouts — Mark Portugal (87)
Wins — Mark Portugal (10)
ERA — Bill Swift (3.38)
Saves — Rod Beck (28)

1995
Games — Rod Beck (60)
Innings Pitched — Mark Leiter (195.2)
Complete Games — Mark Leiter (7)
Shutouts — Mark Leiter (1)
Strikeouts — Mark Leiter (129)
Wins — Mark Leiter (10)
ERA — Mark Leiter (3.82)
Saves — Rod Beck (33)

1996
Games — Mark Dewey (78)
Innings Pitched — Allen Watson (185.2)
Complete Games — Mark Gardner (4)
Shutouts — Mark Gardner (1)
Strikeouts — Mark Gardner (145)
Wins — Mark Gardner (12)
ERA — Mark Gardner (4.42)
Saves — Rod Beck (35)

1997
Games — **Julian Tavarez (89)**
Innings Pitched — Shawn Estes (201.0)
Complete Games — Shawn Estes (3)
Shutouts — Shawn Estes (2)
Strikeouts — Shawn Estes (181)
Wins — Shawn Estes (19)
ERA — Shawn Estes (3.18)
Saves — Rod Beck (37)

1998
Games — Robb Nen (78)
Innings Pitched — Mark Gardner (212.0)
Complete Games — Mark Gardner (4)
Shutouts — Mark Gardner (2)
Strikeouts — Mark Gardner (151)
Wins — Kirk Rueter (16)
ERA — Mark Gardner (4.33)
Saves — Robb Nen (40)

1999
Games — Robb Nen (72)
Innings Pitched — Russ Ortiz (207.2)
Complete Games — Russ Ortiz (3)
Shutouts — Shawn Estes (1)
Strikeouts — Russ Ortiz (164)
Wins — Russ Ortiz (18)
ERA — Russ Ortiz (3.81)
Saves — Robb Nen (37)

2000
Games — Felix Rodriguez (76)
Innings Pitched — Livan Hernandez (240)
Complete Games — Livan Hernandez (5)
Shutouts — Shawn Estes/Livan Hernandez (2)
Strikeouts — Russ Ortiz (167)
Wins — Shawn Estes (15)
ERA — Livan Hernandez (3.75)
Saves — Robb Nen (41)

2001
Games — Felix Rodriguez (80)
Innings Pitched — Livan Hernandez (226.2)
Complete Games — Livan Hernandez (2)
Shutouts — Russ Ortiz (1)
Strikeouts — Russ Ortiz (169)
Wins — Russ Ortiz (17)
ERA—— Russ Ortiz (3.29)
Saves—— Robb Nen (45)

2002
Games — Tim Worrell (80)
Innings Pitched — Livan Hernandez (216)
Complete Games — Livan Hernandez (5)
Shutouts — Livan Hernandez (3)
Strikeouts — Jason Schmidt (196)
Wins — Russ Ortiz/Kirk Rueter (14)
ERA—— Kirk Rueter (3.23)
Saves — Robb Nen (43)

bold type denotes led National League.
bold italic type denotes tied for N.L. lead.

NEW YORK/SAN FRANCISCO GIANTS BALLPARKS

Name	First Game	Last Game	Record
First Polo Grounds (110th Street and Sixth Avenue)	May 1, 1883 New York 7, Boston 5	Oct. 13, 1888 Indianapolis 6, New York 4	234-113 (.674)
Oakland Park (Jersey City)	April 24, 1889 Boston 8, New York 7	April 25, 1889 New York 11, Boston 10	1-1 (.500)
St. George Grounds (Staten Island)	April 29, 1889 New York 4, Washington 2	June 14, 1889 New York 14, Philadelphia 4	17-6 (.739)
Second Polo Gounds (155th Street and Eighth Avenue)	July 8, 1889 New York 7, Pittsburgh 5	Sept. 10, 1890 Boston 8, New York 5	66-35 (.653)
Third Polo Grounds (157th Street and Eighth Avenue)	April 22, 1891 Boston 4, New York 3	Sept. 29, 1957 Pittsburgh 9, New York 1	2,963-2,021 (.595)
Hilltop Park (168th Street and Broadway)	April 15, 1911 New York 6, Brooklyn 3	May 30, 1911 New York 3, Brooklyn 0 (2)	20-8 (.714)
Seals Stadium (15th and Bryant)	April 15, 1958 San Francisco 8, Los Angeles 0	Sept. 20, 1959 Los Angeles 8, San Francisco 2	86-68 (.558)
Candlestick Park/ 3Com Park at Candlestick Point (San Francisco)	April 12, 1960 San Francisco 3, St. Louis 1	Sept. 30, 1999 Los Angeles 9, San Francisco 4	1,776-1,398 (.560)
Pacific Bell Park (Third and King)	April 11,2000 Los Angeles 6, San Francisco 5	— —	154-69 (.634)
Totals			5,317-3,739 (.587)

NEW YORK/SAN FRANCISCO GIANTS RECORD BY DECADE

Decade	Won	Lost	Percentage	First-Place Finishes
1880s	503	316	.614	1888, 1889
1890s	711	660	.519	—
1900s	823	645	.561	1904, 1905
1910s	889	597	.598	1911, 1912, 1913, 1917
1920s	890	639	.582	1921, 1922, 1923, 1924
1930s	868	657	.569	1933, 1936, 1937
1940s	724	808	.473	—
1950s	822	721	.533	1951, 1954
1960s	902	704	.562	1962
1970s	794	818	.493	1971
1980s	773	795	.493	1987, 1989
1990s	790	766	.508	1997
2000s	282	202	.581	2000*

*Won pennant as wild card in 2002

Totals	9,771	8,329	.540	23

CAREER INDIVIDUAL BATTING AND PITCHING STATISTICS (WITH GIANTS)

. . . .

A

Name	Born	Died	B	T	Yrs	Seasons	AVG	G	AB	R	H	2B	3B	HR	RBI	TB	BB	SO	SB	CS	SLG	OBP	Games By Position
Glenn Adams	10/4/47		L	R	2	1975-76	.274	130	164	12	45	6	1	4	18	65	12	37	2	0	.396	.326	OF-31
Rick Adams	1/21/59		R	R	1	1985	.190	54	121	12	23	-	2	-	10	34	5	23	0	0	.281	.228	SS-25, 3B-16, 2B-6
Eddie Ainsmith	2/4/1892	9/6/81	R	R	1	1924	.600	10	5	0	3	0	0	0	0	3	0	0	0	-	.600	.600	C-9
Mike Aldrete	1/29/61		L	L	3	1986-88	.285	349	962	121	274	51	5	14	126	377	132	149	13	8	.392	.370	OF-225, 1B-80
Gary Alexander	3/27/53		R	R	3	1975-77	.251	77	195	30	49	5	3	7	27	81	31	51	4	1	.415	.355	C-58, OF-1
Andy Allanson	12/22/61		R	R	1	1993	.167	13	24	3	4	1	0	0	2	5	1	2	0	0	.208	.200	C-8, 1B-2
Ethan Allen	1/1/04	9/15/93	R	R	3	1930-32	.296	224	639	119	189	33	6	13	81	273	28	50	11	-	.427	.328	OF-163
Felipe Alou	5/12/35		R	R	6	1958-63	.286	719	2292	337	655	119	19	85	325	1067	138	308	51	20	.466	.328	OF-659
Jesus Alou	3/24/42		R	R	6	1963-68	.279	633	2242	243	626	74	19	18	174	780	58	162	21	28	.348	.301	OF-584
Matty Alou	12/22/38		L	L	6	1960-65	.260	453	1048	136	272	32	7	12	72	354	59	101	21	9	.338	.304	OF-319, P-1
Joey Amalfitano	1/23/34		R	R	5	1954-55, 60-61, 63	.249	314	876	132	218	30	8	4	58	276	84	114	11	13	.315	.316	2B-166, 3B-82, SS-8, OF-1
Dave Anderson	8/1/60		R	R	2	1990-91	.279	160	326	38	91	10	3	3	19	116	15	55	3	6	.356	.311	SS-92, 1B-19, 2B-19, 3B-13
Rob Andrews	12/11/52		R	R	3	1977-79	.253	281	767	103	194	17	6	3	49	232	84	60	14	8	.302	.324	2B-230, 3B-3, SS-1
Jack Aragon	11/20/15	4/4/88	R	R	1	1941	-	1	0	0	0	0	0	0	0	0	0	0	0	-	-	-	PR
Chris Arnold	11/6/47		R	R	6	1971-76	.237	273	435	47	103	12	5	4	51	137	42	76	1	2	.315	.303	2B-54, 3B-29, C-9, SS-6, OF-4, 1B-1
Morrie Arnovich	11/16/10	7/20/59	R	R	2	1941, 46	.276	86	210	25	58	8	3	2	22	78	23	14	2	0+	.371	.348	OF-62
Rich Aurilia	9/2/71		R	R	8	1995-2002	.279	864	3093	426	862	164	13	113	415	1373	246	465	14	15	.444	.332	SS-819, 2B-11

B

Name	Born	Died	B	T	Yrs	Seasons	AVG	G	AB	R	H	2B	3B	HR	RBI	TB	BB	SO	SB	CS	SLG	OBP	Games By Position
Charlie Babb	2/20/1873	3/20/54	B	R	1	1903	.248	121	424	68	105	15	8	0	46	136	45	-	22	1	.321	.350	SS-113, 3B-8
Charlie Babington	5/4/1895	3/22/57	R	R	1	1915	.242	28	33	5	8	3	-	0	2	13	0	4	-	0	.394	.265	OF-12, 1B-1
Ed Bailey	4/15/31		L	R	4	1961-63, 65	.241	332	930	113	224	26	2	51	167	407	140	154	2	12	.438	.343	C-278, 1B-2, OF-1
Mark Bailey	11/4/61		B	R	2	1990, 92	.152	18	33	1	5	1	0	0	4	9	3	9	0	0	.273	.222	C-8
Al Baird	6/2/1895	11/27/76	R	R	2	1917, 19	.252	48	107	9	27	1	0	0	9	28	7	11	5	-	.262	.298	2B-31, SS-12, 3B-5
Doug Baird	9/27/1891	6/13/67	R	R	1	1920	.125	7	8	1	1	0	0	0	0	1	3	3	0	0	.125	.222	3B-4
Dusty Baker	6/15/49		R	R	1	1984	.292	100	243	31	71	7	2	2	32	91	40	27	4	1	.374	.387	OF-62
Howard Baker	3/1/1888	1/16/64	R	R	1	1915	.000	2	3	0	0	0	0	0	0	0	0	0	0	0	.000	.250	3B-1
Jeff Ball	4/17/69		R	R	1	1998	.250	2	4	0	1	0	0	0	0	1	0	0	0	0	.250	.250	1B-1
Hal Bamberger	10/29/24		L	R	1	1948	.083	7	12	0	1	0	0	0	1	1	2	-	0	0	.083	.154	OF-3
Dave Bancroft	4/20/1891	10/9/72	B	R	5	1920-23, 30	.310	534	2160	397	670	130	30	11	189	893	242	106	48	33+	.413	.382	SS-521, 2B-11
Tom Bannon	5/8/1869	1/26/50	R	R	2	1895-96	.265	39	166	34	44	7	2	0	8	55	8	0	20	1+	.331	.299	OF-23, 1B-16
Babe Barna	3/2/15	5/18/72	L	R	3	1941-43	.241	154	486	55	117	16	8	8	75	173	56	63	6	0	.356	.319	OF-130
Jose Barrios	6/26/57		R	R	1	1982	.158	10	19	2	3	0	0	0	0	3	4	4	-	0	.158	.200	1B-7
Shad Barry	10/27/1878	11/27/36	R	R	1	1908	.149	37	67	5	10	1	1	0	5	13	9	-	1	0	.194	.260	OF-31
Dick Bartell	11/22/07	8/4/95	R	R	8	1935-38, 41-43, 46	.279	835	3074	434	858	167	13	60	293	1231	315	276	35	4+	.400	.355	SS-621, 3B-194, 2B-2
Bob Barton	7/30/41		R	R	5	1965-69	.210	149	315	11	66	6	1	0	11	74	21	44	0	0	.235	.262	C-142
Kevin Bass	5/12/59		B	R	3	1990-92	.249	274	840	93	209	30	8	24	102	327	66	135	16	13	.389	.307	OF-228
Charley Bassett	2/9/1863	5/28/42	R	R	3	1890-92	.245	265	1064	121	261	34	19	4	138	345	71	65	30	-	.324	.301	2B-139, 3B-126
Bill Bathe	10/14/60		R	R	2	1989-90	.250	82	80	6	20	6	0	3	18	32	7	19	0	0	.400	.303	C-15
Kim Batiste	3/15/68		R	R	1	1996	.208	54	130	17	27	6	0	3	11	42	7	33	3	3	.323	.235	3B-25, SS-7
Larry Battam	5/1/1878	1/27/38	-	-	1	1895	.250	2	4	0	1	0	0	0	0	1	2	-	3	-	.250	.500	3B-2
Joe Bean	3/18/1874	2/15/61	R	R	1	1902	.222	48	176	13	39	2	2	0	5	43	5	-	9	-	.244	.247	SS-48
Des Beatty	4/7/1893	10/6/69	R	R	1	1914	.000	2	3	0	0	0	0	0	0	0	0	2	0	-	.000	.000	SS-1, 3B-1
Buck Becannon	8/22/1859	11/5/23	-	-	1	1887	.000	5	5	0	0	0	0	0	0	0	0	0	0	-	.000	.000	3B-1
Beals Becker	7/5/1886	8/16/43	L	R	3	1910-12	.267	293	700	112	187	31	13	10	102	274	94	82	60	-	.391	.356	OF-217, 1B-1
Marty Becker	12/25/1893	9/25/57	B	L	1	1915	.250	17	52	5	13	3	0	0	3	15	2	-	3	6	.288	.278	OF-16
Jake Beckley	8/4/1867	6/25/18	L	L	2	1896-97	.288	63	250	45	72	10	7	6	49	114	11	7+	13	-	.456	.338	1B-62, OF-2
Gene Begley	6/7/1861		-	-	1	1886	.125	5	16	1	2	0	0	0	1	2	1	3	1	-	.125	.176	C-3, OF-2
David Bell	9/14/1972		R	R	1	2002	.261	154	552	82	144	29	2	20	73	237	54	80	1	2	.429	.333	3B-139, 2B-12, OF-3, SS-2

Name	Born	Died	B	T	Yrs	Years	BA	G	AB	R	H	2B	3B	HR	RBI	TB	BB	SO	SB	CS	SLG	OBP	Pos
Marvin Benard	1/20/71	—	L	L	8	1995–2002	.274	845	2559	436	700	135	20	54	256	1019	261	445	84	43	.398	.345	OF-667
Mike Benjamin	11/22/65	—	R	R	7	1989–95	.196	299	637	79	125	26	3	13	51	196	36	142	21	1	.308	.250	SS-170, 3B-67, 2B-41
Todd Benzinger	2/11/63	—	B	R	3	1993–95	.272	202	515	59	140	20	4	16	59	216	32	122	2	1	.419	.314	1B-144, OF-7, 3B-1
Wally Berger	10/10/05	11/30/88	R	R	2	1937–38	.277	75	231	45	64	11	2	12	47	115	20	34	3	—	.498	.343	OF-61
Dave Bergman	6/6/53	—	L	L	3	1981–83	.271	253	406	54	110	16	2	13	51	169	61	50	7	3	.416	.366	1B-152, OF-27
Curt Bernard	2/18/1878	4/10/55	L	R	2	1900–01	.238	43	147	20	35	2	2	0	14	41	13	—	3	—	.279	.309	OF-34, 2B-4, SS-3, 3B-1
Ray Berres	8/31/07	—	R	R	4	1942–45	.215	68	107	9	23	1	0	1	5	27	6	8	0	0+	.252	.263	C-61
Joe Berry	12/31/1894	4/29/76	B	R	2	1921–22	.333	15	6	0	2	0	1	0	2	4	1	1	0	0	.667	.429	2B-7
Damon Berryhill	12/3/63	—	B	R	1	1997	.257	73	167	17	43	8	0	3	23	60	20	29	0	0	.359	.335	C-51, 1B-1
Dick Bertell	11/21/35	—	R	R	1	1965	.188	22	48	1	9	1	0	0	3	10	7	5	0	0	.208	.291	C-22
Bob Bescher	2/25/1884	11/29/42	L	L	1	1914	.270	135	512	82	138	23	4	6	35	187	45	48	36	—	.365	.336	OF-126
Rae Blaemire	2/8/11	12/23/75	R	R	1	1941	.400	2	5	0	2	0	0	0	0	2	0	0	0	—	.400	.400	C-2
Damaso Blanco	12/11/41	—	R	R	3	1972–74	.212	72	33	9	7	1	0	0	8	8	5	6	3	0	.242	.308	3B-26, SS-13, 2B-6
Don Blasingame	3/16/32	—	L	R	2	1960–61	.235	139	524	73	123	12	8	2	31	157	51	54	14	2	.300	.304	2B-133
Buddy Blattner	2/8/20	—	R	R	3	1946–48	.255	189	593	94	151	28	8	11	62	228	80	73	18	2+	.384	.349	2B-155, 3B-11, 1B-1
Marv Blaylock	9/30/29	10/23/93	L	L	1	1950	.000	1	1	0	0	0	0	0	0	0	0	0	0	—	.000	.000	PH
John Boccabella	6/29/41	—	R	R	1	1974	.138	29	80	6	11	2	0	0	5	14	4	6	0	0	.175	.176	C-26
Carl Boles	10/31/34	—	R	R	1	1962	.375	19	24	4	9	0	0	0	6	9	2	6	0	0	.375	.375	OF-7
Barry Bonds	7/24/64	—	L	L	10	1993–2002	.311	1429	4751	1158	1478	294	37	437	1096	3157	1311	739	242	68	.664	.441	OF-1393
Bobby Bonds	3/15/46	—	R	R	7	1968–74	.273	1014	4047	765	1106	188	42	186	552	1936	500	1016	263	63	.478	.356	OF-1005
Zeke Bonura	9/20/08	3/9/87	R	R	1	1939	.321	123	455	75	146	26	6	11	85	217	46	22	1	0	.477	.388	1B-122
Ike Boone	2/17/1897	8/1/58	L	R	1	1922	.500	2	2	2	1	0	0	0	0	1	0	1	0	0	.500	.500	PH
Chris Bourjos	10/16/55	—	R	R	1	1980	.227	13	22	4	5	1	0	1	2	9	7	7	0	0	.409	.292	OF-6
Chick Bowen	7/26/1897	8/9/48	R	R	1	1919	.200	3	5	0	1	0	0	0	2	1	2	0	0	—	.200	.333	OF-2
Frank Bowerman	12/5/1868	11/30/48	R	R	8	1900–07	.246	700	2220	234	547	64	24	8	255	683	92	—	59	—	.308	.287	C-554, 1B-83, 2B-6, SS-5, 3B-3, OF-1, P-1
Ernie Bowman	7/28/35	—	R	R	3	1961–63	.190	165	205	29	39	4	2	1	10	50	17	33	3	3	.244	.252	SS-62, 2B-56, 3B-30
Jack Boyle	3/22/1866	1/7/13	R	R	1	1892	.183	120	436	52	80	8	8	0	32	104	36	41	10	—	.239	.252	C-79, 1B-40, OF-2, SS-2
Jim Boyle	1/19/04	12/24/58	R	R	1	1926	—	1	0	0	0	0	0	0	0	—	0	0	0	—	—	—	C-1
Vic Bradford	3/5/15	6/10/94	R	R	1	1943	.200	6	5	1	1	0	0	0	1	1	1	2	0	0	.200	.200	OF-1
Dave Brain	1/24/1879	5/25/59	R	R	1	1908	.176	11	17	2	3	1	0	0	1	3	3	—	0	—	.176	.176	2B-3, OF-3, 3B-2, SS-1
Fred Brainerd	2/17/1892	4/17/59	R	R	3	1914–16	.195	95	261	32	51	7	2	1	21	65	7	44	6	7+	.249	.261	1B-45, 3B-18, SS-9, 2B-3, OF-1
Jackie Brandt	4/28/34	—	R	R	3	1956, 58–59	.281	253	832	115	234	33	13	23	107	362	58	105	15	8	.435	.327	OF-226, 3B-18, 1B-3, 2B-1
Bob Brenly	2/25/54	—	R	R	9	1981–89	.250	823	2527	312	632	116	6	90	327	1030	308	421	44	38	.408	.333	C-692, 3B-68, 1B-67, OF-6
Roger Bresnahan	6/11/1879	12/4/44	R	R	7	1902–08	.293	751	2499	438	731	135	35	15	291	981	410	—	118	—	.393	.403	C-430, OF-254, 1B-33, SS-8, 3B-7, 2B-1
Eddie Bressoud	5/2/32	—	R	R	6	1956–61	.239	443	1242	132	297	53	15	26	107	458	104	211	3	5	.369	.299	SS-326, 2B-59, 3B-22, 1B-1
Al Bridwell	1/4/1884	1/23/69	L	R	4	1908–11	.283	510	1698	214	480	50	14	0	180	558	225	33	74	—	.329	.372	SS-509
Steve Brodie	9/11/1868	10/30/35	L	R	1	1902	.281	109	416	37	117	8	2	3	42	138	22	—	11	—	.332	.327	OF-109
Dan Brouthers	5/8/1858	8/2/32	L	L	1	1904	.000	2	5	0	0	0	0	0	0	0	0	—	0	—	.000	.000	1B-1
Chris Brown	8/15/61	—	R	R	4	1984–87	.287	308	1064	130	305	49	6	30	138	456	89	156	18	16	.429	.313	3B-291, SS-3
Eddie Brown	7/17/1891	9/10/56	R	R	2	1920–21	.272	73	136	17	37	7	0	0	12	48	4	14	0	0	.353	.292	OF-32
Jake Brown	3/22/48	12/18/81	R	R	1	1975	.209	41	43	9	9	3	3	0	4	12	5	13	0	7	.279	.292	OF-14
Ollie Brown	2/11/44	—	R	R	1	1965–68	.249	281	865	83	215	24	2	20	97	303	61	156	3	—	.350	.303	OF-268
Willard Brown	1866	12/20/1897	R	R	3	1887–89	.242	109	368	37	89	14	2	1	60	110	20	32	17	—	.299	.292	C-103, OF-5, 3B-3
George Browne	1/12/1876	12/9/20	L	R	6	1902–07	.287	720	2874	444	825	82	37	16	216	1029	169	—	137	—	.358	.330	OF-712
Dick Buckley	9/21/1858	12/12/1929	R	—	2	1890–91	.237	145	519	62	123	20	1	6	57	163	34	65	6	—	.314	.293	C-136, 3B-9

Name	Born	Died	B	T	Yrs	Seasons	AVG	G	AB	R	H	2B	3B	HR	RBI	TB	BB	SO	SB	CS	SLG	OBP	Games By Position
Charlie Buelow	1/12/1877	5/4/51	R	R	1	1901	.111	22	72	3	8	4	0	0	4	12	2	-	0	-	.167	.147	3B-17, 2B-2
Bob Burda	7/16/38		L	L	4	1965-66, 69-70	.209	193	254	24	53	11	0	6	37	82	33	25	0	1	.323	.298	1B-71, OF-25
Eddie Burke	10/6/1866	11/26/07	L	R	4	1892-95	.281	399	1633	362	459	62	28	20	210	637	141	113	144	-	.390	.354	OF-340, 2B-59
Frank Burke	2/16/1880	9/17/46	-	R	1	1906	.333	8	9	2	3	1	0	0	0	6	1	-	1	-	.667	.400	OF-4
John Burke	1/27/1877	8/4/50	R	R	1	1902	.154	4	13	0	2	0	0	0	0	2	0	-	-	-	.154	.154	OF-2, P-2
Jesse Burkett	12/4/1868	5/27/53	L	L	1	1890	.309	101	401	67	124	23	13	4	60	185	33	52	14	-	.461	.366	OF-90, P-21
Ellis Burks	9/11/64		R	R	3	1998-2000	.312	284	930	169	290	46	6	60	214	528	144	166	20	7	.568	.404	OF-256
George Burns	11/24/1889	8/15/66	R	R	11	1911-21	.290	1362	5311	877	1541	267	82	34	458	2074	631	440	334	123+	.391	.368	OF-1356, 3B-1
Oyster Burns	9/6/1864	11/11/28	R	R	1	1895	.307	33	114	21	35	5	3	1	25	49	14	6	10	-	.430	.388	OF-32, 1B-1
Buster Burrell	12/22/1866	5/8/62	R	R	1	1891	.094	15	53	5	5	0	0	0	2	5	3	12	2	-	.094	.158	C-15, OF-1
Brett Butler	6/15/57		L	L	3	1988-90	.293	471	1784	317	523	69	22	13	123	675	246	195	125	55	.378	.381	OF-466
Frank Butler	7/18/1860	7/10/45	L	L	1	1895	.273	5	22	5	6	0	0	0	2	7	1	-	0	-	.318	.304	OF-5
C	Born	Died	B	T	Yrs	Seasons	AVG	G	AB	R	H	2B	3B	HR	RBI	TB	BB	SO	SB	CS	SLG	OBP	Games By Position
Enos Cabell	10/8/49		R	R	1	1981	.255	96	396	41	101	20	0	2	36	129	10	47	6	7	.326	.274	1B-69, 3B-22
Sam Calderone	2/6/26		R	R	2	1950, 53	.268	69	112	13	30	3	0	0	20	36	3	9	0	0+	.321	.287	C-64
Jim Callahan	1/12/1879	3/9/68	R	R	1	1902	.000	1	4	0	0	0	0	0	0	0	3	3	0	-	.000	.200	OF-1
Jay Canizaro	7/4/73		R	R	2	1996, 99	.232	55	138	16	32	6	1	3	17	49	10	40	1	2	.355	.287	2B-39, SS-7
Jose Cardenal	10/7/43		R	R	2	1963-64	.050	29	20	4	1	0	0	0	2	2	1	4	2	1	.050	.174	OF-18
Roger Carey	-		-	-	1	1887	.000	1	4	0	0	0	0	0	0	0	0	-	0	-	.000	.000	2B-1
Mark Carreon	7/19/63		R	L	4	1993-96	.289	327	938	123	271	59	4	36	169	446	65	106	3	4	.475	.338	1B-157, OF-101
Kid Carsey	10/22/1870	3/29/60	R	R	1	1899	.333	5	18	2	6	0	0	0	1	7	2	-	2	-	.389	.400	3B-3, SS-2
Blackie Carter	9/30/02	9/10/76	R	R	2	1925-26	.190	6	21	4	4	1	0	0	1	8	1	1	0	0+	.381	.227	OF-5
Gary Carter	4/8/54		R	R	1	1990	.254	92	244	24	62	10	0	9	27	99	25	31	1	1	.406	.324	C-80, 1B-3
Joe Carter	3/7/60		R	R	1	1998	.295	41	105	15	31	7	0	7	29	59	6	13	0	-	.562	.322	OF-17, 1B-16
Ed Caskin	12/30/1851	10/9/24	R	R	3	1883-84, 86	.236	196	738	97	174	22	3	2	81	208	48	81	0+	-	.282	.282	SS-178, 2B-13, C-7
Foster Castleman	1/1/31		R	R	4	1954-57	.221	170	462	43	102	19	3	17	51	178	65	65	2	1	.385	.254	3B-117, 2B-8, SS-3
Orlando Cepeda	9/17/37		R	R	9	1958-66	.308	1114	4178	652	1286	226	22	226	767	2234	259	636	92	46	.535	.352	1B-872, OF-231, 3B-4
Hal Chase	2/13/1883	5/18/47	L	R	1	1919	.284	110	408	58	116	17	7	5	45	162	17	40	16	-	.397	.318	1B-107
Lou Chiozza	5/17/10	2/28/71	L	R	3	1937-39	.239	214	760	83	182	21	5	10	58	243	41	47	14	-	.320	.278	3B-124, 2B-34, OF-28, SS-8
Bill Cissell	1/3/04	3/15/49	R	R	1	1938	.268	38	149	19	40	6	0	2	18	52	6	11	1	-	.349	.297	2B-33, 3B-6
John Clapp	7/17/1851	12/18/04	R	R	1	1883	.178	20	73	6	13	5	0	0	5	13	5	4	-	-	.178	.231	C-16, OF-5
Jack Clark	11/10/55		R	R	10	1975-84	.277	1044	3731	597	1034	197	30	163	595	1780	497	556	60	44	.477	.359	OF-995, 1B-6, 3B-4
Roy Clark	5/11/1874	11/1/25	L	R	1	1902	.145	21	76	4	11	1	0	0	3	12	-	-	5	-	.158	.156	OF-20
Will Clark	3/13/64		L	L	8	1986-93	.299	1160	4269	687	1278	249	37	176	709	2129	506	744	52	41	.499	.373	1B-1124
Willie Clark	8/16/1872	11/13/32	L	-	3	1895-97	.283	211	766	110	217	32	18	1	124	288	57	18+	27	-	.376	.346	1B-195, OF-7, 3B-1
Artie Clarke	5/6/1865	11/14/49	R	R	2	1890-91	.214	149	569	72	122	14	10	0	70	156	47	54	49	-	.274	.279	C-78, OF-35, 3B-21, 3B-15, SS-1
Boileryard Clarke	10/18/1868	7/29/59	R	R	1	1905	.180	31	50	2	9	0	0	1	4	12	4	-	1	-	.240	.241	1B-15, C-12
Royce Clayton	1/2/70		R	R	5	1991-95	.249	506	1790	179	445	72	18	18	184	607	133	343	66	26	.339	.302	SS-499, 3B-1
Elmer Cleveland	9/15/1862	10/8/13	R	R	1	1888	.235	9	34	6	8	0	2	2	5	18	3	1	1	-	.529	.297	3B-9
Ty Cline	6/15/39		L	L	2	1967-68	.237	180	413	55	98	11	8	2	32	128	20	39	2	3	.310	.275	OF-107, 1B-24
Gil Coan	5/18/22		L	R	2	1955-56	.143	13	14	2	2	0	0	0	2	2	0	2	0	0	.143	.143	OF-6
Andy Cohen	10/25/04	10/29/88	R	R	3	1926, 28-29	.281	262	886	108	249	36	10	14	114	347	43	34	6	-	.392	.317	2B-230, SS-14, 3B-4
Jimmie Coker	3/28/36	10/29/91	R	R	1	1963	.200	4	5	0	1	0	0	0	0	1	2	-	0	-	.200	.333	C-2
Craig Colbert	2/13/65		R	R	2	1992-93	.215	72	163	12	35	7	2	2	21	52	12	35	1	0	.319	.266	C-45, 3B-10, 2B-4
Darnell Coles	6/2/62		R	R	1	1991	.214	11	14	1	3	0	0	0	0	3	0	2	0	0	.214	.214	OF-3, 1B-1
Pete Compton	9/28/1889	2/3/78	L	L	1	1918	.217	21	60	5	13	0	1	0	5	15	5	4	2	-	.250	.277	OF-19
Frank Connaughton	1/1/1869	12/1/42	R	R	1	1896	.260	88	315	53	82	11	3	2	43	95	25	7	22	-	.302	.319	SS-54, OF-30
Joe Connell	1/16/02	9/21/77	L	L	1	1926	.000	2	1	0	0	0	0	0	0	0	0	0	0	-	.000	.000	PH
Joe Connolly	6/4/1896	3/30/60	R	R	1	1921	.000	4	2	0	0	0	0	0	0	0	0	0	0	0	.000	.200	OF-1
Roger Connor	7/1/1857	1/4/31	L	L	11	1883-89, 91-94	.319	1120	4346	946	1388	242	131	76	786	2120	578	276	161+	-	.488	.402	1B-1002, 2B-68, OF-38, 3B-14

Name	Born	Died	B	T	Yrs	Seasons	AVG	G	AB	R	H	2B	3B	HR	RBI	TB	BB	SO	SB	CS	SLG	OBP	Games By Position
Jack Conway	7/30/19	6/11/93	R	R	1	1948	.245	24	49	8	12	2	1	1	3	19	5	10	0	—	.388	.315	2B-13, SS-6, 3B-3
Jimmy Cooney	8/24/1894	8/7/91	R	R	1	1919	.214	5	14	3	3	0	0	0	1	3	0	0	0	—	.214	.214	SS-4, 2B-1
Claude Cooper	4/1/1892	1/21/74	L	L	1	1913	.300	27	30	11	9	4	0	0	4	13	4	6	3	—	.433	.382	OF-15
Walker Cooper	1/8/15	4/11/91	R	R	4	1946-49	.276	360	1232	162	340	50	11	63	243	601	76	92	3	4+	.488	.322	C-324
Tommy Corcoran	1/4/1869	6/25/60	R	R	1	1907	.265	62	226	21	60	9	2	0	24	73	7	—	9	—	.323	.288	2B-62
Pete Cote	8/30/02	10/17/87	—	R	1	1926	.000	2	1	0	0	0	0	0	0	0	0	0	0	—	.000	.000	PH
Dick Cramer	—	8/12/1885	—	—	1	1883	.000	2	6	0	0	0	0	0	0	0	0	5	—	—	.000	.143	OF-2
Del Crandall	3/5/30		R	R	1	1964	.231	69	195	12	45	8	0	3	11	64	22	21	0	3	.328	.309	C-65
Sam Crane	1/2/1854	6/26/25	R	R	1	1890	.000	4	12	0	0	0	0	0	0	0	0	2	1	—	.000	.000	2B-2, 1B-1, OF-1
Pat Crawford	1/28/02	1/25/94	L	R	2	1929-30	.286	90	133	24	38	6	2	6	41	66	18	7	1	—	.496	.375	2B-18, 1B-8, 3B-1
Pete Cregan	4/13/1875	5/18/45	R	R	1	1899	.000	1	2	0	0	0	0	0	0	0	0	—	0	—	.000	.000	OF-1
Felipe Crespo	3/5/73		B	R	2	2000-01	.259	129	197	25	51	7	1	8	39	84	17	49	4	3	.426	.329	1B-29, 2B-10, OF-31
Hughie Critz	9/17/00	1/10/80	R	R	6	1930-35	.255	676	2803	380	715	91	29	20	204	924	111	128	23	0	.330	.285	2B-658
Buddy Crump	11/29/01	9/7/76	L	L	1	1924	.000	2	4	0	0	0	0	0	0	0	1	—	0	0	.000	.000	OF-1
Hector Cruz	4/2/53		R	R	2	1978-79	.212	95	222	21	47	8	1	6	25	75	24	46	0	2	.338	.291	OF-59, 3B-16
Jacob Cruz	1/28/73	11/26/14	L	L	3	1996-98	.210	52	105	13	22	4	0	3	13	35	15	30	1	1	.333	.317	OF-34
Al Cuccinello	11/8/07		R	R	1	1935	.248	54	165	27	41	7	1	4	20	62	—	20	0	—	.376	.262	2B-48, 3B-2
Tony Cuccinello	11/8/07	9/21/95	R	R	1	1940	.208	88	307	26	64	9	2	5	36	92	16	42	1	0	.300	.248	2B-47, 3B-37
Dick Culler	1/15/15	6/16/64	R	R	1	1949	.000	7	1	0	0	0	0	0	0	0	1	—	0	0	.000	.500	SS-7
Jack Cummings	4/1/04	10/5/62	R	R	4	1926-29	.349	86	126	15	44	11	1	4	27	69	12	16	0	—	.548	.410	C-45
Bill Cunningham	7/30/1895	9/26/53	R	R	3	1921-23	.297	204	508	69	151	24	4	8	72	207	20	21	9	8	.407	.326	OF-159, 2B-4, 3B-1
Harry Curtis	2/19/1883	8/1/51	—	R	1	1907	.222	6	9	2	2	0	0	0	1	2	2	—	2	—	.222	.364	C-6
D																							
Bill Dahlen	1/5/1870	12/5/50	R	R	4	1904-07	.240	579	1978	240	475	84	10	10	244	609	233	—	111	—	.308	.328	SS-578, OF-1
Ed Daily	9/7/1862	10/21/1891	R	R	1	1890	.133	4	15	2	2	1	1	0	1	3	0	4	0	—	.200	.133	OF-3, P-2
Harry Danning	9/6/11		R	R	10	1933-42	.285	890	2971	363	847	162	26	57	397	1232	187	217	13	—	.415	.330	C-801, 1B-1
Alvin Dark	1/7/22		R	R	7	1950-56	.292	933	3794	605	1106	205	30	98	429	1665	213	257	41	19+	.439	.334	SS-887, 2B-26, OF-17, 3B-8, P-1
Jim Davenport	8/17/33		R	R	13	1958-70	.258	1501	4427	552	1142	177	37	77	456	1624	382	673	16	25	.367	.318	3B-1130, SS-219, 2B-112, 1B-3, OF-1
Chili Davis	1/17/60		B	R	7	1981-87	.267	874	3148	432	840	144	20	101	418	1327	361	578	95	62	.422	.340	OF-824
Eric Davis	5/29/62		R	R	2	2001	.205	74	156	17	32	7	3	4	22	57	13	38	1	1	.365	.269	OF-74
George Davis	8/23/1870	10/17/40	B	R	10	1893-1901, 03	.332	1096	4303	838	1427	227	98	53	816	2009	399	66+	354	—	.467	.393	SS-635, 3B-426, 1B-17, 2B-10, OF-10
Harry Davis	7/19/1873	8/11/47	R	R	2	1895-96	.276	71	257	44	71	11	11	2	56	110	33	20	17	—	.428	.369	OF-40, 1B-30
Ira Davis	7/8/1870	12/21/42	—	—	1	1899	.235	6	17	3	4	1	1	0	2	7	0	—	1	—	.412	.235	SS-3, 1B-2
John Davis	7/15/15		R	R	1	1941	.214	21	70	8	15	3	0	0	5	18	8	12	0	—	.257	.295	3B-21
Kiddo Davis	2/12/02	3/4/83	R	R	4	1933, 35-37	.257	276	668	103	172	38	5	9	57	247	51	46	13	—	.370	.312	OF-200
Russ Davis	9/13/69		R	R	1	2000-01	.259	133	347	43	90	18	1	16	41	158	26	78	1	3	.455	.314	1B-6, 3B-89
Pat Deasley	11/17/1857	4/1/43	R	R	3	1885-87	.274	125	468	52	128	16	2	0	64	148	22	39	5+	—	.316	.308	C-108, OF-17, 3B-7, SS-2
Steve Decker	10/25/65		R	R	4	1990-92, 96	.219	166	452	35	99	11	1	9	45	139	38	87	0	1	.308	.282	C-138, 1B-3, 3B-2
Rob Deer	9/29/60		R	R	2	1984-85	.183	91	186	27	34	5	1	11	23	74	30	81	1	2	.398	.297	OF-46, 1B-10
Ivan DeJesus	1/9/53		R	R	1	1987	.200	9	10	0	2	0	0	0	1	2	0	2	0	—	.200	.200	SS-9
Bill DeKoning	12/19/18	7/26/79	R	R	1	1945	.000	3	1	0	0	0	0	0	0	0	0	1	0	—	.000	.000	C-2
Jim Delahanty	6/20/1879	10/17/53	R	R	1	1902	.231	7	26	3	6	1	0	0	3	7	—	—	0	—	.269	.259	OF-7
Wilson Delgado	7/15/75		B	R	4	1996-99	.259	59	112	12	29	4	1	0	6	35	7	19	2	0	.313	.320	SS-33, 2B-18
Frank Demaree	6/10/10	8/30/58	R	R	3	1939-41	.299	287	1055	139	315	45	8	18	141	430	115	80	7	—	.408	.370	OF-279
Jerry Denny	3/16/1859	8/16/27	R	R	2	1890-91	.214	118	453	50	97	19	7	3	43	139	28	65	13	—	.307	.269	3B-110, SS-7, 2B-1
Jim Devine	10/5/1858	1/11/05	—	—	1	1886	.000	1	3	0	0	0	0	0	0	0	0	1	0	—	.000	.000	OF-1
Mickey Devine	5/9/1892	10/1/37	R	R	1	1925	.273	21	33	6	9	3	0	0	4	12	2	3	0	0	.364	.314	C-11, 3B-1
Art Devlin	10/16/1879	9/18/48	R	R	8	1904-11	.268	1116	3766	525	1011	139	44	10	439	1268	496	51+	266	—	.337	.365	3B-1097, SS-9, 1B-6, 2B-6

Name	Born	Died	B	T	Yrs	Seasons	AVG	G	AB	R	H	2B	3B	HR	RBI	TB	BB	SO	SB	CS	SLG	OBP	Games By Position
Josh Devore	11/13/1887	10/6/1954	L	L	6	1908-13	.283	431	1437	265	406	45	27	7	118	526	184	183+	141	-	.366	.372	OF-397
Al DeVormer	8/19/1891	8/29/1966	R	R	1	1927	.248	68	141	14	35	5	3	0	21	46	11	11	1	1	.326	.312	C-54, 1B-3
Alex Diaz	10/5/68		B	R	1	1998	.129	34	62	5	8	1	0	0	5	10	0	15	3	1	.161	.129	OF-21
Johnny Dickshot	1/24/10	11/4/97	R	R	1	1939	.235	10	34	3	8	0	0	0	5	8	5	5	0	-	.235	.333	OF-10
Chuck Diering	2/5/23		R	R	1	1952	.174	41	23	7	4	1	1	0	2	7	4	3	0	2+	.304	.296	OF-36
Dick Dietz	9/18/41		R	R	6	1966-71	.262	536	1634	200	428	80	5	62	271	704	318	366	2	6	.431	.384	C-486
Vince DiMaggio	9/6/12	10/3/86	R	R	1	1946	.000	15	25	2	0	0	0	0	0	0	2	5	0	0	.000	.074	OF-13
Cozy Dolan	12/23/1889	12/10/58	R	R	1	1922	-	1	-	-	-	-	-	-	-	-	-	-	-	-	-	-	PR
Mike Donlin	5/30/1878	9/24/33	L	L	6	1904-06, 08, 11, 14	.333	431	1495	231	498	70	34	18	218	690	103	6+	75	-	.462	.380	OF-375, 1B-1
Jim Donnelly	7/19/1865	3/5/15	R	R	1	1897	.188	23	85	19	16	3	2	0	11	19	9	6	6	-	.224	.266	3B-23
Red Dooin	6/12/1879	5/14/52	R	R	2	1915-16	.206	61	141	10	29	2	2	0	9	35	3	18	0	2+	.248	.222	C-61
Mickey Doolan	5/7/1880	11/1/51	R	R	1	1916	.235	18	51	4	12	3	1	1	3	20	2	4	1	-	.392	.264	SS-16, 2B-2
Mike Dorgan	10/2/1853	4/26/09	R	R	5	1883-87	.281	425	1674	255	470	68	21	3	234	589	70	131	31+	-	.352	.311	OF-396, P-15, C-12, 1B-6, 2B-3
Jack Doyle	10/25/1869	12/31/58	R	R	8	1892-95,	.306	741	2861	446	875	157	28	16	476	1136	193	57+	254	-	.397	.355	1B-477, C-91, OF-84, 2B-44, 3B-27, SS-26, 2B-1
Larry Doyle	7/31/1886	3/1/74	L	R	13	1907-16, 18-20	.292	1622	5995	906	1751	275	117	67	725	2461	576	245+	291	27+	.411	.359	2B-1591
Chuck Dressen	9/20/1898	8/10/66	R	R	1	1933	.222	16	45	3	10	4	0	0	3	14	1	4	0	-	.311	.239	3B-16
Dan Driessen	7/29/51		L	R	2	1985-86	.228	69	197	24	45	10	0	3	22	64	21	26	0	0	.325	.302	1B-53
Frank Duffy	10/14/46		R	R	1	1971	.179	21	28	4	5	0	0	0	2	5	0	10	0	0	.179	.179	SS-6, 2B-1, 3B-1
Jack Dunn	10/6/1872	10/22/28	R	R	3	1902-04	.244	242	780	88	190	38	4	1	70	239	46	-	36	-	.306	.291	SS-73, 3B-71, OF-51, 2B-30, P-4
Shawon Dunston	3/21/63		R	R	4	1996,98,2001-02	.270	278	671	70	181	29	5	18	67	274	18	115	12	3	.408	.295	OF-115, SS-88, 1B-2, 2B-1
Jim Dwyer	1/3/50		L	L	1	1978	.225	73	173	22	39	9	2	5	22	67	28	29	6	0	.387	.327	OF-36, 1B-29
Ben Dyer	2/13/1893	8/7/59	R	R	2	1914-15	.217	14	23	5	5	0	1	0	0	7	4	4	1	0+	.304	.357	SS-7, 3B-6, 2B-1

E

Name	Born	Died	B	T	Yrs	Seasons	AVG	G	AB	R	H	2B	3B	HR	RBI	TB	BB	SO	SB	CS	SLG	OBP	Games By Position
Bob Elliott	11/26/16	5/4/66	R	R	1	1952	.228	98	272	33	62	6	2	10	35	102	36	20	1	0	.375	.323	OF-65, 3B-13
Randy Elliott	6/5/51		R	R	1	1977	.240	73	167	17	40	5	1	7	26	68	8	24	0	2	.407	.275	OF-46
Charlie English	4/8/10	8/31/96	R	R	1	1936	.000	6	1	0	0	0	0	0	0	0	0	0	0	-	.000	.000	2B-1
Gil English	7/2/09		R	R	2	1931-32	.217	62	212	22	46	7	5	2	19	69	6	23	0	-	.325	.239	3B-42, SS-23
Angel Escobar	5/12/65		B	R	1	1988	.333	3	3	1	1	0	0	0	0	1	0	0	0	0	.333	.333	3B-1, SS-1
Bobby Estalella	8/23/74		R	R	2	2000-01	.227	135	392	56	89	27	4	17	63	175	68	120	3	0	.446	.343	C-134
Dude Esterbrook	6/20/1857	4/30/01	R	R	3	1885-86, 90	.266	256	1029	139	274	48	12	5	116	361	22	79	25+	-	.351	.284	3B-207, 1B-45, OF-4
Bobby Etheridge	11/25/42		R	R	2	1967, 69	.244	96	246	26	60	16	2	2	25	86	26	38	0	0	.350	.330	3B-76, SS-1
Darrell Evans	5/26/47		L	R	8	1976-83	.255	1094	3728	534	952	159	19	142	525	1575	605	475	55	37	.422	.358	3B-697, 1B-312, OF-81, SS-22
Steve Evans	2/17/1885	12/28/43	L	L	1	1908	.500	2	2	0	1	0	0	0	0	1	0	-	0	-	.500	.500	OF-1
Hoot Evers	2/8/21	1/25/91	R	R	1	1954	.091	12	11	1	1	0	0	1	3	4	0	6	0	0	.364	.091	OF-4
Joe Evers	9/10/1891	1/4/49	R	R	1	1913	-	1	0	0	0	0	0	0	0	0	0	0	0	-	-	-	PR
Buck Ewing	10/17/1859	10/20/06	R	R	9	1883-89, 91-92	.306	734	2957	643	905	122	109	47	459	1386	211	194	178+	-	.469	.353	C-475, 3B-82, 1B-76, OF-64, 2B-40, SS-12, P-7

F

Name	Born	Died	B	T	Yrs	Seasons	AVG	G	AB	R	H	2B	3B	HR	RBI	TB	BB	SO	SB	CS	SLG	OBP	Games By Position
Rikkert Faneyte	5/31/69		R	R	3	1993-95	.173	72	127	10	22	7	1	0	8	31	16	42	1	0	.244	.266	OF-46
Paul Faries	2/20/65		R	R	1	1993	.222	15	36	6	8	2	1	0	4	12	1	4	2	0	.333	.237	2B-7, SS-4, 3B-1
Bob Farley	11/15/37		L	L	1	1961	.100	13	20	3	2	0	0	0	1	2	3	5	0	0	.100	.217	OF-3, 1B-1
Doc Farrell	12/26/01	12/20/66	R	R	5	1925-27, 29	.282	199	547	56	154	27	2	5	77	200	37	51	6	1+	.366	.332	SS-106, 3B-37, 2B-29
Duke Farrell	8/31/1866	2/15/25	B	R	3	1894-96	.285	262	904	108	258	43	24	6	161	367	92	40	22	-	.406	.356	C-200, 3B-36, SS-13, 1B-6
Mike Felder	11/18/61		B	R	2	1991-92	.275	277	670	95	184	23	9	4	41	237	51	60	35	10	.354	.327	OF-212, 2B-4, 3B-3
Pedro Feliz	4/27/77		R	R	3	2000-02	.239	169	373	38	89	13	2	9	35	133	16	78	2	1	.357	.269	3B-134, SS-1, OF-1

Player	Born	Died	B	T	Yrs	Seasons	AVG	G	AB	R	H	2B	3B	HR	RBI	TB	BB	SO	SB	CS	SLG	OBP	Games By Position
Jocko Fields	10/20/1864	10/14/50	R	R	1	1892	.273	21	66	8	18	4	2	0	5	26	9	10	2	-	.394	.368	OF-11, C-10
Steve Filipowicz	6/28/21	2/21/75	R	R	2	1944-45	.203	50	153	24	31	7	1	2	23	46	7	20	0	0	.301	.242	OF-41, C-1
Jim Finigan	8/19/28	5/16/81	R	R	1	1958	.200	23	25	3	5	2	0	0	1	7	3	5	0	0	.280	.310	2B-8, 3B-4
Bill Finley	10/4/1863	10/6/12	-	-	1	1886	.182	13	44	2	8	0	0	0	-	8	5	8	2	0	.182	.200	C-8, OF-8
Matty Fitzgerald	8/31/1880	9/22/49	R	R	2	1906-07	.286	11	21	3	6	1	0	0	5	7	3	-	-	-	.333	.286	C-9
Tom Fleming	11/20/1873	12/26/57	L	L	1	1899	.208	22	77	9	16	1	1	0	4	19	0	-	1	-	.247	.218	OF-22
Art Fletcher	1/5/1885	2/6/50	R	R	12	1909-20	.275	1321	4766	602	1311	193	65	21	584	1697	167	306+	152	20+	.356	.318	SS-1240, 3B-39, 2B-33
Paul Florence	4/22/00	5/28/86	B	R	1	1926	.229	76	188	19	43	4	3	2	14	59	23	12	2	-	.314	.322	C-76
Ray Foley	6/23/06	3/22/80	R	R	1	1928	.000	2	1	0	0	0	0	0	0	0	0	1	0	-	.000	.500	PH
Tim Foli	12/8/50	-	R	R	1	1977	.228	104	368	30	84	17	3	4	27	119	11	16	2	4	.323	.247	SS-102, 2B-1, 3B-1, OF-1
Elmer Foster	8/15/1861	7/22/46	L	R	2	1888-89	.143	39	140	17	20	3	2	0	10	27	12	21	15	-	.193	.226	OF-39, 3B-1
George Foster	12/1/48	-	R	R	3	1969-71	.279	54	129	14	36	6	1	4	13	56	8	33	0	1	.434	.319	OF-45
Pop Foster	4/8/1878	4/16/44	R	R	3	1898-1900	.284	147	497	77	141	18	9	3	77	186	31	-	7	-	.374	.331	OF-117, 3B-11, SS-10, 2B-5
Reddy Foster	8/1864	12/19/08	-	-	1	1896	.000	1	1	0	0	0	0	0	0	0	0	0	0	-	.000	.000	PH
Charlie Fox	10/7/21	-	R	R	1	1942	.429	3	7	1	3	0	0	0	0	3	0	2	0	-	.429	.500	C-3
Herman Franks	1/4/14	-	L	R	1	1949	.667	1	3	1	2	0	0	0	0	2	0	0	0	-	.667	.667	C-1
Lonny Frey	8/23/10	-	L	R	1	1948	.255	29	51	6	13	1	0	0	6	17	4	6	0	1	.333	.309	OF-4
Charlie Frisbee	2/2/1874	11/7/54	B	R	1	1900	.154	4	13	2	2	1	0	0	3	3	2	-	0	-	.231	.267	OF-4
Frankie Frisch	9/9/1898	3/12/73	B	R	8	1919-26	.321	1000	4053	701	1303	180	77	54	524	1799	280	139	224	74+	.444	.367	2B-622, 3B-347, SS-53
Tito Fuentes	1/4/44	-	B	R	9	1965-67, 69-74	.262	1054	3823	417	1000	152	33	34	306	1320	216	405	63	32	.345	.304	2B-842, SS-165, 3B-62
Shorty Fuller	10/10/1867	4/11/04	R	R	5	1892-96	.237	508	1880	325	446	50	19	3	184	543	242	100	114	-	.289	.326	SS-504, 3B-2, OF-2, 2B-1
Chick Fullis	2/27/04	3/28/46	R	R	5	1928-32	.303	295	818	170	248	40	6	11	78	333	65	53	22	-	.407	.360	OF-203, 2B-10
G	Born	Died	B	T	Yrs	Seasons	AVG	G	AB	R	H	2B	3B	HR	RBI	TB	BB	SO	SB	CS	SLG	OBP	Games By Position
Len Gabrielson	2/14/40	-	L	R	2	1965-66	.261	182	509	63	133	13	5	8	42	180	47	99	4	-	.354	.324	OF-144, 1B-11
Augie Galan	5/25/12	12/28/93	B	R	1	1949	.059	39	17	1	1	1	0	0	2	2	5	3	0	-	.118	.273	1B-3, OF-1
Al Gallagher	10/19/45	-	R	R	4	1970-73	.260	332	953	98	248	36	8	11	104	333	103	133	6	3	.349	.332	3B-293
Andres Galarraga	6/18/61	-	R	R	1	2001	.288	49	156	17	45	12	1	7	35	80	13	49	3	2	.513	.351	1B-41
John Ganzel	4/7/1874	1/14/59	R	R	1	1901	.215	138	526	42	113	13	3	2	66	138	20	-	6	-	.262	.255	1B-138
Joe Garagiola	2/12/26	-	L	R	1	1954	.273	5	11	1	3	2	0	0	1	5	1	2	0	0	.455	.308	C-3
Al Gardella	1/11/18	-	L	L	1	1945	.077	16	26	2	2	0	0	0	0	2	4	3	0	0	.077	.226	1B-8, OF-1
Danny Gardella	2/26/20	-	L	L	2	1944-45	.268	168	542	74	145	12	3	24	85	235	57	68	2	-	.434	.344	OF-119, 1B-15
Art Gardner	9/21/52	-	L	L	1	1978	.000	3	2	0	0	0	0	0	0	0	0	2	0	1	.000	.000	PH
Billy Gardner	7/19/27	-	R	R	2	1954-55	.207	121	295	36	61	15	1	4	24	90	19	38	0	-	.305	.261	SS-43, 3B-40, 2B-17
Phil Garner	4/30/49	-	R	R	1	1988	.154	15	13	0	2	0	0	0	1	2	3	3	0	-	.154	.214	3B-2
Gil Garrido	6/26/41	-	R	R	1	1964	.080	14	25	1	2	0	0	0	0	2	2	7	1	0	.080	.148	SS-14
Alex Gaston	3/12/1893	2/8/79	R	R	4	1920-23	.196	62	97	7	19	3	1	0	10	27	2	20	-	0	.278	.220	C-49
Gary Gearhart	8/10/23	-	L	R	1	1947	.246	73	179	26	44	9	0	6	17	71	17	30	-	-	.397	.315	OF-44
Harvey Gentry	5/27/26	-	L	L	1	1954	.250	5	4	0	1	0	0	0	0	1	1	0	0	0	.250	.400	PH
Bill George	1/27/1865	8/23/16	R	L	3	1885-87	.206	29	107	14	22	0	1	0	11	26	1	11	4	-	.243	.213	OF-10, P-17
Joe Gerhardt	2/14/1855	3/11/22	R	R	3	1885-87	.172	236	829	87	143	23	9	0	73	184	46	110	8+	-	.222	.216	2B-235, 3B-1
Charley Gettig	12/1870	4/11/35	R	R	4	1896-99	.241	126	377	48	91	16	2	0	47	111	28	0+	12	-	.294	.302	OF-25, 2B-21, 3B-19, SS-12, 1B-5, C-1, P-42
George Gibson	7/22/1880	1/25/67	R	R	2	1917-18	.179	39	84	1	15	4	0	0	5	19	7	2	1	-	.226	.242	C-39
Russ Gibson	5/6/39	-	R	R	3	1970-72	.210	54	138	5	29	7	2	2	16	43	9	29	0	0	.312	.259	C-50
Billy Gilbert	6/21/1876	8/8/27	R	R	4	1903-06	.247	493	1574	208	389	39	7	3	145	451	170	-	103	-	.287	.340	2B-487
Jack Gilbert	9/4/1875	7/7/41	-	-	1	1898	.250	1	4	0	1	0	0	0	1	1	0	-	1	-	.250	.250	OF-1

	Born	Died	B	T	Yrs	Seasons	AVG	G	AB	R	H	2B	3B	HR	RBI	TB	BB	SO	SB	CS	SLG	OBP	Games By Position
Tookie Gilbert	4/4/29	6/23/67	L	R	2	1950, 53	.203	183	482	52	98	15	2	7	48	138	57	65	4	0+	.286	.299	1B-155, 3B-1
Pete Gillespie	11/30/1851	5/5/10	L	R	5	1883-87	.283	474	1935	311	547	69	33	6	253	700	71	145	54+	-	.362	.310	OF-474, 3B-1
Jim Gladd	10/2/22	11/8/77	R	R	1	1946	.091	11	11	0	1	0	0	0	1	4	4	4	0	-	.091	.167	C-4
Dan Gladden	7/7/57		R	R	4	1983-86	.281	348	1258	196	353	50	11	16	110	473	117	185	94	44	.376	.347	OF-316
Jack Glasscock	7/22/1859	2/24/47	R	R	2	1890-91	.296	221	881	137	261	44	15	1	121	338	77	19	83	-	.384	.362	SS-221
Kid Gleason	10/26/1866	1/2/33	B	R	5	1896-1900	.270	641	2647	374	716	66	21	6	345	842	148	13+	162	-	.318	.312	2B-660, SS-10, 3B-3, OF-1
Ed Glenn	10/1875	12/6/11	R	R	1	1898	.250	2	4	1	1	0	0	0	0	1	3	-	1	-	.250	.250	SS-2
Al Glossop	7/23/15	7/2/91	B	R	2	1939-40	.203	37	123	19	25	3	1	5	11	43	14	18	1	-	.350	.290	2B-34
Randy Gomez	2/4/57		R	R	1	1984	.167	14	30	0	5	0	5	0	6	8	3	-	0	-	.200	.200	C-14
Mike Gonzalez	9/24/1890	2/19/77	R	R	3	1919-21	.215	82	195	22	42	7	0	0	8	49	24	10	4	0+	.251	.311	C-62, 1B-10
Ed Goodson	1/25/48		L	R	6	1970-75	.273	324	1006	92	275	44	2	25	140	398	50	98	4	2	.396	.311	1B-147, 3B-114
Tom Goodwin	7/27/68		L	R	1	2002	.260	78	154	23	40	5	2	1	17	52	14	25	16	2	.338	.321	OF-53, 3B-1
Sid Gordon	8/13/17	6/17/75	R	R	8	1941-43, 46-49, 55	.278	760	2565	385	714	102	32	90	393	1150	356	174	14	-	.448	.368	3B-360, OF-317, 1B-42, 2B-3
George Gore	5/3/1857	9/16/33	L	R	5	1887-89, 91-92	.582	479	922	414	537	74	25	12	179	697	279	127	117	-	.756	.686	OF-478
Hank Gowdy	8/24/1889	8/1/66	R	R	5	1910-11, 23-25	.321	198	445	54	143	21	7	8	76	202	63	30	4	0+	.454	.408	C-162, 1B-7
Mike Grady	12/23/1869	12/3/43	R	R	3	1898-1900	.287	262	849	147	244	45	17	5	130	338	101	-	49	-	.398	.363	C-141, 3B-42, OF-39, 1B-23, SS-14, 2B-2
Jack Graham	12/24/16		L	L	1	1946	.219	100	270	34	59	6	4	14	47	115	23	37	1	-	.426	.280	OF-62, 1B-7
Moonlight Graham	11/9/1876	8/25/65	L	L	1	1905	-	1	0	0	0	0	0	0	0	0	0	-	-	-	-	-	OF-1
Eddie Grant	5/21/1883	10/5/18	L	L	3	1913-15	.247	202	494	60	122	10	2	0	40	136	34	43	6+	-	.275	.295	3B-92, 2B-28, SS-23, 1B-1
George Grantham	5/20/00	3/16/54	L	R	1	1934	.241	32	29	5	7	2	0	1	4	12	8	6	0	-	.414	.405	1B-4, 3B-2
Mickey Grasso	5/10/20	10/15/75	R	R	2	1946, 55	.125	15	24	1	3	0	0	0	1	3	3	3	0	0+	.125	.222	C-15
David Green	12/4/60		R	R	1	1985	.248	106	294	36	73	10	2	5	20	102	22	58	6	5	.347	.301	1B-78, OF-12
Pug Griffin	4/24/1896	10/12/51	L	R	1	1920	.250	5	4	0	1	0	0	0	0	1	2	2	0	-	.250	.400	OF-2
Sandy Griffin	7/19/1858	6/5/26	R	R	1	1884	.177	16	62	7	11	2	2	0	6	13	1	19	0	-	.210	.190	OF-16
Roy Grimes	9/11/1893	9/13/54	R	R	1	1920	.158	26	57	5	9	0	2	0	3	10	3	8	1	-	.175	.200	2B-21
Dick Groat	11/4/30		R	R	1	1967	.171	34	70	4	12	1	0	0	4	15	6	7	0	-	.214	.237	SS-24, 2B-1
Heinie Groh	9/18/1889	8/22/68	R	R	7	1912-13, 22-26	.276	451	1600	253	441	83	12	9	155	575	181	86	22	16+	.359	.349	3B-404, 2B-14, SS-8
Brad Gulden	6/10/56		L	R	1	1986	.091	17	22	2	2	0	0	0	0	2	5	5	0	-	.091	.167	C-10
Cesar Gutierrez	1/26/43		R	R	2	1967, 69	.182	33	44	8	8	1	0	0	0	9	6	6	2	0	.205	.294	SS-19, 3B-7, 2B-1
Edwards Guzman	9/11/76		R	L	2	1999-2001	.215	75	130	20	28	6	0	3	7	40	5	20	0	0	.308	.241	C-27, 3B-12, 1B-7, 2B-3, OF-2
H																							
Bert Haas	2/8/14		R	R	1	1949	.260	54	104	12	27	2	3	1	10	38	5	8	0	-	.365	.294	1B-23, 3B-11
Bill Haeffner	7/8/1894	1/27/82	R	R	1	1928	.000	1	1	0	0	0	0	0	0	0	0	0	-	-	.000	.000	C-2
Tom Hafey	7/12/13	10/2/96	R	R	1	1939	.242	70	256	37	62	10	1	6	26	92	10	44	1	-	.359	.271	3B-70
Odell Hale	8/10/08	6/9/80	R	R	1	1941	.196	41	102	13	20	3	0	0	9	23	18	13	1	-	.225	.317	2B-29
Bob Hall	12/20/1878	12/1/50	-	R	1	1905	.333	1	3	1	1	0	0	0	0	1	0	-	0	-	.333	.333	OF-1
Mel Hall	9/16/60		L	L	1	1996	.120	25	25	1	3	0	0	0	0	4	1	4	0	-	.120	.154	OF-4
Tom Haller	6/23/37		L	R	7	1961-67	.248	761	2368	301	587	82	15	107	320	1020	311	380	10	20	.431	.335	C-719, OF-11, 1B-4
Jim Hamby	7/29/1897	10/21/91	R	R	2	1926-27	.182	55	55	6	10	1	0	0	5	12	7	7	1	-	.218	.274	C-20
Darryl Hamilton	12/3/64		L	L	2	1997-98	.281	222	827	143	232	42	5	6	69	302	120	114	24	18	.365	.371	OF-214
Frank Hankinson	4/29/1856	4/5/11	R	R	2	1883-84	.226	199	726	84	164	29	13	4	73	231	42	97	-	-	.318	.268	3B-198, OF-2
Jack Hannifin	2/25/1883	10/27/45	R	R	3	1906-08	.221	67	181	20	40	7	4	0	18	58	17	-	7	-	.320	.288	1B-29, SS-15, 3B-13, 2B-3, 2B-1
Scott Hardesty	1/26/1870	10/29/44	-	-	1	1899	.222	22	72	4	16	0	0	0	4	16	1	-	2	-	.222	.233	SS-20, 1B-2
George Harper	6/24/1892	8/18/78	L	R	1	1927-28	.320	164	540	96	173	20	6	18	94	259	94	31	8	-	.480	.421	OF-160
John Harrell	11/27/47		R	R	1	1969	.500	6	6	0	3	0	0	0	3	3	2	-	1	-	.500	.625	C-2
Gail Harris	10/15/31		L	L	3	1955-57	.228	181	526	57	120	16	4	22	68	210	39	84	1	0	.399	.281	1B-147
Vic Harris	3/27/50		B	R	2	1977-78	.219	122	265	36	58	16	0	3	25	83	30	60	2	1	.313	.298	2B-37, SS-33, 3B-9, OF-9

Name	Born	Died	B	T	Yrs	Seasons	BA	G	AB	R	H	2B	3B	HR	RBI	TB	BB	SO	SB	CS	SLG	OBP	Pos
Jack Harshman	7/12/27		L	R	3	1948, 50, 52	.143	17	42		6			2		12	4	9	0	0+	.286	.217	1B-12, P-2
Jim Ray Hart	10/30/41		R	R	11	1963–73	.282	1001	3425	488	965	135	27	157	526	1625	341	521	17	15	.474	.347	3B-683, OF-264
Chick Hartley	8/22/1880		R	R	1	1902	.000	4	13		0								0	–	.000	.000	OF-1
Grover Hartley	7/2/1888	10/19/64	R	R	6	1911–13, 24–26	.263	122	194	18	51	6	2	0	17	61	16	10	10	0+	.314	.319	C-109, 1B-9
Fred Hartman	4/25/1868	11/11/38	R	R	2	1898–99	.262	173	649	82	170	19	16	3	104	230	37	–	13	–	.354	.302	3B-173
Gabby Hartnett	12/20/00	12/20/72	R	R	1	1941	.300	64	150	20	45	5	0	5	26	65	12	14	0	0+	.433	.352	C-34
Clint Hartung	8/10/22		R	R	6	1947–52	.238	196	378	42	90	10	6	14	43	154	25	112	0	–	.407	.285	OF-45, 1B-1, P-112
Mickey Haslin	10/31/10		R	R	2	1937–38	.285	58	144	21	41	4	0	3	20	54	13	7	1	–	.375	.344	3B-19, 2B-17, SS-9
Gil Hatfield	1/27/1855	5/27/21	–	–	3	1887–89	.190	62	237	30	45	4	0	1	24	52	11	34	17	16+	.219	.226	SS-37, 3B-18, 2B-1, OF-1, P-6
George Hausmann	2/11/16		R	R	3	1944–45, 49	.268	301	1136	173	304	35	13	3	78	374	120	77	10	–	.329	.338	2B-289
Charlie Hayes	5/29/65		R	R	4	1988–89, 98–99	.246	216	609	72	150	17	1	18	110	223	67	106	5	2	.366	.320	3B-107, 1B-65, OF-5
Ray Hayworth	1/29/04		R	R	1	1939	.231	5	13	1	3	0	0	0	0	3	0	1	0	–	.231	.231	C-2
Fran Healy	9/6/46		R	R	2	1971–72	.214	92	192	22	41	7	0	3	19	57	28	48	1	1	.297	.314	C-65
Francis Healy	6/29/10		R	R	3	1930–32	.220	27	41	8	9	2	0	0	4	11	2	8	0	–	.268	.256	C-16
Jim Hegan	8/3/20	6/17/84	R	R	1	1959	.133	21	30	0	4	0	0	0	0	5	1	10	0	–	.167	.161	C-21
William Heine	9/22/00	9/2/76	L	R	1	1921	.000	2	2		0	0	0	0	0	0	0	0	0	0	.000	.000	2B-1
Tom Heintzelman	11/3/46		R	R	2	1977–78	.216	29	37	2	8	0	2	0	6	15	2	5	0	0	.405	.256	2B-5, 3B-3, 1B-2
Bob Heise	5/12/47		R	R	2	1970–71	.218	80	165	17	36	5	1	2	22	46	5	14	0	0	.279	.241	SS-36, 2B-29, 3B-4
Ed Hemingway	5/8/1893	7/5/69	B	R	1	1917	.320	7	25	3	8	1	0	0	1	11	2	1	2	–	.440	.370	3B-7
Dave Henderson	7/21/58		R	R	1	1987	.238	15	21	2	5	2	0	0	0	7	8	5	2	0	.333	.448	OF-9
Ken Henderson	6/15/46		B	R	8	1965–72	.256	674	2155	316	551	101	17	61	270	869	283	359	59	19	.403	.342	OF-630, 3B-3, 1B-1
Jack Hendricks	4/9/1875	5/13/43	L	L	2	1902	.231	8	26	8	6	2	0	0	0	8	2	2	2	–	.308	.286	OF-7
Butch Henline	12/20/1894	10/9/57	R	R	1	1921	.000	1	1	0	0	0	0	0	0	0	0	–	–	0	.000	.000	PH
John Henry	9/2/1863	6/11/39	–	L	1	1890	.243	37	144	19	35	6	0	0	16	41	7	12	12	–	.285	.278	OF-37
Larry Herndon	11/3/53		R	R	6	1976–81	.267	682	2128	244	568	76	39	24	186	794	131	352	60	40	.373	.309	OF-640
Tom Herr	4/4/56		B	R	1	1991	.250	32	60	6	15	1	1	0	7	18	13	7	2	0	.300	.384	2B-15, 3B-3
Buck Herzog	7/9/1885	9/4/53	R	R	7	1908–09, 11–13, 16–17	.259	602	2006	318	519	77	30	8	179	680	195	125	131	16+	.339	.324	3B-324, 2B-210, OF-30, SS-23
Jack Hiatt	7/27/42		R	R	5	1965–69	.239	290	661	63	158	26	2	18	102	242	132	175	0	0	.366	.366	C-142, 1B-63, OF-2
Charlie Hickman	3/4/1876	4/19/34	R	R	2	1900–01	.297	239	879	109	261	39	23	13	153	385	32	–	15	–	.438	.322	3B-135, OF-57, SS-23, 2B-7, 1B-2, P-9
Mahlon Higbee	8/16/01	4/7/68	R	R	1	1922	.400	3	10	2	4	0	0	0		7	0	2	0	0	.700	.400	OF-3
Glenallen Hill	3/22/65		R	R	3	1995–97	.268	358	1274	174	341	83	8	54	217	602	91	280	38	12	.473	.319	OF-320
Marc Hill	2/18/52		R	R	6	1975–80	.226	431	1201	94	272	39	1	23	139	382	141	151	1	5	.318	.308	C-399, 1B-4, 3B-1
Chuck Hiller	10/1/34		L	R	5	1961–65	.241	429	1471	198	354	52	13	13	111	457	124	126	13	11	.311	.300	2B-399, 3B-1
Bobby Hofman	10/5/25	4/5/94	R	R	7	1949, 52–57	.248	341	670	81	166	22	2	32	101	296	70	94	1	3+	.442	.319	2B-85, 1B-49, 3B-45, C-26
Shanty Hogan	3/21/06	4/7/67	R	R	5	1928–32	.311	618	2015	205	627	99	7	48	333	884	143	122	4	–	.439	.357	C-562
Walter Holke	12/25/1892	10/12/54	B	L	4	1914, 16–18	.277	277	970	109	269	33	13	3	95	337	50	96	33	–	.347	.313	1B-277
James Holmes	1/28/1869	8/6/32	L	R	1	1897	.268	79	306	51	82	8	6	1	44	105	18	–	30	–	.343	.309	OF-77, SS-1
Rogers Hornsby	4/27/1896	1/5/63	R	R	1	1927	.361	155	568	133	205	32	9	26	125	333	86	38	9	–	.586	.445	2B-155
Joe Hornung	6/12/1857	10/30/31	R	R	1	1890	.238	120	513	62	122	18	0	0	65	150	12	37	39	–	.292	.255	OF-77, 1B-36, 3B-5, SS-2
Steve Hosey	4/2/69		R	R	2	1992–93	.259	24	58	6	15	2	2	1	7	20	1	16	1	1	.345	.271	OF-19
Jim Howarth	3/7/47		L	L	4	1971–74	.217	152	226	27	49	6	1	1	16	60	26	29	3	2	.265	.298	OF-65, 1B-5
Shorty Howe			–	–	2	1890, 93	.203	20	69	5	14	0	0	0	6	14	3	2	4	–	.203	.236	2B-18, 3B-2
Bill Howerton	12/12/21		L	R	1	1952	.067	11	15	2	1	1	0	0	2	2	3	2	0	–	.133	.222	OF-3
Trenidad Hubbard	5/11/64		R	R	1	1996	.207	10	29	3	6	0	0	0	2	11	2	5	0	–	.379	.258	OF-9
Johnny Hudson	6/30/12	11/7/70	R	R	1	1945	.105	28	171	18	18	11	0	0	6	19	10	41	0	–	.000	.083	3B-5, 2B-2
John Humphries	11/12/1861	11/29/33	L	L	2	1883–84	.063	49	16	1	1	0	0	0	0	1	0	–	0	–	.111	.155	C-40, OF-12
Randy Hundley	6/1/42		R	R	2	1964–65	.063	8				0	0	1			0	5	0	–	.063	.063	C-8
Bill Hunnefield	1/5/1899	8/28/76	B	R	1	1931	.270	64	196	23	53	5	0	0	17	61	9	16	3	–	.311	.302	2B-56, SS-5

Name	Born	Died	B	T	Yrs	Seasons	AVG	G	AB	R	H	2B	3B	HR	RBI	TB	BB	SO	SB	CS	SLG	OBP	Games By Position
Ron Hunt	2/23/41		R	R	3	1968-70	.262	393	1374	221	360	59	4	11	110	460	173	117	16	10	.335	.345	2B-357, 3B-17
Herb Hunter	12/25/1896	7/25/70	L	R	1	1916	.250	21	28	3	7	0	0	1	4	10	0	5	0	-	.357	.250	3B-5, 1B-2

I

Name	Born	Died	B	T	Yrs	Seasons	AVG	G	AB	R	H	2B	3B	HR	RBI	TB	BB	SO	SB	CS	SLG	OBP	Games By Position
Monte Irvin	2/25/19		R	R	7	1949-55	.296	653	2160	322	639	84	28	84	393	1031	310	179	27	7+	.477	.384	OF-585, 1B-104, 3B-7
Mike Ivie	8/8/52		R	R	4	1978-81	.281	336	1023	114	287	50	7	42	172	477	93	166	9	3	.466	.341	1B-251, OF-46, 3B-4, 2B-1

J

Name	Born	Died	B	T	Yrs	Seasons	AVG	G	AB	R	H	2B	3B	HR	RBI	TB	BB	SO	SB	CS	SLG	OBP	Games By Position
Ray Jablonski	12/17/26	11/25/85	R	R	2	1957-58	.264	189	535	65	141	30	2	21	103	238	48	97	2	2	.445	.324	3B-70, 1B-6, OF-1
Jim Jackson	11/28/1877	10/9/55	R	R	1	1902	.182	35	110	14	20	5	0	1	13	27	15	-	6	-	.245	.280	OF-34
Travis Jackson	11/2/03	7/27/87	R	R	15	1922-36	.291	1656	6086	833	1768	291	86	135	929	2636	412	565	71	13+	.433	.335	SS-1326, 3B-307, 2B-1, OF-1
Merwin Jacobson	3/7/1894	1/13/78	L	L	1	1915	.083	8	24	0	2	0	0	0	0	2	1	5	0	-	.083	.120	OF-5
Art Jahn	12/2/1895	1/9/48	R	R	1	1928	.276	10	29	7	8	1	0	1	7	12	2	5	0	-	.414	.323	OF-8
Bernie James	9/2/05	8/1/94	B	R	1	1933	.224	60	125	22	28	2	1	1	10	35	8	12	5	3	.280	.271	2B-26, SS-6, 3B-5
Chris James	10/4/62		R	R	1	1992	.242	111	248	25	60	10	4	5	32	93	14	45	2	-	.375	.282	OF-62
Skip James	10/21/49		L	L	2	1977-78	.167	51	36	8	6	2	0	0	6	8	6	8	1	0	.222	.286	1B-36
Stan Javier	1/9/64		B	R	4	1996-99	.282	460	1464	225	413	69	10	17	151	553	175	239	73	16	.378	.360	OF-416, 1B-3
Tex Jeanes	12/19/00	4/5/73	R	R	1	1927	.300	20	20	5	6	0	0	0	7	6	2	2	0	-	.300	.364	OF-6, P-1
Marcus Jensen	12/14/72		B	R	2	1996-97	.161	39	93	9	15	3	0	2	7	21	15	30	0	0	.226	.278	C-35
Brian Johnson	1/8/68		R	R	2	1997-98	.253	155	487	53	123	15	3	24	61	216	42	93	0	3	.444	.319	C-150, 1B-2, OF-1
Elmer Johnson	6/12/1884	10/31/66	R	R	1	1914	.167	11	12	0	2	0	0	0	0	3	1	3	0	-	.250	.231	C-11
Erik Johnson	10/11/65		R	R	2	1993-94	.222	9	18	1	4	2	0	0	0	6	3	5	0	0	.333	.222	2B-4, SS-2, 3B-1
Frank Johnson	7/22/42		R	R	6	1966-71	.211	196	436	47	92	4	2	4	43	112	37	60	2	2	.257	.273	OF-68, 1B-36, 3B-36, SS-5, 2B-3
Wallace Johnson	12/25/56		B	R	1	1983	.125	7	8	0	1	0	0	0	1	1	0	0	0	0	.125	.125	2B-1
Greg Johnston	2/12/55		L	L	1	1979	.203	42	74	5	15	2	0	1	7	20	2	17	2	0	.270	.224	OF-17
Jimmy Johnston	12/10/1889	2/14/67	R	R	1	1926	.232	37	69	11	16	2	0	0	5	16	6	5	5	-	.232	.293	OF-14
Chris C. Jones	12/16/65		R	R	1	1998	.189	43	90	14	17	2	1	2	10	27	8	28	2	1	.300	.250	OF-29
Chris D. Jones	7/13/57		L	L	1	1986	.000	3	1	0	0	0	0	0	0	0	0	0	0	-	.000	.000	PH
Dax Jones	8/4/70		R	R	1	1996	.172	34	58	7	10	2	0	0	7	17	8	12	2	2	.293	.273	OF-33
Jim Jones	12/25/1876	5/6/53	R	R	2	1901-02	.229	88	340	26	78	15	4	0	24	101	17	-	9	2	.297	.266	OF-87, P-1
Tracy Jones	3/31/61		R	R	1	1989	.186	40	97	5	18	4	0	0	12	22	5	14	2	1	.227	.225	OF-30
Buck Jordan	1/16/07	3/18/93	L	R	1	1927, 29	.286	7	7	1	2	1	0	0	0	2	0	3	0	-	.286	.286	1B-1
Spider Jorgensen	11/3/19		L	R	2	1950-51	.193	52	88	10	17	0	0	2	12	23	8	4	0	0+	.261	.260	OF-11, 3B-6
Von Joshua	5/1/48		L	L	2	1975-76	.305	171	663	88	202	30	12	7	45	277	36	95	21	13	.418	.340	OF-152
Bill Joyce	9/21/1865	5/8/41	L	R	3	1896-98	.292	303	1061	236	310	44	24	18	198	456	200	14+	80	-	.430	.404	3B-169, 1B-132, 2B-2
Ed Jurak	10/24/57		R	R	1	1989	.238	30	42	2	10	0	0	0	1	10	5	5	0	0	.238	.319	SS-6, 3B-5, 2B-4, OF-2, 1B-1
Billy Jurges	5/9/08	3/3/97	R	R	7	1939-45	.264	744	2595	298	685	69	21	23	266	865	262	195	14	-	.333	.331	SS-575, 3B-133, 2B-1

K

Name	Born	Died	B	T	Yrs	Seasons	AVG	G	AB	R	H	2B	3B	HR	RBI	TB	BB	SO	SB	CS	SLG	OBP	Games By Position
Alex Kampouris	11/13/12	5/29/93	R	R	2	1938-39	.247	156	469	58	116	21	3	10	66	173	57	91	0	-	.369	.329	2B-141, 3B-11
Ray Katt	5/9/27		R	R	6	1952-57	.228	336	848	80	193	22	4	25	94	298	64	126	2	1	.351	.282	C-325
Benny Kauff	1/5/1890	11/17/61	L	L	5	1916-20	.287	564	2029	305	582	102	33	29	274	837	207	208	103	33+	.413	.353	OF-559
Tony Kaufmann	12/16/00	6/4/82	R	R	1	1929	.031	39	32	18	1	0	0	0	0	1	6	4	3	-	.031	.184	OF-16
Bob Kearney	10/3/56		R	R	1	1979	-	1	0	0	0	0	0	0	0	0	0	0	0	0	-	1.000	C-1
Willie Keeler	3/3/1872	1/1/23	L	L	3	1892-93, 1910	.322	40	87	17	28	5	0	1	13	38	11	5	9	-	.437	.398	3B-14, OF-5, 2B-2, SS-2
Duke Kelleher	9/30/1893	9/28/47	-	R	1	1916	-	1	0	0	0	0	0	0	0	0	0	0	0	-	-	-	C-1

Player	Born	Died	B	T	Yrs	Seasons	AVG	G	AB	R	H	2B	3B	HR	RBI	TB	BB	SO	SB	CS	SLG	OBP	Games By Position
George Kelly	9/10/1895	10/13/84	R	R	11	1915-17, 19-26	.301	1136	4213	608	1270	218	52	123	762	1961	277	503	54	43+	.465	.345	1B-919, 2B-132, P-1
King Kelly	12/31/1857	11/8/1894	R	R	1	1893	.269	20	67	9	18	3	2	0	15	18	6	5	3	-	.284	.329	C-17, OF-1
Terry Kennedy	6/4/56		L	R	3	1989-91	.252	301	829	56	209	44	0	10	73	285	77	125	2	5	.344	.316	C-282, 1B-4
Jeff Kent	3/7/68		R	R	6	1997-2002	.297	900	3434	570	1021	247	22	175	689	1837	364	659	57	29	.535	.368	2B-854, 1B-70
Buddy Kerr	11/6/22		R	R	7	1943-49	.256	843	2952	315	756	117	19	28	269	995	252	210	38	-	.337	.315	SS-820, 3B-18
Pete Kilduff	4/4/1893	2/14/30	R	R	1	1917	.205	31	78	12	16	3	0	0	12	22	4	11	2	-	.282	.244	2B-21, SS-5, 3B-1
Red Killefer	4/13/1885	9/4/58	R	R	1	1916	1.000	2	1	0	1	0	0	0	1	1	0	0	0	-	1.000	1.000	PH
Jim King	8/27/32		L	L	1	1958	.214	34	56	8	12	2	1	2	8	22	10	8	0	-	.393	.333	OF-15
Lee King	12/26/1892	9/16/67	R	R	4	1919-22	.247	173	409	60	101	19	6	7	52	153	40	52	4	9+	.374	.314	OF-131, 1B-6
Mike Kingery	3/29/61		L	R	2	1990-91	.256	196	317	37	81	9	3	0	32	96	27	40	7	1	.303	.314	OF-133, 1B-6
Dave Kingman	12/21/48		R	R	4	1971-74	.224	409	1242	177	278	55	9	77	217	582	138	422	37	19	.469	.301	1B-213, 3B-140, OF-38, P-2
Bob Kinsella	1/5/1899	12/30/51	L	R	2	1919-20	.250	4	12	1	3	0	0	0	1	3	1	5	1	0+	.250	.250	OF-4
Kinsler			-	-	1	1893	.000	1	3	1	0	0	0	0	0	0	1	1	0	-	.000	.250	OF-1
Jay Kirke	6/16/1888	8/31/68	L	R	1	1918	.250	17	56	5	14	0	0	0	3	15	1	3	0	-	.268	.263	1B-16
Willie Kirkland	2/17/34		L	L	3	1958-60	.261	394	1396	171	364	68	19	57	189	641	129	239	20	12	.459	.323	OF-375
Joe Klinger	8/2/02	7/31/60	R	R	1	1927	.400	3	5	0	2	0	0	0	0	2	0	2	0	-	.400	.400	OF-1
Clyde Kluttz	12/12/17	5/12/79	R	R	2	1945-46	.283	78	230	25	65	14	1	4	22	91	15	11	0	-	.396	.327	C-59
Jimmy Knowles	9/1856	2/11/12	-	-	1	1892	.153	16	59	9	9	1	0	2	7	10	6	8	2	-	.169	.231	3B-15, SS-1
Brad Kocher	1/16/1888	1/13/65	R	R	2	1915-16	.158	38	76	4	12	2	1	0	3	16	2	11	0	-	.211	.179	C-33
Pip Koehler	1/16/02	12/8/86	R	R	1	1925	.000	12	2	1	0	0	0	0	0	0	1	1	0	-	.000	.000	OF-3
Len Koenecke	1/18/04	9/17/35	L	R	1	1932	.255	42	137	33	35	5	0	4	14	52	11	13	3	0	.380	.311	OF-35
Mark Koenig	7/19/04	4/22/93	B	R	2	1935-36	.282	149	454	47	128	16	0	4	44	156	21	22	0	-	.344	.314	2B-72, SS-31, 3B-18
Brad Komminsk	4/4/61		R	R	1	1990	.200	8	5	2	1	0	0	0	0	1	2	2	0	0	.200	.333	OF-7
Wally Kopf	7/10/1899	4/30/79	B	B	1	1921	.333	2	3	0	1	0	0	0	0	1	0	0	0	-	.333	.500	3B-2
Ernie Krueger	12/27/1890	4/22/76	R	B	1	1917	.000	8	10	0	0	0	0	0	0	0	4	4	0	-	.000	.000	C-5
Harvey Kuenn	12/4/30	2/28/88	R	R	5	1961-65	.280	515	1785	240	500	74	13	25	173	675	185	144	13	13	.378	.348	OF-364, 3B-117, 1B-18, SS-1
Duane Kuiper	6/19/50		L	R	4	1982-85	.255	271	514	48	131	12	3	0	42	149	72	47	2	4	.290	.346	2B-146, 1B-1
Randy Kutcher	4/20/60		R	R	2	1986-87	.233	85	202	35	47	10	2	7	17	82	12	46	7	5	.406	.276	OF-57, SS-14, 3B-6, 2B-5

L

Player	Born	Died	B	T	Yrs	Seasons	AVG	G	AB	R	H	2B	3B	HR	RBI	TB	BB	SO	SB	CS	SLG	OBP	Games By Position
Joe Lafata	8/3/21		L	L	3	1947-49	.229	127	236	31	54	3	2	5	34	76	24	42	0	0	.322	.300	1B-49, OF-19
Mike Laga	6/14/60		L	L	2	1989-90	.191	40	47	5	9	2	0	3	11	20	2	13	0	0	.426	.224	1B-14
Dick Lajeskie	1/8/26	8/15/76	R	R	1	1946	.200	6	10	3	2	0	0	0	0	2	3	2	0	-	.200	.385	2B-4
Tom Lampkin	3/4/64		L	R	2	1995-96	.245	131	253	34	62	10	0	7	38	93	29	30	3	5	.368	.323	C-70, OF-6
Rick Lancellotti	7/5/56		L	L	1	1986	.222	15	18	2	4	0	0	2	6	10	7	7	0	0	.556	.222	1B-1, OF-1
Hobie Landrith	3/16/30		L	R	3	1959-61	.246	223	544	59	134	28	0	6	59	180	78	41	1	5	.331	.341	C-209
Don Landrum	2/16/36		L	R	1	1966	.186	72	102	9	19	4	0	1	7	26	9	18	1	-	.255	.252	OF-54
Hal Lanier	7/4/42		R	R	8	1964-71	.229	1101	3514	283	803	105	20	8	262	972	131	413	10	9	.277	.256	SS-620, 2B-419, 3B-83, 1B-5
Norm Larker	12/27/30		L	L	1	1963	.071	19	14	0	1	0	0	0	0	1	2	2	0	0	.071	.188	1B-11
Arlie Latham	3/15/1860	11/29/52	R	R	1	1909	.000	4	2	0	0	0	0	0	0	0	0	-	1	-	.000	.000	2B-2
Tacks Latimer	11/30/1877	4/24/36	R	R	1	1898	.294	5	17	1	5	1	0	0	1	6	0	-	0	-	.353	.294	C-4, OF-2
Billy Lauder	2/23/1874	5/20/33	R	R	2	1902-03	.257	233	877	93	225	33	1	1	97	263	24	-	38	-	.300	.276	3B-229, OF-4
Garland Lawing	8/29/19	9/27/96	R	R	1	1946	.167	8	12	2	2	2	0	0	0	2	0	3	0	-	.167	.167	OF-4
Les Layton	11/18/21		R	R	1	1948	.231	63	91	14	21	4	4	2	12	39	6	21	1	-	.429	.278	OF-20
Tony Lazzeri	12/6/03	8/6/46	R	R	1	1939	.295	13	44	7	13	0	0	1	8	16	7	6	0	-	.364	.392	3B-13
Freddy Leach	11/23/1897	12/10/81	L	R	3	1929-31	.310	368	1470	239	456	71	24	27	179	656	68	48	17	9	.446	.341	OF-344
Jalal Leach	3/14/69		L	L	1	2002	.267	47	180	30	48	10	3	3	9	73	23	22	7	3	.406	.353	OF-44
Rick Leach	5/4/57		L	L	1	1990	.293	78	174	24	51	13	0	2	16	70	21	20	0	2	.402	.369	OF-52, 1B-7, 2B-1
Fred Lear	4/7/1894	10/13/55	R	R	1	1920	.253	31	87	12	22	0	1	1	7	27	8	15	0	2	.310	.316	3B-24, 2B-1

Name	Born	Died	B	T	Yrs	Seasons	AVG	G	AB	R	H	2B	3B	HR	RBI	TB	BB	SO	SB	CS	SLG	OBP	Games By Position
Al Lefevre	9/16/1898	1/21/82	R	R	1	1920	.148	17	27	5	4	0	1	0	0	6	0	13	0	0	.222	.148	SS-9, 2B-6, 3B-1
Hank Leiber	1/17/11	11/8/93	R	R	7	1933-38, 42	.287	531	1838	257	527	92	21	53	319	820	154	184	3	-	.446	.342	OF-468, P-1
Johnnie LeMaster	6/19/54		R	R	11	1975-85	.225	986	3089	313	695	109	19	21	220	905	235	542	93	49	.293	.280	SS-954, 2B-2, 3B-2
Bob Lennon	9/15/28		L	L	2	1954, 56	.172	29	58	8	10	0	0	0	1	11	4	29	0	0	.190	.226	OF-21
Jeffrey Leonard	9/22/55		R	R	8	1981-88	.275	789	2946	381	809	139	24	99	435	1293	184	586	115	42	.439	.317	OF-752, 1B-6
Mark Leonard	8/14/64		L	R	5	1990-92, 94-95	.235	158	306	36	72	17	2	8	38	117	39	68	0	2	.382	.322	OF-86
Sam Leslie	7/26/05	1/21/79	L	L	8	1929-33, 36-38	.295	438	1030	123	304	53	11	17	148	430	69	51	4	-	.417	.339	1B-218, OF-1
Darren Lewis	8/28/67		R	R	5	1991-95	.249	496	1824	280	455	55	23	9	126	583	165	203	138	50	.320	.312	OF-479
Mark Lewis	11/30/69		R	R	1	1997	.267	118	341	50	91	14	6	10	42	147	23	62	3	2	.431	.318	3B-69, 2B-29
Freddy Lindstrom	11/21/05	10/4/81	R	R	9	1924-32	.318	1087	4242	705	1347	212	63	91	603	1958	263	213	80	10+	.462	.357	3B-776, OF-253, 2B-28, SS-1
Dennis Littlejohn	10/4/54		R	R	3	1978-80	.203	78	222	17	45	7	1	1	15	57	28	53	0	0	.257	.292	C-75
Greg Litton	7/13/64		R	R	4	1989-92	.230	291	614	51	141	26	5	10	71	207	40	132	1	5	.337	.277	2B-79, OF-69, 3B-60, SS-28, 1B-23, C-3, P-1
Mickey Livingston	11/15/14	4/3/83	R	R	3	1947-49	.241	69	162	15	39	6	1	6	24	65	24	21	1	-	.401	.339	C-62
Hans Lobert	10/18/1881	9/14/68	R	R	3	1915-17	.241	204	514	56	124	22	6	1	54	161	35	37	18	15+	.313	.290	3B-144
Whitey Lockman	7/25/26		L	L	13	1945, 47-58	.281	1485	5584	799	1571	216	45	113	543	2216	520	362	41	25+	.397	.343	1B-722, OF-693, 2B-15
Kenny Lofton	5/31/67		L	L	1	2002	.267	47	180	30	48	10	3	3	9	73	23	22	7	3	.406	.353	OF-44
Jack Lohrke	2/25/24		R	R	5	1947-51	.244	317	872	118	213	38	9	22	95	335	106	81	9	0+	.384	.326	3B-213, 2B-60, SS-16
Ernie Lombardi	4/6/08	9/26/77	R	R	5	1943-47	.288	472	1384	129	398	36	2	55	239	603	117	80	1	-	.436	.343	C-356
Dale Long	2/6/26	1/27/91	L	L	1	1960	.167	37	54	4	9	0	0	3	6	18	7	7	0	0	.333	.262	1B-10
Loughran	-	-	-	-	1	1884	.103	9	29	4	3	1	0	0	3	6	7	11	-	-	.207	.278	C-9, OF-1
Terrell Lowery	10/25/70		R	R	1	2000	.441	24	34	13	15	4	0	1	5	22	7	8	1	0	.647	.548	OF-20
Hal Luby	6/13/13	5/4/86	R	R	2	1944	.254	111	323	30	82	10	2	2	35	102	52	15	2	-	.316	.357	3B-65, 2B-45, 1B-1
Trey Lunsford	5/25/79		R	R	1	2002	.667	3	3	0	2	1	0	0	1	3	0	1	0	0	1.000	.667	C-3
Denny Lyons	3/12/1866	1/2/29	R	R	1	1892	.257	108	389	71	100	16	7	8	51	154	59	37	11	-	.396	.355	3B-108
Harry Lyons	3/25/1866	6/30/12	R	R	3	1889, 92-93	.244	148	618	95	151	10	5	0	76	171	49	35	35	-	.277	.300	OF-148

M

Name	Born	Died	B	T	Yrs	Seasons	AVG	G	AB	R	H	2B	3B	HR	RBI	TB	BB	SO	SB	CS	SLG	OBP	Games By Position
Waddy MacPhee	12/23/1899	1/20/80	R	R	1	1922	.286	2	7	2	2	0	0	0	0	4	0	2	0	0	.571	.375	3B-2
Garry Maddox	9/1/49		R	R	4	1972-75	.287	421	1635	221	469	88	20	32	188	693	73	237	59	26	.424	.317	OF-405
Ed Madjeski	7/20/08	11/11/94	R	R	1	1937	.200	5	15	0	3	0	0	0	2	3	0	2	0	-	.200	.200	C-5
Bill Madlock	1/2/51		R	R	3	1977-79	.296	331	1229	183	364	63	6	34	131	541	109	91	40	18	.440	.354	2B-183, 3B-126, 1B-8
Freddie Maguire	5/10/1899	11/3/61	R	R	2	1922-23	.238	46	42	15	10	1	0	0	3	11	2	5	2	0	.262	.273	2B-19, 3B-1
Jack Maguire	2/5/25		R	R	2	1950-51	.250	45	60	9	15	3	1	1	7	23	5	15	0	0+	.383	.308	OF-17, 1B-2
Jim Mahady	4/22/01	8/9/36	R	R	1	1921	-	-	0	0	0	0	0	0	0	0	0	0	0	0	-	-	2B-1
Joe Malay	10/25/05	3/19/89	L	L	2	1933, 35	.160	9	25	0	4	0	0	0	2	4	0	7	0	-	.160	.160	1B-8
Candy Maldonado	9/5/60		R	R	4	1986-89	.256	522	1691	210	433	105	8	59	279	731	128	313	22	18	.432	.308	OF-472, 3B-1
Jim Mallory	9/1/18		R	R	1	1945	.298	37	94	10	28	1	0	0	1	29	6	7	1	-	.309	.340	OF-21
Gus Mancuso	12/5/05	10/26/84	R	R	9	1933-38, 42-44	.270	882	2831	238	765	105	10	36	328	998	250	160	3	-	.353	.329	C-840
Jim Mangan	9/24/29		R	R	1	1956	.100	20	20	2	2	0	0	0	0	2	4	6	0	0	.100	.250	C-15
Charlie Manlove	10/8/1862	2/12/52	R	R	1	1884	.000	3	10	0	0	0	0	0	0	0	0	4	-	-	.000	.000	C-3, OF-1
Les Mann	11/18/1893	1/14/62	R	R	2	1927-28	.281	111	260	42	73	11	2	4	35	100	26	16	4	-	.385	.346	OF-90
Kirt Manwaring	7/15/65		R	R	10	1987-96	.246	709	2135	174	526	83	12	16	207	681	160	339	8	9	.319	.299	C-704
Dave Marshall	1/14/43		L	R	3	1967-69	.245	187	441	49	108	12	2	3	49	133	60	105	3	9	.302	.335	OF-137
Doc (E.H.) Marshall	6/4/06		R	R	4	1929-32	.258	219	658	72	170	21	6	0	61	203	28	28	2	-	.309	.289	SS-119, 2B-69, 3B-8, OF-18, C-16, 1B-2, 2B-1
Doc (W.R.) Marshall	9/22/1875	12/11/59	R	R	2	1904,06	.193	49	119	11	23	4	2	0	9	31	8	-	7	-	.261	.244	
Jim Marshall	5/25/31		L	L	2	1960-61	.234	119	154	24	36	2	2	3	20	51	20	32	0	1	.331	.322	1B-32, OF-8
Willard Marshall	2/8/21		L	R	5	1942, 46-49	.283	686	2534	359	717	86	22	86	370	1105	268	133	13	-	.436	.352	OF-667

Player	Born	Died	B	T	Yrs	Years	AVG	G	AB	R	H	2B	3B	HR	RBI	TB	BB	SO	SB	CS	SLG	OBP	Pos
Frank Martin	2/28/1879	9/30/24	–	–	1	1899	.259	17	54	5	14	2	0	0	1	16	2	21	0	—	.296	.286	3B-17
Jerry Martin	5/11/49		R	R	1	1981	.241	72	241	23	58	5	3	4	25	81	21	52	6	2	.336	.302	OF-64
Joe Martin	8/28/11	9/28/60	R	R	1	1936	.267	15	15	0	4	1	0	0	2	5	0	4	0	—	.333	.267	3B-7
Dave Martinez	9/26/64		L	L	2	1993-94	.244	188	476	51	116	21	4	9	54	172	48	61	9	7	.361	.313	OF-131, 1B-25
Ramon Martinez	10/10/72		R	R	5	1998-2002	.269	368	924	129	249	48	7	20	106	371	85	119	7	10	.402	.335	2B-132, 3B-85, SS-76, 1B-6
Don Mason	12/20/44		L	R	5	1966-70	.204	206	333	58	68	4	2	1	16	79	42	42	2	7	.237	.293	2B-81, 3B-23, SS-11
Gary Matthews	7/5/50		R	R	5	1972-76	.287	594	2175	318	624	100	24	64	296	964	275	312	53	24	.443	.367	OF-584
Mike Mattimore	1859	4/28/31	L	L	1	1887	.250	8	32	5	8	1	0	0	4	9	0	—	1	—	.281	.250	C-2, P-7
Milt May	8/1/50		L	R	4	1980-83	.272	388	1255	94	341	58	2	23	142	472	108	130	1	8	.376	.329	C-362
Buster Maynard	3/25/13	9/7/77	R	R	4	1940, 42-43, 46	.221	224	616	68	136	14	5	14	66	202	46	53	3	—	.328	.275	O-142, 3B-32, 2B-1
Brent Mayne	4/19/68		L	R	2	1998-99	.288	211	597	65	172	32	0	10	71	234	80	112	4	4	.392	.375	C-193
Eddie Mayo	4/15/10		L	R	1	1936	.199	46	141	11	28	4	1	1	8	37	11	12	0	—	.262	.257	3B-40
Willie Mays	5/6/31		R	R	21	1951-52, 54-72	.304	2857	10477	2011	3187	504	139	646	1859	5907	1394	1436	336	98	.564	.386	OF-2749, 1B-56, SS-2, 3B-1
Algie McBride	5/23/1869	1/10/56	L	L	1	1901	.280	68	264	27	74	11	0	2	29	91	12	—	3	—	.345	.312	OF-65
Roger McCardell	8/29/32		R	R	1	1959	.000	4	4	0	0	0	0	0	2	0	0	3	0	0	.000	.000	C-3
Johnny McCarthy	1/7/10	9/13/73	L	L	7	1936-41, 48	.276	423	1150	134	317	45	9	22	166	446	74	84	6	—	.388	.319	1B-271, OF-5, P-1
David McCarty	11/23/69		R	R	2	1995-96	.221	103	195	17	43	4	0	6	26	65	20	47	3	1	.333	.293	1B-53, OF-24
Lew McCarty	11/17/1888	6/9/30	R	R	5	1916-20	.272	288	735	56	200	29	9	3	73	256	60	45	8	0+	.348	.327	C-217
Mike W. McCormick	5/6/17	4/14/76	R	R	1	1950	.000	4	4	0	0	0	0	0	0	2	2	2	0	—	.000	.000	PH
Moose McCormick	2/28/1881	7/9/62	L	L	5	1904, 08-09, 12-13	.289	341	987	140	285	52	20	4	108	389	77	22	24	—	.394	.340	OF-251, 1B-1
Willie McCovey	1/10/38		L	L	19	1959-73, 77-80	.274	2256	7214	1113	1974	308	45	469	1388	3779	1168	1351	24	22	.524	.375	1B-1775, OF-275
Tom McCreery	10/19/1874	7/3/41	B	R	2	1897-98	.258	84	298	51	77	12	8	2	44	111	41	—	18	—	.372	.348	OF-80, 2B-3
Jim McDonald	—		R	R		1902	.333	2	9	0	3	0	0	0	3	3	—	18	0	—	.333	.333	OF-2
Dan McGann	7/15/1871	12/13/10	B	R	6	1902-07	.279	682	2430	360	678	94	42	16	290	904	224	—	151	—	.372	.340	1B-681
Willie McGee	11/2/58		B	R	4	1991-94	.301	444	1602	195	483	81	6	14	148	618	116	253	43	22	.386	.349	OF-415
John McGraw	4/7/1873	2/25/34	L	R	5	1902-06	.242	59	132	15	32	0	0	0	6	32	31	—	9	—	.242	.387	SS-37, 2B-4, OF-3, 3B-2
Bill McKechnie	8/7/1886	10/29/65	B	R	1	1916	.246	71	260	22	64	9	1	0	17	75	8	20	7	—	.288	.266	3B-71
Alex McKinnon	8/14/1856	7/24/1887	–	–	1	1884	.272	116	470	66	128	21	12	4	73	185	8	62	0	—	.394	.285	1B-116
Art McLarney	12/20/08	12/20/84	B	R	1	1932	.130	9	23	2	3	1	0	0	3	4	0	3	0	—	.174	.167	SS-9
Larry McLean	7/18/1881	3/24/21	R	R	3	1913-15	.263	122	262	11	69	10	0	0	27	79	12	14	5	—	.302	.285	C-114
Jack McMahon	10/15/1869	12/30/1894	R	L	2	1892-93	.243	51	177	26	43	11	3	3	28	69	8	9	3	—	.390	.291	1B-36, C-16
George McMillan	—		–	–	1	1890	.143	10	35	4	5	0	0	0	1	5	7	4	1	—	.143	.286	OF-10
Hugh McMullen	12/16/01	5/23/86	B	R	2	1925-26	.179	62	106	19	17	3	1	0	6	22	2	21	1	0+	.208	.194	C-61
Jim McNamara	6/10/65		L	R	2	1992-93	.210	34	81	6	17	1	0	1	10	21	6	26	2	0	.259	.264	C-34
Charlie Mead	4/9/21		L	R	3	1943-45	.245	87	261	18	64	8	1	3	27	83	26	24	3	—	.318	.299	OF-71
Joe Medwick	11/24/11	3/21/75	R	R	3	1943-45	.313	232	906	119	284	48	0	19	141	389	49	40	4	—	.429	.349	OF-219, 1B-3
Francisco Melendez	1/25/64		L	L	2	1987-88	.238	35	42	3	10	3	0	0	4	13	0	5	0	—	.310	.289	1B-11, OF-1
Juan Melo	11/10/76		B	R	1	2000	.077	11	13	0	1	0	0	0	1	1	0	5	0	—	.077	.077	2B-6
Bob Melvin	10/28/61		R	R	3	1986-88	.220	265	787	78	173	35	3	24	83	286	45	159	3	8	.363	.262	C-251, 1B-2, 3B-1
Luis Mercedes	2/15/68		R	R	1	1993	.160	18	25	4	4	2	0	0	3	6	1	3	1	1	.240	.192	OF-5
Win Mercer	6/20/1874	1/12/03	R	R	1	1900	.294	76	248	32	73	4	0	0	27	77	26	—	15	—	.310	.361	3B-19, OF-14, SS-7, 2B-3, P-33
Fred Merkle	12/20/1888	3/2/56	R	R	10	1907-16	.272	1105	3831	504	1042	192	58	48	508	1494	312	414	212	15+	.390	.327	1B-1038, OF-35, 2B-2, 3B-1
John Merritt	10/12/1894	11/3/55	L	R	1	1913	—	1	0	0	0	0	0	0	0	0	0	—	0	—			OF-1
Sam Mertes	8/6/1872	3/11/45	R	R	4	1903-06	.273	507	1853	301	506	96	48	17	323	749	200	—	165	—	.404	.344	OF-505, C-1, 1B-1, SS-1
Roger Metzger	10/10/47		B	R	3	1978-80	.246	197	521	46	128	13	9	0	48	159	38	50	19	4	.305	.297	SS-165, 2B-11, 3B-1
Irish Meusel	6/9/1893	3/1/63	R	R	6	1921-26	.314	765	2969	447	931	148	64	70	571	1417	163	116	46	38+	.477	.349	C-737
Chief Meyers	7/29/1880	7/25/71	R	R	7	1909-15	.301	840	2395	242	722	103	34	14	335	935	231	136+	38	4+	.390	.363	C-769
Bruce Miller	3/4/47		R	R	4	1973-76	.246	196	553	43	136	14	4	1	51	161	30	49	1	2	.291	.285	3B-115, 2B-41, SS-20

Name	Born	Died	B	T	Yrs	Seasons	AVG	G	AB	R	H	2B	3B	HR	RBI	TB	BB	SO	SB	CS	SLG	OBP	Games By Position
Jim Miller	10/2/1880	2/7/37	R	R	1	1901	.138	18	58	3	8	0	0	0	3	8	6	-	-	-	.138	.219	2B-18
Jocko Milligan	8/8/1861	8/29/23	R	R	1	1893	.231	42	147	16	34	5	6	1	25	54	14	14	1	2	.367	.298	C-42
Pete Milne	4/10/25		L	L	3	1948-50	.233	47	60	14	14	2	1	1	9	22	13	13	2	-	.367	.281	OF-10
Eddie Milner	5/21/55		L	L	1	1987	.252	101	214	38	54	14	7	4	19	80	24	33	10	3	.374	.328	OF-84
Damon Minor	1/5/74		L	L	3	2000-02	.229	112	227	37	52	14	0	8	29	82	30	98	9	0	.363	.319	1B-59, 2B-1
Doug Mirabelli	10/18/70		R	R	5	1996-2000	.234	140	359	37	84	19	2	8	43	141	51	95	1	-	.393	.332	C-134
Kevin Mitchell	1/13/62		R	R	5	1987-91	.278	624	2211	351	614	109	17	143	411	1186	264	394	23	25	.536	.355	OF-428, 3B-172, 1B-1, SS-1
Johnny Mize	1/7/13	6/2/93	L	R	5	1942, 46-49	.299	655	2452	473	733	110	16	157	505	1346	340	163	13	-	.549	.384	1B-646
John Monroe	8/24/1898	6/19/56	R	R	2	1921	.143	19	21	4	3	1	0	0	3	6	5	6	4	-	.286	.250	2B-8, SS-1
Willie Montanez	4/1/48		L	L	2	1975-76	.306	195	748	74	229	41	4	10	105	308	60	65	7	4	.412	.358	1B-192
Al Moore	8/4/02	11/29/74	R	R	2	1925-26	.213	30	89	12	19	4	0	0	10	23	6	9	2	1+	.258	.263	OF-22
Eddie Moore	1/18/1899	2/10/76	R	R	1	1932	.264	37	87	9	23	3	0	1	6	29	9	6	1	-	.333	.333	SS-21, 3B-6, 2B-5
Joe Moore	12/25/08		L	R	12	1930-41	.298	1335	5427	809	1615	258	53	79	513	2216	348	247	46	-	.408	.340	OF-1294
Joe Morgan	9/19/43		L	R	2	1981-82	.270	224	771	115	208	35	5	22	92	319	151	97	38	9	.414	.389	2B-207, 3B-3
Howie Moss	10/17/19	5/7/89	R	R	1	1942	.000	7	14	0	0	0	0	0	0	0	4	4	0	-	.000	.000	OF-3
Manny Mota	2/18/38		R	R	1	1962	.176	47	74	9	13	0	1	0	9	14	7	8	3	2	.189	.247	OF-27, 3B-7, 2B-3
Bill Mueller	3/17/71		B	R	6	1996-2000,02	.288	607	2111	333	609	121	8	28	214	830	269	295	15	10	.393	.369	3B-544, 2B-21, 1B-2
Don Mueller	4/14/27		L	R	10	1948-57	.298	1171	4194	492	1248	134	37	65	504	1651	156	137	11	8+	.394	.323	OF-1041
Heinie Mueller	9/16/1899	1/23/75	L	L	2	1926-27	.265	169	495	69	131	12	3	7	48	170	46	29	9	-	.343	.327	OF-137, 1B-1
Ray Mueller	3/8/12	6/29/94	R	R	2	1949-50	.215	60	181	17	39	3	2	5	23	61	13	16	1	-	.337	.268	C-60
Fran Mullins	5/14/57		R	R	1	1984	.218	57	110	8	24	8	0	2	10	38	9	29	3	1	.345	.277	3B-28, SS-28, 2B-4
Bobby Murcer	5/20/46		L	R	2	1975-76	.279	294	1059	153	295	49	6	34	181	458	175	123	21	12	.432	.381	OF-290
Danny F. Murphy	8/11/1876	11/22/55	R	R	2	1900-01	.255	27	94	11	24	1	0	0	6	25	9	9	4	-	.266	.320	2B-27
Danny J. Murphy	9/10/1864	12/14/15	-	-	1	1892	.115	8	26	2	2	1	0	0	0	3	5	4	-	-	.115	.258	C-8
Frank Murphy	4/16/1875	11/4/12	R	-	1	1901	.162	35	130	10	21	3	3	0	8	24	6	8	2	-	.185	.199	2B-23, OF-12
Pat Murphy	1/2/1857	5/16/27	-	R	4	1887-90	.220	86	309	34	68	9	2	1	21	84	24	28	7	-	.272	.276	C-83, OF-3, SS-1
Yale Murphy	11/11/1869	2/14/06	L	R	3	1894-95, 97	.239	130	472	100	113	12	4	0	45	133	80	36+	35	-	.282	.350	SS-60, OF-53, 3B-11, 2B-4, 1B-1
Calvin Murray	7/30/71		R	R	4	1999-2002	.240	240	551	90	132	28	3	8	52	190	64	96	18	11	.345	.325	OF-164
Red Murray	3/4/1884	12/4/58	R	R	8	1909-15, 17	.268	881	2968	407	796	124	63	22	444	1112	221	186+	239	3+	.375	.319	OF-812, C-1
Rich Murray	7/6/57		R	R	2	1980,83	.216	57	204	19	44	4	2	4	25	68	11	51	2	1	.333	.256	1B-56
George Myatt	6/14/14		L	R	2	1938-39	.278	65	223	34	62	4	1	3	13	77	20	19	12	-	.345	.337	3B-33, SS-24
Glenn Myatt	7/9/1897	8/9/69	L	R	1	1935	.222	13	18	2	4	0	1	0	6	9	0	3	0	-	.500	.222	C-4

N

Name	Born	Died	B	T	Yrs	Seasons	AVG	G	AB	R	H	2B	3B	HR	RBI	TB	BB	SO	SB	CS	SLG	OBP	Games By Position
Offa Neal	6/5/1876	4/12/50	L	R	1	1905	.000	4	13	0	0	0	0	0	0	0	0	-	0	-	.000	.000	3B-3, 2B-1
Tom Needham	5/17/1879	12/13/26	R	R	1	1908	.209	54	91	8	19	3	0	0	11	22	12	-	0	-	.242	.301	C-47
Candy Nelson	1849	9/4/10	L	R	1	1887	.000	1	2	0	0	0	0	0	0	0	0	-	0	-	.000	.000	3B-1
Ray Nelson	8/4/1875	1/8/61	R	R	1	1901	.200	39	130	12	26	2	0	0	7	28	10	-	3	-	.215	.257	3B-39
Charlie Newman	11/5/1868	11/23/47	R	R	1	1892	.333	3	12	1	4	0	0	0	0	4	2	0	3	-	.333	.429	OF-3
Roy Nichols	3/3/21		R	R	1	1944	.222	11	9	3	2	1	0	0	0	3	2	2	0	-	.333	.364	2B-1, 3B-1
Steve Nicosia	8/6/55		R	R	2	1983-84	.309	63	165	13	51	11	2	2	25	72	11	16	1	1	.436	.352	C-50
Bert Niehoff	5/13/1884	12/8/74	R	R	1	1918	.261	7	23	3	6	0	0	0	1	6	0	4	0	1	.261	.261	2B-7
Bob Nieman	1/26/27	3/10/85	R	R	1	1962	.300	30	30	9	9	0	0	0	3	14	4	0	0	-	.467	.323	OF-3
Donell Nixon	12/31/61		R	R	2	1988-89	.291	154	244	38	71	5	0	1	21	79	21	42	21	11	.324	.347	OF-110
Ray Noble	3/15/19	5/9/98	R	R	3	1951-53	.218	107	243	31	53	6	1	9	40	88	25	41	1	0	.362	.291	C-87
Matt Nokes	10/31/63		L	R	1	1985	.208	19	53	3	11	2	0	2	5	19	1	9	0	0	.358	.222	C-14
Bill North	5/15/48		B	R	3	1979-81	.250	316	1006	182	252	34	5	7	61	317	203	190	129	51	.315	.376	OF-282

O

Name	Born	Died	B	T	Yrs	Seasons	AVG	G	AB	R	H	2B	3B	HR	RBI	TB	BB	SO	SB	CS	SLG	OBP	Games By Position
Ken Oberkfell	5/4/56		L	R	1	1989	.319	83	116	17	37	5	1	2	15	50	8	8	0	1	.431	.363	3B-38, 1B-7, 2B-7
Tom O'Brien	2/20/1873	2/4/01	-	-	1	1899	.297	150	573	100	170	21	10	6	77	229	44	-	23	-	.400	.347	OF-127, 3B-21, SS-2, 1B-1, 2B-1
Danny O'Connell	1/21/27	10/2/69	R	R	3	1957-59	.246	236	728	107	179	33	5	10	51	252	89	80	10	5	.346	.328	2B-180, 3B-59

Player	Born	Died	B	T	Yrs	Seasons	AVG	G	AB	R	H	2B	3B	HR	RBI	TB	BB	SO	SB	CS	SLG	OBP	Games By Position
Jimmy O'Connell	2/11/01	11/11/76	L	R	2	1923-24	.270	139	356	66	96	13	4	8	57	141	45	48	9	4	.396	.352	OF-93, 1B-8, 2B-1
Ken O'Dea	3/16/13	12/17/85	L	R	3	1939-41	.209	159	282	29	59	10	2	6	40	91	34	51	0	–	.323	.294	C-75
Lefty O'Doul	3/4/1897	12/7/69	L	L	3	1928, 33-34	.314	275	760	125	239	32	8	26	127	365	77	32	12	–	.480	.378	OF-195
Bob O'Farrell	10/19/1896	2/20/88	R	R	5	1928-32	.266	395	871	113	232	47	10	11	143	332	125	100	6	–	.381	.358	C-337
Hal O'Hagen	9/30/1873	1/14/13	–	–	1	1902	.143	26	84	5	12	2	1	0	8	16	2		3	–	.190	.163	1B-18, OF-8
Bill O'Hara	8/14/1883	6/15/31	L	R	1	1909	.236	115	360	48	85	9	3	0	30	103	41	31	31	–	.286	.314	OF-111
Al Oliver	10/14/46	–	L	L	1	1984	.298	91	339	27	101	19	2	0	34	124	20	2	2	2	.366	.337	1B-82
Nate Oliver	12/13/40	–	R	R	1	1968	.178	36	73	13	13	2	0	0	1	15	7	13	0	1	.205	.189	2B-14, SS-13, 3B-1
Tom O'Malley	12/25/60	–	L	R	3	1982-84	.260	240	726	68	189	28	5	7	72	248	87	88	2	7	.342	.339	3B-207, 2B-1, SS-1
Mickey O'Neil	4/12/00	4/8/64	R	R	1	1927	.132	16	38	2	5	2	0	0	3	5	5	2	0	–	.132	.233	C-16
John O'Neill	–	–	–	R	2	1899, 1902	.000	4	15	0	0	0	0	0	0	0	0	–	0	–	.000	.000	C-4
Tip O'Neill	5/25/1858	12/31/15	R	R	1	1883	.197	23	76	8	15	3	1	0	5	18	3	15	3	–	.237	.228	OF-7, P-19
Jack Onslow	10/13/1888	12/22/60	R	R	1	1917	.250	9	8	1	2	1	0	0	3	3	1	0	1	–	.375	.250	C-9
Steve Ontiveros	10/26/51	–	B	R	4	1973-76	.266	311	775	77	206	34	1	8	74	266	122	103	2	0	.343	.366	3B-171, 1B-32, OF-18
Joe Orengo	11/29/14	7/24/88	R	R	1	1941, 43	.216	160	518	51	112	19	4	10	54	169	64	95	2	–	.326	.302	1B-82, 3B-59, SS-9, 2B-6
Jim O'Rourke	9/1/1850	1/8/19	R	R	8	1885-89, 91-92, 1904	.299	807	3232	592	966	170	60	21	446	1319	235	176+	153+	–	.408	.346	OF-655, C-130, 3B-40, 1B-7, 2B-2
Tom O'Rourke	10/1865	7/19/29	–	–	1	1890	.000	2	7	1	0	0	0	0	0	0	0	1	–	–	.000	.125	C-2
Dave Orr	9/29/1859	6/3/15	R	R	1	1883	.000	1	3	0	0	0	0	0	0	0	0	0	–	–	.000	.000	OF-1
John Orsino	4/22/38	–	R	R	2	1961-62	.275	43	131	9	36	5	2	4	16	57	8	24	0	0	.435	.317	C-41
Mel Ott	3/2/09	11/21/58	L	R	22	1926-47	.304	2730	9456	1859	2876	488	72	511	1860	5041	1708	896	89	–	.533	.411	OF-2313, 3B-256, 2B-5
Phil Ouellette	11/10/61	–	B	R	1	1986	.174	10	23	1	4	0	0	0	0	4	3	3	0	0	.174	.269	C-9
Henry Oxley	1/4/1858	10/12/45	–	–	1	1884	.000	2	4	0	0	0	0	0	0	0	2	0	0	–	.000	.200	C-2
P	**Born**	**Died**	**B**	**T**	**Yrs**	**Seasons**	**AVG**	**G**	**AB**	**R**	**H**	**2B**	**3B**	**HR**	**RBI**	**TB**	**BB**	**SO**	**SB**	**CS**	**SLG**	**OBP**	**Games By Position**
Jose Pagan	5/5/35	–	R	R	7	1959-65	.242	655	2042	215	494	69	12	19	178	644	150	278	40	27	.315	.294	SS-613, 3B-19, OF-13, 2B-4
Rick Parker	3/20/63	–	R	R	2	1990-91	.223	67	121	19	27	5	0	2	15	38	11	20	6	1	.314	.288	OF-39, 2B-2, 3B-1, SS-1
John Patterson	2/11/67	–	B	R	4	1992-95	.215	228	564	74	121	16	5	5	52	162	35	113	22	7	.287	.260	2B-138, OF-5
Pat Patterson	1/29/01	10/1/77	R	R	1	1921	.400	23	35	5	14	0	0	1	5	17	2	5	0	–	.486	.432	3B-14, SS-7
Gene Paulette	5/26/1891	2/8/66	R	R	1	1911	.167	12	12	1	2	0	0	0	1	2	0		0	–	.167	.167	1B-7, 3B-1, SS-1
Homer Peel	10/10/02	–	R	R	2	1933-34	.243	105	189	23	46	1	0	2	15	55	15	12	0	0	.291	.299	OF-55
Dan Peltier	6/30/68	–	L	L	1	1996	.254	31	59	3	15	2	0	2	9	17	7	9	0	0	.288	.333	1B-13, OF-1
Marty Perez	2/28/47	–	R	R	1	1976	.259	93	332	37	86	13	1	2	26	107	30	28	3	4	.322	.320	2B-89, SS-5
Tony Perezchica	4/20/66	–	R	R	3	1988, 90-91	.220	34	59	4	13	4	1	0	4	19	5	15	0	1	.322	.281	SS-15, 2B-14
Cap Peterson	8/15/42	5/16/80	R	R	5	1962-66	.235	244	429	43	101	16	1	7	44	142	27	85	2	–	.331	.281	OF-91, 2B-9, 3B-6, 1B-4, SS-3
Joe Pettini	1/26/55	–	R	R	4	1980-83	.203	188	344	38	70	5	2	1	20	82	33	53	10	4	.238	.273	SS-106, 3B-40, 2B-34
Fred Pfeffer	3/17/1860	4/10/32	R	R	1	1896	.143	4	14	1	2	0	0	0	4	2	2	1	0	–	.143	.200	2B-4
Monte Pfyl	5/11/1884	10/18/45	L	L	1	1907	–	1	0	0	0	0	0	0	0	0	1	–	0	–	–	–	1B-1
Dave Philley	5/16/20	–	B	R	1	1960	.164	39	61	5	10	0	0	1	7	13	6	14	0	0	.213	.239	OF-10, 3B-3
Dick Phillips	11/24/31	–	R	R	1	1962	.000	5	3	0	0	0	0	0	0	0	1		0	0	.000	.250	1B-1
J.R. Phillips	4/29/70	–	L	L	4	1993-96	.194	133	310	32	60	10	1	13	40	111	21	100	2	2	.358	.245	1B-104, OF-1
Mike Phillips	8/19/50	–	L	R	3	1973-75	.222	173	418	40	93	9	5	3	30	121	26	58	5	8	.289	.268	3B-68, 2B-43, SS-43
Gracie Pierce	–	8/28/1894	R	R	1	1883	.081	18	62	3	5	0	0	0	3	7	1	9	4	–	.113	.095	3B-18, 2B-1
Sandy Piez	10/13/1892	12/29/30	R	R	1	1914	.375	37	8	9	3	0	1	0	5	7	0		0	–	.625	.375	OF-4
Joe Pignatano	8/4/29	–	R	R	1	1962	.200	7	5	2	1	0	0	1	6	5	4		0	0	.200	.556	C-7
Jess Pike	7/31/15	3/28/84	L	R	1	1946	.171	16	41	4	7	1	1	0	2	13	6	9	0	–	.317	.277	OF-10
Joe Pittman	1/1/54	–	R	R	1	1984	.227	17	22	2	5	0	0	0	2	5	0	6	1	1	.227	.227	SS-6, 2B-5, 3B-2

Name	Born	Died	B	T	Yrs	Seasons	AVG	G	AB	R	H	2B	3B	HR	RBI	TB	BB	SO	SB	CS	SLG	OBP	Games By Position
Hugh Poland	1/19/13	3/30/84	L	R	1	1943	.083	4	12	1	1	0	1	0	2	3	1	0	0	—	.250	.154	C-4
Dante Powell	8/25/73		R	R	3	1997-98,01	.327	49		14				4	23		11		1	—	.469	.411	OF-39
Les Powers	11/5/09	11/13/78	L	L	1	1938	.000	2	3	0	0	0	0	0	0	0	0	1	0	—	.000	.000	PH
Joe P. Price	4/10/1897	1/15/61	R	R	1	1928	.000	1	1	0	0	0	0	0	0	0	0	1	0	—	.000	.000	PH
Ron Pruitt	10/21/51		R	R	2	1982-83	.400	6	5	2	2	1	0	0	2	3	1	1	0	0	.600	.500	C-1, OF-1
John Puhl	1/10/1876	8/24/00	-	-	2	1898-99	.182	3	11	1	2	0	0	0	1	2	0	—	0	—	.182	.182	3B-3

Q

Name	Born	Died	B	T	Yrs	Seasons	AVG	G	AB	R	H	2B	3B	HR	RBI	TB	BB	SO	SB	CS	SLG	OBP	Games By Position
Luis Quinones	4/28/62		B	R	1	1986	.179	71	106	13	19	1	3	0	11	26	3	17	3	1	.245	.202	SS-33, 3B-31, 2B-8

R

Name	Born	Died	B	T	Yrs	Seasons	AVG	G	AB	R	H	2B	3B	HR	RBI	TB	BB	SO	SB	CS	SLG	OBP	Games By Position
John Rabb	6/23/60		R	R	3	1982-84	.218	96	188	20	41	10	7	4	23	65	19	51	2	1	.346	.290	C-37, 1B-13, OF-11
Dave Rader	12/26/48		L	R	6	1971-76	.262	583	1795	193	471	75	7	22	161	626	182	125	5	2	.349	.330	C-560
John Rainey	7/26/1864	11/11/12	L	R	1	1887	.293	17	58	6	17	3	0	0	12	20	6	6	0	1	.345	.349	3B-17
Gary Rajsich	10/28/54		L	L	1	1985	.165	51	91	5	15	6	0	0	10	21	17	22	0	1	.231	.296	1B-23
Cody Ransom	2/17/76		R	R	2	2001-02	.200	16	10	3	2	0	0	1	1	2	1	6	0	0	.200	.273	SS-9
Jeff Ransom	11/11/60		R	R	3	1981-83	.190	26	79	10	15	1	0	0	6	19	11	15	0	0	.241	.289	C-25
Earl Rapp	5/20/21	2/13/92	L	R	1	1951	.091	13	11	0	1	0	0	0		1	2	3	0	0	.091	.231	PH
Goldie Rapp	2/6/1892	7/1/66	B	R	1	1921	.215	58	181	21	39	9	1	0	15	50	15	13	3	11	.276	.276	3B-56
Bill Rariden	2/4/1888	8/28/42	R	R	3	1916-18	.239	290	800	58	191	24	5	1	71	228	112	64	8	—	.285	.332	C-282
Johnny Rawlings	8/17/1892	10/16/72	R	R	2	1921-22	.275	174	615	86	169	21	9	2	60	214	41	34	11	10	.348	.320	2B-163, 3B-5, SS-1
Glenn Redmon	1/11/48		R	R	1	1974	.235	7	17	0	4	3	0	0	4	7	3	0	0	0	.412	.278	2B-4
Jeff Reed	11/12/62		L	R	3	1993-95	.236	182	335	33	79	8	0	7	28	108	47	60	0	—	.322	.330	C-112
Randy Reese	2/7/04	1/10/66	R	R	4	1927-30	.281	331	1142	166	321	47	11	14	111	432	51	107	21	—	.378	.312	OF-120, 3B-84, 2B-70, 1B-8, SS-6
Joe Regan	7/12/1872	11/18/48	R	R	1	1898	.200	2	5	1	1	0	0	0	2	1	0	—	0	—	.200	.200	OF-2
Jessie Reid	6/1/62		L	L	1	1987-88	.100	8	10	1	1	0	0	0	1	4	0	6	0	0	.400	.182	OF-3
Ken Reitz	6/24/51		R	R	1	1976	.267	155	577	40	154	21	1	5	66	192	24	48	5	4	.333	.296	3B-155, SS-1
Nap Reyes	11/24/19	9/15/95	R	R	4	1943-45,50	.284	279	931	90	264	35	11	13	110	360	44	62	5	—	.387	.316	3B-153, 1B-107, OF-3
Bobby Rhawn	2/13/19	6/9/84	R	R	2	1947-48	.263	63	118	26	31	5	1	2	13	44	23	9	4	—	.373	.383	2B-16, SS-14, 3B-12
Dusty Rhodes	5/13/27		L	L	7	1952-57,59	.253	576	1172	146	296	44	10	54	207	522	131	196	3	2	.445	.328	OF-297
Gene Richards	9/29/53		L	L	1	1984	.252	87	135	18	34	4	0	0	4	38	18	28	5	3	.281	.340	OF-26
Paul Richards	11/21/08	5/4/86	R	R	3	1933-35	.181	100	166	14	30	4	0	0	13	34	18	21	0	—	.205	.261	C-77
Danny Richardson	1/25/1863	9/12/26	R	R	7	1884-89,91	.258	696	2736	439	707	101	35	24	353	950	173	176	148+	+	.347	.303	2B-483, OF-141, 3B-36, SS-29, P-15
Hardy Richardson	4/21/1855	1/14/31	R	R	1	1892	.214	64	248	36	53	11	5	2	34	80	21	26	14	—	.323	.275	2B-33, OF-17, 1B-9, SS-6
Bill Rigney	1/29/18		R	R	8	1946-53	.259	654	1966	281	510	78	14	41	212	739	208	206	25	4+	.376	.330	2B-245, 3B-163, SS-149, 1B-1
Ernest Riles	10/2/60		L	R	3	1988-90	.264	293	644	91	170	22	5	18	89	256	64	109	1	8	.398	.331	3B-123, 2B-59, SS-49, OF-5
Armando Rios	9/13/71		L	L	4	1998-2001	.279	292	706	111	197	41	8	33	131	355	92	153	13	8	.503	.360	OF-238, 1B-1
Jimmy Ripple	10/14/09	7/16/59	L	R	4	1936-39	.286	417	1361	190	389	65	8	23	185	539	114	63	6	—	.396	.341	OF-341
Dave Robertson	9/25/1889	11/5/70	L	L	7	1912, 14-17, 19,22	.285	561	1968	254	560	65	30	30	217	775	59	189	70	27+	.394	.305	OF-501, 1B-1
Craig Robinson	8/21/48		R	R	2	1975-76	.143	44	42	8	6	2	0	0	2	8	5	10	0	1	.190	.234	2B-16, SS-13, 3B-2
Jack Robinson	7/15/1880	7/22/21	-	R	1	1902	.000	4	9	0	0	0	0	0	2	0	2	—	1	—	.000	.000	C-3
Andre Rodgers	12/2/34		R	R	4	1957-60	.242	206	594	69	144	25	8	13	66	224	69	129	3	2	.377	.321	SS-145, 3B-29, 1B-6, OF-2
Eric Rodin	2/5/30	1/4/91	R	R	1	1954	.000	5	6	0	0	0	0	0	0	0	2	2	0	0	.000	.000	OF-3
Jose Rodriguez	2/23/1894	1/21/53	R	R	3	1916-18	.166	58	145	17	24	0	3	0	17	30	14	4	8	—	.207	.239	2B-42, 1B-15, 3B-2
Ron Roenicke	8/19/56		B	L	1	1985	.256	65	133	23	34	9	1	3	13	54	35	27	6	2	.406	.411	OF-35
Wally Roettger	8/28/02	9/14/51	R	R	1	1930	.283	121	420	51	119	15	5	5	51	159	25	29	1	—	.379	.324	OF-114
Jimmy Rosario	5/5/45		B	R	2	1971-72	.222	99	194	27	43	6	6	0	13	51	33	35	7	5	.263	.335	OF-68

Name	Born	Died	B	T	Yrs	Seasons	AVG	G	AB	R	H	2B	3B	HR	RBI	TB	BB	SO	SB	CS	SLG	OBP	Games By Position
Goody Rosen	8/28/12	4/6/94	L	L	1	1946	.281	100	310	39	87	11	4	5	30	121	48	32	2	–	.390	.377	OF-84
Harry Rosenberg	6/22/09	4/13/97	R	R	1	1930	.000	9	5	1	0	0	0	0	0	0	0	4	0	–	.000	.167	OF-3
Edd Roush	5/8/1893	3/21/88	L	L	4	1916, 27-29	.298	340	1252	183	373	51	15	17	128	505	86	43	29	0	.403	.343	OF-299
Johnny Rucker	1/15/17	8/7/85	L	R	6	1940-41, 43-46	.272	705	2617	354	711	105	39	21	214	957	109	248	35	3	.366	.301	OF-607
Ken Rudolph	12/29/46		R	R	2	1974-77	.254	68	173	12	44	3	0	0	10	47	22	18	1	0	.272	.338	C-67
Rudy Rufer	10/28/26		R	R	2	1949-50	.077	22	26	2	2	0	0	0	2	2	2	1	1	0	.077	.143	SS-15
Blondy Ryan	1/4/06	11/28/59	R	R	4	1933-34, 37-38	.239	289	1009	93	241	32	6	6	102	303	41	141	3	–	.300	.269	SS-197, 3B-68, 2B-30
Connie Ryan	2/27/20	1/3/96	R	R	1	1942	.185	11	27	4	5	0	0	0	2	5	4	3	1	–	.185	.290	2B-11
S																							
Mike Sadek	5/30/46		R	R	8	1973, 75-81	.226	383	813	88	184	30	4	5	74	237	108	97	6	6	.292	.317	C-356, OF-1
Ebba St. Claire	8/5/21	8/22/82	B	R	1	1954	.262	20	42	5	11	1	0	2	6	18	12	7	0	1	.429	.426	C-16
Ron Samford	2/28/30		R	R	1	1954	.000	12	5	2	0	0	0	0	0	0	0	1	0	0	.000	.000	2B-3
Alejandro Sanchez	2/14/59		R	R	1	1984	.195	41	41	3	8	0	1	0	2	10	0	12	2	3	.244	.195	OF-11
Rey Sanchez	10/5/67		R	R	1	1998	.285	109	316	44	90	14	2	2	30	114	16	47	0	0	.361	.325	SS-76, 2B-36
Deion Sanders	8/9/67		L	L	1	1995	.285	52	214	29	61	9	5	5	18	95	18	42	8	6	.444	.341	OF-52
Reggie Sanders	12/1/67		R	R	1	2002	.250	140	505	75	126	23	6	23	85	230	47	121	18	6	.455	.324	OF-137
Andres Santana	2/5/68		B	R	1	1990	.000	6	2	0	0	0	0	0	1	0	0	0	0	0	.000	.000	SS-3
F.P. Santangelo	10/24/67		B	R	1	1999	.260	113	254	49	66	17	3	3	26	98	53	54	12	4	.386	.406	OF-81, 2B-11, 3B-3, SS-1
Benito Santiago	3/9/65		R	R	2	2001-02	.270	259	955	95	258	49	9	22	119	391	50	151	9	6	.409	.305	C-255, 1B-2
Bill Sarni	9/19/27	4/15/83	R	R	1	1956	.231	78	238	16	55	9	3	5	23	85	20	31	0	1	.357	.291	C-78
Mackey Sasser	8/3/62		L	R	1	1987	.000	2	4	0	0	0	0	0	0	0	0	0	0	0	.000	.000	C-1
Hank Sauer	3/17/17		R	R	3	1957-59	.251	228	629	74	158	22	0	39	123	299	84	103	1	0	.475	.339	OF-98
Skeeter Scalzi	6/16/13	8/25/84	R	R	1	1939	.333	11	18	3	6	0	0	0	0	6	3	2	1	–	.333	.429	SS-5
Mort Scanlon	3/18/1861	12/29/28	–	–	1	1890	.000	3	10	0	0	0	0	0	0	0	2	5	1	–	.000	.167	1B-3
Steve Scarsone	4/11/66		R	R	4	1993-96	.247	281	722	98	178	39	4	20	80	285	57	225	5	8	.395	.302	2B-129, 3B-80, 1B-24, SS-2
Ray Schalk	8/12/1892	5/19/70	R	R	1	1929	.000	5	2	0	0	0	0	0	0	0	0	1	0	–	.000	.000	C-5
Bobby Schang	12/7/1886	8/29/66	R	R	1	1915	.143	12	21	1	3	1	0	0	1	3	4	5	0	–	.143	.280	C-6
Mike Schemer	11/20/17	4/22/83	L	L	2	1945-46	.330	32	109	10	36	3	1	1	10	44	6	1	2	–	.404	.365	1B-27
Hank Schenz	4/11/19	5/12/88	R	R	1	1951	–	8	0	1	0	0	0	0	0	0	0	0	0	0	–	–	PR
Admiral Schlei	1/12/1878	1/24/58	R	R	3	1909-11	.230	148	379	35	87	14	1	0	38	103	54	11+	8	–	.272	.326	C-138
Bob Schmidt	4/22/33		R	R	4	1958-61	.252	310	924	94	233	39	4	27	112	361	72	135	0	6	.391	.306	C-303
Red Schoendienst	2/2/23		B	R	2	1956-57	.301	149	588	74	177	20	7	11	47	244	38	18	3	3	.415	.343	2B-142
Dick Schofield	1/7/35		B	R	2	1965-66	.197	112	395	43	78	10	1	2	19	96	35	52	2	4	.243	.263	SS-101
Hank Schreiber	7/12/1891	2/23/68	R	R	1	1921	.333	6	6	2	2	0	0	0	2	3	1	1	0	–	.333	.429	2B-2, SS-2, 3B-1
Pop Schriver	7/11/1865	12/27/32	R	R	1	1895	.315	24	92	16	29	5	0	1	16	36	9	10	3	–	.391	.376	C-18, 1B-6
Bob Schroder	12/30/44		L	R	4	1965-68	.217	138	221	29	48	5	1	0	12	55	23	21	1	0	.249	.291	2B-61, SS-13, 3B-7
Bob Seeds	2/24/07	10/28/93	R	R	3	1938-40	.284	200	624	86	177	22	6	18	94	265	59	83	1	–	.425	.346	OF-166
Kip Selbach	3/24/1872	2/17/56	L	R	2	1900-01	.313	266	1025	187	321	58	18	5	124	430	117	–	44	–	.420	.384	OF-266
Scott Servais	6/4/67		R	R	2	1999-2000	.272	76	206	22	56	10	0	5	21	81	15	32	0	0	.393	.330	C-94, 1B-1
Cy Seymour	12/9/1872	9/20/19	L	L	10	1896-1900, 06-10	.285	727	2561	300	731	94	27	22	345	945	152	25+	96	–	.369	.325	OF-556, 1B-4, 2B-1, 3B-1, P-139
Tillie Shafer	3/22/1889	1/10/62	B	R	4	1909-10, 12-13	.273	283	776	138	212	24	14	5	83	279	105	80+	60	–	.360	.360	3B-119, 2B-55, SS-49, OF-17
Spike Shannon	2/7/1878	5/16/40	B	R	3	1906-08	.253	308	1140	180	288	19	7	2	79	327	144	–	64	–	.287	.336	OF-305
Jack Sharrott	8/13/1869	12/31/27	–	R	3	1890-92	.224	46	147	22	33	5	2	1	21	45	1	17	9	–	.306	.230	OF-12, P-36
Danny Shay	11/8/1876	12/1/27	–	R	1	1907	.190	35	79	10	15	1	0	0	6	21	12	–	5	–	.266	.297	2B-13, SS-9, OF-2
Jim Sheehan	6/3/13		R	R	1	1936	.000	1	4	0	0	0	0	0	0	0	0	2	0	–	.000	.000	C-1
Tommy Sheehan	11/6/1877	5/22/59	R	R	1	1900	.000	2	2	0	0	0	0	0	0	0	0	0	0	–	.000	.000	SS-5
Pat Sheridan	12/4/57		L	R	1	1989	.205	70	161	20	33	3	4	3	14	53	13	45	4	1	.329	.264	OF-66
Tsuyoshi Shinjo	1/28/72		R	R	1	2002	.238	118	362	42	86	15	3	9	37	134	24	46	5	0	.370	.294	OF-117

Player	Born	Died	B	T	Yr	Seasons	BA	G	AB	R	H	2B	3B	HR	RBI	TB	BB	SO	SB	CS	SLG	OBP	Position
Ralph Shinners	10/4/1895	7/23/62	R	R	2	1922–23	.243	89	148	21	36	5	2	0	15	45	23	3	5		.304	.277	OF-43
Ed Sicking	3/30/1897	8/30/78	R	R	3	1918–20	.217	98	281	22	61	7	1	0	24	70	21	8	2+		.249	.262	3B-52, 2B-33, SS-12
Norm Siebern	7/26/33		L	R	1	1967	.155	46	58	6	9	1	0	0	4	12	13	0	0		.207	.319	1B-15, OF-2
Mike Slattery	11/26/1866	10/16/04	L	L	2	1888–89	.251	115	439	57	110	14	6	2	47	142	31	28	–		.323	.279	OF-115
Scottie Slayback	10/5/01		R	R	1	1926	.000	2	8	0	0	0	0	0	0	0	0	0	–		.000	.000	2B-2
Bruce Sloan	10/4/14	9/24/73	L	L	1	1944	.269	59	104	7	28	4	0	0	9	37	8	0	–		.356	.350	OF-21
Aleck Smith	1871	7/9/19	–	R	2	1901, 06	.151	42	106	5	16	0	0	0	8	16	–	3	–		.151	.159	C-33, 1B-3, OF-1
Billy Smith	7/14/53		B	R	1	1981	.180	36	61	6	11	0	0	0	5	14	9	16	0		.230	.286	SS-21, 2B-5, 3B-3
Chris Smith	7/18/57		B	R	1	1983	.328	22	67	13	22	6	0	0	11	33	12	0	0		.493	.392	1B-15, OF-4, 3B-1
Earl Smith	2/14/1897	6/8/63	L	R	5	1919–23	.296	315	795	91	235	29	11	21	132	349	40	11	6+		.439	.367	C-261, 2B-1
Elmer Smith	3/23/1868	11/3/45	L	L	1	1900	.260	85	312	47	81	9	7	2	34	110	24	14	–		.353	.313	OF-83
Harry Smith	5/15/1890	4/1/22	R	L	1	1914–15	.179	39		7		1	0	0	5	9	13		1+		.231	.333	C-22
Heinie Smith	10/24/1871	6/25/39	R	R	2	1901–02	.250	147	540	51	135	21	3	1	37	165	18	33	–		.306	.274	2B-145, P-2
Jimmy Smith	5/15/1895	1/1/74	B	R	2	1917	.229	36	96	12	22	5	0	0	9	29	9	6	1+		.302	.295	2B-29, SS-7
Mike Smith	11/16/04	5/31/81	L	R	1	1926	.143	7	14	0	2	0	0	0	0	2	0	0	–		.143	.143	OF-1
Red Smith	5/18/04	3/8/78	R	R	1	1927	–	1	0	0	0	0	0	0	0	0	0	0	–		–	–	C-1
Reggie Smith	4/2/45		B	R	1	1982	.284	106	349	51	99	11	0	18	56	164	46	7	0		.470	.367	1B-99
Duke Snider	9/19/26		L	R	1	1964	.210	91	167	16	35	7	0	4	17	54	22	0	0		.323	.302	OF-43
Fred Snodgrass	10/19/1887	4/5/74	R	R	8	1908–15	.278	788	2640	410	735	128	37	10	310	967	345	201	12+		.366	.362	OF-690, 1B-55, C-7, 2B-3, 3B-3
J.T. Snow	2/26/68		B	L	6	1997–2002	.266	855	2779	411	739	161	9	100	464	1218	420	8	13		.438	.363	1B-832
Cory Snyder	11/11/62		R	R	1	1992	.269	124	390	48	105	22	2	14	57	173	23	4	4		.444	.310	OF-70, 1B-27, 3B-2, 2B-4, SS-3
Frank Snyder	5/27/1893	1/5/62	R	R	8	1919–26	.278	731	2212	208	615	96	23	42	317	883	162	210	15	14+	.399	.327	C-686
Mose Solomon	12/8/00	6/25/66	L	L	1	1923	.375	2	8	0	3	0	0	0	1	4	1	0	–		.500	.375	OF-2
Pete Sommers	10/26/1866	7/22/08	R	R	1	1890	.106	17	47	4	5	0	1	0	3	8	4	1	–		.170	.176	C-11, 1B-5, OF-2
Bill Sorrell	10/14/40		R	R	1	1967	.176	17	17	1	3	0	1	0	3	5	4	2	–		.235	.300	OF-5
Billy Southworth	3/9/1893	11/15/69	L	L	3	1924–26	.285	253	870	142	248	38	6	14	110	340	90	28	19+		.391	.352	OF-223
Bob Speake	8/22/30		L	L	2	1958–59	.195	81	82	9	16	3	0	3	11	28	14	8	1		.341	.313	OF-10
Horace Speed	10/4/51		R	R	1	1975	.133	17	15	2	2	0	0	0	2	3	1	3	0		.200	.188	OF-9
Chris Speier	6/28/50		R	R	10	1971–77, 87–89	.248	1114	3730	445	924	153	27	70	409	1341	466	519	35		.360	.331	SS-910, 2B-116, 3B-81, 1B-2
Daryl Spencer	7/13/29		R	R	6	1952–53, 56–59	.242	719	2542	296	616	102	16	74	287	972	259	320	10	5	.382	.312	SS-370, 2B-306, 3B-57
Roy Spencer	2/22/00	2/8/73	R	R	1	1936	.278	19	18	3	5	1	0	0	3	6	3	0	–		.333	.350	C-14
Vern Spencer	2/4/1894	6/3/71	L	L	1	1920	.200	45	140	15	28	2	3	0	19	36	17	4	3		.257	.258	OF-40
Harry Spilman	7/18/54		L	R	3	1986–88	.259	181	224	21	58	13	1	4	39	85	39	1	1		.379	.333	1B-34, 3B-15, C-4, OF-2, 2B-1
Al Spohrer	12/3/02	7/17/72	R	R	1	1928	.000	2	2	0	0	0	0	0	0	0	0	0	–		.000	.000	C-2
General Stafford	7/9/1868	9/18/23	R	R	5	1893–97	.274	270	1043	175	286	29	11	8	147	361	91	88+	78		.346	.332	OF-142, 2B-110, 3B-8, SS-8, 1B-1
Heinie Stafford	11/1/1891	1/29/72	R	R	1	1916	.000	1	1	0	0	0	0	0	0	0	0	0	–		.000	.000	PH
Eddie Stanky	9/3/16	6/6/99	R	R	2	1950–51	.274	297	1042	203	285	42	7	22	94	407	271	113	17	5+	.391	.423	2B-291
Jigger Statz	10/20/1897	3/16/88	R	R	2	1919–20	.244	37	90	7	22	5	2	0	11	28	5	2	1+		.311	.284	OF-30, 2B-5
Jim Steels	5/30/61		L	L	1	1989	.083	13	12	0	1	0	0	0	2	4	2	0	0		.083	.214	1B-3, OF-1
Casey Stengel	7/30/1890	9/29/75	L	L	3	1921–23	.349	177	490	91	171	20	15	12	93	257	42	40	10	5	.524	.400	OF-142
Rennie Stennett	4/5/51		R	R	3	1980–81	.242	158	484	42	117	13	4	6	44	143	25	37	6	5	.295	.279	2B-130
Joe Stephenson	6/30/21		R	R	1	1943	.250	9	24	4	6	1	0	0	9	7	0	5	0		.292	.250	C-6
John Stephenson	4/13/41		L	R	1	1969–70	.129	70	70	5	9	3	0	0	4	12	2	11	0		.171	.153	C-18, 1B-1, OF-1
Glen Stewart	9/29/12	2/11/97	R	R	1	1940	.138	29	29	1	4	1	0	0	0	5	1	2	0		.172	.167	3B-6, SS-5
Milt Stock	7/11/1893	7/16/77	R	R	2	1913–14	.259	122	382	54	99	18	1	3	42	128	36	22	13		.335	.323	3B-113, SS-8
Joe Strain	4/30/54		R	R	2	1979–80	.260	144	446	53	116	14	3	1	28	135	23	31	9	6	.303	.296	2B-109, 3B-7, SS-1
Sammy Strang	12/16/1876	3/13/32	B	R	5	1901, 05–08	.272	510	1459	220	397	59	18	12	144	528	254	110	–		.362	.380	3B-168, OF-157, SS-21, 1B-7

Name	Born	Died	B	T	Yrs	Seasons	AVG	G	AB	R	H	2B	3B	HR	RBI	TB	BB	SO	SB	CS	SLG	OBP	Games By Position
Darryl Strawberry	3/12/62		L	L	1	1994	.239	29	92	13	22	3	1	4	17	39	19	22	0	3	.424	.369	OF-27
Bill Stuart	8/28/1873	10/14/28	-	-	1	1899	.000	1	3	0	0	0	0	0	0	0	0	-	0	-	.000	.000	2B-1
Guy Sularz	11/7/55		R	R	4	1980-83	.218	108	206	21	45	4	1	1	12	54	23	23	4	1	.262	.297	SS-43, 2B-36, 3B-24
Champ Summers	6/15/46		L	R	2	1982-83	.231	99	147	18	34	5	0	4	22	51	23	25	0	1	.347	.335	OF-32, 1B-3
T																							
John Tamargo	11/7/51		B	R	2	1978-79	.224	66	152	13	34	7	1	3	14	52	22	15	0	-	.342	.322	C-48
Don Taussig	2/19/32		R	R	1	1958	.200	39	50	10	10	0	0	1	4	13	3	8	0	0	.260	.245	OF-123
Bill Taylor	12/30/29		L	R	4	1954-57	.211	132	142	13	30	6	0	6	22	54	5	34	0	0	.380	.238	OF-12
Bob Taylor	3/20/44		R	R	1	1970	.190	63	84	12	16	0	0	0	10	22	12	13	0	-	.262	.292	OF-26, C-1
Zack Taylor	7/27/1898	9/19/74	R	R	1	1927	.233	83	258	28	60	7	3	0	21	73	17	20	2	-	.283	.280	C-81
Fred Tenney	11/26/1871	7/3/52	L	L	2	1908-09	.247	257	958	144	237	28	3	5	79	286	124	-	25	-	.299	.334	1B-254
Bill Terry	10/30/1898	1/9/89	L	L	14	1923-36	.341	1721	6428	1120	2193	373	112	154	1078	3252	537	449	56	6+	.506	.392	1B-1579, OF-15
Wayne Terwilliger	6/27/25		R	R	2	1955-56	.255	94	275	29	70	17	1	1	18	92	36	47	2	4	.335	.341	2B-84, 3B-1, SS-1
Nick Testa	6/29/28		R	R	1	1958	-	1	0	0	0	0	0	0	0	0	0	0	0	0	-	-	C-1
Henry Thielman	10/3/1880	9/2/42	R	R	1	1902	.111	6	9	0	1	0	0	0	0	1	2	-	1	-	.111	.273	OF-3, P-2
Derrel Thomas	1/14/51		B	R	3	1975-77	.263	373	1318	212	347	39	23	16	111	480	132	152	53	37	.364	.330	2B-237, OF-81, SS-27, 3B-7, 1B-3
Herb Thomas	5/26/02	12/4/91	R	R	1	1927	.176	13	17	2	3	1	1	0	1	6	1	1	0	-	.353	.222	OF-3, SS-1
Valmy Thomas	10/21/28		R	R	2	1957-58	.253	151	384	44	97	15	3	9	47	145	29	53	1	0	.378	.305	C-149
Gary Thomasson	7/29/51		L	L	6	1972-77	.254	604	1677	233	426	81	22	38	201	665	203	301	42	11	.397	.335	OF-362, 1B-156
Fresco Thompson	6/6/02	11/20/68	R	R	1	1926,34	.556	3	9	1	5	0	0	0	1	5	2	0	0	-	.556	.636	2B-2
Hank Thompson	12/8/25	9/30/69	L	R	8	1949-56	.267	906	2925	482	781	103	33	129	477	1337	483	330	31	14+	.457	.371	3B-655, OF-102, 2B-83, SS-2
Robby Thompson	5/10/62		R	R	11	1986-96	.257	1304	4612	671	1187	238	39	119	458	1860	439	987	103	62	.403	.322	2B-1279, SS-1
Scot Thompson	12/7/55		L	L	2	1984-85	.275	184	356	38	98	12	1	1	37	115	32	36	5	3	.323	.335	1B-111, OF-6
Bobby Thomson	10/25/23		R	R	9	1946-53, 57	.277	1135	4223	648	1171	192	56	189	704	2042	360	477	31	11+	.484	.334	OF-922, 3B-177, 2B-9
Jim Thorpe	5/28/1887	3/28/53	R	R	7	1913-19	.216	152	291	46	63	11	7	2	21	94	15	57	11	2+	.323	.255	OF-92
Mike Tiernan	1/21/1867	11/9/18	L	L	13	1887-99	.311	1476	5906	1313	1834	256	162	106	851	2732	747	318+	428	-	.463	.388	OF-1474, P-5
Rusty Tillman	8/29/60		R	R	1	1988	.250	4	4	1	1	0	0	0	3	4	2	0	0	-	1.000	.500	OF-1
Johnny Tobin	9/15/06	8/6/83	R	R	1	1932	.000	1	1	0	0	0	0	0	0	0	0	0	0	0	.000	.000	PH
Tony Torcato	10/25/79		L	R	1	2002	.273	5	11	0	3	1	0	0	0	4	0	2	0	0	.364	.273	OF-3
Yorvit Torrealba	7/19/78		R	R	2	2001-02	.286	56	140	17	40	10	0	2	16	58	14	20	5	0	.414	.352	C-56
Red Tramback	11/1/15	12/28/79	L	L	1	1940	.250	2	4	0	1	0	0	0	0	1	1	1	0	-	.250	.400	OF-1
Red Treadway	4/28/20	5/26/94	L	R	2	1944-45	.266	138	394	54	105	9	4	4	28	134	33	24	5	-	.340	.323	OF-98
Alex Trevino	8/26/57		R	R	1	1985	.217	57	157	17	34	10	3	6	19	64	20	24	0	0	.408	.305	C-55, 3B-1
Manny Trillo	12/25/50		R	R	2	1984-85	.238	223	852	81	203	37	5	7	61	267	65	99	2	0	.313	.292	2B-216, 3B-5
Dasher Troy	5/8/1856	3/30/38	R	R	1	1883	.215	85	316	37	68	7	5	0	20	85	9	33	-	-	.269	.237	2B-73, SS-12
Ty Tyson	6/1/1892	8/16/53	R	R	2	1926-27	.283	140	494	64	140	23	3	4	52	181	25	47	11	-	.366	.318	OF-133
U																							
George Ulrich	6/5/1869		-	-	1	1896	.178	14	45	4	8	1	0	0	4	9	1	7	0	-	.200	.196	OF-11, 3B-3
Jose Uribe	1/21/59		B	R	8	1985-92	.241	985	2992	299	721	98	34	19	213	944	248	418	72	46	.316	.299	SS-969, 2B-1
V																							
Mike Vail	11/10/51		R	R	1	1983	.154	18	26	1	4	1	0	0	3	5	0	7	0	0	.192	.154	1B-4, OF-2
George Van Haltren	3/30/1866	9/29/45	L	L	10	1894-1903	.321	1221	4906	973	1575	194	88	29	604	2032	486	87	320	-	.414	.382	OF-1212, P-5
John Vander Wal	4/29/66		L	L	1	2001	.252	49	139	19	35	6	1	3	20	52	26	38	1	2	.374	.370	OF-41, 1B-1
Pat Veltman	3/24/06	10/1/80	R	R	3	1928-29, 32	.200	5	5	2	1	0	0	0	0	3	1	1	0	0	.600	.500	C-1, OF-1
Max Venable	6/6/57		L	R	5	1979-83	.222	302	608	72	135	15	8	7	48	187	58	93	38	11	.308	.290	OF-189
Johnny Vergez	7/9/06	7/15/91	R	R	5	1931-34	.258	501	1719	197	443	84	12	42	223	677	121	222	14	-	.394	.307	3B-490, SS-1
Ozzie Virgil Sr.	5/17/33		R	R	4	1956-57, 66,69	.235	142	328	35	77	3	3	6	35	104	18	39	4	4	.317	.275	3B-78, OF-26, C-13, 1B-5, 2B-2, SS-1

W	Born	Died	B	T	Yrs	Seasons	AVG	G	AB	R	H	2B	3B	HR	RBI	TB	BB	SO	SB	CS	SLG	OBP	Games By Position
Jose Vizcaino	3/26/68		R	R	1	1997	.266	151	568	77	151	19	7	5	50	199	48	87	8	8	.350	.323	SS-147, 2B-5
Ham Wade	12/20/1880	7/21/68	R	R	1	1907	-	1	0	0	0	0	0	0	0	0	0	-	0	-	-	-	OF-1
Heinie Wagner	9/23/1880	3/20/43	R	R	1	1902	.214	17	56	4	12	1	0	0	2	13	0	-	0	-	.232	.214	SS-17
Leon Wagner	5/13/34		L	R	3	1958-59, 69	.285	172	362	51	103	13	3	18	59	176	45	59	1	0	.486	.364	OF-86
Dick Wakefield	5/6/21	8/26/85	L	R	1	1952	.000	3	2	0	0	0	0	0	0	0	1	1	0	0	.000	.333	PH
Curt Walker	7/3/1896	12/9/55	L	R	2	1920-21	.272	72	206	30	56	13	5	3	35	88	16	11	4	3	.427	.324	OF-62
Frank Walker	9/22/1894	9/16/74	R	R	1	1925	.222	39	81	12	18	2	0	1	5	22	9	11	1	1	.272	.300	OF-21
Joe Wall	7/24/1873	7/17/36	L	L	2	1901-02	.409	10	22	2	9	2	0	0	1	11	2	-	0	-	.500	.458	OF-4, C-2
John Montgomery Ward	3/3/1860	3/4/25	L	R	9	1883-89, 93-94	.279	1070	4461	828	1245	136	57	17	546	1546	218	200	332+	8	.347	.313	SS-594, 2B-325, OF-115, 3B-5, P-43
John Warner	8/15/1872	12/21/43	L	R	8	1896-01, 03-04	.255	623	2088	238	532	52	16	3	197	625	98	7+	49	-	.299	.288	C-606, 1B-3, OF-1
Bennie Warren	3/2/12	5/11/94	R	R	2	1946-47	.162	42	74	7	12	1	1	4	8	27	14	22	0	-	.365	.295	C-33
Libe Washburn	6/16/1874	3/22/40	B	L	1	1902	.444	6	9	1	4	0	0	0	0	4	2	-	1	-	.444	.545	OF-3
Mark Wasinger	8/4/61		R	R	2	1987-88	.268	47	82	17	22	3	0	1	3	28	8	14	2	0	.341	.333	3B-22, 2B-10, SS-2
George Watkins	6/4/00	6/1/70	L	R	1	1934	.247	105	296	38	73	18	3	6	33	115	24	34	2	-	.389	.303	OF-81
Roy Weatherly	2/25/15	1/19/91	L	R	1	1950	.261	52	69	10	18	3	3	0	11	27	13	10	0	-	.391	.378	OF-15
Jim Weaver	10/10/59		L	L	1	1989	.200	12	20	2	4	0	0	0	2	7	0	7	1	0	.350	.200	OF-8
Earl Webb	9/17/1897	5/23/65	L	R	1	1925	.000	4	3	0	0	0	0	0	0	0	1	1	0	0	.000	.250	PH
Phil Weintraub	10/12/07	6/21/87	L	L	6	1933-35, 37, 44-45	.293	295	854	137	250	34	13	25	142	385	149	114	2	0	.451	.398	1B-195, OF-34
Brad Wellman	8/17/59		R	R	5	1982-86	.224	264	638	55	143	23	2	3	58	179	46	116	20	10	.281	.276	2B-167, SS-47, 3B-35
Jimmy Welsh	10/9/02	10/30/70	L	R	2	1928-29	.294	162	605	102	178	29	5	11	62	250	38	33	7	-	.413	.336	OF-152
Lew Wendell	3/22/1892	7/11/53	R	R	2	1915-16	.211	22	38	0	8	1	1	0	5	11	2	9	0	-	.289	.250	C-18
Billy Werber	6/20/08		R	R	1	1942	.205	98	370	51	76	9	2	1	13	92	51	22	9	-	.249	.302	3B-93
Wes Westrum	11/28/22		R	R	11	1947-57	.217	919	2322	302	503	59	8	96	315	866	489	514	10	5+	.373	.353	C-902, 3B-1
Lew Whistler	3/10/1868	12/30/59	-	R	2	1890-91	.262	117	435	66	114	17	14	5	67	174	44	82	12	-	.400	.330	1B-52, SS-33, OF-22, 2B-6, 3B-5
Steve Whitaker	5/7/43		L	R	1	1970	.111	16	27	3	3	1	0	0	4	4	2	14	0	0	.148	.172	OF-9
Bill White	1/28/34		L	L	2	1956, 58	.255	164	537	68	137	24	7	23	63	244	54	77	16	8	.454	.323	1B-141, OF-4
Fuzz White	6/27/18		R	R	1	1947	.231	7	13	3	3	0	0	0	0	3	0	0	0	-	.231	.231	OF-5
Burgess Whitehead	6/29/10	11/25/93	R	R	6	1936-41	.268	650	2512	303	672	76	22	16	182	840	121	98	38	-	.334	.301	2B-557, 3B-75, SS-9
Terry Whitfield	1/12/53		L	L	4	1977-80	.289	514	1529	201	442	77	11	26	138	619	109	206	16	20	.405	.336	OF-425
Art Whitney	1/16/1858	8/15/43	R	R	2	1888-89	.218	219	801	99	175	13	6	2	87	206	64	61	26	-	.257	.276	3B-219, P-1
Floyd Wicker	9/12/43		L	L	1	1971	.143	9	21	3	3	0	0	0	1	3	2	5	0	0	.143	.217	OF-7
Rob Wilfong	9/1/53		L	R	1	1987	.125	8	8	2	1	0	0	0	2	4	1	5	1	0	.500	.222	2B-2
Joe Wilhoit	12/20/1885	9/25/30	L	R	2	1917-18	.292	98	185	22	54	5	5	0	23	69	25	19	4	-	.373	.376	OF-66
Rick Wilkins	6/4/67		L	R	2	1996-97	.239	118	347	37	83	15	0	14	59	140	38	105	0	2	.403	.308	C-99, 1B-7
Bernie Williams	10/8/48		R	R	3	1970-72	.197	88	157	22	31	6	1	4	15	51	21	47	2	2	.325	.292	OF-48
Davey Williams	11/2/27		R	R	6	1949, 51-55	.252	517	1785	235	450	61	10	32	163	627	164	144	6	12+	.351	.315	2B-481
Keith Williams	4/21/72		R	R	1	1996	.250	9	20	0	5	0	0	0	5	5	0	6	0	0	.250	.250	OF-4
Matt Williams	11/28/65		R	R	10	1987-96	.264	1120	4139	594	1092	179	25	247	732	2062	272	872	29	27	.498	.309	3B-1011, SS-119, 1B-13
Walt Wilmot	10/18/1863	2/1/29	B	R	2	1897-98	.244	46	172	24	42	6	2	3	26	61	11	-	5	-	.355	.290	OF-43
Art Wilson	12/11/1885	6/12/60	R	R	6	1908-13	.266	231	403	53	107	21	4	4	54	148	56	43+	11	-	.367	.355	C-218, 1B-3
Artie Wilson	10/28/20		L	R	1	1951	.182	19	22	2	4	0	0	0	1	4	2	1	2	0	.182	.250	2B-3, SS-3, 1B-2
Desi Wilson	5/9/69		L	L	1	1996	.271	41	118	10	32	2	0	0	12	40	12	27	0	2	.339	.338	1B-33
George Wilson	8/30/25	10/29/74	L	R	3	1952-53, 56	.197	126	188	14	37	8	0	3	18	54	10	30	0	0	.287	.237	OF-29, 1B-2
Hack Wilson	4/26/00	11/23/48	R	R	3	1923-25	.276	172	573	90	158	26	16	16	87	264	65	80	9	5	.461	.350	OF-156
Neil Wilson	6/14/35		L	R	1	1960	.000	6	10	0	0	0	0	0	0	0	0	-	0	-	.000	.091	C-6
Parke Wilson	10/26/1867	12/20/34	R	R	7	1893-99	.265	366	1266	194	336	37	15	3	170	412	106	44+	54	-	.325	.322	C-250, 1B-67, SS-19, 3B-18, OF-11, 2B-1

Name	Born	Died	B	T	Yrs	Seasons	AVG	G	AB	R	H	2B	3B	HR	RBI	TB	BB	SO	SB	CS	SLG	OBP	Games By Position
Mickey Witek	12/19/15	8/24/90	R	R	6	1940-43, 46-47	.277	579	2146	239	594	65	9	22	196	743	148	84	7	-	.346	.323	2B-437, SS-89, 3B-38
Jim Wohlford	2/28/51		R	R	3	1980-82	.252	238	511	58	129	21	5	4	56	172	47	68	9	7	.337	.315	OF-131, 3B-1
Ted Wood	1/4/67		L	L	2	1991-92	.181	34	83	5	15	2	0	1	4	20	8	26	0	0	.241	.253	OF-24
Mike Woodard	3/2/60		L	R	3	1985-87	.244	82	180	26	44	4	1	1	15	53	15	13	13	3	.294	.303	2B-54, 3B-2, SS-2
Pete Woodruff	6/1873	-	R	R	1	1899	.246	20	61	11	15	1	0	2	7	24	9	-	3	-	.393	.343	OF-19, 1B-1
Russ Wrightstone	3/18/1893	2/25/69	L	R	1	1928	.160	30	25	3	4	0	0	0	5	7	3	2	0	-	.280	.250	1B-2
Zeke Wrigley	1/18/1874	9/28/52	-	-	1	1899	.200	4	15	1	3	0	0	0	1	3	1	-	1	-	.200	.250	3B-4
Y																							
George Yeager	6/5/1874	7/5/40	R	R	1	1902	.204	38	108	6	22	2	1	0	9	26	11	-	1	-	.241	.277	C-27, 1B-3, OF-1
Babe Young	7/1/15	12/25/83	L	L	7	1936, 39-42, 46-47	.276	543	1798	240	496	88	10	63	311	793	204	117	9	-	.441	.350	1B-386, OF-78
Joel Youngblood	8/28/51		R	R	6	1983-88	.266	602	1470	174	391	62	4	39	183	578	144	246	18	15	.393	.331	OF-201, 3B-153, 2B-73, 1B-7, SS-1
Ross Youngs	4/10/1897	10/22/27	L	R	10	1917-26	.322	1211	4627	812	1491	236	93	42	592	2039	550	390	153	83+	.441	.394	OF-1199, 2B-12
Sal Yvars	2/20/24		R	R	7	1947-53	.243	142	304	29	74	6	0	7	28	101	27	30	0	0+	.332	.305	C-129
Z																							
Elmer Zacher	9/17/1883	12/20/44	R	R	1	1910	-												0	-	-	-	OF-1
Dave Zearfoss	1/1/1868	9/12/45	-	R	3	1896-98	.239	25	71	6	17	1	2	0	6	22	5	5+	2	-	.310	.289	C-25
Heinie Zimmerman	2/9/1887	3/14/69	R	R	4	1916-19	.276	434	1643	182	454	65	25	10	235	599	57	106	44	8+	.365	.301	3B-412, 1B-19, 2B-6
Roy Zimmerman	9/13/16	11/22/91	L	L	1	1945	.276	27	98	14	27	1	0	5	15	43	5	16	0	-	.439	.311	1B-25, OF-1

+ denotes statistics incomplete.

Name	Born	Died	T	Yrs	Seasons	W	L	PCT	ERA	G	GS	CG	ShO	SV	IP	H	ER	HR	BB	SO	Pitchers' Batting AVG	AB	H
A																							
Woody Abernathy	2/1/15	12/5/94	L	2	1946-47	2	2	.500	3.64	16	1	0	0	0	42.0	36	17	5	11	6	.000	8	0
Ace Adams	3/2/12		R	6	1941-46	41	33	.554	3.47	302	7	2	0	49	552.2	541	213	26	224	171	.121	99	12
Kurt Ainsworth	9/9/78		R	2	2001-02	1	2	.333	2.93	8	4	0	0	0	27.2	25	9	2	14	18	.167	6	1
Vic Aldridge	10/25/1893	4/17/73	R	1	1928	4	7	.364	4.83	22	17	3	0	0	119.1	133	64	7	45	33	.275	40	11
Doyle Alexander	9/4/50		R	1	1981	11	7	.611	2.89	24	24	2	1	0	152.1	156	49	11	44	77	.176	51	9
Johnny Allen	9/30/05	3/29/59	R	2	1943-44	5	10	.333	3.74	33	13	3	1	2	125.0	125	52	11	38	57	.053	38	2
Myron Allen	3/22/1854	3/8/24	R	1	1883	0	0	.000	1.13	1	1	1	0	0	8.0	8	1	0	3	0	.000	4	0
Matty Alou*	12/22/38		L	1	1965	0	0	-	0.00	1	0	0	0	0	2.0	3	0	0	3	3	*	*	*
Wilson Alvarez	3/24/70		L	1	1997	4	3	.571	4.48	11	11	0	0	0	66.1	54	33	9	36	69	.130	23	3
Red Ames	8/2/1882	10/8/36	R	11	1903-13	108	77	.584	2.45	282	211	128	15	12	1802.2	1542	490	17	620	1169	.136	587	80
Fred Anderson	12/11/1885	11/8/57	R	3	1916-18	21	23	.477	2.52	94	49	23	4	8	420.2	390	118	9	89	191	.092	119	11
Hub Andrews	8/31/22		R	2	1947-48	0	0	-	4.63	8	0	0	0	0	11.2	17	6	1	4	2	-	0	0
Nate Andrews	9/30/13	4/26/91	R	1	1956	1	0	1.000	6.00	3	2	0	0	0	12.0	17	8	2	4	5	.500	2	1
Johnny Antonelli	4/12/30		L	7	1954-60	108	84	.563	3.13	280	219	86	21	19	1600.2	1437	556	152	528	919	.180	560	101
Luis Aquino	5/19/64		R	1	1995	0	1	.000	14.40	5	0	0	0	0	5.0	10	8	2	2	4	.000	1	0
Rene Arocha	2/24/66		R	1	1997	1	0	1.000	11.32	6	0	0	0	0	10.1	17	13	2	5	7	.000	1	0
Manny Aybar	5/14/72		R	1	2002	1	0	1.000	2.51	15	0	0	0	0	14.1	16	4	1	3	11	.000	1	0
Bill Ayers	9/27/19	9/24/80	R	1	1947	0	3	.000	8.15	13	4	0	0	1	35.1	46	32	7	14	22	.250	8	2
B																							
Lore Bader	4/27/1888	6/2/73	R	1	1912	2	0	1.000	0.90	2	1	1	0	0	10.0	9	1	0	6	3	.000	3	0
Cory Bailey	1/24/71		R	2	1997-98	0	0	.000	6.92	12	0	0	0	0	13.0	17	10	2	5	7	1.000	1	1
Loren Bain	7/4/22	11/24/96	R	1	1945	0	0	-	7.88	3	0	0	0	0	8.0	10	7	1	4	1	.333	3	1
Tom Baker	6/11/13	1/3/91	R	2	1937-38	1	0	1.000	4.37	15	0	0	0	0	35.0	35	17	5	19	11	.222	9	2
Harry Baldwin	6/3/00	1/23/58	R	2	1924-25	3	1	.750	4.41	11	2	1	0	0	34.2	45	17	5	12	5	.364	11	4
Mark Baldwin	10/29/1863	11/10/29	R	1	1893	16	20	.444	4.10	45	39	33	2	2	331.1	335	151	6	141	100	.127	134	17

Name	Born	Died	T	Yr	Years	W	L	PCT	ERA	G	GS	CG	SHO	SV	IP	H	R	ER	BB	SO	BA	AB	H
George Bamberger	8/1/25		R	2	1951–52	0	0	—	12.00	7	0	0	0	0	6.0	10	8	8	3	1	—	0	0
Steve Barber	2/22/39	3/25/85	L	1	1974	0	1	.000	5.27	13	0	0	0	1	13.2	13	8	12	55	73	.234	64	15
Curt Barclay	8/22/31	9/9/61	R	3	1957–59	10	9	.526	3.48	44	29	5	2	0	199.1	214	77	55	199	287	.252	426	94
Jesse Barnes	8/26/1892	7/24/58	R	6	1918–23	82	43	.656	2.92	181	141	80	11	8	1150.1	1169	373	267	268	.110	354	39
Virgil Barnes	3/5/1897	3/11/30	R	9	1919–20, 22–28	59	52	.532	3.53	189	124	57	7	11	1033.2	1106	406	267	12	11	.091	11	1
Bob Barr	12/1856		R		1891		4	.000	5.33	5	4	2	0		27.0	47	16	12	11	.000		
Jim Barr	2/10/48		R	10	1971–78, 82–83	90	96	.484	3.41	394	220	59	20	11	1800.1	1863	682	391	650	.162	513	83
Bob Barthelson	7/15/24	5/17/65	R	1	1944	1	1	.500	4.66	1	1	0	0		9.2	13	5	5	4	.500		
Bill Bartley	1/8/1885		R	1	1903	0	0	—	0.00	1	0	0	0	1	3.0	3	0	0	2	—	1	0
Shawn Barton	5/14/63		L	2	1995–96	4	1	.800	5.13	59	0	0	0	0	52.2	56	30	4	25	.037	27	1
Jose Bautista	7/25/64		R	2	1995–96	6	12	.333	5.18	89	7	0	0	1	170.1	186	98	20	73	.235	17	4
Rod Beck	8/3/68		R	7	1991–97	21	28	.429	2.97	416	0	0	0	199	463.0	404	153	41	393	.300	10	3
Steve Bedrosian	12/6/57		R	2	1989–90	10	13	.435	3.59	108	0	0	0	34	130.1	107	52	93	77	.125	5	1
Roy Beecher	5/10/1884	10/11/52	R	2	1907–08	0	2	.000	4.12	33	3	2	0	0	19.2	28	9	66	23	.077	8	
Joe Beggs	11/4/10	7/19/83	R	2	1947–48	3	3	.500	4.21	31	0	0	2		66.1	83	31	18	104	.143	13	
Ed Begley	1863	7/24/19	—	1	1884	12	18	.400	4.16	31	30	30	0	4	266.0	296	123	99	25	.182	121	22
Hank Behrman	6/27/21	1/20/87	R	1	1949	3	3	.500	4.92	43	4	1	0	0	71.1	64	39	52	58	.077	13	1
Hi Bell	7/16/1897		R	3	1932–34	18	12	.600	3.06	95	19	4	1	13	279.1	304	95	48	191	.110	82	9
Jack Bentley	3/8/1895	10/24/69	L	5	1923–27	40	22	.645	4.35	92	72	36	2	2	539.2	601	261	194	234	.324	299	97
Larry Benton	11/20/1897	4/3/53	R	4	1927–30	50	34	.595	3.66	118	92	51	6	10	750.1	800	305	200	336	.140	258	36
Rube Benton	6/27/1887	12/12/37	L	7	1915–21	66	53	.555	2.79	172	126	60	12	10	1012.2	949	314	211	72	.141	333	47
Juan Berenguer	11/30/54		R	1	1986	2	3	.400	2.70	46	4	0	0	4	73.1	64	22	44	45	.143	7	
Jack Berly	5/24/03	6/26/77	R	1	1931	7	8	.467	3.88	27	11	4	0	0	111.1	114	48	51	259	.171	35	6
Bud Black	6/30/57		L	4	1991–94	34	32	.515	3.95	88	88	5	4	0	539.1	518	237	179	8	.145	179	26
Bob Blewitt	6/28/1877	3/17/58	L	1	1902	0	2	.000	4.82	5	3	2	0	0	28.0	39	15	7	704	.000	10	0
Vida Blue	7/28/49		L	6	1978–81, 85–86	72	58	.554	3.52	179	166	31	1	0	1131.1	1030	442	453	.107	338	36
Clint Blume	10/17/1898	6/12/73	R	2	1922–23	3	0	1.000	3.00	13	2	1	0	0	33.0	29	11	21	4	.167	6	1
Randy Bockus	10/5/60		L	3	1986–88	2	2	.500	4.15	37	0	0	0	0	56.1	59	26	23	31	.125	8	
Brian Boehringer	1/8/69		R	1	2001	0	3	.000	4.19	29	0	0	0	1	34.1	37	16	17	27	.000	3	0
Bobby Bolin	1/29/39		R	9	1961–69	73	56	.566	3.26	345	144	29	10	21	1282.1	1088	465	477	977	.159	372	59
Hank Boney	10/28/03		R	1	1927	0	0	—	2.25	3	2	0	0	0	4.0	4	1	2	0	—	0	0
Greg Booker	6/22/60		R	1	1990	0	0	—	13.50	2	1	0	0	0	2.0	7	3	0	1	—	0	0
Pedro Borbon	12/2/46		R	3	1979	4	3	.571	4.89	30	0	0	0	3	46.0	56	25	13	26	.333	3	1
Bill Bordley	1/9/58		L	1	1980	8	6	.400	4.70	8	8	3	0	0	30.2	34	16	21	11	.167	6	1
Andy Boswell	9/5/1874		R	1	1895	2	2	.500	5.82	5	4	4	0	0	34.0	41	22	22	18	.188	16	3
Kent Bottenfield	11/14/68	2/3/36	R	1	1994	1	0	—	10.80	2	0	0	0	0	1.2	5	2	0	0	—	0	0
Steven Bourgeois	8/4/72		R	1	1996	3	3	.250	6.30	15	5	0	0	0	40.0	60	28	21	17	.273	11	3
Cy Bowen	2/17/1871	1/25/25	R	1	1896	0	2	.000	6.00	2	1	1	0	0	12.0	12	8	9	3	.333	3	1
Frank Bowerman*	12/5/1868	11/30/48	R		1904	0	1	—	9.00	1	0	0	0	0	1.0	3	1	1	0	*	*	*
Bob Bowman	10/3/10	11/22/90	R	1	1941	6	7	.462	5.71	29	6	2	0	3	80.1	100	51	36	25	.048	21	1
Joe Bowman	6/17/10	7/21/97	R	1	1934	5	4	.556	3.61	30	10	3	0	0	107.1	119	43	36	36	.172	29	5
Roger Bowman	8/18/27		L	3	1949, 51–52	2	4	.333	6.31	13	8	8	0	0	35.2	47	25	32	31	.000	3	
Tom Bradley	3/16/47		R	3	1973–75	23	26	.469	4.56	78	61	8	1	0	400.1	421	203	139	221	.143	126	18
Jeff Brantley	9/5/63		R	6	1988–93	29	20	.592	3.24	299	18	0	0	42	505.1	457	182	219	384	.131	61	8
Fred Breining	11/15/55		R	4	1980–83	27	20	.574	3.37	136	42	8	0	0	430.1	422	161	154	255	.150	107	16
Don Brennan	12/2/03	4/26/53	R	1	1937	1	0	1.000	6.75	6	0	0	0	0	9.1	12	7	9	1	.000	1	0
Jack Brewer	7/21/19		R	3	1944–46	9	10	.474	4.36	43	28	10	0	0	216.2	231	105	76	73	.187	75	14
Jamie Brewington	9/28/71		R	1	1995	6	4	.600	4.54	13	13	0	0	0	75.1	68	38	45	45	.217	23	5
Brad Brink	1/20/65		R	1	1994	0	0	—	1.08	6	0	0	0	0	8.1	4	4	3	.000	3	0
Chris Brock	2/5/70		R	2	1998–99	6	8	.429	5.16	32	19	0	0	0	134.1	155	77	48	95	.205	39	8
Troy Brohawn	1/14/73		L	1	2002	0	0	.000	6.35	11	0	0	0	3	5.2	5	4	1	3	.000		0
Ken Brondell	10/17/21		R	1	1944	0	2	.000	8.38	7	2	0	0	0	19.1	27	18	8	1	.000	4	0
Terry Bross	3/30/66		R	1	1993	0	0	—	9.00	2	0	0	0	0	2.0	3	2	2	1	—	0	0
Jim Brown	12/12/1860	4/6/08	—	1	1884	0	1	.000	5.00	1	1	1	0	0	9.0	10	5	8	2	.000	3	0

Name	Born	Died	T	Yrs	Seasons	W	L	PCT	ERA	G	GS	CG	ShO	SV	IP	H	ER	HR	BB	SO	AVG	AB	H
Jumbo Brown	4/30/07	10/2/66	R	5	1937-41	13	12	.520	2.93	150	0	0	0	27	267.1	237	87	13	104	131	.196	46	9
Greg Brummett	4/20/67		R	1	1993	2	3	.400	4.70	8	8	0	0	0	46.0	53	24	9	13	20	.000	15	0
Ron Bryant	11/12/47		L	7	1967, 69-74	57	55	.509	3.90	195	131	23	6	0	908.1	870	394	78	372	502	.166	290	48
Garland Buckeye	10/16/1897	11/14/75	L	1	1928	0	0	-	14.73	1	0	0	0	0	3.2	9	6	1	2	3	.500	2	1
Mike Budnick	9/15/19		R	2	1946-47	2	3	.400	4.04	42	8	0	1	3	100.1	91	45	13	58	42	.292	24	7
Dave Burba	7/7/66		R	4	1992-95	19	18	.514	4.57	171	16	0	0	3	283.1	272	144	28	138	265	.171	35	6
Enrique Burgos	10/7/65		L	1	1995	0	0	-	8.64	5	0	0	0	0	8.1	14	8	0	6	12	-	0	0
John Burke*	1/27/1877	8/4/50	L	1	1902	0	1	.000	5.79	2	1	1	0	0	14.0	21	9	1	9	3	-	*	*
Jesse Burkett*	12/4/1868	5/27/53	L	1	1890	3	10	.231	5.57	20	14	6	0	0	118.0	134	73	3	92	82	*	*	*
John Burkett	11/28/64		R	6	1987, 90-94	67	42	.615	3.83	163	157	10	3	0	997.1	1025	424	84	245	591	.070	302	21
Pete Burnside	7/2/30		L	3	1955, 57-58	2	4	.333	7.00	18	12	2	1	1	54.0	77	42	9	27	24	.071	14	1
Joe Bush	11/27/1892	11/1/74	R	1	1927	2	1	.500	7.50	3	2	1	0	0	12.0	18	10	1	5	6	.500	4	2
Bud Byerly	10/26/20		R	2	1959-60	2	0	1.000	3.86	30	0	0	0	2	35.0	43	15	5	11	17	.000	17	6
C																							
Leon Cadore	11/20/1890	3/16/58	R	1	1924	0	0	-	0.00	2	0	0	0	0	4.0	2	0	0	3	2	.000	0	0
Mike Caldwell	1/22/49		L	3	1974-76	22	25	.468	4.05	119	57	10	2	3	460.0	515	207	38	131	195	.151	126	19
Mark Calvert	9/29/56		R	2	1983-84	3	8	.273	5.71	28	9	1	0	0	69.1	86	44	6	43	19	.000	16	0
Ernie Camacho	2/1/55		R	2	1989-90	3	0	1.000	3.08	21	0	0	0	6	26.1	20	9	2	14	22	.000	1	0
Sal Campfield	2/19/1868	5/16/52	R	1	1896	2	3	.500	4.00	6	2	2	0	0	27.0	31	12	1	6	6	.167	12	2
Ben Cantwell	4/13/02	12/4/62	R	3	1927-28, 37	2	2	.500	4.71	13	4	3	0	0	42.0	52	22	3	12	7	.333	12	4
John Carden	5/19/21	2/8/49	R	1	1946	0	0	-	22.50	2	0	0	0	0	2.0	4	5	0	4	1	-	0	0
Dan Carlson	1/26/70		R	2	1996-97	0	3	.000	5.68	6	0	0	0	0	25.1	33	16	7	10	18	.000	4	0
Steve Carlton	12/22/44		L	1	1986	1	3	.250	5.10	6	6	0	0	0	30.0	36	17	4	16	18	.182	11	2
Bob Carpenter	12/12/17		R	5	1940-42, 46-47	25	19	.568	3.58	76	53	4	4	0	392.1	401	156	37	128	133	.169	130	22
Bill Carrick	9/5/1873	3/7/32	R	3	1898-1900	38	50	.432	4.07	94	88	76	4	1	743.0	939	336	11	235	133	.156	263	41
Don Carrithers	9/15/49		R	4	1970-73	12	14	.462	5.14	121	31	4	1	2	250.1	280	143	23	128	133	.191	68	13
Larry Carter	5/22/65		R	1	1992	1	5	.167	4.64	83	4	1	0	0	33.0	34	17	2	18	21	.200	10	2
Slick Castleman	9/8/13	3/2/98	R	6	1934-39	36	26	.581	4.25	121	79	25	4	2	586.2	644	277	45	223	225	.135	207	28
Red Causey	8/11/1893	11/11/60	R	5	1918-19, 21-22	25	13	.658	3.12	79	37	17	2	3	348.2	324	121	9	120	87	.155	110	17
Leon Chagnon	9/28/02	7/30/53	R	1	1935	0	2	.000	3.52	14	1	0	0	0	38.1	32	15	7	5	16	.000	9	0
Tiny Chaplin	7/13/05	3/25/39	R	3	1928, 30-31	5	8	.385	4.46	47	12	0	0	2	139.1	155	69	10	40	32	.114	35	4
Ken Chase	10/6/13	1/16/85	L	1	1943	4	12	.250	4.11	21	20	4	0	0	129.1	140	59	7	74	86	.214	42	9
Nestor Chavez	7/6/47	3/16/69	R	1	1967	0	0	1.000	0.00	2	0	0	0	0	5.0	4	0	0	3	3	.000	3	0
Virgil Cheeves	2/12/01	5/5/79	R	1	1927	0	0	-	4.26	3	0	0	0	0	6.1	8	3	1	4	7	-	7	0
Don Choate	7/2/38		R	1	1960	0	0	-	2.25	4	0	0	0	0	8.0	7	2	0	4	7	-	1	0
Jason Christiansen	9/21/69		L	2	2001-02	1	1	.500	2.45	31	0	0	0	0	22	20	6	2	7	13	.000	8	0
Randy Bockus	10/5/60		R	3	1986-88	2	3	.667	4.15	37	9	0	0	0	56.1	59	26	5	23	31	.125	8	1
Watty Clark	5/16/02	3/4/72	L	2	1933-34	4	6	.400	5.31	21	9	0	0	0	62.2	81	37	8	16	17	.235	17	4
Dad Clarke	1/7/1865	6/3/11	R	4	1894-97	40	44	.476	4.08	106	80	67	2	3	747.2	924	339	18	157	158	.217	323	70
Bill Clarkson	9/27/1898	8/27/71	R	2	1927-28	3	9	.250	4.58	30	7	2	0	0	92.1	102	47	3	53	31	.050	20	1
Dad Clarkson	8/31/1866	2/5/11	R	1	1891	1	2	.333	2.89	5	2	2	0	0	28.0	24	9	2	18	11	.444	9	4
Dick Coffman	12/18/06	3/24/72	R	4	1936-39	24	14	.632	3.45	163	0	1	1	25	331.0	378	127	15	81	86	.183	71	13
Dick Cogan	12/5/1871	5/2/48	R	1	1900	0	0	-	6.75	2	1	1	0	0	8.0	10	6	0	6	1	.125	8	1
Tom Colcolough	10/8/1870	12/10/19	L	1	1899	4	5	.444	3.97	11	8	7	0	0	81.2	85	36	1	41	14	.270	37	10
Joe Coleman	2/3/47		R	1	1979	2	0	1.000	0.00	5	0	0	0	0	3.2	3	0	2	2	0	-	0	0
Keith Comstock	12/23/55		L	1	1987	0	0	1.000	3.05	15	0	0	0	0	20.2	19	7	1	10	21	.000	1	0
Bill Connelly	6/29/25	11/27/80	R	2	1952-53	5	1	.833	7.10	19	6	0	0	0	52.0	55	41	8	42	33	.235	17	4
Jim Constable	6/14/33		L	4	1956-58, 63	2	1	.667	4.60	32	6	0	0	1	43.0	49	22	3	18	19	.167	6	1
Sandy Consuegra	9/23/20		R	1	1957	0	0	-	2.45	4	0	0	0	0	3.2	7	1	1	1	1	-	0	0
Dennis Cook	10/4/62		L	2	1988-89	3	1	.750	2.43	6	6	2	0	0	37.0	22	10	2	16	22	.100	10	1
Bobby Coombs	2/2/08	10/21/91	R	1	1943	0	1	.000	12.94	9	0	2	0	0	16.0	33	23	1	8	5	.000	2	0
Mort Cooper	3/2/13	11/17/58	R	1	1947	1	5	.167	7.12	8	8	2	0	0	36.2	51	29	7	13	12	.429	14	6

Name	Born	Died	T	Yrs	Seasons	W	L	PCT	ERA	G	GS	CG	ShO	SV	IP	H	ER	HR	BB	SO	AVG	AB	H
Larry Corcoran	8/10/1859	10/14/1891	R	1	1885	2	1	.667	2.88	3	3	2	0	0	25.0	24	8	1	11	10	.357	14	5
Jeff Cornell	2/10/57		R	1	1984	1	3	.250	6.10	23	0	0	0	0	38.1	51	26	4	22	19	.000	4	0
Terry Cornutt	10/2/52		R	2	1977-78	2	2	.333	3.61	29	1	0	0	0	47.1	39	19	4	22	23	.000	1	0
Al Corwin	12/3/26		R	5	1951-55	18	10	.643	3.98	117	22	6	2	5	289.1	289	128	36	156	142	.152	79	12
Roscoe Coughlin	3/15/1868	3/20/51	R	1	1891	3	4	.429	3.84	8	7	6	0	0	61.0	74	26	5	23	22	.130	23	3
Doc Crandall	10/8/1887	8/17/51	R	6	1908-13	67	36	.650	2.89	217	78	48	6	24	1002.2	991	322	38	245	401	.277	426	118
Ed Crane	5/27/1862	9/19/1896	R	4	1888-89, 92-93	37	44	.457	3.79	98	85	73	4	2	755.1	725	318	25	406	373	.240	329	79
Doug Creek	3/1/69		L	2	1996-97	1	4	.200	6.57	66	3	0	0	0	61.2	57	45	12	46	52	.250	4	1
Ray Crone	8/7/31		R	2	1957-58	5	10	.333	4.73	39	18	2	0	0	144.2	166	76	16	53	63	.023	43	1
John Cronin	5/26/1874	7/12/29	R	3	1902-03	11	10	.524	3.13	33	23	19	0	0	229.2	235	80	8	55	102	.180	111	20
John Cumberland	5/10/47		L	3	1970-72	11	10	.524	3.46	61	27	5	2	2	221.0	197	85	28	66	79	.116	69	8
Jack Curtis	3/9/48		L	3	1977-79	17	15	.531	4.45	116	27	4	3	2	260.2	276	129	21	119	170	.163	49	8
Mike Cvengros	12/1/01	8/2/70	L	1	1922	0	1	.000	4.00	4	1	0	0	0	9.0	6	4	1	3	3	.000	3	0

D	Born	Died	T	Yrs	Seasons	W	L	PCT	ERA	G	GS	CG	ShO	SV	IP	H	ER	HR	BB	SO	Pitchers' Batting		
																					AVG	AB	H
John D'Acquisto	12/24/51		R	4	1973-76	18	27	.400	4.68	83	64	6	0	0	376.2	327	196	27	279	271	.133	113	15
Ed Daily*	9/7/1862	10/21/1891	R	1	1890	2	0	1.000	2.25	2	1	1	0	0	16.0	6	4	0	6	0	*	*	*
George Daly	7/28/1887	12/12/57	R	1	1909	0	3	.000	6.00	3	3	3	0	0	21.0	31	14	0	8	8	.111	9	*
Alvin Dark*	1/7/22		R	1	1953	0	0	—	18.00	1	0	0	0	0	1.0	7	2	0	1	0	*	*	*
Danny Darwin	10/25/55		R	2	1997-98	9	13	.409	5.37	43	32	0	0	0	192.2	227	115	28	63	111	.100	60	6
Claude Davenport	5/28/1898	6/13/76	R	1	1920	0	0	—	4.50	1	0	0	0	0	2.0	2	1	0	1	0	.000	1	0
Chick Davies	3/6/1892	9/5/73	L	2	1925-26	2	4	.333	4.11	40	2	0	0	6	96.1	109	44	3	39	32	.167	24	4
George Davies	2/22/1868	9/22/06		1	1893	1	1	.500	6.19	5	1	1	0	0	36.1	41	25	1	13	7	.333	12	4
Jim Davis	9/15/24	12/6/95	L	1	1957	1	0	1.000	6.55	10	0	0	0	0	11.0	13	8	2	8	6	1.000	1	1
Mark Davis	10/19/60		L	5	1983-87	25	45	.357	4.17	230	61	4	2	11	555.0	518	257	67	207	479	.160	119	19
Ron Davis	8/6/55		R	1	1988	1	1	.500	4.67	32	0	0	0	0	17.1	15	9	6	6	15	.000	2	0
Mike Davison	8/4/45		L	2	1969-70	3	5	.375	6.39	32	0	0	0	1	38.0	48	27	4	22	23	.000	1	0
Paul Dean	8/14/13	3/17/81	R	2	1940-41	4	4	.500	3.86	32	7	2	0	0	105.0	118	45	8	32	35	.115	26	3
Wayland Dean	6/20/02	4/10/30	R	2	1924-25	16	19	.457	4.81	59	34	12	1	0	277.0	308	148	22	95	92	.220	91	20
Dummy Deegan	11/16/1874	5/17/57		1	1901	0	0	.000	6.35	2	1	1	0	0	17.0	27	12	0	6	8	.000	5	0
Miguel Del Toro	6/22/72		R	2	1999-2000	2	0	1.000	4.61	23	0	0	0	0	41	41	21	8	11	20	.500	2	1
Rich DeLucia	10/7/64		R	2	1996-97	3	6	.333	5.97	59	0	0	0	0	63.1	68	42	8	31	57	.250	4	1
Al Demaree	9/8/1884	4/30/62	R	5	1912-14, 17-18	36	32	.529	2.60	112	81	34	7	3	660.0	625	191	13	159	238	.118	204	24
Mark Dempsey	12/17/57		R	1	1982	0	0	—	7.94	3	0	0	0	0	5.2	11	5	1	2	4	.000	1	0
Roger Denzer	10/5/1871	9/18/49	R	1	1901	2	6	.250	3.36	11	9	3	0	0	61.2	69	23	2	5	22	.091	22	2
Jim Deshaies	6/23/60		L	1	1993	2	2	.500	4.24	5	4	0	0	0	17.0	24	8	2	6	5	.000	5	0
Jim Devlin	4/16/1866	12/14/00	L	1	1886	0	0	—	18.00	1	0	0	0	0	2.0	3	4	0	4	2	.000	1	0
Mark Dewey	1/3/65		R	3	1990, 95-96	8	4	.667	3.73	119	0	0	0	0	137.2	131	57	12	63	100	.000	9	0
Walt Dickson	12/3/1878	12/9/18	R	1	1910	1	0	1.000	5.46	12	1	0	0	0	29.2	31	18	1	9	9	.250	4	1
Ed Doheny	11/24/1873	12/29/16	L	7	1895-1901	37	69	.349	4.29	123	112	93	1	0	905.0	974	431	11	493	376	.210	366	77
Red Donahue	1/23/1873	8/25/13	R	1	1893	0	0	—	9.00	3	0	0	0	0	5.0	8	5	0	3	1	.000	2	0
Pete Donahue	11/5/00	2/23/88	R	2	1930-31	7	7	.500	6.06	22	12	4	0	0	98.0	149	66	7	22	30	.257	35	9
Mike Dorgan*	10/2/1853	4/26/09	R	2	1883-84	8	7	.533	3.53	15	15	13	0	0	120.0	106	47	5	57	93	*	*	*
Phil Douglas	6/17/1890	8/1/52	R	4	1919-22	42	28	.600	3.15	118	75	36	7	4	656.2	698	230	29	151	180	.172	227	39
Kelly Downs	10/25/60		R	7	1986-92	47	38	.553	3.64	177	110	11	6	2	762.0	705	308	55	267	494	.123	211	26
Dave Dravecky	2/14/56		L	3	1987-89	11	7	.611	3.22	27	27	5	3	0	162.1	156	58	14	45	102	.137	51	7
Clem Dreisewerd	1/24/16		L	1	1948	0	0	—	5.68	4	0	0	0	0	12.2	17	8	3	5	2	.250	4	1
Rob Dressler	2/2/54		R	2	1975-76	4	10	.286	3.99	28	21	1	0	0	124.0	142	55	8	39	39	.114	35	4
Louis Drucke	12/3/1888	9/22/55	R	4	1909-12	18	15	.545	2.90	53	40	21	0	1	317.0	282	102	4	137	201	.178	101	18
Jean Dubuc	9/15/1888	8/28/58	R	1	1919	6	4	.600	2.66	36	5	1	0	3	132.0	119	39	4	37	32	.143	42	6
Jim Duffalo	11/25/35		R	5	1961-65	15	7	.682	3.38	119	14	2	2	6	253.1	215	95	24	125	176	.145	55	8
Jack Dunn*	10/6/1872	10/22/28	R	2	1902, 04	0	3	.000	3.82	4	2	2	0	0	30.2	31	13	1	15	7	*	*	*
Andy Dunning	8/12/1871	6/21/52	R	1	1891	0	1	.000	4.50	1	1	1	0	0	2.0	3	1	1	3	1	.000	0	0
Bull Durham	6/27/1877	6/28/60	R	2	1908-09	0	0	—	4.15	5	0	0	0	1	13.0	17	6	0	3	4	.000	2	0

E	Born	Died	T	Yrs	Seasons	W	L	PCT	ERA	G	GS	CG	ShO	SV	IP	H	ER	HR	BB	SO	AVG	AB	H
																					Pitchers' Batting		
Hugh East	7/7/19	11/2/81	R	3	1941-43	2	6	.250	5.40	19	8	1	0	0	63.1	85	38	5	41	27	.167	24	4
Claude Elliott	11/17/1879	6/21/23	R	2	1904-05	0	2	.000	3.74	13	3	3	0	6	53.0	62	22	5	15	28	.190	21	4
Alan Embree	1/23/70		L	3	1999-2001	6	9	.400	5.19	153	0	0	0	2	138.2	138	80	17	61	127	.000	0	0
Slim Emmerich	9/29/19	9/17/98	R	2	1945-46	4	4	.500	4.85	33	7	1	0	0	104.0	117	56	9	33	28	.120	25	3
Eric Erickson	3/13/1895	5/19/65	R	1	1914	0	1	.000	0.00	1	1	0	0	0	5.0	8	0	0	3	3	.000	1	0
Paul Erickson	12/14/15		R	1	1948	0	0	-	0.00	2	0	0	0	0	1.0	0	0	0	2	1	-	0	0
Dick Estelle	1/18/42		L	2	1964-65	0	2	.333	3.23	12	7	0	0	0	53.0	51	19	3	31	29	.063	16	1
Shawn Estes	2/18/73		L	7	1995-2001	64	50	.561	4.25	160	160	9	6	0	990	945	468	74	521	795	.157	305	48
Roy Evans	3/19/1874	8/15/15	R	1	1902	8	13	.381	3.17	23	17	17	0	0	176.0	186	62	2	58	48	.148	54	8
Buck Ewing*	10/17/1859	10/20/06	R	4	1884-85, 88-89	2	2	.500	3.16	7	3	3	0	0	37.0	42	13	1	19	21	*	*	*
John Ewing	6/1/1863	4/23/1895	R	4	1891	21	8	.724	2.27	33	30	28	5	0	269.1	237	68	0	105	138	.204	113	23
Scott Eyre	5/30/72		L	1	2002	0	0	.000	1.59	21	0	0	0	0	11.2	11	2	0	7	7	.000	0	0

F	Born	Died	T	Yrs	Seasons	W	L	PCT	ERA	G	GS	CG	ShO	SV	IP	H	ER	HR	BB	SO	AVG	AB	H
																					Pitchers' Batting		
Pete Falcone	10/1/53		L	1	1975	12	11	.522	4.17	34	32	3	1	0	190.0	171	88	16	111	131	.062	65	4
Bill Faul	4/21/40		R	1	1970	0	0	-	7.45	7	0	0	0	1	9.2	15	8	1	6	6	.244	41	10
Jim Faulkner	7/27/1899	6/1/62	L	2	1927-28	10	8	.556	3.54	41	9	3	0	2	127.0	144	50	5	46	34	.000	0	0
Charlie Faust	10/9/1880	6/18/15	R	1	1911	0	0	-	4.50	2	0	0	0	0	2.0	2	1	0	0	0	-	0	0
Harry Feldman	11/10/19	3/16/62	R	6	1941-46	35	35	.500	3.80	143	78	22	6	3	666.0	671	281	45	300	254	.172	221	38
Harry Felix	1870	10/17/61	R	1	1901	0	0	-	0.00	1	0	0	0	0	2.0	3	0	0	0	0	.000	1	0
George Ferguson	8/19/1886	9/5/43	R	2	1906-07	5	2	.714	2.32	37	6	5	1	8	116.1	106	30	3	44	69	.182	33	6
Osvaldo Fernandez	11/4/68		R	2	1996-97	10	17	.370	4.70	41	39	2	0	0	228.0	267	119	29	72	137	.068	74	5
Rube Fischer	9/19/16		R	5	1941, 43-46	16	34	.320	5.10	108	41	7	1	4	382.2	416	217	20	222	136	.193	114	22
Leo Fishel	12/13/1877	5/19/60	R	1	1899	0	1	.000	6.00	1	1	1	0	0	9.0	9	6	0	6	6	.250	4	1
Chauncey Fisher	1/8/1872	4/27/39	R	1	1901	0	0	-	15.75	2	1	0	0	0	4.0	11	7	0	2	1	.000	2	0
Don Fisher	2/6/16	7/29/73	R	1	1945	1	0	1.000	2.00	2	1	1	0	0	18.0	12	4	0	7	4	.143	7	1
Eddie Fisher	7/16/36		R	3	1959-61	3	8	.273	6.25	35	7	1	0	2	86.1	104	60	17	19	38	.200	20	4
Jack Fisher	3/4/39		R	1	1963	6	10	.375	4.58	36	12	2	0	0	116.0	132	59	12	38	57	.103	29	3
John Fitzgerald	9/15/33		L	1	1958	0	1	-	3.00	3	2	0	0	0	3.0	19	17	0	10	3	.000	3	0
Freddie Fitzsimmons	7/28/01	11/18/79	R	13	1925-37	170	114	.599	3.54	403	329	150	21	9	2514.1	2607	988	155	670	693	.209	917	192
Carney Flynn	1/23/1875	2/10/47	L	2	1896	0	2	.000	11.81	3	2	1	0	0	10.2	18	14	0	8	4	.500	4	2
Frank Foreman	5/1/1863	11/19/57	L	3	1898	0	1	.000	27.00	2	1	0	0	0	5.2	19	17	0	10	1	.000	3	0
Keith Foulke	10/19/72		R	1	1997	4	5	.167	8.26	11	8	0	0	0	44.2	60	41	9	18	33	.154	13	2
Alan Fowlkes	8/8/58		R	1	1982	4	2	.667	5.19	21	15	1	0	0	85.0	111	49	12	24	50	.115	26	3
Steve Frey	7/29/63		L	2	1994-95	4	4	.500	4.82	53	0	0	0	0	37.1	44	20	7	17	25	-	0	0
Art Fromme	9/3/1883	8/24/56	R	3	1913-15	20	12	.625	3.67	68	25	6	1	2	262.2	269	107	13	75	111	.203	69	14
Aaron Fultz	9/4/73		L	3	2000-02	10	5	.667	4.66	167	0	0	0	2	181.2	184	94	21	68	160	.333	12	4

G	Born	Died	T	Yrs	Seasons	W	L	PCT	ERA	G	GS	CG	ShO	SV	IP	H	ER	HR	BB	SO	AVG	AB	H
																					Pitchers' Batting		
Frank Gabler	11/6/11	11/1/67	R	3	1935-37	11	9	.550	4.06	75	15	5	0	6	230.2	269	104	18	56	73	.188	64	12
Rich Gale	1/19/54		R	1	1982	7	14	.333	4.23	33	29	2	0	0	170.1	193	80	9	81	102	.125	48	6
Mark Gardner	3/1/62		R	6	1996-2001	58	45	.563	4.71	175	147	11	4	0	951.1	981	498	145	312	663	.128	305	39
Bob Garibaldi	3/3/42		R	4	1962-63, 66, 69	0	2	.000	3.08	15	1	0	0	2	26.1	28	9	0	11	14	.000	4	0
Willie Garoni	7/28/1877	9/9/14	R	1	1899	0	1	.000	4.50	3	1	1	0	0	10.0	12	5	0	2	2	.000	4	0
Scott Garrelts	10/30/61		R	10	1982-91	69	53	.566	3.29	352	89	9	4	48	959.1	815	351	74	413	703	.125	232	29
Dinty Gearin	10/15/1897	3/11/59	L	2	1923-24	2	3	.400	2.89	12	5	3	0	0	53.0	53	17	4	26	13	.313	16	5
Johnny Gee	12/7/15	1/23/88	L	3	1944-46	2	4	.333	3.93	19	6	1	0	1	55.0	70	24	3	17	26	.214	14	3
Joe Genewich	1/15/1897	12/21/85	R	3	1928-30	16	16	.500	4.67	65	36	14	2	7	304.1	340	158	25	104	69	.241	116	28
Bill George*	1/27/1865	8/23/16	L	2	1887-88	5	10	.333	4.32	17	16	14	1	0	141.2	144	68	1	100	75	*	*	*
Oscar Georgy	11/25/16		R	1	1938	0	0	-	18.00	1	0	0	0	0	1.0	2	2	0	1	0	-	0	0

Name	Born	Died	T	Yrs	Seasons	W	L	PCT	ERA	G	GS	CG	ShO	SV	IP	H	ER	HR	BB	SO	Pitchers' Batting AVG	AB	H
Les German	6/1/1869	6/10/34	R	4	1893-96	24	27	.471	5.36	69	51	40	1	1	467.0	592	278	20	215	88	.284	243	69
Al Gettel	9/17/17		R	1	1951	1	2	.333	4.87	30	1	0	0	0	57.1	52	31	12	25	36	.083	12	1
Charley Gettig*	12/1870	4/11/35	R	4	1896-99	15	12	.556	4.50	42	26	22	4	1	276.0	345	138	4	110	51	—	—	—
Joe Gibbon	4/10/35		L	4	1966-69	12	13	.480	3.07	110	20	4	0	5	223.0	199	76	12	81	142	.093	43	4
Sam Gibson	8/5/1899	1/31/83	R	1	1932	4	8	.333	4.85	41	5	1	0	3	81.2	107	44	7	30	39	.263	19	5
Paul Giel	2/29/32		R	3	1954-55, 58	8	9	.471	4.18	69	11	1	0	0	178.2	167	83	20	107	106	.065	46	3
Wayne Gomes	1/15/73		R	1	2001	8	0	1.000	8.40	13	0	0	0	0	15	21	14	3	7	17	.000	0	0
Pat Gomez	3/17/68		L	2	1994-95	2	0	.000	4.18	44	0	0	0	0	47.1	39	22	4	32	29	.000	3	0
Ruben Gomez	7/13/27		R	6	1953-58	71	72	.497	3.90	219	186	60	14	2	1253.1	1203	543	125	498	578	.205	430	88
Tom Gorman	3/16/16	8/11/86	L	1	1939	0	0	—	7.20	7	0	0	0	0	5.0	7	4	0	1	2	.000	1	0
Rich Gossage	7/5/51		R	1	1989	2	1	.667	2.68	31	0	0	0	4	43.2	32	13	2	27	24	.000	—	—
Jim Gott	8/3/59		R	3	1985-87	8	10	.444	4.27	65	31	0	0	2	217.1	213	103	14	96	150	.172	64	11
Ted Goulait	8/12/1889	7/15/36	R	1	1912	0	2	—	6.43	1	1	0	0	0	7.0	11	5	0	4	6	.500	2	1
Mark Grant	10/24/63		R	3	1984, 86-87	2	7	.222	4.76	31	19	2	0	2	124.2	128	66	12	45	69	.033	30	1
Kent Greenfield	7/1/02	3/14/78	R	4	1924-27	27	23	.540	4.27	81	50	20	2	0	417.1	449	198	25	160	145	.085	129	11
Kenny Greer	5/12/67		R	1	1995	0	2	.000	5.25	5	0	0	0	2	12.0	15	7	3	5	7	.000	5	0
Hal Gregg	7/11/21	5/13/91	R	1	1952	0	0	.000	4.71	16	4	0	0	1	36.1	42	19	7	17	13	.125	8	1
Tom Griffin	2/22/48		R	3	1979-81	18	15	.545	3.48	123	29	3	1	2	331.1	284	128	25	152	244	.151	73	11
Burleigh Grimes	8/18/1893	12/6/85	R	2	1927	19	8	.704	3.54	39	34	15	0	2	259.2	274	102	12	87	102	.188	96	18
Marv Grissom	3/31/18		R	7	1946, 53-58	31	25	.554	2.88	285	15	4	0	58	543.1	492	174	46	200	314	.119	109	13
Tom Grubbs	2/22/1894	1/28/86	R	1	1920	0	1	.000	7.20	1	4	0	0	0	5.0	9	4	0	3	1	.000	0	0
Harry Gumbert	11/5/09	1/4/95	R	7	1935-41	68	55	.553	4.01	193	144	57	6	3	1113.1	1145	496	73	390	379	.186	397	74
Eric Gunderson	3/29/66		L	2	1990-91	1	2	.333	5.48	9	4	0	0	1	23.0	30	14	2	12	16	.000	0	0
H	Born	Died	T	Yrs	Seasons	W	L	PCT	ERA	G	GS	CG	ShO	SV	IP	H	ER	HR	BB	SO	Pitchers' Batting AVG	AB	H
Bump Hadley	7/5/04	2/15/63	R	1	1941	1	0	1.000	6.23	3	2	0	0	0	13.0	19	9	1	9	4	.000	3	0
Ed Halicki	10/4/50		R	7	1974-80	52	65	.444	3.58	182	151	36	13	1	1027.2	968	409	77	323	691	.165	322	53
Jack Hallett	11/13/14	6/11/82	R	1	1948	2	2	.500	4.50	2	0	0	0	0	4.0	3	2	4	4	3	.000	1	0
Steve Hamilton	11/30/35	12/2/97	L	1	1971	2	2	.500	3.02	39	0	0	0	4	44.2	29	15	7	11	38	.000	2	0
Atlee Hammaker	1/24/58		L	8	1982-85, 87-90	58	59	.496	3.51	214	144	18	6	5	1008.0	971	393	89	258	583	.116	302	35
Bill Hands	5/6/40		R	1	1965	0	2	.000	16.50	4	2	0	0	0	6.0	13	11	0	6	5	.000	0	0
Andy Hansen	11/12/24		R	6	1944-45, 47-50	15	21	.417	4.55	173	38	8	1	9	451.0	457	228	37	188	142	.072	97	7
Red Hardy	1/6/23		R	1	1951	0	0	—	6.75	2	0	0	0	0	1.1	4	1	0	1	0	—	0	0
Al Hargesheimer	11/21/56		R	2	1980-81	5	8	.385	4.32	21	16	0	0	0	93.2	102	45	4	41	46	.185	27	5
Ray Harrell	2/16/12	1/28/84	R	1	1945	0	0	—	4.97	12	0	0	0	0	25.1	34	14	1	14	7	.200	5	1
Jack Harshman*	7/12/27		L	1	1952	0	2	.000	14.21	2	0	0	0	0	6.1	12	10	2	6	6	*	*	*
Clint Hartung	8/10/22		R	4	1947-50	29	29	.500	5.02	112	72	23	3	1	511.1	529	285	56	271	167	*	*	*
Dean Hartgraves	8/12/66		L	1	1998	0	0	—	9.53	5	0	0	0	0	5.2	10	6	1	4	4	.000	0	0
Gil Hatfield*	1/27/1855	5/27/21	R	1	1889	2	4	.333	3.98	6	5	5	0	0	52.0	53	23	2	25	28	.203	123	25
Pink Hawley	12/5/1872	9/19/38	R	1	1900	18	18	.500	3.53	41	38	34	2	0	329.1	377	129	7	89	80	.400	5	2
Bunny Hearn	5/21/1891	10/10/59	L	1	1913	0	1	.000	2.77	2	2	2	0	0	13.0	13	4	0	7	8	*	*	*
Jim Hearn	4/11/21	6/10/98	R	7	1950-56	78	66	.542	3.74	221	186	55	9	3	1242.2	1176	516	121	477	483	.146	424	62
Dave Heaverlo	8/25/50		R	3	1975-77	12	6	.667	3.11	159	0	0	0	3	237.2	239	82	14	67	133	.250	12	3
Bob Hendley	4/30/39		L	2	1964-65	10	11	.476	4.39	38	31	4	1	0	178.1	188	87	24	72	112	.100	50	5
Ed Hendricks	6/20/1885	11/28/30	L	1	1910	0	1	.000	3.75	4	1	1	0	0	12.0	12	5	0	4	2	.000	0	0
Bill Henry	10/15/27		L	4	1965-68	5	5	.500	3.08	105	2	0	0	7	90.2	75	31	6	30	73	.125	8	1
Doug Henry	12/10/63		R	2	1997, 2000	7	6	.538	4.13	102	0	0	0	3	96	44	44	7	62	85	.000	4	0
Dutch Henry	5/12/02	8/23/68	L	3	1927-29	19	18	.514	4.02	89	32	15	1	6	329.0	395	147	20	87	90	.225	102	23
Chuck Hensley	3/11/59		L	1	1986	0	1	—	2.45	11	0	0	0	0	7.1	5	2	2	2	6	—	0	0
Ron Herbel	1/16/38		R	7	1963-69	33	29	.532	3.60	230	78	11	3	5	718.1	756	287	60	221	364	.027	184	5
Fred Herbert	3/4/1887	5/29/63	R	1	1915	1	1	.500	1.06	2	2	2	0	0	17.0	12	2	0	4	6	.167	6	1
Gil Heredia	10/26/65		R	2	1991-92	2	5	.286	4.57	20	8	0	0	0	63.0	59	32	7	23	28	.308	13	4
Livan Hernandez	2/20/75		R	4	1999-2002	45	45	.500	4.44	110	110	12	5	0	746.1	819	368	71	250	484	.254	252	64

Name	Born	Died	T	Yrs	Seasons	W	L	PCT	ERA	G	GS	CG	ShO	SV	IP	H	ER	HR	BB	SO	Pitchers' Batting AVG	AB	H
Roberto Hernandez	11/11/64		R	1	1997	5	2	.714	2.48	28	0	0	0	4	32.2	29	9	2	14	35	.500	2	1
Orel Hershiser	9/16/58	9/22/43	R	1	1998	11	10	.524	4.41	34	34	0	0	0	202.0	200	99	22	85	126	.152	66	10
Larry Hesterfer	6/9/1878	9/22/43	L	1	1901	0	1	.000	7.50	1	1	1	0	0	6.0	15	5	0	3	2	.000	2	0
Joe Heving	9/2/00	4/11/70	R	2	1930-31	8	11	.421	5.11	63	2	0	0	9	132.0	157	75	11	38	63	.200	30	6
Bryan Hickerson	10/13/63		L	4	1991-94	18	18	.500	4.20	153	36	0	0	1	356.0	382	166	44	115	239	.127	71	9
Charlie Hickman*	3/4/1876	4/19/34	R	1	1901	3	5	.375	4.57	9	9	6	0	0	65.0	76	33	1	26	11	*	*	*
Kirby Higbe	4/8/15	5/6/85	R	2	1949-50	2	3	.400	3.91	55	9	0	0	2	115.0	109	50	14	71	55	.105	19	2
Carmen Hill	10/1/1895	1/1/90	R	1	1922	2	1	.667	4.76	8	3	4	0	0	28.1	33	15	0	5	6	.182	11	2
Frank Hiller	7/13/20	1/8/87	R	1	1953	2	1	.667	6.15	19	4	0	0	0	33.2	43	23	6	15	10	.500	4	2
Billy Hoeft	5/17/32		L	2	1963, 66	2	2	.500	4.82	27	1	0	0	0	28.0	30	15	5	13	11	1.000	55	4
Al Holland	8/16/52		L	4	1979-82	19	11	.633	2.56	162	10	0	0	4	319.2	276	91	18	123	247	.073	0	0
Mul Holland	1/6/03	2/16/69	R	1	1927	1	0	1.000	0.00	2	0	0	0	0	2.0	0	0	0	3	0	-	0	0
Chris Hook	8/4/68		R	2	1995-96	5	2	.714	5.89	55	0	0	0	0	65.2	71	43	10	43	44	.200	5	1
Waite Hoyt	9/9/1899	8/25/84	R	2	1918, 32	5	7	.417	3.39	19	12	3	0	0	98.1	103	37	6	25	31	.094	32	3
Bill Hubbell	6/17/1897	8/3/80	R	2	1919-20	1	2	.333	2.05	16	2	3	0	2	48.1	45	11	5	17	11	.154	13	2
Carl Hubbell	6/22/03	11/21/88	L	16	1928-43	253	154	.622	2.98	535	431	260	36	33	3590.1	3461	1188	227	725	1677	.191	1288	246
Willis Hudlin	5/23/06		R	1	1940	0	0	.000	10.80	1	0	0	0	0	5.0	9	6	0	0	1	.000	0	0
Al Huenke	6/26/1891	9/20/74	R	1	1914	0	0	-	4.50	1	1	0	0	0	2.0	2	1	0	0	2	.000	2	0
Walter Huntzinger	2/6/1899	8/11/81	R	3	1923-25	6	3	.667	4.13	40	4	0	0	1	104.2	118	48	6	27	27	.238	21	5

I

Name	Born	Died	T	Yrs	Seasons	W	L	PCT	ERA	G	GS	CG	ShO	SV	IP	H	ER	HR	BB	SO	Pitchers' Batting AVG	AB	H
Hooks Iott	12/3/19	8/17/80	L	1	1947	3	8	.273	5.93	20	9	2	1	0	71.1	67	47	3	52	46	.143	21	3

J

Name	Born	Died	T	Yrs	Seasons	W	L	PCT	ERA	G	GS	CG	ShO	SV	IP	H	ER	HR	BB	SO	Pitchers' Batting AVG	AB	H
Mike Jackson	12/22/64		R	3	1992-94	15	14	.517	2.99	184	0	0	0	7	201.2	157	67	18	68	201	.333	6	2
Larry Jansen	7/16/20		R	8	1947-54	120	86	.583	3.55	283	230	105	17	9	1731.0	1712	683	186	401	826	.153	589	90
Tex Jeanes*	12/19/00	4/5/73	R	1	1927	0	0	-	9.00	19	0	0	0	0	1.0	2	1	0	2	0	*	*	*
Mike Jeffcoat	8/3/59		L	1	1985	0	2	.000	5.32	19	0	0	0	0	22.0	27	13	4	6	10	.000	0	0
Ryan Jensen	9/17/75		R	2	2001-02	14	10	.583	4.46	42	37	1	0	0	214	227	106	9	91	131	.118	68	8
Art Johnson	2/15/1897	6/7/82	L	1	1927	0	0	-	0.00	17	0	0	0	1	3.0	0	0	0	0	0	-	0	0
Don Johnson	11/12/26		R	1	1958	0	1	.000	6.26	17	0	0	0	0	23.0	31	16	2	8	14	.000	2	0
Fred Johnson	3/10/1894	6/14/73	R	2	1922-23	2	2	.500	4.11	5	4	2	0	0	35.0	31	16	5	8	13	.000	10	0
Jerry Johnson	12/3/43		R	3	1970-72	23	19	.548	3.74	148	1	0	0	29	247.2	233	103	18	126	186	.081	37	3
Jim Johnson	11/3/45		L	1	1970	0	0	1.000	8.10	3	0	0	0	0	6.2	8	6	0	5	2	.000	2	0
Youngy Johnson	7/22/1877	8/28/36	R	1	1899	0	0	-	0.00	1	0	0	0	0	2.0	8	0	0	1	1	-	0	0
John Johnstone	11/25/68		R	4	1997-2000	13	15	.464	3.68	192	0	0	0	3	222.1	199	91	30	78	194	.000	6	0
Roy Joiner	10/30/06	12/26/89	L	2	1940	3	2	.600	3.40	30	2	0	0	0	53.0	66	20	8	17	25	.273	11	3
Bumpus Jones	1/1/1870	6/25/38	R	1	1893	0	2	.000	11.25	1	1	0	0	0	4.0	5	5	3	10	1	-	0	0
Gordon Jones	4/2/30	4/25/94	R	2	1957-59	6	4	.600	3.89	52	0	0	0	3	85.2	94	37	9	27	42	.077	13	1
Jim Jones*	12/25/1876	5/6/53	R	1	1901	0	0	-	10.80	2	1	1	0	0	5.0	6	6	0	2	3	*	*	*
Johnny Jones	8/25/1892	6/5/80	R	1	1919	0	0	-	5.40	2	1	0	0	0	6.2	9	4	0	3	3	.000	3	0
Sam Jones	12/14/25	11/5/71	R	3	1959-61	47	37	.560	3.30	126	87	31	7	5	633.0	566	232	48	257	504	.159	201	32
Sheldon Jones	2/2/22	4/18/91	R	6	1946-51	53	51	.510	3.83	199	98	33	4	11	811.2	781	345	79	366	364	.140	242	34
Sherman Jones	2/10/35		R	1	1960	1	1	.500	3.09	16	0	0	0	1	32.0	37	11	3	11	10	.286	7	2
Claude Jonnard	11/23/1897	8/27/59	R	4	1921-24	14	9	.609	3.15	113	4	2	0	16	285.2	285	100	15	87	136	.041	73	3
Bob Joyce	1/14/15	12/10/81	R	1	1946	3	4	.429	5.34	14	7	2	0	0	60.2	79	36	3	20	24	.158	19	3
Ralph Judd	12/7/01	5/6/57	R	2	1929-30	3	0	1.000	3.09	20	0	0	0	0	58.1	62	20	4	14	21	.000	17	0
Jeff Juden	1/19/71		R	1	1996	4	0	1.000	4.10	36	0	0	0	0	41.2	39	19	7	20	35	.000	0	0

K

Name	Born	Died	T	Yrs	Seasons	W	L	PCT	ERA	G	GS	CG	ShO	SV	IP	H	ER	HR	BB	SO	Pitchers' Batting AVG	AB	H
Tim Keefe	1/1/1857	4/23/33	R	6	1885-89, 91	174	82	.680	2.53	272	269	252	22	1	2265.0	1913	637	41	580	1303	.166	913	152

Name	Born	Died	T	Yrs	Seasons	W	L	PCT	ERA	G	GS	CG	ShO	SV	IP	H	ER	HR	BB	SO	AVG	AB	H
George Kelly*	9/10/1895	10/13/84	R	1	1917	1	0	1.000	0.00	1	0	0	0	0	5.0	4	0	0	1	2	*	*	4
Brickyard Kennedy	10/7/1867	9/23/15	R	1	1902	1	4	.200	3.96	6	6	4	0	0	38.2	44	17	0	16	9	.267	15	4
Monte Kennedy	5/11/22	3/1/97	L	8	1946-53	42	55	.433	3.84	249	127	48	7	4	961.0	928	410	67	495	411	.153	301	46
Silver King	1/11/1868	5/21/38	R	2	1892-93	25	28	.472	3.86	58	54	49	1	0	459.1	461	197	19	197	183	.206	180	37
Brian Kingman	7/27/54		R	1	1983	0	0	—	7.71	2	0	0	0	0	4.2	10	4	0	6	4	—	0	0
Dave Kingman*	12/21/48		R	1	1973	0	0	—	9.00	2	0	0	0	0	4.0	3	4	0	6	4	*	*	0
La Rue Kirby	12/30/1889	6/10/61	R	1	1912	1	0	1.000	5.73	3	1	1	0	0	11.0	13	7	0	15	6	.200	5	1
Al Klawitter	4/12/1888	5/2/50	R	2	1909-10	1	2	.500	2.25	7	3	0	0	0	28.0	26	7	0	6	6	.333	9	3
Ron Kline	3/9/32		R	1	1969	0	2	.000	4.09	7	3	0	0	0	11.0	16	5	0	6	7	—	0	0
Frank Knauss	1868	—	L	1	1895	0	2	.000	17.18	1	1	0	0	0	3.2	9	7	0	7	1	.000	—	0
Bob Knepper	5/25/54		L	7	1976-80, 89-90	53	55	.491	3.71	161	146	37	12	0	970.0	989	400	80	336	527	.140	300	42
Alex Konikowski	6/8/28	9/28/97	R	3	1948, 51, 54	2	3	.400	6.93	35	10	0	0	0	49.1	58	38	8	29	20	.000	20	0
Dave Koslo	3/31/20	12/1/75	L	10	1941-42, 46-53	91	104	.467	3.69	332	188	74	15	21	1559.2	1563	639	119	526	596	.109	512	56
Jack Kramer	1/5/18	5/18/95	R	2	1950-51	3	6	.333	4.14	39	10	0	0	0	91.1	102	42	6	42	29	.100	20	2
Jack Kraus	4/26/18	1/2/76	L	1	1946	2	1	.667	6.12	17	1	0	0	0	25.0	25	17	4	15	7	.000	3	0
Red Kress	1/2/07	11/29/62	R	1	1946	0	0	—	12.27	1	0	0	0	0	3.2	5	5	0	1	1	.000	1	0
Mike Krukow	1/21/52		R	7	1983-89	66	56	.541	3.84	186	182	25	5	1	1154.0	1133	493	124	353	802	.164	383	63

Name	Born	Died	T	Yrs	Seasons	W	L	PCT	ERA	G	GS	CG	ShO	SV	IP	H	ER	HR	BB	SO	AVG (Pitchers' Batting)	AB	H
Bob Lacey	8/25/53		L	1	1984	1	3	.250	3.88	34	0	0	0	0	51.0	55	22	5	13	26	.333	6	2
Mike LaCoss	5/30/56		R	6	1986-91	47	49	.490	3.79	171	111	9	3	6	765.0	741	322	47	308	382	.143	217	31
Max Lanier	8/18/15		L	2	1952-53	7	12	.368	4.05	40	16	6	1	5	142.1	132	64	12	68	49	.262	42	11
Dave LaPoint	7/29/59		L	1	1985	7	17	.292	3.57	31	31	2	0	0	206.2	215	82	18	74	122	.167	60	10
Pat Larkin	6/14/60		L	1	1983	0	0	—	4.35	5	0	0	0	0	10.1	13	5	0	3	5	.000	—	0
Don Larsen	8/7/29		R	3	1962-64	12	12	.500	3.86	101	0	0	0	14	158.2	139	68	17	83	108	.189	37	7
Bill Laskey	12/20/57		R	5	1982-86	41	48	.461	3.84	131	109	10	1	1	686.2	697	293	67	190	290	.103	203	21
Gary Lavelle	1/3/49		L	11	1974-84	73	67	.521	2.82	647	3	0	0	127	980.1	910	307	44	382	696	.081	111	9
Tim Layana	3/2/64	6/28/99	R	1	1993	0	0	—	22.50	3	0	0	0	0	2.0	7	5	1	1	1	—	0	0
Roy Lee	9/28/17	11/11/85	L	1	1945	0	2	.000	11.57	3	1	0	0	0	7.0	8	9	3	3	0	.000	1	0
Thornton Lee	9/13/06	6/9/97	L	1	1948	0	3	.000	4.41	11	4	0	1	0	32.2	41	16	3	12	17	.091	11	1
Craig Lefferts	9/29/57		L	3	1987-89	8	15	.348	2.88	178	0	0	0	35	246.2	203	79	22	63	147	.050	20	1
Hank Leiber*	1/17/11	11/8/93	R	1	1942	0	0	—	6.00	1	0	0	0	0	9.0	9	9	0	5	5	*	*	*
Mark Leiter	4/13/63		R	2	1995-96	14	22	.389	4.38	53	51	2	1	0	331.0	336	161	44	105	247	.117	103	12
Dummy Leitner	6/19/1871	2/20/60	R	1	1901	0	2	.000	4.50	2	2	2	0	0	18.0	27	9	0	4	3	.143	7	1
Dick LeMay	8/28/38		L	2	1961-62	3	7	.300	3.98	36	5	0	0	4	92.2	74	41	13	45	59	.077	26	2
Randy Lerch	10/9/54		L	2	1983-84	6	3	.667	4.12	44	4	0	0	2	83.0	89	38	4	44	54	.133	15	2
Don Liddle	5/25/25		L	3	1954-56	20	10	.667	3.64	72	37	9	3	2	274.1	242	111	28	130	121	.184	76	14
Scott Linebrink	8/4/76		R	1	2001	0	0	—	11.57	3	0	0	0	0	2.1	7	3	0	7	5	.000	—	0
Frank Linzy	9/15/40		R	7	1963, 65-70	48	39	.552	2.71	308	1	0	0	78	531.0	510	160	18	177	258	.149	101	15
Dick Littlefield	3/18/26	11/20/97	L	1	1956	4	4	.500	4.08	31	7	0	0	2	97.0	78	44	16	39	65	.083	24	2
Greg Litton*	7/13/64		R	1	1991	0	0	—	9.00	2	0	0	0	0	1.0	2	1	0	3	0	*	*	—
Jake Livingstone	1/1/1880	3/22/49	—	1	1901	0	0	—	9.00	2	2	—	0	0	12.0	26	12	0	7	6	.167	6	1
Billy Loes	12/13/29		R	2	1960-61	9	7	.563	4.43	63	18	3	1	5	160.1	154	79	22	56	83	.167	36	6
Bill Lohrman	5/22/13	9/12/99	R	7	1937-43	59	54	.522	3.69	178	118	45	9	7	940.0	994	385	68	221	316	.146	309	45
Lou Lombardo	11/18/28		L	1	1948	0	0	—	6.75	2	0	0	0	0	5.1	5	4	3	14	2	.000	2	0
Ray Lucas	10/2/08	10/9/69	R	3	1929-31	0	0	—	3.98	10	2	0	0	0	20.1	13	9	0	4	3	.333	3	1
Red Lucas	4/28/02	7/9/86	R	1	1923	0	0	—	0.00	3	0	0	0	1	5.1	9	0	0	3	9	.000	3	0
Dolph Luque	8/4/1890	7/3/57	R	4	1932-35	19	12	.613	3.47	101	5	0	0	16	236.1	258	91	11	69	69	.173	52	9
Mike Lynch	6/28/1880	4/2/27	R	1	1907	3	6	.333	3.38	12	10	7	0	1	72.0	68	27	3	30	34	.296	27	8
Red Lynn	12/27/13	10/21/77	R	2	1939-40	5	3	.625	3.42	59	0	0	0	4	92.0	84	35	6	45	47	.000	10	0

M	Born	Died	T	Yrs	Seasons	W	L	PCT	ERA	G	GS	CG	ShO	SV	IP	H	ER	HR	BB	SO	Pitchers' Batting		
																					AVG	AB	H
Ken MacKenzie	3/10/34		L		1964	0	0	.000	5.00	10	0	0	0	0	9.0	9	5	1	3	2		0	0
Bill Magee	1/11/1868	8/15/22	R	2	1901-02	0	4	.000	5.70	8	6	4	0	0	47.1	61	30	4	12	16	.133	15	2
Sal Maglie	4/26/17	12/28/92	R	7	1945, 50-55	95	42	.693	3.13	221	171	77	20	8	1297.2	1216	451	117	434	654	.143	428	61
Bill Malarkey	11/26/1878	12/12/56	R	1	1908	0	2	.000	2.57	15	0	0	0	2	35.0	31	10	1	10	12	.000	6	0
Leo Mangum	5/24/1896	7/9/74	R	1	1928	0	0	-	15.00	1	1	0	0	0	3.0	6	5	0	5	1	1.000	1	1
Georges Maranda	1/15/32		R	1	1960	1	4	.200	4.62	17	4	0	0	0	50.2	50	26	6	30	28	.167	12	2
Firpo Marberry	11/30/1898	6/30/76	R	1	1936	0	0	.000	0.00	1	0	0	0	0	0.1	1	0	0	1	0	.000	1	0
Joe Margoneri	1/13/30		L	2	1956-57	7	7	.500	4.29	36	15	3	0	0	126.0	132	60	13	70	67	.081	37	3
Juan Marichal	10/20/37		R	14	1960-73	238	140	.630	2.84	458	446	244	52	2	3444.0	3081	1086	315	690	2281	.166	1219	202
Rube Marquard	10/9/1886	6/1/80	L	8	1908-15	103	76	.575	2.85	239	187	99	16	12	1546.0	1420	489	49	430	897	.177	526	93
Renie Martin	8/30/55		R	3	1982-84	10	15	.400	4.41	78	31	1	0	1	259.0	272	127	27	131	114	.309	81	25
Roger Mason	9/18/58		R	3	1985-87	5	8	.385	4.05	21	21	2	0	0	115.2	114	52	10	51	87	.075	40	3
Christy Mathewson	8/12/1880	10/7/25	R	17	1900-16	372	188	.664	2.12	634	550	433	79	28	4771.2	4203	1125	90	843	2499	.214	1679	359
Henry Mathewson	12/24/1886	7/1/17	R	2	1906-07	0	1	.000	4.91	3	1	1	0	2	11.0	8	6	0	14	2	.000	2	0
Mike Mattimore*	1859	4/28/31	L	1	1887	3	3	.500	2.35	7	7	6	1	0	57.1	47	15	2	28	12	*	*	*
Al Maul	10/9/1865	5/3/58	R	1	1901	0	3	.000	11.37	3	3	2	0	0	19.0	39	24	1	8	5	.375	8	3
Ernie Maun	2/3/01	1/1/87	R	1	1924	1	1	.500	5.91	22	0	0	0	0	35.0	46	23	2	10	5	.667	3	2
Bert Maxwell	10/17/1886	12/10/61	R	1	1911	1	2	.333	2.90	4	3	0	0	0	31.0	37	10	0	7	8	.111	9	1
Carl Mays	11/12/1891	4/4/71	R	1	1929	7	2	.778	4.32	37	8	3	0	4	123.0	140	59	8	31	32	.353	34	12
Windy McCall	7/18/25		L	4	1954-57	11	14	.440	3.69	126	14	4	0	12	236.1	218	97	21	88	131	.116	43	5
Randy McCament	7/29/62		R	2	1989-90	1	1	.500	3.80	28	0	0	0	0	42.2	40	18	4	28	17	.250	4	1
Johnny McCarthy*	1/7/10	9/13/73	L	1	1939	0	0	-	7.20	1	0	0	0	0	5.0	8	4	1	2	*	*	*	*
Paul McClellan	2/3/66		R	2	1990-91	3	7	.300	5.26	17	13	1	0	0	78.2	82	46	15	31	46	.174	23	4
Mike McCormick	9/29/38		L	11	1956-62, 67-70	107	96	.527	3.68	357	252	78	19	11	1822.2	1737	745	194	616	1030	.154	572	88
Lindy McDaniel	12/13/35		R	3	1966-68	12	11	.522	3.45	117	3	0	0	9	213.2	202	82	12	64	150	.086	35	3
Sam McDowell	9/21/42		L	2	1972-73	11	10	.524	4.36	46	28	4	0	3	204.1	200	99	16	115	157	.127	71	9
Andy McGaffigan	10/25/56		R	3	1982-83, 90	4	9	.308	4.47	51	16	0	0	2	147.0	146	73	19	44	101	.065	31	2
Bill McGee	11/16/09	2/11/87	R	2	1941-42	8	12	.400	3.94	53	22	3	1	1	210.0	212	92	17	100	81	.133	60	8
Joe McGinnity	3/19/1871	11/14/29	R	7	1902-08	151	88	.632	2.38	300	237	186	26	21	2151.1	1937	568	34	464	787	.180	772	139
Lynn McGlothen	3/27/50	8/14/84	R	2	1977-78	2	9	.182	5.54	26	16	2	0	0	92.2	109	57	9	56	51	.091	22	2
Mickey McGowan	11/26/21		L	1	1948	0	0	-	7.36	3	0	0	0	0	3.2	3	3	1	4	2	.000	1	0
Don McMahon	1/4/30	7/22/87	R	6	1969-74	29	15	.659	3.28	210	0	0	0	36	305.0	236	111	30	121	236	.172	29	5
Tim McNamara	11/20/1898	11/5/94	R	1	1926	0	0	-	9.00	6	0	0	0	0	6.0	7	6	0	4	4	-	0	0
Frank McPartlin	2/16/1872	11/13/43	R	1	1899	0	0	-	4.50	6	1	0	0	0	4.0	4	2	0	2	2	.000	8	0
Hugh McQuillan	9/15/1897	8/26/47	R	6	1922-27	53	44	.546	3.67	138	110	53	7	5	803.0	853	327	47	230	235	.176	279	49
Jouett Meekin	2/21/1867	12/14/44	R	6	1894-99	116	74	.611	4.01	216	207	178	5	2	1741.0	1904	776	53	648	514	.271	734	199
Cliff Melton	1/3/12	7/28/86	L	8	1937-44	86	80	.518	3.42	272	179	65	13	16	1453.2	1446	552	79	431	660	.164	469	77
Jock Menefee	1/15/1868	3/11/53	R	1	1898	0	1	.000	4.82	6	0	0	0	0	9.1	11	5	0	2	3	.000	5	0
Tony Menendez	2/20/65		R	1	1994	0	0	-	21.60	4	0	0	0	0	3.1	8	8	2	2	2	-	0	0
Win Mercer*	6/20/1874	1/12/03	R	1	1900	13	17	.433	3.86	33	29	26	1	2	242.2	303	104	5	58	39	*	*	*
Jose Mesa	5/22/66		R	1	1998	5	3	.625	3.52	32	0	0	0	0	30.2	30	12	1	18	28	-	0	0
Butch Metzger	5/23/52		R	1	1974	1	0	1.000	3.55	10	0	0	0	1	12.2	11	5	0	12	5	-	0	0
Jim Middleton	5/28/1889	1/12/74	R	1	1917	1	1	.500	2.75	13	0	0	0	0	36.0	35	11	1	8	9	.000	8	0
Roscoe Miller	12/2/1876	4/18/13	R	2	1902-03	3	13	.188	4.34	25	17	13	0	0	157.2	178	76	2	35	45	.115	52	6
Stu Miller	12/26/27		R	6	1957-62	47	44	.516	3.16	307	45	8	1	47	804.1	736	282	67	261	506	.110	191	21
Whitey Miller	5/2/15	4/3/91	R	1	1944	0	1	.000	0.00	4	0	0	0	0	5.0	1	0	0	4	2	.000	1	0
Billy Milligan	8/19/1878	10/14/28	L	1	1904	0	0	-	5.40	5	1	1	0	2	25.0	36	15	2	4	6	.111	9	1
Willie Mills	8/15/1877	7/5/14	L	1	1901	0	2	.000	8.44	10	2	2	0	0	16.0	21	15	0	4	3	.167	6	1
Greg Minton	7/29/51		R	13	1975-87	45	52	.464	3.23	552	7	0	0	125	870.1	857	312	33	376	352	.146	103	15
Steve Mintz	11/24/68		R	1	1995	1	2	.333	7.45	14	0	0	0	0	19.1	26	16	4	12	45	.000	3	0
Gino Minutelli	5/23/64		L	1	1993	0	2	.000	3.77	9	0	0	0	0	14.1	7	6	2	15	10	.000	4	0
Clarence Mitchell	2/22/1891	11/6/63	L	3	1930-32	24	17	.585	4.04	59	44	19	0	2	349.2	413	157	23	99	86	.231	130	30

Name	Born	Died	T	Yrs	Seasons	W	L	PCT	ERA	G	GS	CG	ShO	SV	IP	H	ER	HR	BB	SO	Pitchers' Batting AVG	AB	H
Randy Moffitt	10/13/48		R	10	1972-81	35	46	.432	3.68	459	1	0	0	83	682.1	678	279	53	249	397	.143	84	12
Bill Monbouquette	8/11/36		R	1	1968	0	1	.000	3.65	7	0	0	0	0	12.1	11	5	4	2	5	-	0	0
John Montefusco	5/25/50		R	7	1974-80	59	62	.488	3.47	185	175	30	11	1	1182.2	1143	456	90	383	869	.102	363	37
Rich Monteleone	3/22/63		R	1	1994	4	3	.571	3.18	39	0	0	0	0	45.1	43	16	6	13	16	.000	3	0
Ramon Monzant	1/4/33		R	6	1954-58, 60	16	21	.432	4.38	106	32	8	1	0	316.2	330	154	43	134	201	.157	89	14
Jim Mooney	9/4/06	4/27/79	L	2	1931-32	13	11	.542	3.94	39	26	10	3	0	196.1	225	86	19	58	75	.136	66	9
Bobby Moore	11/8/58		R	1	1985	0	0	-	3.24	11	0	0	0	0	16.2	18	6	0	10	10	.000	2	0
Euel Moore	5/27/08	2/12/89	R	1	1935	1	0	1.000	5.63	6	0	0	0	0	8.0	9	5	0	4	3	.000	7	0
Alvin Morman	1/6/69		L	1	1998	0	1	.000	5.14	9	0	0	0	0	7.0	8	4	4	3	7	-	0	0
Bill Morrell	4/9/1893	8/5/75	R	2	1930-31	5	3	.625	4.01	22	7	2	0	0	74.0	91	33	4	28	19	.100	20	2
John Morris	8/23/41		L	3	1972-74	2	1	.667	4.32	31	0	0	0	2	33.1	38	16	3	9	17	.500	2	1
Billy Muffett	9/21/30		R	1	1959	0	0	-	5.40	5	0	0	0	0	6.2	11	4	2	3	3	-	0	0
Terry Mulholland	3/9/63		L	5	1986, 88-89, 95, 97	8	22	.267	5.18	73	43	4	1	1	290.1	334	167	35	90	141	.078	90	7
Van Mungo	6/8/11	2/12/85	R	3	1942-43, 45	18	16	.529	3.76	80	44	9	4	2	373.2	339	156	15	171	211	.206	131	27
Masanori Murakami	5/6/44		L	2	1964-65	5	1	.833	3.43	54	1	0	0	9	89.1	65	34	10	23	100	.125	16	2
Bob Murphy	12/26/1866	-	-	1	1890	1	0	1.000	5.50	3	2	1	0	0	18.0	23	11	0	10	8	.111	9	1

Name	Born	Died	T	Yrs	Seasons	W	L	PCT	ERA	G	GS	CG	ShO	SV	IP	H	ER	HR	BB	SO	Pitchers' Batting AVG	AB	H
Phil Nastu	3/8/55		L	3	1978-80	3	5	.375	4.50	34	15	0	0	0	114.0	123	57	16	48	53	.040	25	1
Joe Nathan	11/22/74		R	3	1999-2000, 02	12	6	.667	4.61	43	29	0	0	1	187.1	174	96	5	109	117	.167	60	10
Art Nehf	7/31/1892	12/18/60	L	8	1919-26	107	60	.641	3.45	226	181	95	12	7	1436.0	1476	550	78	325	415	.230	491	113
Robb Nen	11/28/69		R	5	1998-2002	24	25	.490	2.43	365	0	0	0	206	378.1	297	102	24	113	453	.167	6	1
Bobo Newsom	8/11/07	12/7/62	R	1	1948	0	4	.000	4.21	11	4	0	0	0	25.2	35	12	1	13	9	.429	7	3
Chet Nichols	7/3/1897	7/11/82	R	1	1928	0	0	-	23.63	3	0	0	0	0	2.2	11	7	0	3	1	-	0	0
Rafael Novoa	10/26/67		L	1	1990	0	1	.000	6.75	7	2	0	0	1	18.2	21	14	3	13	14	.200	5	1

Name	Born	Died	T	Yrs	Seasons	W	L	PCT	ERA	G	GS	CG	ShO	SV	IP	H	ER	HR	BB	SO	Pitchers' Batting AVG	AB	H
Walter Ockey	1/4/20	12/4/71	R	1	1944	0	0	-	3.38	2	0	0	0	0	2.2	2	1	0	2	0	.000	0	0
Hank O'Day	7/8/1862	7/2/35	R	1	1889	9	1	.900	4.27	10	10	8	0	0	78.0	83	37	2	35	28	.097	31	3
Billy O'Dell	2/10/33		L	5	1960-64	56	49	.533	3.55	204	118	41	7	7	921.0	912	363	68	276	620	.133	285	38
Joe Oeschger	5/24/1892	7/28/86	R	2	1919, 24	2	1	.667	3.41	15	3	0	0	0	37.0	47	14	1	16	13	.375	8	3
Jack Ogden	11/5/1897	11/9/77	R	1	1918	0	0	-	3.12	5	0	0	0	0	8.2	3	3	0	3	1	.000	1	0
Francisco Oliveras	1/31/63		R	3	1990-92	8	11	.421	3.46	104	10	0	0	5	179.1	157	69	28	53	106	.136	22	3
Randy O'Neal	8/30/60		R	1	1990	1	0	1.000	3.83	26	0	0	0	0	47.0	58	20	3	18	30	.167	6	1
Tip O'Neill*	5/25/1858	12/31/15	R	1	1883	5	12	.294	4.07	19	19	15	0	0	148.0	182	67	5	64	55	*	*	*
Russ Ortiz	6/5/74		R	5	1998-2002	67	44	.604	4.01	154	144	6	0	0	924.2	849	412	91	468	912	.215	154	34
Marty O'Toole	11/27/1888	2/18/49	R	1	1914	1	1	.500	4.24	10	5	2	0	0	34.0	34	16	0	12	13	.300	10	3

Name	Born	Died	T	Yrs	Seasons	W	L	PCT	ERA	G	GS	CG	ShO	SV	IP	H	ER	HR	BB	SO	Pitchers' Batting AVG	AB	H
Emilio Palmero	6/13/1895	7/15/70	L	2	1915-16	0	5	.000	5.93	7	4	1	0	0	27.1	27	18	2	17	16	.143	7	1
Roy Parmelee	4/25/07	8/31/81	R	7	1929-35	40	30	.571	3.87	122	93	38	5	5	709.0	642	305	40	310	367	.199	253	56
Bronswell Patrick	9/16/70		R	1	1999	1	1	1.000	10.13	6	0	0	0	0	5.1	9	6	4	3	6	.000	1	0
Jim Pena	9/17/64		L	1	1992	1	1	.500	3.48	25	2	0	0	0	44.0	49	17	4	20	32	.200	5	1
Jon Perlman	12/13/56		R	1	1987	0	0	-	3.97	10	0	0	0	0	11.1	5	5	1	4	3	-	1	0
Pol Perritt	8/30/1892	10/15/47	R	7	1915-21	68	50	.576	2.58	169	120	66	20	6	964.2	920	277	25	216	348	.138	312	43
Gaylord Perry	9/15/38		R	10	1962-71	134	109	.551	2.96	367	283	125	21	10	2294.2	2061	755	165	581	1606	.129	760	98
Charlie Petty	6/28/1866	-	R	1	1893	5	2	.714	3.33	9	6	4	0	0	54.0	66	20	0	28	12	.318	22	7
Jack Phillips	5/24/19	6/16/58	R	1	1945	0	1	.000	10.38	1	0	0	0	0	4.1	5	5	1	5	0	-	5	1
Bill Phyle	6/25/1875	8/6/53	R	1	1901	7	10	.412	4.27	24	19	16	0	1	168.2	208	80	2	54	62	.200	66	12
Mario Picone	7/5/26		R	3	1947, 52, 54	0	1	.000	6.37	9	2	0	0	0	29.2	34	21	4	18	10	.200	5	1

Name	Born	Died	T	Yrs	Seasons	W	L	PCT	ERA	G	GS	CG	ShO	SV	IP	H	ER	HR	BB	SO	AVG	AB	H
Billy Pierce	4/2/27		L	3	1962-64	22	17	.564	3.54	102	37	10	3	13	310.1	293	122	37	65	157	.198	96	19
Skip Pitlock	11/6/47		L	1	1970	5	5	.500	4.66	18	15	1	0	0	87.0	92	45	13	48	56	.080	25	2
Emil Planeta	1/31/09	2/2/63	R	1	1931	0	0	-	10.13	2	0	0	0	0	5.1	7	6	0	4	0	.000	0	0
Ed Plank	4/9/52		R	2	1978-79	0	0	-	5.23	9	0	0	0	0	10.1	15	6	1	4	2	-	0	0
Norman Plitt	2/21/1893	2/1/54	R	1	1927	1	0	1.000	3.68	3	0	0	0	0	7.1	9	3	0	3	0	.000	0	0
Ray Poat	12/19/17	4/29/90	R	3	1947-49	15	13	.536	4.01	48	31	12	3	0	220.0	223	98	29	81	82	.143	77	11
Joe Poetz	6/22/00	2/7/42	R	1	1926	0	1	.000	3.38	2	1	0	0	0	8.0	8	3	2	2	1	.000	1	0
Lou Polli	7/9/01		R	1	1944	0	2	.000	4.54	19	0	0	0	3	35.2	42	18	3	20	6	.000	6	0
Jim Poole	4/28/66		L	3	1996-98	6	5	.545	5.55	124	0	0	0	0	105.1	126	65	13	47	61	.167	6	1
Ned Porter	5/6/05	6/30/68	R	2	1926-27	0	0	-	2.25	3	0	0	0	0	4.0	5	1	1	1	1	-	0	0
Mark Portugal	10/30/62		R	2	1994-95	15	13	.536	4.03	38	38	2	0	0	241.1	241	108	27	79	150	.260	77	20
John Pregenzer	8/2/35		R	2	1963-64	2	0	1.000	4.88	19	0	0	0	1	27.2	29	15	1	19	13	.000	0	0
Joe Price	11/29/56		R	3	1987-89	4	9	.308	3.74	65	4	0	0	5	110.2	94	46	13	44	101	.063	16	1
Bob Priddy	12/10/39		R	2	1965-66	7	3	.700	3.73	46	3	0	0	0	101.1	94	42	9	30	58	.167	18	3
Hub Pruett	9/1/00	1/28/82	L	1	1930	5	4	.556	4.78	45	8	1	1	0	135.2	152	72	11	63	49	.135	37	5
Miguel Puente	5/8/48		R	1	1970	1	3	.250	8.20	6	4	0	0	0	18.2	25	17	5	11	14	.000	7	0
Ewald Pyle	8/27/10		L	2	1944-45	7	10	.412	4.81	37	22	3	0	0	170.1	168	91	12	72	81	.151	53	8

Q

Name	Born	Died	T	Yrs	Seasons	W	L	PCT	ERA	G	GS	CG	ShO	SV	IP	H	ER	HR	BB	SO	AVG	AB	H
Dan Quisenberry	2/7/53	9/30/98	R	1	1990	0	1	.000	13.50	5	0	0	0	0	6.2	13	10	1	3	2	.000	0	0

R

Name	Born	Died	T	Yrs	Seasons	W	L	PCT	ERA	G	GS	CG	ShO	SV	IP	H	ER	HR	BB	SO	AVG	AB	H
Pat Ragan	11/15/1888	9/4/56	R	1	1919	1	0	1.000	1.59	7	1	1	0	0	22.2	19	4	0	14	7	.429	7	3
Pat Rapp	7/13/67		R	1	1992, 97	1	4	.200	6.28	11	8	0	0	0	43.0	45	30	5	27	31	.000	14	0
Bugs Raymond	2/24/1882	9/7/12	R	3	1909-11	28	27	.509	2.91	75	50	28	3	0	451.0	418	146	10	160	235	.158	146	23
Frank Reberger	6/7/44		R	3	1970-72	13	12	.520	4.79	78	36	5	0	2	295.0	312	157	28	154	190	.232	95	22
Steve Reed	3/11/66		R	2	1992, 98	3	1	.750	1.66	68	1	0	0	0	70.1	43	13	6	22	61	.333	3	1
Bill Reidy	10/9/1873	10/14/15	R	1	1896	0	1	.000	7.62	2	2	1	1	0	13.0	24	11	0	2	19	.000	5	0
Mike Remlinger	3/23/66		L	1	1991	2	1	.667	4.37	8	6	0	1	0	35.0	36	17	5	20	19	.000	7	0
Marshall Renfroe	5/25/36	12/10/70	L	1	1959	0	0	-	27.00	1	1	0	0	0	2.0	3	6	1	3	3	.000	1	0
Rick Reuschel	5/16/49		R	5	1987-91	44	30	.595	3.29	96	90	12	3	0	601.0	600	220	38	141	283	.133	181	24
Frank Riccelli	2/24/53		L	1	1976	1	1	.500	5.63	15	3	0	1	0	16.0	16	10	1	5	11	.167	6	1
Danny Richardson*	1/25/1863	9/12/26	R	3	1885-87	7	3	.700	3.24	56	15	8	0	0	100.0	91	36	0	30	38	*	*	*
Steve Ridzik	4/29/29		R	2	1956-57	6	4	.600	4.01	166	5	0	0	0	119.0	99	53	10	84	66	.242	33	8
Dave Righetti	11/28/58		L	3	1991-93	5	15	.250	4.61	5	4	0	0	28	197.1	201	101	19	81	129	.182	11	2
George Riley	10/6/56		L	1	1984	1	0	1.000	3.99	39	4	0	0	0	29.1	39	13	6	7	12	.100	10	1
Jimmy Ring	2/15/1895	7/6/65	R	1	1926	11	10	.524	4.57	42	23	5	0	2	183.1	207	93	12	74	76	.143	56	8
Allen Ripley	10/18/52		R	2	1980-81	13	14	.481	4.12	26	34	3	0	0	203.1	222	93	15	63	112	.143	70	10
Hank Ritter	10/12/1893	9/3/64	R	3	1914-16	4	1	.800	3.91	28	2	0	0	2	71.1	73	31	4	19	42	.105	19	2
Joe Roa	10/11/71		R	1	1997	2	5	.286	5.21	3	3	0	0	0	65.2	86	38	8	20	34	.133	15	2
John Roach	-	3/1/15	L	1	1887	0	2	.000	11.25	1	1	1	0	0	8.0	18	10	0	4	3	.250	4	1
Dave Roberts	9/11/44		L	1	1979	0	2	.000	2.57	26	1	0	0	3	42.0	42	12	3	18	23	.000	5	0
Rich Robertson	10/14/44		R	6	1966-71	13	14	.481	4.94	86	40	8	1	2	302.1	333	166	31	153	184	.093	86	8
Don Robinson	6/8/57		R	5	1987-91	42	33	.560	3.56	170	92	12	3	14	695.1	671	275	64	195	400	.170	247	42
Jeff Robinson	12/13/60		R	4	1984-87	19	26	.422	3.81	169	34	1	1	18	385.0	372	163	32	142	282	.106	94	10
Felix Rodriguez	12/5/72		R	4	1999-2002	23	12	.657	3.00	274	0	0	0	3	297.1	236	99	21	197	299	.273	11	3
Rich Rodriguez	3/1/63		L	3	1997-99	11	3	.786	3.98	201	0	0	0	3	187.2	194	83	22	69	120	.300	10	3
Rick Rodriguez	9/21/60		R	1	1990	0	0	-	8.10	3	0	0	0	0	3.1	5	3	0	2	2	-	0	0
Kevin Rogers	8/20/68		L	3	1992-94	2	4	.333	3.17	79	0	0	0	0	125.0	118	44	8	47	95	.167	12	2
John Roper	11/21/71		R	1	1995	0	0	-	27.00	1	0	0	0	0	1.0	2	3	0	2	0	-	0	0
Don Rose	3/19/47		R	1	1974	0	0	-	9.00	2	0	0	0	0	1.0	4	1	0	1	2	-	0	0
George Ross	6/27/1892	4/22/35	L	1	1918	0	0	-	0.00	1	0	0	0	0	2.1	2	0	0	3	2	.000	1	0

Name	Born	Died	T	Yrs	Seasons	W	L	PCT	ERA	G	GS	CG	ShO	SV	IP	H	ER	HR	BB	SO	Pitchers' Batting AVG	AB	H
Joe Rosselli	5/28/72		L	1	1995	2	1	.667	8.70	9	5	0	0	0	30.0	39	29	5	20	7	.200	10	2
Frank Rosso	3/1/21	1/26/80	R	1	1944	0	0	-	9.00			0	0	0	4.0	11	4	0	3	1	1.000	1	1
Mike Rowland	1/31/53		R	2	1980-81	1	2	.333	2.74	28	1	1	0	0	42.2	33	13	3	14	16	.400	5	2
Dick Rudolph	8/25/1887	10/20/49	R	2	1910-11	0	1	.000	7.71	4	1	1	0	2	14.0	23	12	0	2	9	.000	2	0
Kirk Rueter	12/1/70		L	7	1996-2002	84	56	.600	4.08	201	199	2	0	0	1169.1	1246	530	142	350	557	.175	377	66
Amos Rusie	5/30/1871	12/6/42	R	8	1890-95, 97-98	234	163	.589	2.89	427	403	372	29	5	3531.2	3100	1134	62	1588	1835	.253	1619	409
Rosy Ryan	3/15/1898	12/10/80	R	6	1919-24	49	36	.576	3.50	171	66	28	1	15	672.0	674	261	21	202	239	.179	207	37
S																							
Ray Sadecki	12/26/40		L	4	1966-69	32	39	.451	3.52	128	96	30	12	0	685.1	652	268	60	220	517	.181	232	42
Slim Sallee	2/3/1885	3/23/50	L	5	1916-18, 20-21	42	23	.646	2.26	109	53	38	4	8	572.2	548	144	16	70	147	.225	178	40
Jack Salveson	1/5/14	12/28/74	R	2	1933-34	3	3	.500	3.65	20	6	2	0	0	69.0	73	28	6	27	26	.211	19	4
Manny Salvo	6/30/13	2/7/97	R	1	1939	4	10	.286	4.63	32	18	4	0	0	136.0	150	70	11	75	69	.098	41	4
Roger Samuels	1/5/61		L	1	1988	0	2	.000	3.47	15	0	0	0	0	23.1	17	9	4	7	22	.000	3	0
Scott Sanderson	7/22/56		R	1	1993	4	2	.667	3.51	11	8	0	0	0	48.2	48	19	12	7	36	.000	14	0
Jack Sanford	5/18/29	11/20/96	R	7	1959-65	89	67	.571	3.61	233	211	54	9	4	1405.2	1289	564	117	491	781	.154	467	72
Bill Sayles	7/27/17		R	1	1943	1	3	.250	4.75	18	3	1	0	0	53.0	60	28	1	23	38	.308	13	4
Dan Schatzeder	12/1/54		L	1	1982	1	4	.200	7.29	13	3	0	0	0	33.1	47	27	3	12	18	.125	8	1
Rube Schauer	3/19/1891	4/15/57	R	4	1913-16	3	13	.188	3.59	60	11	6	0	0	185.1	175	74	6	68	102	.111	45	5
Jason Schmidt	1/23/73		R	2	2001-2002	20	9	.690	3.43	40	40	2	2	0	251.2	205	96	17	106	261	.134	82	11
Crazy Schmit	2/13/1866	10/5/40	L	1	1893	0	2	.000	7.40	4	4	2	0	0	20.2	30	17	0	17	5	.444	9	4
Hal Schumacher	11/23/10	4/21/93	R	13	1931-42, 46	158	121	.566	3.36	391	329	138	27	7	2482.1	2424	926	139	902	906	.202	896	181
Ferdie Schupp	1/16/1891	12/16/71	L	7	1913-19	32	14	.696	2.63	121	51	34	10	3	561.1	441	164	12	193	311	.152	164	25
Jack Scott	4/18/1892	11/30/59	R	6	1922-23, 25-26, 28-29	62	46	.574	3.80	189	94	50	5	13	907.1	947	383	60	234	342	.294	320	94
Tim Scott	11/16/66		R	1	1996	2	2	.500	8.24	20	0	0	0	0	19.2	24	18	5	9	10	.000	1	0
Doc Sechrist	2/10/1876	4/2/50	R	1	1899	0	1	.000		1	0	0	0	0	0.0	0	0	0	2		-	0	0
Jose Segura	1/26/63		R	1	1991	0	1	.000	4.41	11	0	0	0	0	16.1	20	8	1	5	10	-	0	0
Scott Service	2/26/67		R	1	1995	3	1	.750	3.19	28	0	0	0	1	31.0	18	11	4	20	30	-	0	0
Frank Seward	4/7/21		R	2	1943-44	3	3	.500	5.15	26	8	3	0	0	87.1	110	50	8	37	18	.071	28	2
Cy Seymour*	12/9/1872	9/20/19	L	5	1896-1900	61	56	.521	3.75	139	123	104	6	1	1026.0	947	427	25	652	582	*	*	*
Jack Sharrott*	8/13/1869	12/31/27	R	3	1890-92	16	15	.516	2.82	36	28	24	5	0	255.1	211	80	5	124	126	*	*	*
Bob Shaw	6/29/33		R	3	1964-66	24	19	.558	3.25	116	40	6	0	13	360.0	363	130	31	91	226	.082	98	8
Red Shea	11/29/1898	11/17/81	R	2	1921-22	5	5	.500	3.76	20	4	1	0	0	55.0	50	23	4	13	15	.063	16	1
Joe Shipley	5/9/35		R	3	1958-60	0	0	-	5.95	26	1	0	0	0	39.1	39	26	4	29	20	.000	3	0
Ernie Shore	3/24/1891	9/24/80	R	1	1912	0	0	-	27.00	8	0	0	0	0	1.0	8	3	0	1	1	-	0	0
Bill Shores	5/26/04	2/19/84	R	1	1933	2	1	.667	3.93	8	3	1	0	0	36.2	41	16	4	14	20	.273	11	3
Seth Sigsby	4/30/1874	9/15/53	-	1	1893	0	0	-	9.00	1	1	0	0	0	3.0	1	3	0	4	2	.000	1	0
Al J. Smith	10/12/07	4/28/77	L	4	1934-37	32	30	.516	3.84	146	54	15	5	12	485.2	503	207	32	152	201	.144	146	21
Al K. Smith	12/13/03	8/11/95	R	1	1926	0	0	-	9.00	1	0	0	0	0	2.0	4	2	0	2	0	-	0	0
George Smith	5/31/1892	1/7/65	R	4	1916-19	5	8	.385	3.46	31	6	2	0	0	96.1	96	37	2	27	29	.091	22	2
Heinie Smith*	10/24/1871	6/25/39	R	2	1901	0	1	.000	8.10	2	2	1	0	0	13.1	24	12	0	5	5	*	*	*
Colonel Snover	5/16/1895	4/30/69	L	1	1919	0	0	-	1.00	2	1	0	0	0	9.0	7	1	0	3	4	.000	2	0
Steve Soderstrom	4/3/72		R	1	1996	2	0	1.000	5.27	3	3	0	0	0	13.2	16	8	5	6	9	.000	5	0
Don Songer	1/31/00	10/3/62	L	1	1927	3	5	.375	2.86	22	1	0	0	0	50.1	48	16	4	31	9	.300	10	3
Lary Sorensen	10/4/55		R	1	1988	0	1	.000	4.86	12	0	0	0	0	16.2	24	9	4	3	9	.000		0
Elias Sosa	6/10/50		R	3	1972-74	19	12	.613	3.30	147	0	0	0	27	223.2	199	82	15	98	128	.000	33	0
Warren Spahn	4/23/21		L	1	1965	3	4	.429	3.39	16	3	0	0	1	71.2	70	27	8	21	34	.061	33	2
Tully Sparks	12/12/1874	7/15/37	R	1	1902	4	10	.286	3.76	15	13	11	3	0	115.0	123	48	2	40	40	.143	21	3
George Spencer	7/7/26		R	6	1950-55	15	9	.625	4.12	110	9	3	0	9	233.2	207	107	39	97	73	.135	37	5
Glenn Spencer	9/11/05	12/30/58	R	1	1933	0	2	.000	5.13	17	3	0	0	0	47.1	52	27	3	26	14	.122	49	6
Jerry Spradlin	6/14/67		R	1	1999	3	1	.750	4.19	59	0	0	0	0	58.0	59	27	4	29	52	.167	12	2
Al Stanek	12/24/43		L	1	1963	0	0	-	4.73	11	0	0	0	0	13.1	10	7	1	12	5	.000	1	0

Name	Born	Died	T	Yrs	Seasons	W	L	PCT	ERA	G	GS	CG	ShO	SV	IP	H	ER	HR	BB	SO	AVG	AB	H
Ray Starr	4/23/06	2/9/63	R	1	1933	0	1	.000	5.40	6	2	0	0	0	13.1	19	8	0	10	2	.000	3	0
Bob Steele	1/5/1894	1/27/62	L	2	1918-19	3	6	.333	2.74	13	7	5	1	1	69.0	59	21	1	13	24	.273	22	6
Jeff Stember	3/2/58		R	1	1980	0	0	-	3.00	1	1	0	0	0	3.0	2	1	1	2	0	.000	1	0
Steve Stone	7/14/47	12/22/74	R	2	1971-72	11	17	.393	3.53	51	35	6	3	0	234.1	207	92	20	104	148	.059	68	4
Allyn Stout	10/31/04	4/11/70	R	1	1935	1	4	.200	4.91	40	2	0	0	5	88.0	99	48	7	37	29	.133	15	2
Sailor Stroud	5/15/1885	6/14/06	R	2	1915-16	15	11	.577	2.77	51	26	8	0	2	230.2	241	71	4	44	78	.143	70	10
Mike Sullivan	10/23/1866		L	3	1891, 96-97	19	22	.463	4.75	51	41	32	1	2	358.0	395	189	9	150	88	.235	153	36
Tom Sunkel	8/9/12	10/8/86	L	3	1941-43	4	8	.333	4.63	22	14	4	1	0	81.2	76	42	6	56	43	.160	25	4
Max Surkont	6/16/22		R	2	1956-57	2	3	.400	5.63	13	4	1	0	2	38.1	33	24	7	11	26	.111	9	1
Bill Swabach	-		-	1	1887	0	2	.000	5.06	2	2	2	0	0	16.0	27	9	1	6	6	.000	7	0
Russ Swan	1/3/64		L	1	1889-90	0	1	.000	9.00	4	3	0	0	0	9.0	17	9	4	6	3	.000	3	0
Bill Swift	10/27/61		R	3	1992-94	39	19	.672	2.70	81	73	4	3	1	506.2	448	152	34	129	296	.215	163	35
Ad Swigler	9/21/1895	2/5/75	R	1	1917	0	1	.000	6.00	1	1	0	0	0	6.0	7	4	0	8	4	.000	2	0

T

Name	Born	Died	T	Yrs	Seasons	W	L	PCT	ERA	G	GS	CG	ShO	SV	IP	H	ER	HR	BB	SO	AVG	AB	H
Stu Tate	6/17/62		R	1	1989	0	0	-	3.38	2	0	0	0	0	2.2	3	1	0	1	4	-	0	0
Julian Tavarez	5/22/73		R	3	1997-99	13	7	.650	4.34	196	0	0	0	1	228.1	252	110	18	95	123	.133	15	2
Dummy Taylor	2/21/1875	8/22/58	R	9	1900-08	115	103	.528	2.77	270	233	156	20	3	1882.1	1840	579	39	543	759	.145	635	92
Jack Taylor	5/23/1873	2/7/00	R	1	1891	0	0	.000	1.13	1	0	0	0	0	8.0	4	1	0	3	3	.000	2	0
Jim Tennant	3/3/07	4/16/67	R	1	1929	0	0	-	0.00	1	0	0	0	0	1.0	1	0	0	0	1	-	0	0
Jeff Tesreau	3/5/1889	9/24/46	R	7	1912-18	115	72	.615	2.43	247	205	123	27	9	1679.0	1350	453	37	572	880	.216	574	124
Henry Thielman*	10/3/1880	9/2/42	R	1	1902	0	0	.000	1.50	2	2	0	0	0	6.0	8	1	0	6	5	*	*	*
Fay Thomas	10/10/04	8/16/90	R	1	1927	0	0	-	3.31	9	0	0	0	0	16.1	19	6	3	4	11	.000	2	0
Junior Thompson	6/7/17		L	2	1946-47	8	8	.500	2.38	54	1	0	0	4	98.1	72	26	8	67	44	.077	13	1
Mark Thurmond	9/12/56		L	1	1990	2	3	.400	3.34	43	0	0	0	4	56.2	53	21	6	18	24	.000	5	0
Mike Tiernan*	1/21/1867	11/9/18	L	1	1887	1	2	.333	8.69	35	0	0	0	1	19.2	33	19	2	7	3	*	*	*
Cannonball Titcomb	8/21/1866	6/8/50	L	3	1887-89	19	13	.594	3.02	35	35	34	4	0	295.0	244	99	8	99	170	.106	123	13
Andy Tomasic	12/10/19		R	1	1949	0	3	.000	18.00	2	0	0	0	0	5.0	9	10	2	5	2	.000	1	0
Tommy Toms	10/15/51		R	3	1975-77	3	3	.000	5.40	18	0	0	0	0	23.1	33	14	2	9	12	-	0	0
Fred Toney	12/11/1888	3/11/53	R	5	1918-22	63	36	.636	2.81	132	110	60	10	6	880.1	843	275	34	195	213	.206	310	64
Salomon Torres	3/11/72		R	3	1993-95	5	14	.263	5.19	28	23	1	0	0	137.0	145	79	19	68	67	.175	40	7
Ken Trinkle	12/15/19	5/10/76	R	4	1943, 46-48	20	28	.417	3.69	174	19	3	0	19	361.0	363	148	20	178	116	.149	74	11
Bob Tufts	11/2/55		L	1	1981	0	0	-	3.52	11	0	0	0	0	15.1	20	6	0	6	12	.000	1	0

U

Name	Born	Died	T	Yrs	Seasons	W	L	PCT	ERA	G	GS	CG	ShO	SV	IP	H	ER	HR	BB	SO	AVG	AB	H
George Uhle	9/18/1898	2/26/85	R	1	1933	1	1	.500	7.90	6	1	0	0	0	13.2	16	12	1	6	4	.000	5	0

V

Name	Born	Died	T	Yrs	Seasons	W	L	PCT	ERA	G	GS	CG	ShO	SV	IP	H	ER	HR	BB	SO	AVG	AB	H
Carlos Valdez	12/26/71		R	1	1995	0	1	.000	6.14	11	0	0	0	0	14.2	19	10	1	8	7	.000	1	0
Sergio Valdez	9/7/64		R	1	1995	4	5	.444	4.75	13	11	1	0	0	66.1	78	35	12	17	29	.095	21	2
Hy Vandenberg	3/17/06	7/31/94	R	4	1937-40	1	3	.250	5.57	22	6	2	0	1	64.2	75	40	4	40	29	.056	18	1
George Van Haltren*	3/30/1866	9/29/45	L	4	1895-96, 1900-01	1	0	1.000	4.50	5	0	0	0	0	22.0	31	11	1	12	6	*	*	*
William VanLandingham	7/16/70		R	4	1994-97	27	26	.509	4.54	84	81	1	0	0	477.1	470	241	46	220	300	.122	164	20
Ike Van Zandt	2/1876	9/14/08	-	1	1901	0	0	-	7.11	2	0	0	0	0	12.2	16	10	0	8	2	.167	6	1
Ryan Vogelsong	7/22/77		R	2	2000-01	0	3	.000	4.67	17	0	0	0	0	34.2	33	18	5	16	23	.125	8	1
Bill Voiselle	1/29/19		R	6	1942-47	46	52	.469	3.64	137	111	53	7	0	805.2	764	326	66	340	409	.166	265	44
Ed Vosberg	9/28/61		L	1	1990	1	1	.500	5.55	18	0	0	0	0	24.1	21	15	3	12	12	-	0	0

Pitchers' Batting columns: AVG, AB, H

W

	Born	Died	T	Yrs	Seasons	W	L	PCT	ERA	G	GS	CG	ShO	SV	IP	H	ER	HR	BB	SO	Pitchers' Batting AVG	AB	H
Rube Walberg	7/27/1896	10/27/78	L	1	1923	0	0	–	1.80	2	0	0	0	0	5.0	4	1	0	1	0	.000	4	0
Bill Walker	10/7/03	6/14/66	L	6	1927–32	58	49	.542	3.45	161	115	55	9	6	905.2	920	347	68	300	408	.124	298	37
Red Waller	6/16/1883	2/9/15	–	1	1909	0	0	–	0.00	6	0	0	0	0	1.0	3	0	0	0	1	–	–	0
Colin Ward	11/22/60		L	1	1985	0	0	–	4.38	6	2	0	0	0	12.1	10	6	0	7	8	.000	2	0
John Montgomery Ward*	3/3/1860	3/4/25	R	2	1883–84	19	16	.543	2.83	43	30	29	1	0	337.2	350	106	5	49	144	*	*	*
Allen Watson	11/18/70		L	1	1996	8	12	.400	4.61	29	29	2	0	0	185.2	189	95	28	69	128	.231	65	15
Mule Watson	10/15/1896	8/25/49	R	2	1923–24	15	9	.625	3.59	39	31	14	1	0	208.0	239	83	18	45	44	.210	81	17
Red Webb	9/25/24	2/7/96	R	2	1948–49	3	2	.600	3.72	25	3	2	0	0	72.2	68	30	5	31	18	.316	19	6
Ben Weber	11/17/69		R	1	2001	0	1	.000	14.63	9	0	0	0	0	8	16	13	0	4	6	.000	0	0
Jake Weimer	11/29/1873	6/19/28	L	1	1909	0	0	–	9.00	1	0	0	0	0	3.0	7	3	0	0	1	.000	1	0
Mickey Welch	7/4/1859	7/30/41	R	10	1883–92	238	146	.620	2.69	426	412	391	28	4	3579.0	3308	1068	85	1077	1570	.214	1651	353
Huyler Westervelt	10/1/1870	–		1	1894	7	10	.412	5.04	23	18	11	0	0	141.0	170	79	4	76	35	.143	56	8
Art Whitney*	1/16/1858	8/15/43	R	1	1889	0	0	.000	3.00	1	0	0	0	0	6.0	7	2	0	3	*	*	*	*
Ed Whitson	5/19/55		R	3	1979–81	22	30	.423	3.56	74	73	10	3	0	435.0	450	172	22	142	217	.107	131	14
Stump Wiedman	2/17/1861	3/2/05	R	2	1887–88	1	2	.333	2.77	3	3	3	0	0	26.0	27	8	2	10	9	.100	10	1
Hoyt Wilhelm	7/26/23		R	5	1952–56	42	25	.627	2.98	319	0	0	0	41	608.0	532	201	47	269	385	.142	120	17
Charlie Williams	10/11/47		R	7	1972–78	18	16	.529	3.82	237	24	1	0	4	483.0	489	205	31	234	204	.149	74	11
Frank Williams	2/13/58		R	3	1984–86	14	9	.609	3.22	146	1	1	1	4	231.2	188	83	7	107	178	.217	23	5
Jim Willoughby	1/31/49		R	4	1971–74	11	14	.440	3.95	70	28	8	1	4	255.1	269	112	36	61	115	.152	66	10
Trevor Wilson	6/7/66		L	7	1988–93, 95	41	46	.471	3.87	154	115	7	4	0	720.1	657	310	61	300	425	.176	193	34
Hooks Wiltse	9/7/1880	1/21/59	L	11	1904–14	136	85	.615	2.48	339	223	153	27	29	2053.0	1843	565	53	491	948	.215	721	155
Jesse Winters	12/22/1893	6/5/86	R	2	1919–20	1	2	.333	4.24	37	2	0	0	3	74.1	76	35	2	41	20	.000	17	2
Jack Wisner	11/5/1899	12/15/81	R	2	1925–26	2	2	.500	3.69	30	3	2	0	0	68.1	54	28	8	24	18	.118	17	2
Jay Witasick	8/28/72		R	1	2002	1	0	1.000	2.37	44	0	0	0	0	68.2	58	18	3	21	54	.000	5	0
Johnnie Wittig	6/16/14	2/24/99	R	4	1938–39, 41, 43	10	25	.286	4.86	83	39	7	1	4	305.1	342	165	23	161	121	.110	91	10
Tim Worrell	7/5/67		R	2	2001–02	10	7	.588	2.87	153	0	0	0	7	150.1	126	48	7	63	118	.000	5	0
Al Worthington	2/5/29		R	6	1953–54, 56–59	32	45	.416	3.83	209	69	11	3	12	668.0	642	284	70	293	366	.148	183	27
Roy Wright	9/26/33		R	1	1956	0	1	.000	16.88	1	1	0	0	0	2.2	8	5	1	2	0	.000	1	0

Z

	Born	Died	T	Yrs	Seasons	W	L	PCT	ERA	G	GS	CG	ShO	SV	IP	H	ER	HR	BB	SO	Pitchers' Batting AVG	AB	H
Adrian Zabala	8/26/16		L	2	1945, 49	4	7	.364	5.02	26	9	3	1	1	84.1	90	47	7	30	27	.154	26	4
Dom Zanni	3/1/32		R	3	1958–59, 61	2	0	1.000	4.71	18	0	0	0	0	28.2	32	15	4	21	25	.000	2	0
Chad Zerbe	4/27/72		L	3	2000–02	5	0	1.000	3.46	81	1	0	0	0	101.1	99	39	7	32	53	.200	15	3
Walter Zink	11/21/1899	6/12/64	R	1	1921	0	0	–	2.25	2	0	0	0	0	4.0	4	1	0	3	1	.000	1	0

* denotes position player.

A P P E N D I X   C
RECORDS AND HONORS

· ·

NEW YORK/SAN FRANCISCO GIANTS TEAM GAME RECORDS

Batting

At-Bats — 81 at New York, May 31, 1964 (2)

Runs — 29 vs. Philadelphia, June 15, 1887

      Since 1900 — 26 vs. Brooklyn, April 30, 1944 (1)

Runs (Inning) — 13 five times, last at San Diego, July 15, 1997 (7th)

Hits — 31 at Cincinnati, June 9, 1901

Home Runs — 8 at Milwaukee, April 30, 1961 (Willie Mays 4, Jose Pagan 2, Orlando Cepeda 1, Felipe Alou 1)

RBI — 26 vs. Brooklyn, April 30, 1944 (1)

Total Bases — 50 at Los Angeles, May 13, 1958

Stolen Bases — 17 vs. Pittsburgh, May 23, 1890

      Since 1900 — 11 at Boston, June 20, 1912

Most Players Five Or More Hits — 3 at Cincinnati, June 9, 1901 (Kip Selbach - 6, Charlie Hickman - 5, George Van Haltren - 5); at Philadephia, June 1, 1923 (Heinie Groh - 5, Jimmy O'Connell - 5, Ross Youngs - 5)

Scoring In Every Inning — at Philadelphia, June 1, 1923

General

Longest Game (Time, Innings) — 7:23, 23 innings at New York, May 31, 1964 (2)

Longest Game (Time, Nine Innings) — 4:27 vs. Los Angeles, Oct. 5, 2001

NEW YORK/SAN FRANCISCO GIANTS TEAM SEASON RECORDS

Batting
Highest Batting Average — .319 in 1930
Lowest Batting Average — .233 in 1985
At-Bats — 5,650 in 1984
Runs — 959 in 1930
Hits — 1,769 in 1930
Doubles — 307 in 1999
Triples — 103 in 1911
Home Runs — 235 in 2001
RBI — 889 in 2000
Total Bases — 2,628 in 1930
Grand Slams — 7 in 1951, 1954, 1970, 1998, 2000
Pinch Hit Home Runs — 14 in 2001
Pinch Hit Grand Slams — 3 in 1973, 1978
Walks — 729 in 1970
Strikeouts — 1,189 in 1996
Stolen Bases — 415 in 1887
      Since 1900 — 347 in 1911
Caught Stealing — 137 in 1915
Hit By Pitch — 91 in 1903
Sacrifice Hits — 166 in 1904
Sacrifice Flies — 66 in 2000
On-Base Percentage — .369 in 1930
Slugging Percentage — .473 in 1930
Most .300 Batters — 8 in 1921, 1922, 1924, 1930,
      1931

Pitching
Lowest ERA — 1.72 in 1885
      Since 1900 — 2.14 in 1908

Highest ERA — 4.86 in 1995
Complete Games — 141 in 1898
      Since 1900 — 127 in 1904
Shutouts — 30 in 1896
      Since 1900 — 25 in 1908
Strikeouts — 1,089 in 1998
Saves — 50 in 1993

Fielding
Fielding Percentage — .985 in 2000, 2002
Fewest Errors — 90 in 2002
Most Errors — 565 in 1892
      Since 1900 — 439 in 1900
Most Double Plays — 183 in 1987

General
Games — 165 in 1962
Games Won — 106 in 1904
Games Lost — 100 in 1985
Longest Winning Streak — 26 in 1916
Longest Losing Streak — 13 in 1902, 1944
Most Shutout Games Won — 25 in 1908
Most One-Run Games Won — 42 in 1978
Most Games Won In A Month — 29 in September
      1916
Most Games Lost In A Month — 25 in August 1953
Most Players Used — 51 in 1990
Most Pitchers Used — 26 in 1990

NEW YORK/SAN FRANCISCO GIANTS INDIVIDUAL GAME RECORDS

Batting
At-Bats — 10 Jesus Alou at New York, May 31, 1964 (2); Tom Haller at New York, May 31, 1964 (2); Willie Mays at New York, May 31, 1964 (2)
Runs— 6 Mike Tiernan vs. Philadelphia, June 15, 1887; Mel Ott at Philadelphia, Aug. 4, 1934 (2); Mel Ott vs. Brooklyn, April 30, 1944 (1)
Hits — 6 Danny Richardson vs. Philadelphia, June 11, 1887; Jack Glasscock vs. Cincinnati, Sept. 27, 1890; George Davis at Philadelphia, Aug. 15, 1895; Kip Selbach at Cincinnati, June 9, 1901; Dave Bancroft at Philadelphia, June 28, 1920; Frankie Frisch vs. Boston, Sept. 10, 1924 (1); Jesus Alou at Chicago, July 10, 1964; Mike Benjamin at Chicago, June 14, 1995 (13 innings)
Doubles — 3 many times, last Ramon Martinez at Florida, Aug. 16, 2002
Triples — 4 Bill Joyce at Pittsburgh, May 18, 1897
Home Runs — 4 Willie Mays at Milwaukee, April 30, 1961
RBI — 11 Phil Weintraub vs. Brooklyn, April 30, 1944 (1)
Stolen Bases — 5 Dan McGann vs. Brooklyn, May 27, 1904; Josh Devore at Boston, June 20, 1912

Pitching
Innings Pitched — 21 Rube Marquard at Pittsburgh, July 17, 1914
Walks — 16 Bill George vs. Chicago, May 30, 1887 (1)
     Since 1900 — 14 Henry Mathewson vs. Boston, Oct. 5, 1906
Strikeouts — 16 Christy Mathewson at St. Louis, Oct. 3, 1904

NEW YORK/SAN FRANCISCO GIANTS INDIVIDUAL SEASON RECORDS

Batting
Games — 164 Jose Pagan, 1962
Batting Average — .401 Bill Terry, 1930
At-Bats — 681 Joe Moore, 1935
Runs — 146 Mike Tiernan, 1893
     Since 1900 — 139 Bill Terry, 1930
Hits — 254 Bill Terry, 1930
Doubles — 49 Jeff Kent, 2001
Triples — 26 George Davis, 1893
     Since 1900 — 25 Larry Joyce, 1911
Home Runs — 73 Barry Bonds, 2001
RBI — 151 Mel Ott, 1929
Walks — 198 Barry Bonds, 2002
Strikeouts — 189 Bobby Bonds, 1970
Stolen Bases — 111 John Montgomery Ward, 1883
     Since 1900 — 62 George Burns, 1914
On Base Percentage— .582 Barry Bonds, 2002
Slugging Percentage— .863 Barry Bonds, 2001
Pinch Hits — 22 Sam Leslie, 1932
Pinch Hit Home Runs — 4 Ernie Lombardi, 1946; Bill Taylor, 1955; Mike Ivie, 1978; Candy Maldonado, 1986; Ernest Riles, 1990

Hit By Pitch — 26 Ron Hunt, 1970
Sacrifice Hits — 36 Art Devlin, 1907
Sacrifice Flies — 14 J.T. Snow, 2000
Grand Slams — 3 George Kelly, 1921; Sid Gordon, 1948; Wes Westrum, 1951; Willie McCovey, 1967, Jeff Kent, 1997
Game-Winning RBI — 21 Jack Clark, 1982
Hitting Streak — 33 George Davis, 1893
     Since 1900 — 26 Jack Clark, 1978

Pitching
Games — 89 Julian Tavarez, 1997
Games Started — 65 Mickey Welch, 1884
     Since 1990 — 48 Joe McGinnity, 1903
Complete Games — 62 Mickey Welch, 1884
     Since 1900 — 44 Joe McGinnity, 1903
Shutouts — 11 Christy Mathewson, 1908
Innings Pitched — 557.1 Mickey Welch, 1884
     Since 1900 — 434.0 Joe McGinnity, 1903
Walks — 289 Amos Rusie, 1890
     Since 1900 — 128 Jeff Tesreau, 1914

Strikeouts — 345 Mickey Welch, 1884
    Since 1900 — 267 Christy Mathewson, 1903
Wins — 44 Mickey Welch, 1885
    Since 1900 — 37 Christy Mathewson, 1908
Losses — 34 Amos Rusie, 1890
    Since 1900 — 27 Dummy Taylor, 1901
Saves — 48 Rod Beck, 1993
ERA — 1.14 Christy Mathewson, 1909

Consecutive Wins — 19 Tim Keefe, 1888; Rube
    Marquard, 1912
Consecutive Shutouts — 4 Sal Maglie, 1950; Gaylord
    Perry, 1970
Consecutive Scoreless Innings — 46.1 Carl Hubbell,
    1933
Consecutive Walkless Innings — 68.0 Christy
    Mathewson, 1913
Consecutive Hitless Batters— 41 Jim Barr, 1972

NEW YORK/SAN FRANCISCO GIANTS INDIVIDUAL CAREER RECORDS

Batting

Games — 2,857 Willie Mays, 1951-52, 1954-72
Batting Average — .341 Bill Terry, 1923-36
At-Bats — 10,477 Willie Mays, 1951-52, 1954-72
Runs — 2,011 Willie Mays, 1951-52, 1954-72
Hits — 3,187 Willie Mays, 1951-52, 1954-72
Doubles — 504 Willie Mays, 1951-52, 1954-72
Triples — 162 Mike Tiernan, 1887-99
Home Runs — 646 Willie Mays, 1951-52, 1954-72
RBI — 1,860 Mel Ott, 1926-47
Walks — 1,708 Mel Ott, 1926-47
Strikeouts — 1,436 Willie Mays, 1951-52, 1954-72
Stolen Bases — 428 Mike Tiernan, 1887-99
Pinch Hits — 58 Joel Youngblood, 1983-88
Pinch Hit Home Runs — 13 Willie McCovey, 1959-73,
    1977-80
Grand Slams — 16 Willie McCovey, 1959-73, 1977-80

Pitching

Games — 647 Gary Lavelle, 1974-84
Games Started — 550 Christy Mathewson, 1900-16
Complete Games — 433 Christy Mathewson, 1900-16
Shutouts — 79 Christy Mathewson, 1900-16
Innings Pitched — 4,771.2 Christy Mathewson, 1900-
    16
Walks — 1,588 Amos Rusie, 1890-95, 1897-98
Strikeouts — 2,499 Christy Mathewson, 1900-16
Wins — 372 Christy Mathewson, 1900-16
Saves — 206, Rob Nen, 1998-2002
ERA — 2.12 Christy Mathewson, 1900-16
Consecutive Wins — 24 Carl Hubbell, 1936 (16) and
    1937 (8)

NEW YORK/SAN FRANCISCO GIANTS SEASON BATTING LEADERS

Games

Jose Pagan	164	1962
Orlando Cepeda	162	1962
Willie Mays	162	1962
Will Clark	162	1988
Chuck Hiller	161	1962
J.T. Snow	161	1999
Willie McCovey	160	1965
Jim Ray Hart	160	1965
Bobby Bonds	160	1973
Tito Fuentes	160	1973
Darrell Evans	160	1979
Brett Butler	160	1990
Hal Lanier	159	1965
Will Clark	159	1989
Matt Williams	159	1990
Barry Bonds	159	1993
Barry Bonds	159	1997
Jeff Kent	159	2000
Jeff Kent	159	2001

At Bats

Joe Moore	681	1935
Bobby Bonds	663	1970
Hughie Critz	659	1932
Tito Fuentes	656	1973
George Van Haltren	654	1898
Dave Bancroft	651	1922
Joe Moore	649	1936
Alvin Dark	647	1953
Fred Lindstrom	646	1951
Alvin Dark	646	1951
Alvin Dark	644	1954
Bill Terry	643	1932
Bobby Bonds	643	1973

Runs

Mike Tiernan	147	1889
Bill Terry	139	1930
Mel Ott	138	1929
Johnny Mize	137	1947
George Van Haltren	136	1896
Bobby Bonds	134	1970
Rogers Hornsby	133	1927
George Gore	132	1889
Mike Tiernan	132	1890
Mike Tiernan	132	1896
Bobby Bonds	131	1973
Willie Mays	130	1962

Hits

Bill Terry	254	1930
Fred Lindstrom	231	1928
Fred Lindstrom	231	1930
Bill Terry	226	1929
Bill Terry	225	1932
Frankie Frisch	223	1923
Mike Donlin	216	1905
Bill Terry	213	1931
Bill Terry	213	1934
Don Mueller	212	1954
Frankie Frisch	211	1921
Dave Bancroft	209	1922

Doubles

Jeff Kent	49	2001
Jack Clark	46	1978
Barry Bonds	44	1998
Bill Terry	43	1931
Willie Mays	43	1959
George Kelly	42	1921
Bill Terry	42	1932
Jeff Kent	42	2002
Dave Bancroft	41	1922
Alvin Dark	41	1951
Alvin Dark	41	1953
Jeff Kent	41	2000
Larry Doyle	40	1915
Will Clark	40	1992
Jeff Kent	40	1999

Triples

George Davis	27	1893
Larry Doyle	25	1911
Roger Connor	22	1887
Mike Tiernan	21	1890
Mike Tiernan	21	1895
George Van Haltren	21	1896
Buck Ewing	20	1884
Roger Connor	20	1886
Red Murray	20	1912
Bill Terry	20	1931
Willie Mays	20	1957
George Davis	19	1894
George Van Haltren	19	1895

Home Runs

Barry Bonds	73	2001
Willie Mays	52	1965
Johnny Mize	51	1947
Willie Mays	51	1955
Willie Mays	49	1962
Barry Bonds	49	2002
Willie Mays	47	1964
Kevin Mitchell	47	1989
Orlando Cepeda	46	1961
Barry Bonds	46	1993
Barry Bonds	46	2000
Willie McCovey	45	1969
Willie McCovey	44	1963
Matt Williams	43	1994
Mel Ott	42	1929
Barry Bonds	42	1996

RBI

Mel Ott	151	1929
Orlando Cepeda	142	1961
Willie Mays	141	1962
Johnny Mize	138	1947
Barry Bonds	137	2001
George Davis	136	1897
George Kelly	136	1924
Mel Ott	135	1934
Mel Ott	135	1936
Irish Meusel	132	1922
Roger Connor	130	1889
Bill Terry	129	1930
Barry Bonds	129	1996

Extra-Base Hits

Barry Bonds	107	2001
Willie Mays	90	1962
Barry Bonds	88	1993
Barry Bonds	88	1998
Willie Mays	87	1954
Willie Mays	83	1957
Willie Mays	82	1955
Willie Mays	82	1959
Mel Ott	81	1929
Bill Terry	81	1932
Barry Bonds	81	2000
Jeff Kent	81	2000
Jeff Kent	81	2002
Johnny Mize	79	1947
Jack Clark	79	1978
Orlando Cepeda	78	1961

Total Bases

Barry Bonds	411	2001
Bill Terry	392	1930
Willie Mays	382	1955
Willie Mays	382	1962
Willie Mays	377	1954
Bill Terry	373	1932
Willie Mays	366	1957
Barry Bonds	365	1993
Rich Aurilia	364	2001
Johnny Mize	360	1947
Willie Mays	360	1965
Orlando Cepeda	357	1962
Orlando Cepeda	356	1961
Jeff Kent	352	2002
Willie Mays	351	1964

Walks

Barry Bonds	198	2002
Barry Bonds	177	2001
Barry Bonds	151	1996
Barry Bonds	145	1997
Eddie Stanky	144	1950
Willie McCovey	137	1970
Barry Bonds	130	1998
Eddie Stanky	127	1951
Barry Bonds	126	1993
Willie McCovey	121	1969
Barry Bonds	120	1995
Mel Ott	118	1938
Barry Bonds	117	2000
Mel Ott	113	1929
Willie Mays	112	1971

Strikeouts

Bobby Bonds	189	1970
Bobby Bonds	187	1969
Bobby Bonds	148	1973
Dave Kingman	140	1972
Matt Willaims	138	1990
Bobby Bonds	137	1971
Bobby Bonds	137	1972
Bobby Bonds	134	1974
Robby Thompson	133	1989
Jeff Kent	133	1997
Will Clark	129	1988
J.T. Snow	129	2000
Matt Williams	128	1991

Stolen Bases

John Montgomery Ward	111	1887
George Davis	65	1897

John Montgomery Ward	62	1889
George Burns	62	1914
Josh Devore	61	1911
Art Devlin	59	1905
Bill North	58	1979
Red Murray	57	1910
Mike Tiernan	56	1890
Jack Glasscock	54	1890
Eddie Burke	54	1893
Art Devlin	54	1906

Batting Average

Bill Terry	.401	1930
Fred Lindstrom	.379	1930
Bill Terry	.372	1929
Roger Connor	.371	1885
Barry Bonds	.370	2002
Mike Tiernan	.369	1896
Jack Doyle	.367	1894
Rogers Hornsby	.361	1927
Fred Lindstrom	.358	1928
Roger Connor	.357	1883
Mike Donlin	.356	1905
Ross Youngs	.356	1924
Roger Connor	.355	1886
George Davis	.355	1893

On-Base Percentage

Barry Bonds	.582	2002
Barry Bonds	.515	2000

Barry Bonds	.461	1996
Eddie Stanky	.460	1950
Mel Ott	.458	1930
Barry Bonds	.458	1993
Willie McCovey	.453	1969
Mike Tiernan	.452	1896
Bill Terry	.452	1930
Mel Ott	.449	1929
Mel Ott	.449	1939
Rogers Hornsby	.448	1927
Mel Ott	.448	1936
Mike Tiernan	.447	1889

Slugging Percentage

Barry Bonds	.863	2001
Barry Bonds	.799	2002
Barry Bonds	.688	2000
Barry Bonds	.677	1993
Willie Mays	.667	1954
Willie Mays	.659	1955
Willie McCovey	.656	1969
Barry Bonds	.647	1994
Willie Mays	.645	1965
Mel Ott	.635	1929
Kevin Mitchell	.635	1989
Willie Mays	.626	1957
Bill Terry	.619	1930
Barry Bonds	.617	1999
Willie Mays	.615	1962
Barry Bonds	.615	1996

NEW YORK/SAN FRANCISCO GIANTS SEASON PITCHING LEADERS

Games

Julian Tavarez	89	1997
Mike Jackson	81	1993
Felix Rodriguez	80	2001
Tim Worrell	80	2002
Robb Nen	79	2001
Greg Minton	78	1982
Mark Dewey	78	1996
Robb Nen	78	1998
Gary Lavelle	77	1984
Mark Davis	77	1985
Rod Beck	76	1993
Felix Rodriguez	76	2000
Doug Henry	75	1997
Greg Minton	74	1984
Scott Garrelts	74	1985
Gary Lavelle	73	1977
Greg Minton	73	1983
Rod Beck	73	1997
Tim Worrell	73	2001

Games Started

Mickey Welch	65	1884
Tim Keefe	64	1886
Amos Rusie	62	1890
Amos Rusie	62	1892
Mickey Welch	59	1886
Amos Rusie	57	1891
Tim Keefe	56	1887
Mickey Welch	55	1885
Mickey Welch	52	1883
Amos Rusie	52	1893
Tim Keefe	51	1888
Amos Rusie	50	1894

Complete Games

Mickey Welch	62	1884
Tim Keefe	62	1886
Amos Rusie	58	1892
Mickey Welch	56	1886
Amos Rusie	56	1890
Mickey Welch	55	1885
Tim Keefe	54	1887
Amos Rusie	52	1891
Amos Rusie	50	1893
Tim Keefe	48	1888

Mickey Welch	47	1888
Mickey Welch	46	1883
Silver King	46	1892

Shutouts

Christy Mathewson	11	1908
Carl Hubbell	10	1933
Juan Marichal	10	1965
Joe McGinnity	9	1904
Tim Keefe	8	1888
Christy Mathewson	8	1902
Christy Mathewson	8	1905
Christy Mathewson	8	1907
Christy Mathewson	8	1909
Jeff Tesreau	8	1914
Jeff Tesreau	8	1915
Juan Marichal	8	1969

Innings Pitched

Mickey Welch	557.1	1884
Amos Rusie	548.2	1890
Tim Keefe	540.0	1886
Amos Rusie	532.0	1892
Amos Rusie	500.1	1891
Mickey Welch	500.0	1886
Mickey Welch	492.0	1895
Amos Rusie	482.0	1893
Tim Keefe	478.2	1887
Amos Rusie	444.0	1894
Tim Keefe	434.1	1888
Joe McGinnity	434.0	1903

Walks

Amos Rusie	289	1890
Amos Rusie	267	1892
Amos Rusie	262	1891
Amos Rusie	218	1893
Cy Seymour	213	1898
Amos Rusie	200	1894
Ed Crane	189	1892
Silver King	174	1892
Jouett Meekin	171	1894
Cy Seymour	170	1899
Cy Seymour	164	1897
Mickey Welch	163	1886

Strikeouts

Mickey Welch	345	1884
Amos Rusie	341	1890
Amos Rusie	337	1891
Tim Keefe	333	1888
Tim Keefe	291	1886
Amos Rusie	288	1892
Mickey Welch	272	1886
Christy Mathewson	267	1903
Christy Mathewson	259	1908
Mickey Welch	258	1885
Juan Marichal	248	1963
Juan Marichal	240	1965

Wins

Mickey Welch	44	1885
Tim Keefe	42	1886
Mickey Welch	39	1884
Christy Mathewson	37	1908
Amos Rusie	36	1894
Tim Keefe	35	1887
Tim Keefe	35	1888
Joe McGinnity	35	1904
Mickey Welch	33	1886
Amos Rusie	33	1891
Amos Rusie	33	1893
Jouett Meekin	33	1894
Christy Mathewson	33	1904

Losses

Amos Rusie	34	1890
Amos Rusie	31	1892
Bill Carrick	27	1899
Dummy Taylor	27	1901
Ed Crane	24	1892
Silver King	24	1892
Dad Clarke	24	1896
Mickey Welch	23	1883
Amos Rusie	23	1895
Mickey Welch	22	1886
Bill Carrick	22	1900
Rube Marquard	22	1914

Winning Percentage (15 decisions)

Hoyt Wilhelm	.833	1952
Sal Maglie	.818	1950
Joe McGinnity	.814	1904
Hooks Wiltse	.813	1904
Carl Hubbell	.813	1936
Doc Crandell	.810	1910
Larry Jansen	.808	1947

Christy Mathewson	.806	1909
Juan Marichal	.806	1966
Mickey Welch	.800	1885
Sal Maglie	.793	1951
Shawn Estes	.792	1997

Saves

Rod Beck	48	1993
Robb Nen	45	2001
Robb Nen	43	2002
Robb Nen	41	2000
Robb Nen	40	1998
Rod Beck	37	1997
Robb Nen	37	1999
Rod Beck	35	1996
Rod Beck	33	1995
Greg Minton	30	1982
Rod Beck	28	1994
Dave Righetti	24	1991
Greg Minton	22	1983
Frank Linzy	21	1965
Greg Minton	21	1981

ERA (1 inning pitched per team game)

Christy Mathewson	1.14	1909
Christy Mathewson	1.28	1905
Christy Mathewson	1.43	1908
Fred Anderson	1.44	1917
Tim Keefe	1.58	1885
Joe McGinnity	1.61	1904
Carl Hubbell	1.66	1933
Mickey Welch	1.66	1885
Tim Keefe	1.74	1888
Fred Toney	1.84	1919
Pol Perritt	1.88	1917
Christy Mathewson	1.89	1910

Opponent Batting Average
(1 inning pitched per team game)

Tim Keefe	.195	1888
Christy Mathewson	.200	1909
Bobby Bolin	.200	1968
Christy Mathewson	.200	1908
Cannonball Titcomb	.201	1888
Tim Keefe	.201	1885
Juan Marichal	.202	1966
Amos Rusie	.203	1892
Mickey Welch	.203	1885
Jeff Tesreau	.204	1912
Juan Marichal	.205	1965
Christy Mathewson	.205	1905

NEW YORK/SAN FRANCISCO GIANTS SEASON FIELDING LEADERS

Putouts

Pitcher
Juan Marichal	33	1968
Christy Mathewson	32	1904
Joe McGinnity	31	1903
Rube Marquard	31	1911
Gaylord Perry	31	1968

Catcher
Tom Haller	864	1965
Benito Santiago	830	2001
Dick Dietz	820	1870
Tom Haller	797	1966
Tom Haller	797	1967
Tom Haller	739	1964
Kirt Marwaring	739	1993

First Base
George Kelly	1,759	1920
George Kelly	1,642	1922
Walter Holke	1,635	1917
Fred Tenney	1,624	1908
Bill Terry	1,621	1927

Second Base
Burgess Whitehead	442	1936
Eddie Stanky	407	1950
Kid Gleason	403	1899
Mickey Witek	401	1943
Burgess Whitehead	394	1937

Shortstop
Dave Bancroft	405	1922
Dave Bancroft	396	1921
Travis Jackson	354	1928
George Davis	349	1898
Dick Bartell	339	1935

Third Base
Art Devlin	203	1908
Art Devlin	191	1909
Billy Lauder	189	1902
Charlie Hickman	183	1900
George Davis	181	1893

Outfield
Bobby Thomson	488	1949
Willie Mays	448	1954
Willie Mays	429	1958
Willie Mays	429	1962
Willie Mays	422	1957
Brett Butler	420	1990
Willie Mays	415	1956
Willie Mays	407	1955
Brett Butler	407	1989
Chili Davis	404	1982

Assists

Pitcher
Christy Mathewson	141	1908
Amos Rusie	138	1892
Amos Rusie	129	1890
Joe McGinnity	127	1904
Christy Mathewson	116	1904
Christy Mathewson	116	1905

Catcher
Chief Meyers	154	1910
Chief Meyers	150	1914
Buck Ewing	149	1889
Bill Rariden	144	1916
Buck Ewing	143	1888
Frank Bowerman	143	1902
Chief Meyers	143	1913

First Base
Bill Terry	137	1932
Willie McCovey	134	1970
Bill Terry	128	1930
J.T. Snow	122	1999
Will Clark	119	1990

Second Base
Rogers Hornsby	582	1927
Burgess Whitehead	552	1936
Hughie Critz	541	1933
Frankie Frisch	537	1924
Burgess Whitehead	514	1937

Shortstop

Dave Bancroft	579	1922
Art Fletcher	565	1917
Dick Bartell	559	1936
Travis Jackson	552	1929
Travis Jackson	547	1928

Third Base

Darrell Evans	369	1979
Art Devlin	355	1906
Heinie Zimmerman	349	1917
Darrell Evans	348	1978
Fred Lindstrom	340	1928

Outfield

George Van Haltren	31	1897
George Van Haltren	31	1899
Fred Snodgrass	31	1911
Red Murray	30	1909
George Van Haltren	29	1894
Cy Seymour	29	1908
Josh Devore	29	1911
George Van Haltren	28	1900
Ross Youngs	28	1922
George Van Haltren	26	1895

Fielding Percentage

Pitcher

Hal Schumacher	1.000	1935
Russ Ortiz	1.000	1999
Livan Hernandez	1.000	2000
Russ Ortiz	1.000	2000
Kirk Rueter	1.000	2000
Livan Hernandez	1.000	2001
Kirk Rueter	1.000	2001
Kirk Rueter	1.000	2002
Ryan Jensen	1.000	2002
Jason Schmidt	1.000	2002
Christy Mathewson	.992	1901
Dummy Taylor	.991	1904
Christy Mathewson	.991	1906

Catcher

Wes Westrum	.999	1950
Kirt Manwaring	.998	1993
Tom Haller	.997	1967
Shanty Hogan	.996	1931
Bob Brenly	.995	1986
Brent Mayne	.995	1999
Benito Santiago	.995	2002

First Base

J.T. Snow	.999	1998
Will Clark	.997	1991
Bill Terry	.996	1935
Johnny Mize	.996	1947
J.T. Snow	.996	1999

Second Base

Tito Fuentes	.993	1973
Hal Lanier	.991	1966
Joe Morgan	.991	1981
Robby Thompson	.989	1989
Robby Thompson	.989	1990

Shortstop

Buddy Kerr	.982	1946
Chris Speier	.982	1975
Rich Aurilia	.980	2002
Hal Lanier	.979	1968
Rich Aurilia	.979	1998
Bill Jurges	.978	1942

Third Base

Heinie Groh	.983	1924
Jim Davenport	.978	1959
Heinie Groh	.975	1923
Bill Mueller	.974	2000
David Bell	.973	2002
Chris Brown	.971	1985
Matt Williams	.970	1993

Outfield

Darren Lewis	1.000	1993
Marvin Benard	.997	2000
Monte Irvin	.996	1951
Bobby Bonds	.994	1971
Joe Medwick	.993	1944
Von Joshua	.993	1975
Darren Lewis	.993	1994
Wally Roettger	.992	1930
Willie Mays	.991	1962
George Burns	.990	1919
Felipe Alou	.990	1961

NEW YORK/SAN FRANCISCO GIANTS CAREER BATTING LEADERS

Games

Willie Mays	2,857	1951-52, 1954-72
Mel Ott	2,730	1926-47
Willie McCovey	2,256	1959-73, 1977-80
Bill Terry	1,721	1923-36
Travis Jackson	1,656	1922-36
Larry Doyle	1,622	1907-16, 1918-20
Jim Davenport	1,501	1958-70
Whitey Lockman	1,485	1945, 1947-56, 1957-58
Mike Tiernan	1,476	1887-99
Barry Bonds	1,429	1993-2002
George Burns	1,362	1911-21
Joe Moore	1,335	1930-41

At-Bats

Willie Mays	10,477	1951-52, 1954-72
Mel Ott	9,456	1926-47
Willie McCovey	7,214	1959-73, 1977-80
Bill Terry	6,428	1923-36
Travis Jackson	6,086	1922-36
Larry Doyle	5,995	1907-16, 1918-20
Mike Tiernan	5,906	1887-99
Whitey Lockman	5,584	1945, 1947-56, 1957-58
Joe Moore	5,427	1930-41
George Burns	5,311	1911-21
George Van Haltren	4,906	1894-1903
Art Fletcher	4,766	1909-20

Runs

Willie Mays	2,011	1951-52, 1954-72
Mel Ott	1,859	1926-47
Mike Tiernan	1,313	1887-99
Barry Bonds	1,158	1993-2002
Bill Terry	1,120	1923-36
Willie McCovey	1,113	1959-73, 1977-80
George Van Haltren	973	1894-1903
Roger Connor	946	1883-89, 1891, 1893-94
Larry Doyle	906	1907-16, 1918-20
George Burns	877	1911-21
George Davis	838	1893-1901
Travis Jackson	833	1922-36

Hits

Willie Mays	3,187	1951-52, 1954-72
Mel Ott	2,876	1926-47
Bill Terry	2,193	1923-36
Willie McCovey	1,974	1959-73, 1977-80
Mike Tiernan	1,834	1887-99

Travis Jackson	1,768	1922-36
Larry Doyle	1,751	1907-16, 1918-20
Joe Moore	1,615	1930-41
George Van Haltren	1,575	1894-1903
Whitey Lockman	1,571	1945, 1947-56, 1957-58
George Burns	1,541	1911-21
Ross Youngs	1,491	1917-26

Doubles

Willie Mays	504	1951-52, 1954-72
Mel Ott	488	1926-47
Bill Terry	373	1923-36
Willie McCovey	308	1959-73, 1977-80
Barry Bonds	294	1993-2002
Travis Jackson	291	1922-36
Larry Doyle	275	1907-16, 1918-20
George Burns	267	1911-21
Joe Moore	258	1930-41
Mike Tiernan	256	1887-99
Will Clark	249	1986-93
Jeff Kent	247	1997-2002

Triples

Mike Tiernan	162	1887-99
Willie Mays	139	1951-52, 1954-72
Roger Connor	131	1883-89, 1891, 1893-94
Larry Doyle	117	1907-16, 1918-20
Bill Terry	112	1923-36
Buck Ewing	109	1883-89, 1891-92
George Davis	98	1893-1901
Ross Youngs	93	1917-26
George Van Haltren	88	1894-1903
Travis Jackson	86	1922-36
George Burns	82	1911-21
Frankie Frisch	77	1919-26

Home Runs

Willie Mays	646	1951-52, 1954-72
Mel Ott	511	1926-47
Willie McCovey	469	1959-73, 1977-80
Barry Bonds	437	1993-2002
Matt Williams	247	1987-96
Orlando Cepeda	226	1958-66
Bobby Thomson	189	1946-53, 1957
Bobby Bonds	186	1968-74
Will Clark	176	1986-93
Jeff Kent	175	1997-2002
Jack Clark	163	1975-84

Johnny Mize	157	1942, 1946-49
Jim Ray Hart	157	1963-73

RBI

Mel Ott	1,860	1926-47
Willie Mays	1,859	1951-52, 1954-72
Willie McCovey	1,388	1959-73, 1977-80
Barry Bonds	1,096	1993-2002
Bill Terry	1,078	1923-36
Travis Jackson	929	1922-36
Mike Tiernan	851	1887-99
George Davis	816	1893-1901
Roger Connor	786	1883-89, 1891, 1893-94
Orlando Cepeda	767	1958-66
George Kelly	762	1915-17, 1919-26
Matt Williams	732	1987-96

Extra-Base Hits

Willie Mays	1,289	1951-52, 1954-72
Mel Ott	1,071	1926-47
Willie McCovey	822	1959-73, 1977-80
Barry Bonds	768	1993-2002
Bill Terry	640	1923-36
Mike Tiernan	524	1887-99
Jim Davenport	522	1958-70
Travis Jackson	512	1922-36
Orlando Cepeda	474	1958-66
Will Clark	462	1986-93
Larry Doyle	459	1907-16, 1918-20
Matt Williams	451	1987-96
Roger Connor	445	1883-89, 1891, 1893-94

Total Bases

Willie Mays	5,907	1951-52, 1954-72
Mel Ott	5,041	1926-47
Willie McCovey	3,779	1959-73, 1977-80
Bill Terry	3,253	1923-36
Barry Bonds	3,157	1993-2002
Mike Tiernan	2,732	1887-99
Travis Jackson	2,636	1922-36
Larry Doyle	2,461	1907-16, 1918-20
Oralndo Cepeda	2,234	1958-66
Whitey Lockman	2,216	1945, 1947-58
Joe Moore	2,216	1930-41
Roger Connor	2,186	1883-89, 1891, 1893-94

Walks

Mel Ott	1,708	1926-47
Willie Mays	1,393	1951-52, 1954-72
Barry Bonds	1,311	1993-2002
Willie McCovey	1,168	1959-73, 1977-80

Mike Tiernan	747	1887-99
George Burns	631	1911-21
Darrell Evans	605	1976-83
Roger Connor	578	1883-89, 1891, 1893-94
Larry Doyle	576	1907-16, 1918-20
Ross Youngs	550	1917-26
Bill Terry	537	1923-36
Whitey Lockman	520	1945, 1947-58

Strikeouts

Willie Mays	1,436	1951-52, 1954-72
Willie McCovey	1,351	1959-73, 1977-80
Bobby Bonds	1,016	1968-74
Robby Thompson	987	1986-96
Mel Ott	896	1926-47
Matt Williams	872	1987-96
Will Clark	744	1986-93
Barry Bonds	739	1993-2002
Jim Davenport	673	1958-70
Jeff Kent	659	1997-2002
Orlando Cepeda	636	1958-66
Jeffrey Leonard	586	1981-88

Stolen Bases

Mike Tiernan	428	1887-99
George Davis	354	1893-1901
Willie Mays	336	1951-52, 1954-72
George Burns	334	1911-21
John Montgomery Ward	332	1883-89, 1893-94
George Van Haltren	320	1894-1903
Larry Doyle	291	1907-16, 1918-20
Art Devlin	266	1904-11
Bobby Bonds	263	1968-74
Jack Doyle	254	1892-95, 1898-1900, 1902
Barry Bonds	242	1993-2002
Red Murray	239	1909-17

Batting Average (2,000 plate appearances)

Bill Terry	.341	1923-36
George Davis	.332	1893-1901
Ross Youngs	.322	1917-26
Frankie Frisch	.321	1919-26
George Van Haltren	.321	1894-1903
Roger Connor	.319	1883-89, 1891, 1893-94
Fred Lindstrom	.318	1924-32
Irish Meusel	.314	1921-26
Shanty Hogan	.311	1928-32
Mike Tiernan	.311	1887-99
Barry Bonds	.311	1993-2002
Dave Bancroft	.310	1920-23, 1930

On-Base Percentage (2,000 plate appearances)

Barry Bonds	.461	1993-2002
Mel Ott	.414	1926-47
Roger Bresnahan	.403	1902-08
Roger Connor	.402	1883-89, 1891, 1893-94
Ross Youngs	.399	1917-26
Bill Terry	.393	1923-36
George Davis	.393	1893-1901
Mike Tiernan	.392	1887-99
Johnny Mize	.389	1942, 1946-49
Monte Irvin	.389	1949-55
Willie Mays	.386	1951-52, 1954-72
George Van Haltren	.385	1894-1903

Slugging Percentage (2,000 plate appearances)

Barry Bonds	.664	1993-2002
Willie Mays	.564	1951-52, 1954-72
Johnny Mize	.549	1942, 1946-49
Kevin Mitchell	.536	1987-91
Orlando Cepeda	.535	1958-66
Jeff Kent	.535	1997-2002
Mel Ott	.533	1926-47
Willie McCovey	.524	1959-73, 1977-80
Bill Terry	.506	1923-36
Will Clark	.499	1986-93
Matt Williams	.498	1987-96
Roger Connor	.488	1883-89, 1891, 1893-94

NEW YORK/SAN FRANCISCO GIANTS CAREER PITCHING LEADERS

Games

Gary Lavelle	647	1974-84
Christy Mathewson	634	1900-16
Greg Minton	552	1975-87
Carl Hubbell	535	1928-43
Randy Moffitt	459	1972-81
Juan Marichal	458	1960-73
Amos Rusie	427	1890-95, 1897-98
Mickey Welch	426	1883-92
Rod Beck	416	1991-97
Freddie Fitzsimmons	403	1925-37
Jim Barr	394	1971-78, 1982-83
Hal Schumacher	391	1931-42, 1946

Complete Games

Christy Mathewson	433	1900-16
Mickey Welch	391	1883-92
Amos Rusie	371	1890-95, 1897-98
Carl Hubbell	260	1928-43
Tim Keefe	251	1885-89, 1891
Juan Marichal	244	1960-73
Joe McGinnity	186	1902-08
Jouett Meekin	178	1894-99
Dummy Taylor	156	1900-01, 1902-08
Hooks Wiltse	153	1904-14
Freddie Fitzsimmons	150	1925-37
Hal Schumacher	138	1931-42, 1946

Games Started

Christy Mathewson	550	1900-16
Juan Marichal	446	1960-73
Carl Hubbell	431	1928-43
Mickey Welch	412	1883-92
Amos Rusie	403	1890-95, 1897-98
Freddie Fitzsimmons	329	1925-37
Hal Schumacher	329	1931-42, 1946
Gaylord Perry	283	1962-71
Tim Keefe	269	1885-89, 1891
Mike McCormick	252	1956-62, 1967-70
Joe McGinnity	237	1902-08
Dummy Taylor	233	1900-01, 1902-08

Shutouts

Christy Mathewson	79	1900-16
Juan Marichal	52	1960-73
Carl Hubbell	36	1928-43
Amos Rusie	29	1890-95, 1897-98
Hal Schumacher	29	1931-42, 1946
Mickey Welch	28	1883-92
Hooks Wiltse	27	1904-14
Jeff Tesreau	27	1912-18
Joe McGinnity	26	1902-08
Tim Keefe	22	1885-89, 1891
Freddie Fitzsimmons	21	1925-37
Johnny Antonelli	21	1954-60
Gaylord Perry	21	1962-71

Innings Pitched

Christy Mathewson	4,771.2	1900-16
Carl Hubbell	3,590.1	1928-43
Mickey Welch	3,579.0	1883-92
Amos Rusie	3,522.2	1890-95, 1897-98
Juan Marichal	3,444.0	1960-73
Freddie Fitzsimmons	2,514.1	1925-37
Hal Schumacher	2,482.1	1931-42, 1946
Gaylord Perry	2,294.2	1962-71
Tim Keefe	2,270.0	1885-89, 1891
Joe McGinnity	2,151.1	1902-08
Hooks Wiltse	2,053.0	1904-14
Dummy Taylor	1,882.1	1900-01, 1902-08

Walks

Amos Rusie	1,585	1890-95, 1897-98
Mickey Welch	1,077	1883-92
Hal Schumacher	902	1931-42, 1946
Christy Mathewson	843	1900-16
Carl Hubbell	725	1928-43
Juan Marichal	690	1960-73
Freddie Fitzsimmons	670	1925-37
Cy Seymour	652	1896-1900
Jouett Meekin	648	1894-99
Red Ames	620	1903-13
Mike McCormick	616	1956-62, 1967-70
Gaylord Perry	581	1962-71

Strikeouts

Christy Mathewson	2,499	1900-16
Juan Marichal	2,281	1960-73
Amos Rusie	1,819	1890-95, 1897-98
Carl Hubbell	1,677	1928-43
Gaylord Perry	1,606	1962-71
Mickey Welch	1,570	1883-92
Tim Keefe	1,278	1885-89, 1891
Red Ames	1,169	1903-13
Mike McCormick	1,030	1956-62, 1967-70
Bobby Bolin	977	1961-69
Hooks Wiltse	948	1904-14
Johnny Antonelli	919	1954-60

Wins

Christy Mathewson	372	1900-16
Carl Hubbell	253	1928-43
Mickey Welch	240	1883-92
Juan Marichal	238	1960-73
Amos Rusie	233	1890-95, 1897-98
Tim Keefe	173	1885-89, 1891
Freddie Fitzsimmons	170	1925-37
Hal Schumacher	158	1931-42, 1946
Joe McGinnity	151	1902-08
Hooks Wiltse	136	1904-14
Gaylord Perry	134	1962-71
Larry Jansen	120	1947-54

Losses

Christy Mathewson	188	1900-16
Amos Rusie	163	1890-95, 1897-98
Carl Hubbell	154	1928-43
Mickey Welch	147	1883-92
Juan Marichal	140	1960-73
Hal Schmuchaer	121	1931-42, 1946
Freddie Fitzsimmons	114	1925-37
Gaylord Perry	109	1962-71
Dave Koslo	104	1941-42, 1946-53
Dummy Taylor	103	1900-01, 1902-08
Mike McCormick	96	1956-62, 1967-70
Jim Barr	96	1971-78, 1982-83

Winning Percentage (100 decisions)

Sal Maglie	.693	1945, 1950-55
Tim Keefe	.678	1885-89, 1891
Christy Mathewson	.664	1900-16
Jesse Barnes	.656	1918-23
Doc Crandall	.650	1908-13
Art Nehf	.641	1919-26
Joe McGinnity	.632	1902-08
Juan Marichal	.630	1960-73
Carl Hubbell	.622	1928-43
Mickey Welch	.620	1883-92
Hooks Wiltse	.615	1904-14
Jeff Tesreau	.615	1912-18

Saves

Robb Nen	206	1998-2002
Rod Beck	199	1991-97
Gary Lavelle	127	1974-84
Greg Minton	125	1975-87
Randy Moffitt	83	1972-81
Frank Linzy	78	1963, 1965-70
Robb Nen	77	1998-99
Marv Grissom	58	1946, 1953-58
Ace Adams	49	1941-46
Scott Garrelts	48	1982-91
Stu Miller	47	1957-62
Jeff Brantley	42	1988-93

ERA (1,000 innings pitched)

Christy Mathewson	2.12	1900-16
Joe McGinnity	2.38	1902-08
Jeff Tesreau	2.43	1912-18
Red Ames	2.45	1903-13

Hooks Wiltse	2.48	1904-14
Tim Keefe	2.53	1885-89, 1891
Mickey Welch	2.69	1883-92
Dummy Taylor	2.76	1900-01, 1902-08
Rube Benton	2.79	1915-21
Juan Marichal	2.84	1960-73
Rube Marquard	2.85	1908-15
Doc Crandall	2.89	1908-13

Opponent Batting Average (1,000 innings pitched)

Tim Keefe	.220	1885-89, 1891

Jeff Tesreau	.223	1912-18
Bobby Bolin	.227	1961-69
Amos Rusie	.230	1890-95, 1897-98
Red Ames	.234	1903-13
Christy Mathewson	.236	1900-16
Juan Marichal	.236	1960-73
Mickey Welch	.237	1883-92
Joe McGinnity	.238	1902-08
Gaylord Perry	.238	1962-71
Johnny Antonelli	.239	1954-60
Hooks Wiltse	.241	1904-14

NEW YORK/SAN FRANCISCO GIANTS CAREER FIELDING LEADERS

Putouts

Pitcher

Juan Marichal	287	1960-73
Christy Mathewson	280	1900-16
Freddie Fitzsimmons	185	1925-37
Gaylord Perry	173	1962-71
Amos Rusie	167	1890-95, 1897-98

Catcher

Tom Haller	4,285	1961-67
Chief Meyers	3,849	1909-15
Wes Westrum	3,639	1947-57
Bob Brenly	3,540	1981-88, 1989
Kirt Manwaring	3,516	1987-96

First Base

Bill Terry	15,972	1923-36
Willie McCovey	14,956	1959-73, 1977-80
Will Clark	10,214	1986-93
Roger Connor	10,204	1883-89, 1891, 1893-94
Fred Merkle	10,033	1907-16

Second Base

Larry Doyle	3,316	1907-16, 1918-20
Robby Thompson	2,611	1986-96
Tito Fuentes	1,922	1965-67, 1969-74
Jeff Kent	1,745	1997-2002
Kid Gleason	1,728	1896-1900

Shortstop

Travis Jackson	2,877	1922-36
Art Fletcher	2,411	1909-20
Alvin Dark	1,717	1950-56
George Davis	1,690	1893-1901
Buddy Kerr	1,625	1943-49

Third Base

Art Devlin	1,275	1904-11
Jim Davenport	863	1958-70
Matt Williams	807	1987-96
Fred Lindstrom	804	1924-32
George Davis	595	1893-1901

Outfield

Willie Mays	6,992	1951-52, 1954-72
Mel Ott	4,511	1926-47
George Burns	2,848	1911-21
Barry Bonds	2,584	1993-2002
Joe Moore	2,501	1930-41
George Van Haltren	2,440	1894-1903
Bobby Thomson	2,360	1946-53, 1957
Ross Youngs	2,160	1917-26
Bobby Bonds	2,159	1968-74
Mike Tiernan	2,100	1887-99

Assists

Pitcher

Christy Mathewson	1,500	1900-16
Amos Rusie	836	1890-95, 1897-98
Carl Hubbell	824	1928-43
Freddie Fitzsimmons	731	1925-37
Hal Schumacher	646	1931-42, 1946

Catcher

Chief Meyers	827	1909-15
John Warner	798	1896-1901, 1903-04
Buck Ewing	769	1883-89, 1891-92
Frank Bowerman	707	1900-07
Frank Snyder	575	1919-26

First Base

Bill Terry	1,108	1923-36
Willie McCovey	1,058	1959-73, 1977-80
Will Clark	812	1986-93
Fred Merkle	583	1907-16
George Kelly	552	1915-17, 1919-26

Second Base

Larry Doyle	4,272	1907-16, 1918-20
Robby Thompson	3,704	1986-96
Jeff Kent	2,351	1997-2002
Tito Fuentes	2,343	1965-67, 1969-74
Hughie Critz	2,274	1930-35

Shortstop

Travis Jackson	4,635	1922-36
Art Fletcher	4,387	1909-20
Chris Speier	2,907	1971-77, 1987-89
Jose Uribe	2,756	1985-92
Johnnie LeMaster	2,717	1975-85

Third Base

Art Devlin	2,297	1904-11
Matt Williams	1,979	1987-96
Jim Davenport	1,816	1958-70
Darrell Evans	1,517	1976-83
Fred Lindstrom	1,501	1924-32

Outfield

Mel Ott	256	1926-47
George Van Haltren	224	1894-1903
Willie Mays	193	1951-52, 1954-72
Ross Youngs	192	1917-26
Mike Tiernan	159	1887-99
George Burns	144	1911-21
Red Murray	118	1909-15, 1917
Joe Moore	116	1930-41
Fred Snodgrass	114	1908-15
Jack Clark	94	1975-84

Fielding Percentage

Pitcher

Kirk Rueter	.991	1996-2002
Russ Ortiz	.986	1998-2002
Livan Hernandez	.986	1999-2002
Harry Gumbert	.980	1935-41
Art Nehf	.977	1919-26
Larry Jansen	.977	1947-54

Catcher

Tom Haller	.992	1961-67
Kirt Manwaring	.991	1987-96
Harry Danning	.985	1933-42
Wes Westrum	.985	1947-57
Dave Rader	.985	1971-76

First Base

J.T. Snow	.996	1997-2002
Johnny Mize	.993	1942, 1946-49
George Kelly	.992	1915-17, 1919-26
Bill Terry	.992	1923-36
Will Clark	.992	1986-93

Second Base

Robby Thompson	.983	1986-96
Jeff Kent	.981	1997-2002
Hughie Critz	.976	1930-35
Tito Fuentes	.976	1965-67, 1969-74
Burgess Whitehead	.972	1936-37, 1939-41

Shortstop

Hal Lanier	.982	1964-71
Rich Aurilia	.972	1995-2002
Jose Uribe	.970	1985-92
Chris Speier	.969	1971-77, 1987-89
Buddy Kerr	.967	1943-49

Third Base

Jim Davenport	.964	1958-70
Bill Mueller	.961	1996-2000
Fred Lindstrom	.959	1924-32
Matt Williams	.959	1987-96
Darrell Evans	.948	1976-83

Outfield

Barry Bonds	.982	1993-2002
Don Mueller	.982	1948-57
Willie Mays	.981	1951-52, 1954-72
Mel Ott	.980	1926-47
Bobby Thomson	.980	1946-53, 1957
Whitey Lockman	.978	1945, 1947-58
Felipe Alou	.978	1958-63
Jack Clark	.978	1975-84
Willard Marshall	.976	1942, 1946-49
Bobby Bonds	.976	1968-74

NEW YORK/SAN FRANCISCO GIANTS GAMES BY POSITION LEADERS

Catcher

Wes Westrum	902	1947-57
Gus Mancuso	840	1933-38, 1942-44
Harry Danning	801	1932-42
Chief Meyers	769	1909-15
Tom Haller	719	1961-67

First Base

Willie McCovey	1,775	1959-73, 1977-80
Bill Terry	1,579	1923-36
Will Clark	1,124	1986-93
Fred Merkle	1,038	1907-16
Roger Connor	1,002	1883-89, 1991-94

Second Base

Larry Doyle	1,591	1907-16, 1918-20
Robby Thompson	1,217	1986-96
Jeff Kent	854	1997-2002
Tito Fuentes	842	1965-67, 1969-74
Kid Gleason	660	1896-1900
Hughie Critz	658	1930-35

Shortstop

Travis Jackson	1,326	1922-36
Art Fletcher	1,240	1909-20
Jose Uribe	969	1985-92
Johnnie LeMaster	954	1975-85
Chris Speier	910	1971-77, 1987-89

Third Base

Jim Davenport	1,130	1958-70
Art Devlin	1,097	1904-11
Matt Williams	919	1987-96
Fred Lindstrom	776	1924-32
Darrell Evans	697	1976-83

Outfield

Willie Mays	2,797	1951-52, 1954-72
Mel Ott	2,313	1926-47
Mike Tiernan	1,474	1887-99
Barry Bonds	1,396	1993-2002
George Burns	1,356	1911-21
Joe Moore	1,294	1930-41
George Van Haltren	1,212	1894-1903
Ross Youngs	1,199	1917-26
Don Mueller	1,041	1948-57
Bobby Bonds	1,005	1968-74
Jack Clark	995	1975-84

NEW YORK GIANTS SEASON BATTING LEADERS

Games

Art Devlin	157	1908
George Van Haltren	156	1898
Cy Seymour	156	1908
Fred Tenney	156	1908
Dave Bancroft	156	1922
Bobby Thomson	156	1949
Alvin Dark	156	1951
Spike Shannon	155	1907
Mike Donlin	155	1908
George Burns	155	1915
George Burns	155	1916
George Kelly	155	1920
Rogers Hornsby	155	1927
Joe Moore	155	1935
Willard Marshall	155	1947
Alvin Dark	155	1953

At Bats

Joe Moore	681	1935
Hughie Critz	659	1932
George Van Haltren	654	1898
Dave Bancroft	651	1922
Joe Moore	649	1936
Alvin Dark	647	1953
Fred Lindstrom	646	1951
Alvin Dark	646	1951
Alvin Dark	644	1954
Bill Terry	643	1932
Frankie Frisch	641	1923
Bobby Thomson	641	1949

Runs

Mike Tiernan	147	1889
Bill Terry	139	1930
Mel Ott	138	1929
Johnny Mize	137	1947
George Van Haltren	136	1896
Rogers Hornsby	133	1927
George Gore	132	1889
Mike Tiernan	132	1890
Mike Tiernan	132	1896
John Montgomery Ward	129	1893
George Van Haltren	129	1898
Mike Tiernan	127	1895
Fred Lindstrom	127	1930

Hits

Bill Terry	254	1930
Fred Lindstrom	231	1928
Fred Lindstrom	231	1930
Bill Terry	226	1929
Bill Terry	225	1932
Frankie Frisch	223	1923
Mike Donlin	216	1905
Bill Terry	213	1931
Bill Terry	213	1934
Don Mueller	212	1954
Frankie Frisch	211	1921
Dave Bancroft	209	1922

Doubles

Bill Terry	43	1931
George Kelly	42	1921
Bill Terry	42	1932
Dave Bancroft	41	1922
Alvin Dark	41	1951
Alvin Dark	41	1953
Larry Doyle	40	1915
Fred Lindstrom	39	1928
Bill Terry	39	1929
Fred Lindstrom	39	1930
Bill Terry	39	1930
Dick Bartell	38	1937
Johnny Rucker	38	1941

Triples

George Davis	27	1893
Larry Doyle	25	1911
Roger Connor	22	1887
Mike Tiernan	21	1890
Mike Tiernan	21	1895
George Van Haltren	21	1896
Buck Ewing	20	1884
Roger Connor	20	1886
Red Murray	20	1912
Bill Terry	20	1931
Willie Mays	20	1957
George Davis	19	1894
George Van Haltren	19	1895

Home Runs

Johnny Mize	51	1947
Willie Mays	51	1955
Mel Ott	42	1929
Willie Mays	41	1954
Johnny Mize	40	1948
Mel Ott	38	1932
Mel Ott	36	1938
Willard Marshall	36	1947
Willie Mays	36	1956
Mel Ott	35	1834
Walker Cooper	35	1947
Willie Mays	35	1957

RBI

Mel Ott	151	1929
Johnny Mize	138	1947
George Davis	136	1897
George Kelly	136	1924
Mel Ott	135	1934
Mel Ott	135	1936
Irish Meusel	132	1922
Roger Connor	130	1889
Bill Terry	129	1930
Willie Mays	127	1955
Irish Meusel	125	1923
Rogers Hornsby	125	1927
Johnny Mize	125	1948

Extra-Base Hits

Willie Mays	87	1954
Willie Mays	83	1957
Willie Mays	82	1955
Mel Ott	81	1929
Bill Terry	81	1932
Johnny Mize	79	1947
Bill Terry	77	1930
Mel Ott	76	1932
George Kelly	74	1921
Mel Ott	74	1934
Bill Terry	72	1931
Bobby Thomson	71	1949
Willie Mays	71	1956

Total Bases

Bill Terry	392	1930
Willie Mays	382	1955
Willie Mays	377	1954
Bill Terry	373	1932
Willie Mays	366	1957
Johnny Mize	360	1947
Fred Lindstrom	350	1930

Mel Ott	346	1929
Mel Ott	344	1934
Mel Ott	340	1932
Rogers Hornsby	333	1927
Bobby Thomson	332	1949

Walks

Eddie Stanky	144	1950
Eddie Stanky	127	1951
Mel Ott	118	1938
Mel Ott	113	1929
Mel Ott	111	1936
Mel Ott	109	1942
Wes Westrum	104	1951
Mel Ott	103	1930
Mel Ott	102	1937
Mel Ott	100	1932
Mel Ott	100	1939
Mel Ott	100	1940
Mel Ott	100	1941

Strikeouts

Wes Westrum	93	1951
George Kelly	92	1920
Fred Merkle	80	1914
Bobby Thomson	78	1947
George Burns	74	1913
Bobby Thomson	74	1952
Daryl Spencer	74	1953
George Kelly	73	1921
Wes Westrum	73	1950
Wes Westrum	73	1953
Bill White	72	1956
Travis Jackson	71	1934

Stolen Bases

John Montgomery Ward	111	1887
George Davis	65	1897
John Montgomery Ward	62	1889
George Burns	62	1914
Josh Devore	61	1911
Art Devlin	59	1905
Red Murray	57	1910
Mike Tiernan	56	1890
Jack Glasscock	54	1890
Eddie Burke	54	1893
Art Devlin	54	1906
Buck Ewing	53	1888
Mike Tiernan	53	1891

Batting Average

Bill Terry	.401	1930
Fred Lindstrom	.379	1930
Bill Terry	.372	1929
Roger Connor	.371	1885
Mike Tiernan	.369	1896
Jack Doyle	.367	1894
Rogers Hornsby	.361	1927
Fred Lindstrom	.358	1928
Roger Connor	.357	1883
Mike Donlin	.356	1905
Ross Youngs	.356	1924
Roger Connor	.355	1886
George Davis	.355	1893

On-Base Percentage

Eddie Stanky	.460	1950
Mel Ott	.458	1930
Mike Tiernan	.452	1896
Bill Terry	.452	1930
Mel Ott	.449	1929

Mel Ott	.449	1939
Rogers Hornsby	.448	1927
Mel Ott	.448	1936
Mike Tiernan	.447	1889
Roger Bresnahan	.443	1903
Mel Ott	.442	1938
Bill Joyce	.441	1897
Ross Youngs	.441	1924

Slugging Percentage

Willie Mays	.667	1954
Willie Mays	.659	1955
Mel Ott	.635	1929
Willie Mays	.626	1957
Bill Terry	.619	1930
Johnny Mize	.614	1947
Mel Ott	.601	1932
Mel Ott	.591	1934
Mel Ott	.588	1936
Rogers Hornsby	.586	1927
Walker Cooper	.586	1947
Mel Ott	.583	1938

NEW YORK GIANTS SEASON PITCHING LEADERS

Games

Hoyt Wilhelm	71	1952
Ace Adams	70	1943
Hoyt Wilhelm	68	1953
Amos Rusie	67	1890
Mickey Welch	65	1884
Amos Rusie	65	1892
Ace Adams	65	1944
Ace Adams	65	1945
Tim Keefe	64	1886
Hoyt Wilhelm	64	1956
Ken Trinkle	62	1947
Amos Rusie	61	1891

Games Started

Mickey Welch	65	1884
Tim Keefe	64	1886
Amos Rusie	62	1890
Amos Rusie	62	1892
Mickey Welch	59	1886
Amos Rusie	57	1891
Tim Keefe	56	1887
Mickey Welch	55	1885

Mickey Welch	52	1883
Amos Rusie	52	1893
Tim Keefe	51	1888
Amos Rusie	50	1894

Complete Games

Mickey Welch	62	1884
Tim Keefe	62	1886
Amos Rusie	58	1892
Mickey Welch	56	1886
Amos Rusie	56	1890
Mickey Welch	55	1885
Tim Keefe	54	1887
Amos Rusie	52	1891
Amos Rusie	50	1893
Tim Keefe	48	1888
Mickey Welch	47	1888
Mickey Welch	46	1883
Silver King	46	1892

Shutouts

Christy Mathewson	11	1908
Carl Hubbell	10	1933
Joe McGinnity	9	1904
Tim Keefe	8	1888
Christy Mathewson	8	1902
Christy Mathewson	8	1905
Christy Mathewson	8	1907
Christy Mathewson	8	1909
Jeff Tesreau	8	1914
Jeff Tesreau	8	1915
Tim Keefe	7	1885
Mickey Welch	7	1885
Hooks Wiltse	7	1908
Hal Schumacher	7	1933

Innings Pitched

Mickey Welch	557.1	1884
Amos Rusie	548.2	1890
Tim Keefe	540.0	1886
Amos Rusie	532.0	1892
Amos Rusie	500.1	1891
Mickey Welch	500.0	1886
Mickey Welch	492.0	1895
Amos Rusie	482.0	1893
Tim Keefe	478.2	1887
Amos Rusie	444.0	1894
Tim Keefe	434.1	1888
Joe McGinnity	434.0	1903

Walks

Amos Rusie	289	1890
Amos Rusie	267	1892
Amos Rusie	262	1891
Amos Rusie	218	1893
Cy Seymour	213	1898
Amos Rusie	200	1894
Ed Crane	189	1892
Silver King	174	1892
Jouett Meekin	171	1894
Cy Seymour	170	1899
Cy Seymour	164	1897
Mickey Welch	163	1886

Strikeouts

Mickey Welch	345	1884
Amos Rusie	341	1890
Amos Rusie	337	1891
Tim Keefe	333	1888
Tim Keefe	291	1886
Amos Rusie	288	1892

Mickey Welch	272	1886
Christy Mathewson	267	1903
Christy Mathewson	259	1908
Mickey Welch	258	1885
Cy Seymour	239	1898
Rube Marquard	237	1911

Wins

Mickey Welch	44	1885
Tim Keefe	42	1886
Mickey Welch	39	1884
Christy Mathewson	37	1908
Amos Rusie	36	1894
Tim Keefe	35	1887
Tim Keefe	35	1888
Joe McGinnity	35	1904
Mickey Welch	33	1886
Amos Rusie	33	1891
Amos Rusie	33	1893
Jouett Meekin	33	1894
Christy Mathewson	33	1904

Losses

Amos Rusie	34	1890
Amos Rusie	31	1892
Bill Carrick	27	1899
Dummy Taylor	27	1901
Ed Crane	24	1892
Silver King	24	1892
Dad Clarke	24	1896
Mickey Welch	23	1883
Amos Rusie	23	1895
Mickey Welch	22	1886
Bill Carrick	22	1900
Rube Marquard	22	1914

Winning Percentage (15 decisions)

Hoyt Wilhelm	.833	1952
Sal Maglie	.818	1950
Joe McGinnity	.814	1904
Hooks Wiltse	.813	1904
Carl Hubbell	.813	1936
Doc Crandell	.810	1910
Larry Jansen	.808	1947
Christy Mathewson	.806	1909
Mickey Welch	.800	1885
Sal Maglie	.793	1951
Jouett Meekin	.786	1894
Art Nehf	.778	1924

Saves

Marv Grissom	19	1954
Ace Adams	15	1945
Hoyt Wilhelm	15	1953
Marv Grissom	14	1957
Ace Adams	13	1944
Dick Coffman	12	1938
Hoyt Wilhelm	11	1952
Ace Adams	11	1942
Ken Trinkle	10	1947
Ace Adams	9	1943
Carl Hubbell	8	1934
Jumbo Brown	8	1941
Marv Grissom	8	1955
Hoyt Wilhelm	8	1956

ERA (1 inning pitched per team game)

Christy Mathewson	1.14	1909
Christy Mathewson	1.28	1905
Christy Mathewson	1.43	1908
Fred Anderson	1.44	1917
Tim Keefe	1.58	1885
Joe McGinnity	1.61	1904
Carl Hubbell	1.66	1933
Mickey Welch	1.66	1885
Tim Keefe	1.74	1888
Fred Toney	1.84	1919
Pol Perritt	1.88	1917
Christy Mathewson	1.89	1910

Opponent Batting Average
(1 inning pitched per team game)

Tim Keefe	.195	1888
Christy Mathewson	.200	1909
Christy Mathewson	.200	1908
Tim Keefe	.201	1885
Cannonball Titcomb	.201	1888
Mickey Welch	.203	1885
Amos Rusie	.203	1892
Jeff Tesreau	.204	1912
Christy Mathewson	.205	1905
Mickey Welch	.207	1888
Amos Rusie	.207	1891
Joe McGinnity	.208	1904

NEW YORK GIANTS CAREER BATTING LEADERS

Games

Mel Ott	2,730	1926-47
Bill Terry	1,721	1923-36
Travis Jackson	1,656	1922-36
Larry Doyle	1,622	1907-16, 1918-20
Mike Tiernan	1,476	1887-99
Whitey Lockman	1,393	1945, 1947-56, 1957
George Burns	1,362	1911-21
Joe Moore	1,335	1930-41
Art Fletcher	1,321	1909-20
George Van Haltren	1,221	1894-1903
Ross Youngs	1,211	1917-26
Don Mueller	1,171	1948-57

At-Bats

Mel Ott	9,456	1926-47
Bill Terry	6,428	1923-36
Travis Jackson	6,086	1922-36
Larry Doyle	5,995	1907-16, 1918-20
Mike Tiernan	5,906	1887-99
Whitey Lockman	5,462	1945, 1947-56, 1957
Joe Moore	5,427	1930-41
George Burns	5,311	1911-21
George Van Haltren	4,906	1894-1903
Art Fletcher	4,766	1909-20
Ross Youngs	4,627	1917-26
John Montgomery Ward	4,461	1883-89, 1893-94

Runs

Mel Ott	1,859	1926-47
Mike Tiernan	1,313	1887-99
Bill Terry	1,120	1923-36
George Van Haltren	973	1894-1903
Roger Connor	946	1883-89, 1891, 1893-94
Larry Doyle	906	1907-16, 1918-20
George Burns	877	1911-21
George Davis	838	1893-1901
Travis Jackson	833	1922-36
John Montgomery Ward	828	1883-89, 1893-94
Ross Youngs	812	1917-26
Joe Moore	809	1930-41

Hits

Mel Ott	2,876	1926-47
Bill Terry	2,193	1923-36
Mike Tiernan	1,834	1887-99
Travis Jackson	1,768	1922-36
Larry Doyle	1,751	1907-16, 1918-20
Joe Moore	1,615	1930-41
George Van Haltren	1,575	1894-1903
Whitey Lockman	1,542	1945, 1947-56, 1957
George Burns	1,541	1911-21
Ross Youngs	1,491	1917-26
George Davis	1,427	1893-1901
Roger Connor	1,388	1883-89, 1891, 1893-94

Doubles

Mel Ott	488	1926-47
Bill Terry	373	1923-36
Travis Jackson	291	1922-36
Larry Doyle	275	1907-16, 1918-20
George Burns	267	1911-21
Joe Moore	258	1930-41
Mike Tiernan	256	1887-99
Roger Connor	242	1883-89, 1891, 1893-94
Ross Youngs	236	1917-26
George Davis	227	1893-1901
George Kelly	218	1915-17, 1919-26
Fred Lindstrom	212	1924-32

Triples

Mike Tiernan	162	1887-99
Roger Connor	131	1883-89, 1891, 1893-94
Larry Doyle	117	1907-16, 1918-20
Bill Terry	112	1923-36
Buck Ewing	109	1883-89, 1891-92
George Davis	98	1893-1901
Ross Youngs	93	1917-26
George Van Haltren	88	1894-1903
Travis Jackson	86	1922-36
George Burns	82	1911-21
Frankie Frisch	77	1919-26
Mel Ott	72	1926-47

Home Runs

Mel Ott	511	1926-47
Bobby Thomson	189	1946-53, 1957
Willie Mays	187	1951-52, 1954-57
Johnny Mize	157	1942, 1946-49
Bill Terry	154	1923-36
Travis Jackson	135	1922-36

Hank Thompson	129	1949-56
George Kelly	123	1915-17, 1919-26
Whitey Lockman	111	1945, 1947-56, 1957
Mike Tiernan	107	1887-99
Alvin Dark	98	1950-56
Wes Westrum	96	1947-47

RBI

Mel Ott	1,860	1926-47
Bill Terry	1,078	1923-36
Travis Jackson	929	1922-36
Mike Tiernan	851	1887-99
George Davis	816	1893-1901
Roger Connor	786	1883-89, 1891, 1893-94
George Kelly	762	1915-17, 1919-26
Larry Doyle	725	1907-16, 1918-20
Bobby Thomson	704	1946-53, 1957
George Van Haltren	604	1894-1903
Fred Lindstrom	603	1924-32
Ross Youngs	592	1917-26

Extra-Base Hits

Mel Ott	1,071	1926-47
Bill Terry	640	1923-36
Mike Tiernan	524	1887-99
Travis Jackson	512	1922-36
Larry Doyle	459	1907-16, 1918-20
Roger Connor	445	1883-89, 1891, 1893-94
Bobby Thomson	437	1946-53, 1957
George Kelly	393	1915-17, 1919-26
Joe Moore	390	1930-41
George Burns	383	1911-12
George Davis	378	1893-1901
Willie Mays	378	1951-52, 1954-57

Total Bases

Mel Ott	5,041	1926-47
Bill Terry	3,253	1923-36
Mike Tiernan	2,732	1887-99
Travis Jackson	2,636	1922-36
Larry Doyle	2,461	1907-16, 1918-20
Joe Moore	2,216	1930-41
Roger Connor	2,186	1883-89, 1891, 1893-94
Whitey Lockman	2,176	1945, 1947-56, 1957
George Burns	2,074	1911-21
George Van Haltren	2,051	1894-1903
Bobby Thomson	2,042	1946-53, 1957
Ross Youngs	2,039	1917-26

Walks

Mel Ott	1,708	1926-47
Mike Tiernan	747	1887-99
George Burns	631	1911-21
Roger Connor	578	1883-89, 1891, 1893-94
Larry Doyle	576	1907-16, 1918-20
Ross Youngs	550	1917-26
Bill Terry	537	1923-36
Whitey Lockman	507	1945, 1947-56, 1957
Art Devlin	496	1904-11
Wes Westrum	489	1947-57
George Van Haltren	486	1894-1903
Hank Thompson	483	1949-56

Strikeouts

Mel Ott	896	1926-47
Travis Jackson	565	1922-36
Wes Westrum	514	1947-57
George Kelly	503	1915-17, 1919-26
Bobby Thomson	477	1946-53, 1957
Bill Terry	449	1923-36
George Burns	440	1911-21
Fred Merkle	414	1907-16
Ross Youngs	390	1917-26
Whitey Lockman	354	1945, 1947-56, 1957
Hank Thompson	330	1949-56
Willie Mays	321	1951-52, 1954-57

Stolen Bases

Mike Tiernan	428	1887-99
George Davis	354	1893-1901
George Burns	334	1911-21
John Montgomery Ward	332	1883-89, 1893-94
George Van Haltren	320	1894-1903
Larry Doyle	291	1907-16, 1918-20
Art Devlin	266	1904-11
Jack Doyle	254	1892-95, 1898-1900, 1902
Red Murray	239	1909-17
Frankie Frisch	224	1919-26
Fred Merkle	212	1907-16
Fred Snodgrass	201	1908-15

Batting Average (2,000 plate appearances)

Bill Terry	.341	1923-36
George Davis	.332	1893-1901
Ross Youngs	.322	1917-26
George Van Haltren	.321	1894-1903
Frankie Frisch	.321	1919-26
Roger Connor	.319	1883-89, 1891, 1893-94
Fred Lindstrom	.318	1924-32
Irish Meusel	.314	1921-26
Mike Tiernan	.311	1887-99
Shanty Hogan	.311	1928-32
Willie Mays	.311	1951-52, 1954-57
Dave Bancroft	.310	1920-23, 1930

On-Base Percentage (2,000 plate appearances)

Mel Ott	.414	1926-47
Roger Bresnahan	.403	1902-08
Roger Connor	.402	1883-89, 1891, 1893-94
Ross Youngs	.399	1917-26
George Davis	.393	1893-1901
Bill Terry	.393	1923-36
Mike Tiernan	.392	1887-99
Johnny Mize	.389	1942, 1946-49
Monte Irvin	.389	1949-55
Willie Mays	.387	1951-52, 1954-57
George Van Haltren	.385	1894-1903
Dave Bancroft	.382	1920-23, 1930

Slugging Percentage (2,000 plate appearances)

Willie Mays	.593	1951-52, 1954-57
Johnny Mize	.549	1942, 1946-49
Mel Ott	.533	1926-47
Bill Terry	.506	1923-36
Roger Connor	.488	1883-89, 1891, 1893-94
Bobby Thomson	.484	1946-53, 1957
Irish Meusel	.477	1921-26
Monte Irvin	.477	1949-55
Buck Ewing	.469	1883-89, 1891-92
George Davis	.467	1893-1901
George Kelly	.465	1915-17, 1919-26
Mike Tiernan	.463	1887-99

NEW YORK GIANTS CAREER PITCHING LEADERS

Games

Christy Mathewson	634	1900-16
Carl Hubbell	535	1928-43
Amos Rusie	427	1890-95, 1897-98
Mickey Welch	426	1883-92
Freddie Fitzsimmons	403	1925-37
Hal Schumacher	391	1931-42, 1946
Hooks Wiltse	339	1904-14
Dave Koslo	322	1941-42, 1946-53
Hoyt Wilhelm	319	1952-56
Ace Adams	302	1941-46
Joe McGinnity	300	1902-08
Larry Jansen	283	1947-54

Games Started

Christy Mathewson	550	1900-16
Carl Hubbell	431	1928-43
Mickey Welch	412	1883-92
Amos Rusie	403	1890-95, 1897-98
Freddie Fitzsimmons	329	1925-37
Hal Schumacher	329	1931-42, 1946
Tim Keefe	269	1885-89, 1891
Joe McGinnity	237	1902-08
Dummy Taylor	233	1900-01, 1902-08
Larry Jansen	230	1947-54
Hooks Wiltse	223	1904-14
Red Ames	211	1903-13

Complete Games

Christy Mathewson	433	1900-16
Mickey Welch	391	1883-92
Amos Rusie	371	1890-95, 1897-98
Carl Hubbell	260	1928-43
Tim Keefe	251	1885-89, 1891
Joe McGinnity	186	1902-08
Jouett Meekin	178	1894-99
Dummy Taylor	156	1900-01, 1902-08
Hooks Wiltse	153	1904-14
Freddie Fitzsimmons	150	1925-37
Hal Schmacher	138	1931-42, 1946
Red Ames	128	1903-13

Shutouts

Christy Mathewson	79	1900-16
Carl Hubbell	36	1928-43
Amos Rusie	29	1890-95, 1897-98
Hal Schumacher	29	1931-42, 1946
Mickey Welch	28	1883-92
Hooks Wiltse	27	1904-14
Jeff Tesreau	27	1912-18
Joe McGinnity	26	1902-08
Tim Keefe	22	1885-89, 1891
Freddie Fitzsimmons	21	1925-37
Dummy Taylor	20	1900-01, 1902-08
Pol Perritt	20	1915-21
Sal Maglie	20	1945, 1950-55

Innings Pitched

Christy Mathewson	4,771.2	1900-16
Carl Hubbell	3,590.1	1928-43
Mickey Welch	3,579.0	1883-92
Amos Rusie	3,522.2	1890-95, 1897-98
Freddie Fitzsimmons	2,514.1	1925-37
Hal Schumacher	2,482.1	1931-42, 1946
Tim Keefe	2,270.0	1885-89, 1891
Joe McGinnity	2,151.1	1902-08
Hooks Wiltse	2,053.0	1904-14
Dummy Taylor	1,882.1	1900-01, 1902-08
Red Ames	1,802.2	1903-13
Jouett Meekin	1,741.0	1894-99

Walks

Amos Rusie	1,585	1890-95, 1897-98
Mickey Welch	1,077	1883-92
Hal Schumacher	902	1931-42, 1946
Christy Mathewson	843	1900-16
Carl Hubbell	725	1928-43
Freddie Fitzsimmons	670	1925-37
Cy Seymour	652	1896-1900
Jouett Meekin	648	1894-99
Red Ames	620	1903-13
Tim Keefe	580	1885-89, 1891
Jeff Tesreau	572	1912-18
Dummy Taylor	543	1900-01, 1902-08

Strikeouts

Christy Mathewson	2,499	1900-16
Amos Rusie	1,819	1890-95, 1897-98
Carl Hubbell	1,677	1928-43
Mickey Welch	1,570	1883-92
Tim Keefe	1,278	1885-89, 1891
Red Ames	1,169	1903-13
Hooks Wiltse	948	1904-14
Hal Schumacher	906	1931-42, 1946

Rube Marquard	897	1908-15
Jeff Tesreau	880	1912-18
Larry Jansen	826	1947-54
Joe McGinnity	767	1902-08

Wins

Christy Mathewson	372	1900-16
Carl Hubbell	253	1928-43
Mickey Welch	240	1883-92
Amos Rusie	233	1890-95, 1897-98
Tim Keefe	173	1885-89, 1891
Freddie Fitzsimmons	170	1925-37
Hal Schumacher	158	1931-42, 1946
Joe McGinnity	151	1902-08
Hooks Wiltse	136	1904-14
Larry Jansen	120	1947-54
Jouett Meekin	116	1894-99
Dummy Taylor	115	1900-01, 1902-08
Jeff Tesreau	115	1912-18

Losses

Christy Mathewson	188	1900-16
Amos Rusie	163	1890-95, 1897-98
Carl Hubbell	154	1928-43
Mickey Welch	147	1883-92
Hal Schmuchaer	121	1931-42, 1946
Freddie Fitzsimmons	114	1925-37
Dave Koslo	104	1941-42, 1946-53
Dummy Taylor	103	1900-01, 1902-08
Joe McGinnity	88	1902-08
Larry Jansen	86	1947-54
Hooks Wiltse	85	1904-14
Tim Keefe	82	1885-89, 1891

Winning Percentage (100 decisions)

Sal Maglie	.693	1945, 1950-55
Tim Keefe	.678	1885-89, 1891
Christy Mathewson	.664	1900-16
Jesse Barnes	.656	1918-23
Doc Crandall	.650	1908-13
Art Nehf	.641	1919-26
Joe McGinnity	.632	1902-08
Carl Hubbell	.622	1928-43
Mickey Welch	.620	1883-92
Hooks Wiltse	.615	1904-14
Jeff Tesreau	.615	1912-18
Jouett Meekin	.611	1894-99

Saves

Ace Adams	49	1941-46
Marv Grissom	48	1946, 1953-57
Hoyt Wilhelm	41	1952-56
Carl Hubbell	33	1928-43
Hooks Wiltse	29	1904-14
Christy Mathewson	28	1900-16
Jumbo Brown	27	1937-42
Dick Coffman	25	1952-53
Doc Crandell	24	1908-13
Joe McGinnity	21	1902-08
Dave Koslo	21	1941-42, 1946-53
Ken Trinkle	19	1943, 1946-48

ERA (1,000 innings pitched)

Christy Mathewson	2.12	1900-16
Joe McGinnity	2.38	1902-08
Jeff Tesreau	2.43	1912-18
Red Ames	2.45	1903-13
Hooks Wiltse	2.48	1904-14
Tim Keefe	2.53	1885-89, 1891
Mickey Welch	2.69	1883-92
Dummy Taylor	2.76	1900-01, 1902-08
Rube Benton	2.79	1915-21
Rube Marquard	2.85	1908-15
Amos Rusie	2.89	1890-95, 1897-98
Doc Crandell	2.89	1908-13

Opponent Batting Average (1,000 innings pitched)

Tim Keefe	.220	1885-89, 1891
Jeff Tesreau	.223	1912-18
Amos Rusie	.230	1890-95, 1897-98
Red Ames	.234	1903-13
Christy Mathewson	.236	1900-16
Mickey Welch	.237	1883-92
Joe McGinnity	.238	1902-08
Hooks Wiltse	.241	1904-14
Cy Seymour	.244	1896-1900, 1906-10
Rube Marquard	.248	1908-15
Sal Maglie	.248	1945, 1950-55
Jim Hearn	.249	1950-56

SAN FRANCISCO GIANTS SEASON BATTING LEADERS

Games

Jose Pagan	164	1962
Orlando Cepeda	162	1962
Willie Mays	162	1962
Will Clark	162	1988
Chuck Hiller	161	1962
J.T. Snow	161	1999
Jim Ray Hart	160	1965
Willie McCovey	160	1965
Bobby Bonds	160	1973
Tito Fuentes	160	1973
Darrell Evans	160	1979
Brett Butler	160	1990
Hal Lanier	159	1965
Will Clark	159	1989
Matt Williams	159	1990
Barry Bonds	159	1993
Barry Bonds	159	1997
Jeff Kent	159	2000
Jeff Kent	159	2001

At Bats

Bobby Bonds	663	1970
Tito Fuentes	656	1973
Bobby Bonds	643	1973
Chili Davis	641	1982
Tito Fuentes	630	1971
Barry Bonds	626	1972
Orlando Cepeda	625	1962
Jeff Kent	623	2002
Bobby Bonds	622	1969
Brett Butler	622	1990
Willie Mays	621	1962
Bobby Bonds	619	1971

Runs

Bobby Bonds	134	1970
Bobby Bonds	131	1973
Willie Mays	130	1962
Willie Mays	129	1961
Barry Bonds	129	1993
Barry Bonds	129	2000
Barry Bonds	129	2001
Willie Mays	125	1959
Barry Bonds	123	1997
Barry Bonds	122	1996
Willie Mays	121	1958
Willie Mays	121	1964

Hits

Willie Mays	208	1958
Rich Aurilia	206	2001
Barry Bonds	200	1970
Will Clark	196	1989
Jeff Kent	196	2000
Jeff Kent	195	2002
Orlando Cepeda	192	1959
Brett Butler	192	1990
Orlando Cepeda	191	1962
Willie Mays	190	1960
Willie Mays	189	1962
Orlando Cepeda	188	1958

Doubles

Jeff Kent	49	2001
Jack Clark	46	1978
Barry Bonds	44	1998
Willie Mays	43	1959
Jeff Kent	42	2000
Jeff Kent	41	2002
Will Clark	40	1992
Jeff Kent	40	1999
Willie McCovey	39	1970
Orlando Cepeda	38	1958
Will Clark	38	1989
Barry Bonds	38	1993
Jeff Kent	38	1997

Triples

Willie Mays	12	1960
Willie Mays	11	1958
Larry Herndon	11	1980
Robby Thompson	11	1989
Bobby Bonds	10	1970
Garry Maddox	10	1973
Gary Matthews	10	1973
Von Joshua	10	1975
Derrel Thomas	10	1977
Felipe Alou	9	1963
Willie Mays	9	1964
Hal Lanier	9	1965
Derrel Thomas	9	1975
Larry Herndon	9	1978
Brett Butler	9	1988
Brett Butler	9	1990
Darren Lewis	9	1994

Home Runs

Barry Bonds	73	2001
Willie Mays	52	1965
Willie Mays	49	1962
Barry Bonds	49	2000
Willie Mays	47	1964
Kevin Mitchell	47	1989
Orlando Cepeda	46	1961
Barry Bonds	46	1993
Barry Bonds	46	2002
Willie McCovey	45	1969
Willie McCovey	44	1963
Matt Williams	43	1994

RBI

Orlando Cepeda	142	1961
Willie Mays	141	1962
Barry Bonds	137	2001
Barry Bonds	129	1996
Jeff Kent	128	1998
Willie McCovey	126	1969
Willie McCovey	126	1970
Kevin Mitchell	125	1989
Jeff Kent	125	2000
Willie Mays	123	1961
Barry Bonds	123	1993
Matt Williams	122	1990
Barry Bonds	122	1998

Extra-Base Hits

Barry Bonds	107	2001
Willie Mays	90	1962
Barry Bonds	88	1993
Barry Bonds	88	1998
Willie Mays	82	1959
Barry Bonds	81	2000
Jeff Kent	81	2000
Jeff Kent	81	2002
Jack Clark	79	1978
Rich Aurilia	79	2001
Barry Bonds	79	2002
Orlando Cepeda	78	1961

Total Bases

Barry Bonds	411	2001
Willie Mays	382	1962
Barry Bonds	365	1993
Rich Aurilia	364	2001
Willie Mays	360	1965
Orlando Cepeda	357	1962
Orlando Cepeda	356	1961
Jeff Kent	352	2002

Willie Mays	351	1964
Jeff Kent	350	2000
Willie Mays	350	1958
Willie Mays	347	1963

Walks

Barry Bonds	198	2002
Barry Bonds	177	2001
Barry Bonds	151	1996
Barry Bonds	145	1997
Willie McCovey	137	1970
Barry Bonds	130	1998
Barry Bonds	126	1993
Willie McCovey	121	1969
Barry Bonds	120	1995
Barry Bonds	117	2000
Willie Mays	112	1971
Dick Dietz	109	1970

Strikeouts

Bobby Bonds	189	1970
Bobby Bonds	187	1969
Bobby Bonds	148	1973
Dave Kingman	140	1972
Matt Willaims	138	1990
Bobby Bonds	137	1971
Bobby Bonds	137	1972
Bobby Bonds	134	1974
Robby Thompson	133	1989
Jeff Kent	133	1997
Will Clark	129	1988
J.T. Snow	129	2000

Stolen Bases

Bill North	58	1979
Brett Butler	51	1990
Bobby Bonds	48	1970
Darren Lewis	46	1993
Bobby Bonds	45	1969
Bill North	45	1980
Bobby Bonds	44	1972
Bobby Bonds	43	1973
Brett Butler	43	1988
Bobby Bonds	41	1974
Barry Bonds	40	1996
Johnnie LeMaster	39	1983

Batting Average

Barry Bonds	.370	2002
Willie Mays	.347	1958
Barry Bonds	.336	1993
Jeff Kent	.334	2000

Will Clark	.333	1989		Barry Bonds	.440	2000
Barry Bonds	.328	2001		Barry Bonds	.438	1998
Rich Aurilia	.324	2001		Barry Bonds	.431	1995
Willie McCovey	.320	1969		Dick Dietz	.426	1970
Willie Mays	.319	1960		Barry Bonds	.426	1994
Garry Maddox	.319	1973				
Von Joshua	.318	1975		**Slugging Percentage**		
Orlando Cepeda	.317	1959		Barry Bonds	.863	2001
Willie Mays	.317	1965		Barry Bonds	.799	2002
Chris Brown	.317	1986		Barry Bonds	.688	2000
				Barry Bonds	.677	1993
On-Base Percentage				Willie McCovey	.656	1969
Barry Bonds	.582	2002		Barry Bonds	.647	1994
Barry Bonds	.515	2001		Willie Mays	.645	1965
Barry Bonds	.461	1996		Kevin Mitchell	.635	1989
Barry Bonds	.458	1993		Barry Bonds	.617	1999
Willie McCovey	.453	1969		Willie Mays	.615	1962
Barry Bonds	.446	1997		Barry Bonds	.615	1996
Willie McCovey	.444	1970		Willie McCovey	.612	1970

SAN FRANCISCO GIANTS SEASON PITCHING LEADERS

Games				Jack Sanford	38	1962
Julian Tavarez	89	1997		Juan Marichal	38	1968
Mike Jackson	81	1993		Gaylord Perry	38	1968
Felix Rodriguez	80	2001		Jim Barr	38	1977
Tim Worrell	80	2002		Juan Marichal	37	1965
Robb Nen	79	2001		Gaylord Perry	37	1967
Greg Minton	78	1982		Juan Marichal	37	1971
Mark Dewey	78	1996		Gaylord Perry	37	1971
Robb Nen	78	1998		Jim Barr	37	1976
Gary Lavelle	77	1984		Ed Halicki	37	1977
Mark Davis	77	1985				
Rod Beck	76	1993		**Complete Games**		
Felix Rodriguez	76	2000		Juan Marichal	30	1968
				Juan Marichal	27	1969
Games Started				Gaylord Perry	26	1969
Jack Sanford	42	1963		Juan Marichal	25	1966
Gaylord Perry	41	1970		Juan Marichal	24	1965
Juan Marichal	40	1963		Gaylord Perry	23	1970
Billy O'Dell	39	1962		Juan Marichal	22	1964
Gaylord Perry	39	1969		Bill O'Dell	20	1962
Ron Bryant	39	1973		Gaylord Perry	19	1968
Johnny Antonelli	38	1959		Juan Marichal	18	1963

Juan Marichal	18	1967		Shawn Estes	108	2000
Gaylord Perry	18	1967		John D'Acquisto	102	1976
Juan Marichal	18	1971		Shawn Estes	100	1997
				Jack Sanford	99	1960

Shutouts

Juan Marichal	10	1965		**Strikeouts**		
Juan Marichal	8	1969		Juan Marichal	248	1963
Jack Sanford	6	1960		Juan Marichal	240	1965
Ray Sadecki	6	1968		Gaylord Perry	233	1969
John Montefusco	6	1976		Gaylord Perry	230	1967
Bob Knepper	6	1978		Juan Marichal	222	1966
Juan Marichal	5	1963		Juan Marichal	218	1968
Mike McCormick	5	1967		John Montefusco	215	1975
Juan Marichal	5	1968		Gaylord Perry	214	1970
Gaylord Perry	5	1970		Juan Marichal	206	1964
Jim Barr	5	1974		Ray Sadecki	206	1968
Johnny Antonelli	4	1959		Gaylord Perry	201	1966
Sam Jones	4	1959		Bud Black	201	1991
Mike McCormick	4	1960				
Juan Marichal	4	1964		**Wins**		
Bobby Bolin	4	1966		Juan Marichal	26	1968
Juan Marichal	4	1966		Juan Marichal	25	1963
Juan Marichal	4	1971		Juan Marichal	25	1966
Ron Bryant	4	1972		Jack Sanford	24	1962
John Montefusco	4	1975		Ron Bryant	24	1973
Ed Halicki	4	1976		Gaylord Perry	23	1970
Vida Blue	4	1978		Juan Marichal	22	1965
Ed Halicki	4	1978		Mike McCormick	22	1967
				John Burkett	22	1993
Innings Pitched				Sam Jones	21	1959
Gaylord Perry	328.2	1970		Juan Marichal	21	1964
Juan Marichal	326.0	1968		Gaylord Perry	21	1966
Gaylord Perry	325.1	1969		Juan Marichal	21	1969
Juan Marichal	321.1	1963		Bill Swift	21	1993
Juan Marichal	307.1	1966				
Juan Marichal	299.2	1969		**Losses**		
Juan Marichal	295.1	1965		Ray Sadecki	18	1968
Gaylord Perry	293.0	1967		Gaylord Perry	17	1967
Gaylord Perry	291.0	1968		Jim Barr	17	1973
Jack Sanford	284.1	1963		Mark Davis	17	1984
Johnny Antonelli	282.0	1959		Dave LaPoint	17	1985
Billy O'Dell	280.2	1962		Mike McCormick	16	1959
				Mike McCormick	16	1961
Walks				Juan Marichal	16	1972
Russ Ortiz	125	1999		Jim Barr	16	1977
John D'Acquisto	124	1974		Bob Knepper	16	1980
Ron Bryant	115	1973		Bud Black	16	1991
Shawn Estes	112	1999		Livan Hernandez	16	2002
Russ Ortiz	112	2000				
Pete Falcone	111	1975		**Winning Percentage (15 decisions)**		
Vida Blue	111	1979		Juan Marichal	.806	1966
Sam Jones	109	1959		Shawn Estes	.792	1997

Jack Sanford	.774	1962
John Burkett	.759	1993
Juan Marichal	.758	1963
Juan Marichal	.743	1968
Stu Miller	.737	1961
Mike Caldwell	.737	1974
Scott Garrelts	.737	1989
Billy Pierce	.727	1962
Juan Marichal	.724	1964
Gaylord Perry	.724	1966
Bill Swift	.724	1993

Saves

Rod Beck	48	1993
Robb Nen	45	2001
Robb Nen	43	2002
Robb Nen	41	2000
Robb Nen	40	1998
Rod Beck	37	1997
Robb Nen	37	1999
Rod Beck	35	1996
Rod Beck	33	1995
Greg Minton	30	1982
Rod Beck	28	1994
Dave Righetti	24	1991
Greg Minton	22	1983
Frank Linzy	21	1965
Greg Minton	21	1981

ERA (starters)

Bobby Bolin	1.99	1968
Bill Swift	2.08	1992
Juan Marichal	2.10	1969
Juan Marichal	2.13	1965
Juan Marichal	2.23	1966
Atlee Hammaker	2.25	1983
Scott Garrelts	2.28	1989

Juan Marichal	2.41	1963
Juan Marichal	2.43	1968
Gaylord Perry	2.44	1968
Vida Blue	2.45	1981
Don Robinson	2.45	1988

ERA (relievers)

Bill Henry	1.43	1965
Mike Jackson	1.49	1994
Don McMahon	1.50	1973
Robb Nen	1.50	2000
Frank Linzy	1.51	1967
Robb Nen	1.52	1998
Jeff Brantley	1.56	1990
Felix Rodriguez	1.68	2001
Al Holland	1.76	1980
Rod Beck	1.76	1992
Greg Minton	1.80	1979
Greg Minton	1.83	1982
Bill Henry	2.05	1967
Gary Lavelle	2.06	1977

Opponent Batting Average
(1 inning pitched per team game)

Bobby Bolin	.200	1968
Juan Marichal	.202	1966
Juan Marichal	.205	1965
Bobby Bolin	.211	1966
Scott Garrelts	.212	1989
Bobby Bolin	.214	1965
Gaylord Perry	.214	1967
Juan Marichal	.216	1963
Vida Blue	.217	1981
Bobby Bolin	.220	1964
Ed Halicki	.221	1978
Gaylord Perry	.222	1968
Juan Marichal	.222	1969

SAN FRANCISCO GIANTS CAREER BATTING LEADERS

Games

Willie McCovey	2,256	1959-73, 1977-80
Willie Mays	2,095	1958-72
Jim Davenport	1,501	1958-70
Barry Bonds	1,429	1993-2002
Robby Thompson	1,304	1986-96
Will Clark	1,160	1986-93
Matt Williams	1,120	1987-96
Orlando Cepeda	1,114	1958-66
Chris Speier	1,114	1971-77, 1987-89
Hal Lanier	1,101	1964-71
Darrell Evans	1,094	1976-83
Tito Fuentes	1,050	1965-67, 1969-74

At-Bats

Willie Mays	7,578	1958-72
Willie McCovey	7,214	1959-73, 1977-80
Barry Bonds	4,751	1993-2002
Robby Thompson	4,612	1986-96
Jim Davenport	4,427	1958-70
Will Clark	4,269	1986-93
Orlando Cepeda	4,178	1958-66
Matt Williams	4,139	1987-96
Bobby Bonds	4,047	1968-74
Tito Fuentes	3,823	1965-67, 1969-74
Jack Clark	3,731	1975-84
Chris Speier	3,730	1971-77, 1987-89

Runs

Willie Mays	1,480	1958-72
Barry Bonds	1,158	1993-2002
Willie McCovey	1,113	1959-73, 1977-80
Bobby Bonds	765	1968-74
Will Clark	687	1986-93
Robby Thompson	671	1986-96
Orlando Cepeda	652	1958-66
Jack Clark	597	1975-84
Matt Williams	594	1987-96
Jeff Kent	570	1997-2002
Jim Davenport	552	1958-70
Darrell Evans	534	1976-83

Hits

Willie Mays	2,284	1958-72
Willie McCovey	1,974	1959-73, 1977-80
Barry Bonds	1,478	1993-2002
Orlando Cepeda	1,286	1958-66

Will Clark	1,278	1986-93
Robby Thompson	1,187	1986-96
Jim Davenport	1,142	1958-70
Bobby Bonds	1,106	1968-74
Matt Williams	1,092	1987-96
Jack Clark	1,034	1975-84
Jeff Kent	1,021	1997-2002
Tito Fuentes	1,000	1965-67, 1969-74

Doubles

Willie Mays	376	1958-72
Willie McCovey	308	1959-73, 1977-80
Barry Bonds	294	1993-2002
Will Clark	249	1986-93
Jeff Kent	247	1997-2002
Robby Thompson	238	1986-96
Orlando Cepeda	226	1958-66
Jack Clark	197	1975-84
Bobby Bonds	188	1968-74
Matt Williams	179	1987-96
Jim Davenport	177	1958-70
Chris Speier	153	1971-77, 1987-89

Triples

Willie Mays	76	1958-72
Willie McCovey	45	1959-73, 1977-80
Bobby Bonds	42	1968-74
Larry Herndon	39	1976-81
Robby Thompson	39	1986-96
Jim Davenport	37	1958-70
Will Clark	37	1986-93
Barry Bonds	37	1993-2002
Jose Uribe	34	1985-92
Tito Fuentes	33	1965-67, 1969-74
Jack Clark	30	1975-84
Jim Ray Hart	27	1963-73
Chris Speier	27	1971-77, 1987-89

Home Runs

Willie McCovey	469	1959-73, 1977-80
Willie Mays	459	1958-72
Barry Bonds	437	1993-2002
Matt Williams	247	1987-96
Orlando Cepeda	226	1958-66
Bobby Bonds	186	1968-74
Will Clark	176	1986-93
Jeff Kent	175	1997-2002

Jack Clark	163	1975-84
Jim Ray Hart	157	1963-73
Kevin Mitchell	143	1987-91
Darrell Evans	142	1976-83

RBI

Willie McCovey	1,388	1959-73, 1977-80
Willie Mays	1,350	1958-72
Barry Bonds	1,096	1993-2002
Orlando Cepeda	767	1958-66
Matt Williams	732	1987-96
Will Clark	709	1986-93
Jeff Kent	689	1997-2002
Jack Clark	595	1975-84
Bobby Bonds	552	1968-74
Jim Ray Hart	526	1963-73
Darrell Evans	525	1976-83
J.T. Snow	464	1997-2002

Extra-Base Hits

Willie Mays	911	1958-72
Willie McCovey	822	1959-73, 1977-80
Barry Bonds	768	1993-2002
Jim Davenport	522	1958-70
Orlando Cepeda	474	1958-66
Will Clark	462	1986-93
Matt Williams	451	1987-96
Jeff Kent	444	1997-2002
Robby Thompson	396	1986-96
Darrell Evans	320	1976-83
Jim Ray Hart	319	1963-73

Total Bases

Willie Mays	4,189	1958-72
Willie McCovey	3,779	1959-73, 1977-80
Barry Bonds	3,157	1993-2002
Orlando Cepeda	2,234	1958-66
Will Clark	2,129	1986-93
Matt Williams	2,062	1987-96
Bobby Bonds	1,936	1968-74
Robby Thompson	1,860	1986-96
Jeff Kent	1,837	1997-2002
Jack Clark	1,780	1975-84
Jim Ray Hart	1,625	1963-73
Darrell Evans	1,575	1976-83

Walks

Barry Bonds	1,311	1993-2002
Willie McCovey	1,168	1959-73, 1977-80
Willie Mays	1,032	1958-72
Darrell Evans	605	1976-83
Will Clark	506	1986-93

Bobby Bonds	500	1968-74
Jack Clark	497	1975-84
Chris Speier	466	1971-77, 1987-89
Robby Thompson	439	1986-96
J.T. Snow	420	1997-2002
Jim Davenport	382	1958-70
Jeff Kent	364	1997-2002

Strikeouts

Willie McCovey	1,351	1959-73, 1977-80
Willie Mays	1,115	1958-72
Bobby Bonds	1,016	1968-74
Robby Thompson	987	1986-96
Matt Williams	872	1987-96
Will Clark	744	1986-93
Barry Bonds	739	1993-2002
Jim Davenport	673	1958-70
Jeff Kent	659	1997-2002
Orlando Cepeda	636	1958-66
J.T. Snow	629	1997-2002
Jeffrey Leonard	586	1981-88

Stolen Bases

Bobby Bonds	263	1968-74
Barry Bonds	242	1993-2002
Willie Mays	215	1958-72
Darren Lewis	138	1991-95
Bill North	129	1979-81
Brett Butler	125	1988-90
Jeffrey Leonard	115	1981-88
Robby Thompson	103	1986-96
Chili Davis	95	1981-87
Dan Gladden	94	1983-86
Johnnie LeMaster	93	1975-85
Orlando Cepeda	92	1958-66

Batting Average (2,000 plate appearances)

Barry Bonds	.311	1993-2002
Orlando Cepeda	.308	1958-66
Willie Mays	.301	1958-72
Will Clark	.299	1986-93
Jeff Kent	.297	1997-2002
Brett Butler	.293	1988-90
Gary Matthews	.287	1972-76
Felipe Alou	.286	1958-63
Jim Ray Hart	.282	1963-73
Harvey Kuenn	.280	1961-65
Marvin Benard	.280	1995-99
Jesus Alou	.279	1963-68
Rich Aurilia	.279	1995-2002

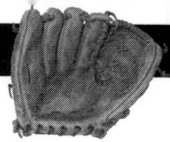

On-Base Percentage (2,000 plate appearances)			Slugging Percentage (2,000 plate appearances)		
Barry Bonds	.461	1993-2002	Barry Bonds	.664	1993-20029
Willie Mays	.384	1958-72	Willie Mays	.553	1958-72
Brett Butler	.381	1988-90	Kevin Mitchell	.536	1987-91
Willie McCovey	.377	1959-73, 1977-80	Orlando Cepeda	.535	1958-66
Will Clark	.373	1986-93	Jeff Kent	.535	1997-2002
Jeff Kent	.368	1997-2002	Willie McCovey	.524	1959-73, 1977-80
Gary Mathews	.367	1972-76	Will Clark	.499	1986-93
J.T. Snow	.363	1997-2002	Matt Williams	.498	1987-96
Jack Clark	.359	1975-84	Bobby Bonds	.478	1968-74
Darrell Evans	.358	1976-83	Jack Clark	.477	1975-84
Kevin Mitchell	.356	1987-91	Jim Ray Hart	.474	1963-73
Bobby Bonds	.356	1968-74	Felipe Alou	.466	1958-63

SAN FRANCISCO GIANTS CAREER PITCHING LEADERS

Games					
Gary Lavelle	647	1974-84	Jack Sanford	54	1959-65
Greg Minton	552	1975-87	Billy O'Dell	41	1960-64
Randy Moffitt	459	1972-81	Bob Knepper	37	1976-80, 1989-90
Juan Marichal	458	1960-73	Ed Halicki	36	1974-80
Rod Beck	416	1991-97	Johnny Antonelli	31	1958-60
Jim Barr	394	1971-78, 1982-83	Sam Jones	31	1959-61
Gaylord Perry	367	1962-71	Vida Blue	31	1978-81, 1985-86
Robb Nen	365	1998-2002	Ray Sadecki	30	1966-69
Scott Garrelts	352	1982-91	John Montefusco	30	1974-80
Bobby Bolin	345	1961-69			
Mike McCormick	330	1958-62, 1967-70	**Shutouts**		
Frank Linzy	308	1963, 1965-70	Juan Marichal	52	1960-73
			Gaylord Perry	21	1962-71
Games Started			Jim Barr	20	1971-78, 1982-83
Juan Marichal	446	1960-73	Mike McCormick	19	1958-62, 1967-70
Gaylord Perry	283	1962-71	Ed Halicki	13	1974-80
Mike McCormick	245	1958-62, 1967-70	Ray Sadecki	12	1966-69
Jim Barr	220	1971-78, 1982-83	Bob Kenpper	12	1976-80, 1989-90
Jack Sanford	211	1959-65	John Montefusco	11	1974-80
Kirk Rueter	199	1996-2002	Bobby Bolin	10	1961-69
Mike Krukow	182	1983-89	Jack Sanford	9	1959-65
John Montefusco	175	1974-80	Sam Jones	7	1959-61
Vida Blue	166	1978-81, 1985-86	Billy O'Dell	7	1960-64
Shawn Estes	160	1995-2001	Vida Blue	7	1978-81, 1985-86
John Burkett	157	1987, 1990-94			
Ed Halicki	151	1974-80	**Innings Pitched**		
			Juan Marichal	3,444.0	1960-73
Complete Games			Gaylord Perry	2,294.2	1962-71
Juan Marichal	244	1960-73	Jim Barr	1,800.1	1971-78, 1982-83
Gaylord Perry	125	1962-71	Mike McCormick	1,741.1	1958-62, 1967-70
Mike McCormick	77	1958-62, 1967-70	Jack Sanford	1,405.2	1959-65
Jim Barr	59	1971-78, 1982-83	Bobby Bolin	1,282.1	1961-69
			John Montefusco	1,182.2	1974-80

Mike Krukow	1,154.0	1983-89
Vida Blue	1,131.1	1978-81, 1985-86
Ed Halicki	1,027.2	1974-80
Atlee Hammaker	1,008.0	1982-90
John Burkett	997.1	1987, 1990-94

Walks

Juan Marichal	690	1960-73
Gaylord Perry	581	1962-71
Mike McCormick	574	1958-62, 1967-70
Shawn Estes	521	1995-2001
Jack Sanford	491	1959-65
Bobby Bolin	477	1961-69
Russ Ortiz	468	1998-2002
Vida Blue	453	1978-81, 1985-86
Scott Garrelts	413	1982-91
Jim Barr	391	1971-78, 1982-83
John Montefusco	383	1974-80
Gary Lavelle	382	1974-84

Strikeouts

Juan Marichal	2,281	1960-73
Gaylord Perry	1,606	1962-71
Bobby Bolin	977	1961-69
Mike McCormick	976	1958-62, 1967-70
John Montefusco	869	1974-80
Mike Krukow	802	1983-89
Shawn Estes	795	1995-2001
Jack Sanford	781	1959-65
Russ Ortiz	712	1998-2002
Vida Blue	704	1978-81, 1985-86
Scott Garrelts	703	1982-91
Gary Lavelle	696	1974-84

Wins

Juan Marichal	238	1960-73
Gaylord Perry	134	1962-71
Mike McCormick	104	1958-62, 1967-70
Jim Barr	90	1971-78, 1982-83
Jack Sanford	89	1959-65
Kirk Rueter	84	1996-2002
Bobby Bolin	73	1961-69
Gary Lavelle	73	1974-84
Vida Blue	72	1978-81, 1985-86
Scott Garrelts	69	1982-91
John Burkett	67	1987, 1990-94
Russ Ortiz	67	1998-2002

Losses

Juan Marichal	140	1960-73
Gaylord Perry	109	1962-71
Jim Barr	96	1971-78, 1982-83

Mike McCormick	94	1958-62, 1967-70
Jack Sanford	67	1959-65
Gary Lavelle	67	1974-84
Ed Halicki	65	1974-80
John Montefusco	62	1974-80
Atlee Hammaker	59	1982-90
Vida Blue	58	1978-81, 1985-86
Bobby Bolin	56	1961-69
Mike Krukow	56	1983-89
Kirk Rueter	56	1996-2002

Winning Percentage (75 decisions)

Juan Marichal	.630	1960-73
John Burkett	.615	1987, 1990-94
Russ Ortiz	.604	1998-2002
Kirk Rueter	.600	1996-2002
Jack Sanford	.571	1959-65
Bobby Bolin	.566	1961-69
Scott Garrelts	.566	1982-91
Shawn Estes	.561	1995-2001
Don Robinson	.560	1987-91
Sam Jones	.560	1959-61
Vida Blue	.554	1978-81, 1985-86
Kelly Downs	.553	1986-92

Saves

Robb Nen	206	1998-2002
Rod Beck	199	1991-97
Gary Lavelle	127	1974-84
Greg Minton	125	1975-87
Randy Moffitt	83	1972-81
Frank Linzy	78	1963, 1965-70
Scott Garrelts	48	1982-91
Stu Miller	46	1958-62
Jeff Brantley	42	1988-93
Don McMahon	36	1969-74
Craig Lefferts	35	1987-89
Steve Bedrosian	34	1989-90

ERA (starters)

Bill Swift	2.70	1992-94
Juan Marichal	2.76	1960-73
Ray Sadecki	2.76	1966-69
Gaylord Perry	2.96	1962-71
Bobby Bolin	3.26	1961-69
Scott Garrelts	3.29	1982-91
Rick Reuschel	3.29	1987-91
Sam Jones	3.30	1959-61
Jim Barr	3.41	1971-78, 1982-83
Trevor Wilson	3.42	1988-95
Mike McCormick	3.44	1958-62, 1967-70
Vida Blue	3.51	1978-81, 1985-86

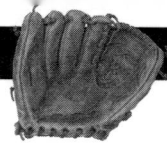

ERA (relievers)				Opponent Batting Average (750 innings pitched)		
Robb Nen	2.43	1998-2002		Bobby Bolin	.227	1961-69
Al Holland	2.56	1979-82		Scott Garrelts	.232	1982-91
Frank Linzy	2.71	1963, 1965-70		Juan Marichal	.236	1960-73
Gary Lavelle	2.82	1974-84		Gaylord Perry	.238	1962-71
Tim Worrell	2.87	2001-02		Jack Sanford	.242	1959-65
Craig Lefferts	2.88	1987-89		Kelly Downs	.245	1986-92
Jeff Johnstone	2.92	1997-99		Ed Halicki	.246	1974-80
Rod Beck	2.97	1991-97		Vida Blue	.246	1978-81, 1985-86
Mike Jackson	2.99	1992-94		Gary Lavelle	.249	1974-84
Felix Rodriguez	3.00	1999-2002		Mike McCormick	.249	1958-62, 1967-70
Stu Miller	3.07	1958-62		Ron Bryant	.252	1967, 1969-74
Bill Henry	3.07	1965-68		John Montefusco	.253	1974-80
				Atlee Hammaker	.253	1982-90

NEW YORK/SAN FRANCISCO GIANTS SEASON GRAND SLAM LEADERS

George Kelly	3	1921		Willie McCovey	3	1967
Sid Gordon	3	1948		Jeff Kent	3	1997
Wes Westrum	3	1951				

NEW YORK/SAN FRANCISCO GIANTS CAREER GRAND SLAM LEADERS

Willie McCovey	16	1959-73, 1977-80		Jeff Kent	7	1997-2002
Barry Bonds	9	1993-2002		Babe Young	5	1936, 1939-47
Willie Mays	8	1951-52, 1954-72		Wes Westrum	5	1947-47
George Kelly	7	1915-17, 1919-26		Jack Clark	5	1975-84
Mel Ott	7	1926-47		Matt Williams	5	1987-96

NEW YORK/SAN FRANCISCO GIANTS SEASON PINCH HIT LEADERS

Sam Leslie	22	1932		Bill Taylor	15	1955
Ken Oberkfell	18	1989		Joel Youngblood	15	1988
Candy Maldonado	17	1986		Marvin Benard	15	1997
Joel Youngblood	16	1986		Felipe Crespo	15	2000
Dusty Rhodes	15	1954		Duane Kuiper	14	1982

NEW YORK/SAN FRANCISCO GIANTS CAREER PINCH HIT LEADERS

Joel Youngblood	58	1983-88	Willie McCovey	51	1959-73, 1977-80
Sam Leslie	57	1929-33, 1936-38	Chris Arnold	41	1971-76
Dusty Rhodes	55	1952-57, 1959			

NEW YORK/SAN FRANCISCO GIANTS HOME RUN RECORDS BY POSITION

Position	New York	San Francisco
Catcher	Walker Cooper (35), 1947	Tom Haller (27), 1966
First Base	Johnny Mize (51), 1947	Orlando Cepeda (46), 1961
Second Base	Rogers Hornsby (26), 1927	Jeff Kent (37), 2002
Shortstop	Alvin Dark (23), 1953	Rich Aurilia (37), 2001
Third Base	Mel Ott (36), 1938	Matt Williams (43), 1994
Left Field	Monte Irvin (24), 1951	Barry Bonds (73), 2001
Center Field	Willie Mays (51), 1955	Willie Mays (52), 1965
Right Field	Mel Ott (42), 1929	Bobby Bonds (39), 1973

NEW YORK/SAN FRANCISCO GIANTS RBI RECORDS BY POSITION

Position	New York	San Francisco
Catcher	Walker Cooper (122), 1947	Dick Dietz (107), 1970
First Base	Johnny Mize (138), 1947	Orlando Cepeda (142), 1961
Second Base	Rogers Hornsby (125), 1927	Jeff Kent (128), 1998
Shortstop	Travis Jackson (101), 1934	Rich Aurilia (97), 2001
Third Base	Mel Ott (116), 1938	Matt Williams (122), 1990
Left Field	Irish Meusel (132), 1922	Barry Bonds (137), 2001
Center Field	Willie Mays (127), 1955	Willie Mays (141), 1962
Right Field	Mel Ott (151), 1929	Jack Clark (103), 1982

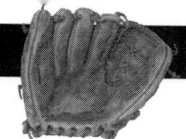

NEW YORK/SAN FRANCISCO GIANTS WITH 10-PLUS DOUBLES, TRIPLES, HOME RUNS AND STOLEN BASES IN A SEASON

Player	Year	2B	3B	HR	SB
Roger Connor	1887	26	22	17	43
Mike Tiernan	1887	13	12	10	28
Roger Connor	1888	15	17	14	27
Roger Connor	1889	32	17	13	21
Mike Tiernan	1889	23	14	10	33
Mike Tiernan	1890	25	21	13	56
Mike Tiernan	1891	30	12	16	53
George Davis	1893	22	27	11	37
Mike Tiernan	1893	19	12	15	26
George Davis	1897	31	10	10	65
Larry Doyle	1911	25	25	13	38
Fred Merkle	1911	24	10	12	49
Irish Meusel	1922	28	17	16	12
Frankie Frisch	1923	32	10	12	29
Ross Youngs	1924	33	12	10	11
Travis Jackson	1929	21	12	21	10
Monte Irvin	1951	19	11	24	12
Willie Mays	1955	18	13	51	24
Willie Mays	1957	26	20	35	38
Willie Mays	1958	33	11	29	31
Willie Kirkland	1960	21	10	21	12
Willie Mays	1960	29	12	29	25
Bobby Bonds	1970	36	10	26	48
Garry Maddox	1973	30	10	11	24
Gary Matthews	1973	22	10	12	17
Robby Thompson	1989	26	11	13	12

Note: From 1886-97 a base runner was credited with a stolen base for advancing a base on a hit or an out made by a teammate.

NEW YORK/SAN FRANCISCO GIANTS NATIONAL LEAGUE BATTING LEADERS

Batting Average
1885 — Roger Connor (.371)
1890 — Jack Glasscock (.336)
1915 — Larry Doyle (.320)
1930 — Bill Terry (.401)
1954 — Willie Mays (.345)
2002 — Barry Bonds (.370)

Runs
1889 — Mike Tiernan (147)
1904 — George Browne (99)
1905 — Mike Donlin (124)
1907 — Spike Shannon (104)
1908 — Fred Tenney (101)
1914 — George Burns (100)
1916 — George Burns (105)
1917 — George Burns (103)
1919 — George Burns (86)
1920 — George Burns (115)
1923 — Ross Youngs (121)
1924 — Frankie Frisch (121)*
1927 — Rogers Hornsby (133)*
1931 — Bill Terry (121)*
1938 — Mel Ott (116)
1942 — Mel Ott (118)
1947 — Johnny Mize (137)
1958 — Willie Mays (121)
1961 — Willie Mays (129)
1969 — Bobby Bonds (120)*
1973 — Bobby Bonds (131)
1988 — Brett Butler (109)
1989 — Will Clark (104)*

Hits
1885 — Roger Connor (169)
1890 — Jack Glasscock (172)*
1909 — Larry Doyle (172)
1915 — Larry Doyle (189)
1923 — Frankie Frisch (223)
1928 — Fred Lindstrom (231)
1930 — Bill Terry (254)
1954 — Don Mueller (212)
1960 — Willie Mays (190)
1990 — Brett Butler (192)*
2001 — Rich Aurilia (206)

Doubles
1903 — Sam Mertes (32)*
1915 — Larry Doyle (40)
1919 — Ross Youngs (31)
1951 — Alvin Dark (41)
1958 — Orlando Cepeda (38)

Triples
1884 — Buck Ewing (20)
1885 — Jim O'Rourke (16)
1886 — Roger Connor (20)
1896 — George Van Haltren (21)*
1911 — Larry Doyle (25)
1931 — Bill Terry (20)
1952 — Bobby Thomson (14)
1954 — Willie Mays (13)
1955 — Willie Mays (13)*
1957 — Willie Mays (20)
1989 — Robby Thompson (11)
1994 — Darren Lewis (9)*

Home Runs
1883 — Buck Ewing (10)
1890 — Mike Tiernan (13)*
1891 — Mike Tiernan (16)*
1909 — Red Murray (7)
1916 — Dave Robertson (12)*
1917 — Dave Robertson (12)*
1921 — George Kelly (23)
1932 — Mel Ott (38)*
1934 — Mel Ott (35)*
1936 — Mel Ott (33)
1937 — Mel Ott (31)*
1938 — Mel Ott (36)
1942 — Mel Ott (30)
1947 — Johnny Mize (51)*
1948 — Johnny Mize (40)*
1955 — Willie Mays (51)
1961 — Orlando Cepeda (46)
1962 — Willie Mays (49)
1963 — Willie McCovey (44)*
1964 — Willie Mays (47)
1965 — Willie Mays (52)
1968 — Willie McCovey (36)
1969 — Willie McCovey (45)

1989 — Kevin Mitchell (47)
1993 — Barry Bonds (46)
1994 — Matt Williams (43)
2001 — Barry Bonds (73)

RBI
1889 — Roger Connor (130)
1897 — George Davis (136)
1903 — Sam Mertes (104)
1904 — Bill Dahlen (80)
1917 — Heinie Zimmerman (102)
1920 — George Kelly (94)*
1923 — Irish Meusel (125)
1924 — George Kelly (136)
1934 — Mel Ott (135)
1942 — Johnny Mize (110)
1947 — Johnny Mize (138)
1951 — Monte Irvin (121)
1961 — Orlando Cepeda (142)
1968 — Willie McCovey (105)
1969 — Willie McCovey (126)
1988 — Will Clark (109)
1989 — Kevin Mitchell (125)
1990 — Matt Williams (122)
1993 — Barry Bonds (123)

Stolen Bases
1887 — John Montgomery Ward (111)
1900 — George Van Haltren (45)*
1905 — Art Devlin (59)*
1914 — George Burns (62)
1919 — George Burns (40)
1921 — Frankie Frisch (49)
1956 — Willie Mays (40)
1957 — Willie Mays (38)
1958 — Willie Mays (31)
1959 — Willie Mays (27)

* denotes tied for N.L. lead.

NEW YORK/SAN FRANCISCO GIANTS NATIONAL LEAGUE PITCHING LEADERS

Games
1886 — Tim Keefe (64)
1893 — Amos Rusie (56)
1900 — Bill Carrick (45)
1901 — Dummy Taylor (45)*
1903 — Joe McGinnity (55)
1904 — Joe McGinnity (51)
1905 — Joe McGinnity (46)*
1908 — Christy Mathewson (56)
1923 — Claude Jonnard, Rosy Ryan (45)*
1926 — Jack Scott (50)
1938 — Dick Coffman (51)*
1942 — Ace Adams (61)
1943 — Ace Adams (70)
1944 — Ace Adams (65)
1946 — Ken Trinkle (48)
1947 — Ken Trinkle (62)
1952 — Hoyt Wilhelm (71)
1953 — Hoyt Wilhelm (68)
1993 — Mike Jackson (81)
1997 — Julian Tavarez (89)

Innings Pitched
1886 — Tim Keefe (535.0)
1893 — Amos Rusie (482.0)
1903 — Joe McGinnity (434.0)
1904 — Joe McGinnity (408.0)
1906 — Joe McGinnity (339.2)
1908 — Christy Mathewson (390.2)
1912 — Christy Mathewson (310.0)
1933 — Carl Hubbell (308.2)
1944 — Bill Voiselle (312.2)
1963 — Juan Marichal (321.1)
1968 — Juan Marichal (326.0)
1969 — Gaylord Perry (325.1)
1970 — Gaylord Perry (328.2)

Complete Games
1886 — Tim Keefe (62)
1893 — Amos Rusie (50)
1899 — Bill Carrick (40)*
1900 — Pink Hawley (34)
1903 — Joe McGinnity (44)
1908 — Christy Mathewson (34)
1910 — Christy Mathewson (27)*
1928 — Larry Benton (28)*
1934 — Carl Hubbell (25)

1964 — Juan Marichal (22)
1968 — Juan Marichal (30)

Shutouts
1888 — Tim Keefe (8)*
1891 — Amos Rusie (6)
1893 — Amos Rusie (4)*
1894 — Amos Rusie (3)*
1895 — Amos Rusie (4)*
1902 — Christy Mathewson (8)*
1904 — Joe McGinnity (9)
1905 — Christy Mathewson (8)
1907 — Christy Mathewson (8)*
1908 — Christy Mathewson (11)
1914 — Jeff Tesreau (8)
1921 — Phil Douglas (3)
1931 — Bill Walker (6)
1933 — Carl Hubbell (10)
1935 — Freddie Fitzsimmons (4)*
1936 — Al Smith (4)*
1950 — Jim Hearn, Larry Jansen, Sal Maglie (5)*
1954 — Johnny Antonelli (6)
1959 — Johnny Antonelli, Sam Jones (4)*
1960 — Jack Sanford (6)
1965 — Juan Marichal (10)
1969 — Juan Marichal (8)
1970 — Gaylord Perry (5)
1976 — John Montefusco (6)*
1978 — Bob Knepper (6)

Strikeouts
1888 — Tim Keefe (335)
1890 — Amos Rusie (341)
1891 — Amos Rusie (337)
1893 — Amos Rusie (208)
1894 — Amos Rusie (195)
1895 — Amos Rusie (201)
1898 — Cy Seymour (239)
1903 — Christy Mathewson (267)
1904 — Christy Mathewson (212)
1905 — Christy Mathewson (206)
1907 — Christy Mathewson (178)
1908 — Christy Mathewson (259)
1911 — Rube Marquard (237)
1937 — Carl Hubbell (159)
1944 — Bill Voiselle (161)

Wins

1886 — Tim Keefe (42)*
1888 — Tim Keefe (35)
1894 — Amos Rusie (36)
1903 — Joe McGinnity (31)
1904 — Joe McGinnity (35)
1905 — Christy Mathewson (31)
1906 — Joe McGinnity (27)
1907 — Christy Mathewson (24)
1908 — Christy Mathewson (37)
1910 — Christy Mathewson (27)
1912 — Rube Marquard (26)*
1919 — Jesse Barnes (25)
1928 — Larry Benton (25)*
1933 — Carl Hubbell (23)
1936 — Carl Hubbell (26)
1937 — Carl Hubbell (22)
1951 — Larry Jansen, Sal Maglie (23)*
1959 — Sam Jones (21)*
1963 — Juan Marichal (25)*
1967 — Mike McCormick (22)
1968 — Juan Marichal (26)
1970 — Gaylord Perry (23)
1973 — Ron Bryant (24)
1993 — John Burkett (22)*

ERA

1885 — Tim Keefe (1.58)
1888 — Tim Keefe (1.74)
1891 — John Ewing (2.27)
1894 — Amos Rusie (2.78)
1897 — Amos Rusie (2.54)
1904 — Joe McGinnity (1.61)
1905 — Christy Mathewson (1.28)
1908 — Christy Mathewson (1.43)
1909 — Christy Mathewson (1.14)
1911 — Christy Mathewson (1.99)
1912 — Jeff Tesreau (1.96)
1913 — Christy Mathewson (2.06)
1917 — Fred Anderson (1.44)
1922 — Phil Douglas (2.63)

1929 — Bill Walker (3.09)
1931 — Bill Walker (2.26)
1933 — Carl Hubbell (1.66)
1934 — Carl Hubbell (2.30)
1936 — Carl Hubbell (2.31)
1949 — Dave Koslo (2.50)
1950 — Jim Hearn (2.49)
1952 — Hoyt Wilhelm (2.43)
1954 — Johnny Antonelli (2.30)
1958 — Stu Miller (2.47)
1959 — Sam Jones (2.83)
1960 — Mike McCormick (2.70)
1969 — Juan Marichal (2.10)
1983 — Atlee Hammaker (2.25)
1989 — Scott Garrelts (2.28)
1992 — Bill Swift (2.08)

Saves

1887 — Mike Tiernan (1)*
1893 — Mark Baldwin (2)*
1903 — Roscoe Miller (3)*
1904 — Joe McGinnity (5)
1905 — Claude Elliott (6)
1906 — George Ferguson (7)
1907 — Joe McGinnity (4)
1908 — Christy Mathewson, Joe McGinnity (5)*
1917 — Slim Sallee (4)
1918 — Fred Anderson (3)*
1922 — Claude Jonnard (5)
1923 — Claude Jonnard (5)
1926 — Chick Davies (6)
1934 — Carl Hubbell (8)
1937 — Cliff Melton (7)*
1938 — Dick Coffman (12)
1940 — Jumbo Brown (7)*
1941 — Jumbo Brown (8)
1944 — Ace Adams (13)
1945 — Ace Adams (15)*
1961 — Stu Miller (17)*

* denotes tied for N.L. lead.

NEW YORK/SAN FRANCISCO GIANTS HALL OF FAME MEMBERS

Significantly Associated With The Giants

Roger Bresnahan — 1945
Orlando Cepeda — 1999
Roger Connor — 1976
George Davis — 1998
Buck Ewing — 1939
Frankie Frisch — 1947
Carl Hubbell — 1947
Monte Irvin — 1973
Travis Jackson — 1982
Tim Keefe — 1964
George Kelly — 1973
Fred Lindstrom — 1976
Juan Marichal — 1983
Rube Marquard — 1971
Christy Mathewson — 1936
Willie Mays — 1979
Willie McCovey — 1986
Joe McGinnity — 1946
John McGraw — 1937
Johnny Mize — 1981
Jim O'Rourke — 1945
Mel Ott — 1951
Gaylord Perry — 1991
Amos Rusie — 1977
Bill Terry — 1954
John Montgomery Ward — 1964
Mickey Welch — 1973
Hoyt Wilhelm — 1985
Ross Youngs — 1972

Spent Part Of Their Career With The Giants

Dave Bancroft — 1971
Jake Beckley — 1971
Dan Brouthers — 1945
Jesse Burkett — 1946
Steve Carlton — 1994
Burleigh Grimes — 1964
Gabby Hartnett — 1955
Rogers Hornsby — 1942
Waite Hoyt — 1969
Willie Keeler — 1939
Mike Kelly — 1945
Ernie Lombardi — 1986
Bill McKechnie — 1962
Joe Medwick — 1968
Joe Morgan 1990
Edd Roush — 1962
Ray Schalk — 1955
Duke Snider — 1980
Warren Spahn — 1973
Casey Stengel — 1966
Hack Wilson — 1979

NEW YORK/SAN FRANCISCO GIANTS RETIRED UNIFORM NUMBERS

(*) —   Christy Mathewson
(*) —   John McGraw
#3 —   Bill Terry
#4 —   Mel Ott
#11 —   Carl Hubbell
#24 —   Willie Mays

#27 —   Juan Marichal
#30 —   Orlando Cepeda
#42 —   Jackie Robinson (retired by all of Major
          League Baseball)
          Last Giant to wear #42: Kirk Rueter, 1996-97
#44 —   Willie McCovey

(*) denotes did not wear uniform number during career.

NEW YORK/SAN FRANCISCO GIANTS HONOR ROLL

Major League Player Of The Decade
(The Sporting News)
1960s — Willie Mays
1990s — Barry Bonds

Major League Player Of The Year
(The Sporting News)
1933 — Carl Hubbell
1954 — Willie Mays
1969 — Willie McCovey
1989 — Kevin Mitchell
2001 — Barry Bonds

National League Most Valuable Player
(Chalmers Award)
1912 — Larry Doyle

National League Most Valuable Player
(Baseball Writers Association of America)
1933 — Carl Hubbell
1936 — Carl Hubbell
1954 — Willie Mays
1965 — Willie Mays
1969 — Willie McCovey
1989 — Kevin Mitchell
1993 — Barry Bonds
2000 — Jeff Kent
2001 — Barry Bonds
2002 — Barry Bonds

National League Most Valuable Player
(The Sporting News)
1930 — Bill Terry
1933 — Carl Hubbell
1936 — Carl Hubbell

National League Player Of The Year
(The Sporting News)
1954 — Willie Mays
1965 — Willie Mays
1969 — Willie McCovey
1973 — Bobby Bonds
1989 — Kevin Mitchell

National League Cy Young Award
(Baseball Writers Association of America)
1967 — Mike McCormick

National League Pitcher Of The Year
(The Sporting News)
1944 — Bill Voiselle
1954 — Johnny Antonelli
1959 — Sam Jones
1967 — Mike McCormick
1973 — Ron Bryant
1978 — Vida Blue

National League Fireman Of The Year
(The Sporting News)
1961 — Stu Miller
2002 — Robb Nen

National League Rookie Of The Year
(Baseball Writers Association of America)
1951 — Willie Mays
1958 — Orlando Cepeda
1959 — Willie McCovey
1973 — Gary Matthews
1975 — John Montefusco

National League Rookie Of The Year
(The Sporting News)
1951 — Willie Mays
1958 — Orlando Cepeda
1959 — Willie McCovey
1965 — Frank Linzy
1972 — Dave Rader
1973 — Gary Matthews
1974 — John D'Acquisto
1975 — John Montefusco
1976 — Larry Herndon
1986 — Robby Thompson

National League Comeback Player Of The Year
1967 — Mike McCormick
1977 — Willie McCovey
1982 — Joe Morgan

National League Silver Slugger Award
(The Sporting News)
1982 — Joe Morgan (2B)
1989 — Will Clark (1B)
      Kevin Mitchell (OF)
      Don Robinson (P)
1990 — Don Robinson (P)
      Matt Williams (3B)

1991 — Will Clark (1B)
1993 — Barry Bonds (OF)
   Robby Thompson (2B)
   Matt Williams (3B)
1994 — Barry Bonds (OF)
   Mark Portugal (P)
   Matt Williams (3B)
1996 — Barry Bonds (OF)
1997 — Barry Bonds (OF)
2000 — Barry Bonds (OF)
   Jeff Kent (2B)
2001 — Barry Bonds (OF)
   Jeff Kent (2B)
   Rich Aurilia (SS)
2002 — Barry Bonds (OF)
   Jeff Kent (SS)

Major League Gold Glove Award
(The Sporting News)
1957 — Willie Mays (OF)

National League Gold Glove Award
(The Sporting News)
1958 — Willie Mays (OF)
1959 — Jackie Brandt (OF)
   Willie Mays (OF)
1960 — Willie Mays (OF)
1961 — Willie Mays (OF)
1962 — Jim Davenport (3B)
   Willie Mays (OF)
1963 — Willie Mays (OF)
1964 — Willie Mays (OF)
1965 — Willie Mays (OF)
1966 — Willie Mays (OF)
1967 — Willie Mays (OF)
1968 — Willie Mays (OF)
1971 — Bobby Bonds (OF)
1973 — Bobby Bonds (OF)
1974 — Bobby Bonds (OF)
1987 — Rick Reuschel (P)
1991 — Will Clark (1B)
   Matt Williams (3B)
1993 — Barry Bonds (OF)
   Kirt Manwaring (C)
   Robby Thompson (2B)
   Matt Williams (3B)
1994 — Barry Bonds (OF)
   Darren Lewis (OF)
   Matt Williams (3B)
1996 — Barry Bonds (OF)
1997 — Barry Bonds (OF)
   J.T. Snow (1B)

1998 — Barry Bonds (OF)
   J.T. Snow (1B)
1999 — J.T. Snow (1B)
2000 — J.T. Snow (1B)

Major League Executive Of The Year
(The Sporting News)
1954 — Horace Stoneham
1978 — Spec Richardson
1987 — Al Rosen

Major League Manager Of The Year
(Associated Press)
1987 — Roger Craig
1993 — Dusty Baker

Major League Manager Of The Year
(The Sporting News)
1951 — Leo Durocher
1954 — Leo Durocher
1971 — Charlie Fox
1997 — Dusty Baker
2000 — Dusty Baker

Major League Manager Of The Year
(United Press International)
1971 — Charlie Fox
1978 — Joe Altobelli
1982 — Frank Robinson

National League Manager Of The Year
(Baseball Writers Association of America)
1993 — Dusty Baker
1997 — Dusty Baker
2000 — Dusty Baker

"Willie Mac" Award
(most inspirational player — selected by team)
1980 — Jack Clark
1981 — Larry Herndon
1982 — Joe Morgan
1983 — Darrell Evans
1984 — Bob Brenly
1985 — Mike Krukow
1986 — Mike Krukow
1987 — Chris Speier
1988 — Jose Uribe
1989 — Dave Dravecky
1990 — Steve Bedrosian
1991 — Robby Thompson
1992 — Mike Felder
1993 — Kirt Manwaring

1994 — no selection
1995 — Mark Carreon
　　　　Mark Leiter
1996 — Shawon Dunston
1997 — J.T. Snow
1998 — Jeff Kent
1999 — Marvin Benard
2000 — Ellis Burks
2001 — Benito Santiago
2002 — David Bell

Dave Dravecky Award
(most inspirational player — selected by fans)
1998 — J.T. Snow

World Series Most Valuable Player
(Babe Ruth Award — selected by the New York chapter of the BBWAA)
1954 — Dusty Rhodes

National League Championship Series
Most Valuable Player
1987 — Jeffrey Leonard
1989 — Will Clark
2002 — Benito Santiago

NEW YORK/SAN FRANCISCO GIANTS NATIONAL LEAGUE ALL-STARS

Players
Ace Adams — 1943
Felipe Alou — 1962
Johnny Antonelli — 1954, 1956, 1957, 1958, 1959
Rich Aurilia — **2001**
Ed Bailey — 1961, **1963**
Dick Bartell — **1937**
Rod Beck — 1993, 1994, 1997
Vida Blue — **1978**, 1981
Barry Bonds — **1993, 1994, 1995, 1996, 1997, 1998,**
2000, **2001, 2002**
Bobby Bonds — 1971, 1973
Jeff Brantley — 1990
Bob Brenly — 1984
Chris Brown — 1986
John Burkett — 1993
Orlando Cepeda — **1959**, 1960, **1961**, 1962, **1963,**
　　　　1964
Jack Clark — 1978, 1979
Will Clark — **1988, 1989, 1990, 1991,** 1992
Walker Cooper — **1946, 1947, 1948**
Harry Danning — 1938, 1939, 1940, 1941
Alvin Dark — **1951**, 1952, **1954**
Jim Davenport — 1962
Chili Davis — 1984, 1986
Dick Dietz — 1970
Shawn Estes — 1997
Darrell Evans — 1983
Scott Garrelts — 1985
Sid Gordon — 1948, 1949
Marv Grissom — 1954

Tom Haller — 1966, 1967
Atlee Hammaker — 1983
Jim Ray Hart — 1966
Jim Hearn — 1952
Carl Hubbell — 1933, 1934, 1935, 1936, 1937,
　　　　1938, 1940, 1941, 1942
Monte Irvin — 1952
Travis Jackson — **1934**
Larry Jansen — 1950, 1951
Sam Jones — 1959
Bill Jurges — 1939, 1940
Jeff Kent — 1999, **2000, 2001**
Buddy Kerr — 1948
Mike Krukow — 1986
Gary Lavelle — 1977, 1983
Hank Leiber — 1938
Jeffrey Leonard — 1987
Whitey Lockman — **1952**
Ernie Lombardi — 1943
Sal Maglie — 1951, 1952
Gus Mancuso — 1935, 1937
Juan Marichal — 1962, 1963, 1964, **1965,** 1966,
　　　　1967, 1968, 1969, 1971
Willard Marshall — 1942, 1947, **1949**
Willie Mays — 1954, 1955, 1956, **1957, 1958,**
　　　　1959, 1960, 1961, 1962, 1963, 1964, **1965,**
　　　　1966, 1967, **1968,** 1969, **1970, 1971**
Mike McCormick — 1960, 1961
Willie McCovey — 1963, 1966, **1968, 1969,**
　　　　1970, **1971**
Joe Medwick — 1944
Cliff Melton — 1942

Stu Miller — 1961
Greg Minton — 1982
Kevin Mitchell — **1989, 1990**
Johnny Mize — **1942, 1946, 1947, 1948, 1949**
John Montefusco — 1976
Joe Moore — 1934, 1935, 1936, 1937, 1938, 1940
Don Mueller — 1954, **1955**
Bobby Murcer — 1975
Robb Nen — 1998, 1999
Lefty O'Doul — 1933
Mel Ott — 1934, 1935, 1936, 1937, **1938**, 1939,
       1940, 1941, **1942**, 1943, 1944
Gaylord Perry — 1966, 1970
Rick Reuschel — 1988, **1989**
Bill Rigney — 1948
Benito Santiago — 2002
Bob Schmidt — 1958
Hal Schumacher — 1933, 1935
Chris Speier — 1972, **1973**, 1974
Eddie Stanky — 1950
Bill Terry — **1933, 1934, 1935**
Robby Thompson — 1988, 1993
Bobby Thomson — 1948, 1949, **1952**
Bill Voiselle — 1944
Wes Westrum — 1952, 53
Burgess Whitehead — 1937
Ed Whitson — 1980
Hoyt Wilhelm — 1953
Dave Williams — 1953
Matt Williams — 1990, **1994, 1995, 1996**

bold type denotes starter

Managers
Roger Craig — 1990
Alvin Dark — 1963
Leo Durocher — 1952, 1955
John McGraw — 1933
Bill Terry — 1934, 1937, 1938

Coaches
Dusty Baker — 1994, 1997, 2001
Roger Craig — 1987, 1988, 1992
Alvin Dark — 1961
Leo Durocher — 1954
Charlie Fox — 1972
Herman Franks — 1966, 1967, 1968
Mel Ott — 1947, 1948
Bill Rigney — 1958
Frank Shellenback — 1952
Bill Terry — 1939

All-Star Game Most Valuable Player
1963 — Willie Mays
1965 — Juan Marichal
1968 — Willie Mays
1969 — Willie McCovey
1973 — Bobby Bonds

All-Star Game Winning Pitcher
1951 — Sal Maglie
1959 (1) — Johnny Antonelli
1961 (1) — Stu Miller
1962 (1) — Juan Marichal
1964 — Juan Marichal
1966 — Gaylord Perry
1981 — Vida Blue

All-Star Game Losing Pitcher
1990 — Jeff Brantley
1993 — John Burkett
1997 — Shawn Estes

All-Star Game Saves
1956 — Johnny Antonelli

All-Star Game Home Runs
1947 — Johnny Mize
1956 — Willie Mays
1960 (2) — Willie Mays
1965 — Willie Mays
1969 — Willie McCovey (2)
1970 — Dick Dietz
1973 — Bobby Bonds
1992 — Will Clark
1998 — Barry Bonds
2002 — Barry Bonds

Honorary Captain
1977 — Willie Mays
1979 — Carl Hubbell
1984 — Willie McCovey
1990 — Juan Marichal
1992 — Willie Mays
1999 — Orlando Cepeda

All-Star Games Hosted By The Giants
1934 — Polo Grounds
1942 — Polo Grounds
1961 (1) — Candlestick Park
1984 — Candlestick Park

Major League All-Star Team
(The Sporting News)

1927 — Rogers Hornsby (2B)
　　　　Travis Jackson (SS)
1928 — Fred Lindstrom (3B)
　　　　Travis Jackson (SS)
1929 — Travis Jackson (SS)
1930 — Fred Lindstrom (3B)
　　　　Bill Terry (1B)
1933 — Carl Hubbell (P)
1934 — Mel Ott (OF)
1935 — Carl Hubbell (P)
　　　　Mel Ott (OF)
1936 — Carl Hubbell (P)
　　　　Mel Ott (OF)
1937 — Dick Bartell (SS)
　　　　Carl Hubbell (P)
1938 — Mel Ott (OF)
1940 — Harry Danning (C)
1942 — Johnny Mize (1B)
1947 — Walker Cooper (C)
　　　　Johnny Mize (1B)
1948 — Johnny Mize (1B)
1951 — Sal Maglie (P)
1954 — Johnny Antonelli (P)
　　　　Alvin Dark (SS)
　　　　Willie Mays (OF)
1957 — Willie Mays (OF)
　　　　Red Schoendienst (2B)
1958 — Willie Mays (OF)
1959 — Johnny Antonelli (P)
　　　　Orlando Cepeda (1B)
　　　　Sam Jones (P)
　　　　Willie Mays (OF)
1960 — Willie Mays (OF)

National League All-Star Team
(The Sporting News)

1961 — Orlando Cepeda (1B)
　　　　Willie Mays (OF)
1962 — Orlando Cepeda (1B)
　　　　Willie Mays (OF)
1963 — Juan Marichal (P)
　　　　Willie Mays (OF)
1964 — Willie Mays (OF)
1965 — Juan Marichal (P)
　　　　Willie Mays (OF)
　　　　Willie McCovey (1B)
1966 — Juan Marichal (P)
　　　　Willie Mays (OF)
1967 — Mike McCormick (P)
1968 — Juan Marichal (P)
　　　　Willie McCovey (1B)
1969 — Willie McCovey (1B)
1970 — Willie McCovey (1B)
1972 — Chris Speier (SS)
1973 — Ron Bryant (LP)
　　　　Bobby Bonds (OF)
1976 — Willie Montanez (1B)
1978 — Vida Blue (LHP)
　　　　Jack Clark (OF)
1988 — Will Clark (1B)
1989 — Kevin Mitchell (OF)
　　　　Will Clark (1B)
1990 — Matt Williams (3B)
1991 — Will Clark (1B)
1993 — Barry Bonds (OF)
　　　　Robby Thompson (2B)
　　　　Matt Williams (3B)
1994 — Barry Bonds (OF)
　　　　Matt Williams (3B)
1996 — Barry Bonds (OF)
1997 — Barry Bonds (OF)
2000 — Barry Bonds (OF)
2001 — Barry Bonds (OF)
2002 — Barry Bonds (OF)
　　　　Jeff Kent (2B)

SAN FRANCISCO GIANTS ALL-DECADE TEAMS
(selected by Bay Area media in 1999)

1960s
Catcher — Tom Haller
First Baseman — Willie McCovey
Second Baseman — Tito Fuentes
Shortstop — Jose Pagan

Third Baseman — Jim Davenport
Outfielder — Willie Mays
Outfielder — Orlando Cepeda
Outfielder — Felipe Alou
Right-Handed Starting Pitcher — Juan Marichal

Left-Handed Starting Pitcher — Mike McCormick
Relief Pitcher — Stu Miller

1970s
Catcher — Mike Sadek
First Baseman — Willie McCovey
Second Baseman — Tito Fuentes
Shortstop — Chris Speier
Third Baseman — Darrell Evans
Outfielder — Willie Mays
Outfielder — Bobby Bonds
Outfielder — Jack Clark
Right-Handed Starting Pitcher — Juan Marichal
Left-Handed Starting Pitcher — Vida Blue
Relief Pitcher — Gary Lavelle

1980s
Catcher — Bob Brenly
First Baseman — Will Clark
Second Baseman — Robby Thompson
Shortstop — Jose Uribe
Third Baseman — Matt Williams
Outfielder — Jeffrey Leonard
Outfielder — Chili Davis
Outfielder — Kevin Mitchell
Right-Handed Starting Pitcher — Mike Krukow
Left-Handed Starting Pitcher — Dave Dravecky
Relief Pitcher — Greg Minton

1990s
Catcher — Kirt Manwaring
First Baseman — Will Clark
Second Baseman — Jeff Kent
Shortstop — Royce Clayton
Third Baseman — Matt Williams
Outfielder — Barry Bonds
Outfielder — Darren Lewis
Outfielder — Willie McGee
Right-Handed Starting Pitcher — John Burkett
Left-Handed Starting Pitcher — Shawn Estes
Relief Pitcher — Rod Beck

SAN FRANCISCO GIANTS ALL-TIME TEAM
(selected by fans in 1999)

Catcher — Tom Haller
First Baseman — Willie McCovey
Second Baseman — Robby Thompson
Shortstop — Chris Speier
Third Baseman — Matt Williams
Left Fielder — Barry Bonds
Center Fielder — Willie Mays
Right Fielder — Bobby Bonds
Utility — Orlando Cepeda
Right-Handed Starting Pitcher — Juan Marichal
Left-Handed Starting Pitcher — Mike McCormick
Relief Pitcher — Rod Beck
Manager — Dusty Baker

SAN FRANCISCO GIANTS 25TH ANNIVERSARY DREAM TEAM
(selected by fans at conclusion of 1981 season)

Catcher — Tom Haller
First Baseman — Willie McCovey
Second Baseman — Tito Fuentes
Shortstop — Johnnie LeMaster
Third Baseman — Jim Davenport
Left Fielder — Gary Matthews
Center Fielder — Willie Mays
Right Fielder — Jack Clark
Utility — Orlando Cepeda
Right-Handed Starting Pitcher — Juan Marichal
Left-Handed Starting Pitcher — Vida Blue
Right-Handed Relief Pitcher — Stu Miller
Left-Handed Relief Pitcher — Al Holland
Manager — Frank Robinson

A P P E N D I X D

POSTSEASON PLAY

- -

NEW YORK/SAN FRANCISCO GIANTS CLINCH DATES

National League Pennant
1888 — Oct. 3
1889 — Oct. 5
1904 — Sept. 22
1905 — Sept. 30
1911 — Oct. 4
1912 — Sept. 26
1913 — Sept. 27
1917 — Sept. 24
1921 — Sept. 28
1922 — Sept. 25
1923 — Sept. 28
1924 — Sept. 27
1933 — Sept. 19
1936 — Sept. 24
1937 — Sept. 30
1951 — Oct. 3
1954 — Sept. 20
1962 — Oct. 3

National League West Division
1971 — Sept. 30
1987 — Sept. 28
1989 — Sept. 27
1997 — Sept. 27
2000 — Sept. 21

National League Wild Card
2002 — Sept. 28

NEW YORK/SAN FRANCISCO GIANTS IN POSTSEASON PLAY

Division Series

1997 (Giants lost to Florida Marlins 3 games to 0)
Sept. 30 — Marlins 2, Giants 1 (at Miami)
Oct. 1 — Marlins 7, Giants 6 (at Miami)
Oct. 3 — Marlins 6, Giants 2 (at San Francisco)

2000 (Giants lost to New York Mets 3 games to 1)
Oct. 4 — Giants 5, Mets 1 (at San Francisco)
Oct. 5 — Mets 5, Giants 4 (10 innings) (at San

Francisco)
Oct. 7—— Mets 3, Giants 2 (13 innings) (at New York)
Oct. 8 — Mets 4, Giants 0 (at New York)

2002 (Giants defeated Atlanta Braves 3 games to 2)
Oct. 2 — Giants 8, Braves 5 (at Atlanta)
Oct. 3 — Braves 7, Giants 3 (at Atlanta)
Oct. 5 — Braves 10, Giants 2 (at San Francisco)
Oct. 6 — Giants 8, Braves 3 (at San Francisco)
Oct. 7 — Giants 3, Braves 1 (at Atlanta)

National League Championship Series

1971 (Giants lost to Pittsburgh Pirates 3 games to 1)
Oct. 2 — Giants 5, Pirates 4 (at San Francisco)
Oct. 3 — Pirates 9, Giants 4 (at San Francisco)
Oct. 5 — Pirates 2, Giants 1 (at Pittsburgh)
Oct. 6 — Pirates 9, Giants 5 (at Pittsburgh)

1987 (Giants lost to St. Louis Cardinals 4 games to 3)
Oct. 6 — Cardinals 5, Giants 3 (at St. Louis)
Oct. 7 — Giants 5, Cardinals 0 (at St. Louis)
Oct. 9 — Cardinals 6, Giants 5 (at San Francisco)
Oct. 10 — Giants 4, Cardinals 2 (at San Francisco)
Oct. 11 — Giants 6, Cardinals 3 (at San Francisco)
Oct. 13 — Cardinals 1, Giants 0 (at St. Louis)
Oct. 14 — Cardinals 6, Giants 0 (at St. Louis)

1989 (Giants defeated Chicago Cubs 4 games to 1)
Oct. 4 — Giants 11, Cubs 3 (at Chicago)
Oct. 5 — Cubs 9, Giants 5 (at Chicago)
Oct. 7 — Giants 5, Cubs 4 (at San Francisco)
Oct. 8 — Giants 6, Cubs 4 (at San Francisco)
Oct. 9 — Giants 3, Cubs 2 (at San Francisco)

2002 (Giants defeated St. Louis Cardinals 4 games to 1)
Oct. 9 — Giants 9, Cardinals 6 (at St. Louis)
Oct. 10 — Giants 4, Cardinals 1 (at St. Louis)
Oct. 12 — Giants 5, Cardinals 4 (at San Francisco)
Oct. 13 — Giants 4, Cardinals 3 (at San Francisco)
Oct. 14 — Giants 2, Cardinals 1 (at San Francisco)

Temple Cup

1894 (Giants defeated Baltimore Orioles 4 games to 0)
Oct. 4 — Giants 4, Orioles 1 (at Baltimore)
Oct. 5 — Giants 9, Orioles 6 (at Baltimore)
Oct. 6 — Giants 4, Orioles 1 (at New York)
Oct. 8 — Giants 16, Orioles 3 (at New York)

World Series

1888 (Giants defeated St. Louis Browns 6 games to 4)
Oct. 16 — Giants 2, Browns 1 (at New York)
Oct. 17 — Browns 3, Giants 0 (at New York)
Oct. 18 — Giants 4, Browns 2 (at New York)
Oct. 19 — Giants 5, Browns 3 (at Brooklyn)
Oct. 20 — Giants 6, Browns 4 (8 innings) (at New York)
Oct. 22 — Giants 12, Browns 5 (8 innings) (at Philadelphia)
Oct. 24 — Browns 7, Giants 5 (8 innings) (at St. Louis)
Oct. 25 — Giants 11, Browns 3 (at St. Louis)
Oct. 26 — Browns 14, Giants 11 (10 innings) (at St. Louis)
Oct. 27 — Browns 18, Giants 7 (at St. Louis)

1889 (Giants defeated Brooklyn Bridegrooms 6 games to 3)
Oct. 18 — Bridegrooms 12, Giants 10 (8 innings) (at New York)
Oct. 19 — Giants 6, Bridegrooms 2 (at Brooklyn)
Oct. 22 — Bridegrooms 8, Giants 7 (8 innings) (at New York)
Oct. 23 — Bridegrooms 10, Giants 7 (6 innings) (at Brooklyn)

Oct. 24 — Giants 11, Bridegrooms 3 (at Brooklyn)

Oct. 25 — Giants 2, Bridegrooms 1 (11 innings) (at New York)

Oct. 26 — Giants 11, Bridegrooms 7 (at New York)

Oct. 28 — Giants 16, Bridegrooms 7 (at Brooklyn)

Oct. 29 — Giants 3, Bridegrooms 2 (at New York)

1905 (Giants defeated Philadelphia Athletics 4 games to 1)

Oct. 9 — Giants 3, Athletics 0 (at Philadelphia)

Oct. 10 — Athletics 3, Giants 0 (at New York)

Oct. 12 — Giants 9, Athletics 0 (at Philadelphia)

Oct. 13 — Giants 1, Athletics 0 (at New York)

Oct. 14 — Giants 2, Athletics 0 (at New York)

1911 (Giants lost to Philadelphia Athletics 4 games to 2)

Oct. 14 — Giants 2, Athletics 1 (at New York)

Oct. 16 — Athletics 3, Giants 1 (at Philadelphia)

Oct. 17 — Athletics 3, Giants 2 (11 innings) (at New York)

Oct. 24 — Athletics 4, Giants 2 (at Philadelphia)

Oct. 25 — Giants 4, Athletics 3 (10 innings) (at New York)

Oct. 26 — Athletics 13, Giants 2 (at Philadelphia)

1912 (Giants lost to Boston Red Sox 4 games to 3 with 1 tie)

Oct. 8 — Red Sox 4, Giants 3 (at New York)

Oct. 9 — Giants 6, Red Sox 6 (11 innings) (at Boston)

Oct. 10 — Giants 2, Red Sox 1 (at Boston)

Oct. 11 — Red Sox 3, Giants 1 (at New York)

Oct. 12 — Red Sox 2, Giants 1 (at Boston)

Oct. 14 — Giants 5, Red Sox 2 (at New York)

Oct. 15 — Giants 11, Red Sox 4 (at Boston)

Oct. 16 — Red Sox 3, Giants 2 (10 innings) (at Boston)

1913 (Giants lost to Philadelphia Athletics 4 games to 1)

Oct. 7 — Athletics 6, Giants 4 (at New York)

Oct. 8 — Giants 3, Athletics 0 (10 innings) (at Philadelphia)

Oct. 9 — Athletics 8, Giants 2 (at New York)

Oct. 10 — Athletics 6, Giants 5 (at Philadelphia)

Oct. 11 — Athletics 3, Giants 1 (at New York)

1917 (Giants lost to Chicago White Sox 4 games to 2)

Oct. 6 — White Sox 2, Giants 1 (at Chicago)

Oct. 7 — White Sox 7, Giants 2 (at Chicago)

Oct. 10 — Giants 2, White Sox 0 (at New York)

Oct. 11 — Giants 5, White Sox 0 (at New York)

Oct. 13 — White Sox 8, Giants 5 (at Chicago)

Oct. 15 — White Sox 4, Giants 2 (at New York)

1921 (Giants defeated New York Yankees 5 games to 3)

Oct. 5 — Yankees 3, Giants 0 (at Polo Grounds)

Oct. 6 — Yankees 3, Giants 0 (at Polo Grounds)

Oct. 7 — Giants 13, Yankees 5 (at Polo Grounds)

Oct. 9 — Giants 4, Yankees 2 (at Polo Grounds)

Oct. 10 — Yankees 3, Giants 1 (at Polo Grounds)

Oct. 11 — Giants 8, Yankees 5 (at Polo Grounds)

Oct. 12 — Giants 2, Yankees 1 (at Polo Grounds)

Oct. 13 — Giants 1, Yankees 0 (at Polo Grounds)

1922 (Giants defeated New York Yankees 4 games to 0 with 1 tie)

Oct. 4 — Giants 3, Yankees 2 (at Polo Grounds)

Oct. 5 — Giants 3, Yankees 3 (10 innings) (at Polo Grounds)

Oct. 6 — Giants 3, Yankees 0 (at Polo Grounds)

Oct. 7 — Giants 4, Yankees 3 (at Polo Grounds)

Oct. 8 — Giants 5, Yankees 2 (at Polo Grounds)

1923 (Giants lost to New York Yankees 4 games to 2)

Oct. 10 — Giants 5, Yankees 4 (at Yankee Stadium)

Oct. 11 — Yankees 4, Giants 2 (at Polo Grounds)

Oct. 12 — Giants 1, Yankees 0 (at Yankee Stadium)

Oct. 13 — Yankees 8, Giants 4 (at Polo Grounds)

Oct. 14 — Yankees 8, Giants 1 (at Yankee Stadium)

Oct. 15 — Yankees 6, Giants 4 (at Polo Grounds)

1924 (Giants lost to Washington Senators 4 games to 3)

Oct. 4 — Giants 4, Senators 3 (12 innings) at Washington)

Oct. 5 — Senators 4, Giants 3 (at Washington)

Oct. 6 — Giants 6, Senators 4 (at New York)

Oct. 7 — Senators 7, Giants 4 (at New York)

Oct. 8 — Giants 6, Senators 2 (at New York)

Oct. 9 — Senators 2, Giants 1 (at Washington)

Oct. 10 — Senators 4, Giants 3 (12 innings (at Washington)

1933 (Giants defeated Washington Senators 4 games to 1)

Oct. 3 — Giants 4, Senators 2 (at New York)

Oct. 4 — Giants 6, Senators 1 (at New York)

Oct. 5 — Senators 4, Giants 0 (at Washington)

Oct. 6 — Giants 2, Senators 1 (11 innings) (at Washington)

Oct. 7 — Giants 4, Senators 3 (10 innings) (at Washington)

1936 (Giants lost to New York Yankees 4 games to 2)

Sept. 30 — Giants 6, Yankees 1 (at Polo Grounds)
Oct. 2 — Yankees 18, Giants 4 (at Polo Grounds)
Oct. 3 — Yankees 2, Giants 1 (at Yankee Stadium)
Oct. 4 — Yankees 5, Giants 2 (at Yankee Stadium)
Oct. 5 — Giants 5, Yankees 4 (10 innings) (at Yankee Stadium)
Oct. 6 — Yankees 13, Giants 5 (at Polo Grounds)

1937 (Giants lost to New York Yankees 4 games to 1)

Oct. 6 — Yankees 8, Giants 1 (at Yankee Stadium)
Oct. 7 — Yankees 8, Giants 1 (at Yankee Stadium)
Oct. 8 — Yankees 5, Giants 1 (at Polo Grounds)
Oct. 9 — Giants 7, Yankees 3 (at Polo Grounds)
Oct. 10 — Yankees 4, Giants 2 (at Polo Grounds)

1951 (Giants lost to New York Yankees 4 games to 2)

Oct. 4 — Giants 4, Yankees 1 (at Yankee Stadium)
Oct. 5 — Yankees 3, Giants 1 (at Yankee Stadium)
Oct. 6 — Giants 6, Yankees 2 (at Polo Grounds)
Oct. 8 — Yankees 6, Giants 2 (at Polo Grounds)
Oct. 9 — Yankees 13, Giants 1 (at Polo Grounds)
Oct. 10 — Yankees 4, Giants 3 (at Yankee Stadium)

1954 (Giants defeated Cleveland Indians 4 games to 0)

Sept. 29 — Giants 5, Indians 2 (10 innings) (at New York)
Sept. 30 — Giants 3, Indians 1 (at New York)
Oct. 1 — Giants 6, Indians 2 (at Cleveland)
Oct. 2 — Giants 7, Indians 4 (at Cleveland)

1962 (Giants lost to New York Yankees 4 games to 3)

Oct. 4 — Yankees 6, Giants 2 (at San Francisco)
Oct. 5 — Giants 2, Yankees 0 (at San Francisco)
Oct. 7 — Yankees 3, Giants 2 (at New York)
Oct. 8 — Giants 7, Yankees 3 (at New York)
Oct. 10 — Yankees 5, Giants 3 (at New York)
Oct. 15 — Giants 5, Yankees 2 (at San Francisco)
Oct. 16 — Yankees 1, Giants 0 (at San Francisco)

1989 (Giants lost to Oakland Athletics 4 games to 0)

Oct. 14 — Athletics 5, Giants 0 (at Oakland)
Oct. 15 — Athletics 5, Giants 1 (at Oakland)
Oct. 27 — Athletics 13, Giants 7 (at San Francisco)
Oct. 28 — Athletics 9, Giants 6 (at San Francisco)

2002 (Giants lost to Anaheim Angels 4 games to 3)

Oct. 19 — Giants 4, Angels 1 (at Anaheim)
Oct. 20 — Angels 11, Giants 10 (at Anaheim)
Oct. 22 — Angels 10, Giants 4 (at San Francisco)
Oct. 23 — Giants 4, Angels 3 (at San Francisco)
Oct. 24 — Giants 16, Angels 4 (at San Francisco)
Oct. 26 — Angels 6, Giants 5 (at Anaheim)
Oct. 27 — Angels 4, Giants 1 (at Anaheim)

SAN FRANCISCO GIANTS NATIONAL LEAGUE DIVISION SERIES PERFORMERS

Wilson Alvarez - 1997
Rich Aurilia - 2000, 2002
Manny Aybar – 2002
Rod Beck - 1997
Marvin Benard – 1997, 2000
Damon Berryhill – 1997
Barry Bonds – 1997, 2000, 2002
Ellis Burks - 2000
David Bell - 2002
Felipe Crespo - 2000
Russ Davis - 2000
Miguel Del Toro - 2000
Shawon Dunston - 2002
Alan Embree - 2000
Bobby Estalella - 2000
Shawn Estes – 1997, 2000
Scott Eyre - 2002
Pedro Feliz - 2002
Aaron Fultz - 2000, 2002
Mark Gardner - 2000
Tom Goodwin - 2002
Darryl Hamilton – 1997
Doug Henry–– 1997, 2000
Livan Hernandez - 2000, 2002
Roberto Hernandez – 1997
Glenallen Hill–– 1997

Stan Javier – 1997
Jeff Kent – 1997, 2000, 2002
Mark Lewis–– 1997
Kenny Lofton - 2002
Ramon Martinez - 2000, 2002
Doug Mirabelli - 2000
Bill Mueller – 1997, 2000
Calvin Murray - 2000
Robb Nen - 2000, 2002
Russ Ortiz - 2000, 2002
Dante Powell – 1997
Armando Rios - 2000
Felix Rodriguez - 2000, 2002
Rich Rodriguez – 1997
Kirk Rueter – 1997, 2000, 2002
Reggie Sanders - 2002
Benito Santiago - 2002
Jason Schmidt - 2002
Tsuyoshi Shinjo - 2002
J.T. Snow–– 1997, 2000, 2002
Julian Tavarez–– 1997
Yorvit Torrealba - 2002
Jay Witasick - 2002
Tim Worrell - 2002
Jose Vizcaino – 1997

Manager
Dusty Baker — 1997, 2000, 2002

SAN FRANCISCO GIANTS NATIONAL LEAGUE CHAMPIONSHIP SERIES PERFORMERS

Mike Aldrete – 1987
Rich Aurilia - 2002
Jim Barr – 1971
Bill Bathe-- 1989
David Bell - 2002
Barry Bonds - 2002
Bobby Bonds – 1971
Jeff Brantley – 1989
Bob Brenly-- 1987
Ron Bryant-- 1971
Don Carrithers – 1971
Will Clark-- 1987, 1989
John Cumberland – 1971
Chili Davis – 1971
Dick Dietz-- 1971
Kelly Downs – 1987, 1989
Frank Duffy – 1971
Shawon Dunston - 2002
Scott Eyre - 2002
Pedro Feliz - 2002
Tito Fuentes – 1971
Aaron Fultz - 2002
Al Gallagher – 1971
Scott Garrelts-- 1987, 1989
Tom Goodwin - 2002
Steve Hamilton – 1971
Atlee Hammaker-- 1987, 1989
Jim Ray Hart-- 1971
Ken Henderson – 1971
Livan Hernandez - 2002
Jerry Johnson – 1971
Jeff Kent - 2002
Dave Kingman – 1971
Mike Krukow – 1987
Hal Lanier-- 1971
Craig Lefferts-- 1987, 1989
Greg Litton – 1989
Kenny Lofton - 2002
Candy Maldonado – 1987, 1989

Kirt Manwaring – 1989
Juan Marichal – 1971
Ramon Martinez - 2002
Willie Mays – 1971
Willie McCovey-- 1971
Don McMahon – 1971
Bob Melvin-- 1987
Eddie Milner – 1987
Robb Nen - 2002
Donnell Nixon – 1989
Gaylord Perry – 1971
Russ Ortiz - 2002
Felix Rodriguez - 2002
Rick Reuschel – 1987, 1989
Ernest Riles-- 1989
Angel Rosario – 1971
Kirk Rueter - 2002
Reggie Sanders - 2002
Benito Santiago - 2002
Jason Schmidt - 2002
Pat Sheridan – 1989
Tsuyoshi Shinjo - 2002
J.T. Snow - 2002
Chris Speier
– 1971, 1987
Robby Thompson – 1987, 1989
Yorvit Torrealba - 2002
Jose Uribe – 1987, 1989
Matt Williams – 1989
Jay Witasick - 2002
Tim Worrell - 2002
Chad Zerbe - 2002

Managers
Dusty Baker — 2002
Roger Craig — 1987, 1989
Charlie Fox — 1971

SAN FRANCISCO GIANTS NATIONAL LEAGUE CHAMPIONSHIP SERIES BATTING LEADERS

Games

Will Clark	7	1987
Jeffrey Leonard	7	1987
Kevin Mitchell	7	1987
Robby Thompson	7	1987
Jose Uribe	7	1987

At-Bats

Kevin Mitchell	30	1987
Jose Uribe	26	1987
Will Clark	25	1987
Jeffrey Leonard	24	1987
Kenny Lofton	21	2002

Runs

Will Clark	8	1989
Brett Butler	6	1989
Jeffrey Leonard	5	1987
Kevin Mitchell	5	1989
Robby Thompson	5	1989
Barry Bonds	5	2002

Hits

Jeffrey Leonard	10	1987
Will Clark	9	1987
Kevin Mitchell	8	1987
Jose Uribe	7	1987
David Bell	7	2002

Doubles

Will Clark	3	1989
Willie Mays	2	1971
Will Clark	2	1987
Fourteen tied with	1	

Triples

Will Clark	1	1987
Pat Sheridan	1	1987
Robby Thompson	1	1987
Barry Bonds	1	2002
J.T. Snow	1	2002

Home Runs

Jeffrey Leonard	4	1987
Willie McCovey	2	1971
Will Clark	2	1989
Kevin Mitchell	2	1989
Robby Thompson	2	1989
Matt Williams	2	1989
Rich Aurilia	2	2002
Benito Santiago	2	2002

RBI

Matt Williams	9	1989
Will Clark	8	1989
Kevin Mitchell	7	1989
Willie McCovey	6	1987
Benito Santiago	6	2002

Stolen Bases

Robby Thompson	2	1987
Twelve tied with	1	

Batting Average

Will Clark	.650	1989
Willie McCovey	.429	1971
Jeffrey Leonard	.417	1987
David Bell	.412	2002
Will Clark	.360	1987

SAN FRANCISCO GIANTS NATIONAL LEAGUE CHAMPIONSHIP SERIES PITCHING LEADERS

Games

Steve Bedrosian	4	1989
Scott Eyre	4	2002
Felix Rodriguez	4	2002
Tim Worrell	4	2002
Craig Lefferts	3	1987
Don Robinson	3	1987
Jeff Brantley	3	1989

Games Started

Gaylord Perry	2	1971
Dave Dravecky	2	1987
Atlee Hammaker	2	1987
Rick Reuschel	2	1987
Scott Garrelts	2	1989
Rick Reuschel	2	1989
Kirk Rueter	2	2002

Complete Games

Juan Marichal	1	1971
Gaylord Perry	1	1971
Dave Dravecky	1	1987
Mike Krukow	1	1987

Shutouts

Dave Draveky	1	1987

Innings Pitched

Dave Dravecky	15.0	1987
Gaylord Perry	14.2	1971
Scott Garrelts	11.2	1989
Kirk Rueter	11.0	2002
Rick Reuschel	10.0	1987

Strikeouts

Dave Dravecky	14	1987
Gaylord Perry	11	1971
Scott Garrelts	8	1989
Jason Schmidt	8	2002
Atlee Hammaker	7	1987
Joe Price	7	1987

Wins

Tim Worrell	2	2002
Gaylord Perry	1	1971
Dave Dravecky	1	1987
Mike Krukow	1	1987
Joe Price	1	1987
Kelly Downs	1	1989
Scott Garrelts	1	1989
Rick Reuschel	1	1989
Don Robinson	1	1989
Kirk Rueter	1	2002
Jason Schmidt	1	2002

Losses

John Cumberland	1	1971
Juan Marichal	1	1971
Gaylord Perry	1	1971
Dave Dravecky	1	1987
Atlee Hammaker	1	1987
Rick Reuschel	1	1987
Don Robinson	1	1987
Rick Reuschel	1	1989
Jay Witasick	1	2002

Saves

Steve Bedrosian	3	1989
Robb Nen	3	2002

ERA

Dave Dravecky	0.60	1987
Jason Schmidt	1.17	2002
Mike Krukow	2.00	1987
Juan Marichal	2.25	1971
Livan Hernandez	2.84	2002

NEW YORK/SAN FRANCISCO GIANTS WORLD SERIES PERFORMERS

Felipe Alou — 1962
Matty Alou — 1962
Red Ames — 1905, 1911, 1912
Fred Anderson — 1917
Johnny Antonelli — 1954
Rich Aurilia — 2002
Ed Bailey — 1962
Al Baird — 1917*
Tom Baker — 1937*
Harry Baldwin — 1924
Dave Bancroft — 1921, 1922, 1923
Jesse Barnes — 1921, 1922
Virgil Barnes — 1922*, 1923, 1924
Dick Bartell — 1936, 1937
Bill Bathe — 1989
Beals Becker — 1911, 1912
Steve Bedrosian — 1989
David Bell — 2002
Hi Bell — 1933
Jack Bentley — 1923, 1924
Rube Benton — 1917
Wally Berger — 1937
Clint Blume — 1922*
Carl Boles — 1962*
Bobby Bolin — 1962
Barry Bonds — 2002
Frank Bowerman — 1905*
Ernie Bowman — 1962
Jeff Brantley — 1989
Don Brennan — 1937
Roger Bresnahan — 1905
Eddie Brown — 1921*
George Browne — 1905
George Burns — 1912*, 1913, 1917, 1921
Brett Butler — 1989
Slick Castleman — 1936
Red Causey — 1921*
Orlando Cepeda — 1962
Lou Chiozza — 1937
Will Clark — 1989
Watty Clark — 1933*
Dick Coffman — 1936, 1937
Claude Cooper — 1913
Al Corwin — 1951, 1954*
Doc Crandall — 1911, 1912, 1913
Hughie Critz — 1933
Bill Cunningham — 1921*, 1922, 1923
Bill Dahlen — 1905

Harry Danning — 1933*, 1936, 1937
Alvin Dark — 1951, 1954
Jim Davenport — 1962
Kiddo Davis — 1933, 1936
Wayland Dean — 1924
Al Demaree — 1913, 1917*
Art Devlin — 1905, 1911*
Josh Devore — 1911, 1912
Mike Donlin — 1905
Phil Douglas — 1921
Kelly Downs — 1989
Larry Doyle — 1911, 1912, 1913
Chuck Dressen — 1933*
Louis Drucke — 1911*
Jim Duffalo — 1962*
Shawon Dunston — 2002
Claude Elliott — 1905*
Scott Eyre — 2002
Pedro Feliz — 2002
Freddie Fitzsimmons — 1933, 1936
Art Fletcher — 1911, 1912, 1913, 1917
Frankie Frisch — 1921, 1922, 1923, 1924
Art Fromme — 1913*
Aaron Fultz — 2002
Frank Gabler — 1936
Billy Gardner — 1954*
Bob Garibaldi — 1962*
Scott Garrelts — 1989
Alex Gaston — 1921*, 1922*, 1923*
Dinty Gearin — 1923
Paul Giel — 1954*
Billy Gilbert — 1905
Ruben Gomez — 1954
Mike Gonzalez — 1921*
Hank Gowdy — 1923, 1924
Eddie Grant — 1913
Marv Grissom — 1954
Heinie Groh — 1912*, 1922, 1923, 1924
Harry Gumbert — 1936, 1937
Tom Haller — 1962
Atlee Hammaker — 1989
Grover Hartley — 1911*, 1912*, 1913*
Clint Hartung — 1951
Mickey Haslin — 1937*
Jim Hearn — 1951
Livan Hernandez — 2002
Buck Herzog — 1911, 1912, 1913, 1917
Carmen Hill — 1922*

Chuck Hiller — 1962
Walker Holke — 1917
Carl Hubbell — 1933, 1936, 1937
Walter Huntzinger — 1924*
Monte Irvin — 1951, 1954
Travis Jackson — 1923, 1924, 1933, 1936
Bernie James — 1933*
Larry Jansen — 1951
Sheldon Jones — 1951
Claude Jonnard — 1922*, 1923, 1924
Ray Katt — 1954*
Benny Kauff — 1917
George Kelly — 1921, 1922, 1923, 1924
Monte Kennedy — 1951
Terry Kennedy — 1989
Jeff Kent — 2002
Lee King 1922
Mark Koenig — 1936
Alex Konikowski — 1951, 1954*
Wally Kopf — 1921*
Dave Koslo — 1951
Harvey Kuenn — 1962
Mike LaCoss — 1989
Don Larsen — 1962
Craig Lefferts — 1989
Hank Leiber — 1936, 1937
Sam Leslie — 1936, 1937
Don Liddle — 1954
Fred Lindstrom 1924
Greg Litton — 1989
Hans Lobert — 1917*
Whitey Lockman — 1951, 1954
Kenny Lofton — 2002
Jack Lohrke — 1951
Dolf Luque — 1933
Ed Madjeski — 1937*
Sal Maglie — 1951, 1954
Freddie Maguire — 1923
Candy Maldonado — 1989
Gus Mancuso — 1933, 1936, 1937
Kirt Manwaring — 1989
Juan Marichal — 1989
Rube Marquard — 1911, 1912, 1913
Ramon Martinez — 2002
Christy Mathewson — 1905, 1911, 1912, 1913
Ernie Maun — 1924*
Eddie Mayo — 1936
Willie Mays — 1951, 1954, 1962
John McCall — 1954*
Johnny McCarthy — 1937
Lew McCarty — 1917
Harry McCormick — 1912, 1913

Mike McCormick — 1962*
Willie McCovey — 1962
Dan McGann 1905
Joe McGinnity — 1905
Larry McLean — 1913
Hugh McQuillan — 1922, 1923, 1924
Cliff Melton — 1937
Fred Merkle — 1911, 1912, 1913
Sam Mertes — 1905
Irish Meusel — 1921, 1922, 1923, 1924
Chief Meyers — 1911, 1912, 1913
Stu Miller — 1962
Kevin Mitchell — 1989
Joe Moore — 1933, 1936, 1937
Don Mueller — 1951*, 1954
Red Murray — 1911, 1912, 1913
Art Nehf — 1921, 1922, 1923, 1924
Robb Nen — 2002
Bob Nieman — 1962
Donell Nixon — 1989
Ray Noble — 1951
Ken Oberkfell — 1989
Jimmy O'Connell — 1923, 1924*
Billy O'Dell — 1962
Lefty O'Doul — 1933
John Orsino — 1962
Russ Ortiz — 2002
Mel Ott — 1933, 1936, 1937
Jose Pagan — 1962
LeRoy Parmelee — 1933*
Gene Paulette — 1911*
Homer Peel — 1933
Pol Perritt — 1917
Billy Pierce — 1962
Bill Rariden — 1917, 1922*
Johnny Rawlings — 1921, 1922*
Rick Reuschel — 1989
Dusty Rhodes — 1954
Paul Richards — 1933*
Ernest Riles — 1989
Bill Rigney — 1951
Jimmy Ripple — 1936, 1937
Dave Robertson — 1917, 1922*
Don Robinson — 1989
Felix Rodriguez — 2002
Kirk Rueter — 2002
Blondy Ryan — 1933, 1937
Rosy Ryan — 1921*, 1922, 1923, 1924
Slim Sallee — 1917
Jack Salveson — 1933*
Reggie Sanders — 2002
Jack Sanford — 1962

Benito Santiago — 2002
Hank Schenz — 1951
Jason Schmidt — 2002
Hal Schumacher — 1933, 1936, 1937
Ferdie Schupp — 1917
Jack Scott — 1922, 1923
Tillie Shafer — 1912, 1913
Red Shea — 1921*
Pat Sheridan — 1989
Tsuyoshi Shinjo — 2002
Ralph Shinners — 1923*
Al Smith — 1936, 1937
Earl Smith — 1921, 1922
Fred Snodgrass — 1911, 1912, 1913
J. T. Snow — 2002
Frank Snyder — 1921, 1922, 1923, 1924
Billy Southworth — 1924
George Spencer — 1951
Glenn Spencer — 1933*
Eddie Stanky — 1951
Casey Stengel — 1922, 1923
Sammy Strang — 1905
Bill Taylor — 1954*
Dummy Taylor — 1905*
Bill Terry — 1924, 1933, 1936
Jeff Tesreau — 1912, 1913, 1917
Hank Thompson — 1951, 1954
Robby Thompson — 1989
Bobby Thomson — 1951
Jim Thorpe — 1913*, 1917
Fred Toney — 1921

Jose Uribe — 1989
Johnny Vergez — 1933*
Mule Watson — 1923, 1924
Wes Westrum — 1951, 1954
Burgess Whitehead — 1936, 1937
Hoyt Wilhelm — 1954
Joe Wilhoit — 1917
Dave Williams — 1951, 1954
Matt Williams — 1989
Art Wilson — 1911, 1912, 1913
Hack Wilson — 1924
Jay Witasick — 2002
Tim Worrell — 2002
Hooks Wiltse — 1911, 1913
Al Worthington — 1954*
Ross Youngs — 1921, 1922, 1923, 1924
Sal Yvars — 1951
Chad Zerbe — 2002
Heinie Zimmerman — 1917

* denotes eligible for World Series but did not play.

Managers
Dusty Baker — 2002
Roger Craig — 1987
Alvin Dark — 1962
Leo Durocher — 1951, 1954
John McGraw — 1905, 1911, 1912, 1913, 1917,
            1921, 1922, 1923, 1924
Bill Terry — 1933, 1936, 1937

NEW YORK/SAN FRANCISCO GIANTS WORLD SERIES BATTING LEADERS

Games

Larry Doyle	8	1912
Art Fletcher	8	1912
Buck Herzog	8	1912
Fred Merkle	8	1912
Chief Meyers	8	1912
Red Murray	8	1912
Fred Snodgrass	8	1912
Dave Bancroft	8	1921
George Burns	8	1921
Frankie Frisch	8	1921
George Kelly	8	1921
Irish Meusel	8	1921
Johnny Rawlings	8	1921
Ross Youngs	8	1921

Note: Fourteen players have appeared in 7 games.

At-Bats

Larry Doyle	33	1912
Fred Merkle	33	1912
Fred Snodgrass	33	1912
Dave Bancroft	33	1921
George Burns	33	1921
Rich Aurilia	32	2002
Red Murray	31	1912
George Kelly	31	1924
Kenny Lofton	31	2002
Buck Herzog	30	1912
Frankie Frisch	30	1921
George Kelly	30	1921
Johnny Rawlings	30	1921
Frankie Frisch	30	1924
Fred Lindstrom	30	1924
Hack Wilson	30	1924

Runs

Barry Bonds	8	2002
George Kelly	7	1924
Kenny Lofton	7	2002
Buck Herzog	6	1912
Hank Thompson	6	1954
Jeff Kent	6	2002
J.T. Snow	6	2002
Larry Doyle	5	1912
Fred Merkle	5	1912
Red Murray	5	1912

Frankie Frisch	5	1921
Dick Bartell	5	1936
Alvin Dark	5	1951
Rich Aurilia	5	2002

Hits

Buck Herzog	12	1912
Dave Robertson	11	1917
George Burns	11	1921
Monte Irvin	11	1951
J.T. Snow	11	2002
Chief Meyers	10	1912
Red Murray	10	1912
Irish Meusel	10	1921
Johnny Rawlings	10	1921
Frankie Frisch	10	1923
Frankie Frish	10	1924
Fred Lindstrom	10	1924
Alvin Dark	10	1951

Doubles

Buck Herzog	4	1912
Red Murray	4	1912
George Burns	4	1921
Frankie Frisch	4	1924
Larry Doyle	3	1911
Johnny Rawlings	3	1921
Dick Bartell	3	1936
Alvin Dark	3	1951
Chuck Hiller	3	1962
Eighteen tied with	2	

Triples

Twenty-four tied with	1	

Home Runs

Barry Bonds	4	2002
Jeff Kent	3	2002
Benny Kauff	2	1917
Casey Stengel	2	1923
Mel Ott	2	1933
Dusty Rhodes	2	1954
Rich Aurilia	2	2002
Reggie Sanders	2	2002
Thirty-one tied with	1	

RBI

Irish Meusel	7	1921
Irish Meusel	7	1922
Dusty Rhodes	7	1954
Jeff Kent	7	2002
Barry Bonds	6	2002
Reggie Sanders	6	2002
Red Murray	5	1912
Benny Kauff	5	1917
Bill Terry	5	1936
Chuck Hiller	5	1962
Rich Aurilia	5	2002
Benito Santiago	5	2002

Stolen Bases

Josh Devore	4	1912
Art Devlin	3	1905

Frankie Frisch	3	1921
Eleven tied with	2	

Batting Average

Dave Robertson	.500	1917
Heinie Groh	.474	1922
Frankie Frisch	.471	1922
Barry Bonds	.471	2002
Monte Irvin	.458	1951
Bill Terry	.429	1924
Casey Stengel	.417	1923
Alvin Dark	.417	1951
Alvin Dark	.412	1954
J.T. Snow	.407	2002
Buck Herzog	.400	1912
Frankie Frisch	.400	1923

NEW YORK/SAN FRANCISCO GIANTS WORLD SERIES PITCHING LEADERS

Games

Felix Rodriguez	6	2002
Tim Worrell	6	2002
Christy Mathewson	3	1905
Rube Marquard	3	1911
Christy Mathewson	3	1911
Christy Mathewson	3	1912
Jeff Tesreau	3	1912
Pol Perritt	3	1917
Jesse Barnes	3	1921
Phil Douglas	3	1921
Art Nehf	3	1921
Rosy Ryan	3	1923
Jack Bentley	3	1924
Hugh McQuillian	3	1924
Art Nehf	3	1924
Cliff Melton	3	1937
Larry Jansen	3	1951
Don Larsen	3	1962
Billy O'Dell	3	1962
Jack Sanford	3	1962
Jeff Brantley	3	1989
Kelly Downs	3	1989
Craig Lefferts	3	1989
Scott Eyre	3	2002
Robb Nen	3	2002
Chad Zerbe	3	2002

Games Started

Christy Mathewson	3	1905
Christy Mathewson	3	1911
Christy Mathewson	3	1912
Jeff Tesreau	3	1912
Phil Douglas	3	1921
Art Nehf	3	1921
Jack Sanford	3	1962
Twenty-five tied with	2	

Complete Games

Christy Mathewson	3	1905
Rube Marquard	3	1912
Christy Mathewson	3	1912
Art Nehf	3	1921
Christy Mathewson	2	1911
Phil Douglas	2	1921
Carl Hubbell	2	1933
Hal Schumacher	2	1933
Twenty-one tied with	1	

Shutouts

Christy Mathewson	3	1905
Joe McGinnity	1	1905
Christy Mathewson	1	1913
Rube Benton	1	1917
Ferdie Schupp	1	1917

Art Nehf	1	1921
Jack Scott	1	1922
Art Nehf	1	1924
Jack Sanford	1	1962

Innings Pitched

Christy Mathewson	28.2	1912
Christy Mathewson	27.0	1905
Christy Mathewson	27.0	1911
Phil Douglas	26.0	1921
Art Nehf	26.0	1921
Jack Sanford	23.1	1962
Jeff Tesreau	23.0	1912
Carl Hubbell	20.0	1933
Jason Schmidt	14	2002
Art Nehf	19.2	1924
Christy Mathewson	19.0	1913

Strikeouts

Jack Sanford	19	1962
Christy Mathewson	18	1905
Jesse Barnes	18	1921
Phil Douglas	17	1921
Jeff Tesreau	15	1912
Carl Hubbell	15	1933
Jason Schmidt	14	2002
Christy Mathewson	13	1911
Johnny Antonelli	12	1954
Hal Schumacher	11	1936
Christy Mathewson	10	1912
Jack Bentley	10	1924
Carl Hubbell	10	1936

Wins

Christy Mathewson	3	1905
Rube Marquard	2	1912
Jesse Barnes	2	1921
Phil Douglas	2	1921

Carl Hubbell	2	1933
Thirty-four tied with	1	

Losses

Christy Mathewson	2	1911
Christy Mathewson	2	1912
Jeff Tesreau	2	1912
Slim Sallee	2	1917
Art Nehf	2	1921
Jack Bentley	2	1924
Freddie Fitzsimmons	2	1936
Cliff Melton	2	1951
Larry Jansen	2	1951
Jack Sanford	2	1962
Livan Hernandez	2	2002

Saves

Robb Nen	2	2002
Hugh McQuillian	1	1924
Mule Watson	1	1924
Carl Hubbell	1	1937
Sheldon Jones	1	1951
Johnny Antonelli	1	1954
Hoyt Wilhelm	1	1954
Billy O'Dell	1	1962

ERA

Christy Mathewson	0.00	1905
Joe McGinnity	0.00	1905
Jack Scott	0.00	1922
Carl Hubbell	0.00	1933
Rube Marquard	0.50	1912
Johnny Antonelli	0.84	1954
Christy Mathewson	0.95	1913
Rosy Ryan	0.96	1923
Christy Mathewson	1.26	1912
Art Nehf	1.38	1921

APPENDIX E
TRADES

NEW YORK/SAN FRANCISCO GIANTS ALL-TIME TRADES

Date	Transaction
August 12, 1899	Sent Jouett Meekin to Boston Beaneaters in exchange for $3,500 cash.
February 1900	Acquired Frank Bowerman from Pittsburgh Pirates in exchange for cash.
February 1900	Sent Tom O'Brien to Pittsburgh Pirates in exchange for cash.
February 9, 1900	Acquired Win Mercer from Washington Senators in exchange for cash.
February 17, 1900	Acquired Charlie Frisbee and Charles Hickman from Boston Beaneaters in exchange for cash.
February 27, 1900	Acquired Pink Hawley from Cincinnati Reds in exchange for cash.
February 29, 1900	Acquired Kip Selbach from Cincinnati Reds in exchange for cash.
August 8, 1900	Acquired Elmer Smith from Cincinnati Reds in exchange for cash.
December 15, 1900	Acquired Christy Mathewson from Cincinnati Reds in exchange for Amos Rusie.
January 1901	Acquired Heinie Smith from Pittsburgh Pirates in exchange for Ed Doheny.
January 1901	Sent Elmer Smith to Pittsburgh Pirates in exchange for cash.
February 1901	Acquired John Ganzel from Chicago Orphans in exchange for cash.
February 1901	Acquired Sammy Strang from Chicago Orphans in exchange for Jack Doyle.
May 1901	Acquired Bill Magee from St. Louis Cardinals in exchange for Chauncey Fisher.
May 30, 1901	Acquired Algie McBride from Cincinnati Reds in exchange for cash.
July 1901	Acquired Frank Murphy from Boston Beaneaters in exchange for cash.
February 1902	Acquired Jim Delahanty and Jack Doyle from Chicago Cubs in exchange for cash.
July 1902	Sent Rowy Evans and George Wall to Brooklyn Superbas in exchange for cash.
July 1902	Acquired George Browne from Philadelphia Phillies in exchange for cash.
July 1902	Acquired Hal O'Hagen from Chicago Cubs in exchange for Jack Hendricks.
January 1903	Sent Brickyard Kennedy to Pittsburgh Pirates in exchange for cash.
July 1903	Acquired Moose McCormick from Philadelphia Phillies in exchange for cash.
December 12, 1903	Acquired Bill Dahlen from Brooklyn Superbas in exchange for Charlie Babb and John Cronin.

February 1904	Sent Roscoe Miller to Pittsburgh Pirates in exchange for cash.
May 1904	Acquired Doc Marshall from Philadelphia Phillies in exchange for cash.
July 3, 1904	Acquired Mike Donlin from Cincinnati Reds in exchange for Moose McCormick.
August 1904	Acquired Claude Elliott from Cincinnati Reds in exchange for cash.
August 7, 1904	Sent Doc Marshall to Boston Beaneaters in exchange for cash.
August 9, 1904	Sent Moose McCormick to Pittsburgh Pirates in exchange for cash.
January 1905	Sent Jack Wagner to St. Louis Cardinals in exchange for cash.
February 1905	Acquired Sammy Strang from Brooklyn Dodgers in exchange for cash.
April 1905	Sent Bob Hall to Brooklyn Dodgers in exchange for cash.
July 13, 1906	Acquired Spike Shannon from St. Louis Cardinals in exchange for Doc Marshall and Sam Mertes.
July 14, 1906	Acquired Cy Seymour from Cincinnati Reds in exchange for $12,000 cash.
December 3, 1907	Acquired Al Bridwell and Tom Needham from Boston Beaneaters in exchange for Frank Bowerman, George Browne, Bill Dahlen, George Ferguson, Dan McGann and Fred Tenney.
April 1908	Sent Jack Hannifin to Boston Beaneaters in exchange for cash.
May 1908	Acquired Moose McCormick from Philadelphia Phillies in exchange for cash.
July 1908	Acquired Shad Barry from St. Louis Cardinals in exchange for cash.
July 1908	Acquired Dave Brain from Cincinnati Reds in exchange for cash.
July 1908	Sent Spike Shannon to Pittsburgh Pirates in exchange for cash.
December 1908	Sent Tom Needham to Chicago Cubs in exchange for cash.
December 12, 1908	Acquired Red Murray, Bugs Raymond and Admiral Schlei from St. Louis Cardinals in exchange for Roger Bresnahan.
December 1909	Acquired Beals Becker from Boston Beaneaters in exchange for Buck Herzog.
May 8, 1910	Sent Elmer Zacher to St. Louis Cardinals in exchange for cash.
July 22, 1911	Acquired Buck Herzog from Boston Beaneaters in exchange for Al Bridwell and Hank Gowdy.
August 1, 1911	Sent Mike Donlin to Boston Beaneaters in exchange for cash.
December 1911	Sent Art Devlin to Boston Beaneaters in exchange for cash.
May 22, 1913	Acquired Art Fromme and Eddie Grant from Cincinnati Reds in exchange for Red Ames, Josh Devore, Heinie Groh and $20,000 cash.
August 6, 1913	Sent Doc Crandall to St. Louis Cardinals in exchange for Larry McLean.
August 13, 1913	Acquired Doc Crandall from St. Louis Cardinals in exchange for cash.
December 12, 1913	Acquired Bob Bescher from Cincinnati Reds in exchange for Grover Hartley and Buck Herzog. Hartley jumped to Federal League and Herzog was named Cincinnati manager.
January 1915	Acquired Hans Lobert from Philadelphia Athletics in exchange for Al Demaree and Milt Stock.
February 18, 1915	Acquired Pol Perritt from St. Louis Cardinals in exchange for cash.
June 1915	Acquired Bobby Schang from Pittsburgh Pirates in exchange for cash.
July 1915	Acquired Howard Baker from Chicago White Sox in exchange for cash.
August 19, 1915	Acquired Rube Benton from Cincinnati Reds in exchange for $3,000 cash.
August 19, 1915	Sent Fred Snodgrass to Boston Braves in exchange for cash.

December 23, 1915	Acquired Benny Kauff from Brooklyn Tip-Tops (Federal League) in exchange for $35,000 cash.
December 23, 1915	Acquired Bill McKechnie and Bill Rariden from Newark Peppers (Federal League) in exchange for cash.
December 23, 1915	Acquired Edd Roush from Newark Peppers (Federal League) in exchange for $7,500 cash.
February 10, 1916	Acquired Fred Anderson from Buffalo Buffeds (Federal League) in exchange for cash.
July 20, 1916	Acquired Buck Herzog and Red Killefer from Cincinnati Reds in exchange for Christy Mathewson, Bill McKechnie and Edd Roush.
July 23, 1916	Acquired Slim Sallee from St. Louis Cardinals in exchange for $10,000 cash.
August 20, 1916	Acquired Lew McCarty from Brooklyn Dodgers in exchange for Fred Merkle.
August 28, 1916	Acquired Mickey Doolan and Heinie Zimmerman from Chicago Cubs in exchange for Larry Doyle, Herb Hunter and Merwin Jacobson.
April 24, 1917	Sent Jim Thorpe to Cincinnati Reds in exchange for cash. Thorpe was returned to New York on August 1, 1917.
July 31, 1917	Acquired Al Demaree from Chicago Cubs in exchange for Pete Kilduff.
January 8, 1918	Acquired Jesse Barnes and Larry Doyle from Boston Braves in exchange for Buck Herzog.
June 1918	Acquired Bob Steele from Pittsburgh Pirates in exchange for cash.
June 20, 1918	Acquired George Smith from Cincinnati Reds in exchange for cash.
July 15, 1918	Sent George Smith to Brooklyn Dodgers in exchange for cash.
July 25, 1918	Acquired Fred Toney from Cincinnati Reds in exchange for cash.
October 1918	Acquired George Smith from Brooklyn Dodgers in exchange for cash.
October 1918	Sent Jimmy Smith to Boston Braves in exchange for cash.
January 1919	Acquired Lee King from Pittsburgh Pirates in exchange for cash.
February 1919	Sent Al Demaree to Boston Braves in exchange for cash.
February 1919	Acquired Jimmy Smith from Boston Braves in exchange for Walter Holke.
February 1919	Sent Jimmy Smith to Cincinnati Reds in exchange for cash.
February 2, 1919	Acquired Hal Chase from Cincinnati Reds in exchange for Bill Rariden.
May 14, 1919	Sent Eddie Sicking to Philadelphia Phillies in exchange for cash.
May 21, 1919	Acquired Pat Ragan from Boston Braves in exchange for Jim Thorpe.
May 27, 1919	Acquired Joe Oeschger from Philadelphia Phillies in exchange for George Smith.
July 16, 1919	Acquired Frank Snyder from St. Louis Cardinals in exchange for Ferdie Schupp.
July 25, 1919	Acquired Phil Douglas from Chicago Cubs in exchange for Dave Robertson.
August 15, 1919	Acquired Art Nehf from Boston Braves in exchange for Red Causey, Johnny Jones, Joe Oeschger, Mickey O'Neil and $55,000 cash.
February 1920	Acquired Fred Lear from Chicago Cubs in exchange for cash.
June 8, 1920	Acquired Dave Bancroft from Philadelphia Phillies in exchange for Art Fletcher, Billy Hubbell and cash.
July 1920	Sent Jigger Statz to Boston Red Sox in exchange for cash.
July 2, 1920	Sent Eddie Sicking to Cincinnati Reds in exchange for cash.
July 4, 1920	Sent Lew McCarty to St. Louis Cardinals in exchange for cash.
July 27, 1920	Acquired Doug Baird from Brooklyn Dodgers in exchange for cash.
June 1921	Sent John Monroe to Philadelphia Phillies in exchange for cash.
June 1921	Sent Pol Perritt to Detroit Tigers in exchange for cash.
July 1, 1921	Acquired Red Cause, Johnny Rawlings and Casey Stengel from Philadelphia Phillies in exchange for Lee King, Goldie Rapp and Lance Richbourg.

July 25, 1921	Acquired Irish Meusel from Philadelphia Phillies in exchange for Butch Henlin, Curt Walker, Jesse Winters and $30,000 cash.
December 7, 1921	Acquired Heinie Groh from Cincinnati Reds in exchange for George Burns, Mike Gonzalez and $100,000 cash.
April 20, 1922	Acquired Dave Robertson from Pittsburgh Pirates in exchange for cash.
July 30, 1922	Acquired Hugh McQuillan from Boston Braves in exchange for Larry Benton, Fred Toney and $100,000 cash. Toney refused to report and remained Giants property.
July 30, 1922	Sent Rube Benton to Cincinnati Reds in exchange for cash.
June 7, 1923	Acquired Hank Gowdy and Mule Watson from Boston Braves in exchange for Jesse Barnes and Earl Smith.
November 12, 1923	Acquired Joe Oeschger and Billy Southworth from Boston Braves in exchange for Dave Bancroft, Bill Cunningham and Casey Stengel. Bancroft was named Boston manager.
June 5, 1924	Sent Dinty Gearin to Boston Braves in exchange for cash.
April 17, 1925	Acquired Tim McNamara from Boston Braves in exchange for Rosy Ryan.
December 30, 1925	Acquired Joe Beggs from Cincinnati Reds in exchange for Babe Young.
May 11, 1926	Sent Art Nehf to Cincinnati Reds in exchange for cash.
June 14, 1926	Acquired Heinie Mueller from St. Louis Cardinals in exchange for Billy Southworth.
December 20, 1926	Acquired Rogers Hornsby from St. Louis Cardinals in exchange for Frankie Frisch and Jimmy Ring.
January 9, 1927	Acquired George Harper and Butch Henline from Philadelphia Phillies in exchange for Jack Scott and Fresco Thompson.
January 9, 1927	Acquired Burleigh Grimes from Brooklyn Dodgers in exchange for Butch Henline.
February 9, 1927	Acquired Edd Roush from Cincinnati Reds in exchange for George Kelly and cash.
May 25, 1927	Acquired Mickey O'Neil from Washington Senators in exchange for cash.
June 12, 1927	Acquired Larry Benton, Zack Taylor and Herb Thomas from Boston Braves in exchange for Doc Farrell, Kent Greenfield and Hugh McQuillan.
January 10, 1928	Acquired Shanty Hogan and Jimmy Welsh from Boston Braves in exchange for Rogers Hornsby.
February 1928	Sent Zack Taylor to Boston Braves in exchange for cash.
February 11, 1928	Acquired Vic Aldridge from Pittsburgh Pirates in exchange for Burleigh Grimes.
May 1, 1928	Acquired Bob O'Farrell from St. Louis Cardinals in exchange for George Harper.
May 29, 1928	Acquired Russ Wrightstone from Philadelphia Phillies in exchange for Art Jahn.
June 15, 1928	Acquired Joe Genevich from Boston Braves in exchange for Virgil Barnes, Ben Cantwell, Bill Clarkson and Al Spohrer.
October 29, 1928	Acquired Freddy Leach from Philadelphia Phillies in exchange for Lefty O'Doul and cash.
June 14, 1929	Acquired Doc Farrell from Boston Braves in exchange for Jimmy Welsh.
July 14, 1929	Sent Jack Cummings to Boston Braves in exchange for cash.
April 10, 1930	Acquired Wally Roettger from St. Louis Cardinals in exchange for Doc Farrell and Showboat Fisher.
May 15, 1930	Acquired Clarence Mitchell from St. Louis Cardinals in exchange for Ralph Judd.
May 21, 1930	Acquired Hughie Critz from Cincinnati Reds in exchange for Larry Benton.
May 27, 1930	Acquired Ethan Allen and Pete Donohue from Cincinnati Reds in exchange for Pat Crawford.
October 29, 1930	Sent Wally Roettger to Cincinnati Reds in exchange for cash.

March 19, 1932	Sent Freddy Leach to Boston Braves in exchange for $10,000 cash.
October 10, 1932	Acquired Gus Mancuso and Ray Starr from St. Louis Cardinals in exchange for Ethan Allen, Jim Mooney, Bob O'Farrell and Bill Walker.
December 12, 1932	Acquired Gus Dugas and Glenn Spencer from Pittsburgh Pirates in exchange for Freddie Lindstrom, then sent Dugas and Chuck Fullis to Philadelphia Phillies in exchange for Kiddo Davis.
December 29, 1932	Sent Shanty Hogan to Boston Braves in exchange for $25,000 cash.
June 12, 1933	Sent Ray Starr to Boston Braves in exchange for cash.
June 16, 1933	Acquired Watty Clark and Lefty O'Doul from Brooklyn Dodgers in exchange for Sam Leslie.
November 15, 1933	Acquired George Grantham from Cincinnati Reds in exchange for Glenn Spencer.
February 1934	Acquired George Watkins from St. Louis Cardinals in exchange for Kiddo Davis.
May 4, 1934	Sent Fran Healy to St. Louis Cardinals in exchange for cash.
November 1, 1934	Acquired Dick Bartell from Philadelphia Phillies in exchange for Pretzels Pezzullo, Blondy Ryan, Johnny Vergez, George Watkins and cash.
December 1934	Acquired Leon Chagnon from St. Louis Cardinals in exchange for cash.
December 13, 1934	Acquired Kiddo Davis from Philadelphia Phillies in exchange for Joe Bowman.
December 14, 1934	Acquired Mark Koenig and Allyn Stout from Cincinnati Reds in exchange for Billy Myers and cash.
December 19, 1934	Sent Sammy Byrd to Cincinnati Reds in exchange for cash.
August 2, 1935	Acquired Euel Moore from Philadelphia Phillies in exchange for cash.
November 14, 1935	Acquired Dick Coffman from St. Louis Browns in exchange for cash.
December 9, 1935	Acquired Burgess Whitehead from St. Louis Cardinals in exchange for Roy Parmelee, Phil Weintraub and cash.
January 1936	Acquired Johnny McCarthy from Brooklyn Dodgers in exchange for $40,000 cash.
January 17, 1936	Sent Tiny Chaplin to Boston Braves in exchange for cash.
February 20, 1936	Acquired Sam Leslie from Brooklyn Dodgers in exchange for cash.
December 4, 1936	Acquired Mickey Haslin from Boston Braves in exchange for Eddie Mayo.
December 8, 1936	Acquired Lou Chiozza from Philadelphia Phillies in exchange for George Scharein and cash.
June 1937	Acquired Jumbo Brown from Cincinnati Reds in exchange for cash.
June 11, 1937	Acquired Tom Baker from Brooklyn Dodgers in exchange for Freddie Fitzsimmons.
June 15, 1937	Acquired Wally Berger from Boston Braves in exchange for Frank Gabler and $35,000 cash.
June 27, 1937	Acquired Ben Cantwell and Hal Lee from Boston Braves in exchange for cash.
August 4, 1937	Sent Kiddo Davis to Cincinnati Reds in exchange for cash.
December 20, 1937	Sent Al Smith to St. Louis Cardinals in exchange for cash.
March 1938	Acquired Bill Cissell from Philadelphia Athletics in exchange for cash.
June 6, 1938	Acquired Alex Kampouris from Cincinnati Reds in exchange for Wally Berger.
December 6, 1938	Acquired Frank Demaree, Bill Jurges and Ken O'Dea from Chicago Cubs in exchange for Dick Bartell, Hank Leiber and Gus Mancuso.
December 7, 1938	Sent Willie Prall to Chicago Cubs in exchange for cash.
December 11, 1938	Acquired Zeke Bonura from Washington Senators in exchange for Tom Baker, Jim Carlin and $20,000 cash.

May 9, 1939	Acquired Red Lynn from Detroit Tigers in exchange for cash.
August 23, 1939	Acquired Ray Hayworth from Brooklyn Dodgers in exchange for Jimmy Ripple.
April 26, 1940	Sent Zeke Bonura to Washington Senators in exchange for $20,000 cash.
June 15, 1940	Acquired Tony Cuccinello from Boston Braves in exchange for Al Glossop and Manny Salvo.
November 25, 1940	Acquired Joe Orengo from St. Louis Cardinals in exchange for cash.
December 5, 1940	Acquired Bob Bowman from St. Louis Cardinals in exchange for cash.
January 1941	Sent Hy Vandenburg to St. Louis Cardinals in exchange for cash.
January 2, 1941	Acquired Bump Hadley from New York Yankees in exchange for cash.
May 14, 1941	Acquired Bill McGee from St. Louis Cardinals in exchange for Paul Dean, Harry Gumbert and cash.
May 29, 1941	Sent Bump Hadley to Philadelphia A's in exchange for cash.
December 4, 1941	Acquired Hank Leiber from Chicago Cubs in exchange for Bob Bowman.
December 9, 1941	Acquired Bill Werber from Cincinnati Reds in exchange for cash.
December 11, 1941	Acquired Johnny Mize from St. Louis Cardinals in exchange for Bill Lohrman, Johnny McCarthy, Ken O'Dea and $50,000 cash.
February 6, 1942	Acquired Ray Berres from Boston Braves in exchange for cash.
May 5, 1942	Acquired Bill Lohrman from St. Louis Cardinals in exchange for cash.
May 5, 1942	Acquired Gus Mancuso from St. Louis Cardinals in exchange for cash.
April 27, 1943	Acquired Ernie Lombardi from Boston Braves in exchange for Hugh Poland and Connie Ryan.
July 6, 1943	Acquired Joe Medwick from Brooklyn Dodgers in exchange for $50,000 cash.
July 31, 1943	Acquired Dolf Camilli from Brooklyn Dodgers in exchange for Bill Lohrman, Joe Orengo and Bill Sayles. Camilli refused to report and retired.
June 12, 1944	Acquired Johnny Gee from Pittsburgh Pirates in exchange for cash.
June 16, 1945	Acquired Clyde Kluttz from Boston Braves in exchange for Joe Medwick and Ewald Pyle.
January 5, 1946	Acquired Walker Cooper from St. Louis Cardinals in exchange for $175,000 cash.
April 27, 1946	Acquired Goody Rosen from Brooklyn Dodgers in exchange for cash.
May 1946	Acquired Jack Graham from Brooklyn Dodgers in exchange for cash.
May 1, 1946	Acquired Vince DiMaggio from Philadelphia Phillies in exchange for Clyde Kluttz.
June 7, 1947	Acquired Joe Beggs from Cincinnati Reds in exchange for Babe Young.
June 13, 1947	Acquired Mort Cooper from Boston Braves in exchange for Bill Voiselle and cash.
January 16, 1948	Acquired Jack Conway from Cleveland Indians in exchange for cash.
July 30, 1948	Sent Paul Erickson to Pittsburgh Pirates in exchange for cash.
February 26, 1949	Acquired Hank Behrman from Brooklyn Dodgers in exchange for cash.
June 6, 1949	Acquired Kirby Higbe from Pittsburgh Pirates in exchange for Ray Post and Bobby Rhawn.
June 13, 1949	Acquired Ray Mueller from Cincinnati Reds in exchange for Walker Cooper.
August 22, 1949	Sent Johnny Mize to New York Yankees in exchange for $40,000 cash.
December 14, 1949	Acquired Alvin Dark and Eddie Stanky from Boston Braves in exchange for Sid Gordon, Buddy Kerr, Willard Marshall and Red Webb.

March 26, 1950	Acquired Jack Kramer from Boston Braves in exchange for cash.
May 17, 1950	Sent Ray Mueller to Pittsburgh Pirates in exchange for cash.
July 10, 1950	Acquired Jim Hearn from St. Louis Cardinals in exchange for cash.
December 11, 1951	Acquired Chuck Diering and Max Lanier from St. Louis Cardinals in exchange for Eddie Stanky. Stanky was named St. Louis manager.
December 13, 1951	Acquired Jake Schmidt from Philadelphia Phillies in exchange for Jack Lohrke.
April 8, 1952	Acquired Bob Elliott from Boston Braves in exchange for Sheldon Jones and $50,000 cash.
May 8, 1952	Acquired Ted Wilson from Chicago White Sox in exchange for $25,000 cash.
October 13, 1952	Acquired Frank Hiller from Cincinnati Reds in exchange for Gale Henley.
June 15, 1953	Sent Sal Yvars to St. Louis Cardinals in exchange for $12,500 cash.
February 1, 1954	Acquired Johnny Antonelli, Billy Klaus, Don Liddle, Ebba St. Clare and $50,000 cash from Milwaukee Braves in exchange for Sam Calderon and Bobby Thomson.
April 8, 1954	Sent Dave Koslo to Baltimore Orioles in exchange for cash.
December 14, 1954	Acquired Del Wilber from Boston Red Sox in exchange for Billy Klaus.
May 22, 1955	Acquired Sid Gordon from Pittsburgh Pirates in exchange for cash.
March 5, 1956	Acquired Jim Mangan from Pittsburgh Pirates in exchange for cash.
April 16, 1956	Acquired Ray Jablonski and Ray Katt from Chicago Cubs in exchange for Bob Lennon and Dick Littlefield
April 21, 1956	Sent Billy Gardner to Baltimore Orioles in exchange for $20,000 cash.
June 14, 1956	Acquired Jackie Brandt, Dick Littlefield, Bill Sarni, Red Schoendienst and Bob Stephenson from St. Louis Cardinals in exchange for Alvin Dark, Ray Katt, Don Liddle and Whitey Lockman.
October 1, 1956	Acquired Gordon Jones from St. Louis Cardinals in exchange for cash.
October 1, 1956	Acquired Stu Miller from Philadelphia Phillies in exchange for Jim Hearn.
December 13, 1956	Acquired Jackie Robinson from Brooklyn Dodgers in exchange for Dick Littlefield and $30,000 cash. Robinson retired and trade was canceled.
February 26, 1957	Acquired Whitey Lockman from St. Louis Cardinals in exchange for Hoyt Wilhelm.
June 15, 1957	Acquired Ray Crone, Danny O'Connell and Bobby Thomson from Milwaukee Braves in exchange for Red Schoendienst.
December 10, 1957	Acquired Tom Poholsky from Chicago Cubs in exchange for Freddy Rodriguez.
January 28, 1958	Acquired Jim Finigan and $25,000 cash from Detroit Tigers in exchange for Gale Harris and Ozzie Virgil.
March 21, 1958	Sent Don Mueller to Chicago White Sox in exchange for cash.
March 24, 1958	Acquired Foster Castleman from Baltimore Orioles in exchange for $30,000 cash.
April 2, 1958	Acquired Jim King from St. Louis Cardinals in exchange for Ray Katt.
April 3, 1958	Acquired Bob Speake and cash from Chicago Cubs in exchange for Bobby Thomson.
October 5, 1958	Sent Pete Burnside to Detroit Tigers in exchange for cash.
October 8, 1958	Acquired Hobie Landrith, Billy Muffett and Benny Valenzuela from St. Louis Cardinals in exchange for Ernie Broglio and Marv Grissom.
December 3, 1958	Acquired Jack Sanford from Philadelphia Phillies for Ruben Gomez and Valmy Thomas.
February 14, 1959	Sent Whitey Lockman to Baltimore Orioles in exchange for cash.
March 25, 1959	Acquired Don Choate and Sam Jones from St. Louis Cardinals in exchange for Ray Jablonski and Bill White.

June 14, 1959	Acquired Jim Hegan from Philadelphia Phillies in exchange for cash.
November 30, 1959	Acquired Billy Loes and Billy O'Dell from Baltimore Orioles in exchange for Jackie Brandt, Gordon Jones and Roger McCardell.
December 15, 1959	Acquired Don Blasingame from St. Louis Cardinals in exchange for Daryl Spencer and Leon Wagner.
March 29, 1960	Acquired Jim Marshall from Boston Red Sox in exchange for Al Worthington.
April 5, 1960	Acquired Dale Long from Chicago Cubs in exchange for cash.
May 12, 1960	Acquired Dave Philley from Philadelphia Phillies in exchange for cash.
August 22, 1960	Sent Dale Long to New York Yankees in exchange for cash.
September 1, 1960	Sent Dave Philley to Baltimore Orioles in exchange for cash.
October 31, 1960	Acquired Andre Rodgers from Milwaukee Braves in exchange for Alvin Dark.
December 3, 1960	Acquired Harvey Kuenn from Cleveland Indians in exchange for Johnny Antonelli and Willie Kirkland.
April 27, 1961	Acquired Ed Bailey from Cincinnati Reds in exchange for Don Blasingame, Sherman Jones and Bob Schmidt.
October 13, 1961	Sent Jim Marshall to New York Mets in exchange for cash.
October 16, 1961	Sent Billy Loes to New York Mets in exchange for cash.
November 30, 1961	Acquired Don Larsen and Billy Pierce from Chicago White Sox in exchange for Bob Farley, Eddie Fisher, Verle Tiefenthaler and Dom Zani.
December 15, 1961	Acquired Joe Pignatano from Kansas City Athletics in exchange for Jose Tartabull.
April 29, 1962	Acquired Bob Nieman from Cleveland Indians in exchange for cash.
July 13, 1962	Sent Joe Pignatano from New York Mets in exchange for cash.
November 30, 1962	Acquired Joey Amalfitano from Houston Colt .45s in exchange for Dick LeMay and Manny Mota.
December 15, 1962	Acquired Jimmie Coker, Jack Fisher and Billy Hoeft from Baltimore Orioles in exchange for Mike McCormick, Stu Miller and John Orsino.
March 29, 1963	Acquired Jacke Davis from Los Angeles Dodgers in exchange for Charlie Dees.
August 8, 1963	Acquired Norm Larker from Milwaukee Braves in exchange for cash.
October 10, 1963	Sent Jack Fisher to New York Mets in exchange for $30,000 cash.
October 15, 1963	Acquired Amado Samuel from Milwaukee Braves in exchange for cash.
December 3, 1963	Acquired Del Crandell, Bob Hendley and Bob Shaw from Milwaukee Braves in exchange for Ed Bailey, Ernie Bowman and Billy Hoeft.
April 14, 1964	Acquired Duke Snider from New York Mets in exchange for cash.
May 20, 1964	Sent Don Larsen to Houston Colt .45s in exchange for cash.
November 21, 1964	Acquired Jack Hiatt from Los Angeles Dodgers in exchange for Jose Cardenal.
February 1, 1965	Acquired Ed Bailey from Milwaukee Braves in exchange for Billy O'Dell.
February 11, 1965	Acquired Bob Burda and Bob Priddy from Pittsburgh Pirates in exchange for Del Crandall.
May 4, 1965	Acquired Bill Henry from Cincinnati Reds in exchange for Jim Duffalo.
May 12, 1965	Sent Chuck Hiller to New York Mets in exchange for cash.
May 22, 1965	Acquired Dick Schofield from Pittsburgh Pirates in exchange for Jose Pagan.
May 29, 1965	Acquired Dick Bertell and Len Grabrielson from Chicago Cubs in exchange for Ed Bailey, Bob Hendley and Harvey Kuenn.
August 18, 1965	Sent Jack Sanford to California Angels in exchange for cash.
October 1, 1965	Acquired Joe Gibbon and Ozzie Virgil from Pittsburgh Pirates in exchange for Matty Alou.
December 2, 1965	Acquired Don Landrum, Lindy McDaniel and Jim Rittwage from Chicago Cubs in exchange for Randy Hundley.

May 8, 1966	Acquired Ray Sadecki from St. Louis Cardinals in exchange for Orlando Cepeda.
May 11, 1966	Sent Dick Schofield to New York Yankees in exchange for cash.
May 16, 1966	Sent Gil Garrido to Atlanta Braves in exchange for cash.
June 10, 1966	Sent Bob Shaw to New York Mets in exchange for cash.
December 13, 1966	Acquired Ken MacKenzie from St. Louis Cardinals in exchange for Jimmie Coker.
December 13, 1966	Acquired Mike McCormick from Washington Senators in exchange for Cap Peterson and Bob Priddy.
December 14, 1966	Acquired Norm Siebern from California Angels in exchange for Al Gallagher.
April 3, 1967	Acquired Don Bryant from Chicago Cubs in exchange for cash.
May 31, 1967	Acquired Ty Cline from Atlanta Braves in exchange for cash.
June 22, 1967	Acquired Dick Groat from Philadelphia Phillies in exchange for cash.
July 16, 1967	Sent Norm Siebern to Boston Red Sox in exchange for cash.
February 13, 1968	Acquired Ron Hunt and Nate Oliver from Los Angeles Dodgers in exchange for Tom Haller and Frank Kasmeta.
June 27, 1968	Sent Bill Henry to Pittsburgh Pirates in exchange for cash.
July 12, 1968	Acquired Bill Monbouquette from New York Yankees in exchange for Lindy McDaniel.
December 6, 1968	Acquired Charley Smith from New York Yankees in exchange for Nate Oliver.
December 21, 1968	Sent Bill Monbouquette to Houston Astros in exchange for cash. Monbouquette was returned to San Francisco on April 5, 1969.
March 28, 1969	Sent Charley Smith to Chicago Cubs in exchange for cash.
June 10, 1969	Acquired Ron Kline from Pittsburgh Pirates in exchange for Joe Gibbon.
July 5, 1969	Sent Ron Kline to Boston Red Sox in exchange for cash.
August 9, 1969	Acquired Don McMahon from Detroit Tigers in exchange for cash.
September 2, 1969	Sent Cesar Gutierrez to Detroit Tigers in exchange for cash.
December 1, 1969	Sent Bob Schroder to Washington Senators in exchange for cash.
December 5, 1969	Acquired Frank Reberger from San Diego Padres in exchange for Bob Barton, Bobby Etheridge and Ron Herbel.
December 12, 1969	Acquired Dick Simpson and Steve Whitaker from Seattle Pilots in exchange for Bobby Bolin.
December 12, 1969	Acquired Jim Gosger and Bob Heise from New York Mets in exchange for Dave Marshall and Ray Sadecki.
April 4, 1970	Acquired Russ Gibson from Boston Red Sox in exchange for cash.
April 6, 1970	Sent Jack Hiatt to Montreal Expos in exchange for cash.
April 20, 1970	Sent Jim Gosger to Montreal Expos in exchange for cash.
May 19, 1970	Acquired Jerry Johnson from St. Louis Cardinals in exchange for Frank Linzy.
June 9, 1970	Sent Bob Burda to Milwaukee Brewers in exchange for cash.
July 20, 1970	Sent John Cumberland from New York Mets in exchange for Mike McCormick.
December 30, 1970	Acquired Steve Huntz from San Diego Padres in exchange for Bill Frost and Don Mason.
March 23, 1971	Acquired Steve Hamilton from Chicago White Sox in exchange for Steve Huntz.
May 29, 1971	Acquired Frank Duffy and Vern Geishert from Cincinnati Reds in exchange for George Foster.
June 1, 1971	Acquired Floyd Wicker from Milwaukee Brewers in exchange for Bob Heise.
November 29, 1971	Acquired Sam McDowell from Cleveland Indians in exchange for Frank Duffy and Gaylord Perry.
February 2, 1972	Sent Hal Lanier to New York Yankees in exchange for cash.

February 7, 1972	Sent Rich Robertson to Chicago White Sox in exchange for cash. Robertson was returned to San Francisco on March 19, 1972.
April 14, 1972	Sent Dick Dietz to Los Angeles Dodgers in exchange for cash.
May 11, 1972	Acquired Charlie Williams from New York Mets in exchange for Willie Mays.
June 16, 1972	Sent John Cumberland to St. Louis Cardinals in exchange for cash.
November 28, 1972	Acquired Tom Bradley from Chicago Cubs in exchange for Ken Henderson and Steve Stone.
March 6, 1973	Sent Jerry Johnson to Cleveland Indians in exchange for cash.
April 2, 1973	Acquired Greg Minton from Kansas City Royals in exchange for Fran Healy.
April 17, 1973	Sent Jim Ray Hart to New York Yankees in exchange for cash.
June 7, 1973	Sent Sam McDowell to New York Yankees in exchange for cash.
October 25, 1973	Acquired Mike Caldwell from San Diego Padres in exchange for Willie McCovey and Bernie Williams.
December 7, 1973	Sent Juan Marichal to Boston Red Sox in exchange for cash.
April 1, 1974	Acquired John Boccabella from Montreal Expos in exchange for Don Carrithers.
October 14, 1974	Acquired Tom Heintzelman from St. Louis Cardinals in exchange for Jim Willoughby.
October 14, 1974	Acquired Marc Hill from St. Louis Cardinals in exchange for Ken Rudolph and Elias Sosa.
October 22, 1974	Acquired Bobby Murcer from New York Yankees in exchange for Bobby Bonds.
December 6, 1974	Acquired Derrel Thomas from San Diego Padres in exchange for Tito Fuentes and Butch Metzger.
January 29, 1975	Acquired Von Joshua from Los Angeles Dodgers in exchange for cash.
February 28, 1975	Sent Dave Kingman to New York Mets in exchange for $150,000 cash.
May 3, 1975	Sent Mike Phillips to New York Mets in exchange for cash.
May 4, 1975	Acquired Willie Montanez from Philadelphia Phillies in exchange for Garry Maddox.
May 9, 1975	Acquired Luis Gonzalez and Larry Herndon from St. Louis Cardinals in exchange for Ron Bryant.
June 11, 1975	Acquired Craig Robinson from Atlanta Braves in exchange for Ed Goodson.
December 8, 1975	Acquired Ken Reitz from St. Louis Cardinals in exchange for Pete Falcone.
June 2, 1976	Sent Von Joshua to Milwaukee Brewers in exchange for cash.
June 13, 1976	Acquired Darrell Evans and Marty Perez from Atlanta Braves in exchange for Jake Brown, Mike Eden, Willie Montanez and Craig Robinson.
October 20, 1976	Acquired Willie Crawford, John Curtis and Vic Harris from St. Louis Cardinals in exchange for Mike Caldwell, John D'Acquisto and Dave Rader.
December 6, 1976	Sent Glenn Adams to Minnesota Twins in exchange for cash.
December 10, 1976	Acquired Lynn McGlothen from St. Louis Cardinals in exchange for Ken Reitz.
February 11, 1977	Acquired Bill Madlock and Rob Sperring from Chicago Cubs in exchange for Andy Muhlstock, Bobby Murcer and Steve Ontiveros.
March 14, 1977	Acquired Terry Whitfield from New York Yankees in exchange for Marty Perez.
March 26, 1977	Acquired Rob Andrews and cash from Baltimore Orioles in exchange for Willie Crawford and Rob Sperring.
March 31, 1977	Acquired Ken Rudolph from St. Louis Cardinals in exchange for cash.
April 27, 1977	Acquired Tim Foli from Montreal Expos in exchange for Chris Speier.
July 27, 1977	Sent Ken Rudolph to Baltimore Orioles in exchange for cash.
October 20, 1977	Sent Junior Kennedy to Cincinnati Reds in exchange for cash.
October 25, 1977	Sent Frank Riccelli to St. Louis Cardinals in exchange for player to be named later. San Francisco received Jim Dwyer on June 15, 1978, to complete trade.

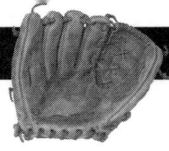
December 7, 1977   Sent Tim Foli to New York Mets in exchange for cash.

February 28, 1978   Acquired Mike Ivie from San Diego Padres in exchange for Derrel Thomas.
March 15, 1978   Acquired Vida Blue from Oakland Athletics in exchange for Mario Guerrero, Dave Heaverlo, Phil Huffman, John Henry Johnson, Gary Thomasson, Alan Wirth and $390,000 cash.
June 15, 1978   Acquired Hector Cruz from Chicago Cubs in exchange for Lynn McGlothen.
June 15, 1978   Acquired Roger Metzger from Houston Astros in exchange for cash.
July 18, 1978   Acquired John Tamargo from St. Louis Cardinals in exchange for Rob Dressler.

March 15, 1979   Sent Jim Dwyer to Boston Red Sox in exchange for cash.
March 27, 1979   Sent Skip James to Milwaukee Brewers in exchange for cash.
June 13, 1979   Acquired Joe Pettini and cash from Montreal Expos in exchange for John Tamargo.

June 28, 1979   Acquired Fred Breining, Al Holland and Ed Whitson from Pittsburgh Pirates in exchange for Bill Madlock, Lenny Randle and Dave Roberts.
June 28, 1979   Acquired Pedro Borbon from Cincinnati Reds in exchange for Hector Cruz.

April 3, 1980   Sent Greg Johnston to Minnesota Twins in exchange for cash.
June 20, 1980   Sent Ed Halicki to California Angels in exchange for cash.
June 20, 1980   Sent Marc Hill to Seattle Mariners in exchange for cash.
December 8, 1980   Acquired Enos Cabell from Houston Astros in exchange for Chris Bourjos and Bob Knepper.
December 12, 1980   Acquired Doyle Alexander from Atlanta Braves in exchange for Craig Landis and John Montefusco.
December 12, 1980   Acquired Jesus Figueroa, Jerry Martin and Mike Turgeon from Chicago Cubs in exchange for Phil Nastu and Joe Strain.

April 20, 1981   Acquired Dave Bergman and Jeff Leonard from Houston Astros in exchange for Mike Ivie.
November 14, 1981   Acquired Duane Kuiper from Cleveland Indians in exchange for Ed Whitson.
December 7, 1981   Acquired Doug Capilla from Chicago Cubs in exchange for Allen Ripley.
December 9, 1981   Acquired Mike Chris and Dan Schatzeder from Detroit Tigers in exchange for Larry Herndon.
December 9, 1981   Sent Dan Schatzeder to Montreal Expos in exchange for cash.
December 11, 1981   Acquired Doe Boyland from Pittsburgh in exchange for Tom Griffin.

March 4, 1982   Acquired Champ Summers from Detroit Tigers in exchange for Enos Cabell.
March 30, 1982   Acquired Andy McGaffigan and Ted Wilborn from New York Yankees in exchange for Doyle Alexander.
March 30, 1982   Acquired Craig Chamberlain, Atlee Hammaker, Rene Martin and Brad Wellman from Kansas City Royals in exchange for Vida Blue and Bob Tufts.
October 15, 1982   Acquired Herman Segelke from Chicago Cubs in exchange for Al Hargesheimer.
December 14, 1982   Acquired Mark Davis, Mike Krukow and Charles Penigar from Philadelphia Phillies in exchange for Al Holland and Joe Morgan.

February 2, 1983   Acquired Chris Smith from Montreal Expos in exchange for Jim Wohlford.
May 25, 1983   Acquired Wallace Johnson from Montreal Expos in exchange for Mike Vail.
August 19, 1983   Acquired Steve Nicosia from Pittsburgh Pirates in exchange for Milt May.
September 30, 1983   Sent Mike Chris to Chicago Cubs in exchange for cash.
December 6, 1983   Acquired Tommy Francis and Joe Pittman from San Diego Padres in exchange for Champ Summers.

February 27, 1984	Acquired Al Oliver from Montreal Expos in exchange for Fred Breining, Andy McGaffigan and Max Venable.
March 24, 1984	Acquired Alejandro Sanchez from Philadelphia Phillies in exchange for Dave Bergman.
August 20, 1984	Acquired Kelly Downs and George Riley from Philadelphia Phillies in exchange for Rene Martin and Al Oliver.
August 31, 1984	Acquired Pat Adams and Mike Treiyillo from Chicago White Sox in exchange for Tom O'Malley.
January 26, 1985	Acquired Jim Gott, Jack McKnight and Augie Schmidt from Toronto Blue Jays in exchange for Gary Lavelle.
February 1, 1985	Acquired David Green, Dave LaPoint, Gary Rajsich and Jose (Gonzalez) Uribe from St. Louis Cardinals in exchange for Jack Clark.
March 24, 1985	Acquired Ed Puikunas and Dan Winters from Oakland Athletics in exchange for Dusty Baker.
April 5, 1985	Acquired Roger Mason from Detroit Tigers for Alejandro Sanchez.
April 17, 1985	Acquired Alex Trevino from Atlanta Braves in exchange for John Rabb.
May 7, 1985	Acquired Mike Jeffcoat and Luis Quinones from Cleveland Indians in exchange for Johnnie LeMaster.
August 1, 1985	Acquired Dan Driessen and player to be named later from Montreal Expos in exchange for Scot Thompson. Montreal returned Bill Laskey on October 24, 1985, to complete trade.
October 7, 1985	Acquired Juan Berenguer, Scott Medvin and Bob Melvin from Detroit Tigers in exchange for Eric King, Dave LaPoint and Matt Nokes. San Francisco received Medvin on December 11, 1985.
October 24, 1985	Acquired Bill Laskey from Montreal Expos in exchange for Alonzo Powell and George Riley.
November 11, 1985	Acquired Colin Ward from Cincinnati Reds in exchange for Bob Buchanan.
December 4, 1985	Acquired player to be named later from Milwaukee Brewers in exchange for David Green. San Francisco received Hector Quinones on December 11, 1985, to complete trade.
December 11, 1985	Acquired Candy Maldonado from Los Angeles Dodgers in exchange for Alex Trevino.
December 11, 1985	Acquired Dave Owen from Chicago Cubs in exchange for Manny Trillo.
December 17, 1985	Acquired Dean Freeland and Eric Pilkington from Milwaukee Brewers in exchange for Rob Deer.
January 23, 1986	Sent Fran Mullins to Cleveland Indians in exchange for cash.
January 8, 1987	Acquired Eddie Milner from Cincinnati Reds in exchange for Timber Mead, Mike Villa and Frank Williams.
March 31, 1987	Acquired Jose Dominquez, Bryan Hickerson and Ray Velasquez from Minnesota Twins in exchange for David Blakley and Dan Gladden.
April 17, 1987	Acquired Tom Meagher and Mark Wasinger from San Diego Padres in exchange for Steve Miller and Colin Ward.
July 4, 1987	Acquired Dave Dravecky, Craig Lefferts and Kevin Mitchell from San Diego Padres in exchange for Chris Brown, Keith Comstock, Mark Davis and Mark Grant.
July 31, 1987	Acquired Don Robinson from Pittsburgh Pirates in exchange for Mackey Sasser and cash.
August 12, 1987	Acquired Rick Reuschel from Pittsburgh Pirates in exchange for Scott Medvin and Jeff Robinson.
September 1, 1987	Acquired Dave Henderson from Boston Red Sox in exchange for Randy Kutcher.
March 19, 1988	Acquired player to be named later from Seattle Mariners in exchange for Rod Scurry. San Francisco received Donell Nixon on June 23, 1988, to complete trade.

March 23, 1988	Acquired Rod Beck from Oakland Athletics in exchange for Charlie Corbell.
June 8, 1988	Acquired Ernest Riles from Milwaukee Brewers in exchange for Jeffrey Leonard.
November 20, 1988	Acquired Wil Tejada from Montreal Expos in exchange for Angel Escobar.
December 8, 1988	Acquired Tracy Jones from Montreal Expos in exchange for Mike Aldrete.
January 24, 1989	Acquired Terry Kennedy from Baltimore Orioles in exchange for Bob Melvin.
March 24, 1989	Acquired Ken Gerhart from Baltimore Orioles in exchange for Francisco Melendez.
May 10, 1989	Acquired Ken Oberkfell from Pittsburgh Pirates in exchange for Roger Samuels.
June 16, 1989	Acquired Pat Sheridan from Detroit Tigers in exchange for Tracy Jones.
June 18, 1989	Acquired Steve Bedrosian and Rick Parker from Philadelphia Phillies in exchange for Dennis Cook, Charlie Hayes and Terry Mulholland.
August 30, 1989	Sent James Steeles to Montreal Expos in exchange for cash.
May 30, 1990	Acquired Francisco Oliveras from Minnesota Twins in exchange for player to be named later. Minnesota received Ed Gustafson on September 26, 1990, to complete trade.
December 4, 1990	Acquired Darren Lewis and player to be named later from Oakland Athletics in exchange for Ernest Riles. San Francisco received Pedro Pena on December 17, 1990, to complete trade.
December 5, 1990	Acquired Johnny Ard and player to be named later from Minnesota Twins in exchange for Steve Bedrosian. San Francisco received Jimmy Williams on December 17, 1990, to complete trade.
December 11, 1991	Acquired Dave Burba, Mike Jackson and Bill Swift from Seattle Mariners in exchange for Kevin Mitchell and Mike Remlinger.
August 7, 1992	Acquired player to be named later from New York Mets in exchange for Kevin Bass. San Francisco received Rob Katzaroff on October 1, 1992, to complete trade.
August 18, 1992	Acquired Brett Jenkins from Montreal Expos in exchange for Gil Heredia.
December 10, 1992	Acquired Paul Faries from San Diego Padres in exchange for Jim Pena.
March 20, 1993	Acquired Steve Scarsone from Baltimore Orioles in exchange for Mark Leonard.
March 31, 1993	Acquired Brian Griffiths from Florida Marlins in exchange for Andres Santana.
April 2, 1993	Acquired Jim McNamara from Florida Marlins in exchange for Jared Juelsgaard.
April 29, 1993	Acquired Luis Mercedes from Baltimore Orioles in exchange for Kevin McGehee.
August 28, 1993	Acquired Jim Deshaies from Minnesota Twins in exchange for Andres Duncan, Aaron Fultz and player to be named later. Minnesota received Greg Brummett on September 1, 1993, to complete trade.
March 25, 1994	Acquired Bob Gamez from California Angels in exchange for Steve Hosey.
March 31, 1994	Acquired Chris Hook and Scott Robinson from Cincinnati Reds in exchange for Adam Hyzdu.
December 24, 1994	Acquired Rich Aurilia and Desi Wilson from Texas Rangers in exchange for John Burkett.
April 22, 1995	Acquired Enrique Burgos from Kansas City Royals in exchange for player to be named later. Kansas City received Brent Cookson on June 25, 1995, to complete trade.
May 20, 1995	Acquired Wilson Delgado and Shawn Estes from Seattle Mariners in exchange for Salomon Torres.
May 20, 1995	Sent Steve Frey to Seattle Mariners in exchange for future considerations.
July 21, 1995	Acquired David McCarty, Ricky Pickett, John Roper, Deion Sanders and Scott Service from Cincinnati Reds in exchange for Dave Burba, Darren Lewis and Mark Portugal.
July 24, 1995	Acquired Luis Aquino from Montreal Expos in exchange for Lou Pote.
October 6, 1995	Acquired Tommy Eason and Jeff Juden from Philadelphia Phillies in exchange for Mike Benjamin.

December 1, 1995	Acquired player to be named later from Texas Rangers in exchange for Rikkert Faneyte. San Francisco received Darryl Kennedy on June 1, 1996, to complete trade.
December 14, 1995	Acquired Doug Creek, Rich DeLucia and Allen Watson from St. Louis Cardinals in exchange for Royce Clayton and player to be named later. St. Louis received Chris Wimmer on January 15, 1996, to complete trade.
May 2, 1996	Acquired player to be named later from Philadelphia Phillies in exchange for J.R. Phillips. San Francisco received cash June 14, 1996, to complete trade.
July 9, 1996	Acquired Jim Poole from Cleveland Indians in exchange for Mark Carreon.
July 26, 1996	Acquired Rick Wilkins from Houston Astros in exchange for Kirt Manwaring and cash.
July 30, 1996	Acquired Kirk Rueter and Tim Scott from Montreal Expos in exchange for Mark Leiter.
November 13, 1996	Acquired Jeff Kent, Julian Tavarez, Jose Vizcaino, player to be named later and cash from Cleveland Indians in exchange for Matt Williams and player to be named later. San Francisco received Joe Roa and Cleveland received Trenidad Hubbard on December 16, 1996, to complete trade.
November 27, 1996	Acquired player to be named later from Kansas City Royals in exchange for Jamie Brewington. San Francisco received Ramon E. Martinez on December 10, 1996, to complete trade.
November 27, 1996	Acquired J.T. Snow from California Angels in exchange for Fausto Macey and Allen Watson.
December 16, 1996	Acquired Mark Lewis from Detroit Tigers in exchange for Jesus Ibarra.
April 14, 1997	Acquired player to be named later from Anaheim Angels in exchange for Rich DeLucia. San Francisco received Travis Thurmond on May 22, 1997, to complete trade.
July 16, 1997	Acquired Brian Johnson from Detroit Tigers in exchange for Marcus Jensen.
July 18, 1997	Acquired Pat Rapp from Florida Marlins in exchange for Brandon Leese and Bobby Rector.
July 29, 1997	Acquired Cory Bailey from Texas Rangers in exchange for Chad Hartvigson.
July 31, 1997	Acquired Wilson Alvarez, Danny Darwin and Roberto Hernandez from Chicago White Sox in exchange for Lorenzo Barcelo, Mike Caruso, Keith Foulke, Bobby Howry, Brian Manning and Ken Vining.
November 11, 1997	Acquired Charlie Hayes and cash from New York Yankees in exchange for Alberto Castillo and Chris Singleton.
November 18, 1997	Acquired Robb Nen from Florida Marlins in exchange for Joe Fontenot, Mick Pageler and Mike Villano.
January 28, 1998	Acquired Jalal Leach and Scott Smith from Seattle Mariners in exchange for David McCarty.
April 27, 1998	Acquired Chris Jones from Arizona Diamondbacks in exchange for Ricky Pickett.
July 24, 1998	Acquired Joe Carter from Baltimore Orioles in exchange for Darin Blood.
July 24, 1998	Acquired Shawon Dunston, Jose Mesa and Alvin Morman from Cleveland Indians in exchange for Jacob Cruz and Steve Reed.
July 31, 1998	Acquired Ellis Burks from Colorado Rockies in exchange for Darryl Hamilton, Jim Stoops and player to be named later. Colorado received Jason Brester on August 17, 1998, to complete trade.
November 10, 1998	Acquired Alan Embree from Arizona Diamondbacks in exchange for Dante Powell.
December 8, 1998	Acquired Felix Rodriguez from Arizona Diamondbacks in exchange for two players to be named later. Arizona received Troy Brohawn and Chris Van Rossum on December 21, 1998, to complete trade.

April 22, 1999	Acquired Jerry Spradlin from Cleveland Indians in exchange for Dan McKinley and player to be named later. Cleveland received Josh Santos on June 27, 1999, to complete trade.
July 24, 1999	Acquired Livan Hernandez from Florida Marlins in exchange for Nate Bump and Jason Grilli.
August 31, 1999	Acquired Joe Messman from Houston Astros in exchange for Stan Javier.
Dec. 12, 1999	Acquired Bobby Estalella from Philadelphia Phillies for Chris Brock.
Dec. 13, 1999	Traded Jerry Spradlin to Kansas City Royals for player to be named (Ken Ray).
March 23, 2000	Acquired Juan Melo from New York Yankees for Wilson Delgado.
July 26, 2000	Acquired Eric Gunderson from Toronto Blue Jays for player to be named.
July 30, 2000	Acquired Doug Henry from Houston Astros for Scott Linebrink.
Nov. 19, 2000	Acquired Tim Worrell from Chicago Cubs for Bill Mueller.
March 27, 2001	Traded Doug Mirabelli to Texas Rangers for cash.
June 29, 2001	Acquired Derek Hasselhoff from Chicago White Sox for Alan Embree.
July 4, 2001	Acquired Brian Boehringer from New York Yankees for Bobby Estalella and Joe Smith.
July 24, 2001	Acquired Andres Galarraga from Texas Rangers for Chris Magruder, Todd Ozias and Erasmo Ramirez.
July 28, 2001	Acquired Wayne Gomes from Philadelphia Phillies for Felipe Crespo.
July 30, 2001	Acquired Jason Schmidt and John Vander Wal from Pittsburgh Pirates for Armando Rios and Ryan Vogelsong.
July 31, 2001	Acquired Jason Christiansen from St. Louis Cardinals for Kevin Joseph and player to be named (Jason Farmer).
Dec. 13, 2001	Acquired Jay Witasick from New York Yankees for John Vander Wal.
Dec. 16, 2001	Acquired Tsuyoshi Shinjo and Desi Relaford from New York Mets for Shawn Estes.
Jan. 25, 2002	Acquired David Bell from Seattle Mariners for Desi Relaford.
April 22, 2002	Traded Calvin Murray to Texas Rangers for cash.
July 28, 2002	Acquired Kenny Lofton from Chicago White Sox for Felix Diaz and Ryan Meaux.
Sept. 3, 2002	Acquired Bill Mueller from Chicago Cubs for Jeff Verplancke.
Dec. 17, 2002	Acquired Damian Moss from Atlanta Braves for Russ Ortiz.

FACTS AND FIGURES, STATS AND STORIES

. . . .

ALL-TIME RECORDS OF CURRENT NATIONAL LEAGUE FRANCHISES

Franchise	First Season	Record	Pct.
New York/San Francisco	1883	9,771-8,329	.540
Brooklyn/Los Angeles	1890	9,047-8,227	.524
Chicago	1876	9,579-9,056	.514
Pittsburgh	1887	9,039-8,631	.512
Cincinnati	1876	8,753-8,540	.506
Houston	1962	2,968-2,900	.506
St. Louis	1892	8,611-8,405	.506
Boston/Milwaukee/Atlanta	1876	9,471-9,417	.501
Montreal	1969	2.605-2,769	.485
Colorado	1993	740-817	.475
New York (Mets)	1962	3,091-3,412	.475
Philadelphia	1883	8,419-9,653	.466
San Diego	1969	2,460-2,921	.457
Florida	1993	706-847	.455
Arizona	1998	440-370	.543
Milwaukee*	1998	345-464	.426

* N.L. totals only (Overall since 1969: 2,545-2,831, .473)

NEW YORK/SAN FRANCISCO GIANTS ALL-TIME OWNERS

John B. Day — Dec. 7, 1882 to Jan. 1893
C.C. Van Cott — Jan. 1893 to Jan. 24, 1895
Andrew C. Freedman — Jan. 24, 1895 to Sept. 9, 1902
John T. Brush — Sept. 9, 1902 to Nov. 26, 1912
Harry N. Hempstead — Nov. 26, 1912 to Jan. 14, 1919
Charles A. Stoneham — Jan. 14, 1919 to Jan. 6, 1936
Horace C. Stoneham — Jan. 15, 1936 to March 2, 1976
Robert A. Lurie — March 2, 1976 to Jan. 12, 1993
Peter A. Magowan — Jan. 12, 1993 to present

NEW YORK/SAN FRANCISCO GIANTS ALL-TIME GENERAL MANAGERS

Charles (Chub) Feeney — 1947-69
Horace Stoneham — 1970-75
Spec Richardson — 1976-80
Tom Haller — 1981-85
Al Rosen — 1985-92
Bob Quinn — 1993-96
Brian Sabean — 1996-present

NEW YORK/SAN FRANCISCO GIANTS ALL-TIME COACHES

Carlos Alfonso — 1992, 1997-2002
Joey Amalfitano — 1972-75
Dusty Baker — 1988-92
Dave Bancroft — 1930-32
Vern Benson — 1980
Bobby Bonds — 1993-96
Bob Brenly — 1992-95
Roger Bresnahan — 1925-28
Rocky Bridges — 1985
Dave Bristol — 1978-79
Don Buford — 1981-84
Jesse Burkett — 1921
George Burns — 1931
Tommy Clarke — 1932-35, 1938
Gene Clines — 1997-2002

Jim Davenport — 1970, 1976-82, 1996
Cozy Dolan — 1922-24
Johnny Evers — 1920
Bill Fahey — 1986-91
Freddie Fitzsimmons — 1949-55
Charlie Fox — 1965-68
Herman Franks — 1949-55, 1958, 1964
Frankie Frisch — 1949
Frank Funk — 1976
Gene Gardner — 2003
Andy Gilbert — 1972-75
Gene Glynn — 2003
Hank Gowdy — 1947-48
Tom Haller — 1977-79
Grover Hartley — 1946

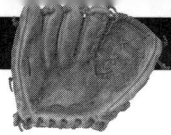

Gabby Hartnett — 1941
Tommy Henrich — 1957
Chuck Hiller — 1985
Sonny Jackson — 1997-2002
Travis Jackson — 1939-40, 1947-48
Larry Jansen — 1954, 1961-71
Hughie Jennings — 1921-25
Bubber Jonnard — 1942-46
Wendell Kim — 1989-96
Red Kress — 1946-49
Arlie Latham — 1909
Cookie Lavagetto — 1964-67
Jim Lefebvre — 1980-82
Joe Lefebvre — 2002-present
Bob Lillis — 1986-96
Whitey Lockman — 1961-64
Juan Lopez — 1999-2002
Peanuts Lowrey — 1967-68
Gordy MacKenzie — 1986-88
Christy Mathewson — 1919-21
Tom McCraw — 1983-85
Don McMahon — 1973-75, 1980-82
John McNamara — 1971-73
Irish Meusel — 1930
Bob Miller — 1985
Clarence Mitchell — 1932-33
Jose Morales — 1986-88
Ray Mueller — 1956
Jack Mull — 1985
Bert Niehoff — 1929

Ivy Olson — 1932
Lefty O'Doul — 1958
Danny Ozark — 1983-84
Salty Parker — 1958-61, 1979
Ron Perranoski — 1997-99
Dick Pole — 1993-97
Bill Posedel — 1959-60
Luis Pujols — 2003
Dave Righetti — 2000- present Wilbert Robinson — 1911-13
Bob Rodgers — 1976
Hank Sauer — 1959
Frank Shellenback — 1950-55
Larry Shepard — 1979
Norm Sherry — 1986-91
Al Smith — 1933
Frank Snyder — 1933-41
Denny Sommers — 1993-94
Billy Southworth, 1933
Herm Starrette — 1977-78, 1983-84
Nick Testa — 1958
Robby Thompson — 2000-01
John Van Ornum — 1981-84
Ozzie Virgil — 1969-72, 1974-75
Wes Westrum — 1958-63, 1968-71
Davey Williams — 1956-57
Bobby Winkles — 1976-77
Ron Wotus — 1998-present
Don Zimmer — 1987

NEW YORK/SAN FRANCISCO GIANTS WIN AND LOSS DATA

Most Wins

106 — 1904
105 — 1905
103 — 1912
103 — 1962
103 — 1993
101 — 1913
99 — 1911
98 — 1908
98 — 1917
98 — 1951

Most Losses

100 — 1985
98 — 1943
96 — 1984
94 — 1996
93 — 1946
91 — 1979
90 — 1899
90 — 1974
90 — 1992
88 — 1902
88 — 1976

Highest Winning Percentage

.759 (85-27) — 1885
.693 (106-47) — 1904
.686 (105-48) — 1905
.682 (103-48) — 1912
.667 (88-44) — 1894
.664 (101-51) — 1913
.659 (83-43) — 1889
.647 (99-54) — 1911
.641 (84-47) — 1888
.636 (98-56) — 1908
.636 (98-56) — 1917
.636 (103-59) — 1993

Lowest Winning Percentage

.353 (48-88) — 1902
.359 (55-98) — 1943
.380 (52-85) — 1901
.383 (62-100) — 1985
.396 (61-93) — 1946
.400 (60-90) — 1899
.407 (66-96) — 1984
.420 (68-94) — 1996
.435 (60-78) — 1900
.435 (67-87) — 1944
.435 (67-87) — 1956

Most Consecutive Wins

26 (26 home, 0 road) — Sept. 7-30 (1), 1916
18 (13 home, 5 road) — June 17-July 4 (2), 1904
17 (14 home, 3 road) — April 25-May 18, 1907
17 (0 home, 17 road) — May 9-29, 1916
16 (11 home, 5 road) — June 19-July 3 (2), 1912
16 (13 home, 3 road) — Aug. 12-27 (2), 1951
15 (7 home, 8 road) — Aug. 11-28, 1936
14 (6 home, 8 road) — June 26 (1)-July 9, 1913
14 (6 home, 8 road) — Sept. 4-16, 1965
13 (8 home, 5 road) — July 20 (1)-Aug. 2, 1905

Most Consecutive Losses

13 (5 home, 8 road) — June 23-July 6, 1902
13 (0 home, 13 road) — Aug. 9-20 (1), 1944
12 (5 home, 7 road) — June 20-July 4 (1), 1900
11 (11 home, 0 road) — Sept. 11 (1)-19, 1940
11 (5 home, 6 road) — April 19 (2)-29, 1951
10 (3 home, 7 road) — June 20-30 (1), 1985
10 (4 home, 6 road) — June 21-30, 1996
9 (9 home, 0 road) — July 15-23, 1939
9 (2 home, 7 road) — April 23-May 1, 1984
9 (3 home, 6 road) — Aug. 24-Sept. 3, 1992

Most Lopsided Wins

29-1 vs. Philadelphia, June 15, 1887
24-0 vs. Buffalo, May 27, 1885
26-2 vs. Philadelphia, June 11, 1887
22-1 vs. Boston, Sept. 10, 1924 (1)
26-8 vs. Brooklyn, April 30, 1944
23-5 at Philadelphia, July 11, 1931 (1)

Most Lopsided Losses

19-0 at Chicago, June 7, 1906
17-0 at Boston, Sept. 17, 1897

NEW YORK/SAN FRANCISCO GIANTS TOP INDIVIDUAL PERFORMANCES

Hit For The Cycle
Mike Tiernan vs. Philadelphia, Aug. 25, 1888
Sam Mertes vs. St. Louis, Oct. 4, 1904 (1)
Chief Meyers vs. Chicago, June 10, 1912
George Burns vs. Pittsburgh, Sept. 17, 1920
Dave Bancroft vs. Philadelphia, June 1, 1921 (2)
Ross Youngs at Boston, April 29, 1922
Bill Terry at Brooklyn, May 29, 1928
Mel Ott at Boston, May 16, 1929
Fred Lindstrom at Pittsburgh, May 8, 1930
Sam Leslie vs. Philadelphia, May 24, 1936
Harry Danning vs. Pittsburgh, June 15, 1940
Don Mueller vs. Pittsburgh, July 17, 1954 (1)
Jim Ray Hart at Atlanta, July 8, 1970
Dave Kingman at Houston, April 16, 1972
Jeffrey Leonard at Cincinnati, June 27, 1985
Candy Maldonado at St. Louis, May 4, 1987
Chris Speier vs. St. Louis, July 9, 1988
Robby Thompson vs. San Diego, April 22, 1991
Jeff Kent at Pittsburgh, May 3, 1999

6 Hits
Danny Richardson vs. Philadelphia, June 11, 1887 Jack
Glasscock vs. Cincinnati, Sept. 27, 1890
George Davis at Philadelphia, Aug. 15, 1895
Kip Selbach at Cincinnati, June 9, 1901
Dave Bancroft at Philadelphia, June 28, 1920
Frankie Frisch vs. Boston, Sept. 10, 1924 (1)
Jesus Alou at Chicago, July 10, 1964
Mike Benjamin at Chicago, June 14, 1995
        (13 innings)

4 Home Runs
Willie Mays at Milwaukee, April 30, 1961

3 Home Runs
Roger Connor at Indianapolis, May 9, 1888
George Kelly at Chicago, Sept. 17, 1923*
George Kelly vs. Cincinnati, June 14, 1924
Mel Ott vs. Boston, Aug. 31, 1930*
Bill Terry vs. Brooklyn, Aug. 13, 1932
Johnny Mize at Boston, April 24, 1947*
Willard Marshall vs. Cincinnati, July 18, 1947*
Wes Westrum vs. Cincinnati, June 24, 1950
Don Mueller vs. Brooklyn, Sept. 1, 1951
Dusty Rhodes vs. St. Louis, Aug. 26, 1953*
Hank Thompson at St. Louis, June 3, 1954*

Dusty Rhodes vs. St. Louis, July 28, 1954*
Willie Mays at Milwaukee, June 29, 1961
Willie Mays at Philadelphia, June 2, 1963
Willie McCovey vs. New York, Sept. 22, 1963*
Willie McCovey at Milwaukee, April 22, 1964*
Willie McCovey vs. New York, Sept. 17, 1966
Gary Matthews vs. Houston, Sept. 25, 1976
Darrell Evans vs. Houston, June 15, 1983
Kevin Mitchell at Pittsburgh, May 25, 1990*
Barry Bonds vs. Cincinnati, Aug. 2, 1994
Barry Bonds at Atlanta, May 19, 2001
Barry Bonds at Colorado, Sept. 9, 2001
Barry Bonds at Colorado, Aug. 27, 2002

* denotes consecutive.

Two Home Runs In One Inning
Hack Wilson at Philadelphia, July 1, 1925 (2) — 3rd
Hank Leiber vs. Chicago, Aug. 24, 1935 — 2nd
Sid Gordon at Cincinnati, July 31, 1949 (2) — 2nd
Willie McCovey vs. Houston, April 12, 1973 — 4th
Willie McCovey at Cincinnati, June 27, 1977 — 6th

Home Run In First Major League At-Bat
Buddy Kerr vs. Philadelphia, Sept. 8, 1943
Whitey Lockman vs. St. Louis, July 5, 1945
Les Layton vs. Chicago, May 21, 1948 (PH)
Hoyt Wilhelm vs. Boston, April 23, 1952
Bill White vs. St. Louis, May 7, 1956
John Montefusco at Los Angeles, Sept. 3, 1974
Johnnie LeMaster vs. Los Angeles, Sept. 2, 1975
Will Clark at Houston, April 8, 1986

Home Runs From Both Sides Of The Plate
Chili Davis vs. Montreal, June 5, 1983
Chili Davis vs. Houston, June 27, 1987
Chili Davis vs. San Diego, Sept. 15, 1987
Kevin Bass vs. Atlanta, Aug. 2, 1992 (2)
Todd Benzinger at Florida, Aug. 30, 1993

No-Hitters
Ed Crane vs. Washington, Sept. 27, 1888
Amos Rusie vs. Brooklyn, July 31, 1891
Christy Mathewson at St. Louis, July 15, 1901
Red Ames at St. Louis, Sept. 14, 1903 (2)
Christy Mathewson at Chicago, June 13, 1905
Hooks Wiltse vs. Philadelphia, July 4, 1908

Red Ames vs. Brooklyn, April 15, 1909
Jeff Tesreau at Philadelphia, Sept. 6, 1912
Rube Marquard vs. Brooklyn, April 15, 1915
Jesse Barnes vs. Philadelphia, May 7, 1922
Carl Hubbell vs. Pittsburgh, May 8, 1929
Mike McCormick at Philadelphia, June 12, 1959
Sam Jones at St. Louis, Sept. 26, 1959
Juan Marichal vs. Houston, June 15, 1963
Gaylord Perry vs. St. Louis, Sept. 17, 1968
Ed Halicki vs. New York, Aug. 24, 1975
John Montefusco at Atlanta, Sept. 29, 1976

Two Complete-Game Victories In One Day
Amos Rusie at Brooklyn, Sept. 28, 1891
    (10-4, 13-5 in 6 innings)
Amos Rusie vs. Washington, Oct. 4, 1892
    (6-4, 9-5)
Cy Seymour vs. Louisville, June 3, 1897
    (6-1, 10-6 in 7 innings)
Joe McGinnity at Boston, Aug. 1, 1903
    (4-1, 5-2)

Joe McGinnity at Brooklyn, Aug. 8, 1903
    (6-1, 4-3)
Joe McGinnity vs. Philadelphia, Aug. 31, 1903
    (4-1, 9-2)
Pol Perritt vs. Philadelphia, Sept. 9, 1916
    (3-1, 3-0)

Nine Consecutive Strikeouts
Mickey Welch vs. Cleveland, Aug. 28, 1884
    (3 in 1st, 3 in 2nd, 3 in 3rd)

Four Strikeouts In One Inning
Ed Crane vs. Chicago, Oct. 4, 1888 — 5th*
Hooks Wiltse at Cincinnati, May 15, 1906 — 5th*
Jerry Spradlin vs. San Diego, July 22, 1999 — 7th

* denotes consecutive.

Three Strikeouts On Nine Pitches
Trevor Wilson vs. Houston, June 7, 1992 — 9th

NEW YORK/SAN FRANCISCO GIANTS TOP INDIVIDUAL SEASONS

50 Home Runs
1947 — Johnny Mize (51)
1955 — Willie Mays (51)
1965 — Willie Mays (52)
2001 — Barry Bonds (73)

40 Home Runs
1929 — Mel Ott (42)
1948 — Johnny Mize (40)
1954 — Willie Mays (41)
1961 — Orlando Cepeda (46)
    Willie Mays (40)
1962 — Wilie Mays (49)
1963 — Willie McCovey (44)
1964 — Willie Mays (47)
1969 — Willie McCovey (45)
1989 — Kevin Mitchell (47)
1993 — Barry Bonds (46)
1994 — Matt Williams (43)
1996 — Barry Bonds (42)
1997 — Barry Bonds (40)
2000 — Barry Bonds (49)
2002 — Barry Bonds (46)

30 Home Runs
1932 — Mel Ott (38)
1934 — Mel Ott (35)
1935 — Mel Ott (31)
1936 — Mel Ott (33)
1937 — Mel Ott (31)
1938 — Mel Ott (36)
1942 — Mel Ott (30)
1947 — Willard Marshall (36)
    Walker Cooper (35)
1948 — Sid Gordon (30)
1956 — Willie Mays (36)
1957 — Willie Mays (35)
1959 — Willie Mays (34)
1962 — Orlando Cepeda (35)
1963 — Willie Mays (38)
    Orlando Cepeda (34)
1964 — Orlando Cepeda (31)
    Jim Ray Hart (31)
1965 — Willie McCovey (39)
1966 — Willie Mays (37)
    Willie McCovey (36)
    Jim Ray Hart (33)
1967 — Willie McCovey (31)

1968 — Willie McCovey (36)
1969 — Bobby Bonds (32)
1970 — Willie McCovey (39)
1971 — Bobby Bonds (33)
1972 — Bobby Bonds (39)
1983 — Darrell Evans (30)
1987 — Will Clark (35)
1990 — Kevin Mitchell (35)
    Matt Williams (33)
1991 — Matt Williams (34)
1993 — Matt Williams (38)
1994 — Barry Bonds (37)
1995 — Barry Bonds (33)
1998 — Barry Bonds (37)
    Jeff Kent (31)
1999 — Barry Bonds (34)
    Ellis Burks (31)
2000 — Jeff Kent (33)
2001 — Rich Aurilia (37)
2002 — Jeff Kent (37)

**40 Home Runs And
40 Stolen Bases**
1996 — Barry Bonds (42 HR, 40 SB)

30 Home Runs And
30 Stolen Bases
1956 — Willie Mays (36 HR, 40 SB)
1957 — Willie Mays (35 HR, 38 SB)
1969 — Bobby Bonds (32 HR, 45 SB)
1973 — Bobby Bonds (39 HR, 43 SB)
1995 — Barry Bonds (33 HR, 31 SB)
1996 — Barry Bonds (42 HR, 40 SB)
1997 — Barry Bonds (40 HR, 37 SB)

50 Home Runs And 20 Stolen Bases
1955 — Willie Mays (51 HR, 24 SB)

100 RBI
1887 — Roger Connor (104)
1889 — Roger Connor (130)
    Danny Richardson (100)
1893 — George Davis (119)
    Roger Connor (105)
    Mike Tiernan (102)
1894 — George Van Haltren (104)
    Jack Doyle (100)
1895 — George Van Haltren (103)
    George Davis (101)
1897 — George Davis (136)
    Kid Gleason (106)
1903 — Sam Mertes (104)
1905 — Sam Mertes (108)
1908 — Mike Donlin (106)
1917 — Heinie Zimmerman (102)
1921 — George Kelly (122)
    Ross Youngs (102)
    Frankie Frisch (100)
1922 — Irish Meusel (132)
    George Kelly (107)
1923 — Irish Meusel (125)
    Frankie Frisch (111)
    George Kelly (103)
1924 — George Kelly (136)
    Irish Meusel (102)
1925 — Irish Meusel (111)
1927 — Rogers Hornsby (125)
    Bill Terry (121)
1928 — Fred Lindstrom (107)
    Bill Terry (101)
1929 — Mel Ott (151)
    Bill Terry (117)
1930 — Bill Terry (129)
    Mel Ott (119)
    Fred Lindstrom (106)
1931 — Mel Ott (115)
    Bill Terry (112)

1932 — Mel Ott (123)
    Bill Terry (117)
1933 — Mel Ott (103)
1934 — Mel Ott (135)
    Travis Jackson (101)
1935 — Mel Ott (114)
    Hank Leiber (107)
1936 — Mel Ott (135)
1938 — Mel Ott (116)
1940 — Babe Young (101)
1941 — Babe Young (104)
1942 — Johnny Mize (110)
1947 — Johnny Mize (138)
    Walker Cooper (122)
    Willard Marshall (107)
1948 — Johnny Mize (125)
    Sid Gordon (107)
1949 — Bobby Thomson (109)
1951 — Monte Irvin (121)
    Bobby Thomson (101)
1952 — Bobby Thomson (108)
1953 — Bobby Thomson (106)
1954 — Willie Mays (110)
1955 — Willie Mays (127)
1959 — Orlando Cepeda (105)
    Willie Mays (104)
1960 — Willie Mays (103)
1961 — Orlando Cepeda (142)
    Willie Mays (123)
1962 — Willie Mays (141)
    Orlando Cepeda (114)
1963 — Willie Mays (103)
    Willie McCovey (102)
1964 — Willie Mays (111)
1965 — Willie Mays (112)
1966 — Willie Mays (103)
1968 — Willie McCovey (105)
1969 — Willie McCovey (126)
1970 — Willie McCovey (126)
    Dick Dietz (107)
1971 — Bobby Bonds (102)
1982 — Jack Clark (103)
1988 — Will Clark (109)
1989 — Kevin Mitchell (125)
    Will Clark (111)
1990 — Matt Williams (122)
1991 — Will Clark (116)
1993 — Barry Bonds (123)
    Matt Williams (110)
1995 — Barry Bonds (104)
1996 — Barry Bonds (129)
1997 — Jeff Kent (121)

    J.T. Snow (104)
    Barry Bonds (101)
1998 — Jeff Kent (128)
    Barry Bonds (122)
1999 — Jeff Kent (101)
2000 — Jeff Kent (125)
    Barry Bonds (106)
2001 — Barry Bonds (137)
    Jeff Kent (106)
2002 — Barry Bonds (110)
    Jeff Kent (108)

40 Wins
1885 — Mickey Welch (44-11)
1886 — Tim Keefe (42-20)

30 Wins
1884 — Mickey Welch (39-21)
1885 — Tim Keefe (32-13)
1886 — Mickey Welch (33-22)
1887 — Tim Keefe (35-19)
1888 — Tim Keefe (35-12)
1891 — Amos Rusie (33-20)
1892 — Amos Rusie (31-31)
1893 — Amos Rusie (33-21)
1894 — Amos Rusie (36-13)
    Jouett Meekin (33-9)
1903 — Joe McGinnity (31-20)
    Christy Mathewson (30-13)
1904 — Joe McGinnity (35-8)
    Christy Mathewson (33-12)
1905 — Christy Mathewson (31-9)
1908 — Christy Mathewson (37-11)

20 Wins
1883 — Mickey Welch (25-23)
1887 — Mickey Welch (22-15)
1888 — Mickey Welch (26-19)
1889 — Tim Keefe (28-13)
    Mickey Welch (27-12)
1890 — Amos Rusie (29-34)
1891 — John Ewing (21-8)
1892 — Silver King (23-24)
1895 — Amos Rusie (23-23)
1896 — Jouett Meekin (26-14)
1897 — Amos Rusie (28-10)
    Jouett Meekin (20-11)
1898 — Cy Seymour (25-19)
    Amos Rusie (20-11)

1901 — Christy Mathewson (20-17)
1904 — Dummy Taylor (21-15)
1905 — Red Ames (22-8)
　　　　Joe McGinnity (21-15)
1906 — Joe McGinnity (27-12)
　　　　Christy Mathewson (22-12)
1907 — Christy Mathewson (24-12)
1908 — Hooks Wiltse (23-14)
1909 — Christy Mathewson (25-6)
　　　　Hooks Wiltse (20-11)
1910 — Christy Mathewson (27-9)
1911 — Christy Mathewson (26-13)
　　　　Rube Marquard (24-7)
1912 — Rube Marquard (26-11)
　　　　Christy Mathewson (23-12)
1913 — Christy Mathewson (25-11)
　　　　Rube Marquard (23-10)
　　　　Jeff Tesreau (22-13)
1914 — Jeff Tesreau (26-10)
　　　　Christy Mathewson (24-13)
1917 — Ferdie Schupp (21-7)

1919 — Jesse Barnes (25-9)
1920 — Fred Toney (21-11)
　　　　Art Nehf (21-12)
　　　　Jesse Barnes (20-15)
1921 — Art Nehf (20-10)
1928 — Larry Benton (25-9)
　　　　Freddie Fitzsimmons (20-9)
1933 — Carl Hubbell (23-12)
1934 — Hal Schumacher (23-10)
　　　　Carl Hubbell (21-12)
1935 — Carl Hubbell (23-12)
1936 — Carl Hubbell (26-6)
1937 — Carl Hubbell (22-8)
　　　　Cliff Melton (20-9)
1944 — Bill Voiselle (21-16)
1947 — Larry Jansen (21-5)
1951 — Sal Maglie (23-6)
　　　　Larry Jansen (23-11)
1954 — Johnny Antonelli (21-7)
1956 — Johnny Antonelli (20-13)
1959 — Sam Jones (21-15)

1962 — Jack Sanford (24-7)
1963 — Juan Marichal (25-8)
1964 — Juan Marichal (21-8)
1965 — Juan Marichal (22-13)
1966 — Juan Marichal (25-6)
　　　　Gaylord Perry (21-8)
1967 — Mike McCormick (22-10)
1968 — Juan Marichal (26-9)
1969 — Juan Marichal (21-11)
1970 — Gaylord Perry (23-13)
1973 — Ron Bryant (24-12)
1986 — Mike Krukow (20-9)
1993 — John Burkett (22-7)
　　　　Bill Swift (21-8)

40 Saves
1993 — Rod Beck (48)
1998 — Robb Nen (40)
2000 — Robb Nen (41)
2001 — Robb Nen (45)
2002 — Robb Nen (43)

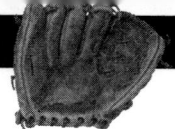

NEW YORK/SAN FRANCISCO GIANTS HITTING AND WINNING STREAKS

Hitting Streaks
33 George Davis, Aug. 3-Sept. 9, 1893 (2)
27 Charlie Hickman, 1900
26 Jack Clark, June 30-July 25, 1978
24 Mike Donlin, June 27 (1)-July 21 (2), 1908
24 Fred Lindstrom, July 28-Aug. 23, 1930
24 Don Mueller, April 14-May 17, 1955
24 Willie McCovey, June 25-July 19, 1963
23 Joe Moore, Aug. 31-Sept. 22 (2), 1934
22 Alvin Dark, July 14-Aug. 7 (2), 1952
22 Willie McCovey, Aug. 17-Sept. 10, 1959
21 Mel Ott, Aug. 15-Sept. 6, 1937
21 Willie Mays, July 27-Aug. 20, 1954
21 Don Mueller, Aug. 22 (2)-Sept. 11, 1954
21 Willie Mays, May 10-June 2 (1), 1957
21 Robby Thompson, May 8-June 1, 1993

Winning Streaks
19 Tim Keefe, June 23-Aug. 10, 1888
19 Rube Marquard, April 11-July 3, 1912*
17 Mickey Welch, July 18-Sept. 4, 1885
16 Carl Hubbell, July 17-Sept. 23, 1936**
16 Jack Sanford, June 17-Sept. 11, 1962
14 Joe McGinnity, April 15-June 8, 1904
13 Christy Mathewson, May 28-July 27, 1909
13 Burleigh Grimes, July 15-Sept. 19, 1927
12 Hooks Wiltse, May 29-Sept. 15, 1904
11 Christy Mathewson, Aug. 10-Sept. 19, 1905
11 Hal Schumacher, May 19-July 10, 1935
11 Sal Maglie, July 21-Sept. 13, 1950
11 Johnny Antonelli, May 25-Aug. 1 (1), 1954
10 Slim Sallee, June 30-Aug. 16, 1917
10 Jesse Barnes, July 4-Aug. 12, 1919
10 Clarence Mitchell, June 26-Sept. 20, 1930
10 Juan Marichal, April 12-May 31, 1966
10 Juan Marichal, May 11-June 23, 1968
10 Vida Blue, June 10-Aug. 4, 1978

* under present-day scoring rules would have been credited with 20 consecutive wins.
** won first eight decisions of 1937 for two-season winning streak of 24 games.

NEW YORK/SAN FRANCISCO GIANTS TOP TEAM HOME RUN PERFORMANCES

Eight Home Runs In A Game
April 30, 1961 — at Milwaukee
    Willie Mays (4), Jose Pagan (2), Felipe Alou (1),
    Orlando Cepeda (1)

Five Home Runs In An Inning
June 6, 1939 — vs. Cincinnati (4th inning)
    Harry Danning, Frank Demaree, Whitey White-
    head, Manuel Salvo, Joe Moore
Aug. 23, 1961 — at Cincinnati (9th inning)
    Orlando Cepeda, Felipe Alou, Jim Davenport,
    Willie Mays, John Orsino

Four Home Runs In An Inning
Aug. 13, 1939 (1) — vs. Philadelphia (4th inning)
    Zeke Bonura, Alex Kampouris, Bill Lohrman, Joe
    Moore
May 28, 1954 — vs. Brooklyn (8th inning)
    Davey Williams, Alvin Dark, Monte Irvin, Bill
    Gardner
July 8, 1956 (1) — vs. Pittsburgh (4th inning)
    Willie Mays, Bobby Thomson, Daryl Spencer,
    Wes Westrum

Three Consecutive Home Runs In An Inning
Aug. 13, 1932 (1) — vs. Brooklyn (4th inning)
    Bill Terry, Mel Ott, Fred Lindstrom
June 6, 1939 — vs. Cincinnati (4th inning)
    Whitey Whitehead, Manuel Salvo, Joe Moore
Aug. 13, 1939 (1) — vs. Philadelphia (4th inning)
    Alex Kampouris, Bill Lohrman, Joe Moore
June 20, 1948 (2) — vs. St. Louis (8th inning)
    Johnny Mize, Willard Marshall, Sid Gordon
June 4, 1949 — vs. Cincinnati (6th inning)
    Whitey Lockman, Sid Gordon, Willard Marshall

Sept. 4, 1953 — vs. Brooklyn (4th inning)
    Wes Westrum, Al Corwin, Whitey Lockman
June 20, 1954 — vs. St. Louis (6th inning)
    Bobby Hofman, Wes Westrum, Dusty Rhodes
July 8, 1956 (1) — vs. Pittsburgh (4th inning)
    Bobby Thomson, Daryl Spencer, Wes Westrum
Aug. 27, 1963 — vs. St. Louis (3rd inning)
    Willie Mays, Orlando Cepeda, Felipe Alou
Aug. 5, 1969 (1) — at Philadelphia (5th inning)
    Dave Marshall, Ron Hunt, Bobby Bonds
July 11, 1982 — at Montreal (2nd inning)
    Reggie Smith, Milt May, Champ Summers
Aug. 2, 1998 — at Philadelphia (2nd inning)
    Ellis Burks, Barry Bonds, Jeff Kent
Aug. 20, 1999 — at Milwaukee (4th inning)
    Ramon Martinez, Barry Bonds, Ellis Burks
Aug. 22, 1999 — at Milwaukee (1st inning)
    Barry Bonds, Jeff Kent, Ellis Burks

Two Grand Slams In A Game
Sept. 5, 1924 (2) — at Philadelphia
    George Kelly and Travis Jackson
July 4, 1938 (2) — vs. Brooklyn
    Dick Bartell and Gus Mancuso
July 13, 1951 — vs. St. Louis
    Wes Westrum and Davey Williams
April 26, 1970 (1) — vs. Montreal
    Willie McCovey and Dick Dietz
Sept. 19, 1998 — vs. Los Angeles
    Bill Mueller and Jeff Kent

Two Pinch-Hit Home Runs In An Inning
June 20, 1954 — vs. St. Louis (6th inning)
    Bobby Hofman and Dusty Rhodes
June 4, 1958 — vs. Milwaukee (10th inning)
    Hank Sauer and Bob Schmidt

BARRY BONDS' MAJOR LEAGUE RECORD
73 HOME RUNS (2001)

No.	Date	Opposing Pitcher (Club)	Stadium	Inning	On Base
1	April 2	Woody Williams (San Diego)	Pacific Bell	5	0
2	April 12	Adam Eaton (San Diego)	Qualcomm	4	0
3	April 13	Jamey Wright (Milwaukee)	Miller	1	1
4	April 14	Jimmy Haynes (Milwaukee)	Miller	5	2
5	April 15	David Weathers (Milwaukee)	Miller	8	0
6*	April 17	Terry Adams (Los Angeles)	Pacific Bell	8	1
7*	April 18	Chan Ho Park (Los Angeles)	Pacific Bell	7	0
8	April 20	Jimmy Haynes (Milwaukee)	Pacific Bell	4	1
9	April 24	Jim Brower (Cincinnati)	Pacific Bell	3	1
10	April 26	Scott Sullivan (Cincinnati)	Pacific Bell	8	1
11	April 29	Manny Aybar (Chicago)	Pacific Bell	4	0

April totals – 11 home runs

No.	Date	Opposing Pitcher (Club)	Stadium	Inning	On Base
12	May 2	Todd Ritchie (Pittsburgh)	PNC	5	1
13	May 3	Jimmy Anderson (Pittsburgh)	PNC	1	1
14	May 4	Bruce Chen (Philadelphia)	Veterans	6	1
15	May 11	Steve Trachsel (New York)	Pacific Bell	4	0
16	May 17	Chuck Smith (Florida)	Pro Players	3	1
17	May 18	Mike Remlinger (Atlanta)	Turner	8	0
18	May 19	Odalis Perez (Atlanta)	Turner	3	0
19	May 19	Jose Cabrera (Atlanta)	Turner	7	0
20	May 19	Jason Marquis (Atlanta)	Turner	8	0
21	May 20	John Burkett (Atlanta)	Turner	1	0
22	May 20	Mike Remlinger (Atlanta)	Turner	7	0
23	May 21	Curt Schilling (Arizona)	Bank One	4	0
24	May 22	Russ Springer (Arizona)	Bank One	9	1
25*	May 24	John Thomson (Colorado)	Pacific Bell	3	0
26	May 27	Denny Neagle (Colorado)	Colorado	1	1
27*	May 30	Robert Ellis (Arizona)	Pacific Bell	2	0
28	May 30	Robert Ellis (Arizona)	Pacific Bell	6	1

May totals – 17 home runs, new major league record for May

No.	Date	Opposing Pitcher (Club)	Stadium	Inning	On Base
29	June 1	Shawn Chacon (Colorado)	Coors	3	1
30	June 4	Bobby Jones (San Diego)	Pacific Bell	4	0
31	June 5	Wascar Serrano (San Diego)	Pacific Bell	3	1
32	June 7	Brian Lawrence (San Diego)	Pacific Bell	7	1
33*	June 12	Pat Rapp (Anaheim)	Pacific Bell	1	0
34	June 14	Lou Pote (Anaheim)	Pacific Bell	6	0
35	June 15	Mark Mulder (Oakland)	Pacific Bell	1	0
36	June 15	Mark Mulder (Oakland)	Pacific Bell	6	0
37	June 19	Adam Eaton (San Diego)	Qualcomm	5	0
38	June 20	Rodney Myers (San Diego)	Qualcomm	8	1
39	June 23	Darryl Kile (St. Louis)	Busch	1	1

June totals – 11 home runs; 39 homers total—new record prior to All-Star Game

40	July 12	Paul Abbott (Seattle)	Safeco	1	0
41	July 18	Mike Hampton (Colorado)	Pacific Bell	4	0
42	July 18	Mike Hampton (Colorado)	Pacific Bell	5	1
43	July 26	Curt Schilling (Arizona)	Bank One	4	0
44	July 26	Curt Schilling (Arizona)	Bank One	5	3
45	July 27	Brian Anderson (Arizona)	Bank One	4	0

July totals – 6 home runs

46	Aug. 1	Joe Beimel (Pittsburgh)	Pacific Bell	1	0
47*	Aug. 4	Nelson Figueroa (Philadelphia)	Pacific Bell	6	1
48	Aug. 7	Danny Graves (Cincinnati)	Cinergy	11	0
49	Aug. 9	Scott Winchester (Cincinnati)	Cinergy	3	0
50	Aug. 11	Joe Borowski (Chicago)	Wrigley	2	2
51*	Aug. 14	Ricky Bones (Florida)	Pacific Bell	6	3
52	Aug. 16	A.J. Burnett (Florida)	Pacific Bell	4	0
53#	Aug. 16	Vic Darensbourg (Florida)	Pacific Bell	8	2
54	Aug. 18	Jason Marquis (Atlanta)	Pacific Bell	8	0
55	Aug. 23	Graeme Lloyd (Montreal)	Olympic	9	0
56	Aug. 27	Kevin Appier (New York)	Shea	5	0
57*	Aug. 31	John Thomson (Colorado)	Pacific Bell	8	1

August totals – 12 home runs

58	Sept. 3	Jason Jennings (Colorado)	Pacific Bell	4	0
59	Sept. 4	Miguel Batista (Arizona)	Pacific Bell	7	0
60	Sept. 6	Albie Lopez (Arizona)	Pacific Bell	2	0
61	Sept. 9	Scott Elarton (Colorado)	Coors	1	0
62	Sept. 9	Scott Elarton (Colorado)	Coors	5	0
63	Sept. 9	Todd Belitz (Colorado)	Coors	11	2
64	Sept. 20	Wade Miller (Houston)	Pacific Bell	5	2
65	Sept. 23	Jason Middlebrook (San Diego)	Qualcomm	2	0
66	Sept. 23	Jason Middlebrook (San Diego)	Qualcomm	4	0
67	Sept. 24	James Baldwin (Los Angeles)	Dodger	7	0
68	Sept. 28	Jason Middlebrook (San Diego)	Pacific Bell	7	0
69*	Sept. 29	Chuck McElroy (San Diego)	Pacific Bell	6	0

September totals – 12 home runs

70	Oct. 4	Wilfredo Rodriguez (Houston)	Enron	9	0
71$	Oct. 5	Chan Ho Park (Los Angeles)	Pacific Bell	1	0
72	Oct. 5	Chan Ho Park (Los Angeles)	Pacific Bell	3	0
73	Oct. 7	Dennis Springer (Los Angeles)	Pacific Bell	1	0

October totals – 4 home runs

* Splash homer into McCovey Cove (9)
\# New Giants' franchise record, surpassing Willie Mays' 52 in 1965
$ New major league record, surpassing Mark McGwire's 70 in 1998

BONDS' BACK-TO-BACK BLITZ

Barry Bonds arguably powered his way to the best back-to-back seasons in major league history in 2001-02, erasing records that were on the books for years by combining power and patience to hit .347 with 119 home runs and 375 walks. How he did it:

2001	AB	H	HR	RBI	Avg.	2002	AB	H	HR	RBI	Avg.
April	75	18	11	22	.240	April	64	24	8	17	.375
May	84	31	17	30	.369	May	72	21	10	16	.292
June	74	22	11	19	.297	June	70	26	7	17	.371
July	86	26	6	15	.302	July	52	19	4	13	.365
Aug.	80	28	12	26	.350	Aug.	76	34	11	25	.447
Sept. +	77	31	16	25	.403	Sept. +	59	25	6	22	.362
Total	480	147	73	137	.306	Total	403	149	46	110	.370

Totals	883	296	119	247	.347

THE 60-HOME RUN CLUB

Player	HR	Year
Barry Bonds	73	2001
Mark McGwire	70	1998
Sammy Sosa	66	1998
Mark McGwire	65	1999
Sammy Sosa	64	2001
Sammy Sosa	63	1999
Roger Maris	61	1961
Babe Ruth	60	1927

ALL-TIME HOME RUN LEADERS

Player	HR
Henry Aaron	755
Babe Ruth	714
Willie Mays	660
Barry Bonds	**613***
Frank Robinson	586
Mark McGwire	583
Harmon Killebrew	573
Reggie Jackson	563
Mike Schmidt	548
Mickey Mantle	536

* Through 2002

CAREER MULTI-HR GAMES

Player	Total
Babe Ruth	72
Mark McGwire	67
Willie Mays	63
Henry Aaron	62
Barry Bonds	**61***

* Through 2002

SINGLE SEASON ON-BASE PERCENTAGE

Player	Year	Pct.
Barry Bonds	2002	.582
Ted Williams	1941	.553
Babe Ruth	1923	.545
Babe Ruth	1920	.532

SINGLE SEASON SLUGGING PERCENTAGE

Player	Year	Pct.
Barry Bonds	2001	.863
Babe Ruth	1920	.847
Barry Bonds	2002	.799

CAREER SLUGGING PERCENTAGE

Player	Pct.
Babe Ruth	.690
Ted Williams	.634
Lou Gehrig	.632
Jimmie Foxx	.609
Barry Bonds	.595*
Rogers Hornsby	.577
Stan Musial	.559
Willie Mays	.557
Mickey Mantle	.557
Henry Aaron	.555

* Through 2002

CAREER RUNS LEADERS

Player	Runs
Rickey Henderson	2,288
Ty Cobb	2,245
Henry Aaron	2,174
Babe Ruth	2,174
Pete Rose	2,165
Willie Mays	2,062
Stan Musial	1,949
Lou Gehrig	1,888
Tris Speaker	1,881
Mel Ott	1,859
Barry Bonds	1,830*
Frank Robinson	1,829

* Through 2002

CAREER WALKS LEADERS

Player	Walks
Rickey Henderson	2,286
Babe Ruth	2,056
Ted Williams	2.019
Barry Bonds	1,922*
Joe Morgan	1,865

* Through 2002

SINGLE-SEASON WALKS LEADERS

Player	Year	Walks
Barry Bonds	198	2002
Barry Bonds	177	2001
Babe Ruth	170	1923

WILLIE MCCOVEY'S NATIONAL LEAGUE CAREER-RECORD 18 GRAND SLAMS

No.	Date	Opposing Pitcher (Club)	Stadium	Inning
1*	June 12, 1960	Carl Willey (Milwaukee)	Candlestick	7th
2	June 22, 1964	John Tsitouris (Cincinnati)	Crosley	6th
3*	Sept. 10, 1965	Ted Abernathy (Chicago)	Candlestick	6th
4	April 27, 1966	Milt Pappas (Cincinnati)	Candlestick	5th
5	April 22, 1967	Ramon Hernandez (Atlanta)	Candlestick	8th
6	Sept. 23, 1967	Juan Pizarro (Pittsburgh)	Candlestick	8th
7	Sept. 27, 1967	Tug McGraw (New York)	Candlestick	3rd
8	May 4, 1968	Larry Jaster (St. Louis)	Candlestick	3rd
9	June 28, 1969	Jack Fisher (Cincinnati)	Crosley	1st
10	Aug. 26, 1969	Jerry Johnson (Philadelphia)	Candlestick	3rd
11	April 26, 1970	Bill Stoneman (Montreal)	Candlestick	1st
12	May 10, 1970	Tug McGraw (New York)	Shea	4th
13	July 21, 1971	Dave Giusti (Pittsburgh)	Three Rivers	9th
14	July 2, 1972	Don Sutton (Los Angeles)	Candlestick	7th
15#	May 19, 1974	Tom Bradley (San Francisco)	Candlestick	5th
16*#	May 30, 1975	Bob Apodaca (New York)	Shea	8th
17	June 27, 1977	Joe Hoerner (Cincinnati)	Riverfront	6th
18	Aug. 1, 1977	Wayne Twitchell (Montreal)	Olympic	3rd

* denotes pinch-hit grand slam.
# denotes as member of San Diego Padres.

CARL HUBBELL'S MAJOR LEAGUE RECORD 24 CONSECUTIVE WINS (1936-37)

No.	Date	Opponent	Score	IP	H	R	ER	BB	SO
1	July 17, 1936	at Pittsburgh	6-0	9.0	5	0	0	0	2
2	July 19, 1936	at Cincinnati	4-3	2.2	0	0	0	2	0
3	July 21, 1936	St. Louis	2-1	10.0	9	1	1	5	3
4	July 30, 1936	Chicago	3-1	9.0	7	1	1	2	3
5	Aug. 2, 1936	Pittsburgh	3-2	9.0	4	2	2	1	2
6	Aug. 8, 1936	at Philadelphia	3-2	9.0	7	2	2	1	3
7	Aug. 15, 1936	Philadelphia	4-1	9.0	9	1	1	1	3
8	Aug. 19, 1936	Brooklyn	3-2	9.0	5	2	2	2	5
9	Aug. 26, 1936	at Cincinnati	6-5	9.0	11	5	5	0	2
10	Aug. 30, 1936	at Chicago	6-1	9.0	7	1	1	1	3
11	Sept. 3, 1936	at St. Louis	2-1	9.0	4	1	1	2	5
12	Sept. 7, 1936	at Philadelphia	6-2	9.0	7	2	2	2	3
13	Sept. 11, 1936	Chicago	5-1	9.0	4	1	1	2	3
14	Sept. 14, 1936	St. Louis	7-5	5.0	6	1	1	0	4
15	Sept. 19, 1936	at Brooklyn	7-1	9.0	4	1	1	1	5
16	Sept. 23, 1936	at Philadelphia	5-4	9.0	8	4	4	1	4
17	April 23, 1937	Boston	3-0	9.0	3	0	0	3	5
18	April 30, 1937	Brooklyn	11-2	9.0	7	2	2	2	9
19	May 4, 1937	Cincinnati	7-6	6.2	9	6	3	3	10
20	May 9, 1937	Chicago	4-1	9.0	7	1	1	2	5
21	May 13, 1937	Pittsburgh	5-2	9.0	6	2	2	0	3
22	May 19, 1937	at St. Louis	4-1	9.0	6	1	1	0	7
23	May 24, 1937	at Pittsburgh	4-3	8.2	10	3	2	3	9
24	May 27, 1937	at Cincinnati	3-2	2.0	0	0	0	0	0
Totals				197.0	145	40	36	36	98
							1.64 ERA		

NEW YORK/SAN FRANCISCO GIANTS FIRSTS

New York (Polo Grounds)
Game — May 1, 1883 (New York 7, Boston 5)
Attendance — 15,000
Lineup — Buck Ewing, C
    Roger Connor, 1B
    John Montgomery Ward, CF
    Pete Gillespie, LF
    Mike Dorgan, RF
    Mickey Welch, P
    Ed Caskin, 2B
    Dasher Troy, SS
    Frank Hankinson, 3B
Hit — Roger Connor (triple) vs. Boston, May 1, 1883 (1st inning off Jim Whitney)
Double — Frank Hankinson vs. Boston, May 1, 1883 (1st inning off Jim Whitney)
Triple — Roger Connor vs. Boston, May 1, 1883
    (1st inning off Jim Whitney)
Home Run — John Montgomery Ward vs. Boston, May 2, 1883 (9th inning off Jim Whitney)
Run — Roger Connor vs. Boston, May 1, 1883
    (1st inning)
RBI — Mike Dorgan vs. Boston, May 1, 1883
    (1st inning)

San Francisco (Seals Stadium)
Game — April 15, 1958 (San Francisco 8, Los Angeles 0)
Attendance — 23,448
Lineup — Jim Davenport, 3B
    Jim King, LF
    Willie Mays, CF
    Willie Kirkland, RF
    Orlando Cepeda, 1B
    Daryl Spencer, SS
    Danny O'Connell, 2B
    Valmy Thomas, C
    Ruben Gomez, P
Hit — Ruben Gomez (single) vs. Los Angeles, April 15, 1958 (3rd inning off Don Drysdale)
Double — Jim King vs. Los Angeles, April 17, 1958 (1st inning off Don Newcombe)
Triple — Bob Schmidt at Los Angeles, April 18, 1958 (6th inning off Carl Erskine)
Home Run — Daryl Spencer vs. Los Angeles, April 15, 1958 (4th inning off Don Drysdale)
Run — Danny O'Connell vs. Los Angeles, April 15, 1958 (3rd inning)
RBI — Jim Davenport vs. Los Angeles, April 15, 1958 (3rd inning)

San Francisco (Candlestick Park)

Game — April 12, 1960 (San Francisco 3, St. Louis 1)

Attendance — 42,269

Lineup — Don Blasingame, 2B
    Jim Davenport, 3B
    Willie Mays, CF
    Willie McCovey, 1B
    Orlando Cepeda, LF
    Willie Kirkland, RF
    Ed Bressoud, SS
    Bob Schmidt, C
    Sam Jones, P

Hit — Orlando Cepeda (triple) vs. St. Louis, April 12, 1960 (1st inning off Larry Jackson)

Double — Willie Mays vs. St. Louis, April 12, 1960 (3rd inning off Larry Jackson)

Triple — Orlando Cepeda vs. St. Louis, April 12, 1960 (1st inning off Larry Jackson)

Home Run — Willie Kirkland vs. St. Louis, April 13, 1960 (3rd inning off Vinegar Bend Mizell)

Run — Don Blasingame vs. St. Louis, April 12, 1960 (1st inning)

RBI — Orlando Cepeda vs. St. Louis, April 12, 1960 (1st inning)

San Francisco (Pacific Bell Park)

Game — April 11, 2000 (Los Angeles 6, San Francisco 5)

Attendance — 40,930

Lineup — Marvin Benard, CF
    Bill Mueller, 3B
    Barry Bonds, LF
    Jeff Kent, 2B
    Ellis Burks, RF
    J.T. Snow, 1B
    Rich Aurilia, SS
    Doug Mirabelli, C
    Kirk Rueter, P

Hit — Bill Mueller (single) vs. Los Angeles, April 11, 2000 (1st inning off Chan Ho Park)

Double — Barry Bonds vs. Los Angeles, April 11, 2000 (1st inning off Chan Ho Park)

Triple — Doug Mirabelli vs. Los Angeles, April 11, 2000 (3rd inning off Chan Ho Park)

Home Run — Barry Bonds vs. Los Angeles, April 11, 2000 (3rd inning off Chan Ho Park)

Run — Bill Mueller vs. Los Angeles, April 11, 2000 1st inning)

RBI — Barry Bonds vs. Los Angeles, April 11, 2000, 1st inning)

NEW YORK GIANTS 1889-90

Following is a look at where the members of the 1889 Giants went on to play in 1890.

Player	1890 Team
Pat Murphy	New York Giants (National League)
Mike Tiernan	New York Giants (National League)
Mickey Welch	New York Giants (National League)
Willard Browne	New York Giants (Players League)
Roger Connor	New York Giants (Players League)
Ed Crane	New York Giants (Players League)
Buck Ewing	New York Giants (Players League)
George Gore	New York Giants (Players League)
Gil Hatfield	New York Giants (Players League)
Tim Keefe	New York Giants (Players League)
Hank O'Day	New York Giants (Players League)
Jim O'Rourke	New York Giants (Players League)
Danny Richardson	New York Giants (Players League)
Art Whitney	New York Giants (Players League)
Mike Slattery	New York Giants (Players League)
Harry Lyons	Rochester Hop Bitters (American Association)
Cannonball Titcomb	Rochester Hop Bitters (American Association)
Elmer Foster	Chicago White Stockings (National League)
John Montgomery Ward	Brooklyn Wonders (Players League)
Bill George	Did Not Play

NEW YORK GIANTS 1889-90

Following is a look at where the members of the 1890 Giants had played in 1889.

Player	1889 Team
Pat Murphy	New York Giants (National League)
Mike Tiernan	New York Giants (National League)
Mickey Welch	New York Giants (National League)
Charley Bassett	Indianapolis Hoosiers (National League)
Dick Buckley	Indianapolis Hoosiers (National League)
Jerry Denny	Indianapolis Hoosiers (National League)
Jack Glasscock	Indianapolis Hoosiers (National League)
Amos Rusie	Indianapolis Hoosiers (National League)
Pete Sommers	Indianapolis Hoosiers (National League)*
Ed Daily	Columbus Colts (American Association)**
Dude Esterbrook	Louisville Colonels (American Association)
Joe Hornung	Baltimore Orioles (American Association)
Jesse Burkett	Did Not Play
Artie Clarke	Did Not Play
Sam Crane	Did Not Play
John Henry	Did Not Play
Shorty Howe	Did Not Play
George McMillan	Did Not Play
Bob Murphy	Did Not Play
Tom O'Rourke	Did Not Play
Mort Scanlan	Did Not Play
Jack Sharrott	Did Not Play
Lew Whistler	Did Not Play

* denotes began 1889 season with Chicago White Stockings (National League) before joining Indianapolis.

** denotes began 1890 season with Brooklyn Gladiators (American Association) before joining Giants.

PLAYERS WHO PLAYED FOR THE GIANTS IN NEW YORK AND SAN FRANCISCO

Players	New York	San Francisco
Joey Amalfitano	1954-55	1960-61
Johnny Antonelli	1954-57	1958-60
Curt Barclay	1957	1958-59
Jackie Brandt	1956	1958-59
Eddie Bressoud	1956-57	1958-61
Pete Burnside	1955, 1957	1958
Jim Constable	1956-57	1958, 1963
Ray Crone	1957	1958
Paul Giel	1954-57	1958
Ruben Gomez	1953-57	1958
Marv Grissom	1946, 1953-57	1958
Ray Jablonski	1957	1958
Whitey Lockman	1945, 1947-56, 1957	1958
Willie Mays	1951-52, 1954-57	1958-72
Mike McCormick	1956-57	1958-62, 1967-70
Stu Miller	1957	1958-62
Ramon Monzant	1954-57	1958, 1960
Danny O'Connell	1957	1958-59
Dusty Rhodes	1952-57	1959
Andre Rodgers	1957	1958-60
Daryl Spencer	1952-53, 1956-57	1958-59
Valmy Thomas	1957	1958
Al Worthington	1953-54, 1956-57	1958-59

Manager	New York	San Francisco
Bill Rigney	1956-57	1958-60, 1976

Coaches	New York	San Francisco
Herman Franks	1949-55	1958, 1964
Larry Jansen	1954	1961-71

BROTHERS WHO PLAYED TOGETHER AS NEW YORK/SAN FRANCISCO GIANTS

Player	Position	Seasons Together
Danny F. Murphy	IF	1901
Frank Murphy	OF	
Christy Mathewson	P	1906-07
Henry Mathewson	P	
Jesse Barnes	P	1919-23
Virgil Barnes	P	
Mort Cooper	P	1947
Walker Cooper	P	
Felipe Alou	OF	1960-63
Matty Alou	OF	
Felipe Alou	OF	1963
Jesus Alou	OF	
Matty Alou	OF	
Jesus Alou	OF	1963-65
Matty Alou	OF	

SAN FRANCISCO GIANTS INTERLEAGUE FIRSTS

When the San Francisco Giants played the Texas Rangers on June 12, 1997, at The Ballpark in Arlington (first pitch 7:11 p.m. CDT), it marked the first interleague game in major league history. Following is a list of interleague firsts accomplished by a San Francisco player:

Feat	Player	Opponent	Date	Location
First Batter	Darryl Hamilton	Texas	June 12, 1997	The Ballpark in Arlington
First Hit	Darryl Hamilton	Texas	June 12, 1997	The Ballpark in Arlington
First Home Run	Stan Javier	Texas	June 12, 1997	The Ballpark in Arlington
First Grand Slam	Rich Aurilia	Anaheim	June 14, 1997	Anaheim Stadium
First N.L. D.H.	Glenallen Hill	Texas	June 12, 1997	The Ballpark in Arlington
First Winning Pitcher	Mark Gardner	Texas	June 12, 1997	The Ballpark in Arlington
First Save	Rod Beck	Texas	June 12, 1997	The Ballpark in Arlington

NEW YORK/SAN FRANCISCO GIANTS GAMES OF 18 INNINGS OR MORE

Innings	Result	Site	Date
23	Giants 8, New York 6	New York	May 31, 1964 (2)
21	Giants 3, Pittsburgh 1	Pittsburgh	July 17, 1914
	Giants 1, Cincinnati 0	Cincinnati	Sept. 1, 1967
18	Giants 9, Pittsburgh 8	Pittsburgh	July 7, 1922
	Giants 1, St. Louis 0	New York	July 2, 1933 (1)
	Pittsburgh 4, Giants 3	Pittsburgh	July 13, 1984 (2)
	Giants 5, Atlanta 4	Atlanta	June 11, 1985
	Diamondbacks 1, Giants 0	San Francisco	May 29, 2001

NEW YORK/SAN FRANCISCO GIANTS HOME ATTENDANCE DATA

Season	Dates	Total Attendance	Average	Season	Dates	Total Attendance	Average
				1908	77	910,000	11,818
				1909	77	783,700	10,178
1883	47	—	—				
1884	56	—	—				
1885	55	—	—	1910	78	511,785	6,561
1886	59	—	—	1911	74	675,000	9,122
1887	63	—	—	1912	74	638,000	8,622
1888	67	—	—	1913	77	630,000	8,182
1889	62	—	—	1914	79	364,313	4,612
				1915	75	391,850	5,225
1890	64	60,667	948	1916	77	552,056	7,170
1891	67	210,568	3,143	1917	78	500,264	6,414
1892	78	130,566	1,674	1918	56	256,618	4,582
1893	69	290,000	4,203	1919	69	708,857	10,273
1894	66	387,000	5,864				
1895	67	240,000	3,582	1920	80	929,609	11,620
1896	65	274,000	4,215	1921	79	973,477	12,322
1897	70	390,340	5,576	1922	78	945,809	12,126
1898	73	206,700	2,832	1923	77	820,780	10,659
1899	73	121,384	1,663	1924	77	844,068	10,962
				1925	76	778,993	10,250
1900	69	190,000	2,754	1926	76	700,362	9,215
1901	68	297,650	4,377	1927	74	858,190	11,597
1902	68	302,875	4,454	1928	77	916,191	11,899
1903	68	579,530	8,523	1929	76	868,806	11,432
1904	82	609,826	7,437				
1905	75	552,700	7,369	1930	78	868,714	11,137
1906	75	402,850	5,371	1931	77	812,163	10,548
1907	75	538,350	7,178	1932	77	484,868	6,297

Season	Dates	Total Attendance	Average
1933	75	604,471	8,060
1934	75	730,851	9,745
1935	77	748,748	9,724
1936	78	837,952	10,743

Season	Dates	Total Attendance	Average
1937	75	926,887	12,697
1938	73	799,633	10,954
1939	74	702,457	9,493
1940	76	747,852	9,840
1941	77	763,098	9,910
1942	78	779,621	9,995
1943	77	466,095	6,053
1944	75	674,483	8,993
1945	77	1,016,468	13,201
1946	77	1,219,873	15,843
1947	76	1,600,793	21,063
1948	77	1,459,269	18,952
1949	77	1,218,446	15,824
1950	76	1,008,878	13,275
1951	78	1,059,539	13,584
1952	77	984,940	12,791
1953	77	811,518	10,539
1954	76	1,155,067	15,198
1955	79	824,112	10,432
1956	77	629,179	8,171
1957	77	653,923	8,493
1958	75	1,272,625	16,968
1959	77	1,442,130	18,729
1960	76	1,795,356	23,623
1961	74	1,390,679	18,793
1962	76	1,556,551	20,481
1963	76	1,568,965	20,644
1964	76	1,500,883	19,748
1965	76	1,542,588	20,297
1966	77	1,651,293	21,445
1967	74	1,237,119	16,718
1968	75	833,594	11,115
1969	74	870,341	11,761
1970	72	728,498	10,118
1971	73	1,088,083	14,905
1972	69	637,327	9,237
1973	74	834,193	11,273
1974	74	519,991	7,027
1975	74	522,925	7,067
1976	73	626,868	8,587
1977	74	700,056	9,460
1978	74	1,740,480	23,520
1979	77	1,456,392	18,914

Season	Dates	Total Attendance	Average
1980	78	1,096,115	14,053
1981	51	632,276	12,398
1982	77	1,200,948	15,597
1983	77	1,251,530	16,254
1984	77	1,001,545	13,007
1985	79	818,697	10,363
1986	78	1,528,748	19,599
1987	79	1,917,863	24,277
1988	79	1,786,482	22,614
1989	79	2,059,829	26,074
1990	80	1,975,571	24,695
1991	81	1,737,479	21,450
1992	79	1,560,998	19,759
1993	81	2,606,354	32,177
1994	59	1,704,608	28,892
1995	72	1,241,500	17,243
1996	80	1,413,687	17,671
1997	80	1,690,831	21,135
1998	80	1,925,634	24,070
1999	81	2,078,365	25,659
2000	81	3,315,330	40,930
2001	81	3,307,686	40,836
2002	81	3,253,203	40,163

Top Polo Grounds Regular Season Crowd
60,747 — vs. Brooklyn, May 31, 1937 (DH)

Top 10 Candlestick Park/3Com Park Regular Season Crowds
61,389 — vs. Los Angeles, Sept. 30, 1999
58,077 — vs. Pittsburgh, April 4, 1994
57,853 — vs. New York, Aug. 14, 1999
57,430 — vs. San Diego, April 8, 1999
56,788 — vs. Los Angeles, July 3, 1998
56,689 — vs. Florida, April 12, 1993
56,679 — vs. Los Angeles, May 9, 1993
56,196 — vs. San Diego, April 10, 1979
56,103 — vs. Los Angeles, May 28, 1978
55,920 — vs. Cincinnati, June 20, 1978

Top 5 Pacific Bell Park Regular Season Crowds
42,005 — vs. Arizona, May 27, 2002
41,991 — vs. Chicago, Aug. 6, 2002
41,980 — vs. Baltimore, June 23, 2002
41,980 — vs. Colorado, July 14, 2002
41,936 — vs. Arizona, July 16, 2002

NEW YORK/SAN FRANCISCO GIANTS SPRING TRAINING DATA
(Spring training records and finishes were not recorded prior to 1948)

Year	Location	Record	N.L. Finish	Year	Location	Record	N.L. Finish
1900	New York, N.Y.	—	—	1940	Winter Haven, Fla.	—	—
1901	New York, N.Y.	—	—	1941	Miami, Fla.	—	—
1902	New York, N.Y.	—	—	1942	Miami, Fla.	—	—
1903	Savannah, Ga.	—	—	1943	Lakewood, N.J.	—	—
1904	Savannah, Ga.	—	—	1944	Lakewood, N.J.	—	—
1905	Savannah, Ga.	—	—	1945	Lakewood, N.J.	—	—
1906	Memphis, Tenn.	—	—	1946	Miami, Fla.	—	—
1907	Los Angeles, Calif.	—	—	1947	Phoenix, Ariz.	—	—
1908	Marlin Springs, Texas	—	—	1948	Phoenix, Ariz.	18-13	4th
1909	Marlin Springs, Texas	—	—	1949	Phoenix, Ariz.	18-14	2nd
1910	Marlin Springs, Texas	—	—	1950	Phoenix, Ariz.	12-18	6th
1911	Marlin Springs, Texas	—	—	1951	St. Petersburg, Fla.	19-12	2nd
1912	Marlin Springs, Texas	—	—	1952	Phoenix, Ariz.	11-16	6th
1913	Marlin Springs, Texas	—	—	1953	Phoenix, Ariz.	14-16	7th
1914	Marlin Springs, Texas	—	—	1954	Phoenix, Ariz.	16-13	4th
1915	Marlin Springs, Texas	—	—	1955	Phoenix, Ariz.	16-11	2nd
1916	Marlin Springs, Texas	—	—	1956	Phoenix, Ariz.	20-15	3rd
1917	Marlin Springs, Texas	—	—	1957	Phoenix, Ariz.	20-14	3rd
1918	Marlin Springs, Texas	—	—	1958	Phoenix, Ariz.	21-11	1st
1919	Gainesville, Fla.	—	—	1959	Phoenix, Ariz.	15-13	3rd
1920	San Antonio, Texas	—	—	1960	Phoenix, Ariz.	13-13	5th
1921	San Antonio, Texas	—	—	1961	Phoenix, Ariz.	15-11	3rd
1922	San Antonio, Texas	—	—	1962	Phoenix, Ariz.	13-13	5th
1923	San Antonio, Texas	—	—	1963	Phoenix, Ariz.	10-17	10th
1924	Sarasota, Fla.	—	—	1964	Phoenix, Ariz.	25-8	2nd
1925	Sarasota, Fla.	—	—	1965	Phoenix, Ariz.	12-8	4th
1926	Sarasota, Fla.	—	—	1966	Phoenix, Ariz.	15-11	3rd
1927	Sarasota, Fla.	—	—	1967	Phoenix, Ariz.	17-9	1st
1928	Augusta, Ga.	—	—	1968	Phoenix, Ariz.	13-17	5th
1929	San Antonio, Texas	—	—	1969	Phoenix, Ariz.	19-7	1st
1930	San Antonio, Texas	—	—	1970	Phoenix, Ariz.	9-7	7th
1931	San Antonio, Texas	—	—	1971	Phoenix, Ariz.	15-11	4th
1932	Los Angeles, Calif.	—	—	1972	Phoenix, Ariz.	9-6	2nd
1933	Los Angeles, Calif.	—	—	1973	Phoenix, Ariz.	13-8	3rd
1934	Miami Beach, Fla.	—	—	1974	Phoenix, Ariz.	12-9	3rd
1935	Miami Beach, Fla.	—	—	1975	Phoenix, Ariz.	12-7	3rd
1936	Pensacola, Fla.	—	—	1976	Phoenix, Ariz.	7-7	7th
1937	Havana, Cuba	—	—	1977	Phoenix, Ariz.	11-15	10th
1938	Baton Rouge, La.	—	—	1978	Phoenix, Ariz.	18-9	1st
1939	Baton Rouge, La.	—	—	1979	Phoenix, Ariz.	14-12	7th

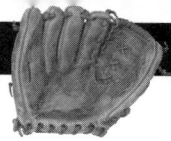

Year	Location	Record	N.L. Finish	Year	Location	Record	N.L. Finish
1980	Phoenix, Ariz.	14-7	1st	1993	Scottsdale, Ariz.	14-17	T11th
1981	Phoenix, Ariz.	14-13	1st	1994	Scottsdale, Ariz.	17-13	5th
1982	Scottsdale, Ariz.	9-14	11th	1995	Scottsdale, Ariz.	12-25	—
1983	Scottsdale, Ariz.	11-13	5th	1996	Scottsdale, Ariz.	12-21	12th
1984	Scottsdale, Ariz.	18-9	1st	1997	Scottsdale, Ariz.	18-15	6th
1985	Scottsdale, Ariz.	14-14	7th	1998	Scottsdale, Ariz.	9-21	15th
1986	Scottsdale, Ariz.	15-12	5th	1999	Scottsdale, Ariz.	13-19	12th
1987	Scottsdale, Ariz.	20-10	2nd				
1988	Scottsdale, Ariz.	16-14	5th	2000	Scottsdale, Ariz	12-17	12th
1989	Scottsdale, Ariz.	13-19	9th	2001	Scottsdale, Ariz	11-20	16th
				2002	Scottsdale, Ariz	16-16	16th
1990	Scottsdale, Ariz.	6-10	12th				
1991	Scottsdale, Ariz.	15-14	6th	Totals		789-717	
1992	Scottsdale, Ariz.	18-13	3rd			(.524 winning percentage)	

SAN FRANCISCO GIANTS FIRST-ROUND DRAFT PICKS (JUNE DRAFT)

1965 — Al Gallagher, IF*
1966 — Bob Reynolds, RHP
1967 — Dave Rader, C*
1968 — Gary Matthews, OF*
1969 — Mike Phillips, IF*
1970 — John D'Acquisto, RHP*
1971 — Frank Riccelli, LHP*
1972 — Rob Dressler, RHP*
1973 — Johnnie LeMaster, IF*
1974 — Terry Lee, IF
1975 — Ted Barnicle, LHP
1976 — Mark Kuecker, IF
1977 — Craig Landis, IF
1978 — Bob Cummings, C
1979 — Scott Garrelts, RHP*
1980 — Jessie Reid, OF*
1981 — Mark Grant, RHP*
1982 — Steve Stanicek, IF
1983 — Jeff Robinson, RHP*
1984 — Alan Cockrell, OF

1985 — Will Clark, IF*
1986 — Matt Williams IF*
1987 — Mike Remlinger, LHP*
1988 — Royce Clayton, IF*
1989 — Steve Hosey, OF*
1990 — Adam Hyzdu, OF
1991 — No selection
1992 — Calvin Murray, OF*
1993 — Steve Soderstrom, RHP*
1994 — Dante Powell, OF*
1995 — Joe Fontenot, RHP
1996 — Matt White, RHP
1997 — Jason Grilli, RHP
1998 — Tony Torcato, IF
1999 — Kurt Ainsworth, RHP
2000 — Boof Bonser, RHP
2001 — Brad Hennessey, RHP
2002 — Matt Cain, RHP

* denotes played for Giants.

Celebrate the Heroes of Baseball
in These Other Acclaimed Titles from Sports Publishing!

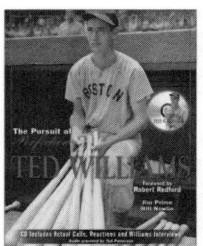